A H F
PSY Y

ORIGINAL CES
AND CONTEMPORARY
RESEARCH

A HISTORY OF PSYCHOLOGY

ORIGINAL SOURCES AND CONTEMPORARY RESEARCH

SECOND EDITION

Ludy T. Benjamin, Jr.

Texas A&M University

McGraw-Hill

Boston, Massachusetts Burr Ridge, Illinois Dubuque, Iowa
Madison, Wisconsin New York, New York San Francisco, California St. Louis, Missouri

McGraw-Hill

A Division of The ***McGraw-Hill*** *Companies*

This book was set in Times Roman by York Graphic Services, Inc.
The editors were Brian L. McKean and LG;
The production supervisor was Richard A. Ausburn.
The cover was designed by Farenga Design Group.
Project supervision was done by York Production Services.
R. R. Donnelley & Sons Company was printer and binder.

A HISTORY OF PSYCHOLOGY:

Original Sources and Contemporary Research

This book is printed on acid-free paper.

5 6 7 8 9 0 QSR/QSR 0 9 8 7 6 5 4 3 2 1

ISBN 0-07-005599-8

Library of Congress Cataloging-in-Publication Data

A history of psychology:original sources and contemporary research/
[edited by] Ludy T. Benjamin, Jr.—2nd ed.
p. cm.
Includes index.
ISBN 0-07-005599-8
1. Psychology—History. I. Benjamin, Ludy T., (date)
BF81.H58 1997
150′ .9—dc20 96-20144

http://www.mhhe.com

ABOUT THE EDITOR

LUDY T. BENJAMIN, JR. is Professor of Psychology at Texas A&M University where he teaches graduate and undergraduate courses in the history of psychology. His published works include 13 books and more than 80 articles in scholarly journals. His historical research has included works on psychology's public image, the development of the first American psychology laboratories, psychology applied to education and business, the psychology of women, and the early organizations of American psychologists. Among his books on the history of psychology are *A History of Psychology in Notes and News* (1989), *Harry Kirke Wolfe: Pioneer in Psychology* (1991), *Essays in the History of American Psychology* (1992), and *A History of Psychology in Letters* (1993). He is currently working on a book on the history of psychology in American business.

Benjamin was elected a Fellow of the American Psychological Association (APA) in 1981 and has served as president of two of APA's divisions, including the Division on the History of Psychology and the Division on the Teaching of Psychology. Currently he serves as a member of the Board of Advisors of the Archives of the History of American Psychology.

In 1984 and 1994 Benjamin received the Distinguished Teaching Award from Texas A&M University, and in 1986 he was awarded the prestigious Distinguished Teaching Award from the American Psychological Foundation. He is author and editor of several books on teaching psychology, including a book on teaching the history of psychology.

Benjamin's interest in the history of psychology grows from a broader interest in American and world history, and he admits that much of his reading for pleasure is on historical subjects. When not engaged as a professor of psychology he enjoys traveling, baseball, theater, and fishing.

This book is dedicated to
the memory of

J. Gilbert McAllister
1904–1993

Who taught his students many things,
especially the importance of thinking for themselves

CONTENTS

PREFACE xiii

1 THE PSYCHOLOGY OF HISTORY AND THE HISTORY OF PSYCHOLOGY: A HISTORIOGRAPHICAL INTRODUCTION 1

2 PHILOSOPHICAL ROOTS OF PSYCHOLOGY: MECHANISM AND EMPIRICISM 22

The Existence of Material Things: The Real Distinction of Mind and Body—*Rene Descartes* **27**

A Prescriptive Analysis of Descartes' Psychological Views—*Robert I. Watson* **34**

On Simple and Complex Ideas—*John Locke* **48**

Tabula Rasa—Its Origins and Implications—*Nicholas G. Petryszak* **53**

3 THE PHYSIOLOGICAL ROOTS OF PSYCHOLOGY 62

The Specific Energies of Nerves—*Johannes Müller* **66**

On the Speech Center—*Paul Broca* **73**

Cortical Localization and Cerebral Dominance: The Work of Paul Broca—*Stanley Finger* **77**

Gall, Flourens, and Phrenology—*Raymond E. Fancher* **81**

4 THE FRENCH CLINICAL TRADITION 88

Treating the Insane—*Philippe Pinel* 93
Hysteria in the Male Subject—*Jean Martin Charcot* 97
Charcot and the Salpêtrière School—*H. F. Ellenberger* 104
Charcot and Freud—*Frank J. Sulloway* 114

5 THE FOUNDING OF SCIENTIFIC PSYCHOLOGY: GUSTAV FECHNER AND WILHELM WUNDT 120

Psychophysics and Mind–Body Relations—*Gustav Theodor Fechner* 127
Biographical Genre and Biographical Archetype: Five Studies of Gustav Theodor Fechner—*Marilyn E. Marshall* 137
Psychical Elements and Compounds—*Wilhelm Wundt* 145
The Establishment of Wundt's Laboratory: An Archival and Documentary Study—*Wolfgang Bringmann, Norma J. Bringmann, and Gustav A. Ungerer* 151
A Reappraisal of Wilhelm Wundt—*Arthur L. Blumenthal* 158

6 E. B. TITCHENER AND STRUCTURALISM 168

The Method and Scope of Psychology—*Edward Bradford Titchener* 172
The Mistaken Mirror: On Wundt's and Titchener's Psychologies—*Thomas H. Leahey* 178
Shared Knowledge: The Experimentalists, 1904–1929—*Laurel Furumoto* 188

7 DARWINIAN INFLUENCES: ADAPTATION AND INDIVIDUAL DIFFERENCES 203

Natural Selection and the Struggle for Existence—*Charles Darwin* 207
Why Darwin Delayed, or Interesting Problems and Models in the History of Science—*Robert J. Richards* 218
Natural Abilities and the Comparative Worth of Races—*Francis Galton* 226
Francis Galton and American Psychology—*Solomon Diamond* 231

8 AMERICAN ANTECEDENTS TO FUNCTIONALISM **240**

The Stream of Thought—*William James* **245**
William James and the Art of Human Understanding—*David E. Leary* **249**
Child Study: The Basis of Exact Education—*G. Stanley Hall* **263**
The Paradox of G. Stanley Hall: Foe of Coeducation and Educator of Women—*Lesley A. Diehl* **266**
Tests of the Senses and Faculties—*James McKeen Cattell* **282**
James McKeen Cattell and the Failure of Anthropometric Mental Testing, 1890–1901—*Michael M. Sokal* **287**

9 FUNCTIONALISM **296**

The Province of Functional Psychology—*James R. Angell* **300**
The Pre-Chicago Association of the Early Functionalists—*Alfred C. Raphelson* **309**
Functionalism, Darwinism, and the Psychology of Women: A Study in Social Myth—*Stephanie A. Shields* **316**

10 ANIMAL EXPERIMENTAL PSYCHOLOGY **335**

The Laws of Learning in Animals—*Edward L. Thorndike* **340**
The Method of Pavlov in Animal Psychology—*Robert M. Yerkes and Sergius Morgulis* **345**
Early Interactions Between Animal Psychologists and Animal Activists and the Founding of the APA Committee on Precautions in Animal Experimentation—*Donald A. Dewsbury* **353**
From Bottle-Fed Chimp to Bottlenose Dolphin: A Contemporary Appraisal of Winthrop Kellogg—*Ludy T. Benjamin, Jr. and Darryl Bruce* **372**

11 BEHAVIORISM **390**

Psychology as the Behaviorist Views It—*John B. Watson* **396**
Struggle for Scientific Authority: The Reception of Watson's Behaviorism, 1913–1920—*Franz Samelson* **402**
The Selling of a Psychologist: John Broadus Watson and the Application of Behavioral Techniques to Advertising—*Kerry W. Buckley* **420**

12 NEOBEHAVIORISM **435**

Cognitive Maps in Rats and Men—*Edward C. Tolman* **441**
Tolman and Tryon: Early Research on the Inheritance of the Ability to Learn—*Nancy K. Innis* **450**
Behavior Theory, Learning, and the Problem of Reinforcement—*Clark L. Hull* **462**
A System of Behavior—*B. F. Skinner* **466**
Engineering Behavior: Project Pigeon, World War II, and the Conditioning of B. F. Skinner—*James H. Capshew* **472**

13 PSYCHOANALYSIS **488**

First Lecture on Psychoanalysis at Clark University: Breuer and the Treatment of Hysteria—*Sigmund Freud* **493**
The Story of "Anna O": A Critical Review with New Data—*H. F. Ellenberger* **499**
The Return of the Repressed: Psychology's Problematic Relations with Psychoanalysis, 1909–1960—*Gail A. Hornstein* **510**

14 GESTALT PSYCHOLOGY **525**

Gestalt Psychology—*Wolfgang Köhler* **530**
One Man Against the Nazis: Wolfgang Köhler—*Mary Henle* **538**
The Gestalt Psychologists in Behaviorist America—*Michael M. Sokal* **545**

15 THE BEGINNINGS OF AMERICAN APPLIED PSYCHOLOGY **557**

Clinical Psychology—*Lightner Witmer* **564**
The Clinical Psychology of Lightner Witmer: A Case Study of Institutional Innovation and Intellectual Change—*John M. O'Donnell* **569**
Psychology and Industrial Efficiency—*Hugo Münsterberg* **584**
Coca-Cola, Caffeine, and Mental Deficiency: Harry Hollingworth and the Chattanooga Trial of 1911—*Ludy T. Benjamin, Jr., Anne M. Rogers, and Angela Rosenbaum* **593**

16 AMERICAN PSYCHOLOGY'S SOCIAL AGENDA: THE ISSUE OF RACE **607**

Race Differences—*Otto Klineberg* **615**
Racial Identification and Preference in Negro Children—*Kenneth B. Clark and Mamie P. Clark* **619**
SPSSI and Race Relations, in the 1950s and After—*Otto Klineberg* **628**
From "Race Psychology" to "Studies in Prejudice": Some Observatlons on the Thematic Reversal in Social Psychology—*Franz Samelson* **633**

INDEX 647

PREFACE

This book is a reader in the history of psychology that covers the field from Descartes and Locke and the rise of modern science through the neobehaviorism of the 1950s. It is unlike any previous reader treating the history of psychology in that it combines primary and secondary sources. In this book, primary sources are original material written by the people whose work is the subject matter of a history of psychology course, individuals such as Pinel, Broca, Charcot, Fechner, Wundt, Darwin, James, Watson, and Freud. Works by each of those individuals and by many others—a total of twenty-seven selections—are included in this book. Secondary sources are the studies written by historians of psychology and other sciences about the individuals and ideas that are the primary sources. In short, primary source material was written by historical figures such as Freud or Darwin, whereas secondary source material was written about such primary work. There are thirty-two secondary source articles included in this reader.

The idea for this book grew out of my own classes in the history of psychology, both undergraduate and graduate, which I have been teaching for more than twenty-five years. Like most faculty, I have used a textbook in teaching those courses because of the integration provided by such books. However, I have two important goals for my classes that cannot be met by the standard textbooks. First, I want my students to read some of the actual primary sources that make up the historical works of psychology. I want them to know what Galton said and how he said it. It is not enough that they read about the marvelous way William James had with words; I want them to read James. Second, I want my students to understand that the history of psychology is an active research specialty in psychology, that the information they are reading in their textbook is the result of some historian's painstaking effort to reconstruct the past, and that those efforts go on every day. They will not learn that by reading about the work of Michael Sokal, or Mary Henle, or Franz Samelson, or Laurel Furumoto in their textbook; they need to read the actual words of those historians.

Those two goals represent the principal rationale for this book, that is, a collection of both primary source literature in the history of psychology and historical research in psychology done within the past twenty-five years. There are, however, other objectives that I wish to accomplish with this book. These objectives can best be introduced historically by reviewing the development of the research specialty of the history of psychology.

History of psychology as a research specialty is a fairly recent development, dating to around 1965. That date is especially important because it marks the beginning of the American Psychological Association's Division on the History of Psychology (Division 26); the founding of the Archives of the History of American Psychology at the University of Akron, now the largest assemblage of manuscript collections in psychology; and the establishment of the *Journal of the History of the Behavioral Sciences,* the first journal devoted largely to research in the history of psychology, as well as other fields in the social sciences. With the special interest group, the increased archival collections, and the journal has come improved historical scholarship, showing a sophistication not prevalent prior to 1960.

Modern researchers recognize the significance of such issues as presentism, historicism, and the role of the social history of science. They use a variety of sources, such as archival records and oral histories, and of techniques, such as prescriptive analysis and citation analysis. Partly this enhanced quality, and quantity, of historical research in psychology is due to the influx of historians of science into the field of behavioral science. But this research also represents the work of psychologists who have left their original specialties to pursue careers in historical work. One of the goals of this book is to make the reader aware of (a) the issues one deals with in doing historical research, (b) the sources available for this research, and (c) the techniques historians of psychology are using. This goal is partially accomplished in the opening chapter on historiography. And it is reinforced throughout the book in the introductions to each chapter and in the secondary source articles, for example, a prescriptive analysis of Descartes' ideas, a comparative study of Fechner biographies, and a citation analysis of Watson's behaviorist ideas.

Another objective of the book is to provide some coverage, where possible, of material that is often omitted from the standard history of psychology textbooks. Thus in the chapter on functionalism, a secondary source article examines the influence of Darwin and the functional psychologists on issues of sex differences and the psychology of women, and the chapter on the physiological roots of psychology includes a selection on phrenology and relates it to the nineteenth-century emphasis on the cortical localization of function. Two new chapters in this edition also address this objective. One treats the beginnings of applied psychology in America, and the other focuses on the psychology of race in the context of American psychologists' attempts to apply psychology to the solution of social problems.

The final objective of this book, and one of the most important, was to assemble some of the most significant literature in the history of psychology. Thus the primary source readings are taken from Darwin's *Origin of Species,* James's *Principles of Psychology,* Locke's *Essay Concerning Human Understanding,* and Fechner's *Elements of Psychophysics*. These selections are lengthy enough that the reader should get a good flavor of the style and substance of the work. Further, the secondary source articles are selected to represent some of the most important historical scholarship in the field. These studies have radically changed our views of Wundt's psychology, of the development of psychoanalysis, and of the spread of behaviorism.

This book is intended for use in history of psychology classes at the upper undergraduate and graduate levels. It is designed to be used as a supplement to one of the existing textbooks in the history of psychology and is broad enough in its coverage so that it can be used with any of a number of leading textbooks. The chapter introductions coupled with the readings, make this a comprehensive text, thus many instructors may find it satisfactory to use this book in place of a textbook.

This edition of the book, like the first one, is organized into sixteen chapters. To keep that number constant and add two new chapters required a combining of other chapters. Thus the separate chapters on mechanism and empiricism in the first edition were combined into one chapter on psychology's philosophical roots, and the separate chapters on Fechner and Wundt were joined as one on the founding of scientific psychology.

The first chapter is totally new for this edition. It replaces a chapter of five readings from the first edition with a comprehensive essay on the historiography of psychology, that is the philosophy and techniques in the history of psychology. The remaining fifteen chapters correspond to chapter titles frequently found in history of psychology textbooks, for example, Physiological Roots of Psychology, Functionalism, Behaviorism, Psychoanalysis. Starting with Chapter 2, each chapter begins with an introduction that provides (a) a historical context for the selections included in that chapter, and (b) some information about the importance of the selections for the topic at hand.

Approximately half of the selections are adapted in some way, and that is especially true of the primary source material because a number of those selections are excerpts from books. The source note for each selection indicates whether it has been reprinted in full or adapted. In some selections where portions were omitted, the footnotes in the remaining portions were renumbered for clarity. The numbers for those footnotes have been placed in parentheses indicating their renumbering.

Of the fifty-nine readings in this book, twenty-four are new to this edition. Those changes are due, principally, to two factors: (a) the continued high quality scholarship in the history of psychology, which has added a number of important articles and books to the field since the first edition was compiled nine years ago, and (b) feedback from my own students and from other instructors using the first edition of this book about which selections proved troublesome. Changes in this new edition have resulted in a more readable set of selections; a better integrated set of readings in each chapter; better coverage of applied psychology by adding a new chapter, but also by including applied work in other chapters, such as John Watson's career in advertising psychology and B. F. Skinner's project to train pigeons to guide a missile to its target; and new coverage of American psychology's efforts in applying the science of psychology to social issues.

The organization of topics in this book and the selection of some of the readings have benefited from the capable advice of my colleagues in the history of psychology and from my students. I want to acknowledge the very helpful assistance of David Baker, Wolfgang Bringmann, Darryl Bruce, Donald Dewsbury, William Hillix, Alfred Kornfeld, David Leary, Donald Polzella, Alfred Raphelson, Elizabeth Scarborough, Stephanie Shields, and George Windholz in reviewing drafts of the first edition and/or the new edition. I owe a very special debt to Michael M. Sokal for his very careful reading of the chapter introductions in the first edition, and for his continued support of this book. Because I have not always followed the advice of these scholars, they cannot be held responsible for any faults in the final product. I am certain, however, that this book is significantly better because of their counsel.

I also want to acknowledge the considerable help of the personnel at McGraw-Hill, particularly my editor, Brian McKean, in making this second edition a reality. I thank Lori Stambaugh for her considerable help in guiding the book through production, and William H. M. Bryant for his help in the final stages of the book.

The index for this book was prepared by Sydney Ellen Schultz, a professional librarian and co-author of the leading textbook on the history of psychology. No one could have created a more useful index and for that I am especially grateful. Of course, I owe a very special debt to the many authors and publishers who have allowed me to reprint their work in this book.

As always I owe a debt of thanks to my wife, Priscilla Benjamin, for her help in a variety of assignments associated with the writing and production of this book.

Finally, I want to thank the many students from my history of psychology classes whose enthusiasm for the subject has made this project, and my involvement in the field, a labor of love. This new edition is significantly improved because of the many helpful suggestions they provided. I hope that this new collection of readings will both instruct and inspire other students with the fascination and intrigue that are part of psychology's history.

Ludy T. Benjamin, Jr.

A HISTORY OF PSYCHOLOGY

ORIGINAL SOURCES AND CONTEMPORARY RESEARCH

CHAPTER 1

THE PSYCHOLOGY OF HISTORY AND THE HISTORY OF PSYCHOLOGY: A HISTORIOGRAPHICAL INTRODUCTION

As noted in the preface to this book, the history of psychology as a research specialty is a little more than thirty years old. In that thirty years, history of psychology interest groups have formed, such as Division 26 of the American Psychological Association, a group of psychologists interested in the history of their field, and Cheiron—the International Society for the History of the Behavioral and Social Sciences—a group of historians, including psychologist-historians, of the social and behavioral sciences. Cheiron has a European counterpart that is one of a number of such organizations to emerge abroad in the past twenty years.

As a venue for publishing the new scholarship in the history of psychology, specialty journals have been created in the past thirty years, such as the *Journal of the History of the Behavioral Sciences,* which is published in the United States, and similar journals in Spain, Italy, England, and Germany. Historians of psychology also publish their work in a variety of historical journals of longer standing such as *Isis* (the quarterly publication of the History of Science Society), the *Journal of the History of Ideas,* and the *American Historical Review,* as well as in related journals such as the *History of Psychiatry, the History of Human Sciences,* and the *Bulletin of the History of Medicine*.

Graduate programs have been established to train students in the theory, methods, and content of the history of psychology. The best known of these programs in North America are located at York University in Canada and the University of New Hampshire. Other traditional programs in the history of science, for example, at the universities of Chicago and Pennsylvania, also allow doctoral students to specialize in the history of behavioral science.

Archival sources in psychology have grown enormously, led by the Archives of the History of American Psychology, the single largest collection of unpublished materials in psychology, located at the University of Akron in Ohio (see Benjamin, 1980; Popplestone & McPherson, 1976). Historians of psychology make extensive use of archival collections all over the world today. And as interest in the History of Psychology has grown, so too has interest in preserving the documents and manuscript collections of psychologists and psychological organizations. Today, the manuscript collections of individual psychologists are more frequently being systematically preserved, as are the collections of organizations such as the American Psychological Association (whose archives are in the Library of Congress) and the Psychonomic Society (whose archives are in the collection at Akron).

With the formation of special groups drawing individuals together with common research interests, the establishment of new journal outlets to publish their research, the formation of new doctoral programs to train students in the new research specialty, and the rapid growth of archival collections providing a rich database for the new research, the history of psychology has emerged as a recognized research specialty in the fields of psychology and the history of science. It is a research field that has been created jointly by psychologists shifting from their original field of training (for example, cognition, development, personality) to historical research and by historians of science shifting to psychology from the more traditional research areas of natural sciences and medicine.

PSYCHOLOGY'S INTEREST IN ITS HISTORY

As a field, psychology has had a long-standing interest in its history. History of psychology courses have been taught since the 1920s, and today such courses are commonly part of the undergraduate and graduate curricula in psychology. Indeed, the history of psychology course is frequently a required course for psychology majors and for doctoral students as well. For example, the American Psychological Association requires all graduates of accredited doctoral programs in professional psychology to have had some instruction in the history of psychology. So why are psychologists so interested in their own history? Such interest does not appear nearly so active in the other sciences.

In trying to answer this question, consider the following quotations from two eminent British historians. One, Robin Collingwood (1946), wrote that the "proper object of historical study . . . is the human mind, or more properly the activities of the human mind" (p. 215). And the other, Edward H. Carr (1961), proposed that "the historian is not really interested in the unique, but what is general in the unique" and that "the study of history is a study of causes; . . . the historian . . . continuously asks the question: Why?" (pp. 80, 113). Thus, according to these historians, to study history is to study the human mind, to be able to generalize beyond the characteristics of a single individual or single event to other individuals and other events, and to be able to answer the "why" of human behavior in terms of motivation, personality, past experience, expectations, and so forth. Historians are not satisfied, for example, with a mere description of the events of May 4, 1970, in which National Guard troops killed four unarmed students on a college campus in Ohio. Description is useful, but it is not the scholarly end product that is sought. By itself, description is unlikely to answer the questions that historians want to answer. They want to understand an event, like the shootings at Kent State University, so completely that they can explain *why* it happened.

Collingwood (1946) has described history as "the science of human nature" (p. 206). In defining history in that way, Collingwood has usurped psychology's definition for itself. One can certainly argue about the scientific nature of history and thus his use of the term *science* in his definition. Whereas historians do not do experimental work, they are engaged in empirical work. And they approach their questions in much the same way that psychologists do, by generating hypotheses and then seeking evidence that will confirm or disconfirm those hypotheses. Thus the intellectual pursuits of the historian and the psychologist are not really very different. And so as psychologists or as students of psychology, we are not moving very far from our own field of interest when we study the history of psychology.

In this book, you will be reading selections from the scholarly works of the individuals working as historians of psychology today. Among other things, you will learn why Charles Darwin may have delayed the publication of his *Origin of Species,* why James McKeen Cattell's intelligence tests failed, why Watsonian behaviorism was not the immediate revolution that many histories have touted it to be. But it is important that you learn more than just what historians have discovered in their research. You should also learn something about the nature of the questions they asked and the methods they used to answer those questions. These are issues of historiography, which is the principal subject of this chapter.

HISTORIOGRAPHY DEFINED

Historiography refers to the philosophy and methods of doing history. Psychology is certainly guided by underlying philosophies and a diversity of research methods. A behaviorist, for example, has certain assumptions about the influence of previous experience, in terms of a history of punishment and reinforcement, on current behavior. And the methods of study take those assumptions into account in the design and conduct of experiments. A psychoanalytic psychologist, on the other hand, has a very different philosophy and methodology in investigating the questions of interest, for example, believing in the influence of unconscious motives and using techniques such as free association or analysis of latent dream content to understand those motives. Historical research is guided in the same way. So in the same way that it helps you understand psychology by knowing something about the philosophies and methods that underlie psychological research, it will help you understand history by knowing something about its philosophy and methods as well.

One of the principal questions in historiography is What is history? That question was mentioned earlier, but more will be said about it in the next section. In answering that question there are related questions to ponder as well such as: What are historical facts, and who or what determines if a fact has historical significance? Is objectivity possible in history? What is the nature of historical inquiry, and what are the different goals of historians? Finally, what are the resources and methods of research that historians use? Each of these questions will be addressed in the discussion that follows. Concluding this chapter will be a brief section on what has been called the "new history" of psychology. Such an introduction to historiography should help you evaluate more fully the content of this book and other histories that you may read.

WHAT IS HISTORY?

You have read that historians have defined their field variously as the study of the human mind, as the study of causes, as the study of behavior, and as the science of human nature, definitions that make history seem indistinguishable from psychology. Whereas these fields have many commonalities, they are not indistinguishable. As noted earlier, both use empirical methods to answer their respective questions. However, psychology, as a science, makes use of the experimental method. That means the psychologist can select variables for manipulation and then study the effects of that manipulation. The experiment is a powerful tool that allows the psychologist to determine cause-and-effect relationships. The historian is also interested in such relationships but must infer them from a reconstruction of past events where all the relevant variables have already been manipulated, in some cases centuries ago. Gilderhus (1992) has written: "For historians, the identification of cause-and-effect relationships establishes meaning and comprehensibility but can never be proven as literally true" (p. 6). History is not a science; however, as Commager (1965) notes, it is "clear that history uses or aspires to use the scientific method. That is, it tests all things which can be tested" (p. 12).

Psychologists typically study contemporary events (behaviors and mental processes), whereas historians study events of the distant past. Both might be interested in the same behavior, but the time frame and the methods are usually distinct. Psychologists are interested in marriage, for example, and they might study marriage using surveys, ex post facto methods, or quasi-experimental designs employing a sample of married couples (or perhaps divorced couples). Historians, on the other hand, would be likely to look at marriage, for example, as an institution in Victorian England, and they would be unable to use any of the methods listed here as part of the arsenal of the psychologist. The questions on marriage that would interest psychologists and historians might be similar: How are mates selected in marriage? At what age do people marry? What roles do wives and husbands play in these marriages? What causes marriages to end? But again, the methods of research and the time frame for the events would be different.

History, then, is the branch of knowledge that attempts to analyze and explain events of the past. The explanatory product is a narrative of those events, a story.

Henry Steele Commager (1965), one of America's most eminent historians, put it this way: "History is a story. That was its original character, and that has continued to be its most distinctive character. If history forgets or neglects to tell a story, it will inevitably forfeit much of its appeal and much of its authority as well" (p. 3). History is about telling stories and about the search for information that allows those stories to be told with considerable accuracy (see Butterfield, 1981). And the building blocks for those stories are facts; they are the information historians seek to be able to tell their stories. Facts are not the whole story, but they are the foundation of all good history. Just what is a fact, and who or what determines which facts have historical significance?

HISTORICAL FACTS AND THEIR SELECTIVITY

In Dragnet, a popular television police drama of the 1950s and 1960s, Detective Joe Friday frequently reminded the witnesses he was interviewing that he was interested only in the facts—"Just the facts, ma'am." Detective Friday, like most people, used the word *fact* to mean some kind of demonstrable truth, some real event whose occurrence cannot be disputed. Yet facts are more elusive, as evidenced in the typical dictionary definition that notes a fact is information that is "presented" as objectively real. Historians present as fact, for example, that an atomic bomb was dropped on the Japanese city of Hiroshima on August 6, 1945. And because of detailed records of that event, as well as many eyewitness accounts, that fact seems indisputable. It is the kind of fact that Carr (1961) has called the "backbone" of history, a fact on which virtually all historians would agree. But there are other kinds of facts.

In addition to the date of the bombing of Hiroshima, historians have presented a number of facts relevant to the decision made by the U.S. government to drop that bomb. Not surprisingly, those facts are more debatable. Thus facts differ in terms of their certainty. Sometimes that is because evidence is incomplete and many inferences have to be made, sometimes it is because evidence is contradictory, and sometimes it is because of bias introduced in the observation or in the interpretation of events. Flawed though they may be, facts are the basis of history. It is the job of the historian to uncover these items of the past and to piece them together in an account that is as accurate as can be constructed.

Not all facts are created equal; a few are of great interest to historians, whereas most are considered to have no historical significance at all. Carr (1961) has expressed it this way: "It is the historian who has decided for his own reasons that Caesar's crossing of that petty stream, the Rubicon, is a fact of history, whereas the crossing of the Rubicon by millions of other people before or since interests nobody at all" (p. 9). He notes that the fact that you crossed the street yesterday is as much a fact as Caesar's crossing the Rubicon, but it is unlikely that anyone will consider your street crossing a historically significant fact. So who determines what historical facts are important? Sometimes monarchs do. Sometimes governments do. Sometimes cultures do. And many times historians do. Thus, historians are selective.

Historians determine which facts they will look for and which facts they will not search out. Of the facts they find, they decide which ones they will use and how they will use them. Consider what we know about ancient Greece in the fifth century b.c. Carr (1961) has argued that our picture of Greece in that time is

> defective, not primarily because so many of the bits have been accidentally lost, but because it is, by and large, the picture formed by a tiny group of people in the city of Athens. We know a lot about what fifth-century Greece looked like to an Athenian citizen; but hardly anything about what it looked like to a Spartan, a Corinthian, or a Theban, not to mention a Persian, or a slave or other non-citizen resident in Athens. Our picture has been preselected and predetermined for us, not so much by accident as by people who were consciously or unconsciously imbued with a particular view and thought the facts which supported that view worth preserving. (p. 12)

Selectivity of facts is a part of contemporary history as well, and it is one of the factors inherent in the historian's concern with objectivity.

OBJECTIVITY IN HISTORY

Psychology was a late arrival in the house of sciences. Partly that was because there were many who agreed with philosopher Auguste Comte that the mind was capable of observing all phenomena but its own. A science of the mind would require that the mind study itself, and philosophers like Comte wondered how that would be possible. Surely psychology could not achieve the objectivity that is required of the other sciences. Whereas psychology is not without its share of subjectivity and bias, it has grown as a science, and its methodologies, particularly ways for controlling confounding variables, have matured in ways that have greatly increased its objectivity. History too has had to face these issues.

Objectivity is a critical goal for the historian. It has been referred to as "that noble dream" and has functioned as the guiding force for history since professional historians arrived on the scene in the nineteenth century (Novick, 1988). Carr (1961) has argued that objectivity is indeed only a dream: "The emphasis on the role of the historian in the making of history tends, if pressed to its logical conclusion, to rule out any objective history at all: history is what the historian makes" (p. 29).

Like psychologists, historians are human too, and they bring to their task a bundle of prejudices, preconceptions, penchants, predispositions, premises, and predilections. Such baggage does not mean that they abandon their hope for objectivity, nor does it mean that their histories are hopelessly flawed. Good historians know their biases. They use their understanding of them to search for evidence in places where they might not otherwise look or to ask questions that they would not ordinarily ask. And when this searching and questioning causes them to confront facts contrary to their own views, they must deal with those facts as they would with facts that are more consistent with their biases.

Bias in history begins at the beginning: "The historian displays a bias through the mere choice of a subject . . ." (Gilderhus, 1992, p. 80). There are an infinite number of historical subjects to pursue. The historian selects from among those, often choosing one of paramount personal interest. The search within that subject begins with a question or questions that the historian hopes to answer, and the historian likely starts with some definite ideas about the answers to those questions.

Bias is manifested in numerous other ways as well. Already noted are the selectivity of facts—a selection controlled to some degree by the historian—and the bias of nationalistic perspective illustrated by the Athenian view of Grecian history as opposed to that history as it might have been told by a Spartan.

Bias is evident too in the data of history. It can occur in primary source material, for example, census records or other government documents, even though such sources are often regarded as quite accurate. Yet such sources are inherently biased by the philosophies underlying the construction of the instruments themselves and the ways in which those instruments are used. Secondary sources too are flawed. Their errors occur in transcription, translation, selection, and interpretation.

Oral histories are filled with biases of the interviewer and the interviewee. Some questions are asked, others are not. Some are answered, others avoided. And memories of events long past are often unreliable. Manuscript collections, the substance of modern archives, are selective and incomplete. They contain the documents that someone decided were worth saving, and they are devoid of those documents that were discarded or lost for a host of reasons, perhaps known only to the discarder.

Biases are indigenous to the historian's high art of interpretation. Some historians have based their interpretations of the past on the context of the present, an error called "presentism" or "Whig history" by Butterfield (1931) or "present-mindedness" by Commager (1965). Not only do presentists seek to interpret the past in terms of the attitudes and values of the present, but they also seek to interpret the past in a way that emphasizes "certain principles of progress in the past and to produce a story which is the ratification if not the glorification of the present" (Butterfield, 1931, p. v). Avoiding this error of interpretation calls for a different approach that Stocking (1965) has labeled "historicism": an understanding of the past in its own context and for its own sake. Such an approach requires historians to immerse themselves in the context of the times they are studying.

These are just some of the hurdles that the historian faces in striving for objectivity. They are not described here to suggest that the historian's task is a hopeless one; instead, they are meant to show the forces against which historians must struggle in attempts at accuracy and objectivity. Daniels (1981) wrote: "The requirements of reasonable objectivity do not rule out individual interpretation and judgment . . . there is no final truth in matters of historical interpretation and explanation" (p. 92). There is only the expectation that the story will be as objective as is possible. Carr (1961) has characterized the striving for this ideal as follows:

> When we call a historian objective, we mean, I think, two things. First of all, we mean that he has the capacity to rise above the limited vision of his own situation in society and in history. . . . Secondly, we mean that he has the capacity to project his vision into the future in such a way as to give him a more profound and lasting insight into the past than can be attained by those historians whose outlook is entirely bounded by their own immediate situation. (p. 163)

In summary, history is a product of selection and interpretation. Knowing that helps us understand why books are usually titled "A History . . ." and not "The History . . .". There are many histories of psychology, and it would be surprising to find any historians so arrogant to presume that their individual narratives constitute "*The* History of Psychology."

THE NATURE OF HISTORICAL INQUIRY

Historians are clearly interested in the past, and for them to do their work some remnants of the past must be found. If no such traces exist, then there can be no history. History begins, as noted earlier, with the collecting of facts. These facts are then placed into some organized whole that allows for a description of the events in question. In this initial phase of historical research the historian is seeking to answer questions like What happened? When did it happen? Who was involved? In the history of psychology, we know that Wilhelm Wundt began laboratory research in psychology at the University of Leipzig in the 1870s. What was the nature of that lab? What was the physical space like? What kinds of equipment did he have? Did students work with him in his research? What kinds of studies were done in the lab? Who were the subjects (usually called observers) in these experiments? These questions are largely descriptive and are typically where the historian would begin in telling the story of Wundt's psychology laboratory.

As noted earlier, historians, however, want to go beyond description. They want to report more than just what happened and who was involved. They want to be able to say "why." This second phase is the riskier part of historical inquiry, but it is essential for the telling of the story. Just as the psychologist wants to go beyond merely describing behavior to offering some explanation for why the behavior occurred, the historian has a similar goal. And like psychological explanations of behavior, historical explanations are riskier because they are more speculative. They often are based on assumptions that exceed the data and on rationales that may or may not be accurate. They draw on the biases discussed earlier, including the historian's underlying assumptions about human motives. The historian is placed in the role of interpreter, trying to make sense of the assembled facts. Hard work and persistence can uncover the facts, but higher skills are needed to excel in interpretation. The great historians, according to Commager (1965), have been the interpreters. And among those, the greatest have been those with exceptional "judgment, originality, imagination, and art" (p. 6). Historian Arthur Schlesinger, Jr. (1963) has argued that it is in interpretation that history as art is evidenced:

> . . . all the elements of artistic form are as organic in historical as in any other kind of literary composition. There are limits on the historian's capacity for invention, but there need be none on his capacity for insight. Written history, after all, is the application of an aesthetic vision to a welter of facts; and both the weight and the vitality of a historical work depend on the quality of the vision. (p. 36)

It was noted earlier that history is about telling stories. Facts and a striving for accuracy of reconstruction of the past place limits on those stories. But history is a literary form, and in interpretation the literary art is manifested.

Gilderhus (1992) has argued that historical inquiry often proceeds to a third phase in which the historian evaluates the consequences of events. Did things turn out well? Ultimately, who benefited from what happened? Would a better result have occurred if the events had happened at a different time or place, or maybe had never happened? Such evaluations, not surprisingly, have led to many disagreements among historians. Still, these evaluations are often part of the intellectual and artistic goals of historical writing.

CONTEMPORARY HISTORICAL RESEARCH

Historical writing is said to have begun in the fifth century B.C. in the works of Herodotus and Thucydides. These earliest of historians sought to learn the facts of past events, albeit recent past events, that would allow them to render accounts of truth. They wrote of great wars, a subject that has remained a principal theme of many subsequent histories. Indeed, until the twentieth century much of the focus of history was on war and governments, that is, on events that were largely political. Individuals, who were the subjects described in these histories, were kings and generals, people who were presumed to be historically important because of the ways in which their actions changed their world. Painters painted these same subjects, composers honored them in their ballads and symphonies, playwrights made them the subjects of the stage, and historians wrote books about them.

Today, history is very different; both the subject matter of histories and the individuals portrayed in those histories are far more diverse than anything early historians would have ever imagined. Historians today still write about the subjects of old, but they also write about common people, people whose lives had no significant impact on a society but whose common lives reveal something important about the nature of life in that society. In the same way that Pieter Brueghel (the Elder) transformed painting in the sixteenth century from portraits of the rich and famous to paintings of the lives of ordinary people, historians of the twentieth century recognized that the standard historical accounts were incomplete. A change in historical philosophy emphasizing social history greatly broadened the definition of history's subject matter. Although much of contemporary historical writing is about politics, wars, and governments, it is also about peoples whose histories have often been unreported, for example, women and African Americans, and about subjects that have rarely been covered, such as art, marriage, agricultural methods, child rearing, and the care of the mentally ill.

One of the subjects of importance in twentieth-century history is the history of science. Although the typical survey courses in American history still give little attention to the history of science and the incredibly important role played by science and technology in shaping history in the past 100 years, history of science scholarship is thriving. And the history of psychology and related behavioral sciences is an important part of the contemporary scene. As noted earlier, a number of the articles reprinted in the subsequent chapters of this book are indicative of today's scholarship in the history of psychology. As background for a better appreciation of those articles, the next two sections discuss the resources and research methods used by these historians.

RESOURCES IN HISTORY

The facts of history can be found in a multitude of places. They are in the books and articles written by historians and others. Those facts come preselected and preinterpreted by the authors, a reality of using secondary sources, as previously noted. The primary sources, although closer to the events in question, are not without their biases. The primary source material ranges widely in kind and includes government documents, business sales records, personal correspondence, patent records, taped or transcribed interviews, diaries, court documents, laboratory notes, patient records, association records, and school documents. And the locations too are many: archives, libraries, schools, corporations, small businesses, courthouses, newspaper files, attics, basements, and garages. In the course of a research project, the historian may search a number of these locations, looking at a variety of records. Let me give you an example from my own research, an investigation of the Coca-Cola court trials in the early 1900s that resulted from a federal government suit against Coca-Cola for marketing a beverage with a deleterious ingredient, namely, caffeine (Benjamin, Rogers, & Rosenbaum, 1991). (This study is reprinted in Chapter 15 of this book.)

I was interested in this case because it marked one of the earliest instances of a psychologist being hired by a large corporation to do psychological research to be used in court. The case began when Harvey Wiley, a chemist and important administrator for the U.S. Department of Agriculture, directed federal agents to seize a shipment of Coca-Cola syrup as it crossed state lines into Tennessee. The trial was scheduled to begin in the spring of 1911, and as the Coca-Cola Company prepared for its defense, it realized that it had no behavioral data on the effects of caffeine on humans. So it hired a recently graduated psychologist, Harry Hollingworth, to do that research. The case progressed through three trials, starting in Chattanooga, followed by another trial before the Appeals Court in Cincinnati, and finally to a 1916 trial before the U.S. Supreme Court.

The search for the information needed to tell that story led to a number of places. The papers of Harry Hollingworth were found at the Archives of the History of American Psychology at the University of Akron in Ohio. Other relevant Hollingworth materials were found at the Nebraska State Historical Society in Lincoln, whose collection included a 600-page unpublished autobiography that Hollingworth had written in 1940. Harvey Wiley's papers were found at the Library of Congress in Washington, D.C. Also there were the papers of James McKeen Cattell, the first psychologist contacted by Coca-Cola to do the research but who declined the offer.

The court records from the three trials were found in National Archives repositories in Atlanta, Chicago, and Washington, D.C. The court record from the Chattanooga trial alone was more than 3,000 pages. Other important documents were found at the Coca-Cola Archives located in Atlanta and in the Coca-Cola papers housed at Emory University, also in Atlanta.

Published sources included the scientific literature on caffeine prior to 1911; biographies of Wiley, including an autobiography; books and articles on the Pure Food and Drug Act of 1906, which was the law used to seize the shipment; histories of the Coca-Cola Company; magazine articles written by Wiley on the dangers of caffeine; the daily local newspaper coverage of the three trials (from microfilm records); Coca-Cola advertisements in magazines from 1906 to 1915; and Hollingworth's own published account of his caffeine studies, as well as the subsequent reviews of those studies and citations of that research in later books and journal articles.

History research is often like detective work; the search for one piece of evidence leads to the search for another and another. One has to follow all leads, some of which produce no useful information. When all the leads have been exhausted, you can analyze the facts to see if they are sufficient for telling the story. In the case of the Coca-Cola trials, that search required almost fifteen years. It was not a full-time effort, but it is indicative of the time typically required in historical studies, particularly those that have produced landmark books.

ARCHIVAL RESEARCH

Contemporary research in the history of psychology makes great use of archival collections. Archival research does not constitute a methodology per se; rather, it is related to research goals, the nature of the archival materials, the finding aids that exist, and the search strategies employed. Undoubtedly the most comprehensive guide to locating a particular manuscript collection is the *National Union Catalog of Manuscript Collections,* a reference guide to collections throughout the United States. Although this reference work contains listings of thousands of collections, it is certainly not complete. Its accuracy depends on archives sending in descriptions of their collections to the *Catalog*'s editor.

Many archives do not do that for their smaller collections, so often those go unlisted.

A number of guides to archival collections exist (see Larsen, 1988), many of them organized by disciplinary field. For example, there is a guide to manuscript collections in psychology and related areas, compiled by Michael Sokal and Patrice Rafail (1982), that describes more than 500 collections in North America. This book is an excellent place to begin searching for archives and manuscript collections; its date, however, means that a number of psychology collections deposited since it was published are not listed. A typical listing from that book is as follows:

Jastrow, Joseph, 1863–1944
Papers, 1875–1961. 995 items and 14 vols.
In Duke University Library (Durham, North Carolina)
Psychologist and professor at the University of Wisconsin. Correspondence, manuscripts of lectures, speeches, prose, and poetry; and copies of published articles, book reviews, and newspaper clippings. Subjects include the Jastrow family of Philadelphia and the Szold family of Baltimore, the University of Wisconsin at Madison, Judaism in Baltimore and Philadelphia, and the Zionist movement. Correspondents include Marcus Jastrow and Henrietta Szold. Card index in the library. Gift, 1959.

Typically, these entries indicate the size of the collection, the range of years covered by the materials, the principal subject matter of the collection, the location of the collection, and whether or not there are any special restrictions on using the collection. The listings in the *National Union Catalog of Manuscript Collections* use a similar format.

All archives have a set of finding aids to help the researcher locate relevant materials. Some finding aids are more comprehensive than others. They include inventories of the various collections, indexes to correspondents, and name and subject indexes that cut across collections in the archives. Still, despite the best of research strategies, good luck is often as important as diligence. As Brozek (1975) has described it, "In comparison with a history based on already published materials, archival research is apt to be a 'higher risk, higher gain' operation" (p. 15). Hill (1993) also has acknowledged the riskiness of archival work: "Investigations in archives simply cannot be predicted. . . . That for me is an attraction, but to others it may seem too indeterminate, too risky" (p. 6). Despite its high-risk nature, archival research provides us with unique value in historical research because the material is itself unique.

Cadwallader (1975) listed the following as the special values of archival labors: unsuspected aspects of history may be discovered, unsuspected personal influences may be revealed, professional politics can be seen to influence personal careers and thus the shape of history, and a more balanced picture of an individual's personality is often revealed through her or his personal correspondence and diaries.

In archival research, one typically begins in one archival collection and then pursues related material through other archives, following wherever the leads suggest going. Collections are rarely, if ever, complete. Some documents relating to important questions are almost always missing. Occasionally, documents that were once part of the collection are missing, sometimes stolen by an unscrupulous "scholar." Some materials may be inaccessible, sealed until a certain time because of donor restrictions. Other problems include finding only one side of a correspondence, a problem partially alleviated by the invention of carbon paper in the 1920s and sometimes solved by finding the other side in another archive.

Perhaps the greatest "problem" in archival research is one of its joys; it is the continual distraction created by materials not related to the research purposes at hand. I refer to this disorder as *Documentus distractus,* a condition that produces disorientation and distortions in time perception. The affected researcher begins to read documents that are wholly irrelevant to the research effort. In its acute form, this disease greatly prolongs the time required for completion of the intended project. The more serious chronic form typically causes the researcher to abandon one project for a new one, which is subsequently abandoned, and so forth, and so forth. Although this problem uses up valuable time in the archives intended for use on the target project, the experienced archival researcher learns to accept it. These distractions often produce discoveries that are quite informative. In my own research, for example, I once pulled two folders from an archival box when I had meant to look at only the first folder. The second was marked "PRT," and reading the few letters it contained led me to discover a secret psychological society founded in 1936 called the Psychological Round Table, a by-invitation-only organization of young, male experimental psychologists, run by a group known as the Secret Six. This secret society still exists today (women were admitted beginning in 1971), meeting annually, and kicking out members once they turn 40 years of age (see Benjamin, 1977).

Sometimes these serendipitous events refuse to be ignored. Gloria Urch (1992) was searching the records in a county historical society when she discovered Rachel Harris, whom she describes as perhaps the only African-American nurse during the United States Civil War era:

> I was looking for something else when I found her photo. . . . I held it for a moment and studied it. . . . I put her photo aside and continued my research. A few minutes later the photo—which I thought I had placed securely on the shelf above me—fell into my lap, and those same eyes were gazing up into mine again. Before I left that day I made a copy of Rachel's photo and obituary and tucked it away. (p. 8)

And that discovery started Urch on her quest to learn about the life and career of this unknown nurse.

Note that the discovery of Rachel Harris began with perhaps a casual interest in finding out a bit more about this nineteenth-century nurse. Intellectual curiosity usually begins the search; the excitement over discovery often comes later. Archival work is a source of great pleasure to historians, a point that is typically difficult for others to realize. The hours spent in these collections go by all too quickly. Often the researcher is waiting at the door when the archive opens in the morning and has to be told to leave at closing time. The hours in between are arguably the most enjoyable for the historical worker. Michael Hill (1993) has described the joys of archival research in this way:

> Archival work appears bookish and commonplace to the uninitiated, but this mundane simplicity is deceptive. It bears repeating that events and materials in archives are not always what they seem on the surface. There are perpetual surprises, intrigues, and apprehensions. . . . Suffice it to say that it is a rare treat to visit an archive, to hold in one's hand the priceless and irreplaceable documents of our unfolding human drama. Each new box of archival material presents opportunities for discovery as well as obligations to treat the subjects of your . . . research with candor, theoretical sophistication, and a sense of fair play. Each archival visit is a journey into an unknown realm that rewards its visitors with challenging puzzles and unexpected revelations. (pp. 6–7)

The papers of important psychologists are spread among archives and libraries all over the world. In the United States, you will find the papers of William James and B. F. Skinner in the collections at Harvard University. The papers of Hugo Münsterberg, a pioneer in the application of psychology to business, can be found at the Boston Public Library. The papers of Mary Whiton Calkins and Christine Ladd-Franklin, important early contributors to experimental psychology, can be found at Wellesley College, and at Vassar College and Columbia University, respectively. The Library of Congress includes the papers of James McKeen Cattell and Kenneth B. Clark. Cattell was one of the founders of American psychology and a leader among American scientists in general, and Clark, an African-American psychologist, earned fame when his research on self-esteem in black children was cited prominently in the U.S. Supreme Court decision that made school segregation illegal (*Brown* vs. *Board of Education,* 1954).

As noted earlier, the single largest collection of archival materials on psychology anywhere in the world is the Archives of the History of American Psychology (AHAP), located at the University of Akron. This archive opened in 1965 and has grown enormously in terms of the size and importance of its collection. Today, it contains the papers of more than 900 individuals and organizations. In addition to extensive manuscript collections of unpublished materials, AHAP contains more than 500 pieces of early psychological apparatus, a large collection of standardized psychological tests, an extensive photo collection, a collection of more than 4,000 films, and a large collection of rare books on the history of psychology. The collection includes the papers of such psychologists as Knight Dunlap, Henry H. Goddard, Harry and Leta Hollingworth, Kurt Koffka, Walter Miles, and Abraham Maslow, and of such organizations as the American Group Psychotherapy Association, the Association for Humanistic Psychology, and the Midwestern Psychological Association.

The archive at Akron, although unique as a central repository for American psychology, is one of many archival collections available to researchers interested in psychology's past. As you read the articles in this book written by researchers in the history of psychology, you will see the pervasive influence of archival materials on contemporary scholarship.

ORAL HISTORY

When the events of interest are historically recent, that is, within the last seventy-five years or so, a source of information for the historian is the oral history. The oral history is an autobiographical account, a personal history, usually in response to an interviewer and recorded on audiotape or videotape. Oral history research

> . . . is a test of other people, of the accuracy of their memories, of their ability to assess their own lives realistically, and of their ability to profit from experience. In a sense it is a test of other people as historians, a test of how well they can deal with their personal histories. But oral history research is also a test of ourselves, of our ability to deserve and win the confidence of other people, of our ability to deal sympathetically but honestly and imaginatively with their memories, and of our ability to deal honestly with ourselves. (Hoopes, 1979, p. 5)

The oral historian, who is the person who will serve as the interviewer, must prepare carefully for the oral history. Following contact with the person to be interviewed, the oral historian collects relevant documents, perhaps including unpublished materials such as correspondence, and asks for names of persons (colleagues, friends, students) who might be contacted prior to the interview. The interviewer should read whatever books and articles are relevant to the subject, including any written by the interviewee and those written about that individual's life or work. At the end of the preparation, the oral historian should be *very familiar* with the facts surrounding the content of the history to be taken. Typically, an outline is prepared that lists the topics and subtopics to be covered in the interview.

The rules for the conduct of the interview can be quite specific (see Hoopes, 1979; Lummis, 1987). They describe acceptable limits for socializing, the balance that must be struck between leading the interview and dominating it, and procedures both for following up on questions to complete the record and for backing off when the interviewee does not wish to pursue discussion in a particular area. Usually a transcript is typed from the tape, in part to protect preservation of the taped material. Often the transcript is sent to the interviewee for editing to promote accuracy (see Baum, 1981).

In short, an oral history is not a casual chat between interviewer and interviewee although some "histories" are taken in that way. An oral history will be as valuable as the preparation that goes into it. Professional oral historians know that and prepare, often for months, for an encounter that may last only a day or two. They are knowledgeable about both the method and the content of the interview. As a result, the quality of their product is significantly better than that of interviewers more casual in their approach.

Some archives, recognizing the unique value of oral histories, have collected these personal accounts. The archives at the University of Akron have a large collection of these histories in psychology. Two collections of approximately 175 oral histories on the subjects of child development and child guidance are housed in the National Library of Medicine in Bethesda, Maryland. Another large collection of more than 100 oral histories of American psychologists can be found in the American Psychological Association Archives, which are part of the collections of the Library of Congress. And a similar collection of tapes and transcripts on more than 100 Canadian psychologists is housed in the Public Archives of Canada in Ottawa, Ontario.

Often oral history data are criticized on the basis of poor reliability. Because the oral history may involve recall of events many years in the past, that recall is suspect. Further, the interviewee is not always forthright in answering questions and may slant answers, even unintentionally, in a self-serving way. That is, the person being interviewed may respond "truthfully," but it will be the truth as he or she wishes to remember it. These problems with oral history data are both significant and controversial. Some historians have argued that both problems—of recall and bias—should be addressed in order to reduce the error in oral histories. They suggest that to deal with errors of recall, one should try to corroborate the testimony with written records or with the testimony from other individuals who would have knowledge of the same events. In terms of the personal bias of the subject, they suggest interviewing other persons who would have reason to hold different biases, thus broadening the perspective on the content in question. Of course, sometimes those cross-checks are not possiblc.

Trevor Lummis (1987) has questioned the critics who have labeled oral history data unreliable. He has argued: "The value of oral evidence as a historical source must ultimately be established within its own authenticity. If it is accepted as authentic only when confirmed by documentary sources then one might as well use the documents" (p. 155). He reminds the critics that documentary evidence is not without its own bias, as we have noted earlier, and that ". . . history does not happen in documents. Human activity happens . . ." (p. 13) before being recorded by someone. And clearly there is opportunity for biases being introduced in that recording. For Lummis and his colleagues in oral history, oral histories provide historical evidence of independent value. These proponents of oral history do not deny the flaws in this method, and they take steps in the evaluation of oral history data to minimize errors of fact and interpretation. Still, they argue for the special value of oral histories as sources for personal feelings and motives, information that may be impossible to recover from any other kind of historical evidence.

In summary, oral history data are valuable in their own right and a complement to other data sources in history. In some cases, they may be the only data, for example, in situations where no written records have been made. They are particularly valuable in revealing personal information about emotions and motives, about self-awareness, and about personality. These important records can significantly enhance the historian's role in the telling of stories.

QUANTITATIVE METHODS

Although quantitative methods have enjoyed popularity in a number of historical fields (see Jarausch & Hardy, 1991), they have become part of the historiography of psychology only in the past twenty-five years. Content analysis and citation analysis are two of the more frequently used quantitative approaches in psychology, and in recent years both have benefited considerably from the convenience of computer analysis.

Content analysis is a method that converts verbal, written, or other kinds of symbolic material into categories and numbers in order that statistical operations might be performed on the material (see Holsti, 1969). The method is typically used to quantify material that is largely qualitative. Although the method is not without its critics, its use has brought some degree of objectivity and meaning to subject areas that were often in great disarray. One begins by formulating a system of classification, that is, a system of categories that are usually mutually exclusive. Those categories should be clearly defined so that there will be good interjudge reliability in determining what material should be included in what categories. Further, the unit of analysis must be specified: words, phrases, sentences, headings, pages, or chapters.

Some examples of historical questions and materials that could be subjected to content analysis are What were the intellectual themes expressed in William James's letters? How did research methodologies change over time in the articles of the *American Journal of Psychology* between 1887 and 1930? What common themes can be found in the presidential addresses for the American Psychological Association from 1892 to 1940? Virtually any written materials can be subjected to content analysis, for example, psychology department catalogs, oral history transcripts, laboratory notes, and introductory psychology textbooks. For an example of its use in psychology, see Cardno's (1965) analysis of Victorian psychology.

In short, the strategy in using content analysis is to choose a content domain of interest, develop appropriate categories for the analysis, decide on the unit of analysis, and then analyze the content domain. Often the analysis reveals features of the material that were not apparent in merely reading that material.

Citation analysis, or citation indexing as it is sometimes called, is the study of relationships of published material through an analysis of citation networks (see Garfield, 1964, 1979). As it is used in history, the purpose is often to discover the influence of a particular publication or publications on subsequent writing in the field or to trace the evolution of ideas through a quantitative analysis of citations. The technique is laborious, is often tedious, and requires access to extensive library sources.

A major development in this field has been the work of the Institute for Scientific Information, located in Philadelphia, which publishes the *Science Citation Index* (begun in 1963) and the *Social Sciences Citation Index* (begun in 1973). Both indexes are cumulated (annually and every five years) and are published six times a year for *SCI* and three times a year for *SSCI*. These indexes reveal the relationships among publications through citations.

Citation analysis can provide one measure of the importance of a particular publication, that is, how frequently the publication is cited. Other questions that could be answered using this technique include In what subfields of psychology is the publication cited? Does the frequency of citations increase or decrease over the years? Thus, from the point of view of the historian, one can get answers to questions about the influence of a particular theory and the evolution of ideas, that is, the issues of intellectual history in psychology.

If you would like to see some examples of how this technique is used in history of psychology research, the following are recommended: Elizabeth Scarborough's (1971) analysis of the influence on contemporary psychology of an 1868 paper on mental reaction time written by F. C. Donders, Josef Brozek's (1980) study of the decay of Wilhelm Wundt's influence on American psychology, and Franz Samelson's (1981) analysis of the influence of John Watson's 1913 behaviorist manifesto (see Chapter 11 of this book).

Other quantitative methods have also been used in historical research in psychology, such as a hypothesis-testing procedure known as *historiometry*. This method is actually more than 100 years old but has been applied to historical questions in psychology in recent years largely through the work of Dean Keith Simonton (1990). He defines historiometry as the use of quantitative techniques to test hypotheses about the behavior of historical individuals. The ultimate goal of historiometry is the discovery of general principles that are descriptive of a certain class of individuals, for example, Nobel Prize winners, generals, composers, and presidents of the American Psychological Association. The method begins with defining a hypothesis in components that are quantifiable and then testing those hypotheses. In Simonton's own work, he has used this technique to investigate the causal relationship between war and scientific discovery, the relationship of creative productivity to age, the factors associated with greatness in American presidents, and the genius and creativity of individuals important in the history of psychology.

THE NEW HISTORY OF PSYCHOLOGY

In the middle of the 1970s, as the history of psychology as a specialty began its second decade, it underwent a change that many would argue reflected an important maturational step for the field (Furumoto, 1989). Research and writing in the history of psychology progressed from ceremonial history to critical history, a change that mirrored historical evolution in other fields as well. The "new history" movement came from both psychologist historians and from historians of science who were working in the history of psychology. They called for a number of changes in the way the history of psychology was being done; most of those changes were conceptual rather than methodological.

First, advocates of the new history called for a more critical history that examined the givens that form the myths of psychology. They cautioned against the fictions that were often created in moments of celebration and ceremony (for example, the 100th anniversary of Wundt's laboratory). They asked for a more objective evaluation of individuals and events and called for histories that adopted new perspectives in looking at familiar subjects. The celebration of the centennial of the American Psychological Association in 1992 is a case in point. As part of the celebration of that event, historian Michael Sokal (1992) wrote an article on the origins of the APA, providing a somewhat unflattering portrait of G. Stanley Hall, APA's founder and first president. Such an article, critical of Hall, likely would not have been written twenty years earlier in the history of psychology. Critical history does not mean character assassination of the idols of psychology's past. Rather, it is a thorough and objective examination of the record, published and unpublished, that allows the chips to fall where they may.

In terms of resources, the new history of psychology has made greater use of archival sources and primary documents. And in terms of philosophy, there has been greater attention to the dangers of interpretive errors, such as presentism. There has also been a much greater interest in intellectual history, that is, focusing on the history of ideas rather than on the great personalities of psychology.

Perhaps of greatest importance, the new history of psychology has adopted what is often called an externalist approach, contrasted with the internalist work of the old history of psychology (Hilgard, Leary, & McGuire, 1991). External histories are those that move outside the narrow confines of the discipline to recognize the broader sociocultural context in which psychology has emerged. For example, one could write a history of business psychology that focused entirely on the early psychologists who did contract research for various businesses. That is, the story would be told by staying solely within that segment of the discipline of psychology. But such an internalist history would be an impoverished one. It would not only misrepresent the history of business psychology in terms of errors of omission but would also distort that history by ignoring a potential host of external variables that shaped what was happening within psychology. Clearly psychology does not exist in a vacuum. What happens in psychology influences events outside psychology and, of greater importance, events outside psychology shape the field considerably. An external history means that the history of psychology is told in the context of the social, cultural, political, economic, and geographic factors that affect it.

The impact of the new history of psychology has been a richer product for both the scholar and the student of history. It has encouraged scholarship in new fields, particularly in social history. And it has emphasized the importance of context in history and the need for psychology to be seen in the context in which it developed.

Many of the contemporary selections reprinted in this book are representative of this new history. As you read these selections, I encourage you to keep in mind the lessons of this chapter. See if you can identify the questions that led the authors to their research. What methods did they use? What are the facts of their stories, and where did they uncover those facts? What archival records were used? What conclusions did they draw, and do those conclusions seem to be supported by the evidence? With your knowledge of historiography, you should have a greater appreciation of the important stories that these historians tell.

REFERENCES

Baum, W. K. (1981). *Transcribing and editing oral histories.* Nashville, TN: American Association for State and Local History.

Benjamin, L. T., Jr. (1977). The Psychological Round Table: Revolution of 1936. *American Psychologist, 32,* 542–549.

Benjamin, L. T., Jr. (1980). Research at the Archives of the History of American Psychology: A case history. In J. Brozek & L. J. Pongratz (Eds.), *Historiography of modern psychology,* (pp. 241–251). Toronto: Hogrefe.

Benjamin, L. T., Jr., Rogers, A. M., & Rosenbaum, A. (1991). Coca-Cola, caffeine, and mental deficiency: Harry Hollingworth and the Chattanooga trial of 1911. *Journal of the History of the Behavioral Sciences, 27,* 42–55.

Brozek, J. (1975). Irons in the fire: Introduction to a symposium on archival research. *Journal of the History of the Behavioral Sciences, 11,* 15–19.

Brozek, J. (1980). The echoes of Wundt's work in the United States, 1887–1977: A quantitative citation analysis. *Psychological Research, 42,* 103–107.

Butterfield, H. (1931). *The Whig interpretation of history.* London: G. Bell & Sons.

Butterfield, H. (1981). *The origins of history.* New York: Basic Books.

Cadwallader, T. C. (1975). Unique value of archival research. *Journal of the History of the Behavioral Sciences, 11,* 27–33.

Cardno, J. A. (1965). Victorian psychology: A biographical approach. *Journal of the History of the Behavioral Sciences, 1,* 165–177.

Carr, E. H. (1961). *What is history?* New York: Random House.

Collingwood, R. G. (1946). *The idea of history.* London: Oxford University Press.

Commager, H. S. (1965). *The nature and the study of history.* Columbus, OH: Charles Merrill.

Daniels, R. V. (1981). *Studying history: How and why* (3rd ed.). Englewood Cliffs, NJ: Prentice Hall.

Furumoto, L. (1989). The new history of psychology. In I. S. Cohen (Ed.), *The G. Stanley Hall lecture series, Vol. 9,* (pp. 8–34). Washington, DC: American Psychological Association.

Garfield, E. (1964). Citation indexing: A natural science literature retrieval system for the social sciences. *American Behavioral Scientist, 7,* 58–61.

Garfield, E. (1979). *Citation indexing: Its theory and application in science, technology, and humanities.* New York: Wiley.

Gilderhus, M. T. (1992). *History and historians: A historiographical introduction* (2nd ed.). Englewood Cliffs, NJ: Prentice-Hall.

Hilgard, E. R., Leary, D. E., & McGuire, G. R. (1991). The history of psychology: A survey and critical assessment. *Annual Review of Psychology, 42,* 79–107.

Hill, M. R. (1993). *Archival strategies and techniques.* Newbury Park, CA: Sage Publications.

Holsti, O. R. (1969). *Content analysis for the social sciences and humanities.* Reading, MA: Addison-Wesley.

Hoopes, J. (1979). *Oral history: An introduction for students.* Chapel Hill: University of North Carolina Press.

Jarausch, K. H., & Hardy, K. A. (1991). *Quantitative methods for historians.* Chapel Hill: University of North Carolina Press.

Larsen, J. C. (Ed.). (1988). *Researcher's guide to archives and regional history sources.* Hamden, CT: Library Professional Publications.

Lummis, T. (1987). *Listening to history: The authenticity of oral evidence.* London: Hutchinson.

Novick, P. (1988). *That noble dream: The "objectivity question" and the American historical profession.* New York: Cambridge University Press.

Popplestone, J. A., & McPherson, M. W. (1976). Ten years at the Archives of the History of American Psychology. *American Psychologist, 31,* 533–534.

Samelson, F. (1981). Struggle for scientific authority: The reception of Watson's behaviorism, 1913–1920. *Journal of the History of the Behavioral Sciences, 17,* 399–425.

Scarborough (Goodman), E. (1971). Citation analysis as a tool in historical study: A case study based on F. C. Donders and mental reaction times. *Journal of the History of the Behavioral Sciences, 7,* 187–191.

Schlesinger, A., Jr. (1963, July). The historian as artist. *Atlantic Monthly, 12,* 35–41.

Simonton, D. K. (1990). *Psychology, science, & history: An introduction to historiometry.* New Haven, CT: Yale University Press.

Sokal, M. M. (1992). Origins and early years of the American Psychological Association, 1890–1906. *American Psychologist, 47,* 111–122.

Sokal, M. M., & Rafail, P. A. (Eds.) (1982). *A guide to manuscript collections in the history of psychology and related areas.* Millwood, NY: Kraus International Publishers.

Stocking, G. W., Jr. (1965). On the limits of 'presentism' and 'historicism' in the historiography of the behavioral sciences. *Journal of the History of the Behavioral Sciences, 1,* 211–218.

Urch, G. (1992, August 9). Seeing the world through Rachel's eyes. *Chicago Tribune,* section 6, p. 8 (as cited in Hill, 1993).

CHAPTER 2

PHILOSOPHICAL ROOTS OF PSYCHOLOGY: MECHANISM AND EMPIRICISM

The Renaissance, which began in the fourteenth century and lasted through the early part of the seventeenth century, started in Italy and spread to the rest of Europe. It represented a revival of interest in, and new approaches to, art, literature, and knowledge, including science. It was the era of Michelangelo and Leonardo Da Vinci, of Shakespeare and Chaucer, and of Copernicus and Galileo. Its importance for science, including the science of psychology, is that the late Renaissance marked an end to the dominance of *rationalism,* a philosophy that sought knowledge through reason and common sense. Replacing rationalism was a belief that knowledge should be acquired through observation and experimentation, a philosophy that signaled the beginning of the *scientific method.* Psychology, as an experimental science, would grow from the post–Renaissance developments in philosophy and from eighteenth- and nineteenth-century physiological studies of the nervous system and sensory mechanisms (discussed in the next chapter).

A new world view emerged from the Renaissance, most significantly due to the work of Galileo Galilei (1564–1642). For Galileo, the universe comprised matter in motion; minute particles of one object come into contact with particles of another object, causing movement or a change in the second object. This view of the world was known as *mechanism,* and because it conceived of the universe as a giant machine, it implied that lawful explanations of the universe were possible. Like any machine, the universe would operate in an orderly way, and if so, its operation could be understood by discovering the laws that governed it. The order and lawfulness meant that actions in the universe could be predicted by understanding the causal relationships within the world. Such a view was an especially important advance for science.

But if humans were part of the universe, could not they also be viewed as machines? The answer was yes according to French philosopher and mathematician René Descartes (1596–1650), who extended the mechanistic view to human behavior. Descartes viewed the human body as a material entity that functioned as a machine, whereas the mind was nonmaterial and free to carry out the functions of consciousness. According to Descartes, however, the mind and body interacted with each other in such a way that not only did the mind influence the body but also the body influenced the mind, a view now referred to as interactive dualism. This idea, radical at the time, provided an excellent explanation for involuntary (reflexive) behavior and voluntary behavior. In adding human actions to the mechanistic world view, Descartes was arguing that human behavior was lawful and that the causes could be understood. He also localized the functions of the mind in the brain, whereas some earlier views had assigned certain mental processes, such as emotion, to such organs as the liver and heart.

Descartes was interested in the nature of the human mind. He proposed that mind consisted of two kinds of ideas: *innate ideas,* such as self and God, and *derived ideas,* which are acquired through experience in the world. Descartes studied the mind through a technique that he called meditation, an introspective approach, that is, an inward looking at the contents of the mind. In his meditative studies, he stressed reason over perception and innate ideas over experience. He was thus both a rationalist and a mechanist, a philosophical combination that some historians (for example, Leahey, 1992) have labeled paradoxical. [Such unlikely philosophical partners have coexisted in other great thinkers such as Issaac Newton (1642–1727), who developed a mechanistic view of the world using rationalist methods in his *Philosophiae Naturalis Principia Mathematica,* published in 1687.] Yet for Descartes, it was his mechanistic views that ultimately contributed to an empirical psychology.

In contrast to Descartes's notion of innate ideas and knowledge by reason stood the British *empiricists,* a group of philosophers who spanned a period of approximately 200 years, beginning with John Locke (1632–1704). Locke rejected the notion of innate ideas and argued forcefully that all ideas were derived from experience. Resurrecting Aristotle's idea of *tabula rasa,* Locke described how experience would write on the blank slate of the mind, thus filling the mind with the sum total of its ideas. Although all ideas were derived from experience, they were not all derived from direct sensory experience; some were the products of the mind from the processes of reflection, or what Locke called the internal operations of the mind. Thus one could know a rose from direct sensory experience, sensing its aroma, color, and texture. But it was also possible to experience the rose when it was not present by reflecting on these earlier experiences. These ideas of reflection were thus derived wholly from the mind and were not the product of any sensory contact of the moment.

Unlike Descartes, Locke was more interested in how the mind works, that is, how it acquires knowledge, than in what it actually knows. He studied that question for twenty years, writing and rewriting his most important work for psychology, *An Essay Concerning Human Understanding,* which was finally published in 1690. Many historians use the publication of that book to mark the formal beginning of British empiricism.

In this classic work, Locke discussed the origin and nature of ideas, drawing distinctions between *simple* and *complex ideas* and *primary* and *secondary qualities*. Simple ideas are derived from either sensory experience or reflection, but complex ideas are the product only of reflection. Primary and secondary qualities he distinguished as follows: Primary qualities are sensory qualities that exist in an object, such as the thorny shape of a rose stem or the whiteness of a feather. Secondary qualities exist in the experiencing individual and are not a part of the object itself, for example, the pain experienced from the rose thorn or the tickle from the feather. That is, the pain is not part of the rose thorn, nor is the tickle part of the feather. Instead, these qualities of sensory experience are part of the individual. Locke's distinction between primary and secondary qualities was especially important for the science of psychology because it recognized experience that was independent of physical objects of the world. In essence, these secondary qualities were products of the mind, and as such they were the very basis of psychological study.

Empiricism continued through the work of George Berkeley (1685–1753), especially in terms of observations on sensory systems such as vision. Berkeley disagreed with Locke's distinction between primary and secondary qualities, arguing that only the latter could really be known to exist. For Berkeley, all knowledge was dependent on the experiencing individual, and qualities of objects existed only as perceived.

Berkeley was followed by David Hartley (1705–1757) and David Hume (1711–1776), whose principal interests were in learning, or what they called *association.* They were particularly interested in how ideas became associated with one another to form the complex ideas about which Locke had written. Both men emphasized contiguity as a fundamental law of association; that is, ideas that were adjacent to one another in space or time were likely to be associated with one another. In their work, they sought to determine the limits of contiguity in forming associations.

Continuing in the empiricist–associationist tradition were the Mills, father James Mill (1773–1836) and his son John Stuart Mill (1806–1873). James Mill recognized that some associations were formed more easily than others and that some were more lasting. His extremely mechanical view of the mind described a set of factors that determined the strength and durability of associations. John Stuart Mill extended his father's work on association, but his most important work for psychology was *A System of Logic,* published in 1843. In this book, Mill argued for the feasibility of a science of psychology.

Whether or not psychology could be a science was a hotly debated topic in Mill's time since many agreed with positivist philosopher Auguste Comte

(1798–1857) that there could be no science of the mind because the mind was not capable of studying its own processes. Although Mill acknowledged that psychology was, in his time, an inexact science, he believed it was as precise as some sciences, such as astronomy, and worthy of study. He called for an empirical, but not experimental, science of psychology. His ideas would later be an important influence on the German philosopher and physiologist Wilhelm Wundt, who would found the first scientific laboratory in psychology.

From Descartes and Locke to John Stuart Mill, the approaches to studying the mind enjoyed an evolution that deepened the emphases of mechanism and empiricism. The British empiricists stressed the role of sensations, the nature of ideas, how those ideas were acquired, and how more complex ideas were formed through associations. These areas of philosophical inquiry would form the basis for the study of consciousness in the experimental psychology that was about to take shape in Germany (the subject of Chapter 5).

THE READINGS

Four selections are presented in this chapter. The first was written by Descartes and published as the sixth meditation in his *Meditations on First Philosophy* (1641). The excerpt is an excellent example of the meditative method and rationalism used by Descartes as he examined daily the existence of the material world. It is not easy reading, partly because of the archaic form of expression, but in it the reader will discover some of Descartes's important views on sensation, imagination, and memory. In trying to ascertain the existence of material things, Descartes was confronted by the unreliability of his senses, both internal and external. He realized that although his senses erred occasionally, they usually functioned without delusion; he reasoned that he could avoid these sensory illusions by relying on information from multiple senses. For Descartes, an understanding of sensation, imagination, and memory were critical if the mind was to know about the state of the body.

The second selection was written by a historian of psychology, Robert I. Watson (1909–1980), who was the founder and first editor of the *Journal of the History of Behavioral Sciences*. In the 1960s, Watson proposed a method to study the history of psychology that he called *prescriptive analysis* (see Watson, 1967), a method that provided a classification system and conceptual framework that could be used historically. It was an approach in the tradition of intellectual history, meaning the history of ideas. Watson selected eighteen dimensions that he believed described the philosophy, content, and methodology of various approaches to psychology. These dimensions, or *prescriptions* as he called them, could be used to describe the major psychological schools (such as behaviorism and psychoanalysis) or the psychological views of an individual. These eighteen prescriptions were arranged in contrasting pairs such as empiricism-rationalism, inductivism-deductivism, mechanism-vitalism, and monism-dualism. Schools or individuals would not be investigated in terms of all eighteen prescriptions. Rather, the analysis would take place only for those issues on which the school or individual took a stance. In the end, psychological systems could be described in terms of their most salient features. Thus on the dimension of molarism-molecularism, Gestalt psychology (see Chapter 14) would be described as molar because of its holistic approach to the study of consciousness ("the whole is different from the sum of its parts"), whereas Titchener's structural school of psychology (see Chapter 6) would be labeled molecular because of its atomistic approach to psychology, an attempt to reduce consciousness to its most basic elements.

In the article in this chapter, Watson (1971) uses his system of prescriptive analysis to present the psychological views of Descartes. The article provides a brief understanding of Watson's method of analysis and an excellent exposition of Descartes's psychological views. Watson compares Descartes with other intellectual giants of the seventeenth century, such as Francis Bacon, Galileo Galilei, William Harvey, and Thomas Hobbes, and concludes that Descartes "was the most significant contributor to psychology that was to be. . . . And it was Descartes, more than any other, who provided the background and formed the problems that were to become salient for psychology" (p. 223).

The third selection in this chapter is one of the most important parts of John Locke's *Essay*. In it he discusses his concepts of simple and complex ideas, focusing on the processes of perception, reflection, and association. As in the Descartes selection, Locke's seventeenth-century prose does not make for easy reading; however, the ideas expressed in this excerpt were crucial in defining the course of empiricist thought and ultimately the new science of psychology.

The final selection is by sociologist Nicholas G. Petryszak who provides a most interesting interpretation of Locke's concept of *tabula rasa*. Petryszak (1981) argues that Locke introduced the concept in order "to resolve two conflicting world views towards which he was equally sympathetic" (p. 16): a belief in divine determination and a belief in individualism. Illustrating the importance of context in historical understanding, Locke's ideas are explored in the social and intellectual milieu of the Enlightenment of the late seventeenth and eighteenth centuries.

REFERENCES

Leahey, T. H. (1992). *A history of psychology: Main currents in psychological thought* (3rd ed.). Englewood Cliffs, NJ: Prentice-Hall.

Petryszak, N. G. (1981). Tabula rasa—Its origin and implications. *Journal of the History of the Behavioral Sciences, 17,* 15–27.

Watson, R. I. (1967). Psychology: A prescriptive science. *American Psychologist, 22,* 435–443.

Watson, R. I. (1971). A prescriptive analysis of Descartes' psychological views. *Journal of the History of the Behavioral Sciences, 7,* 223–248.

The Existence of Material Things: The Real Distinction of Mind and Body

René Descartes

It remains for me to examine whether material things exist. I already know at least the possibility of their existence, in so far as they are the subject-matter of pure mathematics, since in this regard I clearly and distinctly perceive them. For God is undoubtedly able to affect whatever I am thus able to perceive; and I have never decided that anything could not be done by him, except on the ground that it would involve contradiction for me to perceive such a thing distinctly. Further, when I am occupied with material objects, I am aware of using the faculty of imagination; and this seems to imply that they exist. For when I consider carefully what imagination is, it seems to be a kind of application of the cognitive faculty to a body intimately present to it—a body, therefore, that exists.

To explain this, I begin by examining the difference between imagination and pure understanding. For instance, when I imagine a triangle, I do not just understand that it is a figure enclosed in three lines; I also at the same time see the three lines present before my mind's eye, and this is what I call imagining them. Now if I want to think of a chiliagon, I understand just as well that it is a figure of a thousand sides as I do that a triangle is a figure of three sides; but I do not in the same way imagine the thousand sides, or see them as presented to me. I am indeed accustomed always to imagine something when I am thinking of a corporeal object; so I may confusedly picture to myself some kind of figure; but obviously this picture is not a chiliagon, since it is in no way different from the one I should form if I were thinking of a myriagon, or any other figure with very many sides; and it in no way helps me to recognise the properties that distinguish a chiliagon from other polygons. If now it is a pentagon that is in question, I can understand its figure, as I can the figure of a chiliagon, without the aid of imagination; but I may also imagine this very figure, applying my mind's eye to its five sides and at the same time to the area contained by them; and here I clearly discern that I have to make some special effort of mind to imagine it that I do not make in just understanding it; this new mental effort plainly shows the difference between imagination and pure understanding.

I further consider that this power of imagination in me, taken as distinct from the power of understanding, is not essential to the nature of myself, that is, of my mind; for even if I lacked it, I should nevertheless undoubtedly still be the selfsame one that I am; it seems, therefore, that this power must depend on some object other than myself. And if there is a body to which the mind is so conjoined that it can at will apply itself, so to say, to contemplating it, then I can readily understand the possibility of my imagining corporeal objects by this means. The difference between this mode of consciousness and pure understanding would then be simply this: in the act of understanding the mind turns as it were towards itself, and contemplates one of the ideas contained in itself; in the act of imagining, it turns to the body, and contemplates something in it resembling an idea understood by the mind itself or perceived by sense. I can readily understand, I say, that imagination could be performed in this way, if a body exists; and since there does not occur to me any other equally convenient way of explaining it, I form from this the probable conjecture that the body exists. But this is only probable; and, in spite of a careful investigation of all points, I can as yet see no way

Descartes, R. (1641). *Meditationes de prima philosophia.* Adapted from E. S. Haldane and G. R. T. Ross (Trans.), *The philosophical works of Descartes,* Cambridge: Cambridge University Press, 1911, pp. 185–199.

of arguing conclusively from the fact that there is in my imagination a distinct idea of a corporeal nature to the existence of any body.

Besides that aspect of body which is the subject-matter of pure mathematics, there are many other things that I habitually imagine—colours, sounds, flavours, pain, and so on; but none of these are so distinctly imagined. In any case, I perceive them better by way of sensation, and it is from thence that they seem to have reached my imagination, by the help of memory. Thus it will be more convenient to treat of them by treating of sense at the same time; I must see whether I can get any certain argument in favour of the existence of material objects from the things perceived in the mode of consciousness that I call sensation.

I will first recall to myself what kinds of things I previously thought were real, as being perceived in sensation; then I will set out my reasons for having later on called them in question; finally I will consider what to hold now.

In the first place, then: I had sensations of having a head, hands, feet, and the other members that made up the body; and I regarded the body as part of myself, or even as my whole self. I had sensations of the commerce of this body with many other bodies, which were capable of being beneficial or injurious to it in various ways; I estimated the beneficial effects by a sensation of pleasure, and the injurious, by a sensation of pain. Besides pain and pleasure, I had internal sensations of hunger, thirst, and other such appetites; and also of physical inclinations towards gladness, sadness, anger, and other like emotions. I had external sensations not only of the extension, shapes, and movements of bodies, but also of their hardness, heat, and other tangible qualities; also, sensations of light, colours, odours, flavours, and sounds. By the varieties of these qualities I distinguished from one another the sky, the earth, the seas, and all other bodies.

I certainly had some reason, in view of the ideas of these qualities that presented themselves to my consciousness (*cogitationi*), and that were the only proper and immediate object of my sensations, to think that I was aware in sensation of objects quite different from my own consciousness: viz. bodies from which the ideas proceeded. For it was my experience (*experiebar*) that the ideas came to me without any consent of mine; so that I could neither have a sensation of any object, however I wished, if it were not present to the sense-organ, nor help having the sensation when the object was present. Moreover, the ideas perceived in sensation were much more vivid and prominent, and, in their own way, more distinct, than any that I myself deliberately produced in my meditations, or observed to have been impressed on my memory; and thus it seemed impossible for them to proceed from myself; and the only remaining possibility was that they came from some other objects. Now since I had no conception of these objects from any other source than the ideas themselves, it could not but occur to me that they were like the ideas. Further, I remembered that I had had the use of the senses before the use of reason; and I saw that the ideas I formed myself were less prominent than those I perceived in sensation, and mostly consisted of parts taken from sensation; I thus readily convinced myself that I had nothing in my intellect that I had not previously had in sensation.

Again, I had some reason for holding that the body I called "*my* body" by a special title really did belong to me more than any other body did. I could never separate myself entirely from it, as I could from other bodies. All the appetites and emotions I had, I felt in the body and on its account. I felt pain, and the titillations of pleasure, in parts of *this* body, not of other, external bodies. Why should a sadness of the mind follow upon a sensation of pain, and a kind of happiness upon the titillation of sense? Why should that twitching of the stomach which I call hunger tell me that I must eat; and a dryness of the throat, that I must drink; and so on? I could give no account of this except that nature taught me so; for there is no likeness at all, so far as I can see, between the twitching in the stomach and the volition to take food; or between the sensation of an object that gives me pain, and the experience (*cogitationem*) of sadness that arises from the sensation. My other judgments, too, as regards the objects of sensation seemed to have been lessons of nature; for I had convinced myself that things were so, before setting out any reasons to prove this.

Since then, however, I have had many experiences that have gradually sapped the faith I had in the senses. It sometimes happened that towers which had looked round at a distance looked square when close at hand; and that huge statues standing on the roof did not seem large to me looking up from the ground. And there were countless other cases like these, in which I found the external senses to be deceived in their judgment; and not only the external senses, but the internal senses as well. What [experience] can be more intimate than pain? Yet I had heard sometimes, from people who had had a leg or arm cut off, that they still seemed now and then to feel pain in the part of the body that they lacked; so it seemed in my own case not to be quite certain that a limb was in pain, even if I felt pain in it. And to these reasons for doubting I more recently added two more, of highly general application. First, there is no kind of sensation that I have ever thought I had in waking life, but I may also think I have some time when I am asleep; and since I do not believe that sensations I seem to have in sleep come from external objects, I did not see why I should believe this any the more about sensations I seem to have when I am awake. Secondly, I did not as yet know the Author of my being (or at least pretended I did not); so there seemed to be nothing against my being naturally so constituted as to be deceived even about what appeared to myself most true. As for the reasons of my former conviction that sensible objects are real, it was not difficult to answer them. I was, it seemed, naturally impelled to many courses from which reason dissuaded me; so I did not think I ought to put much reliance on what nature had taught me. And although sense-perceptions did not depend on my will, it must not be concluded, I thought, that they proceed from objects distinct from myself; there might perhaps be some faculty in myself, as yet unknown to me, that produced them.

But now that I am beginning to be better acquainted with myself and with the Author of my being, my view is that I must not rashly accept all the apparent data of sensation; nor, on the other hand, call them all in question.

In the first place, I know that whatever I clearly and distinctly understand can be made by God just as I understand it; so my ability to understand one thing clearly and distinctly apart from another is enough to assure me that they are distinct, because God at least can separate them. (It is irrelevant what faculty enables me to think of them as separate.) Now I know that I exist, and at the same time I observe absolutely nothing else as belonging to my nature or essence except the mere fact that I am a conscious being; and just from this I can validly infer that my essence consists simply in the fact that I am a conscious being. It is indeed possible (or rather, as I shall say later on, it is certain) that I have a body closely bound up with myself; but at the same time I have, on the one hand, a clear and distinct idea of myself taken simply as a conscious, not an extended, being; and, on the other hand, a distinct idea of body, taken simply as an extended, not a conscious, being; so it is certain that I am really distinct from my body, and could exist without it.

Further, I find in myself powers for special modes of consciousness, e.g. imagination and sensation; I can clearly and distinctly understand myself as a whole apart from these powers, but not the powers apart from myself—apart from an intellectual substance to inhere in; for the essential (*formali*) conception of them includes some kind of intellectual act; and I thus perceive that they are distinct from me in the way aspects (*modos*) are from the object to which they belong. I also recognise other powers—those of local motion, and change of shape, and so on; these, like the ones I mentioned before, cannot be understood apart from a substance to inhere in; nor, therefore, can they exist apart from it. Clearly these, if they exist, must inhere in a corporeal or extended, not an intellectual substance; for it is some form of extension, not any intellectual act, that is involved in a clear and distinct conception of them. Now I have a passive power of sensation—of getting and recognising the ideas of sensible objects. But I could never have the use of it if there were not also in existence an active power, either in myself or in something else, to produce or make the ideas. This power certainly cannot exist in me; for it presupposes no action of my intellect, and the ideas are produced without my co-operation, and often against my will. The only remaining possibility is that it inheres in some substance other than myself. This must contain all the reality that exists representatively in the ideas produced by this active power; and it must contain it (as I remarked previously) either just as it is represented, or in some higher form. So either this substance is a body—is of corporeal nature—and contains actually whatever is contained representatively in the ideas; or else it is God, or some creature nobler than bodies, and contains the same reality in a higher form. But since God is not deceitful, it is quite obvious that he neither implants the ideas in me by his own direct action, nor yet by means of some creature that contains the representative reality of the ideas not precisely as they represent it, but only in some higher form. For God has given me no faculty at all to discern their origin; on the other hand, he has given me a strong inclination to believe that these ideas proceed from corporeal objects; so I do not see how it would make sense to say God is not deceitful, if in fact they proceed from elsewhere, not from corporeal objects. Therefore corporeal objects must exist. It may be that not all bodies are such as my senses apprehend them, for this sensory apprehension is in many ways obscure and confused; but at any rate their nature must comprise whatever I clearly and distinctly understand—that is, whatever, generally considered, falls within the subject-matter of pure mathematics.

There remain some highly doubtful and uncertain points; either mere details, like the sun's having a certain size or shape, or things unclearly understood, like light, sound, pain, and so on. But since God is not deceitful, there cannot possibly occur any error in my opinions but I can correct by means of some faculty God has given me to that end; and this gives me some hope of arriving at the truth even on such matters. Indeed, all nature's lessons undoubtedly contain some truth; for by nature, as a general term, I now mean nothing other than either God himself, or the order of created things established by God; and by *my* nature in particular I mean the complex of all that God has given *me*.

Now there is no more explicit lesson of nature than that I have a body; that it is being injured when I feel pain; that it needs food, or drink, when I suffer from hunger, or thirst, and so on. So I must not doubt that there is some truth in this. Nature also teaches by these sensations of pain, hunger, thirst, etc., that I am not present in my body merely as a pilot is present in a ship; I am most tightly bound to it, and as it were mixed up with it, so that I and it form a unit. Otherwise, when the body is hurt, I, who am simply a conscious being, would not feel pain on that account, but would perceive the injury by a pure act of understanding, as the pilot perceives by sight any breakages there may be in the ship; and when the body needs food or drink, I should explicitly understand the fact, and not have confused sensations of hunger and thirst. For these sensations of thirst, hunger, pain, etc., are simply confused modes of consciousness that arise from the mind's being united to, and as it were mixed up with, the body.

Moreover, nature teaches me that my body has an environment of other bodies, some of which must be sought for and others shunned.

And from the wide variety of colours, sounds, odours, flavours, degrees of hardness, and so on, of which I have sensations, I certainly have the right to infer that in the bodies from which these various sense-perceptions arise there is corresponding, though perhaps not similar, variety. Again, from the fact that some of these perceptions are pleasant to me and others unpleasant, it is quite certain that my body—or rather myself as a whole, who am made up of body and mind—can be variously affected for good or ill by bodies in its environment.

There are many other beliefs which may seem to be lessons of nature, but which I really derive not from nature but from a habit of inconsiderate judgment; e.g. that a region is empty if there is no occurrence in it that affects my senses; that if a body is (say) hot, it has some property just like my idea of heat; that in a white or green object there is the same whiteness or greenness as in my sensation, and in a sweet or bitter body the same flavour as I taste, and so on; that stars and towers and other distant bodies have just the size and shape they manifest to my senses; and the like. But to avoid an indistinct view of this matter, I must define here more accurately just what I mean by a lesson of nature. I am using "nature" here in a more restricted sense than the complex of everything that God has given me. For this complex includes much that belongs only to the mind—e.g. my seeing that what is once done cannot be undone, and the rest of what I know by the light of nature; I am not speaking here about this. Again, it includes much that has regard only to the body, e.g. a downward tendency; this again I am not now discussing. I am concerned only with what God has given to me considered as a compound of mind and body. It is a lesson of my "nature", in this sense, to avoid what gives me a sensation of pain, and pursue what gives me a sensation of pleasure, and so on. But it does not seem to be also a lesson of nature to draw any conclusion from sense-perception as regards external objects without a previous examination by the understanding; for knowledge of the truth about them seems to belong to the mind alone, not to the composite whole.

Thus, a star has no more effect on my eye than the flame of a small candle; but from this fact I have no real, positive inclination to believe it is no bigger; this is just an irrational judgment that I made in my earliest years. Again, I have a sensation of heat as I approach the fire; but when I approach the same fire too closely, I have a sensation of pain; so there is nothing to convince me that something in the fire resembles heat, any more than the pain; it is just that there must be something in it (whatever this may turn out to be) that produces the sensations of heat or pain. Again, even if in some region there is nothing to affect the senses, it does not follow that there is no body in it. I can see that on these and many other questions I habitually pervert the order of nature. My sense-perceptions were given me by nature properly for the sole purpose of indicating to the mind what is good or bad for the whole of which the mind is a part; and to this extent they are clear and distinct enough. But I use them as if they were sure criteria for a direct judgment as to the essence of external bodies; and here they give only very obscure and confused indications.

I have already examined sufficiently the reason why, in spite of God's goodness, my judgments are liable to be false. But a new problem arises here about the objects that nature shows me I ought to seek or shun; and also as regards the errors I seem to have observed in internal sensations. For instance, a man is deceived by the pleasant taste of some food, and swallows the poison concealed within it. But what his nature impels him to desire is what gives the food its pleasant taste; not the poison, of which his nature knows nothing. All that can be inferred from this is that his nature is not omniscient; and this is not surprising, for a man is a finite thing and his nature has only a finite degree of perfection.

But we quite often go wrong about the things that nature does impel us towards. For instance, sick men long for drink or food that would soon be harmful to them. It might be said that they go wrong because their nature is corrupted; but this does not remove the problem. A sick man is no less God's creature than a healthy man; and it seems just as absurd that God should give him a nature that deceives him.

Now a clock built out of wheels and weights, obeys all the laws of "nature" no less exactly when it is ill-made and does not show the right time, than when it satisfies its maker's wishes in every respect. And thus I may consider the human body as a machine fitted together and made up of bones, sinews, muscles, veins, blood, and skin in such a way that, even if there were no mind in it, it would still carry out all the operations that, as things are, do not depend on the command of the will, nor, therefore, on the mind. Now, if, for instance, the body is suffering from dropsy, it has the dryness of the throat that normally gives the mind the sensation of thirst; and this disposes its nerves and other parts to taking drink, so as to aggravate the disease. But I can easily recognise that this is just as "natural" as it is for a body not so affected to be impelled by a similar dryness of the throat to take drink that will be beneficial to it.

Of course, if I consider my preconceived idea of the use of a clock, I may say that when it does not show the right time it is departing from its "nature". Similarly, if I consider the machine of the human body in relation to its normal operations, I may think it goes astray from its "nature" if its throat is dry at a time when drink does not help to sustain it. But I see well enough that this sense of "nature" is very different from the other. In this sense, "nature" is a term depending on my own way of thinking (*a cogitatione mea*), on my comparison of a sick man, or an ill-made clock, to a conception of a healthy man and a well-made clock; it is something extrinsic to the object it is ascribed to. In the other sense, "nature" is something actually found in objects; so this conception has some degree of truth.

"It may be a merely extrinsic application of a term when, considering a body that suffers from dropsy, we call its nature corrupted because it has a dry throat and yet has no need of drink. But if we consider the compound, the mind united to the body, it is not just a matter of terms; there is a real fault in its nature, for it is thirsty at a time when drink would be hurtful to it. So the question remains: how is it that the divine goodness does not prevent 'nature' (in this sense) from deceiving us?"

I must begin by observing the great difference between mind and body. Body is of its nature always divisible; mind is wholly indivisible. When I consider the mind—that is, myself, in so far as I am merely a conscious being—I can distinguish no parts within myself; I understand myself to be a single and complete thing. Although the whole mind seems to be united to the whole body, yet when a foot or an arm or any other part of the body is cut off I am not aware that any subtraction has been made from the mind. Nor can the faculties of will, feeling, understanding and so on be called its parts; for it is one and the same mind that wills, feels, and understands. On the other hand, I cannot think of any corporeal or extended object without being readily able to divide it in thought and therefore conceiving of it as divisible. This would be enough to show me the total difference between mind and body, even if I did not sufficiently know this already.

Next, I observe that my mind is not directly affected by all parts of the body; but only by the brain, and perhaps only by one small part of that—the alleged seat of common sensibility. Whenever this is disposed in a given way, it gives the same indication to the mind, even if the other parts of the body are differently disposed at the time; of this there are innumerable experimental proofs, of which I need not give an account here.

I observe further that, from the nature of body, in whatever way a part of it could be moved by another part at some distance, that same part could also be moved in the same way by intermediate parts, even if the more distant part did nothing. For example, if ABCD is a cord, there is no way of moving A by pulling the end D that could not be carried out equally well if B or C in the middle were pulled and the end D were not moved at all. Now, similarly, when I feel pain in my foot, I have learnt from the science of physic that this sensation is brought about by means of nerves scattered throughout the foot; these are stretched like cords from there to the brain, and when they are pulled in the foot they transmit the pull to the inmost part of the brain, to which they are attached, and produce there a kind of disturbance which nature has decreed should give the mind a sensation of pain, as it were in the foot. But in order to reach the brain, these nerves have to pass through the leg, the thigh, the back, and the neck; so it may happen that, although it is not the part in the foot that is touched, but only some intermediate part, there is just the same disturbance produced in the brain as when the foot is injured; and so necessarily the mind will have the same sensation of pain. And the same must be believed as regards any other sensation.

Finally, I observe that, since any given disturbance in the part of the brain that directly affects the mind can produce only one kind of sensation, nothing better could be devised than that it should produce that one among all the sensations it could produce which is most conducive, and most often conducive, to the welfare of a healthy man. Now experience shows that all the sensations nature has given us are of this kind; so nothing can be found in them but evidence of God's power and goodness. For example: when the nerves of the foot are strongly and unusually disturbed, this disturbance, by way of the spinal cord, arrives at the interior of the brain; there it gives the mind the signal for it to have a certain sensation, viz. pain, as it were in the foot; and this arouses the mind to do its best to remove the cause of the pain, as being injurious to the foot. Now God might have so made human nature that this very disturbance in the brain was a sign to the mind of something else; it might have been a sign of its own occurrence in the brain; or of the disturbance in the foot, or in some intermediate place; or, in fact, of anything else whatever. But there would be no alternative equally conducive to the welfare of the body. Similarly, when we need drink, there arises a dryness of the throat, which disturbs the nerves of the throat, and by means of them the interior of the brain; and this disturbance gives the mind the sensation of thirst, because the most useful thing for us to know in this whole process is that we then need to drink to keep healthy. And so in other cases.

From all this it is clear that in spite of God's immeasurable goodness, man as a compound of body and mind cannot but be sometimes deceived by his own nature. For some cause that occurs, not in the foot, but in any other of the parts traversed by the nerves from the foot to the brain, or even in the brain itself, may arouse the same disturbance as is usually aroused by a hurt foot; and then pain will be felt as it were in the foot, and there will be a "natural" illusion of sense. For the brain-disturbance in question cannot but produce always the same sensation in the mind; and it usually arises much more often from a cause that is hurting the foot than from another cause occurring somewhere else; so it is in accordance with reason that it should always give the mind the appearance of pain in the foot rather than some other part. Again, sometimes dryness of the throat arises not, as usual, from the fact that drink would be conducive to bodily health, but from some contrary cause, as in dropsy; but it is far better that it should deceive us in that case, than if it always deceived us when the body was in good condition. And so generally.

This consideration is of the greatest help to me, not only for noticing all the errors to which my nature is liable, but also for readily correcting or avoiding them. I know that all my sensations are much more often true than delusive signs in matters regarding the well-being of the body; I can almost always use several senses to examine the same object; above all, I have my memory, which connects the present to the past, and my understanding, which has now reviewed all the causes of error. So I ought not to be afraid any longer that all that the senses show me daily may be an illusion; the exaggerated doubts of the last few days are to be dismissed as ridiculous. In particular, this is true of the chief reason for doubt—that sleep and waking life were indistinguishable to me; for I can now see a vast difference between them. Dreams are never connected by memory with all the other events of my life, like the things that happen when I am awake. If in waking life somebody suddenly appeared and directly afterwards disappeared, as happens in dreams, and I could not see where he had come from or where he went, I should justifiably decide he was a ghost, or a phantasm formed in my own brain, rather than a real man. But when I distinctly observe where an object comes from, where it is, and when this happens; and when I can connect the perception of it uninterruptedly with the whole of the rest of my life; then I am quite certain that while this is happening to me I am not asleep but awake. And I need not have the least doubt as to the reality of things, if after summoning all my senses, my memory, and my understanding to examine them I have no conflicting information from any of these sources. But since practical needs do not always leave time for such a careful examination, we must admit that in human life errors as regards particular things are always liable to happen; and we must recognise the infirmity of our nature.

A Prescriptive Analysis of Descartes' Psychological Views

Robert I. Watson

METHODOLOGICAL PRESCRIPTIONS AT THE BEGINNING OF MODERN SCIENCE

In the Seventeenth Century there was no universally accepted scientific method with experiments and observations methodologically similar being conducted by those interested in science. It almost seemed as if there were as many methods as there were people who thought and wrote about scientific matters. Lacking guidance from a scientific paradigm, each man worked out his particular way of coming to terms with the older speculative traditions.

It was not unnatural that Descartes, and his contemporaries Bacon and Hobbes, each would believe that his particular intellectual formulation was the result of the methods he used. A dogmatic methodism, a belief that technique had an inherent quality of insuring success, was especially prominent in Descartes.

From our vantage point, we can see that along with the others of this time, Descartes had two sets of choices to make—one concerning what was considered to be the major source of knowledge, to follow the rational or the empirical prescription and the other concerning the priority to be given either to general principles or of individual facts, to follow the deductive or the inductive prescription.

Rationalism, his choice in one of these pairs, is a concept with many shades and variations of meaning. In its broadest sense, rationalism is the belief that in thinking logically a man's mind works the same way as does the universe, mak-

Adapted from Watson, R. I. (1971). A prescriptive analysis of Descartes' psychological views, *Journal of the History of the Behavioral Sciences, 7,* 223–248.

ing it possible that ultimately man can understand everything, just as he understood in Descartes's time simple mathematical or physical problems. In the present context, the more specific meaning intended is that of an adherent to the rationalistic prescription who finds the primary, if not the exclusive, source of knowledge to lie in reason.

If, on the other hand, one follows the empirical prescription, knowledge is found in experience. Experience, however, does not come from the senses alone, a narrower doctrine that came to be known as sensationalism. In addition to analysis of sensory experience, often some form of introspective analysis was accepted by the empiricist. To use the formulation of John Locke, the first great modern adherent to empiricism, "reflection" by which we are informed concerning the workings of our minds is operative in addition to the effect of experience. Empiricism, although only counter-dominant, was never completely dormant, and was to receive a strong impetus from the success of the emerging experimental method.

During the period now under consideration, the rationalistic prescription was dominant. Apart from this being a heritage from the past, in earlier periods as well as at the beginning of the modern age, rationalism lent itself more readily than did empiricism to support of religious doctrines since rationalism in lay and religious matters reinforced one and other in their common insistence upon independence from sense perception.[1] This helps to account for the adoption and adaptation of Greek rationalistic systems by Christian theologians. Rationalistic dominance received further support from the increased scope and precision that new mathematical discoveries were beginning to provide at this time. Such was the inspiration of mathematics to the men of this age, that, after Descartes, if a particular philosophical or scientific issue could not be solved mathematically, it would at least be treated in the "spirit of mathematics." What is this spirit? It was to arrive at what were considered to be unchallengeable premises and then proceed to elaborate them by deductive reasoning.

Deductive Rationalism and Descartes

Descartes was deeply interested in the problem of finding precisely the right method to obtain knowledge and thereby to bring about an essential reform. Descartes' solution was intertwined with his conviction of the certainty of the operations of mathematics. The solution of uniting method and mathematics came in a revelation in a very literal sense. It occurred as part of a dream on St. Martin's Eve, 10 November, 1619. One of the insights it gave him was that of applying algebra to geometry—the basic conception of analytic geometry. In effect, this unites algebra to spatial relationships. But it was more than a mathematical advance, tremendous though it was, that occurred that night. There was also another insight—that the method of mathematics could be extended to other fields of knowledge. His aim, however, was not to produce a mathematical interpretation of the universe, but rather to develop a point of view in likeness of mathematics in the way described a moment ago. His first task became the rationalistic one of finding self-evident truths, and once these were established, his second task would be to deduce the other truths that they implied. As did the men of the Middle Ages, he wanted to begin with accepted truths. There was to be this difference: they had begun with accepted truths based on religious pronouncements; he wished to begin with accepted truths based on reasoning.

It is unnecessary with this audience to trace Descartes' sceptical journey to the bed rock of "I think, therefore I am" and his triumphant return with his beloved basic principles, now not matters of mere belief but rationally established truths. One consequence, however, must be indicated. Descartes thereafter was to have a profound faith in the ability of reason to discover the true principles of any problem which he chose to investigate. Never thereafter did he waver in this conviction, never did he even consider that reason might be inadequate for any task to which it legitimately be put (on which ground he excluded little besides revealed dogma).

Descartes supported his rationalism by insisting that the clear, compelling, not to be doubted, and inevitable principles are innate. Before we experience the ideas of God, self, the axioma of mathematics, the figure of the triangle, we have the corresponding ideas. God simultaneously established laws of nature and endowed our minds with them so that, provided we used the right method, we would arrive at them. The innateness of ideas is stated time and again. It is variously spoken of as "certain primary germs of truth implanted by nature"; "naturally existent"; and "imprinted . . . in our minds."

Ideas are not created by the process of thought; rather, they are *discovered* as the content of thought. A clear indication is given when Descartes was challenged by a critic to explain how a man would have an idea of God if he were to be born without the use of his senses and therefore without sensory experience. Descartes answered that he would not only have an idea of God and self, but, since he lacked sense experiences, he would hold them in an even more purified and clear fashion because these ideas existed for him without the adulteration of sense experience. Sources of error found in everyday sensory experience serve to stifle knowledge of innate ideas, a handicap from which a person born without sense would not suffer.

Descartes' earlier statements about innate ideas had given his critics the impression that he was saying that we are born with them in ready-made, complete form. Under their criticism, he modified his view to say that what he meant by innate ideas is the potentiality of thought that is actualized by experience. Innate ideas are not always present; rather, we have the capacity of summoning up such ideas.[2] When we are exposed to extraneous things, it is the faculty of thinking, not those extraneous things themselves, that transmit ideas to our minds. They transmit something which gives "the mind occasion to form these ideas, by means of an innate faculty." An innate idea is a "propensity." To drive home the point, he argued that, just as generosity or disease may run in families, so, too, there may be a familial disposition for certain ideas. Neither ideas nor any other innate characteristic appears full-blown, they await experience to bring them out. Formulation in terms of propensity was something which was later to lend itself readily to adaptation for use in discussing nature versus nurture.

Inept as they are, Descartes held that sense experiences are of some use since they provide the occasions for the arousal of our innate ideas of mathematical entities and other simple natures. The role of perception is that of bringing innate ideas to consciousness. The mind then discovers ideas which it already implicitly possessed.

Descartes' position on innateness of basic principles is in agreement with his dualistic separating of mind and body. In thinking, the mind may function entirely independent of body. When the mind functions in this independent fashion, it has pure ideas, i.e., pure activities as contents of thought without any dependence for their truth upon the world of objects. As would Kant after him, Descartes held that the mind provided the ground for certain structuring principles which were therefore *a priori*.

Knowledge of truth and falsity comes from thinking alone. The senses contribute to the materials of thought but neither sensation alone nor imagination alone could ever assure us of their truth value. Thinking must intervene. Sensory experiences, as he warns again and again, are fallible, and because sensory experiences are omnipresent, it is no easy task for the judgments made by the human mind to be free from their erroneous impressions. This, he admits, makes it hard to follow the rules of correct thinking which occupied so much of his attention in the *Rules for the Direction of the Mind,* and *Dis-*

course of the Method of Rightly Conducting the Reason. But with faithful adherence to these rules, one can do so, Descartes had no doubt. It follows that his was to be a deductive procedure, the beginning of investigation with already formulated principles.

Descartes gives a clear summary statement of how he would use this deductive method, in order to find further principles in his short statement, *Rules for the Direction of the Mind.* Besides intuition, he says, the other fundamental operation of the mind is deduction. Intuition had supplied the first principles of truth safeguarded as to their validity by the already familiar test of clarity so that knowledge comes first from intuition. Deduction that follows is the process of making inferences from this certain knowledge. It is the process whereby the mind allows inferences to be drawn from basic principles in successive steps. These remote deductively derived conclusions have the characteristic of being derived step by step, which intuitive truths do not have.

Descartes relied primarily on deduction but in the broader sense made evident in earlier discussion. No more than to Bacon was deduction as he conceived it dependent upon the Aristotelian syllogism which is useful only in restating that which is already discovered. This dependence upon deduction is not exclusive. He specifically denied the charge that he always deduced particular truths from universal propositions. Instead he said, he always started with particular propositions as he indicated in replying to a critic; he argued that in order to discover the truth, we should always start with particular notions, in order to arrive at general conceptions subsequently, though we may also proceed in the reverse way, after having discovered the universals, deduce other particulars from them. Thus in teaching a child the elements of geometry, we shall certainly not make him understand the general truth that "*when equals are taken from equals the remainders are equal,*" or that "*the whole is greater than its parts,*" unless we show him examples in particular cases. The minds' knowledge then, is such that general propositions are formed from particulars and Descartes cannot be said to exclude induction. Nevertheless, beyond a certain irreducible minimum, he preferred to depend upon deduction.

Descartes, did not, as legend would have it, believe that all physics could be deduced from first principles. "We cannot determine by reason how big these pieces of matter are, how quickly they move, or what circles they describe . . . (this) is a thing we must learn from observation. Therefore, we are free to make any assumptions we like about them so long as all the consequences agree with experience."[3] Hypotheses must be framed and experiments must be used in order to select from among competing equally deductively and rationally plausible interpretations.

The intellect's unaided powers were not enough, "experiments (are) necessary to me in order to justify and support my reasoning." Descartes would experiment—but only to fill out the details, to show from among the alternatives, the way God actually did produce certain effects or to demonstrate from among the possible alternatives the one God has chosen to produce. Experiment, therefore, had a subordinate but acknowledged place in his scheme. As he conceived it, the more advanced the knowledge became, the more necessary experiments became. It not unexpectedly follows that experiment is stressed by Descartes in connection with biological and physiological problems.

To some slight extent, Descartes practiced what he preached. There is evidence that he did make some observations, collected some specimens, and made vivisections.[4] Moreover, he, himself, exhibited his method by exercises in optics and geometry appended for that purpose to the *Discourse.* Neither in these studies nor anywhere else did Descartes, or any other person for that matter, employ his method in all of its details. Instead, he behaved as did other scientists: he discovered experimentally the equality of the sines of the angles of incidence and of refraction in 1626 and only later did he fit it into the deductive proofs of the *Dioptric* first published in 1637.

Looking back over Descartes' rationalistic and deductive system from our vantage point, shows it to be open to serious qualification and criticism. An unvarying system in which each step is laid out in advance may be suitable for exposition of scientific procedures in general terms for the interested reader. It is not a method of scientific discovery because there is no one method of scientific investigation, there are many.

Descartes' method is that of the philosophical system builder rather than that of the scientist. He rejected experimental proof if it could not be assimilated into his system. This explains how he could be so blind as not to be content with Harvey's demonstration that the heart was a contractible muscle and insisted, instead, that the heart was a heated container as it was called for to be by his primary principles. Similarly, after praising Galileo for freeing himself of the errors of the schools and for using mathematics, Descartes went on to say ". . . he has merely sought reasons for certain particular effects without having considered the first causes of nature; and thus he has built without a foundation."[5] He was criticizing Galileo for not having "theoretical" i.e., "metaphysical" presuppositions as a "foundation," for his work, a standpoint that we see to be its precise strength.

The clarity and distinctness of the postulates followed, Descartes held, are important in any deductive system. But then and now, one can argue that they do not tell the whole story. Dependence on self-evident truths is not characteristic of scientific advance. In fact, regarding postulates as tentative, not certain, to be discarded when they disagree with observations or experiments, is a lesson scientists had to learn many times over the centuries. In this methodological sense, Galileo was right and Descartes wrong. In Descartes' hands, the hypothetic-deductive method of Galileo lost its hypothetical to retain only its deductive character.

Despite their defects, Descartes' rational and deductive analysis of the order of nature following mathematical methods was one of the most influential ideas of the Seventeenth Century. It over-shadowed by far Bacon and his adherence to induction and empiricism. With such different views neither could have appreciated the significance of the work of the other. They could not see, as we do from our vantage point, that induction and deduction, and rationalism and empiricism could and would be integrated in the course of scientific endeavour.

DUALISM AND DESCARTES

Against the general scientific background of the early Seventeenth Century and Descartes' methodological and attitudinal conceptions and presuppositions it now becomes appropriate to examine his way of regarding the relationship between mind and body and the nature of mind itself.

Before Descartes, body and mind had not been seen clearly as opposing entities. Influenced by Aristotle, medieval theologians had conceived living bodies as so imbued with soul that no chasm between soul and body could be seen. It was Descartes whose established for all of those who came after to see, the distinction between a spiritual mind and a mechanistic body. Indeed, a sharply defined dualism was a problem that he did much to create.

Descartes conceived of two substances—thought, whose essential character is thinking, and extension (matter), whose essential quality is extensiveness (length, width and depth). With the distinction asserted, it becomes necessary to show how he arrived at this conception.

Cartesian dualism followed directly from his deductive search for certainty. Acceptance of his dictum, "I think therefore I am," made thinking separate from matter, since in the course of his search for certainty, it will be remembered, matter had been recovered at a separate later step.

A host of other arguments supported his absolute distinction between mind and body: matter can easily be divided into parts, while mind cannot: the mind, the independent substance, can "act independently of the brain: for certainly the brain can be of no use in pure thought . . ."; mind moves the body since "the most certain and most evident" experience makes us "immediately aware of its doing so"; [6] and the mind and body can exist apart from one another, and therefore are distinct and separate.

But one argument, above all, was to be important for the future of psychology. This was a distinction between an objective and subjective prescription first given scientific sponsorship by Galileo and to be known from the day of Boyle and Locke[7] as the distinction between primary and secondary qualities.[8]

Without too much attention to the matter, the scholastic philosophers of the past had assumed that in sense perception the mind was directly in touch with real things.[9] To them, things were entities having "qualities" that were inherent in objects. So long as science was content to remain Aristotelian with things being just what they appeared to be, with water being wet, the fire hot, there was no problem. But now Galileo had begun to uncover a new universe, a particular pitch was a certain number of vibrations and water was material particles in motion. The sound of the string, the coolness and wetness of the water, seemed no longer to be properties of water itself. But whence came these properties? The answer was that it must be the mind that heard the sound or felt the water.

This issue was brought into sharp focus by both general scientific developments and by a specific relevant distinction made by Galileo. During these early modern days measurements had been made of weight, size and motion almost to the exclusion of heat, color and sound. The fascination that their mathematical manipulation had for the scientist of the day made the former seem somehow more real than the latter. In the interest of clarifying the nature of the scientific task by setting the limits of physical science and in furthering his mathematical *a priorism*, Galileo made a sharp distinction between the objective and mathematical and the subjective and sensitive world. Discussions occurred in the setting of a consideration of Aristotle's contention that motion is the cause of heat. This Galileo denied, saying that an object or substance has shape, quantity, and motion, and only these. These are the "primary qualities"; they cannot be separated from things. But warmth, (and by a logical extension a color, a taste, a sound and a smell) do not inevitably accompany objects. These are, Galileo said, "mere names, having their location only in the responsive body. . . ." If the sensing persons were taken away, these qualities would no longer exist. These "secondary qualities" do not have the status of physical reality. Take away the sensing person and these qualities disappear. In short, they are qualities of sensation, not of things; they are subject rather than object. They have no reality apart from experience. To Galileo, their subjectivity meant that they are to be banished from natural science.

Galileo had made a highly novel contribution which served to place physical science on a more methodologically objective footing. In the interest of *methodological* objectivity in the physical sciences Galileo was arguing that a *contentual* subjectivity existed concerning the psychology that was to be. Objectivity was being denied to sensory experiences since they were not external to the individual. Instead, sensory experiences were subjective, occurring only within an individual. There is no question that this distinction, useful though it may have been at the time, prolonged the period before psychology was to emerge as a science since the "subjectivity" of sense qualities has been a problem to be overcome ever since.

What was merely a methodological distinction for Galileo, became for Descartes an argument for a dualism of two worlds. In support of the immateriality of the mind, he happily enlisted the distinction between primary and secondary qualities and phrased it that odors, smells, and tastes became mere sensation, "existing in . . . (one's) thought." Bodies exist only in the shape and motion. He goes so far as to say that sensations represent nothing outside of our minds.[10] They are not in the objects, but in our minds. Instead of sensible qualities residing in bodies, actually it is quite possible that sensible qualities and the objects are not at all similar. In approaching fire and first feeling heat, then moving still closer and feeling pain, far from compelling one to believe that "heat" and "pain" are somehow in the fire itself, on the contrary, suggests that they are not. The upshot, then was that secondary qualities were relegated to the mind of the perceiver while primary qualities were the properties of nature and the features of the world requiring mechanical explanation and, to be, by definition, the only essential properties, of the scientific concern.

A rigid separation of body and mind, contrasted and separated entities, was insisted on by Descartes. All reality of the human being, Descartes was saying, is either spatial (body) or conscious (mind). The relationship is disjunctive; what is spatial is not conscious, what is conscious is not spatial. It follows that mind or body each can be studied without reference to the other. The physical world, including body and its mathematically measurable relationships, is in one realm, the mind with its thoughts, sensations and free will is in another. The body's behavior is determined by mechanistic laws, but in the mind there is purpose and freedom of will, making a person's actions subject to praise and blame. As distinguished from body, man's mind then cannot be reduced to an aspect of a mechanical system because man's mind transcends the material world and the efficient causality which governs therein.

Descartes' dualism had important implications for the sciences in general and for psychology in particular. Matter, including body, was to be treated mathematically and explained mechanically. The two substance view, mind and matter, simplified physical science by means of what it excluded, while at the same time, it introduced a major problem for psychology. From the present perspective the effect of dualism was more pernicious than helpful. The dualistic view of psychology, so firmly established by Descartes, was to dominate even into the twentieth century. Ever since Descartes, psychologists have had the problem of dealing with the relation between mind and body. Descartes, himself, offered one solution.

While laboring mightily to separate mind and body, Descartes was acutely aware there was an interaction and union between them. Evidence, so prevalent in nature, that he could not ignore it, attested that the mind influences the body and the body influences the mind. His answer was to postulate a point of interaction—the pineal gland. His choice of what is now known to be a vestigial organ of no functional significance whatsoever, was based entirely on speculative reasoning. The gland's location, deep in the center of the brain, was seen as befitting its central role, while its uniqueness among brain structures in not being divided into hemispheres served to emphasize its unitary nature.

With a point of interaction selected on these grounds, Descartes proceeded to speculate on how it acted to bring about interaction of body and mind. He postulated that the slightest movement of the pineal gland can alter the flow of the animal spirits, and, reciprocally, the animal spirits can alter movements of the gland. According to its direction of inclination, animal spirits are thereby directed which serves to bring about responses in that region. The sources of stimulation for these inclinations of the pineal gland are not only external sense impressions, but also those arising from the two internal senses, the natural appetites (hunger, thirst and the like), and passions (love, hate, fear, etc.).

Selecting a point of interaction, any point of

interaction, however, created the necessity of explaining how mind, a non-material substance, can influence a material body, and *vice versa*. The mind, answered Descartes, directs the *course* of motion flowing through the body without in any way altering the *volume* of motion. In his opinion, this way of understanding the relationship did no violence to the separation of the mental and physical, since, as he saw it, the mind did not exert a physical force. The weakness of this argument is all too obvious today, since we realize this explanation violates that which came to be called the principle of the conservation of momentum. Altering direction is just as much a result of physical energy as is alteration of quantity. Descartes has raised a problem of how the mind and body influenced one another, but had by no means solved it.

He also considered the general nature of the union of mind and body. That there is, in his opinion, a union, he leaves no doubt. This union is not accidental, Descartes insisted.[11] "Accidental," to Descartes, meant something that which, if absent, would still not destroy the object, such as man's clothing which is "accidental" to the man. The relationship is much closer than, say, that of a sailor to a ship. Pain is felt by the mind when the body is hurt which is a more intimate relation than the concern the sailor feels when his ship is damaged. The union of mind and body, it would seem, is an integral one for Descartes.

Although related to body, mind possesses a unity denied to body. If one takes away a part of the body, the body is decreased, but this does not thereby take away part of the mind. Moreover, corporeal objects can be subdivided into parts which is not the case with mind. Instead, mind is united with all parts of the body so as to form a whole. This is to say, the mind is united with an integrated assemblage of organs, which, precisely because the organs are interrelated, makes for a kind of unity.

It now becomes appropriate to focus upon the mind as affected by the body, rather than the reverse, which has been discussed in considering prescriptive influences from physiological problems. Perception, imagination and passion are prominent themes which he uses in this connection.

Sensing has three aspects: (1) the effect on the motions of the bodily organs by external objects; (2) the mental result as in the perception of pain, color or sound, and the like, due to an intermixture of mind and body; and (3) "judgment" made on the basis of the past experiences with things sensed. Since the first has already been discussed in the setting of his physiology, it is the second and third aspects that receive attention. Descartes contends that the first and second aspects, just mentioned, cannot be false. It is the third aspect of judgment which, if not used reflectively, brings about errors which only understanding, and mature understanding at that, can correct.

By introducing the aspect of judgment into discussion of "sense," it is apparent that Descartes is using "sensing" in a manner similar to others who would refer to "perception" of things, that is, the "sensing" of external objects, of hunger, thirst and other natural appetites. In order to avoid terminological confusion the term "perception" will be used hereafter. It is also evident that some perceptions go beyond the body since judgment, which is of the mind, has been introduced in explaining the third level of sensing. As he put it elsewhere, perception is not by sense alone, but involves preconceived opinion exercised upon the sensed object.

Imagination is also related to body. In imagining, the mind contemplates a material form, as distinguished from understanding when the mind employs itself alone. Imagination is not essential since with understanding, but without imagination, one can still find truth. Imagination is sometimes useful, he admits, as a supplemental aid when one is considering material things. The difference between understanding and imagination is shown by the fact that images are produced without contribution on the part of the person and, indeed, sometimes against his will, neither of which characterize understanding.

Much of philosophy before Descartes had emphasized an interest in the contemplative and intellectual, rather than in the active and emotional. In considering "passions" in some detail, Descartes struck a heretofore long neglected note. His was one of the earliest attempts to isolate and to understand the primary constituents of emotional life.

As Descartes conceived the "passions" they concerned more than what we call emotions. "Passion" is derived from the so-called passivity of the mind, a term introduced to stand in contrast with the mind's own initiation of activity through understanding. Passions of the mind, then, arise from bodily movements. The brain was their physiological seat. Descartes admitted that the heart, then accepted by many as their center, is affected by the passions, but that this is a mistake arising from the close connection between animal spirits and blood.

In the broadest sense, every conscious state that arises in the mind occasioned by bodily movements, is a passion. Passions, he indicated, were of three kinds: perceptions referable to the external world, such as the light of a torch and the sound of a bell; appetitive perceptions referable to the body, such as hunger, thirst and other appetites, and perceptions referable to the mind, such as anger and joy. These last, the emotions as such, are those on which Descartes concentrated, that is, those " . . . perceptions, feelings or emotions of the soul (mind) which we specifically relate to it, and which are caused, maintained and fortified by some movement of the animal spirits." These "passions of the mind," the emotions, are those which are referred to the mind alone in the sense that their effects are felt there. For the passions, there is usually no known proximate cause to which they can be attributed as is the case with the perceptions and the appetites. Sadness, a passion, is experienced in the mind itself, and even though, as in all perceptions, there is a physical cause, it cannot be attributed directly to some definite object.

Surprisingly enough, Descartes had a considerable amount to say about the external indices of the passions. He took the position that we can learn about the passions from study of external behavior. He comments on such matters as the effect of the passions on changes of color, in blushing and pallor of the face, and on trembling, languor, fainting, laughter, crying and sighing.

Although objects moving the body are innumerable, he conceived that the passions they excite, affect us only in a limited number of basic ways. His analysis caused him to arrive at six primary passions—admiration (wonder), love, hatred, desire, joy and sadness. Wonder is the intellectual passion, all of the rest are forms of "desire." He was now using this latter term in a broader sense than for the passion of desire itself. Passions, whenever they incite to action, become desires in this broader sense.

Primary passions give rise to related secondary passions. To admiration are related the secondary passions of esteem, contempt, generosity, pride, humility, veneration and disdain. Passions of desire (in the narrower sense) include hope, fear, jealousy, confidence, courage, and cowardice, while from joy and sadness arise derision, envy, anger, shame, regret and joyfulness.

The passions of joy and sadness are the vehicles for his advancing a theory of pleasure and pain. Joy is agreeableness, while sadness is disagreeableness. Pleasure and pain are the predecessors of these passions and serve to produce them. Feelings of pleasure occur when experiencing that which is beneficial, and pain when experiencing that which is harmful.

Joy and sadness come from a consciousness of self-perfection or imperfection. The passions function to incite the mind to consent to "actions which may serve to maintain the body, or to render it in some manner perfect." This call for personal fulfillment and maturity contains more than a hint of what we would today call a self-actualizing approach to personality.

THE MIND AND DESCARTES

At long last, the problem of mind, the salient issue of the emerging psychology, is at hand. The conceptions of the mind's structure, its faculties, its relations to will, the problem of objectivity and primary and secondary qualities will be of major concern. But before considering them, something must be said about the use of meditation as the method for the study of mind.

MEDITATION AS A METHOD FOR THE STUDY OF MIND

It is instructive to compare meditation, as Descartes used it, to the method of introspection which was to be so characteristic of later psychology. From our temporal perspective the classic introspective method has proven to be a cooperative enterprise drawing upon the work of many men in an effort to find the structure of mind. It has been found to proceed by analysis of the contents of this structure into parts according to one schema or another.

In spite of his faith in reason, Descartes clearly took an impatient view about learning from the introspections of others. Meditation was not a collective enterprise. He denied categorically that we need to borrow observations from others concerning the passions because, as he put it, we feel them ourselves. Moreover, Cartesian meditation did not lend itself to molecular analysis of mental states into component parts or aspects. Innate ideas, for example, once achieved, were given to consciousness in all their self-contained unity from which Descartes then proceeded without any attempt to analyse them. So on both counts, Cartesian meditation was dissimilar to the later method of introspection that was to be the dominant method in psychology for a considerable period of time.

THE STRUCTURE OF MIND

Descartes clearly regarded the mind as a substance as previous discussion attests. It was he, along with Hobbes, who made the conception of mind as substance, structure or content prominent on the modern scene. Although the same substance in each case Descartes considered the mind to show different structural emphases—mind as thought, mind as ideas, mind as consciousness and mind as self-consciousness.

Mind as Thought

Time and again, Descartes stressed that mind is identical with thinking. As he put it, "the human mind . . . is a thinking thing, and not extended in length, width, and depth, nor participating in anything pertaining to body." Thought is not a process but a substance, immaterial though it may be. He meant it quite literally when he called it a "thing." The ideational content of the mind, discussed later as still another view, will bring this out even more clearly.

When Descartes wished to be especially precise about thinking as a spiritual substance, or "single agency," he would refer to "understanding" rather than thinking. When the mind is engaged in understanding, the body is an intruder. In these instances, sense, imagination, and memory serve but to obscure and falsify the intuition of ideas of basic principles or their deductive elaboration, giving further support to his contention that a man born without sense would have the greatest appreciation of these ideas. In this restricted meaning, the mind is almost no more than a passive spectator in the world of objects, encapsulated, self-contained and static.

In addition to this narrow meaning just considered in which the mind is in contact with basic principles, Descartes used thinking more broadly to refer to all of which we are consciously aware, including not only "understanding" but also will, imagination and sense, and memory. This broader view comes about when mind in interaction with body is considered. In this perspective, the mind is related to objects—and relation to objects is expressed through the body. The brain, not involved in understanding, now comes into use.

All perceptions, images, emotions and volitions then are related to thinking and aspects of thinking. The mind senses, imagines, remembers, feels emotions and carries out acts of will. The traditional Aristotelian distinction between a sensitive and a rational soul, between sensing and imagining in contrast to thinking, is no longer operative. In effect, the sensitive soul is merged with the thinking mind.

While mind as thinking is fundamental for Descartes, several subsidiary views are discernible in which mind is conceived as ideas, as consciousness and as self-consciousness.

Mind as Ideas

Ideas make up the content of this mind substance for Descartes. There are three kinds of ideas. Above all are the ideas which arise directly from the mind—the innate ideas, those basic, most certain principles, which are the supreme achievement of the mind.

There are also ideas that form a link between the mind and natural objects, the ideas the mind has through sense, memory and imagination. An idea may represent in the mind an object in the world which is its cause. It is not the eye that sees but the mind, although through the intervention of the brain. Ideas of the mind relating to objects, may also be false. Ideas may or may not conform to external reality. Indeed, a major source of human error is to forget that ideas do not always conform to external objects.

Another category of ideas are those manufactured by the mind, such as ideas of imaginary objects which makes sleepers and madmen have ideas of objects which do not exist. We all, he asserts, experience ideas of the mind as being within the mind itself.[12] Such are the passions, the feelings of joy, anger and the like, and perceptions of volition, that is awareness of oneself as willing.

Ideas are not to be confused with images which arise from motion imparted to the senses. Ideas arise from the mind uninfluenced by the body, except as it serves as the instigator to trigger their appearance. But what is sensed cannot give rise to the idea itself and there is no direct correspondence between sensing and ideation.

Mind as Consciousness

The mind underlies consciousness; it is not identical with consciousness. Consciousness is a substance, a thing, an aspect of the structure *of* the mind. Regarding it as a function was yet to appear. The concept of consciousness as substance is neatly illustrated by Descartes' two types of memory—memory of material things leaving traces of preceding excitations on the brain and memory of mental things which leave permanent traces in consciousness itself.

Thought in the extended sense (as differentiated from understanding) covers everything in us of which we are immediately conscious. Ideas in this context are the forms of thoughts. Ideas are immediate awareness of what the mind perceives. Ideas include willing and fearing, for example, since in so doing one perceives, one wills, or one fears.

Awareness is an awareness of consciousness. Despite his acceptance of the potentiality of innate ideas, nothing exists in the mind of which it is not conscious. This follows because the mind contains only thought. Indeed we must be conscious of thought for it to exist. Even infants, he argues, are conscious of their thoughts, although afterwards, they might not remember them. An unconscious mind would have been a contradiction in terms for Descartes. In fostering the prescription of conscious mentalism, he did so without even the slightest consideration of a mental life of which one is unaware, i.e., an unconscious mentalism.

Mind as Self-Consciousness

In advancing his *"cogito ergo sum"* Descartes had made self-consciousness his primary datum. He could conceive of the world being non-existent and of not having a body, but he could not conceive of having a mind which is unaware of itself. Indeed the criterion of truth for things other than the mind is that it be as clear and distinct as that of the mind's own existence.

The mind thinks and it is conscious of itself. Knowledge of self is immediate, and occurs whenever a person first asks himself that particular question, claimed Descartes. The very moment that there is awareness in consciousness, he added, that instant there is awareness of one's own existence.

Descartes also used self-consciousness as an explanatory concept. For example, the continuity of personal identity is used to characterize the waking state and distinguish it from that of sleeping. Self-consciousness also relates to self-evaluation. Self-blame and esteem arise in his opinion through exercise of free will and the control or lack of it we have over our volition. It is for these reasons that a man can be praised or blamed.

Although only a beginning, a concept of unity or self can be found to be emerging in Descartes. The unity of the mind is at the same time the unity of the self. The arguments for unity of mind then become arguments for unity of self as well, although this is a point he did not make explicit.

An important caution must be offered concerning his accounts of mind. Although they were to lead psychologists with different aims and presuppositions than his own toward the particular perspectives just given, Descartes' aim, in contrast, was essentially philosophical, or to be more specific, epistemological. He wished to demonstrate unequivocally that we are thinking beings.

The Faculties of Mind

A conception of mental phenomena as processes or activities, the functional prescription as it shall be called, was also discernible in his thinking although mind as content, the contentual prescription dominated. The functional conception was a tradition traceable at least as far back as Augustine, for whom memory, will and imagination of the mind were to be attributed to their respective faculties, powers or agencies. Faculties were supposed to produce the various mental activities of which human beings were prone. Faculty psychology was a forerunner of functional psychology insofar as it conceived of the mind as having specifiable function or functions.

Descartes specifically claimed authorship of the view that the mind consists of only one thing, the "faculty" of thinking. The mind has unity so that faculties are not parts of that mind since it is one and the same mind which employs itself in these faculties. They are, as he put it, ". . . modes of thinking peculiar to themselves. . . ."

The substantial nature of mind, ". . . a thing that thinks . . ." made it relatively easy for Descartes to espouse a faculty point of view. Hence, his easy reference after the above quoted words to go on ". . . or a thing that has in itself the faculty of thinking.

The faculties useful in cognition are stated by Descartes somewhat casually and inconsistently. One account he gave called for thinking in the form of understanding and imagination, sense and memory. Of these, only understanding can give the truth; the others are auxiliary. Thinking, already familiar as a ". . . power . . . (that is) purely spiritual," uses the bodily-based faculties by applying itself to them or it may cooperate and thus use them. Elsewhere, feeling and willing are also treated as faculties by Descartes. Discussion of willing will be indicative of will as a power.

Will and Its Freedom

Speaking generally two extreme positions may be discerned concerning the freedom of the will. There is the view that, since man possesses a non-material mind or spiritual soul endowed with the power of free choice, he transcends the material world and, therefore, the system of causality. There is the opposed view that would extend the scientific conception of the material universe to include man, in which free will would be seen as an epiphenomenon and freedom of will denied. Between these extremes there is a number of views which would offer qualification and elaborations.

Descartes accepted clearly and unequivocally the reality of the freedom of the will. After stating that all men possess the faculty of willing, he went on to say that it is the power of choosing or not choosing to do a thing. In another place, he referred to judging or refraining from judging as an act of will, which, he adds, is under our control. There is freedom of the will, then, shown in choosing or judging.

This freedom is evident, innate, and found by self-examination claimed Descartes. The very capacity to apply methodic doubt, the starting point of his method, he holds, is evidence of this freedom. In doubting all things, he perceived liberty to do so to exist. Man's freedom of will is received from God. Man's will is free in the same sense and from the same source in God as are miracles, since in both instances, there is a suspension of causality.

But what is the relation of the will to the mind? Despite his repeated references to understanding as the only function of mind, a position that has been accepted as his up to this point, when dealing with the relation of mind to will, he introduces the latter as a faculty. Besides understanding, he now says, there is also the will, in contradiction to his position that mind is pure thought. Statements to the contrary were, he now argues, a matter of emphasis; will is also of the mind. He was perhaps influenced in acceptance of this position by the Church, for to follow its dictates, he had to accept both the will as influencing the mind and its freedom.

His position concerning will as a faculty of the mind is made especially clear when we examine the question of the cooperation and conflict of the will and the understanding. In a setting of considerations of man's ability to distinguish between the true and the false, he argues that error arises from misapplication of the will which consists of extending it beyond understanding. Understanding does not cause errors, incorrect exercise of one's will does. Will exceeds understanding in that we can will many things that we do not understand and therefore err. If we understand (which is God given), we cannot err in willing, but if we do not understand and will nevertheless, we can commit error.

The relation of the will to the passions is important to Descartes because to show how to control the passions is Descartes' didactic and moral aim for considering them. The first step toward this control is to understand them which he believed his book on the passions to give. When passions are aroused, we can divert ourselves until the agitation calms and then, and only then, should we make a judgement as to what is to be done. Then the freely acting mind can influence the workings of the bodily machine by the process of willing which can cause the pineal gland to incline in the manner necessary for the appropriate bodily action.

As distinguished from the passion or desire, will is that which gives or withholds consent to desire. In this context, the principal effect of the passions is to incite the mind to will. The agitation of the animal spirits, especially if it be violent, is of the body, and, just as a clap of thunder must be heard whether we want to or not, so too the mind cannot completely control the passions. The will, however, can quickly gain control of the passions by not permitting their effects to proceed further than the first beginnings. Through the will, the hand that rose to strike in anger can be restrained before the blow is struck; running away in fear can be stopped after the first involuntary movements. Most actions originate with the will, reflex responses being a major class of exceptions. The activity of the will, or rather its failure yet to act, is shown in involuntary action described earlier in connection with the functioning of the nervous system.

In sum, the mind is free since it initiates action through the will and thus transcends causality. Since to be free is to be without laws, Descartes was denying that there can be a science of psychology. The material world was rigidly determined. Physical processes and everything about animals and the bodies of men fall within this material world. The one exception was the human mind which has volition.

Methodological and Contentual Objectivity-Subjectivity

To his successors, Descartes was to be a rich source for various combinations of methodological and contentual objectivity and subjectivity. His conception of matter as extension furthered an objective quantitative science and opened the way to a view of man as a machine. Through his concept of an animal as an automaton and more specifically, through his concept of reflex action, Descartes contributed to the beginnings of both physiological and animal psychology. It was this sort of thinking that led a modern commentator, Randall, to say that Descartes ". . . held to a thoroughly mechanistic biology and psychology."[13] This is true for the latter only if one is thinking of psychology today. It is not true for the centuries between, during which psychology was conceived to be the study of mind. In historical perspective, the psychological side to the story is to prove to be quite a different matter. A non-mechanistic phase in the history of psychology was about to be entered upon because of Descartes. His contentually subjective position concerning the mind, was to dominate in psychology well into the first years of the Twentieth Century. Although Descartes insisted on a contentual subjectivity for the mind, in so doing, he was searching for a methodological objectivity and, hence, his view should not be confused with "subjectivism" in this case. He wanted desperately to attain a truth comparable to the impersonal truth of mathematics. He wished to distinguish the reality of consciousness from the world "outside" of which consciousness is not a part. In consciousness, we each are alone with ourselves. Reality, including other persons, is reached only by an inference, a step in itself that emphasized the distance between subject and object.

Descartes' *Meditations,* as Husserl[14] asserts, is the prototype of philosophical reflection in that he turned within himself for immediate experience. In so doing, he fostered the phenomenological approach which calls for mind to be studied in precisely this fashion.

Descartes must be given credit for a consistent, maintained attempt to examine "the sheer facts of experience" as MacLeod[15] put it recently. Just prior to the quotation MacLeod had explained that two German words, *"Erlebnis"* and *"Erfahrung,"* give a convenient distinction that the English word "experience" does not convey. *"Erlebnis"* refers to present experience, that which is immediately given without reference to origin; *"Erfahrung"* refers to an accumulation of experiences. This makes it possible to speak of Descartes as stressing experience in the sense of "Erlebnis" without implying he was empirical, i.e., depending upon accumulated experience as the source of knowledge which, as is very obvious, he was not. As a consequence of this emphasis, he contributed to a phenomenological point of view. Those who came after Descartes could find in him support for that which they wished to stress, whether it be contentual objectivity or subjectivity or methodological objectivity or subjectivity.

NOTES

Unless otherwise noted, citations to Descartes are the works in Elizabeth S. Haldane & G. R. T. Ross (Trans.), *The philosophical works of Descartes.* (2 vols.) Cambridge: University Press, 1911.

(1) Reichenbach, H. *The rise of scientific philosophy.* Berkeley, Calif.: University of California Press, 1951.

(2) Descartes, R. *Notes directed against a certain programme.* (1648) p. 443.

(3) Descartes, R. *Principles of philosophy. (1644)* In V. Cousin (Ed.), *Oeuvres,* Vol. 3, Paris: Levrault, 1824.
(4) Haldane, Elizabeth S. *Descartes, his life and times.* New York: Dutton, 1905.
(5) Descartes, R. *Letter to Mersenne,* March 1638. In *Oeuvres et lettres.* (Intro. by A. Bridoux.) Paris: Gallimard, 1953, p. 996.
(6) Descartes, R. *Letter to Arnauld.* (1648) In N. K. Smith (Trans.), *Descartes' philosophical writings.* London: Macmillan, 1952, pp. 280–281.
(7) It would seem that the actual term, "primary" and "secondary" in this context was introduced by Robert Boyle in 1666 in his "Origin of Forms and Qualities According to the Corpuscular Philosophy." T. Birch (Ed.), *Works,* Vol. 3, London: Johnson, *et al.* 1773. (1666) Details are given in Sir William Hamilton's edition of the *Works of Thomas Reid, D. D.* (Edinburgh: Machlachlan & Stewart, 1863) Vol. II, p. 825, Note D.
(8) Galileo, G. *Il Saggiatore.* (1623) Quoted in Joan W. Reeves, *Body and mind in Western thought.* London: Penguin Books, 1958, Question 48.
(9) Willey, B. *Seventeenth century background.* London: Chatto & Windus, 1934.
(10) Descartes, R. *Principles of philosophy.* (1644) IX.
(11) Descartes, R. Letter to Regius. (1641) In N. K. Smith (Trans.), *Descartes' philosophical writings.* London: Macmillan, 1952, pp. 269–270.
(12) Haldane, Elizabeth S. *Descartes, his life and times.* New York: Dutton, 1905.
(13) Randall, J.H., Jr., *The career of philosophy: from the Middle Ages to the Enlightenment.* New York: Columbia University Press, 1962, p. 381.
(14) Husserl, E. *Cartesian meditations: an introduction to phenomenology.* The Hague: Nijhoff, 1964. (1936).
(15) MacLeod, R. B. Phenomenology: a challenge to experimental psychology. In T. Wann (Ed.), *Behaviorism and phenomenology: contrasting bases for modern psychology.* Chicago: University of Chicago Press, 1964, pp. 47–78.

On Simple and Complex Ideas

John Locke

OF IDEAS IN GENERAL, AND THEIR ORIGINAL

1. *Idea is the object of thinking.*—Every man being conscious to himself, that he thinks, and that which his mind is applied about, whilst thinking, being the ideas that are there, it is past doubt that men have in their mind several ideas, such as are those expressed by the words, "whiteness, hardness, sweetness, thinking, motion, man, elephant, army, drunkenness," and others: it is in the first place then to be inquired, How he comes by them? I know it is a received doctrine, that men have native ideas and original characters stamped upon their minds in their very first being. This opinion I have at large examined already; and, I suppose, what I have said in the foregoing book will be much more easily admitted, when I have shown whence the understanding may get all the ideas it has, and by what ways and degrees they may come into the mind; for which I shall appeal to every one's own observation and experience.

2. *All ideas come from sensation or reflection.*—Let us then suppose the mind to be, as we say, white paper, void of all characters, without any ideas; how comes it to be furnished? Whence comes it by that vast store, which the busy and boundless fancy of man has painted on it with an almost endless variety? Whence has it

From Locke, J. (1690). *An essay concerning human understanding.* Adapted from edition published by the Open Court Publishing Company, Chicago, 1905. pp. 25–30, 33–36, 90–94.

all the materials of reason and knowledge? To this I answer, in one word, From experience; in that all our knowledge is founded, and from that it ultimately derives itself. Our observation, employed either about external sensible objects, or about the internal operations of our minds, perceived and reflected on by ourselves, is that which supplies our understandings with all the materials of thinking. These two are the fountains of knowledge, from whence all the ideas we have, or can naturally have, do spring.

3. *The object of sensation one source of ideas.*—First. Our senses, conversant about particular sensible objects, do convey into the mind several distinct perceptions of things, according to those various ways wherein those objects do affect them; and thus we come by those ideas we have of yellow, white, heat, cold, soft, hard, bitter, sweet, and all those which we call sensible qualities; which when I say the senses convey into the mind, I mean, they from external objects convey into the mind what produces there those perceptions. This great source of most of the ideas we have, depending wholly upon our senses, and derived by them to the understanding, I call, "sensation."

4. *The operations of our minds the other source of them.*—Secondly. The other fountain, from which experience furnisheth the understanding with ideas, is the perception of the operations of our own minds within us, as it is employed about the ideas it has got; which operations when the soul comes to reflect on and consider, do furnish the understanding with another set of ideas which could not be had from things without; and such are perception, thinking, doubting, believing, reasoning, knowing, willing, and all the different actings of our own minds; which we, being conscious of, and observing in ourselves, do from these receive into our understandings as distinct ideas, as we do from bodies affecting our senses. This source of ideas every man has wholly in himself; and though it be not sense as having nothing to do with external objects, yet it is very like it, and might properly enough be called "internal sense." But as I call the other "sensation," so I call this "reflection," the ideas it affords being such only as the mind gets by reflecting on its own operations within itself. By reflection, then, in the following part of this discourse, I would be understood to mean that notice which the mind takes of its own operations, and the manner of them, by reason whereof there come to be ideas of these operations in the understanding. These two, I say, viz., external material things as the objects of sensation, and the operations of our own minds within as the objects of reflection, are, to me, the only originals from whence all our ideas take their beginnings. The term "operations" here, I use in a large sense, as comprehending not barely the actions of the mind about its ideas, but some sort of passions arising sometimes from them, such as is the satisfaction or uneasiness arising from any thought.

5. *All our ideas are of the one or the other of these.*—The understanding seems to me not to have the least glimmering of any ideas which it doth not receive from one of these two. External objects furnish the mind with the ideas of sensible qualities, which are all those different perceptions they produce in us; and the mind furnishes the understanding with ideas of its own operations.

These, when we have taken a full survey of them, and their several modes, [combinations, and relations,] we shall find to contain all our whole stock of ideas; and that we have nothing in our minds which did not come in one of these two ways. Let any one examine his own thoughts, and thoroughly search into his understanding, and then let him tell me, whether all the original ideas he has there, are any other than of the objects of his senses, or of the operations of his mind considered as objects of his reflection; and how great a mass of knowledge soever he imagines to be lodged there, he will, upon taking a strict view, see that he has not any idea in his mind but what one of these two have imprinted, though perhaps with infinite variety compounded and enlarged by the understanding, as we shall see hereafter.

6. *Observable in children.*—He that attentively considers the state of a child at his first coming into the world, will have little reason to think him stored with plenty of ideas that are to be the matter of his future knowledge. It is by degrees he comes to be furnished with them; and though the ideas of obvious and familiar qualities imprint themselves before the memory begins to keep a register of time or order, yet it is often so late before some unusual qualities come in the way, that there are few men that cannot recollect the beginning of their acquaintance with them: and, if it were worth while, no doubt a child might be so ordered as to have but a very few even of the ordinary ideas till he were grown up to a man. But all that are born into the world being surrounded with bodies that perpetually and diversely affect them, variety of ideas, whether care be taken about it or not, are imprinted on the minds of children. Light and colours are busy at hand every where when the eye is but open; sounds and some tangible qualities fail not to solicit their proper senses, and force an entrance to the mind; but yet I think it will be granted easily, that if a child were kept in a place where he never saw any other but black and white till he were a man, he would have no more ideas of scarlet or green than he that from his childhood never tasted an oyster or a pine-apple has of those particular relishes.

7. *Men are differently furnished with these according to the different objects they converse with.*—Men then come to be furnished with fewer or more simple ideas from without, according as the objects they converse with afford greater or less variety; and from the operations of their minds within, according as they more or less reflect on them. For, though he that contemplates the operations of his mind cannot but have plain and clear ideas of them; yet, unless he turn his thoughts that way, and considers them attentively, he will no more have clear and distinct ideas of all the operations of his mind, and all that may be observed therein, than he will have all the particular ideas of any landscape, or of the parts and motions of a clock, who will not turn his eyes to it, and with attention heed all the parts of it. The picture or clock may be so placed, that they may come in his way every day; but yet he will have but a confused idea of all the parts they are made of, till he applies himself with attention to consider them each in particular.

8. *Ideas of reflection later, because they need attention.*—And hence we see the reason why it is pretty late before most children get ideas of the operations of their own minds; and some have not any very clear or perfect ideas of the greatest part of them all their lives:—because, though they pass there continually, yet like floating visions, they make not deep impressions enough to leave in the mind, clear, distinct, lasting ideas, till the understanding turns inwards upon itself, reflects on its own operations, and makes them the objects of its own contemplation. Children, when they come first into it, are surrounded with a world of new things, which, by a constant solicitation of their senses, draw the mind constantly to them, forward to take notice of new, and apt to be delighted with the variety of changing objects. Thus the first years are usually employed and diverted in looking abroad. Men's business in them is to acquaint themselves with what is to be found without; and so, growing up in a constant attention to outward sensations, seldom make any considerable reflection on what passes within them till they come to be of riper years; and some scarce ever at all.

9. *The soul begins to have ideas when it begins to perceive.*—To ask, at what time a man has first any ideas, is to ask when he begins to perceive; having ideas, and perception, being the same thing. I know it is an opinion, that the soul always thinks; and that it has the actual perception of ideas in itself constantly, as long as it exists; and that actual thinking is as inseparable from the soul, as actual extension is from the

body: which if true, to inquire after the beginning of a man's ideas is the same as to inquire after the beginning of his soul. For by this account, soul and its ideas, as body and its extension, will begin to exist both at the same time.

OF SIMPLE IDEAS

1. *Uncompounded appearances.*—The better to understand the nature, manner, and extent of our knowledge, one thing is carefully to be observed concerning the ideas we have; and that is, that some of them are simple, and some complex.

Though the qualities that affect our senses are, in the things themselves, so united and blended that there is no separation, no distance between them; yet it is plain the ideas they produce in the mind enter by the senses simple and unmixed. For though the sight and touch often take in from the same object, at the same time, different ideas—as a man sees at once motion and colour, the hand feels softness and warmth in the same piece of wax—yet the simple ideas thus united in the same subject are as perfectly distinct as those that come in by different senses; the coldness and hardness which a man feels in a piece of ice being as distinct ideas in the mind as the smell and whiteness of a lily, or as the taste of sugar and smell of a rose: and there is nothing can be plainer to a man than the clear and distinct perception he has of those simple ideas; which, being each in itself uncompounded, contains in it nothing but one uniform appearance or conception in the mind, and is not distinguishable into different ideas.

2. *The mind can neither make nor destroy them.*— These simple ideas, the materials of all our knowledge, are suggested and furnished to the mind only by those two ways above mentioned, viz., sensation and reflection. When the understanding is once stored with these simple ideas, it has the power to repeat, compare, and unite them, even to an almost infinite variety, and so can make at pleasure new complex ideas. But it is not in the power of the most exalted wit or enlarged understanding, by any quickness or variety of thought, to invent or frame one new simple idea in the mind, not taken in by the ways before mentioned; nor can any force of the understanding destroy those that are there: the dominion of man in this little world of his own understanding, being much-what the same as it is in the great world of visible things, wherein his power, however managed by art and skill, reaches no farther than to compound and divide the materials that are made to his hand but can do nothing towards the making the least particle of new matter, or destroying one atom of what is already in being. The same inability will every one find in himself, who shall go about to fashion in his understanding any simple idea not received in by his senses from external objects, or by reflection from the operations of his own mind about them. I would have any one try to fancy any taste which had never affected his palate, or frame the idea of a scent he had never smelt; and when he can do this, I will also conclude, that a blind man hath *ideas* of colours, and a deaf man true, distinct notions of sounds.

3. This is the reason why, though we cannot believe it impossible to God to make a creature with other organs, and more ways to convey into the understanding the notice of corporeal things than those five as they are usually counted, which he has given to man; yet I think it is not possible for any one to imagine any other qualities in bodies, howsoever constituted, whereby they can be taken notice of, besides sounds, tastes, smells, visible and tangible qualities. And had mankind been made with but four senses, the qualities then which are the objects of the fifth sense had been as far from our notice, imagination, and conception, as now any belonging to a sixth, seventh, or eighth sense can possibly be; which, whether yet some other creatures, in some other parts of this vast and stupendous universe, may not have, will be a great presumption to deny. He that will not set himself proudly at the top of all things, but will

consider the immensity of this fabric, and the great variety that is to be found in this little and inconsiderable part of it which he has to do with, may be apt to think, that in other mansions of it there may be other and different intelligible beings, of whose faculties he has as little knowledge or apprehension, as a worm shut up in one drawer of a cabinet hath of the senses or understanding of a man; such variety and excellency being suitable to the wisdom and power of the Maker. I have here followed the common opinion of man's having but five senses, though perhaps there may be justly counted more; but either supposition serves equally to my present purpose.

OF COMPLEX IDEAS.

1. *Made by the mind out of simple ones.*—We have hitherto considered those ideas, in the reception whereof the mind is only passive, which are those simple ones received from sensation and reflection before mentioned, whereof the mind cannot make one to itself, nor have any idea which does not wholly consist of them. [But as the mind is wholly passive in the reception of all its simple ideas, so it exerts several acts of its own, whereby out of its simple ideas, as the materials and foundations of the rest, the other are framed. The acts of the mind wherein it exerts in power over its simple ideas are chiefly these three: (1.) Combining several simple ideas into one compound one; and thus all complex ideas are made. (2.) The second is bringing two ideas, whether simple or complex, together, and setting them by one another, so as to take a view of them at once, without uniting them into one; by which way it gets all its ideas of relations. (3.) The third is separating them from all other ideas that accompany them in their real existence; this is called "abstraction:" and thus all its general ideas are made. This shows man's power and its way of operation to be much the same in the material and intellectual world. For, the materials in both being such as he has no power over, either to make or destroy, all that man can do is either to unite them together, or to set them by one another, or wholly separate them. I shall here begin with the first of these in the consideration of complex ideas, and come to the other two in their due places.] As simple ideas are observed to exist in several combinations united together, so the mind has a power to consider several of them united together as one idea; and that not only as they are united in external objects, but as itself has joined them. Ideas thus made up of several simple ones put together I call "complex;" such as are beauty, gratitude, a man, an army, the universe; which, though complicated of various simple ideas or complex ideas made up of simple ones, yet are, when the mind pleases, considered each by itself as one entire thing, and signified by one name.

2. *Made voluntarily.*—In this faculty of repeating and joining together its ideas, the mind has great power in varying and multiplying the objects of its thoughts infinitely beyond what sensation or reflection furnished it with; but all this still confined to those simple ideas which it received from those two sources, and which are the ultimate materials of all its compositions. For, simple ideas are all from things themselves; and of these the mind can have no more nor other than what are suggested to it. It can have no other ideas of sensible qualities than what come from without by the senses, nor any ideas of other kind of operations of a thinking substance than what it finds in itself: but when it has once got these simple ideas, it is not confined barely to observation, and what offers itself from without; it can, by its own power, put together those ideas it has, and make new complex ones which it never received so united.

3. *Are either modes, substances, or relations.*—Complex ideas, however compounded and decompounded, though their number be infinite, and the variety endless wherewith they fill and entertain the thoughts of men, yet I think

they may be all reduced under these three heads: 1. *Modes*. 2. *Substances*. 3. *Relations*.

4. *Modes.*—First. "Modes" I call such complex ideas which, however compounded, contain not in them the supposition of subsisting by themselves, but are considered as dependences on, or affections of, substances; such are the ideas signified by the words, "triangle, gratitude, murder," &c. And if in this I use the word "mode" in somewhat a different sense from its ordinary signification, I beg pardon; it being unavoidable in discourses differing from the ordinary received notions, either to make new words or to use old words in somewhat a new signification: the latter whereof, in our present case, is perhaps the more tolerable of the two.

5. *Simple and mixed modes.*—Of these modes there are two sorts which deserve distinct consideration. First. There are some which are only variations or different combinations of the same simple idea, without the mixture of any other, as a dozen, or score; which are nothing but the ideas of so many distinct units added together: and these I call "simple modes," as being contained within the bounds of one simple idea. Secondly. There are others compounded of simple ideas, of several kinds, put together to make one complex one; *v.g.*, beauty, consisting of a certain composition of colour and figure, causing delight in the beholder; theft, which, being the concealed change of the possession of any thing, without the consent of the proprietor, contains, as is visible, a combination of several ideas of several kinds; and these "I call mixed modes."

6. *Substances single or collective.*—Secondly. The ideas of substances are such combinations of simple ideas as are taken to represent distinct particular things subsisting by themselves, in which the supposed or confused idea of substance, such as it is, is always the first and chief. Thus, if to substance be joined the simple idea of a certain dull, whitish colour, with certain degrees of weight, hardness, ductility, and fusibility, we have the idea of lead; and a combination of the ideas of a certain sort of figure, with the powers of motion, thought, and reasoning, joined to substance, make the ordinary idea of a man. Now of substances also there are two sorts of ideas, one of single substances, as they exist separately, as of a man or a sheep; the other of several of those put together, as an army of men or flock of sheep; which collective ideas of several substances thus put together, are as much each of them one single idea as that of a man or an unit.

7. *Relation.*—Thirdly. The last sort of complex ideas is that we call "Relation," which consists in the consideration and comparing one idea with another.

Tabula Rasa—Its Origins and Implications

Nicholas G. Petryszak

There is no doubt that the Enlightenment held significant implications for the development of intellectual thought in the Western world. To this end a number of contemporary social historians and scientists contend that social theory as we know it today first emerged during this time.[1] While some students and critics of the Enlightenment have been willing to attribute the origins of social theory to this period in general, others have been more specific and argued that the initial impetus for the emergence of social theory

Adapted from Petryszak, N. G. (1981). Tabula rasa—Its origins and implications. *Journal of the History of the Behavioral Sciences, 17,* 15–27.

originated in the writings of one theorist in particular, John Locke.[2]

In this regard it has been pointed out that Locke's notion of *tabula rasa* contributed the necessary conceptual framework for the development of a science of society. Marvin Harris, for example, has emphatically argued that "Locke's *An Essay Concerning Human Understanding* was the midwife of all those modern behavioral disciplines, including psychology, sociology, and cultural anthropology, which stress the relationship between conditioning, environment and human thought and actions. . . . What Locke attempted to prove was that the human mind at birth was an "empty cabinet" [tabula rasa]. The knowledge or the ideas which the mind later come to be filled are all acquired during the process of . . . enculturation."[3]

The concept of tabula rasa plays a conspicuous role in modern social theory. Undoubtedly, the most pervasive and widespread opinion shared by social scientists today is that man is essentially "a social animal."[4] Most social scientists understand that human behavior is largely formed through social relationships between individuals acting together as members of larger groups.[5] In short, contemporary social theorists emphasize that man's inner nature is a tabula rasa which is fully dependent for its development on the processes of social interaction and socialization.[6]

It is apparent that at present a significant number of social theorists and historians are content in believing that it was John Locke's original intention to demonstrate that human nature is a product of society and the dynamics of socialization.[7] Most, it seems, are also satisfied with the idea that it was Locke's purpose, in developing the concept of tabula rasa, to explain the universe in general, and nature and man in particular, in secular and rational terms. In addition, they are willing to attribute to the concept of tabula rasa the important consequence of undermining Christian mysticism and the belief in Original Sin.[8] Likewise, it is uncritically accepted that Locke built his system of thought, especially his concept of tabula rasa, upon the combined bases of rationalism and experience in order to demonstrate that although man was imperfect, he was nevertheless susceptible to definite improvement through the application of the laws of science to the dimensions of human psychology and socialization as well as through the instituting of programs of social reform. For this reason, it is felt that Locke's emphasis on environmental influences rather than on the inner will in the shaping of the self places him in the modern line. Furthermore, his writings are interpreted as having set the task of education in ensuring that the mind "receives the right impressions, under the right circumstances." On the basis of these particular interpretations Locke is enthusiastically designated by many as the founder of modern pedagogical theory. His concept of tabula rasa is seen as the essential means for rationalizing various social and environmental deterministic solutions to the ills of society.

Despite these prevailing beliefs, it is readily evident when the concept of tabula rasa is examined in terms of the social, religious, and ideological circumstances within which it was written, that Locke's purposes were quite different from those which are commonly assumed today. In fact, it will be argued that Locke formulated the concept of tabula rasa and its related theoretical framework to resolve two conflicting world views towards which he was equally sympathetic. These world views consisted of the belief in divine determination, on the one hand, and the liberal belief in individualism, on the other. Furthermore, on the basis of a critical exegesis of Locke's original writings it is apparent that he did not wish to deny the possibility of the existence of certain biologically innate aspects of human nature, at least as he understood it from a theological nativistic point of view.

These various long-neglected features of Locke's theory of tabula rasa will be explored in the attempt to gain a better understanding of its original meanings and purposes as well as the implications which it holds for certain beliefs, assumptions, and theories popular within the social sciences at the present time. In this respect, this analysis provides the opportunity of determining whether existing theories dealing with concept and theory formation in the social sciences are entirely adequate for explaining the origins of such important and key concepts as tabula rasa. In addition, the question will be dealt with of whether it was Locke's goal to utilize this concept as a means to realize the ideals of rationalism and to provide the groundwork for the development of a science of society. Finally, close attention shall be given to the problem of whether or not the tabula rasa doctrine can be considered as the original impetus to the development of the theory of the social determination of human behavior.

LOCKE AND THE ENLIGHTENMENT

In order to come to terms with the intentions and purposes of Locke's theoretical arguments as related to the concept of tabula rasa, it is first necessary to review the social and ideological context within which he wrote. Locke with other intellectuals in the early period of the Enlightenment of the late seventeenth and eighteenth centuries came to question the traditional, legal, moral, and religious foundations of Western European culture. The Enlightenment is of course older than the eighteenth century and wider than the territory of France. Its overall orientation towards skepticism and science was already widespread in England during the latter half of the seventeenth century and it is in this sense that Locke may be understood as one of its earliest contributors.

While generalizations about the common beliefs shared among theorists of the Enlightenment will be made here, it is nevertheless important to keep in mind that there existed a wide disparity of opinion among them. In many respects it would be difficult to relate such thinkers among others as Locke, David Hume, Adam Ferguson, Baron de Montesquieu, and Jean-Jacques Rousseau to one another, or to the philosophes. As a consequence, it is necessary to qualify any generalization about this body of theorists in a careful and tentative fashion.[9] However, what can be argued is that all of these theorists shared "the spirit of the Enlightenment" which, even in its earliest stages, was expressive of varying levels of inquisitive skepticism towards many traditional beliefs and institutions. The underlying assumption maintained by the Enlightenment thinkers was that the world of reason and the world of phenomena formed a single, unitary structure.[10] It was the articulation of this assumption which initiated the post-Newtonian phase of science by making far-reaching changes in the West's concept of scientific method and its view of nature.[11] The overall revolutionary significance of the Enlightenment consisted of the promotion of the ideal of reason and a secular naturalism which represented a complete reversal of the medieval distrust of the phenomenal world.[12]

One of the chief figures responsible for shifting the general orientation of social thought away from the theories of Descartes and the belief in divine determination was John Locke. Locke's theoretical perspective was directed against metaphysical speculation and the complete reliance on ideas of Divine Will to explain the origins of human thought and action. This does not mean, however, that Locke was intent on undermining the whole credibility of the Christian religion. He set himself the task of understanding how human knowledge was gained without having to rely on the notions of innate ideas implanted by God. The intention of his social theories was to demonstrate that man himself played an important part in the development of human knowledge, moral law, and the law of nature which Locke felt to be synonymous with God's will.[13] Locke sought to solve the rather difficult problem of combining the traditional belief in the divine determination of behavior with the liberal belief in individual freedom and independent initiative of action.

Locke, like the later philosophes, felt it necessary to demonstrate that the natural as well as the human social world conformed to the dictates of human reason; at the same time, he encouraged the reconstruction of European society according to these dictates. The belief of many of the Enlightenment thinkers in a natural science of society was also intimately related to the liberal orientation of their values. To some extent, Locke as well as others shared the idea that society was ruled by predictable, mechanistically determined processes in the form of natural laws. The affirmative belief in natural law was closely linked with their support of the leading liberal ideas of individual freedom and the exemption of man from all forms of arbitrary authority. One of the most striking accomplishments of the Enlightenment theorists was that, in maintaining their liberal ideals of individuality, they seemed to have discovered a concept of social freedom that could reconcile a faith in the orderly, predictable, mechanistically determined operation of society with a commitment to individual liberty.[14] Ideally, the liberal definition of freedom exempted the individual from human authority by subjecting him to the impersonal authority of mechanistic social forces. It was believed that perception and definition of natural law required no aid other than the rational forces of knowledge, which communicated its findings to scientists through sense perception and its supplementary process of logical judgment and inference.[15] This idea was expressed in the famous empirical adage, *"Nihil est in intellectu guod non prius fuit in sensu"* (nothing is in the mind which is not first perceived by the senses.) For this reason it was believed that the realm of nature was opposed, to a greater or lesser degree, to the realm of divine grace and that it was the application of the methods of science which ultimately gave the individual control over the environment. In this sense, the writings of Locke and later intellectuals of the Enlightenment constituted "the intellectual climax to the gradual emancipation of economic and political structures from the framework of feudal Christendom."

Locke's liberal values have been interpreted by many social historians as a leading element in all his theoretical discussions. Theodore Artz and others have emphasized that in Locke's writings there existed a close association between his political ideas and the scientific movement. While he approached social and political questions from the point of view of a seventeenth-century physicist, his emphasis was always on "the liberal side of things.[16] The content of Locke's theories bear the characterizing and distinguishing features of liberal society: individualism, private property, the primacy of economic motives and market relations, utilitarianism, and a separate and supreme realm of positive law."[17]

Also implicit within the social critiques formulated by Locke and other Enlightenment thinkers was the assumption that the prevailing institutions in society were contrary to human nature and thus inhibitive of human growth and development.[18] Human nature was assumed to be innately good and it was the social environment which was responsible for man's aggressive and unjust actions, as well as for the inequalities which could be observed between men.[19] As Lord Morely said, it was believed "that human nature is good, and that the world is capable of being a desirable place and that the evil of the world is the fruit of bad education and bad institutions."[20] Such views about human nature were antithetical to clerical and aristocractic assumptions about human nature of the early- and mid-seventeenth century.[21] It is clear from this that there existed a strong interdependent relationship between the liberal ideals of Locke and other thinkers of the Enlightenment, their theories of man, society, social reform, and their explicit assumptions about man's innate nature.

The question of religion must also be dealt with in the consideration of the overall intellectual orientation of John Locke and the other Enlightenment thinkers. One of the most intense intellectual debates which began in the early period of the Enlightenment was over the question of religion. The "crisis of religious consciousness" in the late seventeenth and early eighteenth centuries would never have developed its distinctive anti-Christian tone if the Church had not been in some sense a political as well as an intellectual force.[22] While some theorists directly criticized the structure and power relationships of the Church, the earlier theorists inclusive of John Locke addressed themselves to the problem of the role which God played in the determination of human thought and action. As a consequence, Locke, as well as others, was faced with the problem of criticizing the then-popular Cartesian world view.

By the mid-seventeenth century, Cartesianism had come to dominate philosophical thought in Western Europe. As a form of methodological inquiry, Cartesianism was applied to a wide range of subjects including history, ethics, and religion. Descartes' method was one of cautious and systematic inquiry aimed at the reductive analysis of complex phenomena into their simplest constituent parts which were explained in terms of truths which are derived from the will of the "Divine Spirit of God."[23] Descartes' discourse of methodological reasoning, given in his famous *Discourse on the Method For Rightly Conducting One's Reason and Seeking Truth in the Sciences* (1637), denied the validity of the axiomatic truths and syllogisms of the scholastics.

Descartes sought to establish a system of rationalism deduced from clear and innate intuitions. His support of the validity of scientific research was complemented by his belief in the existence of fixed and immutable laws of nature, inertia, and the conservation of energy. The material universe, according to Descartes, was ordered by the laws of motion which were determined once and for all by the divine intelligence.[24] In his opinion, man was unique insofar as his nature was characterized by the union of soul and body. Mind, which Descartes saw as equal in importance to man's soul, contained a number of innate ideas. He admitted that ultimately the existence of these innate ideas could be attributed to the hand of God. As he stated, "the whole force of the argument lies in this—that I now would not exist, and possess the nature I have, that nature which puts me in possession of the idea of God, unless God did really exist, the God, the idea of whom is found in me."[25] The laws of nature, man's innate nature, and human ideas were ascribed to the workings of a divine intelligence. He felt that the "idea of God" was innate to the human consciousness. By showing the interrelationship between natural law on the one hand and God on the other, Descartes was able to reconcile to some extent the interests of science and the Church.

Descartes' ideas were subjected to severe criticisms by many social theorists in the late-seventeenth century. The criticism of Descartes originated in the growing discontent of early Enlightenment thinkers with all forms of metaphysical idealism, especially that type of idealism which legitimated the authority of the Church in acting as a mediator between man, the laws of nature, and the ideas which were believed to be innate in human consciousness.[26] Many intellectuals in the initial stages of the Enlightenment increasingly came to believe, contrary to the opinions of Descartes, that man was an individual who played an active role in determining his own behavior and thoughts.

It is within this intellectual climate of liberal individualism, the belief in certain innate features of human nature, and the rejection of the Cartesian paradigm that Locke's theory of tabula rasa must be specifically understood and evaluated.

LOCKE'S THEORY OF TABULA RASA

John Locke's major theoretical contributions were formulated in his well-known *An Essay on*

Human Understanding (1689). In this essay he explained that the mind of a child at birth, rather than being characterized by a number of innate ideas attributable to divine will, was in fact a tabula rasa—a blank slate upon which experience and reflection, derived from senses, wrote their effects. The creation of human knowledge was attributed not completely to divine will, but to experience and its individual interpretation by man. Locke's rejection of the Cartesian notion of innate ideas was in one respect indicative of his liberal world view by which he sought to establish man as a relatively independent actor, able to determine his own affairs and actions although to some extent subject to the influence of God's will. The question nevertheless remains, to what degree might Locke have made use of specific assumptions about the innate features of human nature in order to confirm and legitimize his liberal belief in the autonomy of the individual in the creation of human knowledge on the one hand and on the other, his belief as a Christian that God was the ultimate arbiter of human affairs?

The purpose of Locke's *Essay on Human Understanding* was to inquire into "the origin, certainty, and extent of human knowledge, together with the grounds and degrees of belief, opinion and assent."[27] In rejecting the notion of innate ideas, he argued that "to say, that there are truths imprinted on the soul, which it perceives or understands most; imprinting, if it signify any thing, being nothing else but the making of certain truths to be perceived. For to imprint any thing on the mind, without the mind's perceiving it, seems to me hardly intelligible."[28] Locke added that while there are no innate ideas, there are also no innate moral principles insofar as "the ignorance wherein many men are of them, and the slowness of assent wherewith others receive them, are manifest proofs that they are not innate and such as offer themselves to their view without searching."[29] It was further maintained that knowledge, rather than being based on innate ideas, comes instead from experience. As Locke argues, "our observation employed either about external sensible objects, or about the internal operations of our minds, perceived and reflected on by ourselves, is that which supplies our understandings with all the materials of thinking. These two are the fountains of knowledge, from whence all the ideas we have, or can naturally have do spring."[30] The "human soul" accordingly, "begins to have ideas, when it begins to perceive."[31]

The development of ideas was defined by Locke as a dynamic process in that "in time the mind comes to reflect on its own operations about the ideas got by sensation, and thereby stores itself with a new set of ideas, which I call ideas of reflection. These are the impressions that are made on our senses by outward objects that are intrinsical to the mind, and its own operations, proceeding from powers intrinsical and proper to itself; which when reflected on by itself, becoming also objects of its contemplation."[32]

Despite denying the existence of ideas in the human consciousness since birth, Locke nevertheless admitted that the human mind was characterized by a number of innate faculties which enabled the individual to retain "those simple ideas which from sensation and reflection it hath received."[33] These faculties included perception, contemplation, memory, attention, repetition, pleasure and pain, discerning, comparing, and abstraction."[34] He also believed that the sensing of pleasure and pain played a significant role in the development of the passions which all men share insofar as ". . . we love, desire, rejoice, and hope, only in respect to pleasure; we hate, fear and grieve, only in respect to pain . . . all these passions are moved by things only as they appear to be causes of pleasure and pain . . ."[35] In direct conjunction with this idea of pleasure was the understanding that the "necessity of perceiving true happiness is the foundation of liberty" and is "the greatest good" of intellectual beings.[36] In this fashion Locke purported almost a classical Epicurean view of human nature which maintained that man is motivated by the search for pleasure and the avoidance of pain.[37]

In explaining the origins of man's various faculties, Locke was quite emphatic in pointing out that they were ultimately provided by God in ensuring that man would have the ability to gain knowledge about His good works. He contended that God "furnished man with those faculties, which will serve for the sufficient discerning of all things requisite to the end of such a being. And I doubt not but to show that a man, by the right use of his natural abilities, may, without any innate principles, attain a knowledge of a God, and other things that concern him. God having endowed man with those faculties of knowing which he hath, was no more obliged by his goodness to plant those innate notions in his mind, than that, having given him reasons, hands, and materials, he should build him bridges or houses."[38]

While Locke disclaimed the existence of innate ideas in man as elementary features of human nature, he was at the same time willing to argue that human nature was characterized by certain innate faculties of perception and experience which were given to man, as aspects of his nature by God. It is important to point out from this that Locke in the development of the tabula rasa doctrine was not aloof from using assumptions about the nature of human nature. Nor was he exempt from ascribing the ultimate origins of those innate faculties to the will of God. On the basis of these observations we may justifiably ask the question, already articulated by a number of prominent social historians, whether it is correct to consider Locke's tabula rasa theory as a denial of the role which certain features of man's innate nature may play in the determination of human knowledge and behavior as well as a denial of God's evident intervention in human affairs?[39]

In other major works, Locke also relied on a number of assumptions about the innate features of human nature as well as making overt references to the role which God played in directing human action. His *Essays on the Law of Nature* (1663) was an attempt to define the degree of obligation which the individual had towards natural law. By natural law he meant a "law promulgated by God in a natural way." The binding force of natural law according to this argument was predicated on the interdependent relationship between God, natural law, and human nature. It was assumed that the individual had a moral as well as a natural obligation to natural law. On the one hand, it was felt that there are moral obligations which are binding because they arise from the commands of a superior will, which according to Locke, is the final source of all obligation. Conversely, there are also natural obligations which are binding because they arise from man's innate nature.[40] The essential character of natural law was defined as being "implanted in man's heart by God so that reason can only discover and interpret it."[41] In addition, he asserted that all men are compelled to search out and discover natural laws ". . . since man is very much urged on this part of his duty by an inward instinct."[42] Moreover, man is driven by his own innate nature to seek out the existence of natural law and is compelled by his own nature to obey it. As he explained this point, "For in the first place, it cannot be said that some men are born so free that they are not in the least subject to this law, for this is not a private or positive law created according to circumstances . . . rather it is a fixed and permanent rule of morals, which reason itself pronounces, and which persists being a fact so firmly rooted in the soul of human nature."

Locke, in his discussion of natural law, was again able to reconcile the belief in individual freedom of action with the Christian idea of divine determination by emphasizing that obedience to natural law is dictated by man's individual reason, which is in turn an element of human nature given to man by God. In this instance we see the specific interrelationships which existed between Locke's use of assumptions about human nature, his adamant belief in the liberal ideals of individual freedom, and his determination to avoid overt conflict with the more traditional Church doctrines which asserted that human action, at least to some degree, was ultimately influenced by divine will.

The popular belief maintained today by Marvin Harris and others that Locke's theory of tabula rasa was meant to demonstrate the social determination of human action and the denial of an innate human nature which may affect human behavior is a serious misinterpretation of Locke's actual intentions. The fact is that Locke utilized a whole number of assumptions about man's innate nature to justify his theories about man's ability to reason, his willingness to obey natural law, his right to individual liberty, and the role which God played in human affairs. In general, his social theories exemplify a basic interrelationship between his liberal views on individual liberty and his Christian background. Locke made use of assumptions about human nature to objectify, manifest, and legitimize both his liberal ideals and his Christian beliefs. His rejection of the Cartesian theory of innate ideas did not, in itself, mean that Locke accepted the idea that man is without any form of an innate human nature or that the individual is completely determined by social experience. . . .

NOTES

1. See John H. Abraham, *Origins and Growth of Sociology* (Middlesex, England: Penguin, 1973).
2. John W. Yoltan, *John Locke and the Theory of Ideas* (Oxford: Clarendon Press, 1968).
3. Marvin Harris, *The Rise of Anthropological Theory* (New York: Crowell, 1968), p. 18.
4. Dennis Forcese and Stephen Richer, *Issues In Canadian Society* (Scarborough, Ontario: Prentice-Hall, 1975), p. 7.
5. Leonard Broom and Philip Selznick, *Sociology* (New York: Harper & Row, 1963), p. 15.
6. Robert Nisbet, *The Social Bond* (New York: Knopf, 1950), p. 46.
7. See: James Gibson, *Locke's Theory of Knowledge and Its Historical Relations* (Cambridge, England: University Press, 1960); Ernest L. Tueson, *The Imagination As A Means of Grace—Locke and the Aesthetics of Romanticism* (Berkeley: University of California, 1960); Emile Brehier, *The Seventeenth Century* (Chicago: University of Chicago, 1966); Marvin Harris, *The Rise of Anthropological Theory* (New York: Crowell, 1968); John L. Kraus, *John Locke: Empiricist, Atomist, Conceptualist and Agnostic* (New York: Philosophical Library, 1968); and John W. Yoltan, *Locke and the Compass of Human Understanding* (Cambridge, England: University Press, 1970).
8. Kraus, *John Locke,* pp. 26–27.
9. Daniel W. Rossides, *The History and Nature of Sociological Theory* (Boston: Houghton Mifflin, 1978), p. 47.
10. Ernst Cassirer, *The Philosophy of the Enlightenment* (Boston: Beacon, 1962), p. 29.
11. Peter Gay, *Age of Enlightenment* (NY: Time, 1969).
12. Rossides, *Sociological Theory*, p. 29.
13. See Gordon Hefelbower, *The Relation of John Locke to English Deism* (Chicago: University of Chicago, 1919).
14. Ellen M. Wood, *Mind and Politics* (Berkeley, Calif.: University of California, 1972), p. 177.
15. Cassirer, *The Enlightenment,* p. 39.
16. Frederick B. Artz, *The Enlightenment in France* (Kent, Ohio: Kent University, 1968), p. 12.
17. Crawford B. Macpherson, *The Political Theory of Possessive Individualism* (London: Oxford University, 1962), p. 3.
18. Irving M. Zeitlin, *Ideology and the Development of Sociological Theory* (New Jersey: Prentice-Hall, 1968), p. 3.
19. Shirley Gruner, *Economic Materialism and Social Moralism* (The Hague: Mouton, 1973), pp. 14–15.
20. John R. White, *The Anti-Philosophes* (London: Martin Press, 1970), p. 5.
21. William J. Brandt, *The Shape of Medieval History—Studies in Modes and Perception* (New York: Schoken, 1977).
22. John H. Brumfitt, *The French Enlightenment* (Cambridge, Mass.: Schenkman, 1972), p. 44.
23. Ibid.
24. Norman L. Torrey, *Les Philosophes* (New York: Capricorn, 1960), pp. 12–13.

25. Rene Descartes, *Objections and Replies,* ed. Margaret Wilson (New York: Mentor, 1969), p. 260.
26. Lionel Gossman, *French Society and Culture* (Englewood Cliffs, N.J.: Prentice-Hall, 1972), pp. 76–77.
27. John Locke, *Essay On Human Understanding* (Germany: Scientia Verlage Aalen, 1968), p. 1.
28. Ibid., p. 15.
29. Ibid., p. 35.
30. Ibid., pp. 82–83.
31. Ibid., p. 86.
32. Ibid., pp. 97–98.
33. Ibid., p. 137.
34. Ibid., pp. 137–138.
35. Ibid., p. 234.
36. Ibid., pp. 270–271.
37. Norman W. DeWitt, *Epicurus and His Philosophy* (New York: Paulist Press, 1964), pp. 216–248.
38. Locke, *Essay On Human Understanding,* p. 67.
39. Roland N. Stromberg, *An Intellectual History of Modern Europe* (New York: Prentice-Hall, 1975), p. 113.
40. John Locke, *Essays On the Law of Nature,* ed. William Von Leyden (Oxford: Clarendon, 1954), p. 50.
41. Ibid., p. 95.
42. Ibid., p. 159.

CHAPTER 3

THE PHYSIOLOGICAL ROOTS OF PSYCHOLOGY

The emergence of experimental psychology in the nineteenth century was, to a large extent, the melding of questions from the field of philosophy and methods from the field of physiology. The previous chapter considered the modern philosophical antecedents of psychology, principally in terms of mechanism and empiricism. In this chapter, the focus is on the physiological origins of psychology, largely the work of the nineteenth century. That century was a time of great progress in physiology, particularly with respect to an understanding of the workings of the nervous system.

In 1811, the Scottish anatomist Charles Bell (1774–1842) privately published a booklet in which he stated that the spinal cord was made up of two kinds of nerves—*sensory* (in the dorsal portion of the cord) and *motor* (in the ventral part of the cord). Eleven years later, the French physiologist François Magendie (1783–1855) published a similar statement in a French scientific journal, laying claim to the discovery. That claim of priority angered Bell and his supporters. Magendie countered that he had never read Bell's booklet, which seems likely because Bell is said to have distributed the copies only to select friends. This incident has been judged, with the passage of time, to be one of independent discovery, and the controversy resolved to some extent by labeling the specificity of spinal function as the Bell-Magendie Law.

That discovery was an important one for several reasons. First, it added substantially to the view that specificity existed throughout the nervous system, that is, that different parts of the brain and spinal cord controlled different functions. Second, the work of Bell and Magendie on the spinal cord identified separate sensory and motor systems—separate systems for interpreting stimuli and initiating responses (of obvious importance to the soon-to-be stimulus-response psychologies).

Extending the work on nerve function, the German physiologist Johannes Müller (1801–1858) discovered what would become known as the *doctrine of specific nerve energies.* Müller wrote that there were five kinds of nerves, each type corresponding to a particular sensory system. Thus, visual nerves carried only visual information. For example, the optic nerve can be artificially stimulated by pressure on the eyeball. With this pressure, and the eyes closed, the subject will "see" things (light, color, perhaps movement) because the excitation of visual nerve fibers results in visual perception, regardless of the actual source of stimulation (in this case not light, but mechanical pressure).

Müller was also interested in the speed of nerve conduction. He concluded that because nerve impulses were instantaneous they could never be measured. Yet a few years later, his countryman, Hermann von Helmholtz (1821–1894), using a motor nerve from a frog's leg, was able to measure the speed of conduction and found it to be much slower than imagined (around 50 to 90 meters per second). Helmholtz's discovery meant that mental processes were not instantaneous and that the time required for mental actions might be measured.

As mentioned earlier, one idea that was gaining popularity in the nineteenth century was that different brain areas served different functions, an idea known as *cortical localization of function.* French surgeon Pierre Flourens (1794–1867), whose work partially supported cortical localization though he did not, systematically removed portions of animal brains to observe the subsequent effects on the behavior of those animals. His studies convinced him that the cerebrum was responsible for higher mental processes such as perception, memory, and reasoning, whereas the cerebellum controlled such functions as the coordination of movement. The work of Flourens was extended by another French surgeon, Paul Broca (1824–1880), whose clinical autopsy method allowed him to locate specific functional areas within the cerebrum. Examining the brains of individuals who had lost their ability to speak, Broca found damage in a particular area of the frontal lobe of the cerebrum, an area he believed was responsible for producing speech. Today, neuroscientists refer to that part of the brain as Broca's Area.

Still later in the nineteenth century, researchers began to use mild amounts of electric current to stimulate the neurons of the brain artificially, demonstrating that certain motor and perceptual responses could be reliably produced from stimulation of particular brain areas. There was accompanying research, particularly in the physiology of the sensory systems, that greatly increased our knowledge of perception, especially in the visual and auditory systems—for example, discoveries in color vision, depth perception, sound perception, and touch sensitivity. These studies of sensory physiology, of fundamental importance for the new science of psychology, were largely stimulated by the emphasis the British empiricists placed on the senses in acquiring knowledge.

In short, philosophers had debated the workings of the mind for centuries—questions about the nature of perception, of reason, of learning. The physiologists of the nineteenth century were well equipped in terms of technological and conceptual advances to begin answering those questions, and they did so by reducing the mind to its neurological substrate. Later chapters will have more about that reductionism.

THE READINGS

The readings in this chapter focus on the issue of nervous system specialization, both in terms of neuronal and cortical specificity. The first selection is by Johannes Müller and is the final version of his doctrine of specific nerve energies. This important doctrine was published in his *Handbook of Physiology* in 1838. The second selection, originally published in 1861, is Paul Broca's classic account of his famous patient Leborgne (also known as Tan). Leborgne was unable to speak for the final twenty-one years of his life. After Leborgne's death, Broca's autopsy of his patient's brain revealed a lesion in the left frontal lobe. Broca presented his important finding at a meeting of the Paris Anthropological Society, during which he allowed members to see Leborgne's brain, preserved in a jar.

The remaining two selections are contemporary historical works that treat the issues of cortical localization. The first was written by Stanley Finger, a biopsychologist and author of an excellent history of neuroscience (Finger, 1994), from which this selection is taken. Finger discusses the importance of Broca's work and why it had such a significant impact on the acceptance of cortical localization and on notions of cerebral dominance.

The final selection is by noted historian of psychology Raymond E. Fancher and deals with the subject of phrenology, an eighteenth- and nineteenth-century "science" that proposed that an individual's traits and abilities could be determined by measuring the bumps and indentations on the individual's skull. Those bumps and indentations were supposed to be produced by the growth of the brain tissue underlying those skull areas. Phrenology was a natural extension of the ideas of cortical localization of function, but it did not hold up to scientific scrutiny (see Bakan, 1966; Finger, 1994; Walsh, 1976). Phrenology is often omitted from textbooks on the history of psychology, yet it is clearly a part of psychology's story. It has been variously called the first systematic scientific program of behavioral research (see O'Donnell, 1985), the first applied psychology (a precursor of mental testing and vocational guidance), and the first physiological psychology. In this selection, Fancher tells the interesting tale of Franz Joseph Gall (1758–1828) as a leader of the phrenological movement, and of the work of Flourens in discrediting that movement.

REFERENCES

Bakan, D. (1966). The influence of phrenology on American psychology. *Journal of the History of the Behavioral Sciences*, 2, 200–220.

Finger, S. (1994). *Origins of neuroscience: A history of explorations into brain function.* New York: Oxford University Press

O'Donnell, J. M. (1985). *The origins of behaviorism: American psychology, 1870–1920.* New York: New York University Press.

Walsh, A. A. (1976). Phrenology and the Boston medical community in the 1830s. *Bulletin of the History of Medicine, 50,* 261–273.

The Specific Energies of Nerves

Johannes Müller

The senses, by virtue of the peculiar properties of their several nerves, make us acquainted with the states of our own body, and they also inform us of the qualities and changes of external nature, as far as these give rise to changes in the condition of the nerves. Sensation is a property common to all the senses; but the kind of sensation is different in each: thus we have the sensations of light, of sound, of taste, of smell, and of feeling, or touch. By feeling, or touch, we understand the peculiar kind of sensation of which the ordinary sensitive nerves generally—as, the nervus trigeminus, vagus, glossopharyngeal, and the spinal nerves—are susceptible; the sensations of itching, of pleasure and pain, of heat and cold, and those excited by the act of touch in its more limited sense, are varieties of this mode of sensation. That which through the medium of our senses is actually perceived by the sensorium, is indeed merely a property or change of condition of our nerves; but the imagination and reason are ready to interpret the modifications in the state of the nerves produced by external influences as properties of the external bodies themselves. This mode of regarding sensations has become so habitual in the case of the senses which are more rarely affected by internal causes, that it is only on reflection that we perceive it to be erroneous. In the case of the sense of feeling or touch, on the contrary, where the peculiar sensations of the nerves perceived by the sensorium are excited as frequently by internal as by external causes, it is easily conceived that the feeling of pain or pleasure, for example, is a condition of the nerves, and not a property of the things which excite it. This leads us to the consideration of some general laws, a knowledge of which is necessary before entering on the physiology of the separate senses.

Adapted from Müller, J. (1838). The specific energies of nerves. *Handbook of Physiology*. Translation from B. Rand (1912), *The Classical Psychologists*. Boston: Houghton-Mifflin.

I. In the first place, it must be kept in mind that external agencies can give rise to no kind of sensation which cannot also be produced by internal causes, exciting changes in the condition of our nerves.

In the case of the sense of touch, this is at once evident. The sensations of the nerves of touch (or common sensibility) are those of cold and heat, pain and pleasure, and innumerable modifications of these, which are neither painful nor pleasurable, but yet have the same kind of sensation as their element, though not in an extreme degree. All these sensations are constantly being produced by internal causes in all parts of our body endowed with sensitive nerves; they may also be excited by causes acting from without, but external agencies are not capable of adding any new element to their nature. The sensations of the nerves of touch are therefore states or qualities proper to themselves, and merely rendered manifest by exciting causes external or internal. The sensation of smell also may be perceived independently of the application of any odorous substance from without, the nerve of smell being thrown by an internal cause into the condition requisite for the production of the sensation. This perception of the sensation or odours without an external exciting cause, though not of frequent occurrence, has been many times observed in persons of an irritable nervous system; and the sense of taste is probably subject to the same affection, although it would be always difficult to determine whether the taste might not be owing to a change in the qualities of the saliva or mucus of the mouth; the sensation of nausea, however, which belongs to the sensations of taste, is certainly very often perceived as the result of a merely internal affection of the nerves. The sensations of the sense of vision, namely, color, light, and darkness, are also perceived independently of all external exciting cause. In the state of the most perfect freedom from excitement, the optic nerve has no other sensation than that of darkness. The excited condition of the nerve is manifested, even while the eyes are closed, by the appearance of light, or luminous flashes, which are merely sensations of the nerve, and not owing to the presence of any matter of light, and consequently are not capable of illuminating any surrounding objects. Every one is aware how common it is to see bright colours while the eyes are closed, particularly in the morning when the irritability of the nerves is still considerable. These phenomena are very frequent in children after waking from sleep. Through the sense of vision, therefore, we receive from external nature no impressions which we may not also experience from internal excitement of our nerves; and it is evident that a person blind from infancy in consequence of opacity of the transparent media of the eye, must have a perfect internal conception of light and colours, provided the retina and optic nerve be free from lesion. The prevalent notions with regard to the wonderful sensations supposed to be experienced by persons blind from birth when their sight is restored by operation, are exaggerated and incorrect. The elements of the sensation of vision, namely, the sensations of light, colour, and darkness, must have been previously as well known to such persons as to those of whom the sight has always been perfect. If, moreover, we imagine a man to be from his birth surrounded merely by external objects destitute of all variety of colours, so that he could never receive the impressions of colours from without, it is evident that the sense of vision might nevertheless have been no less perfect in him than in other men; for light and colours are innate endowments of his nature, and require merely a stimulus to render them manifest.

The sensations of hearing also are excited as well by internal as by external causes; for, whenever the auditory nerve is in a state of excitement, the sensations peculiar to it, as the sounds of ringing, humming, &c. are perceived. It is by such sensations that the diseases of the auditory nerve manifest themselves; and, even in less grave, transient affections of the nervous system, the sensations of humming and ringing in the ears afford evidence that the sense of hearing participates in the disturbance.

No further proof is wanting to show that external influences give rise in our senses to no other sensations than those which may be excited in the corresponding nerves by internal causes.

II. The same internal cause excites in the different senses different sensations;—in each sense the sensations peculiar to it.

One uniform internal cause acting on all the nerves of the senses in the same manner, is the accumulation of blood in the capillary vessels of the nerve, as in congestion and inflammation. This uniform cause excites in the retina, while the eyes are closed, the sensation of light and luminous flashes; in the auditory nerve, humming and ringing sounds; and in the nerves of feeling, the sensation of pain. In the same way, also, a narcotic substance introduced into the blood excites in the nerves of each sense peculiar symptoms; in the optic nerves the appearance of luminous sparks before the eyes; in the auditory nerves tinnitus aurium; and in the common sensitive nerves the sensation of ants creeping over the surface.

III. The same external cause also gives rise to different sensations in each sense, according to the special endowments of its nerve.

The mechanical influence of a blow, concussion, or pressure excites, for example, in the eye the sensation of light and colours. It is well known that by exerting pressure upon the eye, when the eyelids are closed, we can give rise to the appearance of a luminous circle; by more gentle pressure the appearance of colours may be produced, and one color may be made to change to another. Children, waking from sleep before daylight, frequently amuse themselves with these phenomena. The light thus produced has no existence external to the optic nerve, it is merely a sensation excited in it. However strongly we press upon the eye in the dark, so as to give rise to the appearance of luminous flashes, these flashes, being merely sensations, are incapable of illuminating external objects. Of this any one may easily convince himself by experiment. I have in repeated trials never been able, by means of these luminous flashes in the eye, to recognize in the dark the nearest objects, or to see them better than before; nor could another person, while I produced by pressure on my eye the appearance of brilliant flashes, perceive in it the slightest trace of real light.

A mechanical influence excites also peculiar sensations of the auditory nerve; at all events, it has become a common saying, "to give a person what will make his ears ring," or "what will make his eyes flash fire," or "what will make him feel," so that the same cause, a blow, produces in the nerves of hearing, sight, and feeling, the different sensations proper to these senses. It has not become a part of common language that a blow shall be given which will excite the sense of smell, or of taste; nor would such sayings be correct; yet mechanical irritation of the soft palate, of the epiglottis and root of the tongue, excites the sensation of nausea. The actions of sonorous bodies on the organ of hearing is entirely mechanical. A sudden mechanical impulse of the air upon the organ of hearing produces the sensation of a report of different degrees of intensity according to the violence of the impulse, just as an impulse upon the organ of vision gives rise to the sensation of light. If the action of the mechanical cause on the organ of hearing be of continued duration, the sound is also continued; and when caused by a rapid succession of uniform impulses, or vibrations, it has a musical character. If we admit that the matter of light acts on bodies by mechanical oscillation (the undulation theory), we shall have another example of a mechanical influence, producing different effects on different senses. These undulations, which produce in the eye the sensation of light, have no such effects on other senses; but in the nerves of feeling they produce the sensation of warmth.

The stimulus of electricity may serve as a second example of a uniform cause giving rise in different nerves of sense to different sensations. A single pair of plates of different metals applied so as to include the eye within the circle excites the sensation of a bright flash of light when the person experimented upon is in a dark room; and, even though the eye does not lie within the circle, if it be not distant from it—as, for example, when one of the plates is applied to one of the eyelids, and the other to the interior of the mouth—the same effect will be produced, owing to a part of the current of electricity being diverted to the eye. A more intense electric stimulus gives rise to more intense sensations of light. In the organ of hearing, electricity excites the sensations of sound. Volta states that, while his ears were included between the poles of a battery of forty pairs of plates, he heard a hissing and pulsatory sound, which continued as long as the circle was closed. Ritter perceived a sound like that of a fiddle G at the moment of the closure of the galvanic circle.

The electricity of friction, developed by the electrical machine, excites in the olfactory nerves the odour of phosphorus. The application of plates of different metals to the tongue gives rise to an acid or a saline taste according to the length of the plates which are applied one above the other beneath the tongue. The facts detailed with regard to the other senses are sufficient to show that these latter phenomena cannot be attributed to decomposition of the salts of the saliva.

The effects of the action of electricity on the nerves of common sensation or feeling, are neither the sensation of light, of sound, of smell, nor of taste, but those proper to the nerves of feeling, namely, the sensations of pricking, of a blow, &c.

Chemical influences also probably produce different effects on different nerves of sense. We have, of course, but few facts illustrating their action on these nerves; but we know that in the sensitive nerves of the skin they excite the different kinds of common sensation—as the sensations of burning, pain, and heat; in the organ of taste, sensations of taste; and, when volatile, in the nerves of smell, the sensations of odors. Without the infliction of great injury on the textures, it is impossible to apply chemical agents to the nerves of the higher senses, sight and hearing, except through the medium of the blood. Chemical substances introduced into the blood act on every nerve of sense, and excite in such a manifestation of its properties. Hence the internal sensations of light and sound, which are well known to result from the action of narcotics.

IV. The peculiar sensations of each nerve of sense can be excited by several distinct causes internal and external.

The facts on which this statement is founded have been already mentioned; for we have seen that the sensation of light in the eye is excited:

1. By the undulations or emanations which from their action on the eye are called light, although they have many other actions than this; for instance, they effect chemical changes, and are the means of maintaining the organic processes in plants.

2. By mechanical influences; as concussion, or a blow.

3. By electricity.

4. By chemical agents, such as narcotics, digitalis, &c. which, being absorbed into the blood, give rise to the appearance of luminous sparks, &c. before the eyes independently of any external cause.

5. By the stimulus of the blood in the state of congestion.

The sensation of sound may be excited in the auditory nerve:

1. By mechanical influences, namely, by the vibrations of sonorous bodies imparted to the organ of hearing through the intervention of media capable of propagating them.

2. By electricity.

3. By chemical influences taken into the circulation; such as narcotics, or alterantia nervina.

4. By the stimulus of the blood.

The sensation of odors may be excited in the olfactory nerves:

1. By chemical influences of a volatile nature—odorous substances.

2. By electricity.

The sensation of taste may be produced:

1. By chemical influences acting on the gustatory nerves either from without or through the medium of the blood; for, according to Magendie, dogs taste milk injected into their blood-vessels, and begin to lap with their tongue.

2. By electricity.

3. By mechanical influences; for we must refer to taste the sensation of nausea produced by mechanically irritating the velum palati, epiglottis, and root of the tongue.

The sensations of the nerves of touch or feeling are excited:

1. By mechanical influences; as sonorous vibrations, and contact of any kind.

2. By chemical influences.

3. By heat.

4. By electricity.

5. By the stimulus of the blood.

V. Sensation consists in the sensorium receiving through the medium of the nerves, and as the result of the action of an external cause, a knowledge of certain qualities or conditions, not of external bodies, but of the nerves of sense themselves; and these qualities of the nerves of sense are in all different, the nerve of each sense having its own peculiar quality or energy.

The special susceptibility of the different nerves of sense for certain influences,—as of the optic nerve for light, of the auditory nerve for vibrations, and so on,—was formerly attributed to these nerves having each a specific irritability. But this hypothesis is evidently insufficient to explain all the facts. The nerves of the senses have assuredly a specific irritability for certain influences; for many stimuli, which exert a violent action upon one organ of sense, have little or no effect upon another: for example, light, or vibrations so infinitely rapid as those of light, act only on the nerves of vision and common sensation; slower vibrations, on the nerves of hearing and common sensation, but not upon those of vision; odorous substances only upon the olfactory nerves. The external stimuli must therefore be adapted to the organ of sense—must be "homogeneous": thus light is the stimulus adapted to the nerve of vision; while vibrations of less rapidity, which act upon the auditory nerve, are not adapted to the optic nerve, or are indifferent to it; for if the eye be touched with a tuning-fork while vibrating, a sensation of tremors is excited in the conjunctiva, but no sensation of light. We have seen, however, that one and the same stimulus, as electricity, will produce different sensations in the different nerves of the senses; all the nerves are susceptible of its action, but the sensations in all are different. The same is the case with other stimuli, as chemical and mechanical influences. The hypothesis of a specific irritability of the nerves of the senses for certain stimuli, is therefore insufficient; and we are compelled to ascribe, with Aristotle, peculiar energies to each nerve,—energies which are vital qualities of the nerve, just as contractility is the vital property of muscle. The truth of this has been rendered more and more evident in recent times by the investigation of the so-called "subjective" phenomena of the senses by Elliot, Darwin, Ritter, Goethe, Purkinje, Tjort. Those phenomena of the senses, namely, are now styled "subjective," which are produced, not by the usual stimulus adapted to the particular nerve of sense, but by others which do not usually act upon it. These important phenomena were long spoken of as "illusions of the senses," and have been regarded in an erroneous point of view; while they are really true actions of the senses, and must be studied as fundamental phenomena in investigations into their nature.

The sensation of sound, therefore, is the peculiar "energy" or "quality" of the auditory nerve; the sensation of light and colours that of the optic nerve; and so of the other nerves of sense. An exact analysis of what takes place in the production of a sensation would of itself have led to this conclusion. The sensations of heat and cold, for example, make us acquainted with the existence of the imponderable matter of caloric, or of peculiar vibrations in the vicinity of our nerves of feeling. But the nature of this caloric cannot be elucidated by sensations, which is in reality merely a particular state of our nerves; it must be learnt by the study of the physical properties of this agent, namely, of the laws of its radiation, its development from the latent state, its property of combining with and producing expansion of other bodies, &c. All this again, however, does not explain the peculiarity of the sensation of warmth as a condition of the nerves. The simple fact devoid of all theory is this, that warmth, as a sensation, is produced whenever the matter of caloric acts upon the nerves of feeling; and that cold as a sensation, results from this matter of caloric being abstracted from a nerve of feeling.

So, also, the sensation of sound is produced when a certain number of impulses or vibrations are imparted, within a certain time, to the auditory nerve: but sound, as we perceive it, is a very different thing from a succession of vibrations. The vibrations of a tuning-fork, which to the ear give the impression of sound, produce in a nerve a feeling or touch the sensation of tickling; something besides the vibrations must consequently be necessary for the production of the sensation of sound, and that something is possessed by the auditory nerve alone. Vision is to be regarded in the same manner. A difference in the intensity of the action of the imponderable agent, light, causes an inequality of sensation at different parts of the retina: whether this action consists in impulses or undulations, (the undulation theory,) or in an infinitely rapid current of imponderable matter, (the emanation theory,) is a question here of no importance. The sensation of moderate light is produced where the action of the imponderable agent on the retina is not intense; of bright light where its action is stronger, and of darkness or shade where the imponderable agent does not fall; and thus results a luminous image of determinate form according to the distribution of the parts of the retina differently acted on. Color is also a property of the optic nerve; and when excited by external light, arises from the peculiarity of the so-called colored rays, or of the oscillations necessary for the production of the impression of color,—a peculiarity, the nature of which is not at present known. The nerves of taste and smell are capable of being excited to an infinite variety of sensations by external causes; but each taste is due to a determinate condition of the nerve excited by the external cause; and it is ridiculous to say that the property of acidity is communicated to the sensorium by the nerve of taste, while the acid acts equally upon the nerves of feeling, though it excites there no sensation of taste.

The essential nature of these conditions of the nerves, by virtue of which they see light and hear sound,—and the essential nature of sound as a property of the auditory nerve, and of light as a property of the optic nerve, of taste, of smell, and of feeling,—remains, like the ultimate causes of natural phenomena generally, a problem incapable of solution. Respecting the nature of the sensation of the color "blue," for example, we can reason no farther; it is one of the many facts which mark the limits of our powers of mind. It would not advance the question to suppose the peculiar sensations of the different senses excited by one and the same cause, to result from the propagations of vibrations of the nervous principle of different rapidity to the sensorium. Such an hypothesis, if at all tenable, would find its first application in accounting for the different sensations of which a single sense is susceptible; for example, in explaining how the sensorium received the different impressions of blue, red, and yellow, or of an acute and a grave tone, or of painful and pleasurable sensations of heat and cold, or of the tastes of bitter, sweet, and acid. It is only with this application that the hypothesis is worthy of regard: tones of different degrees of acuteness are certainly produced by vibrations of sonorous bodies of different degrees of rapidity; and a slight contact of a solid body, which singly excites in a nerve of common sensation merely the simple sensation of touch, produces in the same nerve when repeated rapidly, as the vibrations of a sonorous body, the feeling of tickling; so that possibly a pleasurable sensation, even when it arises from internal causes independently of external influences, is due to the rapidity of the vibrations of the nervous principle in the nerves of feeling.

The accuracy of our discrimination by means of the senses depends on the different manner in which the conditions of our nerves are affected by different bodies; but the preceding considerations show us the impossibility that our senses can ever reveal to us the true nature and essence of the material world. In our intercourse with external nature it is always our own sensations that we become acquainted with, and from them we form conceptions of the properties of external objects, which may be relatively correct; but we can never submit the nature of the objects themselves to that immediate perception to which the state of the different parts of our own body are subjected in the sensorium.

VI. The nerve of each sense seems to be capable of one determinate kind of sensation only, and not of those proper to the other organs of sense; hence one nerve of sense cannot take the place and perform the function of the nerve of another sense.

The sensation of each organ of sense may be increased in intensity till it become pleasurable, or till it becomes disagreeable, without the specific nature of the sensation being altered, or converted into that of another organ of sense. The sensation of dazzling light is an unpleasant sensation of the organ of vision; harmony of colors, an agreeable one. Harmonious and discordant sounds are agreeable and disagreeable sensations of the organ of hearing. The organs of taste and smell have their pleasant and unpleasant tastes and odors; the organ of touch its pleasurable and painful feelings. It appears, therefore, that, even in the most excited condition of an organ of sense, the sensation preserves its specific character. It is an admitted fact that the sensations of light, sound, taste, and odors, can be experienced only in their respective nerves; but in the case of common sensation this is not so evidently the case, for it is a question whether the sensation of pain may not be felt in the nerves of the higher senses—whether, for example, violent irritation of the optic nerve may not give rise to the sensation of pain. This question is difficult of solution. There are filaments of the nerves of common sensation distributed in the nerves of the other organs of sense: the nostrils are supplied with nerves of common sensation from the second division of the nervus trigeminus in addition to the olfactory nerves; the tongue has common sensibility as well as taste, and may retain the one while it loses the other; the eye and organ of hearing likewise are similarly endowed.

To determine this question, it is necessary to institute experiments on the isolated nerves of special sense themselves. As far as such experiments have hitherto gone, they favor the view that the nerves of sense are susceptible of no other kind of sensation than that peculiar to each, and are not endowed with the faculty of common sensibility.

Among the well-attested facts of physiology, again, there is not one to support the belief that one nerve of sense can assume the functions of another. The exaggeration of the sense of touch in the blind will not in these days be called seeing with the fingers; the accounts of the power of vision by the fingers and epigastrium, said to be possessed in the so called magnetic state, appear to be mere fables, and the instances in which it has been pretended to practise it, cases of deception. The nerves of touch are capable of no other sensation than that of touch or feeling. Hence, also, no sounds can be heard except by the auditory nerve; the vibrations of bodies are perceived by the nerves of touch as mere tremors wholly different in its nature from sound; though it is indeed even now not rare for the different modes of action of the vibrations of bodies upon the sense of hearing, and upon that of feeling, to be confounded. Without the organ of hearing with its vital endowments, there would be no such a thing as sound in the world, but merely vibrations; without the organ of sight, there would be no light, color, nor darkness, but merely a corresponding presence or absence of the oscillations of the imponderable matter of light.

VII. It is not known whether the essential causes of the peculiar "energy" of each nerve of sense is seated in the nerve itself, or in the parts of the brain and spinal cord with which it is connected; but it is certain that the central portions of the nerves included in the encephalon are susceptible of their peculiar sensations, independently of the more peripheral portion of the nervous cords which form the means of communication with the external organs of sense.

The specific sensibility of the individual senses to particular stimuli,—owing to which vibrations of such rapidity or length as to produce sound are perceived, only by the senses of hearing and touch, and mere mechanical influences, scarcely at all by the sense of taste,—must be a property of the nerves themselves; but the peculiar mode of reaction of each sense, after the excitement of its nerve, may be due to either of two conditions. Either the nerves themselves may communicate impressions different in quality to the sensorium, which in every instance remains the same; or the vibrations of the nervous principle may in every nerve be the same and yet give rise to the perception of different sensations in the sensorium, owing to the parts of the latter with which the nerves are connected having different properties.

The proof of either of these propositions I regard as at present impossible.

On the Speech Center

Paul Broca

A TWENTY-ONE-YEAR CASE OF APHEMIA PRODUCED BY THE CHRONIC AND PROGRESSIVE SOFTENING OF THE SECOND AND THIRD CONVOLUTIONS OF THE SUPERIOR PORTION OF THE LEFT FRONTAL LOBE

On 11 April 1861 there was brought to the surgery of the general infirmary of the hospice at Bicêtre a man named Leborgne, fifty-one years old, suffering from a diffused gangrenous cellulitis of his whole right leg, extending from the foot to the buttocks. When questioned the next day as to the origin of his disease, he replied only with the monosyllable *tan,* repeated twice in succession and accompanied by a gesture of his left hand. I tried to find out more about the antecedents of this man, who had been at Bicêtre for twenty-one years. I questioned his attendants, his comrades on the ward, and those of his relatives who came to see him, and here is the result of this inquiry.

Since youth he had been subject to epileptic attacks, yet he was able to become a maker of lasts, a trade at which he worked until he was thirty years old. It was then that he lost his ability to speak and that is why he was admitted to the hospice at Bicêtre. It was not possible to discover whether his loss of speech came on slowly or rapidly or whether some other symptom accompanied the onset of this affliction.

When he arrived at Bicêtre he had already been unable to speak for two or three months. He was then quite healthy and intelligent and differed from a normal person only in his loss of articulate language. He came and went in the hospice, where he was known by the name of "Tan." He understood all that was said to him. His hearing was actually very good, but whenever one questioned him he always answered, "Tan, tan," accompanying his utterance with varied gestures by which he succeeded in expressing most of his ideas. If one did not understand his gestures, he was apt to get irate and added to his vocabulary a gross oath ["Sacré nom de Dieu!"] . . . Tan was considered an egoist, vindictive and objectionable, and his associates, who detested him, even accused him of stealing. These defects could have been due largely to his cerebral lesion. They were not pronounced enough to be considered pathological, and, although this patient was at Bicêtre, no one ever thought of transferring him to the insane ward. On the contrary, he was considered to be completely responsible for his acts.

Adapted from Broca, P. (1861). Remarques sur le siège de la faculté du langage articulé, suivies d'une observation d'aphémie. *Bulletin de la Société Anatomiaque de Paris, 6,* 343–357. From Mollie D. Boring (Trans.), in R. J. Herrnstein & E. G. Boring (Eds.), *A sourcebook in the history of psychology.* Cambridge, MA: Harvard University Press, 1965, pp. 223–229.

Ten years after he lost his speech a new symptom appeared. The muscles of his right arm began to get weak, and in the end they became completely paralyzed. Tan continued to walk without difficulty, but the paralysis gradually extended to his right leg; after having dragged the leg for some time, he resigned himself to staying in bed. About four years had elapsed from the beginning of the paralysis of the arm to the time when paralysis of the leg was sufficiently advanced to make standing absolutely impossible. Before he was brought to the infirmary, Tan had been in bed for almost seven years. This last period of his life is the one for which we have the least information. Since he was incapable of doing harm, his associates had nothing to do with him anymore, except to amuse themselves at his expense. This made him angry, and he had by now lost the little celebrity which the peculiarity of his disease had given him at the hospice. It was also noticed that his vision had become notably weaker during the last two years. Because he kept to his bed this was the only aggravation one could notice. As he was not incontinent, they changed his linen only once a week; thus the diffused cellulitis for which he was brought to the hospital on 11 April 1861 was not recognized by the attendants until it had made considerable progress and had infected the whole leg. . . .

The study of this unfortunate person, who could not speak and who, being paralyzed in his right hand, could not write, offered some difficulty. His general state, moreover, was so grave that it would have been cruel to torment him by long interviews.

I found, in any case, that general sensitivity was present everywhere, although it was unequal. The right half of his body was less sensitive than the left, and that undoubtedly contributed to the diminished pain at the site of the diffuse cellulitis. As long as one did not touch him, the patient did not suffer much, but palpation was painful and the incisions that I had to make provoked agitation and cries.

The two right limbs were completely paralyzed. The left ones could be moved voluntarily and, though weak, could without hesitation execute all movements. Emission of urine and fecal matter was normal, but swallowing was difficult. Mastication, on the other hand, was executed very well. The face did not deviate from normal. When he whistled, however, his left cheek appeared a little less inflated than his right, indicating that the muscles on this side of the face were a little weak. There was no tendency to strabismus. The tongue was completely free and normal; the patient could move it anywhere and stretch it out of his mouth. Both of its sides were of the same thickness. The difficulty in swallowing . . . was due to incipient paralysis of the pharynx and not to a paralysis of the tongue, for it was only the third stage of swallowing that appeared labored. The muscles of the larynx did not seem to be altered. The timbre of the voice was natural, and the sounds that the patient uttered to produce his monosyllable were quite pure.

Tan's hearing remained acute. He heard well the ticking of a watch but his vision was weak. When he wanted to see the time, he had to take the watch in his left hand and place it in a peculiar position about twenty centimeters from his right eye, which seemed better than his left.

The state of Tan's intelligence could not be exactly determined. Certainly, he understood almost all that was said to him, but, since he could express his ideas or desires only by movements of his left hand, this moribund patient could not make himself understood as well as he understood others. His numerical responses, made by opening or closing his fingers, were best. Several times I asked him for how many days had he been ill. Sometimes he answered five, sometimes six days. How many years had he been in Bicêtre? He opened his hand four times and then added one finger. That made 21 years, the correct answer. The next day I repeated the question and received the same answer, but, when I tried to come back to the question a third time,

Tan realized that I wanted to make an exercise out of the questioning. He became irate and uttered the oath, which only this one time did I hear from him. Two days in succession I showed him my watch. Since the second hand did not move, he could distinguish the three hands only by their shape and length. Still, after having looked at the watch for a few seconds, he could each time indicate the hour correctly. It cannot be doubted, therefore, that the man was intelligent, that he could think, that he had to a certain extent retained the memory of old habits. He could understand even quite complicated ideas. For instance, I asked him about the order in which his paralyses had developed. First he made a short horizontal gesture with his left index finger, meaning that he had understood; then he showed successively his tongue, his right arm and his right leg. That was perfectly correct, for quite naturally he attributed his loss of language to paralysis of his tongue.

Nevertheless there were several questions to which he did not respond, questions that a man of ordinary intelligence would have managed to answer even with only one hand. At other times he seemed quite annoyed when the sense of his answers was not understood. Sometimes his answer was clear but wrong—as when he pretended to have children when actually he had none. Doubtless the intelligence of this man was seriously impaired as an effect either of his cerebral lesion or of his devouring fever, but obviously he had much more intelligence than was necessary for him to talk.

From the anamnesis and from the state of the patient it was clear that he had a cerebral lesion that was progressive, had at the start and for the first ten years remained limited to a fairly well circumscribed region, and during this first period had attacked neither the organs of motility nor of sensitivity; that after ten years the lesion had spread to one or more organs of motion, still leaving unaffected the organs of sensitivity; and that still more recently sensitivity had become dulled as well as vision, particularly the vision of the left eye. Complete paralysis affected the two right limbs; moreover, the sensitivity of these two limbs was slightly less than normal. Therefore, the principal cerebral lesion should lie in the left hemisphere. This opinion was reinforced by the incomplete paralysis of the left cheek and of the left retina, for, needless to say, paralyses of cerebral origin are crossed for the trunk and the extremities but are direct for the face. . . .

The patient died on 17 April [1861]. The autopsy was performed as soon as possible—that is to say, after 24 hours. The weather was warm but the cadaver showed no signs of putrefaction. The brain was shown a few hours later to the Société d'Anthropologie and was then put immediately into alcohol. It was so altered that great care was necessary to preserve it. It was only after two months and several changes of the fluid that it began to harden. Today it is in perfect condition and has been deposited in the Musée Depuytren. . . .

The organs destroyed are the following: the small inferior marginal convolution of the temporal lobe, the small convolutions of the insula, and the underlying part of the striate body, and, finally, in the frontal lobe, the inferior part of the transverse frontal convolution and the posterior part of those two great convolutions designated as the second and third frontal convolutions. Of the four convolutions that form the superior part of the frontal lobe, only one, the superior and most medial one, has been preserved, although not in its entirety, for it is softened and atrophied, but nevertheless indicates its continuity, for, if one puts back in imagination all that has been lost, one finds that at least three quarters of the cavity has been hollowed out at the expense of the frontal lobe.

Now we have to decide where the lesion started. An examination of the cavity caused by the lack of substance shows at once that the center of the focus corresponds to the frontal lobe. It follows that, if the softening spread out uniformly in all directions, it would have been this lobe in which the disease began. Still we should not be guided solely by a study of the cavity, for we should also keep an eye on the parts that surround it. These parts are very unequally softened and cover an especially variable extent. Thus the second temporal convolution, which bounds the lesion from below, exhibits a smooth surface of firm consistency; yet it is without doubt softened, though not much and only in its superficial parts. On the opposite side on the frontal lobe, the softened material is almost fluid near the focus; still, as one goes away from the focus, the substance of the brain becomes gradually firmer, although the softening extends in reality for a considerable distance and involves almost the whole frontal lobe. It is here that the softening mainly progressed and it is almost certain that the other parts were affected only later.

If one wished to be more precise, he could remark that the third frontal convolution is the one that shows the greatest loss of substance, that not only is it cut transversely at the level of the anterior end of the Sylvian fissure but it is also completely destroyed in its posterior half, and that it alone has undergone a loss of substance equal to about one-half of its total. The second or middle frontal convolution, although deeply affected, still preserves its continuity in its innermost parts; consequently it is most likely that the disease began in the third convolution. . . .

Anatomical inspection shows us that the lesion was still progressing when the patient died. The lesion was therefore progressive, but it progressed very slowly, taking twenty-one years to destroy a quite limited part of the brain. Thus it is reasonable to believe that at the beginning there was a considerable time during which degeneration did not go past the limits of the organ where it started. We have seen that the original focus of the disease was situated in the frontal lobe and very likely in its third frontal convolution. Thus we are compelled to say, from the point of view of pathological anatomy, that there were two periods, one in which only one frontal convolution, probably the third one, was attacked, and another period in which the disease gradually spread toward other convolutions, to the insula, or to the extraventricular nucleus of the corpus striatum.

When we now examine the succession of the symptoms, we also find two periods, the first of which lasted ten years, during which the faculty of speech was destroyed while all other functions of the brain remained intact, and a second period of eleven years, during which paralysis of movement, at first partial and then complete, successively involved the arm and the leg of the right side.

With this in mind it is impossible not to see that there was a correspondence between the anatomical and the symptomological periods. Everyone knows that the cerebral convolutions are not motor organs. Of all the organs attacked, the corpus striatum of the left hemisphere is the only one where one could look for the cause of the paralysis of the two right extremities. The second clinical period, in which the motility changed, corresponds to the second anatomical period, when the softening passed beyond the limit of the frontal lobe and invaded the insula and the corpus striatum.

It follows that the first period of ten years, clinically characterized only by the symptom of aphemia, must correspond to the period during which the lesion was still limited to the frontal lobe.

Cortical Localization and Cerebral Dominance: The Work of Paul Broca

Stanley Finger

SPEECH AND THE FRONTAL LOBE

The first cortical localization that became widely accepted linked fluent, articulate speech to the frontal cortex. The issue of cortical localization of function was being debated in the French learned societies when Paul Broca presented his famous clinical case showing this in 1861. Although many other scientists had previously presented data both for and against the theory, earlier contributions failed to have the impact of Broca's case study.

For example, Jean-Baptiste Bouillaud (1796–1881), a student of Magendie and a respected figure in French science, had long emphasized the use of clinical examinations and autopsy material to support the case for localization of function. In 1825, after examining data from a large number of cases, an approach that clearly distinguished him from his predecessors, he wrote:

> In the brain there are several special organs, each one of which has certain definite movements depending upon it. In particular, the movements of speech are regulated by a special cerebral centre, distinct and independent. Loss of speech depends sometimes on loss of memory for words, sometimes of want of the muscular movements of which speech is composed. . . . Loss of speech does not necessitate want of movements of the tongue, considered as an organ of prehension, mastication, deglutination of food; nor does it necessitate loss of taste. The nerves animating the muscles, which combine in the production of speech arise from the anterior lobes or at any rate possess the necessary communications with them. (Translated in Head, 1926, 13–14)

Adapted from S. Finger (1994). *Origins of neuroscience: A history of explorations into brain function.* New York: Oxford University Press, pp. 36–38, 392–393.

Bouillaud cited Claud-François Lallemand (1790–1854) and Léon Louis Rostan (1790–1866) to bolster his case. In 1820 and 1823, respectively, these men had also reported loss of speech after anterior lobe damage. Bouillaud then argued that lesions elsewhere did not affect fluent speech (see Head, 1926; Ombredane, 1951; Stookey, 1963).

Unfortunately, Bouillaud had two negative factors working against him. First, he had been a founding member of the *Société Phrénologique*. Although he soon questioned Gall's cranioscopy procedures and recommended the use of brain-injured patients to study structure-function relationships, the scientific community remained overly cautious about anything or anyone associated in any way with Gall or phrenology.

Second, Bouillaud's descriptions of the causal lesions, like those of his predecessors and contemporaries, were less than satisfactory. As stated by Adolf Kussmaul (1822–1902) in 1878 (p. 721):

> In order to understand how superficially localizations are recorded even in the writings of the best of the older observers, let one cast a glance at the principle works of such men as Bouillaud, Lallemand and Rostan, to whom, notwithstanding, the pathology of the brain owes so much. They are content to indicate the affected lobe with the general designation, "in front," "behind," "in the middle," etc., and with equally indefinite appreciation of the extent of the lesion. One seldom learns whether the cortex or the white medulla, corpus striatum, centrum, semiovale, etc., was the seat of the lesion.

It should also be noted that not everyone at this time was finding impairments in speech after frontal lobe lesions. For instance, Gabriel Andral (1797–1846) discussed 37 cases of frontal lobe lesions collected at the Charité hospital between 1820 and 1831 and found speech to be seriously impaired in only 21 of these cases. Andral (1840) did not say anything about the side of damage, but he did mention that he also had 14 cases of speech loss who had sustained brain damage posterior to the frontal lobes. These findings left him cautious at best about accepting localization.

Even more disconcerting was the response from Jean Cruveilhier (1791–1874) to Bouillaud's assertions. Cruveilhier stated:

> If it is pathologically demonstrated that a lesion of the anterior lobes is constantly accompanied by a corresponding alteration of speech; on the other hand, if lesions of all parts of the brain other than the anterior lobes never entail speech alterations, the question is solved, and I immediately become a phrenologist. . . . In fact, the loss of the faculty of sound articulation is not always the result of a lesion of the anterior lobes of the brain; moreover, I am able to prove that the loss of the faculty of sound articulation can accompany a lesion of any other part of the brain. (Translated in Riese, 1977, 59)

Thus, rather than being a time of calm, this was a time of controversy and debate, especially in the halls of the French scientific academies. On the whole, the conservatives were on Flourens' side, while the liberals were the localizers (Head, 1926). It was in this far from tranquil environment, with men like Simon Alexandre Ernest Aubertin (1825–1893) arguing for localization and Pierre Gratiolet (1815–1865) taking the opposing position, that an enfeebled Monsieur Leborgne was transferred to Broca's surgical ward. This dying man had been hospitalized for 21 years, and he now showed epilepsy, loss of speech, and right hemiplegia. Broca took it upon himself to examine Leborgne as a test of Bouillaud's and Aubertin's contention that speech loss will always be associated with a large lesion of the anterior lobes.

Six days after Broca saw him, Leborgne died. His brain, which proved to be in poor condition due to infarctions, was removed and presented to the *Société d'Anthropologie* the next day. Broca issued a weak statement about localization at this time, but at a decidedly more animated meeting of the *Société d'Anatomie* later that year, he boldly proclaimed that his case study of Leborgne placed him in firm agreement with the localizationists. Broca was especially careful to emphasize that his localization of a faculty for articulate language in the frontal lobe differed from that proposed by Gall, although both he and the phrenologists believed that articulate speech was an anterior lobe function.

Broca's "conversion" was a true landmark event, and many people who were vacillating about localization accepted the localizationist doctrine after Broca took his stand. As for Monsieur Leborgne, because he had often uttered a word that sounded like "tan," Broca's first and most famous case became known as Tan to the scientific community.

Just why did the case of Tan have so much impact relative to the material presented by Bouillaud, Aubertin, and others who favored localization? The answer to this question probably rests on four important factors that converged in Broca's report (Sondhaus and Finger, 1988). First, Broca's paper contained detail: detail in the case history, detail in its emphasis on articulate speech as opposed to any defect in speech, and detail in trying to find a more circumscribed locus to account for the symptoms. Second, the findings did not support the site of the faculty proposed by the phrenologists. Third, there was a willingness on the part of the scientific community to listen to these ideas at this time; the *Zeitgeist* was right. And fourth, it was Paul Broca, the highly respected scientist, physician, and esteemed head of academic societies, who was now willing to lead the fight for cortical localization of function.

It is worth noting that two more years would pass before Broca would note that the lesion affecting speech was usually on the left side. But even in his 1863 statements, Broca seemed uncomfortable about dealing with the issue of dominance. Perhaps it was because the two sides of the brain looked so similar to him and because, as a scientist, he felt it best always to proceed cautiously. Hence, it was not until 1865 that he addressed this issue in a more direct and meaningful way. Further, while Broca might at first have believed that he was observing an invariant principle when he argued that the center for articulate language resided in the third left frontal convolution, he soon found himself discussing and trying to account for exceptions to this "rule" (Berker, Berker, and Smith, 1986; Finger and Wolf, 1988).

BROCA'S CASE FOR DOMINANCE

In his note in the *Bulletins de la Société d'Anthropologie,* published in May 1863, Paul Broca described eight cases of aphasia, all with lesions on the left side. At the time, this seemed surprising to him. Unlike Marc Dax, Broca could only say that whereas this caught his attention, he could not draw firm conclusions until he had accumulated more facts.

Later that year, Jules Parrott (1829–1883) presented the case of a patient who had a lesion of the right frontal lobe without an articulate language disturbance. Broca recognized that this finding also pointed to the special role of the left hemisphere in speech. Nevertheless, Broca seemed to realize that given how hard it was for the conservative scientific establishment to accept a frontal lobe localization for articulate speech, it was going to be even more difficult to present the novel idea that only the left frontal lobe was essential for this function.

In 1864, Broca described two more patients who had traumatic head injuries on the left side (cited in Duval, 1864). Here he referred to the mounting evidence for left side involvement.

> Numerous observations gathered during the last three years have a tendency to indicate that lesions of the left hemisphere are solely susceptible for causing aphemie. This proposition is no doubt strange, but however perplexing it may be for physiology, it must be accepted if subsequent findings continue to indicate the same view point. (Translated in Berker, Berker, and Smith, 1986, 1066)

In contrast to this relative conservatism, and perhaps now stirred by his knowledge of the Dax findings, Broca's 1865 paper dealt directly and extensively with the issue of left hemispheric dominance for language. This extraordinary paper appeared in the June 15 issue of the *Gazette Hebdomadaire de Médecine et de Chirurgie,* the same journal that published the Marc and Gustave Dax paper less than two months earlier. Broca now took a firm position about left hemispheric dominance for articulate speech, but was careful to add that language was not the exclusive function of the left hemisphere.

> This does not mean to say that the left hemisphere is the exclusive center of the general capacity of language, which consists of establishing a determined relationship between an idea and a sign, nor even of the special capacity of articulate speech, which consists of establishing a determined relationship between an idea and an articulate word. The right hemisphere is not more a stranger than the left hemisphere to this special faculty, and the proof is that the person rendered speech disabled through a deep and extensive lesion of the left hemisphere is, in general, deprived only of the faculty to reproduce the sounds of articulate speech; he understands perfectly the connection between ideas and words. In other words, the capacity to conceive these connections belongs to both hemispheres, and these can, in the case of a malady, reciprocally substitute for each other; however, the faculty to express them by means of coordinated movements in which the practice requires a very long period of training, appears to belong to but one hemisphere, which is almost always the left hemisphere. (Translated in Berker, Berker, and Smith, 1986, 1068)

Armand Trousseau (1864), like Bouillaud, felt that the statistics offered good support for the statements made by Marc Dax and Paul

Broca about the significance of the left side of the brain for speech. He thought the data were also relevant to the question of the seat of the intellect. This view stemmed from his observations of many aphasic patients who showed impairments in general intelligence that went well beyond their language difficulties. Trousseau speculated that the cause of these functional asymmetries might be different blood supplies and other anatomical differences between the hemispheres.

These ideas were acknowledged positively by Jules Gabriel François Baillarger, who postulated that the more rapid growth of the left hemisphere could also explain handedness. In addition, Pierre Gratiolet and François Leuret (1797–1851) had claimed some years earlier that there were differences of a few grams between the two hemispheres during development, with the left hemisphere being the heavier (Gratiolet and Leuret, 1839–1857).

Broca himself accepted these ideas. Hence, in 1865, he made a strong case for the two hemispheres not being innately different from each other, but for the left being more precocious. The implication was that the left hemisphere would be educated first and would take the lead in the acquisition of speech and handedness.

In his 1865 paper, Broca wrote that he believed speech was mediated by the right hemisphere in left-handed people. The concept of reversed dominance was readily accepted, as seen in this quotation from William Gowers 20 years later:

> In left-handed persons the "speech-centre" is usually on the right, and not on the left side of the brain, and the association just mentioned was well exemplified by a left-handed man, who, at the age of thirty-one, became liable to fits which commenced by spasms in the left side of the face, spreading thence to the left arm, without loss of consciousness. Inability to speak preceded each attack for ten minutes, and persisted afterwards for the same time. (1885, 38)

Only in the twentieth century did scientists begin to wonder whether Broca might have been wrong about dominance in left-handed people. In his 1914 review of cerebral functions, Shepherd Ivory Franz stated that the general belief that aphasias in left-handed people are produced by lesions in the right hemisphere was not borne out by case studies. Franz specifically discussed one case in which the author found that a left-handed person developed an aphasia after a lesion of the left frontal lobe. With more time, it was recognized that a majority of left-handed people still have speech localized on the left side of the brain or exhibit more of a "mixed" dominance.

REFERENCES

Andral, G. (1840). *Clinique medicale* (4th ed.) Paris: Fortin, Massonet Cie.

Berker, E. A., Berker, A. H., & Smith, A. (1986). Translation of Broca's 1865 report: Localization of speech in the third frontal convolution. *Archives of Neurology, 43*, 1065–1072.

Duval, A. (1864). Deux cas d'aphemie traumatique, produite par des lesions de la troisieme circonvolution frontale gauche: Diagnostique chirurgical. *Societe de Chirurgerie de Paris Bulletin, 5*, 51–63.

Finger, S., & Wolf, C. (1988). The "Kennard effect" before Kennard: The early history of age and brain lesion effects. *Archives of Neurology, 45*, 1136–1142.

Franz, S. I. (1914). The functions of the cerebrum. *Psychological Bulletin, 11*, 131–140.

Gowers, W. R. (1885). *Epilepsy*. London: William Woods and Co.

Gratiolet, P., & Leuret, F. (1839–1857). *Anatomie comparee du systeme nerveux, consideree dans ses rapports avec l'intelligence* (2 vols; Vol. 2). Paris: J. B. Balliere.

Head, H. (1926). *Aphasia and kindred disorders of speech*. New York: Macmillan.

Kussmaul, A. (1878). Disturbances of speech: An attempt in the pathology of speech. In H. V. Ziemssen (ed.), *Cyclopedia in the practice of medicine*, Vol. 14. New York: Wood.

Ombredane, A. (1951). *L'aphasie et l'elaboration de la pensee explicite*. Paris: Presses Universitaires de France.

Riese, W. (1977). Discussions about cerebral localization in the learned societies of the nineteenth century. In K. Hoops, Y. Lebrun, & E. Buyssens (Eds.), *Selected papers on the history of aphasia*, Vol. 7. Amsterdam: Swets and Zeitling.

Sondhaus, E., & Finger, S. (1988). Aphasia and the C. N. S. from Imhotep to Broca. *Neuropsychology, 2*, 87–110.

Stookey, B. (1963). Jean Baptiste-Bouillaud and Ernest Aubertin: Early studies on cerebral localization and the speech center. *Journal of the American Medical Association, 184*, 1024–1029.

Trousseau, A. (1864). De l'aphasie, maladie decrite recemment sous le nom impropre d'aphemie. *Gazette des Hopitaux, Paris, 37*, 13–14, 25–26, 37–39, 48–50.

Gall, Flourens, and Phrenology

Raymond E. Fancher

The brain did not become an object of major scientific interest until the 1800s, when it became implicated in a sort of pseudoscientific craze that captured the imagination of the general public as much as of scientists. The German physician Franz Josef Gall (1758–1828) played a major role in these developments, as he convincingly demonstrated the general importance of the brain for all of the higher human functions, while also originating the popular nineteenth-century movement known as phrenology. We turn to Gall's story for the origins of an important tradition in brain science that continues today. Although some of Gall's ideas aroused instant suspicion and hostility among "establishment" scientists, he was also quickly recognized as a brilliant anatomist—the greatest since Thomas Willis. Using new and delicate dissection techniques, he confirmed and elaborated upon many of Willis's basic findings regarding gray and white matter. He showed that the two halves of the brain are interconnected by stalks of white matter called commissures, for example, and that other, smaller tracts of white fibers cross over from each side of the brain to connect with the opposite sides of the spinal cord. The latter finding helped explain how damage to one side of the brain could result in paralysis or other debility to the opposite side of the body.

From Fancher, R. E. (1996). *Pioneers of Psychology* (3rd ed.) pp. 75–86. New York: W. W. Norton.

Also the first great *comparative* anatomist of brains, Gall carefully examined the similarities and differences among brains of many different animal species, children, elderly and brain-damaged people, as well as normal human adults. In a general but convincing way, these studies showed that higher mental functions correlated with the size and intactness of the brain in question, particularly its outer surface or cortex. We shall later see that the correlation is imperfect, and can give rise to some misleading assumptions about intellectual differences *within* an adult human population. But Gall demonstrated an undeniable tendency for animals with larger brains to manifest more complex, flexible, and intelligent behavior. More than any other single argument, this demonstration convinced scientists once and for all that the brain was in fact the center of all higher mental activity.

These contributions should have earned Gall a secure and respected place in the history of science. Unfortunately for his reputation, however, he embedded these noncontroversial ideas within another doctrine his followers labeled "phrenology" (meaning "science of the mind", from the Greek root *phrenos,* for "mind"). Not content to stop at the assertion that the higher functions were localized *generally* within the brain, Gall held that discrete psychological "faculties" were housed within specific *parts* of the brain. Moreover, he believed that the bumps and indentations on the surface of an individual skull reflected the size of the underlying brain parts, and hence of the different faculties.

A curious mixture combining a few astute observations with some fanciful logic, phrenology never won the respect of the most orthodox scientists. And when Gall failed to win over the professionals, he appealed increasingly to the general public. Phrenology became very popular, earning Gall and a host of followers a good living; but its popularity only increased the disdain with which it was regarded by many establishment scientists. One prominent figure labeled phrenology a "sinkhole of human folly and prating coxcombry."[1]

Gall's controversial theory had an appropriately idiosyncratic origin in his childhood experience. According to his autobiography, he was irritated as a schoolboy by some fellow students who, while less intelligent than himself (or so he judged them), nevertheless got higher grades because they were better memorizers. As he thought about these exasperating rivals, he realized that they all had one prominent physical characteristic in common: namely, large and protuberant eyes.

At that time, people commonly associated particular facial characteristics with specific psychological qualities. The art of physiognomy—the reading of a person's character in his or her physical features—had been effectively promoted by the Swiss mystic and theologian Johann Kaspar Lavater (1741–1801) in the 1770s, and remained a popular pasttime throughout the 1800s.* But Gall's physiognomic observation took on a new and different significance when he recalled it as an adult, in the context of his emerging view of the brain.

Already convinced that the higher intellectual and psychological qualities were associated with large brains in a general way, he now speculated that perhaps specific parts of the brain were the seats of specific functions or faculties. If one of those parts of the brain happened to be unusually large and well developed, then the specific function it housed should be unusually strong. Thus people with especially good "verbal memories," like his schoolboy rivals, might have particularly well-developed "organs of verbal memory" somewhere in their brains. And Gall believed he knew exactly where this was: in the region of the frontal lobes directly behind the eyes, where the pressure of the enlarged brain caused the eyes to protrude.

After tentatively localizing verbal memory in one part of the brain, Gall naturally began to look for other faculties in other locations. Of course, in an era before CAT (computerized axial tomography) scans and other modern techniques, he had no direct means of observing living people's brains, and so had to make an important but questionable assumption. Just as the brain part responsible for verbal memory causes the eyes to protrude, he argued, so will the conformation of the rest of the brain cause observable irregularities in the skull that surrounds it. Through "craniometry"—the measurement of the physical dimensions of the skull—Gall hoped to draw conclusions about the shape of the brain beneath. Thus he sought correspondence between particular bumps and depressions on the skull and the particular psychological characteristics of the people who had them.

Once embarked on this search, Gall quickly developed further hypotheses. One of his patients, a woman whose strong erotic inclinations earned her the title of "Gall's Passionate Widow," one day conveniently collapsed into

*The youthful Charles Darwin was almost rejected for the post of naturalist aboard the ship H. M. S. *Beagle* in 1831 because the captain thought his nose inappropriately shaped for a seafarer. Later in the century the Italian criminologist Cesare Lombroso (1836–1901) presented an influential physiognomic theory of the "criminal type," part of which still persists today in the myth that evil doers must have shifty eyes and irregular features.

his arms in such a way that his hand supported the back of her neck. Gall could not help but notice that her neck and the base of her skull were unusually thick, leading him to suspect that her cerebellum—the structure at the base of her brain—was unusually well developed. Observations of other people with strong sexual drives convinced Gall that they too had well-developed necks and skull bases, and led him to localize the personality characteristic of "amativeness" in the cerebellum.

Gall's further researches led him to befriend a gang of lower-class boys who did errands for him. After gaining their confidence, he found that the boys' attitudes toward petty theft varied greatly—some expressing an abhorrence of it, and others openly admitting to committing it, even bragging about it. Gall measured the boys' heads, and discovered that the inveterate thieves had prominences just above and in front of their ears, while the honest boys were flat in that region. Thus Gall hypothesized an "organ of acquisitiveness" in the brain beneath. He justified this hypothesis with further cases, including a man with an unusually large bulge in the region who has been repeatedly jailed for theft until he gained insight into his acquisitive nature. Gall reported that when the man realized he could not resist temptation, he decided to become a *tailor* so "he might then indulge his inclination with impunity."[2] (Gall did not explain his antipathy for tailors.)

Through similar observations of other people with outstanding characteristics, Gall localized the qualities of veneration, benevolence, and firmness in separate locations on the top of the brain, love of food and drink just below the organ of acquisitiveness, and a host of other qualities in other regions. While it is easy today to laugh at this phrenological theorizing, we should observe that it did have a certain naive plausibility, and was properly "scientific" in being derived from direct empirical observation. The ultimate weakness of Gall's theory lay in three other factors.

First, Gall incorrectly assumed that the shape of one's skull accurately reflects the shape of the underlying brain. But while recognition of the incorrectness of this "fact" obviously invalidated the phrenologists' practical claims to be able to read character in head shapes, it did not discredit their more basic hypothesis of a relationship between *brain* shapes and character.

A second and more fundamental defect lay in Gall's choice of specific psychological qualities to localize within the brain—a collection of twenty-seven highly specific "faculties" for qualities such as "mirthfulness," "secretiveness," and "philoprogenitiveness" (parental love), in addition to the ones discussed so far. Gall's followers quickly added more, yielding complex configurations like that illustrated in Figure 3-1.[3] Thus phrenologists saw these particular faculties as *basic* to human character, constituting the elemental building blocks out of which all significant personality variations are constructed. But in fact their arbitrary list included complex qualities that were themselves the result of many different interacting factors. The question of just what the basic dimensions of personality variation really are remains in dispute to the present day, but the faculty solution was unquestionably oversimplified. And so long as phrenology lacked an adequate classification of psychological characteristics, its attempts to localize those characteristics in the brain were doomed.

Phrenology's third and fatal defect lay in the feckless methods by which its hypotheses were often tested. Gall always maintained his theory was grounded in observation, a claim literally true but unreflective of the selectivity and arbitrariness of many of the observations. Further, with twenty-seven or more interacting faculties to work with, it became almost ridiculously easy to explain away apparently discrepant observations. When confronted with a huge organ of acquisitiveness in a highly generous person, for example, Gall could claim that a large organ of benevolence (or some other convenient faculty) *counteracted* the acquisitive tendencies that

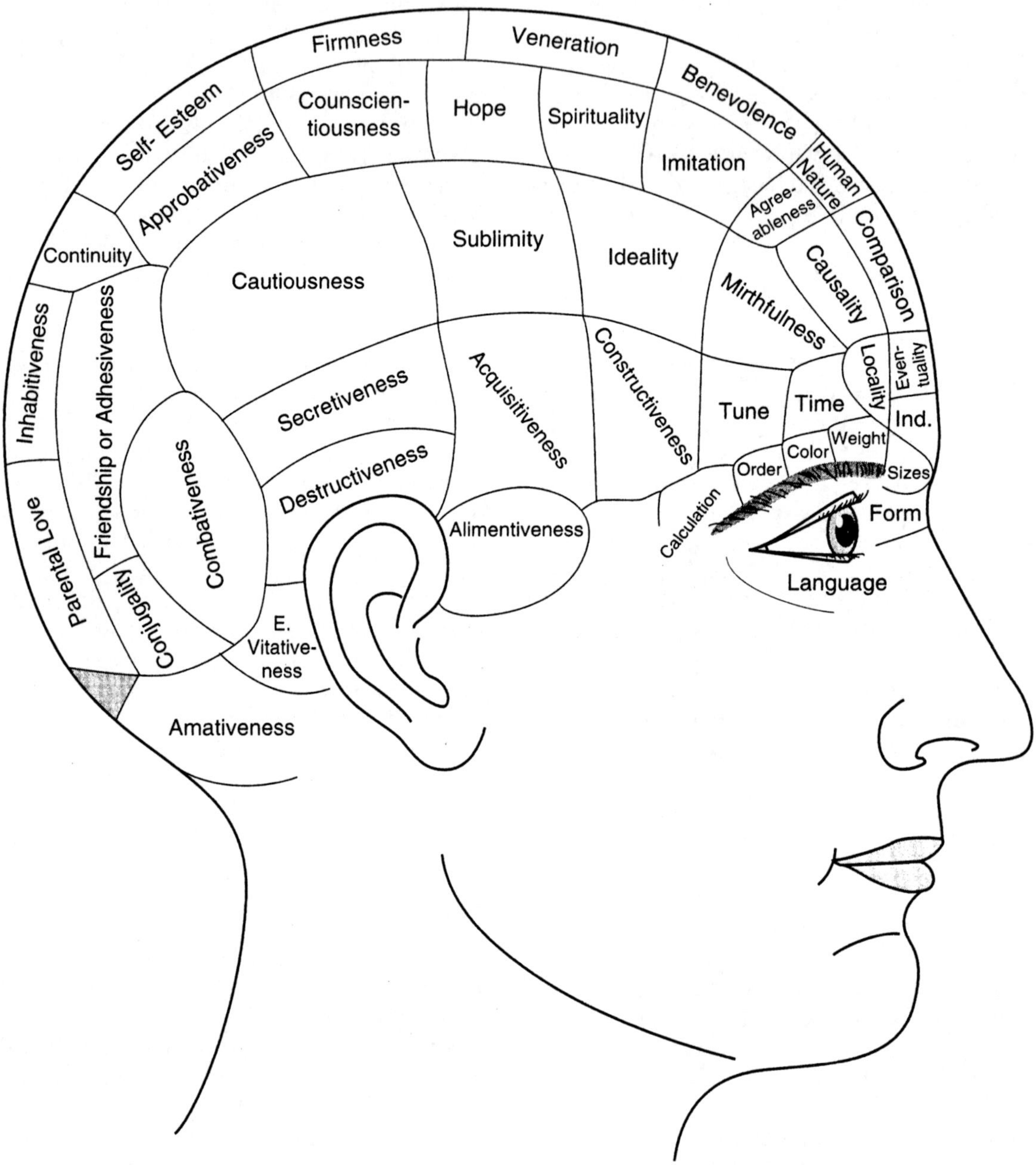

FIGURE 3-1
The phrenological organs.

would otherwise show clearly. Or he could claim that certain organs of the brain became selectively or temporarily impaired by disease, accounting for intermittent alterations in people's behavior. Between the presumably counterbalancing effects of several faculties and the "illnesses" that arbitrarily interfered with some faculties but not others, Gall explained away virtually any observation that ran counter to his theory.

And if Gall was cavalier in his interpretations of evidence, he attracted some followers who raised that tendency to an art form. When a cast of Napoleon's right skull predicted qualities markedly at variance with the emperor's known personality, one phrenologist replied that his dominant side had been the left—a cast of which was conveniently missing. When Descartes's skull was examined and found deficient in the regions for reason and reflection, phrenologists retorted that the philosopher's rationality had always been overrated.

Such tactics, and the promise of easy but "scientific" character analysis, helped phrenology to retain a hold on the public imagination throughout the early and mid-1800s—in much the same way that astrology, biorhythm analysis, and ESP do today. Some practicing phrenologists undoubtedly actually helped some of the clients who flocked to them for readings, using their general knowledge of people (rather than any specific phrenological theories) to offer shrewd advice. But in contrast to the general public, most in the established scientific community regarded phrenology as a joke—exemplified by their widely circulated story that Gall's own skull, when examined after his death, turned out to be twice as thick as the average.

This attitude reflected not only the scientists' disdain for phrenology, but also their respect for a series of experiments conducted in the early 1800s by the young French scientist Pierre Flourens (1794–1867). Flourens's investigations, to which we turn now, ran dramatically counter to several of Gall's hypotheses, and initiated a classic controversy about the nature of the brain that remains alive today.

FLOURENS AND THE DISCREDITING OF PHRENOLOGY

In style and personality, as well as in the course of his career, Flourens contrasted dramatically with Gall. Whereas Gall was always an outsider, never accepted by orthodox scientists, Flourens epitomized the man of the establishment. Born near Montpellier in the south of France, he was graduated from that city's famous medical school at nineteen. He had already published his first scientific article, and won the sponsorship of the famous botanist Augustin de Candolle (1778–1841). Moving to Paris with Candolle's letter of introduction, the young Flourens quickly became a special protégé of Georges Cuvier (1769–1832), the most celebrated scientist in France, known appropriately as the "Dictator of Biology." Cuvier's endorsement guaranteed that Flourens's work would be greeted respectfully—although it was in fact good enough to stand out on its own.

Appalled by the cavalier observational strategies of the phrenologists, Flourens determined to study the functions of the brain strictly by controlled experiment—that is, where particular independent variables would be deliberately and systematically manipulated, and the resulting effects on dependent variables carefully observed. To do this he used the technique of ablation, surgically removing or ablating specific small parts of an animal subject's brain and observing any consequent changes in the behavior or function of the animal after recovery from the surgery. He knew that brain tissue does not regenerate after removal. Thus when he observed specific functions to be permanently missing or altered following an ablation, he hypothesized that the excised brain parts must normally be involved in the production of those functions.

Flourens did not actually invent the brain ablation experiment, but he refined it to a new degree. Showing great surgical skill, he removed more precisely defined areas from the small brains of his animal subjects than his predecessors had been able to do, with a higher survival rate. He always carefully nursed his animals back to as healthy a state as possible before drawing any conclusions, to avoid confusing the transient effects of surgical shock or postoperative complications with the permanent effects of his ablations.

Flourens tested Gall's hypotheses by ablating brain regions associated with particular phrenological faculties. Since he worked with animals, he could most directly investigate those few "faculties" presumably shared by animals and humans. Sexual responsivity obviously qualified, so some of Flourens's earliest and most influential experiments involved ablations of the cerebellum—Gall's "organ or amativeness." His ablations produced alterations of behavior all right, but scarcely of the type that phrenological theory predicted:

> I removed the cerebellum in a young but vigorous dog by a series of deeper and deeper slices. The animal lost gradually the faculty of orderly and regular movement. Soon he could walk only by staggering in zig-zags. He fell back when he wanted to advance; when he wanted to turn to the right he turned to the left. As he made great efforts to move and could no longer moderate these efforts, he hurled himself impetuously forward, and did not fail to fall or roll over. If he found an object in his path, he was unable to avoid it, no matter what means he took; he hurled himself right and left; nevertheless he was perfectly well; when one irritated him he tried to bite; in fact, he bit any object one presented to him when he could reach it, but often he could no longer direct his movements with precision so as to reach the object. He had all his intellectual faculties, all his senses; he was only deprived of the faculty of coordinating and regularizing his movements.[4]

This classic description of a cerebellar lesion, originally published in 1824, has scarcely been improved upon to the present day (though such an experiment would perhaps understandably be frowned upon by animal rights activists today). Flourens clearly established the cerebellum's major role in the integration and "programming" of all the innumerable small muscular movements that make up any organized behavior. Even a simple act like walking requires the proper ordering of thousands of discrete movements, and the cerebellum helps achieve this ordering. Flourens observed that his experimental subjects often moved about as if drunk—and we now know that persistent and heavy alcohol use can in fact produce degenerative changes in the cerebellum, and thus the odd and clumsy walking style of many chronic alcoholics. In sum, Flourens proved that the cerebellum was indeed the center of a specific function—but unfortunately for Gall and phrenology that function bore little relation to "amativeness."

Flourens's ablation studies of the cortex—the brain's surface area implicated by Gall in most of the "higher" faculties—seemed at first even more damaging to phrenology. As Flourens ablated progressively larger sections of cortex from birds, they gradually lost the use of all their senses and their capacity for voluntary action. One pigeon, with its *entire* cortex removed, was kept alive by force feeding and other heroic ministrations, but became completely insensitive to visual or auditory stimulation, and never initiated a movement on its own. Only when prodded or physically disturbed would it move, to resume its customary resting position. In describing this bird's state, Flourens imagined it had lost all capacity for consciousness: "Picture to yourself an animal condemned to perpetual sleep, and deprived even of the faculty of dreaming during this sleep."[5] In his view, the animal had lost its will along with its cortex.

Flourens believed his findings demolished phrenology. Although he had demonstrated localization of a sort, with different functions attributed to the cerebellum and cortex, he believed these separate functions were evenly distributed *within* each organ. As increasingly larger sections of cortex were removed, for example, all of the various sensory and voluntary functions tended to disappear *together*. Flourens argued that if the phrenologists were right and the cortex housed many different specific organs, then small ablations ought to have removed some organs while leaving others intact, producing more specific effects than he had in fact observed.

Actually, Flourens skated on thin ice here, since by his own description he had ablated progressively deeper "slices" of cortex. Any "slice," no matter how shallow, very likely interfered with many different cortical regions at once, thus producing an apparently general effect. Gall, who contemptuously referred to all brain albators as "mutilators," eagerly seized upon this point: "[Flourens] mutilates all the organs at once, weakens them all, extirpates them all at the same time."[6] With hindsight, we know that Gall was correct, and that Flourens did miss important effects of cortical localization.

More enduring, however, have been some of Flourens's other conclusions regarding the cortex's flexibility and plasticity. For example, he observed that sometimes (though not always) ablation-caused deficits improved over time, particularly if the animal was young and the ablations relatively small. Since lost brain tissue does not regenerate, this suggested that intact parts of the brain must somehow be able to take over functions previously served by the ablated portions. The exact limits and conditions of such brain plasticity continue to be explored by scientists today.

Moreover, Flourens's investigations of the brain highlighted the state of integration and harmony that normally prevails among its separate parts. While he conceded a certain "*action propre*" ("specific action") for the cerebellum and cortex considered separately, he also emphasized the cooperation and communication between the two brain parts. Actions initiated by the "will" in the cortex had to be put together and integrated by the cerebellum, and the loss of coordination occasioned by damage to the cerebellum had to be dealt with by voluntary reactions in the cortex. In Flourens's terminology, the *actions propres* of the parts were subject to an overall "*action commune*" ("common action") of the brain acting as a whole. In a conception somewhat reminiscent of Descartes, Flourens saw the brain as the seat of an integrated and harmonious soul.

Flourens's views seemed much more scientifically respectable than phrenology, and were generally accepted by the scientific establishment throughout the middle 1800s. In the 1860s, however, new findings came to light suggesting that even Flourens's meticulous experiments had failed to detect some important localized functions in the cortex, and that he had in some ways overemphasized the unity of brain function.

NOTES

1. Young, R. M. (1970). *Mind, brain and adaptation in the nineteenth century.* Oxford: Clarendon Press, p. 10.
2. Herrnstein, R. J., & Boring, E. G. (Eds.) (1965). *A source book in the history of psychology.* Cambridge, MA: Harvard University Press, p. 212.
3. Diagram adapted from Davies, J. D. (1955). *Phrenology: Fad and science.* New Haven, CT: Yale University Press, p. 6.
4. Olmsted, J. M. D. (1953). Pierre Flourens. In E. A. Underwood (Ed.), *Science, medicine, and history*, (pp. 290–302). New York: Oxford University Press, p. 296.
5. Ibid., p. 293.
6. In Young, *Mind, brain and adaptation*, p. 61.

CHAPTER **4**

THE FRENCH CLINICAL TRADITION

For many decades, the public's prototypical image of a psychologist has been that of a professional involved in the treatment or counseling of clients (see Benjamin, 1986; Wood, Jones, & Benjamin, 1986). And now, for the first time in psychology's history, that image proves to be an accurate one for most psychologists (Stapp, Fulcher, & Wicherski, 1984). Contemporary students possess this clinical image of the field as well and often are surprised in taking a history of psychology course to learn that it is largely about the history of experimental psychology. There are a number of reasons for this narrowness of focus in the history of psychology.

First, many members of the founding generation of psychology as a science were interested in consciousness of the normal mind rather than in psychopathology. It was not that the abnormal mind seemed less interesting; rather, the emphasis on normality stemmed from a reasoned belief that studying normal individuals would lead more rapidly to an understanding of the workings of the mind.

Second, the field of mental illness was a medical field, dominated for centuries by the somatic view that held that psychological disturbances resulted from organic causes. The somatic view would begin to be replaced in the nineteenth century by the psychic view that regarded mental illness as a result of psychological causes, often the result of learning and experience. The tremendous impact of Sigmund Freud's work (see Chapter 13) hastened the acceptability of the psychic view.

Third, the profession of clinical psychology, at least in the United States, is a recent phenomenon. Almost no doctoral programs in clinical psychology existed before World War II, and very small numbers of psychologists were actually heavily involved in clinical work before that time. Further, those that were engaged in clinical psychology functioned chiefly as mental testers; their jobs typically involved assessment and diagnosis, not some kind of psychotherapy. Many of those early clinicians were women, who likely chose that field of psychology when they found the doors of academe closed to them because of their sex.

Fourth, clinical psychology is an applied field, and, as such, it is viewed by many as lying outside the field of scientific psychology. Historically, clinical psychology has been associated with such objectionable notions as demon possession, the occult, and bizarre therapies, and with treatments difficult to evaluate scientifically, such as hypnosis and psychoanalysis. These areas were objectionable for different reasons, but all have added to the scientist's distrust of clinical work.

The topic of psychopathology is an ancient one, dating to the beginnings of speculation about human nature (see Jackson, 1969; Simon, 1972; Simon & Weiner, 1966). This field involved more than just speculation about mental disorders; it included a variety of prescribed treatments as well. In the nineteenth century, when experimental methods were brought to bear on the study of the normal mind, there were those who sought to apply those same methods to the study of psychopathology. One of the pioneers in the field of experimental psychopathology was Emil Kraepelin (1856–1926), a German psychiatrist, who took his medical degree at Leipzig where he studied with Wilhelm Wundt, the founder of the science of psychology (see Chapter 5). Applying methods he learned from Wundt, Kraepelin studied a variety of mental disorders. His research led to his development, in 1883, of a comprehensive taxonomy of psychological disorders, grouping disorders as neuroses and psychoses and naming disorders such as paranoia and manic-depressive psychosis.

Another Wundt student, Lightner Witmer (1867–1956), an American from Philadelphia, returned to his native city to establish the first psychological clinic in the United States in 1896 (see O'Donnell, 1979). That clinic was involved in diagnosis, treatment, and research, and its cases and research were reported regularly in Witmer's own journal, *The Psychological Clinic*. Similar clinic-research facilities were soon opened in conjunction with a number of hospitals, and these clinics were frequently headed by psychologists trained in the new experimental psychology.

Obviously, a history of psychopathology is beyond the scope of this book. Limited treatment is provided in this chapter and in Chapters 13 and 15. For more comprehensive coverage, the reader should consult one or more of the following sources: Alexander & Selesnick (1966), Maher & Maher (1985), Reisman (1991), and Zilboorg (1941). This chapter will focus on views of psychopathology in France in the eighteenth and nineteenth centuries, principally through the work of Philippe Pinel and Jean Martin Charcot.

The tradition of neurological research in France is strong (recall the discussion of Magendie, Flourens, and Broca in the previous chapter.) That tradition, in combination with its progressive views on the treatment of the mentally ill, has made France a country of historical significance in clinical psychology.

Two of the most familiar historical images of treatment of the mentally ill are provided in the eighteenth-century engravings and paintings showing the deplorable conditions at the infamous mental asylum in London known as Bedlam (actually St. Mary of Bethlehem Hospital) and the humane unchaining of the insane in the Bicêtre and Salpêtrière asylums of Paris. The latter accomplishment was due to Philippe Pinel (1745–1826), a French psychiatrist.

The somatic view of mental illness held that because mental disorders were the result of physical causes, they were, in the main, nontreatable. Thus, mental patients were essentially imprisoned, often in chains. Pinel was one of a handful of eighteenth-century physicians who questioned a solely organic interpretation of mental illness and one of the first to put his beliefs to practice. In 1793, in the midst of the French Revolution, he became director of the Bicêtre Asylum and within several months had acquired permission from the asylum's governing board to begin removing the chains from some of the inmates. One of the first inmates to be unchained was an English army officer who had been hospitalized for forty years: "no one had dared to come close to him after the day when, in an attack of fury, he had killed a guard. After two years of remaining calm, following his liberation from the chains, the officer was allowed to leave the hospital" (Zilboorg, 1941, p. 323).

Pinel believed in the possibility of successful treatment, but he acknowledged that recovery was impossible under the conditions he found when he arrived at the Bicêtre Asylum. In addition to removing the chains, Pinel ordered changes in the behavior of his staff and guards: "No man was allowed to strike a maniac even in his own defense. No concessions however humble, nor complaints nor threats were allowed to interfere with the observance of this law. The guilty was instantly dismissed from the service" (Pinel, 1806, pp.90–91). Not only did a number of patients recover sufficiently to be released from the asylum, but the health and quality of life improved dramatically for the inmates. For example, of the 261 patients admitted in the two years before Pinel arrived at the Bicêtre, 152 died within a year of admission, a death rate of 58 percent. In the first two years of Pinel's directorship that rate had dropped to 12 percent (Hothersall, 1995).

Such successes enhanced Pinel's reputation with the Paris hospitals' governing board which, in 1795, appointed him to head La Salpêtrière, an asylum for insane women that housed one of the largest patient populations in all of Europe. Pinel instituted similar changes with similar success in that institution as well, and remained there until his death at age 83. His funeral was an important state affair, attended by the leading political and medical figures of France, and by some of the former patients at the Bicêtre and La Salpêtrière.

Gregory Zilboorg (1941), a historian of medicine, has written that the essence of Pinel's contribution was that his reorganization of hospital procedures made psychotherapy possible. The fame of his success spread to other countries, causing a revolution in care of the mentally ill in the beginning of the nineteenth century. (To understand the influence of Pinel's ideas in America, see Grob, 1994). Without a doubt Pinel's humanitarian practices constitute one of the major landmarks in the history of psychopathology.

THE READINGS

The first selection in this chapter is an excerpt from Pinel's *Treatise on Insanity* (1801), describing some of his hospital practices.

Jean Martin Charcot (1825–1893) was born the year before Pinel's death. As a medical student, Charcot studied at the Salpêtrière Asylum and in 1862, after pursuing a private medical practice, accepted a staff position at that famous hospital. He spent the rest of his life in research and treatment there. By 1870, he had achieved international fame as a neurologist, working on diseases such as poliomyelitis, multiple sclerosis, and epilepsy. Hundreds of Europe's best medical students and physicians flocked to Paris to study with Charcot, among them a 29-year-old Viennese doctor named Sigmund Freud. (Charcot's relationship to Freud is discussed in one of the selections in this chapter and in the introduction to Chapter 13.)

The Salpêtrière population was a treasure house for a student of psychopathology. In the 1870s, Charcot chose to focus on patients he diagnosed as suffering from hysteria, a disorder that was of little interest to his medical colleagues, many of whom viewed hysteria as a patient's pretense of mental illness. But Charcot considered it a serious affliction and spent much of his career at Salpêtrière developing a classification of types of hysteria and working on methods of treatment. He was a flamboyant character, theatrical in his lectures and often given to overstatement. Not surprisingly, he was frequently the center of controversy. The second selection in this chapter is Charcot's description of male hysteria, excerpted from his *Clinical Lectures on Certain Diseases of the Nervous System* (1873).

The two secondary source articles also deal with Charcot. The first is by H. F. Ellenberger (1905–1993), a renowned authority on the history of psychiatry. His article provides a detailed look at Charcot's career at Salpêtrière, including the rapid demise of his confidence and influence toward the end of his life. The final selection from Frank J. Sulloway's biography of Freud (acknowledged by many historians as the best biography ever written on Freud), describes the four and one-half months Freud spent in Charcot's clinic. The emphasis is on Freud's view of the work of Charcot, and its inclusion here is intended to show the importance of the French clinical tradition as an influence on psychoanalysis.

REFERENCES

Alexander, F. G., & Selesnick, S. T. (1966). *The history of psychiatry.* New York: Harper & Row.

Benjamin, L. T. (1986). Why don't they understand us? A history of psychology's public image. *American Psychologist, 41,* 941–946.

Grob, G. N. (1994). *The mad among us: A history of the care of America's mentally ill.* New York: Free Press.
Hothersall, D. (1995). *History of psychology (3rd ed).* New York: Random House.
Jackson, S. W. (1969). Galen—on mental disorders. *Journal of the History of the Behavioral Sciences, 5,* 365–384.
Maher, B. A., & Maher, W. B. (1985). Psychopathology: II. From the eighteenth century to modern times. In G.A. Kimble & K. Schlesinger (Eds.), *Topics in the history of psychology,* Volume 2. Hillsdale, NJ: Erlbaum, pp. 295–329.
Maher, W. B., & Maher, B. A. (1985). Psychopathology: I. From ancient times to the eighteenth century. In G.A. Kimble & K. Schlesinger (Eds.), *Topics in the history of psychology,* Volume 2. Hillsdale, NJ: Erlbaum, pp. 251–294.
O'Donnell, J. M. (1979). The clinical psychology of Lightner Witmer: A case study of institutional innovation and intellectual change. *Journal of the History of the Behavioral Sciences, 15,* 3–17.
Pinel, P. (1806). *A treatise on insanity.* Sheffield: W. Todd. (Originally published in 1801).
Reisman, J. M. (1991). *A history of clinical psychology.* (2nd ed.) New York: Hemisphere.
Simon, B., (1972). Models of mind and mental illness in ancient Greece: II. The Platonic model. *Journal of the History of the Behavioral Sciences, 8,* 389–406.
Simon, B. & Weiner, H. (1966). Models of mind and mental illness in ancient Greece: I. The Homeric model. *Journal of the History of the Behavioral Sciences, 2,* 303–314.
Stapp, J., Fulcher, R., & Wicherski, M. (1984). The employment of 1981 and 1982 doctoral recipients in psychology. *American Psychologist, 39,* 1408–1423.
Wood, W., Jones, M., & Benjamin, L. T. (1986). Surveying psychology's public image. *American Psychologist, 41,* 947–953.
Zilboorg, G. A. (1941). *A history of medical psychology.* New York: Norton.

Treating the Insane

Philippe Pinel

AN INSTANCE ILLUSTRATIVE OF THE ADVANTAGE OF OBTAINING AN INTIMATE ACQUAINTANCE WITH THE CHARACTER OF THE PATIENT

A man, in the vigour of life, confined at Bicêtre, fancied himself to be a king, and always spoke with the voice of command and authority. He had been for sometime at the Hôtel Dieu, where blows and other indignities, received from the keepers, had greatly exasperated his fury. Thus rendered suspicious and unmanageable, it was extremely difficult to fix upon a proper method of treating him. To have recourse to coercive means might still further aggravate his disorder, whilst condescension and acquiescence appeared likely to confirm him in his chimerical pretensions. I determined to wait the further development of his character, and taking advantage of any favourable circumstance that might happen. I was not long kept in suspence. He one day wrote a letter to his wife full of passionate expressions, accusing her with great bitterness of prolonging his detention, in order to enjoy her own entire liberty. He moreover threatened her with all the weight of his vengeance. Before this letter was sent off, he gave it to read to another patient, who reproved his passionate conduct, and remonstrated with him in a friendly manner, for endeavouring, as he did, to make his wife miserable. This remonstrance was kindly received. The letter was not sent, and another, replete with expressions of esteem, was substituted in its place. Mr. Poussin, the governor, saw in the effects of this friendly advice, the evident symptoms of a favourable change which was about to take place. He immediately availed himself of the occasion, and went to the maniac's apartment, where, in the course of conversation, he led him by degrees to the principal subject of his delirium. "If you are a sovereign," observed the governor, "why do you not put an end to your detention; and wherefore do you remain here, confounded with maniacs of every description?" He repeated his visits daily, when he assumed the tone of friendship and kindness. He endeavoured from time to time to convince him of the absurdity of his pretensions, and pointed out to him another maniac, who had for a long time indulged in the conviction that he was invested with sovereign power, and on that account, was now become an object of derision. The maniac was soon shaken in his convictions. In a short time he began to doubt his claim to sovereignty; and, at last, he was entirely convinced of his pretensions being chimerical. This unexpected revolution was accomplished in the course of a fortnight, and after a few months' longer residence in the house, this respectable husband and father was restored to his family.

A CASE OF CONVALESCENT INSANITY AGGRAVATED BY NEGLECT OF ENCOURAGING THE PATIENT'S TASTE FOR THE FINE ARTS

The gloomy and irritable character of maniacs, even when convalescent, is well known. Endowed, in most instances, with exquisite sensibility, they resent with great indignation the slightest appearances of neglect, contempt or indifference, and they forsake for ever what they had before adopted with the greatest ardour and zeal. A sculptor, a pupil of the celebrated Lemoin, was defeated in his endeavours to be admitted a member of the academy. From that moment he sunk into a profound mclancholy, of which the only intermissions consisted in invectives against his brother, whose parsimony he supposed had arrested his career. His extravagance and violence rendered it necessary to con-

From Pinel, P. (1801). *Traite medico-philosophique sur l'alienation mental, ou la manie*. Adapted from D. D. Davis (Trans.), *A treatise on insanity*. Sheffield: W. Todd, 1806, pp. 191–264.

fine him for lunacy. When conveyed to his apartment, he gave himself up to all the extravagances of maniacal fury. He continued in that state for several months. At length a calm succeeded, and he was permitted to go to the interior of the hospital. His understanding was yet feeble, and a life of inactivity was not a little irksome to him. The art of painting, which he had likewise cultivated, presented its renascent attractions to him, and he expressed a desire of attempting portrait painting. His inclination was encouraged and gratified and he made a sketch of the governor and his wife. The likeness was striking; but incapable of much application, he fancied that he perceived a cloud before his eyes. He allowed himself to be discouraged by a conviction of his insufficiency to emulate the models of fine taste, of which the traces were not yet effaced from his memory. The talent which he had discovered, his disposition to exercise it, and the probability of rescueing for his country the abilities of so promising a youth, induced the board of Bicêtre to request of him a pledge of his genius; leaving to him the choice of his subject, that his imagination might not be cramped. The convalescent, as yet but imperfectly restored, shrunk from the task which was thus imposed upon him; requested that the subject might be fixed upon, and that a correct and proper sketch might be given him for a model. His application was evaded, and the only opportunity of restoring him to himself and to his country was thus allowed to escape. He felt exceedingly indignant; considered this omission, as an unequivocal mark of contempt; destroyed all the implements of his art; and with angry haughtiness declared, that he renounced for ever the cultivation of the fine arts. This impression upon his feelings so unintentionally communicated, was so profound, that it was succeeded by a paroxysm of fury of several months' continuance. To this violence again succeded a second calm. But now the brilliant intellect was for ever obscured, and he sunk irrecoverably into a sort of imbecility and reverieism, bordering upon dementia. I ordered him to be transferred to the hospital infirmary, with a view of trying the effects of a few simple remedies, combined with the tonic system of regimen. Familiar and consolatory attentions to him, and such other assistance as his case appeared to suggest, were recurred to, more as they were dictates of humanity than as probable means of recovery. His taste for the fine arts, with his propensity to exertion of any kind, had for ever disappeared. Ennui, disgust with life, his gloomy melancholy and apathy made rapid progress. His appetite and sleep forsook him, and a colliquative diarrhea put an end to his degraded existence.

AN ATTEMPT TO CURE A CASE OF MELANCHOLIA PRODUCED BY A MORAL CAUSE

The fanciful ideas of melancholics are much more easily and effectually diverted by moral remedies, and especially by active employment, than by the best prepared and applied medicaments. But relapses are exceedingly difficult to prevent upon the best founded system of treatment. A working man, during an effervescent period of the revolution, suffered some unguarded expressions to escape him, respecting the trial and condemnation of Louis XVI. His patriotism began to be suspected in the neighborhood. Upon hearing some vague and exaggerated reports of intentions on the part of government agents to prosecute him for disloyalty, he one day betook himself in great tremour and consternation to his own house. His appetite and sleep forsook him. He surrendered himself to the influence of terror, left off working, was wholly absorbed by the subject of his fear; and at length he became fully impressed with the conviction that death was his unavoidable fate. Having undergone the usual treatment at the Hotel Dieu, he was transferred to Bicêtre. The idea of his death haunted him night and day, and he unceasingly repeated, that he was ready to submit to his impending fate. Constant employment at his trade, which was that of a tailor, appeared to me the most probable means of diverting the current of his morbid thoughts. I applied to the board for a small salary for him, in consideration of his repairing the clothes of the other patients of the asylum. This measure appeared to engage his interest in a very high degree. He undertook the employment with great eagerness, and worked without interruption for two months. A favourable change appeared to be taking place. He made no complaints nor any allusions to his supposed condemnation. He even spoke with the tenderest interest of a child of about six years of age, whom it seemed he had forgotten, and expressed a very great desire of having it brought to him. This awakened sensibility struck me as a favourable omen. The child was sent for, and all his other desires were gratified. He continued to work at his trade with renewed alacrity, frequently observing, that his child, who was now with him altogether, constituted the happiness of his life. Six months passed in this way without any disturbance or accident. But in the very hot weather of Messidore (June and July) year 5, some precursory symptoms of returning melancholy began to show themselves. A sense of heaviness in the head, pains of the legs and arms, a silent and pensive air, indisposition to work, indefference for his child, whom he pushed from him with marked coolness and even aversion, distinguished the progress of his relapse. He now retired into his cell, where he remained, stretched on the floor, obstinately persisting in his conviction, that there was nothing left for him but submission to his fate. About that time, I resigned my situation at Bicêtre, without, however, renouncing the hope of being useful to this unfortunate man. In the course of that year, I had recourse to the following expedient with him. The governor, being previously informed of my project, was prepared to receive a visit from a party of my friends, who were to assume the character of delegates from the legislative body, dispatched to Bicêtre to obtain information in regard to Citizen . . . , or upon his innocence, to pronounce upon him a sentence of acquittal. I then concerted with three other physicians whom I engaged to personate this deputation. The principal part was assigned to the eldest and gravest of them, whose appearance and manners were most calculated to command attention and respect. These commissaries, who were dressed in black robes suitable to their pretended office, ranged themselves round a table and caused the melancholic to be brought before them. One of them interrogated him as to his profession, former conduct, the journals which he had been in the habits of reading, and other particulars respecting his patriotism. The defendant related all that he had said and done; and insisted on a definitive judgement, as he did not conceive that he was guilty of any crime. In order to make a deep impression on his imagination, the president of the delegates pronounced in a loud voice the following sentence. "In virtue of the power which has been delegated to us by the national assembly, we have entered proceedings in due form of law, against Citizen . . . and having duly examined him, touching the matter whereof he stands accused, we make our declaration accordingly. It is therefore, by us declared, that we have found the said Citizen . . . a truly loyal patriot; and, pronouncing his acquital, we forbid all further proceedings against him. We furthermore order his entire enlargement and restoration to his friends. But inasmuch as he has obstinately refused to work for the last twelve months, we order his detention at Bicêtre to be prolonged six months from this present time, which said six months he is to employ, with proper sentiments of gratitude, in the capacity of tailor to the house. This our sentence is entrusted to Citizen Poussin, which he is to see executed at the peril of his life." Our commissaries then retired in silence. On the day following the patient again began to work, and, with every expression of sensibility and affection, solicited the return of his child. Having received the impulse of the above stratagem, he worked for some time unremittingly at his trade. But he had completely lost the use of his limbs from having remained so long extended upon the cold flags. His activity, however, was not of long continuance; and its remission concurring with an imprudent disclosure of the above well intended plot, his delirium returned. I now consider his case as absolutely incurable.

THE EFFECTS OF THE COLD AND WARM BATH, AND ESPECIALLY OF THE BATH OF SURPRISE, IN THE CURE OF MANIACAL DISORDERS

A young gentleman, twenty-two years of age, of a robust constitution, was deprived of part of his property by the revolution. He gave way to melancholy, began to look forward to futurity with extreme despondency, and lost his sleep. He was, at length, seized by violent maniacal fury. He was put upon the treatment for acute mania, in the town of his department. With his hands and feet tied he was suddenly immersed in the cold bath. Notwithstanding the violence with which he resisted this treatment, it was practiced upon him for some time. His delirium chiefly consisted in supposing himself to be an Austrian general, and he commonly assumed the tone and manner of a commander. During the process of bathing his fury was greatly exasperated by the mortifying consideration that his rank was neglected and despised. His disorder becoming more and more aggravated by this method, his relations came to the determination to convey him to Paris to be under my care. Upon my first interview with him he appeared exceedingly enraged. To conciliate his favour and obtain his good opinion, I felt the necessity of assenting to his illusive ideas. The bath was never mentioned to him. He was treated with mildness and put upon a diluent regimen, with the liberty of walking at all hours in a pleasant garden. The amusement which he derived from this liberty, exercise and familiar conversation, in which from time to time I engaged him, gradually induced a state of calmness, and towards the end of a month he was not remarkable either for haughtiness or diffidence. In about three months his delirium had completely left him. But towards the autumn of that year, and the spring of the succeeding, some threatening symptoms of a return of his disorder betrayed themselves in his manner and conduct. His looks became more animated, and he was unusually petulant and loquacious. In those circumstances I ordered him a gentle purge to be repeated at intervals, with frequent draughts of whey. He was continued upon this plan for a fortnight. I then advised him to take the warm bath. Not to rouse his former repugnance to bathing, this indication was suggested to him as a practice merely agreeable and conducive to cleanliness. By those means his paroxysms were prevented. To ascertain, however, the permanence of his cure he was detained at my house for a twelve month. Upon his departure he returned into the country, where, for the last two years, he has been occupied partly by literary pursuits, and partly by those of agriculture. No symptom of his delirium has since appeared.

"Cold bathing," says Mr. Haslam, "having for the most part been employed in conjunction with other remedies, it becomes difficult to ascertain how far it may be exclusively beneficial in this disease. The instances in which it had been separately used for the cure of insanity, are too few to enable me to draw any satisfactory conclusions. I may, however, safely affirm, that in many instances, paralytic affections have in a few hours supervened on cold bathing, especially when the patient has been in a furious state, and of a plethoric habit." Dr. Ferriar appears more decidedly favourable to the practice of bathing. In cases of melancholia he advises the cold, and in mania the warm bath. The only case, however, which he adduces in support of the practice must be acknowledged to be equivocal, inasmuch as it was treated, especially in its advanced stages, successively by opium, camphor, purgatives and electricity. General experiments of this nature are, perhaps, more calculated to perpetuate than to dissipate uncertainty. The real utility of bathing in maniacal disorders, remains yet to be ascertained. To establish the practice upon a solid foundation, it must be tried with constant and judicious reference to the different species of insanity. A raving female manic was put upon the use of the warm bath. She bathed twenty five times, great debility was the immediate consequence, and her mania was shortly after succeeded by dementia. I am led to suppose, that the warm bath may be resorted to with more probability of success, as a preventative of approaching maniacal paroxysms.

It has been said, that the bath of surprise has been found a valuable remedy in some cases of insanity which had resisted the effects of the warm bath, the cold shower bath, and other remedies. This superiority of the unexpected application of cold water, has been ascribed to an interruption of the chain of delirious ideas, induced by the suddenness of the shock, and the general agitation of the system experienced from this process. It is well known that the enthusiast Van Helmont, has made some valuable remarks upon the durable effects of sudden immersion in cold water in some cases of mental derangement. His practice was to detain the patient in the bath for some minutes. It may be proper to observe, that this method, however successful in some instances, might in others be extremely dangerous, and that it can only be resorted to with propriety in cases almost hopeless, and where other remedies are ineffectual; such as in violent paroxysms of regular periodical mania, inveterate continued insanity, or insanity complicated with epilepsy.

Hysteria in the Male Subject

Jean Martin Charcot

Gentlemen: We shall study to-day hysteria in the male sex, and in order the better to compass the subject, we shall consider male hysteria more particularly in adolescent subjects, or such as are in the vigor of age and in full maturity, that is to say, in men of from twenty to forty years, and we shall give attention more especially to that intense, very pronounced form which corresponds to what is called in the female great hysteria, or hystero-epilepsy with mixed crises. If I have decided to take up this subject which I have touched upon many times already, it is because we have actually in our clinical service at the present time a truly remarkable collection of patients whom I shall cause to appear before you, and whom I shall study with you. I have for my object especially to make you recognize and prove by your senses the identity of the great neurosis in both sexes, for in the comparison which we shall make as we go on of the symptoms of hysteria major in the female and in the male, everywhere we shall have occasion to remark the most striking similarities, and here and there only, certain differences which as you will see, are of but secondary importance.

Moreover, this question of hysteria in the male subject is one of the questions regarded as of special interest at the present day. In France, during the last few years it has much occupied the attention of physicians. From 1875 to 1880 five inaugural dissertations on hysteria in the male were defended before the Faculty of Paris, and Klein, author of one of these theses written under the direction of Dr. Olivier, succeeded in

From Charcot, J. M. (1873). *Leçons sur les maladies du système nerveux*. In E. P. Hurd (Trans.), *Clinical lectures on certain diseases of the nervous system*. Detroit: G. S. Davis, 1888, pp. 180–194.

compiling eighty cases of this affection. Since then the important publications of Bourneville and his pupils have appeared; of Debove, Raymond, Dreyfus and some others; and all these works tend to prove, among other things, that cases of male hysteria may be met with quite frequently in ordinary practice. Quite recently, male hysteria has been studied in America by Putnam and Walton, principally in connection with and as a sequel of traumatisms, and more especially of railroad accidents. They have recognized, along with Page, who has also interested himself in this question in England, that many of those nervous accidents designated under the name of *railway spine*, and which, in his opinion, might better be called *railway brain*, are in reality, whether appearing in man or in woman, simply hysterical manifestations. It is easy, then, to understand the interest which such a question has to the practical mind of our confreres of the United States. The victims of railroad accidents quite naturally claim damages of the companies. The case goes into court; thousands of dollars are at stake. Now, I repeat, often it is hysteria which is at the bottom of all these nervous lesions. Those neuropathic states, so grave and so tenacious, which present themselves as the sequel of "collisions" of that kind, and which render their victims unable to work or pursue any regular occupation for months and for even years, are often only hysteria, nothing but hysteria. Male hysteria is then worthy of being studied and known by the medico-legalist, for he is often called upon to give his opinion, in matters concerning which great pecuniary interests are at stake, before a tribunal which would be likely to be influenced (and this circumstance renders his task the more difficult) by the disfavor which is still attached to the word hysteria on account of prejudices profoundly rooted. A thorough acquaintance not only with the disease, but also with the conditions under which it is produced, will be on such occasions the more useful from the fact that the nervous disorders often ensue without any traumatic lesion, and simply as a consequence of the psychical nervous shock resulting from the accident; frequently, moreover, they do not come on immediately after the accident, but some time afterwards, when, for instance, one of the victims of the collision, who may have been disabled by fracture of the leg, will have got well after being incapacitated for work for three or four months; another, perhaps, may have been suffering from nervous troubles which are destined to prevent him from working for six months or a year, but which have not reached their full intensity. You see how delicate in such cases is the mission of the medical jurist, and it is this medico-legal side of the question which seems among our American confreres to have awakened a new interest in the study of hysterical neuroses heretofore a little neglected.

In proportion as the disease has been better studied and better known (as habitually happens in similar circumstances), cases become apparently more and more frequent, and at the same time, more easy of analysis. I just told you that four or five years ago, Klein, in his thesis, had collected eighty cases of hysteria in men; today, Batault who is preparing in our hospital service a special work on the subject, has been able to gather together 218 cases of the same kind, none of which belong to our clinic.

Male hysteria is, then, far from being rare. Indeed, gentlemen, if I were to judge from what I see every day among us, these cases are very often misunderstood, even by very distinguished physicians. It is granted that an effeminate young man may, after certain excesses, disappointments, deep emotions, present various phenomena of an hysterical nature, but that a vigorous mechanic, well developed, not enervated by an indolent or too studious mode of life, a fireman of a locomotive, for instance, never before emotional, at least in appearance, may, as the result of a railroad accident, a collision, a car running off from the track, become hysterical just like a woman—all this has never entered into the imagination of some people. Nothing, however, is better proved, and pathology must adjust itself to this new conception, which will hereafter take its place along with other propositions which are today received as demonstrated truths, after having long fought their way through scepticism, and often through ridicule.

There is a prejudice which doubtless contributes much to oppose the diffusion of right knowledge relative to hysteria in the male sex; I refer to the relatively false notion generally entertained of the clinical tableau of this neurosis in the female. In the male, in fact, the disease often presents itself as an affection remarkable by the permanence and tenacity of the symptoms which characterize it. In the female, on the contrary—and this is without doubt that which seems to constitute the capital difference between the two sexes in the estimation of anyone who does not thoroughly and radically know the disease in the female—what is generally believed to be the characteristic feature of hysteria is the instability, the mobility of the symptoms. In hysteria, it is said, observations of the disease in the female being naturally taken as the basis of this opinion, the phenomena are mobile, fugacious, and the capricious march of the affection is often interrupted by scenes of the most unexpected nature. Very well, but, gentlemen, this mobility, this fugaciousness is far from being a universal characteristic of hysteria, even in the female, as I have shown you by numerous examples.

Yes, even in females there are cases of hysteria with durable, permanent phenomena, extremely difficult to modify, and which sometimes resist all medical interference. Cases of this kind are numerous, very numerous, if, indeed, they do not constitute the majority. This is a point to which I shall return shortly. But for the moment I content myself by remarking, only, that the permanence of the hysterical symptoms in the male, and their tenacity often prevent the medical attendants from recognizing their true character. Some, in presence of phenomena which resist all therapeutic modifiers, will believe, I imagine, if there exist sensorial troubles with nervous crises simulating more or less the epileptic fit, that they have to do with an organic localized lesion (lesion en foyer), an intra-cranial neoplasm, or if it is a case of paraplegia, with an organic spinal lesion. Others will willingly admit, or will even affirm, that there can be no question in these cases of an organic alteration, but simply of a dynamic lesion; but in view of symptoms whose tenacity does not comport with the scheme which they have in mind of hysteria, they will think that they have before them a special disease, not yet described, and which merits a place by itself.

A mistake of this kind seems to me to have been committed by M. M. Oppenheim and Thomsen, of Berlin, in a memoir which contains, however, a great number of interesting facts, carefully observed, if not always well interpreted, at least according to my way of thinking. These gentlemen have observed hemi-anaesthesia, sensitive and sensorial, like in all points to that of hysterical patients, in seven observations similar to those of Putnam and Walton. These cases had to do with firemen, conductors, workingmen, victims of railroad or other accidents, all of whom had sustained a blow on the head, a concussion, or a general shock. Alcoholism, lead-poisoning, etc., were not factors in these cases, and the fact was recognized that, according to every probability, there existed no organic lesion in these subjects.

We have here, then, a set of cases quite like those of Putnam and Walton, but differing from the latter in this respect that the German authorities are not willing to concede that these are cases of hysteria, which to their minds constitute something peculiar, some undefined, undescribed pathological state, demanding a new place in the nosological category. The principal arguments which Oppenheim and Thomsen adduce to the support of their thesis are the following: 1. The anaesthesia is obstinate; we do not see there those capricious changes which are characteristic(?) of hysteria. It lasts just as it is for months and for years. 2. Another reason is that the psychical state of the patient is not that of the hysterical. The troubles of this order in these patients have not the changing, mobile traits of hysterical manifestations. The patients are conspicuously depressed, melancholic after a permanent sort, and without great fluctuations in the degree of their melancholy.

It is impossible for me to agree with the conclusions of M. M. Oppenheim and Thomsen, and I hope to show you, gentlemen, 1, that the sensorial hysterical troubles may in the female, even, present a remarkable tenacity, and that in the male it is often so; 2, that in the male in particular, the depression and the melancholic tendency are most commonly observed in the most marked, the least contestable cases of hysteria. We do not indeed ordinarily observe in the male subject, although this is assuredly not a distinctive characteristic of the first order, those caprices, those changes of character and humor, which belong more commonly, but not necessarily, to the hysteria of the female.

But it is time, gentlemen, to bring to end these preliminary remarks, in order to come to the principal object of our lesson today. We shall proceed by clinical demonstration to study together in detail a certain number of perfectly characteristic cases of male hysteria. While thus engaged we shall bring to view the likeness and the differences that exist between the symptoms of hysteria observed in men and those with which we are familiar every day in the corresponding form of the disease in women. Lastly, I intend to present after the manner of a summary, certain general considerations on the great hysteria (hysteria major) as seen in the male sex.

But before coming to my subject proper, I desire briefly to remind you by two examples to what extent in the female the permanent symptoms of hysteria, the hysterical stigmata, as we are wont to call them for convenience, may show themselves fixed, tenacious, and consequently exempt from that proverbial mobility which has been attributed to them, and which some writers regard as characteristic of the disease. I shall not refer now to the six or eight subjects of great hysteria actually assembled in our wards. Certain of them have presented for months and even for years a simple or double anaesthesia which our best and most appropriate therapeutic modifiers can influence only for a few hours. I will limit myself to presenting to you two women who are veritable veterans of hystero-epilepsy, and who now, being rid for several years of their great attacks, and discharged from the medical service, exercise in the hospital the functions of domestics. The first, L. by name, well known in the history of hystero-epilepsy, and noted for the "demoniacal" character which her convulsive crises presented, is today 63 years of age. She entered the Salpêtrière in 1846, and I have not ceased to have her under observation since 1871. At this time she was affected, as she is still today, with a right hemi-anaesthesia, complete, absolute, sensorial and sensitive, with ovaria on the same side, which, during this long period of fifteen years, has never been modified, *even temporarily*, whether by the action many times tried of aesthesiogenous agents, whether by the progress of age and the menopause. Six years ago, at the time when our attention was more particularly directed to the modifications which the visual field undergoes in the hysterical, we detected in this patient the existence in a marked degree of the classic contraction of the visual field, which was pronounced on both sides, but much more so on the right. The repeated examination once or twice every year since then has never failed to reveal the permanence of this contraction.

The other patient, Aurel by name, aged 62 years, and in whom the great seizures, replaced sometimes by certain symptoms of angina pectoris, have only ceased within a dozen of years, presented as far back as 1851, according to a precious note dated that very year, a left hemi-anaesthesia, complete and absolute, sensorial and sensitive, which, as you can observe for yourselves, exists this very day, after a lapse of 34 years. This patient has been under our observation for fifteen years, and never has the hemi-anaesthesia in question ceased to present itself during our often-repeated examinations. The double contraction of the visual field, very plain on both sides, but more pronounced on the left, which the campimetric examination has enabled us at the present time to find, already existed with her five years ago.

This is enough, I think, to show you how stable and permanent in these women are the stigmata of which no one would think of disputing the hysterical nature, and how little this corresponds to the notion, erroneous by reason of being carried too far, which is generally entertained of the evolution of the symptoms of the disease.

I come now to the study of our male hysterics.

Case I.—Rig . . . , aged 44 years, clerk in an oil factory, entered the Salpêtrière May 12, 1884, or about a year ago. He is a large strong man, of firm muscles; was formerly a cooper, and endured without fatigue arduous toil. The hereditary antecedents in this patient are very remarkable. His father is still living, aged 76 years. From the age of 38 to 44 the latter, by reason of disappointments and pecuniary losses, suffered *nervous attacks*, as to the nature of which the patient can give us but little information. His mother died at the age of 63, of asthma. His mother's *great uncle was epileptic*, and died in consequence of a fall into the fire during one of his fits. The *two daughters of this uncle* were also *epileptic*. Rig . . . has had seven brothers and sisters who have never had any nervous diseases. Four are dead; among the three living, one sister is asthmatic. He himself has had nine children, four of whom died young. Of the five who are still living, *one daughter fifteen years old has nervous crises; another, aged ten years, has attacks of hystero-epilepsy* which Dr. Marie has witnessed in this very place; *another daughter is feeble in intelligence*; lastly, two boys present nothing in particular to note.

In the personal antecedents we find the following facts: At the age of 19 or 20 years, the patient was attacked with acute articular rheumatism, without lesions of the heart. The last attack lasted six months, and it is, perhaps, to the rheumatism that we are to attribute the deformation of the hands, which we note in this patient. While a child, he was very timid, his sleep was troubled by dreams and nightmares, and besides he was addicted to somnambulism. He would often rise in the night-time and go to work, and the next morning he would be much surprised to find his job done. This state continued from 12 to 15 years. He married at 28 years of age. We do not find in his antecedents either syphilis or alcoholism, vices from which coopers are not always exempt. He came to Paris when 32 years old, working at first with his father, then employed as shop clerk in an oil refinery.

In 1876, when 32 years of age, he met with his first accident. He cut himself quite deeply with a razor which he was sharpening, as some people are in the habit of doing, by straping it back and forth on the front aspect of the fore arm. A vein was cut, and the blood spurted; under the influence of the hemorrhage and the fright, the patient lost consciousness and fell to the ground. He was a long time in recovering, remaining two months profoundly anaemiated, pale and without power to work.

In 1882, consequently about three years ago, he was lowering a barrel of wine into the cellar, when the cord which held it gave way; the barrel rolled down the stairway and would certainly have crushed him if he had not jumped to one side, he did not, however, save himself sufficiently to avoid a slight wound of the left hand. Despite the fright which he experienced, he was able to get up and help raise the cask. But five minutes afterward, he had an attack of loss of consciousness which lasted twenty minutes. Coming to himself, he was unable to walk, so weak had his limbs become, and he was taken home in a carriage. For two days, it was absolutely impossible for him to work; during the night his sleep was disturbed by frightful visions and interrupted by cries of: help! I am killed! He went over again in dreams the scene in the cellar. He had nevertheless resumed his work, when ten days after the accident, in the middle of the night, he had his first attack of hystero-epilepsy. Since this time, the attacks returned almost regularly every two months; and often in the interval, during the night, whether at the moment of the first sleep or about the time of waking, he would be profoundly disturbed by visions of ferocious animals.

Formerly as he came out of these fits, he remembered that he had been dreaming during the attack, a phenomenon which no longer exists. He imagined that he was in a dark forest pursued by robbers or frightful animals, or the scene of the cellar was acted over again, and he saw wine casks rolling upon him and threatening to crush him. He affirms that never, during these seizures, or in the interval, has he had dreams or hallucinations of a gay or agreeable character.

About this time, he went to St. Anne's Hospital for advice and treatment. The physicians there prescribed for him bromide of potassium, and this medicine (a fact to be noticed) has never had the least influence on the attacks, although administered for a long time till the organism was saturated with it. It was under these conditions that Rig . . . , was admitted to the Salpêtrière, and at his entrance we made note of the following state.

The patient is pale, anaemic, has but little appetite, especially for meat, to which he prefers acid foods; in short, the general condition is far from satisfactory. The *hysterical stigmata* in this patient are very well marked. They consist in *a double anaesthesia in patches* of great extent, for pain (pinching, pricking) and for cold. Sensorial anaesthesia in general does not exist, except to a very mild degree; taste and smell are normal; hearing is nevertheless quite perceptibly blunted, especially in the left ear; the patient hears no better when the sonorous object is applied to the cranium. As far as vision is concerned, the symptoms are much plainer, and alone suffice, in a measure, to enable us to affirm the hysterical nature of the affection. He presents, in fact, on both sides *a notable contraction of the visual field*, more marked, however, on the right. He distinguishes all the colors, but the visual field of the blue is more contracted than that of the red, and passes within the latter, a phenomenon when it is met with, which is quite characteristic, as far as I know, of the visual field of hysterical patients; of this I have many times shown you examples. Lastly, to finish what I say of the permanent stigmata, there exist in Rig . . . *two hysterogenous* points, the one cutaneous, seated below the last right false ribs, the other deeper, in the popliteal space of the right side, at a point where the patient has a cyst, which is the seat of extreme pain of spontaneous origin. There does not exist in this patient any testicular point. Pressure exercised over the spasmogenous points, whether accidentally or voluntarily, produces all the phenomena of the hysterical aura; precordial pain, constriction of the neck, with the sensation of a ball, hissings in the ears, and beatings in the temples, these two last phenomena constituting, as you know, the cephalic aura. Those points whose excitation may provoke the attack with singular facility are, on the other hand, but feebly *spasm-checkers (spasmo-frenateurs)* that is to say, their excitation, even when intense and prolonged, arrests but imperfectly the attack in the process of evolution.

In the mental state of Rig . . . , today as in the past, it is always anxiety, fear, distress, that predominate. He cannot sleep in the dark; in full day he does not like to be alone; he is of excessive sensitiveness, and he experiences great fright at the sight or remembrance of certain animals, such as rats, mice, toads, which he often sees, moreover, in terrifying nightmares, or in hallucinations occurring when half asleep. He is always sad; "I am weary of myself," he says. He manifests a certain mobility of mind characterized by the fact that he can apply himself to nothing, and that he undertakes and abandons with the same facility five or six tasks at a time. He is intelligent and has a fair amount of education. He is, moreover, of a mild disposition, and totally devoid of vicious propensities.

The attacks are spontaneous or provoked. Whatever may be the manner of their origin, they always begin by a keen sensation of smarting or burning in the region of the spasmogenous points, to which succeed first a pain in the epigastrium, then the sensation of constriction of the neck and of a ball, finally the cephalic aura consisting of sibilant noises in the ears, and beatings in the temples. At this moment the patient loses consciousness and the *paroxysm* proper begins. It is divided into *four periods* which are quite clear and distinct. In the first, the patient executes certain epileptiform convulsive movements. Then comes the period of great gesticulations of salutation, which are of extreme violence, interrupted from time to time by an arching of the body which is absolutely characteristic, the trunk being bent bow fashion, sometimes in front (emprosthotonos), sometimes backward (opisthotonos), the feet and head alone touching the bed, the body constituting the arch. During this time the patient utters wild cries. Then comes the third period, called period of passional attitudes, during which he utters words and cries in relation with the sad delirium and terrifying visions which pursue him. Sometimes it is the woods, the wolves, or other frightful animals, sometimes it is the cellar, the stairway, the rolling cask. Finally he regains consciousness, recognizes the persons around him and calls them by name, but the delirium and hallucinations still continue for some time. He looks all around and under the bed for the black beasts which threaten him; he examines his arms, thinking to find there the bites of the animals which he thinks he has felt. Then he comes to himself, and the attack is over, although it is generally sure to be repeated a few minutes later, and so on, till after three or four successive paroxysms, the patient at last completely regains the normal state. Never during the course of these crises has he bitten his tongue or wet his bed.

For more than a year, Rig . . . has been subjected to treatment by static electrization, which, in cases of this kind, as you know, often gives us good results; we have prescribed at the same time all the tonics and reconstituents imaginable. Nevertheless, the phenomena which we have just described, the permanent stigmata and fits, persist just as they were, without appreciable changes; they seem, in short, having already existed almost three years, to be of the kind that undergo very slow modification. We have, however, certainly here, as you will all agree, a case of hystero-epilepsy with mixed crises (epileptiform hysteria) as clearly characterized as possible, and it is plain that the stability of the stigmata, on which we have sufficiently insisted, should not an instant stay our diagnosis.

To conclude this case, so perfectly typical, I will still further call your attention to certain particulars which the clinical analysis has disclosed. In the first place, I will mention particularly the nervous heredity, so strongly pronounced in his family: hysteria in the father (very probable at least); great uncle and cousins-german of the mother epileptic; two daughters, one of whom is hysterical, the other hystero-epileptic. You will frequently, gentlemen, meet with these conditions of heredity in the hysterical male patient, and find them, perhaps, more marked even than in the female.

I must remind you, moreover, how in our patient the hysterical manifestations were developed on the occasion and as the result of an accident which threatened his life. Could the traumatism which was the consequence of the accident (and it was nothing but a trifling wound of the finger) have sufficed of itself to cause the development of the nervous symptoms? This is possible, but I would not affirm it. It is always necessary, alongside of the traumatism, to take account of a factor which very probably has played a more important part in the genesis of these accidents than the wound itself. I refer to the terror experienced by the patient at the moment of the accident, and which found expression shortly afterwards in loss of consciousness followed by temporary paresis of the inferior extremities. This same psychical element is found, apart from the traumatism, in some of the cases described by Putnam, Walton, Page, Oppenheim and Thomsen, where its influence, often predominant, cannot be misunderstood.

Charcot and the Salpêtrière School

H. F. Ellenberger

The Salpêtrière School was strongly organized and headed by a powerful figure, that of the greatest teacher Jean Martin Charcot (1825–1893), a neurologist who had come belatedly to the study of certain mental phenomena. During the years 1870–1893, Charcot was considered to be the great neurologist of his time. He was the consulting physician of kings and princes and patients came to see him "from Samarkand and the West Indies." But celebrity had come to him after long years of incessant and obscure toil, and few of those who marveled at Charcot's extraordinary success realized that it was a belated one reached after many years of strenuous and unnoticed work.

No real biography of Charcot has been written as yet. Most accounts, such as Guillain's book (1), are based on necrologies and depict for the most part the Charcot of the brilliant years. Valuable memories have been recorded by his disciple Souques (2) and particularly by the Russian physician Lyubimov (3) who had been acquainted with Charcot for the last 20 years of Charcot's life.

Charcot was born in Paris, the son of a carriage builder who, it was said, made carriages of great beauty and who was reputed to be more of an artist than an artisan. Very little is known about Charcot's childhood and youth. It is said that he was a cold, silent, shy, and aloof young man who had a speech impediment. He wore a black moustache (the story goes that his first rich patient was referred to him on the condition that he shave off his moustache). As an *interne* (medical resident), the young Charcot was assigned for some time to the Salpêtrière, an old hospital which, at that time, was mainly a medical poor-house for four or five thousand old women. Charcot realized that this hospital sheltered numerous patients with rare or unknown neurologic diseases and would be a gold mine for clinical research. He kept this in mind while he was slowly pursuing his career as an anatomo-pathologist. As a young doctor, he was asked by one of his teachers to be physician and companion to a rich banker traveling to Italy, which gave him an opportunity of getting acquainted with Italy's artistic wealth (4). His medical career was rather slow and laborious. The turning point came in 1862 when, at the age of thirty-six, Charcot was appointed chief physician in one of the Salpêtrière's largest sections and took up his old plans with feverish activity. Case histories were taken, autopsies performed, laboratories opened, while he was building at the same time a team of devoted collaborators. He was inspired by Duchenne (de Boulogne), a neurologist of outstanding genius who had no official position and whom Charcot called his "Master in Neurology" (5,6). Within eight years (1862–1870), Charcot made the discoveries that gave him his position of eminence.

In 1870, Charcot took on the supplementary charge of a special ward which the hospital administration had reserved for a fairly large number of women patients suffering from "convulsions." Some of them were epileptics others were hysterics who had learned to imitate epileptic crises. Charcot strove to discover means of distinguishing between hysterical and epileptic convulsions. He also started to investigate hysteria with the same method he used for organic neurologic diseases and, with his disciple Paul Richer, gave a description of the full blown hysterical crisis (the *grande hystérie*) (7).

In 1878, probably under the influence of Charles Richet, Charcot extended his interest to hypnotism, of which he undertook a purportedly

Ellenberger, H. F. (1965). Charcot and the Salpêtrière school. *American Journal of Psychotherapy, 19,* 253–267.

scientific study (as he had done with hysteria), taking as subjects several of the most gifted of his female hysterical patients. He found that these subjects developed the hypnotic condition through three successive stages: "lethargy," "catalepsy," and "somnambulism," each stage showing very definite and characteristic symptoms. Charcot read his findings at the Académie des Sciences at the beginning of 1882 (8); it was, Janet said, a *tour de force* to have hypnotism accepted by the same Académie which thrice within the past century had condemned it under the name of magnetism. This resounding paper gave magnetism a new dignity, and this heretofore shunned subject became the topic of innumerable publications.

Among Charcot's most spectacular achievements were the investigations on traumatic paralysis (9) which he conducted in 1884 and 1885. In his time, paralysis was generally considered to result from lesions of the nervous system caused by an accident, although the existence of "psychic paralysis" had been postulated in England by B. C. Brodie (10) in 1837 and by Russel Reynolds (11) in 1869. But how could a purely psychologic factor cause paralysis without the patient's awareness of that factor and excluding the possibility of simulation?

Charcot had already analyzed the differences between organic and hysterical paralysis. In 1884, three men afflicted with a monoplegia of one arm consecutive to traumatism were admitted to the Salpêtrière. Charcot first demonstrated that the symptoms of that paralysis, while differing from those of organic paralysis, coincided exactly with the symptoms of hysterical paralysis. The second step was the experimental reproduction of similar states of paralysis under hypnosis. Charcot suggested to some hypnotized subjects that their arms would be paralyzed. The resulting hypnotic paralysis proved to have exactly the same symptoms as the spontaneous hysterical paralysis and the post-traumatic paralysis of the three male patients. Charcot was able to reproduce these conditions segment by segment, and he also suggested their disappearance in the reverse order. The next step was a demonstration of the effect of the trauma. Charcot chose easily hypnotizable subjects and suggested to them that in their waking state, as soon as they were slapped on the back, their arm would become paralyzed. When awakened, the subjects showed the usual post-hypnotic amnesia, and as soon as they were slapped on the back, they were instantly struck with a monoplegia of the arm of exactly the same type as the post-traumatic monoplegia. Finally, Charcot pointed out that in certain subjects living in a state of permanent somnambulism, hypnotic suggestion was not even necessary. They got paralysis of the arm after being slapped on the back, without special verbal suggestion. The mechanism of post-traumatic paralysis seemed thus to be demonstrated. Charcot assumed that the nervous shock following the trauma was a kind of hypnoid state analogous to hypnotism and therefore enabling the development of an autosuggestion of the individual. "I do not think that in any physiopathologic research it would often be possible to reproduce more accurately the condition which one has set onself the task to study," Charcot concluded.

Charcot ranged the hysterical, post-traumatic, and hypnotic paralysis in the group of "dynamic paralysis" in contrast to "organic paralysis" resulting from a lesion of the nervous system. He gave a similar demonstration in regard to hysterical mutism and hysterical coxalgia. Here, too, he reported experimentally, by means of hypnotism, clinical pictures identical with the hysterical conditions. In 1892, Charcot distinguished "dynamic amnesia," in which lost memories can be recovered under hypnosis, from "organic amnesia" where this is impossible (12, 13).

In the last years of his life, Charcot realized that a vast realm existed between that of clear consciousness and that of organic brain physiology. His attention was drawn to "faith healing," and in one of his last articles (14), he stated that he had seen patients going to Lourdes and returning healed from their diseases. He tried to elucidate the mechanism of such cures and anticipated that an increased knowledge of the laws of "faith healing" would result in great therapeutic progresses.

There are many descriptions and pictures of Charcot, but they pertain almost without exception to Charcot at his zenith around 1880 or to the declining Charcot of the last years. The most lively ones were given by Léon Daudet, who had studied medicine at the Salpêtrière and whose father, the novelist Alphonse Daudet, had been Charcot's intimate friend. Here is a condensed excerpt of Léon Daudet's *Memoirs* (15, 16, 17) describing Charcot:

> Charcot was a small, stout and vigorous man with a big head, a bull's neck, a low forehead, broad cheeks. The line of his mouth was hard and meditative. He was clean shaven and kept his straight hair combed back. He somewhat resembled Napoleon and liked to cultivate this resemblance. His gait was heavy, his voice authoritative, somewhat low, often ironical and insisting, his expression extraordinarily fiery.
>
> A most learned man, he was familiar with the works of Dante, Shakespeare, and the great poets; he read English, German, Spanish and Italian. He had a large library full of strange and unusual books.
>
> He was very humane; he showed a profound compassion for animals and forbade any mention of hunters and hunting in his presence.
>
> A more authoritarian man I have never known, nor one who could put such a despotic yoke on people around him. To realize this, one only had to see how he could, from his pulpit, throw a sweeping and suspicious glance at his students and hear him interrupt them with a brief, imperative word.
>
> He could not stand contradiction, however small. If someone dared contradict his theories, he became ferocious and mean and did all he could to wreck the career of the imprudent man unless he retracted and apologized.
>
> He could not stand stupidity. But his need for domination caused him to eliminate the more brilliant of his disciples, so that in the end he was surrounded by mediocre people. As a compensation, he maintained social relationships with artists and poets and gave magnificent receptions.
>
> It was one of his favourite ideas that the share of dream-life in our waking state is much more than just "immense."

Many references to Charcot can be found in the *Diary* of Edmond and Jules de Goncourt (18). These two brothers were known for their biting descriptions and seem to have been particularly antagonistic to Charcot, whom they described as follows:

> Charcot was an ambitious man, envious of any superiority, showing a ferocious resentment against those who declined invitations to his receptions, a despot at the university, hard with his patients to the point of telling them bluntly of their impending death, but cowardly when he himself was ill. He was a tyrant with his children and compelled for instance his son Jean, who wanted to be a seafarer, to become a physician. As a scientist, Charcot was a mixture of genius and charlatan. Most unpleasant was his indiscretion in talking of his patients' confidential matters.

The description given by the Russian physician Lyubimov (3) is so vastly different that one can hardly believe it concerns the same person:

> Beside his extraordinary gift as a teacher, a scientist and an artist, Charcot was extremely humane, devoted to his patients and would not tolerate anything unkind being said about anyone in his presence. He was a poised and sensible man, very circumspect in his judgments, with a quick eye for distinguishing peoples' value. His family life was a harmonious and happy one; his wife, who was a widow with a daughter when he married her, helped him with his work and was active in charitable organizations. He gave great care to the education of his son Jean who had spontaneously chosen to be a physician and whose first scientific publications were a great joy for his father. He enjoyed the devotion of his students and of his patients, so that his patron saint's day, the Saint Mar-

tin on November 11th, was celebrated with entertainments and rejoicing at the Salpêtrière.

One may wonder how Charcot gained that enormous prestige which he enjoyed in the years 1880 to 1890. Several reasons may be distinguished.

Firstly, the Salpêtrière was anything but an ordinary hospital. It was a city within a city in the seventeenth century style, consisting of about 45 buildings with streets, squares, gardens, and an old and beautiful church. It was also a place of historical fame: Saint Vincent de Paul had carried out there his charitable activities; it had later been converted by Louis XIV into an asylum for beggars, prostitutes, and the insane; it was also one of the places where the notorious September Massacres had taken place during the French Revolution and where Pinel had achieved his mental hospital reforms. It was also known from one episode in the classic novel *Manon Lescaut* by the Abbé Prévost. Its thousands of old women had inspired some of Baudelaire's poems. Before Charcot, the Salpêtrière had been little known to medical students, and physicians did not relish the thought of being appointed there. Charcot was now credited with being the scientific wizard who had turned this historical place into a Temple of Science.

That old-fashioned hospital with its antiquated buildings had no laboratories, no examination rooms, no teaching facilities. With his iron will—and with the help of his political connections—Charcot built a treatment, research, and teaching unit. He had carefully chosen his collaborators; he installed consulting rooms for ophthalmology, otolaryngology, and so on, as well as laboratories and a photographic service, later a museum for anatomo-pathology, and finally an outpatient service where men were also admitted, and a large auditorium. Among Charcot's disciples were Bourneville, Pitres, Joffroy, Cotard, Gilles de la Tourette, Meige, Paul Richer, Souques, Pierre Marie, Raymond, Babinski; there is hardly one French neurologist of that time who had not been Charcot's student. On that School, which was his creation, Charcot exerted an absolute domination. Each one of his lectures was carefully recorded by students and published in one or the other of several medical journals he had founded. There came a time when no one could be appointed at the Paris medical faculty without his sanction. The patriotic feeling contributed to Charcot's fame: He and Pasteur were to the French a proof of France's scientific genius, challenging Germany's alleged scientific superiority.

Charcot personified what the French call a "prince de la Science"; he was not only a man of high scientific reputation, but also a powerful and wealthy man. Through his marriage with a rich widow and the very high fees which he charged his patients, he was able to lead the life of the wealthy class. Aside from his villa in Neuilly, he had in 1884 acquired a splendid residence on the Boulevard Saint-Germain which had been decorated according to his own plans. It was a kind of private museum with Renaissance furniture, stained glass windows, tapestries, paintings, antiques, and rare books. He was himself an artist who did excellent drawings and was an expert in painting on china and enamel; he was a keen connoisseur of the history of art (19). He was also a master of French prose and had an exhaustive knowledge of French literature. An infrequent thing at his time, he also knew English, German, and Italian and showed a particular admiration for Shakespeare whom he often quoted in English, and for Dante whom he quoted in Italian. Every Tuesday night, he gave fastuous receptions in his splendid home to the *Tout-Paris* of scientists, politicians, artists, and writers. He was known to be the physician and sometimes the confident of kings and princes. Emperor Pedro II of Brazil, it was said, came to his home, played billiards with him, and attended his lectures at the Salpêtrière.

Charcot was also a very influential figure in English medical circles; at an international Congress which took place in London in 1881, his demonstration on the tabetic arthropathies was received with a storm of applause. He had many admirers in Germany, although he declined invitations to congresses in that country after the Franco-German war of 1870–1871. In Vienna, he was well acquainted with Meynert and Moritz Benedikt. Charcot was very popular in Russia where he had been called several times as consultant physician to the Czar and his family. Russian physicians welcomed him because he relieved them from their strong dependence on German scientists. According to Guillain (1), he arranged an unofficial encounter between Gambetta and the Grand Duke Nikolai of Russia, from which the Franco-Russian alliance was to issue. Charcot travelled extensively; every year he made a carefully planned journey to a different European country, visiting the museums, making drawings, writing travelogues.

Great as it was, Charcot's prestige was still enhanced by a halo of mystery which surrounded him, which had slowly grown after 1870 and reached its peak with his celebrated paper on hypnotism in 1882. He gained the reputation of being a great thaumaturgist. Instances of his quasi-miraculous cures are reported by Lyubimov (3):

> Many patients were brought to Charcot from all over the world, paralytics on stretchers or wearing complicated apparatuses. Charcot ordered the removal of these appliances and told the patients to walk. There was, for instance, a young lady who had been paralyzed for years. Charcot bade her stand up and walk, which she did under the astounding eyes of her parents and of the Mother Superior of the Convent in which she had been staying. Another young lady was brought to Charcot with a paralysis of both legs. Charcot found no organic lesion; the consultation was not yet over when the patient stood up and walked back to the door where the cabman, who was waiting for her, took off his hat in amazement and crossed himself.

In the eyes of the public, Charcot was the man who had explored the abysses of the human mind, hence his nickname "Napoleon of Neuroses." He had come to be identified with the discovery of hysteria, hypnotism, dual personality, catalepsy, and somnambulism. Strange things were said about his hold on the Salpêtrière's hysterical young women and about happenings there. Jules Claretie (20) relates that during a patients' ball at the Salpêtrière, it happened that a gong was inadvertently sounded, whereupon many hysterical women instantaneously fell into catalepsy and kept the attitudes in which they found themselves when the gong was sounded. Charcot was also the man whose searching gaze penetrated the depths of the past and who retrospectively interpreted works of art, giving modern neurologic diagnoses on cripples represented by painters (21). He founded a journal, the *Iconographie de la Salpêtrière*, followed by the *Nouvelle Iconographie de la Salpêtrière*, probably the first journals to combine art and medicine. Charcot was also considered to have found a scientific explanation for demoniac possession which, he assumed, was nothing but a form of hysteria; he also interpreted this condition retrospectively in works of art (22). He was known for his collection of rare old works on witchcraft and possession, some of which he had reprinted in a book series titled *The Diabolical Library*.

All these features contributed to the incomparable fascination exerted by Charcot's *séances* at the Salpêtrière. Tuesday mornings were devoted to examining new, heretofore unseen patients in the presence of physicians and students who enjoyed seeing Charcot display his clinical acumen, the assurance and swiftness with which he was able to disentangle the most complicated case histories and arrive at a diagnosis, even of rare diseases. But the greatest attraction were his solemn lectures on Friday mornings, each of which had been prepared with the utmost care. The large auditorium was filled to capacity with physicians, students, writers and a curious crowd long before the beginning of the lectures. The podium was always decorated afresh with pictures and anatomic schemata pertaining to the day's lecture. Charcot, his bearing reminiscent of Napoleon or Dante, entered at ten o'clock, often accompanied by an illustrious foreign visitor and a group of assistants who sat down in the first rows. Amidst the absolute silence of the audience, he started speaking in a low pitch and gradually raised his voice, giving sober explanations which he illustrated with skillful colored chalk drawings on the blackboard. With an inborn acting talent, he imitated the behavior, mimicry, the gait, the voice of a patient afflicted with the disease he was talking about, after which the patient was brought in. The patient's entrance was sometimes also spectacular. When Charcot lectured on tremors, three or four women were introduced wearing hats with long feathers which, by their quivering made it possible to distinguish the specific characteristics of tremors in various diseases (23). The interrogation took the form of a dramatic dialogue between Charcot and the patient. Most spectacular were the lectures which he gave about hysteria and hypnotism. Another of Charcot's innovations was the use of photographic projections, a procedure which at that time was unusual for medical teaching. The lecture was concluded with a discussion of the diagnosis and a recapitulation stating the lecture's main points, and both were models of lucidity and concision. The lecture lasted for two hours, but the audience, it was said, never found it too long, even when it concerned rare organic brain diseases (4). Lyubimov points to the difference between Charcot's lectures and those of Meynert which he had also attended in Vienna and which left him exhausted and confused, whereas he left Charcot's lectures with a feeling of exhilaration.

It is easy to understand the spell-binding effect which Charcot's teaching exerted on laymen, on many physicians, and especially on foreign visitors such as Sigmund Freud, who spent four months at the Salpêtrière in 1885–1886. Other visitors were more skeptical. The Belgian physician Delboeuf, whose interest in Charcot's work had brought him to Paris in the same period as Freud, was soon assailed by the strongest doubts when he saw how carelessly experiments with hysterical patients were carried out. On his return to Belgium, he published a strongly critical account of Charcot's methods (24).

Those visitors who came to see Charcot in Paris for a short visit and were envious of him, were often unaware that he was surrounded by a host of powerful enemies. He was stamped as an atheist by the clergy and the Catholics (one of the reasons being that he had the nuns at the Salpêtrière replaced by lay nurses), but some atheists found him too spiritualist. He was publicly accused of charlatanism by the magnetists (25). He also had fierce enemies in political and society circles (as is obvious from the *Diary* of the Goncourt brothers). Among neurologists, some who had remained his admirers as long as he remained on the solid ground of neuropathology, deserted him when he shifted to the study of hypnotism and to spectacular experiments with hysterical patients. Lyubimov tells how the German neurologist Westphal expressed deep concern about the new turn taken by Charcot's research after visiting him in Paris. In America, he was attacked on the same grounds by Bucknill; Beard, while admitting that Charcot had made "serious mistakes," nonetheless proclaimed that he still respected him "as a man of genius and a man of honour" (26). Charcot also had to wage a continuous battle against the Nancy School in which he was steadily losing ground to his opponents. Bernheim sarcastically proclaimed that among thousands of patients whom he had hypnotized, only one displayed the three stages described by Charcot—a woman who had spent three years at the Salpêtrière.

Charcot also met with undying hatred on the part of some of his medical colleagues and particularly on the part of his former disciple Bouchard, an ambitious man 12 years his junior. Worse still, a few of his seemingly loyal disciples duped him by showing him more and more extraordinary manifestations which they rehearsed with patients and then demonstrated to him. It is true that many of his disciples never participated in such activities, but no one apparently dared warn him; he had been extremely cautious for a long time, but eventually La Rochefoucauld's maxim applied to him also: "deception always goes further than suspicion." According to Guillain, Charcot began to feel strong doubts toward the end of his life and was thinking of taking up again the entire study of hypnotism and hysteria, which death prevented him from doing. The secret enemy, who was so well acquainted with his medical condition and who for years sent him anonymous letters depicting his angina pectoris and announcing his impending death (23, 27) most likely belonged to the medical circle around Charcot.

The extreme opinions prevailing about Charcot, the fascination he exerted on the one hand, and the fierce enmities he aroused on the other, made it extremely difficult in his lifetime to make a true assessment of the value of his work and, contrary to expectations, the passing of time has not made his task much easier. It is therefore necessary to distinguish the various fields of his activity. First, it is often forgotten that Charcot, as an internist and anatomo-pathologist, made valuable contributions to the knowledge of pulmonary and kidney diseases and that his lectures on diseases of old age were for a long time a classic of what is now called "geriatrics." Second, in neurology, which was his "second career," he made outstanding discoveries upon which his lasting fame will undisputedly rest: delineation of disseminated sclerosis, amyotrophic lateral sclerosis ("Charcot's disease"), locomotor ataxia and its peculiar arthropathies ("Charcot's joints"), his work on cerebral and medullar localizations, on aphasia, and so on.

On the other hand, it is most difficult to evaluate objectively what could be called Charcot's "third career," that is, his exploration of hysteria and hypnotism. As happens with many scientists, he lost control of the new ideas which he had formulated and was carried away by the movement he had created.

Pierre Janet has well shown which were Charcot's methodologic errors in that field (28): The first was his excessive concern with delineating specific disease entities, choosing as model type those cases which showed as many symptoms as possible; he assumed that the other cases were incomplete forms. Since this method had proved fruitful for neurology, Charcot took it for granted that the same would hold true for mental conditions as well. He thus gave arbitrary descriptions of the *grande hystérie* and the *grand hypnotisme*. A second error was to oversimplify the descriptions of these disease entities in order to make them more intelligible to his students. A third fatal error was Charcot's lack of interest in his patients' backgrounds and in the ward life at the Salpêtrière. He hardly ever made rounds; he saw his patients in his hospital examination room while his collaborators, who had examined them, reported to him. Charcot never suspected that his patients were often visited and magnetized on the wards by incompetent people. Janet has shown that the alleged "three stages of hypnosis" were nothing but the result of training which Charcot's patients underwent at the hands of magnetizers. Seeing that the early history of magnetism and hypnotism was forgotten, Charcot—even more than Bernheim—believed that all the manifestations he noted in his hypnotized patients were new discoveries.

Another fact which from the start distorted Charcot's investigations in dynamic psychiatry was the peculiar collective spirit which pervaded the Salpêtrière. This closed community sheltered not only crowds of old women, but comprised also special wards for hysterical patients, some of them young, pretty, and cunning: nothing could be more eminently propitious to the development of mental contagion. These women were the star attractions, utilized to demonstrate clinical cases to the students and in Charcot's lectures given in the presence of the *Tout-Paris*. Due to Charcot's paternalistic attitude and his despotic treatment of students, his staff never dared contradict him; they therefore showed him what they believed he wanted to see. After rehearsing the demonstrations, they showed the subjects to Charcot who was careless enough to discuss their cases in the patients' presence. A most peculiar atmosphere of mental suggestion developed between Charcot, his collaborators, and his patients which would certainly be worthy of an accurate sociologic analysis.

Janet has pointed out that Charcot's description of hysteria and hypnotism were based on a very limited number of patients. The *prima donna*, Blanche Wittmann, deserves more than an anecdotic mention. The role of patients in the elaboration of dynamic psychiatry has been all too neglected and would also be worthy of intensive investigation. Unfortunately, it is very difficult to gather relevant information in retrospect.

We know nothing of Blanche Wittmann's origin and background prior to her admission to the ward for hysterical patients at the Salpêtrière. According to Baudouin (29), she was young when she arrived there and rapidly became one of Charcot's most renowned subjects and was nicknamed *la reine des hystériques*. She was often exhibited to demonstrate the "three stages of hypnosis," of which she was not only the type, but the prototype, according to Frederick Myers who had seen her (30). Baudouin states that she is the woman in full hysterical crisis, depicted between Charcot and Babinski in Bouillet's famous painting; she can also be recognized in several pictures in the *Iconographie de la Salpêtrière* and elsewhere. She was authoritarian, capricious, and unpleasant toward the other patients and toward the personnel.

For some unknown reason, Blanche Wittman left the Salpêtrière and was admitted at the Hôtel Dieu where she was investigated by Jules Janet, Pierre Janet's brother (31). After achieving the "first stage of hypnosis," that is, lethargy, Jules Janet modified the usual technique and saw the patient in a quite new condition: a new personality, "Blanche II," emerged, showing herself much more balanced than "Blanche I." The new personality disclosed that she had been permanently present and conscious, hidden behind "Blanche I," and that she was always aware of everything which occurred during the many demonstrations when she had acted out the "three stages of hypnosis" and was supposed to be unconscious. Myers noted that "it is strange to reflect for how many years the dumbly raging Blanche II has thus assisted at experiences to which Blanche I submitted with easy complacence."

Jules Janet kept Blanche Wittmann in her second state for several months and found that she was remarkably (and apparently lastingly) improved by his treatment. What later happened to Blanche Wittmann has been succinctly reported by Baudouin: She returned to the Salpetrière where she was given a job in the photographic laboratory; later, when a laboratory of radiology was opened, she was employed there. She was still authoritarian and capricious; she denied her past history and became angry when she was asked about that period of her life. Since the dangers of radiology were not yet known, she became one of the first victims of the radiologist's cancer. Her last years were a calvary which she crossed without showing the least hysterical symptom. She had to suffer one amputation after another and died a martyr of Science.

Coming back to Charcot's third career, it contributed more than anything else to his contemporary fame. The writer T. de Wyzewa (32), in an obituary he wrote on Charcot, said that in a few centuries his neurologic work may be forgotten, but that he would stand in the memory of mankind as the man who had revealed to the world an unsuspected realm of the mind. It is through that breakthrough, and not due to his literary works (which have remained unpublished) that Charcot exerted a powerful influence on literature. As stated by de Monzie (33), he was the starting point of a whole tradition of psychiatrically oriented writers such as Alphonse Daudet and his son Léon Daudet, Zola, Maupassant,

Huysmans, Bourget, Claretie, and later Pirandello and Proust, not to speak of many authors of popular novels. Charcot himself was the model for a specific character in many novels and plays in the 1890's: the great scientist of world renown impavidly pursuing his uncanny research in the abyss of the human mind.

An American visitor who saw Charcot at the beginning of 1893 noticed that, while his intellectual strength was as lively as ever, his physical health was greatly shaken (34). He kept working feverishly until August 15, 1893, when he left for a vacation with two of his favorite disciples, Debove and Strauss, intending to visit the Vézelay churches. He died unexpectedly in his hotel room in the night of August 16 and was given a state funeral in Paris on August 19. In spite of the deluge of praise which was lavished on his memory, his fame soon waned. The publication of his complete works, which had been planned in 15 volumes, was abandoned after Volume 9 had appeared in 1894. According to Lyubimov, Charcot had left a considerable amount of literary works: memoirs, illustrated travelogues, critical studies on philosophic and literary works, all of which he did not want published in his lifetime. Lyubimov adds that Charcot's true personality could not be known before their publication. However, none of these writings have ever been printed. Charcot's son Jean (1867–1936), who had studied medicine to please his father, gave up this profession a few years later and made himself famous as a seafarer and explorer of the South Pole (35, 36). Charcot's precious library was donated by his son to the Salpêtrière (37) and gradually fell into the most pitiful state of neglect, as did the Musée Charcot.

The evil that men do lives after them;
The good is oft interred with their bones.

So it was with Charcot. It did not take long before his glory was transformed into the stereotype of the despotic scientist whose belief in his own superiority blinded him into unleashing a psychic epidemic. One year after Charcot's death, Léon Daudet, who had been a medical student on his ward, published a satirical novel, *Les Morticoles* (38), which gave fictitious names to prominent physicians and ridiculed the Paris medical world. Charcot was depicted under the name of "Foutange" and Bernheim was called "Boustibras"; faked hypnotical *séances* at the Hôpital Typhus" with "Rosalie" (portraying Blanche Wittmann) were described in a caricatural manner. Another malevolent account of Charcot's Salpêtrière was later given by Axel Munthe (39) in his autobiographic novel *The Story of San Michele*.

Jules Bois, who was well acquainted with Charcot, relates that during the last months of his life, the old man expressed his pessimism in regard to the future of his work, which he felt would not survive him for long (40). In fact, less than ten years had elapsed before Charcot was largely forgotten and disowned by most of his disciples. His successor Raymond, while giving lip service to Charcot's work on neuroses, himself belonged to the organicist trend in neurology. One of Charcot's favorite disciples, Joseph Babinski, who had made himself known during Charcot's lifetime by his experiments in transferring hysterical symptoms with a magnet from one patient to another (41, 42) now became the main protagonist of a radical reaction against Charcot's concept of hysteria. Hysteria, he claimed, was nothing but the result of suggestion, and it could be cured by "persuasion" (42). The name "hysteria" itself was replaced by that of "pithiatisme" coined by Babinski. Guillain (1) reports that when he was a resident at the Salpêtrière in 1899, that is six years after Charcot's death, there still were a few of Charcot's hysterical female patients who would, for a small remuneration, act out for the students the full-fledged attack of the *grande hystérie*. But hysterical patients eventually disappeared from the Salpêtrière.

As years went by, Charcot's neurologic discoveries were taken for granted and his name became associated with a regrettable episode in the long history of the Salpêtrière. In 1925, his centennial was celebrated at the Salpêtrière with a strong emphasis on his neurologic achievements and a few rapid apologies about the *légère défaillance* (the slight lapse) which his work on hysteria and hypnotism had been. Psychoanalysts, however, praised him in that regard as a "precursor of Freud." In 1928, a group of Paris surrealists, in their endeavor to counteract all accepted ideas of their time, decided to celebrate the discovery of Charcot's hysteria, "the greatest poetical discovery of the end of the 19th century" (43).

Several years later, the author of the present [article], then a medical student at the Salpêtrière, met a very old woman patient who had spent almost her entire life there and had known Charcot and his school; she kept talking to herself and had hallucinations in which she was hearing all these men speaking in turn. These voices from the past, which had never been recorded but still resounded in the disturbed mind of that wretched old woman, were all that was surviving of the glory that had been Charcot's Salpêtrière.

REFERENCES

1 Guillain, G. *J. M. Charcot (1825–1893). Sa vie, son oeuvre*. Paris, Masson, 1955.

2 Souques, A. Charcot intime. *Press Med.*, 33(I): 693–698, 1925.

3 Lyubimov, A. *Profesor Sharko, Nautshnobiografitshesky etiud*. St. Petersburg, Tip. Suvorina, 1894.

4 Levillain, F. Charcot et l'Ecole de la Salpêtrière. *Revue Encylopédique*, 1894, pp. 108–115.

5 Guillain, G. L'Oeuvre de Duchenne (de Boulogne). *Etudes Neurologiques*, 3e série, Paris, Masson, 1929, pp. 419–448.

6 Guilly, P. *Duchenne (de Boulogne)*. Thèse méd., Paris, 1936.

7 Richer, P. *Etudes cliniques sur l'hystéro-épilepie ou Grande Hystèrie*. Paris, Delahaye & Lecrosnier, 1881 (with many pictures).

8 Charcot, J. M. Sur les divers états nerveux déterminés par l'hypnotisation chez les hystériques. *C. R. Acad. Sci.* 94(I): 403–405, 1882.

9 ———. *Oeuvres Complètes. Leçons sur les maladies du Système Nerveux*, 3. Paris, Progrès Médical, 1890, pp. 299–359.

10 Brodie, B. C. *Lectures illustrative of certain local nervous affections*. London, 1837.

11 Reynolds, R. Remarks on paralyses and other disorders of motion and sensation, dependent on ideas. *Brit. Med. J.*, 2: 493–495, 1869.

12 Charcot, J. M. Sur un cas d'amnésie rétroantérograde, probablement d'origine hystérique. *Rev. Méd.* 12: 81–96, 1892.

13 Souques, *A. Rev. Méd.* 12: 267–400, 867–881, 1892. Follow-ups to Charcot (12).

14 Charcot, J. M. La Foi qui guérit. *Arch. Neurol.* 25: 72–87, 1893.

15 Daudet, Léon. *Souvenirs des milieux littéraires, politiques, artistiques et médicaux de 1885 à 1905*. 2e série: *Devant la douleur*. Paris, 1917, pp. 4–15.

16 ———. *Les Oeuvres et les Hommes*. Paris, Nouvelle Librairie Nationale, 1922, pp. 197–243.

17 ———. *Quand mon père vivait. Souvenirs inédits sur Alphonse Daudet*. Paris, Grasset, 1940, pp. 113–119.

18 De Goncourt, E. and J. *Journal. Mémoires de la vie littéraire*. Paris, Fasquelle & Flammarion, 4 vol., 1956 (see particularly vol. 3).

19 Meige, H. Charcot artiste. *Nouvelle Iconographie de la Salpêtrière*, 11: 489–516, 1898.

20 Claretie, J. *La Vie à Paris, 1881*. Paris, Havard, 1882, p. 128 –129.

21 Charcot, J. M., and Richer, P. *Les Difformes et les malades dans l'art*. Paris, Lecrosnier & Babé, 1889.

22 ———. *Les Démoniaques dans l'art*. Paris, Delahaye & Lecrosnier, 1887.

23 Féré, Ch. J. M. Charcot et son oeuvre. *Revue des Deux Mondes*. 122: 410–424, 1894.

24 Delboeuf, J. De l'Influence de l'imitation et de l'éducation dans le somnambulisme provoqué. *Revue Philosophique*. 22: 146–171, 1886 (II).

25 Bué in *Le Magnétisme humain. Congrés International de 1889*. Paris, Georges Carré, 1890, pp. 333–334, 338–339.

26 Beard, G. M. *The Study of Trance, Muscle-Reading and Allied Nervous Phenomena in Europe*

and America, with a Letter on the Moral Character of Trance Subjects and a Defence of Dr. Charcot. New York, 1882.
27 Hahn, G. Charcot et son influence sur l'opinion publique. *Revue des Questions Scientifiques* 2e série, 6(II): 230–261, 353–379, 1894.
28 Janet, P. J. M. Charcot, son oeuvre psychologique. *Revue Philosophique*, 39: 569–604, 1895.
29 Baudouin, A. Quelques souvenirs de la Salpêtrière. *Paris-Méd.*, 15 (I) May 23, No. 21, X–XIII, 1925.
30 Myers, F. *Human personality and its survival of bodily death.* London, Longmans, Green & Co., 1903, vol. 1, p. 447.
31 Janet, J. L'Hystérie et l'hypnotisme, d'après la théorie de la double personnalité. *Revue Scientifique (Revue Rose),* 3e série, 15: 616–623, 1888.
32 *Le Figaro*, Tuesday, August 17, 1893.
33 De Monzie, A. Discours au Centenaire de Charcot. *Rev. Neurol.*, 32(I), 1925 (special issue for Charcot's centennial).
34 Withington, C. F. A last glimpse of Charcot at the Salpêtrière. *Boston Med. and Surg. J.*, 129: 207, 1893.
35 Anonymous. *Jean-Baptiste Charcot.* Paris, Yacht-Club de France, 1937.
36 Dupouy, A. *Charcot.* Paris, Plon, 1938.
37 Charcot, J.-B. Discours pronouncé à l'inauguration de la bibliothèque de son père. *Bull. Méd.*, vol. 21, Nov. 23, 1907.
38 Daudet, Léon. *Les Morticoles.* Paris, Charpentier, 1894.
39 Munthe, A. *The Story of San Michele.* New York, Duffin, 1929, Chapter XVII.
40 Bois, J. *Le Monde invisible.* Flammarion, s.d., pp. 185–192.
41 Babinski, J. *Recherches servant à établir que certaines manifestations hystériques peuvent être tranférées d'un sujet à l'autre sous l'influence de l'aimant.* Paris, Delahaye & Lecrosnier, 1886.
42 ———. Définition de l'Hystérie. *Rev. Neurol*, 9: 1074–1080, 1901.
43 Aragon & Breton. Le cinquantenaire de l'hystérie (1878–1928). *La Révolution Surréaliste*, 4: 20–22, 1928.

Charcot and Freud

Frank J. Sulloway

It was a decisive moment in Freud's life when he applied for and won a government-sponsored traveling fellowship open to the junior *Sekundarärzte* at the Vienna General Hospital. The fellowship, which was allotted to him in June of 1885 by the university's Faculty of Medicine, carried with it an automatic six-month leave of absence from his post at the hospital. In his proposal, Freud had announced his intention to study with Charcot in Paris. His narrow victory over his sole rival candidate—by thirteen votes to eight—was accomplished, so his friend Fleischl later told him, only upon "Brücke's passionate intercession, which had caused a general sensation."[1] Freud was in Paris from 13 October 1885 to 28 February 1886, and he spent seventeen of these twenty weeks in attendance at Charcot's clinic.

Jean Martin Charcot (1825–93) was then at the height of the varied medical career that had led him to the study of neurology, and his stature in French medicine was equaled only by that of the great Louis Pasteur.[2] Son of a carriage builder, Charcot had become by the 1880s a consulting physician to the most prominent royal families in Europe. And from all over the world ordinary patients and physicians flocked to the Salpêtrière in Paris in order to seek his

Adapted from Sulloway, F. J. (1979). *Freud: Biologist of the mind.* New York: Basic Books, pp. 28–35.

medical advice. Charcot was charismatic and authoritarian and enjoyed a legendary reputation even in his own lifetime. He was especially famed for the miraculous cures in which the power of his commandment alone repeatedly enabled paralytic individuals (no doubt largely hysterics) to throw off their crutches and walk.

Also a highly cultured man, Charcot was particularly at home with art and literature. He read widely in the English, German, Spanish, and Italian languages and enjoyed quoting Shakespeare and Dante, his two favorite authors, in their native tongues. In social circles he was also well known for the spectacular receptions and parties at his palatial home on the Boulevard Saint-Germain, where Freud himself was several times a guest (*Letters*, pp. 194–96, 206–8).

Almost every prominent French neurologist in the late nineteenth century studied at one time or another under Charcot at the famous Salpêtrière. This huge medical complex included some forty-odd buildings devoted largely to the care of older women. There Charcot had gradually built up numerous research laboratories in the various major medical disciplines. He had also created the necessary teaching facilities for instructing medical students about the many unique neurological disorders then common among the Salpêtrière's several thousand patients. It is perhaps worth noting that Freud found the laboratory conditions at the Salpêtrière rather unsatisfactory for his own neuroanatomical needs—compared at least with what he was used to—and he eventually gave up, on this account, his plans to pursue anatomical studies of infantile brains while in Paris (Jones 1953:210–11).

Like Freud, hundreds of other foreigners came yearly to visit this "Mecca of neurology" and to attend Charcot's famous Tuesday and Friday lectures on the subject of nervous diseases. The Tuesday lectures were extemporaneous and consisted of Charcot's on-the-spot diagnoses of ailing patients brought to him without prior consultation from the well-stocked wards of the Salpêtrière. It was an unforgettable performance about which Freud, in speaking of "the magic" of Charcot's great personality, later warmly reminisced in his Preface to the German translation of these lectures (Freud 1892–94, *S.E.,I:*135–36). In contrast to the Tuesday lectures, those given on Fridays were models of highly organized learning and lucidity; and Charcot rarely failed to keep his packed audience spellbound throughout the two hours that he customarily devoted to each major neurological disease.

Charcot had begun his medical career in pathological anatomy. As a young intern at the Salpêtrière, where he had served for a short time in the course of his medical training, he had been fascinated by the many strange and seemingly incurable neurological afflictions he had encountered there. He had vowed to himself then and there that he would someday return to study in more detail this neglected world of medical treasures; and in 1862, at the age of thirty-seven, he finally honored that vow, coming back to the Salpêtrière as head of one of its major divisions.

By 1870, Charcot was concentrating on the problem of how to distinguish hysterical from epileptic convulsions. With his disciple and assistant Paul Richer, he succeeded in providing a formal clinical description of the stages that, in his view, characterized the "hysterical crisis" (*grande hystérie*). His approach, while extremely important in the scientific understanding of hysteria, was also symptomatic of the dubious "type" concept of disease then popular in French medicine. Although the type concept had formerly proved useful in Charcot's anatomically based neurological work, it later brought him into considerable discredit when he attempted to apply it to the more problematic phenomena of hysteria.

By 1878, Charcot had taken up the study of hypnotism—a bold step in his medical career, since in France, as elsewhere, the whole subject had been in considerable scientific disrepute for almost a century (ever since the debates over mesmerism in the 1780s). Four years later, in 1882, Charcot delivered a paper on hypnotism at the *Académie des Sciences* in which he personally endorsed the phenomenon of hypnotism as genuine and provided a detailed description of the hypnotic trance as occurring in three sequential stages ("lethargy," "catalepsy," and "somnambulism"). Charcot's paper created a sensation. It also brought about a complete reversal within France of the negative attitude in official science toward mesmerism or "animal magnetism"—a subject that the *Académie des Sciences* itself had twice formally condemned.[3]

By the mid-1880s, when Freud went to Paris to study with Charcot, the latter had just begun his famous researches on the subject of traumatic paralyses. In 1884 and 1885, Charcot had shown that these traumatic paralyses were distinct symptomatically from organic ones, and he had succeeded in *artificially* reproducing such nonorganic paralyses with the use of hypnosis. He subsequently established a similar medical distinction between traumatic and organic amnesia. Before his death in 1893, Charcot's interests in the psychopathology of disease even caused him to consider the psychological mechanism of faith healing (Charcot 1893). It is no wonder, then, that the neurologist whose work on hypnotism and hysteria in the 1880s enthralled both the French medical community and a generation of novelists and playwrights eventually received the nickname "Napoleon of Neuroses" (Ellenberger 1970:95).

Charcot exerted an immediate and profound influence upon Freud, who later named his eldest son after this important figure in his life. His first personal impression of Charcot, whom Freud met a week after reaching Paris, readily conveys his fascination:

> At ten o'clock, M. Charcot arrived, a tall man of fifty-eight [in fact, only a month shy of sixty], wearing a top hat, with dark, strangely soft eyes (or rather, one is; the other is expressionless and has an inward cast), long wisps of hair stuck behind his ears, clean shaven, very expressive features with full protruding lips—in short, like a worldly priest from whom one expects a ready wit and an appreciation of good living. . . . I was very much impressed by his brilliant diagnosis and the lively interest he took in everything, so unlike what we are accustomed to from our great men with their veneer of distinguished superficiality. (*Letters*, p. 175)

By the end of November (a month later), Freud was even more ecstatic in singing the praises of Charcot. "I think I am changing a great deal," he wrote to his future bride. "Charcot, who is one of the greatest physicians and a man whose common sense borders on genius, is simply wrecking all my aims and opinions. I sometimes come out of his lectures as from out of Notre Dame, with an entirely new idea about perfection. . . . Whether the seed will ever bear fruit, I don't know; but what I do know is that no other human being has ever affected me in the same way" (*Letters*, pp. 184–85).

It is nevertheless odd that, by the beginning of December, Freud was at the point of returning to Vienna, as Jones (1953:208) has reported on the basis of an unpublished letter to Martha Bernays. Freud's reasons seem to have been two-fold: his inability to carry out his planned work on the anatomy of the brain and his disappointment over a lack of personal contact with Charcot, to whom Freud was just another face in a large crowd of foreign visitors. But fortunately the idea occurred to Freud at about this time of offering his services to Charcot as German translator for the third volume of Charcot's *Leçons sur les maladies du système nerveux* (1887). In a formal letter of request to Charcot, Freud humorously commented, "Concerning my capacity for this undertaking it must be said that I only have motor aphasia in French but not sensory aphasia" (quoted in Jones 1953:209).

Charcot received Freud's proposal warmly. Thanks to the latter's proficiency as a translator, the German volume was published only seven months later—even before the French original—under the title *Neue Vorlesungen über die Krankheiten des Nervensystems insbesondere über Hysterie* (New Lectures on the Diseases of the Nervous System, Particularly on Hysteria, 1886). Charcot rewarded Freud's labors by giving him a complete leather-bound set of his works inscribed "*À Monsieur le Docteur Freud, excellents souvenirs de la Salpêtrière Charcot.*" (Freud library, New York). Finally, as a result of this translation arrangement, Freud entered into a much closer relationship with Charcot and his circle of personal friends and was soon invited to attend the splendid parties given by Charcot at his home.

It was, of course, Charcot's demonstrations concerning hysteria and hypnotism—many of which, Freud later recalled, had initially provoked in him and others "a sense of astonishment and an inclination to scepticism"—that really captured Freud's imagination during his four-and-a-half-month stay in Paris (*Autobiography*, 1925*d, S.E., 20*:13). These dramatic demonstrations—particularly those of hypnotism—first revealed to Freud the remarkable circumstance that multiple states of consciousness could simultaneously coexist in one and the same individual without either state apparently having knowledge of the other. Charcot and his disciples had used such demonstrations not only for illustrating the psychogenic nature of hysterical paralyses but also as an aid to understanding the phenomenon of "split personality" (or *double conscience*). As Freud later commented about such hypnotic experiments: "I received the profoundest impression of the possibility that there could be powerful mental processes which nevertheless remained hidden from the consciousness of men" (*Autobiography*, 1925d, S.E., 20.:17; see also 1893*f, S.E., 3*:22).

With regard to the specific problem of hysteria, Charcot, who seems to have believed that the theory of *organic* nervous diseases was virtually complete, had accordingly begun full-time work upon this long-puzzling malady in the period immediately preceding Freud's visit to the Salpêtrière. Later, on the occasion of Charcot's death in 1893, Freud described what was known about this disease before Charcot's medical intervention, with the following words: "This, the most enigmatic of all nervous diseases, for the evaluation of which medicine had not yet found a serviceable angle of approach, had just then fallen into thorough discredit; and this discredit extended not only to the patients but to the physicians who concerned themselves with the neurosis. It was held that in hysteria anything was possible, and no credence was given to a hysteric about anything." Charcot's personal achievement in elucidating this protean disease, Freud added, was comparable to, but on a somewhat smaller scale than, Philippe Pinel's (1745–1826) famous liberation of the madmen from their chains at the Salpêtrière almost a century before. "The first thing that Charcot's work did," Freud said in summing up Charcot's medical revolution, "was to restore its dignity to the topic. Little by little, people gave up the scornful smile with which the patient could at that time feel certain of being met. She was no longer necessarily a malingerer, for Charcot had thrown the whole weight of his own authority on the side of the genuineness and objectivity of hysterical phenomena" ("Charcot," 1893*f, S.E., 3*:19).

A series of more specific medical discoveries had also soon emerged from Charcot's intensive work on hysteria. Three of these, in particular, Freud later stressed as having profoundly affected his own thinking on the problem that, in many ways, launched him into his psychoanalytic career.

To begin with, Charcot had shown how the peculiar mechanism of traumatic-hysterical dysfunctions was to be understood from the remarkable fact that identical symptoms could be *induced artificially* by means of suggestions given to hysterical patients during a state of hypnosis. Furthermore, the analogy of hypnotically induced paralysis was all the more convincing as a key to such hysterical dysfunctions when one learned that these impairments were not always manifested immediately. Rather, the patient might return home apparently unharmed by a frightening experience, only to suffer a severe dysfunction several days or even weeks later.

In a like manner, Charcot had persuasively demonstrated that "hysterically prone" individuals could be put into a hypnotic trance and, without any suggestion at all, be induced to simulate paralytic dysfunctions after receiving a light blow to an arm or a leg. Charcot and his assistants explained this phenomenon by assuming that, in these patients, the power of external suggestion had simply been replaced by that of *auto*suggestion. All such subconscious hypnotic suggestions, Charcot believed, were dependent upon an idea or a series of ideas somehow isolated psychically from normal waking consciousness—the ego—and yet firmly planted within a second region of the mind in what he described as "the fashion of parasites" (Charcot 1887:335–37). Freud concluded: "[Charcot] succeeded in proving, by an unbroken chain of argument, that these paralyses were the result of ideas which had dominated the patient's brain at moments of a special disposition" (1893*f*, S.E., *3*:22). In other words, Charcot was the first to understand the hitherto hidden *mechanism* of hysterical phenomena, and he did so, moreover, in proto-Freudian terms.

Implicit in Charcot's first major medical generalization about hysteria was his second—namely, the *psychogenic nature of hysterical symptoms*. "M. Charcot was the first to teach us that to explain hysterical neurosis we must apply to psychology" (Freud 893*c*, *S.E.*, *I*:171); and Freud also commented on how foreign Charcot's clinical and psychological approach to neurological problems had at first seemed to a physician like himself, trained in the Germanic tradition, with its emphasis on a physiological interpretation of symptoms.[4] At the same time, Freud encountered in Charcot's clinical emphasis a refreshing subordination of theory to medical facts. In one of his favorite anecdotes about Charcot, Freud tells how he once dared to contradict the master on some medical point with the remark: "But that can't be true, it contradicts the Young-Helmholtz theory"—to which Charcot unhesitatingly replied, "*La théorie, c'est bon, mais ça n'empêche pas d' exister* ['Theory is good; but it doesn't prevent things from existing']" (Freud 1893*f*, *S.E.*, *3*:13).

Freud deemed Charcot's third and last major contribution to the scientific understanding of hysteria to be his emphatic *rejection of the common notion that this disease is always caused by the female hysteric's disturbed sexual organization*. In his 1888 article "Hysteria" for Villaret's *Handwörterbuch der gesamten Medizin* (Encyclopedic Handbook of Medicine), Freud later exhibited the ironic imprint of Charcot's influence by giving as his principal argument against the sexual etiology of hysteria Charcot's own insistence that this disease could be found in children *before the onset of puberty* (a denial of infantile sexuality) and that severe cases were unquestionably found in the male sex. (Charcot had further fixed the ratio of male to female hysteria at roughly I:20. See Freud 1888*b*, *S.E.*, *I*:50–51).

In addition to working on his translation of Charcot's lectures while in Paris, Freud began an ingenious study on the psychogenic nature of traumatic hysterical paralyses. He later credited Charcot with the basic idea, but as Jones (1953: 233) rightly points out, other contemporary evidence indicates that the major inspiration, although implied in Charcot's overall teachings, was really Freud's own. Freud's idea was to show, using clinical material available to him at the Salpêtrière, that *hysterical* paralyses are largely independent of the regular anatomical distributions governing known instances of *organic* paralysis. For example, he observed that organic cerebral paralyses regularly affected a distal segment (the hand) more than they did a proximal one (the shoulder), but that in hysterical paralysis this was not always true (1893*c*, *S.E.*, *I*:162–63). In short, the functional lesions of hysterical paralysis appeared to follow a layman's notion of paralysis, not the laws of neuroanatomy. Hysteria, Freud concluded, "*behaves as though anatomy did not exist or as though it had no knowledge of it*" (*S.E.*, *I*:169).

NOTES

(1) Unpublished letter to Martha Bernays, 23 June 1885; cited by Jones 1953:76.

(2) With the possible exception of Guillain (1955, trans. 1959), no adequate biographical treatment of Charcot yet exists. This surprising lacuna in the history of medicine is perhaps related to the sharp reversal of medical opinion after Charcot's death regarding the reliability of his famous researches on hypnotism and hysteria. The following account of his life and work relies heavily upon Ellenberger (1970: 89–101), who has composed a brief but multifaceted portrait of Charcot on the basis of many scattered recollections by contemporaries who knew and worked with him. See also Jones (1953:185–86, 207–8, 226–29) for a more anecdotal account, based largely upon Freud's letters to his fiancée, Martha Bernays, written during his stay in Paris; and *Letters*, pp. 171–211.

(3) See Ellenberger (1970:57–85) and Darnton (1968) for informative treatments of the life of Franz Anton Mesmer and the subsequent history of the mesmerism and hypnotism movements.

(4) Preface to Freud's translation of Charcot's *Tuesday Lectures* (1892–94), *S.E., I*: 134–35.

REFERENCES

Charcot, J. M. (1887). *Lecons sur les maladies du systeme nerveux, faites a la Salpêtrière*, III. In *Oeuvres completes* (1888–94, 3).

Charcot, J. M. (1893). "La Foi qui guerit." *Archives de Neurologie, 25,* 72–87.

Darnton, R. (1968). *Mesmerism and the End of the Enlightenment in France.* Cambridge, Mass.: Harvard University Press.

Ellenberger, H. F. (1970). *The Discovery of the Unconscious: The History and Evolution of Dynamic Psychiatry.* New York: Basic Books; London: Allen Lane.

Freud, S. (1888*b*). "Aphasia," "Gehirn," "Hysterie," and "Hysteroepilepsie." In *Handworterbuch der gesamten Medizin*, I. Edited by Albert Villaret. Stuttgart: Ferdinand Enke. (Unsigned; authorship uncertain.)

Freud, S. (1892–94). "Preface and Footnotes to the Translation of Charcot's "*Tuesday Lectures*." In *Standard Edition, 1*, 131–143.

Freud, S. (1893*c*). "Some Points for a Comparative Study of Organic and Hysterical Motor Paralyses." In *Standard Edition, 1*, 157–172.

Freud, S. (1893*f*). "Charcot." In *Standard Edition, 3*, 9–23.

Freud, S. (1925*d*). *An Autobiographical Study.* In *Standard Edition, 20,* 3–70.

Freud, S. (1960*b*). *Letters of Sigmund Freud.* Selected and edited by Ernst L. Freud. Translated by Tania and James Stern. New York: Basic Books; London: Hogarth Press, 1961.

Guillain, G. (1955). *J. M. Charcot, 1825–1893: Sa vie, son oeuvre.* Paris: Masson et Cie. *Trans.*: Guillain (1959).

Jones, E. (1953). *The Life and Work of Sigmund Freud.* Vol. I: *The Formative Years and the Great Discoveries, 1856–1900.* New York: Basic Books; London: Hogarth Press.

CHAPTER 5

THE FOUNDING OF SCIENTIFIC PSYCHOLOGY: GUSTAV FECHNER AND WILHELM WUNDT

Recall, from Chapter 2, John Locke's distinction between primary and secondary qualities. That distinction acknowledged the existence of experience that was independent of the physical objects of the world. As psychology sought to establish itself as a scientific discipline, it was important that human perception and physical stimulation not be perfectly correlated. If such a relationship existed, meaning that changes in physical stimuli always resulted in similar changes in the perception of those stimuli, then it meant that perception (and, more broadly, psychology) and physical stimuli were the same. Under those circumstances, there would be no need for psychology; human perception would be wholly explained by the laws of the discipline of physics.

But how was it possible to compare the physical world with the psychological world? (The reader should recognize that question as a version of the centuries-old mind–body problem.) One answer to that question came to Gustav Theodor Fechner (1801–1887) on the morning of October 22, 1850, while he was lying in bed. He reasoned that mind could be studied by recording an individual's reactions to known changes in physical stimulation. This approach, which Fechner labeled *psychophysics,* allowed the comparison of the psychological world and the physical world. Fechner made two other important discoveries. First, he demonstrated that there was not a one-to-one correspondence between changes in the physical world (stimuli) and changes in the psychological world (the perception of those stimuli). Second, he demonstrated that although the relationship between stimuli and perceptions was not linear, it was predictable; that is, the psychological and physical worlds are lawfully related.

This relationship had already been anticipated in the work of Ernst Weber

(1795–1878), a German physiologist whose initial contributions on touch sensitivity were published in 1834. He studied the relative sensitivity of various areas of the skin through a technique he called the *two-point threshold* (in which two blunt needles are applied at variable distances apart, for example, 1 inch or 2 inches, to various areas of the skin, and subjects are asked to report whether they feel one point of stimulation or two). He also investigated muscle sensations, conducting a series of experiments in which subjects made comparative judgments of small weights. Weber was able to discover the minimum weight change required for the subject to say another weight was heavier or lighter. This difference became known as the *difference threshold* or *just noticeable difference* (jnd). Weber made an extremely important discovery in these weight studies, noting that although the size of the difference threshold between two weights differed according to the size of the weights, the ratio of the change in weight to the base weight was constant. In other words, a 50-gram weight might have to be raised to 55 grams before the subject could reliably say that the weight was heavier. That would mean, given the constant ratio that Weber observed, that a 500-gram weight would have to be increased by 50 grams to be judged heavier. He noted a similar constant relationship in his studies on the perception of tones, leading him to describe that relationship in a simple but profound formula that many psychologists regard as the first statement of a psychological law.

For Weber, these studies were a means of understanding the physiology of sensory systems. It is not known whether Fechner was aware of the earlier work of Weber or not; some sources, such as Edna Heidbreder (1933), say that Fechner did not know of Weber's work until after he had begun his own studies. Whether he knew of Weber's studies or not, Fechner appreciated the value of such measurements for the study of the mind, and it led him to search for methods that would measure mental states as they corresponded to changes in the physical world. In 1860, he published one of the most important books in the history of psychology, *Elements of Psychophysics,* a treatise of such consequence that it has led some historians of psychology to name Fechner as the founder of scientific psychology (for example, Boring, 1950; Adler, 1977). Fechner's book laid out the conceptual issues in measuring the physical and psychological worlds, described a set of methods of undertaking that measurement, and reported his own psychophysical work, including his derivation of a logarithmic law that predicted stimulus–perception relationships better than the earlier law of Weber. Fechner achieved better precision because he realized that the values of physical stimuli increase at a much faster rate than the corresponding psychological perceptions. However, both laws held for only the intermediate range of stimuli and did not predict well when sensory values were extreme. Fechner's 1860 book proved of great influence in psychology, both conceptually and methodologically, as evidenced by the late nineteenth-century work of Wilhelm Wundt and Hermann Ebbinghaus in Germany, and Charles S. Peirce and George Trumbull Ladd in the United States.

Although Fechner's role for the science of psychology is an important one, he is not the popular favorite for "founder of the new science." That honor is typically accorded to Wilhelm Wundt (1832–1920), who established one of the earliest psychology laboratories, indeed, perhaps the first psychology laboratory in the world, in Leipzig, Germany, in 1879. But the laboratory founding, albeit important, is not the reason most historians acknowledge Wundt as founder. According to historian Thomas Leahey (1991), "Wundt is the founder because he wedded physiology to philosophy and made the resulting offspring independent. He brought the empirical methods of physiology to the questions of philosophy and also created a new, identifiable role—that of the psychologist, separate from the roles of philosopher, physiologist, or physician" (p. 55). Another historian, John O'Donnell (1985), has referred to Leipzig as the place where psychology was initially manufactured, and argues that Wundt's central role in the development of psychology "derives not from any scientific discovery that bears his name eponymously but rather from his heroic propagandizing for experimentalism" (p. 16). Wundt's plans for psychology gestated for more than twenty years before the Leipzig laboratory was founded.

Wundt graduated from the University of Heidelberg in 1855, finishing at the top of his medical school class. After a short time in Berlin, where he worked with the famous physiologist Johannes Müller, Wundt returned to Heidelberg to work as Helmholtz's assistant. There he published his first book, on muscular movements and sensations, in 1858. A second book followed in 1862 entitled *Contributions to the Theory of Sense Perception.* It was in this book that Wundt laid out his plans for psychology, an experimental science that would uncover the facts of consciousness. At this time he was teaching a course on experimental physiology that included some psychological material. By 1867, the title of Wundt's course had become "Physiological Psychology," and out of these lectures emerged his most important work for the founding of psychology, the *Principles of Physiological Psychology* (1873–1874). This work went through six editions in Wundt's lifetime and is clearly among the most important publications in the history of psychology. It was a compendium of all the research to that date related to Wundt's vision of an experimental psychology. In the preface to that work, he made his vision clear, noting that it was his intention to establish psychology as a new domain of science.

In 1874, Wundt took a position at Zurich University, but he stayed there only a year before accepting a newly established professorship in philosophy at the University of Leipzig. There he would remain for the rest of his life, establishing the laboratory in 1879 and the first psychological journal, *Philosophische Studien,* two years later in 1881. It was the beginning of an academic Mecca for psychology that would draw students from all over Europe, particularly Germany and Austria, and from the United States and Canada. In his career, Wundt directed the doctoral theses of sixty-six students in psychology. That number included such famous individuals as Hugo Münsterberg, Edward Bradford Titchener, and Emil Kraepelin.

In the latter half of the nineteenth century, it was not uncommon for American students to go abroad for their graduate education (see Sokal, 1981). Of

Wundt's psychology students, sixteen came from Canada and the United States (see Benjamin, Durkin, Link, Vestal, & Acord, 1992). That number included Lightner Witmer, who founded the first psychological clinic in the United States at the University of Pennsylvania (see Baker, 1988; O'Donnell, 1979); Walter Dill Scott, who was one of the pioneers of industrial psychology (see Ferguson, 1976); Edward Wheeler Scripture, who would distinguish himself in speech pathology; Charles H. Judd, whom many consider to be the founder of educational psychology; Harry Kirke Wolfe, whose undergraduate psychology laboratory at the University of Nebraska produced an inordinately large number of graduates who went on to become eminent psychologists (see Benjamin, 1991); and James McKeen Cattell, who founded the psychology laboratories at the University of Pennsylvania and Columbia University (see Sokal, 1980). The first two Americans to earn doctoral degrees in psychology from Wundt were Cattell and Wolfe, both graduating in 1886. Cattell and two other Americans who visited Wundt's laboratory, William James and G. Stanley Hall, we will discuss in Chapter 8. (See Hillix & Broyles [1980] for an example of the academic lineage of Wundt in contemporary American psychology.)

For Wundt, psychology was the study of *immediate experience,* that is, experience devoid of any cultural, social, or linguistic interpretations. The more biased experience was called *mediate experience,* meaning it was mediated by these processes of learning. Immediate experience was basic, unfettered by learning, and this was the experience that Wundt studied initially. His research sought to create experiences in a laboratory setting that could be repeated, independently verified by others, and were thus subject to systematic study. A principal method of study in Wundt's laboratory was verbal report, in which the subjects (observers, as they were usually called) reported on what they saw, heard, felt, and so on (the German term was *Selbstbeobachtung*). Many textbooks call this technique introspection, but that is probably not a good word to describe what Wundt was asking his subjects to do. (See Blumenthal, 1975, in this chapter, and Leahey, 1981, in the next chapter for further explanations of various introspection techniques.) In employing this verbal report technique, Wundt laid down explicit criteria for its use, including the requirement that stimulus variables be altered in various trials to discover how such manipulations affected the subject's experience. These subject reports were primarily quantitative, unlike the qualitative emphases of E. B. Titchener's introspections (see Chapter 6), and dealt mostly with sensory dimensions such as intensity and duration (Danziger, 1980). Other methods were also used, including the psychophysical techniques of Fechner and certain physiological techniques.

About half the research studies conducted in Wundt's laboratory were on sensory processes and perception, topics that occupied much of the early work in psychology (recall the empiricist emphasis on that area). But there were also studies of reaction time, learning (association), attention, and emotion.

Having defined the subject matter of psychology as the study of immediate experience, Wundt mapped out the goals of psychology as the analysis of experience into its component elements. Those elements were of two kinds: sensations and feelings. This atomistic approach sought to reduce experience to its most basic elements. But Wundt's plan was more than just the delineation of a psychological periodic table. In addition to determining what constituted an element of experience, he was interested in discovering how these basic elements combined to form what he called psychic compounds.

Other emerging experimental psychologies developed in opposition to Wundtian psychology, at laboratories in Würzburg, Berlin, Frankfurt, and Vienna. Some argued with Wundt about the validity of his reductionistic approach, favoring instead an approach that analyzed experience at a more global level. Others dissented over methodological issues, for example, arguing for other introspective procedures. Still others argued about what topics were or were not appropriate to study in the fledgling science of psychology.

In the end, Wundt's psychology, as well as that of his contemporaries, was replaced by newer psychological approaches. Although parts of his psychological system exist in modern psychology (see Blumenthal, 1975, in this chapter), we continue to remember him primarily for his vision in seeing the promise of a science of psychology and then taking the truly giant steps required in the nineteenth century to establish the discipline. It is true that Wundt built on the work of those philosophers and physiologists who came before him, just as a mason mixes gravel and cement, but it was Wundt who fashioned those elements into the concrete blocks of psychology and laid them in place to form a new scientific structure.

THE READINGS

The initial selection is an excerpt from Fechner's *Elements of Psychophysics,* in which he discusses his ideas on mind and body that gave rise to psychophysics. He defines his concepts concerning stimuli and sensations, and describes the concept and tasks of psychophysics. The selection was translated from the original German by Helmut Adler, a leading authority on Fechnerian psychology.

The second article was written by Marilyn E. Marshall of Carleton University of Canada. Among contemporary historians of psychology, she is generally acknowledged as one of the principal authorities on the life and work of Fechner (see Marshall, 1969, 1974a, 1974b). In her article, she writes about the use of biographical material as a tool in the history of science, comparing five different biographical studies of Fechner. This article is important, not only for what it says about Fechner but also for what it says about the relationship between biography and history. In short, it is a most useful lesson in historiography.

The third selection, from Wundt's *Outlines of Psychology,* which he published in 1896, is one of the many Wundt works that have been translated into English. It deals with the descriptions of psychical elements and compounds, and was intended as a concise statement of his approach to psychology. It is the second of the primary source articles for this chapter.

Knowledge of Wundt has increased considerably in the past couple of decades. Partly this new vision was facilitated by the attention given to the celebration, in 1979, of the centennial of Wundt's laboratory, but it is also the result of two other factors. First, historians of psychology have begun to read Wundt in the original German rather than the English translations. Not only has this scholarship resulted in a new image of Wundt's theoretical system in psychology, but it has portrayed a breadth of interest (for example, his writings on culture, law, art, language, history, and religion) that has been missing from biographical and theoretical accounts of Wundt. Second, these historians have made much use of archival material in Germany associated with Wundt and his contemporaries. The final two selections in this chapter are evidence of this new scholarship.

The first of these two articles on Wundt is an archival study, focusing particularly on the events surrounding the founding of the laboratory in 1879. It was written by Wolfgang and Norma Bringmann and Gustav Ungerer, all of whom have contributed greatly to our understanding of Wundt and his psychology. The second of these articles is by Arthur Blumenthal. One of the earliest articles of the new Wundt scholarship to emphasize the importance of the original German editions, it radically changed what the history books said about Wundt. An especially important part of this article is the section relating Wundt's ideas to contemporary psychology, particularly cognitive psychology. Another look at Wundt's psychology will provided by Thomas Leahey in the next chapter, by comparing him to his student, E. B. Titchener.

REFERENCES

Adler, H. E. (1977). Vicissitudes of Fechnerian psychophysics in America. *Annals of the New York Academy of Sciences, 291,* 21–32.

Baker, D. B. (1988). The psychology of Lightner Witmer. *Professional School Psychology, 3,* 109–121.

Benjamin, L. T., Jr. (1991). *Harry Kirke Wolfe: Pioneer in psychology.* Lincoln: University of Nebraska Press.

Benjamin, L. T., Jr., Durkin, M., Link M., Vestal, M., & Acord, J. (1992). Wundt's American doctoral students. *American Psychologist, 47,* 123–131.

Blumenthal, A. L. (1975). A reappraisal of Wilhelm Wundt. *American Psychologist, 30,* 1081–1088.

Boring, E. G. (1950). *A history of experimental psychology* (2nd ed.). New York: Appleton-Century-Crofts.

Danziger, K. (1980). The history of introspection reconsidered. *Journal of the History of the Behavioral Sciences, 16,* 241–262.

Ferguson, L. W. (1976). The Scott Company. *JSAS Catalog of Selected Documents in Psychology, 6,* 128 (Ms. 1397).

Heidbreder, E. (1933). *Seven psychologies.* New York: Appleton-Century-Crofts.

Hillix, W. A., & Broyles, J. W. (1980). The family trees of American psychologists. In W. G. Bringmann & R. D. Tweney (Eds.), *Wundt studies* (pp. 422–434). Toronto: C. J. Hogrefe.

Leahey, T. H. (1981). The mistaken mirror: On Wundt's and Titchener's psychologies. *Journal of the History of the Behavioral Sciences, 17,* 273–282.

Leahey, T. H. (1991). *A history of modern psychology*. Englewood Cliffs, NJ: Prentice-Hall.

Marshall, M. E. (1969). Gustav Fechner, Dr. Mises, and the comparative anatomy of angels. *Journal of the History of the Behavioral Sciences, 5,* 39–58.

Marshall, M.E. (1974a). William James, Gustav Fechner, and the question of dogs and cats in the library. *Journal of the History of the Behavioral Sciences, 10,* 304–312.

Marshall, M. E. (1974b). G. T. Fechner: Premises toward a general theory of organisms. *Journal of the History of the Behavioral Sciences, 10,* 438–447.

O'Donnell, J. M. (1979). The clinical psychology of Lightner Witmer: A case study of institutional innovation and intellectual change. *Journal of the History of the Behavioral Sciences, 15,* 3–17.

O'Donnell, J. M. (1985). *The origins of behaviorism: American psychology, 1870–1920.* New York: New York University Press.

Sokal, M. M. (1980). Graduate study with Wundt: Two eyewitness accounts. In W. G. Bringmann & R. D. Tweney (Eds.), *Wundt studies* (pp. 210–225). Toronto: C. J. Hogrefe.

Sokal, M. M. (1981). *An education in psychology: James McKeen Cattell's journal and letters from Germany and England, 1880–1888.* Cambridge, MA: MIT Press.

Psychophysics and Mind-Body Relations

Gustav Theodor Fechner

I. GENERAL CONSIDERATIONS ON THE RELATION OF BODY AND MIND

While knowledge of the material world has blossomed in the great development of the various branches of natural science and has benefited from exact principles and methods that assure it of successful progress, and while knowledge of the mind has, at least up to a certain point, estblished for itself a solid basis in psychology and logic, knowledge of the relation of mind and matter, of body and soul, has up to now remained merely a field for philosophical argument without solid foundation and without sure principles and methods for the progress of inquiry.

The immediate cause of this less favorable condition is, in my opinion, to be sought in the following factual circumstances, which admittedly only make us seek their more remote origins. The relationships of the material world itself we can pursue directly and in accord with experience, as no less the relationships of the inner or mental world. Knowledge of the former, of course, is limited by the reach of our senses and their amplifications, and of the latter by the limitations of everyone's mind; still, these researches go on in such a way that we are able to find basic facts, basic laws, and basic relationships in each of the fields, information which can serve us as a secure foundation and starting point for inference and further progress. The situation is not the same in relating the material and mental worlds, since each of these two inextricably associated fields enters into immediate experience only one at a time, while the other remains hidden. At the moment when we are conscious of our feelings and thoughts, we are unable to perceive the activity of the brain that is associated with them and with which they are in turn associated—the material side is then hidden by the mental. Similarly, although we are able to examine the bodies of other people, animals, and the whole of nature directly in anatomical, physiological, physical, and chemical terms, we are not able to know anything directly about the minds that belong to the former nor of God who belongs to the latter, for the spiritual side is here hidden by the material. There thus remains great latitude for hypothesis and disbelief. Is there really anything revealed, we may ask, once the covers are lifted, and if so, what?

The uncertainty, the vacillation, the argument over these factual issues has so far not allowed us to gain a solid foothold or to find a point of attack for a theory of these relationships, whose factual basis is still in dispute.

And what can be the reason for this singular condition, in which body and mind can be observed, each for itself but never together, in spite of the fact that they belong to each other? Usually we can best observe things which belong together when they occur together. The inviolability of this aspect of the relationship between the mental and material worlds makes us suspect that it is fundamental, that it is rooted in their basic natures. Is there nothing similar that can at least illustrate these facts even though it cannot get to the root of the matter?

Admittedly, we can point to one thing or another. For example, when standing inside a circle, its convex side is hidden, covered by the concave side; conversely, when outside, the concave side is covered by the convex. Both sides belong together as indivisibly as do the mental and material sides of man and can be looked upon as analogous to his inner and outer sides. It is just as impossible, standing in the

From Fechner, G. T. (1860). *Elementen der psychophysik.* Adapted from H. E. Adler (Trans.), *Elements of psychophysics.* New York: Holt, Rinehart and Winston, 1966, pp. 1–18.

plane of a circle, to see both sides of the circle simultaneously as it is to see both sides of man from the plane of human existence. Only when we change our standpoint is the side of the circle we view changed, so that we now see the hidden side behind the one we had seen before. The circle is, however, only a metaphor and what counts is a question of fact.

Now, it is not the task or the intention of this work to enter into deep or penetrating discussions on the basic question of the relationship of body and mind. Let everyone seek to solve this puzzle—insofar as it appears to him as such—in his own way. It will therefore be without prejudice for what follows, if I state my opinion here in a few words, in order not to leave unanswered some possible questions about the general beliefs that formed the starting point of this inquiry and that for me, at least, still form the background. At the same time I am providing something to go by in this field of fluctuating ideas for those who are still seeking a point of view rather than believing that they have found one, even though what I say will not contain anything essential for further progress of this work. In view of the great temptation in starting a work such as this to lose oneself in voluminous and extensive discussions of this sort, and of the difficulty, by no means slight, of avoiding them completely, I hope that I will be forgiven if I limit myself here to the following brief exposition of my position.

To begin with, however, let me add a second illustrative example to the first. The solar system offers quite different aspects as seen from the sun and as observed from the earth. One is the world of Copernicus, the other the world of Ptolemy. It will always be impossible for the same observer to perceive both world systems simultaneously, in spite of the fact that both belong quite indivisibly together and, just like the concave and convex sides of the circle, are basically only two different modes of appearance of the same matter from different standpoints. Here again one needs but to change the point of view in order to make evident the one world rather than the other.

The whole world is full of such examples, which prove to us that what is in fact one thing will appear as two from two points of view; one cannot expect to find things the same from one standpoint and from the other. Who would not admit that it is always thus and cannot be otherwise? Only with respect to the greatest and most decisive example does one deny it or fail to think of it. That is the relationship of the mental and material worlds.

What will appear to you as your mind from the internal standpoint, where you yourself are this mind, will, on the other hand, appear from the outside point of view as the material basis of this mind. There is a difference whether one thinks with the brain or examines the brain of a thinking person. These activities appear to be quite different, but the standpoint is quite different too, for here one is an inner, the other an outer point of view. The views are even more completely different than were the previous examples, and for that reason the differences between the modes of their appearance are immensely greater. For the twofold mode of appearance of the circle or the planetary system was after all basically gained by taking two different external standpoints; whether within the circle or on the sun, the observer remained outside the sweep of the circles outside the planets. The appearance of the mind to itself, on the other hand, is gained from the truly inner point of view of the underlying being regarding itelf, as in coincidence with itself, whereas the appearance of the material state belonging to it derives from a standpoint that is truly external, and not in coincidence.

Now it becomes obvious why no one can ever observe mind and body simultaneously even though they are inextricably united, for it is impossible for anyone to be inside and outside the same thing at one time.

Here lies also the reason why one mind cannot perceive another mind as such, even though one might believe it would be easiest to become aware of the same kind of entity. One mind, insofar as it does not coincide with the other, becomes aware only of the other's material manifestations. A mind can, therefore, gain awareness of another only through the aid of its corporeality, for the mind's exterior appearance is no more than its material nature.

For this reason, too, the mind appears always as unitary, because there exists only the one inner standpoint, whereas every body appears different according to the multitude of external standpoints and the differences among those occupying them.

The present way of looking at these phenomena thus covers the most fundamental relationships between body and mind, as any basic point of view should seek to do.

One more item: body and mind parallel each other; changes in one correspond to changes in the other. Why? Leibniz says: one can hold different opinions. Two clocks mounted on the same board adjust their movement to each other by means of their common attachment (if they do not vary too much from each other); this is the usual dualistic notion of the mind-body relation. It could also be that someone moves the hands of both clocks so that they keep in harmony; this view is occasionalism, according to which God creates the mental changes appropriate to the bodily changes and vice versa, in constant harmony. The clocks could also be adjusted so perfectly from the beginning that they keep perfect time, without ever needing adjustment; that is the notion of prestabilized harmony. Leibniz has left out one point of view—the most simple possible. They can keep time harmoniously—indeed never differ—because they are not really two different clocks. Therewith we can dispense with the common board, the constant adjustment, the artificiality of the original setting. What appears to the external observer as the organic clock with its movement and its works of organic wheels and levers (or as its most important and essential part), appears to the clock itself quite differently, as its own mind with its works of feelings, drives, and thoughts. No insult is meant, if man here be called a clock. If he is called that in one respect, yet he will not be so called in every respect.

The difference of appearance depends not only on the difference of standpoint, but also on the differences among those that occupy it. A blind person does not see any of the exterior world from an external standpoint, though his position is just as favorable as that of a seeing person; and a nonliving clock does not see its interior in spite of its standpoint of coincidence, which is just as favorable as that of a brain. A clock can exist only as external appearance.

The natural sciences employ consistently the external standpoint in their considerations, the humanities the internal. The common opinions of everyday life are based on changes of the standpoints, and natural philosophy on the identity of what appears double from two standpoints. A theory of the relationship of mind and body will have to trace the relationship of the two modes of appearance of a single thing that is a unity.

These are my fundamental opinions. They will not clear up the ultimate nature of body and mind, but I do seek by means of them to unify the most general factual relationships between them under a single point of view.

However, as I mentioned before, it remains open to everyone to seek to effect the same end by another approach, or not to seek to accomplish it at all. Everyone's chosen approach will depend on the context of his other opinions. By arguing backwards, he will have to determine the possibility or impossibility of finding a suitable general relationship himself. At this point it is not important whether he wants to consider body and mind as only two different modes of appearance of the same entity or as two entities brought together externally, or to consider the soul as a point in a nexus of other points of essentially the same or of a different nature, or to dispense entirely with a fundamentally unitary approach. Insofar as an empirical relationship between body and mind is acknowledged and its empirical pursuit is allowed, there is no objection to trying even the most complicated kind of representation. In what follows we shall base our inquiry only on the empirical relationships of body and mind, and in addition adopt for use the most common expressions for the designation of these facts, though they are expressed more in the terms of a dualistic approach than my own monistic one. Translation from one to the other is easy.

This does not mean, however, that the theory which will be developed here will be altogether indifferent to the points of view on the basic relationships of body and mind and without influence upon them, for the contrary is true. Still, one must not confuse the effects that this theory may have some day—and that are partially beginning to take form even now—with the basis of this theory. This basis is indeed purely empirical, and every assumption is to be rejected from the start.

One may well ask whether the possibility of such a basis does not directly contradict the fact, with which we started, that the relationships of body and mind are outside the realm of experience. They are not, however, beyond experience altogether, for only the immediate relationships are beyond immediate experience. Our own interpretation of the general relation of body and mind already has had the support of common experiences with these relationships, even if they do not strike everyone who comes to this work with preconceived notions as necessary. What follows will show how we can draw quite as much on special experiences, which can serve us partly to orient ourselves in the area of meditated relationships and partly to provide a foundation for deductions regarding immediate relationships.

Indeed, we could not rest content with this general point of view, even if it were generally accepted. The proof, the fertility, and the depth of a universal law do not depend on the general principles but on the elementary facts. The law of gravitation and the molecular laws (which undoubtedly include the former) are elementary laws; were they thoroughly known and the whole range of their implications exhausted, we would have a theory of the material world in its most general form. Similarly we must seek to form elementary laws of the relationship of the material and the mental world in order to gain a durable and developed theory instead of a general opinion, and we will only be able to do this, here as elsewhere, by building on a foundation of elementary facts.

Psychophysics is a theory that must be based on this point of view.

II. THE CONCEPT AND THE TASK OF PSYCHOPHYSICS

Psychophysics should be understood here as an exact theory of the functionally dependent relations of body and soul or, more generally, of the material and the mental, of the physical and the psychological worlds.

We count as mental, psychological, or belonging to the soul, all that can be grasped by introspective observation or that can be abstracted from it; as bodily, corporeal, physical, or material, all that can be grasped by observation from the outside or abstracted from it. These designations refer only to those aspects of the world of appearance, with whose relationships psychophysics will have to occupy itself, provided that one understands inner and outer observation in the sense of everyday language to refer to the activities through which alone existence becomes apparent.

In any case, all discussions and investigations of psychophysics relate only to the apparent phenomena of the material and mental worlds, to a world that either appears directly through introspection or through outside observation, or that can be deduced from its appearance or grasped as a phenomenological relationship, category, association, deduction, or law. Briefly, psychophysics refers to the *physical* in the sense of physics and chemistry, to the *psychical* in the sense of experiential psychology, without referring back in any way to the nature of the body or of the soul beyond the phenomenal in the metaphysical sense.

In general, we call the psychic a dependent function of the physical, and vice versa, insofar as there exists between them such a constant or lawful relationship that, from the presence and changes of one, we can deduce those of the other.

The existence of a functional relationship between body and mind is, in general, not denied; nevertheless, there exists a still unresolved dispute over the reasons for this fact, and the interpretation and extent of it.

With no regard to the metaphysical points of this argument (points which concern rather more the so-called essence than the appearance), psychophysics undertakes to determine the actual functional relationships between the modes of appearance of body and mind as exactly as possible.

What things belong together quantitatively and qualitatively, distant and close, in the material and in the mental world? What are the laws governing their changes in the same or in opposite directions? These are the questions in general that psychophysics asks and tries to answer with exactitude.

In other words, but still with the same meaning: what belong together in the inner and outer modes of appearance of things, and what laws exist regarding their respective changes?

Insofar as a functional relationship linking body and mind exists, there is actually nothing to prevent us from looking at it and pursuing it from the one direction rather than from the other. One can illustrate this relationship suitably by means of a mathematical function, an equation between the variables x and y, where each variable can be looked upon at will as a function of the other, and where each is dependent upon the changes of the other. There is a reason, however, why psychophysics prefers to make the approach from the side of the dependence of the mind on the body rather than the contrary, for it is only the physical that is immediately open to measurement, whereas the measurement of the psychical can be obtained only as dependent on the physical—as we shall see later. This reason is decisive; it determines the direction of approach in what follows.

The materialistic reasons for such a preference we need not discuss, nor are they meaningful in psychophysics, and the dispute between materialism and idealism over the essential nature of the dependency of one on the other remains alien and immaterial to psychophysics, since it concerns itself only with the phenomenal relationships.

One can distinguish immediate and mediated relationships of dependency or direct and indirect functions relating body and mind. Sensations are in a directly dependent relationship to certain processes in our brains as far as the one is determined by the other or has the other as its immediate consequence; but sensations are merely in a mediated relationship to the external stimulus, which initiates these processes only via the intervention of a neural conductor. All our mental activity has dependent upon it an immediate activity in our brain, or is accompanied immediately by brain activity, or else directly causes the activity, of which the effects then are transmitted to the external world via the medium of our neural and effector organs.

The mediated functional relationships of body and mind fulfill completely the concept of a functional relationship only under the supposition that the mediation enters into the relationship, since omission of the mediation leads to the absence of the constancy or lawfulness of the relationship of body and mind, which exists by virtue of this mediation. A stimulus then releases proper sensations only when a living brain does not lack the living nerves to transmit the effect of the stimulus to the brain.

As far as the psychic is to be considered a direct function of the physical, the physical can be called the carrier, the factor underlying the psychical. Physical processes that accompany or underlie psychical functions, and consequently stand in a direct functional relationship to them, we shall call psychophysical.

Without making any assumptions about the nature of psychophysical processes, the question of their substrate and form we may leave undecided from the start. There is a twofold reason why we may dispense with this question right away: first, because the determination of the general principles of psychophysics will involve the handling only of quantitative relations, just as in physics, where qualitative depend on earlier quantitative relationships; and second, because we will have to give no special consideration to psychophysical processes in the first part, under the plan of work which follows immediately.

By its nature, psychophysics may be divided into an outer and an inner part, depending on whether consideration is focused on the relationship of the psychical to the body's external aspects, or on those internal functions with which the psychic are closely related. In other words, the division is between the mediated and the immediate functional relationships of mind and body.

The truly basic empirical evidence for the whole of psychophysics can be sought only in the realm of outer psychophysics, inasmuch as it is only this part that is available to immediate experience. Our point of departure therefore has to be taken from outer psychophysics. However, there can be no development of outer psychophysics without constant regard to inner psychophysics, in view of the fact that the body's external world is functionally related to the mind only by the mediation of the body's internal world.

Moreover, while we are considering the regular relations of external stimulus and sensation, we must not forget that the stimulus, after all, does not awaken our sensations directly, but only via the awakening of those bodily processes within us that stand in direct relation to sensation. Their nature may still be quite unknown, the inquiry regarding their nature may be neglected for the present (as already stated), but the fact that they do exist must be affirmed and referred to often, whenever it comes to the point of taking dead aim and following up those lawful relationships which are our immediate concern in outer psychophysics. Similarly, even though the body's activities, which are directly subject to the activity of our will and obey it, are still totally unknown, we should not forget that the effect of the will on the outer world can only be achieved via just such activities. We thus have implicitly to interpolate everywhere the unknown intermediate link that is necessary to complete the chain of effects.

Psychophysics, already related to psychology and physics by name, must on the one hand be based on psychology, and on the other hand promises to give psychology a mathematical foundation. From physics outer psychophysics borrows aids and methodology; inner psychophysics leans more to physiology and anatomy, particularly of the nervous system, with which a certain acquaintance is presupposed. Unfortunately, however, inner psychophysics has not profited so far from recent painstaking, exact, and valuable investigations in this field to the extent it should. Inner psychophysics undoubtedly will do this one day, once these investigations (and those from the different kind of attack on which this work is based) have succeeded to the point of reaching a common meeting ground, where they will be able to cross-fertilize each other. That this is not yet the case to any extent indicates only the incomplete state in which our theory finds itself.

The point of view from which we plan to attack our task is as follows: Even before the means are available to discover the nature of the processes of the body that stand in direct relation to our mental activities, we will nevertheless be able to determine to a certain degree the quantitative relationship between them. Sensation depends on stimulation; a stronger sensation depends on a stronger stimulus; the stimulus, however, causes sensation only via the intermediate action of some internal process of the body. To the extent that lawful relationships between sensation and stimulus can be found, they must include lawful relationships between the stimulus and this inner physical activity, which obey the same general laws of interaction of bodily processes and thereby give us a basis for drawing general conclusions about the nature of this inner activity. Indeed, later discussion will show that, in spite of all our ignorance of the detailed nature of psychophysical processes there exists, for those aspects which are concerned with the more important relationships of ordinary mental life, a basis which within limits already allows us to form certain and sufficient conceptions of the fundamental facts and laws which define the connection of outer to inner psychophysics.

Quite apart from their import for inner psychophysics, these lawful relationships, which may be ascertained in the area of outer psychophysics, have their own importance. Based on them, as we shall see, physical measurement yields a psychic measurement, on which we can base arguments that in their turn are of importance and interest.

III. A PRELIMINARY QUESTION

For the present the discussion of all obscure and controversial questions of inner psychophysics—and almost the whole of inner psychophysics at this time consists of such questions—will be postponed along with the discussion of inner psychophysics itself. Later experience will provide us with the means for the answers. Nevertheless, one of these questions will at least have to be touched upon briefly at the start. This point, which concerns the future of the whole of psychophysics, we take up now in order to answer it to the extent that it can be answered in general, leaving everything else for later discussion.

If we classify thinking, willing, and the finer esthetic feelings as higher mental activities, and sensations and drives as lower mental activities, then, at least in this world—leaving the question of the next world quite open—the higher mental activities can go on no less than the lower without involving physical processes or being tied to psychophysical processes. No one could think with a frozen brain. There can be just as little doubt that a specific visual sensation or auditory sensation can only come about because of specific activities of our nervous system. No one questions this. The idea of the sensory side of the mind is actually based on the conception that there exists an exact connection between it and corporeality. Great doubt exists, however, as to whether each specific thought is tied to just as specific a process in the brain and, if not, whether brain activity as a whole suffices for thinking and the higher mental activities in general, without the necessity for a special type or direction of physiological process in the brain in order for these processes to take place in a specific way and direction. Indeed, it seems that the essential difference between the higher and lower mental spheres (distinguished by some as soul and mind in their narrower senses) is sought precisely in this point.

If we now assume that the higher mental activities are really exempt from a specific relationship to physical processes, there would still be their general relationship, which may be granted to be real, and which would be subject to the consideration and investigation of inner psychophysics. This general relationship will, in any case, be subject to general laws, including common principles, still to be discovered. Indeed, their discovery should always remain the most important of the tasks of inner psychophysics. One of the next chapters . . . will lead us to a consideration of just such conditions.

A metaphor: thought may be regarded as part of the stream of bodily processes itself, and may be real only in terms of these processes, or it may need this stream only for steering as an oarsman steers his boat, raising only some incidental ripples with his oar. The conditions and laws of the river must be taken into account in both instances when the flow or progress of thought is concerned, though in each case from a quite different point of view, to be sure. Even the freest navigation* is subject to laws, as to the nature of the elements and the means that serve it. Similarly, psychophysics will find it necessary, in any case, to deal with the relationship of higher mental activity to its physical base. From what point of view, however, and to what extent, psychophysics will one day have itself to decide.

For the time being everyone should try to confine the conception and the scope of inner psychophysics as much as he can until the force and limitations of facts compel him to abandon the attempt. In my opinion, which as of now has to be considered as a mere opinion, there are no boundaries in this respect.

Indeed, I feel that the experience of harmony and melody, which undoubtedly have a higher character than single tones, is based on the ratios of the vibrations that themselves underlie the separate sensations, and that these ratios can change only in exact relationship to the manner in which the single tones are sounded together or follow one another. Thus, harmony and melody suggest to me only a higher relation, and not one lacking a special relationship of dependency between the higher mental sphere and its physical basis. Indeed everything seems to agree with this suggestion so easily pursued and extended. However, neither the pursuit nor even the assertion of this matter is relevant here at the start.

IV. CONCEPTS CONCERNING SENSATION AND STIMULUS

In the present incomplete state of psychophysical investigations, there would be little profit in an enumeration, definition, and classification of all the psychological conditions that could at some time form their subject matter. At first we shall occupy ourselves mainly with sensory experiences in the common meaning of the word experience, making use of the following distinctions in nomenclature.

I intend to distinguish between intensive and extensive sensations, depending on whether they concern the sensory perception of something whose magnitude can be judged intensively or extensively. For example, I shall include as an intensive sensation the sensation of brightness, as an extensive sensation the perception of a spatial extent by sight or touch; and accordingly I shall distinguish between the intensive and extensive magnitude of a sensation. When one object appears to us brighter than another, we call the sensation it arouses intensively greater; when it appears larger than another we call it extensively greater. This is merely a matter of definition and implies, as generally understood, no specific measure of sensation.

With every sensation whatsoever, intensive as well as extensive, magnitude and form may be distinguished, although in the case of intensive sensations magnitude is often called strength and form quality. With sounds, the pitch, even though it is a quality of the sound, has also a quantitative aspect insofar as we can distinguish a higher from a lower pitch.

E. H. Weber—and undoubtedly quite to the point—calls the spatial sense, or the capacity or sense whereby we arrive at extensive sensations (as the term is used here), a general sense. Those senses that give rise to intensive sensations he calls special senses. The former sensations cannot, like the latter, arise from the impression of single independent nerve fibers or their respective ramifications (sensory circles), but can do so only by a coordination of the impressions of several fibers, wherein the strength and quality of the impression as well as the number and arrangement of the nerve centers are essential to fix the size and form of the extensive sensation. His discussions of this matter are very apt contributions to the clarification of the general relationship of the senses. At present it suffices to

*Trans. Note: A reference to free navigation as a political problem—for example, free navigation on the Rhine.

have pointed out the foregoing difference in the circumstances on which intensive and extensive sensations depend. In fact, these brief preliminary discussions are intended only to introduce the discussion of appropriate measures of sensitivity and sensation, and therefore do not enter into the theory of sensations to any greater extent than this purpose warrants.

Because of their different natures and the different conditions upon which they depend, it is necessary to make a special examination of the laws governing extensive and intensive sensations. One might think that the magnitude of extensive sensations, or the extensive size of sensations, depended on the number of sensory circles stimulated, according to the same laws and corresponding to the way in which the magnitude of intensive sensations depends on the intensity of stimulation; but this is both incorrect to assume a priori and impossible to prove as yet. Our future investigations will preferably concern themselves, though not exclusively, with the intensive sensations, and in the main are so to be understood, unless the contrary is apparent from the added adjective *extensive* or from the context.

Next to the distinction between extensive and intensive sensations we may consider the distinctions between objective and common sensations and between the so-called positive and negative sensations. Objective sensations, such as sensations of light and sound, are those that can be referred to the presence of a source external to the sensory organ. Changes of the common sensations, such as pain, pleasure, hunger, and thirst, can, however, be felt only as conditions of our own bodies. For this relationship the reader is also referred to Weber's classic work in his treatise on touch and common sensations.

As positive and negative sensations it is usual to contrast such sensations as warmth and cold, pleasure and pain, which share the characteristic that the manner of their arousal or the relation to that which gives rise to them includes an antithesis. For example, the sensation of cold originates and increases through the withdrawal of heat, whereas warmth arises through the addition of heat. The sensation of pleasure is connected with a seeking of the cause of its arousal, just as dislike is connected with the opposite tendency.

While such designations as positive and negative sensations may be allowed in the usage of common language, one should not fail to note that the so-called negative sensations have nothing negative about them psychologically. They do not represent a lack, a lessening, a removal of sensations. On the contrary, they may be as violent, or even more so, than the so-called positive sensations, and are able to manifest themselves or give rise to just as strong positive effects on the body. For example, the sensation of freezing can cause a shaking of the whole body, and that of pain can cause crying besides other vigorous movements of the body.

The term *stimulus,* in its narrow sense, refers only to means of arousing the body, the excitation of intensive sensations. To the extent that stimuli belong to the outside world, they are external stimuli; insofar as they belong to the internal world of the body, they are internal stimuli. The former concept can be explained factually by recording external stimuli, such as light and sound; the latter concept will first need closer examination and may then perhaps be at least partially eliminated. A murmuring in our ears can start through the external influences of oscillations of the air, which a waterfall sends to our ears. A similar murmur can originate without outside influence through causes within our body. These are in general unknown; yet insofar as they produce the equivalent of the effect of an outside stimulus, they must be considered its equivalent. From this point of view it will often suit us to treat these unknown, but admittedly (according to their effects) factual, internal bodily sources of sensations under the same concepts, standpoints, and formulas as the external sources.

If the mind were affected only by external and internal excitations to the extent that their effects reach a specific part of the body, then all sensations would, as far as we grant their dependence on the body, be only results of activities of the body. Thus even the innermost conditions of the body would fall under the concept of stimuli. If, on the other hand, it is essentially the case that sensations are only accompanied by bodily activities in a functional relationship, it would not be proper to include such simultaneously conditioned sensations with directly determined sensations. Only those stimuli that serve to cause sensations should be included, if one does not wish to mix two different kinds of things. In the meanwhile we do not immediately have to come to a decision. These diverse opinions have no influence on our factual observations, as long as we consider the existence and magnitude of internal stimuli only according to their equivalent effects as compared to external stimuli and take them into account as such. At this time internal stimuli are an unknown *x* as to their location and quality, although they enter despite this limitation into the phenomenal sphere with a quantitative effect that is comparable to that of an external stimulus. The internal stimulus derives its name and value from this effect.

Some things, like weights, to which one would hesitate to give the meaning of stimulus in everyday life, will be classed as such without misgivings, as far as they give rise to tactile pressure, or weight, when lifted. On the other hand, a generalization of the word stimulus to the causes by which extensive sensations are evoked in us has its drawbacks, especially inasmuch as little clarity exists so far about these causes. We perceive, with our eyes closed, a black visual field of a certain extent, even without the addition of external causes, and, by specially focusing our attention, we can become conscious of a certain extent of our body surface, even without being touched by calipers or other instruments. Added outside stimulation partially sets the boundaries of these natural sensation fields, partially determines their form, and partially provides a basis for judging relative size and distance, without, however, giving rise to the sensation of space. This sensation seems to be rooted in the inborn coordination and organic connections of active nerves, or of their central endings although nothing certain has been decided about the matter so far. If it is still possible to talk of a stimulus in this connection, we could do so only with respect to the coordination of the internal excitation of these nerves. Since these, however, are probably conditions that occur simultaneously with the sensation, this expression [the sensation of space] would again become unsuitable. Experience can also, aided by movements, take part in the judging of extents—as some like to emphasize. This is not the place, however, to go any deeper into this still rather obscure matter, where only the definitions of words are concerned.

One can say, disregarding this obscurity and the question of the extent to which the term *stimulus* is appropriate, that the magnitude of the stimulus in intensive sensations is replaced in the extensive case by the number of active sensory circles insofar as the perceived extension decreases or increases as a dependent function. Thus, in relation to quantitatively depedent relationships, this number can be brought under a common, though rather general, point of view. One cannot assert in this way, however, that the law by which they are dependent is the same in both cases, or that the magnitude of the extensive sensation does not depend on other circumstances besides that number. Indeed, these points are themselves the object of important psychophysical investigations.

Under the application of most outer forces on which sensations are dependent, the sensation increases, after it once becomes noticeable, as the force acting on it is increased continually and in the same direction, and decreases with the lessening of the force continually until unnoticeable. With regard to some sensations, however, such as warmth and pressure on the skin, the organism is so constituted that a sensation arises only by reason of a difference from a given average or normal influence, such as the normal skin temperature or normal air pressure. This sensation then increases in both directions but with different characteristics, as a sensation of warmth or cold, pressure or tension, depending on whether one increases the influence above this point or reduces it below this point. In this case one would correctly regard as the stimulus, not the absolute magnitude of the acting force, but its positive or negative deviation from the point that divides the sensations of contrasting character, the point at which no sensation exists. We could call the former a positive, the latter a negative stimulus.

As far as the interrelationship of stimulus and sensation is to be considered, stimuli are always assumed to be effective under comparable circumstances, unless the contrary is expressly mentioned or can be seen from the context. This comparability can, however, be nullified by a different mode of stimulation, as well as by a differing condition of the subject or the organ at the time the stimulus impinges. The concept of differential sensitivity relates to this condition. . . .

For the sake of brevity one says of a stimulus which evokes a sensation, as well as of a stimulus difference which is accompanied by a difference in sensations, that they are felt more strongly or weakly, according to whether the sensation or difference in sensations is stronger or weaker. This is also an expression that must be allowed to serve us without giving rise to misunderstanding.

Biographical Genre and Biographical Archetype: Five Studies of Gustav Theodor Fechner

Marilyn E. Marshall

Shortly after the hero of Virginia Woolf's *Orlando* turns into a woman to a terrific blast of trumpets, Mrs. Woolf's fictional biography slows to an unusual crawl. She writes: "It was November. After November, comes December, then January, February, March and April. After April comes May. June, July, August follow. Next is September. Then October, and so behold, here we are back at November again, with a whole year accomplished" (Woolf, 1928, p. 172).

Mrs. Woolf admits that "this method of writing biography . . . is a little bare perhaps" (*ibidem,* p. 172) but what is the biographer to do if his subject, like Orlando, just sits down and merely thinks for twelve months? (*ibidem,* p. 173). "There is nothing for it but to recite the calendar, tell one's beads, blow one's nose, stir the fire, look out of the window, until she has done" (*ibidem*).

This fable for biographers[1] suggests that the sort of life which a biographical subject leads influences the character of the work which can be written about him. In what follows, I will consider several biographical studies of Fechner, a man who did little but think and write, not merely for months, but for years on end. My focus will be, first, on differentiating among the works to illustrate something of the range and variability of the biographies, and second, on suggesting that it is not only the life of the subject which influences the character of a biography, nor the well-discussed interaction between character of biographer and subject, but further,

Marshall, M. E. (1980). Biographical genre and biographical archetype: Five studies of Gustav Theodor Fechner. *Storia e Critica Della Psicologia, 1,* 197–210.

the expectations which biographers have of what the subject's life should have been. To what extent may our available portraits of Fechner be drawn to conform to the outlines of generalized models of what biography should be, of what the life of an important nineteenth century scientist should have been?

Table 1 contains an outline summary of five biographical studies of Fechner. These include the most comprehensive and interesting of the some twenty-five biographical and personal studies of which I am aware. They are listed in order of priority of publication, and this comes close to being an order according to weight as well. I have characterized each briefly, first according to the profession of the author and his relation to Fechner, and second according to the author's professed or apparent motive in writing the biography;[2] third is my estimate of the author's interpretational emphasis; finally, I have given the gist of the biographical technique used and the source materials referred to. I suggest these dimensions of classification because each may influence the kind of data, data arrangement, and interpretation of data given by the authors; and each, consequently, affects the historian's use of the proffered material. I cannot talk here about each dimension for each biography, but will rather sample, sip, and taste in my narrative.

First, let me give you an idea of the kind of information on which I based these summary statements. With respect to Number 1, for example, to describe the author's motive tersely as "widow's wish" may strike you as unlikely, but Kuntze (1892) writes at the end of his Preface: "The decision to write the biography was not an easy one for me . . . Yet Fechner's widow did not cease to urge me, and to comply with her wishes I dared attempt the work" (Kuntze, 1892, p. 361). Kuntze, Fechner's nephew, lived in the Fechner household as a stepson for some 50 years, and was thus in an admirable position to supply details of Fechner's domestic life and habits. Indeed, all subsequent biographers are dependent on Kuntze for such information.

The one other biographical study to treat of Fechner's personality in any detail is Number 5, a psycho-historical example. I have referred to Hermann's (1926) motive as "didactic (scientific)" because his purpose is to show psychoanalytic constructs, and his own theory of scientific creativity, illustrated in (and explanatory of) the life and writings of Fechner. At this juncture, let me pursue a sample dilemma in the use of biography. The dilemma is the common one of finding two different interpretations of the same data by different biographers. The illustration will also serve to support my use of the term "psychoanalytic" to describe Hermann's interpretational emphasis, and my disapproving phrase, "highly selective," to modify Hermann's technique.

Hermann tells a story with a (to us) familiar ring and a familiar vocabulary. When Fechner was five, his youngest sister was born (a fact taken from Kuntze); the father baptized the new baby, and the next day the father died (another fact); Fechner, at five, was ripe for the resolution of the Oedipus conflict (permit me to call this theory); would the association of baby's birth and father's death not inhibit the later normal development of Fechner's libido, asks Hermann? Moreover would not the impressionable child be burdened with over-abundant guilt feelings? (Hermann, 1926). These questions are hypotheses in rhetorical clothing. Given the paucity of evidence which Hermann offers for the link between putative cause and effect, one is not surprised when Hermann shifts the scene abruptly in his next sentence to Leipzig, *nineteen* years later: "Then the mother decided to move to Leipzig . . . in order to remove Fechner from the influence of doubtful friends" (*ibidem,* p. 10). Please note, *en passant,* that the nineteen years which separated trauma from evidence of pathology and which Hermann ignores, were not, in Fechner's case, empty years of Orlando—like sitting and thinking.

TABLE 1:
DESCRIPTIVE SUMMARY OF FIVE FECHNER BIOGRAPHIES

Reference	Profession and relation to G. T. Fechner	Motive	Emphasis	Technique	Sources
Kuntze, J. E. Gustav Theodor Fechner (Dr. Mises). Leipzig: Breitkopf & Härtel, 1892, 316 pp.	German jurist, historian of law, Fechner's nephew	commemorative (personal), "widow's wish"	Christian, German nationalism	chronologically "interwoven" critical and personal, emphasis on latter	conversation over 50 years, Fechner's personal archive, knowledge of Fechner's work
Lasswitz, K. *Gustav Theodor Fechner,* Stuttgart, Fromann, 1896, 206 pp.	German historian of philosophy and science (atomism), author of imaginative (science) fiction; no personal relation indicated but responsible for a revival of Fechner's philosophical works after 1900	didactic (social)	wedding of natural science and Weltanschauung	sequential life and work first treated chronologically; Fechner's world picture is treated topically	the "life" part of a "life and work" derives from Kuntze; knowledge of Fechner's works
Wundt, W. Gustav *Theodor Fechner,* Leipzig: Engelmann, 1901. In Wundt, *Reden und Aufsätze.* Leipzig: Kröner, 1913, 89 pp.	German psychologist, colleague and friend of Fechner	commemorative (official) for Leipzig University and Royal Saxon Academy of Sciences	new foundation for psychological science and metaphysics	topical arrangement, on "The Origin of Life," on "Life and Consciousness," on "Psychophysics," etc., addenda on "Personal memories," Fechner's relation to the philosophy of his time, "Fechner's philosophical method"	Fechner diary and archive available, but probably not used; knowledge of works and personal contact
Hall, G. S. "Gustav Theodor Fechner". In Hall, *Founders of American Psychology*. New York: D. Appleton & Co., 1912, 52 pp.	American psychologist, slight and ambivalent personal contact	didactic (descriptive historical)	science supplemented by myth	quasi-chronological account of life and works	almost completely derivative of Lasswitz and Wundt
Hermann, I. "Gustav Theodor Fechner. Eine psychoanalytische Studie über individuelle Bedingtheiten wissenschaftlicher Ideen." *Imago, XI,* 1926, 62 pp.	German analyst, author of articles and books on psychogenesis of scientific creativity	didactic (scientific)	psychoanalytic biography	highly selective look at highly selected works	Kuntze biography, Fechner's own writings

Who were these questionable friends? One was Martin Schulze, and on and off he shared lodgings with Fechner. He was a quasi-mad young wanderer with bare feet and rucksack, a poet, a lover of nature, and a hater of the artificialities of society and intellectualism. He ended his days in an asylum around 1850. Fechner and Schulze tramped and camped together, met in the evenings together with a circle of close friends which included young Christian Weisse. Under Schulze's influence Fechner admits to becoming completely uninterested in science; Schulze made Fechner's occupation with science a burden and created an inner schism in his life. Fechner offers this information in a clever portrait which he wrote of Schulze, which Kuntze (1892) prints in one of his biographical chapters. Kuntze, however, titles this chapter "The Sinister Friend," on the basis of his own vivid memory of Schulze from the point of view of a small and terrified child, and from the widow's memory of Schulze's daemonic guise.

The title of that chapter is enough for Hermann! He has seen in Kuntze that the mother moved to Leipzig to save her son from an undesirable friend, that his friend exercised a sinister fascination over Fechner. Hermann insinuates forthwith, a homosexual relationship between Fechner and Schulze. He reaps further support for Fechner's homosexuality quoting from a letter written to Fechner by another friend, Rüffer: "You want to believe that you could mean something to me! Dear brother, you could not mean something to me, you do already, you have always done, and not just something, but much! It is strange, Müller is on the whole opener toward me than towards you. . . . But for him I feel a different love than for you; the latter I would like to compare with the irresistible feeling with which a woman is attracted to a man. I feel that I must lean on your strength and on your character, so as not to lose my balance. . . . Be assured that neither a Schulze, Nauwerk, nor a Weisse can love you as I do—not even Müller or Spielberg. See, a thousand ties hold me to you, the tenderest of which is that of a brother, because we embrace one mother with childlike love, and because your sisters are mine" (Hermann, 1926, p. 10; from Kuntze, 1892, p. 36).

Now Hermann copied this letter from Kuntze and placed it in his own text in conjunction with the sinister Schulze and the mother's move to Leipzig (Hermann, 1926, p. 10). But Hermann committed a distortion which could mislead the unwitting reader. He did not copy the letter in full. It is a quarrelmending letter which begins: "Although I felt ashamed after your letter and your generous offer to consider everything undone and to belong to me again with the old loyal friendship proven over seven years, this shame gave place to joy. . . . I think it was good that such a storm arose" (Kuntze, 1892, p. 36). The passage omitted by Hermann, I believe, offers two potentially important pieces of information: first, Rüffer was not a new Leipzig friend whom Fechner's mother might question out of ignorance, but one of seven years (and apparently adored by Fechner's mother as if he were her own son); second, the two friends had recently quarrelled. Perhaps some part of the effusive adoration expressed in the letter is explicable in terms of the recent emotional storm.

While Hermann takes Rüffer's letter as evidence of Fechner's homosexuality, connecting it with the idea of a sinister friend, Kuntze places the letter in an entirely different context. It is in a passage which tells of the play of Fechner, the child, turning into the academic activity of a maturing youth, of Fechner's magical attractiveness to his peers because of his readiness for fun and his rich ideas, of the fact that all his old school friends shared lodgings with him at one time or another" (Kuntze, 1892, p. 35). Kuntze introduces the Rüffer letter, saying: "The era still stood under the sign of "friendship"; in each park a sentimental altar was erected to "friendship"; subjective intimacy reigned in the companionable life of feeling, and corresponding to this was the ability to pour out one's sentiments in letters" (*ibidem*).

I submit that placed in the context given by Kuntze, Rüffer's letter may be interpreted as an expressive example of the subjective intimacy which was so much a part of the romantic ideal, as a Saxon counterpart to the extravagant expressions of love common to the Victorian period elsewhere, rather than as automatic evidence of homosexuality. Kuntze, under the widow's eye in 1892, would scarcely have printed the letter had he believed it indicated anything but friendship and the old student ideal, *inter amicos omnia communia.* Sexual maladaptation was, in Kuntze's world, simply not yet a part of the archetype of the great man, nor was the tracing of greatness to childhood woes a part of the biographical model which dominated the *genre.*

The fact that Kuntze and Hermann operated under two different models of what biography should be is illustrative of a change in the style of biography which occurred in the early twentieth century"[3] Of the five portraits outlined, only Hermann's may be considered a twentieth century work, in the sense that it attends specifically to the relation between the character of the man and his writings. Hermann's view is the Freudian one, that Fechner's works were effects of the dynamics of his personality formed by Fechner's early experiences. This is not the view of the usual nineteenth century biographer who is interested in the man and his work, but rarely analyzes the relation between the two.[4] The biographies of Hall, Lasswitz, and Wundt present the image of Fechner retiring to his study to write, but we learn little of the relation between man and work. Even the voluminous chronicle of Kuntze, which actually *contains* the data necessary to a study of the relation between man and product, emphasizes neither this relationship nor the process of intellectual development, which is another characteristic of post-Freudian biography. To the contrary, Kuntze takes pains to establish an *anti*-developmentalist scheme for his biography, insisting that Fechner's ideas and gifts: "Were all so well developed in his youth that his life can hardly be considered as a progressive development, but rather as the actualization and sorting out of an already existing resource" (Kuntze, 1892, p. 314).

All five of our portraits escape the twentieth century debunking trend in biography, which is traced by many historians to Lytton Strachey's *Eminent Victorians.* Though much earlier Cromwell advised Mr. Lely to paint him warts and all, and though biographers followed this lead toward realistic portraiture, it was not the wart on which attention was focused, and well through the nineteenth century the biographer was wont to block out disagreeable facts about his subject. Great men tended to be seen as uniformly good and virtuous men.

Of the violent countertrend in biography which occurred after the century's turn, one historian has written: "Biography became for a while a dance of impish glee around scores of broken altars. No eminence was safe as long as dynamite or crowbars were anywhere to be obtained, and the search for flaws became so relentless that the price of microscopes tripled" (Johnson, 1937, p. 478). In one sense, Hermann's vision of Fechner's youthful homosexuality might be seen as consistent with this debunking trend, for it does erode the rather stiff and unidimensionally academic portraits of the earlier studies. But Hermann was not trying to bring Fechner down to the level of ordinary man by showing his warts. On the contrary, he was trying to enshrine him as a great man, on the theory that sexual maladaptation is a correlate of scientific creativity. To paraphrase Strachey, this may be not so much debunk as plain bunk.

Before turning altogether from the topic of debunking, let me draw your attention to the biographical study of G. Stanley Hall. Hall's portrait (1912) is uniformly complimentary in good nineteenth century style. When he writes of his personal contact with Fechner, it is as follows, blandly: "I lived near him for an academic year, and called occasionally (introduced by a card from Wundt), as a student who was trying to understand psycho-physics. Once our conversation drifted to Slade, and he told me of a solid wooden ring put over a solid spool-head much too big for it and of another wooden ring on the one upright leg of a tripod table, and also of a message written between two sealed slates, at which both he and his wife, who was always present at our interviews, shook their heads and expressed doubt. He sent me to Zöllner who showed me these things, and asked impressively how they could be done save in a space of more than three dimensions" (Hall, 1912, p. 167).

Now contrast this saltless porridge with Hall's account of the same events in a letter which he wrote to William James: "Fechner is a curiosity. His eyelids are strangely fringed and he has had a number of holes, square and round, cut, Heaven knows why, in the iris of each eye—and is altogether a bundle of oddities in person and manners. He has forgotten all the details of his *Psychophysik*; and is chiefly interested in theorizing how knots can be tied in endless strings, and how words can be written on the inner side of two slates sealed together. He . . . wants me to go to Zöllner and talk to him about American spiritualism, but I have not been. Fechner is tedious enough, and I hear Zöllner is more so" (James, 1920, p. 18). This is a more familiar and bumptious Hall, and it leaves little doubt that he entertained negative feelings about Fechner. But he left these out of his biographical portrait, for they were infra dig with respect to the portraiture of the period, and to the sober celebratory spirit of *Founders*.

I have left until last the excellent biographical sketches of Lasswitz and Wundt, perhaps because they appear generally to be unproblematic. In them the author intrudes positively into the life and the work of his subject. In the case of Lasswitz, this is because his interpretational bias, to see in all of Fechner the attempt to wed science and metaphysics, coincides with Fechner's own ubiquitous aim. Lasswitz's motive, to offer a materialist dominated public a paragon of a spiritual leader (Lasswitz, 1896, p. 4), does not prevent him from exercising his skill as an historian of atomism. He writes comfortably and fluently about the physical foundations of Fechnerian philosophy, something which few others have accomplished (but see Schreier, 1979).

In the case of Wundt, too, his psychological bias proves an advantage, giving him a scientific context from which he offers superb, if general, critiques of Fechner's methods and materials. Furthermore, Wundt's own problems of advancement within the nineteenth century German academy sensitized him to several professional blows suffered by Fechner early in his career, which the intimate, Kuntze, fails altogether to mention. And though Wundt does not emphasize personality in this official biography, he manages at moments to bring the reader closer to the man, Fechner, than do his other biographers. One remarkable and uniquely Wundtian insight is that Fechner, who loved conversation and controversy, spoke of his ideas publicly only when they were perfected. For example, the entire *Kollektivmasslehre* was discovered by Wundt when he was ordering Fechner's papers after his death. "Nobody had known of the existence of this work, neither Frau Fechner nor any of his friends and colleagues, yet he had carried the plan with him for approximately twenty years and had been occupied with its elaboration for almost a decade" (Wundt, 1913, p. 315). Such are the fine moments in biography, when the skeleton of history begins to pick up flesh.

Though their treatments of Fechner are generally accurate with respect to the evidence of Fechner's own pen, Lasswitz and Wundt both reveal idiosyncratic biases which emerge in their evaluation of Fechner's response to spiritism, and they differ, consequently, in their treatment of Fechner's involvement in the famous Leipzig seances of 1877. Lasswitz, whose image of the great scientist embraces a natural interest in the poetic and mystical, describes Fechner as a zealous participant in the seances of the American medium, Henry Slade (Lasswitz, 1896, p. 106). Wundt, whose own participation in one such seance brought him much ire and grief (Marshall & Wendt, 1980), describes Fechner as an almost unwilling participant in the Slade affair (Wundt, 1913, p. 340). Both views are over-generalizations, for Fechner vacillated. He had indeed previously refused sittings with Slade and attended one without knowing that it was going to occur, but he also attended a second by design and with keen anticipation. Wundt's image of the great scientist took him further to portray Fechner, if not as a skeptic, at least as suspending judgment about the alleged facts of spiritism. Quoting a paragraph from Fechner's diary of 1877, Wundt writes that Fechner's impressions of Slade's performances were overwhelmingly unfavorable, indicating only slick conjuring (Wundt, 1913, pp. 340–341). But Wundt's selectivity in quotation is misleading, for Fechner continues, in the same passage, to say that in spite of his doubts he believes there is something in the facts of spiritism. Furthermore, after hearing the reports of J. F. C. Zöllner and W. Weber on their even more wonderful experiences with Slade, Fechner, on hearsay evidence from his admired colleagues, and in spite of his own earlier admonition that one should struggle against a spiritistic interpretation of Slade's phenomena, confessed that he had been convinced by the facts.

CONCLUSION

He who writes about the use of biography in history usually believes that biography somehow should be a part of the historical enterprise. In closing, this author wishes to make her view on this matter explicit. An important part of the task of the historian of psychology is the analysis of works—famous, infamous, remembered, and all-but-forgotten—which have tried to explain the nature of human experience and action. These writings are the artifacts left by centuries of creative intellectual effort. Most of the authors are now dead, and I agree with the literary critics who write that the work exists, but, "The tears shed or unshed, the personal emotions are gone and cannot be reconstructed" (Wellek, Warren, 1942–1956, p. 80). This suggests that the most intimate parts of the lives of scientists will remain outside the bounds of the task (and the capability) of the historian of science. Yet the historian's task can not end with an understanding of the content of individual works, for there is really no work or artifact *an sich,* no independent entity, which is its own sole context. Every work is severally determined by social, economic, cultural, and intellectual contexts, and it is necessary to know these in order to evaluate a single work with fidelity. Most frequently, it is biography, imperfect and incomplete though it be, which serves as the connecting link between scientific work and context. When available, it is thus indispensable as a tool in historical study.

Even should we grant that some of the meanings of some writings can be gleaned by studying the single work, any historian with a penchant for the study of intellectual development and change will be led eventually to compare several works by the same author. And as soon as two works by the same man are viewed side by side, the historical enterprise fades into the biographical. For one is then dealing with relations between ideas put forward over a greater or lesser time span, and the relation between these ideas may make sense only with reference to the development of personality, by which I mean the complex accumulation over time of special experiences, temperamental value biases, and traditions unique to individual people.

The use of biography in historical study is not unproblematic, however, and it was to a sampling of problems which this paper turned. By now, readers will recognize that this essay—this bagatelle—in no way represents an attempt at scholarly analysis of the Fechnerian biographical corpus. My remarks were aimed in a meta-biographical direction. That is, they were intended to show some characteristics of biography in general, and they should be construed as an invitation to extend the range of vision with which the historian of psychology views his biographical source materials. I would suggest that this extension of vision is salutary not only in the case of biographical material. The autobiography, the diary, the sermon, the essay, the letter, indeed, the scientific text itself, are in any period written according to particular commonly (if not consciously) accepted models which govern literary *genres* in particular periods; and an awareness of these particularities is necessary if the sources are to lead rather than to mislead scholarship.

Finally, when we deal with outstanding men, as we almost inevitably do in biography, we must also ask to what extent the painted biographical picture is a likeness of the particular man, and to what extent the portrait is merely a likeness of a generalized and temporally parochial, or individually idiosyncratic, model of what great men should be like. To my knowledge, there has been little systematic work done on the history of the concept of the great man in science or social science—nothing, at least, to compare with the study of the hero in literary history. It strikes me as a potentially exciting enterprise, and one which could benefit the sometimes fraught interface of biography and history.[5]

NOTES

1 This is Leon Edel's happy description in his very helpful *Literary Biography* (1957).

2 I have followed the two-fold classification suggested by Harold Nicolson (1927).

3 For a survey of these trends in English literature, see Johnson (1937).

4 For a discussion of this characteristic, see Fiedler (1952).

5 Such a study would lead to many questions of interest to both psychologists and historians, not least among these the extent to which the hero of literary history and the hero of science share attributes within a given period, or the extent to which the generalized biographical model may become a self-fulfilling prophecy for individual scientists, leading to what Ernst Kris (1953) calls "enacted biography."

REFERENCES

Edel, L. (1957). *Literary biography. The Alexander Lectures,* 1955–1956. Toronto: University of Toronto Press.

Fiedler, L. A. (1952). Archetype and signature: A study of the relationship between biography and poetry. *Sewanee Review, 60,* 253–273.

Hall, G. S. (1912). *Founders of American psychology.* New York: D. Appleton & Co.

Hermann, I. (1926). Gustav Theodor Fechner. Eine Psychoanalytische Studie über individuelle Bedingtheiten wissenschaftlicher Ideen. *Imago. Zeitschrift für Anwendung der Psychoanalyse auf den Geisteswissenschaften, 2,* 9–70.

James, H., ed. (1920). *The letters of William James.* Boston: The Atlantic Monthly Press.

Johnson, E. (1937). *One mighty torrent. The drama of biography.* New York: Macmillan, 1955.

Kris, E. (1953). *Psychoanalytic explorations in art.* London: Allen & Unwin.

Kuntze, J. E. (1892). *Gustav Theodor Fechner. Ein deutsches Gelebrtenleben.* Leipzig: Breitkopf & Härtel.

Lasswitz, K. (1896). *Gustav Theodor Fechner.* Stuttgart: Fromann, 1902.

Marshall, M. E., Wendt, R. A. (1980). Wundt spiritism and the nature of science. In *Wundt studies,* eds. W. Bringmann and R. Tweney (Göttingen: Hogrefe).

Nicolson, H. (1927). *The development of English biography. Hogarth Lectures, No. 4.* London: Hogarth.

Strachey, L. (1918). *Eminent Victorians.* New York: G. P. Putnam's Sons.

Wellek, R., Warren, A. (1942–1956). *Theory of literature.* New York: Harcourt, Brace & World.

Woolf, V. (1928). *Orlando. A biography.* New York: Penguin Books, 1946.

Psychical Elements and Compounds

Wilhelm Wundt

I. PSYCHICAL ELEMENTS

1. All the contents of psychical experience are of a composite character. It follows, therefore, that *psychical elements,* or the absolutely simple and irreducible components of psychical phenomena are the products of analysis and abstraction. This abstraction is rendered possible by the fact that the elements are in reality united in different ways. If an element, *a,* is connected in one case with the elements *b, c, d,* . . . and in another case with *b', c', d',* . . . it is possible to abstract it from all the other elements, because none of them is always united with it. If, for example, we hear a simple tone of a certain pitch and intensity, it may be located now in this direction, now in that, and may be heard at different times in connection with various other tones. But since the direction is not constant, or the accompanying tone in all cases the same, it is possible to abstract from these variable elements, and we have the single tone as a psychical element.

2. As a result of psychical analysis, we find that there are *psychical elements of two kinds,* corresponding to the *two factors* contained in immediate experience, namely, to the objective contents of experience and to the experiencing subject. The elements of the objective contents we call *sensational elements,* or simply *sensations*: such are a tone, or a particular sensation of heat, cold, or light, if in each case we neglect for the moment all the connections of these sensations with others, and also all their spacial and temporal relations. The subjective elements, on the other hand, are designated as *effective elements,* or *simple feelings.* We may mention as examples, the feelings accompanying sensations of light, sound, taste, smell, heat, cold, or pain, the feelings aroused by the sight of an agreeable or disagreeable object, and the feelings arising in a state of attention or at the moment of a volitional act. Such simple feelings are in a double sense products of abstraction: every such feeling is connected in reality with an ideational element, and is furthermore a component of a psychical process which occurs in time, during which the feeling itself is continually changing.

3. The actual contents of psychical experience always consist of various combinations of sensational and affective elements, so that the specific character of a given psychical process depends for the most part, not on the nature of its elements, so much as on their union into a composite psychical compound. Thus, the idea of an extended body or of a rhythm, an emotion, and a volition, are all *specific* forms of psychical experience. But their character as such is as little determined by their sensational and affective elements as are the chemical properties of a compound body by the properties of its chemical elements. *Specific* character and *elementary* nature of psychical processes are, accordingly, two entirely different concepts. Every psychical element is a specific content of experience, but not every specific content is at the same time a psychical element. Thus, spacial and temporal ideas, emotions, and volitional acts, are specific, but not elementary processes.

4. Sensations and simple feelings exhibit certain common attributes and also certain characteristic differences. They have in common *two determinants,* namely, *quality* and *intensity.* Every simple sensation and every simple feeling has a definite *qualitative* character that marks it off from all other sensations and feelings; and this quality must always have some degree of *intensity.* Our *designations* of psychical elements

From Wundt, W. (1896). *Grundriss der Psychologie.* Leipzig: Engelmann. From C. H. Judd (Trans.), *Outlines of psychology.* New York: Gustav Sechert, 1902, pp. 32–41, 100–103.

are based entirely upon their qualities; thus, we distinguish such sensations as blue, grey, yellow, warmth and cold, or such feelings as grave, cheerful, sad, gloomy, and sorrowful. On the other hand, we always express the differences in the intensity of psychical elements by the same quantitative designations, as weak, strong, medium strong, and very strong. These expressions are in both cases class-concepts which serve for a first superficial arrangement of the elements, and each expression embraces an unlimitedly large number of concrete elements. Language has developed a relatively complete stock of names for the qualities of simple sensations, especially for colors and tones. Names for the qualities of feelings and for degrees of intensity are far behind in number and precision. Certain attributes other than quality and intensity, such as distinctness and indistinctness, are sometimes classed with quality and intensity as fundamental attributes. But since clearness, obscurity, etc., . . . always arise from the interconnection of psychical compounds, they can not be regarded as determinants of psychical elements.

5. Made up, as it is, of the *two* determinants, quality and intensity, every psychical element must have a certain *degree of intensity* from which it is possible to pass, by continual gradations, to every other degree of intensity in the same quality. Such gradations can be made in only *two* directions: one we call *increase* in intensity, the other *decrease.* The degrees of intensity of every qualitative element, form in this way a single dimension, in which, from a given point, we may move in two opposite directions, just as from any point in a straight line. This fact in regard to intensity may be expressed in the general statement: *The various intensities of every psychical element form a continuity of one dimension.* The extremities of such a continuity we call the *minimal* and *maximal sensations,* or the *minimal* or *maximal feelings,* as the case may be.

In contrast with this uniformity in intensities, *qualities* have more variable attributes. Every quality may, indeed, be assigned a place in a definite continuity of similar qualities in such a way that it is possible to pass uninterruptedly from a given point in this continuous series to any other point. But the various continuities of different qualities, which we may call *systems of quality,* exhibit differences both in the variety of possible gradations and in the number of directions of gradation. With reference to these two kinds of variations in systems of quality, we may distinguish, on the one hand, *homogeneous* and *complex systems,* and on the other hand, *one-dimensional, two-dimensional,* and *many-dimensional* systems of quality. Within a homogeneous system, only such small differences are possible, that generally there has never arisen any practical need of distinguishing them by different names. Thus, we distinguish only *one* quality of pressure, of heat, of cold, or of pain, only *one* feeling of pleasure or of excitement, although, in intensity, each of these qualities may have many different grades. It is not to be inferred from this fact that in each of these systems there is really only *one* quality. The truth is that in these cases the number of different qualities is merely very limited; if we were to represent the system geometrically, we should probably never reduce it to a *single* point. Thus, for example, sensations of pressure from different regions of the skin show, beyond question, small qualitative differences which are great enough to make it possible for us to distinguish clearly any point of the skin from others at some distance from it. Such differences, however, as arise from contact with a sharp or dull point, or from a rough or smooth body, are not to be regarded as different qualities. They always depend on a large number of simultaneous sensations, and without the various combinations of these sensations into composite psychical compounds, the impressions mentioned would be impossible.

Complex systems of quality differ from those we have been discussing, in that they embrace a large number of clearly distinguishable elements between which all possible intermediate forms exist. In this class we must include the tonal system and color system, the systems of smells and tastes; and among the complex feeling systems we must include those which form the subjective complements of these sensational systems, such as the systems of tonal feelings, color feelings, etc. It is probable also that many systems of feelings belong here, which are objectively connected with composite impressions, but are as feelings, simple in character; such are the various feelings of harmony or discord which correspond to various combinations of tones. The differences in the *number of dimensions* have been determined with certainty only in the case of two or three sensational systems. Thus, the tonal system is one-dimensional. The ordinary color system, which includes the colors and their transitional qualities to white, is two-dimensional; while the complete system of light sensations, which includes also the dark color-tones and the transitional qualities to black, is three-dimensional.

6. In regard to the relations discussed thus far, sensational elements and affective elements agree in general. They differ, on the other hand, in certain essential attributes which are connected with the fact that sensations are immediately related to objects, while feelings are immediately related to the subject.

1) When varied in a single dimension, sensational elements exhibit *pure qualitative differences,* which are always in the *same direction* until they reach the possible limits of variation, where they become *maximal differences.* Thus, in the color system, red and green, blue and yellow, or in the tonal system, the lowest and highest audible tones, are the maximal differences and are at the same time purely qualitative differences. Every affective element, on the contrary, when continuously varied in the proper direction of quality, passes gradually into a feeling of *opposite quality.* This is most obvious in the case of those affective elements which are regularly connected with certain sensational elements, as for example, tonal feelings or color feelings. As sensations, a high and low tone present differences that approach more or less the maximal differences of tonal sensation; the corresponding tonal feelings are opposites. In general, then, *series of sensational qualities are bounded at their extremes by maximal differences; series of affective qualities are bounded by maximal opposites.* Between affective opposites is a middle-zone, where the feeling is not noticeable at all. It is, however, frequently impossible to demonstrate this indifference-zone, because, while certain simple feelings disappear, other affective qualities remain, or new ones may arise. The latter case appears most commonly when the passing of the feeling into the indifference-zone depends on a change in sensations. Thus, in the middle of the musical scale, those feelings disappear which correspond to the high and low tones, but the middle tones have independent affective qualities of their own which appear clearly only when the other complicating factors are eliminated. This is to be explained by the fact that a feeling which corresponds to a certain sensational quality is, as a rule, a component of a complex affective system, in which it belongs at the same time to various dimensions. Thus, the affective quality of a tone of given pitch belongs not only to the dimension of pitch feelings, but also to that of feelings of intensity, and finally to the different dimensions in which the clang character of tones may be arranged. A tone of middle pitch and intensity may, in this way, lie in the indifference-zone so far as feelings of pitch and intensity are concerned, and yet have a very marked clang feeling. The passage of affective elements through the indifference-zone can be directly observed only when care is taken to abstract from other accompanying affective elements. The cases most favorable for this observation are those in which the accompanying elements disappear entirely or almost entirely. Wherever such an indifference-zone appears without complication with other effective elements, we

speak of the state as *free from feelings,* and of the sensations and ideas present in such a state, as *indifferent.*

2) Feelings which have specific, and at the same time simple and irreducible quality, appear not only as the subjective complements of simple sensations, but also as the characteristic attendants of composite ideas or even of complex ideational processes. Thus, there is a simple tonal feeling which varies with the pitch and intensity of tones, and there is also a feeling of harmony which, regarded as a feeling, is just as irreducible as the tonal feeling, but varies with the character of compound clangs. Still other feelings, which may in turn be of the most various kinds, arise from melodious series of clangs. Here, again, each single feeling taken by itself at a given moment, appears as an irreducible unit. Simple feelings are, then, much more various and numerous than simple sensations.

3) The various pure sensations may be arranged in a number of separate systems, between the elements of which there is no qualitative relation whatever. Sensations belonging to different systems are called *disparate*. Thus, a tone and a color, a sensation of heat and one of pressure, or, in general, any two sensations between which there are no intermediate qualities, are disparate. According to this criterion, each of the four special senses (smell, taste, hearing, and sight) has a closed, complex sensational system, disparate from that of the other senses; while the general sense (touch) contains four homogeneous sensational systems (sensations of pressure, heat, cold, and pain). All simple feelings, on the other hand, form a single interconnected manifold, for there is no feeling from which it is not possible to pass to any other, through intermediate forms or through indifference-zones. But here too we may distinguish certain systems the elements of which are more closely related, as, for example, feelings from colors, tones, harmonies and rhythms. These are, however, not absolutely closed systems, for there are everywhere relations either of likeness or of opposition to other systems. Thus, feelings such as those from sensations of moderate warmth, from tonal harmony, and from satisfied expectation, however great their qualitative differences may be, are all related in that they belong to the general class of "pleasurable feelings." Even closer relations exist between certain single affective systems, as for example, between tonal feelings and color feelings, where the feelings from deep tones seem to be related to those from dark colors, and feelings from bright colors to those from high tones. When in such cases a certain relationship is ascribed to the sensations themselves, it is probably due entirely to a confusion of the accompanying feelings with the sensations.

This third distinguishing characteristic shows conclusively that the source of the feelings is *unitary* while that of the sensations, which depend on a number of different, and in part distinguishable, conditions, is not unitary. Probably this difference in the character of the sources of feeling and sensations is directly connected, on the one hand, with the relation of the feelings to the unitary subject, and, on the other hand, with the relation of sensations to the great variety of *objects*.

6a. It is only in modern psychology that the terms "sensation" and "feeling" have gained the meanings assigned to them in the definitions above given. In older psychological literature these terms were sometimes used indiscriminatingly, sometimes interchanged. Even yet sensations of touch and sensations from the internal organs are called feelings by physiologists, and the sense of touch itself is known as the "sense of feeling." This corresponds, it is true, to the original significance of the word, where feeling is the same as touching, and yet, after the differentiation has once been made, a confusion of the two terms should be avoided. Then again, the word "sensation" is used even by psychologists to mean not only simple, but also composite qualities, such as compound clangs and spacial and temporal ideas. But since we have the entirely adequate word "idea" for such compounds, it is more advantageous to limit the word sensation to sense qualities which are psychologically simple. Finally the term "sensation" has sometimes been restricted so as to mean only those impressions which come directly from external sense stimuli. For the psychological attributes of a sensation, however, this circumstance is entirely indifferent, and therefore, such a definition of the term is unjustifiable.

The discrimination between sensational elements and affective elements in any concrete case is very much facilitated by the existence of indifference-zones in the feelings. Then again it follows from the fact that feelings range between opposites rather than mere differences, that feelings are much the more variable elements of our immediate experience. This changeable character, which renders it almost impossible to hold an effective state constant in quality and intensity, is the cause of the great difficulties that stand in the way of the exact investigation of feelings.

Sensations are present in all immediate experiences, but feelings may disappear in certain special cases, because of their oscillation through an indifference-zone. Obviously, then, we can, in the case of sensations, abstract from the accompanying feelings, but we can never abstract from sensations in the case of feelings. In this way two false views may easily arise, either that sensations are the *causes* of feelings, or that feelings are a particular species of sensations. The first of these opinions is false because affective elements can never be derived from sensations as such, but only from the attitude of the subject, so that under different subjective conditions the same sensation may be accompanied by different feelings. The second view, that feelings are a particular species of sensations, is untenable because the two classes of elements are distinguished, on the one hand by the immediate relation of sensations to objects and of feelings to the subject, and on the other hand, by the fact that the former range between maximal differences, the latter between maximal opposites. Because of the objective and subjective factors belonging to all psychical experience, sensations and feelings are to be looked upon as real and equally essential, though everywhere interrelated, elements of psychical phenomena. In the interrelation of the two groups of elements, the sensational elements appear as the more constant; they alone can be isolated through abstraction, by referring them to external objects. It follows, therefore, of necessity that in investigating the attributes of both kinds of elements, we must start with the sensations. Simple sensations, in the consideration of which we abstract from the accompanying affective elements, are called *pure sensations*. . . .

II. PSYCHICAL COMPOUNDS

1. By "psychical compound" we mean any composite component of our immediate experience which is marked off from other contents of this experience by characteristics peculiarly its own, in such a way that it is recognized as a relatively independent unity and is, when practical necessity demands it, designated by a special name. In developing such a name, language has followed the general rule that only *classes* and the most important *species* into which phenomena may be grouped shall have special designations. Thus such terms as idea, emotion, volitional act, etc., designate general classes of psychical compounds, such terms as visual idea, joy, anger, hope, etc., designate special species included in these classes. So far as these designations are based upon actual, distinguishing characteristics, they have a certain value for psychological analysis. But in granting this, we must avoid from the first, *two* presuppositions to which the existence of these names might easily mislead us. The first is, that a psychical compound is an absolutely independent content of immediate experience. The second is, that certain compounds, as for example, ideas, have the *nature of things*. The truth is that compounds are only *relatively* independent units. Just as they are made up of various elements, so they themselves unite to form a complete interconnection, in which relatively simple compounds may continually combine to form more composite ones. Then, again, compounds, like the psychical elements contained in them, are never things, but *processes* which change from moment to mo-

ment, so that it is only through deliberate abstraction, which is, indeed, indispensable for the investigation in many cases, that they can be thought of as constant at any given moment. . . .

2. All psychical compounds may be resolved into psychical elements, that is, into pure sensations and simple feelings. The two kinds of elements behave, however, in an essentially different manner, in keeping with the special properties of simple feelings. . . . The sensational elements found by such a resolution, always belong to one of the sensational systems already considered. The effective elements, on the other hand, include not only those which correspond to the pure sensations contained in the compounds, but also those due to the interconnection of the elements into a compound. The systems of sensational qualities, accordingly, remain the same, no matter how many varieties of compounds arise, while the systems of simple affective qualities continually increase. Furthermore, it is a general principle valid for all psychical compounds, whether they are composed of sensations only, of feelings only, or of combinations of both sensations and feelings, that *the attributes of psychical compounds are never limited to those of the elements that enter into them.* It is true rather that *new* attributes, peculiar to the compounds themselves, always arise as a result of the combination of these elements. Thus, a visual idea has not only the attributes of the light sensations and sensations of ocular position and movements contained in it, but it has also the attribute of spacial arrangement of the sensations, a factor not present in the elements themselves. Again a volition is made up not only of the ideas and feelings into which its single acts may be resolved, but there result also from the combination of these single acts, new affective elements which are specifically characteristic of the complex volition. Here, again, the combinations of sensational and affective elements are different. In the first case, on account of the constancy of the sensational systems, no new sensations can arise, but only peculiar *forms of their arrangement.* These forms are the *extensive spacial* and *temporal manifolds.* When, on the other hand, affective elements combine, *new simple feelings* arise, which unite with those originally present to make *intensive* affective units of composite character.

3. The classification of psychical compounds is naturally based upon the character of the elements that enter into them. Those composed entirely or chiefly of sensations are called *ideas,* those consisting mainly of affective elements, *affective processes.* The same limitations hold here as in the case of the corresponding elements. Although compounds are more the products of immediate discrimination among actual psychical processes than are the elements, still, there is in all exactness no pure ideational process and no pure affective process, but in both cases we can only abstract to a certain extent from one or the other component. As in the case of the two kinds of elements, so here, we can neglect the accompanying subjective states when dealing with ideas, but we must always presuppose some idea when giving an account of the affective processes.

We distinguish, accordingly, three chief forms of *ideas*: 1) intensive ideas, 2) spacial ideas, 3) temporal ideas; and three forms of *affective processes:* 1) intensive affective combinations, 2) emotions, 3) volitions. Temporal ideas constitute a sort of link between the two kinds of compounds, for certain feelings play an important part in their formation.

REFERENCES

Kant, Anthropologie, 2nd. Bk. Herbart, Textbook of Psychology, §68 and 95. (Differentiation of the concepts sensation and feeling in the present-day sense.)

Horwicz, Psychologische Analysen auf physiolog. Grundlage, 2 vols., 1872–1878.

Wundt, Ueber das Verhältniss der Gefühle zu den Vorstellungen, Vierteljahrsschr. f. wiss. Philos., III, 1879. (Also in Essays, 1885).

The Establishment of Wundt's Laboratory: An Archival and Documentary Study

Wolfgang G. Bringmann, Norma J. Bringmann, and Gustav A. Ungerer

Traditionally, the academic year 1879–80 has been regarded as the period during which Wundt's laboratory became a reality. Researches at the Wilhelm Wundt Archive in Leipzig and the Dresden State Archive fully support this claim. All in all, the year 1879 was an auspicious one for Wundt. On January 1 of that year, his regular salary was increased by about twenty-five percent to 5,400 Marks annually (Fensch, 1977). On January 26, his son Max was born, who, like his sister Lorle before him, would serve as a research subject for his father's studies of language development.

AN IMPORTANT PETITION

Perhaps encouraged by events, Wundt submitted a petition to the Royal Saxon Ministry of Education on March 24, in which he requested a regular budget for the "establishment and support" of a collection of "psychophysical apparatus." Wundt's long letter to his superiors tells us a great deal about the development of his viewpoint concerning the function of a university laboratory.

> The undersigned had contemplated already at that time (1875) to connect psychophysical practica with his lectures . . . in order to instruct those of his students who were particularly interested in psychology in the techniques of conducting their own psychophysical research work. He believed, however, that he should carry out these plans only after he had convinced himself that such practical activities were desirable.

Adapted from Bringmann, W. G., Bringmann, N. J., & Ungerer, G. A. (1980). The establishment of Wundt's laboratory: An archival and documentary study. In W. G. Bringmann & R. D. Tweney (Eds.), *Wundt studies: A centennial collection.* Toronto: C. J. Hogrefe, pp. 123–159.

After having taught at Leipzig for nearly four years and having been able to stimulate interest in psychological research through the teaching of the seminar (*Psychological Society*), Wundt believed that the time had come to begin offering courses in psychological research tehniques.

> Since the seminars on theoretical aspects of psychological research, taught by the undersigned, have attracted a significant enrollment, it has become ever clearer to him that they need to be supplemented by a practical introduction to the basic psychophysical research methods. (March 24).

In his petition Wundt also declared his willingness to donate his own collection of equipment to the university in exchange for an annual stipend of "600 Marks . . . for the establishment and maintenance of a set of psychophysical apparatus." Although the sum requested by Wundt was trifling, his request was denied due to "financial exigencies."

It almost looks as if Wundt had given up hope for his laboratory, because he did not offer his *Psychological Society* during the Summer Semester, as had been his habit since 1877. Instead he scheduled his seminar course in logic (*Logical Society*). However, in the Winter Catalogue for 1878–80, the psychological seminar was again listed (1879):

> *Psychological Society*. Monday 7–9 p.m. (*private* and *gratis*).

Since it was a *private* course, students needed Wundt's permission to enroll but the word *gratis* indicated that no fee was to be charged.

An Eyewitness Account

Information about what took place in this seminar during the Winter Semester of 1879–80 has been provided by an eyewitness—G. Stanley

Hall (1840–1926). Hall is generally considered to be Wundt's first American student, although, having already received his doctorate at Harvard University, he was not formally enrolled at Leipzig. In Hall's autiobiography, *Life and Confessions of a Psychologist* (1924), he comments:

> I also attended Wundt's seminary, in which his method was then to assign readings, expecting each to report in detail. He took incessant notes, so that in a sense we read for him; and I have thought this method was the key for the vast erudition which marks his publications. (p. 204).

Despite his sarcasm, Hall was to copy the format of Wundt's seminar course in later years at Clark University, even including the Monday night schedule. Hall's report also indicates that the *Psychological Society* did not include any opportunities for practical psychological research.

THE LABORATORY

Wundt has provided considerable information about the early days of his laboratory, which will be quoted in chronological order. The earliest account is contained in another petition to the ministry, dated April 4, 1882, in which Wundt once again summarized the history of his institute.

> The undersigned began . . . to offer a practical seminar activity in addition to his theoretical seminar during the Winter Semester of 1879–80.

This practical seminar, as Wundt calls it to distinguish it from the *Psychological Society*, was not listed in the catalogue at all. Wundt provides the same information to the Austrian philosopher Jerusalem, who had inquired about the origin of Wundt's institute (1892):

> The main dates about the institute are quickly collected. In the Winter of 1879–80 it was opened first as a private undertaking. Stanley Hall and Max Friedrich . . . were the first participants. . . . Initially the institute had only *one* single room at its disposal. (February 2).

The official history of Wundt's laboratory, which he wrote on the occasion of the 500th anniversary of Leipzig University, is slightly more explicit (1909):

> Following the psychological seminars, which during the first semesters were held in the form of a colloquium, dealing with the topics of the formal lecture, individual students began to occupy themselves in this room in the Konvict with research investigations. (p. 1).

This interestingly suggests that the actual practical research of Wundt's institute was originated by his students. It is noteworthy that Wundt gives credit to his students for helping him to get his laboratory started. His comment may only have been a matter of courtesy on his part. On the other hand, Wundt may have known what most teachers of psychology eventually discover. It is dangerous to inspire students with your ideas about research or practical professional services, because they will eventually expect you to practice what you preach. While these and other accounts of the early laboratory vary, it is clear that Wundt regarded the inofficial practical research activities as the actual beginning of his institute. The practical research activities took place in the classroom on the third floor of the *Konvikt* building which has been assigned to Wundt in the summer of 1876.

Although G. Stanley Hall was eager to minimize his association with Wundt, he provides independent support for the existence of Wundt's laboratory in his autiobiography (1924):

> . . . Wundt at Leipzig . . . had only lately been elected full professor there . . . and his laboratory was but little organized. . . . I participated as subject in several of the experiments. But as the laboratory was open only in the afternoon and especially because I felt it necessary to ground myself

> in physiology, I left Wundt and spent most of the day in the laboratory of Professor Ludwig, who gave me a problem in myology working with me a great deal. . . . Wundt was an indefatigable worker and we rarely saw him outside the laboratory, although, even here he spent little time and did little work. . . . He impressed me as rather inept in the use of his hands. (p. 205).

While Hall is obviously biased in almost all that he has to say about Wundt and his small laboratory, he nevertheless confirms its independent existence. His comparison with Ludwig's Physiological Institute is meaningless, when one considers that Carl Ludwig (1816–1895) had come to Leipzig a decade before Wundt and was able to move into a special laboratory building which had been constructed at the cost of nearly 200,000 Marks (Stieda, 1909).

Dissertation Research

According to Wundt, the first research project completed under his supervision in the laboratory was the dissertation of Max Friedrich on *The duration of simple and complex apperceptions* (1881). . . . Friedrich, who was by training a mathematician and not a philosopher, acknowledged that his work was carried out "under the direction of Professor Dr. Wundt." The preliminary research was begun in "early December" of 1879 and Wundt, Hall and Friedrich were the first participants. The data collection continued in early January of 1880 and ended along with the winter semester in early March. Despite Hall's claims that Wundt did not spend much time in the laboratory, we discover that he participated in the data collection on no less than 16 occasions between January 17 and March 5. We also find that Hall participated in the data collection only on an irregular basis. In conclusion, an approximate date can be fixed for the beginning of the actual work in Wundt's laboratory in the *Konvikt*. The earliest time is "early December," the latest suitable date would be January 17, when Wundt, Hall, Tischer and Friedrich participated as experimental subjects.

MY PSYCHOPHYSICAL LABORATORY

It has been suggested by Boring that Wundt was not really aware of the establishment of his laboratory, and that he chose the 1879 date randomly many years later when he was writing the history of his institute (Boring, 1965). Nothing could be further from the truth, as we can learn from a letter of recommendation written by Wundt for Hall on June 18, 1880. Hall used this letter in securing his appointment at Johns Hopkins University, and a copy has been found in the papers of Coit Gilman (1831–1908). Wundt penned the recommendation in Latin letters rather than in the traditional German script which he used for most of his writing (1880a):

> I have come to know Dr. G. Stanley Hall well through frequent personal contact during his extended stay in Leipzig as a man of comprehensive philosophical knowledge, great scientific interests and solid independent judgment. In particular, Mr. Hall has been able to gain a rare knowledge of the German scientific literature not only in psychology but also in the related subjects of sensory- and neurophysiology.

As far as Hall's participation in the laboratory is concerned, Wundt states generously:

> He has participated in the work of my psychophysical laboratory during the winter semester of 1879–80 and the summer semester of 1880 with great industry and success. (June 18).

Additional evidence that Wundt regarded his "humble" facilities on the third floor of the *Konvikt* as a laboratory can be found in correspondence between Wundt and Kraepelin dated August 4 and October 14, 1880.

EXPANSION AND RECOGNITION

The Philosophical Studies

Once Wundt had his own laboratory facilities in which his students were conducting independent psycho-physical research, it comes as no surprise that he soon founded his own journal, the *Philosophical Studies*. Considerable new information about the origin of Wundt's journal has been discovered in his correspondence with the noted psychiatrist Emil Kraepelin (1880b):

> Your comment about a journal of psychology, which you regard as desirable has much interested me, especially since I have had similar ideas. . . . I have currently a number of investigations on the time sense . . . for which I do not yet have a place of publication. . . . The best physiological journals pursue other interests as a rule, and a philosophical journal . . . does not have the necessary space for such topics. . . . If the project should become reality in any form, I would like to count on your collaboration. (August 4).

Wundt later elaborated some of his plans for such a project to Kraepelin (1880c):

> The plan of a psychological journal, which you suggested, has come closer to realization. After due deliberation, I think it would be best to extend the scope of the journal to the whole field of psychology and related subject areas. . . . I also think it would be best if the journal would initially print only original research . . . and not reviews of other research. (October 14).

Wundt had apparently talked to his publisher and many details were already worked out (1880d):

> The individual issues are to appear in an informal order . . . and the publication is to depend on available material. The publisher has declared himself willing to provide an honorarium of 40 Marks and 40 reprints of each article. I would like to bring out articles in the first issue which represent the different fields which the journal is to cover. (December 17, 1880).

Wundt announced his plans to publish "*Psychological Studies*: in January of 1881. The main purpose of the new journal was to publish experiments "which over the last several years have been carried out in my laboratory." The title of the journal was already changed by August 4 of the same year to *Philosophische Studien*. It seems possible that the change in title was due to the fact that a journal called *Psychologische Studien* was already in existence, and, moreover, dealt with the obnoxious topic of spiritism and other parapsychological phenomena (Wundt, 1927). The first number of the *Philosophische Studien,* containing a long article by Wundt on psychological methods and the Friedrich dissertation, was published in October of 1881. The first volume, however, was not completed until 1883.

Institute for Experimental Psychology

By April, 1882, Wundt felt sufficiently confident of the solid accomplishments of his laboratory to compose yet another petition for university support of his work. The lengthy missive began with a history of the laboratory (1882):

> Already at that time (1875), the undersigned had contemplated the eventual foundation of a seminar for experimental psychology, in which students could be instructed through practica in carrying out their own research. However, he had thought it best to delay specific petitions in this direction until his teaching at the university had produced the conditions necessary for such a seminar activity. Accordingly, the undersigned started a practical seminar program about two years ago during the winter semester of 1879–80 and in publicly announced practica beginning with the summer semester of 1880.

Wundt also reported that he had supported the experimental work of his students out of his own pocket. Thus, he had been forced to limit the areas in which research could be carried out to those for which his personal research equipment was suitable. He had apparently been able to attract quite a few students.

> To these practica in experimental psychology a larger number of students than the undersigned had originally expected have been attracted. These include not only students who are special-

izing in philosophy. Many students in the sciences and mathematics have actively participated in the psycho-physical research as well.

Wundt also mentioned that he had supervised a significant number of dissertations which were published in his own journal.

> As far as the achievements of the Seminar for Experimental Psychology during the last two years are concerned, the undersigned would like to mention several pertinent dissertations, which were accepted by the College of Arts and Sciences and which have been published in the *Philosophical Studies* by him. (April 4).

Wundt also complained that the large anatomical drawings, which he had initially obtained as lecture illustrations for small classes, were totally inappropriate for his big lecture classes which exceeded 250 students. Finally, Wundt asked the Royal Ministry of Culture and Public Education to add the "*Institute of Experimental Psychology*" to the number of academic institutes of Leipzig University. He also requested approval of an annual budget of 900 Marks for this institute.

This letter contains a whole chapter of psychological history. Wundt used the name *Institute* for the first time as a synonym for *Seminar*. His eloquent petition, however, was only partially successful. The Ministry thanked him for his efforts, refused the establishment of a regular budget, but agreed to provide the requested 900 Marks for the current year. Official recognition was not mentioned.

A Famous Visitor

Recognition of a somewhat different type came late in the fall in the form of a personal visit by William James (1840–1910), who had just returned from a trip to Prague to see Carl Stumpf (1882):

> I stayed in Berlin a week, in Leipzig five days, in Liege two and a half days with Delboeuf. In each place I heard all the university lectures that I could and spoke with several of the professors. From some I got very good hints as to how not to lecture. Helmholtz, for example, gave me the very worst lecture I ever heard in my life except one (that one was by our most distinguished American mathematician). The lecture I heard in Prague from Mach was on the same elementary subject as Helmholtz's and one of the most artistic lectures I ever heard. Wundt in Leipzig impressed me very agreeably personally. He has a ready smile and is entirely unaffected and unpretending in his manner. I heard him twice and was twice in his laboratory. He was very polite but showed no desire for further acquaintance. (November 26).

James' letter makes it very clear that Wundt's laboratory was in full existence at that time. His comments about Wundt's accessibility are in agreement with the observations of Hall, who in 1879 had found Wundt "very accessible and free to talk about everything." One also gains the impression that James is somewhat unhappy about his favorable impression of Wundt, because he was certainly familiar with Stumpf's intense personal dislike of Wundt and his work.

Call To Breslau

Wundt was considered for an appointment at Breslau University, as we discover in a letter to his friend Siegfried Brie (1883):

> The news in your letter surprised me to a high degree. It is the first word that they have thought of me in Breslau. Here, I heard only a short time ago that Paulssen in Berlin or Windelband in Strassburg had been recommended. Everyone here is of the opinion that the Prussian government does not like to call anyone from Leipzig . . . because in Prussia the system of academic calls seems to have been replaced by bureaucratic promotions. It would be a joy for my wife and myself to renew our friendship with you and your family, since we have no one as close as you in Leipzig. You know, of course, that my working conditions here in

> Leipzig are not the best. It is also doubtful if the Saxon government will make an effort to keep me.

Wundt was in a difficult position. He and his family enjoyed their friendship with the Brie family, but were not all that eager to leave Leipzig, as we find out in the next section of the letter.

> I very much doubt that any personal activity on my side will help the call. Secondly, I am in these matters a fatalist. I prefer to let events approach me and if they do not work out, I regard it as proof that they should not have occurred at all. (January 27).

Nevertheless, the formal call was received and communicated by Wundt to his superiors together with a list of conditions which could help him decide to stay in Leipzig.

Reward and Recognition

The first bonus for deciding not to leave his position in Leipzig was a nearly forty percent raise in salary from 5400 to 7500 Marks a year (Fensch, 1977). In addition, the local administrators in Leipzig were instructed to:

> place the immediately adjacent small auditorium at his (Wundt's) disposal in addition to the room, which he has used until now in the *Konvikt* building, and to carry out the minor changes in construction according to his wishes.

The minor changes desired by Wundt were, in fact, quite substantial as we can see in the drawings submitted by the architect and approved by the University. A total of 1614 Marks was expended to turn two old classrooms and a hallway into quite a respectable laboratory. The following changes were made (Drucker, 1883):

(a) The hallway area in front of classroom number V on the third floor of the *Konvikt* building was separated by walls and turned into an office-waiting room. Part of it was to be used as a darkroom.

(b) The new classroom, which had been assigned to Wundt (Number III) on the same floor was divided into two workrooms by the construction of a dividing wall.

(c) Storm windows and screens were installed on all windows.

(d) The walls and ceilings were painted with waterbase paint. All woodwork was painted with oil paint.

(e) Connections for gas light were installed in all rooms and hallways and all rooms were connected with electrical lines.

(f) Three new cabinets, five tables and 12 cane-bottom chairs were added to the existing furnishings of the laboratory (August 1).

Altogether the enlarged laboratory of Wundt consisted of two large (Rooms 1 and 7) and five small rooms (2, 3, 4, 5 and 6) providing approximately 1000 square feet of space (Bringmann & Ungerer, 1980). Incidentally, the original storage room, which had been assigned to Wundt in 1876 (Fensch, 1977), now served as his university office (Room 1), except for a small section (Rooms 3 and 4) which was used as darkroom and for equipment storage.

The assignment and equipment of a permanent home for the laboratory was followed on June 26, 1883 by the inclusion of Wundt's Laboratory among the *regular* academic institutes of Leipzig University (Fensch, 1977). The new seminar was called *Institute for Experimental Psychology*. It also received a regular annual budget at that time. The Winter Catalogue of Leipzig University for 1883–1884 contains the information that Wundt's private laboratory had officially become the 26th institute or seminar of the university (1883–84):

> 26. *Institute for Experimental Psychology (Convict Building),* Professor Dr. Wilhelm Wundt, Director, 6 Goethestraβe. Cand math. G. Lorenz, Famulus, 6 Salomonstraβe.

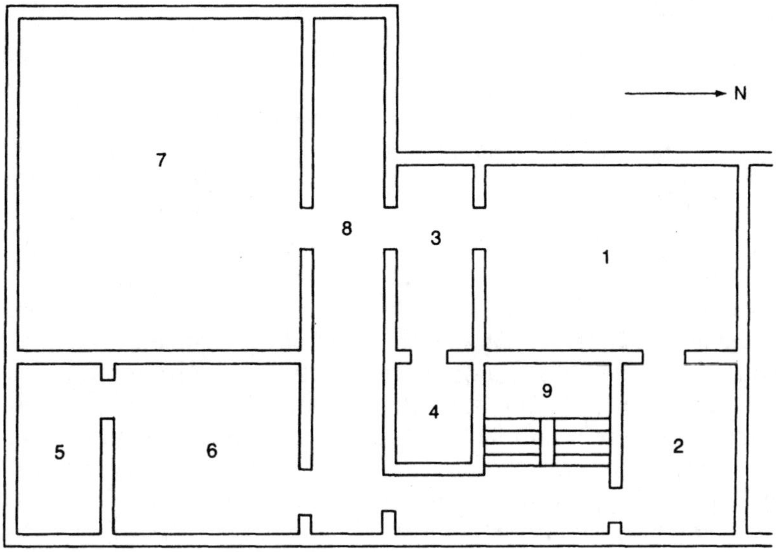

1. Classroom # 5
2. Conference room
3. Waiting room
4. Darkroom
5. Workroom (Laboratory)
6. Workroom (Laboratory)
7. Classroom # 4
8. Hallway
9. Staircase

FIGURE 1
Floorplan of Wundt's Leipzig laboratory.

REFERENCES

Boring, E. G. On the subjectivity of important historical dates: Leipzig 1879. *Journal of the History of the Behavioral Sciences,* 1965, 1, 5–10.

Bringmann, W., & Ungerer, G. A. An archival journey in search of Wilhelm Wundt. In L. Pongratz & J. Brozek (Eds.) *Historiography of psychology.* Göttingen: Hogrefe, 1980.

Drucker, R. Personal communication, October 31, 1979.

Fensch, D. Zur Rolle Wilhelm Wundt's bei der Institutionalisierung der Psychologie in Leipzig. *Psychologie-Historische-Manuskripte,* 1977, 1, 60–66.

Friedrich, M. Über die Apperceptionsdauer bei einfachen und zusammengesetzten Vorstellungen. *Philosophische Studien,* 1883 (1881), 1, 38–77.

Hall, G. S. *Life and confessions of a psychologist.* New York: Appleton, 1924.

Stieda, W. *Die Entwicklung der Universität Leipzig in ihrem tausendsten Semester.* Leipzig: Hirzel, 1909.

Wundt, E. *Wilhelm Wundts Werk.* München: Beck, 1927.

Wundt, W. Letter of recommendation for G. S. Hall, June 18, 1880a. (Clark U.).

Wundt, W. to E. Kraepelin, August 4, 1880b. (Tübingen U.).

Wundt, W. to E. Kraepelin, October 14, 1880c. (Tübingen U.).

Wundt, W. to E. Kraepelin, December 17, 1880d. (Tübingen U.).

Wundt, W. to Ministry of Education, April 4, 1882.

Wundt, W. to W. Jerusalem, February 2, 1892. (Tübingen U.).

Wundt, W. *Das Institut für experimentelle Psychologie.* Leipzig: Hirzel, 1909.

A Reappraisal of Wilhelm Wundt

Arthur L. Blumenthal

Approximately 100 years ago, in an era of intellectual ferment, events of marked consequence took place in the history of psychology. It was in the decade of the 1870s that the first handbook of experimental psychology appeared, followed soon by the founding of the first formal laboratory of experimental psychology. Both were the achievements of Wilhelm Wundt, ever since recognized as experimental psychology's great patron, though later barred from any role that might remotely resemble sainthood. Soon after the wave of "new" psychologists spread out from Wundt's laboratory, a series of intellectual revolutions largely erased from memory the content of Wundtian psychological theory.

Now that the movement set in motion by Wundt has come through its first century, it would seem fitting to mark the centenary by briefly turning back, reexamining psychology's historical foundations, and paying homage to the founding father. There is, however, another reason for review, being less ceremonial and clearly more interesting. To put it simply, the few current Wundt-scholars (and some do exist) are in fair agreement that Wundt as portrayed today in many texts and courses is largely fictional and often bears little resemblance to the actual historical figure (cf. Blumenthal, 1970; Bringmann, Balance, & Evans, 1975; Mischel, 1970).

Naturally, it might be suspected that the above radical statement is only the nit-picking of a few antiquarians obsessed with minor matters of interpretation. But alas, such is not the case. These are claims about the very fundamentals of Wundt's work, often asserting the opposite of what has been a standard description prevailing over much of the past century. Yet, if popular historical accounts of Wundt are in need of serious correction, then one might again ask whether Wundt still turns out to be irrelevant and of little interest. This article is addressed to that question, and its answers will, I suspect, contain some surprises for many readers.

There is another question that immediately follows upon these claims. It is, How could such historical misinterpretations have arisen? This is surely a fascinating question but one requiring separate treatment. For the moment merely take note that Wundtian anecdotes have long been passed down from author to author without worthy recourse to original sources, and, also, that it is common in intellectual history for later schools of thought to foster distortions and misinterpretations of earlier ones—psychology, of course, offering numerous opportunities. For now, let us examine the fundamentals of Wundt's psychology that have, for better or worse, been disguised or lost in the course of history's machinations.

WUNDT'S METHOD

The basic premise in Wundtian psychology is that the only certain reality is immediate experience. Proceeding from this premise, Wundt had accepted the following goals for all science: the construction of explanations of experience and the development of techniques for objectifying experience. By the latter, he meant that the scientist attempts to communicate and reproduce his experiences in others in standardized ways; thus it becomes possible to perform tests that lead to public agreement about phenomena and to agreement about their explanation. This was commonplace for Wundt and is found at the outset of many of his texts.

In the natural sciences, as Wundt continues, it is the attributes of experience derived from ex-

Blumenthal, A. L. (1975). A reappraisal of Wilhelm Wundt. *American Psychologist, 30,* 1081–1088.

ternal objects and energies that are subjected to tests, explanations, and public agreement. But in the case of psychology, it is the attributes of experience derived from the processes of the experiencing subject that are made the object of tests, explanations, and public agreement. These psychological entities include experienced memory and perceptual capacities, fluctuations of attention or alertness, ranges of our sensitivities, etc. In the jargon of today, we would without hesitation say "human information-processing capacities."

Yet it is this subtle division between the physical and the psychological sciences that has led to innumerable textbook treatments of Wundt as a mind-body dualist, and that is one of history's glaring distortions. For if you read Wundt, in almost any of his texts, you will discover that his rejection of mind-body dualism is as emphatic a statement on the matter as you are likely ever to encounter. He often said that psychology cannot be defined as the science of the mind because there are no objects called "minds" that are distinct from objects called "bodies," a scenario that appears repeatedly in his works.

Although physiologists and psychologists study one and the same organism, Wundt viewed them as analyzing and objectifying different experiences derived from different vantage points. This is now usually called the "double-aspect" resolution of the mind-body problem. And Wundt's use of the phrase "psychophysical parallelism" referred to this same view, though again it unfortunately led many later reviewers to the mind-body–dualism interpretation. Rather, it referred to the separate orientations of physiology and psychology where it is separate *methodologies,* in the sense of separate types of observations, that here run in parallel.

Another serious problem of misinterpretation concerns Wundt and *introspection.* Contrary to frequent descriptions, Wundt was not an introspectionist as that term is popularly applied today. The thrust behind his entire experimental program was the claim that progress in psychology had been slow because of reliance on casual, unsystematic introspection, which had led invariably to unresolvable debates. In several books and monographs (in particular, 1888 and 1907) Wundt argued that armchair introspection could in principle, never succeed, being a logical impossibility as a scientific technique. The 1907 monograph was a severe critique of the Würzburg psychologists for their return to an earlier style of unverifiable introspection.

Wundt promoted the cause of experimental psychology more through accomplishments in his laboratory than through polemics. From its outset, the Wundtian program followed the general conceptions of experimental science and the requirement that private experience be made public and replicable, in this case for the study of perception, attention, memory, etc. To be sure, there were some disagreements, conflicting data, and unsupported speculations in those days, just as there are today.

Wundt's adherence to the canons of experimental procedure was so strict that, in fact, it sharply limited his use of experiments in psychology. Thus, in the case of most "higher" mental processes such as language or concept formation, he felt that true experiments were not feasible. Instead, these topics must, he argued, be studied through techniques of historical and naturalistic observation and also of logical analysis. This Wundt did by examining the social-cultural products of human mental activity, making logical inferences about the underlying processes. In the case of language, for example, he went deeply into the technical study of linguistics (Blumenthal, 1970). So in these ways, a large part of Wundt's psychological work is not experimental.

WUNDT'S THEORETICAL SYSTEM

But so far these are methodological matters and do not speak to the essence of Wundt's psychological theory. What emerged as the paradigm psychological phenomenon in his theoretical system would now be described as selective volitional attention. It is why he identified his psychology as "voluntaristic" to distinguish it from other schools (see especially Wundt, 1896b). He did not use the label "structuralist" which was proffered and perpetuated by Titchener and James.

Mischel (1970) has recently surveyed Wundt's writings, detailing Wundt's grounding in volitional-motivational processes. Yet it was with apparent forceful impact on later historical interpretation that Titchener (1908) had given short shrift to this theme, at the very heart of Wundtian psychology, because of the overtones of continental idealist philosophy in notions of volition. Titchener's longest period of formal education came at Oxford, and not surprisingly he maintained certain biases toward the British empiricist-sensationist tradition, even though that tradition was anathema to Wundt's views, and more than any other topic the brunt of Wundt's polemical writings.

Without giving supportive citation, Boring (1950) states that Wundt had opposed the implication of an active volitional agent in psychology. But now Mischel (1970) with extensive citation has shown, on the contrary, that volition-motivation is a central, primary theme in Wundt's psychology. Briefly, that theme runs as follows: To explain a volitional act on the basis of its motives is different from the explanation of occurrences in the physical sciences, and "volitional activities are the type in terms of which all other psychological phenomena are to be construed" (Wundt, 1908, Vol. 3, p. 162).

Wundt's studies of volition, in turn, amounted to an elaborate analysis of selective and constructive attentional processes (often summarized under the term *apperception*), which he localized in the brain's frontal lobes. Other psychological processes (perceptions, thoughts, memories) are, according to Wundt, generally under the control of the central attentional process.

It is on this basis that Wundt claimed another point of separation between psychology and physics—a difference between psychological and physical causality (see especially, Wundt, 1894). In the case of physics, actions and events obey inviolable laws; but in the case of psychosocial phenomena, actions are *made* by an active agent with reference to rule systems.

Wundt acknowledged the principle of the conservation of energy and, consequently, the theoretical possibility of reducing psychological observations to physiological or physical descriptions. Still, he argued, these physical sciences would then describe the act of greeting a friend, eating an apple, or writing a poem in terms of the laws of mechanics or in terms of physiology. And no matter how fine-grained and complicated we make such descriptions, they are not useful as descriptions of psychological events. Those events need be described in terms of intentions and goals, according to Wundt, because the actions, or physical forces, for a given psychological event may take an infinite variety of physical forms. In one notable example, he argued that human language cannot be described adequately in terms of its physical shape or of the segmentation of utterances, but rather must be described as well in terms of the rules and intentions underlying speech. For the ways of expressing a thought in language are infinitely variable, and language is governed by creative rules rather than fixed laws (Wundt, 1900–1920).

MECHANISM OR ORGANISM?

These distinctions lead to a related and consistent theme in Wundt's writings concerning what he called "the false materialization of mental processes," which he found prevalent in other schools of psychology, especially associationism. His reactions against associationism were directed mostly at the form it had assumed in mid-19th-century Germany in Herbart's psychology.

Herbart, you may recall, had atomized mental processes into elemental ideas that became associated into compounds according to classical associationist descriptions. Wundt considered that approach to be a mere primitive analogy to systems of physical mechanics, and he argued at length that those systems teach little about the interrelations of psychological processes (Wundt, 1894). For those systems were oblivious to what he felt was the essential distinction between psychological and physical causality; they portrayed mental processes as if they were a "mere field of billiard balls" colliding and interacting with each other, where central control processes are lacking.

Boring's widely repeated assertion that Wundt turned to chemistry for his model seems clearly inaccurate to the serious reader of Wundt. However, the Wundtian mental-chemistry cliché did become popular among later textbook writers. Wundt did in his early years make brief, passing reference to J. S. Mill's use of a chemical analogy to describe certain perceptual processes, namely, that one cannot determine the quality of water (i.e., "wetness") from the separate qualities of oxygen and hydrogen. Similarly, the qualities of a perception are not directly given in its underlying elements.

But Wundt points out that this analogy does not go far enough, and by the end of the century he is describing it as a false analogy because the chemical synthesis is, in the final analysis, wholly determined by its elements while the psychological synthesis is "truly a new formation, not merely the result of a chemical-like formation." And, "J. S. Mill's discussion in which the mental formation is conceived as a 'psychic chemistry' leaves out its most significant aspect—the special creative character of psychic syntheses" (Wundt, 1902, p. 684). What the chemical analogy lacks is the independent, constructive, attentional process which in the psychological case is the source of the synthesis.

Wundt did, of course, write chapters on elementary sensory-perceptual processes and elemental affective processes, but with the emphasis on *process*. And he acknowledged that a major part of any scientific methodology involved analysis of a system into component processes. Further, he stressed that these elements were to be taken as hypothetical constructs. Such elemental processes would never actually be observed, he thought, in pure isolation but would always be aspects or features of larger images or configurations.

Here Wundt used the German word *Gebilde*. For a translation, the dictionary (*Cassell's*) gives us the following choices: either "creation," "product," "structure," "formation," "system," "organization," "image," "form," or "figure." But in the few English translations of Wundt, we find the word "compound," unfortunately again suggesting the analogy to chemistry. "Compound" is a conceivable choice, but in the context of Wundt's configurational system it seems not the best term. Another example: Wundt's "whole or unified mental impression" (*Gesamtvorstellung*) is unfortunately translated as "aggregate ideas."

In the following note in an obscure book, published in 1944, Wundt's own son, Max Wundt, rebutted the caricature of his father's work as a psychology of mental elements:

> One may follow the methodologically obvious principle of advancing from the simple to the complicated, indeed even employing the approach that would construct the mind from primitive mechanical elements (the so-called psychology of mental elements). In this case, however, method and phenomena can become grossly confused. . . . Whoever in particular ascribes to my father such a conception could not have read his books. In fact, he had formed his scientific views of mental processes in reaction against a true elementistic psychology, namely against that of Herbart, which was dominant in those days. (p. 15).

To confound matters further, the later movement toward holism in Gestalt psychology placed Wundt in a contrastive position and again portrayed him as an elementalist and associationist in ways not characteristic of his intentions. True, there is always a chapter titled "Associations" in Wundt's texts—but it is a far cry from the serial linkages of atomistic ideas found among many associationists. Wundt's "associations" are "structural integrations," "creative syntheses," "fusions," and "perceptual patternings."

Wundt's later students, including Sander, Krueger, and Volkelt, renamed their school *Ganzheit* psychology or roughly "holistic psychology," and throughout the 1920s and 1930s the old Wundtian institute at Leipzig was a center for theorists with a holistic bent. Wundt's journal, the *Psychologische Studien,* which had ceased publication upon his retirement, was then reactivated with the title, *Neue Psychologische Studien.* It was the central organ of the *Ganzheit* psychologists; however, its articles primarily followed Wundt's interests in the "higher" mental processes and hence were mostly nonexperimental investigations.

Werner (1948) has written that Wundt represented the halfway mark in the transition from Herbart's atomism to the Gestaltist's holism. But from the point of view of Wundt's voluntaristic psychology, the essential central control processes were of no more primacy to the Gestaltists than to Herbart—both conceived a rather passive organism, one that is controlled by external or independent forces such as the a priori self-organizing qualities of sensory fields. Both, in sharp contrast to Wundt, appealed to physics for models and theories.

MODERN RECONSTRUCTIONS

Now to describe Wundt's psychology in more detail, and to consider its present relevance, I want to outline some six current trends that could be viewed as reconstructions of Wundt's psychology in modern clothing:

First, Wundt's central emphasis on volitional processes bears noteworthy resemblance to the modern work on "cognitive control" as found, for example, in extensive research by Gardner, Klein, Holzman, and their associates (cf. Gardner, Holzman, Klein, Linton, & Spence, 1959). Both traditions used notions of different styles of attention deployment to explain a variety of perceptual and thought processes (sometimes even involving the same materials, e.g., the Müller-Lyer illusion).

The recent research, employing factor analyses of a variety of performance tasks, has determined two independent variables of cognitive control, which Gardner et al. call "field-articulation" and "scanning." These can be defined, as well, simply by substituting a similar description found in Wundt's psychology texts, as follows: First, in corresponding order, is Wundt's mental "clearness" process that concerns the focusing or emphasizing of a single item of experience. Wundt described this as "apperceptive synthesis" where variations from broad to narrow syntheses may occur. The second variable is a mental "distinctiveness" process which is the marking off of an item of experience from all others. Wundt described this as "apperceptive analysis," a relating and comparing function. The discovery and testing of nearly identical attention deployment factors in recent times occurred independently of the old Wundtian psychology. And too, the recent studies make frequent use of elaborate personality theories that were unavailable to Wundt.

Second, detailed comparisons have been made recently between the development of psycholinguistics in the 1960s and that of Wundtian psycholinguistics at the turn of the century (Blumenthal, 1970). Both the modern transformational grammarians after Chomsky and the Wundtian psycholinguists at the turn of the century trace their notions of language back to the same historical sources (e.g., to Humboldt). The psycholinguistic issues debated in the 1960s often parallel those debated at the turn of the century, such as the opposition between taxonomic and generative descriptions of language. Very briefly, Wundt's analysis of language usage depicts the transformation of simultaneous configurations of thought into sequential representations in language symbols by means of the scanning activities of attention (Wundt, 1900–1920, Vol. 1).

A *third* reconstruction concerns abnormal psychology. Among his students, the one who maintained the longest intellectual association with Wundt was the psychiatrist Emil Kraepelin (see Fischel, 1959). Kraepelin's (1919) attentional theory of schizophrenia is an application of Wundtian psychology, an explanation of schizophrenias as abnormalities of the attention deployment (apperception) process. It conceives certain abnormalities of behavior as resulting from flaws in the central control process that may take the form of either highly reduced attentional scanning, or highly erratic scanning, or extremes of attentional focusing. Kraepelin proposed that abnormalities in simple perceptual tests should show up in schizophrenic individuals corresponding to these particular control-process distortions.

The modern attentional theory of schizophrenia is a direct revival of the Kraepelinian analysis, as noted, for example, in an extensive review by Silverman (1964). As in the Kraepelinian descriptions, abnormalities of behavior result from disruptions of the central attentional processes where there is either highly reduced or highly erratic attentional scanning and focusing. And these mental changes, again, are indicated by divergent performances in simple perceptual tests.

Fourth is Wundt's three-factor theory of affect, which was developed by analogy to his formulations of multidimensional descriptions of certain areas of sensory experience. For the description of emotional experience, he used these three bipolar affective dimensions: *pleasant versus unpleasant, high arousal versus low arousal,* and *concentrated attention versus relaxed attention.* Wundt had adopted the first two dimensions from earlier writers on the topic of emotion. The third dimension reflects his characteristic emphasis on the process of attention.

Around the turn of the century, an intensive sequence of investigations to relate these dimensions to unique bodily response patterns did not meet with popular success. However, years later, when factor analysis became available, statistical studies of affective and attitudinal behavior again yielded factors that parallel those of Wundt rather closely (cf. Burt, 1950; Osgood, Suci, & Tannenbaum, 1957; Schlosberg, 1954; and several others reviewed by Strongman, 1973). Osgood's three dimensions are described as "good-bad," "active-passive," and "strong-weak." Schlosberg's dimensions are "pleasantness-unleasantness," "high-low activation," and "attention-rejection."

Emotions and affects held an important place in Wundt's system because they were postulated as the constituents of volition. Further, Wundt suggested that almost every experience (perception, thought, or memory) has an affective component. Thus, affect became the basis for his explanation of pattern recognition: a melody, for instance, produces a very similar emotional configuration as it is transformed to other keys or played on other instruments. Wundt speculated that affect was the by-product of the act of apperceptive synthesis, and as such it was always on the periphery of consciousness. That is, we can never focus our attention upon an emotion, but can only focus on objects or memories that produce an emotional aura in immediate experience.

Fifth, the study of selective attention has been at the core of much of the recent work on human information processing (e.g., Broadbent, 1958; Kahneman, 1973; Moray, 1970; Neisser, 1967). It is impossible here to relate this highly complex field to the early Wundtian psychology other than to note the prominence of attention in both and that the time variable is central to both. Space permits mention of only two examples:

The seminal investigations of Sperling (1960) concerning perceptual masking are one example. Sperling took direct inspiration from Wundt's 1899 monograph on the use of tachistoscopes in psychological research in which Wundt came to the following three conclusions about the perception of extremely brief stimuli: (1) the effective duration of a percept is not identical with the duration of the stimulus—but rather reflects the duration of a psychological process; (2) the relation between accuracy of a perception and stimulus duration depends on pre- and postexposure fields (which may induce what we now call masking); and (3) central processes, rather than peripheral sense organ aftereffects, determine these critical times. Wundt's observations spurred a body of early research, and those early data are now relevant to a large body of similar modern investigations.

Perhaps the most frequently employed technique in Wundt's laboratory was that of reaction-time measurement. This was the direct adoption of a program suggested earlier by Donders (1868–1869). Essentially, inferences were made about human information-processing capacities on the basis of measured performance times under systematically varied performance conditions. This program has now, in post-mid-20th century, been widely and successfully revived. It is well illustrated, for instance, in the seminal studies of Sternberg (1970) on the attentional scanning of immediate-memory images, in which Sternberg draws the relation between his work and the earlier Donders program.

For a *sixth* and final comparison, I must refer to what Wundt called his deepest interest, which resulted in a 10-volume work titled *Völkerpsychologie: Eine Untersuchung der Entwicklungsgestze von Sprache, Mythus, und Sitte*. An English version of this title could be *Cultural Psychology: An Investigation of the Developmental Laws of Language, Myth, and Morality.** Appearing from 1900 through 1920, this series contains two books on language, three on myth and religion, one on art, two on society, one on law, and one on culture and history. If there is a current work by another author that is conceptually close to these volumes, it is Werner's (1948) *Comparative Psychology of Mental Development,* today read in some circles of developmental psychologists.

Following Wundt, Werner described an *organismic* psychology that is in opposition to *mechanistic* psychologies. He also drew parallels, as did Wundt, between the development of individuals and of societies. And Werner acknowledged indebtedness to Wundt. But in Wundt's *Völkerpsychologie* there is, again, greater emphasis on volitional and attentional processes in the analysis of the development of human culture; he theorized that those central mental processes had emerged as the highest evolutionary development, and that they are the capacities that set men above other animals. It is the highly developed selective-attention capacities that, as he claimed, enabled mankind to make a consistent mental advance and to develop human culture. For without these capacities, men would forever be at the mercy of sporadic thoughts, memories, and perceptions.

WUNDT'S HISTORICAL CONTEXTS

Wundt was not a mere encyclopedist or compiler of volumes, contrary to many descriptions. It was typical of him, however, always to compare and to contrast his system with other schools of thought, ancient and modern. Perhaps in that sense he could be considered an encyclopedist. True, most of his works begin with a long recital of his antecedents and the antecedents of rival positions.

Wundt's motivation for scholarly productivity should not be surprising, considering the strong family traditions that lay behind him (and that went unrecognized by most historical writ-

* *Völkerpsychologie* has also been translated as "folk psychology," "psychology of peoples," and "ethnic psychology." Wundt quite deliberately avoided the terms *sociology* and *anthropology* because they were then heavily identified with the mid-19th-century positivism of Auguste Comte and related Anglo-French trends, which Wundt opposed. Some later writers on the history of psychology erroneously stated that the *Völkerpsychologie* is available in English translation. They apparently mistook a different and simpler one-volume work that E. Schaub (1916) translated as *Elements of Folk Psychology.*

ers). Recent researchers (Bringmann et al., 1975) claim that no other German intellectual has a family tree containing as many ancestors engaged in intellectual pursuits. On his father's side were historians, theologians, economists, and geographers. On his mother's side were natural scientists and physicians. Two of his ancestors had been rectors of the University of Heidelberg.

To conclude, I wish to draw an outline of the streams of history in which Wundt lived and worked. Historians have often defined a few broad, alternating cultural epochs in the 19th century. At some risk in using a much-abused word, one might call each a "zeitgeist"—a time that favored a particular cultural style. These periods begin with the dominant romanticism and idealism early in the century, largely a German-inspired ethos shared by Kant, Humboldt, Schopenhauer, Goethe, Hegel, and Fichte, to mention a few. In that era, philosophy, science, religion, and art were often combined into something called "nature-philosophy." Such an integration was exemplified in the pantheistic writings of Gustav Fechner, an exotic latecomer to the romantic movement and an important source of inspiration for Wundt. (In several ways, Wundt's 10-volume *Völkerpsychologie* reflects the spirit of the old nature-philosophy.)

Around the mid-19th century, a positivist and materialist movement grew dominant by vigorously rejecting the previous idealism. There then appeared the influential Berlin Physical Society, the mechanistic psychology of Herbart, the behavioristic linguistics of the so-called *Junggrammatiker* linguists, and Comtean positivist sociology, among other examples across the disciplines. At the peak of this movement, academicians became methodology conscious to the extreme. The taxonomic methods of biology were imported into the social sciences. There was often a downgrading of "mentalism" in favor of "physicalism" and "environmentalism."

Then, toward the end of the 19th century came a resurgence of the romanticist-idealist outlook, particularly in continental Europe. It has been described either as neoromanticism, neoidealism, or neo-Kantianism. H. Stuart Hughes (1958) has provided a summarization in his influential book, *Consciousness and Society: The Reorientation of European Social Thought, 1890–1930*. At around the time of World War I, this movement went into sharp decline, being displaced by a rebirth and rise in popularity of positivism and behaviorism which subsequently dominated many intellectual circles well into the 20th century.

Wundt's psychology rose and fell with the late-19th-century neoidealism. His core emphasis on volition and apperception comes straight from the earlier German idealist philosophy. It is not surprising that this should be so, for as a youth he was deeply inspired by the romanticist-idealist literature and nature-philosophy (Wundt, 1920). Certainly his intellectual development also included the influence of mid-19th-century positivism, especially in his promotion of experimental psychology. Yet, during that positivist period, he had remained largely unrecognized as a psychological theorist. The popular success of his theoretical system seems coordinated with the beginnings of neoidealist reorientations, and his system became fully formed in the *Grundriss* of 1896 (and later editions; Wundt, 1896a).

But unfortuntately for Wundt, zeitgeist support disappeared rapidly in the early 20th century; definitions of psychology were then changing, and his works were soon meaningless to a newer generation. Few, especially outside Germany, understood any more what the old term *apperception* had once referred to.

Strange as it may seem, Wundt may be more easily understood today than he could have been just a few years ago. This is because of the current milieu of modern cognitive psychology and of the recent research on human information processing. Yet this new understanding does require serious study of Wundt in the original German. Most current textbook summaries of Wundt useable!

grew out of a time when early behaviorist and positivist movements were eager to encourage a break with the past, hence giving understandably little effort to careful description of the enormous body of writings they were discarding. Simplistic historical accounts resulted.

Today much of the history of Wundt remains to be told, both of his personal development and of his psychological system. It is well worth telling.

REFERENCES

Blumenthal, A. L. *Language and psychology: Historical aspects of psycholinguistics.* New York: Wiley, 1970.

Boring, E. G. *A history of experimental psychology.* New York: Appleton-Century-Crofts, 1950.

Bringmann, W. G., Balance, W., & Evans, R. B. Wilhelm Wundt 1832–1920: A biographical sketch. *Journal of the History of the Behavioral Sciences,* 1975, *11,* 287–297.

Broadbent, D. *Perception and communication.* New York: Pergamon, 1958.

Burt, C. The factorial study of emotions. In M. Reymert (Ed.), *Feelings and emotions.* New York: McGraw-Hill, 1950.

Donders, F. Over de snelheid van psychische processen. *Tweede Reeks,* 1868–1869, II, 92–120. (Trans. by W. Koster as On the speed of mental processes, In *Acta Psychologica,* 1969, *30,* 412–431.)

Fischel, W. Wilhelm Wundt und Emil Kraepelin. *Karl Marx Universität Leipzig, Beiträge zur Universität Geschichte,* 1959, *1.*

Gardner, R. W., Holzman, P. S., Klein, G. S., Linton, H., & Spence, D. P. Cognitive control: A study of individual consistencies in cognitive behavior. *Psychological Issues,* 1959, Monograph 4.

Hughes, H. S. *Consciousness and society: The reorientation of European social thought, 1890–1930.* New York: Knopf, 1958.

Kahneman, D. *Attention and effort.* Englewood Cliffs, N.J.: Prentice-Hall, 1973.

Kraepelin, E. *Dementia praecox and paraphrenia* (Trans. by M. Barclay from selected writings of Kraepelin). Chicago: Chicago Medical Book, 1919.

Mischel, T. Wundt and the conceptual foundations of psychology. *Philosophical and Phenomenological Research,* 1970, *31,* 1–26.

Moray, N. *Attention.* New York: Academic Press, 1970.

Neisser, U. *Cognitive psychology.* New York: Appleton-Century-Crofts, 1967.

Osgood, C., Suci, G., & Tannenbaum, P. *The measurement of meaning.* Urbana: University of Illinois Press, 1957.

Schlosberg, H. Three dimensions of emotion. *Psychological Review,* 1954, *61,* 81–88.

Silverman, J. The problem of attention in research and theory in schizophrenia. *Psychological Review,* 1964, *71,* 352–379.

Sperling, G. The information available in brief visual presentations. *Psychological Monographs,* 1960, *74* (11, Whole No. 498).

Sternberg, S. Memory-scanning: Mental processes revealed by reaction-time experiments. In J. Antrobus (Ed.), *Cognition and affect.* Boston: Little, Brown, 1970.

Strongman, K. T. *The psychology of emotion.* New York: Wiley, 1973.

Titchener, E. B. *The psychology of feeling and attention.* New York: Macmillan, 1908.

Werner, H. *The comparative psychology of mental development.* New York: Science Editions, 1948.

Wundt, M. *Die Wurzeln der deutschen Philosphie in Stamm und Rasse.* Berlin: Junker and Dunnhaupt, 1944.

Wundt, W. Selbstbeobachtung und innere Wahrnehmung. *Philosophische Studien,* 1888, *4,* 292–309.

Wundt, W. Ueber psychische Kausalität und das Prinzip des psychophysichen Parallelismus. *Philosophische Studien,* 1894, *10,* 1–124.

Wundt, W. *Grundriss der Psychologie.* Leipzig: Engelmann, 1896 (10th ed., 1911). (Trans. by C. Judd of 1896 and 1907 editions as *Outlines of psychology.*) (a)

Wundt, W. Ueber die Definition der Psychologie. *Philosophische Studien, 1*896, *12,* 1–66 (b)

Wundt, W. Zur Kritik tachistokopischer Versuche. *Philosophische Studien,* 1899, *15,* 287–317.

Wundt, W. *Völkerpsychologie: Eine Untersuchung der Entwicklungsgesetze von Sprache, Mythus, und Sitte* (10 vols.). Leipzig: Engelmann, 1900–1920.

Wundt, W. *Grundzüge der physiologischen Psychologie* (Vol. 2). Leipzig: Engelmann, 1902 (5th ed.).

Wundt, W. Ueber Ausfrageexperimente und ueber Methoden zur Psychologie des Denkens. *Psychologische Studien,* 1907, *3,* 301–360.

Wundt, W. *Logik* (3 vols.). Leipzig: Engelmann, 1908.

Wundt, W. *Erlebtes und Erkanntes.* Stuttgart: Krohner, 1920.

CHAPTER 6

E. B. TITCHENER AND STRUCTURALISM

The previous chapter noted that nearly a quarter of Wundt's doctoral students in psychology were from North America. These psychologists returned to transform American psychology from philosophical discourse to an experimental science, and they did so by founding psychology laboratories at the University of Pennsylvania (1887), University of Nebraska (1889), Columbia University (1890), Catholic University (1891), Cornell University (1891), Harvard University (1891), Yale University (1892), Stanford University (1893), University of Minnesota (1894), Smith College (1895), University of California (1896), Wesleyan University (1897), New York University (1900), and Northwestern University (1900). Although these new laboratories were founded by Wundt's students, who used the various scientific methods they had learned in their study at Leipzig, the brand of psychology practiced at those universities was not readily identified with Wundt's conceptual position. Instead, a very narrow version of Wundtian psychology in the United States was largely, but not exclusively, represented in the psychology of his British student, Edward Bradford Titchener (1867–1927), who arrived at Cornell University in Ithaca, New York, in 1892.

The laboratory at Cornell had been founded one year earlier, as noted above, by another of Wundt's students, Frank Angell, who left after a year to begin a similar laboratory at Stanford University. Titchener began to build his laboratory in the Leipzig tradition and soon established himself as one of the foremost psychologists in the United States. In the thirty-five years of his professional career, he wrote more than two hundred articles and books and trained more than fifty doctoral students in his brand of psychology. Many of those students would found laboratories of their own (for example, Margaret Floy Washburn at Vassar College, and Walter B. Pillsbury at the University of Michigan).

Titchener would name his system of psychology *structuralism* because of its emphasis on discovering the elemental structure of consciousness. Conceptually, that focus of his system was similar to one of the goals of Wundtian psychology although Wundt never used the label *structuralism* to refer to his psychology. Indeed, Wundt was not the atomist that most histories of psychology have described him to be (recall the selection from Wundt in the previous chapter and the article by Blumenthal in that same chapter). For the past sixty years, textbooks on the history of psychology have been treating the psychological systems of Wundt and Titchener as if they were the same, often discussing them together in a chapter entitled "Structuralism." Titchener may have contributed to that confusion, as some authors have suggested, by his selective translations of Wundt's writings. Indeed, most of the Wundt read by American psychologists in the early part of the twentieth century was the Wundt that was translated by Titchener and his colleagues.

Before he went to Leipzig, Titchener was schooled at Oxford University in the traditions of British associationism. His extremely reductionistic approach to the study of consciousness can be traced to those influences. In essence, his system of psychology represented only the bottom level of Wundtian psychology in a hierarchy that sought to explain mental processes fully. For Wundt, such explanation required an understanding of the processes of apperception and creative synthesis. He recognized that there was more to consciousness than an aggregate of sensory and emotional elements. The previous chapter includes some of Wundt's (1896) thoughts on these issues:

> The actual contents of psychical experience always consist of various combinations of sensational and affective elements, so that the specific character of a given psychical process depends for the most part, not on the nature of its elements, so much as on their union into a composite psychical compound. (p. 33)

Wundt studied psychical elements as part of his systematic approach to psychology, but he recognized the importance of higher-order processes and wrote much about their role in understanding consciousness. There is a more holistic nature to his system, a fact recognized by his students who succeeded him at Leipzig, who named their psychology *Ganzheit psychology,* roughly translated as holistic psychology. Do not misread these comments to mean that Wundt was a Gestalt psychologist (see Chapter 14). He was not; but his system had more in common with the Gestalt approach than has been traditionally believed.

As indicated earlier, Titchener defined his psychology in the narrowest of terms. He mostly rejected child psychology, abnormal psychology, and any studies on animals. His experimental science was built largely on *introspection,* a technique that proved to be of little use in those areas of study. It was narrower still, in comparison to Wundt, because of Titchener's adherence to positivism, for he agreed with Auguste Comte that unobservable processes had no place in science. Whereas Wundt sought to explain consciousness by invoking some hypothetical mental processes, Titchener avoided the mentalistic dilemma by focusing his efforts on a purely descriptive science.

But American psychology was not satisfied with description. Influenced by the pragmatism of Charles S. Peirce and John Dewey, and the evolutionary ideas of Charles Darwin, many American psychologists were asking questions about the *why* of consciousness. As Rand B. Evans (1972) has described it, these other psychologists were interested in the questions of what consciousness *is for,* whereas Titchener was interested in what consciousness *is*. It was this difference in approach that led Titchener to label the opposition's views as *functionalism* (see Chapter 9) because of its emphasis on the functions of consciousness, as contrasted to his emphasis on the structure of consciousness.

Cornell became the stronghold for this descriptive psychology, protecting its purity from the infidels that made up most of American psychology. Titchener's disagreements led him to abandon the American Psychological Association (founded in 1892), to which most of his colleagues belonged, and to form his own organization in 1904, usually referred to as "The Experimentalists" or "Titchener's Experimentalists." The annual meetings of this group were essentially by invitation only. It was another attempt by Titchener to deal with psychology exclusively on his own terms.

Few of Titchener's students became disciples although many continued to espouse the appropriate ideas in his presence (E. G. Boring may have been his most loyal student). When Titchener died of a brain tumor at age 60, structuralism died with him. His system of psychology is not a part of contemporary psychology; his many research articles, so carefully conceived and executed, are no longer cited in the literature. Current references to him are almost always of a historical nature. But these statements are not meant to imply that his legacy is nonexistent. He was a model scientist when psychology needed such models to break its bonds with philosophy. That contribution was manifested in several ways, but is nowhere more evident than in the success of Titchener's four volumes of *Experimental Psychology*.

Those books were published between 1901 and 1905. Two were for the psychology instructor and two for the student. Two volumes dealt with quantitative studies, and two focused on qualitative studies. Collectively they were known as "The Manuals" or "Titchener's Manuals." And they were used to train an entire generation of American psychology students, not just those at Cornell, in the methods of this new science. Titchener was an excellent scientist who modeled and communicated the integrity of scientific investigation better than any psychologist of his day. His manuals certainly rank among the most important books in the history of psychology. Oswald Külpe, a psychologist who frequently battled Titchener on theoretical grounds, called Titchener's *Experimental Psychology* "the most erudite psychological work in the English language" (Boring, 1950, p. 413).

THE READINGS

The initial selection in this chapter is from Titchener's *Text-book of Psychology,* which he published in 1910. It begins with a discussion of Titchener's distinction between mind and consciousness and continues with a discussion of the method of psychology (introspection) and the scope of psychology.

In this chapter, two selections are written by historians of psychology. The first, by Thomas H. Leahey, a psychologist at Virginia Commonwealth University, compares the psychologies of Wundt and Titchener, noting the frequent mistaking of Titchener as a clone of Wundt and the reasons for such mistakes. In the years since Leahey wrote this article, textbooks have improved markedly in their descriptions of the differences in these two men. Still, the myth that "Titchener was merely Wundt in America" appears in print with dismaying frequency, especially in introductory psychology textbooks. So clearly Leahey's lesson is still needed.

The second selection, by Laurel Furumoto of Wellesley College, recounts the history of Titchener's organization, the Experimentalists, mentioned earlier. Furumoto's account is excellent narrative history, grounded in an exhaustive search of archival materials and a deep understanding of the social and academic structures from which the exclusionary organization developed. It describes Titchener as a man possessed by his desire to control experimental psychology and obsessed with his determination to keep his private club free of women. From the initial meeting in 1904 until his death in 1927, Titchener succeeded in keeping women experimental psychologists from attending these important meetings. In doing so, Furumoto (1988) notes that he deprived women "of establishing collegial ties and of being part of an informal communication network, essential for scientific research" (pp. 94–95). And, she adds, "Experimental psychology, in turn, was deprived of women's participation, contributions, and point of view, as Titchener's discriminatory policy effectively relegated them to the periphery of the field" (p. 95). Together, these two articles contribute much to our understanding of Titchener as a psychologist and as a man.

REFERENCES

Boring, E. G. (1950). *A history of experimental psychology* (2nd ed.). New York: Appleton-Century-Crofts.

Evans, R. B. (1972). Titchener and his lost system. *Journal of the History of the Behavioral Sciences, 8,* 168–180.

Furumoto, L. (1988). Shared knowledge: The Experimentalists, 1904–1929. In J. G. Morawski (Ed.), *The rise of experimentation in American psychology,* (pp. 94–113). New Haven, CT: Yale University Press.

Wundt, W. (1896). *Outlines of psychology.* New York: Gustav Sechert.

The Method and Scope of Psychology

Edward Bradford Titchener

§5. MENTAL PROCESS, CONSCIOUSNESS AND MIND

The most striking fact about the world of human experience is the fact of change. Nothing stands still; everything goes on. The sun will someday lose its heat; the eternal hills are, little by little, breaking up and wearing away. Whatever we observe, and from whatever standpoint we observe it, we find process, occurrence; nowhere is there permanence or stability. Mankind, it is true, has sought to arrest this flux, and to give stability to the world of experience, by assuming two permanent substances, matter and mind: the occurrences of the physical world are then supposed to be manifestations of matter, and the occurrences of the mental world to be manifestations of mind. Such an hypothesis may be of value at a certain stage of human thought; but every hypothesis that does not accord with the facts must, sooner or later, be given up. Physicists are therefore giving up the hypothesis of an unchanging, substantial matter, and psychologists are giving up the hypothesis of an unchanging, substantial mind. Stable objects and substantial things belong, not to the world of science, physical or psychological, but only to the world of common sense.

We have defined mind as the sum-total of human experience considered as dependent upon the experiencing person. We have said, further, that the phrase 'experiencing person' means the living body, the organised individual; and we have hinted that, for psychological purposes, the living body may be reduced to the nervous system and its attachments. Mind thus becomes the sum-total of human experience considered as dependent upon a nervous system. And since human experience is always process, occurrence, and the dependent aspect of human experience is its mental aspect, we may say, more shortly, that mind is the sum-total of mental processes. All these words are significant. 'Sum total' implies that we are concerned with the whole world of experience, not with a limited portion of it; 'mental' implies that we are concerned with experience under its dependent aspect, as conditioned by a nervous system; and 'processes' implies that our subject-matter is a stream, a perpetual flux, and not a collection of unchanging objects.

From Titchener, E. B. (1910). *A textbook of psychology*. New York: Macmillan, pp. 15–30.

It is not easy, even with the best will possible, to shift from the common-sense to the scientific view of mind; the change cannot be made all in a moment. We are to regard mind as a stream of processes? But mind is personal, my mind; and my personality continues throughout my life. The experiencing person is only the bodily organism? But, again, experience is personal, the experience of a permanent self. Mind is spatial, just as matter is? But mind is invisible, intangible; it is not here or there, square or round.

These objections cannot be finally met until we have gone some distance into psychology, and can see how the scientific view of mind works out. Even now, however, they will weaken as you look at them. Face that question of personality. Is your life, as a matter of fact, always personal? Do you not, time and again, forget yourself, lose yourself, disregard yourself, neglect yourself, contradict yourself, in a very literal sense? Surely, the mental life is only intermittently personal. And is your personality, when it is realised, unchanging? Are you the same self in childhood and manhood, in your working and in your playing moods, when you are on your best behaviour and when you are freed from restraint? Surely, the self-experience is not only intermittent, but also composed, at different times, of very different factors. As to the other question: mind is, of course, invisible, because sight is mind; and mind is intangible, because touch is mind. Sight-experience and touch-experience are dependent upon the experiencing person. But common sense itself bears witness, against its own belief, to the fact that mind is spatial: we speak, and speak correctly, of an idea in our head, a pain in our foot. And if the idea is the idea of a circle seen in the mind's eye, it is round; and if it is the visual idea of a square, it is square.

Consciousness, as reference to any dictionary will show, is a term that has many meanings. Here it is, perhaps, enough to distinguish two principal uses of the word.

In its first sense, consciousness means the mind's awareness of its own processes. Just as, from the common-sense point of view, mind is that inner self which thinks, remembers, chooses, reasons, directs the movements of the body, so is consciousness the inner knowledge of this thought and government. You are conscious of the correctness of your answer to an examination question, of the awkwardness of your movements, of the purity of your motives. Consciousness is thus something more than mind; it is "the perception of what passes in a man's own mind";[1] it is "the immediate knowledge which the mind has of its sensations and thoughts."[2]

In its second sense, consciousness is identified with mind and 'conscious' with 'mental.' So long as mental processes are going on, consciousness is present; as soon as mental processes are in abeyance, unconsciousness sets in. "To say I am conscious of a feeling, is merely to say that I feel it. To have a feeling is to be conscious; and to be conscious is to have a feeling. To be conscious of the prick of the pin, is merely to have the sensation. And though I have these various modes of naming my sensation, by saying, I feel the prick of a pin, I feel the pain of a prick, I have the sensation of a prick, I have the feeling of a prick, I am conscious of the feeling; the thing named in all these various ways is one and the same."[3]

The first of these definitions we must reject. It is not only unnecessary, but it is also misleading, to speak of consciousness as the mind's awareness of itself. The usage is unnecessary, because, as we shall see later, this awareness is a matter of observation of the same general kind as observation of the external world; it is misleading, because it suggests that mind is a personal being, instead of a stream of processes. We shall therefore take mind and consciousness to mean the same thing. But as we have the two different words, and it is convenient to make some distinction between them, we shall speak of mind when we mean the sum-total of mental processes occurring in the life-time of an individual, and we shall speak of consciousness when we mean the sum-total of mental processes occurring *now*, at any given 'present' time. Consciousness will thus be a section, a division, of the mind-stream. This distinction is, indeed, already made in common speech: when we say that a man has 'lost consciousness,' we mean that the lapse is temporary, that the mental life will shortly be resumed; when we say that a man has 'lost his mind,' we mean—not, it is true, that mind has altogether disappeared, but certainly that the derangement is permanent and chronic.

While, therefore, the subject-matter of psychology is mind, the direct object of psychological study is always a consciousness. In strictness, we can never observe the same consciousness twice over; the stream of mind flows on, never to return. Practically, we can observe a particular consciousness as often as we wish, since mental processes group themselves in the same way, show the same pattern of arrangement, whenever the organism is placed under the same circumstances. Yesterday's high tide will never recur, and yesterday's consciousness will never recur; but we have a science of psychology, as we have a science of oceanography.

§6. THE METHOD OF PSYCHOLOGY

Scientific method may be summed up in the single word 'observation'; the only way to work in science is to observe those phenomena which form the subject-matter of science. And observation implies two things: attention to the phenomena, and record of the phenomena; that is, clear and vivid experience, and an account of the experience in words or formulas.

In order to secure clear experience and accurate report, science has recourse to experiment. An experiment is an observation that can be repeated, isolated and varied. The more frequently you can *repeat* an observation, the more likely are you to see clearly what is there and to describe accurately what you have seen. The more strictly you can *isolate* an observation, the easier does your task of observation become, and the less danger is there of your being led astray by irrelevant circumstances, or of placing emphasis on the wrong point. The more widely you can *vary* an observation, the more clearly will the uniformity of experience stand out, and the better is your chance of discovering laws. All experimental appliances, all laboratories and instruments, are provided and devised with this one end in view: that the student shall be able to repeat, isolate and vary his observations.

The method of psychology, then, is observation. To distinguish it from the observation of physical science, which is inspection, a looking-at, psychological observation has been termed introspection, a looking-within. But this difference of name must not blind us to the essential likeness of the methods. Let us take some typical instances.

We may begin with two very simple cases. (1) Suppose that you are shown two paper discs: the one of an uniform violet, the other composed half of red and half of blue. If this second disc is rapidly rotated, the red and blue will mix, as we say, and you will see a certain blue-red, that is, a kind of violet. Your problem is, so to adjust the proportions of red and blue in the second disc that the resulting violet exactly matches the violet of the first disc. You may repeat this set of observations as often as you like; you may isolate the observations by working in a room that is free from other, possibly disturbing colours; you may vary the observations by working to equality of the violets first from a two-colour disc that is distinctly too blue, and secondly from a disc that is distinctly too red. (2) Suppose, again, that the chord *c-e-g* is struck, and that you are asked to say how many tones it contains. You may repeat this observation; you may isolate it, by working in a quiet room; you may vary it, by having the chord struck at different parts of the scale, in different octaves.

It is clear that, in these instances, there is practically no difference between introspection and inspection. You are using the same method that you would use for counting the swings of a pendulum, or taking readings from a galvanometer scale, in the physical laboratory. There is a difference in subject-matter: the colours and the tones are dependent, not independent experiences: but the method is essentially the same.

Now let us take some cases in which the material of introspection is more complex. (1) Suppose that a word is called out to you, and that you are asked to observe the effect which this stimulus produces upon consciousness: how the word affects you, what ideas it calls up, and so forth. The observation may be repeated; it may be isolated,—you may be seated in a dark and silent room, free from disturbances; and it may be varied,—different words may be called out, the word may be flashed upon a screen instead of spoken, etc. Here, however, there seems to be a difference between introspection and inspection. The observer who is watching the course of a chemical reaction, or the movements of some microscopical creature, can jot down from moment to moment the different phases of the observed phenomenon. But if you try to report the changes in consciousness, while these changes are in progress, you interfere with consciousness; your translation of the mental experience into words introduces new factors into that experience itself. (2) Suppose, again, that you are observing a feeling or an emotion: a feeling of disappointment or annoyance, an emotion of anger or chagrin. Experimental control is still possible; situations may be arranged, in the psychological laboratory, such that these feelings may be repeated, isolated and varied. But your observation of them interferes, even more seriously than before, with the course of consciousness. Cool consideration of an emotion is fatal to its very existence; your anger disappears, your disappointment evaporates, as you examine it.

To overcome this difficulty of the introspective method, students of psychology are usually recommended to delay their observation until the process to be described has run its course, and then to call it back and describe it from memory. Introspection thus becomes retrospection; introspective examination becomes *post mortem* examination. The rule is, no doubt, a good one for the beginner; and there are cases in which even the experienced psychologist will be wise to follow it. But it is by no means universal. For we must remember (*a*) that the observations in question may be repeated. There is, then, no reason why the observer to whom the word is called out, or in whom the emotion is set up, should not report at once upon the first stage of his experience: upon the immediate effect of the word, upon the beginnings of the emotive process. It is true that this report interrupts the observation. But, after the first stage has been accurately described, further observations may be taken, and the second, third and following stages similarly described; so that presently a complete report upon the whole experience is obtained. There is, in theory, some danger that the stages become artificially separated; consciousness is a flow, a process, and if we divide it up we run the risk of missing certain intermediate links. In practice, however, this danger has proved to be very small; and we may always have recourse to retrospection, and compare our partial results with our memory of the unbroken experience. Moreover, (*b*) the practised observer get into an introspective habit, has the introspective attitude ingrained in his system; so that it is possible for him, not only to take mental notes while the observation is in progress, without interfering with consciousness, but even to jot down written notes, as the histologist does while his eye is still held to the ocular of the microscope.

In principle, then, introspection is very like inspection. The objects of observation are different; they are objects of dependent, not of independent experience; they are likely to be transient, elusive, slippery. Sometimes they refuse to be observed while they are in passage; they must be preserved in memory, as a delicate tissue is preserved in hardening fluid, before they can be examined. And the standpoint of the observer is different; it is the standpoint of human life and of human interest, not of detachment and aloofness. But, in general, the method of psychology is much the same as the method of physics.

It must not be forgotten that, while the method of the physical and the psychological sciences is substantially the same, the subject-matter of these sciences is as different as it can well be. Ultimately, as we have seen, the subject-matter of all the sciences is the world of human experience; but we have also seen that the aspect of experience treated by physics is radically different from the aspect treated by psychology. The likeness of method may tempt us to slip from the one aspect to the other, as when a textbook of physics contains a chapter on vision and the sense of colour, or a text-book of physiology contains paragraphs on delusions of judgement; but this confusion of subject-matter must inevitably lead to confusion of thought. Since all the sciences are concerned with the one world of human experience, it is natural that scientific method, to whatever aspect of experience it is applied, should be in principle the same. On the other hand, when we have decided to examine some particular aspect of experience, it is necessary that we hold fast to that aspect, and do not shift our point of view as the enquiry proceeds. Hence it is a great advantage that we have the two terms, introspection and inspection, to denote observation taken from the different standpoints of psychology and of physics. The use of the word introspection is a constant reminder that we are working in psychology, that we are observing the dependent aspect of the world of experience.

Observation, as we said above, implies two things: attention to the phenomena, and record of the phenomena. The attention must be held at the highest possible degree of concentration; the record must be photographically accurate. Observation is, therefore, both difficult and fatiguing; and introspection is, on the whole, more difficult and more fatiguing than inspection. To secure reliable results, we must be strictly impartial and unprejudiced, facing the facts as they come, ready to accept them as they are, not trying to fit them to any preconceived theory; and we must work only when our general disposition is favourable, when we are fresh and in good health, at ease in our surroundings, free from outside worry and anxiety. If these rules are not followed, no amount of experimenting will help us. The observer in the psychological laboratory is placed under the best possible external conditions; the room in which he works is fitted up and arranged in such a way that the observation may be repeated, that the process to be observed may stand out clearly upon the background of consciousness, and that the factors in the process may be separately varied. But all this care is of no avail, unless the observer himself comes to the work in an even frame of mind, gives it his full attention, and is able adequately to translate his experience into words.

§ 7. THE SCOPE OF PSYCHOLOGY

If mind is the sum-total of human experience considered as dependent upon the experiencing person, it follows that each one of us can have direct acquaintance only with a single mind, namely, with his own. We are concerned in psychology with the whole world of human experience; but we are concerned with it solely under its dependent aspect, as conditioned by a nervous system; and a nervous system is a particular thing, possessed by a particular individual. In strictness, therefore, it is only his own mind, the experience dependent upon his own nervous system, that each of us knows at first-hand; it is only to this limited and individual subject-matter that the method of experimental introspection can be directly applied. How, then, is a scientific psychology possible? How can psychology be anything more than a body of personal beliefs and individual opinions?

The difficulty is more apparent than real. We have every reason to believe, not only in general that our neighbours have minds like our own, that is, are able like ourselves to view experience in its dependent aspect, but also in detail that human minds resemble one another precisely as human bodies do. Within a given race there is much apparent diversity of outward form: differences in height and figure, in colour of hair and eyes, in shape of nose and mouth. We notice these differences, because we are obliged in everyday life to distinguish the persons with whom we come in contact. But the resemblances are more fundamental than the differences. If we have recourse to exact measurements, we find that there is in every case a certain standard or type to which the individual more or less closely conforms and about which all the individuals are more or less closely grouped. And even without measurement we have evidence to the same effect: strangers see family likenesses which the members of the family cannot themselves detect, and the units in a crowd of aliens, Chinese or Negroes, look bewilderingly alike.

Now all of our main social institutions rest upon the assumption that the individuals of whom society is composed possess minds, and possess minds that are of the same sort. Language, religion, law and custom,—they one and all rest upon this assumption, and they one and all bear testimony that the assumption is well grounded. Would a man invent language in order to talk to himself? Language implies that there are more minds than one. And would the use of a common speech be possible if minds were not essentially alike? Men differ in their command of language, as they differ in complexion, or in liability to disease; but the general use of language testifies to a fundamental likeness of mental constitution in us all.

Hence the psychologist is fully justified in believing that other men have minds of the same kind as his own, and in basing psychology upon the introspective reports furnished by a number of different observers. These reports show, in point of fact, just what we should expect them to show: a fundamental agreement, and a great variety of detail,—the mental differences grouping themselves, as we have seen that physical differences group themselves, about a central type or standard.

If, however, we attribute minds to other human beings, we have no right to deny them to the higher animals. These animals are provided with a nervous system of the same pattern as ours, and their conduct or behaviour, under circumstances that would arouse certain feelings in us, often seems to express, quite definitely, similar feelings in them. Surely we must grant that the highest vertebrates, mammals and birds, have minds. But the lower vertebrates, fishes and reptiles and amphibia, possess a nervous system of the same order, although of simpler construction. And many of the invertebrates, insects and spiders and crustaceans, show a fairly high degree of nervous development. Indeed, it is difficult to limit mind to the animals that possess even a rudimentary nervous system; for the creatures that rank still lower in the scale of life manage to do, without a nervous system, practically everything that their superiors do by its assistance. The range of mind thus appears to be as wide as the range of animal life.

The plants, on the other hand, appear to be mindless. Many of them are endowed with what we may term sense-organs, that is, organs differentiated to receive certain forms of stimulus, pressure, impact, light, etc. These organs are analogous in structure to the sense-organs of the lower animal organisms: thus, plant "eyes" have been found, which closely resemble rudimentary animal eyes, and which—if they belonged to animals—might mediate the perception of light: so that the development of the plant-world has evidently been governed by the same general laws of adaptation to environment that have been at work in the animal kingdom. But we have no evidence of plant-consciousness.

Just as the scope of psychology extends beyond man to the animals, so does it extend from the individual man to groups of men, to societies. The subject-matter of psychology is human experience considered as dependent upon the individual. But since the individuals of the same race and epoch are organised in much the same way, and since they live together in a society where their conduct affects and is affected by the conduct of others, their view of experience under its dependent aspect naturally becomes, in certain main features, a common or general view; and this common view is embodied in those social institutions to which we have referred above,—in language, religion, law and custom. There is no such thing as a collective mind, or a national mind, or a social mind, if we mean by mind some immaterial being; but there is a collective mind, if we mean by it the sum-total of human experience considered as dependent upon a social group of similar individuals. The study of the collective mind gives us a psychology of language, a psychology of myth, a psychology of custom, etc.; it also gives us a differential psychology of the Latin mind, of the Anglo-Saxon mind, of the Oriental mind, etc.

And this is not all: the scope of psychology extends, still further, from the normal to the abnormal mind. Life, as we know, need not be either complete or completely healthy life. The living organism may show defect, the lack of a limb or of a sense-organ; and it may show disorder and disease, a temporary or a permanent lapse from health. So it is with mind. The consciousnesses of those who are born deaf or blind are defective; they lack certain sensations and images that are normally present. In dreaming and the hypnotic state, during intoxication, after prolonged sleeplessness or severe strain of any kind, we have illustrations of temporary mental derangement. And the various forms of insanity—mania, melancholia, dementia—are forms of permanent mental disorder.

Derangement of the social mind may be studied in the various panics, fads, epidemics of speculation, of false belief, etc., which occur from time to time even in the most highly civilised societies. The mob consciousness stands to a healthy social consciousness very much as dreaming to the waking life. Permanent disorder of the social mind means the downfall of society.

All these various fields of psychology may be cultivated for their own sake, on account of their intrinsic interest and value; they must, indeed, be so cultivated, if psychology is to progress. At the same time, their facts and laws often throw light upon the problems of normal human psychology. Suppose, for instance, that a man, blind from his birth, is rendered able to see by a surgical operation. He must learn to use his eyes, as a child learns to walk. And the gradual perfecting of his vision, the mistakes and confusions to which he is liable, all the details of his visual education, form a storehouse of facts upon which the psychologist can draw when he seeks to illustrate the development of the perception of space in the normal mind,—the manner in which we come to judge of the distance of objects from ourselves and from one another, of their direction, and of their size and shape. Instructive, also, are those forms of mental unsoundness which consist in the derangement of a single group of processes. The various types of morbid fear—agoraphobia, the fear of being alone in open spaces; neophobia, the fear of everything that is new; phobophobia, the nervous dread of being afraid—are only exaggerated forms of experiences that most of us have had. The sanest man will feel lost when he passes, suddenly, from a quiet country life to the bustle of a large town; we are all a little timid when we enter a strange community; we have all been afraid that on such-and-such an occasion we shall show our nervousness. Similarly, the self-importance of paranoia is merely an exaggeration of the pleased self-consciousness, the self-complacency, that we often observe in others and, if we are honest, must often detect in ourselves. In all these instances, the strong lines of the caricature may help us to a more correct picture of the normal consciousness.

NOTES

1. John Locke, *An Essay Concerning Human Understanding,* [1690] Bk. II., Ch. i., §19.
2. Dugald Stewart, *Outlines of Moral Philosophy,* [1793]. Pt. I., Section i., §7.
3. James Mill, *Analysis of the Phenomena of the Human Mind,* [1829] Vol. I., Ch. v. Mill uses the word "feeling" to denote what we have called "mental process."

The Mistaken Mirror: on Wundt's and Titchener's Psychologies

Thomas H. Leahey

It is widely believed by American psychologists that Edward Bradford Titchener was a loyal pupil of Wilhelm Wundt who acted as a kind of English-speaking double for the founder of psychology. Only recently have historians of psychology begun to cast doubt on this belief,[1] but no one has as yet explored the systematic differences between the psychologies of Wundt and Titchener. The present paper has a twofold pur-

Leahey, T. H. (1981). The mistaken mirror: On Wundt's and Titchener's psychologies. *Journal of the History of the Behavioral Sciences, 17,* 273–282.

pose. The first is historical, to demonstrate that Titchener was not Wundt's double, and to explore some of the sources of the modern misconception. The second is systematic, for Titchener and Wundt represent two different metatheoretical orientations that transcend commonly recognized psychological, and even scientific systems. We will then find that Titchener does have a mirror image in a most surprising place.

A SKETCH OF WUNDTIAN PSYCHOLOGY

Wundt's psychology was produced by a wide-ranging mind and developed over a long lifetime, and so cannot be briefly summarized. Most important for present purposes, however, was Wundt's division of mental phenomena into inner and outer phenomena. The distinction is most easily grasped today in the study of language, since it resembles Chomsky's distinction of deep and surface structure. According to Wundt, a sentence consists of a set of visual or auditory sensations given in consciousness. However, underlying the sentence are certain cognitive processes whose operations in the speaker produce the sentence, or analyze it and extract the meaning for the hearer. These processes are the inner phenomena of language.[2] We may note in passing that although there is some similarity between Wundt's distinction of inner phenomena and outer phenomena and Chomsky's deep and surface structures, Wundt's formulation is more psychological. Wundt treats a sentence as a consciously given experience produced by general cognitive processes; Chomsky treats a sentence as embodying abstract and specifically linguistic structures.

For Wundt the distinction of inner and outer phenomena was not limited to language, however. In all its aspects, the mind could be viewed as a set of conscious experiences produced jointly by external stimuli and various higher mental processes. The most important of those processes was apperception, which served a number of mental functions according to Wundt. It was responsible for attention: we apperceive those stimuli we want to attend to, but only incompletely apprehend others. It was responsible for perceptual grouping: "word" is more than a collection of letters because apperception synthesizes them into a more meaningful whole. It was also responsible, reciprocally, for analysis: "word" can be analyzed into four letters because we can focus our attention on each of its elements. Apperception played a similar role in sentence production and comprehension.

A complete understanding of the mind required study of both outer and inner mental phenomena, and Wundt adopted two methods appropriate to each study. The first method, applicable to outer phenomena, is the better known to modern psychologists. It is Wundt's so-called physiological psychology. For Wundt, physiological psychology was the study of individual human consciousness by means of self-observation. I avoid the more widely used term introspection, for as Blumenthal has pointed out, Wundt did not ask his subjects to introspect in the commonly used Cartesian sense, in which introspection is an intensely analytical reflection on a remembered event experienced without experimental control.[3] Wundt harshly criticized his student Külpe for adopting such a procedure.[4] Self-observation as used by Wundt was a simple report of an experience not too different from procedures used by modern, thoroughly 'objective,' anti-introspective, cognitive psychologists.[5]

The second method, appropriate to inner mental phenomena, is much less well known. It is Wundt's *Völkerpsychologie*.[6] Wundt believed that "(we) cannot experiment upon mind itself, but only upon its outworks, the organs of sense and movement . . ."[7] However, ". . . fortunately for science there are other sources of objective psychological knowledge which become accessible at the very point where the experimental method fails us. These are certain products of the common mental life," especially language, myth, and custom, which form the subject matter of *Völkerpsychologie,* "our chief source of information regarding the general psychology of the complex mental processes."[8] These phenomena expand the range of human experience by including historical experience, and Wundt thought that by comparing primitive and complex societies we could trace the development of mind. A complete psychology thus had to include physiological psychology as a direct study of outer mental phenomena given in consciousness, and *Völkerpsychologie* as an indirect study of the inner phenomena of mind.

The most important goal of psychology, given Wundt's framework, was an explanation of human consciousness. Self-observation produced a descriptive classification of conscious experience, or outer phenomena, but this is only the first stage for psychological science. The second stage would be an explanation of the facts of immediate experience by reference to indirectly known, voluntarily controlled cognitive processes, such as attention.[9] Furthermore, psychological explanation was to resemble historical explanation. Wundt believed that the mind was creative, which meant that reported experience could not be predicted from initial conditions, as in physics. Instead, a psychologist could show that an experience, once reported, was an orderly product of sensation and the operation of cognitive processes, as the historian shows an event to be an orderly product of a situation and human action.[10] We may note that Sigmund Freud shared this same historical orientation.[11]

TITCHENER'S SYSTEM CONTRASTED WITH WUNDT'S

We may let Titchener speak for himself:

> Wundt . . . accepts . . . a whole array of explanatory terms: consciousness, attention, association—perception, emotion, memory, imagination. If only he had the insight to throw them all away! Wundt possessed, in fact, just one clear concept, the concept of sensation. . . . All the rest were foggy from much argument . . . we ourselves are getting rid of the theory-ridden terms piecemeal . . . and it will be long before experimental psychology is finally free of them.[12]

We find that Titchener was not afraid to criticize his teacher in the broadest and harshest terms. It is clear from this passage that Titchener viewed much of Wundt's system as unnecessary, overspeculative, and even unscientific.

The most obvious of Titchener's excisions is the entire *Völkerpsychologie;* Titchener had nothing like it, and did little to bring it to the attention of others. He himself, like another of Wundt's students, Oswald Külpe, essayed a direct experimental attack on the higher mental processes.[13] However, and herein lies the crucial difference between Titchener and Wundt, Titchener did not view cognitive processes as underlying and giving rise to conscious experience, but as completely analyzable complexes of conscious sensations to be reduced to their elemental constituents.

Titchener acknowledged his own system to be a kind of sensationism, a meaning-free description of the elements of consciousness, in contrast to Wundt's voluntarism. Wundt emphasized the voluntary activity of mind, especially in the process of apperception, but Titchener preferred pure sensationism. To define sensationism, he quoted, and appeared to accept, Baldwin's definition: "the theory that all knowledge originates in sensations; that all cognitions, even reflective ideas and so-called intuitions, can be traced back to the elementary sensations."[14]

The three original tasks expected of this sensationistic psychology were: to discover and catalogue the simplest sensations given in consciousness; to discover how these sensations were connected; and to discover, for both sensations and connections, their underlying physiological processes. The method by which the first two tasks were to be accomplished may best be termed analytical or anatomical introspection. Unlike Wundt's, Titchener's subjects did not just briefly report an experimentally controlled experience, they had to dissect it, attempting to discover the sensation-elements given at that moment in consciousness. Titchener's analytic introspection was similar to the methods adopted by Külpe at Würzburg, which Wundt himself criticized as a return to the philosophical introspection he had abandoned. Titchener also discarded Wundt's goal of a psychological explanation of mind in favor of a physiological one.

Let us consider an example—attention. For Wundt, attention was one aspect of the cognitive process of apperception, whose operation gave rise to various conscious phenomena. Titchener, however, pleads for a "simplification of the psychology of attention." He would rather have "a psychology of clearness—considering clearness as an attribute of sensation."[15] Titchener's key move is this: It is not that some sensations are clear *because* they are attended to, but that we say we have attended to some sensations *because* we find them clear in our consciousness. Where Wundt had explained sensory clarity by appealing to the process of attention, Titchener argued that "attention" is just a descriptive label given to what we experience with clarity. Titchener's analysis also applies to the feeling of effort that Wundt held accompanied active attention. Titchener writes: "When I am trying to attend I . . . find myself frowning, wrinkling my forehead etc. All such . . . bodily sets and movements give rise to characteristic sensations. Why should not these sensations be what we call 'attention'."[16] Attention for Titchener is something of a rationalization after the fact of an experience, in that it is only a label we apply to clear sensations accompanied by certain bodily sets that indicate effort.

Titchener did away with Wundt's distinction between inner and outer aspects of mind. Titchener attempted to turn Wundt's inner cognitive processes into descriptive attributes of the outer, conscious, region of mind as bundles of sensations. In short, Titchener wanted psychology primarily to describe conscious facts, not explain them. Explanation of mental events Titchener referred to physiology, by linking conscious experience to its substrate in the material processes of the brain. In any event, terms such as apperception were given no explanatory role.

In his latest work, Titchener's descriptive emphasis was sharpened. He abandoned the search for elements and their connections in consciousness in favor of phenomenological description, and he abandoned the goal of explanation altogether, be it physiological or psychological. In a letter to Adolf Meyer written in 1918, Titchener declares, "I don't *explain* or *causally relate* at all at all! . . . Causality I regard as mythological,—if you mean by it anything more than correlation."[17] Titchener thus departed even further from Wundt, but the change only strengthened existing differences.

Given Titchener's background, that Titchener is not Wundt's double should not surprise us. After all, he was an Englishman, and Fritz Ringer has shown how great was the intellectual gulf between English and German intellectual Zeitgeiste. Although Titchener studied with Wundt, Titchener's earlier grounding in philosophy in England undoubtedly kept him from absorbing the Wundtian paradigm, and predisposed him to accept the Machian positivism espoused by some, but not all, young German psychologists such as Külpe and Ebbinghaus. The founding Gestalt psychologists, on the other hand, rejected positivism.[18] So when he set out on his own, he reverted to what he knew. In his *An Outline of Psychology,* Titchener wrote that "the general standpoint of the book is that of the traditional English psychology."[19] The differences between Titchener and Wundt are more than a matter of historical accident, however. Titchener sought a descriptive psychology and Wundt and explanatory psychology. This brings us to the systematic side of our problem.

DESCRIPTIVE AND EXPLANATORY SCIENCE

In his recent study of behaviorism, Brian Mackenzie argues that the behaviorist's acceptance of positivism created an excessive commitment to experimental method as the savior of psychology.[20] For example, John B. Watson in his famous 1913 paper urged that psychologists should temporarily avoid studies of complex mental processes, but that "As our methods become better developed it will be possible to undertake investigations of more and more complex forms of behavior."[21] There is no mention of better theory, only 'refined' method. Titchener wrote on the same topic: "We may have absolute confidence in our method . . . there is not the slightest doubt that the patient application of the experimental method will presently solve the problems of feeling and attention."[22] Titchener and Watson were equally committed to good experimental method, although to different methods, as the surety of scientific progress. If Mackenzie's analysis of behaviorism can be applied to Titchener, we should find evidence of positivism in Titchener as well as Watson.

Titchener's most extended treatment of his philosophy of science is given in the posthumously published *Systematic Psychology: Prolegomena*. Titchener here affirmed his descriptive orientation: "Institutional science . . . is descriptive and not explanatory; it stops short of the 'why' of things." Titchener "denies that science has anything to do with explanation, with Why and Because." He seems to reduce natural law to simple correlation "expressing" "covariation among phenomena" which cannot be sharply distinguished from a "law of facts."[23] This attitude is further confirmed by the letter to Meyer printed in the 1972 edition of *Systematic Psychology*, quoted above. The synthesis of laws into a theory "never transcends description, a shorthand description which . . . brackets together a multitude of related facts."[24] Just as terms such as "force" and "cause" are retained by physics because they are convenient, while protesting "against [their] mythical power of explanation," psychology may still use "memory" and "imagination" while disavowing "common sense ideas as both superfluous and misleading. . . ."[25]

In saying all this, Titchener advocated the radical positivism of Ernst Mach and other nineteenth-century positivist philosophers, a tradition of which Titchener was well aware. He cited Mach, for example, to the effect that " 'the grand universal laws of physics . . . are not essentially different from descriptions'."[26] Mach advocated a completely descriptive approach to physics, and rejected the use of any purely theoretical terms, such as "atom," on the grounds of unobservability. Mach's positivism is more radical than later logical positivism, which admitted theoretical terms to science as long as they were empirically defined.

Wundt, on the other hand, was one of those German academic mandarins described by Ringer for whom the word "positivism" was a term of opprobrium. Titchener himself noted that Wundt was a voluntarist, not a sensationist. Wundt believed descriptive psychology to be incomplete and felt that explanation was the proper goal of science. In the explanatory psychology he sought "the chief emphasis is laid on the way in which immediate experience arises in the subject, so that a variety of explanatory psychology results which attributes to those subjective activities not referred to external objects, a position as independent as that assigned to ideas. This variety has been called *Voluntaristic psychology*, because of the importance that must be conceded to volitional processes . . ."[27] Furthermore, in contrast to Titchener, Wundt believed in "an *independent psychical causality*," compatible with, but "different from" the physical causality of physiology. Alongside "*laws of nature*" there exist "*laws of psychical phenomena*."[28] Titchener did not "causally relate at all" beyond mere correlation, while Wundt listed six causal laws of the mind in his *Outlines of Psychology*.[29]

The issue between Wundt and Titchener was what to do with the data of psychology. They agreed that psychology's data were the facts of conscious experience, but they completely disagreed on what needed to be explained. For Wundt, what we experience in consciousness is the outcome of deeper mental processes not directly subject to self-observation. The goal of psychology, therefore, was to use the data of individual (physiological psychology) and collective (*Völkerpsychologie*) experience to discover the hidden cognitive processes. These processes could be used to scientifically explain the facts of experience, which in turn provide evidence for the existence and operation of the cognitive processes.

Titchener, on the other hand, as a positivist, believed that what was not observable was not admissable in science, including the so-called cognitive processes for which Titchener rebuked Wundt in the passage quoted [earlier] . . . . As purely theoretical, nonobservable terms, apperception, memory, attention, and so on were for Titchener essentially mythical. Titchener began, like Wundt, with the facts of experience, but instead of seeing them as evidence of the workings of mental processes, as in need of explanation, he saw them as the rock bottom bed of science. The facts of experience were not to be explained, held Titchener, but were to be used to explain the supposed processes of apperception and attention. As we have seen, Wundt said a sensation is clear because we attended to its source; the clear sensation is evidence of the process of attention. According to Titchener, however, people have learned to say they attended to something because the sensation was clear. In Titchener's view, the myth of attention is a sort of rationalization or label attached to clear sensation. The explanation of sensory clarity for Titchener would come from revealing the physiology of clarity. And then, in good positivist fashion, one observable fact, sensory clarity, would be explained by another observable fact, a brain-process; nowhere would one need to introduce an unobservable cognitive process of apperception or attention.

We may conclude, then, that underlying the distinct psychological systems of Wundt and Titchener are two different philosophies of science. For Wundt, scientific psychology should be causal and explanatory, accounting for the facts of immediate experience by showing how they depend on the operation of complex, inner mental processes. For Titchener, on the other hand, scientific psychology should be correlational and descriptive, accounting for the facts of immediate experience by showing how they depend on (nonpsychological) nerve processes, or, later, by simply describing regularities in experience. Titchener is not Wundt's double, in method, theory, or philosophy of science. Why then, is he so often believed to be Wundt's double?

MISTAKING TITCHENER FOR WUNDT

As Henry Veatch has remarked, scientists are a very present-minded group,[30] and psychologists are no exception. A useful example of modern psychologists' misunderstanding of their own past may be found in Ulric Neisser's recent *Cognition and Reality*.[31] Neisser is an interesting case, for although he did much to found contemporary information-processing cognitive psychology with his 1967 *Cognitive Psychology*,[32] he now opposes much of what the movement has become. He is familiar with a fair amount of very early psychological research,[33] and in some respects his current orientation resembles Wundt's.[34] Nevertheless, in his recounting of the failures of introspective psychology, he makes a number of erroneous charges. He attributes much of the failure of early mentalistic psychology to its employment of "a special form of introspection," in which the mind's activities are observed. He has in mind the analytic introspection of Külpe or Titchener, not Wundt's self-report. He also writes that "the introspectionists had no theory of cognitive development."[35] This is essentially true of Wundt's physiological psychology and Titchener's system, but Neisser seems unaware of *Völkerpsy-*

chologie, Wundt's tool for studying cognitive development. Such conflating of Wundt and Titchener into a single "introspective psychology" is typical of the beliefs of psychologists today.

As is typical of the present-minded scientist, Neisser cites neither Titchener nor Wundt, but seems to draw his information from unnamed "(t)extbooks in the history of psychology."[36] Blumenthal has already pointed to textbooks as a source of ignorance about the true Wundt: "American textbook accounts of Wundt now present highly inaccurate and mythological accounts of the man and his work."[37] The classic history is, of course, E. G. Boring's *History of Experimental Psychology.*[38] Boring treats Wundt as something of a British associationist. Association is given more space than apperception. Creative synthesis is said to be "not too different" from J. S. Mill's mental chemistry, a passive process of association determined by the elements themselves. The *Völkerpsychologie* is given no more than a mention. Titchener is described as "an Englishman who represented the German psychological tradition in America."[39]

More recent texts have done little to correct, and much to further distort, Boring's description of Wundt. Duane Schultz, for example, in his popular work, explicitly equates Wundt and Titchener, which at least Boring did not do: "The orthodox Wundtian brand of . . . psychology was transplanted to the United States by Wundt's most devoted pupil, E. B. Titchener, and underwent its fullest development at his hands." Schultz's presentation of Wundt closely follows Boring, and he writes that "A knowledge of Wundt's psychology provides a reasonably accurate picture of Titchener's system"[40] although the two are not identical. In his text, William Sahakian titles his section on Titchener, "Titchener: Wundt in America."[41] He fails to go beyond Boring in his brief consideration of Wundt's system, and describes the *Völkerpsycholgie* only on the basis of the *Elements of Folk Psychology*[42] which has little in common with the developed *Völkerpsycholgie*. Daniel Robinson gives neither Wundt nor Titchener their own sections in his text. His presentation of Wundt is sketchy, not even mentioning the *Völkerpsychologie,* while his treatment of Titchener is almost nonexistent. He does say that Titchener's system was "not far removed from" Wundt's. Both are criticized for having "no theory worth the name."[43] This is true of Titchener, though given his descriptive orientation he would not find it troubling, but it is certainly untrue of Wundt. His theory of attention, for example, is a worthy rival to any modern account, as I have argued earlier.[44] Watson's *Great Psychologists* treats Wundt at some length, unlike other texts after Boring, but it shares the same difficulties as the others.[45] The most extreme equation of Wundt and Titchener is found in Fred Keller's *Definition of Psychology*: "Titchener's system was so close to Wundt's and so much easier to describe, that we shall not here dwell on . . . Wundt. . . ."[46] The thinking reader should be left wondering how two things can be identical but one be "much simpler" than the other.

To the extent that working psychologists know Wundt only through textbook accounts, as Neisser seems to, they will confuse Titchener with Wundt, as the texts do. With Blumenthal, I believe that textual distortions of Wundt's psychology are the major reason for Wundt's low status today. A contributing factor is the lack of translations of Wundt's volumes on *Völkerpsychologie.* Enough of his works on individual psychology are available in English that Americans can get an accurate picture of that side of Wundt's work, but until Blumenthal's *Language and Psychology* none of the important *Völkerpsychologie* was available. Finally, the rise of American behaviorism made unacceptable any form of mentalistic psychology, to the point where differences among mentalists became blurred. This blurring has been continued by behaviorism's antihistorical bias. Behaviorism was launched in a fervor of optimism that the past could be forgotten in pursuit of the utopian future, so that accurate historical scholarship was deemed irrelevant:[47] history was not taught at Walden Two.[48]

STRANGE BEDFELLOWS IN DESCRIPTION

Titchener is not Wundt's mirror-image: he does not accurately reflect Wundt's psychology. However, we should bear in mind that a mirror image has a peculiar characteristic: every detail of the original is faithfully reflected, but the whole scene is reversed. If we look, we may find a living psychologist who *is* Titchener's mirror double.

This psychologist espouses a system which, unlike methodological behaviorism, does not rule mental events out of psychology, but like Titchener on attention, writes that "what one feels or introspectively observes are conditions of one's own body," not explanatory cognitive processes. As Titchener optimistically and directly studied the higher mental processes, so today this writer's psychology "does . . . not reject any . . . 'higher mental processes';" but it has taken the lead in investigating their conditions. Like Titchener, he cites Ernst Mach favorably, writing that science is a search for "lawful relations among the events in nature." Like Titchener, he reduces cause to correlation between independent and dependent variables: "The old 'cause-and-effect connection' becomes a 'functional relation'." In short, although this psychologist admits that we can talk about attention, memory, and other mental processes, he considers them myths that explain nothing, and adopts an essentially descriptive stance.

Space limitations preclude further exposition of the similarities between Titchener's system and this new one. Some readers may have guessed Titchener's double, B. F. Skinner, the father of radical behaviorism.[49] I believe that Titchener and Skinner do stand in a true mirror-image relation: both adopt the same descriptive, Machian, philosophy of science and both adopt the same view of conscious phenomena, as sensations which we learn to label in different ways. The emphases in each system, however, are entirely different. Skinner cannot deny the possibility of a mentalistic psychology like Titchener's, but he certainly denies its scientific status, since it cannot predict and control behavior.[50] Titchener did not want psychology to be useful; Skinner does. Nevertheless, each adopts a radically positivist approach to science, as something that has as little to do with theory as possible.[51] On the contrary, both think that psychology should deal in exact objective description. It is an attitude equally applicable to mentalism or behaviorism.

Finally, we may note a personal similarity between the two. In 1914, Titchener, whose system was shortly to be erased by behaviorism, wrote at the end of his reply to Watson: ". . . introspective psychology . . . will go quietly about its task . . . declining, with the mild persistence natural to matters of fact—either to be eliminated or ignored."[52] In 1963, after hearing the death-knell of behaviorism pronounced by Sigmund Koch,[53] Skinner said that he finds trends in psychology "still running away from me," but that nevertheless his "science of behavior is moving very rapidly and powerfully . . . it justifies itself by its success in dealing with the subject matter."[54] Whether Skinner's dogged optimism will prove any more justified than Titchener's remains to be seen.

Positivism, however, is a philosophy of science that has been tried and found wanting. Mach's radical positivism, which motivated both Titchener's and Skinner's descriptive psychologies, was long ago superseded by logical positivism, which in turn has been rejected by contemporary philosophers of science. [55] Studies by N. R. Hanson and Thomas Kuhn have shown that no scientific system can be theory-free even if the effort is made,[56] and Edwin Burtt has observed that "there is an exceedingly subtle and insidious danger in positivism," for in trying to avoid theoretical "metaphysics," which is impossible, the positivist's "metaphysics will be held uncritically because it is unconscious."[57] Secret theory replaces explicit theory. Titchener and Skinner both accepted positivism and sought theory-free descriptive psychologies. Titchener's failed, and it is now only an historical curiosity. The cognitive revolt against behaviorism may give radical behaviorism the same fate.[58]

NOTES

1. Arthur Blumenthal, "A Reappraisal of Wilhelm Wundt," *American Psychologist* 30 (1975): 1081–1088.
2. See the fragment of Wundt's *Völkerpsychologie* translated by Arthur Blumenthal in his *Language and Psychology* (New York: Wiley, 1970), pp. 20–31, and Blumenthal's preceding commentary.
3. Blumenthal, speaking in a discussion session on "European Influence Upon American Psychology," in *The Roots of American Psychology,* ed. R. W. Rieber and K. Salzinger (*Annals of the New York Academy of Sciences* 291 [1977]: 1–394), pp. 66–73. The best English discussion of Wundt's strictures on proper experimental method is Wilhelm Wundt, *Principles of Physiological Psychology* Vol. I, trans. E. B. Titchener (London: Swan Sonnenschein; New York: Macmillan, 1910). pp. 4–6. Wundt's views on method, description, and explanation have been discussed by Theodore Mischel, "Wundt and the Conceptual Foundations of Psychology," *Philosophy and Phenomenological Research* 31 (1900): 1–26. But Mischel persists in identifying, incorrectly, Wundt's and Titchener's views on introspection (p. 13); for a corrective, see Kurt Danziger, "The Positivist Repudiation of Wundt," *Journal of the History of the Behavioral Sciences* 15 (1979): 205–230.
4. Good English accounts of Wundt's criticisms of Külpe may be found in the first edition of Robert S. Woodworth, *Experimental Psychology* (New York: Holt, 1938), pp. 784–786 and in George Humphrey, *Thinking* (New York: Science Editions, 1963), pp. 106–132.
5. See, for example, George Sperling, "The Information Available in Brief Visual Presentation," *Psychological Monographs* 74, whole number 498 (1960) which uses one of Wundt's own visual apperception tasks; or E. Colin Cherry, "Some Experiments on the Recognition of Speech, with One and Two Ears," *Journal of the Acoustic Society of America* 26 (1953): 554–559, which asks subjects to attend and describe auditory information.
6. Wilhelm Wundt, *Völkerpsychologie,* 10 vols. (Leipzig: Englemann, 1900–1920).
7. Wundt, *Lectures on Human and Animal Psychology* (London: Swan Sonnenschein; New York: Macmillan, 1894), p. 10.
8. Wundt, *Principles of Physiological Psychology,* p. 4.
9. Wundt, *Outlines of Psychology,* trans. Charles Judd (Leipzig: Englemann; London: Williams and Norgate; New York: Gustav E. Stechert, 1897; reprint ed., St. Clair Shores, Mich.: Scholarly Press), pp. 11–15.
10. Wundt, *Introduction to Psychology,* trans. Rudolph Pintner (London: Allen, 1912; reprint ed., New York: Arno, 1973), pp. 166–167.
11. Sigmund Freud, "The Psychogenesis of a Case of Homosexuality in a Woman," in *Collected Papers* (London: Hogarth Press, 1953), pp. 202–231; see pp. 226–227.
12. Edward Bradford Titchener, "Experimental Psychology: A Retrospect," *American Journal of Psychology* 36 (1925): 313–323, p. 318.
13. Titchener, *Lectures on the Elementary Psychology of the Thought Processes* (New York: Macmillan, 1909; reprint ed., New York: Arno, 1973).
14. Ibid., p. 23.
15. Titchener, *Lectures on the Elementary Psychology of Feeling and Attention* (New York: Macmillan; reprint ed., New York: Arno, 1973), p. 209.
16. Titchener, *Experimental Psychology,* vol. I (New York: Macmillan, 1901), p. 109.
17. Titchener, in Appendix to reprint edition of *Systematic Psychology: Prolegomena* (New York: Macmillan, 1929; reprinted ed., Ithaca and London: Cornell University Press, 1972), p. 273. See also Rand B. Evans, "E. B. Titchener and His Lost System," *Journal of the History of the Behavioral Sciences* 11 (1972): 334–341.
18. For the comparison of English and German intellectual environments, see Fritz K. Ringer, *The De-*

cline of the German Mandarins (Cambridge, Mass.: Harvard University Press, 1969); for the appeal of positivism to Titchener and others, see Danziger, "The Positivist Repudiation of Wundt;" on the Gestalt psychologists, see Michael Wertheimer, "Max Wertheimer: Gestalt Prophet." Presidential address to Division 26, annual meeting of the American Psychological Association, Toronto, Ontario, August 31, 1978.

19. Edward Bradford Titchener, *An Outline of Psychology* (New York: Macmillan, 1897), p. vi.
20. Brian Mackenzie, *Behaviorism and the Limits of Scientific Method* (London: Routledge and Kegan Paul, 1977).
21. John B. Watson, "Psychology as the Behaviorist Views It," *Psychological Review* 20 (1913): 158–176, p. 175.
22. Titchener, *Lectures on Feeling and Attention,* p. 317.
23. Titchener, *Prolegomena,* pp. 65, 56, and 61.
24. Ibid., p. 63.
25. Ibid., pp. 57–58.
26. Ibid., p. 63.
27. Wundt, *Outlines,* p. 12.
28. Ibid., p. 320.
29. Ibid., pp. 321–328. A shorter list is given in his *Introduction,* pp. 154–198.
30. Henry B. Veatch, "Science and Humanism" in *Theories in Contemporary Psychology,* 2nd ed., ed. Melvin Marx and Felix Goodson (New York: Macmillan, 1976), pp. 61–66.
31. Ulric Neisser, *Cognition and Reality* (San Francisco: Freeman, 1976).
32. Neisser, *Cognitive Psychology* (New York: Appleton-Century-Crofts, 1967).
33. Elizabeth Spelke, William Hirst, and Neisser, "Skills of Divided Attention," *Cognition* 4 (1976): 215–230.
34. Thomas H. Leahey, "Something Old, Something New: Wundt and Contemporary Theories of Attention," *Journal of the History of the Behavioral Sciences* 15 (1979): 242–252.
35. Neisser, *Cognition and Reality,* pp. 1–3.
36. Ibid., p. 2.
37. Blumenthal, *Language and Psychology,* p. 11.
38. Edwin G. Boring, *History of Experimental Psychology,* 2nd ed. (New York: Appleton-Century-Crofts, 1950).
39. Ibid., p. 410.
40. Duane Schultz, *A History of Modern Psychology,* 2nd ed. (New York: Academic Press, 1975), both quotes p. 83.
41. William Sahakian, *History and Systems of Psychology* (New York: Schenkman, 1975), p. 352.
42. Wilhelm Wundt, *Elements of Folk Psychology* (London: George Allen, 1916).
43. Daniel Robinson, *An Intellectual History of Psychology* (New York: Macmillan, 1976), pp. 329–333.
44. Leahey, "Something Old, Something New."
45. Robert Watson, *The Great Psychologists,* 3rd ed. (New York: Lippincott, 1971). The most recent, fourth edition (1978) contains an improved presentation of Wundt's psychology, but still calls Titchener "Wundt's most faithful pupil," who "in most respects . . . held to the tradition of Wundt," giving his "master's" ideas "a systematic explictness" (pp. 413–414).
46. Fred S. Keller, *The Definition of Psychology,* 2nd ed. (Englewood Cliffs, N.J.: Prentice-Hall, 1973), p. 19.
47. Joseph R. Royce, "Pebble Picking vs. Boulder Building," *Psychological Reports* 16 (1965): 447–450.
48. Reinforcement history is not the same as history as usually understood. Reinforcement creates a certain present state in the organism that disposes it to respond in a certain way. Ideally, this state could be known without knowing the actual reinforcement history (i.e., through neurophysiological state-description or behavioral testing). In this context, history is not seen as a developmental process but only as a means of changing an organism's (or a society's) momentary state.
49. The first two quotes came from Burrhus F. Skinner, *About Behaviorism* (New York: Knopf, 1974), pp. 216 and 223; the second two came from Skinner, *Science and Human Behavior* (New York: Macmillan, 1953), pp. 13 and 23.
50. Skinner, *About Behaviorism* p. 165.
51. Compare Skinner's "Are Theories of Learning Necessary?" *Psychological Review* 57 (1950): 193–216, to Titchener's comments on Wundt's "theory ridden terms" quoted above (see note 12).
52. Titchener, "On Psychology as the Behaviorist Views It," *Proceedings of the American Philosophical Society* 53 (1914): 1–17, p. 17.

53. Sigmund Koch, "Psychology and Emerging Conceptions of Knowledge as Unitary," in *Behaviorism and Phenomenology,* ed. T. W. Wann (Chicago: University of Chicago Press, 1964).
54. Skinner, Speaking in the "Discussion of Koch" (note 53), in *Behaviorism and Phenomenology, p. 42.*
55. Frederick Suppe, "The Search for Philosophic Understanding of Scientific Theories," in *The Structure of Scientific Theories,* ed. F. Suppe (Urbana: University of Illinois Press, 1974), pp. 3–254. See also Peter Achinstein, *Concepts of Science* (Baltimore: Johns Hopkins Press, 1968) for a rigorous analysis of positivism.
56. Norwood Russell Hanson, *Patterns of Discovery* (Cambridge: Cambridge University Press, 1958) and *Observation and Explanation* (New York: Harper Torchbooks, 1971). Thomas S. Kuhn, *The Structure of Scientific Revolutions,* enl. ed., (Chicago: University of Chicago Press, 1970).
57. Edwin A. Burtt, *The Metaphysical Foundations of Modern Science,* rev. ed., (1932; reprint ed., Garden City, N.Y.: Doubleday Anchor, 1954), p. 229.
58. An extended analysis of the effects of positivism on psychology will be given in my "The Myth of Operationism," *Journal of Mind and Behavior,* in press. The question of whether cognitive psychology represents a real revolt against behaviorism and positivism is explored at length in my *A History of Psychology* (Englewood Cliffs, N.J.: Prentice Hall, 1980), chap. 13, esp. pp. 371–376 and chap. 15, esp. pp. 392–394.

Shared Knowledge: The Experimentalists, 1904–1929

Laurel Furumoto

"For many years I wanted an experimental club—no officers, the men moving about and handling (apparatus), the visited lab to do the work, no women, smoking allowed, plenty of frank criticism and discussions, the whole atmosphere experimental, the youngsters taken in on an equality with the men who have arrived."[1] Thus, in 1904, shortly after his thirty-seventh birthday, Cornell's E. B. Titchener described his vision of a society for the advancement of experimental psychology in a letter to a colleague at Harvard, Hugo Münsterberg.

In this chapter, I will examine the early history of this small, elite scientific society and the life and career of the psychologist who inaugurated it. The story has relevance to the history of experimentation in that it illustrates very clearly how one psychologist's cognitive authority came to be exerted in a particular social arrangement which had significant consequences for the subfield of experimental psychology.[2] Titchener's personality exhibited a peculiar admixture of erudition, charm, and dogged insistence, which often enabled him to lead and control those in his immediate environment very effectively. While in the eyes of many of his contemporaries the force of these personal qualities may have elevated him to a level somewhat larger than life, the obedience he commanded from his students and associates would not have been possible in the absence of mutually held values. An instructive example of this is provided by the exclusion of women from Titchener's society. Although Titchener originated the policy, it seems implausible that it could have been maintained without the tacit approval of the other members. The impact of this exclusion was to deprive women in the field of the op-

Furumoto, L. (1988). Shared knowledge: The Experimentalists, 1904–1929. In J. G. Morawski (Ed.), *The rise of experimentation in American psychology,* (pp. 94–113). New Haven, CT: Yale University Press.

portunity of establishing collegial ties and of being part of an informal communication network, essentials for scientific research.[3] Experimental psychology, in turn, was deprived of women's participation, contributions, and point of view, as Titchener's discriminatory policy effectively relegated them to the periphery of the field.

Titchener's club, begun in 1904, came to be called "the Experimentalists," and for more than twenty years, until his death in 1927, he dictated how it was run. Attendance was by invitation only to the heads of psychology laboratories, primarily in elite eastern universities. In addition to men who had arrived, a select group of youngsters—promising advanced graduate students and junior faculty—were invited from the chosen laboratories.

Titchener insisted that the meetings be kept informal; he frowned on the reading of papers, encouraging instead reports of work in progress, discussion, and hands-on demonstration of apparatus. The only subject matter welcomed for inclusion was that which Titchener considered legitimate psychology. This excluded from consideration mental testing and comparative and applied psychology, among other things. Titchener vigilantly enforced two other practices: no prohibition against smoking and no women at meetings. Finally, Titchener did not want what went on in the meetings to be disseminated publicly. He was opposed to publishing proceedings, and when in the early years of the group some published notes did appear, he expressed his displeasure to those responsible.

Information on Titchener's background, personality, and the way in which he came to conceptualize psychology is provided in the following section, with the intent of shedding some light on his reasons for sponsoring the Experimentalists and his insistence that the group observe a certain protocol. It is useful to keep in mind the observation of one historian of psychology that the originator of the Experimentalists was a breed apart from his American colleagues: "Titchener was not typical of those who founded American experimental psychology in the 1890's. He maintained the image of a 19th century aristocratic Oxford scholar when others were rapidly moving toward the image of modern twentieth century man."[4]

E. B. TITCHENER

Origins, Education, and Cornell

E. B. Titchener was born in 1867 in Chichester, a town seventy miles south of London, close to the English coast. He was a descendant of an old, respected family, counting among his paternal ancestors a great grandfather who was a mayor of Chichester and a grandfather who was an influential barrister.[5] However, when Titchener was in adolescence, both his father and his paternal grandfather died, and soon after the family found itself financially bereft. Nevertheless, Titchener was able to further his education by earning a scholarship to a public preparatory school. He subsequently spent five years at Oxford, where he took his A.B. degree. The first four years he devoted to studying classics and philosophy, making his way by means of scholarships and summer jobs; the fifth he spent in the laboratory of the physiologist Burdon Sanderson, who was apparently responsible for suggesting to Titchener that he study psychology with Wundt.[6]

Titchener followed the suggestion to study with the German scion of experimental psychology, spending two years in Leipzig, where he earned his doctorate in 1892. Frank Angell, an American graduate student with whom Titchener struck up a cordial friendship during his first year of study in Germany, was to play an important role in bringing Titchener to the United Sates. In the fall of 1891 Angell went to Cornell to set up a psychological laboratory, but after only one year resigned from his position to accept a job at Stanford, which was just opening its doors. His admiration for Titchener's abilities prompted Angell to recommend Titchener as his replacement at Cornell.[7] Titchener apparently had an opportunity to return to Oxford, in addition to the offer of a position from Cornell. Moreover, there were serious drawbacks to Cornell. Aside from necessitating leaving England to live in the American wilderness, which Ithaca surely was in the 1890s, Titchener had doubts about Cornell's stature as an academic institution. Howard C. Warren, who was studying in Leipzig at the time that Titchener was completing his doctorate, remembered "the day when Titchener received the call to Cornell; we were in Wundt's lecture hall . . . waiting for the lecturer, and T. asked me whether Cornell really ranked as a first class university."[8]

It seems that it was the lure of the laboratory which tipped the scales in favor of Cornell. Many years later Titchener confided to a younger colleague, "When I had the choice between creating my subject at Oxford, with no chance of a laboratory, and coming here, I came here."[9] E. G. Boring, who took his Ph.D. with Titchener in 1914, also considered the laboratory to have been the decisive factor influencing Titchener's decision: "In those days a laboratory was a laboratory, Titchener . . . often said; and . . . [Titchener] only twenty-five years old, hurried to Ithaca, New York, with its laboratory, as an assistant professor of psychology. He never left Cornell; and within psychology Cornell and Titchener (became) almost interchangeable words,"[10]

A vivid impression of the legendary psychologist toward the end of his career is conveyed in the recollections of Titchener's nephew, written for the *Cornell Alumni News* in the late 1960s. The author, who was the son of Titchener's sister, had become well acquainted with his uncle in his years as an undergraduate at Cornell during the early 1920s. First and foremost in his reminiscences was "the code by which Uncle Bradford guided his life—the code of the British gentleman. . . . That code, carried out to the point of brusqueness, dictated at one extreme, absolute intellectual integrity, and at the other, rigid rules of etiquette."[11] Another central feature of Titchener's image his nephew recalled was that of the British intellectual, who had gained the reputation of being the best-informed individual in any gathering. And, in his nephew's opinion, "he worked very hard to maintain that status. The result was that his students and colleagues regarded him with a mixture of fear and reverence."[12]

Psychology as Experimentation

To understand Titchener's stance on a variety of issues surrounding the question of what could legitimately be thought of as psychology requires an appreciation of how he conceptualized the emerging discipline. In this regard it is important to note that Titchener embraced a positivist philosophy in which psychology was conceived as wholly a natural science. He discovered positivism while a student in Leipzig and became one of a group of younger psychologists, which included Külpe and Ebbinghaus, that adopted this perspective. In doing so, Titchener placed himself squarely in opposition to Wundt, whose adherence to German idealist philosophy led him to espouse a model of psychology "which had at most one foot in the camp of the natural sciences."[13]

Titchener's commitment to positivist philosophy is revealed by his adoption of experimentation as the criterion for judging what was and what was not psychology. Very early in his career, he came to construe the role of experimentation in psychology in a way vastly different from Wundt. For Titchener, "the experimental method made a scientific psychology possible. For him questions that could not be explored using the method were not properly part of psychology."[14] In Titchener's own words, "*Experimental psychology* is just psychology; the science which describes 'mental' processes, and enumerates their conditions."[15] One of his earliest Ph.D. students, Walter Pillsbury, in an assessment of Titchener's psychology, characterized his former adviser's attitude toward experimentation as follows:

> When he came to America the extension of the experimental method became his dominant interest. He was full of enthusiasm for the laboratory and all that went with it. From the first year at Cornell he began to gather apparatus and plan new pieces for the investigations of his students. . . . He believed in the possession of apparatus and its use: He practically laid down the law for the laboratory that there is no psychology without introspection and little useful introspection without experimental aids.[16]

For Titchener, then, advancing experimentation was equivalent to advancing psychology, and there is evidence that during his early years at Cornell he was intently pursuing this aim. It is most clearly manifested in his manuals of experimental psychology, which set forth for the student and the instructor alike the background, subject matter, and methods of the psychological enterprise as interpreted by their author. It is also apparent in Titchener's idea of a club that would bring together established experimentalists and novices so that the latter would be appropriately inducted into the field, as defined by Titchener. In the following section, I will consider these endeavors of Titchener's to institutionalize psychology as experimentation.

Promoting Experimental Psychology

In his lengthy obituary of Titchener, E. G. Boring included a detailed account of the life and career of his doctoral adviser and long-time mentor. Commenting on the decade of the nineties at Cornell, Boring acclaimed it one of "remarkable accomplishment" for Titchener. In addition to building up the laboratory, directing the work of several graduate students, and giving lectures to undergraduates, he also found time for an impressive amount of scientific work and writing. He produced sixty-two articles and two books by the end of 1900 and was heavily involved in translating works by Wundt and Külpe.[17]

The manuals. The next decade was marked by a decline in Titchener's rate of publication, which Boring attributed to his involvement in a major undertaking, preparing the four volumes of his *Experimental Psychology.* These laboratory manuals, two addressed to the student and two to the instructor, represented an enormous investment of time and energy. Titchener himself worked out in the laboratory all the experiments contained in the manuals, devising procedures requiring only simple apparatus that would be available even to psychology laboratories with limited means. He revised instructions, added cautions, and modified procedures until students performing the experiments were able to obtain unequivocal results. As Boring notes, this achievement necessitated "a tremendous amount of careful, laborious work in the laboratory."[18]

The manuals were much more than a collection of painstakingly devised laboratory exercises; they also included an exhaustive up-to-date compilation of the psychological literature, which has been referred to as encyclopedic. Quoting again from Pillsbury's 1928 article on Titchener's psychology: "At the time the volumes were published they gave a summary of the results on topics treated that had probably not been equalled in any language. It is still a very useful work of reference. . . . If one desires today to look into any of the topics discussed, the literature up to the date of publication can be found accurately stated and evaluated there."[19] The companion student and instructor manuals having to do with qualitative methods were published in 1901.[20] The other two manuals, which deal with quantitative methods, occupied Titchener for several years more, appearing in 1905.[21] Boring tersely, yet candidly, summed up the motivation behind this herculean labor thus: "What Titchener wanted to do was to establish psychology as a science."[22] In fact, the manuals can be seen as Titchener's bid to spread the word throughout the English-speaking academic world that psychology was an experimental science. As the manuals were approaching completion, Titchener launched another project, different in nature but with the same goal of promoting psychology as an experimental science.

The Club. In a printed form letter dated 15 January 1904, Titchener appealed to a select group of psychologists for their assistance in organizing "an American society for the advancement of Experimental Psychology."[23] While asserting that the field of experimental psychology in America now stood second, if to any country, only to Germany, Titchener nevertheless believed that there existed "a serious need of organization and consolidation of forces."[24] In his view, "Not only would the directors of laboratories benefit by interchange of ideas and discussion of programmes; but the younger men also—and this is a point upon which I desire to lay especial weight—would realize, by association, the community of their interests, the common dangers to which their profession is exposed, and their responsibilities to the science."[25]

Titchener disavowed any desire "to interfere with the existing American Psychological Association."[26] While crediting the twelve-year-old association (hereafter APA) with having "done admirable work for American psychology at large," he said he believed it to be "evident that the opportunities which it offers for scientific and social intercourse have not met the special requirements of Experimental Psychology."[27] Foreshadowing the restrictions that the society was to adopt regarding who it would accept as members and what was acceptable as subject matter, Titchener recommended that the club's membership "be confined to men who are working in the field of experimental psychology" and "that its discussions be confined to subjects investigated by the experimental method."[28] He expressed the hope that his readers would approve of his scheme and assured them: "The intention underlying these proposals is, very simply, that the experimentalists shall come together for a couple of days every year, to talk, think, and act nothing but Experimental Psychology."[29]

THE EXPERIMENTALISTS

Titchener, along with certain other experimental psychologists, notably Lightner Witmer at the University of Pennsylvania, had long been dissatisfied with the APA. In fact, six years prior to Titchener's proposal, Witmer had launched an abortive attempt to found a new society limited exclusively to experimentalists. G. Stanley Hall, who had only a few years earlier hosted the founding meeting of the APA at Clark University, had written to Titchener about Witmer's plan: "A line from Witmer says that he wants to join you, me and others in forming a new Psychological organization which shall put the lab on a proper basis and exclude half breeds and extremists. Do you want to consider it?"[30] Although tentative plans were laid for an organizational meeting at Clark over the Christmas holidays, Witmer did not succeed in establishing a society of experimentalists. In his account of Witmer's failed attempt, historian of psychology C. James Goodwin comments that, ironically, it was Titchener himself who proved to be the chief stumbling block. It seems that Titchener dissuaded both Hall and Witmer from going ahead with the plan for a new society because he wished to avoid public repudiation of the APA, which the establishment of a rival society would signify. Titchener at the time suggested an alternative plan to another colleague, which, as Goodwin observes, "was virtually identical to what eventually emerged in 1904. . . . He had 'advised informal friendly gatherings of experimentalists by personal invitation, at the leading laboratories, year by year, the inviter presiding'."[31]

So it is clear that, as early as 1898, Titchener and some other psychologists were distinctly unhappy with the APA and were thinking about the possibility of forming another professional interest group. What were the grounds for their disaffection? Titchener's quarrel with the APA is often traced to its failure to respond to his request that it oust a member whom Titchener believed to be guilty of plagiarism. This led to Titchener's resignation from the APA in protest in the mid-1890s. However, Goodwin points to a more fundamental difficulty with the APA, one that Titchener shared with other experimentalists:

> It was dominated by interests other than those of experimental psychology, which Titchener took to mean the study of the basic units of human conscious experience, analyzed through the use of experimental and introspective procedures. The most notable of these other interests was philosophy. . . . Other topics outside the boundaries of Titchener's definition of 'experimental' were, for example, mental testing, child study, abnormal psychology, and animal psychology. All of these were of interest to American psychologists.[32]

Despite the long-standing displeasure of many experimental psychologists with the APA, approximately half of the fifteen responses to Titchener's form letter in 1904 expressed reservations about creating a rival society. Hugo Münsterberg was among those who questioned the need for a new psychological association. He suggested instead that Titchener rejoin the APA, confessing, "I am unable to see what two psychological associations can do in this country side by side."[33] Münsterberg foresaw a major problem in trying to hold two psychological meetings each year in different locations. Reminding Titchener that in the United States the distances that had to be traveled to meetings were so great "that no one cares to make such long trips too often," he also worried that there were too few psychologists in the country to support two meetings.[34] Münsterberg observed that there had already been "this year a regrettable conflict between the Psychological Association, which met at St. Louis, and the Philosophical Association which met at Princeton."[35] There were grounds for the concern of Münsterberg and several others that a new association might imperil the APA. The APA's twelfth annual meeting, to which he referred, had been held in a high school and had been very poorly attended, featuring just twelve papers, as compared with twenty-six the year before.

Titchener, undeterred by the objection that his proposed society would pose a threat to the already none too robust APA, issued another form letter approximately three weeks after the first. He began by claiming that "the large proportion of favourable answers" he had received "shows that the need of such an organization is keenly felt" and indicated that there was "pretty general agreement" about the features that the new society should have, listing them as follows:

> **(1)** no fees; no officers; organization as simple as possible;
> **(2)** membership small; meetings entirely informal;
> **(3)** for the present at least, membership confined to men;
> **(4)** for the present at least, no affiliation to any existing society;
> **(5)** meetings to be held at the larger university laboratories;
> **(6)** place and date of meetings to be so chosen as to avoid conflict with the meetings of other scientific societies;
> **(7)** special effort to be directed towards the encouragement of graduate students and the younger independent workers in Experiemental Psychology;
> **(8)** papers, demonstrations, symposia, etc., to be strictly confined to subjects investigated by the experimental method.[36]

Granting that all these points would be "entirely open to discussion among those who accept[ed] membership in the society," Titchener asked his correspondents to indicate whether they would be willing to become active members and whether they could attend a meeting at Ithaca during the Easter vacation.[37]

That first meeting was rather sparsely attended compared with those in later years, and most of those attending (seven out of twelve), were affiliated with the host institution. It attracted representatives from the laboratories of only four other institutions—Yale, Pennsylvania, Clark, and Michigan.[38] However, the Cornell gathering was significant in that it established guidelines for future meetings, as the Experimentalists continued to meet each spring until 1928 with the exception of one year during World War I (1918). Although the group had no officers, each year there was a host, the head of one of the participating laboratories. The host sent out invitations to the heads of the other laboratories, who, in turn, invited and brought along with them some of their staff and advanced graduate students. The meetings were run informally, emphasized discussion of work in progress, and, as Titchener had envisioned, provided an unparalleled opportunity for young men just entering the profession to become acquainted with those who were already well established.[39]

Not only was the society an important communication network and source of contacts within the profession, it also, on more than one occasion, engaged in decision making that affected the profession as a whole. Two notable cases were the recommendation to the APA that it abandon the plan to host the International Congress of Psychology, which emanated from the 1910 meeting of the Experimentalists at Johns Hopkins[40] and the plans for the role of psychology in the war effort, which were formulated at the Harvard meeting in 1917.[41]

A prominent feature of the group was what Boring has labeled "Titchener's insistent regnancy. . . . Always Titchener dominated the group."[42] For example, hosts consulted Titchener about whom to invite, and, according to Boring, Titchener "was virtually the arbiter of invitations. Not only were there certain persons in certain years who were understood to be ostracized from Titchener's presence; there were also those whose status as experimentalists lay in doubt."[43] Thus it was with trepidation that Columbia's Robert S. Woodworth was invited to the 1922 meeting hosted by Raymond Dodge at Wesleyan. Boring reports that Woodworth "was in Titchener's bad graces" because, finding he could not attend the meeting at Cornell in 1920, he had posted Titchener's invitation to him on the bulletin board at Columbia "with the added query 'Who wants to go?' In Titchener's view one did not do that with invitations."[44]

As for the fate of those who strayed from the straight and narrow path of what Titchener viewed as psychology, the experience of Gordon Allport is instructive. In his autobiographical sketch, Allport tells of his single encounter with Titchener, which occurred in the early 1920s when he was a graduate student at Harvard doing his dissertation under the direction of Herbert S. Langfeld:

> I had been invited to attend the select gathering of his group of experimentalists, which met at Clark University . . . . just as I was finishing my thesis. After two days of discussing problems in sensory psychology Titchener allotted three minutes to each visiting graduate to describe his own investigations. I reported on traits of personality and was punished by the rebuke of total silence from the group, punctuated by a glare of disapproval from Titchener. Later Titchener demanded of Langfeld, "Why did you let him work on that problem?"[45]

Boring, who was host for the Clark meeting, also vividly recalled the incident and Titchener's total dismissal of Allport and his work: "There was a long discussion of David Katz's modes of appearance of colors, and after that Langfeld was asked for a report and he put up Gordon Allport to tell about his analysis of personality. Allport's communication was followed by a long silence, and then Titchener said 'As we were saying, the modes of appearance of colors are . . .'."[46]

Exclusion of Women

In addition to assuming an uncompromising stance in regard to matters of decorum and what counted as legitimate psychology, Titchener rigidly enforced a ban on women at meetings of the Experimentalists. At the time the group began, there were about two hundred scientists in North America who identified themselves as psychologists, a little over 10 percent of whom were women.[47] Of course not all the women would have qualified as experimentalists, but there were several, including some of Titchener's own students, who did. In fact, if one consults the list of fifty-six psychologists who took their doctorates with Titchener, which was appended to the obituary by Boring, one finds that slightly over one-third were women.[48] And of the group of eleven students who took their degrees with Titchener prior to the advent of the Experimentalists in 1904, six were women.

The abundance of women among Titchener's doctoral students could be attributed to institutional factors. In the 1890s, at a time when many universities were unwilling to admit women as Ph.D. candidates, Cornell not only admitted them, but, what was even more unusual, regarded them as eligible for fellowships.[49] However, it appears that Titchener was not merely tolerating an institutional policy that brought many women graduate students to Cornell. There is evidence in the prefaces of his two instructor's manuals of experimental psychology that he found many of his women students credible as potential experimentalists. In the preface to the first manual he acknowledged it as "a product of the laboratory," embodying "the work of a long roll of students."[50] Of the few students whose names he selected for mention, half (three out of six) were women. Similarly, in the preface to the second manual, he gave particular thanks to nineteen of his students, ten of whom were women.

At least two of his early woman students are known to have developed into full-fledged experimental psychologists: Margaret Floy Washburn (Ph.D. 1894) and Eleanor Acheson McCulloch Gamble (Ph.D. 1898). Washburn, who became a professor at Vassar College, was unquestionably the more eminent of the two, her research achievements winning her the distinction of being the second woman ever elected to the National Academy of Sciences, in 1931.[51] Gamble also became a respected experimental psychologist who held a professorship at Wellesley College and continued her research, teaching, and writing despite an increasingly severe visual handicap which rendered her almost blind by the time of her sudden death at the age of sixty-five. Writing to a younger male colleague in 1907, Titchener, who was not lavish in his compliments, referred to Gamble as "an old pupil of mine, and a very good psychologist."[52] Yet, the existence of accomplished women experimentalists among his own former students and elsewhere notwithstanding, Titchener felt impelled to prohibit women from his experimental club. This gesture exemplified a gender-biased attitude painfully familiar to educated women in that era who were seeking access to the academic and scientific professions in general and to psychology in particular.[53]

The first form letter distributed by Titchener in mid-January 1904 was somewhat ambiguous regarding the status of women in the Experimentalists, stating: "that . . . membership be confined to men who are working in the field of experimental psychology."[54] The word *men* could have been interpreted generically in the context of the letter. In the next form letter, sent out in early February, Titchener outlined the features of his new society, and the third point in the list left no room for doubt: "For the present at least, membership confined to men."[55] As can be seen from the quote at the beginning of this chapter, Titchener's letter to Münsterberg in late January was also explicit about excluding women from his proposed club. Titchener's incoming correspondence during January and February 1904 contains only three letters which refer to the plan to exclude women from the group: two psychologists mildly questioned the policy, and one strongly endorsed it. But the bulk of the correspondence was silent on the issue.

E. C. Sanford at Clark felt caught in a dilemma, because he knew that there were women experimental psychologists who should be invited to the meetings, yet feared that their presence would be an inhibiting influence on the men.

> The question with regard to women in the association is a poser. Several of them on scientific grounds have full right to be there and might feel hurt (in a general impersonal way) if women are not asked. On the other hand they would undoubtedly interfere with the smoking and to a certain extent with the general freedom of a purely masculine assembly. Would it be possible to give them also the chance to say whether they would like to come—assuring them by a personal note that transactions would not come off except in a partially smoke-charged atmosphere?[56]

While in basic agreement with Titchener's proposal for the new society, a psychologist at the University of Toronto, August Kirschmann, did express some sympathy for the plight of the women: "I find it a little hard on ladies who take an interest in Experimental Psychology if we exclude them altogether."[57] Lightner Witmer also regretted that the ban on women meant "excluding a number of very capable experimentalists" yet felt compelled to support it, explaining his position as follows:

> I am quite positive in my objection to inviting women. . . . I am sure from my experience, that you cannot run an informal meeting of men and women. . . . We want a small vigorous association where we can speak our minds with perfect freedom. . . . The larger and more heterogeneous the organization the more likely is vigorous discussion to be misinterpreted and to be taken as an offence by individuals who may happen to be attacked. I think that the presence of women in the organization adds greatly to this danger, owing to the personal attitude which they usually take even to scientific discussions. I favor a small association, no invited guests, and no women members.[58]

There was thus virtually no opposition from his correspondents to Titchener's policy of excluding women from the Experimentalists' meetings, even though it was freely admitted by Titchener and others—including Sanford, Kirschmann, and Witmer—that there were several women who in terms of scientific credentials warranted inclusion. Furthermore, as mentioned earlier, Titchener himself had numerous women doctorate students, beginning with his first graduate student at Cornell, Margaret Floy Washburn.

Titchener never explained why women were unacceptable as members of his society. That he wanted above all to have free, informal interchange between older and younger men in the area of experimental psychology, with the goal of socializing the next generation into the profession, seems clear. Sanford and Witmer both suggest that the presence of women would interfere with this process, and it is a fair assumption that Titchener thought so too.

The exclusionary policy remained in effect throughout Titchener's lifetime with, it seems, little, if any, protest from the other men in the group. Only two recorded incidents from the early years of the society could be interpreted as challenges to his position, and even these are open to other interpretations. The first involved James Rowland Angell of the University of Chicago. Angell, invited to the inaugural meeting of the Experimentalists, did not attend. He did contribute a paper, however, and perhaps it is significant that it was written by a woman graduate student, Matilde Castro.[59] The other incident took place at the meeting held at the University of Pennsylvania in 1907. Titchener later described the event in a letter to Münsterberg, telling him that James Leuba, a professor at Bryn Mawr College, had sent some of his women students to the meeting. Titchener indicated to Münsterberg that the "girls" were "promptly turned out," and he dismissed the whole incident as a "sheer misunderstanding."[60]

The only unambiguous protest to Titchener's exclusionary policy came from Christine Ladd-

Franklin, a woman who was unquestionably qualified to be a member of the group in terms of scientific credentials. Twenty years Titchener's senior, Ladd-Franklin had completed her doctoral studies in mathematics and logic at Johns Hopkins in 1882.[61] Soon after, she had developed an interest in the topic of vision and had published a paper on binocular vision in 1887, in the first volume of the *American Journal of Psychology*.[62] In 1891–92 she had had the opportunity to study in Europe, carrying out experimental work on vision in the laboratory of G. E. Müller in Göttingen. She had also traveled to Berlin, where she had worked in Helmholtz's laboratory and attended the lectures of Arthur König. By the conclusion of her year of study, Ladd-Franklin had worked out her own theory of color vision, an evolutionarily based model, which she had presented to the International Congress of Psychology in London.

Her marriage to Fabian Franklin, a member of the mathematics faculty at Johns Hopkins, just after she had completed her doctoral work there, had foreclosed the possibility of an academic career. In that era married women were not viewed by institutional authorities as suitable candidates for those academic positions that were open to women.[63] Only through persistent effort was Ladd-Franklin able to secure appointments to teach some courses in her areas of specialization at Johns Hopkins and at Columbia, albeit intermittently and on a part-time basis. But in spite of her marginal institutional base, she managed to remain active in scientific pursuits throughout her lifetime, promoting her theory of color vision, conducting research on vision, attending and giving papers at meetings, and publishing. She was labeled "a remarkable woman" by one of her younger colleagues at Columbia, R. S. Woodworth.[64] He was impressed not only by "her keen logical mind" and "power of criticism," but also by her vitality, the zeal with which she promoted her views, and "her cheerful aggressiveness."[65]

Ladd-Franklin began corresponding with Titchener in 1892, as soon as he arrived in the United States to take up his post at Cornell. Both were endowed with dominating personalities, which would be pitted against each other twenty years later in a contest over the policy of exclusion of women from the Experimentalists. In 1912 Ladd-Franklin, perhaps the most outspoken of the women psychologists of that era in her feminist views, reacted incredulously when Titchener first barred her from a meeting of the Experimentalists that she wanted to attend.[66] She had written to ask if she might present a paper at his April meeting. "I am particularly anxious to bring my views up, once in a while, for hand-to-hand discussion before experts, and just now I have especially a paper which I should like very much to read before your meeting of experimental psychologists. I hope you will not say nay!"[67]

Titchener's reply has not been preserved, but the surviving evidence suggests that he wrote informing Ladd-Franklin that women were not welcome to attend the Experimentalists' meetings. Her next letter to Titchener conveys her indignant reaction to this discriminatory practice: "I am shocked to know that you are still—at this year—excluding women from your meeting of experimental psychologists. It is such a very old-fashioned standpoint!"[68] She also pointed out how irrational it was for Titchener to invite to that year's meeting at Clark University "the students of G. Stanley Hall, who are not in the least experimentalists and exclude the women who are doing particularly good work in the experimental laboratory of Professor Baird."[69] She was also unwilling to accept the notion that it was legitimate to exclude women from the meetings because they would interfere with the men's smoking: "Have your smokers separated if you like (tho I for one always smoke when I am in fashionable society), but a scientific meeting (however personal) is a public affair, and it is not open to you to leave out a class of fellow workers without extreme discourtesy."[70]

Although Ladd-Franklin failed to persuade Titchener to let her attend the Experimentalists' gathering at Clark, she did not admit defeat on the matter. Two years later the Experimentalists decided to meet at Columbia, where Ladd-Franklin was teaching courses in logic and color vision. Shortly before the meeting, she wrote to Titchener, thanking him for having referred to her as belonging to the group of psychologists that "had some logic in them."[71] In view of this compliment, she considered it all the more contradictory that Titchener should persist in excluding her from his Experimentalists' meetings: "Is this then a good time, my dear Professor Titchener, for you to hold to the medieval attitude of not admitting me to your coming psychological conference in New York—at my very door? So unconscientious, so immoral,—worse than that—so unscientific!"[72] It seems that Ladd-Franklin was permitted to attend one session at the Columbia meeting. At the others, according to Boring's account, "tradition was kept supreme."[73] In spite of the fact that Ladd-Franklin persisted in protesting Titchener's policy until at least 1916, when she attempted to enlist John B. Watson in her cause, tradition indeed remained supreme.[74]

Nor did the group rush to open its doors to women immediately after Titchener died in 1927. In 1928, the committee of five charged with the task of developing a plan for reorganizing the society hesitated to break with the traditional ban on women members. Although two women—Margaret Floy Washburn and June Etta Downey—were discussed favorably, the committee "decided not to prejudice this issue" and declined to elect any women that year.[75] The next year the organizing committee was enlarged, and in 1929 it met at Princeton, where several important decisions were made regarding the future of the society. In keeping with tradition, the society was to be restricted to experimental psychologists meeting "for the purpose of informal discussion."[76] However, in a break with the past, the group also decided "that there should be no restriction of membership with regard to sex."[77]

The Experimentalists reconstituted themselves as the Society of Experimental Psychologists at the Princeton meeting. The charter group consisted of twenty-six members, among them Washburn and Downey. Downey, a professor and chair of the Department of Psychology and Philosophy at the University of Wyoming, was never to attend a meeting; in her mid-fifties when elected, she died suddenly just three years later.[78] Washburn, a professor at Vassar College, was in her late fifties when admitted to the society. Although she had the opportunity to host the society for its 1931 meeting, her participation in the group was cut short when, in 1937, she suffered an incapacitating cerebral stroke from which she never recovered.[79]

By the late thirties, then, neither of the women elected to the society in 1929 remained in the group, and no other woman had been elected to membership. This dearth of women in the society was not a temporary phenomenon. A group photo taken in 1947, twenty years after Titchener's death, when the society met at Princeton, shows thirty-nine psychologists, all men.

In fact, it was not until 1958 that another woman, Eleanor J. Gibson, was admitted to the society. And as recently as the early 1970s, the membership list of the organization showed only one more woman, Dorothea Jameson Hurvich, added to the rolls in 1970. In both cases, their spouses had belonged to the group for over a decade before they were elected to membership,[80] which suggests that sponsorship and access to the communication network of the group provided by a spouse were key ingredients in their election to membership.

In summary, the elite society organized by E. B. Titchener in 1904 to promote psychology as an experimental science provided an important communication network and opportunities for contact among a select group of established and neophyte psychologists. Collegial relationships were fostered, and knowledge was shared at the annual meetings. The gatherings also, on more than one occasion, served as a forum for decision making that would affect the larger profession. For over two decades, Titchener dominated this group, insisting, among other things, that the subject matter of the meetings be confined strictly to what he defined as experimental psychology. Also by Titchener's fiat, and with the acquiescence of the other members, certain groups of psychologists, such as women and those not considered experimentalists, were excluded from the meetings. The evidence suggests that this prolonged policy of social ostracism took a heavy toll on women's participation and advancement in experimental psychology. Deprived because of their gender of the collegial ties and informal communication so vital to the successful pursuit of experimental work, they faced virtually insurmountable obstacles to advancing their careers as scientists.

The cost to experimental psychology of losing women as practitioners is more difficult to assess. I would like to suggest, however, that by excluding women, the subfield may have deprived itself of a perspective recently articulated by a group of women scholars who regard it as a distinctively, but not exclusively, feminine approach to knowledge. What Belenky, Clinchy, Goldberger, and Tarule describe as "women's ways of knowing" stand in sharp contrast to the masculine approach to scientific knowledge (epitomized by Titchener), with its emphasis on objectivity, detachment, control, and domination.[81] The epistemological orientation associated with this masculine approach, which Belenky and her colleagues call "separate knowing," is tough-minded, being based on impersonal procedures for establishing truth. The more typically feminine epistemological orientation that Belenky and her co-workers call "connected knowing," is an approach that places a premium on learning through empathy and involves intimacy and equality between the self and the object of study. If Titchener's group had allowed participation by women, with their special ways of knowing, who is to say how profoundly different the subfield of experimental psychology might have become? But to imagine that is another story.

NOTES

1. Letter from E. B. Titchener to Hugo Münsterberg, 1 Feb. 1904, Münsterberg Papers, Boston Public Library.
2. For an inquiry into how the epistemological authority of scientific specialists is brought to bear in social arrangements inside and outside science, see Kathryn Pyne Addelson, "The Man of Professional Wisdom," in *Discovering Reality: Feminist Perspectives on Epistemology, Metaphysics, Methodology, and Philosophy of Science,* ed. Sandra Harding and Merrill B. Hintikka (Dordrecht: Reidel, 1983), pp. 165–86.
3. For an insightful discussion of how women scientists are hindered in their research role by restricted access to the informal communication system in science and to informal contacts among colleagues, see Barbara F. Reskin, "Sex Differentiation and the Social Organization of Science," *Social Inquiry* 48 (1978): 6–37.
4. Arthur L. Blumenthal, "Shaping a Tradition: Experimentalism Begins," in *Points of View in the Modern History of Psychology,* ed. Claude E. Buxton (Orlando, Fla.: Academic Press, 1985), p. 71.
5. Rand B. Evans, "Edward Bradford Titchener: A Sketch" (brochure printed by the American Psychological Association to accompany a photographic exhibit on E. B. Titchener, 1 Nov. 1972–1 Apr. 1973, and an exhibit of memorabilia, Apr. 1973–1 Oct. 1973, located in the headquarters of the APA, Washington, D.C.), p. 1.
6. Ibid., p. 2.
7. Frank Angell, "Titchener at Leipzig, *Journal of General Psychology* 1 (1928): 198.
8. Howard C. Warren, in *A History of Psychology in Autobiography,* vol. 1, ed. Carl Murchison (Worcester, Mass.: Clark University Press, 1930), p. 451.
9. Titchener to Hunter, 24 Jan. 1907, Titchener Papers, Department of Manuscripts and University Archives, Cornell University Libraries.

10. Edwin G. Boring, "Edward Bradford Titchener 1867–1927." *American Journal of Psychology* 38 (1927): 493.
11. Raymond F. Howes, "Recollections of E. B. Titchener," *Cornell Alumni News,* Apr. 1969, p. 20.
12. Ibid., pp. 21–22.
13. Kurt Danziger, "The Positivist Repudiation of Wundt," *Journal of the History of the Behavioral Sciences* 15 (1979): 205. For other recent scholarship that discusses the differences between Wundtian and Titchenerian psychology, see Arthur L. Blumenthal, "Wilhelm Wundt: Psychology as the Propaedeutic Science," in *Points of View in the Modern History of Psychology,* ed. Claude E. Buxton (Orlando, Fla.: Academic Press, 1985), pp. 19–50; Thomas H. Leahey, "The Mistaken Mirror: On Wundt's and Titchener's Psychologies," *Journal of the History of the Behavioral Sciences* 17 (1981): 273–82; and Ryan D. Tweney and Stephen A. Yachanin, "Titchener's Wundt," in *Wundt Studies: A Centennial Collection,* ed. Wolfgang G. Bringmann and Ryan D. Tweney (Toronto: C. J. Hogrefe, 1980), pp. 380–95.
14. Tweney and Yachanin, "Titchener's Wundt," p. 388.
15. E. B. Titchener, "Some Current Problems in Experimental Psychology," *Natural Science* 4 (1894):446.
16. W. B. Pillsbury, "The Psychology of Edward Bradford Titchener," *Philosophical Review* 37 (1928): 97.
17. Boring, "Titchener," p. 494.
18. Ibid., p. 497.
19. Pillsbury, "Psychology of Titchener," pp. 99–100.
20. E. B. Titchener, *Experimental Psychology: A Manual of Laboratory Practice,* vol. 1, *Qualitative Experiments,* part 1, *Students' Manual;* part 2, *Instructor's Manual* (London: Macmillan, 1901).
21. E. B. Titchener, *Experimental Psychology: A Manual of Laboratory Practice,* vol. 2, *Quantitative Experiments,* part 1. *Students's Manual;* part 2, *Instructor's Manual,* (London: Macmillan, 1905)..
22. Boring, "Titchener," p. 497.
23. "E. B. Titchener and the Beginnings of the Society of Experimental Psychologists," *Newsletter of the Division of the History of Psychology: American Psychological Association* 13, no. 2 (1981): 17.
24. Ibid.
25. Ibid.
26. Ibid.
27. Ibid.
28. Ibid.
29. Ibid.
30. Quoted by C. James Goodwin, "On the Origins of Titchener's Experimentalists," *Journal of the History of the Behavioral Sciences,* 21 (1985): 386.
31. Ibid.
32. Ibid., p. 384.
33. Münsterberg to Titchener, 30 Jan. 1904, Titchener Papers.
34. Ibid.
35. Ibid.
36. "Titchener and the Society of Experimental Psychologists," p. 18.
37. Ibid.
38. C. H. Judd, "Meeting of Experimental Psychologists at Cornell University," *Journal of Philosophy, Psychology and Scientific Methods* 1 (1904): 238–40.
39. Edwin G. Boring, "The Society of Experimental Psychologists: 1904–1938," *American Journal of Psychology* 51 (1938): 410–21.
40. See Pillsbury to Titchener, 26 Apr. 1910, Titchener Papers.
41. See Robert M. Yerkes, ed., *Psychological Examining in the United States Army,* Memoirs of the National Academy of Sciences, vol. 15 (Washington: Government Printing Office, 1921), p. 7.
42 Boring, "Society of Experimental Psychologists," p. 410.
43. Ibid.
44. Ibid., p. 415.
45. Gordon W. Allport, in *A History of Psychology in Autobiography,* vol. 5, ed. Edwin G. Boring and Gardner Lindzey (New York: Appleton-Century-Crofts, 1967), p. 9.
46. Edwin G. Boring, "Titchener's Experimentalists," *Journal of the History of the Behavioral Sciences* 3 (1967): 323.
47. For an account of these early women psychologists, see Laurel Furumoto and Elizabeth Scarbor-

ough, "Placing Women in the History of Psychology: The First American Women Psychologists," *American Psychologist* 41 (1986): 35–42.
48. Boring, "Titchener," p. 506.
49. For discussions of the struggles of women to gain access to graduate education in the late nineteenth century, see Margaret W. Rossiter, *Women Scientists in America: Struggles and Strategies to 1940* (Baltimore: Johns Hopkins University Press, 1982), and Elizabeth Scarborough and Laurel Furumoto, *Untold Lives: The First Generation of American Women Psychologists* (New York: Columbia University Press, 1987).
50. Titchener, *Experimental Psychology,* vol. 1, part 2, p. vii.
51. See Scarborough and Furumoto, *Untold Lives,* pp. 91–107, for an account of Washburn's life and career.
52. Titchener to Hunter, 24 Jan. 1907, Titchener Papers.
53. For detailed accounts of the obstacles confronting women aspiring to careers in the sciences and more particularly the social sciences and psychology in the late nineteenth and early twentieth centuries, see Rossiter, *Women Scientists,* (for women scientists, in general), Rosalind Rosenberg, *Beyond Separate Spheres: Intellectual Roots of Modern Feminism* (New Haven: Yale University Press, 1982) (for women in the social sciences), and Scarborough and Furumoto, *Untold Lives* (for women psychologists).
54. "Titchener and the Society of Experimental Psychologists," p. 17.
55. Ibid., p. 18.
56. Edmund C. Sanford to Titchener, 19 Jan. 1904, Titchener Papers.
57. August Kirschmann to Titchener, 5 Mar. 1904, Titchener Papers.
58. Lightner Witmer to Titchener, 25 Jan. 1904, Titchener Papers.
59. C. H. Judd, "Meeting of Experimental Psychologists," p. 240.
60. Titchener to Münsterberg, 29 Feb. 1908, Münsterberg Papers.
61. Johns Hopkins refused to grant her the degree she had earned because she was a woman. On the occasion of its fiftieth anniversary in 1926, it belatedly awarded Ladd-Franklin the Ph.D. For a fuller account of Ladd-Franklin's life and experience at Johns Hopkins, see Elizabeth Scarborough and Laurel Furumoto, *Untold Lives,* pp. 119–24.
62. Christine Ladd-Franklin, "A Method for the Experimental Determination of the Horopter," *American Journal of Psychology* 1 (1887): 99–111.
63. See Scarborough and Furumoto, *Untold Lives,* pp. 71–90, for a more detailed discussion of the marriage-versus-career dilemma faced by highly educated women in the late nineteenth and early twentieth centuries.
64. R. S. Woodworth, "Christine Ladd-Franklin," *Science* 71 (1930): 307.
65. Ibid.
66. See Scarborough and Furumoto, *Untold Lives,* pp. 109–12, for an account of Ladd-Franklin's feminist stance.
67. Christine Ladd-Franklin to Titchener, undated, Christine Ladd-Franklin and Fabian Franklin Papers, Butler Library, Columbia University.
68. Ladd-Franklin to Titchener, undated, Christine Ladd-Franklin and Fabian Franklin Papers.
69. Ibid.
70. Ibid.
71. Ladd-Franklin to Titchener, 21 Mar. 1914, Christine Ladd-Franklin and Fabian Franklin Papers.
72. Ibid.
73. Boring, "Society of Experimental Psychologists," p. 414.
74. See John B. Watson to Ladd-Franklin, 14 Apr. 1916 and 18 Apr. 1916, Christine Ladd-Franklin and Fabian Franklin Papers.
75. Boring, "Society of Experimental Psychologists," p. 417.
76. Ibid., p. 418.
77. Ibid.
78. For a fuller account of Downey's life and career, see Christina Van Horn and Laurel Furumoto, "June Etta Downey: The Psychologist, the Poet, and the Person" (Unpublished manuscript).
79. See Scarborough and Furumoto, *Untold Lives,* pp. 91–107.
80. "Report of the Society of Experimental Psychologists, Inc., 1971–72." David Krech Papers, Archives of the History of American Psychology, University of Akron, Ohio.
81. Mary Field Belenky, Blythe McVicker Clinchy,

Nancy Goldberger, and Jill Mattuck Tarule, *Women's Ways of Knowing: The Development of Self, Voice, and Mind* (New York: Basic Books, 1986). For an analysis of the gendered nature of science, see Evelyn Fox Keller, *Reflections on Gender and Science* (New Haven: Yale University Press, 1985), and the insightful review of Keller's book by Jill G. Morawski, "Toward Science without Gender," *Contemporary Psychology* 31 (1986): 95–96.

CHAPTER 7

DARWINIAN INFLUENCES: ADAPTATION AND INDIVIDUAL DIFFERENCES

On November 24, 1859, Charles Darwin's book, *On the Origin of Species,* appeared in the bookshops of London. At the end of the day, all 1,250 copies of the first printing had been sold. It was an appropriate beginning for the book that would be judged by many scholars to be the most influential work published in the last four hundred years. Its influence has been enormous in many fields of inquiry, and psychology is no exception.

At the age of 22, Charles Darwin (1809–1882) signed on as a naturalist aboard *H.M.S. Beagle,* a small British ship scheduled for a scientific voyage around the world. That voyage of five years would change Darwin and the world. In the last year of that voyage, he began to organize his many notes toward eventual publication. He began his writing immediately after his return to England, completing first the five volumes of his *Zoology of the Voyage of H.M.S. Beagle* and then, in 1839, his journal entitled *The Voyage of the Beagle.* Early in the course of this writing, Darwin began to think about the transformation of species, an idea that had been part of scientific conjecture for many years. His own data from the *Beagle* voyage, and the impetus of reading Thomas Malthus's essay on population, provided the basis for his revolutionary book on the theory of evolution by natural selection. Malthus argued that human populations grew geometrically, whereas the availability of food resources increased only arithmetically. That meant that people would eventually face a struggle for food and other resources. This insight would help Darwin understand how natural selection worked. Darwin began his writing on that theory around 1840 and by 1844 had produced a manuscript of approximately two hundred pages. Yet he did not publish those ideas until nearly twenty years after he first began work on them. The reasons for this twenty-year delay and the interesting story surrounding the writing of the *Origin* are discussed in one of the selections in this chapter.

The idea of evolution was not original with Darwin. In a 1794 book *Zoonomia,* his grandfather, Erasmus Darwin (1731–1802), a physician and biologist, had written about attempts at adaptation producing evolution of animal species. These ideas anticipated the evolutionary theory of Jean Baptiste Lamarck (1744–1829), whose *Philosophie Zoologique,* published in 1809, argued for a behavioral theory of evolution. In other words, learned behaviors that proved adaptive were passed to subsequent generations. (Lamarck's ideas remained influential through most of the nineteenth century but fell into disrepute at the beginning of the twentieth century. However, some recent work in the field of evolutionary theory has revived them.) Evolutionary ideas existed outside of biology as well. Charles Darwin's good friend, Charles Lyell (1797–1875), an eminent geologist, had published an evolutionary account of the transformations in the geology of the earth.

These intellectual forces set the stage for a theory that could explain the growing fossil, botanical, and zoological evidence that was inconsistent with a Genesis account of the origin of species, and Darwin was to generate that theory (see Gruber, 1981). His extensive and meticulous work as the *Beagle* naturalist led Darwin to propose natural selection as the mechanism for evolution. Changes in species occurred through random variations. Certain of those variations would be better suited to changing demands in the environment, and those animals and plants would be more likely to survive. Darwin's theory gave new importance to the notion of variation and individual differences and provided an understanding of their role in species adaptation to the environment.

These ideas were influential in Freud's psychoanalytic theory (see Chapter 13), but nowhere were they more important than in American functional psychology, a psychology built on an emphasis on individual differences and their importance for adaptation (see Chapters 8 and 9). Further, Darwin's work significantly strengthened the field of comparative psychology by linking humans with the rest of the animal kingdom (see Chapter 10). Of particular importance in that respect was his 1872 book entitled *The Expression of the Emotions in Man and Animals,* which described the similarity in form and function of emotional expressions in humans and other animals.

Darwin's theory also had a great impact on his cousin, Francis Galton (Erasmus Darwin was Galton's grandfather as well). Galton (1822–1911) was an explorer, statistician, inventor, and scientist, who made significant contributions to many fields, including psychology. His interests were incredibly diverse. For example, he studied fingerprints, the geographic distribution of beauty, the efficacy of prayer, word associations, twins, paranoia, cuckoos, animal hearing, correlation, and intelligence. He even taught himself to perform arithmetical calculations using odors substituted for numbers (see Galton, 1894).

Galton is probably best remembered for his founding of *eugenics*, an ideology that proposed improvement of the human race by selectively mating those individuals who possessed the most desirable characteristics. Needless to say, such ideas produced considerable controversy in and out of the scientific community.

Within a few days of the publication of Darwin's *Origin,* Galton wrote to his cousin:

> Pray let me add a word of congratulations on the completion of your wonderful volume. . . . I have laid it down in the full enjoyment of a feeling that one rarely experiences after boyhood days, of having been initiated into an entirely new province of knowledge which, nevertheless, connects itself with other things in a thousand ways. (as cited in Fancher, 1979, pp. 261–262)

The social implications of Darwin's book were especially important to Galton as he began his studies of eminent individuals and the reasons for their eminence. He concluded, through statistical studies, that eminence occurred among the members of certain families too frequently to be explained by the influence of the environment. He published his findings in his most famous book, *Hereditary Genius,* which appeared in 1869. Returning the compliment he had received, Darwin wrote to Galton:

> I have only read about 50 pages of your book . . . but I must exhale myself, else something will go wrong in my inside. I do not think I have ever in my life read anything more interesting and original. . . . You have made a convert of an opponent in one sense, for I have always maintained that, excepting fools, men do not differ in intellect, only in zeal and hard work. (as cited in Fancher, 1979, p. 268)

Galton argued in his book that, like physical traits, natural abilities (that is, psychological traits such as judgment, intelligence, sociability) were inherited. The next logical step was the improvement of the human race by a eugenics program that ensured the "best kind" of people. In 1884, he established a laboratory in the Natural History Museum in the South Kensington district of London, where for six years he collected anthropometric measurements (visual acuity, strength of grip, color vision, hearing acuity, hand preference, span of arms, and so on) to support his views of the distribution of abilities and physical characteristics. Solomon Diamond (1977) has argued that all of Galton's work in psychology arose from one concern: "how we might best manipulate the forces of evolution to mankind's advantage" (p.52). Eugenics was thus a practical program to accelerate the progress of evolution.

As noted earlier, the legacy of Darwin and Galton is an important one for psychology, especially for the American school of psychology known as *functionalism.* Consciousness was viewed by this school as having evolutionary significance; obviously it aided an organism's ability to adapt to the environment. Deriving from the concept of evolutionary adaptation was an emphasis on the processes of psychological adjustment, a belief that selection of behavioral acts was determined by the consequences of those actions and a focus on the value of studying individual differences (Kendler,1987). Those emphases would characterize the work of many American psychologists, such as William James, G. Stanley Hall, James McKeen Cattell, and Edward L. Thorndike (all of whom are discussed in the next three chapters).

THE READINGS

In this chapter, there are two primary source selections, one from Darwin and the other from Galton. The two secondary source articles also treat the work and influence of those two scientists. The first selection, from Darwin's *Origin of Species,* includes the introduction to the book as well as the third chapter dealing with the struggle for existence. Pay special attention to the hesitancy and caution of Darwin's language in the introduction to the *Origin.* The second selection, from Galton's *Hereditary Genius,* includes the preface and introductory chapter of the book as well as an excerpt from the end of the book treating the "comparative worth of different races, " a section that discusses some of Galton's views on eugenics.

One of the long-standing questions in the history of science is why Darwin delayed so long in publishing his theory (see Gould, 1977). Not surprisingly, many explanations have been offered. In the third selection, the historian of science Robert J. Richards attempts a definitive answer and, in doing so, discusses what makes for an interesting question in science and what historiographical models can be best used to answer those questions.

The final selection is by Solomon Diamond, a distinguished psychologist who has written much in the field of intellectual history. In this article, Diamond looks at the influence of Galton's ideas in American psychology, focusing especially on James McKeen Cattell and Joseph Jastrow. The influence of both Darwin and Galton on American psychology will become even more evident in the following three chapters of this book.

REFERENCES

Diamond, S. (1977). Francis Galton and American psychology. *Annals of the New York Academy of Sciences,* 291, 47–55.

Fancher, R. E. (1979). *Pioneers of psychology,* New York: W. W. Norton & Co.

Galton, F (1894). Arithmetic by smell. *Psychological Review,* 1, 61–62.

Gould, S. J. (1977). *Ever since Darwin.* New York: W. W. Norton & Co.

Gruber, H. (1981). *Darwin on man: A psychological study of scientific creativity* (2d ed.). Chicago: University of Chicago Press.

Kendler, H. H. (1987). *Historical foundations of modern psychology.* Chicago: Dorsey Press.

Natural Selection and the Struggle for Existence

Charles Darwin

INTRODUCTION

When on board H.M.S. 'Beagle,' as naturalist, I was much struck with certain facts in the distribution of the organic beings inhabiting South America, and in the geological relations of the present to the past inhabitants of that continent. These facts, as will be seen in the latter chapters of this volume, seemed to throw some light on the origin of species—that mystery of mysteries, as it has been called by one of our greatest philosophers. On my return home, it occurred to me, in 1837, that something might perhaps be made out on this question by patiently accumulating and reflecting on all sorts of facts which could possibly have any bearing on it. After five years' work I allowed myself to speculate on the subject, and drew up some short notes; these I enlarged in 1844 into a sketch of the conclusions, which then seemed to me probable: from that period to the present day I have steadily pursued the same object. I hope that I may be excused for entering on these personal details, as I give them to show that I have not been hasty in coming to a decision.

My work is now (1859) nearly finished; but as it will take me many more years to complete it, and as my health is far from strong, I have been urged to publish this Abstract. I have more especially been induced to do this, as Mr. Wallace, who is now studying the natural history of the Malay archipelago, has arrived at almost exactly the same general conclusions that I have on the origin of species. In 1858 he sent me a memoir on this subject, with a request that I would forward it to Sir Charles Lyell, who sent it to the Linnean Society, and it is published in the third volume of the Journal of that Society. Sir C. Lyell and Dr. Hooker, who both knew of my work—the latter having read my sketch of 1844—honoured me by thinking it advisable to publish, with Mr. Wallace's excellent memoir, some brief extracts from my manuscripts.

This Abstract, which I now publish, must necessarily be imperfect. I cannot here give references and authorities for my several statements; and I must trust to the reader reposing some confidence in my accuracy. No doubt errors will have crept in, though I hope I have always been cautious in trusting to good authorities alone. I can here give only the general conclusions at which I have arrived, with a few facts in illustration, but which, I hope, in most cases will suffice. No one can feel more sensible than I do of the necessity of hereafter publishing in detail all the facts, with references, on which my conclusions have been grounded; and I hope in a future work to do this. For I am well aware that scarcely a single point is discussed in this volume on which facts cannot be adduced, often apparently leading to conclusions directly opposite to those at which I have arrived. A fair result can be obtained only by fully stating and balancing the facts and arguments on both sides of each question; and this is here impossible.

I much regret that want of space prevents my having the satisfaction of acknowledging the generous assistance which I have received from very many naturalists, some of them personally unknown to me. I cannot, however, let this opportunity pass without expressing my deep obligations to Dr. Hooker, who, for the last fifteen years, has aided me in every possible way by his large stores of knowledge and his excellent judgment.

In considering the Origin of Species, it is quite conceivable that a naturalist, reflecting on the mutual affinities of organic beings, on their embryological relations, their geographical dis-

From Darwin, C. (1859). *On the origin of species by means of natural selection.* New York: D. Appleton, 1892, pp. 1–4, 48–61.

tribution, geological succession, and other such facts, might come to the conclusion that species had not been independently created, but had descended, like varieties, from other species. Nevertheless, such a conclusion, even if well founded, would be unsatisfactory, until it could be shown how the innumerable species inhabiting this world have been modified, so as to acquire that perfection of structure and coadaptation which justly excites our admiration. Naturalists continually refer to external conditions, such as climate, food, &c., as the only possible cause of variation. In one limited sense, as we shall hereafter see, this may be true; but it is preposterous to attribute to mere external conditions, the structure, for instance, of the woodpecker, with its feet, tail, beak, and tongue, so admirably adapted to catch insects under the bark of trees. In the case of the mistletoe, which draws its nourishment from certain trees, which has seeds that must be transported by certain birds, and which has flowers with separate sexes absolutely requiring the agency of certain insects to bring pollen from one flower to the other, it is equally preposterous to account for the structure of this parasite, with its relations to several distinct organic beings, by the effects of external conditions, or of habit, or of the volition of the plant itself.

It is, therefore, of the highest importance to gain a clear insight into the means of modification and coadaptation. At the commencement of my observations it seemed to me probable that a careful study of domesticated animals and of cultivated plants would offer the best chance of making out this obscure problem. Nor have I been disappointed; in this and in all other perplexing cases I have invariably found that our knowledge, imperfect though it be, of variation under domestication, afforded the best and safest clue. I may venture to express my conviction of the high value of such studies, although they have been very commonly neglected by naturalists.

From these considerations, I shall devote the first chapter of this Abstract to Variation under Domestication. We shall thus see that a large amount of hereditary modification is at least possible; and, what is equally or more important, we shall see how great is the power of man in accumulating by his Selection successive slight variations. I will then pass on to the variability of species in a state of nature; but I shall, unfortunately, be compelled to treat this subject far too briefly, as it can be treated properly only by giving long catalogues of facts. We shall, however, be enabled to discuss what circumstances are most favourable to variation. In the next chapter the Struggle for Existence amongst all organic beings throughout the world, which inevitably follows from the high geometrical ratio of their increase, will be considered. This is the doctrine of Malthus applied to the whole animal and vegetable kingdoms. As many more individuals of each species are born than can possibly survive; and as, consequently, there is a frequently recurring struggle for existence, it follows that any being, if it vary however slightly in any manner profitable to itself, under the complex and sometimes varying conditions of life, will have a better chance of surviving, and thus be *naturally selected*. From the strong principle of inheritance, any selected variety will tend to propagate its new and modified form.

This fundamental subject of Natural Selection will be treated at some length in the fourth chapter; and we shall then see how Natural Selection almost inevitably causes much Extinction of the less improved forms of life, and leads to what I have called Divergence of Character. In the next chapter I shall discuss the complex and little known laws of variation. In the five succeeding chapters, the most apparent and gravest difficulties in accepting the theory will be given: namely, first, the difficulties of transitions, or how a simple being or a simple organ can be changed and perfected into a highly developed being or into an elaborately constructed organ; secondly, the subject of Instinct, or the mental powers of animals; thirdly, Hybridism, or the infertility of species and the fertility of varieties when intercrossed; and fourthly, the imperfection of the Geological Record. In the next chapter I shall consider the geological succession of organic beings throughout time; in the twelfth and thirteenth; their geographical distribution throughout space; in the fourteenth, their classification or mutual affinities, both when mature and in an embryonic condition. In the last chapter I shall give a brief recapitulation of the whole work, and a few concluding remarks.

No one ought to feel surprise at much remaining as yet unexplained in regard to the origin of species and varieties, if he make due allowance for our profound ignorance in regard to mutual relations of the many beings which live around us. Who can explain why one species ranges widely and is very numerous, and why another allied species has a narrow range and is rare? Yet these relations are of the highest importance, for they determine the present welfare, and, as I believe, the future success and modification of every inhabitant of this world. Still less do we know of the mutual relations of the innumerable inhabitants of the world during the many past geological epochs in its history. Although much remains obscure, and will long remain obscure, I can entertain no doubt, after the most deliberate study and dispassionate judgment of which I am capable, that the view which most naturalists until recently entertained, and which I formerly entertained—namely, that each species has been independently created—is erroneous. I am fully convinced that species are not immutable; but that those belonging to what are called the same genera are lineal descendants of some other and generally extinct species, in the same manner as the acknowledged varieties of any one species are the descendants of that species. Furthermore, I am convinced that Natural Selection has been the most important, but not the exclusive, means of modification. . . .

STRUGGLE FOR EXISTENCE

Before entering on the subject of this chapter, I must make a few preliminary remarks, to show how the struggle for existence bears on Natural Selection. It has been seen in the last chapter that amongst organic beings in a state of nature there is some individual variability: indeed I am not aware that this has ever been disputed. It is immaterial for us whether a multitude of doubtful forms be called species or sub-species or varieties; what rank, for instance, the two or three hundred doubtful forms of British plants are entitled to hold, if the existence of any well-marked varieties be admitted. But the mere existence of individual variability and of some few well-marked varieties, though necessary as the foundation for the work, helps us but little in understanding how species arise in nature. How have all those exquisite adaptations of one part of the organisation to another part, and to the conditions of life, and of one organic being to another being, been perfected? We see these beautiful co-adaptations most plainly in the woodpecker and the misletoe; and only a little less plainly in the humblest parasite which clings to the hairs of a quadruped or feathers of a bird; in the structure of the beetle which dives through the water: in the plumed seed which is wafted by the gentlest breeze; in short, we see beautiful adaptations everywhere and in every part of the organic world.

Again, it may be asked, how is it that varieties, which I have called incipient species, become ultimately converted into good and distinct species, which in most cases obviously differ from each other far more than do the varieties of the same species? How do those groups of species, which constitute what are called distinct genera, and which differ from each other more than do the species of the same genus, arise? All these results, as we shall more fully see in the next chapter, follow from the struggle for life. Owing to this struggle, variations, however slight, and from whatever cause proceeding, if they be in any degree profitable to the individuals of a species, in their infinitely complex relations to other organic beings and to their physical conditions of life, will tend to the preservation of such individuals, and will generally be inherited by the offspring. The offspring, also, will thus have a better chance of surviving, for, of the many individuals of any species which are periodically born, but a small number can survive. I have called this principle, by which each slight variation, if useful, is preserved, by the term Natural Selection, in order to mark its relation to man's power of selection. But the expression often used by Mr. Herbert Spencer of the Survival of the Fittest is more accurate, and is sometimes equally convenient. We have seen that man by selection can certainly produce great results, and can adapt organic beings to his own uses, through the accumulation of slight but useful variations, given to him by the hand of Nature. But Natural Selection, as we shall hereafter see, is a power incessantly ready for action, and is as immeasurably superior to man's feeble efforts, as the works of Nature are to those of Art.

We will now discuss in a little more detail the struggle for existence. In my future work this subject will be treated, as it well deserves, at greater length. The elder DeCandolle and Lyell have largely and philosophically shown that all organic beings are exposed to severe competition. In regard to plants, no one has treated this subject with more spirit and ability than W. Herbert, Dean of Manchester, evidently the result of his great horticultural knowledge. Nothing is easier than to admit in words the truth of the universal struggle for life, or more difficult—at least I have found it so—than constantly to bear this conclusion in mind. Yet unless it be thoroughly engrained in the mind, the whole economy of nature, with every fact on distribution, rarity, abundance, extinction, and variation, will be dimly seen or quite misunderstood. We behold the face of nature bright with gladness, we often see superabundance of food; we do not see or we forget, that the birds which are idly singing round us mostly live on insects or seeds, and are thus constantly destroying life; or we forget how largely these songsters, or their eggs, or their nestlings, are destroyed by birds and beasts of prey; we do not always bear in mind, that, though food may be now superabundant, it is not so at all seasons of each recurring year.

The Term, Struggle for Existence, Used in a Large Sense

I should premise that I use this term in a large and metaphorical sense including dependence of one being on another, and including (which is more important) not only the life of the individual, but success in leaving progeny. Two canine animals, in a time of dearth, may be truly said to struggle with each other which shall get food and live. But a plant on the edge of a desert is said to struggle for life against the drought, though more properly it should be said to be dependent on the moisture. A plant which annually produces a thousand seeds, of which only one on an average comes to maturity, may be more truly said to struggle with the plants of the same and other kinds which already clothe the ground. The misletoe is dependent on the apple and a few other trees, but can only in a far-fetched sense be said to struggle with these trees, for, if too many of these parasites grow on the same tree, it languishes and dies. But several seedling misletoes, growing close together on the same branch, may more truly be said to struggle with each other. As the misletoe is disseminated by birds, its existence depends on them; and it may metaphorically be said to struggle with other fruit-bearing plants, in tempting the birds to devour and thus disseminate its seeds. In these several senses, which pass into each other, I use for convenience' sake the general term of Struggle for Existence.

Geometrical Ratio of Increase

A struggle for existence inevitably follows from the high rate at which all organic beings tend to increase. Every being, which during its natural lifetime produces several eggs or seeds, must suffer destruction during some period of its life, and during some season or occasional year, otherwise, on the principle of geometrical increase, its numbers would quickly become so inordinately great that no country could support the product. Hence, as more individuals are produced than can possibly survive, there must in every case be a struggle for existence, either one individual with another of the same species, or with the individuals of distinct species, or with the physical conditions of life. It is the doctrine of Malthus applied with manifold force to the whole animal and vegetable kingdoms; for in this case there can be no artificial increase of food, and no prudential restraint from marriage. Although some species may be now increasing, more or less rapidly, in numbers, all cannot do so, for the world would not hold them.

There is no exception to the rule that every organic being naturally increases at so high a rate, that, if not destroyed, the earth would soon be covered by the progeny of a single pair. Even slow-breeding man has doubled in twenty-five years, and at this rate, in less than a thousand years, there would literally not be standing-room for his progeny. Linnaeus has calculated that if an annual plant produced only two seeds—and there is no plant so unproductive as this—and their seedlings next year produced two, and so on, then in twenty years there would be a million plants. The elephant is reckoned the slowest breeder of all known animals, and I have taken some pains to estimate its probable minimum rate of natural increase; it will be safest to assume that it begins breeding when thirty years old, and goes on breeding till ninety years old, bringing forth six young in the interval, and surviving till one hundred years old; if this be so, after a period of from 740 to 750 years there would be nearly nineteen million elephants alive, descended from the first pair.

But we have better evidence on this subject than mere theoretical calculations, namely, the numerous recorded cases of the astonishingly rapid increase of various animals in a state of nature, when circumstances have been favourable to them during two or three following seasons. Still more striking is the evidence from our domestic animals of many kinds which have run wild in several parts of the world; if the statements of the rate of increase of slow-breeding cattle and horses in South America, and latterly in Australia, had not been well authenticated, they would have been incredible. So it is with plants; cases could be given of introduced plants which have become common throughout whole islands in a period of less than ten years. Several of the plants, such as the cardoon and a tall thistle, which are now the commonest over the wide plains of La Plata, clothing square leagues of surface almost to the exclusion of every other plant, have been introduced from Europe and there are plants which now range in India, as I hear from Dr. Falconer, from Cape Comorin to the Himalaya, which have been imported from America since its discovery. In such cases, and endless others could be given, no one supposes, that the fertility of the animals or plants has been suddenly and temporarily increased in any sensible degree. The obvious explanation is that the conditions of life have been highly favourable, and that there has consequently been less destruction of the old and young, and that nearly all the young have been enabled to breed. Their geometrical ratio of increase, the result of which never fails to be surprising, simply explains their extraordinarily rapid increase and wide diffusion in their new homes.

In a state of nature almost every full-grown plant annually produces seed, and amongst animals there are very few which do not annually pair. Hence we may confidently assert, that all plants and animals are tending to increase at a geometrical ratio,—that all would rapidly stock every station in which they could any how exist,—and that this geometrical tendency to increase must be checked by destruction at some period of life. Our familiarity with the larger domestic animals tends, I think, to mislead us: we see no great destruction falling on then, but we do not keep in mind that thousands are annually slaughtered for food, and that in a state of nature an equal number would have somehow to be disposed of.

The only difference between organisms which annually produce eggs or seeds by the thousand, and those which produce extremely few, is, that the slow-breeders would require a few more years to people, under favourable conditions, a whole district, let it be ever so large. The condor lays a couple of eggs and the ostrich a score, and yet in the same country the condor may be the more numerous of the two; the Fulmar petrel lays but one egg, yet it is believed to be the most numerous bird in the world. One fly deposits hundreds of eggs, and another, like the hippobosca, a single one; but this difference does not determine how many individuals of the two species can be supported in a district. A large number of eggs is of some importance to those species which depend on a fluctuating amount of food, for it allows them rapidly to increase in number. But the real importance of a large number of eggs or seeds is to make up for much destruction at some period of life; and this period in the great majority of cases is an early one. If an animal can in any way protect its own eggs or young, a small number may be produced, and yet the average stock be fully kept up; but if many eggs or young are destroyed, many must be produced, or the species will become extinct. It would suffice to keep up the full number of a tree, which lived on an average for a thousand years, if a single seed were produced once in a thousand years, supposing that this seed were never destroyed, and could be ensured to germinate in a fitting place. So that, in all cases, the average number of any animal or plant depends only indirectly on the number of its eggs or seeds.

In looking at Nature, it is most necessary to keep the foregoing considerations always in mind—never to forget that every single organic being may be said to be striving to the utmost to increase in numbers; that each lives by a struggle at some period of its life; that heavy destruction inevitably falls either on the young or old, during each generation or at recurrent intervals. Lighten any check, mitigate the destruction ever so little, and the number of the species will almost instantaneously increase to any amount.

Nature of the Checks to Increase

The causes which check the natural tendency of each species to increase are most obscure. Look at the most vigorous species; by as much as it swarms in numbers, by so much will it tend to increase still further. We know not exactly what the checks are even in a single instance. Nor will this surprise any one who reflects how ignorant we are on this head, even in regard to mankind, although so incomparably better known than any other animal. This subject of the checks to increase has been ably treated by several authors, and I hope in a future work to discuss it at considerable length, more especially in regard to the feral animals of South America. Here I will make only a few remarks, just to recall to the reader's mind some of the chief points. Eggs or very young animals seem generally to suffer most, but this is not invariably the case. With plants there is a vast destruction of seeds, but, from some observations which I have made it appears that the seedlings suffer most from germinating in ground already thickly stocked with other plants. Seedlings, also, are destroyed in vast numbers by various enemies; for instance, on a piece of ground three feet long and two wide, dug and cleared, and where there could be no choking from other plants, I marked all the seedlings of our native weeds as they came up, and out of 357 no less than 295, were destroyed, chiefly by slugs and insects. If turf which has long been mown, and the case would be the same with turf closely browsed by quadrupeds, be let to grow, the more vigorous plants gradually kill the less vigorous, though fully grown plants; thus out of twenty species growing on a little plot of mown turf (three feet by four) nine species perished, from the other species being allowed to grow up freely.

The amount of food for each species of course gives the extreme limit to which each can increase; but very frequently it is not the obtaining food, but the serving as prey to other animals, which determines the average numbers of a species. Thus, there seems to be little doubt that the stock of partridges, grouse, and hares on any large estate depends chiefly on the destruction of vermin. If not one head of game were shot during the next twenty years in England, and, at the same time, if no vermin were destroyed, there would, in all probability, be less game than at present, although hundreds of thousands of game animals are now annually shot. On the other hand, in some cases, as with the elephant, none are destroyed by beasts of prey; for even the tiger in India most rarely dares to attack a young elephant protected by its dam.

Climate plays an important part in determining the average numbers of a species, and periodical seasons of extreme cold or drought seem to be the most effective of all checks. I estimated (chiefly from the greatly reduced numbers of nests in the spring) that the winter of 1854–5 destroyed four-fifths of the birds in my own grounds; and this is a tremendous destruction, when we remember that ten per cent, is an extraordinarily severe mortality from epidemics with man. The action of climate seems at first sight to be quite independent of the struggle for existence; but in so far as climate chiefly acts in reducing food, it brings on the most severe struggle between the individuals, whether of the same or of distinct species, which subsist on the same kind of food. Even when climate, for instance extreme cold, acts directly, it will be the least vigorous individuals, or those which have got least food through the advancing winter, which will suffer most. When we travel from south to north, or from a damp region to a dry, we invariably see some species gradually getting rarer and rarer, and finally disappearing; and the change of climate being conspicuous, we are tempted to attribute the whole effect to its direct action. But this is a false view; we forget that each species, even where it most abounds, is constantly suffering enormous destruction at some period of its life, from enemies or from competitors for the same place and food; and if these enemies or competitors be in the least degree favoured by any slight change of climate, they will increase in numbers; and as each area is already fully stocked with inhabitants, the other species must decrease. When we travel southward and see a species decreasing in numbers, we may feel sure that the cause lies quite as much in other species being favoured, as in this one being hurt. So it is when we travel northward, but in a somewhat lesser degree, for the number of species of all kinds, and therefore of competitors, decreases northwards; hence in going northwards, or in ascending a mountain, we far oftener meet with stunted forms, due to the *directly* injurious action of climate, than we do in proceeding southwards or in descending a mountain. When we reach the Arctic regions, or snow-capped summits, or absolute deserts, the struggle for life is almost exclusively with the elements.

That climate acts in main part indirectly by favouring other species, we clearly see in the prodigious number of plants which in our gardens can perfectly well endure our climate, but which never become naturalised, for they cannot compete with our native plants nor resist destruction by our native animals.

When a species, owing to highly favourable circumstances, increases inordinately in numbers in a small tract, epidemics—at least, this seems generally to occur with our game animals—often ensue; and here we have a limiting check independent of the struggle for life. But even some of these so-called epidemics appear to be due to parasitic worms, which have from some cause, possibly in part through facility of diffusion amongst the crowded animals, been disproportionally favoured: and here comes in a sort of struggle between the parasite and its prey.

On the other hand, in many cases, a large stock of individuals of the same species, relatively to the numbers of its enemies, is absolutely necessary for its preservation. Thus we can easily raise plenty of corn and rape-seed, &c., in our fields, because the seeds are in great excess compared with the number of birds which feed on them; nor can the birds, though having a superabundance of food at this one season, increase in number proportionally to the supply of seed, as their numbers are checked during winter; but any one who has tried, knows how troublesome it is to get seed from a few wheat or other such plants in a garden: I have in this case lost every single seed. This view of the necessity of a large stock of the same species for its preservation, explains, I believe, some singular facts in nature such as that of very rare plants being sometimes extremely abundant, in the few spots where they do exist; and that of some social plants being social, that is abounding in individuals, even on the extreme verge of their range. For in such cases, we may believe, that a plant could exist only where the conditions of its life were so favourable that many could exist together, and thus save the species from utter destruction. I should add that the good effects of intercrossing, and the ill effects of close interbreeding, no doubt come into play in many of these cases; but I will not here enlarge on this subject.

Complex Relations of All Animals and Plants to Each Other in the Struggle for Existence

Many cases are on record showing how complex and unexpected are the checks and relations between organic beings, which have to struggle together in the same country. I will give only a single instance, which, though a simple one, interested me. In Staffordshire, on the estate of a relation, where I had ample means of investigation, there was a large and extremely barren heath, which had never been touched by the hand of man; but several hundred acres of exactly the same nature had been enclosed twenty-five years previously and planted with Scotch fir. The change in the native vegetation of the planted part of the heath was most remarkable, more than is generally seen in passing from one quite different soil to another; not only the proportional numbers of the heath-plants were wholly changed, but twelve species of plants (not counting grasses and carices) flourished in the plantations, which could not be found on the heath. The effect on the insects must have been still greater, for six insectivorous birds were very common in the plantations, which were not to be seen on the heath; and the heath was frequented by two or three distinct insectivorous birds. Here we see how potent has been the effect of the introduction of a single tree, nothing whatever else having been done, with the exception of the land having been enclosed, so that cattle could not enter. But how important an element enclosure is, I plainly saw near Farnham, in Surrey. Here there are extensive heaths, with a few clumps of old Scotch firs on the distant hilltops: within the last ten years large spaces have been enclosed, and self-sown firs are now springing up in multitudes, so close together that all cannot live. When I ascertained that these young trees had not been sown or planted, I was so much surprised at their numbers that I went to several points of view, whence I could examine hundreds of acres of the unenclosed heath, and literally I could not see a single Scotch fir, except the old planted clumps. But on looking closely between the stems of the heath, I found a multitude of seedlings and little trees which had been perpetually browsed down by the cattle. In one square yard, at a point some hundred yards distant from one of the old clumps, I counted thirty-two little trees; and one of them, with twenty-six rings of growth, had, during many years tried to raise its head above the stems of the heath, and had failed. No wonder that, as soon as the land was enclosed, it became thickly clothed with vigorously growing young firs. Yet the heath was so extremely barren and so extensive that no one would ever have imagined that cattle would have so closely and effectually searched it for food.

Here we see that cattle absolutely determine the existence of the Scotch fir; but in several parts of the world insects determine the existence of cattle. Perhaps Paraguay offers the most curious instance of this; for here neither cattle nor horses nor dogs have ever run wild, though they swarm southward and northward in a feral state; and Azara and Rengger have shown that this is caused by the greater number in Paraguay of a certain fly, which lays its eggs in the navels of these animals when first born. The increase of these flies, numerous as they are, must be habitually checked by some means, probably by other parasitic insects. Hence, if certain insectivorous birds were to decrease in Paraguay, the parasitic insects would probably increase; and this would lessen the number of the navel-frequenting flies—then cattle and horses would become feral, and this would certainly greatly alter (as indeed I have observed in parts of South America) the vegetation: this again would largely affect the insects; and this, as we have just seen in Staffordshire, the insectivorous birds, and so onwards in ever-increasing circles of complexity. Not that under nature the relations will ever be as simple as this. Battle within battle must be continually recurring with varying success; and yet in the long-run the forces are so nicely balanced, that the face the nature remains for long periods of time uniform, though assuredly the merest trifle would give the victory to one organic being over another. Nevertheless, so profound is our ignorance, and so high our presumption, that we marvel when we hear of the extinction of an organic being; and as we do not see the cause, we invoke cataclysms to desolate the world, or invent laws on the duration of the forms of life!

I am tempted to give one more instance showing how plants and animals, remote in the scale of nature, are bound together by a web of complex relations. I shall hereafter have occasion to show that the exotic Lobelia fulgens is never visited in my garden by insects, and consequently, from its peculiar structure, never sets a seed. Nearly all of orchidaceous plants absolutely require the visits of insects to remove their pollen-masses and thus to fertilise them. I find from experiments that humble-bees are almost indispensable to the fertilisation of the heartsease (Viola tricolor), for other bees do not visit this flower. I have also found that the visits of bees are necessary for the fertilisation of some kinds of clover: for instance, 20 heads of Dutch clover (Trifolium repens) yielded 2,290 seeds, but 20 other heads protected from bees produced not one. Again, 100 heads of red clover (T. pratense) produced 2,700 seeds, but the same number of protected heads produced not a single seed. Humble-bees alone visit red clover, as other bees cannot reach the nectar. It has been suggested that moths may fertilise the clovers; but I doubt whether they could do so in the case of the red clover, from their weight not being sufficient to depress the wing-petals. Hence we may infer as highly probable that, if the whole genus of humble-bees became extinct or very rare in England, the hearts-ease and red clover would become very rare, or wholly disappear. The number of humble-bees in any district depends in a great measure on the number of field-mice, which destroy their combs and nests; and Col. Newman, who has long attended to the habits of humble-bees, believes that "more than two-thirds of them are thus destroyed all over England." Now the number of mice is largely dependent on, as everyone knows, on the number of cats; and Col. Newman says, "Near villages and small towns I have found the nests of humble-bees more numerous than elsewhere, which I attribute to the number of cats that destroy the mice." Hence it is quite credible that the presence of a feline animal in large numbers in a district might determine, through the intervention first of mice and then of bees, the frequency of certain flowers in that district!

In the case of every species, many different checks, acting at different periods of life, and during different seasons or years, probably come into play; some one check or some few being generally the most potent; but all will concur in determining the average number or even the existence of the species. In some cases it can be shown that widely-different checks act on the same species in different districts. When we look at the plants and bushes clothing an entangled bank, we are tempted to attribute their proportional numbers and kinds to what we call chance. But how false a view is this! Every one has heard that when an American forest is cut down, a very different vegetation springs up; but it has been observed that ancient Indian ruins in the Southern United States, which must formerly have been cleared of trees, now display the same beautiful diversity and proportion of kinds as in the surrounding virgin forest. What a struggle must have gone on during long centuries between the several kinds of trees, each annually scattering its seeds by the thousand; what war between insect and insect—between insects, snails, and other animals with birds and beasts of prey—all striving to increase, all feeding on each other, or on the trees, their seeds and seedlings, or on the other plants which first clothed the ground and thus checked the growth of the trees! Throw up a handful of feathers, and all fall to the ground according to definite laws; but how simple is the problem where each shall fall compared to that of the action and reaction of the innumerable plants and animals which have determined, in the course of centuries, the proportional numbers and kinds of trees now growing on the old Indian ruins!

The dependency of one organic being on another, as of a parasite on its prey, lies generally between beings remote in the scale of nature. This is likewise sometimes the case with those which may be strictly said to struggle with each other for existence, as in the case of locusts and grass-feeding quadrupeds. But the struggle will almost invariably be most severe between the individuals of the same species, for they frequent the same districts, require the same food, and are exposed to the same dangers. In the case of varieties of the same species, the struggle will generally be almost equally severe, and we sometimes see the contest soon decided: for instance, if several varieties of wheat be sown together, and the mixed seed be resown, some of the varieties which best suit the soil or climate, or are naturally the most fertile, will beat the others and so yield more seed, and will consequently in a few years supplant the other varieties. To keep up a mixed stock of even such extremely close varieties as the variously-coloured sweet-peas, they must be each year harvested separately, and the seed then mixed in due proportion, otherwise the weaker kinds will steadily decrease in number and disappear. So again with the varieties of sheep: it has been asserted that certain mountain-varieties will starve out other mountain-varieties, so that they cannot be kept together. The same result has followed from keeping together different varieties of the medicinal leech. It may even be doubted whether the varieties of any of our domestic plants or animals have so exactly the same strength, habits, and constitution, that the original proportions of a mixed stock (crossing being prevented) could be kept up for half-a-dozen generations, if they were allowed to struggle together, in the same manner as beings in a state of nature, and if the seed or young were not annually preserved in due proportion.

Struggle for Life Most Severe between Individuals and Varieties of the Same Species

As the species of the same genus usually have, though by no means invariably, much similarity in habits and constitution, and always in structure, the struggle will generally be more severe between them, if they come into competition with each other, than between the species of distinct genera. We see this in the recent extension over parts of the United States of one species of swallow having caused the decrease of another species. The recent increase of the missel-thrush in parts of Scotland has caused the decrease of the song-thrush. How frequently we hear of one species of rat taking the place of another species under the most different climates! In Russia the small Asiatic cockroach has everywhere driven before it its great congener. In Australia the imported hive-bee is rapidly exterminating the small, stingless native bee. One species of charlock has been known to supplant another species; and so in other cases. We can dimly see why the competition should be most severe between allied forms, which fill nearly the same place in the economy of nature; but probably in no one case could we precisely say why one species has been victorious over another in the great battle of life.

A corollary of the highest importance may be deduced from the foregoing remarks, namely, that the structure of every organic being is related, in the most essential yet often hidden manner, to that of all the other organic beings, with which it comes into competition for food or residence, or from which it has to escape, or on which it preys. This is obvious in the structure of the teeth and talons of the tiger; and in that of the legs and claws of the parasite which clings to the hair on the tiger's body. But in the beautifully plumed seed of the dandelion, and in the flattened and fringed legs of the water-beetle, the relation seems at first confined to the elements of air and water. Yet the advantage of plumed seeds no doubt stands in the closest relation to the land being already thickly clothed with other plants; so that the seeds may be widely distributed and fall on unoccupied ground. In the water-beetle, the structure of its legs, so well adapted for diving, allows it to compete with other aquatic insects, to hunt for its own prey, and to escape serving as prey to other animals.

The store of nutriment laid up within the seeds of many plants seems at first sight to have no sort of relation to other plants. But from the strong growth of young plants produced from such seeds, as peas and beans, when sown in the midst of long grass, it may be suspected that the chief use of the nutriment in the seed is to favour the growth of the seedlings, whilst struggling with other plants growing vigorously all around.

Look at a plant in the midst of its range, why does it not double or quadruple its numbers? We know that it can perfectly well withstand a little more heat or cold, dampness or dryness, for elsewhere it ranges into slightly hotter or colder, damper or drier districts. In this case we can clearly see that if we wish in imagination to give the plant the power of increasing in number, we should have to give it some advantage over its competitors, or over the animals which prey on it. On the confines of its geographical range, a change of constitution with respect to climate would clearly be an advantage to our plant; but we have reason to believe that only a few plants or animals range so far, that they are destroyed exclusively by the rigour of the climate. Not until we reach the extreme confines of life, in the Arctic regions or on the borders of an utter desert, will competition cease. The land may be extremely cold or dry, yet there will be competition between some few species, or between the individuals of the same species, for the warmest or dampest spots.

Hence we can see that when a plant or animal is placed in a new country amongst new competitors, the conditions of its life will generally be changed in an essential manner, although the climate may be exactly the same as in its former home. If its average number are to increase in its new home, we should have to modify it in a different way to what we should have had to do in its native country; for we should have to give it some advantage over a different set of competitors or enemies.

It is good thus to try in imagination to give to any one species an advantage over another. Probably in no single instance should we know what to do. This ought to convince us of our ignorance on the mutual relations of all organic beings; a conviction as necessary, as it is difficult to acquire. All that we can do, is to keep steadily in mind that each organic being is striving to increase in a geometrical ratio; that each at some period of its life, during some season of the year, during each generation or at intervals, has to struggle for life and to suffer great destruction. When we reflect on this struggle, we may console ourselves with the full belief, that the war of nature is not incessant, that no fear is felt, that death is generally prompt, and that the vigorous, the healthy, and the happy survive and multiply.

Why Darwin Delayed, or Interesting Problems and Models in the History of Science

Robert J. Richards

In October of 1836, Charles Darwin returned from his five-year voyage on the *Beagle*. During his travel around the world, he appears not to have given serious thought to the possibility that species were mutable, that they slowly changed over time. But in the summer and spring of 1837, he began to reflect precisely on this possibility, as his journal indicates: "In July opened first notebook on 'Transformation of Species'—Had been greatly struck from about Month of previous March on character of S. American fossils—& species on Galapagos Archipelago. These facts [are the] origin (especially latter) of all my views."[1] Darwin's views on evolution really only began to congeal some six months after his voyage. In the summer of 1837, he started a series of notebooks in which he worked on the theory that species were transformed over generations. In his first, second, and most of his third transmutation notebooks, he constructed several mechanisms, most of a Lamarckian variety, to account for the evolutionary process.[2] In September of 1838, a bit over a year and a half after he first began to reflect on the meaning of his South American findings, he chanced to read Thomas Malthus's *Essay on Population;* and this, as he related in his *Autobiography,* gave him "a theory by which to work."[3] Darwin credited Malthus with having furnished him the key to his formulation of the principle of natural selection—the principle that not only transformed species but also our very understanding of life. But here a problem arises for the historian of science, and it is this problem that I would like to consider.

Richards, R. J. (1983). Why Darwin delayed, or interesting problems and models in the history of science. *Journal of the History of the Behavioral Sciences, 19,* 45–53.

THE PROBLEM OF DARWIN'S DELAY

Darwin read Malthus in late September of 1838, and his notebooks show that immediately thereafter he had the essence of what has become known as the theory of evolution by natural selection.[4] Yet he did not publish his discovery in complete form until the *Origin of Species* appeared in 1859, over twenty years later. Certainly he was not slow to recognize the importance of his conception. In 1844 he wrote out a large essay sketching his theory, and had a fair copy made.[5] (Part of this essay was read, along with a paper by Alfred Wallace, before the Linnean Society in 1858 as the first public announcement of the discovery.) When he had finished the 1844 essay, he made arrangements with his wife for its posthumous publication, in case he should die before revealing his great idea.[6] Darwin thus harbored few doubts about the significance of his discovery. What, then, caused him to delay publication of a theory that is perhaps the most intellectually and socially important theory of the nineteenth century, and arguably among the most important scientific conceptions of all time?

In discussing this problem I would like principally to do two things: first, to mention the several kinds of explanation that have been given for Darwin's delay, spending some time on one in particular; and second, to consider the reasons an historian of science might tackle a problem such as this—in general to offer a few reflections on the nature of the history of science, its problems, and its methods.

Explanations of Darwin's Delay

Darwin's delay may not seem like an important or historically significant problem. To see why it is, however, suggests that our first inquiry ought to be historiographic: what makes a problem in history of science interesting in the first place? But before touching on this, I would like to outline the various explanations that have been given for Darwin's delay. This will provide some concrete examples for discussing the larger problem of interesting problems.

The first sort of explanation derives from the conventional interpretation of the hypothetical-deductive method in science: it holds that Darwin formulated his hypothesis in 1838 and then set out collecting facts to support it, which took him twenty years. Charles Coulston Gillispie adopts this account in his *Edge of Objectivity:*

> [Darwin] was held back from publication, and even from giving himself joyfully to his conclusions, by a fear of seeming premature. This went beyond scientific caution in Darwin. It is, perhaps, a disease of modern scholarship to hold back the great work until it can be counted on to overwhelm by sheer factual mass. [7]

Another explanatory strategy is a variant on the first. It contends that Darwin required the services of several correspondents and associates—among whom were Charles Lyell, Joseph Hooker, and Thomas Huxley—to gather facts for him, since he was ill a good deal of the time after his return to England and, really, was a bit lazy. To coordinate others to do one's bidding while one is indisposed would, of course, take time. Gertrude Himmelfarb in her *Darwin and the Darwinian Revolution,* adds that Darwin was concomitantly attempting to convince his friends of the truth of his theory, but with little success. She implies that he failed for good reasons, since his theory lacked cogency and his arguments were crude.[8]

A third kind of explanation supposes that Darwin was hardly indolent or lazy. Rather, it was because of his work agenda that he was not able to get to his species book more quickly. Indeed, during the twenty years in question, he brought out: *Journal of Researches of the Voyage of H. M. S. Beagle* (1839 and revised in 1845); five volumes of *Zoology of the Voyage of H. M. S. Beagle* (1840–1843), which he edited; three volumes of the *Geology of the Voyage of the Beagle* (1842–1846); and almost thirty papers and reviews.

In 1846 he began an eight-year study of barnacles, resulting in four volumes completed in 1854.[9] The barnacle project seduced Darwin. He initially planned merely to do a little study of one species and ended up investigating the whole group of Cirripedia. His work on barnacles has been singled out as both a necessary stage in preparation for the *Origin of Species* and a significant cause of its delay. Thomas Huxley, in looking back on his friend's accomplishment, wrote to Darwin's son Francis: "Like the rest of us, he had no proper training in biological science, and it has always struck me as a remarkable instance of his scientific insight, that he saw the necessity of giving himself such training, and of his courage, that he did not shirk the labour of obtaining it."[10] Thus, so the explanation goes, he had to fit himself out as a real biologist before he felt confident to tackle the species theory.

A fourth explanation points out that at the time Darwin finished the sketch of his theory in 1844, Robert Chambers published, anonymously his *Vestiges of the Natural History of Creation.* This book advanced an evolutionary hypothesis, but was extremely speculative and often silly—neither trait slipping past the attention of Darwin's scientific community. J. W. Burrow argues that Chambers's book would have cooled any enthusiasm Darwin might have had for quickly publishing his ideas: "Darwin regarded *The Vestiges* as rubbish, and Huxley reviewed it devastatingly, but the fear of being taken for simply another evolutionary speculator haunted Darwin and enjoined caution in announcing his views and patience in marshalling his evidence."[11]

A fifth explanation looks to the impact Darwin presumably anticipated his theory as having. It was, after all, materialistic; it assumed the rise of human reason and morality out of animal intelligence and instinct. Howard Gruber, in his *Darwin on Man,* divines that "Darwin sensed that some would object to seeing rudiments of human mentality in animals, while others would recoil at the idea of remnants of animality in man."[12] Darwin closed the link between humankind and animals, and thus chained himself to the dread doctrine of materialism. Stephen Gould, supporting Gruber's argument, finds evidence for this reconstruction in Darwin's early notebooks, which

> include many statements showing that he espoused but feared to expose something he perceived as far more heretical than evolution itself: philosophical materialism—the postulate that matter is the stuff of all existence and that all mental and spiritual phenomena are its by-products. No notion could be more upsetting to the deepest traditions of Western thought than the statement that mind—however complex and powerful—is simply a product of brain.[13]

The proffered hypothesis suggests, then, that Darwin was acutely sensitive to the social consequences of equating human beings with animals and therefore mind with brain, and that he thus shied from publicly revealing his views until the intellectual climate became more tolerable.[14]

The social-psychological approach, of which this last explanation discreetly makes use, is more overtly appealed to in another kind of explanation, the psychoanalytic. Some psychoanalysts emphasize that Darwin suffered from a variety of illnesses during his later adulthood—he was always taking the waters and different kinds of faddish cures for his nervousness, palpitations, exhaustion, headaches, and gastrointestinal eruptions.[15] Anyone examining the letters written to Darwin, from about 1840 till his death in 1882, is struck by what seems their invariable salutation: "Dear Darwin, sorry to hear you've been ill." The analyst Rankine Good interprets Darwin's maladies as neurotic symptoms, expressing an unconscious hate for his father:

> His illness was compounded of depressive, obsessional anxiety, and hysterical symptoms which, for the most part, co-existed, though he appears to have gone through phases when one or other group of symptoms predominated for a time. Further, there is a wealth of evidence that unmistakably points to these symptoms as a distorted expression of the aggression, hate, and resentment felt at an unconscious level, by Darwin towards his tyrannical father. . . . The symptoms represent in part, the punishment Darwin suffered for harboring such thoughts about his father. For Darwin did revolt against his father. He did so in a typical obsessional way (and like most revolutionaries) by transposing the unconscious emotional conflict to a conscious intellectual one—concerning evolution. Thus if Darwin did not slay his father in the flesh, then in his *Origin of Species* and *Descent of Man,* he certainly slew the Heavenly Father in the realm of natural history.[16]

Hamlet-like, then, Darwin hesitated to commit the symbolic murder of his despised father; he could not quite bring himself to plunge in the knife that the *Origin* represented.

A somewhat less dramatic explanation looks to Darwin's social and professional, rather than filial, relationships. Michael Ruse, in his recent book *The Darwinian Revolution,* sets some previous accounts within a sociological framework. He argues:

> The true answer [for his delay] has to be sought in Darwin's professionalism. . . . Darwin was not an amateur outsider like Chambers. He was part of the scientific network, a product of Cambridge and a close friend of Lyell, and he knew well the dread and the hatred most of the network had for evolutionism. . . . When telling Hooker of his evolutionism, Darwin confessed that it was like admitting to a murder. It was a murder—the purported murder of Christianity, and Darwin was not keen to be cast in this role. Hence the Essay of 1844 went unpublished.[17]

In order to protect his status as a professional, a status that presumably included defending the faith, Darwin laid down his pen.

INTERESTING PROBLEMS AND MODELS IN THE HISTORY OF SCIENCE

The Context of Interesting Problems

I have mentioned some seven different explanations for Darwin's delay, but not yet the one I wish to propose. Before considering that, let me suggest why a question such as Darwin's delay is historically interesting in the first place. Historians of science, as well as philosophers of science, scientists, and other scholars want to work on interesting problems—not just interesting because of personal idiosyncracies, but problems that are in some sense objectively interesting, interesting in terms of their disciplines.

What, then, makes for an interesting problem in history of science? There are at least three contexts in which a problem can become historically interesting. The first is that of normal expectations. Initially those expectations derive from present circumstances. The historian might note, for instance, that in the contemporary period scientists rush to publish important discoveries, a feature of the modern temper vividly illustrated by James Watson's *Double Helix*. In this light, Darwin's delay becomes puzzling. But most historians do not regard the present context as the controlling one. The question is, what would be the expectation for a mid-nineteenth-century scientist? If it is presumed that Victorian intellectual life ambled at a more leisurely pace or that the social convention for scientists of the period was to publish their big books as the summation of a career's work—the usual practice during the Renaissance—then a solution is had for what turns out to be not a very interesting problem after all. But in Darwin's case, we know that neither of these explanations rings true. He published fairly rapidly and often throughout his career. And consider the keen anguish he felt when he got the letter from Alfred Wallace in 1858 announcing the discovery of virtually the same theory that he had been toiling over some twenty years—this feeling of intellectual emasculation clearly demonstrates that Darwin feared being anticipated as much as any present-day scientist. The problem of his delay again becomes interesting—in terms both of our general expectations for scientific practice and expectations for the professional situation of the nineteenth-century scientist.

A second context determining interest is that of scholarship: if other historians have treated a problem as interesting, ipso facto it becomes so—for the moment at least. In the case of Darwin's delay, scholars have, simply by dint of their explanatory attempts, made it a problem of interest. Anyone undertaking a comprehensive analysis of Darwin's accomplishment must therefore contend with the problem, if only to show that it is historically intractable or actually not very interesting—interesting, that is, in either the first or the third sense I have in mind.

The third context that determines the interest invested in a problem is provided by a particular scientific theory or a nexus of theories constituting a scientific movement. In this context, interest becomes a function both of the importance of the theory, or theories, and of the proximity of the problem to such a reference base. Thus a problem even at the heart, say, of the major theory of an obscure physiologist should hold little interest for the historian of science—unless the theory and problem are representative of some larger and more significant movements in science. Nor should it be of interest to the historian of science *as such* to discover whether Darwin was really neurotic—except that the question bears on the origin and development of his theory of evolution.

This last contextual control implies that the present-day state of science ultimately fixes those problems of interest for the historian. Some scholars would find this suggestion destructive of the historical ideal, which, they believe, requires the reconstruction of the past only on it own terms, without use of present conceptual resources. To aim for less would be to indulge in Whig history, the unwarranted reading of contemporary ideas, motives, social conditions, and interests into the past.[18] But the historicist ideal can be realized in neither practice nor theory. The historian is ineluctably a product of his or her time and therefore must bring to the study of the past the conceptual equipment of the present. Any historical analysis, explicitly or implicitly, steps off from the present. Every historian of science initially learns, for instance, the contemporary meaning of the concept of science itself, and in its light regressively traces the evolutionary descent of its past embodiments. Of course, the sensitive historian seeks continually to enrich the concept of science, recognizing that though ancient practices and notions evolved into those of the present, they may appear structurally very different—just as eohippus seems worlds apart from the modern horse.

In terms of this third context, Darwin's delay is certainly interesting. For the very fact of delay suggests either something not finished, something left undone for the theory to be logically acceptable, or something about the theory that made it unacceptable in the scientific and social climate of Victorian England. In either case, the problem beckons because it hints that there is something about Darwin's theory that we have not yet considered; and to understand its origins, development, structure, and impact, this something needs to be recovered.

Models in History of Science

Assuming that the historian has an interesting problem—and perhaps now it will be granted that Darwin's delay is interesting—what approach should be taken in attempting to resolve it? Initially, there seem to be two options.

Historians of science seem innately disposed to one of two basic approaches, internalism or externalism. Internalists focus on the development of scientific ideas and theories, tracing their internal logic and conceptual linkages. In extreme form, internalists treat the historical movement from one set of ideas to another much as Platonic philosophers, weaving together the logical forms of ideas while ignoring their physical and social embodiments. Externalists, by contrast, embed scientific ideas and theories in the human world, in the minds of scientists who move in a variety of interlocking societies. In the extreme, externalists cloak themselves in Durkheim or Freud; they suppose that ideas reflect only social relationships or psychological complexes. Of the several approaches to the problem of Darwin's delay, Gillispie clearly represents the internalist perspective, while Good represents the externalists; the others cluster more or less closely to one of these poles.

Historians disposed toward internalism or externalism specify their tendencies by adopting—usually unreflectively—an historiographic model, in light of which they articulate their subject. In this respect they function much like scientists. For historians, after all, do formulate theories, construct hypotheses, gather evidence, and, of necessity, employ models. Historiographic models comprise sets of assumptions concerning the nature of science, its developmental character, and the modes of scientific knowing. That historians *must* use models can be argued a priori: without antecedent conceptions about the character of science, they would have no idea where to look for their subject matter, nor could they define its limits or determine what evidence would be relevant. That models have in fact been used can be established easily by an empirical survey of histories of science since the Renaissance.[19] So, for instance, a model familiar to most is Thomas Kuhn's paradigm model of science. Gillispie, more traditionally, employs a revolutionary model (not to be confused with Kuhn's conception of scientific revolutions). This model, introduced by historians in the eighteenth century, assumes that a discipline must undergo a fundamental upheaval to put it on the road to modern science—before the revolution (for example, that produced in physics by Galileo) there was not science; afterward scientists gradually laid a path of scientific truth leading right up to the modern age. A more recently formulated model, which has considerable advantage over the others available, is a natural selection model of scientific evolution. It treats conceptual systems as comparable to biological species, and regards this evolution as ultimately determined by a natural selection of scientific ideas against a variety of intellectual environments.

I will not rehearse here the whole litany of models available to the historian of science, but simply point out that some are more congenial to those of internalist temper, others to those of externalist, while a few will appeal to historians whose attitudes about the issue are a healthy mix. It is the latter class of models, the ones suitable to those of hybrid sentiment, that, I believe, will generally be the most successful. This is not merely because extreme positions—that of the hard-headed internalist or the soft-minded externalist—are generally to be avoided. Barry Goldwater once admonished, with some justice, that extremism in the cause of truth is no vice. These starkly restrictive approaches should be avoided because they lead historians down some very dark byways.

The internalists forget that ideas alone are causally impotent—one idea cannot, of itself, generate another. Moreover, the connections among sets of historically developed scientific ideas are not usually logical, at least not in any deductive sense. It is breathing human beings who produce ideas. Ideas become historically linked only by passing through embodied minds, which respond to logical implication and evidentiary support, of course, but also to emotion, prejudice, class attitudes, and, sometimes perhaps, oedipal anxieties. Hence, to deal with their subject—the growth of scientific ideas—historians of science cannot neglect the explanatory strategies of social, political, and cultural historians.

Extreme externalists, say of the Durkheimian or Marxian variety, those who interpret scientific ideas as totally determined by social structures (and who seem to ply their trade these days mostly in Edinburgh)[20] can be terminally infected, and, if gentlemen, will succumb to a simple *reductio* argument: their thesis of social determinism must also be determined; but why should we listen to those who take a position from extrinsic compulsion instead of relevant good reason? Even the less extreme sorts often forget that the most intimate society to which the scientist belongs and whose attitudes he or she most readily adopts is that of other scientists. Externalists thus usually ignore something that their own assumptions imply: that scientists are enculturated to respond to the logical and objective character of theories and evidence. Demonstrations of logical consistency and empirical confirmation usually bear the most weight, even for the natural philosophers of ages past. This suggests, incidentally, that well-trained historians of science will also know the more detailed workings of the science they profess to chronicle, as well as be apprised of what contemporary philosophers have had to say about the logical character of theories and explanations in science.

Hybrids between the internalists and the externalists enjoy advantage over both. They can adjust their considerations to the structure of the problem with which they are concerned. That is, they will be ready to construe the problem in terms of the internal structure of the science, which should logically be their first step, or in terms of external influences, if the evidence warrants. Usually they will find both approaches, in different measures, necessary. And this for a simple reason, which I will briefly mention and which will return us to the problem at hand, Darwin's delay.

DARWIN'S DELAY AGAIN

In arriving at a possible solution to the perplexity of Darwin's delay, one must recognize a critical difficulty which always faces the historian: scientific theories and the activities of scientists are overdetermined. A multitude of factors impinge on the scientist, and the historian must apportion different conceptual and causal weightings to these factors. It is conceivable, and I think likely, that most of the explanations mentioned earlier for Darwin's delay have some merit. The factors they isolate did bear on his delay. The mistake usually made, however, is to assume that one explanation is *the* explanation. Having offered this caveat, let me suggest which inhibiting factor did cause Darwin no end of difficulty and which, therefore, must be accorded considerable conceptual weight.

In reading several natural theological discussions of animal instinct in the early 1840s, Darwin came upon one particular example that the natural theologians made much of—the "wonderful" instincts of worker bees and slave-making ants. Only God, they argued, could have endowed the hive bee with a geometer's knowledge of how to construct perfect hexagonal cells, or *Formica rufescens* with the gentleman's unerring sense of what other species would make the best domestic servants.[21] What struck Darwin about these instincts—actually whole sets of related innate behaviors—was that they were exhibited by sterile castes of insects. The account of instinctive behavior on which he had been working in the early 1840s—which likened the fixed patterns of instinct to anatomical structures and argued that both could be explained by natural selection—seemed precluded for neuter insects, since they left no progeny that could inherit profitable variations.

That this quickly loomed as a critical difficulty for the validity of his theory of evolution by natural selection can be fairly estimated from the annotations Darwin left in the margins of those natural theological treatises he was reading in the 1840s.[22] Moreover, in the *Origin of Species,* he stated flatly that he initially thought the problem of instincts of neuter insects "fatal to my whole theory."[23] This was precisely the kind of stumbling block—a conceptual failure at the heart of this theory—that would cause him to hesitate in publishing his views.

Manuscript evidence indicates that Darwin discovered this difficulty in 1843.[24] Shortly thereafter he attempted to construct several possible explanations compatible with the theory of natural selection. But these were weak, and he knew it. In his 1844 essay Darwin sketched several potential objections to his theory, and then, with a soft note of triumph, proceeded to answer them. Conspicuously absent, however, was any mention of that difficulty he thought fatal to his theory—he had no explanation for it. Further evidence shows that the problem of neuter insects continued to plague him. In 1848 he composed a four-page manuscript detailing the problem of the instincts of neuter insects, and concluded that it was "the greatest *special* difficulty I have met with."[25]

Even after Darwin sat down, in 1856, to begin work on a manuscript that would be, he hoped, the definitive description and justification of his theory of evolution by natural selection, he still had not settled on one explanation of the wonderful instincts of social insects. In fact, he proposed several, only one of which contained elements of what we now accept as the correct explanation—kin selection: the idea that selection does not work on the individual, but on the whole hive or nest in competition with other communal groups of the same species. Darwin came to recognize the solution to his difficulty and to flesh it out only in late December of 1857, as he wrote what would become the chapter on instinct in the *Origin of Species*.[26] In the very act of writing the chapter, he resolved the difficulty he regarded as threatening the existence of his theory. In the explanation of Darwin's delay, much conceptual weight must thus be given to his struggles with the wonderful instincts of neuter insects. And this, I believe, is a good part of the solution to an interesting problem in the history of science.

NOTES

1 Charles Darwin, "Journal," ed. Gavin de Beer, in *Bulletin of the British Museum (Natural History),* Historical Series 2 (1959): 7.

2 Gavin de Beer edited and transcribed "Darwin's Notebooks on Transmutation of Species" and "Pages Excised by Darwin," in *Bulletin of the British Museum (Natural History),* Historical Series 2 and 3 (1960, 1967). For an account of Darwin's early theories about evolution, see Sandra Herbert, "The Place of Man in the Development of Darwin's Theory of Transmutation," *Journal of History of Biology* 7 (1974): 217-258; 10 (1977): 243–273; David Kohn, "Theories to Work By: Rejected Theories, Reproduction and Darwin's Path of Natural Selection," *Studies in History of Biology* 4 (1980): 67–170; Camille Limoges, *La Selection Naturelle* (Paris: Presses Universitaires de France, 1970); and Robert Richards, "Influence of Sensationalist Tradition on Early Theories of the Evolution of Behavior," *Journal of History of Ideas* 40 (1979): 85–105.

3 Charles Darwin, *Autobiography,* ed. Nora Barlow (New York: Norton, 1969), p.120.

4 Darwin, "Third Notebook on Transmutation," MS pp. 134–135 (de Beer, "Excised Pages," pp. 162–163).

5 The essay is transcribed in *The Foundations of the Origin of Species,* ed. Francis Darwin (Cambridge: Cambridge University Press, 1909).

6 Charles Darwin, *The Life and Letters of Charles Darwin,* ed. Francis Darwin, 2 vols. (New York: D. Appleton, 1891), 1:377–379.

7 Charles Coulston Gillispie, *The Edge of Objectivity* (Princeton, NJ: Princeton University Press, 1960), p. 312.

8 Gertrude Himmelfarb, *Darwin and the Darwinian Revolution* (New York: Norton, 1968), pp. 126–146, 203–215, 312–352.

9 Charles Darwin, *A Monograph of the Sub-Class Cirripedia,* 4 vols. (London: Ray Society, 1851–1854).

10 Thomas Huxley to Francis Darwin, quoted in *Life and Letters of Charles Darwin,* 1:315.

11 J. W.Burrow, "Editor's Introduction," in Charles Darwin, *The Origin of Species* (Baltimore: Penguin Books, 1968), p.32.

12 Howard Gruber, *Darwin on Man* (New York: Dutton, 1974), p 202.

13 Stephen Gould, "Darwin's Delay," in his *Ever Since Darwin* (New York: Norton, 1977), p. 24. Silvan Schweber, in "The Origin of the *Origin* Revisited." *Journal of History of Biology* 10 (1977): 310–315, concurs with Gruber and Gould that fear of materialism was a considerable restraining influence on Darwin.

14 In "Instinct and Intelligence in British Natural Theology: Some Contributions to Darwin's Theory of the Evolution of Behavior," *Journal of History of Biology* 14 (1981): 193–230. I have taken specific exception to this explanation of Darwin's delay.

15 Ralph Colp, Jr., gives an extensive account of Darwin's illness in *To Be an Invalid* (Chicago: University of Chicago Press, 1977).

16 Rankine Good, "The Life of the Shawl," *Lancet* (9 January 1953): 106.

17 Michael Ruse, *The Darwinian Revolution* (Chicago: University of Chicago Press, 1979), p. 185.

18 Whiggish history was carefully diagnosed in Herbert Butterfield's *The Whig Interpretation of History* (New York: Norton, 1965; originally published, 1931). There he described it as "the tendency in many historians to write on the side of Protestants and Whigs, to praise revolutions provided they have been successful, to emphasise certain principles of progress in the past and to produce a story which is the ratification if not the glorification of the present."

19 I have offered such a survey in "Natural Selection and Other Models in the Historiography of Science," in *Scientific Inquiry and the Social Sci-*

ences: A Volume in Honor of Donald T. Campbell, ed. Marilynn B. Brewer and Barry E. Collins (San Francisco: Jossey-Bass, 1981), pp 37–76.

20 See, for example, the work of the Edinburgh sociologists of science David Bloor, *Knowledge and Social Imagery* (London: Routledge and Kegan Paul, 1976), and Barry Barnes, *Interests and the Growth of Knowledge* (London: Routledge and Kegan Paul, 1977).

21 Darwin's authority for the habits of social insects was the work of two natural theologians and premier entomologists, William Kirby and William Spence, in their *Introduction to Entomology,* 2nd ed., 4 vols. (London: Longman, Hurst, Rees, Orme, and Brown, 1818); see especially vol. 2.

22 I have discussed these annotations in "Instinct and Intelligence."

23 Charles Darwin, *On the Origin of Species* (London: Murray, 1959), p. 236.

24 From Darwin's reading notebooks, we know that he read Kirby and Spence's *Introduction to Entomology* in 1843 (see the transcription of these notebooks by Peter Vorzimmer, "The Darwin Reading Notebooks [1838–1860]," *Journal of History of Biology* 10 [1977]: 130). On p. 55 of vol. 2 of the work, where Kirby and Spence describe some of the wonderful instincts of worker bees, Darwin scribbled his frustration in the margin: "Neuters do not breed! How instinct acquired." Darwin's books are held in the Manuscript Room of Cambridge University Library.

25 Darwin's four-page manuscript is in container-book #73, held in the Manuscript Room of Cambridge University Library.

26 The manuscript version of what Darwin abridged into the *Origin of Species* has been published by R. C. Stauffer as *Charles Darwin's Natural Selection: Being the Second Part of His Big Species Book Written From 1856 to 1858* (Cambridge: Cambridge University Press, 1975).

Natural Abilities and the Comparative Worth of Races

Francis Galton

INTRODUCTORY

I propose to show in this book that a man's natural abilities are derived by inheritance, under exactly the same limitations as are the form and physical features of the whole organic world. Consequently, as it is easy, notwithstanding those limitations, to obtain by careful selection a permanent breed of dogs or horses gifted with peculiar powers of running, or of doing anything else, so it would be quite practicable to produce a highly-gifted race of men by judicious marriages during several consecutive generations. I shall show that social agencies of an ordinary character, whose influences are little suspected, are at this moment working towards the degradation of human nature, and that others are working towards its improvement. I conclude that each generation has enormous power over the natural gifts of those that follow, and maintain that it is a duty we owe to humanity to investigate the range of that power, and to exercise it in a way that, without being unwise towards ourselves, shall be most advantageous to future inhabitants of the earth.

I am aware that my views, which were first published four years ago in *Macmillan's Magazine* (in June and August 1865), are in contradiction to general opinion; but the arguments I then used have been since accepted, to my great gratification, by many of the highest authorities on heredity. In reproducing them, as I now do, in a much more elaborate form, and on a greatly enlarged basis of induction, I feel assured that, inasmuch as what I then wrote was sufficient to earn the acceptance of Mr. Darwin ("Variation

From Galton, F. (1869). *Hereditary genius*. New York: D. Appleton, 1891, pp. 1–5, 343–350.

under Domestication," ii. 7), the increased amount of evidence submitted in the present volume is not likely to be gainsaid.

The general plan of my argument is to show that high reputation is a pretty accurate test of high ability; next to discuss the relationships of a large body of fairly eminent men—namely, the Judges of England from 1660 to 1868, the Statesmen of the time of George III., and the Premiers during the last 100 years—and to obtain from these a general survey of the laws of heredity in respect to genius. Then I shall examine, in order, the kindred of the most illustrious Commanders, men of Literature and of Science, Poets, Painters, and Musicians, of whom history speaks. I shall also discuss the kindred of a certain selection of Divines and of modern Scholars. Then will follow a short chapter, by way of comparison, on the hereditary transmission of physical gifts, as deduced from the relationships of certain classes of Oarsmen and Wrestlers. Lastly, I shall collate my results, and draw conclusions.

It will be observed that I deal with more than one grade of ability. Those upon whom the greater part of my volume is occupied, and on whose kinships my argument is most securely based, have been generally reputed as endowed by nature with extraordinary genius. There are so few of these men that, although they are scattered throughout the whole historical period of human existence, their number does not amount to more than 400, and yet a considerable proportion of them will be found to be interrelated.

Another grade of ability with which I deal is that which includes numerous highly eminent, and all the illustrious names of modern English history, whose immediate descendants are living among us, whose histories are popularly known, and whose relationships may readily be traced by the help of biographical dictionaries, peerages, and similar books of reference.

A third and lower grade is that of the English Judges, massed together as a whole, for the purpose of the prefatory statistical inquiry of which I have already spoken. No one doubts that many of the ablest intellects of our race are to be found among the Judges; nevertheless the *average* ability of a Judge cannot be rated as equal to that of the lower of the two grades I have described.

I trust the reader will make allowance for a large and somewhat important class of omissions I have felt myself compelled to make when treating of the eminent men of modern days. I am prevented by a sense of decorum from quoting names of their relations in contemporary life who are not recognised as public characters, although their abilities may be highly appreciated in private life. Still less consistent with decorum would it have been, to introduce the names of female relatives that stand in the same category. My case is so overpoweringly strong, that I am perfectly able to prove my point without having recourse to this class of evidence. Nevertheless, the reader should bear in mind that it exists; and I beg he will do me the justice of allowing that I have not overlooked the whole of the evidence that does not appear in my pages. I am deeply conscious of the imperfection of my work, but my sins are those of omission, not of commission. Such errors as I may and must have made, which give a fictitious support to my arguments, are, I am confident, out of all proportion fewer than such omissions of facts as would have helped to establish them.

I have taken little notice in this book of modern men of eminence who are not English, or at least well known to Englishmen. I feared, if I included large classes of foreigners, that I should make glaring errors. It requires a very great deal of labour to hunt out relationships, even with the facilities afforded to a countryman having access to persons acquainted with the various families; much more would it have been difficult to hunt out the kindred of foreigners. I should have especially liked to investigate the biographies of Italians and Jews, both of whom appear to be rich in families of high intellectual breeds. Germany and America are also full of interest. It is a little less so with respect to France, where the Revolution and the guillotine made sad havoc among the progeny of her abler races.

There is one advantage to a candid critic in my having left so large a field untouched; it enables me to propose a test that any well-informed reader may easily adopt who doubts the fairness of my examples. He may most reasonably suspect that I have been unconsciously influenced by my theories to select men whose kindred were most favourable to their support. If so, I beg he will test my impartiality as follows:—Let him take a dozen names of his own selection, as the most eminent in whatever profession and in whatever country he knows most about, and let him trace out for himself their relations. It is necessary, as I find by experience, to take some pains to be sure that none, even of the immediate relatives, on either the male or female side, have been overlooked. If he does what I propose, I am confident he will be astonished at the completeness with which the results will confirm my theory. I venture to speak with assurance, because it has often occurred to me to propose this very test to incredulous friends, and invariably, so far as my memory serves me, as large a proportion of the men who were named were discovered to have eminent relations, as the nature of my views on heredity would have led me to expect. . . .

THE COMPARATIVE WORTH OF DIFFERENT RACES

If we could raise the average standard of our race only one grade, what vast changes would be produced! The number of men of natural gifts equal to those of the eminent men of the present day, would be necessarily increased more than tenfold, . . . because there would be 2,423 of them in each million instead of only 233; but far more important to the progress of civilization would be the increase in the yet higher orders of intellect. We know how intimately the course of events is dependent on the thoughts of a few illustrious men. If the first-rate men in the different groups had never been born, even if those among them who have a place in my appendices on account of their hereditary gifts, had never existed, the world would be very different to what it is. . . .

It seems to me most essential to the well-being of future generations, that the average standard of ability of the present time should be raised. Civilization is a new condition imposed upon man by the course of events, just as in the history of geological changes new conditions have continually been imposed on different races of animals. They have had the effect either of modifying the nature of the races through the process of natural selection, whenever the changes were sufficiently slow and the race sufficiently pliant, or of destroying them altogether, when the changes were too abrupt or the race unyielding. The number of the races of mankind that have been entirely destroyed under the pressure of the requirements of an incoming civilization, reads us a terrible lesson. Probably in no former period of the world has the destruction of the races of any animal whatever, been effected over such wide areas and with such startling rapidity as in the case of savage man. In the North American Continent, in the West Indian Islands, in the Cape of Good Hope, in Australia, New Zealand, and Van Diemen's Land, the human denizens of vast regions have been entirely swept away in the short space of three centuries, less by the pressure of a stronger race than through the influence of a civilization they were incapable of supporting. And we too, the foremost labourers in creating this civilization, are beginning to show ourselves incapable of keeping pace with our own work. The needs of centralization, communication, and culture, call for more brains and mental stamina than the average of our race possess. We are in crying want for a greater fund of ability in all stations of life; for neither the classes of statesmen, philosophers, artisans, nor labourers are up to the modern complexity of their several professions. An extended civilization like ours comprises more interests than the ordinary statesmen or philosophers of our present race are capable of dealing with, and it exacts more intelligent work than our ordinary artisans and labourers are capable of performing. Our race is overweighted, and appears likely to be drudged into degeneracy by demands that exceed its powers. If its average ability were raised a grade or two, our new classes . . . would conduct the complex affairs of the state at home and abroad as easily as our present [classes] . . . when in the position of country squires, are able to manage the affairs of their establishments and tenantry. All other classes of the community would be similarly promoted to the level of the work required by the nineteenth century, if the average standard of the race were raised.

When the severity of the struggle for existence is not too great for the powers of the race, its action is healthy and conservative, otherwise it is deadly, just as we may see exemplified in the scanty, wretched vegetation that leads a precarious existence near the summer snow line of the Alps, and disappears altogether a little higher up. We want as much backbone as we can get, to bear the racket to which we are henceforth to be exposed, and as good brains as possible to contrive machinery, for modern life to work more smoothly than at present. We can, in some degree, raise the nature of man to a level with the new conditions imposed upon his existence, and we can also, in some degree, modify the conditions to suit his nature. It is clearly right that both these powers should be exerted, with the view of bringing his nature and the conditions of his existence into as close harmony as possible.

In proportion as the world becomes filled with mankind, the relations of society necessarily increase in complexity, and the nomadic disposition found in most barbarians becomes unsuitable to the novel conditions. There is a most unusual unanimity in respect to the causes of incapacity of savages for civilization, among writers on those hunting and migratory nations who are brought into contact with advancing colonization, and perish, as they invariably do, by the contact. They tell us that the labour of such men is neither constant nor steady; that the love of a wandering, independent life prevents their settling anywhere to work, except for a short time, when urged by want and encouraged by kind treatment. Meadows says that the Chinese call the barbarous races on their borders by a phrase which means "hither and thither, not fixed." And any amount of evidence might be adduced to show how deeply Bohemian habits of one kind or another, were ingrained in the nature of the men who inhabited most parts of the earth now overspread by the Anglo-Saxon and other civilized races. Luckily there is still room for adventure, and a man who feels the cravings of a roving, adventurous spirit to be too strong for resistance, may yet find a legitimate outlet for it in the colonies, in the army, or on board ship. But such a spirit is, on the whole an heirloom that brings more impatient restlessness and beating of the wings against cage-bars, than persons of more civilized characters can readily comprehend, and it is directly at war with the more modern portion of our moral natures. If a man be purely a nomad, he has only to be nomadic, and his instinct is satisfied; but no Englishmen of the nineteenth century are purely nomadic. The most so among them have also inherited many civilized cravings that are necessarily starved when they become wanderers, in the same way as the wandering instincts are starved when they are settled at home. Consequently their nature has opposite wants, which can never be satisfied except by chance, through some very exceptional turn of circumstances. This is a serious calamity, and as the Bohemianism in the nature of our race is destined to perish, the sooner it goes the happier for mankind. The social requirements of English life are steadily destroying it. No man who only works by fits and starts is able to obtain his living nowadays; for he has not a chance of thriving in competition with steady workmen. If his nature revolts against the monotony of daily labour, he is tempted to the public-house, to intemperance, and, it may be, to poaching, and to much more serious crime: otherwise he banishes himself from our shores. In the first case, he is unlikely to leave as many children as men of more domestic and marrying habits, and, in the second case, his breed is wholly lost to England. By this steady riddance of the Bohemian spirit of our race, the artisan part of our population is slowly becoming bred to its duties, and the primary qualities of the typical modern British workman are already the very opposite of those of the nomad. What they are now, was well described by Mr. Chadwick, as consisting of "great bodily strength, applied under the command of a steady, persevering will, mental self-contentedness, impassibility to external irrelevant impressions, which carries them through the continued repetition of toilsome labour, 'steady as time.' "

It is curious to remark how unimportant to modern civilization has become the once famous and thoroughbred looking Norman. The type of his features, which is, probably, in some degree correlated with his peculiar form of adventurous disposition, is no longer characteristic of our rulers, and is rarely found among celebrities of the present day; it is more often met with among the undistinguished members of highly-born families, and especially among the less conspicuous officers of the army. Modern leading men in all paths of eminence, as may easily be seen in a collection of photographs, are of a coarser and more robust breed; less excitable and dashing, but endowed with far more ruggedness and real vigour. Such also is the case, as regards the German portion of the Austrian nation; they are far more high-caste in appearance than the Prussians, who are so plain that it is disagreeable to travel northwards from Vienna, and watch the change; yet the Prussians appear possessed of the grater moral and physical stamina.

Much more alien to the genius of an enlightened civilization than the nomadic habit, is the impulsive and uncontrolled nature of the savage. A civilized man must bear and forbear, he must keep before his mind the claims of the morrow as clearly as those of the passing minute; of the absent, as well as of the present. This is the most trying of the new conditions imposed on man by civilization, and the one that makes it hopeless for any but exceptional natures among savages, to live under them. The instinct of a savage is admirably consonant with the needs of savage life; every day he is in danger through transient causes; he lives from hand to mouth, in the hour and for the hour, without care for the past or forethought for the future: but such an instinct is utterly at fault in civilized life. The half-reclaimed savage, being unable to deal with more subjects of consideration than are directly before him, is continually doing acts through mere maladroitness and incapacity, at which he is afterwards deeply grieved and annoyed. The nearer inducements always seem to him, through his uncorrected sense of moral perspective, to be incomparably larger than others of the same actual size, but more remote; consequently, when the temptation of the moment has been yielded to and passed away, and its bitter result comes in its turn before the man, he is amazed and remorseful at his past weakness. It seems incredible that he should have done that yesterday which to-day seems so silly, so unjust, and so unkindly. The newly-reclaimed barbarian, with the impulsive, unstable nature of the savage, when he also chances to be gifted with a peculiarly generous and affectionate disposition, is of all others the man most oppressed with the sense of sin.

Now it is a just assertion, and a common theme of moralists of many creeds, that man, such as we find him, is born with an imperfect nature. He has lofty aspirations, but there is a weakness in his disposition, which incapacitates him from carrying his nobler purposes into effect. He sees that some particular course of action is his duty, and should be his delight; but his inclinations are fickle and base, and do not conform to his better judgment. The whole moral nature of man is tainted with sin, which prevents him from doing the things he knows to be right.

The explanation I offer of this apparent anomaly, seems perfectly satisfactory from a scientific point of view. It is neither more nor less than that the development of our nature, whether under Darwin's law of natural selection, or through the effects of changed ancestral habits, has not yet overtaken the development of our moral civilization. Man was barbarous but yesterday, and therefore it is not to be expected that the natural aptitudes of his race should already have become moulded into accordance with his very recent advance. We, men of the present centuries, are like animals suddenly transplanted among new conditions of climate and of food: our instincts fail us under the altered circumstances.

My theory is confirmed by the fact that the members of old civilizations are far less sensible than recent converts from barbarism, of their nature being inadequate to their moral needs. The conscience of a negro is aghast at his own wild, impulsive nature, and is easily stirred by a preacher, but it is scarcely possible to ruffle the self-complacency of a steady-going Chinaman.

The sense of original sin would show, according to my theory, not that man was fallen from a high estate, but that he was rising in moral culture with more rapidity than the nature of his race could follow. My view is corroborated by the conclusion reached at the end of each of the many independent lines of ethnological research—that the human race were utter savages in the beginning; and that, after myriads of years of barbarism, man has but very recently found his way into the paths of morality and civilization.

Francis Galton and American Psychology

Solomon Diamond

Karl Pearson has told us that Galton's motto was *Whenever you can, count.*[40] He followed it with extraordinary persistence. For example, having had his portrait painted at 60 and again at 81, he could report that each artist had touched the brush to canvas about 20,000 times, although the first used slow, methodical strokes, and the second (in the impressionist era) made flurries of quick dabs.[29] The habit of counting repetitive acts is also a conspicuous behavior of many American psychologists. I have been told that at a round table of distinguished persons, one of our present conferees skillfully increased the rate of finger-wagging by a long-winded participant, by reinforcing each such gesture with a nod of his head. This is not in itself proof of Galton's enduring influence, but it does illustrate the fact that American psychology is largely imbued with the essence of Galtonism: the conviction that any significant problem can be stated in terms which make it accessible to quantitative study. That conviction was the foundation for each of Galton's many important contributions. Some that have had very wide application in the work of other psychologists are these:

Diamond, S. (1977). Francis Galton and American psychology. *Annals of the New York Academy of Sciences, 291,* 47–55.

(1) The method of word association,[19] which first opened the way to quantitative analysis of the higher thought processes and individual dynamics.

(2) The introduction of test batteries,[24] to arrive at a many-sided assessment of abilities for a given person.

(3) Systematic use of the questionnaire,[20] out of which all inventory-type tests were developed.

(4) Use of the normal distribution for purposes of classification,[15] which has been a boon to the sophisticated, as well as devising the system of scoring by percentile ranks,[25] which has made it possible for us to communicate with the unsophisticated.

(5) The method of twin comparison,[18] which, aside from its special application to the problem of nature vs. nurture, is notable as the first use of a control group in psychological research, since Galton compared results based on pairs of identical twins with those based on fraternal twins.

(6) Finally, and most important in this abbreviated list, the concepts of regression[26] and correlation,[27] which opened up new possibilities for the analysis of complex phenomena which, like heredity, are dependent on multiple influences.

In early textbooks and manuals of experimental psychology Galton's name is cited most often in connection with Galton's whistle, Galton's bar, or Galton's weights. These products of his anthropometric research were to be found in almost every laboratory in which students were trained in the psychophysical methods. His more important innovations in experimental design and statistical analysis of data were assimilated more slowly, but without them it would have been a far more difficult task to give psychology its new direction, that is, to change it from a normative science, which had been conceived as the propaedeutic basis for philosophy, into a functional science of behavior, independent of philosophy.

Cattell was the most important conduit of Galton's influence on American psychology. His fellow psychologists ranked him second in importance only to William James.[8] When Galton died, only five months after the passing of James, Cattell wrote that these were the two greatest men he had known.[10] In later years he said flatly that Galton was the greatest man he ever knew.[12,13] Rating scientists for distinction was a serious matter to Cattell, and he would not have made such a judgment without due deliberation.

Since Cattell had both G. Stanley Hall and Wundt as his formal teachers, we cannot assess his relationship to Galton without reviewing the full course of his university studies. In 1880 Cattell, not yet 20, heard Lotze at Göttingen.[45] After an interlude of study at Paris and Geneva, he spent a semester at Leipzig, where he heard both Wundt and Heinze. After this double exposure to the new psychology, he planned to continue his work under Lotze,[44] but this plan was upset by Lotze's unexpected death. In 1882, Cattell enrolled at Johns Hopkins Univesity, Baltimore, Md., and won a scholarship with an essay on Lotze's philosophy. There were no psychology courses during the first semester, and his principal interests then were team sports and personal experimentation with drugs. Then Hall was brought in, and Cattell enrolled in his laboratory course along with John Dewey, Joseph Jastrow, and E. M. Hartwell. Except for Cattell, they were all to complete doctorates at Johns Hopkins. In Hall's laboratory, Cattell performed the pioneer experiment on the time required to recognize letters. The next year Cattell left Johns Hopkins because of what he perceived, probably correctly, as double-dealing on Hall's part.[43] He returned to Leipzig and Wundt, *faute de mieux*.

The results of the experiment performed at Johns Hopkins are included in Cattell's first article in the *Philosophische Studien*.[5] The clue to the fact that it was not performed at Leipzig is in the initials of the observers who participated. They include J. D. for Dewey, E. H. for Hartwell, and G. H. for Hall. One can only speculate as to what extent Cattell's resentment toward Hall, to what extent Wundt's jealousy of other laboratories, contributed to the failure to mention where the experiment had been performed.

Cattell was justly proud of this experiment, but he is not strictly accurate in the claim that it was the first to be concerned with individual differences, and to make no appeal to introspection. This point is not trivial, because it is so often said that interest in individual differences was an autocthonous development of American soil. In 1879 Obersteiner, a collaborator of Exner at Vienna, published an account of reaction-time experiments in which he emphasized the importance of differences between individuals.[39] He found no difference between the sexes, said that members of the serving class are less consistent in performance, and that extremely long times are an indication of mental derangement. Since this article appeared in English, it might well have been known to Cattell, and was almost certainly known to Hall, before Cattell did his experiment. Furthermore, in 1883 Galton's friend Romanes reported an experiment in which the subjects were allowed 20 seconds to read a short printed paragraph and were then required to write down all they could remember.[42] Although all the subjects were "accustomed to much reading," they showed "a positively astonishing difference . . . with respect to the rate at which they were able to read." Romanes also remarked that the swifter readers generally retained more of the content than the slow readers. Even at this early date, therefore, Cattell and America had no monopoly on psychological research in individual differences, or on using objective criteria of performance.

At Leipzig, Cattell broke precedent by rejecting the introspective problem which Wundt assigned to him, and he was permitted to continue work on his own problem. This time he used far more elegant apparatus of his own design—the gravity tachistoscope and the voice-key—and the work was carried on in his own rooms "in part because Wundt would not allow the testing in his laboratory of individuals who could not profit from introspection."[40]

After Leipzig, Cattell spent the greater part of two years in England. He participated in a stillborn effort to establish a psychological laboratory at Cambridge,[46] but worked chiefly at Galton's laboratory, which had originally been established at the International Health Exhibition. Cattell states that he helped set it up in its new quarters at the South Kensington Museum of Science and that he and Galton "began in cooperation the preparation of a book of instructions for a laboratory course in psychology."[12] It was an ideal learning situation. The famous article "Mental Tests and Measurements" was the outgrowth of this experience, and the recommendation in it that all students should take a battery of anthropometric tests followed a line of thought which Galton had initiated much earlier.[16] The battery of tests described was an amplified version of the Galton program, which had been fitted to a level of public tolerance. But the most important outcome was the fact that Walker points out, that Cattell's psychology courses were the first "to make consistent and systematic use of statistical methods."[51] It was a sharp turn from the Leipzig orientation, for, as Walker also states, "It does not appear that Wundt himself was committed to a belief in the statistical treatment of the results of experimentation." It was from Galton that Cattell acquired that faith which caused it to be said, supposedly first by Titchener, that "Cattell's god is Probable Error."[52]

Galton was a figure with whom Cattell could readily identify. Both men had a flair for mechanical invention, and they also shared an obvious pride of membership in that natural aristocracy of talent which even Thomas Jefferson[37] recognized as deserving of recognition. By calling Galton the greatest man he ever knew, Cattell, who was probably conscious of the many points of resemblance, was not lowering his own stature. His career might have been quite different had it not happened that, as Lyman Wells put it, his "formative years brought him into contact with another exceptional man through whom his interests were fixed upon the quantitative properties of the human mind."[52] It is clear that Cattell profited from his contact with Galton immeasurably more than from his contact with Wundt, and American psychology profited as a result.

Joseph Jastrow was another conduit of Galton's influence.[36] He inherited no silver spoon, and had no opportunity to study abroad. While still a student he began earning money by writing papers of a popular scientific character. Thus he was launched on his career as a popularizer of scientific psychology, whose own contributions were of secondary importance. The titles of some of his early papers show the Galton influence already at work: some peculiarities in the age statistics of the United States;[30] Composite portraiture;[31] The longevity of great men;[32] The dreams of the blind;[33] Eye-mindedness and earmindedness.[34]

In 1888, Cattell returned from England to a chair at the University of Pennsylvania, Jastrow received an appointment at Wisconsin, and Hall and Sanford went from Johns Hopkins to newly founded Clark University. Almost overnight America had four active psychology laboratories in place of one.

With a means of livelihood at last assured, Jastrow took leave the following spring for his first trip abroad. Characteristically, on his return he published a series of articles on "Aspects of Modern Psychology."[35] He said of Galton's work that it "could not readily be classified in the psychological activity of any country," but formed "a unique chapter of science, interesting no one more deeply than the students of scientific psychology." He described American psychology as characterized by "a readiness to introduce innovations whenever circumstances will allow, and . . . utilizing the freedom . . . of intellectual and educational youthfulness." With hindsight we may read these statements to mean that Galton was laying down new lines for psychology, and only the Americans were free enough from the restraints of traditional university disciplines to follow in the path he indicated.

Jastrow was active in the AAAS, and he was asked to organize the psychology exhibit for the World's Columbian Exposition, which opened in Chicago in 1893. Galton's influence was dominant in shaping the result, which Jastrow later described as "the first attempt to introduce tests to the American public."[37] The Official Directory[54] informed all visitors that "any one who wishes can have, by the payment of a small fee, various tests applied and can be measured and recorded upon cards which are given to the person, while the record is made upon the charts and tables hanging on the walls of the laboratory." It was as if Galton's anthropometric laboratory had been transported to Chicago. Popplestone[41] points out that the lack of any historical record of the public response compels us to wonder if the affair may not have been a dud, perhaps because it was located in a remote corner of the vast Exposition grounds. Whatever the public response may have been, this mobilization of all the current techniques of testing surely stimulated additional interest among psychologists themselves.

Even before the Exposition opened, Titchener[49] deplored the manner in which the exhibit confused anthropometrics with psychology, using the very argument which had driven Cattell to experiment in his own rooms: that a psychological experiment presupposes introspectively practiced observers. "It is one of the commonest errors," he wrote, "that since we are all using our minds, in some way or another, everyone is qualified to take part in psychological experimentation. As well maintain, that because we eat bread, we are all qualified to bake it." His protest was futile. Soon most of the new psychology laboratories, though they might be headed by Wundt's former students, were busy with anthropometrics. Titchener[50] in desperation wrote to Galton to solicit aid to repulse the invasion. "You would speak with authority," he wrote, "as you could not be suspected of wanting to undervalue Anthropometry. Unless some sort of protest is made, the American laboratories will all run over into anthropometrical statistics: which are, of course, valuable—but not psychology." The appeal is testimony to the high prestige that Galton enjoyed, but he must have been amused to be thus solicited to assist in throttling his own creation to defend the purity of experimental psychology.

Madison Bentley, then a student at Cornell, later said of this period that among the "adventitious" factors that shaped the careers of young psychologists might be the "worship of a Wundt or a Galton."[1] Among the partisans of Galton we must count Terman and Thorndike. Terman wrote in his autobiography: "Of the founders of modern psychology, my greatest admiration is for Galton."[47] Thorndike wrote: "Excellent work can surely be done by men with widely different notions of what psychology should be, the best work of all perhaps being done by men like Galton, who gave little or no thought to what it is or should be."[48]

The case of Woodworth is most interesting.[53] If we say, with Boring,[4] that "it is almost true that American psychology was personified in the person of Cattell," we may add that it is equally true that his student Woodworth personified the shift of orientation without which such a statement could not approach validity. Woodworth's undergraduate teacher in philosophy directed him to study science, as a preparation for philosophy; when later he abandoned philosophy in favor of a career in psychology, he spent more than five years of apprenticeship as a physiologist, to complete the preparation; yet he found in Cattell, whose attention went to the probable error and not to the brain, "the chief of all (his) teachers in giving shape to (his) psychological thought and work." This epitomizes the development of American psychology during the last quarter of the nineteenth century. Having begun the study of psychology as a propaedeutic to philosophy, it was soon caught up in the fascination of research on the physiology of brain, nerves, sense organs, and muscle, but then transferred its principal energies to the study of behavior, including especially the quantitative study of competence in all its manifestations. Psychology was able to pass through the two earlier phases because of the fluidity of the new universities, one consequence of which was that instruction in "mental science" passed from the hands of the college presidents, who almost invariably had theological training, into the hands of specialists. If we wish to claim the third phase as distinctively American, we shall have to give Galton a posthumous grant of American citizenship. We must ask whether the swift progress of individual psychology in the United States is not to be explained by the absence of the restraints on such development which were imposed by the more rigid university structure in Europe, at least as much as by the presence of stronger motivating forces in that direction.

In 1904, when the world met at St. Louis, psychology had another chance to speak to the nation. On that occasion Cattell not only rejected mentalism, in his statement that "it is no more necessary for the subject to be a psychologist than it is for the vivisected frog to be a physiologist," but he also rejected all limiting definitions for the new science, declaring that psychology consists of what psychologists wish to do "*qua* psychologists."[9] It was the first time that psychology had been defined broadly enough to include Cattell's true mentor, Galton.

By the time of the entry of the United States into World War I, the study of individual differences accounted for well over half of all work reported at meetings of the APA,[11] if we omit papers of historical and philosophical nature, which had by then declined from the largest to the smallest category. American psychologists had developed the skills which they put to work in the war effort.

In 1929, Cattell presided over the International Congress at New Haven, Conn. It was neither in his nature nor in the American character to acknowledge the full extent of our indebtedness to foreign mentors. "Wundt and Galton," he said, "are the foreign psychologists whom we most honor, but it may be that if neither of them had lived psychology in America would be much what it is."[13] Boring[2] concurred in part, writing that "it is an open question as to how much [Galton] influenced Cattell and the American tradition of individual psychology and the mental tests." In the revised edition of his history[3] this passage is omitted, and we read instead: "Perhaps it is true that America, while giving homage to Wundt, has overlooked Galton, to whom it owes a greater debt." Let us consider some of the reasons why we have been so much more ready to give homage to one than to the other.

The rise of American psychology was linked with the reform of American higher education, which was signaled in 1869 by the election of a chemist, Charles Eliot, as president of Harvard University. The theological domination of the colleges was to give way to an industrial-scientific orientation. The German universities were taken as models. Their great strength was in their laboratories, which had originated with Liebig's chemical laboratory at Giessen in 1824, and had subsequently provided the basis for Germany's world leadership in physiology. For a young man seeking a job in the expanding system of American universities, experience in a German laboratory was like money in the bank. Students of chemistry and physiology flocked to Germany. Psychologists were a minuscule group, but when they heard of a psychology laboratory at Leipzig, it became their Mecca. Even those who disliked what they found there were victims of the cognitive dissonance effect. After a young man spends several years of effort to earn a degree in a foreign country, all the while yearning for a sweetheart back home, and then returns triumphantly to a prestigious job and chances of advancement, he is unlikely to say that another course of study might have been more satisfying. Wundt was more than a prophet: he really led his American students into the promised land. Galton, on the other hand, was a man who lacked university status in a country which lacked a psychology laboratory, and where the leading universities were still primarily devoted to educating country divines who might make a hobby of science. Americans might read his books and articles with excitement, but there was no economic inducement to acclaim him as a leader.

It is universally agreed that all Galton's work in psychology radiated from one dominant concern: to learn how we might best manipulate the forces of evolution to mankind's advantage. While philosophers battled over the ethical implications of natural selection, or attempted to subordinate it to a cosmic drive toward higher forms of existence, Galton the pragmatist turned his attention to the phenomenon of variation, as providing the means by which we might accelerate the process. The anthropometric laboratory he set up at great personal expense was a device to tease the public into providing the data he needed for his research. His interest in individual differences was therefore derivative, not primary, but the resulting anthropometric work attracted the interest of psychologists. His ideas about evolution were more correct than Spencer's, and his ideas on the mechanism of heredity were more correct than Darwin's, but they had little following. It was Spencer who was almost universally regarded as the grand theorist of evolution. The American historian Fiske[14] had ranked Spencer's achievement with that of Newton, and the British zoologist Mitchell[38] compared him to Descartes and declared that his writings "may be regarded as the *Principes de la Philosophie* of the 19th century."

Galton's influence derived wholly from his genius in quantitative investigation. He arrived at the concepts of regression and correlation because they were peculiarly appropriate to the study of heredity, and thus also to the study of any complex phenomenon that is influenced in its quantitative manifestation by a large number of causal factors. Indeed, it has proved even more valuable for econometrics than for anthropometrics. No rival claims of priority, no record of independent discovery by others, dims the brilliance of this discovery. For Cattell to have said that American psychology might have been much the same without Galton is an understandable expression of vanity, but it is difficult to see how a historian can concur in that judgment. As we have seen, Boring did retreat from it.

The principal focus of this paper has been on Galton's positive contributions. There was also a negative aspect, of which we are all aware. Galton's advocacy of eugenics provided racists with a rationale for genocide which has been extensively exploited in the United States. When, however, we assess the degree of his culpability on this issue, we should not attribute to him opinions that were not his own. His views, as he himself remarked,[28] were often misrepresented. I shall discuss briefly some aspects of his thinking which are usually overlooked.

(1) It was not in Galton's manner of thinking to condemn a whole race as inferior. Once, after hearing a paper about the "dealings of colonists with aborigines," he said in discussion (which was reported in the third person) that "ethnologists were apt to look upon race as something more definite than it really was. He presumed it meant no more than the average of the characteristics of all the persons who were supposed to belong to the race, and this average was continually varying."[21] He went on to indicate regret that Englishmen did not, like the ancient Romans, live more closely with the populations of the subject colonies, and make them more welcome in England. The notion of racial "purity" had no place in Galton's scheme of eugenics.

(2) Galton was always more interested (as Pearson[40] points out with obvious regret) in raising high intelligence rather than in eliminating low intelligence, which he was much more willing to leave to the slow processes of natural selection. He never subscribed to the theory of degeneration, which was popular so late in the nineteenth century, and which was the basis of the direction which the eugenic movement took after Galton's death.

(3) He always insisted that the great need was for research, to acquire a knowledge of heredity which would be a sufficient basis for wise eugenic practices (or, as we would now say, for informed genetic counseling). He fully recognized the danger of even well-intentioned programs based on inadequate knowledge. He said, for example, in 1884: "Our present ignorance of the conditions by which the level of humanity may be raised is so gross, that I believe if we had some dictator of the Spartan type, who exercised absolute power over marriages . . . and who acted with the best intentions, he might perhaps do even more harm than good to the race."[23]

(4) Finally, Galton was fully aware of the need for attention to environmental influences, both in research on heredity and in efforts to improve society. The conclusion of his study of twins, in which he defined the nature-nurture issue, was stated thus: "Nature prevails enormously over nurture when the differences in nurture do not exceed what is commonly to be found among persons of the same rank of society and in the same country."[18] He perfectly appreciated the statistical fact that more genetic gold can be mined from the great masses of the disadvantaged than from the thin layer of those who have risen to distinction.[26] That is why he could claim that "the sterling values of nurture, including all kinds of sanitary improvements," were "powerful auxiliaries" to his cause.[17] He also emphasized that "it cannot be too strongly hammered into popular recognition that a well-developed human being, capable in mind and body, is an expensive animal to rear."[28] To rear, be it noted, not to breed.

On the occasion of the conference on which this volume is based, it is especially fitting to recall one more expression of Galton's recognition of the power of environment: "The most likely nest . . . for self-reliant natures is to be found in States founded and maintained by emigrants."[22] Surely this is one reason why American psychology displayed what Jastrow called "a readiness to introduce innovations." Galton's innovative methods for the study of human capacities were accepted as a part of psychology, and they helped to give American psychology its distinctive character. It seems quite unlikely that the same development could have taken place in anything like the same time span without Galton's influence.

REFERENCES

1 Bentley, M. 1936. In *History of Psychology in Autobiography*. C. Murchison, Ed. Vol. 3: 53–67. Clark University Press. Worcester, Mass.

2 Boring, E. G. 1929. *A History of Experimental Psychology*. D. Appleton-Century Co. New York, N.Y.

3 Boring, E. G. 1950. *A History of Experimental Psychology*. 2nd edit. Appleton-Century-Crofts. New York, N.Y.

4 Boring, E. G. 1950. The influence of evolutionary theory upon American psychological thought. In *Evolutionary Thought in America*. S. Persons, Ed.: 267–298.

5 Cattell, J. McK. 1885. Ueber die Zeit der Erkennung und Bennenung von Schriftzeichen, Bildern und Farben. *Philosophische Studien* 2:635–650.

6 Cattell, J. McK. 1886. Psychometrische Untersuchungen. I. Apparate und Methoden. *Philosophische Studien* 3: 305–335.

7 Cattell, J. McK. 1890. Mental tests and measurements. *Mind* 15: 373–380.

8 Cattell, J. McK. 1903. Statistics of American psychologists. *Amer. J. Psychol.* 14: 310–328.

9 Cattell, J. McK. 1904. The conceptions and methods of psychology, *Popular Science Monthly* 66: 176–186.

10 Cattell, J. McK. 1911. Francis Galton. *Popular Science Monthly* 78: 309–311.

11 Cattell, J. McK. 1917. Our psychological association and research. *Science* 45: 275–284.

12 Cattell, J. McK. 1928. Early psychological laboratories. In *Feelings and Emotions,* the Wittenberg Symposium. M. L. Reymert, Ed.: 427–433. Clark University Press. Worcester, Mass.

13 Cattell, J. McK. 1929. *Psychology in America.* Address of the president of the Ninth Int. Congr. of Psychology. Science Press. New York, N.Y.

14 Fiske, J. 1874. *Outlines of Cosmic Philosophy.* 2 vols. Macmillan & Co. London, England.

15 Galton, F. 1869. *Hereditary Genius.* Macmillan & Co. London, England.

16 Galton, F. 1874. Proposal to apply for anthropological statistics from schools. *J. Anthropol. Inst.* 3: 308–311.

17 Galton, F. 1873. Hereditary improvement. *Fraser's Mag.* NS 7: 116–130.

18 Galton, F. 1876. The history of twins, as a criterion of the relative powers of nature and nurture. *J. Anthropol. Inst.* 5: 391–406.

19 Galton, F. 1879. Psychometric experiments. *Brain* 2: 149–162.

20 Galton, F. 1880. Statistics of mental imagery. *Mind* 5: 301–318.

21 Galton, F. 1882. *J. Anthropol. Inst.* 11: 352–353.

22 Galton, F. 1883. *Inquiries into Human Faculty and Its Development:* 82 Macmillan & Co. New York. N.Y.

23 Galton, F. 1884. *Record of Family Faculties.* Macmillan & Co. London, England.

24 Galton, F. 1885. On the anthropometric laboratory of the late International Health Exhibition. *J. Anthropol. Inst.* 14: 205–219.

25 Galton, F. 1885. Some results of the anthropometric laboratory. *J. Anthropol. Inst.* 14: 275–287.

26 Galton. F. 1885. Types and their inheritance. *Science* 6: 268–274.

27 Galton, F. 1888. Co-relations and their measurement, chiefly from anthropometric data. *Proc. Roy. Soc.* 45: 135–145.

28 Galton, F. 1903. The Daily Chronicle (London). July 29. Excerpts in K. Pearson. 1930. *The Life, Letters and Labours of Francis Galton.* The University Press. Cambridge, England. Vol. IIIA: 252–253.

29 Galton, F. 1905. Number of strokes of the brush in a picture. *Nature* 72: 198.

30 Jastrow, J. 1885. *Science* 5: 461–464.

31 Jastrow, J. 1885. *Science* 6: 165–168.

32 Jastrow, J. 1886. *Science* 8: 294–296.

33 Jastrow, J. 1888. *New Princeton Rev.* 5: 18–24.

34 Jastrow, J. 1888. *Popular Science Monthly* 33: 597–608.

35 Jastrow, J. 1890. Aspects of modern psychology. In *Epitomes of Three Sciences.* H. Oldenberg, J. Jastrow and C. H. Cornill. 59–100. The Open Court Publishing Co. Chicago, Ill.

36 Jastrow, J. 1930. In *History of Psychology in Autobiography.* C. Murchison. Ed.: 2:297–331. Clark University Press. Worcester, Mass.

37 Jefferson, T. 1925. Letter dated Oct. 28, 1818. In *Correspondence of John Adams and Thomas Jefferson.* P Wilstach, Ed. The Bobbs-Merrill Co. Indianapolis, Ind.

38 Mitchell, P. C. 1910. Evolution. In *Encyclopedia Brittanica.* 11th edit. 10: 22–37. The University Press. Cambridge, England

39 Obersteiner, H. 1879. Experimental researches on attention. *Brain* 1: 439–453.

40 Pearson, K. 1914–1930. *The Life, Letters and Labours of Francis Galton.* 3 vols. in 4. The University Press. Cambridge, England.

41 Popplestone, J. A. 1976. The psychological exhibit at the Chicago World's Fair of 1893. Paper presented at the meeting of the Western Psychol. Assoc. Los Angeles, Calif. April, 1976.

42 Romanes, G. J. 1883. *Mental Evolution in Animals.* Kegan Paul & Co., London, England.

43 Ross, D. 1972. *G. Stanley Hall: The Psychologist as Prophet.* Chicago University Press. Chicago, Ill.

44 Sokal, M. M. 1969. Influences on a young psychologist: James McKeen Cattell, 1880–1890. Paper presented at mtg. of the History of Science Society. Washington, D.C., December, 1969.

45 Sokal, M. M. 1971. The unpublished autobiography of James McKeen Cattell. *Amer. Psychol.* 26: 626–635.

46 Sokal, M. M. 1972. Psychology at Victorian Cambridge—the unofficial laboratory of 1887–1888. *Proc. Amer. Phil. Soc.* 116: 145–147.

47 Terman, L. M. 1932. In *History of Psychology in Autobiography.* C. Murchison, Ed.: 2: 297–331. Clark University Press, Worcester, Mass.

48 Thorndike, E. L. 1936. In *History of Psychology in Autobiography.* C. Murchison. Ed.: 3: 263–270. Clark Universtity Press, Worcester, Mass.

49 Titchener, E. B. 1893. Anthropometry and experimental psychology. *Phil. Rev.* 2: 187–192.

50 Titchener, E. B. 1898. Letter to Francis Galton, dated 18 IV 1898. Copy in Archives of the History of American Psychology, The University of Akron. Akron, Ohio.

51 Walker, H. M. 1929. *Studies in the History of Statistical Method.* Williams & Wilkins Co. Baltimore, Md.

52 Wells, F. L. 1944. James McKeen Cattell: 1860–1944. *Amer. J. Psychol.* 57 270–275.

53 Woodworth, R. S. 1932. In *History of Psychology in Autobiography.* C. Murchison, Ed.: 2: 359–380. Clark University Press. Worcester, Mass.

54 World's Columbian Exposition. 1893. Official Directory. Chicago, Ill.

CHAPTER 8

AMERICAN ANTECEDENTS TO FUNCTIONALISM

The first three psychology laboratories in the United States were founded by William James, G. Stanley Hall, and James McKeen Cattell. On both conceptual and methodological grounds, the psychology of each of those men contributed greatly to the founding of functionalism.

William James (1842–1910) earned his medical degree from Harvard in 1869. Although he had no course work in scientific psychology, he had spent some time in 1867–68 in Europe, visiting the laboratories of Fechner, Helmholtz, and Wundt. In 1875, James established a demonstrational laboratory at Harvard to accompany a course he was teaching on the relations between psychology and physiology (see Harper, 1949; Perry, 1935). Because it was not a laboratory used for original research, many historians discount its priority among American psychology laboratories.

That honor is often given to G. Stanley Hall (1844–1924), a student of James's at Harvard, where he earned in 1878 what is often labeled the first psychology doctorate in the United States. Following his graduation, Hall went to Leipzig, where he studied briefly with Wundt and more extensively with the physiologist Karl Ludwig. Hall also studied for a time with Helmholtz in Berlin. His first full-time position was at Johns Hopkins University, where he founded a psychology laboratory in 1883. One of his graduate students at Johns Hopkins was James McKeen Cattell (1860–1944).

Cattell and Hall did not get along (see Sokal, 1982), so Cattell went to Leipzig, where he earned his doctorate with Wundt in 1886. A year later, he established the psychology laboratory at the University of Pennsylvania. He took a leave of absence the next year and went to England where for a while he worked in Francis Galton's laboratory (recall Diamond's article in the previous chapter regarding Galton's substantial influence on Cattell).

The content of James's, Hall's, and Cattell's scientific work all reflected, in one way or another, Darwinian concerns for function, development, adaptation, and individual differences, and many later psychologists—especially those who called themselves functionalists, partly in response to Titchener's attempt to limit psychology's scope—followed their lead. But their contributions to the emergence of a science of psychology went beyond the intellectual. Each proved to be a major spokesperson for psychology, explaining—sometimes selling—psychology to students, educators, businesses, and the general public. Word about the *new psychology,* this laboratory science that had seemingly evolved so suddenly from the merger of philosophy and physiology, needed to reach those in the university community as well as those in the world outside of academe (see Benjamin, 1986). James's principal contribution in this regard was through a book that he took twelve years to write.

In 1890, Henry Holt Company published James's two-volume work, *The Principles of Psychology*. It was James's assemblage of the world's psychological knowledge as only James could write it. Many historians consider it the best-written book in the history of psychology, and indeed James's prose is masterful (in comparison with his famous author-brother, Henry, it was said that William was a psychologist who wrote like a novelist, whereas Henry was a novelist who wrote like a psychologist.) James's *Principles* became popular reading in colleges at the end of the nineteenth century, and later many eminent psychologists, for example, Edward L. Thorndike, would say that they were drawn into a career in psychology after reading it. The opening line of the book is "Psychology is the Science of Mental Life," and in the nearly 1,400 pages that followed, James explained what was known about the mind *and* lauded the great potential for human understanding that was promised by a scientific approach to psychology. It was that promise of psychology as a natural science that was so enormously influential in recruiting many of the next generation of psychologists.

The success of the *Principles* encouraged Holt to produce a version of the book that was more appropriate in size for classroom use. So in 1892, Holt published James's *Psychology: Briefer Course,* which was only slightly more than a third the length of the *Principles* (people referred to the large work as "James" and the briefer version as "Jimmy").

The Darwinian influences are clear in James's writing. He argued that the content of consciousness was not as important as what consciousness does for the organism, and, according to James, what it does is to enhance the organism's capability of adapting to the environment. It accomplishes that by its role in choice; that is, it enables the organism to decide among choices and motivates the organism toward making a particular choice—one that has survival value. In short, consciousness has evolved because it has survival value.

Hall and Cattell played roles very different from that of James in the beginnings of the new psychology in the United States. Both published a great deal, but neither produced any written work that would shape psychology in the way James did with the *Principles*. Instead, their role was more of organization, founding, promotion, application, and even entrepreneurship. Hall founded the first psychology journal in the United States in 1887 (the *American Journal of Psychology)* and the American Psychological Association in 1892. He founded three other journals as well: *Pedagogical Seminary* (now published as the *Journal of Genetic Psychology*), the *Journal of Religious Psychology*, and the *Journal of Applied Psychology*. He is remembered for bringing Sigmund Freud to the United States for his only visit; Freud lectured at Clark University (where Hall was president) on the occasion of its twentieth anniversary in 1909.

Although Hall had diverse interests in psychology and related fields, he might best be characterized as a developmental psychologist. For much of his career, he wrote about developmental topics—his two-volume magnum opus on adolescence (1904); his many publications on child study; and his 1922 book on the psychology of aging, written when he was 78. The ideas of Darwin and Galton figured prominently in Hall's research and writing. In one of his two autobiographies, Hall (1923) recalled that when as a young boy he heard about Darwin's theory, he greeted it as music to his ears.

Hall's *recapitulation theory* was a direct outgrowth of Darwinian evolution. It stated that in the course of development, from embryo to old age, every human repeated all the stages of development that had existed in the course of human evolution. Thus an evolutionary account of the human race was available by a detailed study of the life course of humans. An understanding of these developmental stages was particularly important for schoolteachers and reflected Hall's interest in child study.

Hall was one of the first to promote the application of psychology outside the university. In describing the new psychology he wrote, "The one chief and immediate field of application for all this work is its application to education" (Hall, 1894, p. 718). Using new experimental methods, psychology could learn all there was to know about the child—about sensory capabilities, physical characteristics, sense of humor, religious ideas, memory, play, attention span, and so forth. With this new knowledge, education would be no longer guesswork but a science. Pedagogical techniques could be planned and used in such a way as to be maximally effective for all kinds of students. Not all of Hall's colleagues agreed with his claims about the applicability of psychology to education, but he persisted in his efforts for two decades as part of the child study movement, a national movement he initiated (see Davidson & Benjamin, 1987). One of the by-products of Hall's work in child study was that he gave American psychology a new research method—the questionnaire. Hall did not invent the questionnaire, but his extensive use of the technique greatly popularized it, making it part of the methodological arsenal of the functionalists.

Cattell began his psychology research as a graduate student at Johns Hopkins, where he used reaction time tasks to measure the speed of mental operations. He completed those studies in Leipzig. His greatest influence, by his own acknowledgment, was not Hall or Wundt but Galton. From Wundt, he acquired a set of research methods, whereas Galton provided him with his scientific goal: "The measurement of the psychological differences between people" (Sokal, 1982, p. 327). (The influence of Galton was evident even in Cattell's offer to pay $1,000 each to his seven children if they would marry the sons or daughters of college professors.)

Cattell coined the term *mental test* and for more than a decade worked on a program of anthropometric mental testing designed to predict mental abilities from physical and sensory characteristics. It was a failure that essentially signaled the end of his research career. Instead, he turned to his editing duties, mostly to the weekly journal *Science,* which he had purchased from Alexander Graham Bell in 1894. As editor of this prestigious publication, Cattell became one of the most visible persons in science and the first psychologist to be admitted to the National Academy of Sciences. He used his position to promote psychology among the natural sciences, and he promoted it well. There is no denying that psychology made far greater strides in the scientific community in the first quarter of the twentieth century than would have been possible without Cattell's influence.

Although Cattell had abandoned his own testing research, he did not leave the field altogether. His students at Columbia were involved with mental testing, most notably Edward L. Thorndike. Further, in the 1920s, Cattell founded the Psychological Corporation, then and now one of the principal publishers of psychological tests.

THE READINGS

There are six selections in this chapter. The first is taken from the chapter entitled "The Stream of Thought" in James's *Principles*. In the opening paragraph of this selection, James takes issue with the psychology of Wundt, arguing that thought, and not sensation, is the starting point for a science of psychology. In this excerpt, James's emphasis is on selective perception and the ways in which the senses and the mind select particular stimuli from the vast array comprising the perceptual environment. He shows that selective attention is about choice and about the adaptive significance of choice.

The second selection, by historian David E. Leary of the University of Richmond, is closely tied to the selection from James's own pen. The focus of Leary's article is on James's view of human understanding and how that view was shaped by James's training and sensibility as an artist. Leary, who has written much about the use of metaphor in scientific thinking and writing, shows how James's metaphors defined his philosophical and psychological thinking.

G. Stanley Hall is the subject of the next two selections. The first was published by Hall in 1894 in a popular magazine of the day. In it he describes child study as a program of research destined to make education a science. The article is an excellent example of the combination of science and zeal that was characteristic of Hall and of the child study movement. That article is followed by a contemporary historical piece, written by Lesley A. Diehl, that describes Hall's view of women in relationship to his recapitulation theory of development and the influence of his work on the beginnings of psychology's interest in sex differences. Diehl's analysis of Hall takes the form of an investigation of the paradox of his opposition to coeducation and his education of women graduate students at Clark University.

The final two selections are about James McKeen Cattell and his work in mental testing. The first of these, published by Cattell in 1893, is a review of the "new psychology" and the work on mental testing, much of it pioneered by Cattell. The article which appeared in an education journal, extols the virtues of mental testing for teachers. The last article is by Michael M. Sokal, a historian of science at Worcester Polytechnic Institute. He is the acknowledged authority on Cattell and an expert, as well, on the history of mental testing (see Sokal, 1987). He describes Cattell's anthropometric mental testing program, Galton's influence on that work, and, ultimately, why Cattell's program failed as a measure of intelligence.

Together, these six selections provide a view of the beginnings of the new psychology in America and the influences borrowed from England in the writings of Darwin and Galton.

REFERENCES

Benjamin, L. T. (1986). Why don't they understand us? A history of psychology's public image. *American Psychologist, 41,* 941–946.

Davidson, E. S., & Benjamin, L. T. (1987). A history of the child study movement in America. In J. Glover & R. Ronning (Eds.), *Historical foundations of educational psychology.* New York: Plenum Press, pp. 41–60.

Hall, G. S. (1894, August). The new psychology as a basis of education. *Forum,* pp. 688–702.

Hall, G. S. (1923). *The life and confessions of a psychologist.* New York: D. Appleton.

Harper, R. S. (1949). The laboratory of William James. *Harvard Alumni Bulletin, 52,* 169–173.

Perry, R. B. (1935). *The thought and character of William James* (2 vols.). Boston: Little Brown.

Sokal, M. M. (1982). James McKeen Cattell and the failure of anthropometric mental testing. 1890–1901. In W. R. Woodward & M. G. Ash (Eds.). *The problematic science: Psychology in nineteenth-century thought.* New York: Praeger, pp. 322–345.

Sokal, M. M. (Ed.) (1987). *Psychological testing and American society, 1890–1930.* New Brunswick, NJ: Rutgers University Press.

The Stream of Thought

William James

We now begin our study of the mind from within. Most books start with sensations, as the simplest mental facts, and proceed synthetically, constructing each higher stage from those below it. But this is abandoning the empirical method of investigation. No one ever had a simple sensation by itself. Consciousness, from our natal day, is of a teeming multiplicity of objects and relations, and what we call simple sensations, are results of discriminative attention, pushed often to a very high degree. It is astonishing what havoc is wrought in psychology by admitting at the outset apparently innocent suppositions, that nevertheless contain a flaw. The bad consequences develop themselves later on, and are irremediable, being woven through the whole texture of the work. The notion that sensations, being the simplest things, are the first things to take up in psychology is one of these suppositions. The only thing which psychology has a right to postulate at the outset is the fact of thinking itself, and that must first be taken up and analyzed. If sensations then prove to be amongst the elements of the thinking, we shall be no worse off as respects them than if we had taken them for granted at the start.

The first fact for us, then, as psychologists, is that thinking of some sort goes on. I use the word thinking . . . , for every form of consciousness indiscriminately. If we could say in English 'it thinks,' as we say 'it rains' or 'it blows,' we should be stating the fact most simply and with the minimum of assumption. As we cannot, we must simply say that *thought goes on.*

Adapted from James, W. (1890). *Principles of psychology*. New York: Henry Holt & Co., pp. 224–225, 283–290.

FIVE CHARACTERS IN THOUGHT

How does it go on? We notice immediately five important characters in the process, of which it shall be the duty of the present chapter to treat in a general way:

1) Every thought tends to be part of a personal consciousness.

2) Within each personal consciousness thought is always changing.

3) Within each personal consciousness thought is sensibly continuous.

4) It always appears to deal with objects independent of itself.

5) It is interested in some parts of these objects to the exclusion of others, and welcomes or rejects—*chooses* from among them, in a word—all the while. . . .

The last peculiarity of consciousness to which attention is to be drawn is this first rough description of its stream in that *It is always interested more in one part of its object than in another, and welcomes and rejects, or chooses, all the while it thinks.*

The phenomena of selective attention and of deliberative will are of course patent examples of this choosing activity. But few of us are aware how incessantly it is at work in operations not ordinarily called by these names. Accentuation and Emphasis are present in every perception we have. We find it quite impossible to disperse our attention impartially over a number of impressions. A monotonous succession of sonorous strokes is broken up into rhythms, now of one sort, now of another, by the different accent which we place on different strokes. The simplest of these rhythms is the double one, tick-tóck, tick-tóck, tick-tóck. Dots dispersed on a surface are perceived in rows and groups. Lines separate into diverse figures. The ubiquity of the distinctions, *this* and *that, here* and *there, now* and *then,* in our minds is the result of our laying the same selective emphasis on parts of place and time.

But we do far more than emphasize things, and unite some, and keep others apart. We actually *ignore* most of the things before us. Let me briefly show how this goes on.

To begin at the bottom, what are our very senses themselves but organs of selection? Out of the infinite chaos of movements, of which physics teaches us that the outer world consists, each sense-organ picks out those which fall within certain limits of velocity. To these it responds, but ignores the rest as completely as if they did not exist. It thus accentuates particular movements in a manner for which objectively there seems no valid ground; for, as Lange says, there is no reason whatever to think that the gap in Nature between the highest sound-waves and the lowest heat-waves is an abrupt break like that of our sensations; or that the difference between violet and ultra violet rays has anything like the objective importance subjectively represented by that between light and darkness. Out of what is in itself an undistinguishable, swarming *continuum,* devoid of distinction or emphasis, our senses make for us, by attending to this motion and ignoring that, a world full of contrasts, of sharp accents, of abrupt changes, of picturesque light and shade.

If the sensations we receive from a given organ have their causes thus picked out for us by the conformation of the organ's termination, Attention, on the other hand, out of all the sensations yielded, picks out certain ones as worthy of its notice and suppresses all the rest. Helmholtz's work on Optics is little more than a study of those visual sensations of which common men never become aware—blind spots, *muscœ volitantes,* after-images, irradiation, chromatic fringes, marginal changes of color, double images, astigmatism, movements of accommodation and convergence, retinal rivalry, and more besides. We do not even know without special training on which of our eyes an image falls. So habitually ignorant are most men of this that one may be blind for years of a single eye and never know the fact.

Helmholtz says that we notice only those sensations which are signs to us of *things.* But what are things? Nothing, as we shall abundantly see, but special groups of sensible qualities, which happen practically or æsthetically to interest us, to which we therefore give substantive names, and which we exalt to this exclusive status of independence and dignity. But in itself, apart from my interest, a particular dust-wreath on a windy day is just as much of an individual thing, and just as much or as little deserves an individual name, as my own body does.

And then, among the sensations we get from each separate thing, what happens? The mind selects again. It chooses certain of the sensations to represent the thing most *truly,* and considers the rest as its appearances, modified by the conditions of the moment. Thus my table-top is named *square,* after but one of an infinite number of retinal sensations which it yields, the rest of them being sensations of two acute and two obtuse angles; but I call the latter *perspective* views, and the four right angles the *true* form of the table, and erect the attribute squareness into the table's essence, for æsthetic reasons of my own. In like manner, the real form of the circle is deemed to be the sensation it gives when the line of vision is perpendicular to its centre—all its other sensations are signs of this sensation. The real sound of the cannon is the sensation it makes when the ear is close by. The real color of the brick is the sensation it gives when the eye looks squarely at it from a near point, out of the sunshine and yet not in the gloom; under other circumstances it gives us other color-sensations which are but signs of this—we then see it looks pinker or blacker than it really is. The reader knows no object which he does not represent to himself by preference as in some typical attitude, of some normal size, at some characteristic distance, of some standard tint, etc., etc. But all these essential characteristics, which together form for us the genuine objectivity of the thing and are contrasted with what we call the subjective sensations it may yield us at a given moment, are mere sensations like the latter. The mind chooses to suit itself, and decides what particular sensation shall be held more real and valid than all the rest.

Thus perception involves a twofold choice. Out of all present sensations, we notice mainly such as are significant of absent ones; and out of all the absent associates which these suggest, we again pick out a very few to stand for the objective reality *par excellence*. We could have no more exquisite example of selective industry.

That industry goes on to deal with the things thus given in perception. A man's empirical thought depends on the things he has experienced, but what these shall be is to a large extent determined by his habits of attention. A thing may be present to him a thousand times, but if he persistently fails to notice it, it cannot be said to enter into his experience. We are all seeing flies, moths, and beetles by the thousand, but to whom, save an entomologist, do they say anything distinct? On the other hand, a thing met only once in a lifetime may leave an indelible experience in the memory. Let four men make a tour in Europe. One will bring home only picturesque impressions—costumes and colors, parks and views and works of architecture, pictures and statues. To another all this will be non-existent; and distances and prices, populations and drainage-arrangements, door- and window-fastenings, and other useful statistics will take their place. A third will give a rich account of the theatres, restaurants, and public balls, and naught beside; whilst the fourth will perhaps have been so wrapped in his own subjective broodings as to tell little more than a few names of places through which he passed. Each has selected, out of the same mass of presented objects, those which suited his private interest and has made his experience thereby.

If, now, leaving the empirical combination of objects, we ask how the mind proceeds *rationally* to connect them, we find selection again to be omnipotent. We shall see that all Reasoning depends on the ability of the mind to break up the totality of the phenomenon reasoned about, into parts, and to pick out from among these the particular one which, in our given emergency, may lead to the proper conclusion. Another predicament will need another conclusion, and require another element to be picked out. The man of genius is he who will always stick in his bill at the right point, and bring it out with the right element—'reason' if the emergency be theoretical, 'means' if it be practical—transfixed upon it. I here confine myself to this brief statement, but it may suffice to show that Reasoning is but another form of the selective activity of the mind.

If now we pass to its æsthetic department, our law is still more obvious. The artist notoriously selects his items, rejecting all tones, colors, shapes, which do not harmonize with each other and with the main purpose of his work. That unity, harmony, 'convergence of characters,' as M. Taine calls it, which gives to works of art their superiority over works of nature, is wholly due to *elimination*. Any natural subject will do, if the artist has wit enough to pounce upon some one feature of it as characteristic, and suppress all merely accidental items which do not harmonize with this.

Ascending still higher, we reach the plane of Ethics, where choice reigns notoriously supreme. An act has no ethical quality whatever unless it be chosen out of several all equally possible. To sustain the arguments for the good course and keep them ever before us, to stifle our longing for more flowery ways, to keep the foot unflinchingly on the arduous path, these are characteristic ethical energies. But more than these; for these but deal with the means of compassing interests already felt by the man to be supreme. The ethical energy *par excellence* has to go farther and choose which *interest* out of several, equally coercive, shall become supreme. The issue here is of the utmost pregnancy, for it decides a man's entire career. When he debates, Shall I commit this crime? choose that profession? accept that office, or marry this fortune?—his choice really lies between one of several equally possible future Characters. What he shall *become* is fixed by the conduct of this moment. Schopenhauer, who enforces his determinism by the argument that with a given fixed character only one reaction is possible under given circumstances, forgets that, in these critical ethical moments, what consciously *seems* to be in question is the complexion of the character itself. The problem with the man is less what act he shall now choose to do, than what being he shall now resolve to become.

Looking back, then, over this review, we see that the mind is at every stage a theatre of simultaneous possibilities. Consciousness consists in the comparison of these with each other, the selection of some, and the suppression of the rest by the reinforcing and inhibiting agency of attention. The highest and most elaborated mental products are filtered from the data chosen by the faculty next beneath, out of the mass offered by the faculty below that, which mass in turn was sifted from a still larger amount of yet simpler material, and so on. The mind, in short, works on the data it receives very much as a sculptor works on his block of stone. In a sense the statue stood there from eternity. But there were a thousand different ones beside it, and the sculptor alone is to thank for having extricated this one from the rest. Just so the world of each of us, howsoever different our several views of it may be, all lay embedded in the primordial chaos of sensations, which gave the mere *matter* to the thought of all of us indifferently. We may, if we like, by our reasonings unwind things back to that black and jointless continuity of space and moving clouds of swarming atoms which science calls the only real world. By all the while the world *we* feel and live in will be that which our ancestors and we, by slowly cumulative strokes of choice, have extricated out of this, like sculptors, by simply rejecting certain portions of the given stuff. Other sculptors, other statues from the same stone! Other minds, other worlds from the same monotonous and inexpressive chaos! My world is but one in a million alike embedded, alike real to those who may abstract them. How different must be the worlds in the consciousness of ant, cuttle-fish, or crab!

But in my mind and your mind the rejected portions and the selected portions of the original world-stuff are to a great extent the same. The human race as a whole largely agrees as to what it shall notice and name, and what not. And among the noticed parts we select in much the same way for accentuation and preference or subordination and dislike. There is, however, one entirely extraordinary case in which no two men ever are known to choose alike. One great splitting of the whole universe into two halves is made by each of us; and for each of us almost all of the interest attaches to one of the halves; but we all draw the line of division between them in a different place. When I say that we all call the two halves by the same names, and that those names are *'me'* and *'not-me'* respectively, it will at once be seen what I mean. The altogether unique kind of interest which each human mind feels in those parts of creation which it can call *me* or *mine* may be a moral riddle, but it is a fundamental psychological fact. No mind can take the same interest in his neighbor's *me* as in his own. The neighbor's me falls together with all the rest of things in one foreign mass, against which his own *me* stands out in startling relief. Even the trodden worm, as Lotze somewhere says, contrasts his own suffering self with the whole remaining universe, though he have no clear conception either of himself or of what the universe may be. He is for me a mere part of the world; for him it is I who am the mere part. Each of us dichotomizes the Kosmos in a different place.

William James and the Art of Human Understanding

David E. Leary

It has long been noted that William James, one of the founders of philosophical pragmatism as well as psychological science, had the sensibility of an artist. It has also been suggested that his artistic sensibility made a tangible difference in the crafting of his thought, both in philosophy and in psychology. G. Stanley Hall (1891), for instance, said that James was "an impressionist in psychology" whose "portfolio" (*The Principles of Psychology,* W. James, 1890/1983c) contained many stimulating and even brilliant "sketches" (Hall, 1891, p. 585). Later, James Jackson Putnam (1910) averred that James was "through and through an artist" (p. 842), and John Dewey (1910) stated that he was "an artist who gave philosophical expression to the artist's sense of the unique" (p. 507). Still later, George Santayana (1930) referred to James's "pictorial cosmology" (p. 252), and Ralph Barton Perry (1935) wrote about his "pictorial manner of philosophizing" (Vol. 2, p. 684).

It may surprise some to learn that James not only had the sensibility of an artist, but that his first vocation (as he himself called it) was to be an artist. This was no whimsical aspiration. From a young age, James drew very capably and persistently, he studied art in American and European museums with great avidity and insight, and at the age of 18, he committed himself to an apprenticeship with William Morris Hunt, one of the major painters in America. As testimony to his ability, the well-known artist John La Farge, who had been an apprentice to Hunt at the same time as James, asserted that James "had the promise of being a remarkable, perhaps a great, painter" (La Farge, 1910, p. 8).

Leary, D. E. (1992). William James and the art of human understanding. *American Psychologist, 47,* 152–160.

Recently, Jacques Barzun (1983, 1985), Daniel Bjork (1983, 1988), and Howard Feinstein (1984) have suggested some of the possible consequences of James's artistic ability, aesthetic interests, and abbreviated artistic career for his subsequent work in psychology and philosophy. Their scholarship is extremely valuable, but it has left many unresolved questions and issues to be explored. For instance, Barzun (1985) argued that "the Jamesian mind is artist first and last" (p. 909), but he did not articulate in concrete detail what this meant, nor did he relate his thesis to James's own particular artistic experiences. Feinstein (1984), whose detailed and fascinating research has provided grist for many mills (including my own), was primarily concerned with the emotional antecedents and consequences of James's turn away from his early artistic vocation and with the effects of these emotional factors (rather than artistic factors per se) on the development of James's thought. Even Bjork, who has examined the extent to which James, the psychologist, was a "compromised artist" (Bjork, 1983, pp. 15–36) and has portrayed the center of James's subsequent vision (Bjork, 1988), has not analyzed many of the tangible ways in which James's artistic background and sensitivities affected the development of his specific premises and doctrines. Nor has he pursued his insight that James often articulated his thought in terms of metaphors drawn from the arts.

Through the aid of such metaphors, drawn by James from the realm of the arts, I will introduce and illustrate my thesis in the next section. This thesis is simply that James's artistic sensibility and experience were critically important in the development of his psychological and philosophical thought and, more particularly, in the articulation of a view of human understanding that was fundamental to his psychology and philosophy. This view of human understanding, I will argue, underlay how James characterized all thought, ranging from the philosophical and psychological through the common-sensical and scientific. It also influenced the way in which he thought about and formulated his own specific psychological and philosophical doctrines. To underscore its centrality as a fundamental motif throughout all his work, I shall begin by reviewing the ways in which—and the artistic metaphors through which—James characterized philosophy and philosophizing over the course of his career. Subsequently, I shall turn my attention to James's view of human understanding, its development, and its further articulation and application in his psychology.

JAMES'S PORTRAIT OF PHILOSOPHY

The heuristic goal of philosophy, according to James, is to achieve the most all-encompassing view, or perspective, possible. In practice, however, "no philosophy can ever be anything but a summary sketch, a picture of the world in abridgment, a foreshortened bird's-eye view of the perspective of events" (James, 1909/1977, p. 9). Because no single person or group can achieve a view that is all-inclusive, James (1876/1978b) defined philosophical study as "the habit of always seeing an alternative," of gaining and changing "mental perspective," like a connoisseur walking around a three-dimensional statue (p. 4).

Just as Plato once described science as the search for likely stories, James (1905/1978a) said that the philosopher searches for "more or less plausible pictures" (p. 143). Concepts are "views taken on reality," he suggested (James, 1910/1979, p. 200), and "philosophies are only pictures of the world which have grown up in the minds of different individuals" (quoted in Myers, 1986, p. 570). If you want to understand anyone's philosophical system, James argued, you should "place yourself . . . at the centre of [that person's] philosophic vision." When you do, "you understand at once all the different things it makes [that person] write or say. But keep outside [that vision] . . . and of course you fail" (James, 1909/1977, p. 117). For "philosophy is more a matter of passionate vision than of logic. . . . Logic only find[s] reasons for the vision afterwards" (p. 81). Given this conviction, it is not surprising that James felt that "a man's vision is the great fact about him" (p. 14).

Although James had a special affinity for the notion that philosophers "paint" their views (see, e.g., James 1907/1975b, p. 275; 1903–1904/1988), he was not indelibly wedded to the painting metaphor. On occasion he characterized his system of thought, instead, as a "mosaic philosophy" in which the picture of reality was composed of myriad little pieces or aspects of reality (James, 1912/1976, pp. 22, 42). The mosaic, James said, would never be completed, for "every hour of human life" can add a new aspect, achieved from a novel perspective, guided by a distinctive interest, thus enlarging the "picture gallery" of human life (p. 83). Because "of no concrete bit of experience was an exact duplicate ever framed" (James, 1910/1979, p. 76), he insisted that truth should be conceptualized "to mean everywhere, not duplication, but addition" (James, 1909/1975a, p. 41). The full truth about the universe, which includes the experiences and conceptual constructions of humans within it, cannot possibly be known—it will not even exist—until all its aspects have been created.

JAMES'S PORTRAIT OF HUMAN UNDERSTANDING

The preceding review of James's metaphorical descriptions of philosophy and philosophizing should serve as an apt introduction to his view of human understanding in general. This view was solidly grounded in the analyses presented in his masterpiece, *The Principles of Psychology* (1890/1983c), and these psychological analyses were based, in turn, on insights gained or corroborated through his experiences as a fledgling artist and artist's apprentice and through his reading of Ralph Waldo Emerson, William Wordsworth, and others.

Before discussing these experiences, I want to provide a "charcoal sketch" (to use a Jamesian term) of two major features in James's portrait of human understanding. Stated most simply, these features (or claims) are (a) that all knowledge, including science, is ultimately based on the finding of analogy, which is to say, on the finding of an appropriate, enlightening comparison or metaphor; and (b) that the analogies or metaphors in any field of knowledge, including science, are (or should be) always changing rather than fixed. In the words of his much-beloved Emerson, they should be "fluxional" rather than "frozen" (Emerson, 1837/1983a, p. 55; 1844/1983c, p. 463; on these important points, see James, 1890/1983c, pp. 500, 753–754; 984; Leary, 1987, pp. 326–327; 1988; 1990a, pp. 19–20, 45–47). In other words, James felt that the analogies, comparisons, or metaphors that provide the means of human understanding are partial and temporary in their utility, and that they should be changed as newer aspects of reality come to the fore in the stream of experience. For James, a staunch empiricist, there was always a new way to experience any reality and a new way to categorize any experience. Although a given analogy may provide useful insight into experience and reality, it can never provide a truly definitive and final view of it. His convictions in this regard pertained perforce to his philosophy of science. "Any bit of scientific research," he wrote, "becomes an angle and place of vantage from which arguments are brought to bear" (James, 1885/1987b, pp. 383–384). Whenever a scientific theory is taken as "definitive," it cuts off other vantage points and hence becomes "perspectiveless and short" (James, 1896/1986a, p. 136).

For example, if one wishes to understand the nature of the mind, it might be helpful to note that the mind is like a machine in a number of regards, and it may prove fruitful to explicate the ways in which, and the degrees to which, this is the case. But James would insist that the mind is not identical, structurally or functionally, with any known machine, including the most sophisticated computer of our own day. The use of other analogies will be necessary to elucidate the mind's other, perhaps neglected aspects.

Another way to express James's belief—a belief that he began to articulate in the 1870s—is to say that we humans can understand things, events, and experiences only from and through the viewpoint of other things, events, and experiences. This belief or thesis by no means rules out valid and reliable human understanding. On the contrary, if in addition to noting parallels among a variety of phenomena, we abstract and name the specific similarities that account for these parallels, we can develop reasonable and coherent arguments regarding the aptness of particular analogies and of the theories based on them. Such arguments will sometimes result in quite reliable inferences. Crafting such arguments, James pointed out, is something that occupies both scientists and philosophers: Disconfirming or verifying them is something at which scientists excel, and leaving analogical or metaphorical insights in their more complex, "unresolved," but highly suggestive form accounts for the genius and fertile works of poets, artists, and others (see James, 1890/1983c, pp. 984–988). Whatever the various uses to which analogies and metaphors can be put, James emphasized that the offering of what he called "similar instances," far from being "a perverse act of thought," is "the necessary first step" in any type of human understanding, whether scientific or nonscientific (p. 987).

It should also be noted, because it will underscore the *art* involved (according to James) in creative cognition, that the conjuring of "similar instances" was, for him, a very subtle affair. Some individuals, and not others, are unusually adept at this task. As he stated in *The Principles of Psychology*, *"some people are far more sen-*

sitive to resemblances, and far more ready to point out wherein they consist, than others are" (James, 1890/1983c, p. 500). Indeed, he was convinced that "*a native talent for perceiving analogies is . . . the leading fact in genius of every order*" (p. 500). For whereas most people "have no eyes but for those aspects of things which [they] have already been taught to discern," creative individuals are precisely those who further human understanding by noting analogies that others "could never cogitate alone," although they may recognize and appreciate them once they are pointed out, whether by Shakespeare, Newton, Darwin, Tolstoy, or some other genius (p. 420). (The persons I have just named were some of James's favorite examples of genius. See James, 1890/1983c, pp. 984–988).

DEVELOPMENT OF JAMES'S PORTRAIT OF HUMAN UNDERSTANDING

James's theory of what I shall call the *art of human understanding*—the art of grasping similarities among phenomena and of thus forging perceptual patterns and conceptual categories out of the flux or chaos of experience—evolved in the 1870s from a very rich mixture of his own reading and experience. The reading, as I have argued elsewhere (Leary, 1988), included especially the work and thought of Ralph Waldo Emerson and William Wordsworth—for instance, Emerson's essays on "The American Scholar" (1837/1983a), "Art" (1841/1983b), and "The Poet" (1844/1983c), and Wordsworth's long poem, "The Excursion" (1814/1977). It also included works by Robert Browning, Johann Wolfgang von Goethe, and Nathaniel Hawthorne. The experience, as opposed to the reading, that formed the basis for James's insight and belief had more to do with his efforts and encounters with art, and it started long before his time as a painter and artist's apprentice. Here is the way that his brother, the novelist Henry James (1913/1983b), subsequently described the youthful William: "As I catch W. J.'s image, from far back, at its most characteristic, he sits drawing and drawing, always drawing . . . and not as with a plodding patience . . . but easily, freely and . . . infallibly" (p. 118). This image is repeated in Henry's various reminiscences, and it is a picture that emerges from other sources as well, not least from William's own drawing notebooks (many fine examples of James's drawings are reproduced in Feinstein, 1984). From early in life, James showed a remarkable aptitude with a pencil and a strong inclination to give free rein to it. In addition, first in New York City, then in Europe, and finally in Newport, Rhode Island, James took lessons and developed the obvious abilities that he had. Supplementing the exercise and development of his own talent, he also showed a distinctive interest and an unusual sensitivity as an observer of art. Throughout his life he was a curious and omnivorous museum visitor, often attracted to what was new and experimental.[1]

In this context, James was persuaded at the age of 18 to become an artist, and he committed himself wholeheartedly to an apprenticeship in Newport, Rhode Island, with the highly regarded painter, William Morris Hunt (on this period of James's life, see Bjork, 1988, pp. 22–36; Feinstein, 1984, pp. 103–145; Perry, 1935, Vol. 1, pp. 190–201). Significantly, this was James's first commitment to any field of study or potential career. In explaining his decision to his father, he said that he continually received from his "intercourse with art . . . spiritual impressions the intensest and purest I know." Not only was he inclined toward art, he said, but life "would be embittered if I were kept from it." With foresight he added, "That is the way I feel *at present*. Of course I may change" (quoted in Perry, 1935, Vol. 1, pp. 199–200).

The following year was full of the explorations, discoveries, and trials of apprenticeship, enhanced in significant ways by the friendship and ideas of his fellow apprentice, John La Farge. La Farge was seven years older than

William and much more experienced than either William or William's younger brother Henry, who often accompanied him to Hunt's studio. As Henry (1914/1983a) later recalled, La Farge quickly became "quite the most interesting person we knew" (p. 287). Although Hunt was clearly "a figure unmistakable" (p. 279) from whom William learned a great deal, La Farge became "the figure of figures" for both William and Henry (p. 289). "An embodiment of the gospel of aesthetics" (p. 290), La Farge "opened up . . . prospects and possibilities that made the future flush and swarm" (p. 287). Besides introducing them to Browning and Balzac, who were to influence William and Henry respectively, he represented for William a continuation of the visual and intellectual challenges presented earlier by Delacroix. He also encouraged Henry to turn from dabbling in art to committing himself seriously to writing. As La Farge's Newport paintings show, he was already guided by his later-renowned proposition that, in human consciousness or experience, subjectivity is intertwined with the supposedly objective, material world. One critic who has speculated on La Farge's influence on William and Henry (Adams, 1985) expressed it this way:

> La Farge's paintings created a new relation between the artist and his subject. His paintings unite the external world with subjective inner experience to the point where subject and object, the viewer and the thing seen, merge into one. Perception ceases to lead to solid, substantive qualities but culminates instead in feelings of transition and relation—in ever-changing gradations of light, focus, interest, and emotion, in continually fluctuating perceptual nuances, which never become fixed or solid. (Adams, 1987, p. 30)

William was so struck by the technical and conceptual issues with which La Farge was struggling at that time that he remembered and discussed them with La Farge—to La Farge's amazement—almost 50 years later (La Farge, 1910). Although James's subsequent "psychology of consciousness" was no doubt multiply determined, Gay Wilson Allen (1967) had good reason to suggest that La Farge was among those who influenced its development (p. 69).[2]

Despite the creative energy and growth produced during this apprenticeship, by the fall of 1861 James had left Hunt's studio, given up his aspiration to an artistic career, and moved with his family to Cambridge, Massachusetts. He entered Lawrence Scientific School at Harvard University, thus starting down the path that led to his accomplishments and renown in psychology and philosophy.

Much has been written about James's one-year apprenticeship. In particular, there has been a great deal of speculation about James's motives for giving up his calling to become an artist, despite plentiful evidence of his interest and ability; but in fact, little is known for certain. That his father was not happy about his choice of vocation is abundantly clear, and this almost certainly played a role in James's decision (see especially Feinstein, 1984, pp. 140–145). However, it is also plausible, as Perry (1935, Vol. 1, p. 200), and Bjork (1988, pp. 30–31) have suggested, that James simply concluded that he could not become a painter of the very first rank, and hence turned to science, another of his (and his father's) many interests. In any case, as his brother Henry (1914/1983a) put it, "nothing . . . could have been less logical, yet at the same time more natural, than that William's interest in the practice of painting should have suddenly and abruptly ceased" (p. 300). There was in the event "no repining at proved waste" on William's part (pp. 300–301), perhaps because on a deeper level there was no waste. As Henry (1913/1983b) had noted earlier, William "flowered in every [seeming] waste" (p. 117). And indeed, with hindsight, I would argue that his year-long stay in Newport was a tutorial for his later philosophical and scientific work, not a detour on the way to it.

Whatever factors were involved, the motives and rationale for James's turn from art to science are less important than the fact that he had such a formative exposure to art and painting.[3] This experience, building on his native artistic aptitude, prepared him to be sympathetic and responsive, in the 1860s and 1870s, to Emerson's and Wordsworth's ideas regarding the nature of human thought. In James's own rendition, as in Emerson's and Wordsworth's, the notion that human understanding is basically analogical or metaphorical was often expressed with visual imagery. It wasn't simply that humans can apply different analogies or metaphors; rather, humans can assume different viewpoints and achieve new perspectives. As a former artist, James felt the rightness of Emerson's and Wordsworth's claims. He was deeply and intimately aware that one can come to see things anew, to notice fresh aspects, and to create novel possibilities in reality. As Wordsworth put it in "The Excursion," which James read and reread in the early 1870s much as Charles Darwin had done to similar effect in the early 1840s (see Perry, 1935, Vol. 1, pp. 338–339, 355), the mind has an "excursive power" to "wander about" the world, viewing it from this and now that vantage point, thus shaping its "prospects" (Wordsworth, 1814/1977, pp. 155, 173). Even what is taken to be normal reality needs to be learned, as James came to realize. As he put it quite tellingly in *The Principles of Psychology* (1890/1983c), just as "in poetry and the arts, someone has to come and tell us what aspects we may single out" (p. 420), so too all humans "must go through a long education of the eye and ear before they can perceive the realities which adults perceive" (p. 724). Ideally, the labels for reality that are thus stamped in our mind through this long education will be fluxional rather than frozen. Unfortunately, this proves often not to be the case, so that we become all too conventional or literal in our mentality. As a result, James said, "if we lost our stock of labels we should be intellectually lost in the midst of the world" (p. 420). Human understanding, he realized, depends on such labels, whose meanings are derived (or were derived long ago) from their analogical relations. It can be advanced, however, only with the exchange of these labels for new concepts and terms, grounded in new views of reality.

FURTHER ARTICULATION AND APPLICATION OF JAMES'S VIEW OF HUMAN UNDERSTANDING IN PSYCHOLOGY

James's belief in the analogical or metaphorical foundations of knowledge is richly illustrated in his psychological writings. His treatment of thought or consciousness as a stream instead of a chain or train is well-known (see James, 1890/1983c, chap. 9), and his discussion of other psychological topics is similarly informed by underlying analogies and metaphors. The ultimate metaphors that founded and framed his psychological thinking, and that came to undergird his philosophical pragmatism, pluralism, and radical empiricism, were the Darwinian metaphors of variation, selection, and function. All psychological states and actions, according to James, are products of spontaneous variation or selection in terms of their consequential utility. This functionalist orientation has influenced many other American psychologists and has structured much of the theoretical argumentation in modern psychology. Unfortunately, it has in some respects become frozen, despite James's advocacy of a fluxional approach to human and scientific understanding, and it is often taken (in one or another of its contemporary versions) as a definitively authoritative portrait of human nature.

I have discussed this elsewhere (Leary, 1990a, pp. 20–21, 47–49). The point here is that James's own psychology (not to mention his philosophy) reflected and reinforced his view of human understanding. James used analogies and metaphors throughout his works, not simply as ways of expressing his ideas, but as ways of constructing them. He often drew on his artistic experiences in his attempt to understand and explain psychological phenomena as well as in his attempt to pursue philosophical reflection. In fact, the frequency with which he drew on his artistic experience in important, often critical, passages is noteworthy. Insofar as these passages often have to do with the nature of human cognition and understanding, which he conceived from the start on the model of artistic experience, this is not surprising. But his use of artistic experience as a source of metaphorical referents suggests a basic principle of human cognition—that humans tend, naturally enough, to draw their most telling analogies from their own experience. In other words, they use what is familiar to understand the less familiar.

In this section I quote at length from various passages in *The Principles of Psychology* (1890/1983c) to demonstrate sufficiently how James often used a transparently artistic analogy to reach, explicate, and defend a point. In these passages, note how often the notion of *perspective,* of seeing from a different angle or within a different context, was crucial for James, and attend to his frequent references to what he had learned as an artist. For instance, looking forward to his chapter on perception, James wrote,

> We shall see how inveterate is our habit of not attending to sensations as subjective facts, but of simply using them as stepping-stones to pass over to the recognition of the realities whose presence they reveal. The grass out of the window now looks to me of the same green in the sun as in the shade, and yet a painter would have to paint one part of it dark brown, another part bright yellow, to give its real sensational effect. We take no heed, as a rule, of the different way in which the same things look and sound and smell at different distances and under different circumstances. The sameness of the *things* is what we are concerned to ascertain; and any sensations that assure us of that will probably be considered in a rough way to be the same with each other. . . . What appeals to our attention far more than the absolute quality or quantity of a given sensation is its *ratio* to whatever other sensations we may have at the same time. When everything is dark a somewhat less dark sensation makes us see an object white. (pp. 225–226)

Further on:

> If the assumption of "simple ideas of sensation" recurring in immutable shape is so easily shown to be baseless, how much more baseless is the assumption of immutability in the larger masses of our thought! For there it is obvious and palpable that our state of mind is never precisely the same. Every thought we have of a given fact is, strictly speaking, unique, and only bears a resemblance of kind with our other thoughts of the same fact. When the identical fact recurs, we *must* think of it in a fresh manner, see it under a somewhat different angle, apprehend it in different relations from those in which it last appeared. . . . From one year to another we see things in new lights. What was unreal has grown real, and what was exciting is insipid. (p. 227).

In summing up at the end of his critical "Stream of Thought" chapter, in a famous passage that articulated his view of human understanding as well as anything he ever wrote, James wrote,

> Looking back, then, over this review, we see that the mind is at every stage a theatre of simultaneous possibilities. Consciousness consists in the comparison of these with each other, the selection of some, and the suppression of the rest by the reinforcing and inhibiting agency of attention. . . . The mind, in short, works on the data it receives very much as a sculptor works on his block of stone. In a sense the statue stood there from eternity. But there were a thousand different ones beside it [within the same block of stone], and the sculptor alone is to thank for having extricated this one from the rest. Just so the world of each of us, howsoever different our several views of it may be, all lay embedded in the primordial chaos of sensations, which gave the mere *matter* to the thought of all of us indifferently. . . . Other sculptors, other statues from the same stone! Other minds, other worlds from the same monotonous

and inexpressive chaos! My world is but one in a million alike embedded, alike real to those who may abstract them. How different must be the worlds in the consciousness of ant, cuttle-fish, or crab! (p. 277)

The selection of one possible statue, of one possible view of the world, rather than another was intricately and deeply related, for James, to the interests of each person. The concept of *interest* is thus fundamental to James's psychology and philosophy, and in particular to his view of human understanding. The next passage provides James's definition of interest. It should be clear that the artistic analogies that he used in this passage are not secondary; rather, they reflect the most fundamental way in which he conceived this important concept.

> Millions of items of the outward order are present to my senses which never properly enter into my experience. Why? Because they have no *interest* for me. *My experience is what I agree to attend to.* Only those items which I *notice* shape my mind—without selective interest, experience is an utter chaos. Interest alone gives accent and emphasis, light and shade, background and foreground—intelligible perspective, in a word. It varies in every creature, but without it the consciousness of every creature would be a gray chaotic indiscriminateness, impossible for us even to conceive. . . . The interest itself, though its genesis is doubtless perfectly *natural, makes* experience more than it is made by it. (pp. 380–381)

To underscore how fundamental this concept of interest is, recall that in James's psychology, interest directs attention, attention directs selection, and selection confers coherence on each level of psychological functioning—the perceptual, the conceptual, the practical, the aesthetic, and the moral (see James, 1890/1983c, pp. 273–278).[4] Interest, then, defined as "intelligible perspective," underlies the art of human understanding.

James supplied a nice example of the application of this art:

> Let four men make a tour in Europe. One will bring home only picturesque impressions—costumes and colors, parks and views and works of architecture, pictures and statues. To another all this will be non-existent; and distances and prices, populations and drainage-arrangements, door- and window-fastenings, and other useful statistics will take their place. A third will give a rich account of the theatres, restaurants, and public balls, and naught beside; whilst the fourth will perhaps have been so wrapped in his own subjective broodings as to tell little more than a few names of places through which he passed. Each has selected, out the same mass of presented objects, those which suited his private interest and has made his experience thereby. (pp. 275–276)

Many other passages could be cited, making the same point. For instance, in a passage already quoted in part, James wrote,

> Men have no eyes but for those aspects of things which they have already been taught to discern. Any one of us can notice a phenomenon after it has once been pointed out, which not one in ten thousand could ever have discovered for himself. . . .*The only things which we commonly see are those which we preperceive* [those for which we are on the lookout], and the only things which we preperceive are those which have been labelled for us, and the labels stamped into our mind. (p. 420)[5]

After discussing the perception of likeness, which is to say, the perception of analogies or metaphors, James said,

> If the reader feels that this faculty [of perceiving similarities] is having small justice done it. . . . I think I emphasize it enough when I call it one of the ultimate foundation-pillars of the intellectual life. (p. 500)

Not surprisingly, James drew on his sensibilities and experience as an artist and artist's apprentice throughout his chapter on perception, pointing out (for instance) that the "eye-picture" created by stimuli impinging on the optic nerve is quite different from the mind-picture that is produced, the mind somehow correcting for the angle of vision and substituting a concept of the object as it would appear from a hypothetically ideal vantage point (James, 1890/1983c, p. 724). Similarly, in the chapter on space perception, James discussed what is now called brightness and size constancy. In one passage he explicitly referred to the training that underlay his psychological insights:

> Usually we see a sheet of paper as uniformly white, although a part of it may be in shadow. But we can in an instant, if we please, notice the shadow as local color. A man walking towards us does not usually seem to alter his size; but we can, by setting our attention in a peculiar way, make him appear to do so. The whole education of the artist consists in his learning to see the presented signs as well as the represented things. No matter what the field of view *means,* he seeks it also as it *feels*—that is, as a collection of patches of color bounded by lines—the whole forming an optical diagram of whose intrinsic proportions one who is not an artist has hardly a conscious inkling. The ordinary man's attention passes *over* them to their import; the artist's turns back and dwells *upon* them for their own sake. "Don't draw the thing as it *is,* but as it *looks!*" is the endless advice of every [art] teacher to his pupil; forgetting that what "is" is what it would also "look," provided it were placed in what we have called the "normal" [that is, the ideal] situation for vision. (pp. 874–875)[6]

In his chapter on the perception of reality, in which the psychology of belief was his central concern, James went beyond the usual focus on things and distinguished very effectively among a number of different worlds—the world of sensory things, the world of scientific qualities and forces, the world of ideal relations and abstract truths, the world of "idols of the tribe," the various supernatural worlds of religious belief, the innumerable worlds of individual opinion, and the worlds of "sheer madness and vagary" (pp. 920–922). "*Every object we think of gets at last referred to one world or another of this or of some similar list,*" he wrote (p. 922).

> Propositions concerning the different worlds are made from "different points of view"; and in this more or less chaotic state the consciousness of most thinkers remains to the end. Each world *whilst it is attended to* is real after its own fashion; [but] the reality lapses with the attention. (p. 923)

I need not remind you that attention is directed by interest, which for James is a natural, individuating factor. Thus, he said,

> *The fons et origo [that starting point and foundation] of all reality, whether from the absolute or the practical point of view, is . . . subjective, is ourselves. . .* Reality, starting from our Ego, thus sheds itself from point to point. . . . It only fails when the connecting thread is lost. A whole system may be real, if it only hang to our Ego by one immediately *stinging* term. (pp. 925–926)

What is felt and understood to be real, then, is what is of "stinging" interest, which according to James's definition of interest is whatever is linked to a compelling intelligible perspective.[7]

As the fundamental role of perspective in James's thought becomes clearer, his later reduction of the self or ego to a point of view or field of vision, in the years after the publication of *The Principles of Psychology,* begins to make increasing sense (see Leary, 1990b, pp. 116–117).[8] In this little-known development of his thought, James came to depict the individual ego, not human understanding alone, in terms of the fundamental artistic concept of perspective. From the present historical vantage point, one can see how this largely unexplored extension of his thought was consistent with his career-long reliance on the concept of perspective. Starting from his earliest definition of philosophy as "the possession of mental perspective" (James, 1876/1978b, p. 4), James had infused his principles of psychology with his perspectivalist vision, and he went on subsequently to develop versions of philosophical pragmatism, pluralism, and radical empiricism that were equally premised on the assumption that there is always another view to be had. Together with many other artistic insights and metaphors, this belief in the fundamental reality of alternative and supplemental perspectives permeated James's entire system of thought.

CONCLUSION

I have argued that William James's portrait of human understanding was influenced, as he put it, by "the whole drift of my education" (James, 1902/1985, p. 408). In particular, it was influenced in a deep and lasting way by his artistic sensitivity, experience, and training. On the basis of this view of human understanding, James felt that it was perfectly legitimate—even necessary—to use analogies and metaphors, often from the realm of the arts, in the development of his psychological and philosophical doctrines. It also led him to organize his major psychological work in a very distinctive manner.[9]

Given this background and orientation, it is not surprising that James came to understand the place and type of his psychology and philosophy, in relation to previous and alternative modes of thought, in explicitly artistic terminology. His system of thought, he said, was "romantic" rather than "classic" (James, 1901/1986b, pp. 193–194). His views, he explained, were concrete, uncouth, complex, overflowing, open-ended, and incomplete. On the one hand, they lacked the "clean pure lines and noble simplicity" typical of the abstract constructions of the "classic-academic" approach, but on the other, they were consonant with the art of human understanding as he comprehended it (see James, 1907/1975b, pp. 16–17; 1910/1979, pp. 76–79).

The fact that his view of human understanding was based on his experience as an artist may help explain why James's psychology and philosophy, grounded as they are on this view of human understanding, have attracted the attention and respect of so many artists and humanists—not to mention scientists and psychologists—to the present day.[10] As James (1897/1987a) once said of someone else's work, his own works do not "violate" the "deepest instincts" of artists (p. 536).

Perhaps the leading artist in James's life was his brother Henry James, Jr., the novelist. It is interesting to note that Henry published a novel, *The Tragic Muse* (1890/1988), in the same year that William published *The Principles of Psychology*. William himself suggested that this concurrence made 1890 a banner year for American literature (James, 1920, p. 299). Not purely by chance, Henry's novel dealt with the world of art.[11] In his own inimitable language (H. James, 1906–1908/1934), the "pictorial fusion" of the novel brings together a "multiplication of aspects" (p. 85) that denies any "usurping [specially privileged] consciousness" (p. 90). The overlap of Henry's and William's motifs has often been noted. I use Henry's quotation here simply to provide a context for saying that I do not intend my view of William James's art of human understanding, and of its impact on his system of thought, to have any undue privilege over other perspectives on the development of his thought. Both James and his work are incredibly rich and overdetermined. But I do believe that the particular aspect of William James's life and work that I have pointed out in this article is important and needs to be fused into our picture of this remarkable and influential person.

NOTES

1 James's fascination with, and close study of, the paintings of Eugène Delacroix in Paris—at thirteen years of age—is a relevant example (see Bjork, 1988, pp. 14–19). There is good reason to suppose that his ruminations on the works of Delacroix stimulated his thinking about the lack of any clear distinction between the subjective and objective poles in experience. This was an

important concern of his later work. At the other end of his life, perhaps the best example of his continuing openness to novelty in art was his joyful astonishment at the work of Matisse and Picasso (see Stein, 1933/1960, p. 80). Clearly, his awareness that modes of representation and understanding are liable to change was nurtured and sustained by his familiarity with art. If he sometimes expressed regret about his lack of formal education, he could nonetheless have agreed with his brother Henry that, for them, "the great rooms of the Louvre" were "educative, formative, fertilizing, in a degree which no other 'intellectual experience' . . . could pretend . . . to rival" (H. James, 1913/1983b, p. 197). My argument here is that James's shortcomings in terms of mathematics and logic, which formal education would have corrected, were more than counterbalanced by the insights he gained from art. As his "master" William Morris Hunt (1875–1883/1976) said with considerable foresight, at least as regards James, "mathematics . . . don't develop a person like painting" (p. 86).

2 Allen (1967) also claimed that "it would be futile to attempt to trace any lasting influence of William Hunt on his life," although Hunt's school of painting was consonant with James's later insights (p. 69). Without asserting any singularity of influence, I think that Allen's claim is exaggerated. Hunt's (1875–1883/1976) repeated admonishments to his students contained many hints of James's later doctrines (e.g., regarding the centrality of experience and the primacy of action), and James himself suggested how sensitive and retentive he was with regard to these hints by periodically referring to "the endless advice of every [art] teacher to his pupil" (James, 1890/1983c, p. 875). Indeed, James's portrait of philosophy echoed his teacher's dictum that painting is "the *only universal language!* All nature is creation's picture-book!" (Hunt, 1875–1883/1976, p. 73).

3 After leaving Newport, James kept his drawing alive for another decade before he claimed to have let it "die out" (quoted in Perry, 1935, Vol. 1, p. 330). He regretted this loss of serious drawing, but he maintained his interest in art, with some fluctuations, throughout his life. As he told his brother in 1872, he envied Henry's belonging to "the world of art" because "away from it, as we live, we sink into a flatter, blanker kind of consciousness, and indulge in an ostrich-like forgetfulness of all our richest potentialities." These potentialities, he said, "startle us now and then when by accident some rich human product, pictorial, literary, or architectural slaps us with its tail" (quoted in Perry, 1935, Vol. 1, p. 327). At critical points in 1868, 1873–1874, 1882, and 1892, art "slapped" him into important meditations. This remains a largely untold story.

4 James's critical concept of selection was not drawn solely from Darwinian thought. Rather, his artistic experience prepared the way for his acceptance of this Darwinian principle and its application on all levels of psychological phenomena. As he wrote in an unpublished manuscript on the psychology of aesthetics, there is an "analogy between art and life in that by both, results are reached only by selection & elimination." Quoting Robert Louis Stevenson, he went on to say that "there is but one art—to omit" (James, ca. 1894). The importance of selection in James's psychology was unambiguously expressed when he asserted that "selection is the very keel on which our mental ship is built" (James, 1890/1983c, p. 640).

5 James articulated a version of this principle in his first psychological essay, in which he pointed out that "a layman present at a shipwreck, a battle, or a fire is helpless. . . . But the sailor, the fireman, and the general know directly at what point to take up the business. They 'see into the situation' . . . with their first glance" (James, 1878/1983a, p. 15).

6 This "endless advice" about drawing a thing as it looks was obviously given to James by his art teacher. In the very first of his published talks on painting and drawing, Hunt (1875–1883/1976) proclaimed, "You are to draw *not reality, but the appearance of reality!*" (p. 3).

7 Not only reality, but also its meaning and worth are a matter of perspective. As James (1899/1983b) wrote in an essay that expressed the heart of his thought: "Some years ago, whilst journeying in the mountains of North Carolina, I passed by a large number of 'coves'. . . . The impression on my mind was one of unmitigated squalor. . . . I said to the mountaineer who was driving me:

"What sort of people are they who have to make these new clearings?' 'All of us,' he replied; 'why, we ain't happy here unless we are getting one of these coves under cultivation.' I instantly felt that I had been losing the whole inward significance of the situation. . . . When *they* looked on the hideous stumps, what they thought of was personal victory. . . . I had been as blind to the peculiar ideality of their conditions as they certainly would also have been to the ideality of mine, had they had a peep at my strange indoor academic ways of life at Cambridge" (pp. 133–134). "Neither the whole of truth, nor the whole of good, is revealed to any single observer, although each observer gains a partial superiority of insight from the peculiar position in which he stands" (p. 149).

8 Having extended perspectivism to his treatment of the self or ego, James came to understand personal identity and religious conversion as involving, respectively, a centering or changing of one's perspective (James, 1902/1985, pp. 161–162). Beyond that, he came to understand "the Absolute" as the sum of all actual perspectives, nonhuman as well as human, and thus to suggest that even the Absolute is open to continual development, as more pictures of reality are created by its constituent points of view (1909/1977, pp. 130–131, 139–144; 1899/1983d, p. 4; 1902/1985, pp. 409–414). This led Santayana (1913/1940) to comment, with perhaps more justification than he knew, that James's God was "a sort of . . . struggling artist" (p. 210).

9 The organization of *The Principles of Psychology* (James, 1890/1983c) has baffled many psychologists and critics. In fact, this organization makes reasonably good sense if one assumes James's artistic point of view. After getting preliminary discussions out of the way in the first eight chapters, James provided an overview of his psychology of consciousness (or "our study of the mind from within," as he called it on p. 219) in the "Stream of Thought" chapter. This chapter, James said, is "like a painter's first charcoal sketch upon his canvas, in which no niceties appear" (p. 220). Then, after reviewing the various levels of psychological functioning in this chapter, James went on in subsequent chapters to fill in his charcoal sketch with more detailed treatments of the various aspects of his system, proceeding from the most general (consciousness of self) to the most circumscribed (the will) of the mind's experiences. Although his scheme does not account completely for the placement of each chapter, it makes sense of the book's overall organization.

10 Besides the various roles that he played in establishing the physiological, behavioral, cognitive, and therapeutic traditions in contemporary psychology, James profoundly influenced individuals all across the cultural landscape—individuals as disparate as Bernard Berenson, Niels Bohr, Jorge Luis Borges, John Dewey, W. E. B. DuBois, Nelson Goodman, Helen Keller, Walter Lippmann, Stephen Pepper, Oliver Sacks, Gertrude Stein, and Wallace Stevens. Another such person, Alfred North Whitehead, the great mathematician, philosopher, and historian of science, considered James to be one of the four major thinkers in the entire Western tradition, along with Plato, Aristotle, and Leibniz (see Whitehead, 1938, pp. 3–4). Whitehead (1956) noted that when the foundations of the modern worldview were blown apart by various discoveries at the turn of this century, William James was one of the few intellectuals prepared and able to withstand the blow (p. 272), and James withstood it without having to change his way of thinking.

11 Art and artists in modern society—especially painting and painters—provided frequent topics, themes, motifs, and devices in Henry's work (e.g., H. James, 1868–1897/1956; 1874–1909/1984; see also Bowden, 1956; Holland, 1964; Hopkins, 1961; Ward, 1965; Winner, 1967, 1970). The importance of art, particularly painting, in Henry's conceptual scheme is strongly suggested by his assertion that "the analogy between the art of the painter and the art of the novelist is, so far as I am able to see, complete" (H. James, 1884/1987, p. 188).

REFERENCES

Adams, H. (1985). William James, John La Farge, and the foundations of radical empiricism. *American Art Journal, 17,* 60–67.

Adams, H. (1987). The mind of John La Farge. In H. Adams, (Ed.), *John La Farge* (pp. 11–77). New York: Abbeville Press.

Allen, G. W. (1967). *William James: A biography.* New York: Viking Press.

Barzun, J. (1983). *A stroll with William James.* New York: Harper & Row.

Barzun, J. (1985). William James: The mind as artist. In S. Koch & D. E. Leary (Eds.), *A century of psychology as science* (pp. 904–910). New York: McGraw-Hill.

Bjork, D. W. (1983). *The compromised scientist: William James in the development of American psychology.* New York: Columbia University Press.

Bjork, D. W. (1988). *William James: The center of his vision.* New York: Columbia University Press.

Bowden, E. T. (1956). *The themes of Henry James: A system of observation through the visual arts.* New Haven, CT: Yale University Press.

Dewey, J. (1910). William James. *Journal of Philosophy, Psychology and Scientific Methods, 7,* 505–508.

Emerson, R. W. (1983a). The American scholar. In J. Porte (Ed.), *Essays and lectures* (pp. 51–71). New York: Library of America. (Original work published 1837)

Emerson, R. W. (1983b). Art. In J. Porte (Ed.), *Essays and lectures* (pp. 429–440). New York: Library of America. (Original work published 1841)

Emerson, R. W. (1983c). The poet. In J. Porte (Ed.), *Essays and lectures* (pp. 445–468). New York: Library of America. (Original work published 1844)

Feinstein, H. M. (1984). *Becoming William James.* Ithaca, NY: Cornell University Press.

Hall, G. S. (1891). Review of William James's *Principles of psychology. American Journal of Psychology, 3,* 578–591.

Holland, L. B. (1964). *The expense of vision: Essays on the craft of Henry James.* Princeton, NJ: Princeton University Press.

Hopkins, V. (1961). Visual art devices and parallels in the fiction of Henry James. *Modern Language Association Publications, 76,* 561–574.

Hunt, W. M. (1976). *On painting and drawing* (H. M. Knowlton, Ed.). New York: Dover (Original two-volume work published 1875–1883)

James, H., Jr. (1934). *The art of the novel: Critical prefaces* (R. P. Blackmur, Ed.). New York: Scribner. (Original works published 1906–1908)

James, H., Jr. (1956). *The painter's eye* (J. L. Sweeney, Ed.). Cambridge, MA: Harvard University Press (Original works published 1868–1897)

James, H., Jr. (1983a). Notes of a son and brother. In F. W. Dupee (Ed.), *Autobiography* (pp. 237–544). Princeton, NJ: Princeton University Press. (Original work published 1914)

James, H., Jr. (1983b). A small boy and others. In F. W. Dupee (Ed.), *Autobiography* (pp. 1–236). Princeton, NJ: Princeton University Press. (Original work published 1913)

James, H., Jr. (1984). *Tales of art and life* (H. Terrie, Ed.). Schenectady, NY: Union College Press. (Original works published 1874–1909)

James, H., Jr. (1987). The art of fiction. In R. Gard (Ed.). *The critical muse: Selected literary criticism* (pp. 186–206). London: Penguin Books. (Original work published 1884)

James, H., Jr. (1988). *The tragic muse.* New York: Viking Penguin. (Original work published 1890)

James, W. (ca. 1894). *Manuscript on psychology of aesthetics.* In William James Papers, File 4393. Houghton Library, Harvard University, Cambridge, MA.

James, W. (1920). *The letters of William James* (Vol. 1; Henry James III, Ed.). Boston: Atlantic Monthly Press.

James, W. (1975a). *The meaning of truth: A sequel to "pragmatism."* Cambridge, MA: Harvard University Press. (Original work published 1909)

James, W. (1975b). *Pragmatism: A new name for some old ways of thinking.* Cambridge, MA: Harvard University Press. (Original work published 1907)

James, W. (1976). *Essays in radical empiricism.* Cambridge, MA: Harvard University Press. (Original work published 1912)

James, W. (1977). *A pluralistic universe.* Cambridge, MA: Harvard University Press. (Original work published 1909)

James, W. (1978a). Preface to Harald Höffding's *Problems of philosophy.* In *Essays in philosophy* (pp. 140–143). Cambridge, MA: Harvard University Press. (Original work published 1905)

James, W. (1978b). The teaching of philosophy in our colleges. In *Essays in philosophy* (pp. 3–6). Cambridge, MA: Harvard University Press. (Original work published 1876)

James, W. (1979). *Some problems of philosophy.* Cambridge, MA: Harvard University Press.

(Original manuscript incomplete and unpublished at James's death in 1910)

James, W. (1983a). Brute and human intellect. In *Essays in psychology* (pp. 1–37). Cambridge, MA: Harvard University Press. (Original work published 1878)

James, W. (1983b). On a certain blindness in human beings. In *Talks to teachers on psychology and to students on some of life's ideals* (pp. 132–149). Cambridge, MA: Harvard University Press. (Original work published 1899)

James, W. (1983c). *The principles of psychology.* Cambridge, MA: Harvard University Press. (Original work published 1890)

James, W. (1983d). *Talks to teachers on psychology and to students on some of life's ideals.* (Cambridge, MA: Harvard University Press. (Original work published 1899)

James, W. (1985). *The varieties of religious experience.* Cambridge, MA: Harvard University Press. (Original work published 1902)

James, W. (1986a). Address of the president before the Society for Psychical Research. In *Essays in psychical research* (pp. 127–137). Cambridge, MA: Harvard University Press. (Original work presented 1896).

James, W. (1986b). Frederic Myers's service to psychology. In *Essays in psychical research* (pp. 192–202). Cambridge, MA: Harvard University Press. (Original work published 1901)

James, W. (1987a). Review of George Santayana's *The sense of beauty.* In *Essays, comments, and reviews* (pp. 536–539). Cambridge, MA: Harvard University Press. (Original work published 1897)

James, W. (1987b). Review of Josiah Royce's *The religious aspect of philosophy.* In *Essays, comments, and reviews* (pp. 383–388). Cambridge, MA: Harvard University Press. (Original work published 1885)

James, W. (1988). Introduction: Philosophies paint pictures. In *Manuscript essays and notes* (pp. 3–6). Cambridge, MA: Harvard University Press. (Original work written 1903–1904)

La Farge, J. (1910, September 2). A new side of Prof. James. *The New York Times,* p. 8.

Leary, D. E. (1987). Telling likely stories: The rhetoric of the New Psychology, 1880–1920. *Journal of the History of the Behavioral Sciences. 23,* 315–331.

Leary, D. E. (1988, August). *Poetry and science: Wordsworth's influence on Darwin and James.* Paper presented at the 96th Annual Convention of the American Psychological Association, Atlanta, GA.

Leary, D. E. (1990a). Psyche's muse: The role of metaphor in the history of psychology. In D. E. Leary (Ed.), *Metaphors in the history of psychology* (pp. 1–78). New York: Cambridge University Press.

Leary, D. E. (1990b). William James on the self and personality: Clearing the ground for subsequent theorists, researchers, and practitioners. In M. G. Johnson & T. B. Henley (Eds.), *Reflections on The Principles of Psychology: William James after a century* (pp. 101–137). Hillsdale, NJ: Erlbaum.

Myers, G. E. (1986). *William James: His life and thought.* New Haven, CT: Yale University Press.

Perry, R. B. (1935). *The thought and character of William James* (Vols. 1 and 2). Boston: Little, Brown.

Putnam, J. J. (1910). William James. *Atlantic Monthly, 106,* 835–848.

Santayana, G. (1930). Brief history of my opinions. In G. P. Adams & W. P. Montague (Eds.), *Contemporary American philosophy* (Vol. 2, pp. 239–257). New York: Scribner.

Santayana, G. (1940). The genteel tradition in American philosophy. In *Winds of doctrine: Studies in contemporary opinion* (pp. 186–215). New York: Scribner. (Original work published 1913)

Stein, G. (1960). *The autobiograpy of Alice B. Toklas.* New York: Vintage Books. (Original work published 1933)

Ward, J. A. (1965). Picture and action: The problem of narration in James's fiction. *Rice University Studies, 51,* 109–123.

Whitehead, A. N. (1938). *Modes of thought.* New York: Macmillan.

Whitehead, A. N. (1956). *Dialogues of Alfred North Whitehead.* (L. Price, Ed.), New York: New American Library.

Winner, V. H. (1967). Pictorialism in Henry James's theory of the novel. *Criticism, 9,* 1–21.

Winner, V. H. (1970). *Henry James and the visual arts.* Charlottesville: University Press of Virginia.

Wordsworth, W. (1977). The excursion. In J. O. Hayden (Ed.), *The poems* (Vol. 2, pp. 35–289). Harmondsworth, Middlesex, England: Penguin. (Original work published 1814)

Child-Study: The Basis of Exact Education

G. Stanley Hall

The study of children is now attempted by very different methods, for purposes quite diverse, and with all degrees of scientific exactness. The points of view here taken, and the literature, now numbering many hundred titles, are so new that I can find nowhere any attempt at a general survey of the various lines of work now under way to aid me in presenting such an outline as the editor of "The Forum" has requested; while new material is accumulating so fast and the future promises so much that any attempt to map out the field even by a text-book could have only temporary value.

That so considerable a part of the work has been done in this country, which, if it has not had a large share in the development of the physical sciences, now shows signs of making up its arrears by advancing several branches of the great science of man, is a fact well befitting a republic, new and without tradition, which most needs to take a fresh, free look at every aspect of human nature, which alone is true and to which school, as well as church, state and family, must conform to be true, good or stable. The future of the movement depends largely upon long, hard work yet to be done and requires the coöperative effort of many people—teachers, parents and men of science, whose efforts may now be coördinated in a national society, the organization of which was projected last July in Chicago.

Most of this vast and growing material has been wrought out by investigators who made little attempt to coördinate their work with what others had done. The doctors, the anthropologists, the psychologists, parents and teachers, have each given little attention to each other's work.

The first study on the contents of children's minds was made in Berlin in 1869 and showed as astonishing ignorance of things every child ought and was supposed to know. By the liberality of Mrs. Quincy Shaw I was enabled to make comprehensive studies in 1880 of a large number of Boston children just after they had entered the lowest grade of the primary school. The tactful and experienced questioners were convinced that fourteen per cent of these six-year old children had never seen the stars and had no idea about them; that thirty-five per cent had never been into the country; that twenty per cent did not know that milk came from cows; fifty-five per cent did not know that wooden things came from trees; that from thirteen to fifteen per cent did not know the colors, green, blue and yellow, by name; that forty-seven per cent had never seen a pig; sixty per cent had never seen a robin; from thirteen to eighteen per cent did not know where their cheek, forehead or throat was, and fewer yet knew elbow, wrist, ribs, etc. More than three-fourths of all the children had never seen to know them any of the common cereals, trees, or vegetables growing. These subjects were chosen because most of them constitute the material of school primers or elementary instruction which this new science of ignorance shows must make mere verbal cram of much matter of instruction. What idea can the eighteen per cent of children who thought a cow no larger than its picture get from all instruction about hide, horns, milk, etc? Country children excel in this kind of knowledge, and, while they know less, know it better and have greater power of concentration. In Annaberg, Germany, careful and repeated studies of such general and local items, about one hundred in all, like the Boston tests, are now made the natural basis of the school-work of the first year or two. Color tests have been made by H. K. Wolfe, Professor Barnes, Mrs. Hicks, and others. Wolfe examined many children between

From Hall, G. S. (1893). Child-study: The basis of exact education. *Forum, 16,* 429–441.

five and seventeen years of age as to power of discriminating and naming colors, and found the order of knowledge to be white, black, red, blue, yellow, green, pink, orange, violet.

Here, too, might be mentioned the interesting studies on colored hearing and number forms by Miss Calkins and others, on the individuality of numerals by Miss Whiting, which not only explain anomalies more common than was thought but tell how to meet them; and the statistical study of six species of lies children are prone to. T. L. Bolton tested memory-span for numbers up to nine places and found that memory-span increased with age rather than intelligence, that it was better in girls than boys, that it measures power of prolonged and concentrated attention, that the first stage of forgetfulness is loss of order, that if the number of ideas is too great it is overestimated and that they are forgotten inversely as they are removed from the beginning of the series.

The theological and religious life of children has been investigated in large numbers of children. These studies show that the sky is the chief field for religious ideas, that God, angels, heaven, are very distinctly imagined, connected with stars, clouds and thunder in the most material way. For example, God is a big blue man who pours rain out of big buckets, thumps clouds to make thunder, puts the sun and moon to bed, takes dead people, birds and even broken dolls up there, distributes babies, and is closely related to Santa Claus. This infant philosophy although intimidated and broken through at every point and on the ebb at the beginning of school life, is very persistent, though as hard for an adult to get at as for an electric light to study shadows. Barnes found that from seven to ten years of age there began to be occasional vague questionings and doubts about early conceptions which had hitherto been accepted without question or comment, that doubt grew with age and culminated at the age of thirteen or fourteen when criticism was more severe than later. Barnes has studied also the delicate subject of feelings and ideas of sex in children. Miss A. E. Wyckoff has studied constitutionally bad spellers.

This entire class of studies shows how easily school-work may miscarry, how supremely important the imagination is for this stage of child life, how large a part imitation and the struggle to be and do like older people play. The work of Mr. Russell, which is described above, belongs here and promises to be of great value. We want also minute objective studies, such as any intelligent mother or teacher could make if they would focus their attention on one subject, such as fear, shame, anger, pity, the phenomena of crying, unusual manifestations of will, traits made worse or better by school, effects of defect and physical malformation, of wise or unwise religious teaching, or any of the remarkable periodicities so common and described by Siegert, who thinks every kind of growth is zig-zag toward its goal, and that bright children have periods of muddle. We cannot here speak of exceptional children or pedagogical pathology, as it has been called by Strumpel, and worked out by Nicolay, Siegert, and others, nor of the studies made upon blind, deaf, idiot, criminal children; these last would make a chapter by themselves. Human nature at this stage is so vastly complex that only those of unusual attainments and genius can study it as a whole. It is clear that boys and girls are now being understood in a new light which may lead to much reconstruction of school methods and matter.

Passing now to the ephebic stage of youth we find that adolescence is a physiological second-birth; new traits and diseases, organs, and cells are developed; boys and girls become independent, must devote themselves to others and to causes; the life of the individual terminates and that of the race begins; the religious sense is deepened, and almost every religious cult has marked this period by its most solemn ceremonials. Dr. Burnham has well stated the great increase of vitality and energy at this period when nature gives man his capital of life force, and Dr. Daniels has now shown both by statistics and psychology how closely it is related to regeneration, in a religious sense. The great danger is that the lower elements will be developed in excess or disproportion. But nothing is so educable as love. It can attach itself, as recent morbid studies show, to almost any act or object; it can suck up all that is vile in the environment, or it can climb Godward up the stages of a heavenly ladder, as Plato describes in the "Symposium." Excitement young men must have, which like a breeze swelling new sails brings the new nerve tissue and faculties into activity without which they atrophy. If there is no enthusiasm, deep and strong interests in intellectual and moral fields, passion is stronger. The two are in a sense physiological or kinetic equivalents, and if the young man vents this erethic tendency during the adolescent decade in drink or vice, he will really be, as so many youth absurdly affect, apathetic, stoical, indifferent, and ashamed of enthusiasm. Alas for our academic youth if they lose freshness, and *naiveté,* and college freshmen become poised men of the world instead of being a little green and awkward. It is to be hoped that those who think that there is an increase of vice among boys in our high and preparatory schools in recent years, are mistaken.

Very few systematic studies have been made of collegians in this country, except the systematic weighing and measuring connected with gymnastics. Mr. Drew collected 356 love poems in student papers and published interesting figures of the features and traits of the beloved most often referred to. Eleven professors in larger Eastern colleges asked their seniors to answer four questions concerning their philosophical electives, points of interest therein, etc.; the returns are full of interest but cannot be presented in any composite-portrait way. College sentiment and opinion seem to be more and more influential; college teams and captains can keep order where faculties fail; student ideals are the best material for prophecy. The student chooses for himself not only what to study but whether to study or not. Inside academic administration is a kind of psychological engineering applied to the sentiments and ideals of later adolescence. A body of select young men taught by select professors, exempt from all practical life, brought in contact with the choicest minds of all time, ought to exhibit in the spontaneous drift of their disinterested ideals the dominant drift of the *volks*-soul; with a peculiar fascination, all their own, they are perhaps most of all things in the world interesting and worthy of study. Student life has its own laws quite apart from a curriculum and is for many more important than it. If its tone deteriorates, as it does in occasional periods and institutions, the whole *morale* of the place may decay.

This paper closes with a practical suggestion for farther work here—that one or two of the largest colleges cause a well trained and tactful man to devote his time to the study and improvement of college life, calling freely upon others to coöperate. Abundant material for a study of the natural history of students is afforded by the more than 200 college periodicals now published in this country. Sentiment and custom might be acted on by occasional lectures on the history of student life from the Middle Ages down. The corps, codes of honor, fraternities, sports, occupations, etc.; the tabulation of choices of study with reasons therefor; essays, and now the daily themes as at Harvard, the religious life and needs of students—a new problem lately forced upon many college preachers; and, above all, habitual intimacy with students and personal acquaintance on the ball ground and in the study;—these suggest a new field and method which might be called the higher anthropology.

The Paradox of G. Stanley Hall: Foe of Coeducation and Educator of Women

Lesley A. Diehl

Recent feminist scholarship in the area of sex differences (e.g., Rosenberg, 1982; Shields, 1975) has established that the origin of the question of feminine character within psychology predated psychoanalytic theory and can be found in the late 19th- and early 20th-century functionalist movement. Such scholarship, acknowledging the impact of an intellectual climate dominated by Darwinism on the formation of psychological theory, also asserts the significance of Victorian social attitudes in shaping the profession's attitudes toward women. In addition, these analyses along with those provided earlier by Schwendinger and Schwendinger (1971), Smith-Rosenberg and Rosenberg (1973), and Trecker (1974) imply a causal link between the genesis of scientific thought within such a social milieu and contemporary social sciences' biases about women's nature, calling attention to "the tenacity of the 'scientific' arguments, not their eventual defeat" (Trecker, 1974, p. 365).

Among the functionalists discussed by both Rosenberg and Shields, G. Stanley Hall emerges as significant in the study of woman's psychological makeup. In light of Hall's prolific writings in psychology and education and in popular magazines about woman's nature, it is surprising that he has not received more consideration among feminist scholars interested in the origin and development of the topic of sex differences.

Most accounts of Hall's contributions to functionalist psychology treat him as one of the many functionalists interested in shaping the emergence of the new American psychology (e.g., Boring, 1929/1950; Watson, 1978). Not surprisingly, these accounts portray Hall as well as his contemporaries as being concerned with the major themes of functionalism, that is, mental functions and adaptive processes. Even the most complete biographical study of Hall, provided by Ross in 1972, omits mention of his interest in sex differences and woman's nature, topics of significance to his theory of development, and provides no information on his role as leader of the early 20th-century movement against coeducation. Though these accounts accurately portray Hall's relationship to the emergence and development of American psychology, they provide little insight into Hall's significance in shaping psychology's perspectives on women. Furthermore, mainstreaming Hall into functionalist psychology ignores the significance that Hall himself accorded to the issue of women's nature, evidenced in the considerable time he devoted to the topic in his writings.

The present article discusses the significance of Hall to the development of psychology's perspective on sex differences and woman's nature by exploring the paradox of Hall as both opponent of coeducation and educator of women graduate students. The evolution of this paradox and its resolution by Hall can be understood by examining the three areas of Hall's professional eminence—as psychologist, educational theorist, and president of Clark University.

Diehl, L. A. (1986). The paradox of G. Stanley Hall: Foe of coeducation and educator of women. *American Psychologist, 41,* 868–878.

RECAPITULATION AND THE NATURE OF WOMAN

Hall's recapitulation theory was the direct outcome of the impact of Darwinian evolutionary principles on Hall's attempts to understand mental development. That Darwin provided the basis for all of Hall's research and theorizing in psychology is apparent in Hall's (1923) confession. "As soon as I first heard it in my youth I think I must have been almost hypnotized by the word "evolution," which was music to my ear and seemed to fit my mouth better than any other" (p. 357).

So important was evolution to Hall that he argued that it, rather than physics, should form the basis for science and be understood as the genesis of democracy and government (Hall, 1923). He saw in evolution a great organizing principle uniting the phylogenetic emergence of the species with the ontogenetic development of a single individual. Evolutionary recapitulation in Hall's theory assumed that "every child, from the moment of conception to maturity, recapitulates, very rapidly at first, and then more slowly, every stage of development through which the human race from its lowest animal beginnings has passed" (Hall, 1923, p. 380).

Prenatally, recapitulation called for rapid fetal change from a single-celled organism to a newborn parallel in maturity to mammals lower than humans on the phylogenetic scale. In childhood, Hall saw evidence of the expression of savage impulses, cruelty, and immorality representative of earlier, less civilized stages of human development, or of contemporary temperament produced in primitive societies (Hall, 1904b). Not only was recapitulation viewed as a necessary outcome of the evolution of humans, but the expression of primitive impulses was deemed cathartic by Hall. Thus, Hall's view of education for the child was pedocentric, that is, encouraged the schools and teachers to construct an atmosphere that encouraged the expression of these impulses in order that they would not be carried into adulthood (Hall, 1904b).

Hall did not create a unique theory of psychological nature, however. Before him, Galton (1907) had used evolutionary doctrine to argue for psychological sex differences. Few 19th-century functionalists argued with the use of Darwinism to account for the contention that men and women possessed inherently different natures and were, therefore, suited for vastly different roles—man as competitive and creative genius, and woman as mother of the species. As an extension of Geddes and Thomson's (1890) view of the sexes, many functionalists asserted that men were more active (katabolic) and variable than women, who were more passive (anabolic) and generic. Not only were men believed to differ more among themselves than were women, they were viewed as the agents introducing variability into offspring. Brain weight and brain size differences between men and women were employed as concrete expressions of the relationship between evolutionary structural and mental functional change (Ellis, 1894; Gould, 1981; Hall 1904a; Shields, 1975). Therefore, Hall drew little criticism from his colleagues for the manner in which he incorporated evolution into his theory of psychological development. Although 19th-century functionalists believed that human mental abilities were the product of evolution, few had articulated as clearly as did Hall evolution's impact on ontogenetic development and, therefore, its significance in creating and sustaining differentiation between the sexes.

Although Hall had written extensively about sex differences in the late 1800s, his concentration on recapitulation in infants and children and his interest in developing data to support his theory had directed most of his energy into child study and the use of his questionnaire method. Although his child-centered education found some favor with educators, psychologists became critical of his methodology and of his inability to tie collected data to his theory. The publication of *Adolescence: Its Psychology and Its Relations to Physiology, Anthropology, Sociology, Sex, Crime, Reli-*

gion and Education in 1904 focused Hall's interest on the critical period of puberty and specifically on the significance of sex differentiation for psychological development. This two-volume work was widely read and reviewed, although not favorably by some leading psychologists (e.g., Thorndike, 1904). Other functionalists were directing their research toward principles of learning and the development of testing materials while Hall continued to elaborate on a general developmental theory for which he had little supporting data (Siegel & White, 1982). However, because Hall had in the past attended to education for the young, *Adolescence* received some acceptance among educators and, because of its chapter topics (e.g., "Diseases of Body and Mind," "Juvenile Faults, Immorality, and Crimes," "Social Instincts and Institutions"), among those who were working with adolescents in institutions and clinics.

In his chapter entitled "Adolescent Girls and Their Education," Hall applied recapitulation theory to adolescent development, presenting a view of female development derived from evolutionary doctrine. The adolescent girl, according to Hall, could be looked upon as the springboard for the future evolution of the species, for she was "at the top of the human curve from which the higher super-man of the future is to evolve, while man is phylogenetically by comparison a trifle senile, if not decadent" (Hall, 1904a, p. 561). Thus, Hall asserted the importance of adolescence, age 14 or 15 through age 25 (Hall, 1905), as a critical period in the progression of civilization. As such, the biological differentiation of the sexes at puberty seemed to necessitate educational and role separation beginning in adolescence. Hall was well aware that the 19th-century battle against coeducation had been lost. Therefore, he focused on the need for separation of the sexes in adolescence only, a period during which he felt women were highly susceptible to reproductive organ damage. Puberty prepared a woman for her natural function of motherhood, to which, Hall felt, she should single-mindedly devote herself. That some women did not understand this need was not surprising to Hall, for the "hidden" but "all-pervasive" nature of the female reproductive organs could conceal their functioning from the individual woman as well as from science (Hall, 1904a, p. 562).

Woman's place within Hall's theory, as in the theories of many other functionalists, was that of mother of the species. She alone could determine by her reproductive abilities whether the race would grow, flourish, and progress or whether it would cease to exist. Her interest in motherhood assured the production of men of genius and of more daughters to bear more children. In contemporary terms, she was a baby factory; in Hall's eyes she was "by nature more typical and a better representative of the race and less prone to specialization" (Hall, 1904a, p. 562). Woman was closer in psychological nature to the child than was man, and she was at all stages of development a perennial adolescent, possessing larger lower brain centers presumably to more adequately govern the maternal functions of milk production, fertility, natality, and general nurturing (Hall, 1904a). Did Hall see her as inferior to man? Hall would quickly have answered "no" to such a question, asserting that if the two sexes could be compared, woman was superior, at least in a moral sense: "The glorified madonna ideal shows us how much more whole and holy it is to be a woman than to be an artist, orator, professor, or expert" (Hall, 1904a, p. 646).

Despite Hall's attempts to couch his views of women in positive and often religious terms, some feminists took issue with his theory (e.g., Thomas, 1901), not because, as Hall believed, all feminists viewed the sexes as identical, but because Hall's insistence that woman's biological nature fitted her only for motherhood denied her access to the same social, economic, and political considerations given to men. Hall often misrepresented feminist positions on the nature of women and often used his interpretation of their views to argue his own position. For example Hall (1908) charged feminists with viewing the menstrual function as "immodest" and suggested that they denied young girls the right to complain of monthly pain (p. 10240). Because Hall was extremely well read, his interpretation of feminist ideology was probably a misrepresentation of their views. Hall (1904a) revealed some awareness that feminists differed among themselves by referring to "the cranky and extreme left wing of this movement, which strives to theoretically ignore and practically escape the monthly function" (p. 609). Unlike most of his conservative and like-minded colleagues, Hall was more than willing to label feminism his enemy and to label those psychologists who did not share his perspective on women as feminists. When Helen Bradford Thompson Woolley chose to interpret her research findings on the mental traits of the sexes in terms of early environmental influences, Hall (1904a) labeled her thinking "feminist" and dismissed her interpretation as absurd in the light of evolutionary doctrine (p. 565).

Not only did some feminists find Hall's theory an impediment to social change for women, but feminist concerns over women's rights had, by the end of the 19th century, found their way into psychological theorizing. Some functionalists, particularly those at Chicago and Columbia, as the result of their exposure to and sympathy with reform movements such as urban and social reform and the women's rights movement, began to focus their understanding of the development of adult sex differences on the role played by social institutions in creating and sustaining sex differentiation (Rosenberg, 1982). Thus, psychologists such as Dewey, Angell, and later Thorndike were willing to entertain interpretations of sex differences in terms of social construction. In turn, they produced women graduate students such as Helen Bradford Thompson Woolley and Hollingworth, whose research on sex differences pointed to the significance of social and educational variables in shaping adult sex differences.

The desire on the part of younger functionalists at Chicago and Columbia to experiment with possible social reconstructions of woman's role was particularly offensive to Hall, not because his recapitulation theory denied modifiability of the organism by environmental factors, but because Hall questioned the desirability of alterations that might interfere with woman's primary role as mother of the race. The view of woman as mother was for Hall almost a religious as well as a scientific principle, and one he chose to translate into political, social, and educational terms:

> As the foliage of delicate plants first shows the early warmth of spring, and the earliest frost of autumn, so the impressible, susceptible organization of woman appreciates and exhibits far sooner than that of man the manifestation of national progress or decay. (Hall, 1904a, p. 571)

The most serious challenge to the role of woman as mother was perceived by Hall to be found in the turn-of-the-century movement toward coeducation for women. Whereas social reformers, feminists, and some of Hall's functionalist colleagues applauded the higher education of women, Hall felt education was one social modification that had far-reaching detrimental implications for the nature of men and women, and especially for family life. Much of Hall's writing and many of his speeches before professional and lay audiences alike in the early 1900s discussed the application of recapitulation theory in the home and the school. The focus of many of these discussions was the significance of proper education for motherhood as well as education for adolescent boys and girls.

COEDUCATION AND WOMEN

By 1900, 98 percent of public high schools were coeducational and the question of mixed-sex classrooms was viewed by many as a dead issue in all areas of the country but the South (Woody, 1929/1974). However, arguments about the education of boys and girls, particularly during adolescence, continued well into the 20th century, for although coeducation was a practical reality in most grade schools and high schools, the presence of women in colleges and universities had had a relatively short history by the turn of the century. Some observers viewed their presence as due less to a resolution of the coeducational controversy in terms of educational wisdom or sexual equality and more to the financial crises that plagued many institutions during the 1870s, resulting in the opening of college doors to women students (MacMechan, 1903; Woody, 1929/1974).

By virtue of undergraduate degrees obtained from coeducational institutions, women's colleges, or coordinate colleges, women presented credentials for graduate study, and numerous institutions during the 1890s allowed women into postgraduate work. The fate of these women was far from equal to that of their male counterparts. For example, although Mary Calkins completed all necessary requirements for her doctorate at Harvard, the school refused to confer the degree upon her (Stevens & Gardner, 1982). Women who were granted graduate degrees, for example, at Chicago, Columbia, Cornell, and Clark, found traditional advanced degree positions in teaching, administration, and research closed to them (Bryan & Boring, 1944; Woody, 1929/1974). Instead, women were encouraged to take positions in two areas deemed appropriate for the career-minded professional woman: social welfare work and teaching in women's colleges. Because these positions denied women professionals access to the usual means of recognition in professional fields, research publication, and recognition by professional organizations or the university, these well-trained and capable young women fell into professional oblivion. Recent efforts (e.g., Stevens & Gardner, 1982) to document their impact on psychology suggest that, because they occupied peripheral positions in academe, their contributions to theory and research often went unrecognized.

The presence of women in colleges and universities, rather than settling the issue of higher education for women as was hoped by advocates of women's education (e.g., Thomas, 1901, 1908), seemed to rekindle the fires of controversy over the issue of coeducation. For example, after 10 years as a coeducational institution, Chicago in 1902 proposed segregation in order to improve its reputation and establish itself as a research center (Rosenberg, 1982; Woody, 1929/1974). Concerned about the "feminizing" effect of women on men students, institutions such as Chicago were more comfortable with presenting the issue of segregation as a matter of educational philosophy rather than as a matter of political expediency or public image.

Regardless of whether the question of the presence of women in colleges was a matter of educational philosophy or merely financial necessity, the rationale against coeducation in the early 20th century often took the form of arguments "reheated" from their original 19th-century serving. Not surprisingly, in light of Hall's recapitulation theory of development, Hall became the spokesperson for the anticoeducational movement as revived in the early 1900s. Derived from and united by recapitulation theory, Hall's arguments had the appearance of being more scientific than those of his predecessors. In actuality, Hall simply rehashed what had gone before, adding the appeal of his position as an educational and psychological authority and extending his influence by selecting parents' groups as his audience and writing in popular magazines as well as educational journals. Although some people viewed Hall as being 20 years behind the times (e.g., "Notes and News," 1902), both the *Educational Review* and the

Proceedings of the National Education Association, from 1903 through 1906, published numerous letters, essays, and reports discussing the issue of coeducation. In 1903 and again in 1904, Hall addressed the issue of coeducation at the annual meetings of the National Education Association, receiving both favorable and unfavorable responses to his remarks.

If some of the educational establishment chose to see Hall's views as antiquated, his appeal to parents afforded him a more sympathetic audience, for it was during the early 1900s Hall aired his stance on coeducation in various popular magazines, such as *Harper's* and the *Ladies Home Journal.* Some of the articles provided advice to parents on how to handle problems with adolescents (e.g., Hall, 1900, 1907a). Others extolled the virtues of motherhood (e.g., Hall, 1909d). All of them connected coeducation with problems of decay in relationships, in the family and nationally. In all of his writings as well as his speeches on education, Hall affected an expression (probably successfully) of sympathetic understanding of what it is to feel the responsibilities and joys of motherhood. His professed sympathy with womanhood was the basis of his persuasive arguments that coeducation undermined woman's role and thereby destroyed the future of the race. Before the National Congress of Mothers in 1905, Hall concluded his remarks in the following manner:

> I do not know, and I do not suppose any one knows, whether the Holy Mother knew Chaldee or Greek, or whether she even knew how to read, but the whole world has united in reverence of her because she illustrates the complete glory of motherhood. (p. 27)

The premises of Hall's argument against coeducation were derived from three concerns of recapitulation: (a) that adolescence was a critical period in the development of the reproductive organs in women, (b) that the adolescent male needed freedom to engage in cathartic expression of his savage impulses, and (c) that natural sexual differentiation during adolescence was the basis for later attraction between the sexes.

Concern over the development of women's reproductive organs had received the most attention in the 19th-century coeducational movement. Edward Clarke (1873) had argued that the development of women's reproductive organs during adolescence left little power for the tasks of schooling and that education for women could result in arrested development of the reproductive system. Like Clarke, Hall appealed to medical authorities to testify to the damage done to women's reproductive organs by too much mental activity, especially in competition with men. The net result of overexposure in the classroom would be loss of mammary function, followed by lack of interest in motherhood, decreased fertility, and the production, of few and sickly children, if any (Hall, 1904a).

Because many of the proponents of coeducation were not persuaded by the medical testimony, which consisted mostly of opinion and not fact, they discounted it. Hall, too, felt the need to support his arguments about the physical damage caused by coeducation with empirical data. Therefore, he employed his questionnaire approach to assess the health of college women. The results, admitted Hall, were disappointing. Undaunted by the evidence provided using his own instrument, Hall rejected the questionnaire method as a legitimate way of assessing the effects of coeducation, saying that women would often lie about health matters in order to not "bias their education" and, he concluded, the effects of coeducation on health were not really measurable although they were, in his opinion, "probably great and common" (Hall, 1904a, p. 586).

According to Hall, the truest measures of the effects of education on the development of the reproductive organs were the reduced number of marriages among female college graduates and the smaller number of children produced. In order to keep up the species, Hall (1904a) contended, each woman would need to produce at least six children, and the college woman produced far fewer than this. Therefore, the real victim of coeducation was the bachelor woman who had "overdrawn her account with heredity" (Hall, 1904a, p. 633). Although Hall described her as fine in body and mind, he felt that she, having fallen "a conscious prey to the gospel of the feminists" (Hall, 1904a, p. 611), would eventually become bitter when she discovered that she could not keep up with the intellectual capabilities of her male counterparts. Hall (1904a) warned that a bachelor woman was really neither male nor female, neither masculine nor feminine, but "agamic," a third sex produced by the removal of sex from the female (p. 622). Thus, Hall saw her as a sterile accident of evolution, doomed not to reproduce more of her kind.

Hall's position on the abnormality of the unmarried female hints at concerns of female sexuality being expressed by sexologists such as Ellis and Westphal in the late 19th century (Faderman, 1981). Whether or not Hall entertained any notion of female sexuality outside the realm of heterosexual expression, he chose not to mention such a possibility. However, Hall clearly perceived the avoidance of heterosexuality on the part of women as a threat to the continuation of the species and, therefore, as aberrant. In addition, Hall laid the cause for such avoidance at the feet of education.

According to Hall, if women were to be educated at all, they should be educated to motherhood. He suggested (1904a) that the mothers of most great men were of "strong mind" though not highly educated (p. 573). In arguing against the coeducation of girls, Hall (1908) insisted that he was not taking a step backward in the "great movement of emancipation and the higher education of women" (p. 10243), but rather that he had begun to examine the kind of education fully suited to women. Ironically, though Hall often found himself at odds with social feminists on the issue of the professionalization of the domestic sphere in the form of home economics and social welfare work, he and some feminists shared the view that women in these areas of professional concern could positively influence family and societal matters (M. P. Ryan, 1979). Thus, Hall considered appropriate training for women to include both education that taught about motherhood and education leading to a professionalization of nurturing qualities, such as social work, home economics, and elementary school teaching, as long as such professions did not replace motherhood.

Recapitulation would also be adversely affected in the male if he were exposed to an educational environment that discouraged the development of his masculine nature. In an attempt to recapture the path of evolutionary development for the male, Hall argued that nature also decreed the separation of adolescent boys from feminine influence. Hall supported the Boy Scouts and the reading of masculinizing books such as the Tarzan series as ways of allowing expression of adolescent male savage impulses. To encourage boys to become gentlemanly though exposure to girls was anathema to Hall, for it denied recapitulatory catharsis and would result in a wild or feminized adult male. Hall held female teachers responsible for the wildness in adult men, even suggesting that no man would beat his wife if he had "been flogged early," a task easily undertaken by a male teacher (Hall, 1908, p. 10239). In general Hall (1903) felt that women teachers did not belong in the high school, for it was during adolescence that boys needed the firm hand of a man and a model to emulate.

Some educators were in close agreement with Hall on this issue (e.g., Barnes, 1912), as his ideas represented an extension of growing social concern over perceived declining masculinity in the American male (Filene, 1975). The issue of women teachers in the high school had wide ramifications for the teaching profession. In

1904, the Male Teachers' Association of New York City filed with the *Educational Review* a report arguing for male teachers in the high schools. The report suggested that boys could not grow into manhood without the firm and forceful presence of a male and without a masculine ideal ("Report of the Male Teachers' Association," 1902). Female teachers were under attack in many school systems, and school officials and parents alike applauded when they married or had children and left the schools (Sohen, 1972).

Hall's case against coeducation included the assertion that recapitulation called for separation of the sexes in adolescence (adolescence lasted for 10 to 15 years) also because segregation of the sexes was responsible for sexual attraction. Overexposure of the sexes in adolescence often resulted in "contempt or disillusionment in both men and women" (Hall, 1908, p. 10243) and was responsible for slovenly appearance in women and a disgust for women and sex in men (Hall, 1904a, 1911). Women clearly were responsible for the lack of attraction between the sexes because women's competitiveness with men and failure to hold motherhood as the basis for sexual relations, both the outcome of education, resulted in the early 20th-century American males finding their female counterparts unattractive.

WOMEN AT CLARK

The question of the position of women at Clark arose often during Hall's years there, and his handling of the issue through his position as president appears to be a clear expression of his anticoeducational policy as well as his theoretical bias about the nature of women. An examination of Hall's policies and his treatment of women graduate students at Clark shows that apparent departures from a firmly established policy against coeducation during adolescence, which included college and graduate years, were not failures of his theory nor did they represent a change of mind on Hall's part, but rather they may be interpreted as political and economic moves enacted in such a way as to leave his original biases about the nature and education of women wholly intact.

As at other universities and colleges, Clark's entertainment of the question of allowing women to enroll in graduate programs was representative of a general movement following the Civil War toward higher education for women. As already discussed, the financial crises of the 1870s encouraged increasing enrollments, and many institutions found that economic necessity dictated the development of coeducational policy. In addition, proponents of higher education for women and of coeducation found voice through the establishment of women's colleges and through the opening of coeducational institutions such as Chicago and Michigan. Thus, it was merely a matter of time before women would present respectable baccalaureate degrees for entrance into graduate programs.

In the 1890s institutions such as Yale, Brown, Harvard, Chicago, and Johns Hopkins allowed graduate admission to women (Woody, 1929/1974). In the case of Harvard, however, female students became candidates for Radcliffe degrees, an indication that coeducation was not yet firmly established. From the academic year 1892–1893 to the year 1919–1920, the number of women students enrolled in graduate programs in public and private institutions increased from 484 to 5,775 (Woody, 1929/1974). As pointed out by Woody, however, the prevailing opinion of women in graduate programs was that they were intellectually inferior to their male counterparts in creative work areas.

Although the large increase in three decades is impressive, it appears that the "prevailing opinion" about women dictated their career opportunities and development more than did the women's credentials. In psychology, for example, Stevens and Gardner (1982) found that early 20th-century women psychologists found work primarily in small colleges and universities, and especially in women's colleges. Stevens and Gardner concluded that these career moves isolated women from the "old boy" networks so useful in furthering careers and in attaining a student following. Furthermore, commensurate with their traditional socialization, women psychologists gravitated toward social issues areas and applied psychology areas sometimes trivialized by historians of psychology (Rosenberg, 1982; Stevens & Gardner, 1982).

Thus, although the decade beginning the 20th century can be viewed as representing a freeing up of anti-coeducational policies in both undergraduate and graduate programs, two matters continued to plague the woman PhD. First, there remained serious educational policy questions about the appropriate education for women. Second, the professional woman found few opportunities in which she could exercise her newly obtained graduate degree. Thus, it is not Clark's policy on women graduate students that is worthy of attention here, but rather the process, under the direction of Hall, by which Clark University changed its stance on women that provides insight into how Hall, an avowed enemy of coeducation, headed a university that graduated a substantial number of women PhDs.

The question of the presence of undergraduate women in the college (as differentiated from the university) did not arise in Clark's early years because, as Hall (undated) suggested, it was the founder's (Jonas Clark's) intention to exclude women as students. Hall acknowledged that Clark fully intended to establish a university department for women, but only when money could be made available to establish it in a building of its own. Furthermore, Jonas Clark wanted this money to come from private endowments and not from the Clark estate. On September 26, 1889, the Board of Trustees, with Hall as secretary, voted that, in accordance with Clark's original plans for a separate university department for women, "the subject of the admission of women be postponed until the University shall receive such endowment as will enable the corporation to make suitable provision for that purpose" (Hall, undated, p. 2).

Hall served as chief administrative officer of the university from its founding in 1888 until 1920 and during those years often served as interpreter of Jonas Clark's intentions to the Board of Trustees. There is little question that Hall attempted to govern the institution in an autocratic manner. This manner coupled with the financial problems at Clark and the "raid" on Clark faculty by the University of Chicago resulted in the resignation of many faculty and students early in Clark's history (Rosenberg, 1982; Ross, 1972). It is clear, too, that Hall successfully bent the will of the Board of Trustees in accordance with his own desires and perspectives on higher education. An examination of documents and letters to and from the president's office during Hall's tenure reveal him to have been a clever politician, intensely aware of the temper of the times and the position of Clark, a fledging institution plagued by major financial difficulties (*G. Stanley Hall Papers,* 1888–1920).

However, exceptional women (as determined by Hall) were admitted to special courses in the university, such policy having been enacted by the board in 1896. In the years following, not only did women enter special courses, but graduate degrees were also conferred upon women. In 1908, $500 was granted for a "retiring room" for women (Hall, undated).

In 1909 Hall felt it necessary to deal more specifically with university policy on women. The issue arose primarily because the college and the university had been called by the Boston Chamber of Commerce to answer questions as to what Clark was accomplishing for the "public weal" that would exempt the university from taxation (Hall, undated). In addition, according to Hall (undated), Carnegie and Rockefeller money could be made available to Clark depending on Clark's record as a pioneer in educational policy.

Ever in touch with public sentiment and recognizing the university's need for tax exemption as well as for financial backing from the private sector, Hall (undated) drafted a memorandum to the board outlining the past status of women at Clark and proposing future educational policy on women. The policy, proposed by Hall and adopted by the board, recommended that women, as in the past, not be admitted to take the bachelor's nor any other undergraduate degree at Clark, but that those women already in individual classes in the college be allowed to remain so as to "call less attention" (p. 6). Furthermore, an Educational Department was to be established. This department was to be formed from the Child Bureau and the Saturday classes that had been established to serve teachers. The Educational Department would be allowed to grant master's degrees to women, but women were to be excluded from other master's programs. The founding of such a department would, according to the memorandum, "exclude them too from the Main Building and the Chemical Building and segregate them after this year to one floor in the new building and to the Educational Department" (p. 7). This move by Hall was a recognition of the role the university might play in establishing good relations with public schools in teacher training. His intention was that this department would be interpreted as providing service to education and to the public, thereby assuring Clark of tax exemption. In addition, Hall (undated) asserted, "On general principles too, it seems undesirable, especially in view of the present state of public sentiment on the woman question, to take steps that are liable to result in calling public attention to any discrimination against women" (p. 7).

That Hall was making some concessions to public opinion was clear, for in a letter in 1909 to a friend and board member, Col. George Bullock, he wrote

> I am strongly opposed to giving women the slightest foothold in the College. . . . On the other hand, as to the Doctor's degree, of which we have given an average of one in ten years, I am inclined to think that, if we still continue to leave that open, it would save us a good deal of pounding by feminists; and by depriving it we would needlessly shut off possible bequests from women sho [sic] have bourne a pretty large part in the endowment of Universities. (Hall, 1909a)

Hall was willing to alter his educational policy on women to meet the exigencies of public opinion and financial need.

Not only would the establishment of the Educational Department ensure tax exemption, but Hall (undated) felt that Clark's record on education would warrant endowments "from several wealthy women who are deeply interested in this work" (p. 9). Finally, the door was left open to admitting women to the PhD program, but not without personal reservation on Hall's part:

> My own hope is that we may find some way to dispense with the presence of all women in the University proper (outside the Educational Department) except a few very exceptional ones of rare promise and efficiency for science. (Hall, 1909b)

From 1896, when exceptional women were admitted to graduate study, until Hall stepped down as president in 1920, approximately 150 women students enrolled in courses of study at Clark. The first graduate degrees to women were granted in 1907 to Louise Ellison, Edith Dixon, and Caroline Osborne; Osborne was the first woman to be granted a PhD from Clark in 1908 (File on Hall's Students, 1888–1920). During Hall's years as president, almost 50% of the women scholars in graduate study at Clark received graduate degrees. In keeping with Hall's policy, many of the master's degrees were in education, but many were in such fields as psychology, biology, physics, history, foreign relations, and chemistry (File on Hall's Students, 1888–1920). Although Clark drew to it such eminent scholars as Mary Calkins and Phyllis Blanchard, most of the women from Clark were no more successful in obtaining positions in universities or in research institutions than were their sisters who obtained advanced degrees from other institutions. Like other women with graduate degrees, the Clark women obtained positions in teaching and in social welfare work, positions Hall had advocated as the natural lot for scholarly women.

Ironically, however, Hall's attempts to isolate women within the Educational Department were obviously unsuccessful, not because he was overruled by the board or by the faculty at Clark, for Hall himself was responsible for admissions to Clark. Requests for admission to graduate study were submitted to the president's office. There is little evidence from the records of that office that Hall treated the inquiries about graduate study from women any differently than those from men (Presidential Papers). None of the letters to women who had requested entrance to the university used board policy as a way of excluding them from graduate study.

Individuals within the profession who were critical of Hall's psychology were willing to admit that Hall created an atmosphere of learning at Clark that allowed for open and flexible intellectual development for its students. The financial and organizational crisis in the early years of Clark forced Hall back into the classroom, and he set up Monday evening seminars, which, according to both W. C. Ryan (1939) and Tanner (1908), were significant in creating an atmosphere of learning that encouraged the best from each student. Although these seminars were not required and the number and composition of students varied from week to week, students approached them with great enthusiasm. Hall allowed exchange of ideas from the participating students; his major function was to summarize what had been said during the evening.

Hall appeared to place few restrictions on topics for investigation, and it appears that this freedom extended even into research concerning women. For example, the *Topical Syllabi* developed by women students through the Child Study Institute included questionnaires entitled "The Developmental Value of Women's Special Work" (Boggs, 1909a) and "The Monthly Period" (Brown, 1899). Theses and dissertations also revealed interest in women: "Wages of Women Workers in Department and Retail Stores" (Waite, 1913), "An Introduction to the Modern History of the Education of Women" (Wood, 1911), and "The Adolescent Girl" (Blanchard, 1919). That these studies incorporated Hall's biases is unquestionable. Blanchard's (1919) dissertation on adolescent girls, later published in book form, was an extension and elaboration of Hall's work on adolescence with additional incorporation of psychoanalytic theory. However, it would be incorrect to assume that Hall was insistent that psychological study at Clark use only his theoretical orientation. The graduate research in psychology included work in human and animal learning, physiological psychology, introspection, and psychoanalysis. Although Hall was criticized for looseness in his psychological theorizing (Thorndike, 1904), this characteristic may have been of benefit to his student's intellectual freedom and development.

Additionally surprising in light of his stance on women was Hall's support of and personal interest in a number of women students and a woman staff member, Amy Tanner. Tanner, who obtained her PhD from the University of Chicago and who had worked with John Dewey, was granted a fellowship at Clark in 1907. She wrote to Hall to ask his advice as to whether she should continue in teaching and come to Clark or go into social work, having been offered a position in the South (Tanner, 1907). Hall's reply to her, if there was one, has been lost or was not issued out of the president's office. The latter would seem to have been the case because Tanner's request was personal. She did come to Clark, but her interest in social work and her indecision about her career choice continued to plague her throughout her years there.

For all but her last two years at Clark, Tanner was on annual appointment as an honorary fellow or as a research assistant to Hall. In May of

1916 she requested that she be put on staff, having completed her ninth year of service at Clark (Tanner, 1916). Hall supported her request, and she was placed on the continued list; half her salary came from the university, where she was his assistant, and the other half came from the Children's Institute, where she was lecturer. In the latter position Tanner came as close as any woman to being a university colleague of Hall.

Hall's support of Tanner extended beyond her position and duties at Clark and included his numerous attempts to get her poetry and translations of French fairy tales published. Although his efforts were unsuccessful, he was instrumental in the publication and promotion of a second edition of her book, *The Child* (1904), written prior to her arrival at Clark.

The relationship between Hall and Tanner had its difficult moments, however. After granting her authority to order equipment for the Children's Institute, Hall submitted her order to Sanford, chair of psychology, for review, a move that Tanner resented. She expressed her disapproval in a letter to Hall suggesting that if her judgment were not deemed "trustworthy enough to be taken as final . . . it was best not to have me doing the ordering at all" (Tanner, 1909). She further recommended that all future agreements and arrangements as to her position be put in writing. In his reply Hall (1909c) assured her that he had utmost confidence in her, but had wanted to make certain that there would be no laboratory duplication with psychology; his reply was given, as she had requested, in writing.

Tanner left Clark in 1918 to go into settlement house work in the Italian (Shrewsbury Street) district of Worcester. Her reason for leaving Clark, according to Hall (1918) was "solely because she was (with too much ground, alas) dissatisfied that women were not recognized in the university, and that she was the only one who has ever done any teaching here." It is probable that Hall correctly expressed Tanner's reasons for leaving, but his professed sympathy with her position on women at Clark can be viewed only as openly hypocritical in the light of his role in establishing the university's policies. Although he extended to Tanner a colleaguelike status, her position as a Saturday lecturer within the Child Study Institute was commensurate with Hall's perspective on women in education. In correspondence between himself and Tanner (e.g., Hall, 1907b), Hall often expressed sympathy for the difficulty women had in obtaining positions in universities), yet this sympathy must be considered somewhat superficial; Hall's pronouncements on women's education and womanly career pursuits expressed the kinds of sentiments that kept the doors to male-dominated professions closed to women.

Despite the duplicity in his relationship with Tanner, his support for her was strong. Perhaps he did not view this support as a violation of his philosophy on women; he had often stated that child study was to be a science undertaken by women because he believed them to be the best observers of children, and Tanner's position was primarily within the Children's Institute.

Hall appeared to be generally supportive of the women students at Clark and was as unreserved in his praise for them as he was for the men students. His favorite student was Phyllis Blanchard, to whom he often referred as his best research assistant in his 32 years at Clark. Hall clearly saw Blanchard as a case of the apple not falling far from the tree, as her work on adolescence reinforced his earlier interest in the area. Other women students asked for and obtained support from Hall even after they had left Clark. Lucinda Pearl Boggs, who attended Clark for only one summer, frequently wrote to Hall and obtained his endorsement of her extension course in home life offered through the University of Illinois in 1909 ("Lecture and Correspondence," undated). Bogg's respect for Hall and his for her were apparently the result of Hall's having converted her from feminist philosophy (Boggs, 1909b). This "conversion" stimulated her interest in a social psychology of the home and resulted in the home life courses, which were similar to others offered around the country and were the forerunners of the professionalization of the domestic sphere by way of the discipline of home economics.

Although Hall's educational policies at Clark were consistent with his psychological theory and educational doctrine on sex differences, his treatment of women graduate students appeared to contain little that was connected with his educational and psychological position on women. Indeed, it is somewhat surprising that Hall provided higher education for women in an institution over which he clearly maintained considerable control.

RESOLUTION

In view of Hall's theoretical perspective on women that led to an orientation against coeducation, his enrollment of women into graduate programs at Clark is particularly confusing. But there is little to suggest that it was a problem for Hall. Nowhere in his correspondence with potential women students nor in his treatment of women at Clark is there any evidence that Hall considered their presence a violation of his presidential pronouncements on graduate study for women. Scholars examining the Clark experience have remarked on the excellence of training obtained at Clark (W. C. Ryan, 1939), and some contemporary feminist scholars have suggested that at the beginning of the 20th century the two schools most open to women were Clark and Cornell (Rosenberg, 1982). Thus, unlike President Harper at Chicago, Hall apparently saw no damage to Clark's reputation or public image resulting from admitting women to the graduate programs. In fact, so highly did Hall laud the Clark education that visitors from Europe were led to the erroneous conclusion that the only real graduate education in the United States was at Clark (Ross, 1972).

The resolution of the paradox of Hall as an enemy of coeducation and a teacher of women may be found, in part, in Hall's perspective on the women at Clark. Many of the women graduate students were single women and thus might be considered in that category of bachelor women to which Hall referred in *Adolescence*. Such women were for Hall "individuals," that is, not representative of most women. In terms of variability, Hall must have perceived them as abnormal, as women who would not produce children and, thus, who were terminal products of evolution (Hall, 1904a; Trecker, 1974). Thus, it is possible to resolve the paradox by referring to Hall's perception that the women at Clark had an unusual aptitude for scholarship. (It should be noted, however, that although the majority of the women who studied at Clark were unmarried, about 40% were not.) Although alumni information on these women does not indicate how many of them produced children, few had families when they were enrolled at Clark (File on Hall's Students, 1888–1920; Clark University Library, 1930, 1940, 1951).

Another explanation, not necessarily contradictory to that just offered, is based on Hall's perspective on the kinds of careers appropriate to women. An examination of the careers of the women graduates of Clark suggests that they fared as poorly as did graduates from other institutions in obtaining positions in university teaching and research. Many of the Clark women graduates found positions in teaching, mostly in public and private schools in the elementary grades (Clark University Library, 1930, 1940, 1951). Women who obtained university or college positions were located in women's colleges and not in coeducational institutions. Equally likely as employment for Clark graduates were private or public social and welfare agencies. Within the area of psychology, the best-known graduate of Clark is probably Phyllis Blanchard, who remained until her retirement at the Child Guidance Clinic in Philadelphia. Many Clark women graduates found employment in private practice in psychology or in consulting work with hospitals and other agencies (Clark University Library, 1930, 1940, 1951). Although there is no evidence to suggest that Hall directed women into these areas, he would not have had to do so because there were few positions open to professionally trained women in traditional male academe (Woody, 1929/1974). Thus, Hall educated his women students for careers considered to be appropriate for females, so this education did not violate his perspective on women's nature.

Finally, the possible attitudes of the women themselves must be considered. It is clear that women like Bradford Thompson Woolley at Chicago and Hollingworth at Columbia entered their institutions with questions about women's psychological makeup, questions stimulated by their sympathy with social reform movements (Rosenberg, 1982). In addition, these women entered institutions where they found instructors who shared their perspectives on sex differences. Most likely there was a similar correspondence between the views of the women entering Clark and those of G. Stanley Hall. Surely these students would not have been unaware of Hall's well-known views on women. Thus, if the women of Clark questioned the traditional status of women, perhaps such questioning began after the Clark years, for the atmosphere at Clark would not have been particularly sympathetic to feminist positions on women's education or legal status.

In short, the significance of such a suggestion for the resolution of Hall's apparent paradox is that Hall would not have been exposed to women with feminist sympathies, unlike the men at Chicago and Columbia (Rosenberg, 1982). Therefore, he would have been able to maintain correspondence between an educational policy that dictated education for motherhood and womanly careers, such as education and social work, and his position as an educator engaged in providing just such an education to women who behaved according to his theoretical notions of womanhood. The only evidence to suggest that Hall was ever directly challenged by a woman graduate student on feminist issues is found in L. P. Bogg's letter (1909b) to him, and in this case Hall converted her to his perspective, meriting him her gratitude; he later assumed the role of her mentor in establishing her career in the social psychology of the home. If any of the Clark women were feminists, their sympathies with women's issues in the early 20th century have remained undiscovered for more than a half century.

Conversely, there is no evidence to suggest that Hall's exposure to women graduate students at Clark changed his view of women or that he ever viewed these women as other than exceptions. In 1922, Hall published *Senescence* (Hall, 1922b), a work dedicated to the later years of development. In it, he reasserted his view of sex differences, suggesting again the eternal adolescence of the female and her generic nature. In a final work before his death in 1924, Hall commented on the newest woman, the flapper. The freedom of the flapper was not viewed by Hall as a departure from his theory on woman's nature, but rather as the "bud of a new and better womanhood" (Hall, 1922a, p. 780), one that would assert anew the distinction between the sexes.

In conclusion, the paradox under investigation in this article can be resolved by the underlying consistency that emerges from an examination of the many ways Hall chose to understand the nature of women. Hall's developmental theory clearly necessitated an educational stance against coeducation, a stance he was willing to take by proposing and enacting educational policy that encouraged the professional development of women in accordance with traditional womanly virtues. In this effort, he was helped by a social-educational system that barred women from the usual areas of male professional advancement. Thus, Hall emerges as unique only in that he may be viewed as the 19th-century bridge to the development of 20th-century social sciences' perspectives on women's nature. Until recently these perspectives have remained grounded within the 19th-century patriarchal structures of womanhood often found as unconscious biases within the theoretical perspectives on sex differences proposed by Hall and other early functionalists. A more complete understanding of the enduring nature of these perspectives on women is necessary and could be accomplished through an examination of the early Clark women graduates within their chosen professions.

REFERENCES

Barnes, E. (1912). The feminizing of culture. *Atlantic Monthly, 109,* 770–776.

Blanchard, P. (1919). *The adolescent girl.* Unpublished doctoral dissertation, Clark University, Worcester, MA.

Boggs, L. P. (1909a). The development value of women's special work. Topical syllabi. In *G. Stanley Hall papers.* (Available from Clark University Archives, Goddard Library, Clark University, Worcester, MA)

Boggs, L. P. (1909b, September 27). [Letter to Hall]. In *G. Stanley Hall papers.* (Available from Clark University Archives, Goddard Library, Clark University, Worcester, MA)

Boring, E. G. (1950). *A history of experimental psychology.* New York: Appleton-Century-Crofts. (Original work published 1929)

Brown, A. (1899). The monthly period. Topical syllabi. In *G. Stanley Hall papers.* (Available from Clark University Archives, Goddard Library, Clark University, Worcester, MA)

Bryan, A. I. & Boring, E. G. (1944). Women in American psychology: Prolegomenon. *Psychological Bulletin, 41,* 447–454.

Clark University Library. (1930, May). *Alumni directory* (No. 76). Worcester, MA: Author.

Clark University Library. (1940, June). *Alumni directory* (Vol. 9, No. 1). Worcester, MA: Author.

Clark University Library. (1951, April). *Alumni directory* (No. 201). Worcester, MA: Author.

Clark, E. (1873). *Sex in education: Or, a fair chance for the girls.* Boston: Osgood.

Ellis, H. (1894). *Man and woman: A study of human secondary sexual characteristics.* New York: Scribner's.

Faderman, L. (1981). *Surpassing the love of men.* New York: Morrow. [File on Hall's students]. (1888–1920). (Available from Clark University Archives, Goddard Library, Clark University, Worcester, MA)

Filene, P. G. (1975). *Him/her self: Sex roles in modern America.* New York: Mentor Books.

G. Stanley Hall Papers. (1888–1920). (Available from Clark University Archives, Goddard Library, Clark University, Worcester, MA)

Galton, F. (1907). *Inquiries into the human faculty and its development.* London: Dent.

Geddes, P. & Thomson, J. A. (1890). *The evolution of sex.* New York: Scribner & Welford.

Gould, S. J. (1981). *The mismeasure of man.* New York: Norton.

Hall, G. S. (1900, August). The awkward age. *Appleton's Magazine,* pp. 149–156.

Hall, G. S. (1903). Coeducation in the high school. *Addresses and Proceedings of the National Education Association,* 446–460.

Hall, G. S. (1904a). *Adolescence: Its psychology and its relations to physiology, anthropology, sociology, sex, crime, religion and education* (Vols. 1 & 2). New York: Appleton.

Hall, G. S. (1904b, June 27–July 1). Coeducation. *Addresses and Proceedings of the National Education Association.* 538–542.

Hall, G. S. (1905). New ideals of motherhood suggested by child study. *Report of the National Congress of Mothers,* 14–27.

Hall, G. S. (1907a, September). How and when to be frank with boys. *Ladies' Home Journal.*

Hall, G. S. (1907b, February 3). [Letter to Tanner]. In *G. Stanley Hall papers.* (Available from Clark University Archives, Goddard Library, Clark University, Worcester, MA)

Hall, G. S. (1908). Feminization in school and home. *World's Work, 16,* 10237–10244.

Hall, G. S. (1909a, November 20). [Letter to Bullock]. In *G. Stanley Hall papers.* (Available from Clark University Archives, Goddard Library, Clark University, Worcester, MA)

Hall, G. S. (1909b, November 27). [Letter to Bullock]. In *G. Stanley Hall papers.* (Available from Clark University Archives, Goddard Library, Clark University, Worcester, MA)

Hall, G. S. (1909c, December 20). [Letter to Tanner]. In *G. Stanley Hall papers.* (Available from Clark University Archives, Goddard Library, Clark University, Worcester MA)

Hall, G. S. (1909d, June). A man's adventure in domestic industry. *Appleton's Magazine,* pp. 677–683.

Hall, G. S. (1911). *Educational problems* (Vol. 2). New York: Appleton.

Hall, G. S. (1918, August 8). [Letter to Ellis]. In *G. Stanley Hall papers.* (Available from Clark University Archives, Goddard Library, Clark University, Worcester, MA)

Hall, G. S. (1922a, June). Flapper americana novissima. *Harper's,* pp. 771–780.

Hall, G. S. (1922b). *Senescence.* New York: Appleton.

Hall, G. S. (1923). *Life and confessions of a psychologist.* New York: Appleton.

Hall, G. S. (undated). [Memorandum in re women students at Clark]. In *G. Stanley Hall papers.* (Available from Clark University Archives, Goddard Library, Clark University, Worcester, MA)

Lecture and correspondence courses on home life [Brochure on course offered by L. P. Boggs at Urbana, IL]. (undated). In *G. Stanley Hall papers.* (Available from Clark University Archives, Goddard Library, Clark University, Worcester, MA)

MacMechan, A. (1903). Of girls in a Canadian college. *Atlantic Monthly, 92,* 402–406.

Notes and News: Dr. Hall on high school conditions. (1902). *Educational Review, 28,* 323–324.

Presidential papers. In *G. Stanley Hall papers.* (Available from Clark University Archives, Goddard Library, Clark University, Worcester, MA)

Report of the Male Teachers' Association of New York City. (1902). *Educational Review, 23,* 323–324.

Rosenberg, R. (1982). *Beyond separate spheres: Intellectual roots of modern feminism.* New Haven, CT: Yale University Press.

Ross, D. (1972). *G. Stanley Hall: The psychologist as prophet.* Chicago: University of Chicago Press.

Ryan, M. P. (1979). *Womanhood in America: From colonial times to the present* (2nd ed.). New York: New Viewpoints.

Ryan, W. C. (1939). *Studies in early graduate education.* New York: The Carnegie Foundation, Merrymount Press.

Schwendinger, J. & Schwendinger, H. (1971). Sociology's founding fathers: Sexists to a man. *Journal of Marriage and the Family, 33,* 783–799.

Shields, S. (1975). Functionalism, Darwinism, and the psychology of women. *American Psychologist, 30,* 739–754.

Siegel, A. W., & White, S. H. (1982). The child study movement: Early growth and development of the symbolized child. In H. W. Reese (Ed.), *Advances in child development and behavior* (Vol 17, pp. 233–285). New York: Academic Press.

Smith-Rosenberg, C., & Rosenberg, C. (1973). The female animal: Medical and biological views of woman and her roles in nineteenth century America. *Journal of American History, 60,* 350–352.

Sohen, J. (1972). *The new woman in Greenwich Village.* New York: Quadrangle.

Stevens, G., & Gardner. S. (1982). *The women of psychology: Vol I. Pioneers and innovators.* Cambridge, MA: Schenkman.

Tanner, A. (1904). *The child: This thinking, feeling, and doing.* Chicago: Rand McNally.

Tanner, A. (1907, July 17). [Letter to Hall]. In *G. Stanley Hall papers.* (Available from Clark University Archives, Goddard Library, Clark University, Worcester, MA)

Tanner, A. (1908). *History of Clark University through the interpretation of the will of the founder.* Unpublished manuscript. (Available from Clark University Archives, Goddard Library, Clark University, Worcester, MA)

Tanner, A. (1909, December 16). [Letter to Hall]. *In G. Stanley Hall papers.* (Available from Clark University Archives, Goddard Library, Clark University, Worcester, MA)

Tanner, A. (1916, May 22). [Letter to Hall]. *In G. Stanley Hall papers.* (Available from Clark University Archives, Goddard Library, Clark University, Worcester, MA)

Thomas, M. C. (1901). Should the higher education of women differ from that of men? *Educational Review, 21,* 1–10.

Thomas, M. C. (1908). Present tendencies in women's college and university education. *Educational Review, 35,* 64–85.

Thorndike, E. (1904). The newest psychology. *Educational Review, 28,* 217–227.

Trecker, J. L. (1974). Sex, science, and education. *American Quarterly, 26,* 352–366.

Waite, M. A. (1913). *Wages of women workers in department and retail stores.* Unpublished master's thesis, Clark University, Worcester, MA.
Watson, R. I. (1978). *The great psychologists* (4th ed.). New York: Lippincott.
Wood, I. (1911). *An introduction to the modern history of the education of women.* Unpublished master's thesis, Clark University, Worcester, MA.
Woody, T. A. (1974). *A history of women's education in the U.S.* New York: Octagon Books. (Original work published 1929)

Tests of the Senses and Faculties

James McKeen Cattell

Tests of the senses and faculties concern the teacher from three points of view. In the first place, those who wish to contribute to the advancement of psychology will find here a convenient opening. In the second place, such tests give a useful indication of the progress, condition, and aptitudes of the pupil. In the third place, the carrying out of the tests might serve as a means of training and education.

The senses and faculties have been studied hitherto by men of science, who have mostly made the determinations upon themselves. This is a necessary beginning, but now that methods have been elaborated, it is very desirable that the measurements should be extended so as to include different classes of persons. There are no individuals better suited for such experiments than the pupils in our schools. They are classified according to age, acquirements, and sex, and the teacher has considerable knowledge of their ability, character, and heredity. A careful investigation of the variation in the senses and faculties under such conditions would at the present time be an important contribution to science. In so far as experiment can be used in the study of mind, scientific progress is assured. The traditional psychology is vague and inexact, and cannot rank as co-ordinate with physical science. But when we regard the history of the several physical sciences, we see that they too at one time consisted of inexact descriptions, artificial classifications, dubious anecdotes, and verbal explanations. With the introduction of experiment and measurement astrology has become astronomy, allchemy has become chemistry, and natural history has become natural science. Physical sciences, such as astronomy, in which measurements could be readily undertaken were the first to be developed, while those, such as electricity, in which it is difficult to make measurements, are still backward. Matter in motion is more readily subject to experiment when passive than when organic and living. Physics has consequently preceded biology in its development. But the progress of biology has recently been rapid, and it will be found that nearly all advances have been due to the application of experiment and measurement. As the living organism is more complex and changeable than inert matter, so the mind is more complicated, protean, and inaccessible than the body. It is natural, therefore, that psychology should be the last science to be weaned by philosophy and to begin an independent growth. Those who have followed the recent development of psychology know that this has been the result of experiment and measurement. Each new application of experimental methods subserves the advancement of psychology, and the very backwardness of the science gives the teacher an opportunity to contribute to its progress.

From Cattell, J. McK. (1893). Tests of the senses and faculties. *Educational Review, 5,* 257–265.

When our knowledge of the normal variation of mental processes has been somewhat further increased, its determination will give useful indications of individual condition, progress, and ability. In conjunction with the ordinary school examination such tests would show whether the course of study is improving or blunting the fundamental processes of perception and mental life. Tests made at the beginning and end of the day, week, and session would show whether the student is exhausted by the required curriculum. They could be used in comparing different systems of education, different schools, the advantages of city and country, etc. They would show whether girls are able, without injury to health, to follow the same courses of study as boys. Careful tests must almost of necessity be introduced into the public schools. If attendance be made compulsory, the state is undoubtedly responsible for any bad consequences which could be avoided. Thus if the eyesight of a student be injured, so as to involve a loss of ability to earn a living, the state would, under our present laws, probably be liable for damages. In many cases tests which could readily be made would indicate disease, especially of the nervous system, long before it becomes apparent to common observation. The tendency to certain diseases counterindicate certain employments. Thus a very large percentage of women teachers become insane; consequently those having neuropathic tendencies should not enter on this profession. One boy in twenty is color blind, and this defect, which is never discovered by the individual himself, but may be determined by the teacher in one minute, unfits him for work so far separated as that of the railway signal man or of the artist. As our knowledge increases we shall, on the one hand, be able to indicate very early in the life of the child tendencies to insanity and other diseases, to dipsomania and other vices, and to crime, and precautions may be taken which will limit the range of these abnormal tendencies in the individual, and prevent their spreading in the race. On the other hand, valuable qualities may be early discovered and developed. Special aptitudes will not be lost through unsuitable surroundings and uncongenial work, but the child may be led to the course of life in which he will be most happy and most useful. Many tendencies are likely to be eliminated or increased in offspring according to the marriage of the parents. While instinct is probably a better guide to suitable marriage than scientific principles, it cannot be denied that parents and the conventions of society have much to do with the conditions under which choice is made. Somewhat of the backwardness of the dark ages may be due to the fact that many of the best men were celibates. If a code of honor (such as obtains in some aristocracies, and prevents its members from marrying below their rank) could be developed, and directed toward eliminating degenerative tendencies, and developing valuable traits, the race would be greatly strengthened and perfected.

Such experiments on the senses and faculties would not only advance our knowledge of the mind, and serve as a useful criterion in many ways, but they would also be a valuable training for the pupil. The senses and faculties would be developed as well as measured. In the child and savage every sensation from without is apt to distract the attention and lead to some movement. In the language of physiology, afferent impulses are immediately converted into efferent, and nothing is stored up within. Education seeks to prevent such dispersion, and the importance of manual training and laboratory work for this purpose is now universally admitted. The senses and faculties are trained wherever the student makes special movements and independent observations, but the direction in which these should be undertaken remains an open question. It should be remembered that a laboratory course, as in chemistry, is intended rather for training the pupil than for learning about the combinations of elements, etc. It is, in fact, a course in experimental psychology as much as a course in experimental physics. It can only be decided after practical trial whether a laboratory course expressly directed to studying the senses and faculties would serve better or worse than a physical or biological science as a means of training. Such tests certainly require the most complete abstraction and concentration, and every wandering of the attention is at once betrayed by the experiments themselves. The stimulus of competition and of the effort to improve will certainly secure the interest of the student. It may be found that the experiments will become too much of a "game." But they require a steady hand, undimmed senses, and a clear mind, and any effort to secure these cannot but benefit the student. Those who have marked the improvement in health of students in the English universities as they train for a boat race must wish that some such healthy competition could be more widespread in schools and colleges.

In this paper suitable tests can be indicated only; the teacher who wishes to study methods and results must work over special books and papers.* Experiments can be made in an hour which would leave a record of permanent value both to science and to the individual student. If the experiments be regarded as a means of training and made part of the school curriculum, and an hour a week throughout the year be devoted to them, much more can be accomplished. In this case the senses may be taken up in order, beginning, say, with vision. The sharpness of sight may be easily measured by determining the distance at which a printed page can be read. If the sharpness be defective an oculist should be consulted, as the difficulty is usually mechanical and may be readily corrected. Each eye should be tested separately, as one eye is often defective, and an excess of strain is needlessly thrown on the better eye. Color blindness may be detected by letting the student select all the green shades from a heap of colored wools, and more exactly determined by matching colors on revolving wheels. The size of the field of vision may be mapped out by letting the observer look at a fixed point and determining how far in every direction letters can be read and colors seen.

The error in perceiving size may be tested by drawing a line as nearly as possible the length of a standard line, and in perceiving intensity by matching shadows or revolving wheels. The perception of size, distance, and solidity with one and with two eyes may be studied, and its exactness measured. If time permit contrast and after-images may be observed, and the individual variation determined. Useful training in subjective observation may be obtained by noticing that things not looked at directly are seen double, and by observing entoptic phenomena. These are various images due to the structure of the eye. They are often discovered by the individual, and lead him to think that his eyes are failing.

The sharpness of hearing may be tested by determining the distance at which the ticking of a watch can be heard. The test should be made for each ear separately. The range of pitch which can be heard varies considerably with different individuals, and this may be determined. The accuracy with which small differences in pitch can be distinguished and with which intervals can be adjusted should be measured. Time is often misspent by girls who learn to play the piano mechanically with no ear for music. The exactness with which distance and direction can be recognized with the ear may be measured. Learning to distinguish the simple tones in a complex sound is a useful training.

Touch may be tested and trained by determining how far apart two points must be in order that they may be recognized as two when they touch the skin. This distance differs greatly in different parts of the body. Taste and smell are neglected senses, and ones peculiarly open to education. Considering its importance to

*We are fortunate in having the recent psychologies of Professor James and Professor Ladd. Those who know German should also read Professor Wundt's *Physiologische Psychologie*. Mr. Galton's *Inquiries into Human Faculty* and other writings are of special interest. Professor Jastrow has given in the *Educational Review* (II:442) an excellent example of tests on memory and association.

comfort and health, cooking is a backward art, and our housewives should be trained to distinguish and value small differences. If good water could be distinguished from bad by the average individual as well as it is by the horse, many cases of typhoid fever and diphtheria would be avoided. The same holds for smells, which are invaluable criteria of unhygienic surroundings. The sense of temperature could also be trained so that one may know when a room becomes overheated, and may distinguish subjective from objective causes. The organic changes within the body are obscure and not easy to observe and study, but they are of enormous importance. To recognize correctly the need for fresh air, food, sleep, rest, and exercise would be an acquirement whose value cannot be overstated. If the causes leading to *malaise* and *bien être,* tedium and comfort, could be learned and the mode of living adjusted accordingly, the value of life and all the institutions of society would be affected.

Movement and its perception offer a valuable series of tests. The strength of the grasp of the hand and the rate at which a blow can be struck should be measured. These are convenient tests of bodily condition, and a difference between two hands is often characteristic. The tremor of the hand and the sway of the body give early and important indications of overstrain. The way we judge movements by their extent, their force, and their time should be studied, and the accuracy of discrimination measured. It is easy to find how much difference there must be between two weights, in order that their difference may be noticed.

Feelings of pleasure and pain may be tested in such a course, and possibly elementary aesthetic perceptions trained. It would be a great gain if students could learn to appreciate simplicity and taste in dress and surroundings. The colors and their combinations liked best and least may be determined, as also shapes, relative sizes, etc. A corresponding experiment may be made for the combinations of tones used in speech and music. The pressure or temperature which just hurts may be determined.

Leaving the senses and turning to the faculties we find that imagination, memory, and the association of ideas may be tested. Thus a series of questions can be framed the answers to which will throw light on the mental imagery of the pupil. The thoughts of some are accompanied by vivid pictures, others think more in sounds or movements. Some can call up a scene so as to see all the details before them, others only remember the relations. Such differences are highly characteristic, and indicate special aptitudes which should not be disregarded. The accuracy of ordinary observation may be tested by requiring the student to draw the plan of the hall of the schoolhouse; or to give an account of some event, say something that happened in the school the day before. Casual observation will be found very defective, and the student will learn that but little reliance can be placed on stories of extraordinary events, or even on the testimony in a court of justice. He may also learn to distinguish clearly what he in fact knows, and what he surmises and invents. If so he will have acquired nothing more valuable in his whole school course. Memory may be tested by reading a passage aloud, and requiring the student to write down afterward as much as he can remember. It can be measured more exactly by reading a series of numerals, and determining how many can be remembered. The experiment may be varied by choosing a series of numerals greater than can be remembered on hearing once and determining how often it must be repeated in order that it may be learned. The same series may be used a day or a week afterward; the greater rapidity with which it is learned indicates unconscious memory, and the experiment may be arranged to measure the rate of forgetting. The rate at which a simple sensation fades from the memory may also be determined. The range of consciousness may be measured by uncovering objects for a very short time and determining how much the student can perceive simultaneously. The association of ideas may be studied by giving a word to the class, and letting them write down what idea or other word is suggested by it. The train of ideas for twenty seconds may be recorded. Questions may also be arranged in such a manner that the answers will throw light on the acquirements and interests of the student.

The time of mental processes is a useful text. The accuracy with which an interval of time can be judged is a somewhat different matter; it may be tested readily by giving the student an interval, say one minute, and letting him note when an equal period has elapsed. The time passing before a movement can be made in answer to a stimulus may be measured, but it is so short that delicate apparatus is required. The time needed to see and name series of colors, letters, and words should be found. An educated man can read words making sentences in about half the time that he can read disconnected words. The absolute and relative times are consequently a good test of progress in learning to read. The rate of reading foreign languages measures familiarity with the language. The time of mental processes, such as translating words from one language to another, adding or multiplying digits, remembering the country in which a city is situated, or the author of a book, may be measured readily by letting the student make ten trials in succession. The time in coming to a decision or in making a judgment may also be measured. In normal mental life the attention waxes and wanes and the duration of this rhythm may be measured.

In conjunction with these mental tests certain anthropometric data should be secured. Such are the height, weight, breathing capacity, the color of eyes and hair, etc. Age and sex and the nationality and position of the parents should always be noted. If possible it will be well to record what diseases the student has suffered, as also the age, state of health, etc., of his brothers and sisters, his parents, and other near relatives.

This series of tests of the senses and faculties by no means exhausts such as may be made to advantage. Those wishing to undertake more advanced work will seek to study and measure mental time, intensity and extensity, and the correlation of these magnitudes. But all the tests enumerated here may be made by an intelligent teacher on even the youngest school children, and without expensive or complicated apparatus. It may seem surprising that, with the exception of a few isolated tests, this has not as yet been attempted anywhere; but it must be remembered that experimental psychology is a recent study even in our universities. The first laboratory for research work was established by Professor Wundt at Leipzig in 1879, and the second by Dr. G. Stanley Hall at Baltimore in 1882. The first course in which students carried out a series of experiments in the laboratory was given by the writer in 1888. Now, however, the teacher can prepare himself for such work in most of the leading universities—at Harvard, Yale, Columbia, Pennsylvania, Cornell, Clark, Brown, Washington, Chicago, Wisconsin, Michigan, Indiana, Nebraska, Stanford, and Toronto. The rapid extension of the study of experimental psychology in American universities leads to the expectation that tests of the senses and faculties will soon be undertaken in many schools, and will perhaps be made part of the regular curriculum.

James McKeen Cattell and the Failure of Anthropometric Mental Testing, 1890–1901

Michael M. Sokal

CATTELL'S PROGRAM FOR ANTHROPOMETRIC MENTAL TESTING

On January 1, 1889, Cattell was appointed to a professorship of psychology at the University of Pennsylvania that he later claimed (erroneously) to be the world's first. His father's advocacy and his European scientific pedigree played a part in this high honor to a twenty-nine-year-old youth. Within a year, he had established a laboratory, begun to train students, and sketched out a research program on "mental tests and measurements," which coined the term now in common use.[1] He explicitly ignored the simple measurements of bodily dimensions that had been so much a part of Galton's program; instead, he concentrated on procedures to examine both physiological and psychological characteristics. These tests, carried out sporadically on his students at the University, were dynamometer pressure, rate of movement, sensation areas, pressure causing pain, least noticeable difference in weight, reaction time to sound, time for naming colors, bisection of a 50 cm line, judgment of 10 seconds' time, and number of letters remembered on one hearing.

Cattell was clearly skillful in parlaying this simple program into a major institutional and eventually public commitment. He effectively alluded to Helmholtzian science with the term "mental energy," flimsily applied to the tasks measuring strength of squeeze and rate of arm movement in the first two tests above. The ideology of evolution was also invoked by his claim that the tests "would be of considerable value in discovering the constancy of mental processes, their interdependence, and their variation under different circumstances." Galton himself amplified this point in a series of comments, comparing Cattell's testing to "sinking shafts . . . at a few critical points." He admitted that one goal of Cattell's procedures was exploratory, to determine "which of the measures are the most instructive."[2] Cattell also hinted at a public need when he commented that the tests might "perhaps [be] useful in regard to training, mode of life or indication of disease."

Cattell was not the only American to sense a public need to be tapped by mental testing in the 1890s. By that decade, scientists working in physical anthropometry began to claim that they could measure "The Physical Basis of Precocity and Dullness," and though their claim was disputed,[3] their studies continued throughout the decade. Within the discipline just beginning to identify itself as psychology, testing boomed. At Clark University, for example, Edmund C. Sanford extended his colleague Franz Boas's anthropometric studies of school children.[4] At the University of Nebraska, Harry K. Wolfe, the second American doctoral student of Wundt in experimental psychology, urged the adoption of mental tests in the local public schools. Like Cattell, he admitted that he was not sure what he was studying, and he reminded teachers "not [to] be uneasy because the meaning of any peculiarities is obscure."[5] At Yale, another of Wundt's students, Edward Wheeler Scripture, tried out various mental testing procedures and even published a paper on fencing as an indication of mental ability.[6]

Most important from the viewpoint of legitimating the new discipline in the public eye was the work of Joseph Jastrow. He had earned a Ph.D. with G. Stanley Hall at Johns Hopkins in 1886. He began corresponding with Francis Galton about his anthropometric interest in

Adapted from Sokal, M. M. (1982). James McKeen Cattell and the failure of anthropometric mental testing, 1890–1901. In W. R. Woodward & M. G. Ash (Eds.), *The problematic science: Psychology in nineteenth-century thought*. New York: Praeger, pp. 322–345.

1887, and he became professor of psychology at the University of Wisconsin in 1888. By 1890, his concern with mental testing paralleled Cattell's; early in 1892 he published a proposal for "Some Anthropological and Psychological Tests on College Students" based almost completely on Galton's program.[7] He also used tests to investigate sex differences and clashed with Mary Whiton Calkins, the distinguished Wellesley psychologist, as to the meaning of the differences his tests revealed.[8]

Under Jastrow's direction in 1893, the two streams of interest in anthropometric mental testing converged at the World's Columbian Exposition in Chicago. At this World's Fair, Frederic Ward Putnam, Curator of the Peabody Museum of American Archaeology and Ethnology at Harvard University, planned a Department of Ethnology to include a Section on Physical Anthropology under the direction of Franz Boas. Part of Boas's plan was to carry out a program of anthropometric measurements on the visitors to the Fair, including as many foreign visitors as possible, and the members of the Indian tribes brought to Chicago for the occasion. Jastrow, Boas, and Putnam saw no reason why the program should be limited to physical anthropometry and extended it to include mental tests.[9] The result was to be an outgrowth of Galton's Anthropometric Laboratory, and Jastrow wrote to Galton in 1892, asking for suggestions as to procedures and apparatus. He even went before the preliminary meeting of the American Psychological Association and "asked the cooperation of all members for the Section of Psychology at the World's Fair and invited correspondence on the matter."[10] Using a schedule of tests that resembled Galton's and Cattell's, Jastrow tested thousands of individuals with the help of the army of graduate student volunteers he had assembled for the occasion.

Despite this flurry of interest in testing that he had in large part set off, Cattell was unable to devote much time to this work between 1891 and 1894. About the time he published his "Mental Tests and Measurements" paper, he began to commute to New York from Philadelphia to lecture a day or so a week at Columbia College. In 1891, Cattell moved to Columbia and so had to give up his program of testing at Pennsylvania. He devoted the next three years to establishing the psychological laboratory at Columbia, completing two major experimental studies[11] and planning the *Psychological Review*. He did find time to review books on anthropometry of interest to psychologists and to prepare a popular article on mental testing at the invitation of the editor of the *Educational Review*.[12]

In January, 1893, Cattell wrote to the President of Columbia "concerning the possibility of using tests of the senses and faculties in order to determine the condition and progress of students, the relative value of different courses of study, etc." Beneath his rationale for educational efficiency, he had to admit that he did not have specific tests designed for specific purposes; he compared his program of testing with the work of researchers in electricity 50 years earlier: "they believed that practical applications would be made, but knew that their first duty was to obtain more exact knowledge." He carried this argument to its Baconian conclusion: "The best way to obtain the knowledge we need is to make the tests, and determine from the results what value they have."[13]

It was not, however, until September 1894 that Cattell finally received authorization for the testing program he wanted. He was granted permission to examine every student on entering Columbia College and the Columbia School of Mines for the next four years, and in fact he tested students throughout the 1890s and into the twentieth century. Cattell, his junior colleague Livingston Farrand, and all their graduate students were deeply involved in the testing program, which soon began to attract national attention. The scope of their reputation may be appreciated from the diversity of their audiences. Cattell and Farrand described their work in papers presented at meetings of the New York

Schoolmasters' Association, The New York Academy of Sciences, the American Psychological Association, and the American Association for the Advancement of Science.[14] The day had yet to come when errors in the Scholastic Aptitude Test were front-page news, but the clipping service to which Cattell subscribed certainly kept busy.

The schedule of tests that Cattell prepared at Columbia was explicitly concerned with both physical and mental measurements. Cattell stressed again that he did not "wish to draw any definite conclusions from the results of the tests made so far" because they were "mere facts." However, like the positivist he was, he noted that "they are quantitative facts and the basis of science." He concluded with the pragmatic resolution that "there is no scientific problem more important than the study of the development of man, and no practical problem more urgent than the application of our knowledge to guide this development." The questions he hoped to answer were:

> To what extent are the several traits of body, of the senses and of mind interdependent? How far can we predict one thing from our knowledge of another? What can we learn from the tests of elementary traits regarding the higher intellectual and emotional life?[15]

Within a few years, Cattell's testing program provided answers to at least the last two of these questions, but these were to be extremely disappointing to him.

Perhaps the weakness of his testing program stemmed from the ad hoc manner in which Cattell adapted Wundt's reaction-time experiment into a testing instrument. The technical details are of interest in appreciating just what he was offering to society. The experimenter, now called a tester, sits at the left in front of a Hipp chronoscope, which measures time intervals accurately to milliseconds. . . . The subject or person being tested sits . . . in front of a Cattell gravity chronograph, with a Cattell lip key in his mouth. The experiment or test begins when the experimenter, or tester, pulls the string . . . to start the mechanism of the chronoscope and then closes the switch. . . . The closing of the switch completes an electric circuit that starts the hands of the chronoscope revolving and allows the screen of the chronograph to fall, thus revealing a card to the subject, on which is printed a stimulus. He then responds verbally in a previously agreed-upon way, thus opening the lip key and breaking the electric circuit, which stops the hands of the chronoscope. The experimenter, or tester, then reads the reaction time directly from the chronoscope dials.[16]

The transformation of an experimental situation into a testing one brought with it several major innovations. Wundt required that his subjects introspect while carrying out the reaction, while Cattell arranged his tests so that those being tested did not have to introspect at all. To be sure, Wundt's use of this technique did not resemble the systematic introspection developed by Edward B. Titchener, and both he and Cattell were concerned primarily with the reaction time itself as self-contained datum, rather than as an adjunct to a subject's mental observations. Titchener, in fact, complained in print when Jastrow adopted Cattell's approach to the reaction-time experiment at the Chicago World's Fair.[17] In any event, by adopting only the mechanics of Wundt's procedures while ignoring his broader concerns, Cattell was acting no differently with respect to his German teacher than did the American historians who studied with Ranke or the American chemists who studied with Liebig.[18] Paradoxically, what they lost by oversimplifying their European models the Americans gained back in social usefulness.

PROFESSIONAL JUDGMENTS ABOUT MENTAL TESTING

Interest in mental testing in the United States reached a peak in December 1895, when the

American Psychological Association, meeting under Cattell's presidency, appointed a committee "to consider the feasibility of cooperation among the various psychological laboratories in the collection of mental and physical characteristics." The committee took upon itself the task to "draw up a series of physical and mental tests which are regarded as especially appropriate for college students."[19] It consisted of Cattell, Jastrow, Sanford, and two other psychologists: James Mark Baldwin of Princeton University and Lightner Witmer of the University of Pennsylvania. Witmer had been Cattell's student at Pennsylvania and had earned a Ph.D. with Wundt, at Cattell's insistence. He then succeeded Cattell to the chair of psychology at Pennsylvania, and in many ways his approach to psychology was similar to Cattell's.[20] Baldwin, by contrast, was broadly educated in philosophy and, though he had experimented, was not convinced that the laboratory provided the best approach to an understanding of individuals. Instead, he worked on broader questions and in 1895 had published his *Mental Development in the Child and the Race*.[21] As such, he was the only member of the committee to come to the problem of testing without a commitment to an anthropometric approach to the study of human differences.

The committee presented a preliminary report in December 1896 and a detailed report in December 1897, and both accounts stressed mental anthropometry as a preferred method. Sanford, for example, wrote that he "approved the Columbia schedule as it stands." Jastrow did recognize that at least three categories of tests could be developed, namely, those of "(a) the senses, (b) the motor capacities, and (c) the more complex mental processes." But he argued that the last category should be ignored and that "it is better to select, even if in part arbitrarily, on part of a certain sense capacity" than a broader aspect of mental life.[22]

But the report of the committee was not unanimous. Baldwin presented a minority report in which he agreed that tests of the senses and motor abilities were important, but he argued that such essentially physiological tests had received too great a place in a schedule developed by a committee of the American Psychological Association. He asked for additional tests of the higher mental processes and discussed several possible approaches that could be used in testing memory. He concluded by arguing for "giving the tests as psychological a character as possible.[23]

Baldwin's criticisms of the anthropometric tests were the first, but not the last. Some of the critiques took the form of attacks on the assumptions made by the testers. Hugo Münsterberg, for example, director of the psychological laboratory at Harvard, wrote about the "danger" of believing that psychology could never help educators. More directly, he attacked Scripture's work and the scientific assumptions that underlay much of the test, claiming that "I have never measured a psychical fact, I have never heard that anyone has measured a psychical fact, I do not believe that in centuries to come a psychical fact will ever be measured."[24] To be sure, there were other reasons for Münsterberg's attack,[25] and it went beyond the criticisms that most psychologists would make of what the testers were doing. Furthermore, it was not directed at Scripture solely as a tester and, if Baldwin's criticisms were taken seriously, it was not clear that the testers were trying to measure psychological quantities. But to deny that psychological processes were in principle measureable was to undercut the positivistic assumption of Cattell that quantifiable data was the only type worthy of scientific attention.

Other critics were to compare Cattell's tests to others then being developed in France by Alfred Binet and his collaborators, which were explicitly concerned with the higher mental processes.[26] Cattell knew of Binet—who was a cooperating editor of the *Psychological Review*—and of his work. He even cited Binet's work in his major paper on anthropometric tests.

There he noted that he and his coauthor "fully appreciate the arguments urged by . . . M. M. Binet and Henri in favor of making tests of a strictly psychological character, "but he stressed that "measurements of the body and of the senses come as completely within our scope as the higher mental processes." They went even further, noting that "if we undertake to study attention or suggestibility we find it difficult to measure definitely a definite thing."[27] In other words, Cattell's stress on quantification led him to avoid investigating that which was difficult to quantify and to concentrate on what he could measure. His positivistic Baconianism therefore had him avoid what he knew was more important, or at least what his colleagues told him was more important, to focus on that which he could work with easily. He was like a man who lost a quarter one night in the middle of the block, but who looked for it at the corner, because that was where the light was better.

One psychologist who compared Cattell's work with Binet's was Stella Emily Sharp, a graduate student of Edward Bradford Titchener at Cornell. In 1898, she published her doctoral dissertation in which she compared the theories of "individual psychology"—the phrase is Binet's—of the American and French testers. In it, she stressed that "the American view is founded upon no explicit theory," a conclusion with which Cattell would have agreed entirely, and presented Binet's view as the belief that "the complex mental processes . . . are those the variations of which give most important information in regard to those mental characteristics whereby individuals are commonly classed." She did not describe her classification scheme but informally tried out some of Binet's suggested procedures on several of her graduate student classmates. For example, she asked them to remember sentences (rather than Cattell's series of letters) and to describe a picture that they had seen sometime before (rather than reproduce the length of a line seen earlier). Her results for some tests seemed to form "a basis of a general classification of the individuals," but she also found that "a lack of correspondences in the individual differences observed in the various tests was quite as noticeable as their presence." She therefore concluded that she had demonstrated the "relative independence of the particular mental activities under investigation" and hence the uselessness of Binet's procedures. But she went further. If Binet's tests did not give a good picture of the variations among individuals, she argued, then "mental anthropometry," which lacked any theoretical superstructure, could not yield results of any value either.[28]

Sharp's results are still quoted today,[29] but other events of the late 1890s had more to do with the failure of anthropometric mental testing. At least two were personal. At Yale, Scripture's personality had led him into conflicts with most of his colleagues and in the last years of the decade he was too busy fighting for his academic life to continue testing. Jastrow, meanwhile, had given up his struggle to publish the results of his testing program; this effort had led to conflicts with the officials at the Exposition and contributed to his nervous breakdown in the mid-1890s.[30] Scripture's and Jastrow's abandonment of anthropometric mental testing left Cattell and Witmer the only prominent psychologists working in the area, and Witmer's attention was soon focused on narrow applications of tests in his clinical psychology. Cattell was therefore left alone with his tests, which he continued throughout the decade, and by the late 1890s he was able to subject the data he collected to a new form of analysis. And this analysis, carried out by one of his graduate students, led most directly to the failure of his testing program.

Clark Wissler was an 1897 graduate of Indiana University who had come to Columbia as a graduate student primarily to work with Cattell on his anthropometric testing program. At Columbia, he was especially impressed by Franz Boas, the distinguished anthropologist whom Cattell had brought to the University, and soon grew interested in the anthropological implications of Cattell's work. He later had an important career as an anthropologist, but his studies with Boas in the late 1890s had a more immediate effect. Cattell was mathematically illiterate—his addition and subtraction were often inaccurate—but Boas, with a Ph.D. in physics, was mathematically sophisticated. Cattell knew that Galton had developed mathematical techniques to measure how closely two sets of data were related, or were correlated, and he made sure that Wissler learned these procedures from Boas. He then had Wissler apply these techniques to the data collected during his decade-long testing program at Columbia.[31]

Wissler calculated the correlation between the results of any one of Cattell's tests and the grades the students tested earned in their classes; and between the grades earned in any class and those earned in any other. His results showed that there was almost no correlation among the results of the various tests. For example, in calculating the correlation between the results of the reaction-time test and the marking-out-A's test,[32] Wissler found that 252 students took both tests, and he measured the correlation between the results of the two tests as −0.05. Consequently, despite the fact that the two tests might appear to be closely related "an individual with a quick reaction-time [was] no more likely to be quick in marking out the A's than one with a slow reaction-time." Furthermore, Wissler's analysis showed that there was no correlation between the results of any of Cattell's tests and the academic standing of any of the students tested. In contrast, Wissler found that academic performance in most subjects correlated very well with that in other subjects. Even "the gymnasium grade, which [was] based chiefly on faithfulness in attendance, correlated with the average class standing to about the same degree as one course with another."[33] In all, Wissler's analysis struck most psychologists as definitive and, with it, anthropometric mental testing, as a movement, died.

Cattell, of course, abandoned his career as an experimental psychologist, but he continued his activity within the American psychological community. For example, in the 1920s he founded The Psychological Corporation. From about 1900 on, he was better known as an editor and as an entrepreneur of science than he was as a psychologist. In many ways, his later career is more interesting than his earlier one, though as his experience with The Psychological Corporation shows, it may not have been any more successful.[34]

THE INFLUENCE OF THE MENTAL TESTING MOVEMENT

But despite the death of the anthropometric movement as such, anthropometric testing itself—in many ways a product of nineteenth-century philosophy of science—continued into the first years of the twentieth century. America at that time was engaged in what has been called "The Search for Order."[35] Millions of new immigrants—most with cultural backgrounds totally different from those of the early nineteenth century—were flocking to the New World. The rapid industrialization of the period and the rise of the new professions placed a heavy premium on a standardized work style and on the development of formalized criteria for judging applicants for universities and jobs. Many citizens looked to education as an ordering, and Americanizing, process, and compulsory education laws were enacted by 1900. The rising concern for the welfare, and evil influence, of the delinquent, dependent, and defective classes led to the rapid growth of institutions to serve their needs and to protect the public from them.[36]

In such an atmosphere of social concern, mental testing was seen to be too valuable a tool to be completely abandoned, even if anthropometric mental testing was shown to have extreme limitations. On one level, specialized anthropometric tests, designed for specialized uses, were found to be useful. Even one of Titchener's students, who was studying the sense of hearing and techniques for evaluating it, had to admit that they served "practical purposes" when designed carefully. In many ways, the clinical psychology developed by Witmer in the late 1890s illustrates the point perfectly. After all, in diagnosing what are today called sensory disorders and learning disabilities, Witmer applied the tests developed by Cattell and others in particularly appropriate ways. Similarly, Scripture's best-known student—Carl E. Seashore—merely developed a set of specialized tests relating to the sense of hearing when he constructed his widely used tests of musical talent.[37] In these ways anthropometric mental tests, especially designed to focus on specific sensory problems, played (and continue to play) a major role in bringing order to American society and, especially to American education.

On another level, however, the continued use of anthropometric tests in the early twentieth century was much less successful. Though testing worked when applied narrowly, it yielded essentially useless results when the testers set larger goals. One can readily see eugenical implications in Cattell's goals for his early tests. Similarly, Jastrow believed that his tests demonstrated the proper spheres of activity for each of the sexes. Others used anthropometric tests to justify, and argue for, their own ideas as to the proper relations between the races.[38] More prosaically, though still on a large scale, Frank Parsons in the early 1900s established a vocational guidance bureau in Boston with a goal of helping young men find the profession for which they were best suited. Here he used tests of the "delicacy of touch, nerve, sight and hearing reactions, association time, etc." And as late as 1908, Parsons argued that reaction-time tests had a great value for judging an "individual's probable aptitudes and capacities."[39]

More important for psychology was the work of Henry H. Goddard, a Clark Ph.D. and student of G. Stanley Hall. In 1906, after several years of teaching psychology at a small state college, he became director of the psychological laboratory at the Vineland, New Jersey, Training School for the Feeble-Minded. There he worked with children who would today be called retarded or developmentally disabled. To obtain some estimate of the children's abilities, he used various anthropometric techniques—more than five years after Wissler's analysis was published. Although he did not find this approach very helpful, he continued to employ it for lack of another. Finally, in the last years of the decade, he traveled to France and there discovered in detail the full range of the work of Binet and his colleagues. When he brought this knowledge back to America, his English version of Binet's tests finally supplanted anthropometric mental testing, at least outside its narrower applications.[40] Thereby, Goddard introduced a new testing movement, which has done much to shape modern America. But that is another story . . .

NOTES

(1) James McKeen Cattell, "Mental Tests and Measurements," *Mind 15* (1890):373–81.

(2) Ibid., pp. 373, 379–81.

(3) William T. Porter, "The Physical Basis of Precocity and Dullness," *Transactions of the Academy of Science of St. Louis* 6 (1893): 161–81; Franz Boas, "On Dr. William Townsend Porter's Investigation of the Growth of School Children of St. Louis," *Science* 1 (1895):225–30.

(4) For example, Arthur MacDonald, "Mental Ability in Relation to Head Circumference, Cephalic Index, Sociological Conditions, Sex, Age, and Nationality," unpublished paper, Arthur MacDonald files, U.S. Office of Education papers, U.S. National Archives, Washington, D.C. See also Michael M. Sokal, "Anthropometric Mental Testing in Nineteenth-Century America," James Allen Young, "Height, Weight, and Health: Anthropometric Study of Human Growth in Nineteenth-Century American Medicine," *Bulletin of the History of Medicine* 53 (1979): 214–43; Elizabeth Lomax, "Late Nineteenth-Century American Growth Studies: Objectives, Methods and Outcomes," unpublished paper, Fifteenth International Congress of the History of Science, Edinburgh, Scotland, August 1977.

(5) Sokal, M. M., "Anthropometric Mental Testing in Nineteenth-Century America," unpublished Sigma Xi national, Lecture, 1979–81; Harry K. Wolfe, "Simple Observations and Experiments: Mental Tests and Their Purposes," *NorthWestern Journal of Education* 7 (1896): 36–37.

(6) Edward W. Scripture, "Tests of Mental Ability as Exhibited in Fencing," *Studies from the Yale Psychological Laboratory* 2 (1894):114–19; Michael M. Sokal, "The Psychological Career of Edward Wheeler Scripture," *Historiography of Modern Psychology: Aims, Resources, Approaches,* ed. Josef Brožek and Ludwig J. Pongratz (Toronto: C. J. Hogrefe, 1980), pp. 255–78.

(7) For example, Joseph Jastrow to Galton, August 19, 1887, Galton papers; Joseph Jastrow, "Some Anthropometric and Psychologic Tests on College Students; A Preliminary Survey," *American Journal of Psychology* 4 (1892): 420–28.

(8) Joseph Jastrow, "A Study in Mental Statistics," *New Review* 5 (1891):559–68; Mary Whiton Calkins, "Community of Ideas of Men and Women," *Psychological Review* 3 (1896):426–30. Cf. Laurel Furumoto, "Mary Whiton Calkins (1863–1930)," *Psychology of Women Quarterly* 5 (1980):55–68.

(9) World's Columbian Exposition, *Official Catalogue, Department M Ethnology: Archaeology, Physical Anthropology, History, Natural History, Isolated and Collective Exhibits* (Chicago: W. B. Conkey, 1893).

(10) Jastrow to Galton, July 17, 1892. Galton papers; Michael M. Sokal (ed.), "APA's First Publication: Proceedings of the American Psychological Association, 1892–1893," *American Psychologist 28* (1973):277–92.

(11) James McKeen Cattell and George S. Fullerton, *On the Perception of Small Differences, with Special Reference to the Extent, Force and Time of Movement,* Publications of the University of Pennsylvania, Philosophical Series, no. 2 (Philadelphia: University of Pennsylvania, 1892): James McKeen Cattell and Charles S. Dolley, "On Reaction-Times and the Velocity of the Nervous Impulse," *Proceedings of the National Academy of Sciences 7* (1896):393–415.

(12) James McKeen Cattell, "Psychological Literature: Anthropometry," *Psychological Review* 2 (1895):510–11; James McKeen Cattell, "Tests of the Senses and Faculties," *Education Review* 5 (1893):257–65.

(13) Cattell to Seth Low, January 30, 1893, James McKeen Cattell collection, Columbia University Archives, New York, NY

(14) Sokal, "Anthropometric Mental Testing."

(15) James McKeen Cattell and Livingston Farrand, "Physical and Mental Measurements of the Students of Columbia University," *Psychological Review* 3 (1896):618–48.

(16) Michael M. Sokal, Audrey B. Davis, and Uta C. Merzbach, "Laboratory Instruments in the History of Psychology," *Journal of the History of the Behavioral Sciences* 12 (1976):59–64.

(17) Edward B. Titchener, "Anthropometry and Experimental Psychology," *Philosophical Review 2* (1893):187–92.

(18) George G. Iggers, "The Image of Ranke in American and German Historical Thought," *History and Theory* 2 (1962):17–33; Margaret W. Rossiter, *The Emergence of Agricultural Science: Justus Liebig and the Americans, 1840–1880* (New Haven, Conn.: Yale University Press, 1975). Cf. Sokal, "Foreign Study before Fulbright: American Students at European Universities in the Nineteenth Century," unpublished Sigma Xi National Lecture, 1979–81.

(19) Edmund C. Sanford, "The Philadelphia Meeting of the American Psychological Association" *Science* 3 (1896):119–21.

(20) John O'Donnell, "The Clinical Psychology of Lightner Witmer: A Case Study of Institutional Innovation and Intellectual Change," *Journal of the History of the Behavioral Sciences* 15 (1979):3–17.

(21) James Mark Baldwin, *Mental Development in the Child and the Race: Methods and Processes* (New York: Macmillan, 1895).

(22) Sanford to Baldwin, December 7, 1896, Cattell papers; James Mark Baldwin, James McKeen Cattell, and Joseph Jastrow, "Physical and

Mental Tests," *Psychological Review 5* (1898): 172–79.

(23) Baldwin et al., "Physical and Mental Tests."

(24) Hugo Münsterberg, "The Danger from Experimental Psychology," *Atlantic Monthly* 81 (1898):159–67.

(25) Matthew Hale, Jr., *Human Science and Social Order: Hugo Münsterberg and the Origins of Applied Psychology* (Philadelphia: Temple University Press, 1980); Sokal, "The Psychological Career of Edward Wheeler Scripture."

(26) Alfred Binet and Victor Henri, "La psychologie individuelle," *L'Annee psychologique* 2 (1895): 411–15.

(27) Cattell and Farrand, "Physical and Mental Measurements."

(28) Stella Emily Sharp, "Individual Psychology: A Study in Psychological Method," *American Journal of Psychology* 10 (1898):329–91.

(29) See Richard J. Herrnstein and Edwin G. Boring (ed.), *A Source Book in the History of Psychology* (Cambridge: Harvard University Press, 1965), pp. 438–42.

(30) Sokal, "The Psychological Career of Edward Wheeler Scripture," Joseph Jastrow, autobiography, *A History of Psychology in Autobiography,* vol. 1, edited by Carl Murchison (Worcester: Clark University Press, 1930), pp. 135–62. Cf. Jastrow, correspondence with Frederic Ward Putnam, 1891–1900, Frederic Ward Putnam papers, Harvard University Archives, Cambridge, Massachusetts.

(31) Clark Wissler, "The Contribution of James McKeen Cattell to American Anthropology," *Science* 99 (1944):232–33; James McKeen Cattell, "Memorandum for Miss Helen M. Walker," undated note, Cattell papers.

(32) Individuals were presented with a ten-by-ten array of one hundred letters in which were scattered ten A's. The time required to strike out all A's was measured.

(33) Clark Wissler, "The Correlation of Mental and Physical Tests," *Psychological Review Monograph Supplements 3,* no. 6 (1901).

(34) Sokal, M. M. "The Origins of the Psychological Corporation." *Journal of the History of the Behavioral Science 17* (1981):54–67.

(35) Robert H. Wiebe, *The Search for Order, 1877–1920* (New York: Hill and Wang, 1967).

(36) This paragraph summarizes many years of scholarship in the social history of American ideas. See Wiebe, *The Search for Order;* Henrika Kuklick, "The Organization of Social Science in the United States," *American Quarterly* 28 (1976):124–41; Burton J. Bledstein, *The Culture of Professionalism: The Middle Class and the Development of Higher Education in America* (New York: Norton, 1978).

(37) Benjamin Richard Andrews, "Auditory Tests," *American Journal of Psychology* 15 (1904): 14–56; O'Donnell, "The Clinical Psychology of Lightner Witmer," Audrey B. Davis and Uta C. Merzbach, *Early Auditory Studies: Activities in the Psychology Laboratories of American Universities,* Smithsonian Studies in History and Technology, no. 31 (Washington: Smithsonian Institute Press, 1975).

(38) R. Meade Bache, "Reaction Time with Reference to Race," *Psychological Review* 2 (1895): 475–86; Anna Tolman Smith, "A Study of Race Psychology," *Popular Science Monthly* 50 (1896): 354–60; Arthur MacDonald, "Colored Children—A Psycho-Physical Study," *Journal of the American Medical Association* 32 (1899): 1140–44. Cf. Charles S. Johnson and Horace M. Bond, "The Investigation of Racial Difference Prior to 1910," *Journal of Negro History* 3 (1934): 328–39.

(39) Frank Parson, "The Vocation Bureau: First Report to Executive Committee and Trustees, May 1st, 1908," as reprinted in John M. Brewer, *History of Vocational Guidance: Origins and Early Development* (New York: Harper and Brothers, 1942), pp. 303–8.

(40) Henry H. Goddard, *The Research Department: What It Is, What It Is Doing, What It Hopes to Do* (Vineland, New Jersey: The Training School 1914).

CHAPTER 9

FUNCTIONALISM

Previous chapters made frequent references to functionalism, first concerning its opposition to Titchener's structuralism, second with regard to its debt to the writings of Darwin and Galton, and third in terms of the conceptual and methodological base provided by early American psychologists—James, Hall, and Cattell. This chapter will describe this school of psychology as it became identified with the University of Chicago.

In her classic book, *Seven Psychologies,* Edna Heidbreder (1933) wrote, "In functionalism, American psychology made its first definite and organized stand against domination by the Titchenerian, or Wundtian, school" (p. 201). A similar point is made by D. P. Schultz and S. E. Schultz (1996), who state that "functionalism [was] the first uniquely American system of psychology" (p. 124). To call it "uniquely American" is not to deny the influence from England but to say that, as a system of psychology, it took root in American soil. In truth, functionalism was never a "school," at least not in the sense that that label could be applied to a much more systematized position like structuralism (see Krantz, 1969; O'Donnell, 1985). There was no single leader, as Titchener was for his school, nor was there a common conceptual and methodological base that defined functionalism (Hilgard, 1987). Nevertheless, functionalism, or more accurately, several functionalisms, characterized much of American psychology in the early part of the twentieth century. Although it lacked the focus of structuralism, its impact was much more substantial.

As noted in Chapter 6, functionalism arose in opposition to Titchener's structuralism. Indeed, Titchener (1898) gave the school its name in an article he wrote that contrasted his approach to psychology with what he saw as an emerging approach that emphasized the functions of consciousness. Titchener did not deny the importance of the questions the functionalists were asking, but he did believe they were premature. For Titchener, function could not be understood without a complete understanding of structure. Drawing on his training in the field of biology, Titchener argued that the work on anatomy had to precede physiology. The initial step was to dissect the organism (consciousness), identifying the various structures (mental elements); then, once the structures were known, the next appropriate step was to investigate their functions (the mental operations of consciousness). Titchener warned his psychological colleagues that they must guard against being seduced by the attractiveness of functional questions and adhere to what was, for him, the natural order of science and the only proper way for scientific psychology to proceed.

It was against those restrictions and absolute certainty that the functionalists rebelled. James Rowland Angell (1869–1949), one of the most influential of the functionalists, used his presidential address before the annual meeting of the American Psychological Association to deal with those issues. According to Angell (1907), functionalism "gains its vitality primarily perhaps as a protest against the exclusive excellence of another starting point for the study of the mind." (p. 61). Angell was not denying the validity of the structural approach, only objecting to its claim for exclusivity.

The functionalists were happy to coexist with their structural colleagues, although the reverse cannot be said to be true. The controversy fueled many psychological conversations around the turn of the century, but by 1905 functionalism had become the dominant view in American psychology (Leahey, 1992). Its formal beginning is often traced to a decade earlier, when John Dewey (1859–1952) published his classic article on the *reflex arc concept* (Dewey, 1896). Dewey had studied with G. Stanley Hall at Johns Hopkins, where he earned his doctoral degree in 1884. Two years later, he published a textbook on psychology, but it was not a treatise on functionalist psychology—those ideas were yet to materialize in Dewey's thought. By the time he arrived at the University of Chicago in 1894, however, he was convinced of the artificiality of the atomistic approach to the study of consciousness. Studies of reflexive behavior involved analysis of the reflex into its component elements, namely, *stimulus* (sensation) and *response* (movement). Dewey opposed such reductionism, arguing that the *reflex arc* was a continuous whole that must be studied in that form. Using the example of a child seeing a candle flame and then reaching for it, he noted that the structuralist approach was to view the sensation (seeing) as the initial part of the act and the movement (reaching) as the second part of the act. Dewey argued that the act was not divisible and, indeed, that it was not clear that the second part followed from the first. For example, head movements and eye movements are an integral part of the looking process. Further, the interplay between sensory functioning and motor processes is critical to the reaching response so that coordinated movements can be made using visual and kinesthetic feedback. So the two interact, rather than one following from the other. In this way they form a conscious event that must be studied as the entity (whole) that it is. Acts, such as the child reaching for a flame, occur in a functional context and must be studied in that framework.

The reflex arc paper was Dewey's last important contribution to psychology; thereafter he turned most of his energies to his involvement in what became known as the progressive education movement. His successor in psychology at the University of Chicago was James Rowland Angell, who had been his student as an undergraduate. Angell did graduate work with William James and went to Germany for his doctorate in psychology. Although he completed all of his course work, the degree was never awarded because he never finished rewriting his dissertation into better German, as his doctoral committee had requested.

Under Angell's administration of psychology at Chicago, functionalism became a more formalized position. The laboratory there was the site of an active research program whose studies defined functional psychology. Much of this research appeared in Angell's textbook, *Psychology,* (1904) the first textbook written from a functionalist perspective, although it was not a statement of the functionalist position. He made that philosophical statement in his APA presidential address, mentioned earlier.

The functionalist research at Chicago was much more directed to learning as an area of investigation, in contrast to the work on sensation-perception that was characteristic of the structuralists. The functional psychologists certainly researched perceptual questions (for example, Harvey Carr's 1935 book on space perception), but the learning investigations were more prominent in their laboratories. Physiological studies were more prevalent, an emphasis that had come from Angell himself, and animal studies at Chicago became commonplace (for example, the work of Carr, John B. Watson, and Walter Hunter) because of the methodological eclecticism.

The functionalists used the method of introspection, but not in the microanalytic way it was employed by the structuralists. In addition to that method and the physiological techniques, they used mental tests, questionnaires, and experimental techniques in which stimulus–response relationships were studied. Thus, they broadened the goals of psychology, added greatly to the list of accepted methodologies, and significantly expanded the domain of psychological inquiry to include animal studies, studies on children, and even studies on the mentally ill.

THE READINGS

The first selection in this chapter is the APA presidential address that Angell delivered in 1906 (published in 1907). It is considered to have spelled out the philosophical base for functional psychology in the way that Titchener's (1898) article had done for structuralism. In his article, Angell states that at the time of that writing, functional psychology was "little more than a point of view, a program, an ambition" (p. 61). But he was being much too modest. The program begun by Dewey at Chicago, and continued by Angell, had already made functionalism into the dominant theme of American psychology.

The second selection is by Alfred C. Raphelson, a historian of psychology at the University of Michigan at Flint. It is an intellectual history of John Dewey that traces the evolution of Dewey's ideas in the influence of George S. Morris, Charles S. Peirce, and G. Stanley Hall. It also presents an interesting case for why the functionalist movement came to fruition at the University of Chicago.

The third selection, by psychologist Stephanie A. Shields, deals with the historical roots of the psychology of women in the ideas of Darwin and those psychologists involved in functionalism. With the Shields's selection and the article by Lesley A. Diehl in the previous chapter, the reader should get a detailed view of the history of psychology's concern with sex differences, a topic typically omitted from most history of psychology textbooks.

In summary, the three selections in this chapter trace the intellectual development of Dewey that gave rise to the founding of the functionalist school at the University of Chicago; show how Angell, at the height of functionalism, described the functional approach; and illustrate psychology's views on women as rooted in Darwinian and functionalist thought.

REFERENCES

Angell, J. R. (1904). *Psychology*. New York: Henry Holt.

Angell, J. R. (1907). The province of functional psychology. *Psychological Review, 14,* 61–91.

Carr, H. A. (1935). *An introduction to space perception*. New York: Longmans, Green.

Dewey, J. (1896). The reflex arc concept in psychology. *Psychological Review, 3,* 357–370.

Heidbreder, E. (1933). *Seven psychologies*. New York: Appleton-Century-Crofts.

Hilgard, E. R. (1987). *Psychology in America: A historical survey*. San Diego: Harcourt, Brace, Jovanovich.

Krantz, D. L. (Ed.) (1969). *Schools of psychology: A symposium*. New York: Appleton-Century-Crofts.

Leahey, T. H. (1992). *A history of psychology: Main currents in psychological thought* (3rd ed.). Englewood Cliffs, NJ: Prentice-Hall.

O'Donnell, J. M. (1985). *The origins of behaviorism: American psychology, 1870–1920*. New York: New York University Press.

Schultz, D. P. & Schultz, S. E. (1996). *A history of modern psychology* (6th ed.). San Diego: Harcourt, Brace.

Titchener, E. B. (1898). The postulates of a structural psychology. *Philosophical Review, 7,* 449–465.

The Province of Functional Psychology

James Rowland Angell

Functional psychology is at the present moment little more than a point of view, a program, an ambition. It gains its vitality primarily perhaps as a protest against the exclusive excellence of another starting point for the study of the mind, and it enjoys for the time being at least the peculiar vigor which commonly attaches to Protestantism of any sort in its early stages before it has become respectable and orthodox. The time seems ripe to attempt a somewhat more precise characterization of the field of functional psychology than has as yet been offered. What we seek is not the arid and merely verbal definition which to many of us is so justly anathema, but rather an informing appreciation of the motives and ideals which animate the psychologist who pursues this path. His status in the eye of the psychological public is unnecessarily precarious. The conceptions of his purposes prevalent in non-functionalist circles range from positive and dogmatic misapprehension, through frank mystification and suspicion up to moderate comprehension. Nor is this fact an expression of anything peculiarly abstruse and recondite in his intentions. It is due in part to his own ill-defined plans, in part to his failure to explain lucidly exactly what he is about. Moreover, he is fairly numerous and it is not certain that in all important particulars he and his confrères are at one in their beliefs. The considerations which are herewith offered suffer inevitably from this personal limitation. No psychological council of Trent has as yet pronounced upon the true faith. But in spite of probable failure it seems worth while to hazard an attempt at delineating the scope of functionalist principles. I formally renounce any intention to strike out new plans; I am engaged in what is meant as a dispassionate summary of actual conditions.

Whatever else it may be, functional psychology is nothing wholly new. In certain of its phases it is plainly discernible in the psychology of Aristotle and in its more modern garb it has been increasingly in evidence since Spencer wrote his *Psychology* and Darwin his *Origin of Species*. Indeed, as we shall soon see, its crucial problems are inevitably incidental to any serious attempt at understanding mental life. All that is peculiar to its present circumstances is a higher degree of self-consciousness than it possessed before, a more articulate and persistent purpose to organize its vague intentions into tangible methods and principles.

A survey of contemporary psychological writing indicates, as was intimated in the preceding paragraph, that the task of functional psychology is interpreted in several different ways. Moreover, it seems to be possible to advocate one or more of these conceptions while cherishing abhorrence for the others. I distinguish three principal forms of the functional problem with sundry subordinate variants. It will contribute to the clarification of the general situation to dwell upon these for a moment, after which I propose to maintain that they are substantially but modifications of a single problem.

I

There is to be mentioned first the notion which derives most immediately from contrast with the ideals and purposes of structural psychology so-called. This involves the identification of functional psychology with the effort to discern and portray the typical *operations* of consciousness under actual life conditions, as over against the attempt to analyze and describe its elementary

From Angell, J. R. (1907). The province of functional psychology. *Psychological Review, 14,* 61–91.

and complex *contents*. The structural psychology of sensation, *e.g.*, undertakes to determine the number and character of the various unanalyzable sensory materials, such as the varieties of color, tone, taste, etc. The functional psychology of sensation would on the other hand find its appropriate sphere of interest in the determination of the character of the various sense activities as differing in their *modus operandi* from one another and from other mental processes such as judging, conceiving, willing and the like.

In this its older and more pervasive form functional psychology has until very recent times had no independent existence. No more has structural psychology for that matter. It is only lately that any motive for the differentiation of the two has existed and structural psychology—granting its claims and pretensions of which more anon—is the first, be it said, to isolate itself. But in so far as functional psychology is synonymous with descriptions and theories of mental action as distinct from the materials of mental constitution, so far it is everywhere conspicuous in psychological literature from the earliest times down.

When the structural psychologists define their field as that of mental *process,* they really preëmpt under a fictitious name the field of function, so that I should be disposed to allege fearlessly and with a clear conscience that a large part of the doctrine of psychologists of nominally structural proclivities is in point of fact precisely what I mean by one essential part of functional psychology, *i.e.,* an account of psychical operations. Certain of the official exponents of structuralism explicitly lay claim to this as their field and do so with a flourish of scientific rectitude. There is therefore after all a small but nutritious core of agreement in the structure-function apple of discord. For this reason, as well as because I consider extremely useful the analysis of mental life into its elementary forms, I regard much of the actual work of my structuralist friends with highest respect and confidence. I feel, however, that when they use the term structural as opposed to the term functional to designate their scientific creed they often come perilously near to using the enemy's colors.

Substantially identical with this first conception of functional psychology, but phrasing itself somewhat differently, is the view which regards the functional problem as concerned with discovering how and why conscious processes are what they are, instead of dwelling as the structuralist is supposed to do upon the problem of determining the irreducible elements of consciousness and their characteristic modes of combination. I have elsewhere defended the view that however it may be in other sciences dealing with life phenomena, in psychology at least the answer to the question 'what' implicates the answer to the questions 'how' and 'why.'

Stated briefly the ground on which this position rests is as follows: In so far as you attempt to analyze any particular state of consciousness you find that the mental elements presented to your notice are dependent upon the particular exigencies and conditions which call them forth. Not only does the affective coloring of such a psychical moment depend upon one's temporary condition, mood and aims, but the very sensations themselves are determined in their qualitative texture by the totality of circumstances subjective and objective within which they arise. You cannot get a fixed and definite color sensation for example, without keeping perfectly constant the external and internal conditions in which it appears. The particular sense quality is in short functionally determined by the necessities of the existing situation which it emerges to meet. If you inquire then deeply enough what particular sensation you have in a given case, you always find it necessary to take account of the manner in which, and the reasons why, it was experienced at all. You may of course, if you will, abstract from these considerations, but in so far as you do so, your analysis and description is manifestly partial and incomplete. Moreover, even when you do so abstract and attempt to describe certain isolable sense qualities, your descriptions are of necessity couched in terms not of the experienced quality itself, but in terms of the conditions which produced it, in terms of some other quality with which it is compared, or in terms of some more overt act to which the sense stimulation led. That is to say, the very description itself is functionalistic and must be so. The truth of this assertion can be illustrated and tested by appeal to any situation in which one is trying to reduce sensory complexes, *e.g.*, colors or sounds, to their rudimentary components.

II

A broader outlook and one more frequently characteristic of contemporary writers meets us in the next conception of the task of functional psychology. This conception is in part a reflex of the prevailing interest in the larger formulae of biology and particularly the evolutionary hypotheses within whose majestic sweep is nowadays included the history of the whole stellar universe; in part it echoes the same philosophical call to new life which has been heard as pragmatism, as humanism, even as functionalism itself. I should not wish to commit either party by asserting that functional psychology and pragmatism are ultimately one. Indeed, as a psychologist I should hesitate to bring down on myself the avalanche of metaphysical invective which has been loosened by pragmatic writers. To be sure pragmatism has slain its thousands, but I should cherish scepticism as to whether functional psychology would the more speedily slay its tens of thousands by announcing an offensive and defensive alliance with pragmatism. In any case I only hold that the two movements spring from similar logical motivation and rely for their vitality and propagation upon forces closely germane to one another.

The functional psychologist then in his modern attire is interested not alone in the operations of mental process considered merely of and by and for itself, but also and more vigorously in mental activity as part of a larger stream of biological forces which are daily and hourly at work before our eyes and which are constitutive of the most important and most absorbing part of our world. The psychologist of this stripe is wont to take his cue from the basal conception of the evolutionary movement, *i.e.*, that for the most part organic structures and functions possess their present characteristics by virtue of the efficiency with which they fit into the extant conditions of life broadly designated the environment. With this conception in mind he proceeds to attempt some understanding of the manner in which the psychical contributes to the furtherance of the sum total of organic activities, not alone the psychical in its entirety, but especially the psychical in its particularities—mind as judging, mind as feeling, etc.

This is the point of view which instantly brings the psychologist cheek by jowl with the general biologist. It is the presupposition of every philosophy save that of outright ontological materialism that mind plays the stellar rôle in all the environmental adaptations of animals which possess it. But this persuasion has generally occupied the position of an innocuous truism or at best a jejune postulate, rather than that of a problem requiring, or permitting, serious scientific treatment. At all events, this was formerly true.

It is not unnatural perhaps that the frequent disposition of the functional psychologist to sigh after the flesh-pots of biology should kindle the fire of those consecrated to the cause of a pure psychology and philosophy freed from the contaminating influence of natural science. As a matter of fact, alarms have been repeatedly sounded and the faithful called to subdue mutiny. But the purpose of the functional psychologist has never been, so far as I am aware, to scuttle the psychological craft for the benefit of biology. Quite the contrary. Psychology is still for a time at least to steer her own untroubled course. She is at most borrowing a well-tested compass which biology is willing to lend and she hopes by its aid to make her ports more speedily and more surely. If in use it prove treacherous and unreliable, it will of course go overboard.

This broad biological ideal of functional psychology of which we have been speaking may be phrased with a slight shift to emphasis by connecting it with the problem of discovering the fundamental utilities of consciousness. If mental process is of real value to its possessor in the life and world which we know, it must perforce be by virtue of something which it does that otherwise is not accomplished. Now life and world are complex and it seems altogether improbable that consciousness should express its utility in one and only one way. As a matter of fact, every surface indication points in the other direction. It may be possible merely as a matter of expression to speak of mind as in general contributing to organic adjustment to environment. But the actual contributions will take place in many ways and by multitudinous varieties of conscious process. The functionalist's problem then is to determine if possible the great types of these processes in so far as the utilities which they present lend themselves to classification.

The search after the various utilitarian aspects of mental process is at once suggestive and disappointing. It is on the one hand illuminating by virtue of the strong relief into which it throws the fundamental resemblances of processes often unduly severed in psychological analysis. Memory and imagination, for example, are often treated in a way designed to emphasize their divergences almost to the exclusion of their functional similarities. They are of course functionally but variants on a single and basal type of control. An austere structuralism in particular is inevitably disposed to magnify differences and in consequence under its hands mental life tends to fall apart; and when put together again it generally seems to have lost something of its verve and vivacity. It appears stiff and rigid and corpse-like. It lacks the vital spark. Functionalism tends just as inevitably to bring mental phenomena together, to show them focalized in actual vital service. The professional psychologist, calloused by long apprenticeship, may not feel this distinction to be scientifically important. But to the young student the functionalistic stress upon community of service is of immense value in clarifying the intricacies of mental organization. On the other hand the search of which we were speaking is disappointing perhaps in the paucity of the basic modes in which these conscious utilities are realized.

III

The third conception which I distinguish is often in practice merged with the second, but it involves stress upon a problem logically prior perhaps to the problem raised there and so warrants separate mention. Functional psychology, it is often alleged, is in reality a form of psychophysics. To be sure, its aims and ideals are not explicitly quantitative in the manner characteristic of that science as commonly understood. But it finds its major interest in determining the relations to one another of the physical and mental portions of the organism.

It is undoubtedly true that many of those who write under functional prepossessions are wont to introduce frequent references to the physiological processes which accompany or condition mental life. Moreover, certain followers of this faith are prone to declare forthwith that psychology is simply a branch of biology and that we are in consequence entitled, if not indeed obliged, to make use where possible of biological materials. But without committing ourselves to so extreme a position as this, a mere glance at one familiar region of psychological procedure will disclose the leanings of psychology in this direction.

The psychology of volition affords an excellent illustration of the necessity with which descriptions of mental process eventuate in physiological or biological considerations. If one take the conventional analysis of a voluntary act drawn from some one or other of the experiences of adult life, the descriptions offered generally portray ideational activities of an anticipatory and deliberative character which serve to initiate immediately or remotely certain relevant expressive movements. Without the execution of the movements the ideational performances would be as futile as the tinkling cymbals of Scripture. To be sure, many of our psychologists protest themselves wholly unable to suggest why or how such muscular movements are brought to pass. But the fact of their occurrence or of their fundamental import for any theory of mental life in which consciousness is other than an epiphenomenon, is not questioned.

Moreover, if one considers the usual accounts of the ontogenesis of human volitional acts one is again confronted with intrinsically physiological data in which reflexes, automatic and instinctive acts, are much in evidence. Whatever the possibilities, then, of an expurgated edition of the psychology of volition from which should be blotted out all reference to contaminating physiological factors, the actual practice of our representative psychologists is quite otherwise, and upon their showing volition cannot be understood either as regards its origin or its outcome without constant and overt reference to these factors. It would be a labor of supererrogation to go on and make clear the same doctrine as it applies to the psychology of the more recondite of the cognitive processes; so intimate is the relation between cognition and volition in modern psychological theory that we may well stand excused from carrying out in detail the obvious inferences from the situation we have just described.

Now if someone could but devise a method for handling the mind-body relationships which would not when published immediately create cyclonic disturbances in the philosophical atmosphere, it seems improbable that this disposition of the functional psychologist to inject physiology into his cosmos would cause comment and much less criticism. But even parallelism, that most insipid, pale and passionless of all the inventions begotten by the mind of man to accomplish this end, has largely failed of its pacific purpose. It is no wonder, therefore, that the more rugged creeds with positive programs to offer and a stock of red corpuscles to invest in their propagation should also have failed of universal favor.

This disposition to go over into the physiological for certain portions of psychological doctrine is represented in an interesting way by the frequent tendency of structural psychologists to find explanation in psychology substantially equivalent to physiological explanation. Professor Titchener's recent work on *Quantitative Psychology* represents this position very frankly. It is cited here with no intent to comment disparagingly upon the consistency of the structuralist position, but simply to indicate the wide-spread feeling of necessity at certain stages of psychological development for resort to physiological considerations.

Such a functional psychology as I have been presenting would be entirely reconcilable with Miss Calkins' 'psychology of selves' (so ably set forth by her in her presidential address last year) were it not for her extreme scientific conservatism in refusing to allow the self to have a body, save as a kind of conventional biological ornament. The real psychological self, as I understand her, is pure disembodied spirit—an admirable thing of good religious and philosophic ancestry, but surely not the thing with which we actually get through this vale of tears and not a thing, before which psychology is under any obligation to kowtow.

It is not clear that the functional psychologist because of his disposition to magnify the significance in practice of the mind-body relationships is thereby committed to any special theory of the character of these relationships, save as was said a moment since, that negatively he must seemingly of necessity set his face against any epiphenomenalist view. He might conceivably be an interactionist, or a parallelist or even an advocate of some wholly outworn creed. As a matter of fact certain of our most ardent functionalists not only cherish highly definite articles of faith as regards this issue, they would even go so far as to test functional orthodoxy by the acceptance of these tenets. This is to them the most momentous part of their functionalism, their holy of holies. It would display needless temerity to attempt within the limitations of this occasion a formulation of doctrine wholly acceptable to all concerned. But I shall venture a brief reference to such doctrine in the effort to bring out certain of its essentials.

The position to which I refer regards the mind-body relation as capable of treatment in psychology as a methodological distinction rather than a metaphysically existential one. Certain of its expounders arrive at their view by means of an analysis of the genetic conditions under which the mind-body differentiation first makes itself felt in the experience of the individual. This procedure clearly involves a direct frontal attack on the problem.

Others attain the position by flank movement, emphasizing to begin with the insoluble contradictions with which one is met when the distinction is treated as resting on existential differences in the primordial elements of the cosmos. Both methods of approach lead to the same goal, however, *i.e.*, the conviction that the distinction has no existence on the genetically lower and more naif stages of experience. It only comes to light on a relatively reflective level and it must then be treated as instrumental if one would avoid paralogisms, antinomies and a host of other metaphysical nightmares. Moreover, in dealing with psychological problems this view entitles one to reject as at least temporarily irrelevant the question whether mind *causes* changes in neural action and conversely. The previous question is raised by defenders of this type of doctrine if one insists on having such a query answered. They invite you to trace the lineage of your idea of causality, insisting that such a searching of one's intellectual reins will always disclose the inappropriateness of the inquiry as formulated above. They urge further that the profitable and significant thing is to seek for a more exact appreciation of the precise conditions under which consciousness is in evidence and the conditions under which it retires in favor of the more exclusively physiological. Such knowledge so far as it can be obtained is on a level with all scientific and practical information. It states the circumstances under which certain sorts of results will appear.

One's view of this functionalistic metaphysics is almost inevitably colored by current philosophical discussion as to the essential nature of consciousness. David Hume has been accused of destroying the reality of mind chiefly because he exorcised from it relationships of various kinds. If it be urged, as has so often been done, that Hume was guilty of pouring out the baby with the bath, the modern philosopher makes good the disaster not only by pouring in again both baby and bath, but by maintaining that baby and bath, mind and relations, are substantially one. Nor is this unity secured after the manner prescribed by the good Bishop Berkeley. At all events the metaphysicians to whom I refer are not fond of being called idealists. But the psychological functionalist who emphasizes the instrumental nature of the mind-body distinction and the metaphysician who regards mind as a relation are following roads which are at least parallel to one another if not actually convergent.

Whether or not one sympathizes with the views of that wing of the functionalist party to which our attention has just been directed it certainly seems a trifle unfair to cast up the mind-body difficulty in the teeth of the functionalist as such when on logical grounds he is no more guilty than any of his psychological neighbors. No courageous psychology of volition is possible which does not squarely face the mind-body problem, and in point of fact every important description of mental life contains doctrine of one kind or another upon this matter. A literally pure psychology of volition would be a sort of hanging-garden of Babylon, marvelous but inaccessible to psychologists of terrestrial habit. The functionalist is a greater sinner than others only in so far as he finds necessary and profitable a more constant insistence upon the translation of mental process into physiological process and conversely.

IV

If we now bring together the several conceptions of which mention has been made it will be easy to show them converging upon a common point. We have to consider (1) functionalism conceived as the psychology of mental operations in contrast to the psychology of mental elements; or, expressed otherwise, the psychology of the how and why of consciousness as distinguished from the psychology of the what of consciousness. We have (2) the functionalism which deals with the problem of mind conceived as primarily engaged in mediating between the environment and the needs of the organism. This is the psychology of the fundamental utilities of consciousness; (3) and lastly we have functionalism described as psychophysical psychology, that is the psychology which constantly recognizes and insists upon the essential significance of the mind-body relationship for any just and comprehensive appreciation of mental life itself.

The second and third delineations of functional psychology are rather obviously correlated with each other. No description of the actual circumstances attending the participation of mind in the accommodatory activities of the organism could be other than a mere empty schematism without making reference to the manner in which mental processes eventuate in motor phenomena of the physiological organism. The overt accommodatory act is, I take it, always sooner or later a muscular movement. But this fact being admitted, there is nothing for it, if one will describe accommodatory processes, but to recognize the mind-body relations and in some way give expression to their practical significance. It is only in this regard, as was indicated a few lines above, that the functionalist departs a trifle in his practice and a trifle more in his theory from the rank and file of his colleagues.

The effort to follow the lead of the natural sciences and delimit somewhat rigorously—albeit artificially—a field of inquiry, in this case consciousness conceived as an independent realm, has led in psychology to a deal of excellent work and to the uncovering of much hidden truth. So far as this procedure has resulted in a focusing of scientific attention and endeavor on a relatively narrow range of problems the result has more than justified the means. And the functionalist by no means holds that the limit of profitable research has been reached along these lines. But he is disposed to urge in season and out that we must not forget the arbitrary and self-imposed nature of the boundaries within which we toil when we try to eschew all explicit reference to the physical and physiological. To overlook this fact is to substitute a psychology under injunction for a psychology under free jurisdiction. He also urges with vigor and enthusiasm that a new illumination of this preëmpted field can be gained by envisaging it more broadly, looking at it as it appears when taken in perspective with its neighboring territory. And if it be objected that such an inquiry however interesting and advantageous is at least not psychology, he can only reply; psychology is what we make it, and if the correct understanding of mental phenomena involves our delving in regions which are not at first glance properly mental, what recks it, provided only that we are nowhere guilty of untrustworthy and unverifiable procedure, and that we return loaded with the booty for which we set out, and by means of which we can the better solve our problem?

In its more basal philosophy this last conception is of course intimately allied to those appraisals of mind which emphasize its dominantly social characteristics, its rise out of social circumstances and the pervasively social nature of its constitutive principles. In our previous intimations of this standpoint we have not distinguished sharply between the physical and the social aspect of environment. The adaptive activities of mind are very largely of the distinctly social type. But this does not in any way jeopardize the genuineness of the connection upon which we have been insisting between the psychophysical aspects of a functional psychology and its environmental adaptive aspects.

It remains then to point out in what manner the conception of functionalism as concerned with the basal operations of mind is to be correlated with the other two conceptions just under discussion. The simplest view to take of the relations involved would apparently be such as would regard the first as an essential propaedeutic to the other two. Certainly if we are intent upon discerning the exact manner in which mental process contributes to accommodatory efficiency, it is natural to begin our undertaking by determining what are the primordial forms of expression peculiar to mind. However plausible in theory this conception of the intrinsic logical relations of these several forms of functional psychology, in practice it is extremely difficult wholly to sever them from one another.

Again like the biological accommodatory view the psychophysical view of functional psychology involves as a rational presupposition some acquaintance with mental processes as these appear to reflective consciousness. The intelligent correlation in a practical way of physiological and mental operations evidently involves a preliminary knowledge of the conspicuous differentiations both on the side of conscious function and on the side of physiological function.

In view of the considerations of the last few paragraphs it does not seem fanciful nor forced to urge that these various theories of the problem of functional psychology really converge upon one another, however divergent may be the introductory investigations peculiar to each of the several ideals. Possibly the conception that the fundamental problem of the functionalist is one of determining just how mind participates in accommodatory reactions, is more nearly inclusive than either of the others, and so may be chosen to stand for the group. But if this vicarious duty is assigned to it, it must be on clear terms of remembrance that the other phases of the problem are equally real and equally necessary. Indeed the three things hang together as integral parts of a common program.

The functionalist's most intimate persuasion leads him to regard consciousness as primarily and intrinsically a control phenomenon. Just as behavior may be regarded as the most distinctly basic category of general biology in its functional phase so control would perhaps serve as the most fundamental category in functional psychology, the special forms and differentiations of consciousness simply constituting particular phases of the general process of control. At this point the omnipresent captious critic will perhaps arise to urge that the knowledge process is no more truly to be explained in terms of control than is control to be explained in terms of knowledge. Unquestionably there is from the point of view of the critic a measure of truth in this contention. The mechanism of control undoubtedly depends on the cognitive processes, to say nothing of other factors. But if one assumes the vitalistic point of view for one's more final interpretations, if one regards the furtherance of life in breadth and depth and permanence as an end in itself, and if one derives his scale of values from a contemplation of the several contributions toward this end represented by the great types of vital phenomena, with their apex in the moral, scientific and aesthetic realms, one must certainly find control a category more fundamental than the others offered by psychology. Moreover, it may be urged against the critic's attitude that even knowledge itself is built up under the control mechanism represented by selective attention and apperception. The basic character of control seems therefore hardly open to challenge.

One incidential merit of the functionalist program deserves a passing mention. This is the one method of approach to the problem with which I am acquainted that offers a reasonable and cogent account of the rise of reflective consciousness and its significance as manifested in the various philosophical disciplines. From the vantage point of the functionalist position logic and ethics, for instance, are no longer mere disconnected items in the world of mind. They take their place with all the inevitableness of organic organization in the general system of control, which requires for the expression of its immanent meaning *as psychic* a theoretical vindication of its own inner principles, its modes of procedure and their results. From any other point of view, so far as I am aware, the several divisions of philosophical inquiry sustain to one another relations which are almost purely external and accidental. To the functionalist on the other hand they are and must be in the nature of the case consanguineous and vitally connected. It is at the point, for example, where the good, the beautiful and the true have bearing on the efficacy of accommodatory activity that the issues of the normative philosophical sciences become relevant. If good action has no significance for the enriching and enlarging of life, the contention I urge is futile, and similarly as regards beauty and truth. But it is not at present usually maintained that such is the fact.

These and other similar tendencies of functionalism may serve to reassure those who fear that in lending itself to biological influences psychology may lose contact with philosophy and so sacrifice the poise and balance and sanity of outlook which philosophy undertakes to furnish. The particular brand of philosophy which is predestined to functionalist favor cannot of course be confidently predicted in advance. But anything approaching a complete and permanent divorce of psychology from philosophy is surely improbable so long as one cultivates the functionalist faith. Philosophy cannot dictate scientific method here any more than elsewhere, nor foreordain the special facts to be discovered. But as an interpreter of the psychologist's achievements she will always stand higher in the functionalist's favor than in that of his colleagues of other persuasions, for she is a more integral and significant part of his scheme of the cosmos. She may even outgrow under his tutelage that 'valiant inconclusiveness' of which the last of her long line of lay critics has just accused her.

A sketch of the kind we have offered is unhappily likely to leave on the mind an impression of functional psychology as a name for a group of genial but vaguer ambitions and good intentions. This, however, is a fault which must be charged to the artist and to the limitations of time and space under which he is here working. There is nothing vaguer in the program of the functionalist when he goes to his work than there is in the purposes of the psychologist wearing any other livery. He goes to his laboratory, for example, with just the same resolute interest to discover new facts and new relationships, with just the same determination to verify and confirm his previous observations, as does his colleague who calls himself perhaps a structuralist. But he looks out upon the surroundings of his science with a possibly greater sensitiveness to its continuity with other ranges of human interest and with certainly a more articulate purpose to see the mind which he analyzes as it actually is when engaged in the discharge of its vital functions. If his method tempts him now and then to sacrifice something of petty exactitude, he is under no obligation to yield, and in any case he has for his compensation the power which comes from breadth and sweep of outlook.

So far as he may be expected to develop methods peculiar to himself—so far, indeed, as in genetic and comparative psychology, for example, he has already developed such—they will not necessarily be iconoclastic and revolutionary, nor such as flout the methods already devised and established on a slightly different foundation. They will be distinctly complementary to all that is solid in these. Nor is it in any way essential that the term functionalism should cling to this new-old movement. It seems at present a convenient term, but there is nothing sacrosanct about it, and the moment it takes unto itself the pretense of scientific finality its doom will be sealed. It means to-day a broad and flexible and organic point of view in psychology. The moment it becomes dogmatic and narrow its spirit will have passed and undoubtedly some worthier successor will fill its place.

The Pre-Chicago Association of the Early Functionalists

Alfred C. Raphelson

It is generally agreed among those who write of its history, that American psychology made its first distinctive stand against European psychology in the form of functionalism. There may, indeed, have been individuals who differed on matters of concepts, methods or goals, but before 1900, no distinctly "American" school had emerged.

The historians often emphasize that it was no mere coincidence that this new viewpoint first appeared at the University of Chicago.They argue that the time was ripe for the emergence of a "native" psychology, and, as Roback, for example put it:

> . . . It was only fit that such should spring up in a region of comparatively recent settlement and far inland. . . . About half way from each coast and therefore relatively free from foreign influences . . . the University of Chicago . . . was a brand new university, founded only the same year Titchener . . . arrived in America. To this day, this University represents American initiative and enterprise rather than tradition and dignity. . . . If the location is typically American, with its bustling packing houses, political machines, etc., the particular brand of psychology which would issue, therefore, would be expected to correspond to the American genius which is characterized by action, utility and practicality? . . .[1]

Raphelson, A. C. (1973). The pre-Chicago association of the early functionalists. *Journal of the History of the Behavioral Sciences, 9,* 115–122.

The story is then detailed how John Dewey (1859–1952) was invited to come to Chicago in 1894 as the Chairman of the Department of Philosophy, how he found James H. Tufts (1862–1942) already there and interested in psychological topics. Within a year George H. Mead (1863–1931) and James R. Angell (1867–1949) arrived, the latter to take charge of the psychological laboratory. These men brought to Chicago backgrounds in philosophy, the new psychology of Germany as well as interests in ethics, education, sociology and political science. Furthermore, they were unusually effective teachers. Largely because of their combined effect, the University of Chicago emerged as a flourishing center of psychological activity that in a few years appeared to take a form that justifiably could be called a "school of thought."

One need not quarrel with the above facts to point out, however, that though functional psychology did develop at Chicago as a set of ideas, it was not mere "fate" that determined that its originators happened to appear on the staff of that new university. Another way of looking at the history of any set of ideas is to consider, in addition to the immediate circumstance of its creation, how it happened that at a certain place and point in time, a particular group of men with particular interests and experiences happened to become joined in a fertile intellectual enterprise.[2] This social-psychological approach is often neglected in detailing the history of new ideas and their innovators. In the case of these early functionalists, their association clearly preceded their meeting at Chicago and reflected the influences of the specific character of philosophy and psychology as it was taught at Johns Hopkins University and the University of Michigan.

In the late 1870's the newly-organized Johns Hopkins University was seeking someone to add to its philosophy staff. The Trustees, after looking in vain toward Europe, invited three Americans to lecture in Baltimore in alternative semesters. The invitations went to Charles S. Peirce (1839–1914), G. Stanley Hall (1844–1924) and George S. Morris (1840–1889). Three more diverse thinkers and personalities could hardly have been found.[3]

The backgrounds of Peirce and Hall are well known. It will be useful, however, to briefly consider their diversity to set in perspective the intellectual environment created at Johns Hopkins by their overlapping presence with Morris. Peirce had been recommended by William James who had been first offered the position but had turned it down after considering it favorably for some time. Peirce had lectured on several occasions at Harvard and had had, of course, a great influence on James. He was well inclined toward mathematics and the natural sciences. However, Peirce's personality showed a strong trend toward emotional instability which was expressed in a quarrelsomeness that had precluded his receiving a permanent academic post. As a matter of fact, he had been employed since 1859 by the United States Coast Survey and kept that position during his part-time lectureship at Johns Hopkins.

G. Stanley Hall had been educated at Williams College and the Union Theological Seminary but had discovered he was not made to be a minister. He then became interested in the "new" psychology being offered by Wundt and was about to leave for Leipzig when he was offered a part-time position teaching English at Harvard. While there he was able to carry out graduate work with James and earned what is usually considered the first American doctorate in psychology in 1878. Hall then went to Germany where he absorbed the new work going on in physiology as well as in Wundt's laboratory in Leipzig. After returning to America, he received the call from Johns Hopkins to offer a series of lectures on the new experimental psychology.

Morris had also studied at the Union Theological Seminary but had decided upon a career in philosophy rather than the ministry. He studied further in Germany for several years becoming greatly influenced by German Idealism—especially Hegel, Kant, and Schilling. Although he did not earn a doctoral degree, his articles and translations earned him a good reputation as a philosopher. In 1870 Morris accepted a position as head of the Department of Modern Languages and Literature at the University of Michigan . . . this despite his reputation as a philosopher.[4]

Morris was the first of the three to arrive on the Hopkins scene. During the spring term of 1878, he gave twenty lectures on the history of philosophy. The next spring he returned to give ten lectures on historical and practical ethics. In 1881, he was then offered a three year appointment as a lecturer on the condition that he would remain at Johns Hopkins at least one semester a year. He was to alternate with Peirce who would lecture on logic and Hall who would offer work in the new German physiological psychology.

The Johns Hopkins University, in the 1880's, was an institute offering only advanced study, so the three lecturers were guaranteed a good group of students. As a matter of fact, the particular group they were to meet in the philosophy courses included a number who would become quite successful members of the American academic scene. Among them were Joseph Jastrow, James McKeen Cattell, H. H. Donaldson, E. C. Sanford, Fred M. Taylor, and John Dewey.

Morris, although perceived by the Hopkins community as being intelligent, accessible and cooperative, was not comfortable with the philosophical climate that was being created there. Being a Hegelian idealist with a strong religious interest, Morris did not fit in with "the exaggerated scientism" he found. The students were well-informed about the physiological and experimental side of psychology Hall presented and were impressed with this orientation. Hall had also set up a small laboratory which enabled the students to experience first hand the new methods. Peirce's lectures strongly reinforced Hall's presentations. Morris, on the other hand, saw philosophy's function in the curriculum as acting as a "liberalizing agency . . . preventing the . . . narrowing tendencies of extreme specialism . . . and to serve the public aim of the University by producing leaders capable of recognizing the true ideals and intelligently directing the nation's energies to their accomplishment."[5] He was not convinced that an empirical psychology had a claim to be called philosophy. But Morris' views, perhaps due to his less forceful style and personality, could not hold their own in face of the combined empirical and pragmatic orientations of Hall and Peirce.

In 1884, the Johns Hopkins trustees ended the part-time lecturer arrangement by appointing Hall professor of Psychology and Pedagogy. At Michigan, the chairmanship of the Department of Philosophy had become vacant and it was offered to Morris. Morris accepted it and immediately wrote to one of his most brilliant students at Hopkins to offer him an instructorship at a salary of $900. John Dewey accepted the position and together they proceeded to change the orientation and scope of the instruction of both philosophy and psychology at Michigan.[6]

It was not altogether surprising that Dewey accepted Morris' offer. He had been greatly influenced by his work with Morris. The experience had led the young man into German Idealism, and despite his later deviation, had left a very definite mark on his thought. Dewey himself once remarked that regardless of their differences, he would be happy to believe that Morris' teaching had an enduring influence on him.[7]

But Dewey was also greatly impressed with Hall's arguments that while psychology and philosophy were closely related, psychology had to be worked out on the basis of the new experimental approach that he had observed at Leipzig and Berlin. Experiment would replace the older idealistic and rational approaches to the questions raised by the mental philosophers. At Michigan Dewey devoted his full energies to developing this new approach.[8]

During his first term (1884–1885) Dewey offered a course in Empirical Psychology using Sully's *Outline of Psychology* (1884), Special Topics (Physiological, Comparative, and Morbid Psychology), and a third course covering special topics in psychology and philosophy with reference to the history of philosophy in Great Britain. In subsequent terms he introduced courses in experimental, speculative and historical psychology. Sully's text was soon replaced with a printed syllabus which was his own digest of the new field. This work, published in 1887 under the title, *Psychology,* was Dewey's first book and became the standard text at Michigan for the next ten years.[9]

It is, in many ways, a curious book which attempts to integrate the older idealistic epistemology with the new empirical development in psychological research. The twenty-six year old Dewey was groping and in this book is discovered straddling the two positions. Introspection is the preferred method. The works of Helmholtz, Hering, Wundt, Volkmann and Stumpf are all cited. Sensation is stressed, reaction patterns are described and the concept of habit is extensively employed. There are discussions of other adaptive mechanisms (e.g. will, feeling, intuition) which became important features of the functional psychology that was still a dozen years away. For these reasons perhaps Brett was correct when he described the text as "the first grey dawn of that tomorrow for which the psychology of the American colleges was waiting."[10]

It was only a "first" dawn, however, for the text fell back on an older metaphysics to support the new science. This strange mixture gave the book an uncomfortably disorganized appearance. Mind, for example, is denied existence as an entity but is mentioned as "causing attention." The units of mental life had to be accounted for and Dewey saw no other way except to evoke the activity of the self defined somewhat vaguely as "the activity of synthesis upon sensation." Sensation itself is the "elementary consciousness which arises from the reaction of the soul upon a nervous impulse conducted to the brain from the affection of some sensory nerve-ending by a physical stimulus." Every "concrete act of knowledge involves an intuition of God for it involves a unity of the real and the ideal, of the objective and the subjective."[11]

It was not until Dewey read James' *Principles of Psychology* (1890) that he was helped from the fence on which he perched with his text. So certain was James in his endorsement of the empirically-oriented new psychology, that Dewey felt encouraged to abandon the idealistic psychology completely in favor of a more empirical and objective functionalism. This was, of course, more clearly expressed in 1896, in his landmark paper, "The Reflex Arc Concept in Psychology."[12]

In 1888 Dewey accepted a position at the University of Minnesota. His association with Michigan, however, was only interrupted by this appointment. During a spring vacation in 1889, Morris, who had gone camping, caught pneumonia and died. Dewey was immediately recalled and made head of the department of philosophy. He remained at Michigan for five years and began to devote more of his attention to philosophy and his growing interest in education.[13]

At Michigan Dewey found ample stimulation for his new interest in education. It had one of the earliest chairs in education in this country. A regular program of statewide high school visitations by faculty members had been established and Dewey made many trips to determine the preparation given college-bound students. As an early member of the Schoolmaster Club, he cooperated in bringing secondary and higher educational practices together. These experiences led him to study the educative process from the standpoint of psychology. He frequently spoke throughout the state at teachers' meetings on such topics as attention, memory, imagination, habit and thinking and their relation to teaching and learning. In his *Applied Psychology* (1889), written with J. A. McLellan of the University of Toronto, he presented these concepts in a practical manner that appeared appropriate to the problems of education.[14]

Dewey, as head of the department, did not neglect the psychological tradition he had begun. Though no longer interested in teaching these subjects, he did bring in competent people to handle their instruction. He immediately engaged James H. Tufts (1862–1942) to offer the psychology courses. Tufts was not specifically trained in psychology and was, as a matter of fact, to make his reputation in philosophy through his translation of Windleband's influential *History of Philosophy* (1893). Originally a New Englander, Tufts completed his undergraduate work at Amherst (A.B. 1884) and Yale (B.D. 1889) and later (1892) took a doctorate at Freiberg. During the two years he was in Ann Arbor, Tufts formed a deep personal and intellectual friendship with Dewey that lasted throughout their lives.[15]

During the academic years 1889–90 and 1890–91 Tufts offered the courses in general and physiological psychology. At that time there were only eight psychology laboratories established in America. In 1890 Dewey encouraged

Tufts to establish one at Michigan. He managed to collect some pieces of equipment and set them up on the top floor of the old medical building. Three hours a week were devoted to elementary studies of reaction time, color, Weber's Law, and physiological exercises. One of the students enrolled in this laboratory course was James R. Angell, son of the University's president.[16]

Angell received his undergraduate and masters training at Michigan, electing most of his work in the philosophy department. His first psychology was gained from reading Dewey's text. He also took ethics, aesthetics, metaphysics and Hegel's logic under Dewey and history of philosophy under Tufts. In his autobiographical sketch, Angell writes

> . . . most rewarding of all in the year following my graduation, which I spent as a graduate student at Michigan, a seminar with Dewey in William James' freshly published *Principles of Psychology*. The book unquestionably affected my thinking for the next 20 years more profoundly than any other. . . . During this period, I greatly increased my obligations to Dewey and to Tufts, both later my colleagues for many years at the University of Chicago. For my intellectual awakening, for many basic elements in my subsequent habits of thought, and for endless kind and helpful acts in later years, I am under the deepest obligation to John Dewey, whose simplicity of character, originality, and virility of mind, brought him the unqualified affection, admiration, and devotion of thousands of students. . . .[17]

On Dewey's recommendation, Angell left Michigan in 1891 to study at the Harvard Graduate School under William James, Josiah Royce, and George Herbert Palmer. He also undertook more intense laboratory work in the one that James had set up but had turned over to Hugo Münsterberg.[18]

In 1891 Tufts left Michigan for a position as assistant professor of philosophy at the newly established University of Chicago. It was necessary for Dewey to replace him with two instructors in order to handle the increasing number of students enrolled in philosophy and psychology. One instructor was engaged to handle the psychology offerings and the other to handle the philosophy courses. George H. Mead (1863–1931) was brought in for the psychology part.[19]

Mead had been reared in the orthodox tradition of his minister father who had himself descended from a long line of Puritan clergymen. As a young man, however, Mead had been sufficiently influenced by contemporary naturalistic thought to have succeeded in refuting the dogma of the church to his own satisfaction. After completing his undergraduate work he matriculated at Harvard, where he studied under James and Royce and also served as tutor for the James children for over a year. In the fall of 1888 he went to Germany to study at Leipzig and Berlin. While at Leipzig Mead met G. Stanley Hall, who convinced the young man (as he had Dewey and others at Johns Hopkins) that physiological psychology was the direction in which he should move. Mead soon came to see that he should make a specialty of this area,

> . . . because in America . . . poor, bated, unhappy Christianity, trembling for its life, claps the gag into the mouth of Free Thought and says, "Hush, hush, not a word or nobody will believe in me any more. He (Mead) thinks it will be hard for him to get a chance to utter any ultimate philosophical opinions savouring of independence. In physiological psychology, on the other hand, he has a harmless territory in which he can work quietly without drawing down upon himself the anathema and excommunication of all-patent Evangelicanism. . . ."[20]

Mead was ready and willing, therefore, to accept Dewey's offer to give the work in physiological psychology. A single-unit room was obtained where Mead carried out laboratory instruction for three years. Dewey was quite enthusiastic about this work and informed the students that all introspective psychology had come to an end. The "new psychology" was what Mead was offering. One student, recalling the experience years later, remembered only the tedious routine of dissecting frogs. Tradition has associated only one "empirical" outcome with Mead's laboratory. While preparing and shellacking a brain, Mead allowed it to catch fire, which in turn, spread to the laboratory walls before being brought under control.[21]

In 1894, the University of Chicago, at the urging of Tufts, approached Dewey with an offer of the chairmanship of the Department of Philosophy. One of the main reasons that Dewey accepted the offer was that work in pedagogy and psychology were included in the department. Thus, the assignment was compatible with all three of the major interests he had developed at Michigan. In addition, he would be able to renew his friendship with Tufts. Mead agreed to move to Chicago with Dewey.[22]

The next year Dewey called Angell to Chicago to direct the psychology laboratory. After leaving Harvard, Angell had gone to Europe intending to study with Wundt at Leipzig. Wundt's laboratory, however, was filled so he went to Berlin to work with Paulsen, Ebbinghaus and Helmholtz and later to Halle to work with Erdmann in psychology and Vaihinger in philosophy. Before completing his doctorate, he accepted a position at the University of Minnesota, where he taught the elementary psychology courses and set up a modest laboratory. Angell was at Minnesota when he received the offer from Dewey at Chicago. Though the officials at Minnesota urged him to stay, he could not resist the opportunity to have as colleagues men like Dewey, Tufts and Mead, the men who had inspired him so at Michigan. It was a decision that he never had cause to regret.[23]

In this manner, then, the four men who formed the main nucleus of the Chicago school of functionalism came to be together. Dewey's article, "The Reflex Arc Concept in Psychology," that first stated the main thesis of functionalism was published two years (1896) after the four were joined as a group at Chicago.

Ben-David and Collins, in their study of social factors in the origins of a new science, have argued that "ideas are not self-generating, and even if potentially fertile, have to be carried from person to person and implanted in some special way in order to give rise to new generation."[24] The necessary ideas for the development of a new scientific prescription or paradigm are usually available over a relatively prolonged time period and in several places. Since only a few of these potential beginnings eventually lead to further growth, it can be argued that fruition occurs only where and when individuals become involved with a new idea not only as intellectual content but as a means of establishing a new intellectual identity that redefines an entire problem area.[25]

The point of view, then, that developed at Chicago can be better understood if one takes into account the intellectual experiences Dewey had at Johns Hopkins and their subsequent development at Michigan. The empiricism of Hall and the pragmatism of Peirce were worked through to supplant the idealism of Morris that initially attracted him. His involvement in questions of statewide education reinforced Dewey's growing sense of the importance of the role played by mental processes in adaptation. At Michigan he found the vital support he needed from a group of young and stimulating colleagues and students. A new intellectual context began to form and the group gave it the social reinforcement it needed to take on a new identity.

Chicago provided the fertile intellectual climate that was needed to bring to fruition this new thought. A new institution, it was founded upon enthusiasm for, as well as a vision of, a new kind of American intellectual environment. This spirit encouraged the innovative thinking of this group of men who had a past association of proven mutual stimulation and commonality of ideas. They looked to Chicago as an opportunity to continue their association in hopes that it would be satisfying to them and fruitful for American scholarship. Chicago did not fail them nor they Chicago. The results of their association, which drew heavily upon their past collaboration, gave very quickly that university an illustrious beginning as it also gave American psychology a history of its own.

NOTES

1. Roback, A. A., *History of American Psychology,* rev. ed. (New York: Collier Books, 1964), p. 238.
2. See for example, Ben-David, Joseph and Collins, Randall, "Social Factors in the Origins of a New Science: The Case of Psychology," *Amer. Sociol. Rev.,* 1966, 51, 451–464.
3. Hawkins, Hugh, *Pioneer: A History of the Johns Hopkins University, 1874–1889* (Ithaca, New York: Cornell University Press, 1960) pp. 187–210. All references to the Johns Hopkins University experiences of Morris, Hall and Peirce are taken from these pages.
4. Hinsdale, Burke A., *History of the University of Michigan,* Isaac N. Demmon (ed.) (Ann Arbor, Mich.:1906), p. 245.
5. Hawkins, op. cit., p. 199.
6. Parker, Dewitt H. and Vibbert, Charles B., "The Department of Philosophy," in *The University of Michigan: An Encyclopedic Survey, v.* II, W. B. Shaw (ed.) (Ann Arbor: University of Michigan Press, 1944) pp. 672–73; Dewey, Jane, "Biography of John Dewey," in Paul A. Schlipp (ed.) *The Philosophy of John Dewey,* (New York: Tudor Publishing Co., 1951), p. 19.
7. Dewey, Jane, op. cit., pp. 18–19; Hawkins, op. cit., pp. 269–270.
8. Ibid.
9. Parker and Vibbert, op. cit., p. 673.
10. Roback, op. cit., pp. 115–118; Allport, Gordon W., "Dewey's Individual and Social Psychology," in P. A. Schlipp (ed.) *Philosophy of John Dewey,* op. cit., pp. 266–267.
11. Pillsbury, Walter B., "John Dewey, 1859–1952," *Nat. Acad. Sci. Bio. Mem.,* 1957, 30, 113.
12. Allport, op. cit., p. 267.
13. Parker and Vibbert, op. cit., pp. 673–674.
14. Ibid., Dewey, Jane, op. cit., pp. 26–27.
15. Dewey, Jane, op. cit., p. 24; *Calendar, University of Michigan,* Ann Arbor, Michigan, 1884–1892.
16. Pillsbury, Walter B., "The Department of Psychology" in *The University of Michigan: An Encyclopedic Survey, v.* II, W. B. Shaw (ed.) (Ann Arbor: University of Michigan Press, 1940). p. 709; Morris, Amos R., "Machines Aid in the Teaching of English," *Mich. Alum.,* 1929, 35, 322.
17. Angell, James R., "Autobiographical Sketch" in *A History of Psychology in Autobiography,* C. Murchinson (ed.) (New York: Russell and Russell, 1961) pp. 5–6.
18. Ibid., pp. 6–7.
19. Pillsbury, W. B., "The Department of Psychology," op. cit. p. 709; Parker and Vibbert, op. cit., p. 674; Dewey, Jane, op. cit., p. 25.
20. Letter from Henry Northrup Castle, dated February, 1889, Leipzig, Germany, quoted in Wallace, David, "Reflections on the Education of George Herbert Mead," *Amer. Journ. Sociol.,*1967, 72, 406.
21. Lamont, Corliss (ed.) *Dialogue on John Dewey* (New York: Horizon Press, 1954) pp. 19–20; Pillsbury, "The Department of Psychology," op. cit., pp. 709–710.
22. Dewey, Jane, op. cit., p. 27; Pillsbury, "The Department of Psychology," op. cit., p. 710.
23. Angell, op. cit., pp. 10–12; Pillsbury, "The Department of Psychology," op. cit., p. 710.
24. Ben-David and Collins, op. cit., p. 452.
25. Ibid.

Functionalism, Darwinism, and the Psychology of Women: A Study in Social Myth

Stephanie A. Shields

The psychology of women is acquiring the character of an academic entity as witnessed by the proliferation of research on sex differences, the appearance of textbooks devoted to the psychology of women, and the formation of a separate APA division, Psychology of Women. Nevertheless, there is almost universal ignorance of the psychology of women as it existed prior to its incorporation into psychoanalytic theory. If the maxim "A nation without a history is like a man without a memory" can be applied, then it would behoove the amnesiacs interested in female psychology to investigate its pre-Freudian past.

This article focuses on one period of that past (from the latter half of the 19th century to the first third of the 20th) in order to clarify the important issues of the time and trace their development to the position they occupy in current psychological theory. Even a limited overview leads the reader to appreciate Helen Thompson Woolley's (1910) early appraisal of the quality of the research on sex differences:

> There is perhaps no field aspiring to be scientific where flagrant personal bias, logic martyred in the cause of supporting a prejudice, unfounded assertions, and even sentimental rot and drivel, have run riot to such an extent as here. (p. 340).

THE FUNCTIONALIST MILIEU

Although the nature of woman had been an academic and social concern of philosopher psychologists throughout the ages, formal psychology (its inception usually dated 1879) was relatively slow to take up the topic of female psychology. The "woman question" was a social one, and social problems did not fall within the sharply defined limits of Wundt's "new" psychology. The business of psychology was the description of the "generalized adult mind," and it is not at all clear whether "adult" was meant to include both sexes. When the students of German psychology did venture outside of the laboratory, however, there is no evidence that they were sympathetic to those defending the equality of male and female ability (cf. Wundt, 1901).

It was the functionalist movement in the United States that fostered academic psychology's study of sex differences and, by extension, a prototypic psychology of women. The incorporation of evolutionary theory into the practice of psychology made the study of the female legitimate, if not imperative. It would be incorrect to assume that the psychology of women existed as a separate specialty within the discipline. The female was discussed only in relation to the male, and the function of the female was thought to be distinctly different from and complementary to the function of the male. The leitmotiv of evolutionary theory as it came to be applied to the social sciences was the evolutionary supremacy of the Caucasian male. The notion of the supplementary, subordinate role of the female was ancillary to the development of that theme.

The influence of evolutionary theory on the psychology of women can be traced along two major conceptual lines: (a) by emphasizing the biological foundations of temperament, evolutionary theory led to serious academic discussion of maternal instinct (as one facet of the general topic of instinct); and (b) by providing a theoretical justification of the study of individ-

Adapted from Shields, S. A. (1975). Functionalism, Darwinism, and the psychology of women: A study in social myth. *American Psychologist, 30,* 739–754.

ual differences, evolutionary theory opened the door to the study of sex differences in sensory, motor, and intellectual abilities. As a whole, the concept of evolution with its concomitant emphasis on biological determinism provided ample "scientific" reason for cataloging the "innate" differences in male and female nature.

This articles examines three topics that were of special significance to the psychology of women during the functionalist era: (a) structural differences in the brains of males and females and the implications of these differences for intelligence and temperament, (b) the hypothesis of greater male variability and its relation to social and educational issues, and (c) maternal instinct and its meaning for a psychology of female "nature." As the functionalist paradigm gave way to behaviorism and psychoanalytic theory, the definition and "meaning" of each of these issues changed to fit the times. When issues faded in importance, it was not because they were resolved but because they ceased to serve as viable scientific "myths" in the changing social and scientific milieu. As the times change, so must the myths change.

THE FEMALE BRAIN

The topic of female intelligence came to 19th-century psychology via phrenology and the neuroanatomists. Philosophers of the time (e.g., Hegel, Kant, Schopenhauer) had demonstrated, to their satisfaction, the justice of woman's subordinate social position, and it was left to the men of science to discover the particular physiological determinants of female inadequacy. In earlier periods, woman's inferiority had been defined as a general "state" intimately related to the absence of qualities that would have rendered her a male and to the presence of reproductive equipment that destined her to be female. For centuries the mode of Eve's creation and her greater guilt for the fall from grace had been credited as the cause of woman's imperfect nature, but this was not an adequate explanation in a scientific age. Thus, science sought explanations for female inferiority that were more in keeping with contemporary scientific philosophy.

Although it had long been believed that the brain was the chief organ of the mind, the comparison of male and female mental powers traditionally included only allusions to vague "imperfections" of the female brain. More precise definition of the sites of these imperfections awaited the advancement of the concept of cortical localization of function. Then, as finer distinctions of functional areas were noted, there was a parallel recognition of the differences between those sites as they appeared in each sex.

At the beginning of the 19th century, the slowly increasing interest in the cerebral gyri rapidly gathered momentum with the popularization of phrenology. Introduced by Franz Joseph Gall, "cranioscopy," as he preferred to call it, postulated that the seat of various mental and moral faculties was located in specific areas of the brain's surface such that a surfeit or deficiency could be detected by an external examination of the cranium. Phrenology provided the first objective method for determining the neurological foundation of sex differences in intelligence and temperament that had long been promulgated. Once investigation of brain structure had begun, it was fully anticipated that visible sex differences would be found: Did not the difference between the sexes pervade every other aspect of physique and physiological function? Because physical differences were so obvious in every other organ of the body, it was unthinkable that the brain could have escaped the stamp of sex.

Gall was convinced that he could, from gross anatomical observation, discriminate between male and female brains, claiming that "if there had been presented to him in water, the fresh brains of two adult animals of any species, one male and the other female, he could have distinguished the two sexes" (Walker, 1850, p. 317). Gall's student and colleague, Johann Spurzheim, elaborated on this basic distinction by noting that the frontal lobes were less developed in females, "the organs of the perceptive faculties being commonly larger than those of the reflective powers." Gall also observed sex differences in the nervous tissue itself, "confirming" Malebranche's belief that the female "cerebral fibre" is softer than that of the male, and that it is also "slender and long rather than thick" (Walker, 1850, p. 318). Spurzheim also listed the cerebral "organs" whose appearance differed commonly in males and females: females tended to have the areas devoted to philoprogenetiveness and other "tender" traits most prominent, while in males, areas of aggressiveness and constructiveness dominated. Even though cranioscopy did not survive as a valid system of describing cortical function, the practice of comparing the appearance of all or part of the brain for anatomical evidence of quality of function remained one of the most popular means of providing proof of female mental inferiority. Most comparisons used adult human brains, but with the rise of evolutionary theory, increasing emphasis was placed on the value of developmental and cross-species comparisons. The argument for female mental inferiority took two forms: some argued that quality of intellect was proportional to absolute or relative brain size; others, more in the tradition of cortical localization, contended that the presence of certain mental qualities was dependent upon the development of corresponding brain centers.

The measurement of cranial capacity had long been in vogue as one method of determining intellectual ability. That women had smaller heads than men was taken by some as clear proof of a real disparity between male and female intelligence. The consistently smaller brain size of the female was cited as another anatomical indicator of its functional inferiority. More brain necessarily meant better brain; the exception only proved this rule. Alexander Bain (1875) was among those who believed that the smaller absolute brain size of females accounted for a lesser mental ability. George Romanes (1887) enumerated the "secondary sex characteristics" of mental abilities attributable to brain size. The smaller brain of women was directly responsible for their mental inferiority, which "displays itself most conspicuously in a comparative absence of originality, and this more especially in the higher levels of intellectual work" (p. 655). He, like many, allowed that women were to some degree compensated for intellectual inferiority by a superiority of instinct and perceptual ability. These advantages carried with them the germ of female failure, however, by making women more subject to emotionality.

Proof of the male's absolute brain-size superiority was not enough to secure his position of intellectual superiority, since greater height and weight tended to offset the brain-size advantage. Reams of paper were, therefore, dedicated to the search for the most "appropriate" relative measures, but results were equivocal: if the ratio of brain weight to body weight is considered, it is found that women possess a proportionately larger brain than men; if the ratio of brain surface to body surface is computed, it is found to favor men. That some of the ratios "favored" males while others "favored" females led some canny souls to conclude that there was no legitimate solution to the problem. That they had ever hoped for a solution seems remarkable; estimates of brain size from cranial capacity involve a large margin of error because brains differing as much as 15 percent have been found in heads of the same size (Elliott, 1969, p. 316).

Hughlings Jackson has been credited as the first to regard the frontal cortex as the repository of the highest mental capacities, but the notion must have held popular credence as early as the 1850s because that period saw sporadic references to the comparative development of the frontal lobes in men and women. Once the function of the frontal lobes had been established, many researchers reported finding that the male possessed noticeably larger and more well-developed frontal lobes than females. The neuroanatomist Hischke came to the conclusion in 1854 that woman is *homo parietalis* while man is *homo frontalis* (Ellis, 1934). Likewise, Rudinger in 1877 found the frontal lobes of man in every way more extensive than those of women, and reported that these sex differences were evident even in the unborn fetus (Mobius, 1901).

At the turn of the century, the parietal lobes (rather than the frontal lobes) came to be regarded by some as the seat of intellect, and the necessary sex difference in parietal development was duly corroborated by the neuroanatomists. The change in cerebral hierarchy involved a bit of revisionism:

> the frontal region is not, as has been supposed smaller in woman, but rather larger relatively. . . . But the parietal lobe is somewhat smaller, [furthermore,] a preponderance of the frontal region does not imply intellectual superiority . . . the parietal region is really the more important. (Patrick, 1895, p. 212).

Once beliefs regarding the relative importance of the frontal and parietal lobes had shifted, it became critical to reestablish congruence between neuroanatomical findings and accepted sex differences. Among those finding parietal predominance in men were Paul Broca, Theodore Meynert, and the German Rudinger (see Ellis, 1934, p. 217).

Other neuroanatomical "deficiencies" of the female were found in (a) the area of the corpus callosum, (b) the complexity of the gyri and sulci, (c) the conformation of gyri and sulci, and (d) the rate of development of the cortex of the fetus (Woolley, 1910, p. 335). Franklin Mall (1909) objected to the use of faulty research methods that gave spurious differences the appearance of being real. Among the most serious errors he noted was the practice of making observations with a knowledge of the sex of the brain under consideration.

The debate concerning the importance of brain size and anatomy as indicators of intelligence diminished somewhat with the development of mental tests; nevertheless, the brain-size difference was a phenomenon that many felt obligated to interpret. Max Meyer (1921) attempted to settle the matter by examining the various measures of relative difference that had been employed. After finding these methods far too equivocal, he concluded, in the best behavioristic terms, that sex differences in intelligence were simply "accidents of habits acquired."

Characteristics of the female brain were thought not simply to render women less intelligent but also to allow more "primitive" parts of human nature to be expressed in her personality. Instinct was thought to dominate woman, as did her emotions, and the resulting "affectability" was considered woman's greatest weakness, the reason for her inevitable failure. Affectability was typically defined as a general state, the manifestation of instinctive and emotional predispositions that in men were kept in check by a superior intellect.

One of the most virulent critics of woman was the German physiologist Paul Mobius (1901), who argued that her mental incapacity was a necessary condition for the survival of the race. Instinct rendered her easily led and easily pleased, so much the better for her to give her all to bearing and rearing children. The dependence of woman also extracted a high price from man:

> All progress is due to man. Therefore the woman is like a dead weight on him, she prevents much restlessness and meddlesome inquisitiveness, but she also restrains him from noble actions, for she is unable to distinguish good from evil. (p. 629)

Mobius observed that woman was essentially unable to think independently, had strong inclinations to be mean and untrustworthy, and spent a good deal of her time in an emotionally unbalanced state. From this he was forced to conclude that: "If woman was not physically and mentally weak, if she was not as a rule rendered harmless by circumstances, she would be extremely dangerous" (Mobius, 1901, p. 630). Diatribes of this nature were relatively common German importations; woman's severest critics in this country seldom achieved a similar level of acerbity. Mobius and his ilk (e.g., Weininger, 1906) were highly publicized and widely read in the United States, and not a little of their vituperation crept into serious scientific discussions of woman's nature. For example, Porteus and Babcock (1926) resurrected the brain-size issue, discounting the importance of size to intelligence and instead associating it with the "maturing of other powers." Males, because of their larger brains, would be more highly endowed with these "other powers," and so more competent and achieving. Proposals such as these, which were less obviously biased than those of Mobius, Weininger, and others, fit more easily into the current social value system and so were more easily assimilated as "good science" (cf. Allen, 1927, p. 294).

THE VARIABILITY HYPOTHESIS

The first systematic treatment of individual differences in intelligence appeared in 1575. Juan Huarte attributed sex differences in intelligence to the different humoral qualities that characterized each sex, a notion that had been popular in Western thought since ancient Greece. Heat and dryness were characteristic of the male principle, while moisture and coolness were female attributes. Because dryness of spirit was necessary for intelligence, males naturally possessed greater "wit." The maintenance of dryness and heat was the function of the testicles, and Huarte (1959) noted that if a man were castrated the effects were the same "as if he had received some notable dammage in his very braine" (p. 279). Because the principles necessary for cleverness were only possessed by males, it behooved parents to conduct their life-style, diet, and sexual intercourse in such a manner as to insure the conception of a male. The humoral theory of sex differences was widely accepted through the 17th century, but with the advent of more sophisticated notions of anatomy and physiology, it was replaced by other, more specific, theories of female mental defect: the lesser size and hypothesized simpleness of the female brain, affectability as the source of inferiority, and complementarity of abilities in male and female. It was the developing evolutionary theory that provided an overall explanation for why these sex differences existed and why they were necessary for the survival of the race.

The theory of evolution as proposed by Darwin had little to say regarding the intellectual capacity of either sex. It was in Francis Galton's (Charles Darwin's cousin) anthropometric laboratory that the investigation of intellectual differences took an empirical form (Galton, 1907). The major conclusion to come from Galton's research was that women tend in all their capacities to be inferior to men. He looked to common experience for confirmation, reasoning that:

> If the sensitivity of women were superior to that of men, the self interest of merchants would lead to their being always employed; but as the reverse is the case, the opposite supposition is likely to be the true one. (pp. 20–21).

This form of logic—women have not excelled, therefore they cannot excel—was often used to support arguments denigrating female intellectual ability. The fact of the comparative rarity of female social achievement was also used as "evidence" in what was later to become a widely debated issue concerning the range of female ability.

Prior to the formulation of evolutionary theory, there had been little concern with whether deviation from the average or "normal" occurred more frequently in either sex. One of the first serious discussions of the topic appeared in the early 19th century when the anatomist

Meckel concluded on pathological grounds that the human female showed greater variability than the human male. He reasoned that because man is the superior animal and variability a sign of inferiority, this conclusion was justified (in Ellis, 1903, p. 237). The matter was left at that until 1871. At that time Darwin took up the question of variability in *The Descent of Man* while attempting to explain how it could be that in many species males had developed greatly modified secondary sexual characteristics while females of the same species had not. He determined that this was originally caused by the males' greater activity and "stronger passions" that were in turn more likely (he believed) to be transmitted to male offspring. Because the females would prefer to mate with the strong and passionate, sexual selection would insure the survival of those traits. A tendency toward greater variation per se was not thought to be responsible for the appearance of unusual characteristics, but "development of such characters would be much aided, if the males were more liable to vary than the females" (Darwin, 1922, p. 344). To support this hypothesis of greater male variability, he cited recent data obtained by anatomists and biologists that seemed to confirm the relatively more frequent occurrence of physical anomaly among males.

Because variation from the norm was already accepted as the mechanism of evolutionary progress (survival and transmission of adaptive variations) and because it seemed that the male was the more variable sex, it soon was universally concluded that the male is the progressive element in the species. Variation for its own sake took on a positive value because greatness, whether of an individual or a society, could not be achieved without variation. Once deviation from the norm became legitimized by evolutionary theory, the hypothesis of greater male variability became a convenient explanation for a number of observed sex differences, among them the greater frequency with which men achieved "eminence." By the 1890s it was popularly believed that greater male variability was a principle that held true, not only for physical traits but for mental abilities as well:

> That men should have greater cerebral variability and therefore more originality, while women have greater stability and therefore more "common sense," are facts both consistent with the general theory of sex and verifiable in common experience. (Geddes & Thomson, 1890, p. 271).

Havelock Ellis (1894), an influential sexologist and social philosopher, brought the variability hypothesis to the attention of psychologists in the first edition of *Man and Woman*. After examining anatomical and pathological data that indicated a greater male *variational tendency* (Ellis felt this term was less ambiguous than *variability),* he examined the evidence germane to a discussion of range of intellectual ability. After noting that there were more men than women in homes for the mentally deficient, which indicated a higher incidence of retardation among males, and that there were more men than women on the roles of the eminent, which indicated a higher incidence of genius among males, he concluded that greater male variability probably held for all qualities of character and ability. Ellis (1903) particularly emphasized the wide social and educational significance of the phenomenon, claiming that greater male variability was "a fact which has affected the whole of our human civilization" (p. 238), particularly through the production of men of genius. Ellis (1934) was also adamant that the female's tendency toward the average did not necessarily imply inferiority of talent; rather, it simply limited her expertise to "the sphere of concrete practical life" (p. 436).

The variability hypothesis was almost immediately challenged as a "pseudo-scientific superstition" by the statistician Karl Pearson (1897). Though not a feminist, Pearson firmly believed that the "woman question" deserved impartial, scientific study. He challenged the idea of greater male variability primarily because he thought it contrary to the fact and theory of evolution and natural selection. According to evolutionary theory (Pearson, 1897), "the more intense the struggle the less is the variability, the more nearly are individuals forced to approach the type fittest to their surroundings, if they are to survive" (p. 258). In a "civilized" community one would expect that because men have a "harder battle for life," any difference in variation should favor women. He took Ellis to task by arguing it was (a) meaningless to consider secondary sex characteristics (as Ellis had done) and, likewise, (b) foolish to contrast the sexes on the basis of abnormalities (as Ellis had done). By redefining the problem and the means for its solution, he was able to dismiss the entire corpus of data that had been amassed: "the whole trend of investigations concerning the relative variability of men and women up to the present seems to be erroneous" (Pearson, 1897, p. 261). Confining his measurements to "normal variations in organs or characteristics not of a secondary sexual character," he assembled anthropometric data on various races, from Neolithic skeletons to modern French peasants. He also challenged the adequacy of statistical comparison of only the extremes of the distribution, preferring to base his contrasts on the dispersion of measures around the mean. Finding a slight tendency toward greater female variability, he concluded that the variability hypothesis as stated remained a "quite unproven principle."

Ellis countered Pearson in a lengthy article, one more vicious than that ordinarily due an intellectual affront. Pearson's greatest sins (according to Ellis) were his failure to define "variability" and his measurement of characteristics that were highly subject to environmental influence. Ellis, of course, overlooked his own failure to define variability and his inclusion of environmentally altered evidence.

In the United States the variability hypothesis naturally found expression in the new testing movement, its proponents borrowing liberally from the theory of Ellis and the statistical technique of Pearson. The favor that was typically afforded the hypothesis did not stem from intellectual commitment to the scientific validity of the proposal as much as it did from personal commitment to the social desirability of its acceptance. The variability hypothesis was most often thought of in terms of its several corollaries: (a) genius (seldom, and then poorly, defined) is a peculiarly male trait; (b) men of genius naturally gravitate to positions of power and prestige (i.e., achieve eminence) by virtue of their talent; (c) an equally high ability level should not be expected of females; and (d) the education of women should, therefore, be consonant with their special talents and special place in society as wives and mothers.

Woman's Education

The "appropriate" education for women had been at issue since the Renaissance, and the implications of the variability hypothesis favored those who had been arguing for a separate female education. Late in the 18th century, Mary Wollstonecraft Godwin (1759–1797) questioned the "natural" roles of each sex, contending that for both the ultimate goal was the same: "the first object of laudable ambition is to obtain a character as a human being, regardless of the distinction of sex" (Wollstonecraft, 1955, p. 5). Without education, she felt, women could not contribute to social progress as mature individuals, and this would be a tragic loss to the community. Though not the first to recognize the social restrictions arbitrarily placed on women, she was the first to hold those restrictions as directly responsible for the purported "defective nature" of women. She emphasized that women had never truly been given an equal chance to prove or disprove their merits. Seventy years later, John Stuart Mill (1955) also took up the cause of women's education, seeing it as one positive action to be taken in the direction of correcting the unjust social subordination of women. He felt that what appeared as woman's intellectual inferiority was actually no more than the effort to maintain the passive-dependent role relationship with man, her means of support:

> When we put together three things—first, the natural attraction between the sexes; secondly, the wife's entire dependence on the husband . . . and lastly, that the principal object of human pursuit, consideration, and all objects of social ambition, can in general be sought or obtained by her only through him, it would be a miracle if the object of being attractive to men had not become the polar star of feminine education and formation of character. (pp. 232–233)

Although Mill objected to fostering passivity and dependency in girls, other educators felt that this was precisely their duty. One of the more influential of the 19th century, Hannah More, rejected outright the proposal that women should share the same type of education as men, because "the chief end to be proposed in cultivating the understanding of women" was "to qualify them for the practical purposes of life" (see Smith, 1970, p. 101). To set one's sights on other than harmonious domesticity was to defy the natural order. Her readers were advised to be excellent women rather than indifferent men; to follow the "plain path which Providence has obviously marked out to the sex . . . rather than . . . stray awkwardly, unbecomingly, and unsuccessfully, in a forbidden road" (Smith, 1970, pp. 100–101). Her values were constant with those held by most of the middle class, and so her *Strictures on the Modern System of Female Education* (More, 1800) enjoyed widespread popularity for some time.

By the latter part of the century, the question had turned from whether girls should be educated like boys to how much they should be educated like boys. With the shift in emphasis came the question of coeducation. One of the strongest objections to coeducation in adolescence was the threat it posed to the "normalization" of the menstrual period. G. Stanley Hall (1906) waxed poetic on the issue:

> At a time when her whole future life depends upon normalizing the lunar month, is there not something not only unnatural and unhygienic, but a little monstrous, in daily school associations with boys, where she must suppress and conceal her instincts and feelings, at those times when her own promptings suggest withdrawal or stepping a little aside to let Lord Nature do his magnificent work of efflorescence. (p. 590).

Edward Clarke (see Sinclair, 1965, p. 123) had earlier elucidated the physiological reason for the restraint of girls from exertion in their studies: by forcing their brains to do work at puberty, they would use up blood later needed for menstruation.

Hall proposed an educational system for girls that would not only take into consideration their delicate physical nature but would also be tailored to prepare them for their special role in society. He feared that women's competition with men "in the world" would cause them to neglect their instinctive maternal urges and so bring about "race suicide." Because the glory of the female lay in motherhood, Hall believed that all educational and social institutions should be structured with that end in mind. Domestic arts would therefore be emphasized in special schools for adolescent girls, and disciplines such as philosophy, chemistry, and mathematics would be treated only superficially. If a girl had a notion to stay in the "male" system, she should be able to, but, Hall warned, such a woman selfishly interested in self-fulfillment would also be less likely to bear children and so be confined to an "agamic" life, thus failing to reproduce those very qualities that made her strong (Hall, 1918).

Throughout Hall's panegyric upon the beauties of female domestic education, there runs an undercurrent of the *real* threat that he perceived in coeducation, and that was the "feminization" of the American male. David Starr Jordan (1902) shared this objection but felt that coeducation would nevertheless make young men more "civilized" and young women less frivolous, tempering their natural pubescent inclinations. He was no champion of female ability though, stressing that women "on the whole, lack originality" (p. 100). The educated woman, he said, "is likely to master technic rather than art; method, rather than substance. She may know a good deal, but she can do nothing" (p. 101). In spite of this, he did assert that their training is just as serious and important as that of men. His position strongly favored the notion that the smaller range of female ability was the cause of lackluster female academic performance.

The issue of coeducation was not easily settled, and even as late as 1935, one finds debates over its relative merits *(Encyclopedia of the Social Sciences,* 1935, pp. 614–617).

The Biological Bases of Sex Differences

The variability hypothesis was compatible not only with prevailing attitudes concerning the appropriate form of female education but also with a highly popular theory of the biological complementarity of the sexes. The main tenet of Geddes and Thomson's (1890) theory was that males are primarily "catabolic," females "anabolic." From this difference in metabolism, all other sex differences in physical, intellectual, and emotional makeup were derived. The male was more agile, creative, and variable: the female was truer to the species type and therefore, in all respects, less variable. The conservatism of the female insured the continuity of the species. The author stressed the metabolic antecedents of female conservatism and male differentiation rather than variational tendency per se, and also put emphasis on the complementarity of the two natures:

> The feminine passivity is expressed in greater patience, more open-mindedness, greater appreciation of subtle details, and consequently what we call more rapid intuition. The masculine activity lends a greater power of maximum effort, of scientific insight, or cerebral experiment with impressions, and is associated with an unobservant or impatient disregard of minute details, but with a more stronger grasp of generalities. (p. 271)

The presentation of evolutionary theory anchored in yin-yang concepts of function represents the most positive evaluation of the female sex offered by 19th-century science. Whatever woman's shortcomings, they were necessary to complete her nature, which itself was necessary to complete man's: "Man thinks more, woman feels more. He discovers more, but remembers less; she is more receptive, and less forgetful" (Geddes & Thomson, 1890, p. 271).

Variability and the Testing Movement

Helen Thompson (later Woolley) put Geddes and Thompson's and other theories of sex differences in ability to what she felt was a crucial experimental test (see Thompson, 1903). Twenty-five men and 25 women participated in nearly 20 hours of individual testing of their intellectual, motor, and sensory abilities. Of more importance than her experimental results (whether men or women can tap a telegraph key more times per minute has lost its significance to psychology) was her discussion of the implications of the resulting negligible differences for current theories of sex differences. She was especially critical of the mass of inconsistencies inherent in contemporary biological theories:

> Women are said to represent concentration, patience, and stability in emotional life. One might logically conclude that prolonged concentration of attention and unbiased generalization would be their intellectual characteristics, but these are the very characteristics assigned to men. (p. 173)

In the face of such contradictions, she was forced to conclude that "if the author's views as to the mental differences of sex had been different, they might as easily have derived a very different set of characteristics" (pp. 173–174).

Thompson singled out the variability hypothesis for special criticism, objecting not only to the use of physical variation as evidence for intellectual variation but also to the tendency to minimize environmental influences. She held that training was responsible for sex differences in variation, and to those who countered that it is really a fundamental difference of instincts and characteristics that determines the differences in training, she replied that if this were true, "it would not be necessary to spend so much time and effort in making boys and girls follow the lines of conduct proper to their sex" (p. 181).

Thompson's recommendation to look at environmental factors went unheeded, as more and more evidence of woman's incapability of attaining eminence was amassed. In the surveys of eminent persons that were popular at the turn of the century, more credence was given to nature (à la Hall) than nurture (à la Thompson) for the near absence of eminent women (Cattell, 1903; Ellis 1904). Cattell (1903) found a ready-made explanation in the variability hypothesis: "Women depart less from the normal than man," ergo "the distribution of women is represented by a narrower bell-shaped curve" (p. 375). Cora Castle's (1913) survey of eminent women was no less critical of woman's failure to achieve at the top levels of power and prestige.

One of the most significant individuals to take up the cause of the variability hypothesis was Edward Thorndike. Much of the early work in the testing movement was done at Columbia University, which provided the perfect milieu for Thorndike's forays into the variability problem as applied to mental testing and educational philosophy. Thorndike based his case for the acceptance of the variability hypothesis on the reevaluation of the results of two studies (Thompson, 1903; Wissler, 1901) that had not themselves been directed toward the issue. Thorndike insisted that greater male variability only became meaningful when one examined the distribution of ability at the highest levels of giftedness. Measurement of more general sex differences could only "prove that the sexes are closely alike and that sex can account for only a very small fraction of human mental differences in the abilities listed" (Thorndike, 1910, p. 185). Since the range of female ability was narrower, he reasoned, the talents of women should be channeled into fields in which they would be most needed and most successful because "this one fundamental difference in variability is more important than all the difference between the average male and female capacities" (Thorndike, 1906):

> Not only the probability and the desirability of marriage and the training of children as an essential feature of woman's career, but also the restriction of women to the mediocre grades of ability and achievement should be reckoned with by our educational systems. The education of women for . . . professions . . . where a very few gifted individuals are what society requires, is far less needed than for such professions as nursing, teaching, medicine, or architecture, where the average level is the essential. (p. 213)

He felt perfectly justified in this recommendation because of "the patent fact that in the great achievements of the world in science, as, invention, and management, women have been far excelled by men" (Thorndike, 1910, p. 35). In Thorndike's view, environmental factors scarcely mattered.

Others, like Joseph Jastrow (1915), seemed to recognize the tremendous influence that societal pressure had upon achievement. He noted that even when women had been admitted to employment from which they had previously been excluded, new prejudices arose: "allowances and considerations for sex intrude, favorably or unfavorably; the avenues of preferment, though ostensibly open are really barred by invisible barriers of social prejudice" (pp. 567–568). This was little more than lip service because he was even more committed to the importance of variational tendency and its predominance over any possible extenuating factors: the effects of the variability of the male and the biological conservatism of the female "radiates to every distinctive aspect of their contrasted natures and expressions" (p. 568).

A small but persistent minority challenged the validity of the variability hypothesis, and it is not surprising that this minority was composed mainly of women. Although the "woman question" was, to some degree, at issue, the larger dispute was between those who stressed "nature" as the major determinant of ability (and therefore success) and those who rejected nature and its corollary, instead emphasizing the importance of environmental factors. Helen Thompson Woolley, while remaining firmly committed to the investigation of the differential effects of social factors of each sex, did not directly involve herself in the variability controversy. Leta Stetter Hollingworth, first a student and then a colleague of Thorndike's at Teachers College of Columbia University, actively investigated the validity of the hypothesis and presented sound objections to it. She argued that there was no real basis for assuming that the distribution of "mental traits" in the population conforms without exception to the Gaussian distribution. The assumption of normality was extremely important to the validity of the variability hypothesis, because only in a normal distribution would a difference in variability indicate a difference in range. It was the greater range of male ability that was used to "prove" the ultimate superiority of male ability. Greater range of male ability was usually verified by citing lists of eminent persons (dominated by men) and the numbers and sex of those in institutions for the feebleminded (also dominated by men). Hollingworth (1914) saw no reason to resort to biological theory for an explanation of the phenomenon when a more parsimonious one was available in social fact. Statistics reporting a larger number of males among the feebleminded could be explained by the fact that the supporting data had been gathered in institutions, where men were more likely to be admitted than women of an equal degree of retardation. That better ability of feebleminded women to survive outside the institutional setting was simply a function of female social role:

> Women have been made and are a dependent and non-competitive class, and when defective can more easily survive outside of institutions, since they do not have to compete *mentally* with normal individuals, as men do, to maintain themselves in the social *milieu*. (Hollingworth, 1914, p. 515)

Women would therefore be more likely to be institutionalized at an older age than men, after they had become too old to be "useful" or self-supporting. A survey of age and sex ratios in New York institutions supported her hypothesis: the ratio of females to males increased with the age of the inmates (Hollingworth, 1913). As for the rarity of eminence among women, Hollingworth (1914) argued that because of the social role of women was defined in terms of housekeeping and child-rearing functions, "a field where eminence is not possible," and because of concomitant constraints placed on the education and employment of women by law, custom, and the demands of the role, one could not possible validly compare the achievements of women with those of men who "have followed the greatest possible range of occupations, and have at the same time procreated unhindered" (p. 528). She repeatedly emphasized (Hollingworth, 1914, 1916) that the true potential of woman could only be known when she began to receive social acceptance of her right to choose career, maternity, or both.

Hollingworth's argument that unrecognized differences in social training had misdirected the search for *inherent* sex differences had earlier been voiced by Mary Calkins (1896). Just as Hollingworth directed her response particularly at Thorndike's formulation of the variability hypothesis, Calkins objected to Jastrow's (1896) intimations that one finds "greater uniformity amongst women than amongst men" (p. 431).

Hollingworth's work was instrumental in bringing the variability issue to a crisis point, not only because she presented persuasive empirical data to support her contentions but also because this was simply the first major opposition that the variability hypothesis had encountered. Real resolution of this crisis had to await the development of more sophisticated testing and statistical techniques. With the United States' involvement in World War I, most testing efforts were redirected to wartime uses. This redirection effectively terminated the variability debate, and although it resumed during the postwar years, the renewed controversy never attained the force of conviction that had characterized the earlier period. "Variational tendency" became a statistical issue, and the pedagogic implications that had earlier colored the debate were either minimized or disguised in more egalitarian terms.

After its revival in the mid-1920s, investigation of the variability hypothesis was often undertaken as part of larger intelligence testing projects. Evidence in its favor began to look more convincing than it ever had. The use of larger samples, standardized tests, and newer methods of computing variation gave an appearance of increased accuracy, but conclusions were still based on insubstantial evidence of questionable character. Most discussions of the topic concluded that there were not enough valid data to resolve the issue and that even if those data were available, variation within each sex is so much greater than the difference in variation between sexes that the "meaning" of the variability hypothesis was trivial (Shields, Note 1).

MATERNAL INSTINCT

The concept of maternal instinct was firmly entrenched in American psychology before American psychology itself existed as an entity. The first book to appear in the United States with "psychology" in its title outlined the psychological sex differences arising from the physical differences between men and women. Differences in structure were assumed to imply differences in function, and therefore differences in abilities, temperament, and intelligence. In each sex a different set of physical systems was thought to predominate: "In man the arterial and cerebral system prevail, and with them irritability; in women the venous and ganglion systems and with them plasticity and sensibility" (Rausch, 1841, p. 81). The systems dominant in woman caused her greatest attributes to lie in the moral sphere in the form of love, patience, and chastity. In the intellectual sphere, she was not equally blessed, "and this is not accidental, not because no opportunity has offered itself to their productive genius . . . but because it is their highest happiness to be mothers" (Rausch, 1841, p. 83).

Although there was popular acceptance of a maternal instinct in this country, the primary impetus for its incorporation into psychology came by way of British discussion of social evolution. While the variability hypothesis gained attention because of an argument, the concept of maternal instinct evolved without conflict. There was consistent agreement as to its existence, if not its precise nature or form. Typical of the evolutionary point of view was the notion that woman's emotional nature (including her tendency to nurturance) was a direct consequence of her reproductive physiology. As Herbert Spencer (1891) explained it, the female's energies were directed toward preparation for pregnancy and lactation, reducing the energy available for the development of other qualities. This resulted in a "rather earlier cessation of individual evolution" in the female. Woman was, in essence, a stunted man. Her lower stage of development was evident not only in her inferior mental and emotional powers but also in the resulting expression of the parental instinct. Whereas the objectivity of the male caused his concern to be extended "to all the relatively weak who are dependent upon him" (p. 375), the female's propensity to "dwell on the concrete and proximate rather than on the abstract and remote" made her incapable of the generalized protective attitude assumed by the male. Instead, she was primarily responsive to "infantile helplessness."

Alexander Sutherland (1898) also described a parental instinct whose major characteristic (concern for the weak) was "the basis of all other sympathy," which is itself "the ultimate basis of all moral feeling" (p. 156). Like his contemporaries (e.g., McDougall, 1913, 1923; Shand, 1920; Spencer, 1891), Sutherland revered maternal sentiment but thought the expression of parental instinct in the male, that is, a protective attitude, was a much more significant factor in social evolution, an attitude of benevolent paternalism more in keeping with Victorian social ethic than biological reality. The expression of the parental instinct in men, Sutherland thought, must necessarily lead to deference toward women out of "sympathetic regard for women's weakness." He noted that male protectiveness had indeed wrought a change in the relations between the sexes, evident in a trend away from sexual motivations and toward a general improvement in moral tone, witness the "large number of men who lead perfectly chaste lives for ten or twenty years after puberty before they marry," which demonstrated that the "sensuous side of man's nature is slowly passing under the control of sympathetic sentiments" (p. 288).

Whatever facet of the activity that was emphasized, there was common agreement that the maternal (or parental) instinct was truly an instinct. A. F. Shand (1920) argued that the maternal instinct is actually composed of an ordered "system" of instincts and characterized by a number of emotions. Despite its complexity, "maternal love" was considered to be a hereditary trait "in respect not only of its instincts, but also of the bond connecting its primary emotions, and of the end which the whole system pursues, namely, the preservation of the offspring" (p. 42). The sociologist L. T. Hobhouse (1916) agreed that maternal instinct was a "true" instinct, "not only in the drive but in some of the detail." He doubted the existence of a corresponding paternal instinct, however, since he had observed that few men have a natural aptitude with babies.

The unquestioning acceptance of the maternal instinct concept was just as prevalent in this country as it was in Britain. William James (1950) listed parental love among the instincts of humans and emphasized the strength with which it was expressed in women. He was particularly impressed with the mother-infant relationship and quoted at length from a German psychologist concerning the changes wrought in a woman at the birth of her child: "She has, in one word, transferred her entire egoism to the child, and lives only in it" (p. 439). Even among those who employed a much narrower definition of instinct than James, maternal behavior was thought to be mediated by inherent neural connections. R. P. Halleck (1895) argued that comparatively few instincts are fully developed in humans, because reason intervenes and modifies their expression to fit the circumstances. Maternal instinct qualified as a clear exception, and its expression seemed as primitive and unrefined as that of infants' reflexive behavior.

Others (e.g., Jastrow, 1915; Thorndike, 1914a, 1914b) treated instinct more as a quality of character than of biology. Edward Thorndike (1911) considered the instincts peculiar to each sex to be the primary source of sex differences: "it appears that if the primary sex characters—the instincts directly related to courtship, love, child-bearing, and nursing—are left out of account, the average man differs from the average woman far less than many men differ from one another" (p. 30). Thorndike taught that the tendency to display maternal concern was universal among women, although social pressures could "complicate or deform" it. He conceded that males share in an instinctive "good will toward children," but other instincts, such as the "hunting instinct," predominated (Thorndike, 1914b).

He was so sure of the innate instinctual differences between men and women that it was his contention (Thorndike, 1914b) that even "if we should keep the environment of boys and girls absolutely similar these instincts would produce sure and important differences between the mental and moral activities of boys and girls" (p. 203). The expression of instincts therefore was thought to have far-reaching effects on seemingly unrelated areas of ability and conduct. For example, woman's "nursing instinct," which was most often exhibited in "unreasoning tendencies to pet, coddle, and 'do for' others," was also "the chief source of woman's superiorities in the moral life" (Thorndike, 1914a, p. 203). Another of the female's instinctive tendencies was described as "submission to mastery":

> Women in general are thus by original nature submissive to men in general. Submissive behavior is apparently not annoying when assumed as the instinctive response to its natural stimulus. Indeed, it is perhaps a common satisfier. (Thorndike, 1914b, p. 34)

The existence of such an "instinct" would, of course, validate the social norm of female subservience and dependence. An assertive woman would be acting contrary to instinct and therefore contrary to *nature*. There is a striking similarity between Thorndike's description of female nature and that of the Freudians with their mutual emphasis on woman's passivity, dependency, and masochism. For Thorndike, however, the *cause* of such a female attitude was thought to be something quite different from mutilation fears and penis envy.

The most vocal proponent of instinct, first in England and later in this country, was William McDougall (1923). Unlike Shand, he regarded "parental sentiment" as a primary instinct and did not hesitate to be highly critical of those who disagreed with him. When his position was maligned by the behaviorists, his counterattack was especially strong:

> And, when we notice how in so many ways the behavior of the human mother most closely resembles that of the animal-mother, can we doubt that . . . if the animal-mother is moved by the impulse of a maternal instinct, so also is the woman? To repudiate this view as baseless would seem to me the height of blindness and folly, yet it is the folly of a number of psychologists who pride themselves on being strictly "scientific" (p. 136)

In McDougall's system of instincts, each of the primary instincts in humans was accompanied by a particular emotional quality. The parental instinct had as its primary emotional quality the "tender emotion" vaguely defined as love, tenderness, and tender feeling. Another of the primary instincts was that of "pairing," its primary emotional quality that of sexual emotion or excitement, "sometimes called love—an unfortunate and confusing usage" (p. 234). Highly critical of what he called the "Freudian dogma that all love is sexual," McDougall proposed that it was the interaction of the parental and pairing instincts that was the basis of heterosexual "love." "Female coyness," which initiated the courtship ritual, was simply the reproductively oriented manifestation of the instincts of self-display and self-abasement. The appearance of a suitable male would elicit coyness from the female, and at that point the male's parental instinct would come into play:

> A certain physical weakness and delicacy (probably moral also) about the normal young woman or girl constitute in her a resemblance to a child. This resemblance . . . throws the man habitually into the protective attitude, evokes the impulse and emotion of the parental instinct. He feels that he wants to protect and shield and help her in every way. (p. 425)

Once the "sexual impulse" had added its energy to the relationship, the young man was surely trapped, and the survival of the species was insured. McDougall, while firmly committed to the importance of instinct all the way up the evolutionary ladder, never lost his sense of Victorian delicacy: while pairing simply meant reproduction in lower animals, in humans it was accorded a tone of gallantry and concern.

The fate of instinct at the hands of the radical behaviorists is a well-known tale. Perhaps the most adamant, as well as notorious, critic of the instinct concept was J. B. Watson (1926). Like those before him who had relied upon observation to prove the existence of maternal instinct, he used observation to confirm its nonexistence:

> We have observed the nursing, handling, bathing, etc. of the first baby of a good many mothers. Certainly there are no new ready-made activities appearing except nursing. The mother is usually as awkward about that as she can well be. The instinctive factors are practically nil. (p. 54)

Watson attributed the appearance of instinctive behavior to the mother's effort to conform to societal expectations of her successful role performance. He, like the 19th-century British associationist Alexander Bain, speculated that not a little of the mother's pleasure in nursing and caring for the infant was due to the sexually stimulating effect of those activities.

Even the most dedicated behaviorists hedged a bit when it came to discarding the idea of instinct altogether. Although the teleology and redundancy of the concept of instinct were sharply criticized, some belief in "instinctive activity" was typically retained (cf. Dunlap, 1919–1920). W. B. Pillsbury (1926), for example, believed that the parental instinct was a "secondary" instinct. Physical attraction to the infant guided the mother's first positive movements toward the infant, but trial and error guided her subsequent care. Instinct was thought of as that quality which set the entire pattern of maternal behavior in motion.

In time instinct was translated into *drive* and *motivation*, refined concepts more in keeping with behavioristic theory. Concomitantly, interest in the maternal instinct of human females gave way to the study of mothering behavior in rodents. The concept of maternal instinct did find a place in psychoanalytic theory, but its definition bore little resemblance to that previously popular. Not only did maternal instinct lose the connotation of protectiveness and gentility that an earlier generation of psychologists had ascribed to it, but it was regarded as basically sexual, masochistic, and even destructive in nature (cf. Rheingold, 1964).

THE ASCENDANCY OF PSYCHOANALYTIC THEORY

The functionalists, because of their emphasis on "nature," were predictably indifferent to the study of social sex roles and cultural concepts of masculine and feminine. The behaviorists, despite their emphasis on "nurture," were slow to recognize those same social forces. During the early 1930s, there was little meaningful ongoing research in female psychology: the point of view taken by the functionalists was no longer a viable one, and the behaviorists with their emphasis on nonsocial topics (i.e., learning and motivation) had no time for serious consideration of sex differences. While the functionalists had defined laws of behavior that mirrored the society of the times, behaviorists concentrated their efforts on defining universal laws that operated in any time, place, or organism. Individual differences in nature were expected during the functionalist era because they were the sine qua non of a Darwinian view of the world and of science. The same individual differences were anathema to early learning-centered psychology because, no longer necessary or expedient, they were a threat to the formulation of universal laws of behavior.

In the hiatus created by the capitulation of functionalism to behaviorism, the study of sex differences and female nature fell within the domain of psychoanalytic theory—the theory purported to have all the answers. Freudian theory (or some form of it) had for some years already served as the basis for a psychology of female physiological function (cf. Benedek & Rubenstein, 1939). The application of principles popular in psychiatry and medicine (and their inescapable identification with pathology) to academic psychology was easily accomplished. Psychoanalytic theory provided psychology with the first comprehensive theoretical explanation of sex differences. Its novelty in that respect aided its assimilation.

Psychology proper, as well as the general public, had been well-prepared for a biological, and frankly sexual, theory of male and female nature. Havelock Ellis, although himself ambivalent and even hostile toward Freudian teachings, had done much through his writing to encourage openness in the discussion of sexuality. He brought a number of hitherto unmentionable issues to open discussion, couching them in the commonly accepted notion of the complementarity of the sexes, thus insuring their popular acceptance. Emphasis on masculinity and femininity as real dimensions of personality appeared in the mid-1930s in the form of the Terman Masculinity-Femininity Scale (Terman & Miles, 1968). Although Lewis Terman himself avoided discussion of whether masculinity and femininity were products of nature or nurture, social determinants of masculinity and femininity were commonly deemphasized in favor of the notion that they were a type of psychological secondary sexual characteristic. Acceptance of social sex role soon came to be perceived as an indicator of one's mental health.

The traps inherent in a purely psychoanalytic concept of female nature were seldom recognized. John Dewey's (1957) observation, made in 1922, merits attention, not only for its accuracy but because its substance can be found in present-day refutations of the adequacy of psychoanalytic theory as an explanation of woman's behavior and "nature":

> The treatment of sex by psycho-analysts is most instructive, for it flagrantly exhibits both the consequences of artificial simplification and the transformation of social results into psychic causes. Writers, usually male, hold forth on the psychology of women, as if they were dealing with a Platonic universal entity, although they habitually treat men as individuals, varying with structure and environment. They treat phenomena which are peculiarly symptoms of civilization of the West at the present time as if they were the necessary effects of fixed nature impulses of human nature. (pp. 143–144)

The identification of the psychology of women with psychoanalytic theory was nearly complete by the mid-1930s and was so successful that many psychologists today, even those most deeply involved in the current movement for a psychology of women, are not aware that there was a psychology of women long before there was a Sigmund Freud. This article has dealt only with a brief period in that history, and then only with the most significant topics of that period. Lesser issues were often just as hotly debated, for example, whether there is an innate difference in the style of handwriting of men and women (cf. Allen, 1927; Downey, 1910).

And what has happened to the issues of brain size, variability, and maternal instinct since the 1930s? Where they are politically and socially useful, they have an uncanny knack of reappearing, albeit in an altered form. For example, the search for central nervous system differences between males and females has continued. Perhaps the most popular form this search has taken is the theory of prenatal hormonal "organization" of the hypothalamus into exclusively male or female patterns of function (Harris & Levine, 1965). The proponents of this theory maintain an Aristotelian view of woman as an incomplete man:

> In the development of the embryo, nature's first choice or primal impulse is to differentiate a female. . . . The principle of differentiation is always that to obtain a male, something must be added. Subtract that something, and the result will be a female. (Money, 1970, p. 428)

The concept of maternal instinct, on the other hand, has recently been taken up and refashioned by a segment of the woman's movement. Pregnancy and childbirth are acclaimed as important expressions of womanliness whose satisfactions cannot be truly appreciated by males. The idea that women are burdened with "unreasoning tendencies to pet, coddle, and 'do for' others" has been disposed of by others and replaced by the semiserious proposal that if any "instinctive" component of parental concern exists, it is a peculiarly male attribute (Stannard, 1970). The variability hypothesis is all but absent from contemporary psychological work, but if it ever again promises a viable justification for existing social values, it will be back as strongly as ever. Conditions which would favor its revival include the renaissance of rugged individualism or the "need" to suppress some segment of society, for example, women's aspirations to positions of power. In the first case the hypothesis would serve to reaffirm that there are those "born to lead," and in the latter that there are those "destined to follow."

Of more importance than the issues themselves or their fate in contemporary psychology is the recognition of the role that they have played historically in the psychology of women: the role of social myth. Graves (1968, p. v) included among the functions of mythologizing that of justification of existing social systems. This function was clearly operative throughout the evolutionist-functionalist treatment of the psychology of women: the "discovery" of sex differences in brain structure to correspond to "appropriate" sex differences in brain function; the biological justification (via the variability hypothesis) for the enforcement of woman's subordinate social status; the Victorian weakness and gentility associated with maternity; and pervading each of these themes, the assumption of an innate emotional, sexless, unimaginative female character that played the perfect foil to the Darwinian male. That science played handmaiden to social values cannot be denied. Whether a parallel situation exists in today's study of sex differences is open to question.

REFERENCE NOTE

1. Shields, S. A. *The variability hypothesis and sex differences in intelligence.* Unpublished manuscript, 1974. (Available from Department of Psychology, Pennsylvania State University.)

REFERENCES

Allen, C. N. Studies in sex differences. *Psychological Bulletin,* 1927, *24,* 294–304.

Bain, A. *Mental science.* New York: Appleton, 1875.

Benedek, T., & Rubenstein, B. B. The correlations between ovarian activity and psychodynamic processes. II. The menstrual phase. *Psychosomatic Medicine, 1939, 1,* 461–485.

Calkins, M. W. Community of ideas of men and women. *Psychological Review,* 1896, *3,* 426–430.

Castle, C. A. A statistical study of eminent women. *Columbia Contributions to Philosophy and Psychology,* 1913, 22(27).

Cattell, J. McK. A statistical study of eminent men. *Popular Science Monthly,* 1903, *62,* 359–377.

Darwin, C. *The descent of man* (2nd ed.). London: John Murray, 1922. (Originally published, 1871; 2nd edition originally published, 1874.)

Dewey, J. *Human nature and conduct.* New York: Random House, 1957.

Downey, J. E. Judgment on the sex of handwriting. *Psychological Review,* 1910, *17,* 205–216.

Dunlap, J. Are there any instincts? *Journal of Abnormal and Social Psychology,* 1919–1920, *14,* 307–311.

Elliott, H. C. *Textbook of neuroanatomy* (2nd ed.). Philadelphia: Lippincott, 1969.

Ellis, H. *Man and woman: A study of human secondary sexual characters.* London: Walter Scott; New York: Scribner's, 1894.

Ellis, H. Variation in man and woman. *Popular Science Monthly, 1903, 62,* 237–253.

Ellis, H. *A study of British genius.* London: Hurst & Blackett, 1904.

Ellis, H. *Man and woman, a study of secondary and*

tertiary sexual characteristics (8th rev. ed.). London: Heinemann, 1934.
Encyclopedia of the Social Sciences. New York: Macmillan, 1935.
Galton, F. *Inquiries into the human faculty and its development.* London: Dent, 1907.
Geddes, P., & Thomson, J. A. *The evolution of sex.* New York: Scribner & Welford, 1890.
Graves, R. Introduction. In *New Larousse encyclopedia of mythology* (Rev. ed.). London: Paul Hamlyn, 1968.
Hall, G. S. The question of coeducation. *Munsey's Magazine,* 1906, *34,* 588–592.
Hall, G. S. *Youth, its education, regimen and hygiene.* New York: Appleton, 1918.
Halleck, R. *Psychology and psychic culture.* New York: American Book, 1895.
Harris, G. W., & Levine, S. Sexual differentiation of the brain and its experimental control. *Journal of Physiology,* 1965, *181,* 379–400.
Hobhouse, L. *Morals in evolution.* New York: Holt, 1916.
Hollingworth, L. S. The frequency of amentia as related to sex. *Medical Record,* 1913, *84,* 753–756.
Hollingworth, L. S. Variability as related to sex differences in achievement. *American Journal of Sociology,* 1914, *19,* 510–530.
Hollingworth, L. S. Social devices for impelling women to bear and rear children. *American Journal of Sociology,* 1916, *22,* 19–29.
Huarte, J. *The examination of mens wits* (trans. from Spanish to Italian by M. Camilli; trans. from Italian to English by R. Carew). Gainesville, Fla.: Scholars' Facsimiles and Reprints, 1959.
James, W. *The principles of psychology.* New York: Dover, 1950.
Jastrow, J. Note on Calkins' "Community of ideas of men and women." *Psychological Review,* 1896, *3,* 430–431.
Jastrow, J. *Character and temperament.* New York: Appleton, 1915.
Jordan, D. S. The higher education of women. *Popular Science Monthly,* 1902, *62,* 97–107.
Mall, F. P. On several anatomical characters of the human brain, said to vary according to race and sex, with especial reference to the weight of the frontal lobe. *American Journal of Anatomy,* 1909, *9,* 1–32.
McDougall, W. *An introduction to social psychology* (7th ed.). London: Methuen, 1913.
McDougall, W. *Outline of psychology.* New York: Scribner's, 1923.
Meyer, M. *Psychology of the other-one.* Columbia: Missouri Book, 1921.
Mill, J. S. *The subjection of women.* London: Dent, 1955.
Mobius, P. J. The physiological mental weakness of woman (A. McCorn, Trans.). *Alienist and Neurologist, 1901, 22,* 624–642.
Money, J. Sexual dimorphism and homosexual gender identity. *Psychological Bulletin,* 1970, *74,* 425–440.
More, H. *Strictures on the modern system of female education. With a view of the principles and conduct prevalent among women of rank and fortune.* Philadelphia, Pa.: Printed by Budd and Bertram for Thomas Dobson, 1800.
Patrick, G. T. W. The psychology of women. *Popular Science Monthly, 1895, 47,* 209–225.
Pearson, K. Variation in man and woman. In *The chances of death* (Vol. 1). London: Edward Arnold, 1897.
Pillsbury, W. B. *Education as the psychologist sees it.* New York: Macmillan, 1926.
Porteus, S., & Babcock, M. E. *Temperament and race.* Boston: Gorham Press, 1926.
Rausch, F. A. *Psychology; Or, a view of the human soul including anthropology* (2nd rev. ed.). New York: Dodd, 1841.
Rheingold, J. *The fear of being a woman.* New York: Grune & Stratton, 1964.
Romanes, G. J. Mental differences between men and women. *Nineteenth Century,* 1887, *21,* 654–672.
Shand, A. F. *The foundations of character.* London: Macmillan, 1920.
Sinclair, A. *The better half: The emancipation of the American woman.* New York: Harper & Row, 1965.
Smith, P. *Daughters of the promised land.* Boston: Little, Brown, 1970.
Spencer, H. *The study of sociology.* New York: Appleton, 1891.
Stannard, U. Adam's rib, or the woman within. *Trans Action,* 1970, *8,* 24–35.
Sutherland, A. *The origin and growth of the moral*

instinct (Vol. 1). London: Longmans, Green, 1898.

Terman, L., & Miles, C. C. *Sex and personality*. New York: Russell and Russell, 1968.

Thompson, H. B. *The mental traits of sex*. Chicago: University of Chicago Press, 1903.

Thorndike, E. L. Sex in education. *The Bookman*, 1906, *23*, 211–214.

Thorndike, E. L. *Educational psychology*. (2nd ed.). New York: Teachers College, Columbia University, 1910.

Thorndike, E. L. *Individuality*. Boston: Houghton Mifflin, 1911.

Thorndike, E. L. *Educational psychology* (Vol. 3). New York: Teachers College, Columbia University, 1914. (a)

Thorndike, E. L. *Educational psychology briefer course*. New York: Teachers College, Columbia University, 1914. (b)

Walker, A. *Woman physiologically considered*. New York: J. & H. G. Langley, 1850.

Watson, J. B. Studies on the growth of the emotions. In *Psychologies of 1925*. Worcester, Mass.: Clark University Press, 1926.

Weininger, O. *Sex and character* (trans.). London: Heinemann, 1906.

Wissler, C. The correlation of mental and physical tests. *Psychological Review Monograph Supplements*, 1899–1901, *3* (6, Whole No. 16).

Wollstonecraft, M. *A vindication of the rights of woman*. New York: Dutton, 1955.

Woolley, H. T. Psychological literature: A review of the recent literature on the psychology of sex. *Psychological Bulletin*, 1910, *7*, 335–342.

Wundt, W. *Ethics*. Vol. 3: *The principles of morality, and the departments of the moral life* (M. F. Washburn, Trans.). London: Sonnenschein, 1901.

CHAPTER 10

ANIMAL EXPERIMENTAL PSYCHOLOGY

The next chapter considers behaviorism, probably the most important school of thought in the history of American psychology. In starting its conceptual revolution, behaviorism borrowed from functionalism. But of equal importance was the legacy from animal psychology. This chapter focuses on animal work, not in the sense of providing a history of animal psychology but for providing the context necessary to understand its contributions to behaviorism.

Once Darwin had removed humans from their lofty perch and placed them with the rest of the animal kingdom, the study of animal behavior took on a new meaning. In 1882, the year of Darwin's death, George Romanes (1848–1894), an English biologist, published his *Animal Intelligence,* a book that is considered by many historians as the first textbook on comparative psychology. Romanes studied both vertebrates and invertebrates, attempting to compare their mental processes, which he investigated by his technique of *introspection by analogy*. That means that in observing animals he would try to understand their behavior by asking himself what he would do in a similar situation. Not surprisingly, his book was considerably anthropomorphic.

C. Lloyd Morgan (1852–1936), another of the English biologists influenced by Darwin, objected to the practice of Romanes and others attributing human faculties, such as reason, to animals lower in the phylogenetic scale, when in fact such attributions might not be warranted. In his 1894 book, *Introduction to Comparative Psychology,* Morgan stated what has become known as Morgan's Canon: that in explaining animal behavior, a higher mental process should not be invoked if the behavior can be adequately explained by a lower mental process. Although Morgan insisted on parsimonious explanations for animal behavior, he did not object to introspection by analogy and used the method himself. However, he also performed experiments with animals in their natural settings, an important step forward for animal psychology.

Whereas Romanes, Morgan, and others sought to explain the mental processes of animals, the German biologist Jacques Loeb (1859–1924), who did much of his research in the United States, was arguing that much animal behavior occurred without regard to any mental activity. He introduced his concept of *tropism,* meaning a response that occurred involuntarily to a stimulus. He noted that plants turned their leaves toward the sun in an automatic response (heliotropism) and argued that much animal behavior could be explained in a similar fashion. For the behaviorists, Loeb's ideas had special appeal: "If the actions of lower organisms can be explained without reference to mental events, why cannot human behavior be explained in the same way." (Kendler, 1987, p. 153).

In opposition to Loeb, an American psychologist, Edward L. Thorndike (1874–1949), sought to show the relationship between mental processes in lower animals and those in humans. Thorndike, whose interests in animal behavior were attributed to C. Lloyd Morgan, began his animal research career testing baby chicks in mazes set up in the basement of William James's home. He later moved from Harvard University to Columbia University, where he continued his animal research in Cattell's laboratories, taking his doctorate in psychology there in 1898. His dissertation, entitled "Animal Intelligence," described his maze studies with chicks and his now-classic puzzle box experiments with cats and dogs. Thorndike constructed fifteen puzzle boxes in which the animals were placed (see Burnham, 1972). Each box required a different response for escape. Once the animal had made the correct response and had escaped from the box, it was rewarded with food. Thorndike found that his animal subjects learned to escape the boxes in a trial-and-error fashion (which he took as evidence against the operation of mental processes in animals); the correct responses were gradually learned, whereas those responses that did not lead to escape were gradually eliminated from the animal's behavior in the box. From this he formulated his *law of effect,* which is today recognized as the forerunner of the *law of reinforcement:*

> Any act which in a given situation produces satisfaction becomes associated with that situation, so that when the situation recurs the act is more likely than before to recur also. Conversely, any act which in a given situation produces discomfort becomes disassociated from the situation, so that when the situation recurs the act is less likely than before to recur. (Thorndike, 1905, p. 203)

The first part of that law describes the effects of what has come to be called reinforcement, and the second part the effects of punishment. Much later, Thorndike eliminated the second part when research showed that punishment suppressed stimulus–response connections but did not necessarily weaken them (this subsequent version is called the *truncated law of effect*).

Thorndike was a busy researcher and a prolific writer throughout his career, publishing more than five hundred works, a number of those books. But his animal research was confined to the early years of his career, and was largely abandoned by 1911 as he pursued his interests in educational psychology and mental testing (see O'Donnell, 1985). Nevertheless, his animal work ranks among his most important work, both methodologically and theoretically. It would play a very influential role in the rise of learning research and the dominance of learning theory throughout the reign of behaviorism (see Chapters 11 and 12). Further, Thorndike was among the first scientists (some historians say the first) to conduct research with animals in a laboratory setting. His procedures served as models for much of the early animal psychology in the United States (Gottlieb, 1979).

Some histories of psychology label Thorndike a functionalist, others see him as a behaviorist. He denied membership in either. His placement in this chapter is meant to show his work as intermediate between the two.

While Thorndike was watching his animals escape from the puzzle boxes, a Russian physiologist was beginning to explore what he termed a *psychic reflex*—the salivation that could be elicited in an animal upon presenting a stimulus, when that stimulus had been previously paired with food. Ivan Pavlov (1849–1936) spent the last thirty-four years of his life working out the various facets of what we call *classical conditioning* (or Pavlovian conditioning). Independent of Thorndike, he and his co-workers discovered the principle of reinforcement and many other learning phenomena such as extinction, spontaneous recovery, generalization, discrimination, conditioned inhibition, conditioned emotional reactions, and higher-order conditioning (see Windholz, 1990). Once his work became known to American psychologists, around 1909, it proved to be an important influence for those looking to move psychology away from mentalism to a more objective study of observable behavior.

Unlike Romanes, who had attributed much consciousness to animals, Thorndike found little evidence for animal consciousness in his puzzle-box studies. Consistent with that view was Loeb's emphasis on animal tropisms, which discarded any need for assuming animal consciousness. Pavlov's work added weight to this view as well. He rejected the mentalism of psychology (indeed, he rejected all of psychology until the last few years of his life) and called for a total explanation of the higher mental processes in terms of physiological processes. Perhaps, as the behaviorists would soon assert, psychology could discard the mind and provide a wholly scientific account based on observable behavior and physiology.

THE READINGS

The first selection in this chapter is on the psychology of learning, written by Edward L. Thorndike. In it he discusses his laws of effect, exercise, and readiness in the context of his animal studies. It is an elegant statement of this classic early work in learning.

The second selection is on Pavlov's work, but it was not written by Pavlov. Instead, it is the article published in the *Psychological Bulletin* in 1909 that first introduced American psychologists to the work of Pavlov. The authors are Robert M. Yerkes (1876–1956), a pioneer researcher in animal behavior, and a Russian student, Sergius Morgulis. In spite of Pavlov's negative views toward psychology, it was a paper that would generate considerable interest, particularly for behaviorist John B. Watson (whose use of it is described in the next chapter).

The third selection is by Donald A. Dewsbury, a historian of psychology at the University of Florida, whose research has focused on the history of the study of animal behavior. In this article, he traces concerns about the humane treatment of animals in the history of animal experimentation, beginning with the Victorian antivivisectionist movement. He presents the animal research views of Darwin, Romanes, James, Angell, Dewey, Yerkes, and Pavlov, and focuses on a controversial study published in 1907 by John Watson (the subject of the next chapter) that a *New York Times* editorial described as torture. In this excellent review, Dewsbury describes the long and intertwined history of psychology's animal researchers and their critics, concluding with a description of the formation of the American Psychological Association's Committee on Animal Experimentation.

The final selection is by Ludy T. Benjamin, Jr., the editor of this book, and Darryl Bruce, a cognitive psychologist at St. Mary's University in Nova Scotia, whose historical research has focused on comparative psychology, particularly the work of Karl Lashley. This selection describes the work of comparative psychologist Winthrop Kellogg (1898–1972), who was educated in functional psychology, receiving his doctorate at Columbia University in 1929, where he worked with Robert Woodworth and animal researcher Carl Warden. In his early research at Indiana University, Kellogg used Pavlovian conditioning studies in dogs to investigate the nature of learning; however, a move to Florida in 1950 introduced a dramatic shift in his research to the study of porpoises and their use of echolocation. This article describes both of those research programs and their importance for comparative psychology. However, the focus of the article is on a single study conducted in 1931–1932, in which Winthrop and Luella Kellogg raised their infant son with an infant chimpanzee. The nine-month study was an *experimentum crucis,* the kind of grand experiment that Franz Brentano, a contemporary of Wundt, had argued was critical for the advancement of the science of psychology. The highly controversial experiment sought to answer the nature–nurture question by determining how human a chimp could become when raised like a child in a human environment. Like most crucial experiments, it was incapable of fully answering the grand question that it tackled; however, it was an imaginative and well-controlled undertaking that has continued to generate discussion in psychology.

REFERENCES

Burnham, J. C. (1972). Thorndike's puzzle boxes. *Journal of the History of the Behavioral Sciences, 8,* 159–167.

Gottlieb, G. (1979). Comparative psychology and ethology. In E. Hearst (Ed.), *The first century of experimental psychology,* pp. 147–173. Hillsdale, NJ: Lawrence Erlbaum.

Kendler, H. H. (1987). *Historical foundations of modern psychology.* Chicago: Dorsey Press.

Morgan, C. L. (1894). *An introduction to comparative psychology.* London: Walter Scott.

O'Donnell, J. M. (1985). *The origins of behaviorism: American psychology, 1870–1920.* New York: New York University Press.

Thorndike, E. L. (1905). *The elements of psychology.* New York: A. G. Seiler.

Watson, J. B. (1907). Kinaesthetic and organic sensations: Their role in the reactions of the white rat to the maze. *Psychological Review Monograph Supplements, 8(33),* 1–100.

Windholz, G. (1990). Pavlov and the Pavlovians in the laboratory. *Journal of the History of the Behavioral Sciences, 25,* 64–74.

The Laws of Learning in Animals

Edward L. Thorndike

SAMPLES OF ANIMAL LEARNING

The complexities of human learning will in the end be best understood if at first we avoid them, examining rather the behavior of the lower animals as they learn to meet certain situations in changed, and more remunerative, ways.

Let a number of chicks, say six to twelve days old, be kept in a yard (YY of Figure 1) adjoining which is a pen or maze (A B C D E of Figure 1). A chick is taken from the group and put in alone at A. It is confronted by a situation which is, in essence, *Confining walls and the absence of the other chicks, food and familiar surroundings.* It reacts to the situation by running around, making loud sounds, and jumping at the walls. When it jumps at the walls, it has the discomforts of thwarted effort, and when it runs to B, or C, or D, it has a continuation of the situation just described; when it runs to E, it gets out and has the satisfaction of being with the other chicks, of eating, and of being in its usual habitat. If it is repeatedly put in again at A, one finds that it jumps and runs to B or C less and less often, until finally its only act is to run to D, E, and out. It has formed an association, or connection, or bond, between the situation due to its removal to A and the response of going to E. In common language, it has learned to go to E when put at A—has learned the way out. The decrease in the useless running and jumping and standing still finds a representative in the decreasing amount of time taken by the chick to escape. The two chicks that formed this particular association, for example, averaged three and a half minutes (one about three and the other about four) for

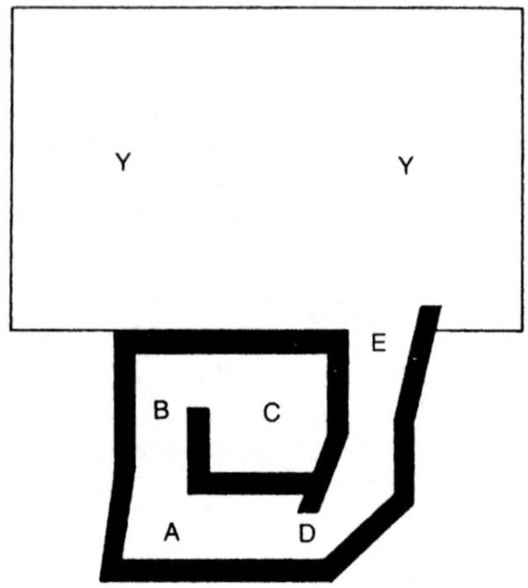

FIGURE 1

their first five trials, but came finally to escape invariably within five or six seconds.

The following schemes represent the animal's behavior (1) during an early trial and (2) after the association has been fully formed—after it has learned the way out perfectly. A graphic representation of the progress from an

1
BEHAVIOR IN AN EARLY TRIAL

Situation	Responses	Resulting States of Affairs
As described above, in the text	To chirp, etc.	Annoying continuation of the situation and thwarting of the inner tendencies.
	To jump at various places.	" " "
	To run to B.	" " "
	To run to C.	" " "
	To run to D.	" " "
	To run to E.	Satisfying company, food and surroundings.

Adapted from Thorndike, E. L. (1913). *Educational psychology: The psychology of learning,* Volume 2. New York: Teachers College Press, pp. 6–16. Copyright © 1913 by Teachers College Press. Adapted and reprinted by permission of the publisher.

2
BEHAVIOR IN A TRIAL AFTER LEARNING

Situation	Responses	Resulting States of Affairs
Same as in (1).	To run to E.	Satisfying as above.

early trial to a trial after the association has been fully formed is given in the following figures, in which the dotted lines represent the path taken by a turtle in his fifth (Figure 2) and fiftieth (Figure 3) experiences in learning the way from the point A to his nest. The straight lines represent walls of boards. Besides the useless movements, there were, in the fifth trial, useless stoppings. The time taken to reach the nest in the fifth trial was seven minutes; in the fiftieth, thirty-five seconds. The figures represent typical early and late trials, chosen from a number of experiments on different individuals in different situations, by Dr. R. M. Yerkes, to whom I am indebted for permission to use these figures.

Let us next examine a somewhat more ambitious performance than the mere discovery of the proper path by a chick or turtle. If we take a box twenty by fifteen by twelve inches, replace its cover and front side by bars an inch apart, and make in this front side a door arranged so as to fall open when a wooden button inside is turned from a vertical to a horizontal position, we shall have means to observe such. A kitten, three to six months old, if put in this box when hungry, a bit of fish being left outside, reacts as follows: It tries to squeeze through between the bars, claws at the bars and at loose things in and out of the box, stretches its paws out between the bars, and bites at its confining walls. Some one of all these promiscuous clawings, squeezings, and bitings turns round the wooden button, and the kitten gains freedom and food. By repeating the experience again and again, the animal gradually comes to omit all the useless clawings, and the like, and to manifest only the particular impulse (e.g., to claw hard at the top of the button with the paw, or to push against one side of it with the nose) which has resulted successfully. It turns the button around without delay whenever put in the box. It has formed an association between the situation, *confinement in a box of a certain appearance,* and the response of *clawing at a certain part of that box in a certain definite way.* Popularly speaking, it has learned to open a door by turning a button. To the uniniti-

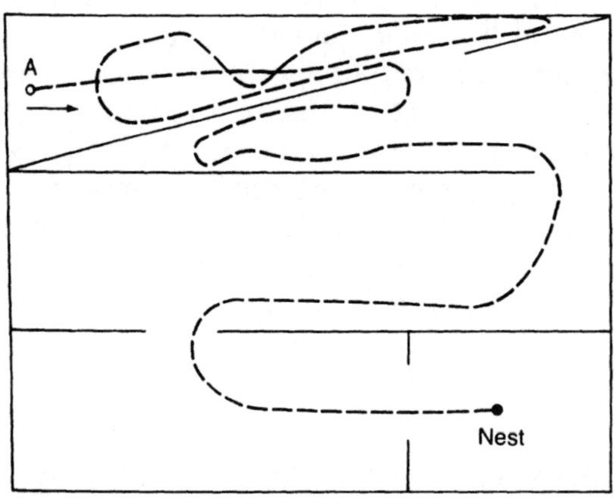

FIGURE 2
The path taken by a turtle in finding his way from A to his nest, in his 5th trial.

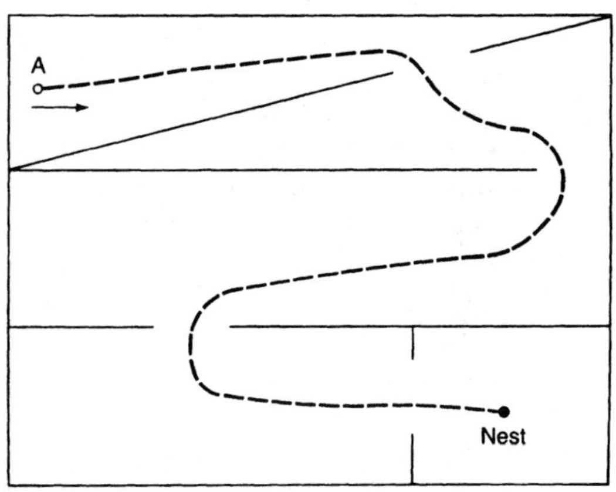

FIGURE 3
The path taken by a turtle in finding his way from A to his nest, in his 50th trial.

ated observer the behavior of the six kittens that thus freed themselves from such a box would seem wonderful and quite unlike their ordinary accomplishments of finding their way to their food or beds, but the reader will realize that the activity is of just the same sort as that displayed by the chick in the pen. A certain situation arouses, by virtue of accident or, more often, instinctive equipment, certain responses. One of these happens to be an act appropriate to secure freedom. It is stamped in connection with that situation. Here the act is clawing at a certain spot instead of running to E, and is selected from a far greater number of useless acts.

In the examples so far given there is a certain congruity between the 'set' associated with the situation and the learning. The act which lets the cat out is hit upon by the cat while, as we say, trying to get out, and is, so to speak, a likely means of release. But there need be no such congruity between the 'set' and the learning. If we confine a cat, opening the door and letting it out to get food only when it scratches itself, we shall, after enough trials, find the cat scratching itself the moment it is put into the box. Yet in the first trials it did not scratch itself in order to get out, or indeed until after it had given up the unavailing clawings and squeezings, and stopped to rest. The association is formed with such an 'unlikely' or 'incongruous' response as that of scratching, or licking, or (in the case of chicks) pecking at the wing to dress it, as truly as with a response which original nature or previous habit has put in connection with the set of the organism toward release, food, and company.

The examples chosen so far show the animal forming a single association, but such may be combined into series. For instance, a chick learns to get out of a pen by climbing up an inclined plane. A second pen is then so arranged that the chick can, say by walking up a slat and through a hole in the wall, get from it into pen No. 1. After a number of trials the chick will, when put in pen No. 2, go at once to pen No. 1, and thence out. A third pen is then so arranged that the chick, by forming another association, can get from it to pen No. 2, and so on. In such a series of associations the response of one brings the animal into the *situation* of the next, thus arousing its response, and so on to the end. Three chicks thus learned to go through a sort of long labyrinth without mistakes, the 'learning' representing twenty-three associations.

The learning of the chick, turtle, and kitten in the cases quoted is characterized negatively by the absence of inferential, ratiocinative thinking; and indeed by the absence of effective use of 'ideas' of any sort. Were the reader confined in a maze or cage, or left at some distance from home, his responses to these situations would almost certainly include many ideas, judgments, or thoughts about the situation; and his acts would probably in large measure be led up to or 'mediated' by such sequences of ideas as are commonly called reasoning. Between the annoying situation and the response which relieves the annoyance there might for the reader well intervene an hour of inner consideration, thought, planning, and the like. But there is no evidence that any ideas about the maze, the cage, the food, or anything else, were present to determine the acts of the chicks or kittens in question. Their responses were made directly to the situation as sensed, not *via* ideas suggested by it. The three cases of learning quoted are adequately accounted for as the strengthening and weakening of bonds between a situation present to sense and responses in the nervous system which issue then and there in movement. The lower animals do occasionally show signs of ideas and of their influence on behavior, but the great bulk of their learning has been found explainable by such direct binding of acts to situations, unmediated by ideas.

CHARACTERISTICS OF ANIMAL LEARNING

These cases, and the hundreds of which they are typical, show the laws of readiness, exercise, and effect, uncomplicated by any pseudo-aid from imitation, ideo-motor action, or superior faculties of inference. There are certain states of affairs which the animal welcomes and does nothing to avoid—its satisfiers. There are others which it is intolerant of and rejects, doing one thing or another until relieved from them. Of the bonds which the animal's behavior makes between a situation and responses those grow stronger which are accompanied by satisfying states of affairs, while those accompanied by annoyance weaken and disappear. Exercise strengthens and disuse weakens bonds. Such is the sum and substance of the bulk of animal learning.

These cases exemplify also five characteristics of learning which are secondary in scope and importance only to the laws of readiness, exercise, and effect.

The first is the fact of *multiple response to the same external situation.* The animal reacts to being confined in the pen in several ways, and so has the possibility of selecting for future connection with that situation one or another of these ways. Its own inner state changes when jumping at the wall at B produces a drop back into the pen, so that it then is less likely to jump again—more likely to chirp and run. Running to C and being still confronted with the confining walls may arouse an inner state which impels it to turn and run back. So one after another of the responses which, by original nature or previous learning, are produced by the confining walls *plus* the failure of the useless chirpings, jumpings, and runnings, are made.

This principle of *Multiple Response or Varied Reaction* will be found to pervade at least nine-tenths of animal and human learning. As ordinarily interpreted, it is not universal, since, even if only one response is made, the animal may change its behavior—that is, learn—either by strengthening the connection so as to make that response more surely, more quickly, and after a longer interval of disuse; or by weakening the connection so as to be more likely to do nothing at all in that situation, inactivity being a variety of response which is always a possible alternative. If we interpret variety of reaction so as to include the cases where an animal either makes one active response or is inactive—that is, either alters what it was doing when the situation began to act, or does not alter what it was doing—the principle of varied response is universal in learning.

The second of the five subsidiary principles is what we may call the law of the learner's *Set* or *Attitude* or *Adjustment* or *Determination.* The learning cannot be described adequately in a simple equation involving the pen and a chick taken abstractly. The chick, according to his age, hunger, vitality, sleepiness and the like, may be in one or another attitude toward the external situation. A sleepier and less hungry chick will, as a rule, be 'set' less toward escape-movements when confined; its neurones involved in roaming, perceiving companions and feeding will be less ready to act; it will not, in popular language, 'try so hard to' get out or 'care so much about' being out. As Woodworth says in commenting upon similar cases of animal learning:

> In the first place we must assume in the animal an adjustment or determination of the psychophysical mechanism toward a certain end. The animal desires, as we like to say, to get out and to reach the food. Whatever be his consciousness, his behavior shows that he is, as an organism, set in that direction. This adjustment persists till the motor reaction is consummated; it is the driving force in the unremitting efforts of the animal to attain the desired end. His reactions are, therefore, the joint result of the adjustment and of stimuli from various features of the cage. Each single reaction tends to become associated with the adjustment. [Ladd and Woodworth, 1911, p. 551.]

The principle that in any external situation, the responses made are the product of the 'set' or 'attitude' of the animal, that the satisfyingness or annoyingness produced by a response is conditioned by that attitude, and that the 'successful' response is by the law of effect connected with that attitude as well as with the external situation *per se*—is general. Any process of learning is conditioned by the mind's 'set' at the time.

Animal learning shows also the fact, which becomes of tremendous moment in human learning, that one or another element of the situation may be prepotent in determining the response. For example, the cats with which I experimented, would, after a time, be determined by my behavior more than by other features of the general situations of which that behavior was a part; so that they could then learn, as they could not have done earlier, to form habits of response to signals which I gave. Similarly, a cat that has learned to get out of a dozen boxes—in each case by pulling some loop, turning some bar, depressing a platform, or the like—will, in a new box, be, as we say, 'more attentive to' small objects on the sides of the box than it was before. The connections made may then be, not absolutely with the gross situation as a total, but predominately with some element or elements of it. Thus, it makes little or no difference whether the box from which a cat has learned to escape by turning a button, is faced North, South, East, or West; and not much difference if it is painted ten per cent blacker or enlarged by a fifth. The cat will operate the mechanism substantially as well as it did before. It is, of course, the case that the animals do not, as a thoughtful man might do, connect the response with perfect strictness just to the one essential element of the situation. They can be much more easily confused by variations in the element's concomitants; and in certain cases many of the irrelevant concomitants have to be supplied to enable them to give the right response. Nevertheless they clearly make connections with certain parts or elements or features of gross total situations. Even in the lower animals, that is, we find that the action of a situation is more or less separable into the action of the elements that compose it—that even they illustrate the general *Law of Partial Activity*—that a part or element or aspect of a situation may be prepotent in causing response, and may have responses bound more or less exclusively to it regardless of some or all of its accompaniments.

If a cat which has never been confined in a box or cage of any sort is put into a box like that described a few pages back, it responds chiefly by trying to squeeze through the openings, clawing at the bars and at loose objects within the box, reaching out between the bars, and pulling at anything then within its grasp. In short, it responds to this artificial situation as it would by original nature to confinement, as in a thicket. If a cat which has learned to escape from a number of such boxes by manipulating various mechanical contrivances, is confined in a new box, it responds to it by a mixture of the responses originally bound to confining obstacles and of those which it has learned to make to boxes like the new one.

In both cases it illustrates the *Law of Assimilation* or *Analogy* that to any situations, which have no special original or acquired response of their own, the response made will be that which by original or acquired nature is connected with some situation which they resemble. For S_2 to resemble S_1 means for it to arouse more or less of the sensory neurones which S_1 would arouse, and in more or less the same fashion.

The last important principle which stands out clearly in the learning of the lower animals is that which I shall call *Associative Shifting*. The ordinary animal 'tricks' in response to verbal signals are convenient illustrations. One, for example, holds up before a cat a bit of fish, saying, "Stand Up." The cat, if hungry enough, and not of fixed contrary habit, will stand up in response to the fish. The response, however, contracts bonds also with the total situation, and hence to the human being in that position giving that signal as well as to the fish. After enough trials, by proper arrangement, the fish can be omitted, the other elements of the situation serving to evoke the response. Association may later be further shifted to the oral signal alone. With certain limitations due to the necessity of getting an element of a situation attended to, a response to the total situation A B C D E may thus be shifted to B C D E to C D E, to D E, to E. Moreover, by adding to the situation new elements F, G, H, etc., we may, subject to similar limitations, get *any response of which a learner is capable* associated with *any situation to which he is sensitive*. Thus, what was at the start utterly without power to evoke a certain response may come to do so to perfection. Indeed, the situation may be one which at the start would have aroused an exactly opposite response. So a monkey can be taught to go to the top of his cage whenever you hold a piece of banana at the bottom of it.

These simple, semi-mechanical phenomena—multiple response, the coöperation of the animal's set or attitude with the external situation, the predominant activity of parts or elements of a situation, the response to new situations as to the situations most like them, and the shifting of a response from one situation to another by gradually changing a situation without disturbing the response to it—which animal learning discloses, are the fundamentals of human learning also. They are, of course, much complicated in the more advanced stages of human learning, such as the acquisition of skill with the violin, or of knowledge of the calculus, or of inventiveness in engineering. But it is impossible to understand the subtler and more planful learning of cultivated men without clear ideas of the forces which make learning possible in its first form of directly connecting some gross bodily response with a situation immediately present to the senses. Moreover, no matter how subtle, complicated, and advanced a form of learning one has to explain, these simple facts—the selection of connections by use and satisfaction and their elimination by disuse and annoyance, multiple reaction, the mind's set as a condition, piecemeal activity of a situation, with prepotency of certain elements in determining the response, response by analogy, and shifting of bonds—will, as a matter of fact, still be the main, and perhaps the only, facts needed to explain it.

The Method of Pavlov in Animal Psychology

Robert M. Yerkes and Sergius Morgulis

About eight years ago Professor J. P. Pawlow,* Director of the physiological department of the Institute of Experimental Medicine in St. Petersburg, devised and introduced into his great research laboratory an ingenious and valuable new method of investigating the physiology of the nervous system in its relations to the so-called psychic reactions of organisms. This method—now widely known as the Pawlow salivary reflex method—has been extensively employed by Pawlow and his students in St. Petersburg. Recently it has been introduced into the Psychological Institute of Berlin by Nicolai, a former student of Pawlow. It consists in the quantitative study of those modifications of the salivary reflex which are conditioned by complex receptive and elaborative processes (psychic reactions) in the central nervous system.

*J. P. Pawlow is, of course, Ivan P. Pavlov. The spelling is due to the differences between the Russian and English alphabets. (Ed. note)

Inasmuch as practically all of the results of the method have been published in Russia, it has seemed to us important that a general description of the technique of the method, together with a statement of certain of the important results which it has yielded, should be published at this time in English. Our purposes in preparing this article were two: first, to present a body of facts which is of great importance to both physiologists and animal psychologists; and second, to familiarize American investigators with the salivary reflex method and hasten the time when it shall be as advantageously used in this country as it now is in Russia.

The materials for this discussion we have obtained chiefly from six papers. Of these the first four are, in the main, general accounts of the method and its results from the strikingly different points of view and interests of Pawlow and Nicolai. The papers of Selionyi and Orbeli are admirable reports of facts. . . . We are indebted to Professor Pawlow for a number of the titles included in this list and also for a thorough revision and correction of the bibliography.

Our discussion naturally falls into four parts: (1) A general description of the method of its application, from the standpoints of Pawlow, Nicolai, and Selionyi; (2) an expository summary of the study of the auditory reactions of the dog as reported by Selionyi; (3) a similar summary of Orbeli's study of the visual reactions of the dog; and (4) a general summary of the results of the method.* To give a complete account of the investigations of the St. Petersburg laboratory—for already more than forty papers have been published—would be possible only if each paper were dismissed with a sentence or two. We have preferred to consider two representative papers in some detail instead of mentioning several casually.

*The section of Orbeli's study of visual reactions has been omitted. (Ed. note)

DESCRIPTION OF THE SALIVARY REFLEX METHOD

The salivary reflex (secretion of saliva) occurs under two strikingly different conditions: (*a*) when the mouth is stimulated by certain chemical processes (the specific stimuli for secretion); and (*b*) when the animal is stimulated by sights, sounds, odors, temperatures, touches which have been present previously in connection with stimuli of the first class. The environment of the dog may be said to consist of two sets of properties, the essential and non-essential. Essential, for a given reaction, are those stimulating properties of an object which regularly and definitely determine that reaction of the organism; non-essential, for the reaction in point, are those properties of an object which only in a highly variable and inconstant manner condition the reaction. The chemical property of food, whereby it acts upon the receptors of the mouth of the dog, is an 'essential' property, for it invariably causes a salivary reflex. The appearance of the same food—its lightness, color, etc.—is a 'non-essential,' for it may or may not cause the reflex. Pawlow has termed reflexes in response to 'essential' properties 'unconditioned,' and those in response to 'non-essential' properties 'conditioned.'

It was Pawlow's idea that the perfectly constant and dependable 'unconditioned' salivary reflex might be used to advantage as a basis for the investigation of those complex nervous processes one of whose expressions is a 'conditioned' reflex of the same glands. Since many, if not all, changes in the nervous system gain expression in one way or another, through the salivary reflex, why not, Pawlow asks, investigate these processes by observing their relation to this particular reflex? That there was nothing novel in this idea is evident when we recollect that numerous reflexes have been used, by other investigators, for the study of psychic reactions. Respiration, heartbeat, and certain secretory changes have been studied, in this connection, with varying success. But what Pawlow may claim, apparently, is the discovery of that particular reflex which seems to be best adapted for the investigation of complex nervous processes.

The technique of the method we shall describe, with the help of two figures which have been re-drawn from Nicolai. The first of these figures represents a dog prepared for experiments in accordance with the method used in St. Petersburg. The second of the figures represents the modification of experimental technique which has been devised by Nicolai in Berlin.

The experimental procedure is as follows. A normally active and healthy dog of vigorous salivary reaction having been selected, the duct of one of the salivary glands—the parotid for example—is exposed on the outer surface of the cheek and a salivary fistula is formed. The wound heals completely within a few days and the dog exhibits no signs of discomfort or inconvenience. Those who have used the method insist, indeed, that their animals are perfectly normal in all respects. In further preparation for the study of the salivary reflex a small glass funnel is fastened over the opening to the duct with Mendelejeff cement. To this funnel is attached a tube which conducts the saliva to a graduate.

Three methods of measuring the quantity of saliva secreted are in use. (1) As the secretion flows from the tube into a graduate the drops are counted, and if the experimenter so desires, an additional measurement may subsequently be obtained by readings from the scale of the graduate. (2) The saliva is permitted, as Figure 1 shows, to flow through a short tube into a graduate bottle and the amount of the secretion is then determined by reading the scale on the bottle. This method necessitates the replacing of the partially filled bottle by a clean one and the careful cleaning of the funnel between experiments. (3) A small metal canula, inserted in the duct of the gland, is connected by a heavy walled rubber tube with a small glass tube. The saliva drops from this tube upon the lever of a Marey tambour, as is shown in Figure 2. As it falls drop by drop upon this lever a record is made upon a smoked drum. From this record the experimenter may read the quantity of the secretion in drops and the rate of flow, *i.e.*, how many drops fell in a given interval. This graphic method of recording the salivary reaction is Nicolai's improvement on the Pawlow method as used in Russia. In addition to enabling the experimenter to obtain more detailed and accurate data concerning the reaction, it has the important advantage of permitting him to withdraw from the experiment room during the experiments. This is desirable because his presence is likely to influence the dog in unexpected and undesirable ways.

FIGURE 1

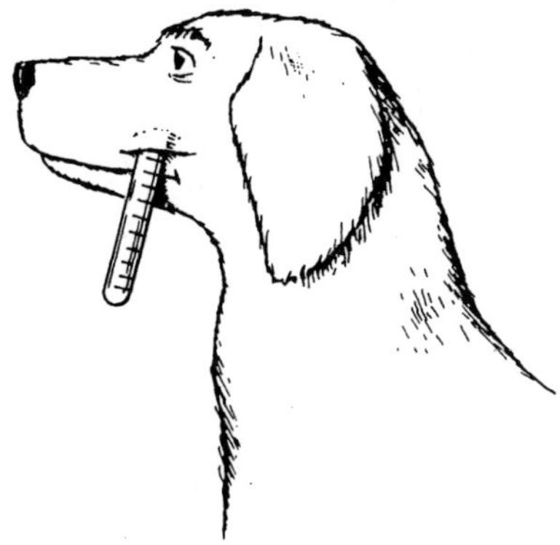

The Pawlow method lends itself readily to the investigation of many psychic reactions. In order to get clearly in mind the remaining essential points of experimental procedure we may consider its application to the study of visual discrimination of colors. A dog, which has been selected for observation and in which a salivary fistula has been created, is subjected to a course of training to establish a 'conditioned' reflex on the basis of visual stimulation. This is accomplished by showing the animal a particular color—say green—at intervals and at the same time giving it food. After numerous repetitions of this procedure the visual stimulus becomes the sign of food and induces the salivary reflex

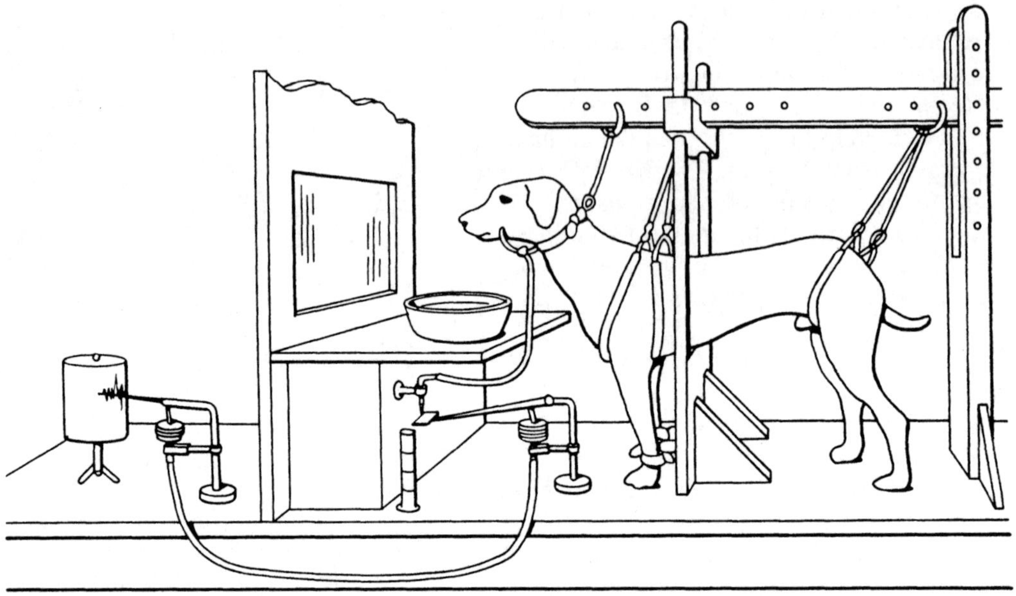

FIGURE 2

in the absence of the food. An animal so trained is ready for experiments on the discrimination of colors. If it appears that no color except green produces the 'conditioned' reflex, there is reason to believe that the dog perceives green as distinct from the other colors.

Pawlow devised and employs this method not for the study of psychic phenomena, as Nicolai proposes to do, but simply as a means of approach to the physiology of the nervous system. Of his insistence upon the objective point of view the following quotation from his Huxley lecture is excellent proof. "Up to the present time the physiology of the eye, the ear, and other superficial organs which are of importance as recipients of impressions has been regarded almost exclusively in its subjective aspect; this presented some advantages, but at the same time, of course, limited the range of inquiry. In the investigation of the conditioned stimuli in the higher animals, this limitation is got rid of and a number of important questions in this field of research can be at once examined with the aid of all the immense resources which experiments on animals place in the hands of the physiologist. . . . The investigation of the conditioned reflexes is of very great importance for the physiology of the higher parts of the central nervous system. Hitherto this department of physiology has throughout most of its extent availed itself of ideas not its own, ideas borrowed from psychology, but now there is a possibility of its being liberated from such evil influences. The conditioned reflexes lead us to the consideration of the position of animals in nature: this is a subject of immense extent and one that must be treated objectively."

Although psychology—or rather psychologists—deserves all of the criticisms which the physiologists have made, students of animal behavior and comparative psychology should not allow Pawlow's attitude to discourage them. Nor should they be slow to appreciate the immediate importance, and promise for the advancement of their science, of the Pawlow method and its results. That it can be used to advantage by animal psychologists, as well as by those physiologists for whom the psychic phenomenon is merely an unescapable nuisance, is obvious.

Already Nicolai has ably discussed the relations of the method to psychological problems. He contends, with reason, that the salivary reflex method possesses the four essential characteristics of a scientific method in psychology: (*a*) it is general, in its applicability to the study of psychic processes; (*b*) it is constant; (*c*) it permits accurate measurement; and (*d*) it is specific.

Undoubtedly the method may be applied to the study of various aspects of sensation and the mutual relations of sensations, to memory and ideation, to the formation of judgments and will acts. Its obvious limitation appears in the number of organisms with which it may be employed. Evidently it can not be used for the study of animals which lack salivary glands, and even among those animals which do possess these glands there are many which surely would not lend themselves satisfactorily to the method. It seems, therefore, as if Pawlow's method were especially important in animal psychology as a means to the intensive study of the mental life of a limited number of mammals. The dog evidently is especially well suited to the experiments.

SELIONYI'S STUDY OF AUDITORY REACTIONS

With this brief general sketch of the method and its purposes in mind we may turn to the investigation reported by Selionyi. In order, we shall state the problem, the principal points of method, and the results of his study of the auditory reactions of the dog.

The initial purpose of the work was to determine, by means of one form of the Pawlow method, how great must be the difference in the quality or the intensity of two auditory stimuli in order that they shall produce perceivably different effects upon the auditory apparatus of the dog. The problem as it presented itself to the investigator was primarily one of the physiology of the nervous system, and secondarily one of animal psychology.

Starting with the familiar fact that sounds which have been associated with food may under certain conditions stimulate the salivary reflex, Selionyi first of all, as a necessary preliminary to his research, attempted to ascertain whether certain unusual or unfamiliar sounds, as well as those which have become familiar through their association with food, cause the secretion of saliva. He discovered that only 'familiar' sounds—those which the dog has learned to recognize as significant—have this effect as a rule.

No dogs were used for the investigation whose salivary reaction was not vigorous. An animal after having been tested for its normal reaction and prepared for the experiments by the creation of a salivary fistula, was trained until a definite 'conditioned' reflex appeared in connection with some particular sound. Repeatedly, in the training experiments, this sound was produced near the dog at the instant food was given. Sometimes the two stimuli were presented simultaneously; sometimes the sound preceded the food by five to thirty seconds. The combined action of the stimuli was permitted to continue for thirty to sixty seconds. This procedure was repeated at intervals of ten to thirty minutes, on a number of different days, until the sound, when given alone, would rapidly bring about the secretion of saliva. This usually occurred after twenty to forty repetitions. A particular sound—of definitely determined pitch, intensity, and quality—was thus rendered significant and 'familiar.' It now differed from other distinguishably different sounds in that it had its specific salivary reflex, whereas they caused no reaction.

During these training tests it is extremely important, Selionyi points out, that the experimenter make no unusual movements or otherwise produce conditions which may regularly and markedly stimulate the dog, else these irrelevant stimuli may become associated with food and spoil the result of the training experiment.

In all of the experiments the experimenter has to guard against irregularities of condition. If he moves too quickly or if he holds himself too rigidly quiet, as the inexperienced worker is likely to do, the dog is disturbed and the salivary reaction modified.

The sounds whose influence was carefully observed by Selionyi were produced by an organ, by organ pipes, and by two whistles one of which (a tuning pipe) gave a number of tones of different pitch and the other a rattling sound.

A dog whose normal salivary reaction had been carefully observed and in which the habit of responding to a certain sound had been developed was placed in an apparatus similar to that of Figure 2. The 'familiar' sound was then produced and the reaction noted. The experimenter took account of both the quantity and the quality of the saliva. A quantitative expression for the former was obtained either by counting the drops as they left the fistula or by measuring the secretion in a graduate. The quality (viscidity) was determined by a measurement of the rate of flow through a capillary tube. Some ten minutes after the 'familiar' sound, an 'unfamiliar' sound whose influence upon the reaction the experimenter wished to discover, was given in the same way, and the reaction was again observed. After another interval, the 'familiar' sound was repeated. Thus, for the purpose of comparison, the observer obtained reactions to both kinds of stimuli in rapid succession. The experimenter noted the interval (latent period) between application of a stimulus and the appearance of the first drop of saliva, and he collected and measured the saliva which was secreted between stimulations as well as immediately after the application of each stimulus.

The sample record reproduced herewith will serve to illustrate the results obtained by this procedure.

In order to render a translation of Selionyi's summary of results intelligible it will be necessary to define a number of the terms which he employs.

TABLE
EXPERIMENT 54: 'MARGARET'

Familiar sound, A, of Tuning Pipe.
Unfamiliar sound, A, of Tuning Pipe and 'Rattling' Whistle.

Time	Sound	Duration of Stim.	Quantity of Saliva in Drops
4:25	Unfamiliar	1′40″	0
4:55	Familiar	30″	15
5:05	Familiar	20″	5
5:19	Unfamiliar	2′15″	0
5:29	Familiar	30″	9

A 'conditioned reflex' is a reaction (salivary in this case) to a stimulus which is only secondarily and indirectly a condition of the reflex. (For example, the sight of meat may produce a 'conditioned' salivary reflex.)

An 'unconditioned reflex' is a reaction to a stimulus which regularly and constantly conditions the reflex. (For example, food placed in the mouth causes an 'unconditioned' salivary reflex.)

A 'familiar' stimulus (sound, in this investigation) is one which experience has taught the animal to respond to as if it were the precursor of food. It is in fact a sound which produces a 'conditioned reflex' ordinarily.

An 'unfamiliar' stimulus is one which the animal has not been trained to respond to.

A 'fundamental reflex' is one which is caused by a 'familiar' sound.

An 'additional reflex' is one which is caused by an 'unfamiliar' sound which differs from the 'familiar' sound only in pitch.

A 'partial reflex' is one which is caused by some part of a complex 'familiar' sound. As, for example, when one tone of a 'familiar' chord causes a reflex.

In reading the summary of Selionyi's results it is important that the reader remember (1) that conditioned reflexes die out with repetition. (2)

That edible substances, when used as stimuli repeatedly, produce a constantly diminishing secretion of saliva, whereas inedible substances, when used repeatedly, produce a constantly increasing secretion. (3) That the secretion in response to edible substances increases as the interval between stimuli is lengthened, whereas the secretion to inedible substances diminishes as the interval is lengthened. Selionyi states that he made use mostly of edible substances. He did, however, at times make use of weak acid solutions as a substitute for food.

1 Separate sounds are received by the auditory apparatus of the dog as distinct stimuli even when they differ from one another by only a quarter of a tone.

2 Sounds which differ from one another only very slightly in quality are received as distinct stimuli.

3 A conditioned reflex of definite intensity is specific of (results from) a sound ("familiar") of a given pitch which has become its stimulus.

4 'Unfamiliar' sounds which differ from the 'familiar' sound by a slight variation in pitch, produce in some dogs 'additional' reflexes which are much less intense than the reflex to the 'familiar' sound.

5 Even comparatively slight changes in the quality of 'familiar' sounds result in a diminution and disappearance of the fundamental salivary reflex.

6 Sounds which differ from one another very little in pitch (the quality and intensity remaining constant) may become the stimuli for the secretion of saliva of different degrees of viscidity: some cause the flow of liquid saliva; others, of viscid saliva.

7 The specificity of conditioned reflexes for the sounds which induce them may persist for two months.

8 Diminishing the strength of the 'familiar' sound causes the weakening or even the complete disappearance of its conditioned reflex.

9 A 'familiar' sound, which very gradually reaches such an intensity that a conditioned reflex would ordinarily result from it, fails to call forth its reflex if it was too weak at the beginning.

10 Separate components of a complex sound which conditions a 'fundamental' reflex, will produce reflexes (the so-called partial reflexes) at a certain relative intensity.

11 The intensity of partial reflexes depends upon the relative intensity of the sounds by which they are induced. The more intense the partial sound, the stronger is the partial reflex. A single tone of a familiar chord of three tones, of the same quality and intensity, produces a less intense partial reflex than do two tones of the same chord.

12 Each partial sound has its specific partial reflex just as each 'familiar' tone has its fundamental reflex.

13 The substitution of an irrelevant tone for one element of a 'familiar' chord tends to inhibit the reflex.

14 The addition of an irrelevant sound to the 'familiar' sound tends to inhibit the conditioned reflex.

15 The degree of inhibition is directly related to the intensity of the new or inhibiting sound.

16 Simultaneous stimulation by two sounds, each of which produces, when alone, the conditioned reflex (in connection with a non-conditioned reflex which is induced by the same food substance) brings about different results according to the character of the sound. In some cases the reflex which is thus produced is equal in intensity to the reflex caused by one of the two sounds; in other cases it is of considerably less intensity.

17 Under certain conditions of excitability or permanency, a conditioned reflex which has been worn out by repetitions may spontaneously reappear at the end of the interval which separated the previous repetitions.

18 The statement that a worn-out conditioned reflex may be restored by any unconditioned stimulus must be recognized as false.

19 The wearing out, by repetitions, of a fundamental reflex to a particular sound tends also to weaken the reflex to a second sound, which occurs in connection with the same non-conditioned reflex as the first sound.

20 The wearing out of an 'additional' reflex causes a slight weakening—in an acute experiment—of the fundamental reflex with which it is associated.

21 The wearing out of a fundamental reflex—in an acute experiment—causes a complete loss of the additional reflex which is associated with it.

22 The wearing out of a partial reflex—in an acute experiment—causes some weakening of the fundamental reflex.

23 The wearing out of one partial reflex causes the wearing out of another of the same intensity as the first. This phenomenon is observable in an acute as well as in a chronic experiment (at least in those cases in which the partial sounds are of the same quality).

24 By subjecting additional and partial reflexes to wear by repetition in a chronic experiment, and by simultaneously reinforcing the fundamental conditioned reflex by means of a non-conditioned reflex, it is possible to destroy completely the additional and partial reflexes while retaining the fundamental reflex in its full original intensity.

25 The independent restoration of two partial reflexes which have disappeared in a chronic experiment by reason of the repetition of one of them comes about differently. At the time when the partial reflex which was subjected to the influence of repetition has not yet reappeared the other partial reflex is fully expressed.

26 'Unfamiliar' sounds which differ from a 'familiar' sound only very slightly in pitch, when given before the 'familiar' sound tend to inhibit its reflex.

27 A 'familiar' sound, the conditioned reflex of which had been worn out, produces an inhibitory effect upon the unworn reflex of another 'familiar' sound, when it is given simultaneously with the latter sound. . . .

LAWS OF CONDITIONED REFLEXES AND CONCLUSIONS CONCERNING THE RELATIVE IMPORTANCE OF THE SENSES OF THE DOG

The work in Pawlow's laboratory has rendered it possible to formulate a number of laws concerning the conditioned reflex. We shall mention only three of the most important of these, as examples.

Law I. A conditioned reflex can be worn out or destroyed by repetition of its conditioning stimulus or stimulus complex. Whereas at first a particular sound, sight, or odor which is indicative of food causes the secretion of several drops of saliva, after a few repetitions at short intervals and without the presentation of food to the dog it causes no secretion. This wearing out of the conditioned reflex serves to distinguish it from the unconditioned reflex.

Law II. The destruction of a conditioned reflex by repetition does not influence other conditioned reflexes. For example, the wearing out of the conditioned reflex to the sight of a particular kind of food leaves unmodified the reflex to the odor of the food.

Law III. Irrelevant stimuli (a sudden noise, a new object in the environment, etc.) produce a depressing effect upon conditioned reflexes. In regard to the nature of their influence, they may be conveniently classed in two groups: (1) those that temporarily diminish or even suspend the activity of the conditioned reflex, but lose this retarding effect after a few repetitions; (2) those which at first tend to reduce the intensity of the reflex and finally inhibit it completely. . . .

Finally we may be permitted to quote from Nicolai his conclusions concerning the relation of the Pawlow method to animal psychology.

> The Pawlow salivary reflex is a relatively complicated process which is connected only indirectly

with the exciting stimulus and for the occurrence of which the idea of eating is always necessary.

Pawlow's salivary reflex method gives us a better explanation of the manner in which a dog learns spontaneously [than do most other methods], but it remains to be shown how far the learning can be carried. In the solving of related questions, the method does not seem to be superior to Kalischer's training method, and the latter is much the more convenient.

One can show experimentally that a dog learns by subsuming certain new ideas under general ideas which he has already acquired in the course of the experiment. ▲

Early Interactions Between Animal Psychologists and Animal Activists and the Founding of the APA Committee on Precautions in Animal Experimentation

Donald A. Dewsbury

Psychologists studying animals and animal rights activists are engaged in an ideological and political struggle over the use of nonhuman animals in research. Whereas the researchers believe animal use is justified because of its implications for both health applications and the accumulation of new knowledge, activists believe much research is trivial or inhumane. The struggle is often presented as a recent phenomenon, unparalleled in earlier times. In some respects, such as the scope of activity and attention in the media, this may be true. However, opposition to animal research developed during the 19th century, reached one peak near the turn of the present century, and has been continuous, though less visible, throughout the century. Although they have been refined considerably, the fundamental arguments on both sides of the issue during the earlier antivivisection peak and the recent animal rights peak were essentially the same. Although it is clear that the earlier antivivisectionist movement was targeted especially against physiologists, it is less well known that it involved animal psychologists as well. I shall show that some of the founding fathers of psychology, including William James, G. Stanley Hall, Ivan Pavlov, and John B. Watson, were affected by the controversy over vivisection.

Dewsbury, D. A. (1990). Early interactions between animal psychologists and animal activists and the founding of the APA Committee on Precautions in Animal Experimentation. *American Psychologist, 45,* 315–327.

THE DEVELOPMENT OF THE HUMANE AND ANTIVIVISECTION MOVEMENTS

If one is to understand the attitudes of critics toward animal research in psychology, it is important to understand something of the general development and context of the humane and antivivisection movements. The latter two must be differentiated, as adherents to the two approaches often differed substantially in their attitudes toward research (see Sperling, 1988). The movement evolved gradually during the 19th century, primarily in Great Britain (see French, 1975; Niven, 1967; Sechzer, 1981; Turner, 1980). In 1822 a bill providing penalties for cruelty to animals was prepared by Richard Martin and was approved in Parliament. The Society for the Prevention of Cruelty to Animals was founded in London on June 16, 1824. It became the Royal Society (RSPCA) in 1840 at Queen Victoria's command.

In the meantime, experimental physiology, relying heavily on animal subjects, developed in continental Europe during the middle of the century. Frenchmen Claude Bernard and Francois

Magendie were among the leaders in this effort. The movement crossed the English channel and received considerable attention with the publication of the first manual of experimental physiology in English, written by John Scott Burdon Sanderson (1873), a student of Bernard, and three colleagues.

The Victorian antivivisection movement developed out of the humane movement, under the leadership of Frances Power Cobbe, an Englishwoman who had led the fight against vivisection in Italy. Frustrated with the failure of the RSPCA to move against vivisection, Cobbe founded the Society for the Protection of Animals Liable to Vivisection (or the "Victoria Street Society") on December 2, 1875.

Cobbe arranged for the introduction to Parliament of a bill limiting vivisection in May 1875. This was met with another bill, introduced Lyon Playfair and others and supported by Burdon Sanderson and Charles Darwin, that promised much less restriction. A Royal Commission was formed to study the situation. Finally, the Cruelty to Animals Act of 1876 received Royal Assent on August 15. The act provided protection for all vertebrate animals, requiring licensing of experimenters, providing for inspection of facilities, and limiting animal use in teaching. This may be regarded as the prototype of much later legislation in various countries. The antivivisectionists were not satisfied with the Act and called for the complete abolition of all vivisection.

Experimental physiology, the humane movement, and the antivivisection movement developed in the United States a little after those in England. A bill forbidding cruelty to animals passed the New York State legislature in 1828. Similar laws were soon passed in Massachusetts, Connecticut, and Wisconsin. On April 21, 1866, the American Society for the Prevention of Cruelty to Animals (ASPCA) was founded by Henry Bergh, the son of a New York shipbuilder. George T. Angell founded the Massachusetts Society for the Prevention of Cruelty to Animals (MSPCA) on March 31, 1867. Caroline Earle White, who had founded the Pennsylvania Society for the Prevention of Cruelty to Animals in 1866, organized the American Anti-Vivisection Society in Philadelphia in 1883. Agitation against vivisection was continuous. In 1894 the State of Massachusetts passed a law banning vivisection in elementary and secondary schools.

In 1896 a bill to limit vivisection in the District of Columbia was introduced by Senator James McMillan (see Gossel, 1985). Senator Jacob Gallinger, a physician sympathetic to the antivivisection cause, chaired the hearings. This activity stimulated the organization of workers in the medical community, involving both the American Medical Association and the National Academy of Sciences, led by William H. Welch, to fight the bill. Although the bill passed the committee, neither it nor its two successors, in 1898 and 1899, passed the Senate.

The Washington hearings and various other incidents, including attacks against the Rockefeller Institute in New York in 1908, led scientists to take the antivivisectionist attacks more seriously. In 1908 the AMA Council on the Defense of Medical Research was formed, with a physiologist who exerted much influence on psychology, Walter Bradford Cannon (see Yerkes, 1946), as its chair. The group functioned actively with Cannon as its chair for 17 years. During this time Cannon published numerous articles in defense of vivisection in medical research (e.g., Cannon, 1912; see Benison, Barger, & Wolfe, 1987).

The antivivisection movement received favorable exposure in some elements of the press. John Ames Mitchell, editor of the New York-based *Life* magazine, a satirical weekly, was especially active in mounting a campaign against vivisection (Mott, 1957). In brief reports, satirical pieces, and cartoons, scientists engaged in vivisection were portrayed as cruel and inhumane, and animals often were shown gaining revenge.

Animal psychology developed in the United States and elsewhere at the very end of the 19th century and beginning of the 20th century, as this antivivisection activity was in full swing. It seems inevitable that although criticism was directed primarily against physiologists, it should touch psychologists as well.

ATTITUDES TOWARD ANIMAL USE

British Evolutionists and Their Attitudes Toward Animals and Legislation

The evolution of comparative psychology can be traced largely to the work of 19th century evolutionists in Great Britain. Their correspondence reveals a conflict typical of many current-day scientists: between a love of animals on the one hand and a belief in the value of scientific research on the other. As a rule, these were individuals with a true affection for animals, to which they often were close, but who also believed in the value of physiology for human welfare; they were puzzled that criticism of the use of animals in science exceeded criticism of the use of animals in sport.

There is abundant evidence that Charles Darwin was a true animal lover. In his autobiography, Darwin (1887/1958) noted that "I was as a boy humane" (p. 26) and he detailed various representative instances. He was a regular donor to the Royal Society for the Prevention of Cruelty to Animals (Clark, 1984). In editing a book on Darwin's life and letters, his son Frances cited various incidents consistent with this view (F. Darwin, 1896). He noted that his father's strong feeling in regard to human and animal suffering was "one of the strongest feelings in his nature" (p. 377). "He returned one day from his walk pale and faint from having seen a horse ill-used, and from the agitation of violently remonstrating with the man" (p. 377). His eldest son, William, recalled an incident wherein his father initiated a prosecution and secured a conviction against a farmer in his neighborhood who had starved some sheep (Clark, 1984). Although one might suspect these authors of some bias, the same cannot be said of antivivisectionist Frances Power Cobbe, who was a neighbor of Darwin for a while. Of his treatment of an old pony, Cobbe wrote that "His gentleness to this beast and incessant efforts to keep flies from his head, and his fondness for his dog Polly . . . were very pleasing traits in his character" (Cobbe, 1894, pp. 444–445).

Darwin struggled with issues of vivisection, but came out in its support. In an 1871 letter he noted that "it is justifiable for real investigations on physiology; but not for mere damnable and detestable curiosity. It is a subject that makes me sick with horror, so I will not say another word about it, else I shall not sleep tonight" (quoted in F. Darwin, 1896, p. 378). It was thus not without conflict that Darwin gave evidence before the Royal Commission on Vivisection in November, 1875. In 1875 Darwin wrote to Lord Playfair that "I am not personally concerned, as I never tried an experiment on a living animal, nor am I a physiologist; but I know enough to see how ruinous it would be to stop all progress in so grand a science[s] as Physiology" (quoted in F. Darwin, 1903, p. 436). In January of that year he wrote to his daughter both that he would "gladly punish severely any one who operated on an animal not rendered insensible" and that "if stringent laws are passed . . . physiology, which has been until within the last few years at a standstill in England, will languish or quite cease" (quoted in F. Darwin, 1896, p. 380). However, Darwin did not agree with a view becoming popular today that the only justification for animal work lies in immediate applicability. He wrote to Lauder Brunton that he agreed with almost everything in a published letter "except with some passages which appear to imply that no experiments should be tried unless some immediate good can be predicted, and this is a gigantic mistake contradicted by the whole history of science" (quoted in F. Darwin, 1903, p. 441). In the letter to his daughter, Darwin raised another issue common in the writing of the British evolutionists—puzzlement over the willingness of the populace to countenance animal suffering inflicted in the name of sport but to be restrictive of scientific endeavors. Of the Playfair bill, which he supported, Darwin wrote to J. D. Hooker that "the object is to protect animals, and at the same time not to injure Physiology" (quoted in F. Darwin, 1896, p. 381).

On April 18, 1881, the *Times* of London published a letter concerning vivisection written by Darwin to Frithiof Holmgren of Uppsala (Darwin, 1881). Again, Darwin noted on the one hand that "I have all my life been a strong advocate for humanity to animals" and that "physiology cannot possibly progress except by means of experiments on living animals" (p. 10). Darwin was critical of the 1876 Act and cited work by both Pasteur and Virchow as illustrating the benefits of animal research. The following day the seventh Earl Shaftesbury, an antivivisectionist, transmitted to the *Times* a reply from Cobbe (Cobbe, 1881a). She accused Darwin of having "fallen into some errors, which, in the case of a man of his celebrated accuracy, are not a little remarkable" (p. 8). The two agreed that there were abuses on the Continent, but disagreed concerning the need for regulation in Britain. Darwin replied on April 22, 1881, criticizing Magendie's "cruel experiments" but noting that the Royal Commission could not document any abuse against British physiologists (quoted in F. Darwin, 1896, p. 384). Again Cobbe replied the following day, noting that "it is impossible for a man to devote his life to such a practice without experiencing a growing ardour for scientific curiosity and a corresponding recklessness and callousness respecting the suffering which the gratification of that curiosity may involve" (Cobbe, 1881b, p. 8). In her autobiography, Cobbe reflected on how vivisectors corrupted Darwin "till the deplorable spectacle was exhibited of a man who would not allow a fly to bite a pony's neck, standing forth before all Europe (in his celebrated letter to Professor Holmgren of Sweden) as the advocate of vivisection" (Cobbe, 1894, p. 449).

Darwin's protege, George John Romanes, may be credited with writing the first influential textbook in comparative psychology, *Animal Intelligence* (Romanes, 1882). His approach resembled that of Darwin. Indeed, he joined the fray just discussed with a letter to the *Times* published on April 25, 1881, noting that he was "a lover of animals" (Romanes, 1881, p. 10) but defending the research of Burdon Sanderson, in whose laboratory he had worked, and which had been attacked by Cobbe in her letter of April 23. Romanes contrasted concern about vivisection with the phenomenon whereby "rabbits are put to death in spring traps by torture as atrocious as the wildest delirium of an anti-vivisector could imagine" (p. 10). In an 1877 letter to Darwin he noted that "there are more rabbits expressly bred every year for trapping than could be vivisected in all the physiological laboratories in Europe during the next thousand years" (quoted in E. Romanes, 1896, p. 61). In 1881 Romanes attended the International Medical Congress and worked with the Physiology Section for a resolution on vivisection. He wrote to Darwin to enlist his support and suggested that they might publish a piece together (in E. Romanes, 1896). Though sympathetic, Darwin was unable to contribute at that time.

Thomas Henry Huxley, "Darwin's bulldog" in the debates over evolution, shared these views on animals and vivisection. In an 1874 letter Huxley noted that "personally, indeed I may say constitutionally, the performance of experiments upon living and conscious animals is extremely disagreeable to me, and I have never followed any line of investigation in which such experiments are required" (quoted in L. Huxley, 1900, p. 463). Leonard Huxley, his son, noted that "Like Charles Darwin, he was very fond of animals, and our pets in London found him an indulgent master" (L. Huxley, 1900, p. 466). Like Darwin, however, Huxley also supported vivisection, writing that "I am of the opinion that the practice of performing experiments on living animals is not only reconcilable with true humanity, but under certain circumstances is imperatively demanded by it" (L. Huxley, 1900, p. 468).

Herbert Spencer was both less visible than his fellow evolutionists and apparently less favorably inclined to animal experimentation. Cobbe (1894) noted that "he has never (to his honor be it remembered!) pronounced a word in favor of painful experiments on animals" (p. 443). Spencer endorsed a statement from the American Humane Association supporting the legislation to restrict vivisection in the District of Columbia (Shortall, Rowley, Coan, & Leffingwell, 1897).

William James: The Risks of Moderation

The attitudes and conflicts displayed by the British evolutionists can be seen as well in the writings of that prototypical psychologist, William James. Questions of ethics were of great importance to James (see Rambo, 1980), and this is as apparent in his writing on animal experimentation as anywhere else. James was a complex man and his views on animal research were both complex and moderate, leading to some rejection from both sides.

James's initial statements on vivisection appear in two notes in *The Nation* published at the time of the passage of the British Cruelty to Animals Act, in 1875 and 1876 (in Burkhardt, Bowers, & Skrupskelis, 1987). In the former he captured a common view effectively and efficiently in true Jamesian style, "Vivisection, in other words, is a painful duty" (quoted in Burkhardt et al., 1987, p. 11). James believed that scientific investigation is a critical part of human nature:

> Man lives for sciences as well as bread. . . . To taboo vivisection is then the same thing as to give up seeking after a knowledge of physiology; in other words, it is sacrificing a human intellectual good, and all that flows from it, to a brute and corporeal good. (quoted in Burkhardt et al., 1987, p. 11)

Like Darwin, James opposed limiting investigations to those with a promise of immediate benefits to human health. Commenting in 1876 on what he believed to be the worst aspect of the British Act, James noted that "it only legitimates such experimental investigations as are made with the express purpose of relieving human suffering. A flatter ignorance of the motives of science, or of the conditions under which discoveries useful to man have hitherto been made, cannot be conceived" (quoted in Burkhardt et al., 1987, pp. 18–19). In 1875 he noted that "we still absolutely and totally deny the expediency of any legislative regulation of the matter" (quoted in Burkhardt et al., 1987, p. 11).

At the same time, however, James also took vivisectors to task, condemning some reported animal uses as "revolting excesses" (quoted in Burkhardt et al., 1987, p. 12). In fact, he detected superficiality on both sides of the issue. James agreed that "advocates of humanity have a good field open to them in trying to restrict the amount of *useless* vivisection" (quoted in Burkhardt et al., 1987, p. 12). He was especially opposed to repeated use of animals in educational settings for mere dramatic effect. James believed that such demonstrations dulled the senses of the students. He believed that the SPCA could do some good in working to encourage limitations on classroom demonstrations.

In 1909 James permitted publication in the *New York Evening Post* and elsewhere of his letter to Sidney Taber, a lawyer with the Vivisection Reform Society. Although James's views were rather moderate, he thus incurred the wrath of various physiologists, most notably his former student, Walter Bradford Cannon (see also Benison et al., 1987). On the side of the physiologists, James noted that "much of the talk against vivisection is, in my opinion, as idiotic as the talk in defence of it is uncandid" (quoted in Burkhardt et al., 1987, p. 191). Furthermore, he believed that the "fear of state rules and inspectors on the part of the investigators is . . .

well founded" (p. 192). However, James took investigators to task for opposing all regulation. James believed that investigators had to be responsible to some authority and that they opposed such regulation. Again, he especially opposed the use of animals in classroom demonstrations. James concluded that as long as physiologists refused responsibility for the incorporation of ethical standards in vivisection, the antivivisection agitation, "with all its expensiveness, idiocy, bad temper, untruth, and vexatiousness" (p. 192) would continue.

Cannon replied immediately, contending that most large laboratories have explicit rules governing vivisection and presenting a list of five such rules. Cannon noted that investigators do not oppose all regulation and, in fact, the Harvard Medical School, of which James was a graduate, had a "Committee on Animals, with plenary powers to control the conditions of research and to discharge instantly any employe [sic] guilty of inhumanity to the laboratory animals" (Cannon, 1909a, p. 2). James replied on May 28 urging that the American Physiological Association should be "frankly admitting that experiments on live animals are an atrocious necessity" and developing means of effective regulation (James, 1909a). James urged that the most effective way for Cannon to thwart antivivisectionist criticisms was to become an energetic advocate of reform within the scientific community. James admitted ignorance of the existing rules and wrote that he was glad to learn of them, but that he believed them formulated as the reaction to agitation. He reflected unfavorably on his own use of animals in classroom demonstrations in the 1870s. Again, James expressed concern about both sides. In his reply on June 4, Cannon (1909b) asserted that there is no evidence of wrongdoing in laboratories and affirmed the need for animal use in demonstrations. In his reply, James reasserted the need for "some positive *ethical expression of a mandatory sort* on the part of your committee as contrasted with mere repelling of accusations" (James, 1909b, p. 1). In a letter to W. W. Keen the next month, Cannon (1909c) noted that James had admitted being unaware of the regulations under which laboratories operated and lamented that anything he, Cannon, wrote would not receive the attention given James's writings. Four months later, in another letter to Keen, Cannon (1909d) noted with some vexation that, even though he had corrected James on the matter of the existence of regulations, James had permitted use of his original letter in a small pamphlet produced by the Vivisection Reform Society.

The conflict erupted again in February 1910. James, apparently misinterpreting Cannon's letter, told a reporter from the *New York Herald* that "the AMA was about to assume disciplinary control over experimental research" (in Benison et al., 1987, p. 201). Cannon (1910a) wrote to James that even after he told a reporter that James's statement was an incorrect inference from what he had written, the *New York Herald* stated that James still maintained that the AMA was about to publish disciplinary rules. Cannon then dissociated the AMA from the rules clearly and unambiguously. He also noted "that in an antivivisection 'chamber of horrors' in New York City, your name is posted with others in large letters on the wall as having expressed opposition to vivisection" (Cannon, 1910a). On February 13, Cannon (1910b) replied to James's reply with the hope that "this may be the last (letter) we need to exchange on this distressing subject" (p. 4).

Other Psychologists's Views on Issues Related to Animal Research

Numerous other psychologists expressed views on animal research. As most were involved, to one degree or another, it is perhaps not surprising that most, although not all, supported animal studies.

T. Wesley Mills, of McGill University, founded the first Association for the Study of Comparative Psychology in 1886 and was an early American Psychological Association (APA) member. He addressed the American Humane Association in Philadelphia on October 27, 1892 (Mills, 1893). Mills was concerned with the development of humane feelings toward animals and suggested that never before in history had there been greater knowledge or better treatment of animals and that this was due to the advancement of science. Because of this, he proposed that "it will be wise for all societies with a humane object to think well before interfering with scientific investigations of any kind" (Mills, 1893, p. 48).

James Rowland Angell, the 15th president of the APA, addressed the ethical questions related to animal research in two articles (Angell, 1907a, 1910).He concluded that "we find no obstacle to the practice of animal experimentation in any intuitive moral convictions, nor in the traditional morality of our own race" (Angell, 1910, p. 203).

In two related articles, John Dewey (1926, 1931) addressed the ethics of animal experimentation. Dewey took a strong stand, regarding experimentation as more than a right, but as a duty. He defended two moral principles as follows:

> 1. Scientific men are under definite obligation to experiment upon animals so far as that is the alternative to random and possibly harmful experimentation upon human beings, and so far as such experimentation is a means of saving human life and of increasing human vigor and efficiency.
>
> 2. The community at large is under definite obligations to see to it that physicians and scientific men are not needlessly hampered in carrying on the inquiries necessary for an adequate performance of their important social office of sustaining human life and vigor. (Dewey, 1926, p. 343)

Robert M. Yerkes (1946) took a dim view of

> the propaganda and ill-advised restrictive proposals of that small minority of our fellow citizens who make a fetish or a religion of "antivivisection" and who sometimes act as though other organisms are more worthy of considerate treatment and preservation from accident or disease than is man. (p. 143)

In 1895 University of Chicago President William Rainey Harper referred criticisms of the University Experimental Station to C. O. Whitman, an important proto-ethologist and a later APA member. The criticisms were published in *Anti-Vivisection,* a publication of the Illinois Anti-Vivisection Society, based in Aurora. Although there was no vivisection being done at the Station, Whitman (1895) suggested that the critic "study Pasteur and see how much suffering such experiments have saved the world. I am surprised that people who know absolutely nothing about our purpose should presume to send you such lengthy protests" (p. 2).

Some took a softer line. Animal behaviorist and APA member Samuel Jackson Holmes (1911) believed that "lower" animals have minds and that "it would be unfortunate if we were mistaken in regarding them as automata and should proceed to cut them up in a ruthless fashion on that assumption" (pp. 7–8).

Perhaps the strongest critic was John Bascom, author of perhaps the earliest North American textbook in comparative psychology (Bascom, 1878) and President of the University of Wisconsin. In conjunction with the 1897 hearings on legislation to limit vivisection in the District of Columbia, Bascom wrote to Senator Gallinger: "I am much interested in the success of the bill in restriction of vivisection. I have given the subject attention, and believe that humanity will be promoted by it and knowledge in no way restricted" (Bascom, 1897, p. 3). In a letter originally sent to the *Springfield Republican* and later published in the *Journal of Zoophily,* Bascom (1903) wrote,

> Considering the uncertainty and costly nature of the knowledge gained by vivisection, and the great abuse the practice has suffered, its opponents demand that animals should not be sub-

> jected to this suffering except in view of some definite and important question to be answered; that the pain involved in such an investigation should be reduced to its lowest possible terms; that experiments once satisfactorily made should not be indefinitely repeated; and that vivisection should not be left in the hands of every tyro acquiring the rudiments of knowledge. (p. 28)

The statement has a contemporary ring.

MEDIA ATTACKS AFFECTING PSYCHOLOGISTS

As has been true of the animal rights movement, those in the earlier antivivisection movement were successful in bringing media pressure on psychologists.

G. Stanley Hall: The Trials of a University President

G. Stanley Hall, the APA's first President, was not an animal researcher and apparently made few pronouncements regarding animal research. In his role as a university administrator, however, Hall faced a media problem similar to those faced by many occupying such positions more recently (Hall, 1927; Koelsch, 1987; Ross, 1972). Hall was the first President of Clark University when it opened its doors in the fall of 1889. Jonas Clark, who provided the funds for the university, apparently offended Austin P. Cristy, editor of the *Worcester Telegram.* The *Telegram* attacked Clark University at every opportunity, and the vivisection question provided such an opening. The opening article on March 9, 1890, carried seven headlines including "Dogs Vivisected," "Scientific Torture at Clark University," "Helpless Animals Are Killed by Inches," "Cruelty Is Reduced to a Fine Art," and "Dumb Victims Writhe Under the Cruel Knife" ("Dogs Vivisected," 1890). A series of similar articles followed during March and April. That of March 23 carried headlines including "Docents' Devilish Devices," "Jack the Ripper and Mr. Hyde in a Chamber of Torture," and " 'Devildoms of Spain' Rivaled by 'Science' of Today" ("Docents' Devilish Devices," 1890). Hall's primary response was to call in George T. Angell of the MSPCA to inspect the facilities. Hall adopted an open-door policy, similar to that recommended later by both Cannon and the APA, inviting Angell to attend every operation performed at Clark. After sending two of his best agents to investigate, Angell gave the University a clean bill of health (Angell, 1890). The attacks continued, with the MSPCA added as a target (A "Careful Investigation," 1890). Clark physiologist C. F. Hodge also issued a pamphlet on the subject; he later published an analysis of the vivisection question (Hodge, 1896).

John B. Watson and the Antivivisectionists

The primary target of the press was John B. Watson. The press was often unkind to Watson, as when the *Chicago Daily News* reported his field research on terns under the headline "Unclad U. of C. Man Hears Birds Talking" (1907).

Watson completed his doctoral dissertation, *Animal Education: An Experimental Study of the Psychical Development of the White Rat, With the Growth of its Nervous System* at the University of Chicago in 1903. Watson described the ways in which the rats of varying ages learned puzzle-box problems, reported on anatomical study of the brains of rats of different ages, and attempted to correlate structure with function. *The Nation* reviewed it, calling the work "a definite step in the advance of our knowledge of the correlation between cerebral structure and psychic function" (Staff, 1904b, p. 137). *The Athenaeum* criticized only the writing style (Staff, 1904a, p. 435). Yerkes (1904) called it "a valuable piece of work" (p. 71). According to Cohen's (1979) much-maligned biography of Watson,

> *Life* seized on the story, spurred on by angry antivivisectionists. It pilloried Watson. He was criticized in print and caricatured in cartoons as a killer of baby rats. And all to what end? To see how the animals could learn their way round a maze. (p. 36)

Despite a search of the relevant sources, I have thus far been unable to document this incident as described by Cohen, nor has he been able to provide relevant references.

A more sustained controversy emerged in 1906–1907; this appears to have been the most substantial press attack on animal psychology during the period now under consideration. The APA met together with the American Association for the Advancement of Science (AAAS) and several other organizations in New York City, December 27–29, 1906. Watson presented a paper entitled "Kinaesthetic Sensations: Their Role in the Reactions of White Rats to the Hampton Court Maze." The abstract was published in *Psychological Bulletin* (Watson, 1907a) and the complete article was published in full in the May 1907 issue of the *Psychological Review Monograph Supplements* (Watson, 1907b). The immediate objective of the research was to determine the sensory bases used by rats in negotiating mazes. The long-term rationale was to develop a functional approach to the study of defective minds. After first determining the performance in the maze by rats with full sensory capacity, Watson selectively eliminated sensory channels and examined the effect on maze performance. Among the surgical operations used by Watson were the removal of the eyes, destruction of the tympanic membrane, removal of the olfactory bulbs, cutting of the vibrissae, and anesthetization of the soles of the rats' feet. All surgery was done under ether anesthesia. Watson noted the apparent total absence of shock from the surgery. Anesthetization of the soles of the feet was accomplished by spraying them with ethyl chloride. One trained, blind rat was studied by applying collodion to the anterior portion of the snout. The results were striking. Watson reported that "none of these subtractions of sense data prevented normal reactions in animals which had already learned the maze, nor lengthened the time of learning" (1907a, p.212). However, by rotating the entire maze through an angle, Watson disturbed performance in rats that had learned the maze. He concluded that kinesthetic sensations were critical to maze performance. Finally, Watson studied a single rat that had been deprived of its eyes, olfactory bulbs, and vibrissae. Once it recovered, this rat too was able to learn and negotiate the maze.

The *New York Times* of December 30, 1906, reported Watson's paper in a manner that can only be considered as pejorative ("Vivisection Described," 1906). Two AAAS presentations were described in a single article. The headline pertaining to Watson's paper read "Vivisection Described/Prof. Watson Tells of Gradually Depriving a Rat of its Senses to Test a Theory." The *Times* reported, "An experiment tending to establish the existence in rats of sixth sense unknown to man was described" (p. 6). After summarizing several of Watson's manipulations, as if done sequentially to a single rat, the report continued, "the professor proceeded to freeze its feet. Still it emerged from its prison. Finally he covered its head completely with collodion and even then it threaded the maze" (p. 6). Later, the *Times* noted, "Dr. Watson asked the section to believe that the rat must possess a sense of direction which may be shared by other animals" (p. 6). The *Times* opined that "his recital of what he did to the rat in any other place would probably have caused a sensation" (p. 6).

A separate article appeared next to the primary report ("Vivisection in Illinois," 1906). The headline read "Vivisection in Illinois/Prof. Watson Can Be Prosecuted if His Subject Felt Pain." In it, the *Times* reported an interview with John L. Shortall, President of the Illinois Humane Society, concerning the fine points of the Illinois anticruelty laws and whether or not Watson might be prosecuted for his research. Shortall concluded that "if an anaesthetic was used and if the experiment was done in the interest of science the charge of cruelty could not be sustained in court" (p. 6), a conclusion counter to the more sensationalistic headline.

On December 31, the *Times* followed up its story with a headline reading "Little Vivisection Here/Authorities, However, Decry Publicity as Hampering Research" (1906). Interviews with various unnamed local scientists asserted the absence of similar research in the New York area. One authority decried the difficulty of conducting animal research in Massachusetts because of the popular outcry against the use of living animals. The *Times* moved the matter to the editorial page the next day ("Torture to No Purpose," 1907). Supporting vivisection in relation to medical benefits, the editorial proceeded "to condemn the torturing of animals merely to gratify an idle or mistaken curiosity as to what they will do when subjected to this or that ingenious mutilation" (p. 8). The utility of the study was the particular target of the attack. The *Times* alleged that Watson's aim was to seek a sixth sense. It concluded that the experiments could not accomplish this and that success would have no obvious utility in any event. Interestingly, the *Times* noted that it is the enemies of research that use the term "vivisection," "so called chiefly because the name is offensive and carries an implication of cruelty" (p. 8). However, "vivisection" was the first word of the first headline the *Times* used in reporting the case—and not on the editorial page. On January 5, the *Times* printed a letter from a G. W. Wishard (1907). He concluded, "I do not see that Prof. Watson has proved anything new by torturing the rat" (p. 8).

The *New York Tribune* of December 30 reported Watson's paper in a manner similar to that of the *New York Times,* although reporting mice as having been the subjects ("Mice May have Sixth Sense," 1906). On January 1, the *New York Evening Journal* picked up the story with the headline "To Prosecute Rat Scientist for Cruelty" (1907), stating that at the instigation of Robert Gifford, of the Illinois Engineering Company, the matter had been turned over to the Illinois Humane Society (p. 3).

The Nation used language similar to that of the *Times* in attacking Watson's research in their issue of January 3 (Staff, 1907c). The writer noted, "We must protest against the torture of animals for merely trivial investigation. . . . This cruelty was so nearly purposeless as to be wholly unjustifiable" (p. 2). Although *Life* covered the meeting, it did not address Watson's presentation (Staff, 1907b). The editors repaired this oversight by reprinting an open letter to Watson from David Belais, President of the New York City Humane Society (Belais, 1907). He wrote, "The mere recital of your methods sounds like a chapter from the Dark Ages" (p. 561). The cartoon shown in Figure 1 originated in *Life*.

The antivivisectionist *Journal of Zoophily* predictably pilloried Watson (Staff, 1907a). They contended that Watson planned similar studies on monkeys and humans and noted,

> Now, if the same experiments were tried on the inspired Watson himself the results would be better, as he could tell us all about it. But he prefers to keep his eyes in his own head. So would the rats. (p. 28)

In an article summarizing the New York AAAS meeting in *Science,* Hayford (1907) did not mention the Watson incident but noted that "the reports in the press were simply scandalous" (p. 44).

On January 9, Watson (1907c) wrote to Robert Yerkes of the "brutal attack" on him in *The Nation.* He wrote that H. H. Donaldson would reply in *Science* and James Mark Baldwin would reply in *The Nation.* Watson wrote, "I didn't want to present that paper in N.Y. fearing just what I got, but Angell and Mead wanted some representation of the work here and I had nothing else ready" (p. 1). I have found no record of a defense from Donaldson. Baldwin, the APA's sixth President and a witness to some of Watson's research, defended it in the January 24 issue of *The Nation* (Baldwin, 1907). He pointed out that Watson's aim was the study of the evolution of intelligence, not the discovery

DREAM OF THE MEDICAL VIVISECTIONIST CRANK WHO WANTONLY AND CRUELLY OPERATED ON RATS, TO SEE THE EFFECT, FROM A "SCIENTIFIC" VIEW-POINT, OF THE LOSS OF THE DIFFERENT SENSES.

FIGURE 1.
Cartoon Satirizing John B. Watson's Experiments on the Role of Sensory Modalities in Maze Learning*

of a sixth sense. Baldwin corrected some of the erroneous reporting, noting that ethyl chloride, not "freezing," was used to anesthetize the feet, that all surgery was done under anesthesia, and that recovered animals were indistinguishable from controls. On January 9, James Rowland Angell (1907b) wrote to James McKeen Cattell asking him to publish in *Science* a correction to the inaccurate reports. Angell himself addressed the issue in the broader context of the vivisection question in two later articles (Angell, 1907a, 1910). In the *Journal of Zoophily* (Staff, 1907d), Angell was criticized for his efforts.

As might be expected, there was fallout at the University of Chicago. President H. P. Judson was contacted by Shortall and others, and Judson referred the matter to Angell, Watson's department head (Judson, 1907a). In his January 17 reply, Angell (1907c) defended Watson with words remarkably similar to those of Baldwin. He noted that

> as regards the operations themselves I may say that they were conducted under the most scrupulous conditions of anesthesis and asepsis—a fact guaranteed by the almost immediate recovery of

*This cartoon was attributed to the publishers of *Life* and was published in the *Journal of Zoophily,* 1907, *16*(6), p. 65.

> the animals, their prodigious appetites and their prompt return to play with their companions. (p. 3)

Judson referred the matter to other departments as well, as a reply from R. R. Bensley (1907) of the Department of Anatomy testifies. In the meantime, on January 24, Rose Fay Thomas, President of the Anti-Cruelty Society of Chicago, sent a 12-page letter to Judson bitterly criticizing Watson and his alleged plans to extend the research to monkeys (Thomas, 1907a). Judson supported his faculty in a letter to Thomas on February 1 (Judson, 1907b). Thomas replied with a 14-page diatribe critical of the departments of both psychology and anatomy and stating that she believed Angell to "juggle with the truth" (Thomas, 1907b). In his reply, Judson (1907c) again defended his faculty and noted that Angell "is incapable of anything of the sort" (p. 1).

Understandably, in the published article Watson (1907b) was very careful in discussing his treatment of the rats. On page 1 he justified vivisection in relation to the value of previous work by physiologists and psychologists. He repeatedly noted the difficulty of the naive observer in discriminating operated from unoperated animals. Watson wrote,

> Much has been written about the artificiality, the abnormality—yes, even the brutality of the present "laboratory" method in animal psychology. However well founded they may be in certain cases, these criticisms cannot with justice be urged against the present set of tests. (p. 13)

In his *History of the Humane Movement,* Niven (1967) noted that "biographers . . . rarely mention whether the subject of the biography had affection and sympathy for animals" (p. 22). As seen earlier with respect to Darwin and Huxley, that was not the case for the sons of British evolutionists. Nor was it the case for the son of John B. Watson. James B. Watson (Hannush, 1987) noted that "Dad was loving to animals and very sensitive to their needs" (p. 141). He noted further that "he was given to disliking people because they were insensitive or bores or demonstrated cruelty to animals or children. To him they were sadistic. That's something he couldn't stand" (p. 144). Of course, we know little of the ontogeny of this recollection.

Ivan P. Pavlov: Contrasting Perspectives

Like others, Pavlov appears to have struggled with the issue of vivisection and its justification. He was called "humane with his animals" by Gantt (1928, p. 21). Pavlov wrote that feelings of pity are at the foundation of the antivivisection movement, "But the experimenter also has this feeling" (quoted by Gantt, 1928, p. 21). Pavlov justified his work because "the human mind has no other means of becoming acquainted with the laws of the organic world except by experiments and observations on living animals" (p. 21). Like other authors, he contrasted animal use in science with that in hunting. His biographer, B. P. Babkin (1949) quoted Pavlov:

> When I dissect and destroy a living animal, I hear within myself a bitter reproach that with rough and blundering hand I am crushing an incomparable artistic mechanism. But I endure in the interest of truth, for the benefit of humanity." (p. 162)

On a monument at the Institute of Experimental Medicine to the dogs used in his experiments Pavlov had carved, "The dog, man's helper and friend from pre-historic times, may justly be offered as a sacrifice to science; but let this always be done without unnecessary suffering" (in Cuny, 1965, p. 25).

An English antivivisectionist, Emilie A. L. Lind-af-Hageby, lectured in the United States on several occasions. Cannon (1913) noted that she had been found guilty in litigation of false statements on one visit. He recognized her as an excellent public speaker (Benison et al., 1987). She discussed Pavlov's work in an address published in the annual report of the American Anti-Vivisection Society. She noted that Pavlov "has denounced the ordinary methods of vivisection on the ground of inutility" (Lind-af-Hageby, 1909, p. 37). "He is now spending his life trying to reform vivisection" (p. 37). Nevertheless, she proceeded to criticize Pavlov for the "revolting" things going on in his laboratory and his lack of understanding of animals. She concluded, "I have presented to you this instance to show you that even ideal vivisection, as it is called, is far from ideal; and that it is difficult for any vivisectionist to make the conditions humane and painless" (p. 38).

Cannon (1909e) described an antivivisection exhibit on Fifth Avenue in New York. He noted that on the walls "there are two entirely fanciful pictures of Pawlow dogs, representing them, quite falsely, as wasted, miserable creatures, sick unto death" (p. 2102). Antivivisectionists remain critical of Pavlov's work and of its use as a model of human abnormal behavior (Kuker-Reines, 1982).

In 1908, *Life* described Pavlov's work on the digestive glands and concluded sarcastically that "The Physical Researchers probably enjoyed it, so it was not a useless experiment" (Staff, 1908, p. 551). Earlier, a note ridiculing Pavlov's work concluded, "The professor seems to be a humane man. Otherwise he would most likely have tied a tin can to the dog's tail, also" (Staff, 1902a, p. 457).

Pavlov's most notable critic was George Bernard Shaw, who devoted a whole book chapter to his criticism (Shaw, 1947). Shaw called Pavlov "the Pontifex Maximus in biological science" and contended that "he was in fact the prince of pseudoscientific simpletons" (p. 202). After criticizing Pavlov's work, Shaw concluded,

> The existing law is clear on the point that if you keep a dog you must not illtreat it; and as Pavlov not only illtreated his dogs horribly but assumed that as a scientist he could do so with impunity, he brought the police up against the very troublesome public question of how far they should tolerate, and even enforce, practices which both common law and common sense class as criminal and detestable. (p. 212)

A famous piece comparing Pavlov and Shaw was written by H. G. Wells (1927). He had recently visited Pavlov and compared him favorably to Shaw:

> You put it in as a problem rather after the fashion of "The Doctor's Dilemma"; if "A" is drowning on one side of a pier and "B" is equally drowning on the other, and you have one life belt and cannot otherwise help, to which of the two would you throw it? Which would I save, Pavloff or Shaw?
>
> I do not think it would interest the reader to give my private answer. But while I was considering it I was manifestly obliged to ask myself, "What is the good of Shaw?" And what is the good of Pavloff? Pavloff is a star which lights the world, shining above a vista hitherto unexplored. Why should I hesitate with my life belt for one moment? (p. 1)

This article was cited by B. F. Skinner (1976) as influential in his decision to give up literature and turn to psychology.

The Press and the Research of Other Animal Psychologists

Similar criticisms, though on a smaller scale, were directed at other animal psychologists. *Life* reprinted an article on Edward L. Thorndike opining that "the public looks upon Professor Thorndike, not as the discovering Columbus of a new scientific continent, but as a cold-blooded wretch who is endeavoring to cloak his fiendish crimes with the wrap of false science" (Staff, 1902b, p. 168). Leffingwell (1901) listed Jacques Loeb's laboratory course in a critical survey of American courses with vivisection. Adele M. Fielde conducted a long series of studies on the behavior of ants; the work was summarized by Casson (1905). Some of the experiments involved terminal food deprivation and others entailed deliberate maltreatment of a nest to permit examination of the consequences. A protest was lodged in the *Journal of Zoophily* (Staff, 1905). Perhaps all of this should not be surprising; Thomas Jefferson also was criticized for vivisection (Miller, 1960).

EFFECTS OF THE CONTROVERSIES

In many of these cases, the criticism had minimal effects on the work being conducted. Surely, the time and emotional involvement of the investigators in defending their work decreased their effectiveness in doing it, as in the case of Walter B. Cannon (Yerkes, 1946). Perhaps the most extreme effect of antivivisectionist concern can be seen in the Bell–Magendie controversy (Gallistel, 1981; Sechzer, 1983). In the pre-anesthetic era, the important discovery of the differentiation of sensory and motor function in the dorsal and ventral roots of the spinal cord was made accurately by Francois Magendie in France. The Briton, Sir Charles Bell, was more sensitive to animal concerns and, as a consequence, did more modest experiments that led to erroneous conclusions.

Other effects were more subtle. Thus, in 1916, animal behaviorist and APA member, Herbert Spencer Jennings, was denied use of a house for a laboratory by the President of Johns Hopkins University because of its proximity to the main street and vulnerability to antivivisectionists (Kingsland, 1987).

These events had effects outside animal research as well. Thus, as the child study movement developed in the United States, some of the resistance was encountered because critics accused practitioners of perpetrating a form of human "vivisection" (Zenderland, 1988).

ANTIVIVISECTION: THE FALLOW PERIOD

The antivivisection movement has been continuous throughout the century. However, the scene was relatively quiet during the long period between the burst of activity around the turn of the century and the onset of the second wave of activity, which can be dated from the publication of Peter Singer's *Animal Liberation* publications (1973, 1975).

Nevertheless, activity did continue, as a few examples will show. Thus, Cannon (1922) editorialized against an antivivisectionist initiative in Colorado. In the mid-1930s there was an initiative against the use of pound animals led by actress Irene Castle McLaughlin (McLaughlin, 1935). Articles regarding renewed antivivisection activity were written by Ivy and Carlson (1941), Whipple, Luckhardt, and Reed (1944), and Manchester (1950).

For the most part, however, I have found little criticism of behavioral research during this period. Storm (1951) wrote critically of behavioral work by Benson Ginsburg, Robert M. Yerkes, and Hans Selye. Jules Masserman received at least one letter critical of his work on cats (Brewer, 1945).

The 1976 criticism of the behavioral studies of Lester Aronson at the American Museum of Natural History in New York signaled the renewal of more extensive criticism of the use of animals in behavioral research (in Wade, 1976).

THE FOUNDING OF THE APA COMMITTEE ON PRECAUTIONS IN ANIMAL EXPERIMENTATION

The APA Committee on Animal Experimentation was formed at the instigation of Walter B. Cannon, who addressed a letter to the APA Council in 1924 (Bentley, 1925). The immediate stimulus for Cannon's action appears to have been an article published by future APA President Calvin P. Stone (1923) in the *Journal of Comparative Psychology*. Surgery was conducted and although it appeared virtually certain that anesthetics were used, Stone neglected to mention the use of anesthetics in his article. In letters to both Robert M. Yerkes (Cannon, 1924a) and editor Knight Dunlap (Cannon, 1924b), Cannon was critical of Stone's report and pointed out that the article left all open to attacks from antivivisectionists. On February 2, 1925, APA President Madison Bentley appointed a committee on animal experimentation, consisting of Robert M. Yerkes of Yale as the chair, with Paul Thomas Young of the University of Illinois and Edward C. Tolman of the University of California, Berkeley, as committee members (Bentley, 1925). Some correspondence from the early years of the committee survives in the Yerkes papers at the Sterling Library of Yale University. Each of the committee members expressed reservations about their roles on the committee, and each tried to resign part way through his term. Nevertheless, the committee remained intact through 1930. Young appears to have been the most active member as he collected materials and presented concrete suggestions; he became chair of the committee in 1928, with Yerkes and Tolman remaining as committee members.

The committee elected to take a low-profile approach to the issues of animal experimentation. The primary accomplishment was the adoption of the American Medical Association (AMA) regulations on animal use in experimentation and the preparation of cards with these rules, which were to be posted in laboratories of animal psychology. Two of these cards survive in the Yerkes papers.

At the 1925 APA meeting in Ithaca, New York, attended only by Young from the committee, five resolutions were adopted by the APA at the instigation of the committee (Young, 1928). These resolutions originated in a letter from Young to Yerkes (Young, 1925). The first was the acceptance of the AMA regulations. The second concerned an "open door" policy toward officials of humane societies. The third requested the cooperation of journal editors in enforcing the code for animal experimentation recommending that editors "decline to publish manuscripts descriptive of experiments which violate the code of animal experimentation adopted by the Association" (Young, 1928, p. 489). The fourth resolution concerned classroom use of animals. The final resolution concerned the appointment of the Committee on Precautions in Animal Experimentation as a standing committee. After the APA meeting Young wrote to Yerkes that "at the meeting no great interest was shown in the report" (Young, 1926, p. 1).

From the beginning, the committee served the dual function served by today's APA Committee on Animal Research and Ethics (CARE): both promulgating standards for animal use and working to ensure that humane animal research could be continued. Young (1930) published in the *Psychological Bulletin* a note highlighting the need for such activity, as a bill had been introduced to make animal experimentation illegal in the State of Illinois. In 1931 the new committee, composed of C. J. Warden, E. G. Wever, and W. T. Heron, urged APA members to protest a new bill introduced into the U.S. Senate that would have made it illegal to experiment on dogs within the District of Columbia (Warden, Wever, & Heron, 1931). The beat went on.

ANIMAL RIGHTS AND ANTIVIVISECTION

The current agitation over animal use in experiments is unprecedented with respect to the scope and extent of media coverage. The topic of animal experimentation has become common in newspapers and magazines and on radio and television. The movement is sufficiently complex and recent to make evaluation in a historical framework difficult. Furthermore, as there is a wide spectrum of opinion on both sides of the issues, it is impossible to discuss a single position as that of "activists" or "scientists." Clearly, the current animal rights movement is much broader than the earlier antivivisection movement, encompassing such animal uses as product testing, factory farming, and hunting. Many activists have adopted vegetarian life-styles. The current movement has generally evolved out of the activist movements for civil rights for Blacks, protests against the Vietnam War, agitation regarding women's issues, and environmentalist concerns. The belief among many activists is that the rights accorded humans, some of which were won in these movements, should be extended to nonhuman animals.

However, with respect to that very visible aspect of the animal rights movement that is targeted at the use of laboratory animals, the resemblances between the antivivisectionist movement at the turn of the century and the current agitation far exceed the differences. Many critics in both movements have charged that animal research is unnecessary, that alternatives are available, that needless pain and suffering are involved, and that scientists are more concerned with grants and profits than with welfare. Organizations formed by scientists counter by citing instances of important findings resulting from animal research, arguing that there are no viable alternatives for much research, contending that instances of pain and suffering are greatly exaggerated, and showing that many scientists are humane individuals motived by noble goals for their science. As argued by Sperling (1988), "The critique developed by the Victorians . . . anticipated every fundamental issue confronted by the modern movement, from philosophical and moral issues . . . to practical problems, such as presenting alternatives to vivisection in research" (p. 53).

To take one instance, the concept of animal rights, often treated as a new development, was prevalent in the Victorian antivivisection movement. Representative works include Nicholson's (1879) *The Rights of an Animal: A New Essay in Ethics,* Salt's (1894) *Animals' Rights Considered in Relation to Social Progress,* and Hughes's (1901) tongue-in-cheek "Animal and Vegetable Rights." Salt's essay was more wide ranging than much writing of the time, dealing with issues such as the state of domestic animals, the rights of wild animals, the slaughter of animals for food, "sport the most wanton of all violations of animals' rights" (p. viii), and the fur and feather trade, as well as vivisection. An annotated bibliography was provided.

In both movements the critics saw excessive manipulation by scientists and physicians as upsetting the balance of nature and called for a return to all that was more "natural." It is common to read in the current literature that much medical research would be unnecessary if humans would return to a more natural life-style with respect to such matters as diet, exercise, and environmental pollution. The Victorian movement too was opposed to excessive medical intervention with opposition to vaccination a key issue. Kidd (1916) was still able to argue against the germ theory of disease. At the root of much of the disagreement were differing world views concerning humans versus nonhumans and scientific progress versus humanistic concerns.

CONCLUSION

My goal has been to piece together some very scattered fragments in an effort to reconstruct the story of the interactions between early animal psychologists and antivivisectionist activists, rather than to advocate a position. Psychologists, like other in our society at large, differ with respect to their views on these issues. It seems clear that the criticisms of animal research in psychology have been with us for much longer than has often been assumed. Indeed, the critics appear to have been present as long as has the field as a whole. Both critics and defenders may take heart that they share a tradition with their predecessors. Both may find encouragement in noting that their movement has a long history and survives, but may find grounds for pessimism in noting that the same is true for the opposition. It is likely that both psychological animal research and its critics will remain on the scene for some time to come. Perhaps an understanding of the historical framework of the controversy will help each side understand the other, even though they may disagree.

REFERENCES

Angell, G. T. (1890, April 10). George T. Angell on vivisection at the University. *Worcester, Mass. Evening Gazette*.

Angell, J. R. (1907a). The reflections of a layman on vivisection. *World To-day, 12,* 379–383.

Angell, J. R. (1907b, January 9). [Letter to James McKeen Cattell]. (Available from the Manuscript Division of the Library of Congress, Washington, DC)

Angell, J. R. (1907c, January 17). [Letter to H. P. Judson]. (Available from the University of Chicago Library, Chicago, IL)

Angell, J. R. (1910). The ethics of animal experimentation. *Journal of the American Medical Association, 54,* 201–203.

Babkin, B. P. (1949). *Pavlov: A biography.* Chicago: University of Chicago Press.

Baldwin, J. M. (1907, January 24). Professor Watson's experiments on rats defended. *The Nation, 84,* 79–80.

Bascom, J. (1878). *Comparative psychology or, the growth and grades of intelligence.* New York: Putnam's.

Bascom, J. (1897). Letter to Senator Gallinger. In *Hearings before the Senate Committee on the District of Columbia, 54th Congress, 2nd session* (Vol. 3469, Document No. 70., p. 3). Washington, DC: U.S. Government Printing Office.

Bascom, J. (1903). Letter of December 15, 1902. *Journal of Zoophily, 12,* 28.

Belais, D. (1907, April 18). His cruelty to rats. *Life,* 561.

Benison, S., Barger, A. C., & Wolfe, E. L. (1987). *Walter B. Cannon: The life and times of a young scientist.* Cambridge, MA: Harvard University Press.

Bensley, R. R. (1907). [Letter to H. P. Judson]. (Available from the University of Chicago Library, Chicago, IL)

Bentley, M. (1925, February 2). Memorandum upon a committee to consider animal experimentation. (Available from the Yale University Library, New Haven, CT)

Brewer, M. (1945). [Letter to J. H. Masserman]. (Available from the University of Chicago Library, Chicago, IL)

Buckhardt, F. H., Bowers, F., & Skrupskelis (Eds.). (1987). *Essays, comments, and reviews: William James.* Cambridge, MA: Harvard University Press.

Cannon, W. B. (1909a, May 25). [Letter to William James]. (Available from the Harvard University Library, Cambridge, MA)

Cannon, W. B. (1909b, June 4). [Letter to William James]. (Available from the Harvard University Library, Cambridge, MA)

Cannon, W. B. (1909c, July 13). [Letter to W. W. Keen]. (Available from the American Philosophical Society Library, Philadelphia, PA)

Cannon, W. B. (1909d, November 12). [Letter to W. W. Keen]. (Available from the American Philosophical Society Library, Philadelphia, PA)

Cannon, W. B. (1909e). An antivivisection exhibition. *Journal of the American Medical Association, 53,* 2102–2103.

Cannon, W. B. (1910a, February 11). [Letter to William James]. (Available from the Harvard University Library, Cambridge, MA)

Cannon, W. B. (1910b, February 13). [Letter to William James]. (Available from the Harvard University Library, Cambridge, MA)

Cannon, W. B. (1912). Animal experimentation and its benefits to mankind. *Journal of the American Medical Association, 58,* 1829–1837.

Cannon, W. B. (1913). The Washington antivivisection congress. *Journal of the American Medical Association, 61,* 2244–2245.

Cannon, W. B. (1922). The antivivisection initiative in Colorado. *Journal of the American Medical Association, 78,* 1895–1896.

Cannon, W. B. (1924a, January 22). [Letter to Robert M. Yerkes]. (Available in the Yale University Library, New Haven, CT)

Cannon, W. B. (1924b, February 16). [Letter to Knight Dunlap]. (Available in the library of Harvard University, Cambridge, MA)

A "careful investigation." (1890, April 27). *Worcester Sunday Telegram.*

Casson, H. N. (1905). New wonders of ant life. *Munsey's Magazine, 33,* 235–241.

Clark, R. W. (1984). *The survival of Charles Darwin: A biography of a man and an idea.* New York: Random House.

Cobbe, F. P. (1881a, April 19). Mr. Darwin and vivisection. *Times of London,* p. 8.

Cobbe, F. P. (1881b, April 23). Mr. Darwin on vivisection. *Times of London,* p. 8.

Cobbe, F. P. (1894). *Life of Frances Power Cobbe* (Vol. 2). Boston: Houghton Mifflin.

Cohen, D. (1979). *J. B. Watson: The founder of behaviourism.* London: Routledge & Kegan Paul.

Cuny, H. (1965). *Ivan Pavlov: The man and his theories.* New York: Eriksson.

Darwin, C. (1881, April 18). Mr. Darwin on vivisection. *Times of London,* p. 10.

Darwin, C. (1958). *The autobiography of Charles Darwin* (1809–1881). New York: Harcourt, Brace. (Original work published 1887)

Darwin, F. (Ed.). (1896). *The life and letters of Charles Darwin* (Vol. 2). New York: Appleton.

Darwin: F. (Ed.). (1903). *More letters of Charles Darwin* (Vol. 2). New York: Appleton.

Dewey, J. (1926). The ethics of animal experimentation. *Atlantic Monthly, 138,* 343–346.

Dewey, J. (1931). "Ethics of animal experimentation." *Hygeia, 9,* 118–120.

Docents' devilish devices. (1890, March 23). *Worcester Sunday Telegram.*

Dogs vivisected. (1890, March 9). *Worcester Sunday Telegram.*

French, R. D. (1975). *Antivivisection and medical science in Victorian society.* Princeton, NJ: Princeton University Press.

Gallistel, C. R. (1981). Bell, Magendie, and the proposals to restrict the use of animals in neurobehavioral research. *American Psychologist, 36,* 357–360.

Gantt, W. H. (1928). Ivan P. Pavlov: A biographical sketch. In W. H. Gantt (Ed.), *I. P. Pavlov's lectures on conditioned reflexes* (pp. 11–31). New York: Liveright.

Gossel, P. P. (1985). William Henry Welch and the antivivisection legislation in the District of Columbia, 1896–1900. *Journal of the History of Medicine and Allied Sciences, 40,* 397–419.

Hall, G. S. (1923). *Life and confessions of a psychologist.* New York: Appleton.

Hannush, M. J. (1987). John B. Watson remembered: An interview with James B. Watson. *Journal of the History of the Behavioral Sciences, 23,* 137–152.

Hayford, J. F. (1907). The New York meeting of the American Association for the Advancement of Science. *Science, 25,* 41–50.

Hodge, C. F. (1896). The vivisection question. *Popular Science Monthly, 49,* 614–624, 774–785.

Holmes, S. J. (1911). *The evolution of animal intelligence.* New York: Holt.

Hughes, R. (1901, November). Animal and vegetable rights. *Harper's Monthly Magazine,* 852–853.

Huxley, L. (Ed.). (1900). *Life and letters of Thomas Henry Huxley.* New York: Appleton.

Ivy, A. C. & Carlson, A. J. (1941). Renewed opposition to animal experimentation. *The Humanist, 1,* 84–89.

James, W. (1909a, May 28). [Letter to W. B. Cannon]. (Available from the Harvard University Library, Cambridge, MA)

James, W. (1909b, June 7). [Letter to W. B. Cannon]. (Available from the Harvard University Library, Cambridge, MA)

Judson, H. P. (1907a, January 12). [Letter to James Rowland Angell]. (Available from the University of Chicago Library, Chicago, IL)

Judson, H. P. (1907b, February 1). [Letter to Mrs. Theodore Thomas]. (Available from the University of Chicago Library, Chicago, IL)

Judson, H. P. (1907c, February 13). [Letter to Mrs. Rose Fay Thomas]. (Available from the University of Chicago Library, Chicago, IL)

Kidd, B. E. (1916). Do germs cause disease? Some flaws in the theory. *Journal of Zoophily, 25*(1), 61–62, 77–78.

Kingsland, S. (1987). A man out of place: Herbert Spencer Jennings at Johns Hopkins, 1906–1938. *American Zoologist, 27,* 807–817.

Koelsch, W. A. (1987). *Clark University 1887–1987: A narrative history.* Worcester, MA: Clark University Press.

Kuker-Reines, B. (1982).*Psychological experiments on animals.* Boston, MA: New England Anti-Vivisection Society.

Leffingwell, A. (1901). *The vivisection question.* New Haven: Tuttle, Morehouse & Taylor.

Lind-af-Hageby, E. (1909). Address to the American Anti-Vivisection Society. *Twentieth annual report of the American Anti-Vivisection Society for the Year 1908* (pp. 26–42). Philadelphia, PA: American Anti-Vivisection Society.

Little vivisection here. (1906, December 31). *New York Times,* p. 5.

Manchester, W. (1950, June 6). The great vivisection dog fight. *Look,* pp. 22–27.

McLaughlin, I. C. (1935). [Transcript of a radio interview with Mr. Bob White of WCFL, February 22, 1935]. (Available from the University of Chicago Library, Chicago, IL)

Mice may have sixth sense. (1906, December 30). *New York Tribune,* p. 4.

Miller, J. C. (1960). *The Federalist era 1789–1801.* New York: Harper.

Mills, T. W. (1893). The cultivation of humane ideas and feelings. *Popular Science Monthly, 43,* 46–51.

Mott, F. L. (1957). *A history of American magazines 1885–1905.* Cambridge, MA: Harvard University Press.

Nicholson, E. B. (1879). *The rights of an animal: A new essay in ethics.* London: C. Kegan Paul.

Niven, C. D. (1967). *History of the humane movement.* London: Johnson.

Rambo, L. R. (1980). Ethics, evolution, and the psychology of William James. *Journal of the History of the Behavioral Sciences, 16,* 50–57.

Romanes, E. (1896). *The life and letters of George John Romanes.* London: Longmans, Green.

Romanes, G. J. (1881, April 25). Vivisection. *Times of London,* p. 10.

Romanes, G. J. (1884). *Animal intelligence.* New York: Appleton.

Ross, D. (1972). *G. Stanley Hall: The psychologist as prophet.* Chicago: University of Chicago Press.

Salt, H. S. (1894). *Animals' rights considered in relation to social progress.* New York: Macmillan.

Sanderson, J. B. (Ed.). (1873). *Handbook for the physiological laboratory.* London: J. & A. Churchill.

Sechzer, J. A. (1981). Historical issues concerning animal experimentation in the United States. *Social Science & Medicine, 15F,* 13–17.

Sechzer, J. A. (1983). The ethical dilemma of some classical animal experiments. *Annals of the New York Academy of Sciences, 406,* 5–12.

Shaw, G. S. (1947). *Everybody's political what's what?* New York: Dodd, Mead.

Shortall, J. G., Rowley, F. H., Coan, T. M. & Leffingwell, A. (1897). Statement. In *Hearings before the Senate Committee on the District of Columbia, 54th Congress, 2nd session* (Vol. 3469, Document No. 70, p. 3) Washington, DC: U.S. Government Printing Office.

Singer, P. (1973). Animal liberation. *New York Review of Books, 20*(5), 17–21.

Singer, P. (1975). *Animal liberation.* New York: Avon.

Skinner, B. F. (1976). *Particulars of my life.* New York: McGraw Hill.

Sperling, S. (1988). *Animal liberators: Research and morality.* Berkeley, CA: University of California Press.

Staff. (1902a, November 27). Science. *Life,* p. 457.

Staff. (1902b, February 27). Relating to Thorndike. *Life,* p. 168.

Staff. (1904a). [Review of *Animal Education*]. *The Athenaeum,* No. 3988, p. 435.

Staff. (1904b, February 18). [Review of *Animal Education*]. *The Nation,* p. 137.

Staff. (1905). Untitled. *Journal of Zoophily, 14*(6), 61.

Staff. (1907a). Fun for Watson. *Journal of Zoophily, 16*(3), 28.

Staff. (1907b, January 27). At the anthropological station. *Life, 49,* p. 137.

Staff. (1907c, January 3). [Untitled editorial on Watson's research]. *The Nation, 84,* p. 2.

Staff. (1907d). Chicago savant flays anti-vivisection. *Journal of Zoophily, 16*(6), 69.

Staff. (1908, May 2). An amusing experiment. *Life, 51,* 551.

Stone, C. P. (1923). Further study of sensory functions in the activation of sexual behavior in the young male albino rat. *Journal of Comparative Psychology, 3,* 469–473.

Storm, M. (1951). *Rights of animals: An appeal to human beings.* Mexico: Privately printed.

Thomas, R. F. (1907a, January 24). [Letter to H. P. Judson]. (Available from the University of Chicago Library, Chicago, IL)

Thomas, R. F. (1907b, February 11). [Letter to H. P. Judson]. (Available from the University of Chicago Library, Chicago, IL)

To prosecute rat scientist for cruelty. (1907, January 1). *New York Evening Journal,* p. 3.

Torture to no purpose. (1907, January 1). *New York Times,* p. 8.

Turner, J. (1980). *Reckoning with the beast.* Baltimore: Johns Hopkins University Press.

Unclad U. of C. man hears birds talking. (1907, July 29). *Chicago Daily News,* p. 1.

Vivisection described. (1906, December 30). *New York Times,* p. 5.

Vivisection in Illinois. (1906, December 30). *New York Times,* p. 5.

Wade, N. (1976). Animal rights: NIH cat sex study brings grief to New York Museum, *Science, 194,* 162–167.
Warden, C. J., Wever, E. G., & Heron, W. T. (1931). [Annual report of the APA Committee on Precautions in Animal Experimentation]. (Available in the Yale University Library, New Haven, CT)
Watson, J. B. (1903). *Animal education: An experimental study of the psychical development of the white rat.* Chicago: University of Chicago Press.
Watson, J. B. (1907a). Kinaesthetic sensations: Their role in the reactions of the white rat to the Hampton Court maze. *Psychological Bulletin, 4,* 211–212.
Watson, J. B. (1907b). Kinaesthetic and organic sensations: Their role in the reactions of the white rat to the maze. *Psychological Review Monograph Supplements, 8*(33), 1–100.
Watson, J. B. (1907c, January 9). [Letter to Robert M. Yerkes]. (Available from the Yale University Library, New Haven, CT)
Wells, H. G. (1927, November 13). Mr. Wells appraised Mr. Shaw. *New York Times Magazine,* pp. 1–2, 16.
Whipple, G. H., Luckhardt, A. B., & Reed, C. I. (1944). Renewed antivivisection threat. *Federation Proceedings, 3,* 277–280.
Whitman, C. O. (1895, February 19). [Letter to W. Harper]. (Available from the University of Chicago Library, Chicago, IL)
Wishard, G. W. (1907, January 5). Groping for a sixth sense. *New York Times,* p. 8.
Yerkes, R. M. (1904). Animal education. *Journal of Comparative Neurology and Psychology, 14,* 70–71.
Yerkes, R. M. (1946). Walter Bradford Cannon 1871–1945. *Psychological Review, 53,* 137–146.
Young, P. T. (1925, October 23). [Letter to Robert M. Yerkes]. (Available in the Yale University Library, New Haven, CT)
Young, P. T. (1926, February 22). [Letter to Robert M. Yerkes]. (Available in the Yale University Library, New Haven, CT)
Young, P. T. (1928). Precautions in animal experimentation. *Psychological Bulletin, 25,* 487–489.
Young, P. T. (1930). Precautions in animal experimentation. *Psychological Bulletin, 27,* 119–120.
Zenderland, L. (1988). Education, evangelism, and the origins of clinical psychology: The child-study legacy. *Journal of the History of the Behavioral Sciences, 24,* 152–165.

From Bottle-Fed Chimp to Bottlenose Dolphin: A Contemporary Appraisal of Winthrop Kellogg

Ludy T. Benjamin, Jr. and Darryl Bruce

Winthrop Niles Kellogg was born in 1898 in Mount Vernon, New York, and died in 1972 in Fort Lauderdale, Florida. He spent approximately 40 of those 74 years actively engaged in research, a career that produced more than 130 publications, including two books assured as classics by their primacy in their respective areas, if not in fact by their quality as experimental investigations. Those books are *The Ape and the Child* (Kellogg and Kellogg, 1933), and *Porpoises and Sonar* (Kellogg, 1961) and both were ground-breaking projects in psychology. It is the purpose of this paper to explore the background of those two pioneering studies as well as other aspects of Kellogg's science that are often overlooked, for example, his numerous studies of learning and conditioning. Using Kellogg's own published writings, published evaluations of his work, unpublished notes on

Benjamin, L. T., Jr. & Bruce, D. (1982). From bottle-fed chimp to bottlenose dolphin: A contemporary appraisal of Winthrop Kellogg. *The Psychological Record, 32,* 461–482.

his research (chiefly on the porpoise studies), and correspondence and interviews with approximately 35 of his former students and colleagues, this paper provides the following: a biographical sketch; an overview of the diversity of his research interests; detailed comments on the ape and child project, the conditioning work, and the porpoise investigations; and finally, an assessment of Kellogg's place in the history of psychology. While the focus is on Kellogg as a researcher, it is hoped that the reader will also acquire a feeling for Kellogg as a teacher, a mentor, and a person.

WINTHROP KELLOGG AS A STUDENT

Kellogg began his college days at Cornell University in 1916 but left after a year for the Great War in Europe. For 2 years he flew in England and France in the U.S. Army Air Service as part of the American Expeditionary Forces where he earned the prestigious *Croix de Guerre*. After the war he continued his undergraduate work at Indiana University where he met and married Luella Dorothy Agger in 1920. He graduated in 1922, having majored in philosophy and psychology, and for a while tried his hand at several jobs, including a brief time as a journalist. His wife's uncle, Eugene E. Agger, himself a university professor, felt Kellogg's talents and personality were well suited to an academic career and encouraged him to consider such an option. Accordingly, Kellogg enrolled in psychology at Columbia where he received his M.A. degree in 1927 and his doctorate in 1929. His dissertation, which was directed by Robert S. Woodworth, involved a comparison of psychophysical methods (Deese, 1973).

THE INDIANA UNIVERSITY YEARS

Kellogg was an active researcher as a graduate student, publishing five articles in 1928–29 in addition to his dissertation, and only one of those was coauthored. Three more articles appeared in 1930 and another five, the following year. This level of productivity was maintained throughout his academic career. He began that career at Indiana University as an assistant professor in 1929. The following year he was promoted to associate professor, and in 1937, to full professor. Kellogg remained at Indiana until 1950, although there were brief periods elsewhere—summers spent as a visiting faculty member at Columbia University in 1933 and 1934 and at the University of Southern California in 1948, 1959, and 1961. In addition, most of the 1931–32 academic year was spent at Orange Park, Florida, as the result of a research leave funded by the Social Science Research Council. It was during that period that the ape and child study was conducted. However, the time at Indiana was devoted largely to research on conditioning and learning. This research was carried out in a special dog conditioning laboratory, a facility which was completed in 1936 and proudly described by Kellogg (1938a) in an article in the *American Journal of Psychology*.

Still, he did research on other topics, sometimes with students, sometimes on his own. At least a few of these studies deserve mention to illustrate the versatility of Kellogg as scientist. As mentioned previously, his earliest work was on psychophysics and that research was essentially completed at Columbia, although one additional study was published during his time at Indiana. Single studies appeared on a variety of topics such as fear in rats, mice, and birds (1931a), advertising (1932a), emotion as it affects muscular steadiness (1932b), fetal activity (1941), and a learning curve for flying an airplane (1946). The latter paper was the result of studies conducted in 1939–40 for the Civil Aeronautics Authority as the United States prepared for the possibility of war. Kellogg would reenlist for that war, serving in South America and Trinidad.

The diversity of other research at Indiana no doubt reflected student interest. That is not to say that Kellogg was not involved in those projects; indeed, it is most unlikely that he would have supervised any research that he did not view as interesting. Included among these projects was a study on social perception in different racial groups (Kellogg & Eagleson, 1931), research on maze learning in water snakes (Kellogg & Pomeroy, 1936), and an investigation of the true-false question as an aid in studying (Kellogg & Payne, 1938). The source of the last of these studies is easily ascertained. Kellogg was a great believer in the value of objective tests and routinely gave his students in introductory psychology a list of hundreds of true-false questions from which those comprising the final exam would be selected.

There is another feature of Kellogg's publication record that should be mentioned and that is his facility for designing new scientific apparatus, improving extant equipment, designing new data collection procedures, and developing new surgical techniques, the latter primarily for chronic preparations used in his dog conditioning research. His vita includes nearly a dozen publications that deal entirely or in part with these kinds of improvements in research methods. The later pioneering work with porpoises would require that same kind of technical innovation.

THE FLORIDA STATE UNIVERSITY YEARS

Kellogg left Indiana University to accept a position at Florida State University. Apparently for some time he had wanted to move to Florida and sent letters to several universities in the state notifying them of that wish. Florida State University had only recently emerged from its role as a women's college and was eager to begin building a major university. That university made Kellogg an offer, and although it was below the salary he had been receiving at Indiana, he accepted it, moving his family to Tallahassee in the summer of 1950. That move marked the end of the dog conditioning studies and signaled the beginning of a whole new focus of research. After a single paper on conditioning in salt-water fishes (Kellogg, 1952), he turned his attention to the study of porpoises, something that would occupy much of the next 13 years of his life.

Florida State University offered Kellogg a chance to be a major force in shaping the psychology programs there, a leadership role he had not enjoyed at Indiana. Kellogg was something of a loner at Indiana, a fact dictated in part by his personality but also by the nature of his research. He spent his career, particularly the Indiana years, in a time when most of psychology was involved in research derived from one learning theory or another. For Kellogg, science was the product of natural curiosity. He spurned the value of theory because he felt it placed blinders on the scientist causing important findings to go unnoticed or at least to be misinterpreted. This atheoretical position was not very popular at Indiana, nor at many other institutions in the 1930s and 1940s, and it undoubtedly contributed to the fact that Kellogg had only a few doctoral students during his 21 years at Indiana.

Kellogg's situation at Florida State University was very different. He found himself as the senior person in the psychology department, and in terms of his visibility nationally, he was likely one of the most famous professors on the campus at that time. He worked hard to build an excellent doctoral program in psychology and began that task by completely restructuring the undergraduate and master's degree programs. More than anyone else he was responsible for the acquisition of the matching funds from the National Science Foundation (NSF) to build the psychology research building at Florida State, the building that now bears his name. He also aided in the recruitment of new faculty, argued for the needed growth of the department, and in general used his considerable reputation as a scientist and scholar to enhance the psychology programs. At the same time he was conducting a very active research program with his graduate students on the sonar abilities of porpoises.

STANFORD RESEARCH INSTITUTE AND RETIREMENT

In 1963, Kellogg officially retired from Florida State, although he would return to that campus on several occasions in temporary faculty positions. In 1962, however, he began his association with the Stanford Research Institute (SRI) at Menlo Park, California, where he established two large research projects. One was funded by NSF and involved investigations of sonar in sea lions, while the second was funded by the National Institute of Health and involved echolocation in blind humans. The grants were for long-term projects, but it is unlikely that Kellogg ever saw his involvement in the projects beyond the first year or two. He hired two of his doctoral students from Florida State to direct the investigations—Ronald Schusterman for the sea lion studies and Charles Rice for the human echolocation studies. In February of 1965, Kellogg resigned from SRI. He and Luella spent much of their remaining days together traveling to various parts of the world. Their deaths came in the summer of 1972, his on June 22, hers on July 17.

KELLOGG AS COLLEAGUE, EDUCATOR, RESEARCHER

Before discussing Kellogg's major research areas, we provide a brief picture of the personality of this man as described to us by his former students and colleagues. To begin with, we note that the responses from these individuals have been amazingly uniform. Thus it appears that Kellogg was consistent in the way he dealt with people, and he does not seem to have been one way to one person and another way to someone else.

Winthrop Kellogg was a man of strong likes and dislikes who formed impressions of people on initial encounters, impressions that were not easily altered. He has been described as fair in his dealings with others and perhaps naive in his expectation that he would be treated similarly. He had little tolerance for those he viewed as unjust or those whose behavior he viewed as less than ethical and he had clear views about who were the incompetents and scoundrels in science. These negative evaluations often provided Kellogg with the impetus for his own research, thus at times giving it an adversarial quality. He was more than a little egocentric and frequently had difficulty in recognizing validity in positions contrary to his own. Kellogg was an individual with great self-confidence in his professional as well as personal life. Indeed, overconfident might not be too exagerated a description. For example, one of his students, Paul R. Fuller, related an incident in which Kellogg suffered some financial embarrassment from an automobile accident since he did not have collision insurance on his car. "Since he was a skillful and careful driver . . . he surmised that if there were a collision he would not be at fault" (Fuller, Note 1).

Kellogg's manner was often brusque and businesslike. He had little time for casual chatter, particularly with students. He was a workaholic who demanded much from himself and from those around him, whether they were colleagues, students, or social acquaintances. He possessed a good sense of humor, although he did not necessarily appreciate humor from his students, since to him it indicated disrespect for the instructor. He was viewed as a person of great energy and intensity, who brought enthusiasm to much of what he did.

As a teacher, Kellogg received high marks from his students who were impressed by his exhaustive knowledge of the literature in his areas of instruction. He demanded respect from his students which included the requirement that they always address him as Dr. Kellogg. His well-planned lectures were enthusiastic, filled with details on numerous research studies and occasional vignettes about the researchers. While his manner in dealing with students was often curt, he was approachable and not unsympathetic to their problems. Many of his former graduate students felt that Kellogg was one of the best, if not the best, classroom teachers they had experienced. Not only did he make the subject matter interesting, but he communicated an enormous amount of information.

We have already mentioned some of Kellogg's talents as a scientist and his disdain for theory. He was also the very model of scientific integrity in the planning, execution, and reporting of his research. He took all precautions possible to see that extraneous variables were controlled; it was intended that nothing be left to chance. Everything was checked and checked again. He was almost obsessive in some of his research habits such as having extra equipment and tools on hand in the event that some repairs or replacements were needed during the course of an investigation. His laboratory was both orderly in arrangement and immaculately clean. Woe be the student who failed to maintain those standards. One of his students, Robert S. Daniel, has described him as "from the old school of researchers who did everything they could think of to try to prove that their own hypotheses were wrong before they published results" (Daniel, Note 2). Many of those trained by Kellogg acknowledged the debt they owed to him as a model for carrying out exacting, rigorous investigations. His skills in doing empirical research, and the rigor of that work were no doubt partly responsible for Kellogg's reputation as a scientist and his success in obtaining grants throughout his career.

RESEARCH ON THE APE AND THE CHILD AT ORANGE PARK

No investigation in Kellogg's career brought him more attention than did the study involving the rearing of his infant son Donald with an infant chimpanzee, Gua. The study is well documented in the 336 pages that comprise *The Ape and the Child*. Our aim here is to explore the reasons behind the initiation of the study, to discuss some of the difficulties encountered in the conduct of the research, to describe some of the major characteristics of the investigation that set it apart from earlier and later studies, to speculate on the reasons for the eventual termination of the project, and to discuss its importance as a scientific investigation.

The idea for the study emerged in 1927 when Kellogg was still a graduate student at Columbia University. Kellogg and Kellogg (1933) give us that date for the idea but not its source. However, our guess is that it was stimulated by an article on the "wolf children" of India which was published that year in the *American Journal of Psychology* (Squires, 1927). Similar to Itard's "wild boy of Aveyron," the wolf children were two young girls found in a cave inhabited by wolves. These children behaved as though they were wolves, eating and drinking like those animals and making no use of their hands except to crawl around on all fours, which was their method of locomotion. Eventually the girls learned to walk upright, although they could never run. One acquired speech, at least a vocabulary of approximately 100 words, but the other continued only to make grunting noises. Howling noises at night were never extinguished, nor were their human teachers able to break them of the rather distasteful habit of "pouncing upon and devouring small birds and mammals" (Kellogg, 1931b, p. 162). Both girls died at an early age.

Like other feral children, the wolf children were judged to be subnormal in intelligence and it was assumed that their intellectual deficits prevented them from being able to adapt to their new surroundings. This interpretation was common in explaining the problems of adjustment in feral children and was, in fact, the explanation offered by Squires (1927). Kellogg disagreed with that interpretation, and in two replies published in the *American Journal of Psychology* (1931c, 1934), he argued that the wolf children, and others like them, were probably born of normal intelligence. Indeed, it was unlikely that they would otherwise have been capable of survival. From his environmentalistic perspective he contended that these children learned to be wild animals because that was exactly what their environment demanded of them. He believed in the strong impact of early experience and the existence of critical periods in development, and he maintained that the problem with civilizing feral children was the difficulty of overturning the habits learned early in life.

One way to test this hypothesis would be to place a human infant of normal intelligence in an uncivilized environment and to observe systematically its development in that environment. Kellogg noted that while such an experiment would be both morally outrageous and illegal, there was another way, albeit somewhat indirect, to test the environment-heredity question. That was to take a wild animal and place it in the civilized environment of a human home (Kellogg & Kellogg, 1933). Thus began the attempt to produce this unusual experiment.

A decision was made to select an ape, either a chimpanzee or an orangutan, preferably as soon after birth as possible. Kellogg was aware of earlier investigations with apes in civilized surroundings, but none of those instances met the rigorous criteria he would propose for his own experiment. As early as 1909, Lightner Witmer had attempted to teach human language to a chimpanzee, Peter, a retiree from a theatrical act. The experiment was largely a failure, but Witmer (1909) speculated that success might be obtained in future investigations where "chimpanzees will be taken early in life and subjected for purposes of scientific investigation to a course of procedure more closely resembling that which is accorded the human child" (p. 205).

Kellogg wanted to use an experimental subject that was very young, before the animal could acquire a repertoire of infrahuman modes of responding. He wanted a situation that would assure that the animal was *always* treated as a human and never as an animal, particularly a pet. That is, it was not to be fed from a dish on the floor or scratched behind its ears. Interactions with the animal were to be full-time. He objected to arrangements whereby the animal was played with for several hours each day, only to be placed in a cage or otherwise ignored for the remainder of the day. One or more of these situations rendered previous investigations invalid in Kellogg's view.

The plan for Kellogg's experiment was outlined in a *Psychological Review* (1931b) article in which he wrote:

> Suppose an anthropoid were taken into a typical human family at the day of birth and reared as a child. Suppose he were fed upon a bottle, clothed, washed, bathed, fondled, and given a characteristically human environment; that he were spoken to like the human infant from the moment of parturition; that he had an adopted human mother and an adopted human father. . . . The experimental situation *par excellence* should indeed be attained if this technique were refined one step farther by adopting such a baby ape into a human family with one child of approximately the ape's age. (p. 168)

Kellogg ended that article with a statement indicating that arrangements for such an experiment were currently underway. Those arrangements were the culmination of a number of years of discussion, a major issue being whether or not even to undertake the experiment. The matter is mentioned in the preface of *The Ape and the Child:*

> Indeed the enthusiasm of one of us met with so much resistance from the other that it appeared likely we could never come to an agreement upon whether or not we should even attempt such an undertaking. (p. ix)

The preface does not tell us who was who in that statement, but the enthusiasm undoubtedly belonged to Winthrop and the resistance to Luella.

That issue apparently resolved, Kellogg arranged a leave of absence from Indiana University, and with a grant secured from the Social Science Research Council, he, Luella, and infant son Donald moved to Florida, near the Yale Anthropoid Experiment Station at Orange Park. Through a special agreement with Robert Yerkes, they were able to obtain a young female chimpanzee, Gua. Gua was 7 and 1/2 months old when the Kelloggs acquired her. At that time, Donald was 10 months of age. Kellogg regretted the fact that the chimp was not younger, but given the difficulties of acquiring young apes, he had little choice. At the conclusion of the experiment he would assert that the age problem "was of less serious consequence in influencing her 'human' life than might at first have been supposed" (Kellogg & Kellogg, 1933, p. 18).

Luella Kellogg was not the only person to express some misgivings about the project. There were reactions from the public and, less directly, from some of Kellogg's own colleagues within the scientific community. Some individuals objected on the grounds that the experiment was inhumane in its rearing of a human child with an ape sibling. These criticisms also focused on the undesirability of using a young child as an experimental subject for such an extended period of time. A few people objected to the separation of Gua from her mother and the company of those of her own kind.

Further, the study was characterized as sensationalism and publicity-seeking. Kellogg felt his scientific integrity was in question from some of the reactions he received regarding the study. When the book was reviewed by *Time* magazine ("Babe and Ape," 1933), the reviewer referred to the project as a "curious stunt." Writing in 1968, Kellogg reviewed the studies that had reared chimpanzees in human homes and claimed that this kind of research required an investigator of high determination and dedication who could face those who would ridicule the experiment from their base of misunderstanding (Kellogg, 1968a).

Finally, there was another variety of criticism that was not unique to Kellogg's study but was (and is) a common experience for those scientists who chose to work with apes. Robert Yerkes had faced the problem in establishing his anthropoid research station (Hahn, 1971). The objections came from people who could be labeled creationists or anti-Darwinists. They were suspicious of the Kellogg experiments which they viewed as against nature. Some people believed that the Yerkes station was involved in secret crossbreeding experiments between apes and humans, a belief that has persisted into modern times (Riopelle, Note 3). Recall also that Kellogg's experiment was not too distant in time or place from the famous Scopes trial in Tennessee, and any study that purported to look at similarities between apes and humans was no doubt viewed by some as evil. Despite the criticisms, the study was begun on June 26, 1931, when the Kelloggs brought Gua to their home.

For the next 9 months, Winthrop and Luella served as experimenters in a project that demanded 12 hours a day from the two of them, 7 days a week. With a few exceptions necessary "to meet the indispositions of the infants or experimenters," the schedule remained unchanged. Winthrop Kellogg was concerned that the experiment measure up to his demands. There was nothing he could do about the age difference between Donald and Gua, nor about the fact that Gua was not obtained shortly after her birth. Nevertheless, he would conduct his experiment as no other prior investigation with apes. He would maintain identical rearing conditions for his two experimental subjects. Further, he would use a variety of tasks to test his infants, not only on a comparative basis but also in looking at developmental sequences within each of them. Lastly, he would maintain sufficient detachment to be able to evaluate objectively the data he was collecting.

So for 9 months, Donald and Gua were tested daily on such things as blood pressure, memory, body size, scribbling, reflexes, depth perception, vocalization, locomotion, reactions to tickling, strength, manual dexterity, problem solving, fears, equilibrium, play behavior, climbing, obedience, grasping, language comprehension, attention span, and others. The tests were exhaustive, and likely exhausting for the experimenters if not for the subjects. There were occasional baby sitters which gave the experimenters a brief respite from their duties, but those were rare occasions.

The scientific rigor and ingenuity of these tests is readily apparent from the detailed descriptions provided in the book. The reader is also likely to notice the impersonal style in which these tests are reported. If the preface and initial chapter of the book were omitted, the reader might not realize that the authors were describing studies involving their own child. At times one gets the impression of an overzealousness in the pursuit of knowledge. For example, consider the following passage from a chapter that deals with physical differences and similarities:

> The differences between the skulls can be audibly detected by tapping them with the bowl of a spoon or with some similar object. The sound made by Donald's head is somewhat in the nature of a dull thud, while that obtained from Gua's is harsher, like the crack of a mallet upon a wooden croquet or bowling ball. (Kellogg & Kellogg, 1933, p. 25)

While this example is extreme in terms of the specific difference being assessed, it is characteristic of the detachment of most of the authors' descriptions. Indeed, the book, as well as the experiment it reports, is very different from a later publication, *The Ape in Our House* (1951), a report by Cathy Hayes about her chimp-rearing experiences. Her book is filled with anecdotes and makes no pretense of being a scientific investigation.

The Ape and the Child is clearly a book about an ape. It was the chimp who was the primary object of study; she was the experimental subject while Donald served as the control subject. This was a study designed to answer a question that was beyond the scope of other investigations. There were other works that described the young chimpanzee in considerable detail such as the naturalistic observations in *The Great Apes* (Yerkes & Yerkes, 1929) or the physical and physiological studies of Jacobsen, Jacobsen, and Yoshioka (1932). Other researchers, such as Wolfgang Köhler, had looked at problem-solving abilities in chimpanzees, and work on learning and memory had been going on at the Orange Park station since it had opened. But these studies did not permit answers of the kind the Kelloggs sought. At the simplest level, their investigation was an attempt to discover how human a chimpanzee could become when reared in a human environment. In fact, Kellogg's (1931b) *Psychological Review* article published prior to the project was entitled "Humanizing the Ape." But the experiment was much more than that; it was designed to be the definitive investigation explicating the interaction of heredity and environment. As such, it probably succeeded better than any study before its time in demonstrating the limitations heredity placed on an organism regardless of environmental opportunities as well as the developmental gains that could be made in enriched environments.

Our final concern is why the project ended when it did. *Time* magazine's review ("Babe and Ape," 1933) said the following:

> At the end of nine months the Kelloggs demonstrated that environment, particularly psychological environment, is necessary for the development of an individual's inherent abilities. Gua, treated as a human child, behaved like a human child except when the structure of her body and brain prevented her. This being shown, the experiment was discontinued. (p. 44)

However, *Time's* reason, while plausible, is not explicit in the book. Nor is a reason given in two articles that Kellogg would write about the subject toward the end of his career (1968a, 1968b). We are told only that the study was terminated on March 28, 1932, when Gua was returned to the Orange Park primate colony through a gradual rehabilitating process. But as for why, the Kelloggs, who are so specific on so many other points, leave the reader wondering. Several possible reasons, in addition to the one suggested by *Time,* come to mind. First, the schedule that the Kelloggs maintained for the 9 months was so grueling that they may have quit for reasons of fatigue. Second, they may have wanted to use the time remaining to them on leave from Indiana to prepare the book manuscript for publication. Third, Gua was maturing, gaining in strength and, according to Kellogg, becoming less predictable and more difficult to manage. It is possible that the Kelloggs feared Gua might inadvertently harm Donald.

A fourth possibility is suggested by material in the book having to do with the acquisition of language, as well as by comments from several of Kellogg's students. Although the Kelloggs spent considerable time trying to teach Gua some words, she was never able to master them. She was quite adept at vocalizing and possessed a number of distinguishable and meaningful sounds. Gua was an excellent imitator in many respects, but at vocal imitation she was a failure. The Kelloggs noted that she never went through anything resembling the period of babbling common to human infants (see also Kellogg, 1968b). While Gua did not imitate Donald's sounds, the opposite was not true. When Donald was 14 months of age, the Kelloggs first observed him imitating the food bark that Gua would use in the presence of food. Initially he would mimic Gua's calls while she was engaged in such vocalizations, but later he would initiate the sounds wholly on his own.

Remember that Donald was 10 months old when Gua arrived. It was only a short time later that he was able to say her name, one of only three words in his vocabulary at 11 and 1/2 months. By the age of 19 months, Donald's vocabulary still consisted of three words. Actually, he had used six words to that point, but it seemed that as one new word was acquired, one of the other words would be lost. With regard to Donald's expressive vocabulary, the Kelloggs wrote:

> he was therefore less in advance of Gua than he might have been. Indeed it can be safely said that neither really learned to talk during the interval of research.
>
> No doubt the necessity of spending so much time with tests of various sorts was to some extent responsible for this retardation. In addition the opportunity of associating with other children, an advantage possessed by most infants, was in view of the confining nature of the work of comparatively infrequent occurrence. (Kellogg & Kellogg, 1933, p. 281)

In short, the language retardation in Donald may have brought an end to the study. Of course, it is also possible that the project could have been halted for all or some combination of the reasons mentioned.

While on the subject of language, we would like to correct a common misconception of the ape and child study that has been magnified in recent years by the various studies on communication in primates using sign language or other symbols. The Kellogg project is sometimes conceptualized as an effort to teach language to an ape. But as our description indicates, this was not an objective of the study. Language and communication represents only one chapter out of 13 in *The Ape and the Child,* and most of that chapter deals with the development of receptive language.

We have reviewed the ape and child project in some detail because we believe that it played a significant role in Kellogg's professional career, primarily through the public recognition it brought. Some of Kellogg's colleagues in psychology and in the larger scientific community seemed little impressed with the study. Yet the project caught the imagination of much of the public, and as a result, Kellogg was something of a celebrity, famous to some, infamous to others. He is said to have lamented often the popularity of the research, particularly because he felt it caused much of his other work (for example, the dog conditioning studies) to go unnoticed. Following publication of the book in

1933, he did not write on the subject again until the late 1960s, and then in response to the work of the Gardners with Washoe. Nevertheless, he would be queried about those 9 months in Orange Park for the rest of his life.

RESEARCH ON CONDITIONING AND LEARNING AT INDIANA UNIVERSITY

Kellogg's research in conditioning and learning while at Indiana resulted in some 50 published articles. These papers, many of which describe work carried out in the Indiana Conditioning Laboratory, cover a broad range of subjects. Among them are the bilateral transfer of conditioning, the necessity of making a motor response in order to condition that response, learning in dogs suffering varying degrees of cortical loss, the effects of various drugs on learning, the relationship of forward and backward conditioning, spinal conditioning, and the nature of the response in flexion conditioning. As well, there are reports describing methods and apparatus that Kellogg used in his conditioning work. It is outside the intent and scope of this essay to review all of Kellogg's research in this field. Instead, we shall attempt to present its general nature and purpose. This will serve to illustrate further the kind of scientist that Kellogg was and to help us understand what posterity's judgment of him is likely to be.

From the array of problems that Kellogg investigated, one may get the impression that his conditioning research had no focus. However, such an impression is mistaken. His chief concern was the nature of learning, and virtually all of his conditioning work was aimed at illuminating that issue. Kellogg's views on the matter are set out in five articles published in the *Psychological Review* from 1938 through 1940. In retrospect, one can see how his empirical research flowed from the ideas expressed in these papers. This is not to say that they contained a comprehensive theory of learning. Rather, they presented what Kellogg considered to be a scientifically useful conception of learning, that is, one that did not stray far from what could be observed, namely, behavior, and one that generated scientifically researchable questions. Moreover, the articles nicely illustrate Kellogg's atheoretical bias that we mentioned earlier.

The first three papers are the most important. In "An Eclectic View of Some Theories of Learning" Kellogg (1938b) attempted to minimize the differences among four different theories of learning by showing that each simply emphasized different parts of the learning situation and by highlighting continuities among them. Another paper (Kellogg, 1938c) criticized Cason (1937) for defining learning in part as the strengthening of neural connections. The themes of this article were sounded later at greater depth by Kellogg and Britt (1939). They argued for a definition of learning that stressed function (behavior change) and not structure (changes in the nervous system), as Cason had proposed. The major part of the essay raised objections to the structural viewpoint. Essentially, these were that the structural changes underlying learning are hypothetical and that the role played by the nervous system in learning was uncertain. In discussing the latter point, Kellogg and Britt mentioned the evidence of learning in dogs when the cerebral cortex was missing and the possibility of conditioning in spinal animals. Rather prophetically, both topics were ones that Kellogg was later to investigate in depth himself. In any case, it was concluded that a physiological definition of learning was far too speculative and should yield to one that emphasized changes in behavior or function. Behavioral changes were factual and observable; neurological changes amounted to little more than hypothetical inference.

The two final articles in the series (Kellogg, 1939, 1940) were brief replies to criticisms of the earlier papers. Neither reply is particularly substantive, although the latter one is characteristically Kellogg. Chappell (1940) had attacked Kellogg and Britt's (1939) behavioral definition of learning. In response, Kellogg simply reiterated that the existing scientific data did not warrant a definition of learning in terms of changes in the nervous system, and, he concluded, "As far as I am concerned, that is all there is to it" (1940, p. 97).

We have said that a review of Kellogg's empirical work in conditioning and learning is beyond the scope of this essay. Nevertheless, it is appropriate to describe briefly one of the more significant of the learning projects, specifically, conditioning in spinal dogs. For one thing, Kellogg's interest in this problem may be clearly linked to his conceptual concerns about learning since, as noted above, spinal conditioning is explicitly mentioned in the Kellogg and Britt (1939) article. Second, major textbooks of the 1950s and 1960s (Kimble, 1961; Osgood, 1953; Stevens, 1951) gave prominent attention to Kellogg's spinal conditioning work. Third, the work brought Kellogg into controversy. Finally, the spinal conditioning publications indicate how accomplished Kellogg was as an empirical scientist.

The issue was whether dogs whose spinal cords had been transsected could acquire a conditioned response to a limb below the point of transsection. Observations pointing to this possibility had been first described by Culler (1937). Later, Shurrager and Culler (1940) reported data which they felt met the criteria of true motor conditioning and extinction in spinal dogs. The specific response conditioned was a muscle twitch in the exposed semitendinosis muscle in the dog's hind leg. Kellogg's first reference to the Shurrager–Culler data was in an article (Pronko & Kellogg, 1942), that described a muscle twitch in a limb when an electric shock was delivered to another limb. The animals involved were not spinal dogs, but the observation suggested to Kellogg the possibility that Shurrager and Culler's semitendinosis muscle twitch was not a true conditioned response.

Kellogg does not seem to have acted on this possibility immediately. In the years 1946 through 1949, however, he and his students published seven articles and delivered three oral presentations on the problem. The upshot was that spinal conditioning in dogs could not be produced in the Indiana laboratory. The most extensive reports were by Kellogg, Deese, Pronko, and Feinberg (1947) and by Deese and Kellogg (1949). In both articles, Kellogg concluded that the muscle twitch observed by Shurrager and Culler (1940) was actually a basic response to a conditioned electric shock stimulus applied to another part of the body (either to another limb or to the tail) and that an unconditioned electric shock stimulus applied to the limb in question was unnecessary. It was argued further than changes in this muscle twitch with training should be regarded simply as sensitization of a reflex.

Although Shurrager responded to Kellogg's claims (Shurrager, 1947) and continued his interest in the topic (e.g., Dykman & Shurrager, 1956), we shall not follow the story further. Our intent has been to describe the nature and extent of Kellogg's participation in the controversy. One point worth noting is that Shurrager's work was carried out with acute preparations whereas Kellogg's research employed chronic preparations. While it is possible that this was the reason for the difference in their results, we mention the point also as a tribute to Kellogg's laboratory skills. It was no simple matter to keep dogs alive for months after their spinal cords had been transsected. The data published with Deese in 1949 were Kellogg's last word on the problem. Convinced that he had done all the experimental work necessary and that spinal conditioning was not to be found in his animals, he turned to other concerns.

RESEARCH ON PORPOISES AT FLORIDA STATE UNIVERSITY

Shortly after his arrival at Florida State University in 1950, Kellogg began his well-known investigation of the sonar capacity of porpoises.

This project was completed in 1956. But after an interlude of research on other topics Kellogg returned to the study of porpoises (1961–63), this time to their visual and problem-solving abilities. This was his last serious involvement in research. As in our discussion of Kellogg's other research interests, our review of the porpoise investigations is intended to highlight the important features of Kellogg's science and to help us evaluate his position in the history of psychology.

In his investigation of the echolocating capacity of porpoises, Kellogg followed his characteristic ways. To begin with, his interest in porpoises was motivated by simple curiosity about how they were able to navigate so well. Believing that they used sonar, he set out to resolve the matter through experiments and careful observations. Three questions were asked. The first was whether porpoises (actually, bottlenose dolphins) emit sounds that can serve as sonar signals. The answer was that they do, namely, rapidly repeated clicking noises and bird-like whistles. The second question was whether porpoises can decode the echoes from such sounds. Two main things convinced Kellogg of this. One was the structure of the dolphin's ear and the related neuroanatomy. The second was the upper limit to the dolphin's hearing. Kellogg's procedures indicated this limit to be in the neighborhood of 80,000 Hz, although it is now known to be closer to 200,000 Hz or roughly 10 times that of the human.

Our principal concern here is with the third question, namely, the limits of the dolphin's sonar system and whether it is actually used by the animal in navigating and orienting. To obtain data about such matters, a special porpoise pool was constructed on the coast of the Gulf of Mexico and two porpoises were procured for study. We shall sketch the results of a number of experiments that were carried out with these animals.

First, the capacity of the dolphins to detect stimuli was found to be remarkably acute. For example, they emitted sound signals to a stimulus as slight as a single BB shot dropped into the pool. As for sounds on the surface of the water, the minimal stimulus for a similar reaction was a half teaspoon of water dropped from a height of 1.5 m. Objects that were immersed silently, for example, a fish, were sensed in the course of periodic trains of sound pulses emitted by the animals every 15–20 seconds.

In testing discriminative capacity, Kellogg capitalized on the porpoise's preference for spot to mullet as a food fish. Using spots that were half the size of mullets and pitting the two in a choice-discrimination situation, it was shown that the dolphin quickly learned to go directly to the spot. The conclusion preferred by Kellogg was that the animal was discriminating size by means of echolocation.

Further experiments were conducted to buttress this conclusion and to rule out the possible involvement of other sense modalities, notably vision. The latter was considered a possibility even though human visibility in the pool was restricted to about .5 m, the water was quite turbid, and some of the testing sessions were conducted on moonless overcast nights. One of these additional studies offered the dolphin the choice of two fish, both spots. They were lowered into the water simultaneously, and the porpoise began its approach toward them from a distance of roughly 2 m. However, one of the fish was held behind a plate of clear glass. Thus if the porpoise was acting on visual clues, as often as not it should swim toward the obstructed fish and strike the glass. But if it were echolocating, it should unerringly approach and select the unobstructed fish. The results were unequivocal. There were no errors in 202 test trials, and the time to go from the start point to the target point declined over the course of testing.

While other examples of such straightforward experiments giving equally unambiguous outcomes could easily be given, what we have described to this point suffices to illustrate the empirical and nontheoretical character of the entire project. It is emphasized also that this investigation represented pioneering research that demanded a considerable measure of methodological innovation. Kellogg warmed to such demands and functioned best when so challenged. The gathering of data for this project ended in 1956 and a complete account of the work was published as *Porpoises and Sonar* in 1961. Intended for the interested layperson as well as the scientist, the book was more than just an engaging account of the methods, results, and implications of a series of scientific studies. It also successfully captured the spirit and puzzle-solving nature of empirical science.

The second porpoise project (Kellogg & Rice, 1966) investigated the visual and problem-solving abilities of these animals. What makes this project notable are the unpublished research notes that were written as the study progressed. Not only do they allow a richer account of the work, but they afford considerable insight into the Kellogg brand of animal psychology.

By way of an overview of the research, we consider a single porpoise (Paddy) who was trained on a series of form discriminations. The stimuli were always two white patterns each set against a black background. When these patterns were presented below the surface of the water and an errorless training procedure was used, Paddy was typically able to learn the correct member of each pair. To assess the problem-solving ability of the animal, numerous transfer tests of previously learned discriminations were made. A transfer task involved a change in the positive member of an earlier learned discrimination, in the negative member, or in both. In 71% of the transfer problems, Paddy responded correctly on all test trials on the problem. It was therefore concluded that the dolphin can not only use vision but is capable of generalizing from previously learned visual discriminations to the solving of new ones.

We consider now the unpublished research notes. In general, they contain qualitative observations, insights, testing suggestions, and an idea of what happened during the course of the project. Most of them were written by Kellogg and indicate that he played a dominant role in the data gathering phase of the research. Moreover, these notes are not merely cryptic scribbled affairs. They are typed, single spaced, and typically a page in length. In short, they mirror the care and thought with which the project was conducted.

When the published reports and the unpublished materials are taken together, certain features of the project stand out. First, it had a strong comparative slant. In the original grant application, one of the stated objectives was to compare the dolphin's problem-solving ability with that of infra-human primates and human children. Comparative work on a chimpanzee was actually conducted, although in a collaborative manner rather than directly by Kellogg. Unfortunately, the correspondence between the methods of the chimpanzee and Paddy studies was not sufficient to permit the intended comparisons. The point, though, is that the research was distinctly motivated in part by comparative interests.

A review of the research notes reveals that the project was more than a set of experiments. It was also a qualitative, descriptive exploration of the visual and problem-solving behavior of a single, intensively tested animal. The notes are replete with comments about the qualitative aspects of Paddy's activities. The animal's way of solving discrimination problems is often described and not simply its success or lack of success in such problems. Many of the descriptions are quite anthropomorphic, although Kellogg was well aware of this and typically used quotation marks around such comments. These kinds of comments did not appear in the published accounts of his research. There are also interpretations of Paddy's behavior from an emotional and a communicative perspective. In sum, the notes show that Kellogg was an earnest student of the dolphin's behavior.

In a similar vein, he often tried to understand things from the standpoint of the porpoise. Occasionally, this meant getting into the pool with the animal to see how things looked from his angle. In fact, this was how Kellogg discovered a possible source of Paddy's difficulty in solving pattern discrimination problems when the stimuli were presented *above* the waterline. In notes dated July 14, 1962, Kellogg wrote:

> For the first time we made some dives to see what the apparatus looked like from Paddy's standpoint. This probably should have been done on the first day. What we found out was astonishing and I am reluctant to admit we could have gone so far and been so damned dumb.
>
> When there is the slightest ripple in the water, the angle of entry of the refracted light rays is so garbled as to prevent any clear image of objects in the air whatever. . . .
>
> In contrast to all this, the stimulus objects when held a few inches under the water are perfectly clear even without an illuminated background. . . .
>
> Obviously, what we must do is present the stimuli underwater without lights.

Thus, Kellogg often acquired in a first-hand way an understanding of why Paddy behaved as he did.

Our review of the porpoise research has been an extended one. But we have felt this was necessary to convey an idea of the substantive nature of the research and, more important, further understanding of the characteristics of Kellogg's projects in animal and comparative psychology and of Kellogg the scientist.

AN ASSESSMENT OF KELLOGG'S PLACE IN THE HISTORY OF PSYCHOLOGY

To review, Kellogg had two main scientific roles during his career. First, he was a comparative psychologist and a student of animal behavior. This is best exemplified by his research on the chimp and the child and by his study of the echolocating capacity of the porpoise. Second, he investigated conditioning and learning. Particularly notable in this respect was his work on spinal conditioning in dogs. In both of these roles, Kellogg was recognized as an empirical scientist who did well-controlled, thorough experiments and who had a knack for mechanical inventiveness. His interest in theory was minimal and his research was stimulated by fundamental albeit broad questions (e.g., the contributions of heredity and environment to the development of chimpanzee behavior), by previous data (whether from his own or other laboratories), or by plain curiosity.

During his lifetime, Kellogg appears to have been recognized more for his conditioning and learning research than his comparative and animal behavior studies. To understand this, we need to consider the dominant ideas and practices of American animal psychology during the period in which Kellogg was active, 1930–65. These commitments were perhaps well known for they have been written about frequently (e.g., Beach, 1950; Gottlieb, 1979; Lockard, 1971). Accordingly, we mention them only briefly. To begin with, the subject of main interest was learning and the method for its investigation was laboratory experimentation. Kellogg's conditioning and learning projects and his laboratory skills squared perfectly with this tradition. In contrast, there were many other features of American animal psychology with which Kellogg was out of step. The preferred organism for study was the Norway rat. Similarly, the range of behaviors examined was quite limited. For the most part, rats pressed levers or ran in alleyways or mazes. A prominent casualty of the emphasis on learning was inquiry into the sensory capacities of animals. The aim of animal learning research was a theory, preferably mathematical, of behavior or learning in general. Qualitative differences among species were given short shrift. Instead, it was held that species differed mainly quantitatively and that such differences could be recognized simply by changing the constants in the equations of general behavior theory (Hull, 1945). Finally, in keeping with the emphasis on theory, it was felt that empirical science should be guided by the hypothetico-deductive method. In other words, one should generate a hypothesis from a theory and then carry out a laboratory experiment to test the hypothesis and hence the theory. Given this set of commitments, it is clear that Kellogg's professional reputation during his lifetime would have rested on his conditioning and learning research and that his comparative and animal behavior investigations would have placed him out of the mainstream of American animal psychology. Indeed, they may even have diminished his eminence in the eyes of American psychologists. We have noted previously that the professional reception of the ape-child project was lukewarm.

At the same time, much of Kellogg's research was compatible with the methodological practices of ethology, the science of animal behavior that prospered in Europe beginning with the 1930s but which failed to make much headway in America until the 1960s. The approach of ethologists, the ethological attitude, has been summarized by Burghardt (1973) as follows: (1) studying animal behavior that is meaningful given the animal's natural existence; (2) beginning with descriptive studies of an animal's behavior; (3) examining a broad range of species and behaviors; (4) comparing similar behaviors in related species; and (5) avoiding concentrating research on domesticated animals.

One may find evidence of all of these commitments in one part or another of Kellogg's research. Thus, far from concentrating on any one domesticated species, Kellogg worked with a wide range of species (fish, snakes, birds, mice, rats, dogs, porpoises, chimps, and humans), not to mention a variety of behaviors (reflexes, various expressions of sensory capacity in the porpoise, various learned behaviors, and a vast array of developing behaviors in the chimp and the human child). The ape-child investigation is also a prime example of a comparative study, and one that was as much descriptive as experimental. Similar claims could be made for the porpoise research. Moveover, the latter research well illustrates the examination of something meaningful in the natural existence of the porpoise, namely, its sonar capacity.

There are other features of Kellogg the scientist that have a decidedly ethological flavor. In the case of the dolphin, at least, he tried to acquire as thorough a knowledge as possible of the animal's behavior. Often this meant trying to see things from the porpoise's perspective. The earlier-mentioned incident of Kellogg getting into the pool to determine how a visual stimulus appeared to the dolphin is only one of a number of such examples. This sort of thing plus Kellogg's anthropomorphic comments about his animals, his taking a chimp into his home and raising it like a human for 9 months, and his ape-child and porpoise books that were written for the layperson are all reminiscent of the practices of ethologists.

At the same time, Kellogg was far from the complete ethologist. What set him apart from this tradition was exactly what gained him recognition from American psychologists, namely, his investigations of conditioning and learning, his preference for laboratory experimentation, and his zeal for the principle of control. Furthermore Kellogg did not share the ethologists' proclivity toward instinct. All of these points are plainly evident in his work, even in those projects which were most ethological in character. Thus, to the ape-child project, Kellogg brought a considerable environmentalistic bias; and in the porpoise research, he used many learning tasks to assess the sonar and problem-solving abilities of these animals. Finally, control and experimentation marked not only the porpoise research but also the ape-child study; raising a chimp in one's home is by any measure an experiment.

In sum, Kellogg was neither entirely an American animal psychologist nor a European ethologist. Rather, he represented a blend of some of the best commitments of both groups. Interestingly, the contemporary science of animal behavior represents a similar fusion of classic American animal psychology and classic ethology (Dewsbury, 1978). The excesses of both traditions are clearly declining, that is, the American overemphasis on learning and the pursuit of general behavior theory, and the ethological stress on the concept of instinct. As a result of this, a genuine comparative psychology has reasserted itself. Accordingly, from the vantage point of today's science of animal behavior, it is Kellogg's comparative research that seems most significant and enduring, especially his ape-child and porpoise projects.

Of these two, we believe it is the chimp-child study for which Kellogg will be best remembered. We find this quite understandable, for in our opinion, scientists are remembered for their ideas and not their empirical science no matter how good the latter might have been. And while both the ape-child and porpoise projects were major pioneering efforts of empirical science that were done with care, objectivity, thoroughness, concern for control, and ingenuity that few other than Kellogg were capable of, the ape-child work was more than that. It was fundamentally a good idea. First, it tackled a significant problem, namely, the nature-nurture issue. Second, it did so in an imaginative and extremely fruitful way. With the Kelloggs' son Donald serving as the control subject, the experiment was able to answer definitively the question of how human a chimp could become when raised like a human child in a human environment. When one adds in the anthropocentric flavor of the idea and its basic bizarreness in the eyes of many, it is not surprising that the ape-child study still commands recognition. We expect such recognition to continue and to ensure Kellogg a place in any serious history of comparative psychology. We would hope, though, that posterity will also remember him as one who performed important comparative and animal-behavior research in America during a time when it was not very fashionable to do so.

REFERENCE NOTES

1. Fuller, Paul. Personal communication, December 8, 1981.
2. Daniel, Robert S. Personal communication, November 26, 1981.
3. Riopelle, Arthur. Personal communication, January 22, 1982.

REFERENCES

Babe and Ape. 1933. *Time,* June 19, p. 44.

Beach, F. A. 1950. The snark was a boojum. *American Psychologist, 5,* 115–124.

Burghardt, G. M. 1973. Instinct and innate behavior: Toward an ethological psychology. In J. A. Nevin (Ed.), *The study of behavior*. Glenview, Illinois: Scott, Foresman.

Cason, H. 1937. The concepts of learning and memory. *Psychological Review,* 44, 54–61.

Chappell, M. N. 1940. The inadequacy of the Kellogg-Britt definition of learning. *Psychological Review,* 47, 90–94.

Culler, E. 1937. Observations on the spinal dog. *Psychological Bulletin,* 34, 742–743.

Deese, J. 1973. In memoriam, Winthrop Niles Kellogg, 1898–1972. *The Psychological Record,* 23, 423–425.

Deese, J., & Kellogg, W. N. 1949. Some new data on the nature of 'spinal conditioning.' *Journal of Comparative and Physiological Psychology,* 42, 157–160.

Dewsbury, D. A. 1978. *Comparative animal behavior*. New York: McGraw-Hill.

Dykman, R. A. & Shurrager, P. S. 1956. Successive and maintained conditioning in spinal carnivores. *Journal of Comparative and Physiological Psychology,* 49, 27–35.

Gottlieb, G. 1979. Comparative psychology and ethology, In E. Hearst (Ed.), *The first century of experimental psychology*. Hillsdale, New Jersey: Lawrence Erlbaum Associates.

Hahn, E. 1971. *On the side of the apes*. New York: Crowell.

Hayes, C. 1951. *The ape in our house*. New York: Harper & Row.
Hull, C. L. 1945. The place of innate individual and species differences in a natural-science theory of behavior. *Psychological Review,* 52, 55–60.
Jacobsen, C. F., Jacobsen, M. M., & Yoshioka, J. G. 1932. Development of an infant chimpanzee during her first year. *Comparative Psychology Monographs,* 9, No. 41.
Kellogg, W. N. 1931a. A note on fear behavior in young rats, mice, and birds. *Journal of Comparative Psychology,* 12, 117–121.
Kellogg, W. N. 1931b. Humanizing the ape. *Psychological Review,* 38, 160–176.
Kellogg, W. N. 1931c. More about the 'wolf children' of India. *American Journal of Psychology,* 43, 508–509.
Kellogg, W. N. 1932a. The influence of reading matter upon the effectiveness of adjacent advertisements. *Journal of Applied Psychology,* 16, 49–58.
Kellogg, W. N. 1932b. The effect of emotional excitement upon muscular steadiness. *Journal of Experimental Psychology,* 15, 142–166.
Kellogg, W. N. 1934. A further note on the 'wolf children' of India. *American Journal of Psychology,* 46, 149–150.
Kellogg, W. N. 1938a. The Indiana conditioning laboratory. *American Journal of Psychology,* 15, 174–176.
Kellogg, W. N. 1938b. An eclectic view of some theories of learning. *Psychological Review,* 45, 165–184.
Kellogg, W. N. 1938c. Some objections to Professor Cason's definition of learning. *Psychological Review,* 45, 96–100.
Kellogg, W. N. 1939. On the nature of skills—a reply to Mr. Lynch. *Psychological Review,* 46, 489–491.
Kellogg, W. N. 1940. The superfluity of the Chappell critique—a reply. *Psychological Review,* 47, 95–97.
Kellogg, W. N. 1941. A method for recording the activity of the human fetus *in utero,* with specimen results. *Journal of Genetic Psychology,* 58, 307–326.
Kellogg, W. N. 1946. The learning curve for flying an airplane. *Journal of Applied Psychology,* 30, 435–441.
Kellogg, W. N. 1952. "Anxiety" and conditioning in salt-water fishes. *American Psychologist,* 7, 279–280.
Kellogg, W. N. 1961. *Porpoises and sonar*. Chicago: University of Chicago Press.
Kellogg, W. N. 1968a. Chimpanzees in experimental homes. *The Psychological Record,* 18, 489–498.
Kellogg, W. N. 1968b. Communication and language in the home-raised chimpanzee. *Science,* 162, 423–427.
Kellogg, W. N., & Britt, S. H. 1939. Structure or function in the definition of learning? *Psychological Review,* 46, 186–198.
Kellogg, W. N., Deese, J., Pronko, N. H., & Feinberg, M. 1947. An attempt to condition the *chronic* spinal dog. *Journal of Experimental Psychology,* 37, 99–117.
Kellogg, W. N., & Eagleson, B. M. 1931. The growth of social perception in different racial groups. *Journal of Educational Psychology,* 22, 367–375.
Kellogg, W. N., & Kellogg, L. A. 1933. *The ape and the child.* New York: Whittlesey House (McGraw-Hill).
Kellogg, W. N., & Payne, B. 1938. The true-false question as an aid in studying. *Journal of Educational Psychology,* 29, 581–589.
Kellogg, W. N., & Pomeroy, W. B. 1936. Maze learning in water snakes. *Journal of Comparative Psychology,* 21, 275–295.
Kellogg, W. N., & Rice, C. E. 1966. Visual discrimination and problem solving in a bottlenose dolphin. In K. S. Norris (Ed.), *Whales, dolphins, and porpoises.* Berkeley: University of California Press.
Kimble, G. A. 1961. *Hilgard and Marquis' conditioning and learning* (2nd ed.). New York: Appleton-Century-Crofts.
Lockard, R. B. 1971. Reflections on the fall of comparative psychology: Is there a message for us all? *American Psychologist,* 26, 168–179.
Osgood, C. E. 1953. *Method and theory in experimental psychology.* New York: Oxford University Press.
Pronko, N. H., & Kellogg, W. N. 1942. The phenomenon of the muscle twitch in flexion conditioning. *Journal of Experimental Psychology,* 31, 232–238.

Shurrager, P. S. 1947. A comment on 'an attempt to condition the *chronic* spinal dog.' *Journal of Experimental Psychology,* 37, 261–263.

Shurrager, P. S., & Culler, E. 1940. Conditioning in the spinal dog. *Journal of Experimental Psychology,* 26, 133–159.

Squires, P. C. 1927. 'Wolf children' of India. *American Journal of Psychology,* 38, 313–315.

Stevens, S. S. (Ed.). 1951. *Handbook of experimental psychology.* New York: Wiley.

Witmer, L. 1909. A monkey with a mind. *Psychological Clinic,* 3, 179–205.

Yerkes, R. M., & Yerkes, A. W. 1929. *The great apes.* New Haven: Yale University Press.

CHAPTER **11**

BEHAVIORISM

By the beginning of the twentieth century, the new psychology had a firm foothold in American universities. After the founding of Hall's laboratory at Johns Hopkins University in 1883, nearly forty more universities followed suit by 1900. James's *Principles,* having been in print for ten years, had led many new converts to psychology's promised land. That book played an important role in functionalism's establishment as a viable alternative to the more restrictive brand of structural psychology espoused by Titchener.

Although only a decade old in 1900, the University of Chicago was a university on the move, largely due to the efforts of the founding president, William Rainey Harper, who raided the established universities (especially G. Stanley Hall's Clark University) in search of their best faculty talent. Chicago was an exciting place to be at the turn of the century. The biology department included Jacques Loeb (see Chapter 10) and Henry H. Donaldson (1857–1938), an internationally known authority on the human brain who had studied with G. S. Hall at Johns Hopkins. John Dewey and James Rowland Angell were members of the Philosophy Department.

In 1900, John Broadus Watson (1878–1958) arrived at the University of Chicago from his home in Traveler's Rest, South Carolina, having completed his baccalaureate and master's degrees at a southern Baptist college, Furman University. Watson had planned to pursue his doctorate in philosophy but lost interest in Dewey's classes. In Angell, though, he found the new psychology more to his liking. He took classes from Loeb and Donaldson as well, with Angell and Donaldson eventually directing his doctoral dissertation research. Watson's research was a comparative psychological investigation using infant rats of varying ages to study the relationship between neurological development and behavioral complexity. By 1903, the university granted authority for a degree in psychology, separate from philosophy, and the first psychology doctorate was awarded to Watson in that year. His dissertation was entitled, "Animal Education: The Psychical Development of the White Rat" (see Dewsbury's article in Chapter 10). Watson had several job offers upon graduation but elected to stay at Chicago when Angell offered him an assistant professor position in psychology. There he continued his animal research until he was offered a full professorship in the department of psychology at Johns Hopkins in 1908. The offer was too good to refuse.

According to his autobiography, Watson's dissatisfaction with the prevailing psychology of his day began in 1904 when he was at Chicago (Watson, 1936). Influenced by his physiological training, he searched for a way to make his own science more objective. More and more he was troubled by the mentalism of a psychology defined as the study of consciousness. He greatly doubted the validity of the introspective method, preferring the more controlled stimulus–response conditions of his laboratory studies with rats. For Watson, those ideas were expressed in some detail in an address he delivered at Columbia University in 1913 entitled "Psychology as the Behaviorist Views It." A few months later that address was published under the same title in the *Psychological Review,* a journal founded by Cattell and James Mark Baldwin, and edited at the time by Watson. The paper became known as the "Behaviorist Manifesto" and marked the beginning of a revolution in psychology (although not an immediate rebellion—see the Samelson article in this chapter).

Watson's manifesto began:

> Psychology as the behaviorist views it is a purely objective experimental branch of natural science. Its theoretical goal is the prediction and control of behavior. Introspection forms no essential part of its methods, nor is the scientific value of its data dependent upon the readiness with which they lend themselves to interpretation in terms of consciousness. (Watson, 1913, p. 158)

He rebuked not only the structuralists but also the functionalists among whom he had trained. He claimed that he could not distinguish between them, that both were mired in a mentalism that thwarted objective science. In continuing his attack he wrote:

> I do not wish unduly to criticize psychology. It has failed signally, I believe, during the fifty-odd years of its existence as an experimental discipline to make its place in the world as an undisputed natural science. . . . The time seems to have come when psychology must discard all reference to consciousness; when it need no longer delude itself into thinking that it is making mental states the object of observation. (Watson, 1913, p. 163)

Needless to say, those were harsh words from this brash young man who had received his doctorate in psychology only ten years earlier. Regarding Watson's admonition against consciousness and other mentalistic terms, some psychologists have referred to it as "the time when psychology lost its mind."

Watson was not alone in his dissatisfaction with the subjectivism of psychology, and his 1913 paper was by no means the initial appearance of such ideas. The unmistakable rumblings of behaviorism were all too apparent in the earliest days of the twentieth century. Behavioral ideas, in one form or another, were espoused by William McDougall (a British psychologist), Herbert S. Jennings (a biologist), Adolf Meyer (a psychiatrist), Knight Dunlap, and others. Jennings, Meyer, and Dunlap were Watson's colleagues at Johns Hopkins University, and all exerted identifiable influences on Watson's thinking. Indeed, in his autobiography, Dunlap (1932) lamented the fact that Watson had received the credit for behavioristic ideas that were largely Dunlap's. Interestingly, in his own autobiography, Watson (1936) acknowledged Dunlap's priority (see Kornfeld, 1991).

Other early behaviorists included Max F. Meyer (1873–1967), a psychologist at the University of Missouri, whose 1911 book, *The Fundamental Laws of Human Behavior,* attacked introspection and a psychology of subjective states, especially the notion of consciousness. Historian John O'Donnell (1985) has said of Meyer: "Had he been an American working in a more prominent eastern institution and capable of communicating his notions in the evangelical language of a southern Baptist, the name John B. Watson might be less prominent today" (p. 216).

The intellectual roots of behaviorism obviously predate Watson, and they extend beyond the boundaries of psychology into the allied fields of physiology, medicine, and sociology (see Parmelee, 1912). But behaviorism as a movement in psychology belongs to Watson. Some historians, for example, John Burnham (1968), have argued against labeling Watson the *founder* of behaviorism. Burnham prefers to view Watson's role in behaviorism as that of "charismatic leader." Yet that label does not seem to do justice to Watson's role, if it implies that in 1913 the philosophical tenets of behaviorism were already in place in any centralized formulation. Watson's contribution was that he crystallized those scattered ideas into a systematic formulation that was *new*. In Burnham's (1968) words, "Watson combined these elements into a synthesis, the whole of which was greater than its parts" (p. 145). If anyone deserves the label of founder of behavioral psychology, it is John B. Watson. The impact of his words, although not immediate, has been profound in the history of modern psychology.

For Watson, psychology was to be the science of behavior, not mental states. Processes that were not directly observable would have no place in a behavioral psychology. Not only was the subject matter of psychology to be changed, but so were its methods. Introspection was rejected; it was a method that only pretended to produce accurate observations. Watson did recognize the possible value of verbal report from subjects, but only in conjunction with other corroborating observations. Instead, Watson called for more objective forms of observation, with and without the use of scientific instruments. He approved of the reaction time studies and the experimental research of Hermann Ebbinghaus on learning and memory. Further, he approved of some psychological tests, so long as they were not mental tests. Somewhat later, Watson called for extended use of the conditioned reflex method of Pavlov. He noted how it could be used to answer questions that heretofore seemed answerable only by the method of introspection, for example, in determining the range of the visible spectrum to which the human eye is sensitive.

> We start with any intermediate wave length and by the use of the electric shock establish a conditioned reflex. Each time the light appears the reflex occurs. We then increase the length of the wave rather sharply and if the reflex appears we again increase the wave length. We finally reach a point where the reflex breaks down, even when punishment is used to restore it—approximately 760 millimicrons. This wave length represents the human being's spectral range at the red end. We then follow the same procedure with respect to the violet end (397 millimicrons). In this way we determine the individual's range just as surely as if we had stimulated the subject with monochromatic lights varying in wave lengths and asked him if he saw them. (Watson, 1919, pp. 35–36)

Watson followed the publication of his manifesto with his first book, *Behavior: An Introduction to Comparative Psychology* (1914), in which he lauded the value of animal research in psychology and expressed his views about a wholly behavioral psychology. By the time his next book appeared, *Psychology from the Standpoint of a Behaviorist* (1919), he had shifted his work to human infants. In 1919, he was engaged in the most famous research study of his career. Indeed, it is one of the most famous studies in the history of American psychology. With the assistance of a graduate student, Rosalie Rayner (whom he would later marry), Watson sought to demonstrate that fear could be acquired in humans as the result of conditioning, an idea he had proposed in an earlier article (Watson & Morgan, 1917). Using an 11-month-old infant, Albert B., they presented first a white rat (which the infant did not fear) and then a loud noise (which the infant did fear). After repeated pairings, Watson and Rayner (1920) reported that fear had been conditioned to the rat. It was an important claim for Watson because it supported his largely environmentalistic theory of emotion in humans. The success of the conditioning and the generalization of the fear demonstrated that conditioning was a fact, not just in the lives of laboratory dogs but in humans as well. But was the research all that successful? Harris (1979) and others have shown that there were a number of problems with Watson's study: reliance on a single subject, too few stimuli to test for generalization, confounding of classical and operant conditioning procedures, lack of appropriate controls, and irregularity of conditioning trials. Despite the methodological flaws, the conditioning of "Little Albert" was cited often as proof of the power of Watson's psychology.

That classic study was Watson's last as an academic psychologist although he later supervised the research of Mary Cover Jones (see Jones, 1974; Kornfeld, 1989).

Scandal over his affair with Rayner forced him to leave Johns Hopkins at the age of 42. He went to New York City, where he pursued a successful career in advertising and wrote a number of books and articles on psychology for the popular press.

Watson's impact on psychology was substantial, perhaps more so than any other figure in the history of American psychology. Yet the value of his legacy is debated today. In arguing for an objective science of behavior, he eliminated a number of topics that have only begun to reappear in American psychology in the last twenty years, for example, consciousness, thinking, dreaming, and emotion. Some psychologists believe that Watson's philosophy was too radical, that in throwing out what he saw as bad, he also contributed to the elimination of much that was good. They would argue that in the long run he inhibited psychology's progress.

Others would argue that psychology's progress as a science was largely because of Watson, that he was the one figure who demanded a complete break with philosophy and the mentalistic baggage attached to it. Watsonian behaviorism strengthened the role of physiological processes in psychological explanations, expanded psychological methods, and made apparent the ties between animal and human psychology.

Whatever the value of the legacy, Watson's ideas dominated American psychology for more than fifty years through many varieties of behaviorism (see the next chapter). Although the cognitive psychology movement has weakened the stronghold of the behaviorists, they continue to be a major force in contemporary psychology.

THE READINGS

The first selection in this chapter is Watson's famous 1913 paper that started the behaviorist revolution. Histories of psychology have generally reported that the rebellion was immediate, that psychologists were instantly upon Watson's bandwagon, waving the banners of objectivism. But recent historical research (see the second selection in this chapter) suggests that the acceptance of Watson's ideas was much slower in coming. This second selection, by the historian of psychology Franz Samelson, an authority on behaviorism, represents extensive research in the published and unpublished sources of psychology in search of the impact of Watson's ideas and the timetable for their acceptance.

The final selection is by historian of science, Kerry W. Buckley, the author of an excellent biography of Watson (Buckley, 1989). Buckley's article details how Watson, fired from his academic post at Johns Hopkins, brought his behaviorism to the field of advertising. Watson was able to sell his behavioristic psychology to the New York City advertising community, arguing that the goals of psychology—prediction and control—were those of advertising: the ability to predict the effectiveness of advertising campaigns and the ability to control consumer behavior. This article illustrates one of the legacies of American functionalism, namely, the application of scientific psychology, in this case, to business. This topic will be discussed in greater detail in Chapter 15.

REFERENCES

Buckley, K. W. (1989). *Mechanical man: John Broadus Watson and the beginnings of behaviorism.* New York: Guilford Press.

Burnham, J. C. (1968). On the origins of behaviorism. *Journal of the History of the Behavioral Sciences, 4,* 143–151.

Dunlap, K. (1932). Autobiography. In C. Murchison (Ed.), *A history of psychology in autobiography* (Volume 2). Worcester, MA: Clark University Press, pp. 35–61.

Harris, B. (1979). Whatever happened to Little Albert? *American Psychologist, 34,* 151–160.

Jones, M. C. (1974). Albert, Peter, and John B. Watson. *American Psychologist, 29,* 581–583.

Kornfeld, A. D. (1989). Mary Cover Jones and the Peter case: Social learning versus conditioning. *Journal of Anxiety Disorders, 3,* 187–195.

Kornfeld, A. D. (1991). Contributions to the history of psychology: LXXVI. Achievement, eminence, and histories of psychology: The case of Knight Dunlap. *Psychological Reports, 68,* 368–370.

Meyer, M. F. (1911). *The fundamental laws of human behavior.* Boston: Badger.

O'Donnell, J. M. (1985). *The origins of behaviorism: American psychology, 1870–1920.* New York: New York University Press.

Parmelee, M. (1912). *The science of human behavior: Biological and psychological foundations.* New York: Macmillan.

Samelson, F. (1980). J. B. Watson's Little Albert, Cyril Burt's twins, and the need for a critical science. *American Psychologist, 35,* 619–625.

Watson, J. B. (1913). Psychology as the behaviorist views it. *Psychological Review, 20,* 158–177.

Watson, J. B. (1914). *Behavior: An introduction to comparative psychology.* New York: Henry Holt.

Watson, J. B. (1919). *Psychology from the standpoint of a behaviorist.* Philadelphia: J. B. Lippincott.

Watson, J. B. (1936). Autobiography. In C. Murchison (Ed.), *A history of psychology in autobiography* (Volume 3). Worcester, MA: Clark University Press, pp. 271–281.

Watson, J. B., & Morgan, J. J. B. (1917). Emotional reactions and psychological experimentation. *American Journal of Psychology, 28,* 163–174.

Watson, J. B., & Rayner, R. (1920). Conditioned emotional reactions. *Journal of Experimental Psychology, 3,* 1–14.

Psychology as the Behaviorist Views It

John B. Watson

Psychology as the behaviorist views it is a purely objective experimental branch of natural science. Its theoretical goal is the prediction and control of behavior. Introspection forms no essential part of its methods, nor is the scientific value of its data dependent upon the readiness with which they lend themselves to interpretation in terms of consciousness. The behaviorist, in his efforts to get a unitary scheme of animal response, recognizes no dividing line between man and brute. The behavior of man, with all of its refinement and complexity, forms only a part of the behaviorist's total scheme of investigation.

It has been maintained by its followers generally that psychology is a study of the science of the phenomena of consciousness. It has taken as its problem, on the one hand, the analysis of complex mental states (or processes) into simple elementary constituents, and on the other the construction of complex states when the elementary constituents are given. The world of physical objects (stimuli, including here anything which may excite activity in a receptor), which forms the total phenomena of the natural scientist, is looked upon merely as means to an end. That end is the production of mental states that may be 'inspected' or 'observed.' The psychological object of observation in the case of an emotion, for example, is the mental state itself. The problem in emotion is the determination of the number and kind of elementary constituents present, their loci, intensity, order of appearance, etc. It is agreed that introspection is the method *par excellence* by means of which mental states may be manipulated for purposes of psychology. On this assumption, behavior data (including under this term everything which goes under the name of comparative psychology) have no value *per se*. They possess significance only in so far as they may throw light upon conscious states. Such data must have at least an analogical or indirect reference to belong to the realm of psychology.

Indeed, at times, one finds psychologists who are sceptical of even this analogical reference. Such scepticism is often shown by the question which is put to the student of behavior, "what is the bearing of animal work upon human psychology?" I used to have to study over this question. Indeed it always embarrassed me somewhat. I was interested in my own work and felt that it was important, and yet I could not trace any close connection between it and psychology as my questioner understood psychology. I hope that such a confession will clear the atmosphere to such an extent that we will no longer have to work under false pretences. We must frankly admit that the facts so important to us which we have been able to glean from extended work upon the senses of animals by the behavior method have contributed only in a fragmentary way to the general theory of human sense organ processes, nor have they suggested new points of experimental attack. The enormous number of experiments which we have carried out upon learning have likewise contributed little to human psychology. It seems reasonably clear that some kind of compromise must be effected: either psychology must change its viewpoint so as to take in facts of behavior, whether or not they have bearings upon the problems of 'consciousness'; or else behavior must stand alone as a wholly separate and independent science. Should human psychologists fail to look with favor upon our overtures and refuse to modify their position, the behaviorists will be driven to using human beings as subjects and to employ methods of investigation which are exactly comparable to those now employed in the animal work.

Any other hypothesis than that which admits the independent value of behavior material, re-

From Watson, J. B. (1913). Psychology as the behaviorist views it. *Psychological Review, 20,* 158–177.

gardless of any bearing such material may have upon consciousness, will inevitably force us to the absurd position of attempting to *construct* the conscious content of the animal whose behavior we have been studying. On this view, after having determined our animal's ability to learn, the simplicity or complexity of its methods of learning, the effect of past habit upon present response, the range of stimuli to which it ordinarily responds, the widened range to which it can respond under experimental conditions,—in more general terms, its various problems and its various ways of solving them,—we should still feel that the task is unfinished and that the results are worthless, until we can interpret them by analogy in the light of consciousness. Although we have solved our problem we feel uneasy and unrestful because of our definition of psychology we feel forced to say something about the possible mental processes of our animal. We say that, having no eyes, its stream of consciousness cannot contain brightness and color sensations as we know them,—having no taste buds this stream can contain no sensations of sweet, sour, salt and bitter. But on the other hand, since it does respond to thermal, tactual and organic stimuli, its conscious content must be made up largely of these sensations; and we usually add, to protect ourselves against the reproach of being anthropomorphic, "if it has any consciousness." Surely this doctrine which calls for an analogical interpretation of all behavior data may be shown to be false: the position that the standing of an observation upon behavior is determined by its fruitfulness in yielding results which are interpretable only in the narrow realm of (really human) consciousness.

This emphasis upon analogy in psychology has led the behaviorist somewhat afield. Not being willing to throw off the yoke of consciousness he feels impelled to make a place in the scheme of behavior where the rise of consciousness can be determined. This point has been a shifting one. A few years ago certain animals were supposed to possess 'associative memory,' while certain others were supposed to lack it. One meets this search for the origin of consciousness under a good many disguises. Some of our texts state that consciousness arises at the moment when reflex and instinctive activities fail properly to conserve the organism. A perfectly adjusted organism would be lacking in consciousness. On the other hand whenever we find the presence of diffuse activity which results in habit formation, we are justified in assuming consciousness. I must confess that these arguments had weight with me when I began the study of behavior. I fear that a good many of us are still viewing behavior problems with something like this in mind. More than one student in behavior has attempted to frame criteria of the psychic—to devise a set of objective, structural and functional criteria which, when applied in the particular instance, will enable us to decide whether such and such responses are positively conscious, merely indicative of consciousness, or whether they are purely 'physiological.' Such problems as these can no longer satisfy behavior men. It would be better to give up the province altogether and admit frankly that the study of the behavior of animals has no justification, than to admit that our search is of such a 'will o' the wisp' character. One can assume either the presence or the absence of consciousness anywhere in the phylogenetic scale without affecting the problems of behavior by one jot or one tittle; and without influencing in any way the mode of experimental attack upon them. On the other hand, I cannot for one moment assume that the paramecium responds to light; that the rat learns a problem more quickly by working at the task five times a day than once a day, or that the human child exhibits plateaux in his learning curves. These are questions which vitally concern behavior and which must be decided by direct observation under experimental conditions.

This attempt to reason by analogy from human conscious processes to the conscious processes in animals, and *vice versa*: to make consciousness, as the human being knows it, the center of reference of all behavior, forces us into a situation similar to that which existed in biology in Darwin's time. The whole Darwinian movement was judged by the bearing it had upon the origin and development of the human race. Expeditions were undertaken to collect material which would establish the position that the rise of the human race was a perfectly natural phenomenon and not an act of special creation. Variations were carefully sought along with the evidence for the heaping up effect and the weeding out effect of selection; for in these and the other Darwinian mechanisms were to be found factors sufficiently complex to account for the origin and race differentiation of man. The wealth of material collected at this time was considered valuable largely in so far as it tended to develop the concept of evolution in man. It is strange that this situation should have remained the dominant one in biology for so many years. The moment Zoölogy undertook the experimental study of evolution and descent, the situation immediately changed. Men ceased to be the center of reference. I doubt if any experimental biologist today, unless actually engaged in the problem of race differentiation in man, tries to interpret his findings in terms of human evolution, or even refers to it in his thinking. He gathers his data from the study of many species of plants and animals and tries to work out the laws of inheritance in the particular type upon which he is conducting experiments. Naturally, he follows, the progress of the work upon race differentiation in man and in the descent of man, but he looks upon these as special topics, equal in importance with his own yet ones in which his interests will never be vitally engaged. It is not fair to say that all of his work is directed toward human evolution or that it must be interpreted in terms of human evolution. He does not have to dismiss certain of his facts on the inheritance of coat color in mice because, forsooth, they have little bearing upon the differentiation of the *genus homo* into separate races, or upon the descent of the *genus homo* from some more primitive stock.

In psychology we are still in that stage of development where we feel that we must select our material. We have a general place of discard for processes, which we anathematize so far as their value for psychology is concerned by saying, "this is a reflex": "that is a purely physiological fact which has nothing to do with psychology." We are not interested (as psychologists) in getting all of the processes of adjustment which the animal as a whole employs, and in finding how these various responses are associated, and how they fall apart, thus working out a systematic scheme for the prediction and control of response in general. Unless our observed facts are indicative of consciousness, we have no use for them, and unless our apparatus and method are designed to throw such facts into relief, they are thought of in just as disparaging a way. I shall always remember the remark one distinguished psychologist made as he looked over the color apparatus designed for testing the responses of animals to monochromatic light in the attic at Johns Hopkins. It was this: "And they call this psychology!"

I do not wish unduly to criticize psychology. It has failed signally, I believe, during the fifty-odd years of its existence as an experimental discipline to make its place in the world as an undisputed natural science. Psychology, as it is generally thought of, has something esoteric in its methods. If you fail to reproduce my findings, it is not due to some fault in your apparatus or in the control of your stimulus, but it is due to the fact that your introspection is untrained. The attack is made upon the observer and not upon the experimental setting. In physics and in chemistry the attack is made upon the experimental conditions. The apparatus was not sensitive enough, impure chemicals were used, etc. In these sciences a better technique will give reproducible results. Psychology is otherwise. If you can't observe 3–9 states of clearness in attention, your introspection is poor. If, on the other hand, a feeling seems reasonably clear to you, your introspection is again faulty. You are seeing too much. Feelings are never clear.

The time seems to have come when psychology must discard all reference to consciousness; when it need no longer delude itself into thinking that it is making mental states the object of observation. We have become so enmeshed in speculative questions concerning the elements of mind, the nature of conscious content (for example, imageless thought, attitudes, and Bewusseinslage, etc.) that I, as an experimental student, feel that something is wrong with our premises and the types of problems which develop from them. There is no longer any guarantee that we all mean the same thing when we use the terms now current in psychology. Take the case of sensation. A sensation is defined in terms of its attributes. One psychologist will state with readiness that the attributes of a visual sensation are *quality, extension, duration,* and *intensity.* Another will add *clearness.* Still another that of *order.* I doubt if any one psychologist can draw up a set of statements describing what he means by sensation which will be agreed to by three other psychologists of different training. Turn for a moment to the question of the number of isolable sensations. Is there an extremely large number of color sensations—or only four, red, green, yellow and blue? Again, yellow, while psychologically simple, can be obtained by superimposing red and green spectral rays upon the same diffusing surface! If, on the other hand, we say that every just noticeable difference in the spectrum is a simple sensation, and that every just noticeable increase in the white value of a given color gives simple sensations, we are forced to admit that the number is so large and the conditions for obtaining them so complex that the concept of sensation is unusable, either for the purpose of analysis or that of synthesis. Titchener, who has fought the most valiant fight in this country for a psychology based upon introspection, feels that these differences of opinion as to the number of sensations and their attributes, as to whether there are relations (in the sense of elements) and on the many others which seem to be fundamental in every attempt at analysis, are perfectly natural in the present undeveloped state of psychology. While it is admitted that every growing science is full of unanswered questions, surely only those who are wedded to the system as we now have it, who have fought and suffered for it, can confidently believe that there will ever be any greater uniformity than there is now in the answers we have to such questions. I firmly believe that two hundred years from now, unless the introspective method is discarded, psychology will still be divided on the question as to whether auditory sensations have the quality of 'extension,' whether intensity is an attribute which can be applied to color, whether there is a difference in 'texture' between image and sensation and upon many hundreds of others of like character.

The condition in regard to other mental processes is just as chaotic. Can image type be experimentally tested and verified? Are recondite thought processes dependent mechanically upon imagery at all? Are psychologists agreed upon what feeling is? One states that feelings are attitudes. Another finds them to be groups of organic sensations possessing a certain solidarity. Still another and larger group finds them to be new elements correlative with and ranking equally with sensations.

My psychological quarrel is not with the systematic and structural psychologist alone. The last fifteen years have seen the growth of what is called functional psychology. This type of psychology decries the use of elements in the static sense of the structuralists. It throws emphasis upon the biological significance of conscious processes instead of upon the analysis of conscious states into introspectively isolable elements. I have done my best to understand the difference between functional psychology and structural psychology. Instead of clarity, confusion grows upon me. The terms sensation, perception, affection, emotion, volition are used as much by the functionalist as by the structuralist.

The addition of the word 'process' ('mental act as a whole,' and like terms are frequently met) after each serves in some way to remove the corpse of 'content' and to leave 'function' in its stead. Surely if these concepts are elusive when looked at from a content standpoint, they are still more deceptive when viewed from the angle of function, and especially so when function is obtained by the introspection method. It is rather interesting that no functional psychologist has carefully distinguished between 'perception' (and this is true of the other psychological terms as well) as employed by the systematist, and 'perceptual process' as used in functional psychology. It seems illogical and hardly fair to criticize the psychology which the systematist gives us, and then to utilize his terms without carefully showing the changes in meaning which are to be attached to them. I was greatly surprised some time ago when I opened Pillsbury's book and saw psychology defined as the 'science of behavior.' A still more recent text states that psychology is the 'science of mental behavior.' When I saw these promising statements I thought, now surely we will have texts based upon different lines. After a few pages the science of behavior is dropped and one finds the conventional treatment of sensation, perception, imagery, etc., along with certain shifts in emphasis and additional facts which serve to give the author's personal imprint.

One of the difficulties in the way of a consistent functional psychology is the parallelistic hypothesis. If the functionalist attempts to express his formulations in terms which make mental states really appear to function, to play some active rôle in the world of adjustment, he almost inevitably lapses into terms which are connotative of interaction. When taxed with this he replies that it is more convenient to do so and that he does it to avoid the circumlocution and clumsiness which are inherent in any thoroughgoing parallelism. As a matter of fact I believe the functionalist actually thinks in terms of interaction and resorts to parallelism only when forced to give expression to his views. I feel that *behaviorism* is the only consistent and logical functionalism. In it one avoids both the Scylla of parallelism and the Charybdis of interaction. Those time-honored relics of philosophical speculation need trouble the student of behavior as little as they trouble the student of physics. The consideration of the mind-body problem affects neither the type of problem selected nor the formulation of the solution of that problem. I can state my position here no better than by saying that I should like to bring my students up in the same ignorance of such hypotheses as one finds among the students of other branches of science.

This leads me to the point where I should like to make the argument constructive. I believe we can write a psychology, define it as Pillsbury, and never go back upon our definition: never use the terms consciousness, mental states, mind, content, introspectively verifiable, imagery, and the like. I believe that we can do it in a few years without running into the absurd terminology of Beer, Bethe, Von Uexküll, Nuel, and that of the so-called objective schools generally. It can be done in terms of stimulus and response, in terms of habit formation, habit integrations and the like. Furthermore, I believe that it is really worth while to make this attempt now.

The psychology which I should attempt to build up would take as a starting point, first, the observable facts that organisms, man and animal alike, do adjust themselves to their environment by means of hereditary and habit equipments. These adjustments may be very adequate or they may so inadequate that the organism barely maintains its existence; secondly, that certain stimuli lead the organisms to make the responses. In a system of psychology completely worked out, given the response the stimuli can be predicted; given the stimuli the response can be predicted. Such a set of statements is crass and raw in the extreme, as all such generalizations must be. Yet they are hardly more raw and less realizable than the ones which appear in the psychology texts of the day. I possibly might illustrate my point better by choosing an everyday problem which anyone is likely to meet in the course of his work. Some time ago I was called upon to make a study of certain species of birds. Until I went to Tortugas I had never seen these birds alive. When I reached there I found the animals doing certain things: some of the acts seemed to work peculiarly well in such an environment, while others seemed to be unsuited to their type of life. I first studied the responses of the group as a whole and later those of individuals. In order to understand more thoroughly the relation between what was habit and what was hereditary in these responses, I took the young birds and reared them. In this way I was able to study the order of appearance of hereditary adjustments and their complexity, and later the beginnings of habit formation. My efforts in determining the stimuli which called forth such adjustments were crude indeed. Consequently my attempts to control behavior and to produce responses at will did not meet with much success. Their food and water, sex and other social relations, light and temperature conditions were all beyond control in a field study. I did find it possible to control their reactions in a measure by using the nest and egg (or young) as stimuli. It is not necessary in this paper to develop further how such a study should be carried out and how work of this kind must be supplemented by carefully controlled laboratory experiments. Had I been called upon to examine the natives of some of the Australian tribes, I should have gone about my task in the same way. I should have found the problem more difficult: the types of responses called forth by physical stimuli would have been more varied, and the number of effective stimuli larger. I should have had to determine the social setting of their lives in a far more careful way. These savages would be more influenced by the responses of each other than was the case with the birds. Furthermore, habits would have been more complex and the influences of past habits upon the present responses would have appeared more clearly. Finally, if I had been called upon to work out the psychology of the educated European, my problem would have required several lifetimes. But in the one I have at my disposal I should have followed the same general line of attack. In the main, my desire in all such work is to gain an accurate knowledge of adjustments and the stimuli calling them forth. My final reason for this is to learn general and particular methods by which I may control behavior. My goal is not "the description and explanation of states of consciousness as such," nor that of obtaining such proficiency in mental gymnastics that I can immediately lay hold of a state of consciousness and say, "this, as a whole, consists of gray sensation number 350, of such and such extent, occurring in conjunction with the sensation of cold of a certain intensity; one of pressure of a certain intensity and extent," and so on *ad infinitum.* If psychology would follow the plan I suggest, the educator, the physician, the jurist and the business man could utilize our data in a practical way, as soon as we are able, experimentally, to obtain them. Those who have occasion to apply psychological principles practically would find no need to complain as they do at the present time. Ask any physician or jurist today whether scientific psychology plays a practical part in his daily routine and you will hear him deny that the psychology of the laboratories finds a place in his scheme of work. I think the criticism is extremely just. . . .

In concluding, I suppose I must confess to a deep bias on these questions. I have devoted nearly twelve years to experimentation on animals. It is natural that such a one should drift into a theoretical position which is in harmony with his experimental work. Possibly I have put up a straw man and have been fighting that. There may be no absolute lack of harmony between the position outlined here and that of functional psychology. I am inclined to think, however, that the two positions cannot be easily harmonized. Certainly the position I advocate is weak enough at present and can be attacked from many standpoints. Yet when all this is admitted I still feel that the considerations which I have urged should have a wide influence upon the type of psychology which is to be developed in the future. What we need to do is to start work upon psychology, making *behavior,* not *consciousness,* the objective point of our attack. Certainly there are enough problems in the control of behavior to keep us all working many lifetimes without ever allowing us time to think of consciousness *an sich.* Once launched in the undertaking, we will find ourselves in a short time as far divorced from an introspective psychology as the psychology of the present time is divorced from faculty psychology.

Struggle for Scientific Authority: The Reception of Watson's Behaviorism, 1913–1920

Franz Samelson

If retrospectively the appearance of Watson's manifesto was a major historical event, primary sources do not quite reflect it as such. Except for Howard C. Warren's reference to the fact that he had repeatedly urged Watson to publish his position paper, none of the autobiographies of prominent psychologists of the period have marked it as a red letter day. In fact, the dean of psychology's historians, E. G. Boring, in an extended reminiscence of his professional life history, did not find it necessary to recall any encounter with Watson or Watson's ideas, even though his own orientation changed from Titchnerian structuralism to a (behavioral) "physicalism."[1]

INITIAL RESPONSES: THREE THEMES AND SOME HOSTILITY

To be sure, the contemporary literature did not ignore Watson's paper completely; neither did it give his challenge singular prominence. A summary of the events of 1913 in psychology, written by Langfeld for the *American Year Book,* started out by dealing with two other "important discussions" before mentioning the "behaviorist movement"; even then it cited Maurice Parmelee's new book *The Science of Human Behavior* rather than Watson's work. The discussion of Watson's paper came only in the second section, entitled "Psychological Method," and treated it mainly as another attack on introspection. A second overview of the preceding year, the summary on "General Problems: Mind and Body" in the January 1914 *Psychological Bulletin* did open with the question whether psychology was purely a study of behavior, or of mental states and processes, or both; commenting that the behaviorists especially were attracting attention in the debate, it then quoted half a page from Watson's paper before going on, noncommittally, to other views on the issue[2]

Beyond such summaries we find that, in an address on the "Study of Human Behavior" for a June 1913 Eugenics Conference, Robert M. Yerkes had begun to use the term "behaviorist" (apparently coined in late 1912 independently by both Watson and James R. Angell);[3] but his ref-

Adapted from Samelson, F. (1981). Struggle for scientific authority: The reception of Watson's behaviorism, 1913–1920. *Journal of the History of the Behavioral Sciences, 17,* 399–425.

erences were to three recent books: Parmelee's work mentioned above, Max Meyer's book on *The Fundamental Laws of Human Behavior,* and William McDougall's *Introduction to Social Psychology,* not to Watson's paper (with which he was familiar).[4] Apart from some footnote references added on to papers written before the appearance of Watson's article, the first direct response in print came in a short article by Mary W. Calkins, entitled "Psychology and the Behaviorist."[5] Critical of Watson's "vigorous" paper, she expressed her "radical disagreement with [its] main thesis" of the uselessness of introspection, questioned his supporting arguments, and insisted that certain kinds of psychological processes could be studied only by introspection. However, she also expressed much sympathy with the "important truth embedded" in Watson's criticism of the "undue abstractness" of the present psychology as the "study of mental state." Instead, psychology needed to be concerned with "problems of life." The study of behavior by objective methods was indeed important, as long as "behavior" was understood not merely as "mechanical," but meant the study of "self related to environment."[6]

Here we have the emergence of three themes which in one form or another came to predominate in the published reactions to Watson for some time: (1) although Calkins conceded some problems with the method of introspection and granted the legitimacy of objective procedures, she nevertheless maintained the usefulness of introspection as one of the methods of psychology (what we might call the "don't throw out the baby with the bath" argument); (2) she expressed a strong desire to expand the subject matter of psychological study to a concern with real people in the real world (the "relevance" argument, as we might call it today); and (3) accepting the notion of behavior, but questioning Watson's narrow definition of the term, she attempted to redirect Watson's thrust toward her own goal, a special "self psychology" version of a functionalist approach (the "cooptation" theme). It is tempting to argue, by the way, that, taking psychology as a whole, Mary Calkin's view was more nearly prophetic of what psychology would become half a century later than was Watson's narrower position, even though his slogan of the "study of behavior" eventually carried the day.

The other direct, and quite enthusiastic, response to Watson came from Fred L. Wells, perhaps best described as a hybrid experimentalist-clinician working at McLean Hospital for the Insane. Once in the context of a review of Parmelee's book, and again in a summary review of "Dynamic Psychology" for the *Psychological Bulletin,* he put himself into Watson's corner, lauding Watson's "well-aimed blow at the autistic method in psychology. . . ."[7] and quoting with obvious relish some of his attacks on the "pure" psychologists and their lack of concern with human life. "Experimental psychology . . . dodges . . . the more actual and vital questions . . . [and retreats] into a burrow of trivial inquiries . . . ," Wells complained.[8] Yet he, like Calkins (and Angell before them, in an APA address on "Behavior as a Psychological Category," delivered about the time Watson was preparing his paper for publication), argued that at least for practical purposes some use of introspection was unavoidable. Furthermore, the crucial issue to be settled was the meaning of "behavior"; in order to be useful it could not be restricted to activities describable in physical or physiological terms, but had to include "*mental*[!] behavior."[9]

A very brief comment in a review of "Criminology and Delinquency" by Jean Weidensall (who as a student had known Watson at Chicago and was, like Wells, working in a nonacademic setting) concludes the list of references to Watson in the *Psychological Bulletin* of 1913: Though Watson's paper seemed a bit radical, she felt that "in truth [it was outlining] the psychology we shall find most useful."[10]

There were also three brief items in the *Journal of Philosophy, Psychology, and Scientific*

Method. In the last paragraph of a short paper on the definition of Comparative Psychology, Yerkes protested strongly against Watson's attempt to "throw overboard . . . the method of self-observation" and to usurp the science of psychology for the study of behavior, although he supported wholeheartedly the integration of behavior methods into psychology. Angell put in a brief demurrer against Watson's claim, that Angell's research on imagery had justified the dismissal of the image from psychology. And finally philosopher Henry R. Marshall, in a paper asking, "Is Psychology Evaporating?" briefly referred to Thorndike, Watson, and the objective science of behavior which was, in his view, legitimate; but it was not psychology.[11]

In late December 1913 the American Psychological Association held its annual convention at Yale University (which hosted the American Philosophical Association at the same time). APA president H. C. Warren gave an address on "The Mental and the Physical." Rejecting any solution of the metaphysical mind-body problem as premature, he went on to argue for the adoption of a double-aspect view as a working hypothesis. This position required a redefinition of psychology to embrace both inner and outer aspects of experience and made it the "science of the relations between the individual and his environment, [to] be studied either objectively as behavior, or introspectively as events of consciousness."[12]

A page-long summary of Warren's address in the proceedings did not refer to Watson at all. The paper itself contained a number of references to Watson and his position; yet it was clearly not a response to him, but to a problematic which had been debated by psychologists for some time. Warren agreed with Watson that the hope for the future might lie in the study of behavior, since it revealed "dynamic aspects" more than did introspection. But he could not accept an autocratic decree prohibiting introspective study; introspection had produced many results of scientific worth; Watson's critique was too "destructive."[13] In summary, Warren's argument, while different in the specifics, was basically the same as Calkins's: don't throw out the baby of introspection, but accept behavior for the sake of "dynamics," and fashion a "double-aspect" compromise instead of splitting psychology into two different disciplines.

At the same convention, a joint session with the philosophers on the "standpoint of psychology" heard, among others, John Dewey and Hugo Münsterberg refer favorably but briefly to behaviorism. Wishing behaviorism well, Dewey expressed both fear and hope—fear, if "behavior" meant just the mechanics of the nervous system; hope, if it included the "attitudes and responses towards others which cannot be located under the skin. . . ." Münsterberg, in an exposition of his scheme of two psychologies, one "causal" and the other "teleological," expressed the opinion that behaviorism might be successful in an applied psychology derived from the causal approach. In the discussion, Knight Dunlap raised some questions about "delimiting the behaviorist's field. . . ." Earlier that year, Dunlap had presented a talk at Johns Hopkins, in which he distanced himself sharply from Watson and protested against the latter's "extreme doctrine" likely to produce opposition to more moderate innovations.[14]

The earliest recorded reference to Watson's manifesto apparently occurred in a discussion of "four recent tendencies" in psychology, presented by G. Stanley Hall at a Mental Hygiene Conference in April 1913. After introspection and psychoanalysis, "a rich, rank, seething mass of new facts and new ideas, sure to revolutionize . ." psychology, Hall mentioned behaviorism briefly and in rather neutral fashion, obviously quoting or paraphrasing Watson's major thesis. From there he proceeded to an extended discussion of the last tendency, Pavlov's "amazing" work on salivary conditioning, which had barely touched American psychology as yet.[15] The seventy-year old Hall still had his ear to the ground.

The only indication of a "violent reaction"

and "furor"[16] caused by Watson's polemic is found in a short notice reporting on the meeting of the Experimental Psychologists (largely the inner, Titchenerian circle of the academic discipline), held at Wesleyan University in April 1913. It appears that a ""lively discussion" on the introspection and behaviorism developed in one of the sessions. Introspection had been hotly debated—without Watson—at a meeting two years earlier, with Titchener on one side and Dodge and Holt on the other.[17] This time, "the hostility to an identification of psychology with 'behaviorism' was surprisingly unanimous. . . ."[18] That is unfortunately all we know about the meeting.

Concerning the other meeting, the year-end APA convention, Melvin E. Haggerty's report remarked that "in spirit [it] had a decidedly behavioristic tendency. More than half the papers either championed the behavioristic point of view in one or another form or [used] behavioristic methods [in their experiments]. A considerable part of the time the word itself was in the air."[19] Here at last is an indication of an apparently broad-based and positive response to Watson. Yet when we look for specifics (beyond the comments by Dewey, Münsterberg, and Warren), we cannot find, either in the titles or in the texts of the paper abstracts for the convention, any mention of Watson or behaviorism; at least for the modern reader, it turns out to be rather difficult to see which of these papers (with one or two exceptions) were supposed by Haggerty to champion the behaviorist point of view. (Judged by subsequent comments, Haggerty himself sympathized with behaviorism, but he also called Watson's refusal to consider introspective knowledge "the merest folly.")[20] And a different report on the convention, by APA secretary Walter V. Bingham, failed to notice any wave of behaviorism. It only remarked, with some relief, that in spite of the presence of the philosophers at the convention the paper sessions had not produced an inordinate number of philosophical or theoretical papers; instead, it had been a well-balanced program (and, we might add, apparently without major surprises).[21] We shall meet this problem again: after discovering a tantalizing reference to the popularity of behaviorism among a certain group of persons, if we ask just who was involved and how it was expressed, we find the concrete evidence to be very elusive.

A BEHAVIORISTIC UNDERGROUND?

On this note ends our account of the recorded responses to Watson in the first year.[22] They were not overwhelming either in their frequency or their intensity, and furthermore came mainly from authors already in favor of some changes before Watson's appeal. Criticism of introspection was not new; neither was the use of objective methods or the advocacy of the study of behavior, as references to other authors like Meyer, Parmelee, and Thorndike indicate. (As Wells had expressed it, Watson had produced an "unusually concrete statement of a central idea that has always claimed certain adherents among us. . . ."[23])

Was there a behaviorist revolution in the year 1913? The terms "behaviorist" and "behaviorism" had been accepted into professional language; there certainly was some awareness and, on occasion, lively discussion of Watson's contribution to the ongoing debate about the methods and objects of the science. In print, a few direct but mixed reactions agreed with some aspects of Watson's challenge with some enthusiasm while firmly rejecting others. But no reminiscence has described memories of a dramatic encounter with the manifesto; we have not found any contemporary evidence for the conversion of a single individual to Watson's position. While he may have issued a call to revolution, as yet we have seen no clear signs of a mass uprising. But scientific revolutions may take a bit more time. Or perhaps there was a behaviorist "movement," though it was underground, below the printed surface.[24]

Unfortunately, a laborious search of various archival collections has failed to be of much help. Indeed, I have not yet turned up a single letter from the year 1913 containing reactions to Watson's Columbia presentation or its printed version. The only contemporary references came from Watson himself. Sending some reprints of his paper to Yerkes, Watson commented: "I understand that [Yale's Roswell P.] Angier thinks I am crazy. I should not be surprised if this was the general consensus of opinion." (This estimate seems not far off the mark at least in terms of the consensus among the experimentalists, meeting at Wesleyan the following month.) While unfortunately Yerkes's reply is not preserved, Watson's next letter referred to some differences of opinion. At a later date, when the rift between Watson and Yerkes was widening, Yerkes implied that he had held back sharp criticism of the manifesto at the time.[25] And in another place, Watson indicated that James M. Cattell had scolded him for being "too radical."[26]

I have located very few additional pre-war comments (there are more later on) related to behaviorism in various archives: a very positive though brief one by Gilbert V. Hamilton, and two years later a rather solemn declaration by Margaret F. Washburn that she thought "JBW an enemy to psychology." In addition, there is the exchange of critical comments between Titchener, Angell, and Yerkes, reported earlier by Cedric A. Larson and John J. Sullivan.[27]

There are probably three reasons for this disappointing outcome of an extensive archival search. The most obvious one is that the relevant source material may be lost. Still, some of the surviving collections might have been expected to contain references to the allegedly revolutionary events. Thus a second reason, I would suggest, is that—at least by that time—the function of academic correspondence had shifted. It was no longer a scholarly discussion and sharing of views between colleagues about the substantive issues of their field (assuming gratuitously that it had been so in earlier times); it was rather (with some exceptions) a somewhat hurried bureaucratic exchange, dealing mainly with concrete administrative-political problems: jobs, students, technical details of research and publishing activities, arrangements for meetings, etc., topped off by a bit of gossip and brief personal news. The typewriter had come to the office, but not yet the secretary; letters were usually typed, but mostly by their authors (and therefore without copies). In short, writing letters had become a chore. The discussion of substantive psychological issues may have been displaced to oral exchanges at formal meetings and informal visits; major statements on psychological issues were put into print.

And yet, I believe there is a third reason for this lack of references to behaviorism. Watson had said some strongly provocative and offensive things; but criticism of important aspects of the discipline and/or proposals for new directions had appeared before and after 1913, as they have on and off throughout the history of psychology. Usually, they are taken notice of, if coming from authors with some visibility, and may even produce a bit of a stir; some new terms may become fashionable; but then business goes on as usual for the vast majority of psychologists. Their activities are determined by other forces than verbal appeals—as any good behaviorist would know. After all, Watson's initial statement had not contained many concrete suggestions, except for the prohibition on introspective procedures. His main point had been a call for reconceptualization. We shall return to this issue later.

Two additional events occurring at year's end must be mentioned. Watson was elected president of the Southern Society for Philosophy and Psychology; he also became editor of the new *Journal of Experimental Psychology,* started by Warren upon Watson's suggestion.[28] But whether these honors were bestowed on him because of his call to arms or in spite of it (i.e. were based on his reputation as an outstanding young scientist acquired before 1913) is impossible to tell. We can only note that any hostility felt by the establishment was either not intense or not powerful enough to prevent these nominations. . . .

If, on the assumption that publication lag or other reasons delayed the response to Watson's historic paper, we search the psychology journals for the following year in order to find evidence of the full impact, we are in for another disappointment. Apart from registering some of the events and talks of 1913 already described, the *Psychological Bulletin* mentioned Watson or behaviorism hardly at all. . . . Langfeld's survey of the year 1914 in the *American Year Book* noticed no major changes; he reported a continued discussion of the fundamental problem of psychology: the relation of the mental and the physical world, with references to Warren, Holt, Münsterberg, and Prince. Mention of behaviorism remained relegated to the Methods section, according to which "discussion still center[ed] about the question of introspection *versus* behaviorism . . ."; although Watson was still maintaining his radical view, "many psychologists believe in the combination of these two methods. . . ."[29]

By 1915, Watson's first book, *Behavior: An Introduction to Comparative Psychology,* had been published. The introductory chapter had reprinted his 1913 papers with only minor changes; the main text had fleshed out Watson's behaviorist program a bit more in a discussion of instincts, reflexes, and habit development in animal psychology. A short description of the book's content by Langfeld and three special reviews by Carr, Thorndike and Herrick, and Haggerty were quite favorable overall; the longer ones criticized some details and all rejected Watson's more extreme theoretical statements, especially the ban on introspection.[30] In a 1910 APA paper and in the introduction to the 1911 edition of *Animal Intelligence,* Thorndike had argued strongly for the importance of objective studies of behavior. Now he expressed his regret that Watson had not added a chapter on *human* psychology to show that recognized psychologists had, for thirty years, carried out behavioral studies of humans. Watson should have corrected the impression that human psychology had been exclusively an introspective affair. But even Thorndike found it unwise to ignore the special form of observation of themselves humans were capable of; it might "well play some part in science."[31]

Apart from the reviews, few references to Watson or his book can be found in the 1915 *Psychological Bulletin.* In the *Psychological Review* of 1915, Watson's name does not seem to have appeared even once (except on the masthead, as the journal's editor). Only one passing reference to the "behaviorist standpoint" could be located[32] while five of the six issues of the journal contained at least one article dealing with imageless thought, images, or imagery of one sort or another. The 1915 volume of the *Journal of Philosophy, Psychology, and Scientific Method* included a protest by Walter Hunter against Watson's misinterpretation of Hunter's delayed reaction experiment, and a few articles on the issues of consciousness and behavior, with both positive and critical references to Watson.[33] . . .

At year's end of 1916, the twenty-fifth anniversary of the APA and of the *Philosophical Review* elicited a number of papers by renowned psychologists discussing the past, present, and future of their science. In general, these papers treated behaviorism as only one trend among many and dealt with it briefly. Margaret Washburn defended introspection against Watson's attacks. Joseph Jastrow mentioned behaviorism in passing. Pillsbury pointed to the disagreement between Watson and Yerkes regarding animal consciousness. Cattell, while strongly urging the replacement of introspective studies of the mind by experiments on "behavior and conduct," was more concerned with other issues, especially the economics of research support. Dewey's address on the future of social psychology applauded behaviorism as a promising trend, which could—in a twist surprising to modern readers—in combination with McDougall's work on instincts lead to an understanding of the social emergence of mind—not strictly a Watsonian position. Finally G. Stanley Hall, little concerned with theoretical quibbles, speculated in the grand manner about the role of psychology in the cataclysm looming on the horizon: the war, which was soon to disrupt the lives of many psychologists.[34]

The events of the war years did not silence the behaviorism debate completely. And even before that time Watson had expanded his position in his presidential address on the conditioned reflex, begun his observational studies of human infants, and written an early version of the first chapter for his new book on behaviorism.[35] However, the narration of events will conclude with three more indications of Watson's influence, or lack thereof. In 1915, Dunlap's efforts had initiated the formation of an APA Committee on Terminology, charged with producing some agreed-upon definitions of crucial psychological terms. The first installment of this work was published in the 1918 *Psychological Bulletin.* But Watson's position was not represented in these definitions. With the exception of one subcategory, which accepted "behavior" as the "reaction of an organism to the environment" but expressly restricted it to biological usage, all relevant definitions, e.g., of "psychobiological," led back to others containing the words "mental" or "conscious."[36]

The omission of behavioristic views was apparently no accident. The papers of Mary Calkins, one of the committee members, contain a preprint of the committee report, dated September 1917, and bearing some handwritten corrections. Instead of the twenty-eight definitions published in the *Psychological Bulletin,* this document listed twenty-nine items. Number 29 was: "Behaviorism. Identification of *psychology* with the science of *behavior.*" But this definition had been crossed out in ink.[37] The subsequently published version did not include the term behaviorism.

Unfortunately, no correspondence is attached to this preprint. Thus it remains uncertain whether the elimination of Watson's slogan was a bit of skullduggery on the part of one or more committee members, or whether it reflected the result of a mail survey of sixty psychologists in the fall of 1917. Still, in either case this "smoking gun" supports the argument that, five years after his manifesto, any inroads Watson had made in psychology did not lead very far into its center. Even an updated version of the committee's work published in 1922, defining eight varieties of psychology, did not include behaviorism among them. The one closest to it, "Objective Psychology," described in an added note as a "synonym for *Behavior Psychology,*" was defined as "concerned with *mental*[!] *phenomena* expressed in the *behavior* of the organism to the exclusion of *introspective data.*"[38] . . .

This rather detailed (though not exhaustive) account of recorded reactions to Watson stands in definite contrast to some retrospective histories which claim or at least imply that Watson's behaviorism, supported by an anonymous Zeitgeist, quickly swept the field. . . .

IN SEARCH OF EXPLANATIONS

Obviously, this is not the whole story. For instance, although the Terminology Committee of the APA had failed to print a definition of Behaviorism in 1918, the *Encyclopedia Americana* carried a two-page article on "Behavior and Behaviorism" in the same year.[39] Although Watson's 1914 book was never reviewed by *Science,* in spite of Watson's anxious inquiries, Edwin B. Holt had recommended it to his readers as a "valiant and clear-headed volume."[40] And though it turned out to be difficult to identify many probehaviorists in the contemporary records, later sources do indicate that behaviorism had, in the teens, an impact on a number of mainly younger people besides Weiss and

Hunter: Karl S. Lashley, Harold C. Bingham, Melvin E. Haggerty, John F. Dashiell, and a group of Harvard students, among them Floyd H. and Gordon W. Allport, Richard M. Elliott, and Edward C. Tolman. (However, at Harvard the influence had come less from Watson than from Holt, who was teaching a "red-hot behaviorism" at the time,[41] and from Ralph B. Perry).

Neither is this the end of the story of the behaviorist revolution, only of its first phase. But it is high time to ask what all the details reported so far add up to. Perhaps the general drift of this account has not really come as a surprise to the reader. Though I had initially expected a rather different course of events, once I started to think about it I found the emerging story not too surprising either. Nevertheless, it may present difficulties for some traditional explanations: If there was a Zeitgeist, it seems that so far he (or she) communicated mainly like God to Moses, on a one-to-one basis. If the fact that Watson's program was a strictly American product had any influence on its acceptance, so far we have not seen any direct or even indirect reference to it. Fred Wells, Watson's first vocal supporter, was anything but parochial; his writings were sprinkled generously with German, French, and Latin quotes.

Another popular explanation has to do with the acceptance of behaviorism because it was so practical. Although this argument touches on what I believe to be a crucial aspect (and though we have found mostly favorable responses to what was called the "relevance" theme), it puts some complex issues too simply. For instance, the (American) *Journal of Applied Psychology* did not begin publication until 1917; the similarly titled German *Zeitschrift für Angewandte Psychologie* had first appeared in 1907. An *"Institut für Angewandte Psychologie"* had been established in Berlin in 1906, almost a decade before the start of an applied psychology program at Carnegie Institute of Technology. (And the *Journal of Educational Psychology*, appearing in 1910, had been preceded by a decade by the *Zeitschrift für Pädagogische Psychologie und Experimentelle Pädagogik.*) When Titchener had warned, in 1909, against the undesirable developments toward applied psychology, his specific references were to five German psychologists (and one Frenchman: Binet).[42] While such a list may in part reflect Titchener's European orientation, it should also help to scuttle the myth that applied psychology was "ganz amerikanisch," and that the impractical German professors were preoccupied with nothing but abstruse and esoteric speculations of a philosophical nature. Applied psychology had its roots at least as much in Europe as in America. Furthermore, as the European example shows clearly, an applied psychology does not have to be behavioristic at all (unless, of course, we view it through behaviorist eyes).

Another myth should also be laid to rest: that behaviorism developed out of animal psychology because the situation there forced the researcher into a behavioristic stance. As others[43] have pointed out before, this does not seem altogether true. At least some of the major figures in the small group of American animal psychologists did not feel at all compelled by their subject matter to adopt this position. Washburn and Yerkes both rejected Watsonian behaviorism (though Yerkes claimed that in his early days around 1900 he had been a pre-Watsonian Watsonian behaviorist).[44] Carr belongs in this category, too. In fact, in the early twenties we find more philosophers than animal psychologists among those taking a behaviorist stance; the psychologists in this group (Holt, Tolman, Edwin R. Guthrie, and a bit later Clark L. Hull) were more likely to turn to animal work after their conversion than to move in the reverse direction.

Abandoning such obviously post hoc explanations as, at the very least, overstatements, we should look at a different version of explanation, which is not new but in our days has been formulated in Kuhnian terms.[45] It goes like this: Around 1912 the "imageless thought" controversy laid bare an "anomaly" which the existing science could not deal with; this produced a "crisis" which led to the abandonment of the old "paradigm" and the acceptance of a better one, which could account for the anomaly. But this version, too, is at least a gross oversimplification; it seems to fit neither the facts nor Kuhn's theory. The imageless thought controversy was indeed a problem, but one among at least several; only retrospective historians and polemicists have made it into a "crisis." In his original paper, Watson referred to it only in one sentence in a footnote, in which he listed other problems of introspective psychology.[46] Robert S. Woodworth, not a bad scientist, was trying to solve the problem two years later; he did not see it as an anomaly creating a crisis.[47] And Titchener, in my view quite properly, replied to Watson's claims about the failure of introspection that in many scientific areas the results of observations did not always agree; it was reasonable to allow some time to work out the apparent contradictions. After all, his kind of introspection had been introduced less than ten years before, and not fifty, as Watson had asserted.[48] (We might add that after a turn to behavioral methods, the results obtained by different experimenters have not always agreed either). And when we look carefully at Kuhn's argument, we find that anomalies are always around in science. Only rarely do they touch off crises and revolutions.

A (Slow) Perceptual Shift and a Missing Paradigm-Exemplar

I am impressed by the applicability of one of Kuhn's ideas: the change in the way of seeing things involved in paradigm change. Such a shift did occur in, I believe, a fundamental way. It is most visible in the manner psychologists described their methods of observation. In the earlier phase we find again and again the statement that the introspective method constitutes direct and immediate contact with the subject matter, while what we now mean by objective observation was then only an indirect or mediate one.[49] After the revolution, the meanings are reversed: objective observation is the direct contact, while information obtained through introspection, if not altogether impossible or irrelevant, is at best indirect, a tenuous base for fragile inferences from questionable verbal reports. I think this is more than a manner of speaking; it reflects a real change in the way psychologists experienced, or had been trained to experience, their reality. For most psychologists, however, this shift did not seem to occur suddenly, as an "aha" experience with a reversible figure; it took a long time to develop—even if for us, immersed as we are in post-Watson "behavior" language, it is hard to look upon the earlier construction as anything but patently contrived and transparent. But this shift is what Watson, having made it himself, demanded from others. To accept the addition of objective observations and performance measures was not so difficult for many psychologists (as we have heard), because they had said or done so even before Watson.[50] But he rejected such a mixture of methods, such a compromise; he was asking for the reversal in the definition of what was real—this made him appear so radical, and made it difficult for others to follow him.

Besides the crisis-inducing anomaly, another element of Kuhn's theory seems to be missing: the new paradigm. Many people have, in my view, misread Kuhn (helped along by his ambiguities) and assimilated his concept of paradigm to other, more familiar ideas: theories, conceptual systems, viewpoints. But such an understanding turns Kuhn's argument into an old story. What may be novel in Kuhn was his emphasis on the role of the paradigm-exemplar, the specific case of the successful solution of a (crucial) problem, which becomes a relatively concrete model-example for the solution of other problems.[51] But where was Watson's paradigm-exemplar? It was not there.

Should one not cite the conditioned reflex and Pavlov's salivating dogs? Our textbooks often seem to portray the development of modern psychology as an historical chain, from Darwin to Pavlov to Watson, and on to Hull and Skinner. But this compact story is not entirely true. While eventually coming to play the role of paradigm-exemplar (a count of the textbooks reprinting the original line drawing of Pavlov's dog is overdue), the conditioned reflex entered only slowly and in stages into Watson's thinking and did not gain its dominant role until the mid-twenties. Even then, a close look shows the surprising fact that the actual experimental data underlying the diagram, the concrete observations made, were almost nonexistent, as far as Watson and American psychology in general were concerned. After all, Pavlov's dogs lived in a faraway country. Knowledge of them came only through indirect channels, in translations and third-hand reports; some of these reports were imprecise, obscure, or clearly wrong.[52] Did nobody try to replicate the work?

Watson's APA address describing his own and Lashley's observations on motor conditioning was actually based only on pilot studies, which had raised at least as many questions as they had answered. The literature contains no final report of Lashley's elaborate studies of salivary conditioning; a close reading of his progress reports seems to indicate that he gave up the effort because it had failed. (Hilgard and Marquis's classic on conditioning drew a similar conclusion.) As for Watson, he once mentioned briefly an attempt to develop an experimental analogue to reactions to lightning and thunder, by exposing infants to a strong light followed by a loud sound.[53] Subsequently, Watson never referred to this experiment again—had it been a failure too?

The only concrete observation Watson produced (in 1920) was the famous case of "Albert and the rat." But while this case did come to serve as a powerful exemplar, it was not a very solid data-base which could carry a whole theory. It was, after all, an experiment with a sample of one; it also involved some fairly problematic procedures.[54] Some years later, Elsie O. Bregman tried to replicate Watson's experiment in a more systematic manner. As Hilgard and Marquis summed up: "Later experiments have been unsuccessful in duplicating it. . . . The process is not as simple as the story of Albert suggests."[55]

But surely, there must have been other American conditioning studies. Not really. The first bona fide American conditioning experiment with humans was not reported until 1922, by Hulsey Cason; and he did not feel compelled to accept a Watsonian interpretation. The mass of conditioning experiments did not appear until after the translation of Pavlov's work had become available to American psychologists in 1927 and 1928. All Watson had was Little Albert. Yet while he presented a beautiful example of an idea, if one had already accepted this idea, he did not provide solid scientific evidence to a skeptical observer. The actual paradigm-exemplar, as a way of doing things, did not produce the paradigm shift at all; the exemplar came after the formula had been developed, and even then it was more like a diagram than a way of actually doing things.[56]

Here we may have put a finger on one of the places where Watson was hurting, on one of the facts at least partly responsible for the slow rate of conversion of his fellow scientists. What was it, after all, that Watson had to offer them? He had used some strong words in attacking their psychology and had exploited some of their troubles; he had proposed some intriguing ideas. But in spite of his insistence on a new, harder science, objective observations, etc., when it came to experimental data he had very few (apart from his animal studies) to justify his attempt to usurp scientific authority.

Watson's 1913 research program, loose as it was, seems to have been plagued by false leads or experimental failures. The two concrete proposals of 1913, the identification of thinking with subvocal movements and his explanation of affection, in good Freudian fashion, in terms of activity of the sex glands, had been proffered without any empirical evidence. (The two major specifics radical behaviorism eventually became identified with, environmentalism and the conditioned response, did not become central to Watson's system until ten years later.)

Apparently, Watson spent some time trying to collect data on laryngeal movements, but eventually gave up.[57] His first attack on conditioning (still within a limited theoretical context) also seems to have ended with an impasse, and with a shift to observational work on infants. By 1920, not one concrete experimental problem of human psychology had been solved convincingly by Watson and had provided him with a Kuhnian paradigm.

Yet he was addressing professionals who had been trained in the use of introspective methods, and were so training others; who had believed all along that what they were doing was indeed real science, since it involved laboratories, observations, measurements, controlled conditions, etc. Watson was asking these professionals to throw their tools overboard as not scientific, to declare all the hard-won generalizations that filled their textbooks and their lectures to be artifacts of bad methods. This was too much to ask, as we heard one psychologist after another assert in their reaction to Watson. Though obviously they had not yet solved all the difficult problems of mental phenomena, nevertheless they were the professional experts on the mind, on the inner experience of man. All of a sudden they should forswear their claim to this expertise, surrender their scientific authority?

In recent years we have heard some calls for radical changes in psychology or in its specialities. Their reception, with responses ranging from hostility to indifference—even though there are at least *some* anomalies around in our science—should let us empathize with the feelings of the established psychologists of Watson's time. What did Watson have to offer them in return for their renunciation? He promoted a different version of science which, so it seemed to them, would make them lose their professional identity and turn them into either biologists or physiologists. Why should they risk such an exchange?

A New Goal for Psychology

After all, Watson's call for a revolution in psychology had been largely programmatic. His main thrust had aimed at a redefinition of scientific standards and a redirection of psychology. Put simply, this redefinition proceeded on three different levels: First was the change in *method:* the call for objective procedures and the elimination of "unscientific" introspection. This argument, having the most direct impact on the workday of psychologists, drew the largest share of public responses. While the emphasis on objective methods, already widely used and advocated, met with a good deal of sympathy, the total proscription of introspection ran into strong resistance, if only for the intolerant tone of its imposition (even from those not using introspection in their own work, like Thorndike and Yerkes).

The second level concerned the *subject matter* of psychology, changing it from mental contents and/or processes to movement and behavior, with its attendant peripheralism, rejection of central processes, and associated metaphysical connotations. This issue, too, met with considerable debate. Its acceptance required a fundamental figure-ground reversal which was not easy to accomplish and took its time in coming about, although the expansion of the field to problems of "real life" had widespread support in the growing discipline.

I would like to propose, however, that the crucial argument occurred at a third level and dealt with the *goal* for psychology. According to Watson, this goal was to be the "prediction and control of behavior." Here Watson proposed something radical and new for psychology. All textbooks before him had defined psychology's aim in a different way, as description and/or explanation of mental phenomena, their understanding (on occasion including self-understanding, even self-improvement), etc.: the traditional goals of academic science.

Where Watson obtained his formula about prediction and control is not quite clear. Initially I assumed that he had taken a cliché from the natural sciences which he was trying to emulate, but a somewhat cursory search complicated this answer. Most sources I found (discussions of philosophy of science and encyclopedia definitions of "science")[58] did not define science in terms of prediction and control, mentioned prediction only in passing, and were more concerned with the problem raised by positivism: the banishment of causes, description versus explanation. However, the biologist Jacques Loeb had on several occasions described the goal of modern biology as the "control of life-phenomena" and in 1912 even referred to two outcomes, control or quantitative prediction. Watson, who had studied with Loeb at Chicago, may well have derived his novel definition of the goal of psychology from Loeb's ideas.[59] Of course some psychologists had, if only in passing, spoken of control before Watson: William James had once talked about "practical prediction and control" as the aim of all sciences, and about the demand on psychologists from all kinds of managers for "practical rules" for the "control of states of mind."[60] Cattell's famous St. Louis address had eagerly anticipated the "application of systematized knowledge to the control of human nature," to the "control of ourselves and our fellow men."[61] Thorndike had mentioned "control [of man's] acts" in a 1911 essay defining psychology as the study of behavior.[62] Yerkes's 1911 textbook contained, as sixth and final part, a rather abstract discussion of foresight and the control of mental events.[63] And finally, in England William McDougall had published a little book, in which he stated as psychology's aim: "to increase our understanding of, and our power of guidance and control over, the behaviour of men and animals."[64] (Watson knew McDougall's earlier books.)

Still I believe that Watson's treatment of the issue constituted a quantum jump. Only with him did control become a fundamental idea, part of the textbook definition; and it came right at the start, appearing in the second sentence of his 1913 paper (and at least four more times in fourteen pages): The "theoretical goal [of psychology] is the prediction and control of behavior." Why did Watson use this phrase? Why "theoretical goal" why not "practical" goal, or just "the" goal? Did theoretical mean hypothetical, ideal—a goal unreachable in practice? I do not think that this is what Watson tried to say.

Before Watson, the aims of psychology had been seen in terms of the category of pure science, as contrasted to either applied science or art. Of course, most psychologists have had their dreams of glory, in which their science would affect the real world and solve some of its problems. Even defenders of an ascetic science, like Titchener, believed that scientific knowledge would eventually produce its practical fruit and thus justify science to the impure, though true scientists ignored the question of application. But James's brief remark concerned the pressures from the *outside* for practical rules, presumably *derived* from theoretical knowledge. The quote from Cattell referred to the *application* of systematized knowledge. And Yerkes ended his discussion by saying: "Control is the outcome, albeit not the avowed goal, of scientific research. . . . Psychology is *not* the science of mental control."[65] It merely would make it possible. In other words, traditionally the issue was seen as involving two steps: first, the acquisition of knowledge as the task of science, and then its application to practical affairs. What was debatable, and debated, was the desirability, the timing, and the division of labor in such application. Watson saw the issue differently. his phrase "theoretical goal" shows him reshuffling the traditional categories[66]; prediction and control were no longer indirect or second-stage outcomes, but had become the direct focus and criterion of theory development. I think this notion was radically new (for psychology) and provided the fulcrum for the reorientation of psychology in subsequent decades, so that today any psychology major will state what is self-evident to him: that the goal of (behavioristic as well as cognitive) psychology is the prediction and control of behavior.

It is interesting, and somewhat puzzling, that the early reactions to Watson, the more intensive debate over behaviorism in the early twenties, and more recent analyses of Watson's contribution were largely silent on this point.[67] Only Titchener's rebuttal focused on the behaviorist's goal, in his accusation that Watson was trying to create a technology rather than a science. Thorndike's and Carr's reviews of Watson's *Comparative* book, which reprinted the 1913 papers, reacted in passing to this point; yet both seem to have misunderstood it. In part, I believe, the Janus-face of the term *control* is responsible for the lack of discussion. Control could mean control of conditions, precision in experimentation, elimination of unwanted influence; but that was a commonplace. Or it could mean what Watson clearly intended, at least much of the time (he also used a more abstract formula about predicting stimuli from responses and responses from stimuli), and spelled out later: *social control,* i.e., manipulation of human beings for the benefit of society.[68] But the experimental psychologist failed to confront this aspect of behaviorism in their theoretical debate and eventually defined the issue away.

Yet others did get the message. The first text in applied psychology—while not strictly Watsonian—opened on a distinctly behavioristic note. It introduced the ideas of prediction and control, and explained that the change in emphasis from consciousness to behavior may have been due in part to theoretical difficulties (as with imageless though); but it was also due to the demands of practical life.[69] About the same time, John Dewey's address on the need for social psychology linked behaviorism with the development of a social psychology in the service of social control. Reviewing the applications of psychology to industry in 1920, Henry Link cited the Gilbreths, involved in time and motion work in industry, as the "ideal behaviorists" and concluded: "Watson's work is, in fact, the conscious methodology which practically all recent literature in industrial psychology has more or less explicitly *implied.*"[70] Soon after, W. V. Bingham, head of the applied psychology unit at Carnegie Tech, was to complain about this accidental (and to him unfortunate) identification of behaviorism with applied psychology, which made his attempt to separate an applied science from the pure science of psychology more difficult. And Floyd Allport described social psychology as becoming "the study of the social behavior of the individual . . . [needed] for study and control of the socially significant aspects of individual response." He also wrote in his lecture notes: "Responsibilities incident to human control. Practical psychology is essentially behavioristic in method."[71]

CONCLUSION

Such beginnings are part of a larger and complex pattern of developments in the twenties, which is discussed elsewhere.[72] So far, it appears that a less than monolithic mainstream of experimental psychology, debating issues of method and concepts, resisted Watson's advances for a long time, assimilating them gradually in the form of the more abstract S-R formula. Yet in the meantime others, inside and outside psychology, more immediately concerned with problems of social control and helped along by the exigencies and opportunities of World War I, were finding Watson's arguments a convenient or inspiring rationale. Even if they may not have accepted all of his theoretical ideas, Watson had given the discipline a strong push in the direction of technological science.

Certainly, Watson had not singlehandedly transformed psychology. Too many of the specifics of his argument had not been original with him—although the common practice of briefly quoting one or another author's use of "behavioral" definitions of psychology before 1913,[73] in order to demolish Watson's claim to priority, misses the mark. It overlooks the fact that Watson had already in 1907 declared that the "science of behavior" was "thoroughly established."[74] It is true enough that at this time he did not yet apply it to all of psychology; nonetheless, the phrase had been abroad long before 1913. What counted were its corollaries.

But while using ideas from others, as well as appealing to their dissatisfactions with the status quo, Watson had sharpened the arguments into a revolutionary weapon. Provoking a good deal of resistance with his rhetoric, he also discovered the price to be paid for his shift, in 1913, from a strategy of succession to, in Pierre Bourdieu's terms, a high-risk strategy of subversion of established scientific authority.[75] When the shift finally paid off, others reaped the benefits. Watson was no longer a part of the professional community, when eventually the reestablished monopoly of scientific authority had accepted prediction and control as the criterion of positive science and declared only outward manifestations, "behavior," to be legitimate scientific data. Anything mental had become unobservable, an at best problematic inference if not a superstition pure and simple.

In a sense, the present research effort turned out to be a failure. Looking for the sources of behaviorism's powerful appeal to American psychologists, we found more often criticisms or partial acceptance. Did we look in the wrong place? What I had not realized at the outset was that the victory of behaviorism took so much longer in coming about. And at least this scientific revolution did not involve simply conceptual transformations and conversions, but something Kuhn has not talked about—a power struggle in a discipline, affected by events without. Like the other social sciences,[76] the young profession of psychology grew up facing a predicament, in it dependence on a larger clientele, on the one hand, and its desire for autonomy and academic status, on the other—as reflected in the rhetorics of relevance and purity. Eventually, psychology adopted Watson's ingenious solution combining the appeals of hard-headed science, pragmatic usefulness, and ideological liberation.

NOTES

(1) Howard C. Warren, (Autobiography), in *A History of Psychology in Autobiography,* vol. 1, ed. Carl Murchison (Worcester, Mass.: Clark University Press, 1930), p. 462. See also John B. Watson "Psychology as the Behaviorist Views It," *Psychological Review 20* (1913): 158–177. Walter B. Pillsbury recalled, in his autobiography, that he had read Watson's paper while in Germany. However, his only concern was Watson's misinterpretation of a comment Pillsbury had made about Watson's animal lab. See Pillsbury, *A History of Psychology in Autobiography,* vol. 2 (1932), p. 285. Finally, John F. Dashiell's autobiography mentions Watson's "prompt appeal" without giving any specifics (although Dashiell attended Columbia University at the time of Watson's presentation); nor do his early writings show much of a behavioristic influence. Dashiell, (Autobiography), in *A History of Psychology in Autobiography,* vol. 5 (1967), pp. 117–118; and "Spirit and Matter: A Philosophical Tradition," *Journal of Philosophy, Psychology, and Scientific Method* 14 (1917): 66–74. E. G. Boring, *Psychologist at Large* (New York: Basic Books, 1961).

(2) H. S. Langfeld, "Psychology," in *The American Year Book, 1913,* ed. Francis G. Wickware (New York: Appleton, 1914), p. 704; Maurice Parmelee, *The Science of Human Behavior* (New York: Macmillan, 1913); Walter T. Marvin, "General Problems; Mind and Body," *Psychological Bulletin* 11 (1914): 1–7.

(3) Robert M. Yerkes, "The Study of Human Behavior," *Science* 39 (1914): 625–633; James R. Angell, "Behavior as a Category of Psychology," *Psychological Review* 20 (1913): 225–270, pp. 261, 264; for the origin of the term see also Howard C. Warren, "Terminology," *Psychological Bulletin* 11 (1914): 10–11.

(4) Max F. Meyer, *The Fundamental Laws of Human Behavior* (Boston: Badger, 1911); William McDougall, *An Introduction to Social Psychology* (London: Methuen, 1908).

(5) Angell, "Behavior as a Category"; Fredrick J. E. Woodbridge, "The Belief in Sensations," *Journal of Philosophy, Psychology, and Scientific Method* 10 (1913): 599–608; Mary W. Calkins, "Psychology and the Behaviorist," *Psychological Bulletin* 10 (1913): 288–291.

(6) Calkins, "Psychology," p. 289.

(7) Fredrick L. Wells, "Special Reviews" and "Dynamic Psychology," *Psychological Bulletin* 10 (1913): 280–281 and 434–440, p. 434.

(8) Wells, "Special Reviews," p. 281.

(9) James R. Angell, "Behavior as a Psychological Category," (abstract), *Psychological Bulletin* 10 (1913): 48–49; Wells, "Special Reviews," p. 281.

(10) Jean Weidensall, "Criminology and Delinquency," *Psychological Bulletin* 10 (1913): 229–237, p. 232.

(11) Robert M. Yerkes, "Comparative Psychology: A Question of Definitions," *Journal of Philosophy, Psychology, and Scientific Method* 10 (1913): 580–582, p. 581; James R. Angell, "Professor Watson and the Image," *Journal of Philosophy, Psychology, and Scientific Method* 10 (1913): 609; Henry R. Marshall, "Is Psychology Evaporating?" *Journal of Philosophy, Psychology, and Scientific Method* 10 (1913): 710–716.

(12) Howard C. Warren, "The Mental and the Physical," *Psychological Bulletin* 11 (1914): 35–36 (abstract), and *Psychological Review* 21 (1914): 79–100, p. 100.

(13) Ibid., pp. 97, 95.

(14) John Dewey, "Psychological Doctrine and Philosophical Teaching," *Journal of Philosophy, Psychology, and Scientific Method* 11 (1914): 505–511, p. 511; Harold C. Brown, "The Thirteenth Annual Meeting of the American Philosophical Association," *Journal of Philosophy, Psychology, and Scientific Method* 11 (1914): 57–67, p. 65; Knight Dunlap, "Images and Ideas," *Johns Hopkins University Circular* 33 (1914): 25–41.

(15) G. Stanley Hall, "Food and Mind," Mental Hygiene Conference, Boston, 4 April 1913 (typed ms.), p. 3, Box 29, G. Stanley Hall Papers, Clark University Archives. (I am indebted to David E. Leary for making this item available to me.)

(16) John C. Burnham, "On the Origins of Behaviorism," *Journal of the History of the Behavioral Sciences 4* (1968): 143–151.

(17) E. G. Boring, "The Society of Experimental Psychologists; 1904–1938," *American Journal of Psychology* 51 (1938): 410–423.

(18) "Notes and News," *Psychological Bulletin* 10 (1913): 211–212; see also Samuel W. Fernberger, "Convention of Experimental Psychologists," *American Journal of Psychology* 24 (1913): 445; and for a retrospective account in almost the same words, Boring, "The Society," p. 414.

(19) Melvin E. Haggerty, "The Twenty-second Annual Meeting of the American Psychological Association," *Journal of Philosophy, Psychology, and Scientific Method* 11 (1914): 85–109, p. 86.

(20) Melvin E. Haggerty, "The Relation of Psychology and Pedagogy," *Psychological Bulletin* 13 (1916): 55–56, and "Reviews and Abstracts of the Literature," *Journal of Philosophy, Psychology, and Scientific Method* 13 (1916): 470–472, p. 472.

(21) Walter V. Bingham, "Proceedings of the Twenty-second Annual Meeting of the American Psychological Association," *Psychological Bulletin* 11 (1914): 29–35, p. 29.

(22) This account is not exhaustive. For instance, a summary of Watson's manifesto by J. R. Tuttle appeared in the *Philosophical Review* 22 (1913): 674; "Notes and News," *Journal of Educational Psychology* 4 (1913): 180, reported briefly on Watson's Columbia address.

(23) F. L. Wells, "Dynamic Psychology," p. 434.

(24) Howard C. Warren's autobiography (p. 462) recounted two decades later that, although he could not accept Watson's position, "the younger psychologists hailed Watson as a second Moses." Yet specifics supporting and detailing this dramatic image are hard to find in the contemporary record. In "The Origins of Behaviorism," (1979 Ph.D. dissertation) John

O'Donnell discusses at length what he calls Watson's "silent majority" which, however, was not a group converted by the manifesto (as Warren had it), but which had been interested in applied psychology, and thus had been behavioristic, before 1913. But even if there was such a majority for behaviorism, the very fact that its members are hard to track down in the record (even O'Donnell gives us only a few names) indicates their marginal role in the development of the academic discipline, its publications, and its training of students. Finally, O'Donnell's argument, in which applied interests are equated with behaviorism, seems problematical to me; at the very least it proceeds at a more global level of analysis than does the present paper.

(25) J. B. Watson to R. M. Yerkes, 26 March 1913; R. M. Yerkes to J. B. Watson, 16 May 1916, Robert M. Yerkes Papers, Historical Library, Yale Medical Library, New Haven, Conn.

(26) John B. Watson, "Image and Affection in Behavior," *Journal of Philosophy, Psychology, and Scientific Method 10* (1913): 421–428.

(27) Gilbert V. Hamilton to R. M. Yerkes, 22 December 1914. (Hamilton was a former Yerkes student with an M.D. degree, involved in animal research at the time); Margaret F. Washburn to R. M. Yerkes, 26 May 1916, Yerkes Papers. Cedric A. Larson and John J. Sullivan, "Watson's Relation to Titchener," *Journal of the History of the Behavioral Sciences* 1 (1965): 338–354.

(28) "Notes and News," *Psychological Bulletin* 11 (1914): 28, 79.

(29) H. S. Langfeld, "Psychology," in *American Year Book, 1914* (New York: Appleton, 1915), 674.

(30) John B. Watson, *Behavior: An Introduction to Comparative Psychology* (New York: Holt, 1914); H. S. Langfeld, "Text-books and General Treatises," *Psychological Bulletin* 12 (1915): 30–37; Harvey A. Carr, "Special Reviews," *Psychological Bulletin* 12 (1915): 308–312; Edward L. Thorndike and C. Judson Herrick, "Watson's 'Behavior'," *Journal of Animal Behavior* 5 (1915): 462–470; M. E. Haggerty, "Reviews and Abstracts of Literature," *Journal of Philosophy, Psychology, and Scientific Method* 13 (1916): 470–472.

(31) E. L. Thorndike, "The Study of Consciousness and the Study of Behavior," (abstract), *Psychological Bulletin* 8 (1911): 39; Thorndike, *Animal Intelligence* (New York: Macmillan, 1911); Thorndike and Herrick, "Watson's 'Behavior'," p. 464.

(32) George A. Coe, "A Proposed Classification of Mental Functions," *Psychological Review* 22 (1915): 87–98, p. 91.

(33) Walter S. Hunter, "A Reply to Some Criticisms of the Delayed Reaction," *Journal of Philosophy, Psychology, and Scientific Method* 12 (1915): 38–41, Edwin B. Holt, "Response and Cognition," *Journal of Philosophy, Psychology, and Scientific Method* 12 (1915): 38–41; Edwin B. Holt, "Response and Cognition," *Journal of Philosophy, Psychology, and Scientific Method* 12(1915):365–373 and 393–409; C. Judson Herrick, "Introspection as a Biological Method," *Journal of Philosophy, Psychology, and Scientific Method* 12 (1915): 543–551.

(34) Margaret F. Washburn, "Some Thoughts on the Last Quarter Century in Psychology," *Philosophical Review* 26 (1917): 46–55; Joseph Jastrow, "Varieties of Psychological Experience," *Psychological Review* 24 (1917): 249–265; Walter B. Pillsbury, "The New Developments in Psychology in the Past Quarter Century," *Philosophical Review* 26 (1917): 56–59; James M. Cattell, "Our Psychological Association and Research," *Science* 45 (1917): 275–284; John Dewey, "The Need for Social Psychology," *Psychological Review* 24 (1917): 266–277; G. Stanley Hall, "Practical Relations between Psychology and the War," *Journal of Applied Psychology* 1 (1917): 9–16.

(35) John B. Watson, "The Place of the Conditioned Reflex in Psychology," *Psychological Bulletin* 23 (1916): 89–117. Apparently this address did not produce much of a reaction. See H. S. Langfeld to H. Münsterberg, 1 January 1916, Hugo Münsterberg Papers, Boston Public Library; Watson, "An Attempted Formulation of the Scope of Behavior Psychology," *Psychological Review* 24 (1917): 329–352; Watson and John J. B. Morgan, "Emotional Reactions and Psychological Experimentation," *American Journal of Psychology* 28 (1917): 163–174.

(36) Howard C. Warren, Mary W. Calkins, Knight

Dunlap, H. N. Gardiner, and C. A. Ruckmich, "Definitions and Delimitations of Psychological Terms," *Psychological Bulletin* 15 (1918): 89–95, p. 94.

(37) Preprint located in 3P, Mary Whiton Calkins Unprocessed Papers, Wellesley College Archives, Wellesley, Mass.

(38) Warren et al., "Definitions, II," *Psychological Bulletin* 19 (1922): 230–235, p. 231.

(39) Walter B. Pillsbury, "Behavior and Behaviorism," *Encyclopedia Americana* (New York: Encyclopedia Americana Corporation, 1918); 446–448.

(40) See J. B. Watson to J. M. Cattell, 15 January 1915, Cattell Papers, and J. B. Watson to R. M. Yerkes, 27 March 1916, Yerkes Papers; Holt, "Response and Cognition," p. 409n.

(41) Gardner Murphy to Robert S. Woodworth, n.d. (in reply to Woodworth's letter dated 27 October 1932), Robert S. Woodworth Papers, Library of Congress.

(42) E. B. Titchener, "The Past Decade in Experimental Psychology," *American Journal of Psychology* 21 (1910): 404–422.

(43) David Bakan, "Behaviorism and American Urbanization," *Journal of the History of the Behavioral Sciences* 2 (1966): 5–28.

(44) R. M. Yerkes, "Behaviorism and Genetic Psychology," *Journal of Philosphy, Psychology, and Scientific Method* 14 (1917): 154–161, p. 161.

(45) Thomas S. Kuhn, *The Structure of Scientific Revolutions* (Chicago: University of Chicago Press, 1962).

(46) Watson, "Psychology," p. 163n.

(47) Robert S. Woodworth, "A Revision of Imageless Thought," *Psychological Review* 22 (1915): 1–27.

(48) Edward B. Titchener, "On 'Psychology as the Behaviorist Views It,' " *Proceedings of the American Philosophical Society 53* (1914): 1–17, p. 8. See also Kurt Danziger, "The History of Introspection Reconsidered," *Journal of the History of the Behavioral Sciences* 16 (1980): 241–262.

(49) E.g., James R. Angell, *Psychology,* 3rd ed. (New York: Holt, 1906), p. 4; Harvey A. Carr, *Psychology* (New York: Longmans Green, 1926), p. 7.

(50) See Danziger, "History of Introspection," pp. 257–258.

(51) Franz Samelson, "Paradigms, Labels, and Historical Analysis," *American Psychologist* 28 (1973): 1141–1143. See also Brian D. Mackenzie, *Behaviorism and the Limits of Scientific Method* (London: Routledge & Kegan Paul, 1977).

(52) Karl S. Lashley, "Recent Literature of a General Nature on Animal Behavior," *Psychological Bulletin 11* (1914): 269–277, p. 272.

(53) Watson, "The Place of the Conditioned-Reflex"; Karl S. Lashley, "The Human Salivary Reflex and Its Use in Psychology," *Psychological Review* 23 (1916): 445–464; Lashley, "Reflex Secretions of the Human Parotid Gland," *Journal of Experimental Psychology,* 1 (1916): 461–495; Ernest R. Hilgard and Donald G. Marquis, *Conditioning and Learning* (New York: Appleton-Century, 1940), p. 13. Watson and Morgan, "Emotional Reactions," p. 171.

(54) J. B. Watson and Rosalie Rayner, "Conditioned Emotional Reactions," *Journal of Experimental Psychology* 3 (1920): 1–14; J. B. Watson and R. R. Watson, "Studies in Infant Psychology," *Scientific Monthly* 13 (1921): 493–515. For a more detailed discussion, see Franz Samelson, "John B. Watson's Little Albert, Cyril Burt's Twins, and the Need for a Critical Science," *American Psychologist* 35 (1980): 619–625.

(55) Elsie O. Bregman, "An Attempt to Modify the Emotional Attitudes of Infants by the Conditioned Response Technique," *Journal of Genetic Psychology* 45 (1934): 169–198; Hilgard and Marquis, *Conditioning and Learning,* pp. 293, 294.

(56) Hulsey Cason, "The Conditioned Pupillary Reaction," *Journal of Experimental Psychology* 5 (1922): 108–146; Ivan P. Pavlov, *Conditioned Reflexes,* trans. G. V. Anrep (London: Oxford University Press, 1927); Pavlov, *Lectures on Conditioned Reflexes,* trans. W. Horsley Gantt (New York: International Publishers, 1928). Two earlier American conditioning studies do not qualify for inclusion, for different technical reasons: Ignatius A. Hamel, "A Study and Analysis of the Conditioned Reflex," *Psychological Monographs* 27 (1919): No. 1; Florence Mateer, *Child Behavior* (Boston: Badger,

1918). Of course, others had started to *talk* about conditioning (F. L. Wells, "Von Bechterew and Uebertragung," *Journal of Philosophy, Psychology, and Scientific Method* 13 [1916]: 354–356; William H. Burnham, "Mental Hygiene and the Conditioned Reflex," *Pedagogical Seminary* 24 [1917]: 449–488), but that only proves my point. Cf. Hilgard and Marquis, *Conditioning and Learning,* on this issue although their emphasis is different.

(57) J. B. Watson to R. M. Yerkes, 22 October 1915 and 17 February 1916, Yerkes Papers.

(58) For instance, Karl Pearson, *The Grammar of Science,* 2nd ed. (London: Black, 1900).

(59) Jacques Loeb, *Comparative Physiology of the Brain and Comparative Psychology* (New York: Putnam, 1907), p. 287; Loeb, *The Mechanistic Conception of Life* (Chicago: University of Chicago Press, 1912), pp. 3, 196. Philip J. Pauly's recent work on Loeb comes independently to similar conclusions; see his "Jacques Loeb and the Control of Life," unpublished Ph.D. dissertation, Johns Hopkins University, 1980. Of course, in at least a loose sense these ideas go back to Auguste Comte and beyond.

(60) William James, "A Plea for Psychology as a 'Natural Science'," *Philosophical Review* 1 (1892): 146–153, p. 148 (I am indebted to John O'Donnell for this reference).

(61) James M. Cattell, "The Concepts and Methods of Psychology," *Popular Science Monthly* 66 (1904): 176–186, pp. 185, 186.

(62) Thorndike, *Animal Intelligence,* p. 15.

(63) Robert M. Yerkes, *Introduction to Psychology* (New York: Holt, 1911).

(64) William McDougall, *Psychology: The Study of Behavior* (London: Butterworth, 1912), p. 21.

(65) Yerkes, *Introduction to Psychology,* p. 416 (italics added). Thorndike had said: "Science seeks to know the world; the arts, to control it." *The Elements of Psychology* (New York: Seiler, 1905), p. 324.

(66) See Watson's argument that "applied psychology" was a misnomer; "Psychology," p. 169.

(67) Gustav Bergman, "The Contribution of John B. Watson," *Psychological Review* 63 (1956): 265–276; Herrnstein, Introduction to Watson's *Behavior;* Mackenzie, *Behaviorism;* not so John C. Burnham, whose repeated references to the "social control" theme helped to direct my attention to this issue. See also Lucille C. Birnbaum, *Behaviorism: John Broadus Watson and American Social Thought,* unpublished Ph.D. dissertation (Berkeley: University of California, 1965).

(68) John B. Watson, "An Attempted Formulation of the Scope of Behavior Psychology," *Psychological Review* 24 (1917): 329–352 and *Psychology from the Standpoint of a Behaviorist* (Philadelphia: Lippincott, 1919); p. 2. See also Paul T. Young to J. B. Watson, 27 May 1917, P. T. Young Papers.

(69) Harry L. Hollingworth and Albert T. Poffenberger, *Applied Psychology* (New York: Appleton, 1917), pp. 5, 6.

(70) Dewey, "The Need for Social Psychology"; Henry C. Link, "The Application of Psychology to Industry," *Psychological Bulletin* 17 (1920): 335–346, pp. 341, 345 (italics added).

(71) Walter V. Bingham, "On the Possibility of an Applied Psychology," *Psychological Review* 30 (1923): 289–305; Floyd H. Allport, "Social Psychology," *Psychological Bulletin* 17 (1920): 85–94, p. 85; F. H. Allport, Lecture Notes, "Psychology 35; Industrial and Vocational Psychology," (typed, 1923?), Box 3, Walter V. Bingham Papers, University Archives, Carnegie-Mellon University, Pittsburgh, Penn.

(72) Franz Samelson, "Early Behaviorism, Pt. 3. The Stalemate of the Twenties," Paper presented at the 12th annual meeting of Cheiron, Bowdoin College, Brunswick, ME, June 1980; See also F. Samelson, "Putting Psychology on the Map," *Psychology in Social Context,* pp. 101–168.

(73) For instance, O'Donnell, "Origins," p. 537.

(74) John B. Watson, "Comparative Psychology," *Psychological Bulletin* 4 (1907): 208.

(75) Pierre Bourdieu, "The Specificity of the Scientific Field and the Social Conditions of the Progress of Reason," *Social Science Information* 14 no. 6 (1975): 19–47.

(76) Cf. Dorothy Ross, "The Development of the Social Sciences," in *The Organization of Knowledge in Modern America, 1860–1920,* ed. Alexandra Oleson and John Voss (Baltimore: Johns Hopkins University Press, 1979), pp. 107–138.

The Selling of a Psychologist: John Broadus Watson and the Application of Behavioral Techniques to Advertising

Kerry W. Buckley

As 1924 drew to a close, John B. Watson was made a vice-president in the J. Walter Thompson advertising agency. "You place a sort of economic sanction on behaviorism," wrote E. G. Boring of Harvard, "by rising to business heights which must transcend the attainment of any other psychologist."[1] Watson had good reason to feel satisfaction in his accomplishment. Only four years earlier the celebrated founder of behaviorism had been forced to resign from his position in the Psychology Department of Johns Hopkins University under the cloud of an ugly and very public divorce scandal. When he joined the Thompson agency in 1920, his reputation as the founder of a science which had as its object "the prediction and control of behavior" held an undeniable appeal to advertisers.[2] But Watson's successful marketing of psychological expertise did not begin with his venture into advertising. The notion of a psychology whose assumptions and techniques were as applicable in the marketplace as in the laboratory was part of the very fabric of behaviorism itself. Psychology as the behaviorist viewed it was from the beginning a psychology of use. In order to characterize the appeal of behaviorism, both within and outside of the profession of psychology, it is revealing to consider the ways in which its utility was applied by Watson.

Watson was part of a new generation of professionals who came of age around the turn of the century. This socially mobile group found that the very problems created by an expanding industrial economy created additional opportunities for those who could offer solutions to these problems.[3]

When Watson made his behavioral stand public in 1913, he characterized behaviorism as a science that would be useful to "the educator, the physician, the jurist and the businessman."[4] By doing so, he appealed to the professional interests of many psychologists who may have differed with him theoretically. Behaviorism not only became a new school of psychological theory but also demonstrated the means by which the profession of psychology could respond to the needs of a new corporate order. Behavioral psychology would work in harmony with the other branches of natural science in a division of the common labor of establishing "efficient" control over natural phenomena and social activity. Watson considered his brand of psychology to be a particularly American product. In a nation that was becoming more centralized, older forms of social control were seen as sluggish and slow to respond to the accelerating pace of urban life.

Watson's behaviorism helped crystallized fundamental issues that had created a crisis in psychology.[5] Psychologists who attempted to establish connections between the realm of the mind and the world of experience were caught in a dualism that kept them beyond the pale of the emerging professional scientific community. There, such metaphysical concepts as "mind" and "consciousness" were considered outside the bounds of scientific inquiry. Watson resolved this dilemma by restructuring the framework of psychological investigation within the lines of current scientific assumptions. Behaviorism was pragmatic in the sense that it insisted that the proper study of psychology was not mind but behavior and naturalistic in that it was derived directly from animal psy-

Buckley, K. W. (1982). The selling of a psychologist: John Broadus Watson and the application of behavioral techniques to advertising. *Journal of the History of the Behavioral Sciences, 18,* 207–221.

chology. Watson did not separate human beings from the animal kingdom. Behaviorism was positivistic because Watson would not admit for study anything that could not be observed and verified from overt behavior. In short, Watson provided psychology with a theory and a methodology that satisfied the contemporary requirements for achieving status as a science. But in emphasizing the prediction and control of natural phenomena (in this case, human behavior) in the interests of efficiency, order, and progress, behaviorism also satisfied the contemporary requirements for the *uses* of science.[6]

Watson believed social control to be the primary area of application for psychology. Not only were psychologists to predict human behavior, they were also to formulate laws to enable "organized society" to control that behavior. The psychologist was the logical replacement for the clergyman and the politician. Traditional ways of maintaining social order through the church and the political process had been accomplished mainly by "trial and error."[7] Behaviorism would replace such outmoded methods with techniques that would increase efficiency by bringing human behavior under scientific control.[8] The notion of control is the underlying theme connecting the growth of science, technology, and the emerging professions with the expansion of a centralized urban society. The shift of authority and control from older institutions such as the church, the family, and the local community to a bureaucracy of experts that provided services to corporations, public institutions, and social agencies gave rise to a demand for methods of behavior control, to which Watson directed his energies.[9]

Watson looked to the areas of education, business, and industry as the primary beneficiaries of his expertise. The application of psychological techniques to pedagogical method was not new. G. Stanley Hall, William James, and John Dewey had all been interested in the prospects of psychology in the classroom.[10] But Watson, himself once a teacher in rural South Carolina, sought a more comprehensive role for the psychologist in the developing systems of public education. In 1917, he contributed to a symposium which presented "suggestions of modern science concerning education." Watson argued that most biological and psychological problems center around processes of growth and development and emphasize the need for "*predicting, controlling* and *regulating* such development." The task of the laboratory and the school room, according to Watson, was to discover what an individual can instinctively do and what he can be trained to do and then to develop methods that will lead the individual to perform as required by society. As Watson put it: "If it is demanded by society that a given line of conduct is desirable, the psychologist should be able with some certainty to arrange the situation or factors which will lead the individual most quickly and with the least expenditure of effort to perform that task."[11]

Watson lent scientific legitimacy to a growing sentiment among social reformers and educators that the school should take over functions of a socialization formerly assumed by the family. And Watson went even further. He advocated the funding of an experimental nursery that would lead to the establishment of "infant laboratories" in the public school system. In this way mothers of preschool children "could be guided and warned about the way the children were tending to develop," and could receive "expert guidance and intelligent help." The laboratories would also be used to train teachers in child behavior. Watson had nothing but contempt for a "society which permits them [teachers] to *teach* instead of to *guide* the child's development."[12] Not only was Watson emphasizing the role of the school as the agent of social adjustment for the child, but he was also demonstrating the role of psychology in facilitating that adjustment.

While at Johns Hopkins, Watson looked beyond academia for other opportunities to apply his psychological techniques. In 1916 Watson wrote that he had enjoyed "some success" in negotiating with the Baltimore and Ohio Railroad and in acting as a consultant for a life insurance firm.[13] Watson sought to strengthen psychology within academia by demonstrating its usefulness to a large and powerful constituency. He also hoped to bring psychologists' skills to the attention of a potential market. Watson took steps to bring applied psychology into the university curriculum by offering a course on the "Psychology of Advertising." Designed to draw students into the university's courses in "Business Economics," Watson's course taught future managers the value of applied psychology and demonstrated to academic officials the ability of psychology to provide valuable services to the business community.[14]

The United States' involvement in World War I provided an environment for the emergence of a well-defined applied role for psychology. Psychologists gained from the war a reputation for expertise in personnel management and "mental engineering." Through the Committee on Classification of Personnel in the Army and the institution of the Army Alpha and Beta intelligence tests, many psychologists saw possibilities in the large-scale application of psychological skills to problems of personnel management. Watson was part of the group of psychologists that served on the committee, formed by the National Research Council. Headed by Walter Dill Scott (the founder of advertising psychology who was, at the time, affiliated with the Bureau of Salesmanship Research at the Carnegie Institute of Technology), the committee developed the Army intelligence tests, as well as personnel classification and training procedures.[15]

The Army intelligence tests had been given wide publicity during the war. Following the Armistice there was a demand on the part of industry for psychological services. In response to this demand, Walter Dill Scott along with Watson and other members of the Committee organized the Scott Company to offer psychological consulting services to business and industry.[16] In 1921, members of this group and other influential psychologists headed by James McKeen Cattell established the Psychological Corporation. Watson was one of the corporation's original founders and served on its board of directors until 1933. Endorsed by the American Psychological Association, the Psychological Corporation appealed to the professional aspirations of many psychologists. It was Cattell's intention to publicize the achievements of applied psychology and sell those applied skills to the business and industrial community.[17] Other professional interests were also at stake. Robert M. Yerkes wrote to Cattell that "it is urgently important to do something to place the control of psycho-technology in the hands of professional psychologists and to insure its staying there."[18] The Psychological Corporation appealed to the desire of business management to make personnel selection and training as efficient as the industrial machinery had become. Technical problems had been solved; human beings were now the only uncontrolled variable in the production and marketing process.

Watson's experience as an industrial consultant before World War I, his service on the Committee on Classification of Personnel in the Army during the war, and his subsequent association with the Scott Company and the Psychological Corporation provided a context for his enthusiam about the role of an applied psychology. Especially after the war, encouragement from the business community was not lacking. The Western Union Company had called upon Watson to undertake the "study and standardization" of employees who were "not particularly efficient." But Watson was impressed with the success of private consulting firms like the Scott Company and believed that the expansion of opportunities for psychologists lay along that line. In the spring of 1920 he collaborated with Dr. Edward Magruder, a Baltimore physician, in establishing an "Industrial Service Corporation." Its purpose was to provide services relating to personnel selection and management and to conduct "industrial psychological investigations." Watson's object in helping to organize this agency was not only to extend the influence of the psychologist from the laboratory to the marketplace, but also to strengthen the position of the applied psychologist within the profession. In return for Watson's help, Magruder agreed to finance a program at Johns Hopkins "for training Ph.D. men to work in industrial psychology." Watson had "long desired" such a program but had despaired over the difficulty of obtaining funding from the university. Watson was encouraged for his efforts in industrial psychology by Johns Hopkins's President Frank J. Goodnow, but the university would not commit itself to any support other than moral.[19]

Watson's interest in applied psychology was inevitably bound up with his desire for psychology to achieve independent professional goals. For too long, Watson argued, psychology had been a stepchild of philosophy. In a reply to a query from Bertrand Russell, Watson made it clear that he was "trying to get psychology just as far away from philosophy as are chemistry and physics." Sharing with Russell points that he had discussed with psychiatrist Adolf Meyer, Watson wrote that:

> One of the strongest motives I have had in trying to word a simple uncontroversial standpoint in psychology is the fact that students entering our field have to be ruined with logic clipping before they are capable of doing anything. Many of them become word artists, logicians, and pseudo-philosophers and pseudo-clinical psychologists—they will do anything which gives them a chance without being *blocked* by a system. This is the reason for the influx into the field of mental tests, trade tests and the like. But we are using up our reserve material—the world of science goes on and psychology as a science must keep not only in touch with other sciences but also work out advances in fields peculiarly its own. Hence, if we are to keep our students we must have a simpler, more matter-of-fact entrance into psychology. If this is not done now practical and social applications of psychology will never be forthcoming for future use. In other words, technical or applied psychology, like applied chemistry, cannot go on long without research in the laboratory.[20]

Thus Watson made clear the connection between the development of psychology as a science and its uses as a technology. Research was inevitably linked to its application and Watson hoped that an emphasis on practical technique would attract students and ensure the expansion of the profession.

By the spring of 1920, Watson's reputation had achieved international recognition. His professional and academic position seemed, to the envy of his colleagues, secure beyond challenge. Jealous of losing Watson to rival institutions, Johns Hopkins's President Goodnow generously increased Watson's salary. Goodnow assured Watson that his own favorable impression of the behaviorist's work was corroborated by the faculty. He also took pains to convey to Watson that support of the board of trustees as well as the "universal feeling" that it would be "extremely unfortunate" for Johns Hopkins should Watson decide to accept an offer from another university.[21] Yet within a few months, Watson found himself dismissed from academia as the result of a divorce scandal that received national publicity.[22]

Watson had no doubt that he could find a job in the business community. "It will not be as bad as raising chickens or cabbages" he wrote to his colleague, Adolf Meyer. Although he insisted that "both psychology and the university [could] do without [him]," Watson feared that his influence on the profession would be diminished. "I feel that my work is important for psychology," Watson wrote to Meyer, "and that the tiny flame which I have tried to keep burning for the future of psychology will be snuffed out if I go—at least for some time." Yet, Watson continued, "I shall go into commercial work wholeheartedly and burn all bridges."[23]

Watson turned to his friend, sociologist William I. Thomas (who had himself been dismissed from the University of Chicago amid charges of sexual impropriety), who introduced Watson to officials of the J. Walter Thompson advertising agency in New York. The Thompson agency was evidently impressed by Watson's credentials and by the potential of the application of psychological techniques to the business of selling commodities. Thus, Watson's first success as a salesman was the marketing of his scientific expertise as a commodity to be consumed by those whose business it was to motivate and control human behavior.[24]

The creation of a national advertising industry in the 1920s grew as a response to the development of a system of industrial production that was increasingly geared toward the distribution of goods to a national market. The advertising industry attempted to convince businessmen that it could offer a systematic if not scientific method of efficiently marketing products. Advertisers looked to science and especially to psychology to provide techniques that would rationalize the distribution and marketing process.[25] In 1921, the National Association of Advertisers had written to applied psychologist Walter Van Dyke Bingham concerning the "possibility of evolving principles applicable to advertising which could be utilized as a sure guide to success in the making and placing of advertisements."[26] The product that advertisers hoped to sell was a controlled and predictable body of consumers. In order to produce markets of consumers efficiently, advertisers endeavored to discover universal principles to explain the motivation behind consumption. Thus the industry turned to psychologists like Watson who claimed to have the techniques that could be used to predict and control human behavior. Within the Thompson agency, Watson served a dual role. Watson was proof to the business community that the Thompson agency was serious in its commitment to find scientific solutions to marketing problems. In addition, his task as an advertising psychologist was to develop campaigns of mass appeal that would create reliable markets for goods created by mass production.

Soon after joining the Thompson organization, Watson was sent to the field for direct experience in selling the products his company advertised. As he went from one small store to another selling Yuban coffee, he found his task to be a "thankless job." He admitted that he was "shown the door quite frequently," but he found himself to be "learning at a very rapid rate even if in a different school."[27] Upon his return to New York he set about preparing what he called "a 'life program' of experimental work in advertising."[28] After living down the "stigma" of "being an academician," Watson wrote to Bertrand Russell, he hoped to bring his psychological training to bear on problems "connected with markets, salesmanship, public resistances, types of appeals, etc." He considered himself to be "happily at work" with a wider latitude for research than he had had within the university.[29] In fact, he later reflected, he "began to learn that it can be just as thrilling to watch the growth of a sales curve of a new product as to watch the learning curve of animals or men."[30]

By the spring of 1921, Watson explained to Adolf Meyer that he was concerned with "the problems of scientific and practical control of advertising." He was highly critical of the "terrific waste" in the advertising business. "No one knows just what appeals to use," he complained. "It is all a matter of 'instinctive' judgement. Whether I can establish certain principles or not remains to be seen." But advertising offered rich possibilities for applied psychology. If clients could be persuaded to provide research funds, Watson looked forward to a time when "experimentation can be carried out upon a large scale." The prospects were endless. He wrote to Meyer: "We can do many things which have a very direct bearing upon human behavior."[31]

Watson discovered that "the consumer is to the manufacturer, the department stores and the advertising agencies, what the green frog is to the physiologist." For the advertising psychologist the marketplace became the laboratory and the consumer became the experimental subject. Consumption was buying behavior, and as such it was an activity that could be controlled. Watson was determined to develop methods "to keep the consumer headed [his] way. . . ." Not only did he have to discover the consumer's present needs but also to manipulate those needs and to create desires for additional goods and services.[32]

Watson believed that behaviorism was ideally suited for such a task. Since, for Watson, man was "nothing but an organic machine," it ought to be possible "to predict that machine's behavior and to control it as we do other machines."[33] The goal of advertising was not merely the dissemination of information about given products or services. Its purpose was the creation of a society of consumers and the control of the activities of consumption. According to Watson, this could be accomplished by the use of behavioral techniques to condition emotional responses. "To get hold of your consumer," he explained to his advertising colleagues, or better, to make your consumer react, it is only necessary to confront him with either fundamental or conditioned emotional stimuli." In order to effectively sell a given product, one did not have to make false claims or resort to the use of "yellow copy." To insure the appropriate reaction from the consumer, Watson counseled, "tell him something that will tie up with fear, something that will stir up a mild rage, that will call out an affectionate or love response, or strike at a deep psychological or habit need." These "secret and hidden springs of action" were the "powerful genii of psychology," but behavioral techniques were not to be employed randomly in the hope of hitting upon the right stimulus for the desired response. Watson emphasized the need to establish consumer reactions under laboratory conditions. Using sample populations of consumers as subjects, advertisers must refine their techniques scientifically, Watson told his colleagues, "until you feel sure that when you go out on the firing line with your printed message you can aim accurately and with deadly execution."[34]

For Watson and his associates at the J. Walter Thompson Company, behaviorism seemed to offer the universal key to human motivation. A technique that would enable advertisers to influence and shape mass markets over a wide geographical distribution was considered to be essential for continued industrial expansion. Although Watson admitted that he was troubled by the lack of individuality in the emerging mass society, his qualms did not prevent him from exploiting the situation. In fact, he said, "as an advertising man I rejoice; my bread and butter depend on it." It was the universality of human response that made behaviorism possible and its application to advertising highly desirable. "After all," Watson pointed out, "it is the emotional factor in our lives that touches off and activates our social behavior whether it is buying a cannon, a sword or a plowshare—and love, fear and rage are the same in Italy, Abyssinia and Canada."[35]

The visibility of Watson's brand of psychology within the advertising community reflected a fundamental shift in the conception and development of sales campaigns. Until approximately 1910, the dominant attitude among advertisers was one that considered consumers to be motivated by reason or "common sense." Advertisements were designed to educate or inform the public about the usefulness of a given product. Only a small minority of advertisers argued that efforts should be made to persuade and to create desires for new products. There was general agreement, however, that advertising was a combination of chance and shrewd guesses; advertisers considered the creation of a science of advertising unlikely. Although Walter Dill Scott introduced a text on *The Theory of Advertising* (Boston: Small, Maynard) in 1903, professionals considered it "scientific" only in the sense that it classified the rule-of-thumb procedures that had long been in use among advertisers. Yet Scott argued that the "law of suggestion" could be employed to motivate consumers and, in 1908, his *Psychology of Advertising* (Boston: Small, Maynard) discussed the importance of "emotion" and "sympathy" in influencing the consumer's suggestibility to advertising copy. Scott was representative of a growing tendency to regard advertising not as information for a rational consumer but as a method of persuading a nonrational public based on the scientific application of psychological theories.[36]

After 1910, the accent on persuasion rather than information came to dominance within the advertising industry. In an urban-industrial economy based not on scarcity but on constantly expanding production, competition shifted from an emphasis on competing products to an emphasis on competing desires. Not only did brands of similar products compete for markets, but advertisers vied to persuade consumers of the desirability of automobiles, for example, over the competing desires for electric appliances or vacation trips. Within this context, the use of applied psychology in advertising began to grow and the behavioristic viewpoint offered to provide further refinements in sales techniques.

Behaviorism represented a departure from earlier notions of advertising psychology that emphasized an appeal to distinct desires and hence distinct mental categories. The behavioral approach ignored questions of the rationality or irrationality of mind and emphasized instead the malleability of human behavior. Behaviorism was not simply a psychological theory with vague applications to advertising. It was the science of behavior itself, and its methodology aimed at nothing less than a comprehensive control of human action.[37]

In 1932, Henry C. Link (who later became Secretary of the Psychological Corporation) published *The New Psychology of Selling and Advertising*, which included an introduction by Watson. Link noted that a "revolution" had occurred in the method of distributing goods. The consolidation of manufacturing industries and retail outlets indicated by the growth of chain stores had the effect of eliminating the middleman (the small, independent retail outlet) and had opened up vast markets for the distribution of consumer goods. Advertisers had been concerned with overcoming sales resistance, but Link saw the emergence of an advertising psychology that was concerned with the avoidance of sales resistance altogether. With an integrated system of production and distribution, psychologists could help manufacturers "discover and sell articles to which there will be the least resistance" and help advertisers "crystallize the latest wants of consumers into active demand." In his introduction to Link's book, Watson described the extent to which psychology had become established in advertising. Although academic psychology continued to be relevant to those interested in its application, psychology had moved out of the laboratory and into the marketplace. Market research had become an integral part of advertising campaigns and advertisers had instituted their own laboratory studies to test consumer reactions. The "science" of advertising was the "psychology of selling" and advertising had become scientific in the extent to which it had adopted psychological methods.[38]

Psychologists who had established the Psychological Corporation in the hope of attracting business interest organized a Division of Market and Advertising Research in anticipation of corporate demand. In 1934, the Division of Market and Advertising Research had ranked behind the other divisions in the percentage of the Corporation's total profit. But by the next year it had overtaken the lead from the Testing Division and by 1936 its percentage of profit was almost twice that of test sales.[39] As the depressed economy began to approach 1929 levels of prosperity, corporate interests began to shift from problems of production to problems of marketing and distribution. Henry C. Link, who then headed the division, demonstrated that "the *major* problems of selling and advertising demanded consumer studies *in the marketplace. . . .*" Each purchase was seen as "a sample of *buying behavior* of psychological, social and economic significance." The issues addressed by Link were considered by corporation officials to "go to the very heart of most psychological theory and require the best that psychologists have to offer in the way of techniques and ingenuity of their attack." The Corporation's viewpoint was graphically made by its Secretary, Paul S. Achilles: "What makes a million cash registers clatter cheerfully, and what would be the consequences if they ceased? To scorn such problems is to play the ostrich in a society whose betterment depends on scientific effort to solve them."[40]

Under Link's direction, the Marketing and Advertising Division developed a series of programs designed to measure consumer trends and public opinion. The "Psychological Sales Barometer" was created to determine the effectiveness of advertising campaigns for specific lines of products. Based on four thousand individual interviews at two-month intervals in forty-seven locations across the country, these reports were issued on a regular basis to those corporations subscribing to the service.[41]

Demographic information was an important part of Watson's strategy as he attempted to translate behavioral methodology into sales techniques in the development of advertising campaigns. The platform that Watson developed for Johnson and Johnson's Baby Powder serves as a good example of his approach. Watson intended his campaign to appeal to young middle-class mothers who were expecting their first child. The campaign was carefully designed for a demographic cross-section that was selected on the basis of class and race. Blacks were immediately eliminated as being "a decidedly questionable market," and in conducting market surveys, the field investigators "did not visit slum districts." Watson clearly intended to draw his market from the young, white, upwardly mobile middle class. In presenting his sales proposal, Watson made it clear that the advertising agency should attempt to sell several ideas about the product rather than merely to publicize the product itself: for example, its "purity" and "cleanliness," the dangers of infection to infants, and the desirability of using baby powder frequently. In this way Watson hoped to stimulate an anxiety or fear response on the part of the young mothers by creating doubts as to their competence in dealing with questions of infant hygiene. Watson reinforced the implications of his message with the use of testimony by medical experts. This served the dual purpose of testifying to the "scientific" standards of the product as well as appropriating authority on infant care and hygiene from the family to "experts." Without the child care resources of the extended family, the mobile nuclear family was asked to rely upon scientific opinion in the care and feeding of the young. Methods of child care that had passed from one generation to another were dismissed as old-fashioned or unscientific. Advertisers were in the vanguard of mobilizing popular opinion in support of the reliance upon expert advice in areas once dominated by folk wisdom or tradition.[42]

In his popular book on child care published in 1928, Watson minimized the value of parental affection in preparing children to take their place in the industrial world. According to Watson, the demands of a mobile society made it "less. . . expedient to bring up a child in accordance with the fixed molds that our parents imposed upon us." He encouraged the development of children "who, almost from birth, [are] relatively independent of the family situation." Children must learn, wrote Watson, that in the commercial and industrial world, "there is no one there to baby us."[43] The modern child would soon learn that real authority lay not in the family but in the marketplace and in its supporting social institutions. Success depended upon internalizing the values of the corporate order and, according to advertisers, upon the ability to maintain a high level of consumption based not upon need but on a desire to emulate the style of living exemplified by mass advertising.

It was the promotion of style rather than substance that Watson emphasized in the marketing of products. In the case of automobiles, Watson reasoned that since all models were mechanically similar and served the same function, the basis for sales should be a constantly changing design and style that appeared to the wish fulfillment of the consumer.[44] The introduction of style into product design created a superficial impression of novelty that rendered products unfashionable or obsolete before the end of their serviceable life. In the mid-1930s the Research Director of General Motors stated the case clearly: "The whole object of research is to keep everyone reasonably dissatisfied with what he has in order to keep the factory busy in making new things."[45]

Watson emphasized that advertisers must always keep in mind that they were selling "more than a product." There were "idea[s] to sell—prestige to sell—economy to sell—quality to sell, etc. It is never so much as dry, solid or liquid matter."[46] Thus, many of Watson's newspaper and radio campaigns were designed to sell products indirectly, if not covertly. This was accomplished by the use of what seemed to be informative news articles and radio broadcasts which were actually intended to disseminate information that related directly to a line of products. In one newspaper article, Watson discussed the beneficial effects of coffee as a stimulant that increased mental "efficiency."[47] In another case, a radio broadcast sponsored by Pebeco toothpaste featured Watson in a seemingly scientific discussion of salivary glands and their function in digesting food. Watson did not fail to stress the importance of brushing the teeth to stimulate gland activity. But listeners who responded to an offer of additional information received a circular and samples of the sponsor's product.[48] In both instances, Watson's scientific credentials were emphasized to give weight and authority to his message.

Another technique employed by Watson to lend authority to sales campaigns was the use of testimonial advertising. Testimonials had long been used by manufacturers of patent medicines but were generally held in low esteem by most advertisers. But by the 1920s, the successful use of testimonials called for a re-evaluation by the industry. The J. Walter Thompson agency was the leader in the large-scale use of testimonial advertising. Under Watson's direction, the services of such notables as Queen Marie of Rumania and Mrs. Marshall Field were enlisted to endorse the cosmetic qualities of Pond's Cold Cream.[49] Some advertisers protested that the use of paid testimonials endangered the reputation of the industry. But J. Walter Thompson's President, Stanley Resor, defended the practice. Testimonials were directed not to a select audience, he explained, but to the mass market. The target of the advertiser was the tabloid reader who lived vicariously through the public personalities that were manufactured specifically for the reader's consumption. "Hero worship" he argued, was a "social fact." According to Resor, "people are eternally searching for authority. . . ." This "sense of inferiority" on the part of "the masses" was a fact that "no successful editor dares to ignore. . . ."[50]

Watson's successful use of the direct testimonial linked the product with an appeal to authority or a desire for emulation; but he also used what he described as "indirect testimonials." This method employed symbols to stimulate those responses of fear, rage, and love which Watson held to be the fundamental elements of all emotional reactions. Watson had found that brand appeal depended on factors other than usefulness or product reliability. Mass production rendered many competing products indistinguishable in quality and function. In one carefully controlled experiment funded by the Thompson agency, Watson found that smokers with definite brand preferences could not distinguish one brand of cigarettes from another.[51] This reinforced Watson's conviction that the marketing of goods depended not upon an appeal to reason but upon the stimulation of desire, or as a contemporary critic of Watson's put it, upon "the fixation of systematized illusions in the minds of the public necessary to the use and wont of an acquisitive society."[52]

An example of Watson's use of the "indirect testimonial" is an ad campaign that he developed for Pebeco toothpaste. Watson presented the image of a seductively dressed young woman smoking a cigarette. The ad encouraged women to smoke as long as Pebeco toothpaste was used regularly. Smoking was depicted as an act of independence and assertiveness for women; the ad encouraged the young to flout the older generation's social restrictions. Poise, attractiveness, and self-fulfillment were equated with the consumption of products. The ad associated cigarettes with sexuality and seduction and raised fears that attractiveness might be diminished by the effects of smoking on the breath and teeth. Toothpaste was promoted not as a contribution to health and hygiene but as a means of heightening the sexual attraction to the user. Consumers were buying not merely toothpaste, they were buying sex appeal. In this sense, commodities themselves became eroticized.[53]

Watson reigned as the "chief showpiece" of the Thompson agency. Beyond wrought-iron bars of Spanish grillwork, Watson's lavish executive suite afforded a view of crowds of people far below as they made their way along Lexington Avenue toward the maze of streets in downtown Manhattan. From those heights, the prospects of applied psychology must have appeared bright indeed.[54] "I believe you will be happier in business," he wrote to Robert Yerkes. "I did not think that I would be," he continued, "but now I would not go back for the world. . . ." But Watson continued to consult with his former academic colleagues on advertising research projects and looked to them to provide young Ph.D.'s as recruits in the growing army of market researchers.[55]

In addition to the development of advertising campaigns, Watson sought to expand his own role of applied psychologist within the business community. He contributed to the training of salesmen in his own and in his clients' companies. He also argued that behavioral psychology could be useful as a tool in personnel management.[56] Watson maintained that tests could be devised that would measure the performance of office workers. These tests would serve two purposes. By plotting a curve of office production, employees' work output could be measured and controlled. A method of measuring the productivity of individual employees would also retard the emergence of any group solidarity among office workers that might limit production and management control. Watson argued for a role for psychologists within the management structure itself. Heretofore psychologists had acted chiefly as consultants in the preparation of personnel selection tests. For Watson, these tests were useful only as a rough screening device. As a behaviorist, Watson believed it possible to devise managerial techniques that would produce efficient, well-controlled labor from a random selection of workers. A psychologist on the staff of a business organization could standardize the production of office work and assign it to employees in units so that work efficiency could be measured. In words reminiscent of efficiency engineer Frederick W. Taylor, Watson argued for the extension of scientific management from the shop floor to the office. "[T]he main problem to be solved in the office," Watson wrote, "is the problem which has already been solved in the factory, or is in the process of being solved there. It is the problem of getting units of work comparable with the piece work of the factory."[57] Watson was not content with the control of work flow and office routine but insisted that successful management depended on the ability to motivate broad patterns of behavior. Traits considered essential for the successful bureaucrat were neatness, loyalty, subordination, a passive temperament, and compatibility with co-workers.[58] The psychologist's task was to enable management to create "the organizational man" who identified his wishes with those of the bureaucratic hierarchy and who subordinated his life goals to the demands of the corporate order.

During the 1920s and 1930s Watson increasingly turned his efforts toward spreading the behaviorist faith to a mass audience. Through an enormous output of books, magazine articles, and radio broadcasts he was able to establish himself as the public spokesman for the profession of psychology and as an expert on subjects ranging from child rearing to economics. In effect, Watson became the first "pop" psychologist to the rapidly expanding middle class, assuming the role once held by the minister in a more rurally based society. In this sense, his writings were designed not only to inform, but to persuade. His vision of a behavioristic future implied a faith in the blessings of a technocratic society with its values of order and efficiency.[59]

Not long after Watson's promotion to Vice-President in the Thompson agency, culture critic Stuart Chase wrote in a review of Watson's *Behaviorism* that ". . . one stands for an instant blinded with great hope."[60] Watson's promise of a psychology of use was not mere hucksterism but part of the progressive dream. It spoke to an era when science was to become a new religion and the scientific method was to create a binding faith for its practitioners.[61]

Behaviorism was, above all, a radical environmentalism, a faith in the ability to make and shape one's own world, free from the authority of tradition and the dead hand of the past. A "nation of villagers" had found themselves in a society that had rapidly become urbanized and industrialized. Rapid change was the order of the day and the happiness or misery of humankind depended on its willingness to bring the process of change under control. But Watson's insistence that the nature of human behavior was reducible to a set of unambiguous facts appealed to both reformers and reactionaries. If behaviorism represented the freedom to remake the individual, it also posed the possibility of directing human activity into predetermined channels. It was the latter aspect of behaviorism that Watson chose to emphasize. For, as envisioned by Watson, behaviorism was to serve the authority of those who desired a stable and predictable social order.

NOTES

1. E. G. Boring to John B. Watson, 20 January 1925, E. G. Boring Papers, Harvard University Archives, Cambridge, Massachusetts. Cited hereafter as Boring Papers. See also: E. B. Titchener to Watson, 17 January 1925, E. B. Titchener Papers, Cornell University Archives, Ithaca, New York; and Robert M. Yerkes to Watson, 23 January 1925, Robert M. Yerkes Papers, Yale University Medical Library, New Haven, Connecticut. Cited hereafter as Yerkes Papers.
2. John B. Watson, "Psychology as the Behaviorist Views It," *Psychological Review* 20 (1913): 158.
3. For a study of the growth of new professions and social mobility in the nineteenth century, see Burton Bledstein, *The Culture of Professionalism: The Middle Class and the Development of Higher Education in America* (New York: Norton, 1976). A study of the growth of psychology as a profession after 1920 can be found in Donald S. Napoli, *The Architects of Adjustment: The History of the Psychological Profession in the United States* (Port Washington, N.Y.: Kennikat, 1980). Napoli argues that it was their contribution to World War II that finally secured for applied psychologists the professional recognition for which they had been striving.
4. Watson, "Psychology as the Behaviorist Views It," pp. 168–169.
5. Three studies of Watson and behaviorism offer valuable insights into the social and intellectual context of the development of psychology. A study of the advent of behaviorism in light of Thomas Kuhn's theory of scientific revolutions can be found in John C. Burnham, "On the Origins of Behaviorism," *Journal of the History of the Behavioral Sciences* 4 (1968): 143–151. The most thoughtful and complete study to date of the

institutional and professional foundations of behaviorism is John M. O'Donnell, "The Origins of Behaviorism: American Psychology, 1870–1920" (Ph.D. diss., University of Pennsylvania, 1979). A useful analysis of Watson's published writings and their effect on that of his contemporaries is Lucille T. Birnhaum, "Behaviorism: John Broadus Watson and American Social Thought, 1913–1933" (Ph.D. diss., University of California, Berkeley, 1964). In addition, David Cohen's *John B. Watson, The Founder of Behaviorism: A Biography* (London: Routledge and Kegan Paul, 1979) should be noted. However, it suffers from serious flaws of historical inaccuracy and journalistic hyperbole.

6. The argument has been made that, despite its sensational impact, few psychologists were willing to accept Watsonian behaviorism wholeheartedly. (See Franz Samelson, "The Struggle for Scientific Authority: The Reception of Watson's Behaviorism, 1913–1920," *Journal of the History of the Behavioral Sciences* 17 [1981]: 399–425). Many contemporaries, however, were still able to call themselves "behaviorists" without embracing all of Watson's claims. Bertrand Russell, for instance, argued that behaviorism was first of all "a method in psychology and only derivatively a psychological theory." He found it possible to accept the former without accepting the latter. See Bertrand Russell, "An Essay on Behaviorism: A Defense of the Theory that Psychologists Should Observe Impulses Rather than Speculate Upon the Unconscious," *Vanity Fair* 21 (1923): 47, 96, 98. For Russell, Watson's rejection of introspection was essentially a rejection of "unobservables" and was characteristic of the growing positivist trend within the physical sciences. See also Brian D. MacKenzie, *Behaviorism and the Limits of Scientific Method* (London: Routledge and Kegan Paul, 1977).

7. John B. Watson, *Psychology from the Standpoint of a Behaviorist* (Philadelphia: Lippincott, 1919), pp. 1–2, 4.

8. Ibid., p. vii.

9. A suggestive essay on the relation of behaviorism to urban growth is David Bakan, "Behaviorism and American Urbanization," *Journal of the History of the Behavioral Sciences* 2 (1966): 5–28.

10. See Dorothy Ross, *G. Stanley Hall: The Psychologist as Prophet* (Chicago: University of Chicago Press, 1972), pp. 105–107; William James, "Talks to Teachers on Psychology," *Atlantic Monthly* 83 (1899): 155–162; and John Dewey, "Psychology and Social Practice," *Science* 11 (1900): 321–333.

11. John B. Watson, "Practical and Theoretical Problems in Instinct and Habit," in Herbert Spencer Jennings et al. *Suggestions of Modern Science Concerning Education* (New York: Macmillan, 1917), pp. 53–55. Also participating in the symposium were biologist Herbert Spencer Jennings, sociologist William I. Thomas, and psychiatrist Adolf Meyer.

12. Ibid., pp. 77–82.

13. Watson to Yerkes, 31 March 1916; 1 April 1916, Yerkes Papers.

14. Watson to Jacob H. Hollander, 21 March 1917; Hollander to Watson, 22 March 1917; Hollander to Watson, 18 April 1917, John B. Watson Correspondence, Special Collections, Milton S. Eisenhower Library, Johns Hopkins University, Baltimore, Maryland.

15. A complete treatment of the role of psychologists in World War I is found in Thomas Camfield, "Psychologists at War: The History of American Psychology and the First World War" (Ph.D. diss., University of Texas, Austin, 1969). A history of the work of Scott's Committee on the Classification of Personnel in the Army can be found in Leonard W. Ferguson, *The Heritage of Industrial Psychology* (Hartford, Conn.: Finlay, 1962). Studies of intelligence testing in the Army include Daniel J. Kevles, "Testing the Army's Intelligence: Psychologists and the Military in World War I," *Journal of American History* 55 (1968): 565–581; as well as Franz Samelson, "World War I Intelligence Testing and the Development of Psychology," *Journal of the History of the Behavioral Sciences* 13 (1977): 274–282.

16. Information concerning the Scott Company can be found in Leonard W. Ferguson, "Industrial Psychology and Labor," in *Walter Van Dyke Bingham Memorial Program,* ed. Von Haller Gilmer (Pittsburgh: Carnegie Institute of Technology, 1962), pp. 15–21. See also Loren Baritz, *The Servants of Power: A History of the Use of Social Science in American Industry* (New York:

Wiley, 1960), pp. 51–54; and David F. Noble, *America by Design: Science, Technology and the Rise of Corporate Capitalism* (New York: Knopf, 1977), pp. 295–302.

17. Michael M. Sokal, "The Origins of the Psychological Corporation," *Journal of the History of the Behavioral Sciences* 17 (1981): 54–67.

18. Yerkes to Cattell, 29 March 1921, James McKeen Cattell Papers, Manuscript Division, Library of Congress, Washington, D.C. Cited hereafter as Cattell Papers.

19. Watson to Frank J. Goodnow, 30 March 1920; Goodnow to Watson, 31 March 1920, The Ferdinand Hamburger, Jr. Archives of the Johns Hopkins University, Office of the President, Series #115 (Department of Psychology). Cited hereafter as Hamburger Archives. Events that led to Watson's dismissal began soon after the above exchange with President Goodnow; presumably, Watson did not follow through with plans he had worked out with Magruder.

20. Watson to Bertrand Russell, 21 February 1919, Bertrand Russell Papers, Mills Memorial Library, McMaster University, Hamilton, Ontario, Canada. Cited hereafter as Russell Papers. Enclosed with this letter is a six-page typescript of topics discussed by Watson in one of his staff meetings with Adolf Meyer.

21. Goodnow to Watson, 18 March 1920, Hamburger Archives.

22. It is ironic that in the midst of conducting the classic experiment in conditioning and controlling emotional responses (John B. Watson and Rosalie Rayner, "Conditioned Emotional Reactions," *Journal of Experimental Psychology* 3 [1920]: 1–14), the behaviorist became romantically involved with his graduate student and coworker in the investigation, Rosalie Rayner. It was characteristic of Watson to be at once capable of sustained, concentrated, controlled behavior and impulsive, spontaneous outbursts of emotion. But, at least in this case, his defiance of community mores as well as the influence of the powerful Rayner family had disastrous consequences for Watson. An account of the circumstances surrounding Watson's dismissal can be found in Kerry W. Buckley, "Behaviorism and the Professionalization of American Psychology: A Study of John Broadus Watson, 1878–1958" (Ph.D. diss., University of Massachusetts, Amherst, 1982).

23. Watson to Meyer, 13 August 1920, Adolf Meyer Papers, John Broadus Watson Correspondence Series I, Unit 3974, Alan Mason Chesney Medical Archives, Johns Hopkins University, Baltimore, Maryland. Cited hereafter as Meyer Papers.

24. John B. Watson in *The History of Psychology in Autobiography,* vol. 3, ed. Carl Murchison (Worcester, Mass.: Clark University Press, 1936), p. 279. Thomas had been approached earlier by the Thompson agency concerning a study of "the psychology of appeal." Although he was willing to put Watson in contact with the agency, he had serious misgivings about advertising in general. See William I. Thomas to Ethel Sturges Dummer, 3 May 1920, Ethel Sturges Dummer Papers, Schlesinger Library, Radcliffe College, Cambridge, Massachusetts. For information concerning Thomas's dismissal from the University of Chicago, see Morris Janowitz's introduction to William I. Thomas, *On Social Organization and Social Personality* (Chicago: University of Chicago Press, 1966), pp. xiv–xv.

25. Stuart Ewen, *Captains of Consciousness: Advertising and the Social Roots of the Consumer Culture* (New York: McGraw-Hill, 1977), pp. 32–33. For a history of psychology in advertising prior to 1920, see David P. Kuna, "The Psychology of Advertising, 1896–1916" (Ph.D. diss., University of New Hampshire, 1976). See also Otis Pease, *The Responsibilities of American Advertising: Private Control and Public Influence, 1920–1940* (New Haven: Yale University Press, 1958); and A. Michal McMahon, "An American Courtship: Psychologists and Advertising Theory in the Progressive Era," *American Studies* 13 (1972): 5–18.

26. Association of National Advertisers, Inc., Committee on Research to Bingham, 24 October 1921, Walter Van Dyke Bingham Papers, Hunt Library, Carnegie-Mellon University, Pittsburgh, Pennsylvania. Cited hereafter as Bingham Papers.

27. Watson to Mildred V. Bennett, 20 January 1921, John B. Watson file, J. Walter Thompson Company Archives, New York. Cited hereafter as Thompson Archives.

28. Watson to Bingham, 16 April 1921, Bingham Papers.

29. Watson to Russell, 11 October 1921, Russell Papers.
30. Watson, in *Autobiography,* p. 280.
31. Watson to Meyer, 9 April 1921, Meyer Papers.
32. John B. Watson, "The Ideal Executive," speech given to Macy's graduating class of young executives, 20 April 1922, typescript contained in the John Broadus Watson Papers, Manuscript Division, Library of Congress, Washington, D.C. Cited hereafter as Watson Papers.
33. John B. Watson, "Influencing the Mind of Another," speech delivered to the Montreal Advertising Club, 26 September 1935, and reprinted by the J. Walter Thompson Company. Copy contained in Watson Papers.
34. John B. Watson, "Dissecting the Consumer: An Application of Psychology to Advertising," undated typescript, pp. 14, 19, Watson Papers.
35. Watson, "Influencing the Mind of Another."
36. Merle Curti, "The Changing Concept of 'Human Nature' in the Literature of American Advertising," *Business History Review* 41 (1967): 337–345; David P. Kuna, "The Concept of Suggestion in the Early History of Advertising Psychology," *Journal of the History of Behavioral Sciences* 12 (1976): 350–351.
37. Curti, "The Changing Concept of 'Human Nature,' " pp. 345–353. In an interview three years before his death, Watson recalled to John C. Burnham that it was not until the 1940s that the advertising industry as a whole became receptive to the suggestions of psychologists (Pease, *Responsibilities,* p. 171n.). Otis Pease, however, set the widespread acceptance of psychology by advertising as beginning with the Depression (Pease, *Responsibilities,* p. 170), while Merle Curti maintained that the estimation of psychology's effectiveness grew among advertisers during the 1920s and was established as the dominant viewpoint by 1930 (Curti, "The Changing Concept of 'Human Nature'," p. 353). The J. Walter Thompson Company was certainly an industry leader in employing Watson in 1920. Watson's high visibility and success with that firm, no doubt, was a significant factor in convincing other advertisers to follow Thompson's example.
38. Henry C. Link, *The New Psychology of Selling and Advertising* (New York: Macmillan, 1932), pp. vii–xiii.
39. "Report of the Treasurer of the Psychological Corporation for the Year 1936," Cattell Papers.
40. Paul S. Achilles, "The Role of the Psychological Corporation in Applied Psychology," *American Journal of Psychology* 50 (1937): 243.
41. Henry C. Link, "A New Method for Testing Advertising and a Psychological Sales Barometer," *Journal of Applied Psychology* 18 (1934): 1–26.
42. John B. Watson, "What, To Whom, When, Where, How are We Selling?" typescript of a speech delivered to the J. Walter Thompson Company class in advertising, 14 October 1924, Thompson Archives.
43. John B. Watson and Rosalie Rayner Watson, *Psychological Care of Infant and Child* (New York: Norton, 1928), pp. 186, 77.
44. "Dr. John B. Watson Favors Testimonial Advertising," *The American Press* (November, 1928), p. 14, newspaper clipping contained in Watson Papers.
45. James Rorty, *Our Master's Voice: Advertising* (New York: John Day, 1934), p. 233.
46. John B. Watson, "Newspapers and How to Advertise in Them," undated typescript, Watson Papers.
47. "Believes Coffee Only Beneficial Stimulant," Balitmore *Sun,* 3 May 1927.
48. John B. Watson, "Advertising by Radio," *J. Walter Thompson Company News Bulletin* no. 98 (1923): 11–16.
49. "Testimonial Advertising."
50. Pease, *Responsibilities,* pp. 51–56.
51. John B. Watson, "What Cigarettes Are You Smoking and Why?" *J. Walter Thompson Company News Bulletin* no. 88 (1922): 1–15. This was the beginning of the now familiar "blindfold test" in which a client's product is pitted against brand "X." See Watson's obituary in *The Marketing and Social Research Newsletter of the Psychological Corporation* (Summer, 1959): 3–4.
52. Rorty, *Our Master's Voice,* p. 242.
53. "Testimonial Advertising." See also Howard Gadlin, "Private Lives and Public Order: A Critical View of the History of Intimate Relations in the U.S.," *The Massachusetts Review* 17 (1976), p. 324.
54. Kenneth Macgowan, "The Adventure of the Behaviorist," *The New Yorker* (6 October 1928), p. 30.

55. Watson to Yerkes, 2 May 1923, Yerkes Papers. See also Watson to Boring, 28 September 1936 and 24 November 1937; Boring to Watson, 30 September 1936, 5 October 1936, and 27 November 1937, Boring Papers.

56. John B. Watson, "Behaviorist Psychology Applied to Selling," *The Red Barrel* 23 (1934): 20–21.

57. John B. Watson, "The Possibilities and Limitations of Psychology in the Office" (unpublished typescript of an address given before the National Association of Managers, Washington, D.C., 18 May 1922), pp. 9–12. Thompson Archives.

58. Watson, "The Ideal Executive."

59. Lucille T. Birnbaum, "Behaviorism in the 1920s," *American Quarterly* 7 (1955): 15–30.

60. Stuart Chase, review of *Behaviorism* by John B. Watson, New York *Herald Tribune,* 21 June 1925, p. 5. Ironically, Chase later became an outspoken critic of advertising and a leading consumer advocate. See Pease, *Responsibilities,* pp. 98–99.

61. For a discussion of social control as a factor linking the growth of psychology and the progressive movement, see John C. Burnham, "Psychiatry, Psychology and the Progressive Movement," *American Quarterly* 12 (1960): 457–465.

CHAPTER **12**

NEOBEHAVIORISM

Recall Watson's 1913 claim from the previous chapter that the theoretical goal of psychology is the prediction and control of behavior. That goal would be the focus of American psychology during the period from 1930 through 1960, a period that marked the dominance of a view usually labeled *neobehaviorism.* Although Watson had lost his academic position in 1920, he continued to be the principal spokesperson for behaviorism during the 1920s. He certainly was the chief promoter of behavioral psychology with the general public, largely through his many popular writings. Within the psychology of the 1920s, much of conceptual, and even methodological, behaviorism was accepted as the wave of the future. But there were disciples whose displeasure with Watson's radical views led them to propose alternative behavioral psychologies. These psychologies were characterized by an emphasis on theory, operational definitions, animal studies, and the processes underlying learning.

In addition to Watsonian behaviorism, at least four other sources of influence were important to the development of neobehaviorism. One source was a philosophical view known as *logical positivism,* a view of science largely associated with philosophers in Vienna around the time of World War I (see Smith, 1986). As positivists, their emphasis was on knowledge that is objectively determined, but they went beyond the positivism of Auguste Comte and Ernst Mach in arguing for the inclusion of theoretical concepts grounded in observations. They were adamant in their view of the scientific method as the one proper road to knowledge, eschewing other approaches such as philosophy, poetry, and religion.

> Science had proven to be humankind's most powerful means of understanding reality, of producing knowledge, so that the task of epistemology should be to explicate and formalize the scientific method, making it available to new disciplines and improving its practice among working scientists. Thus, the logical positivists purported to provide a formal recipe for doing science, offering exactly what psychologists thought they needed. (Leahey, 1992, p. 323).

For the psychologists of the 1920s and 1930s, this view of science as the one valid route to knowledge strengthened their resolve to create a true science of psychology.

Related to logical positivism was the second influence, the concept of *operationism,* the belief that theoretical constructs had reality only with regard to the operations used to observe or measure those constructs. Popularized by a Harvard physicist, Percy Bridgman (1882–1961), and promoted in psychology by the Harvard psychologist S. S. Stevens (1906–1973), operationism became one of the watchwords of American psychology in the 1930s. Definitions of psychological constructs had to be operational definitions, that is, definitions that specified the objective measures underlying those constructs. Thus, hunger was a scientific construct only if it could be specified in objective measures such as hours of food deprivation or the percentage of body weight reduction. If a construct could not be defined operationally, then it was not a scientific construct and should be discarded.

A third influence was the focus on animal studies, a legacy of functionalism, which was also emphasized in the work of Watson, Thorndike, Pavlov, and others. Use of animal subjects, like the laboratory rat, afforded a number of benefits. First, greater precision could be obtained in experiments because it was possible to control the relevant variables in an animal's life experience better. Second, it was believed that processes, such as perception and learning, were less complex in animals than in humans and that studying a conceptually simpler system could give valuable insights into the more complex human systems.

A fourth influence, also a bequest from functionalism, was an emphasis on learning and a belief that adaptation to the environment was the result of learning. Learning capacity was seen as a sign of adjustive capability, which in turn would become psychology's definition of *intelligence,* that is, the ability to adapt to the environment. Animal learning was the topic of principal interest for the neobehaviorists, who viewed these studies as laying the groundwork for the important questions concerning how humans learn (see Jenkins, 1979).

Watson had called for a scientific psychology capable of prediction and control of behavior. The scientific recipe of the logical positivists, the emphasis on operational definitions, and the advantages of animal subjects promised the achievement of Watson's hope for psychology. The new generation of behaviorists pursued Watson's goal, constructing the grand theories of learning that characterized American psychology in the 1930s and 1940s. Although there are a number of psychologists who made contributions as neobehaviorists, this chapter will focus on the work of three whose influence has been especially important for contemporary psychology: Edward C. Tolman, Clark L. Hull, and B. F. Skinner.

These three psychologists produced some of their most important work in the 1930s, yet their periods of maximum influence have differed. In the 1930s, the theoretical debates on learning surrounded the competing views of Tolman and Hull, with Skinner's work being largely ignored. By the 1940s, Hull's ideas had gained the upper hand, and his theories dominated research in the 1940s and 1950s. By the late 1960s, Hullian learning theory had been supplanted by the operant psychology of Skinner, partly because of the greater applicability of Skinner's ideas to education and modification of problem behavior. The 1970s, with the growing strength of the cognitive revolution, brought new attention to the purposive behaviorism of Tolman.

Edward C. Tolman (1886–1959) published his most important book in 1932, entitled *Purposive Behavior in Animals and Men.* For Tolman, behavior is, in a word, *purposive.* And the purposiveness of behavior is determined by cognitions. How does a behaviorist justify such obviously mentalistic terms?

> Behavior as behavior, that is, as molar, *is* purposive and *is* cognitive. . . . it must nonetheless be emphasized that purposes and cognitions which are thus immediately, immanently, in behavior are wholly objective as to definition. They are defined by characters and relationships which we observe out there in the behavior. (Tolman, 1932, p. 5)

Tolman argued that with experience, an organism builds up expectancies about the environment, and these expectancies are one of the determinants of responding. In essence, according to Tolman, organisms learn what leads to what. He objected to the molecular approach of Watson, who used a limited stimulus–response framework. Tolman called for a model that recognized the existence of intervening variables—processes within the organism that intervened between stimuli and responses. Cognitions were examples of those intervening variables and were scientifically respectable so long as they could be tied to observable referents.

Tolman also objected to Thorndike's notion of trial-and-error learning and to the idea that reinforcement was an important determinant of learning, a view championed by his theoretical rival Hull. Influenced by the Gestalt psychologists (see Chapter 14) and a group of philosopher-psychologists known as the *neorealists,* Tolman proposed that learning occurred because of the accumulation of *sign-Gestalts,* which he viewed as cognitive representations of what leads to what. With experience, these sign-Gestalts were combined into a more complex cognitive structure, a kind of *cognitive map* of the organism's environment (more about that later).

Clark L. Hull (1884–1952) published much of his theoretical work in a series of articles in the *Psychological Review* in the 1930s (see Amsel & Rashotte, 1984). The integration and extension of that work appeared in his 1943 book, *Principles of Behavior*. Throughout much of the 1930s and 1940s, Hull and Tolman debated each other, either in the printed literature or at the annual meetings of the American Psychological Association.

Hull made reinforcement his central concept in accounting for learning. His theory contained several intervening variables, but it was largely a strict stimulus–response psychology, often viewed as more rigorous than Watson's behaviorism. Evidence of that rigor is provided in the complex mathematico-deductive theory of behavior so fully described in his 1943 book. Using a number of postulates and corollaries, stated in logical deductive form, Hull created a theory of behavior that has no peer in the history of psychology, including the psychology of the present. Melvin Marx and W. A. Cronan-Hillix (1987) have described it as follows: "Hull deliberately laid out the system as explicitly as he could in order to expedite empirical checking. This explicitness was probably the most important feature of his systematic endeavor" (p. 317).

The empirical checking began almost immediately, as literally thousands of master's and doctoral students tested some prediction of Hull's grand theory, making him the most frequently cited psychologist in the research of the 1950s. Unlike Tolman, whose theory of learning was vague on several critical issues (a fact admitted by Tolman), Hull made painstaking efforts to spell out his theoretical concepts in precise (often mathematical) detail. Some historians have argued that the domination of Hull's ideas was not owing to their appeal but that they lent themselves so readily to empirical testing.

While Tolman and Hull battled over whether learning involved cognitive maps or stimulus–response associations, the third principal neobehaviorist was beginning his important work. B. F. Skinner (1904–1990) was a radical behaviorist, much in the mold of Watson in his total opposition to mentalism in psychology. Although his early interests were in literature and a career as a writer, he soon abandoned those interests for a devotion to science, which, the reader will remember, the logical positivists had proclaimed was the only valid road to knowledge.

There was no place for intervening variables in Skinner's system of psychology. The inner world of the organism was off limits to the scientist, a view that caused his psychology to be labeled *the psychology of the empty organism.* Skinner saw no need for explanations of behavior that appealed to inner events. Behavior was the result of *consequences,* events that followed particular responses. Psychologists would achieve Watson's goal of prediction and control once they could understand the relationships between responses and the stimulus events that preceded and followed those responses. Environmental events (consequences) alter the probabilities of responses, with some behaviors made more probable and other less probable. Unlike Thorndike in his statement of the law of effect, Skinner made no references to internal states of affairs (satisfaction or annoyance) in his definition of reinforcement. These ideas were spelled out rather clearly in his first book, *The Behavior of Organisms* (1938), which defined the new field of operant conditioning as a model of animal and human learning.

Many of the psychologists of the 1930s and 1940s did not know what to make of Skinner or his work. He criticized the value of theory in a time when theory construction was revered; he tolerated no references to internal states, even in terms of objective behavioral referents; he argued against the necessity of large samples in research and elaborate statistical treatments of data and offered instead studies involving one or two subjects whose data were presented in the form of response rate curves. In 1948, ten years after its publication, his book had sold only approximately five hundred copies, whereas Hull's 1943 book had sold nearly five thousand copies in only five years. All of that would change in the 1960s with the application of Skinner's work to education and clinical psychology.

Today Hull's learning theory is mostly of historical interest. Whereas citations to his work once dominated American psychology, his ideas get little attention today. On the other hand, Skinner's operant psychology continues to have a strong influence on contemporary psychology despite the growth of cognitive psychology, and that growth has, of course, ensured the currency of Tolman's ideas.

THE READINGS

The first selection is from Tolman. It is not taken from his famous 1932 book but is instead from what historians would argue was his most important article, "Cognitive Maps in Rats and Men" (1948). It is an excellent description of years of work in his Berkeley laboratory and of his disagreements with Hull. It also illustrates some of Tolman's social activism as he sought to apply his rat studies to improvement of the social fabric of the world.

The second selection is by Nancy K. Innis, a historian of psychology at the University of Western Ontario, who is working on a biography of Tolman. In this article, Innis looks at the pioneering work of Tolman, and his student Robert Tryon, in a field that would today be labeled behavior genetics. Tolman began this work in the early 1920s, testing rats in mazes for differences in learning ability, and then, via a selective breeding program, further differentiating strains of rats that were "maze bright" and "maze dull." This selection describes this significant research program that sought to discover the role of inheritance in learning abilities.

The third selection is an excerpt from Hull's 1943 book, *Principles of Behavior*. The very nature of that book as an elaborate and heavily interconnected theory makes it difficult to extract a section that is easily understood in isolation. The section selected is from the end of the book and deals with learning and the problems of reinforcement.

The fourth selection is an excerpt from the opening chapter of Skinner's 1938 book, a book that Tolman had predicted would ". . . always have a very important place in the history of psychology" (Thompson, 1988, p. 397). And, indeed it has. In a retrospective review of Skinner's book, written on the fiftieth anniversary of its publication, Travis Thompson (1988) wrote, "Chapter 1 . . . is one of the most masterfully written pieces in psychology. . . ." (p. 398). The selection from Skinner's opening chapter focuses principally on the differences between classical and operant conditioning, or what Skinner called Type S and Type R conditioning. In this excerpt, he explains that he intends to shift the focus on behavior in psychology from behaviors that are elicited (for example, reflexes) to behaviors that are emitted. In doing that, he shifted attention from the antecedents of behavior to an understanding of the consequences of behavior and how manipulations of those consequences could be used to control and predict behavior. In a few short years, Skinner began to understand how his manipulations of consequences could lead to a powerful behavioral technology.

The last of the selections is by Indiana University historian of science, James H. Capshew, whose work includes an interest in the history of technology. In this article, Capshew tells the fascinating story of Skinner's involvement in Project Pigeon, an attempt to develop a missile guidance system using pigeons to direct a World War II missile toward its target. There are many players in this story, including engineers, military brass, researchers from General Mills, and even a physicist named Richard Tolman (the brother of Edward Tolman). This is the tale of an ill-fated project that illustrates creativity, genius, simplicity, comedy, and most of all, the power of Skinner's behavioral technology.

REFERENCES

Amsel, A., & Rashotte, M. E. (1984). *Mechanisms of adaptive behavior: Clark L. Hull's theoretical papers with commentary*. New York: Columbia University Press.

Hull, C. L. (1943). *Principles of behavior*. New York: Appleton-Century-Crofts.

Jenkins, H. M. (1979). Animal learning and behavior theory. In E. Hearst (Ed.), *The first century of experimental psychology*. Hillsdale, NJ: Lawrence Erlbaum, pp. 177–228.

Leahey, T. H. (1992). *A history of psychology: Main currents in psychological thought* (3rd ed.). Englewood Cliffs, N.J.: Prentice-Hall.

Marx, M., & Cronan-Hillix, W. A. (1987). *Systems and theories in psychology* (4th ed.). New York: McGraw-Hill.

Skinner, B. F. (1938). *The behavior of organisms*. New York: Appleton-Century-Crofts.

Smith, L. D. (1986). *Behaviorism and logical positivism:A reassessment of the alliance*. Stanford, CA: Stanford University Press.

Thompson, T. (1988). Benedictus behavior analysis: B. F. Skinner's magnum opus at fifty. *Contemporary Psychology, 33,* 397–402.

Tolman, E. C. (1932). *Purposive behavior in animals and men*. New York: Appleton.

Tolman, E. C. (1948). Cognitive maps in rats and men. *Psychological Review, 55,* 189–208.

Cognitive Maps in Rats and Men

Edward C. Tolman

I shall devote the body of this paper to a description of experiments with rats. But I shall also attempt in a few words at the close to indicate the significance of these findings on rats for the clinical behavior of men. Most of the rat investigations, which I shall report, were carried out in the Berkeley laboratory. But I shall also include, occasionally, accounts of the behavior of non-Berkeley rats who obviously have misspent their lives in out-of-State laboratories. Furthermore, in reporting our Berkeley experiments I shall have to omit a very great many. The ones I *shall* talk about were carried out by graduate students (or underpaid research assistants) who, supposedly, got some of their ideas from me. And a few, though a very few, were even carried out by me myself.

Let me begin by presenting diagrams for a couple of typical mazes, an alley maze and an elevated maze. In the typical experiment a hungry rat is put at the entrance of the maze (alley or elevated), and wanders about through the various true path segments and blind alleys until he finally comes to the food box and eats. This is repeated (again in the typical experiment) one trial every 24 hours and the animal tends to make fewer and fewer errors (that is, blind-alley entrances) and to take less and less time between start and goal-box until finally he is entering no blinds at all and running in a very few seconds from start to goal. The results are usually presented in the form of average curves of blind-entrances, or of seconds from start to finish, for groups of rats.

All students agree as to the facts. They disagree, however, on theory and explanation.

(1) First, there is a school of animal psychologists which believes that the maze behavior of rats is a matter of mere simple stimulus-response connections. Learning, according to them, consists in the strengthening of some of these connections and in the weakening of others. According to this 'stimulus-response' school the rat in progressing down the maze is helplessly responding to a succession of external stimuli—sights, sounds, smells, pressures, etc. impinging upon his external sense organs—plus internal stimuli coming from the viscera and from the skeletal muscles. These external and internal stimuli call out the walkings, runnings, turnings, retracings, smellings, rearings, and the like which appear. The rat's central nervous system, according to this view, may be likened to a complicated telephone switchboard. There are the incoming calls from sense-organs and there are the outgoing messages to muscles. Before the learning of a specific maze, the connecting switches (synapses according to the physiologist) are closed in one set of ways and produce the primarily exploratory responses which appear in the early trials. *Learning,* according to this view, consists in the respective strengthening and weakening of various of these connections; those connections which result in the animal's going down the true path become relatively more open to the passage of nervous impulses, whereas those which lead him into the blinds become relatively less open.

It must be noted in addition, however, that this stimulus-response school divides further into two subgroups.

(a) There is a subgroup which holds that the mere mechanics involved in the running of a maze is such that the crucial stimuli from the maze get presented simultaneously with the correct responses more frequently than they do with any of the incorrect responses. Hence, just on a basis of this greater frequency, the neural connections between the crucial stimuli and the correct responses will tend, it is said, to get strengthened at the expense of the incorrect connections.

Adapted from Tolman, E. C. (1948). Cognitive maps in rats and men. *Psychological Review, 55,* 189–208.

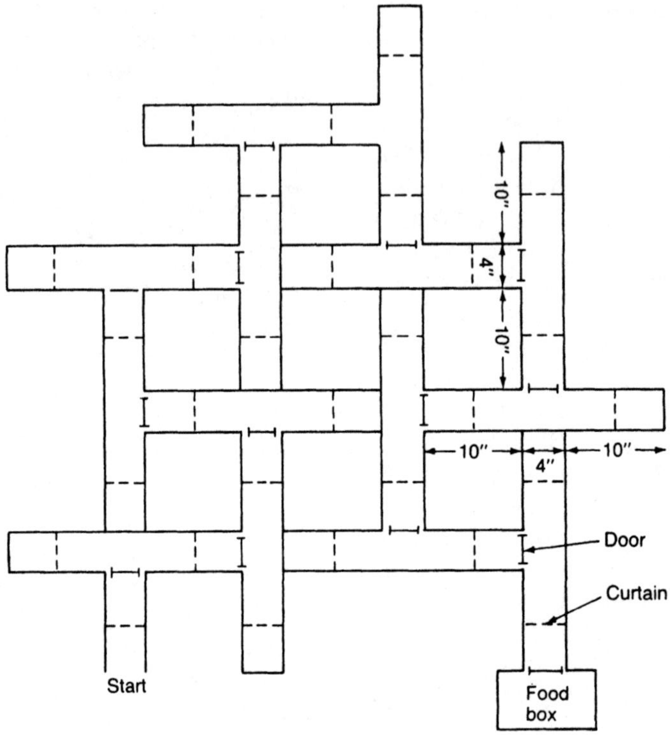

FIGURE 1
Plan of maze: 14-unit T-alley maze.

(b) There is a second subgroup in this stimulus-response school which holds that the reason the appropriate connections get strengthened relatively to the inappropriate ones is, rather, the fact that the responses resulting from the correct connections are followed more closely in time by need-reductions. Thus a hungry rat in a maze tends to get to food and have his hunger reduced *sooner* as a result of the true path responses than as a result of the blind alley responses. And such immediately following need-reductions or, to use another term, such 'positive reinforcements' tend somehow, it is said, to strengthen the connections which have most closely preceded them. Thus it is as if—although this is certainly not the way this subgroup would themselves state it—the satisfaction-receiving part of the rat telephoned back to Central and said to the girl: "Hold that connection; it was good; and see to it that you blankety-blank well use it again the next time these same stimuli come in." These theorists also assume (at least some of them do some of the time) that, if bad results—'annoyances,' 'negative reinforcements'—follow, then this same satisfaction-and-annoyance-receiving part of the rat will telephone back and say, "Break that connection and don't you dare use it next time either."

So much for a brief summary of the two subvarieties of the 'stimulus-response,' or telephone switchboard school.

(2) Let us turn now to the second main school. This group (and I belong to them) may be called the field theorists. We believe that in the course of learning something like a field map of the environment gets established in the rat's brain. We agree with the other school that the rat

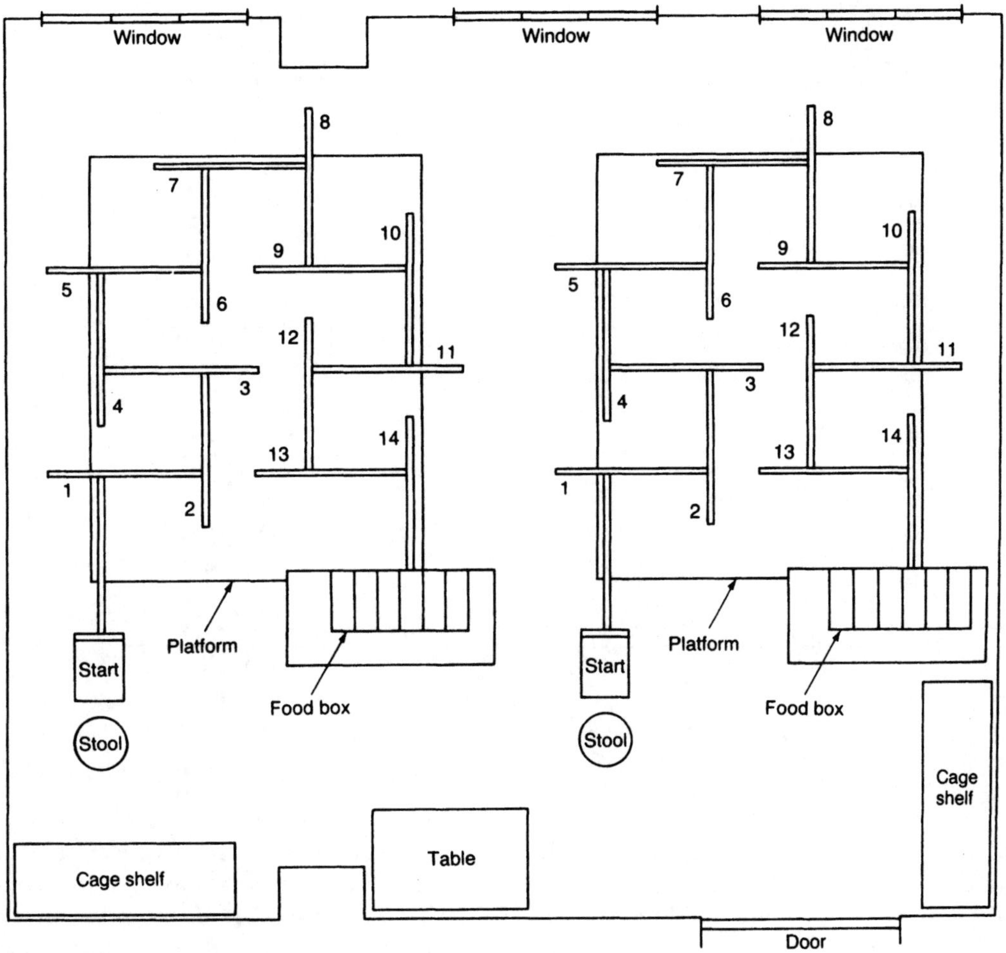

FIGURE 2
14-unit T-elevated mazes.

in running a maze is exposed to stimuli and is finally led as a result of these stimuli to the responses which actually occur. We feel, however, that the intervening brain processes are more complicated, more patterned and more often, pragmatically speaking, more autonomous than do the stimulus-response psychologists. Although we admit that the rat is bombarded by stimuli, we hold that his nervous system is surprisingly selective as to which of these stimuli it will let in at any given time.

Secondly, we assert that the central office itself is far more like a map control room than it is like an old-fashioned telephone exchange. The stimuli, which are allowed in, are not connected by just simple one-to-one switches to the outgoing responses. Rather, the incoming impulses are usually worked over and elaborated in the central control room into a tentative, cognitive-like map of the environment. And it is this tentative map, indicating routes and paths and environmental relationships, which finally de-

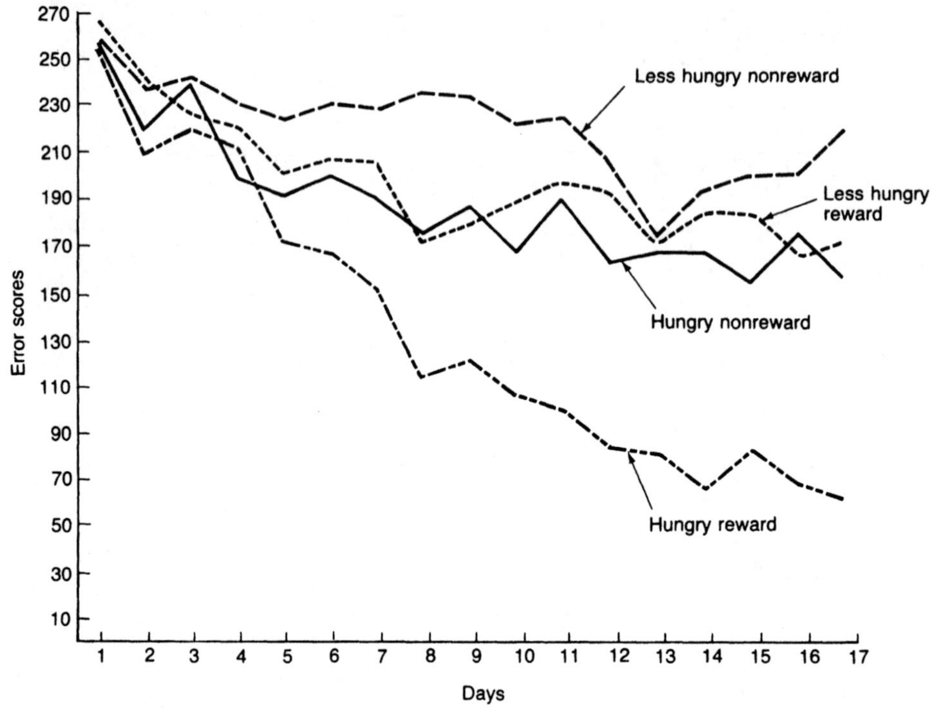

FIGURE 3
Error curves for four groups, 36 rats.

termines what responses, if any, the animal will finally release.

Finally, I, personally, would hold further that it is also important to discover in how far these maps are relatively narrow and strip-like or relatively broad and comprehensive. Both strip-maps and comprehensive-maps may be either correct or incorrect in the sense that they may (or may not), when acted upon, lead successfully to the animal's goal. The differences between such strip maps and such comprehensive maps will appear only when the rat is later presented with some change within the given environment. Then, the narrower and more strip-like the original map, the less will it carry over successfully to the new problem; whereas, the wider and the more comprehensive it was, the more adequately it will serve in the new set-up. In a strip-map the given position of the animal is connected by only a relatively simple and single path to the position of the goal. In a comprehensive-map a wider arc of the environment is represented, so that, if the starting position of the animal be changed or variations in the specific routes be introduced, this wider map will allow the animal still to behave relatively correctly and to choose the appropriate new route.

But let us turn, now, to the actual experiments. The ones, out of many, which I have selected to report are simply ones which seem especially important in reinforcing the theoretical position I have been presenting. This position, I repeat, contains two assumptions: First, that learning consists not in stimulus-response connections but in the building up in the nervous system of sets which function like cognitive maps, and second, that such cognitive maps may be usefully characterized as varying from a narrow strip variety to a broader comprehensive variety.

The experiments fall under five heads: (1) "latent learning," (2) "vicarious trial and error" or "VTE," (3) "searching for the stimulus," (4) "hypotheses" and (5) "spatial orientation."*

1 "LATENT LEARNING" EXPERIMENTS

The first of the latent learning experiments was performed at Berkeley by Blodgett. It was published in 1929. Blodgett not only performed the experiments, he also originated the concept. He ran three groups of rats through a six-unit alley maze, shown in Figure 4. He had a control group and two experimental groups. The error curves for these groups appear in Figure 5. The solid line shows the error curve for Group I, the control group. These animals were run in orthodox fashion. That is, they were run one trial a day and found food in the goal-box at the end of each trial. Groups II and III were the experimental groups. The animals of Group II, the dash line, were not fed in the maze for the first six days but only in their home cages some two hours later. On the seventh day (indicated by the small cross) the rats found food at the end of the maze for the first time and continued to find it on subsequent days. The animals of Group III were treated similarly except that they first found food at the end of the maze on the third day and continued to find it there on subsequent days. It will be observed that the experimental groups as long as they were not finding food did not appear to learn much. (Their error curves did not drop.) But on the days immediately succeeding their first finding of the food their error curves did drop astoundingly. It appeared, in short, that

*The experiments in categories 2, 3, and 4 have been omitted in this adapted version of Tolman's paper. (Ed. note)

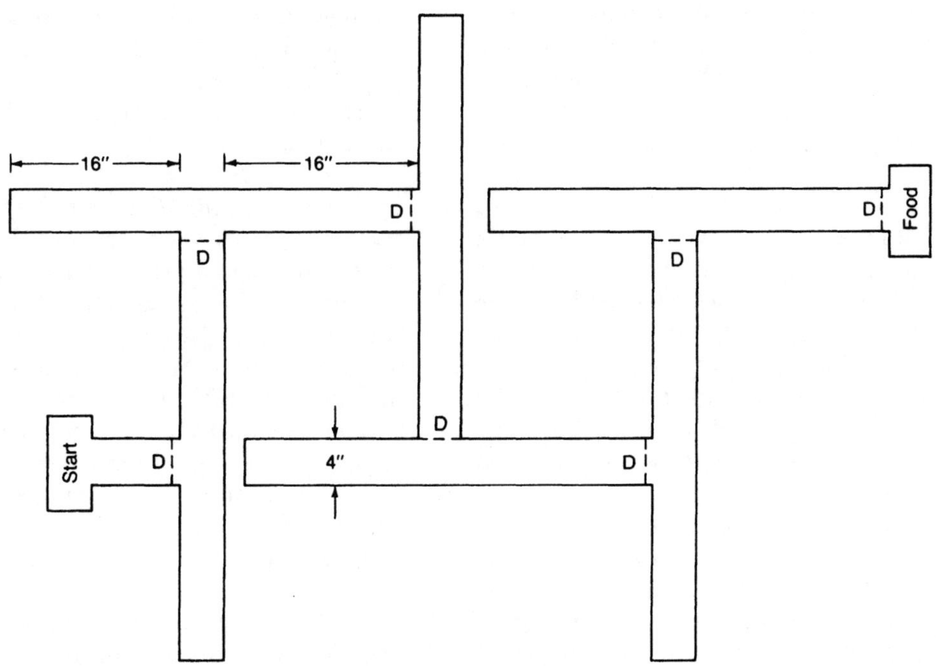

FIGURE 4
6-unit alley T-maze.

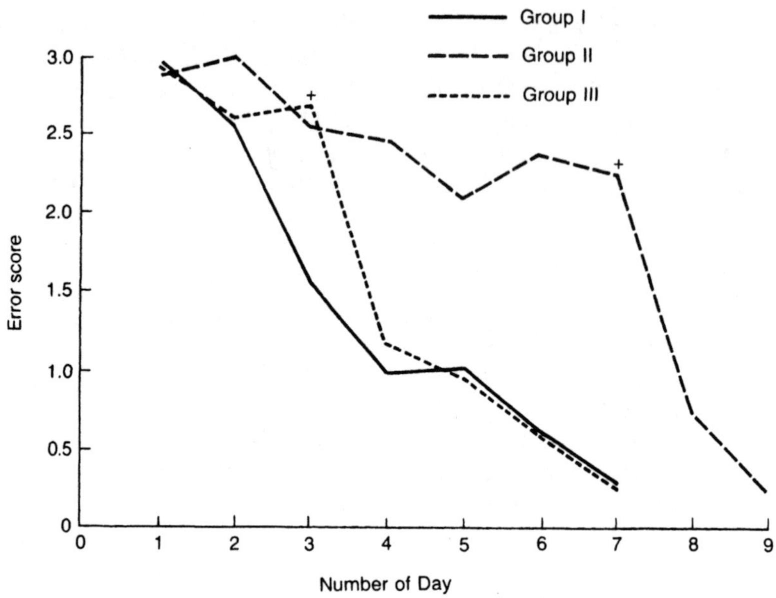

FIGURE 5

during the non-rewarded trials these animals had been learning much more than they had exhibited. This learning, which did not manifest itself until after the food had been introduced, Blodgett called "latent learning." Interpreting these results anthropomorphically, we would say that as long as the animals were not getting any food at the end of the maze, they continued to take their time in going through it—they continued to enter many blinds. Once, however, they knew they were to get food, they demonstrated that during these preceding non-rewarded trials they had learned where many of the blinds were. They had been building up a 'map,' and could utilize the latter as soon as they were motivated to do so.

Honzik and myself repeated the experiments (or rather he did and I got some of the credit) with the 14-unit T-mazes shown in Figure 1, and with larger groups of animals, and got similar results. The resulting curves are shown in Figure 6. We used two control groups—one that never found food in the maze (HNR) and one that found it throughout (HR). The experimental group (HNR-R) found food at the end of the maze from the 11th day on and showed the same sort of a sudden drop.

But probably the best experiment demonstrating latent learning was, unfortunately, done not in Berkeley but at the University of Iowa, by Spence and Lippitt. Only an abstract of this experiment has as yet been published. However, Spence has sent a preliminary manuscript from which the following account is summarized. A simple Y-maze (see Figure 7) with two goal-boxes was used. Water was at the end of the right arm of the Y and food at the end of the left arm. During the training period the rats were run neither hungry nor thirsty. They were satiated for both food and water before each day's trials. However, they were willing to run because after each run they were taken out of whichever end box they had got to and put into a living cage, with other animals in it. They were given four trials a day in this fashion for seven days, two trials to the right and two to the left.

In the crucial test the animals were divided

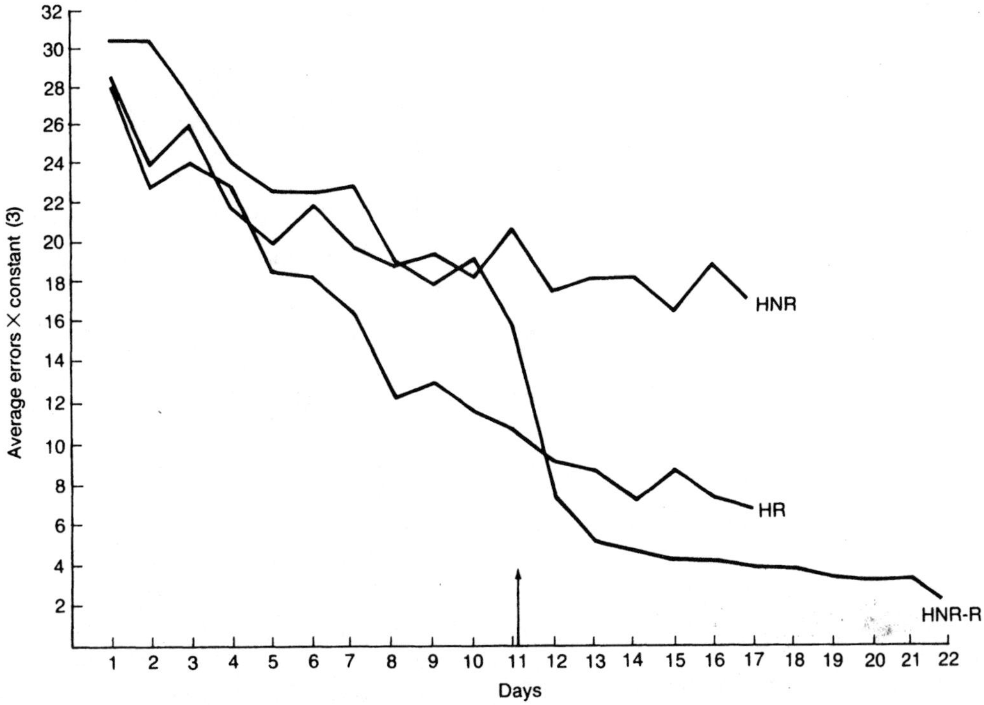

FIGURE 6
Error curves for HR, HNR, and HNR-R.

into two subgroups, one made solely hungry and one solely thirsty. It was then found that on the first trial the hungry group went at once to the left, where the food had been, statistically more frequently than to the right; and the thirsty group went to the right, where the water had been, statistically more frequently than to the left. These results indicated that under the previous non-differential and very mild rewarding conditions of merely being returned to the home cages the animals had nevertheless been learning where the water was and where the food was. In short, they had acquired a cognitive map to the effect that food was to the left and water to the right, although during the acquisition of this map they had not exhibited any stimulus-response propensities to go more to the side which became later the side of the appropriate goal.

There have been numerous other latent learning experiments done in the Berkeley laboratory and elsewhere. In general, they have for the most part all confirmed the above sort of findings. . . .

5 "SPATIAL ORIENTATION" EXPERIMENTS

As early as 1929, Lashley reported incidentally the case of a couple of his rats who, after having learned an alley maze, pushed back the cover near the starting box, climbed out and ran directly across the top to the goal-box where they climbed down in again and ate. Other investigators have reported related findings. All such observations suggest that rats really develop wider spatial maps which include more than the mere trained-on specific paths. In the experiments now to be reported this possibility has been subjected to further examination.

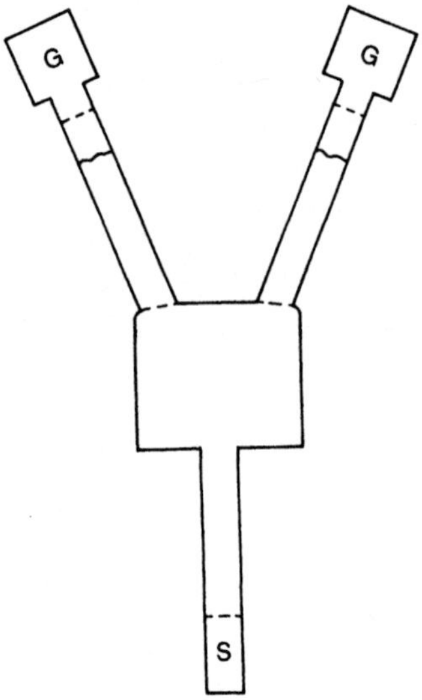

FIGURE 7
Ground plan of the apparatus.

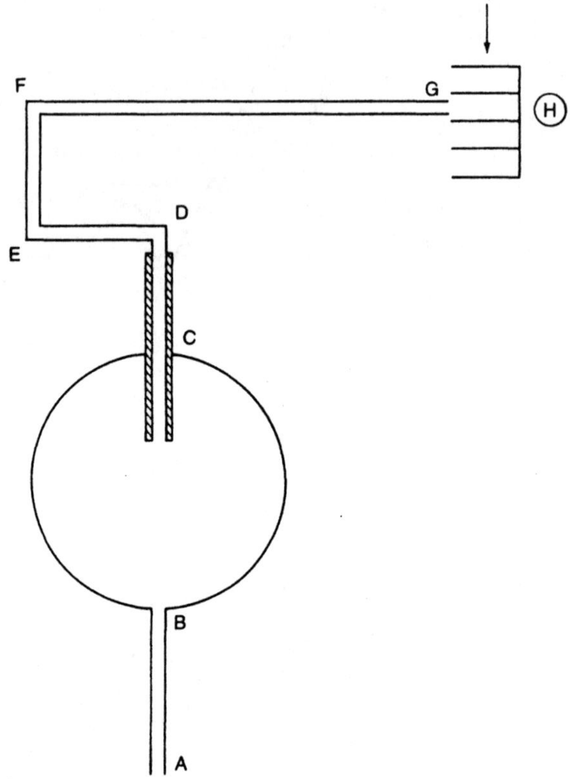

FIGURE 8
Apparatus used in preliminary training.

In the first experiment, Tolman, Ritchie and Kalish (actually Ritchie and Kalish) used the setup shown in Figure 8.

This was an elevated maze. The animals ran from A across the open circular table through CD (which had alley walls) and finally to G, the food box. H was a light which shone directly down the path from G to F. After four nights, three trials per night, in which the rats learned to run directly and without hesitation from A to G, the apparatus was changed to the sun-burst shown in Figure 9. The starting path and the table remained the same but a series of radiating paths was added.

The animals were again started at A and ran across the circular table into the alley and found themselves blocked. They then returned onto the table and began exploring practically all the radiating paths. After going out a few inches only on any one path, each rat finally chose to run all the way out on one. The percentages of rats finally choosing each of the long paths from 1 to 12 are shown in Figure 10. It appears that there was a preponderant tendency to choose path No. 6 which ran to a point some four inches in front of where the entrance to the food box had been. The only other path chosen with any appreciable frequency was No. 1—that is, the path which pointed perpendicularly to the food-side of the room.

These results seem to indicate that the rats in this experiment had learned not only to run rapidly down the original roundabout route but also, when this was blocked and radiating paths presented, to select one pointing rather directly towards the point where the food had been or else at least to select a path running perpendicularly to the food-side of the room.

As a result of their original training, the rats had, it would seem, acquired not merely a strip-map to the effect that the original specifically

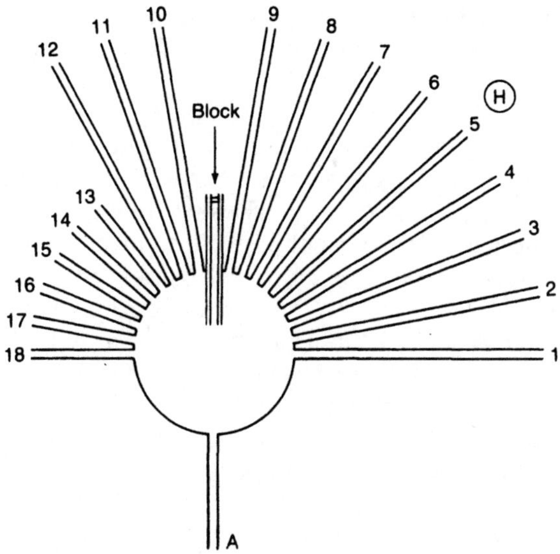

FIGURE 9
Apparatus used in the test trial.

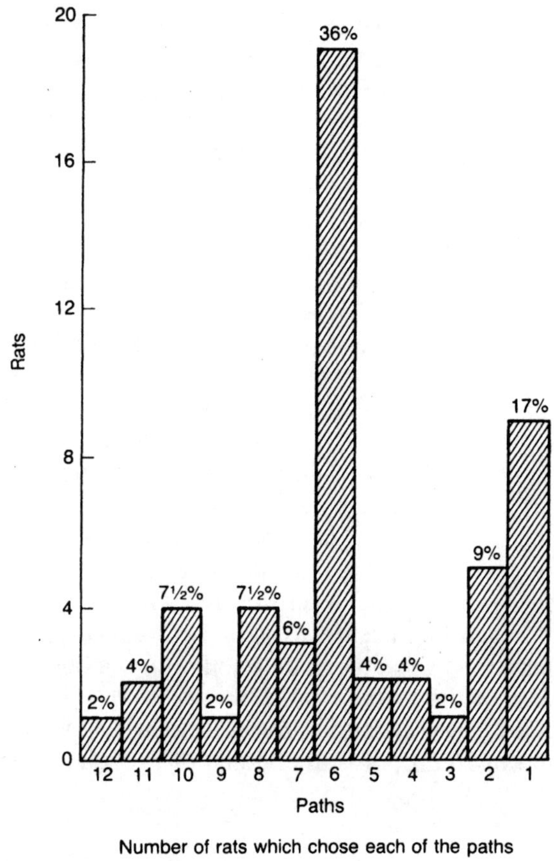

FIGURE 10
Numbers of rats which chose each of the paths. (*From E. C. Tolman, B. F. Ritchie and D. Kalish, Studies in spatial learning. I. Orientation and the short-cut.* J. exp. Psychol., 1946, 36, p. 19.)

trained-on path led to food but, rather, a wider comprehensive map to the effect that food was located in such and such a direction in the room. . . .

This completes my report of experiments. There were the *latent learning experiments,* the *VTE experiments,* the *searching for the stimulus experiment,* the *hypothesis experiments,* and these last *spatial orientation experiments.* . . .

And now, at last, I come to humanly significant and exciting problem: namely, what are the conditions which favor narrow strip-maps and what are those which tend to favor broad comprehensive maps not only in rats but also in men?

There is considerable evidence scattered throughout the literature bearing on this question both for rats and for men. Some of this evidence was obtained in Berkeley and some of it elsewhere. I have not time to present it in any detail. I can merely summarize it by saying that narrow strip-maps rather than broad comprehensive maps seem to be induced: (1) by a damaged brain, (2) by an inadequate array of environmentally presented cues, (3) by an overdose of repetitions on the original trained-on path and (4) by the presence of too strongly motivational or of too strongly frustrating conditions.

It is this fourth factor which I wish to elaborate upon briefly in my concluding remarks. For it is going to be my contention that some, at least, of the so-called 'psychological mechanisms' which the clinical psychologists and the other students of personality have uncovered as the devils underlying many of our individual and social maladjustments can be interpreted as narrowings of our cognitive maps due to too strong motivations or to too intense frustration. . . .

Over and over again men are blinded by too violent motivations and too intense frustrations into blind and unintelligent and in the end desperately dangerous hates of outsiders. And the expression of these their displaced hates ranges all the way from discrimination against minorities to world conflagrations.

What in the name of Heaven and Psychology can we do about it? My only answer is to preach again the virtues of reason—of, that is, broad cognitive maps. And to suggest that the child-trainers and the world-planners of the future can only, if at all, bring about the presence of the required rationality (*i.e.,* comprehensive maps) if they see to it that nobody's children are too over-motivated or too frustrated. Only then can these children learn to look before and after, learn to see that there are often round-about and safer paths to their quite proper goals—learn, that is, to realize that the well-beings of White and of Negro, of Catholic and of Protestant, of Christian and of Jew, of American and of Russian (and even of males and females) are mutually interdependent.

We dare not let ourselves or others become so over-emotional, so hungry, so ill-clad, so over-motivated that only narrow strip-maps will be developed. All of us in Europe as well as in America, in the Orient as well as in the Occident, must be made calm enough and well-fed enough to be able to develop truly comprehensive maps, or, as Freud would have put it, to be able to learn to live according to the Reality Principle rather than according to the too narrow and too immediate Pleasure Principle.

We must, in short, subject our children and ourselves (as the kindly experimenter would his rats) to the optimal conditions of moderate motivation and of an absence of unnecessary frustrations, whenever we put them and ourselves before that great God-given maze which is our human world. I cannot predict whether or not we will be able, or be allowed, to do this; but I *can* say that, only insofar as we *are* able and *are* allowed, have we cause for hope.

Tolman and Tryon: Early Research on the Inheritance of the Ability to Learn

Nancy K. Innis

Psychology and biology have at least one thing in common—the enormous debt owed to Charles Darwin, whose theory of evolution by natural selection is considered by many to be the most important milestone in the history of both fields. The evolution of behavior, therefore, has concerned both biologists and psychologists for some time. Research in what now is called *behavior genetics* began shortly after the turn of the century, when the rediscovery of Mendel's work on genetic transmission in garden peas provided a mechanism for natural selection (see Bateson, 1909/1930, for a contemporary discussion).

Hirsch and McGuire (1982) briefly discussed the history of behavior genetics in the introduction to a volume that reprinted benchmark papers in the area. The early history of the field spanned the entire first half of the century, end-

Innis, N. K. (1992). Tolman and Tryon: Early research on the inheritance of the ability to learn. *American Psychologist, 47,* 190–197.

ing in 1951, when Calvin Hall introduced the term *psychogenetics* to describe what he believed was a new interdisciplinary science, with psychologists and geneticists working together on problems in the genetics of behavior. The name did not catch on, but the field of behavior genetics continued to develop and attract an ardent band of dedicated researchers. The early 1960s were, no doubt, the most exciting years, as research flourished and the discipline finally achieved recognition. Enough had been accomplished for reviews of developments in the field to appear (see, especially, Fuller & Thompson, 1960; McClearn, 1962) and for the organization of two important conferences on behavior genetics, held in 1961 and 1962 (see Hirsch, 1967).

Nevertheless, enthusiasm must have been just as strong during the early decades of this century when the very first studies of the inheritance of behavior were conducted. Two approaches were evident in this early work; one utilized the inbred animals of the pure strains being developed at the time (e.g., by the Wistar Institute), the other involved selective breeding for a particular trait or ability. It is not surprising that the inheritance of the ability to learn was one of the first to be examined. Interest in learning was high at the time, particularly among psychologists. John B. Watson (1913, 1914) was promoting what would become a new school of psychology, *behaviorism,* in which the importance of learning was emphasized. The nature–nurture controversy would soon become full-blown, as those who championed instincts (e.g., William McDougall) were challenged on several fronts.

One of the earliest studies of the inheritance of learning ability was Ada Yerkes's (1916) comparison of maze learning in inbred albino rats (*Mus Norvegicus albinus*) obtained from the Wistar Institute and rats from the local stock. As well as comparing errors and trial times in different mazes, Yerkes obtained measures of the brain weight for each group. A report by Basset (1914) had shown that inbred Wistar rats with lower than average brain weights showed deficits in habit formation. Yerkes's results were inconclusive because of the small number of subjects involved, although there was a tendency for the stock rats to learn more rapidly. Brain weight to body length ratios were slightly lower in the inbred rats. The behavioral differences were ascribed to differences in temperament—the inbred rats were more timid. This finding confirmed the suspicion of Ada's husband, Robert Yerkes (who previously had studied the inheritance of savageness in rats; R. Yerkes, 1913), that differences in emotionality were responsible for the differences in habit formation reported by Basset.

Few psychologists are aware of the seminal role played by learning theorist Edward C. Tolman in selection studies of maze-learning ability, the other (and what would become the more popular) approach to the study of the inheritance of behavior. This article examines Tolman's early concern with the innate determinants of animal behavior and his part in initiating research involving the selective breeding of rats for maze-learning ability. Moreover, even after he turned his attention to more theoretical issues, Tolman continued to promote the inheritance research through his support of Robert Tryon, his student and later his colleague at the University of California.

EDWARD CHACE TOLMAN: EARLY YEARS AT THE UNIVERSITY OF CALIFORNIA (1918–1923)

In 1918, Edward Tolman accepted the position of instructor at the University of California and arrived in Berkeley in September of that year. After earning his doctorate at Harvard under the supervision of Hugo Münsterberg in studies of human memory (Tolman, 1915), Tolman had continued this line of research while on the faculty at Northwestern University. His move to California involved far more than relocating on the other side of the country; it resulted in a major change in the emphasis of Tolman's research, from human to animal psychology.

Tolman had agreed to teach a course in animal psychology when he accepted the Berkeley position, but circumstances delayed this venture. Because of the war, the course was not offered as scheduled in the fall of 1918. He taught army recruits instead. In fact, it was not until the following summer that Tolman acquired his first animals—six white rats, obtained from and housed in the Anatomy Department. Like many rat runners, his first impression was not entirely positive. "I have begun with my rats. At present I am merely playing with them every day. I have six to begin with. I don't like them. They make me feel creepy" (Tolman, July 1919a). His feelings, however, did not deter him; he built cages and by October had 50 rats, two students in his animal behavior course working on projects, and his own research under way (Tolman, October 1919b).

On November 17, 1919, Tolman's application for funding to the Board of Research at the University of California was approved, and he received a grant of $105 "For study of inheritance of unusual ability in learning as exhibited by lower mammals." This was a relatively substantial sum for the time; for example, Tolman's salary his first year in Berkeley was only $1,500. In a footnote to the article reporting the results of the inheritance study, Tolman (1924) credited his colleague, Warner Brown, with the "original impetus which started the problem" (p. 1). Exactly how this came about is not recorded; however, one may speculate that the nature–nurture issue, very topical at the time, was the subject of more than one lively discussion, as psychology faculty and students met each afternoon for tea. Students from that time fondly remember the very positive atmosphere in the department and the free interchange and openness to all ideas, no matter how divergent, that prevailed.

Warner Brown, who had obtained his PhD (with Robert Woodworth) at Columbia during a period when interest in individual differences was strong among James McKeen Cattell's group, had returned to Berkeley to complete a major work on individual differences in suggestibility (Brown, 1916). In general, at that time, concern with individual differences in behavior was of growing importance to psychologists, and individual differences in animal behavior were not to be ignored. Tolman, who had been at Harvard when Ada Yerkes was carrying out her study of the genetics of maze learning, may well have recalled this work in taking the next step—attempting to determine whether individual differences in maze-learning ability could be enhanced by selective breeding, and then attempting to discover the genetic basis of this ability.

The issue of inheritance versus environment was likely an important topic in Tolman's advanced psychology course in the fall of 1920. Among the 12 students in the course was a precocious undergraduate, Zing Yang Kuo, who kept Tolman's interest in the topic of instinct alive over the next few years. Many readers will recognize Kuo as the champion of environmental explanations of behavioral control and recall his work in developmental psychology. At the time, Kuo had barely turned 20 and had been in the United States for only two years. Nevertheless, he was stimulated to respond to those supporting the importance of instinct in psychology and did so by publishing an article denouncing instinct in the *Journal of Philosophy,* early in 1921. In the fall of that year, Tolman held a "voluntary seminar on Instinct" at his home each Thursday evening with a group of handpicked students, including Kuo, who by now was enrolled as Tolman's graduate student (Tolman, 1921). What lively debates must have occurred at those meetings. Kuo's article denouncing instinct resulted in an extended exchange between Tolman and Kuo in the literature (Kuo, 1921, 1922, 1924; Tolman, 1922a, 1923) and played a key role in the broad-based attack on instinct, initiated by Dunlap (1919), that continued throughout the early 1920s.

Many psychologists joined in this assault, which soon resulted in the demise of instinct as a useful construct in explaining behavior.

Tolman credited Brown with getting him started on the inheritance research; however, Tolman's theoretical work at the time indicates that he was very interested in the role of instinct and innate factors in determining behavior (Tolman, 1920). Moreover, although influenced by Watson's behaviorism, Tolman was unwilling to go as far as Watson in rejecting the traditional constructs of psychology, including purpose and cognition. Thus, he began to devise a "new formula for behaviorism" (Tolman, 1922b) that would be both objective and purposive. In the fall of 1919, when he was requesting funds from the Board of Research for his inheritance study, Tolman was also preparing an address for the Berkeley Philosophical Union, which he delivered that December. His topic was "Instinct and Sensitivity," and shortly after the talk, he submitted a related article, "Instinct and Purpose," to the *Psychological Review* (Tolman, 1920). This was the second in what would be a long series of theoretical papers in which Tolman attempted to define objectively the terms of psychology.

Instinct and Purpose

Tolman (1920) used the idea of instinct to show how a purposive psychology could be objective. He presented a "two-level theory of instinct" (p. 233) involving "determining adjustment" and "subordinate acts." Subordinate acts included "all the things we do, not as separate and independent reflexes [e.g., unconditioned responses], but as parts of bigger groups of activity" (p. 220). A determining adjustment "set in readiness the subordinate acts" (p. 220). Depending on the prevailing determining adjustment, a certain random, albeit limited, set of responses (subordinate acts) was activated. Thus, a particular stimulus produced a determining adjustment, which then released a set of relatively random responses that continued until that stimulus was removed (the familiar "persistence until" characteristic of purposive behavior). For Tolman, the "determining adjustment . . . [provided a] theory of instinct," and so purpose, comprising the "interaction of determining adjustment and subordinate acts" (p. 233), involved a completely deterministic mechanism.

The key feature of Tolman's (1920) conceptualization that distinguished it from similar contemporary positions, such as Woodworth's (1918) notion of drive and mechanism, was his emphasis on "the *variability* among the subordinate acts" (p. 223). Although Tolman did not relate the idea of response variability, as he conceptualized it in his theory, to the possibility of selection for particular subordinate acts, the implications are obvious. For Tolman, the relationship between the determining adjustment and the particular set of subordinate acts it released was innate, although the importance of learning was not ignored. In selectively breeding rats for maze-learning ability, one could be selecting for differences in the kinds of subordinate acts that were more likely to be set in readiness by the determining adjustment activated in the maze situation.

Although various maze-learning studies were carried out by Tolman and his students between the summer of 1919 (when he encountered his first white rats) and the summer of 1923 (when he left the University of California at Berkeley for a six-month sabbatical leave in Europe), the inheritance study was by far the most extensive project. With much of his teaching and theoretical efforts during this period centered on innate determinants of behavior, it is easy to understand why the work on the inheritance of maze-learning ability intrigued Tolman. Moreover, he had debates with Zing Yang Kuo to keep his interest in instinct alive; a diligent research assistant, Frederick Adams, to carry out much of the extensive data collection; and another competent student, Barbara Burks (who would later continue to work on the nature–nurture problem with humans; e.g., Burks, 1928), to supervise the computations. (The tedium and time consumption involved in calculating the numerous correlation coefficients necessary for analyzing these data are difficult to imagine by a generation raised with computers.) Tolman also continued to receive financial support from the Board of Research at the University of California ($150 in 1921 and $180 for the construction of mazes in 1922), and in January 1922 the attic of the Psychology Building was remodeled to provide new housing for his growing colony of rats.

INHERITANCE OF MAZE-LEARNING ABILITY IN RATS

Tolman's study was the first experiment to examine the genetic basis of maze learning by breeding distinct lineages of rats selected for their maze performance. The data were reported in 1924 in the *Journal of Comparative Psychology* in an article entitled "The Inheritance of Maze-Learning Ability in Rats," completed just before Tolman began his sabbatical.

Tolman (1924) began the article with a discussion of the implications of this kind of research in general and acknowledged that the study was merely a first report of an extensive, ongoing research program.

> The problem of this investigation might appear to be a matter of concern primarily for the geneticist. None the less, it is also one of very great interest to the psychologist. For could we, as geneticists, discover the complete genetic mechanism of a character such as maze-learning ability—i.e. how many genes it involves, how these segregate, what their linkages are, etc.—we would necessarily, at the same time, be discovering what psychologically, or behavioristically, maze-learning ability may be said to be made up of, what component abilities it contains, whether these vary independently of one another, what their relations are to other measurable abilities, as, say, sensory discrimination, nervousness, etc. The answers to the genetic problem require the answers to the psychological, while at the same time the answers to the former point the way to the latter.
>
> But as far as the present investigation is concerned it must be admitted that only the most elementary answers of either sort have yet been obtained. The preliminary problems of technique and method have proved all important. (p. 1)

The study involved the selective breeding of rats performing very well or very poorly on an enclosed maze with four choice points. Eighty-two rats (41 males and 41 females), albinos from the Anatomy Department stock, formed what Tolman (1924) labeled the "initial or P generation" (p. 2). Their performance on the maze was assessed using three measures—number of errors, perfect runs, and time to complete a trial. A composite score was used in the selection. The top-scoring males and females were mated to begin a *maze-bright* strain, and those scoring lowest were bred to start a *maze-dull* strain. The offspring of these pairs (labeled the F_1 generations) were then tested on the maze, and eight new pairs (siblings from among the highest scoring *bright* males and females and from the lowest scoring *dulls*) were selected to continue each line. The study concluded with the testing of their offspring, the F_2 generation rats.

The performance of the F_1 maze-bright rats improved in comparison with the original unselected group, whereas that of the maze-dull subjects was worse. However, the divergence between the two lineages did not continue; the F_2 maze-bright rats did not perform as well as their F_1 counterparts, whereas the F_2 maze-dull rats were about the same as theirs. Several possibilities for the decline in performance of the F_2 bright strain were considered, including age at testing, environmental conditions, nutrition, and inbreeding. All of these were taken into account in future research.

All in all, the results of the inheritance study were not as clear-cut as Tolman had hoped. In fact, the work pointed to numerous methodological problems. However, adopting the philosophy that we can learn from our mistakes, Tolman began to develop a more rigorous approach to selective breeding research.

A test of individual differences must be both reliable (providing the same result on different occasions) and valid (measuring what you claim it is measuring). Thus, considerable effort was directed toward developing a performance measure that had both high reliability and validity. In order to assess the reliability of the scores obtained, data for the initial group of 82 rats tested on the maze were subjected to a number of statistical treatments, including determining correlations of performance on different runs (e.g., first five and last five runs and odd vs. even runs). All correlations for the error measure were disappointingly low, and even a corrected measure, eliminating extreme scores, resulted in a correlation of only .509. The correlations for time were not much better, and when intercorrelations using all three measures (errors, time, and perfect runs) were computed, the effect of time turned out to be ambiguous.

The validity of the maze for assessing a general maze-learning ability was also of concern, and in a follow-up study Davis and Tolman (1924) compared the performance of white rats on two versions of a maze that was very similar to the one used in the original study (Maze A) and a second maze of a very different configuration (Maze B) and its replica. Correlations of error scores on odd and even trials for individual mazes were consistent with these same correlations for the inheritance study, whereas correlations between each maze and its twin were somewhat higher. As in the previous study, time proved to be an ambiguous measure and the least reliable in comparisons between mazes.

ROBERT CHOATE TRYON: EARLY YEARS AT CALIFORNIA (1924–1932)

Tolman's ability to continue the selection project when he returned to Berkeley following his sabbatical in 1924 was certainly facilitated when Robert Tryon enrolled as his graduate student. Tryon, who had been an undergraduate at Berkeley, had interest and skill in both genetics and statistics—the two areas of expertise most important for work on the inheritance project—and Tolman was eager to get him involved.

During the four years from 1924 until he defended his doctoral dissertation, "Individual Differences at Successive Stages of Learning," in 1928, Tryon, along with others associated with the selection project, worked diligently to overcome the problems made obvious by the original inheritance study. These problems included (a) the reliability and validity of the measures of maze learning, which entailed consideration of both the adequacy of statistical treatments and the generality of the findings from a particular maze; (b) the nature of the initial subject population and the method of selecting mates in future generations; and (c) the control of environmental variables, such as living conditions, diet, and handling. Other concerns were the high cost of the research, both in terms of the care and maintenance of the rats in an expanding colony, and the extensive time and effort necessary for data recording and analysis. Each of the problem areas identified in the original research was addressed before Tryon initiated the decisive study in 1927, a study that would continue for more than a decade and provide data from more than 20 generations of maze-bright and maze-dull rats.

Reliability and Validity of the Behavioral Measures

The reliability coefficients obtained for data from both within and between mazes in the initial research (Davis & Tolman, 1924; Tolman, 1924) were not very large. Tolman and Nyswander (1927) assessed the necessity of obtaining high reliability coefficients in general, and concluded that

> Even though an instrument (as applied) is not precise enough, or consistent enough, to distinguish

> very reliably between all the separate individuals of a population (i.e., gives a low reliability coefficient), it may none the less be reliable enough to distinguish (a) between small groups at the two extremes, or (b) between the mean performances of very large groups even though the latter fall fairly near together on the scale. (p. 428)

Thus, because comparisons between maze-bright and maze-dull rats involved the extreme ends of the population distribution, they felt that the low coefficients obtained might not be a critical problem; however, it would be desirable to use a maze that resulted in higher correlations. Efforts were therefore made to find a maze that led to reliable scores. Rats were trained on seven mazes, each with a different configuration, and odd–even and split-half correlations over trials were computed for the data. Multiple T mazes proved to be the most reliable, and reliability increased with the number of T units in the maze. Turning to the problem of validity, the researchers tried to assess which measure—time, errors, retracings, or perfect runs—would be the best index of learning. Tolman and Nyswander (1927) confirmed that time was an ambiguous index and, after examining the other measures, concluded that "errors" was "the one desirable type of score for measuring learning *per se*." (p. 459)

Genetic Makeup of the Rat Population and Breeding Methods

Tryon started with a new and more heterogeneous breeding stock than the one originally used by Tolman (1924). He chose animals from a large number of litters that had been unrelated for many generations. Tolman was of the opinion that his original population (all albino rats from the Anatomy Department colony) may have been too close genetically and that the inbreeding from the brother–sister matings in his F_1 generation was responsible for the decline in performance of their maze-bright offspring. Tryon continued to use brother–sister matings, but only in alternate generations. (The issue of inbreeding has continued to be a controversial one in the field of behavior genetics; see Hall, 1951; McClearn, 1962.)

Laboratory Procedures—Data Recording, Housing, and Handling

An important concern for researchers using mazes, particularly in studies in which large numbers of animals are tested, has always been the immense amount of time and effort involved in conducting the daily trials (i.e., recording errors and choices in the maze). The most obvious solution to this problem was automation, and with the assistance of Lloyd Jeffress, a psychology student who was very good at gadgetry, Tolman began to construct a self-recording maze. The prototype maze (Tolman & Jeffress, 1925) involved multiple T units, each of which permitted a choice between a cul-de-sac and an arm that led to the next unit. Telegraph keys under treads on the floor of the maze, closed by the rat's weight, activated relays and counters that registered errors and correct choices. The researcher was required only to place the rat in the maze and return at the end of a trial to remove the animal and record the data from the counters. This type of maze was used for a number of different studies by Tolman's students.

An additional factor that had not really been given much attention in the previous work was vitally important for trying to identify genetic differences. If differences in learning are to be accurately attributed to genetic factors, then great care must be taken to ensure that all environmental variables (e.g., housing, handling) are equivalent across groups. Jeffress devised a method whereby rats were housed in cages set in two tiers of shelves positioned on a large, automatic turntable. A rat entered the maze from its cage on the lower level, and when it reached the end of the maze ran into a cage on the upper level, where it received its daily ration of food. The turntable then revolved, allowing the next rat to begin its trial on the maze. When all of the animals had completed the maze, the top set of shelves was exchanged with the bottom set in preparation for the next training trial. Thus it was necessary to handle the rats only to check their body weights, essentially eliminating any experimenter bias in the treatment of the different groups of rats (Tolman, Tryon, & Jeffress, 1929).

Tryon also attempted to control for early differential experience in his selected generations by separating siblings at weaning and housing the offspring of bright and dull parents together until they were tested, at which point they lived in the individual cages on the automatic turntable.

TRYON'S STUDY OF THE GENETICS OF LEARNING ABILITY IN RATS

Tryon took advantage of all of the findings and technical advances described earlier in designing the experimental situation for his inheritance study. He constructed a 17-unit multiple T maze, incorporating the automatic delivery table for housing and running the rats. The self-recording maze units were modified by replacing the telegraph keys with mercury cup contacts under the floor treads, so that data could be recorded using a voltmeter to deflect a pen on a moving strip of paper. This permitted a continuous record of performance, rather than the total scores obtained when counters were used.

Tryon's maze had taken many years and much labor to develop, and he was extremely protective of it. Thus, when the Psychology Department was about to take up residence in the new Life Sciences Building, Tryon approached the move with some trepidation. Sensing his anxiety, some of the graduate students persuaded him to join them on a trip one weekend, and while they were absent, others undertook the move without his knowledge. All went well, and the maze was safely installed on the top floor of Life Sciences, where it would remain in service for many years to come.

Guided by Tolman and Nyswander's (1927) findings on reliability and validity, Tryon chose *errors* (entries into the blind arms of the T-maze units) as his performance measure. The work reported in Tryon's (1928) dissertation was directed at assessing the validity of his measurements by comparing the performance of the parental (P) generation (his original group of rats) on the 17-unit maze and on another quite dissimilar maze in which the animals were run by hand. Correlations between performance in the two situations were always above .80, indicating "that the automatic maze differentiated the animals in some general fundamental ability which is likewise employed in learning another maze" (Tryon, 1929, p. 74).

Tryon's (1929) first published report of the inheritance work dealt with the question Tolman had addressed earlier: "To what degree are individual differences in mental ability (i.e. the ability to learn) due to hereditary factors, and to what degree due to environmental factors?" (p.71). He also maintained that his work had a further objective: "the determination of the genetic mode of inheritance of this ability to learn" (p. 72). In this article, Tryon presented data for two generations of maze-bright and maze-dull rats, showing that the two populations were beginning to diverge.

SUPPORT FOR TRYON'S INHERITANCE PROJECT

By 1927, Tolman had essentially placed the inheritance research in Tryon's hands, and he wanted to make sure that the work would continue under Tryon's supervision after he had completed his doctorate. Funding, of course, was the major problem. In the spring of 1928, Tolman had "a colony of some thousand rats, a caretaker getting $750 and paid assistants amounting to about $800" (Tolman, March 16, 1928). He had spent about $2,700 in the past year for animals alone, some of which had come from his own pocket. Obviously, most of this expense was for the inheritance study, and this work would have to continue for a long time in order to observe enough generations to "work out the genetic laws involved" and permit use of the "bright and dull strains . . . for comparative purposes in all sorts of other problems" (Tolman, March 26, 1931).

Tolman had been trying hard to find funds to pay Tryon once he received his degree. In November 1927, an attempt to get the Board of Research to provide a fellowship for Tryon had been rejected. Tolman even wrote Robert Yerkes for advice on sources of funding, and (whether or not there was a connection) early in 1928, Tryon received word that he had been awarded a National Research Council Fellowship for the coming year.

All of this became important when, in March 1928, Tolman was offered an associate professorship at Harvard. The possibility of being on the Harvard faculty resulted in considerable conflict for Tolman. A Harvard appointment was what he had most desired as a young instructor in his early years at California. Now, 10 years later, he was not so certain. He had risen through the ranks (indeed, had just been recommended for full professor) in a department with congenial colleagues; had attracted a group of productive, intelligent graduate students; and had come to love living in California. Moreover, he was getting close to completing the book in which he would present his theoretical system, and he was afraid that a move would disrupt his writing. Still, the Harvard offer was tempting.

The inheritance project played a central role in the outcome of the job offer, if not in Tolman's actual decision. He wrote to Boring:

> Then there is the specific difficulty of the problem on the Inheritance of Maze-Learning Ability. We have this year got our automatic maze going and it is a humdinger. Tryon has been running it ever since last summer and gets his Ph.D. on the first generation this spring. And he has received a National Research Fellowship for next year to carry it on. . . . I hate to leave him and it behind and I hardly know if he or it would be transportable. (Tolman, March 16, 1928)

Whether Harvard would have moved the maze or built another, we will never know; Tolman decided to remain at Berkeley. Moreover, Tolman used the Harvard offer to get the administration of the University of California to permanently commit funds from the Board of Research to him for a half-time research assistant. From then on, even during the depression, when departmental funding dropped substantially, Tolman always had money for an assistant.

Tryon's work continued; his National Research Fellowship was renewed for a second year, and Tolman was trying "to pull all strings possible" (Tolman, 1931) to get a third year for him. Then in March 1931, Boring once again approached Tolman about coming to Harvard, and again Tolman used the offer to barter—this time to Tryon's decided advantage. Tolman wrote to Boring:

> The deciding point seems to have been that I am just *terribly keen* to have Tryon's homogeneous "bright" and "dull" rats to do more kinds of learning experiments with, and your tentative offer was a way to wangle an assistant professorship for Tryon through the administration and through the department and hence to make possible the final completion of his inheritance problem which will take two or three years more and give me research material for the rest of my few remaining years. (Tolman, March 26, 1931)

Tryon was appointed to the Berkeley faculty in 1931, where he remained until his death in 1967.

FURTHER RESEARCH ON SELECTION FOR MAZE-LEARNING ABILITY

Tryon continued to study succeeding generations of maze-bright and maze-dull rats and found that by the eighth there was virtually no overlap in performance on the multiple T maze. Although, eventually, data for more than 20

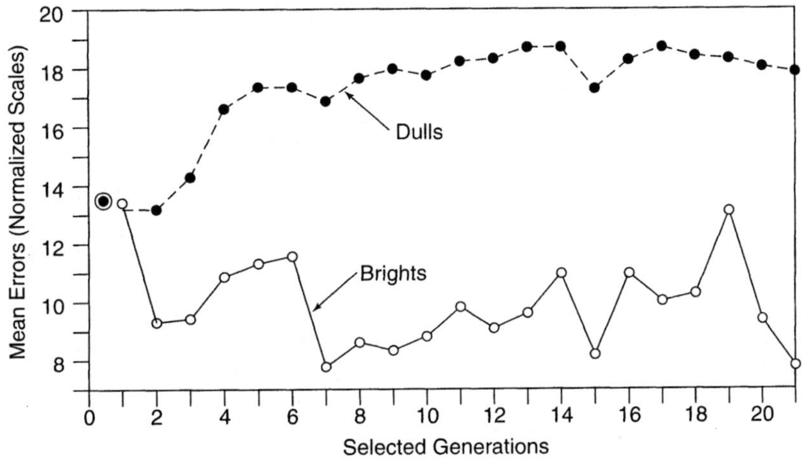

Figure 1
Mean Errors for 21 Generations of Tryon's Maze-Bright and Maze-Dull Rats*

generations were collected, no further divergence between strains was observed, as indicated in Figure 1 (see Tryon, 1940, 1942, and also Hall, 1951, and McClearn, 1962, for summaries of this work).

The Berkeley group was not alone in studying the inheritance of maze learning in selected strains of maze-dull and maze-bright rats. Shortly after Tryon started his study, W. T. Heron began a similar long-term project at the University of Minnesota, even designing a similar automated apparatus (Heron, 1933). Heron was also able to establish distinct bright and dull strains of rats, confirming Tryon's work (Heron, 1935, 1941).

Inevitably, the question of what was being selected—a specific maze-learning ability or some more general learning ability—was addressed. One such study, carried out by another of Tolman's graduate students, I. Krechevsky (later David Krech), used rats from Tryon's colony. Krechevsky (1933) wanted to determine if rats of the bright and dull strains developed different "hypotheses" when faced with an insoluble problem. He found that rats from the maze-bright strain typically adopted spatial hypotheses, whereas those from the maze-dull strain tried nonspatial (visual) solutions. His conclusion was that the so-called bright rats were, in fact, very limited in their response repertoire as a result of their selection history.

In January 1932, Tolman's book, *Purposive Behavior in Animals and Men,* was published. Tolman dedicated the book to *Mus Norvegicus albinus,* the white rat. His attitude toward this small creature had changed markedly in the few short years since he received his first animals. Tolman spent the following academic year on sabbatical leave in Europe, and by the time he returned to Berkeley, his interest in the inheritance project seems to have waned. *Purposive Behavior in Animals and Men* had attracted a good deal of attention to Tolman's theoretical ideas, and he spent more and more time refining these. Moreover, while he was in Austria, discussions with members of the Vienna Circle, particularly Egon Brunswik (whom he helped settle in Berkeley a few years later) had stimulated him in new directions.

However, Tolman continued to maintain a role for hereditary factors in his theory of learn-

*From "The Inheritance of behavior" (p. 213) by G. E. McClearn, 1962, in L. Postman, *Psychology in the Making,* New York: Knopf. Copyright 1962 by Alfred A. Knopf. Reprinted by permission.

ing, incorporating them as part of the set of intervening variables represented by the acronym HATE (Heredity, Age, Training, Endocrine Conditions; see e.g., Tolman, 1938). The H stood for heredity, and Tolman had Tryon just down the hall in Life Sciences to make sure that he remembered.

Finally, even Tryon's involvement with the inheritance project began to dissipate, as he became more interested in his other area of expertise, statistics, and particularly in problems of cluster analysis (see Tryon & Bailey, 1970). However, the Berkeley legacy continued in the work of Tryon's student, Jerry Hirsch, who became a leader in the new field of behavior genetics—for which, incidentally, Hirsch and Tryon (1956) provided the name. But Hirsch abandoned the white rat for a lower organism, the fruit fly, *Drosophila,* which had the advantage of numerous offspring and a rapid turnover of generations.

Although many researchers, including Hirsch, are still active today, the field of behavior genetics seems to have passed its heyday. The excitement experienced during the early years and again with the emergence of a new discipline at the end of the 1950s is gone. Social and political pressures no doubt have played a role in this change in mood; studies of individual differences in behavior are no longer politically correct. Nevertheless, this centennial issue provides an opportunity to review the work of two pioneers—Edward C. Tolman and Robert Tryon, the first researchers to conduct successful selective-breeding studies of the inheritance of maze-learning ability. Perhaps as scientists map the genome over the next decade and interest in genetics revives, there will be another shift in attitude toward behavior genetics. For as Tolman (1924) implied when he began the inheritance project, a complete understanding of maze-learning ability will be achieved only when studies of genetic mechanisms and research on behavioral processes go on hand in hand.

REFERENCES

Basset, G. C. (1914). Habit formation in a strain of genetic albino rats with less than normal brain weight. *Behavior Monographs, 2*(4).

Bateson, W. (1930). *Mendel's principles of heredity.* Cambridge, England: Cambridge University Press. (Original work published 1909)

Brown, W. (1916). Individual and sex differences in suggestibility. *University of California Publications in Psychology, 2,* 291–430.

Burks, B. S. (1928). Statistical hazards in nature–nurture investigations. *Yearbook of the National Society for Studies in Education, 1,* 9–33.

Davis, F. C., & Tolman, E. C. (1924). A note on the correlation between two mazes. *Journal of Comparative Psychology, 4,* 125–135.

Dunlap, K. (1919). Are there any instincts? *Journal of Abnormal Psychology, 14,* 307–311.

Fuller, J. L., & Thompson, W. R. (1960). *Behavior genetics.* New York: Wiley.

Hall, C. S. (1951). The genetics of behavior. In S. S. Stevens (Ed.), *Handbook of experimental psychology* (pp. 304–329). New York: Wiley.

Heron, W. T. (1933). An automatic recording device for use in animal psychology. *Journal of Comparative Psychology, 16,* 149–158.

Heron, W. T. (1935). The inheritance of maze-learning ability in rats. *Journal of Comparative Psychology, 19,* 77–89.

Heron, W. T. (1941). The inheritance of brightness and dullness in maze learning ability in the rat. *Journal of Genetic Psychology, 58,* 41–49.

Hirsch, J. (1967). *Behavior–genetic analysis.* New York: McGraw-Hill.

Hirsch, J., & McGuire, T. (1982). *Behavior–genetic analysis.* Stroudsburg, PA: Hutchinson Ross.

Hirsch J., & Tryon, R. C. (1956). Mass screening and reliable individual measurement in the experimental behavior genetics of lower organisms. *Psychological Bulletin, 53,* 402–410.

Krechevsky, I. (1933). Hereditary nature of "hypotheses." *Journal of Comparative Psychology, 16,* 99–116.

Kuo, Z. Y. (1921). Giving up instincts in psychology. *Journal of Philosophy, 18,* 645–654.

Kuo, Z. Y. (1922). How are our instincts acquired? *Psychological Review, 29,* 344–365.

Kuo, Z. Y. (1924). A psychology without heredity. *Psychological Review, 31,* 427–448.

McClearn, G. E. (1962). The inheritance of behavior. In L. Postman (Ed.), *Psychology in the making* (pp. 144–252). New York: Knopf.

Tolman, E. C. (1915). *Studies in memory.* Unpublished doctoral thesis (submitted to the Department of Philosophy and Psychology), Harvard University.

Tolman, E. C. (1919a, July). *Letter to Mary Chace Tolman.* In Tolman Family Papers, Berkeley, CA.

Tolman, E. C. (1919b, October). *Letter to Mary Chace Tolman.* In Tolman Family Papers, Berkeley, CA.

Tolman, E. C. (1920). Instinct and purpose. *Psychological Review, 27,* 217–233.

Tolman, E. C. (1921, September 18). *Letter to Mary Chace Tolman.* In Tolman Family Papers, Berkeley, CA.

Tolman, E. C. (1922a). Can instincts be given up in psychology? *Journal of Abnormal Psychology, 17,* 139–152.

Tolman, E. C. (1922b). A new formula for behaviorism. *Psychological Review, 29,* 44–53.

Tolman, E. C. (1923). The nature of instinct. *Psychological Bulletin, 20,* 200–216.

Tolman, E. C. (1924). The inheritance of maze-learning ability in rats. *Journal of Comparative Psychology, 4,* 1–18.

Tolman, E. C. (1928, March 16). *Letter to E. G. Boring.* In Boring Papers, Harvard University.

Tolman, E. C. (1931, March 26). *Letter to E. G. Boring.* In Boring Papers, Harvard University.

Tolman, E. C. (1932). *Purposive behavior in animals and men.* New York: Century.

Tolman, E. C. (1938). The determiners of behavior at a choice point. *Psychological Review, 45,* 1–41.

Tolman, E. C., & Jeffress, L. A. (1925). A self-recording maze. *Journal of Comparative Psychology, 5,* 455–463.

Tolman, E. C., & Nyswander, D. B. (1927). The reliability and validity of maze-measures for rats. *Journal of Comparative Psychology, 7,* 425–460.

Tolman, E. C., Tryon, R. C., & Jeffress, L. A. (1929). A self-recording maze with an automatic delivery table. *University of California Publications in Psychology, 4,* 99–112.

Tryon, R. C. (1928). *Individual differences at successive stages of learning.* Unpublished doctoral dissertation, University of California.

Tryon, R. C. (1929). The genetics of learning ability in rats. *University of California Publications in Psychology, 4,* 71–89.

Tryon, R. C. (1940). Genetic differences in maze-learning ability in rats. *Yearbook of the National Society for Studies in Education, 39,* 111–119.

Tryon, R. C. (1942). Individual differences. In F. A. Moss (Ed.), *Comparative psychology.* New York: Prentice Hall.

Tryon, R. C., & Bailey, D. E. (1970). *Cluster analysis.* New York: McGraw-Hill.

Watson, J. B. (1913). Psychology as the behaviorist views it. *Psychological Review, 20,* 158–177.

Watson, J. B. (1914). *Behavior: An introduction to comparative psychology.* New York: Holt.

Woodworth, R. S. (1918). *Dynamic psychology.* New York: Columbia University Press.

Yerkes, A. W. (1916). Comparison of the behavior of stock and inbred albino rats. *Journal of Animal Behavior, 6,* 267–296.

Yerkes, R. M. (1913). The inheritance of savageness and wildness in rats. *Journal of Animal Behavior, 3,* 286–296.

Behavior Theory, Learning, and the Problem of Reinforcement

Clark L. Hull

BEHAVIOR THEORY AND SYMBOLIC CONSTRUCTS

Scientific theories are mainly concerned with dynamic situations, i.e., with the consequent events or conditions which, with the passage of time, will follow from a given set of antecedent events or conditions. The concrete activity of theorizing consists in the manipulation of a limited set of symbols according to the rules expressed in the postulates (together with certain additional rules which make up the main substance of logic) in such a way as to span the gap separating the antecedent conditions or states from the subsequent ones. Some of the symbols represent observable and measurable elements or aggregates of the situation, whereas others represent presumptive intervening processes not directly subject to observation. The latter are theoretical constructs. All well-developed sciences freely employ theoretical constructs wherever they prove useful, sometimes even sequences or chains of them. The scientific utility of logical constructs consists in the mediation of valid deductions; this in turn is absolutely dependent upon every construct, or construct chain, being securely anchored both on the antecedent and on the consequent side to conditions or events which are directly observable. If possible, they should also be measurable.

The theory of behavior seems to require the use of a number of symbolic constructs, arranged for the most part in a single chain. The main links of this chain are represented in Figure (1). In the interest of clarity, the symbolic constructs are accompanied by the more important and relevant symbols representing the objectively anchoring conditions or events. In order that the two types of symbols shall be easily distinguishable, circles have been drawn around the symbolic constructs. It will be noticed that the symbols representing observables, while scattered throughout the sequence, are conspicuously clustered at the beginning and at the end of the chain, where they must be in order to make validation of the constructs possible. Frequent reference will be made to this summarizing diagram throughout the present chapter, as it reveals at a glance the groundwork of the present approach to the behavior sciences.

ORGANISMS CONCEIVED AS SELF-MAINTAINING MECHANISMS

From the point of view of biological evolution, organisms are more or less successfully self-maintaining mechanisms. In the present context *a mechanism is defined as a physical aggregate whose behavior occurs under ascertainable conditions according to definitely statable rules or laws.* In biology, the nature of these aggregates is such that for individuals and species to survive, certain optimal conditions must be approximated. When conditions deviate from the optimum, equilibrium may as a rule be restored by some sort of action on the part of the organism; such activity is described as "adaptive." The organs effecting the adaptive activity of animals are for the most part glands and muscles.

In higher organisms the number, variety, and complexity of the acts required for protracted survival is exceedingly great. The nature of the act or action sequence necessary to bring about optimal conditions in a given situation depends jointly (1) upon the state of disequilibrium or need of the organism and (2) upon the charac-

Adapted from Hull, C. L. (1943). *Principles of behavior*. New York: Appleton-Century-Crofts, pp. 382–389.

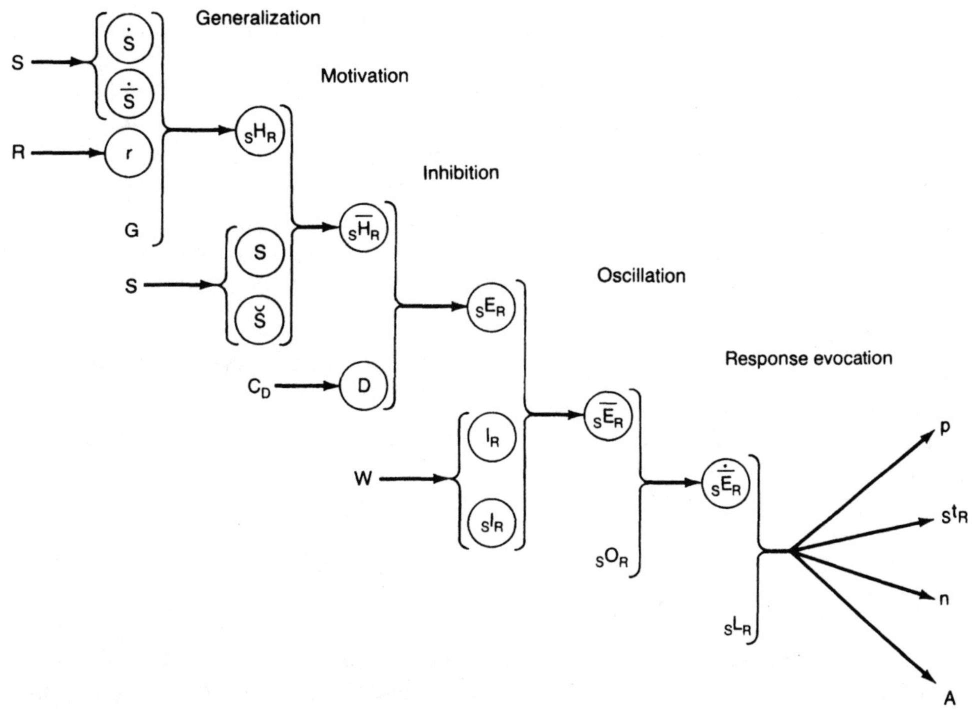

FIGURE (1)
Diagram summarizing the major symbolic constructs (encircled symbols) employed in the present system of behavior theory together with the symbols of the supporting objectively observable conditions and events. In this diagram $\dot{S}$ represents the physical stimulus energy involved in learning; R, the organism's reaction; s, the neural result of the stimulus; $\dot{s}$, the neural interaction arising from the impact of two or more stimulus components; r, the efferent impulse leading to reaction; G, the occurrence of a reinforcing state of affairs; $_SH_R$, habit strength; S, evocation stimulus on the same stimulus continuum as S; $_S\bar{H}_R$, the generalized habit strength; C_D, the objectively observable phenomena determining the drive; D, the physiological strength of the drive to motivate action; $_SE_R$, the reaction potential; W, work involved in an evoked reaction; I_R, reactive inhibition; $_SI_R$, conditioned inhibition; $_S\bar{E}_R$, effective reaction potential; $_SO_R$, oscillation; $_S\dot{\bar{E}}_R$, momentary effective reaction potential; $_SL_R$, reaction threshold; p, probability of reaction evocation; $_St_R$, latency of reaction evocation; n, number of unreinforced reactions to produce experimental extinction; and A, amplitude of reaction. Above the symbols the lines beneath the words *reinforcement, generalization, motivation, inhibition, oscillation,* and *response evocation* indicate roughly the segments of the chain of symbolic constructs with which each process is especially concerned.

teristics of the environment, external and internal. For this reason a prerequisite of truly adaptive action is that both the condition of the organism and that of all relevant portions of the environment must somehow be brought simultaneously to bear on the reactive organs. The first link of this necessary functional *rapport* of the effector organs with organismic needs and environmental conditions is constituted by receptors which convert the biologically more important of the environmental energies (S) into neural impulses (s). For the most part these neural impulses flow to the brain, which acts as a kind of automatic switchboard mediating their efferent flow (r) to the effectors in such a way as to evoke response (R). In this connection there are two important neural principles to be noted.

The first of these principles to be observed is that after the stimulus (S) has ceased to act upon the receptor, the afferent impulse (s) continues its activity for some seconds, or possibly minutes under certain circumstances, though with gradually decreasing intensity. This *perseverative stimulus trace* is biologically important because it brings the effector organ *en rapport* not only with environmental events which are occurring at the time but with the events which have occurred in the recent past, a matter frequently critical for survival. Thus is effected a short-range temporal integration. . . .

The second neural principle is that the receptor discharges and their perservative traces (s) generated on the different occasions of the impact of a given stimulus energy (S) upon the receptor, while usually very similar, are believed almost never to be exactly the same. This lack of uniformity is postulated as due (1) to the fact that many receptors are activated by stimulus energies simultaneously and (2) to "afferent neural interaction." The latter hypothesis states that the receptor discharges interact, while passing through the nervous system to the point where newly acquired receptor-effector connections have their locus, in such a way that each receptor discharge changes all the others to a greater or less extent; i.e., s is changed to $\check{s}_1$, $\check{s}_2$, or $\check{s}_3$, etc., in accordance with the particular combination of other stimulus energies which is acting on the sensorium at the time (see Figure (1)). This type of action is particularly important because the mediation of the responses of organisms to distinctive combinations or patterns of stimuli, rather than to the components of the patterns, is presumably dependent upon it. . . .

The detailed physiological principles whereby the nervous system mediates the behavioral adaptation of the organism are as yet far from completely known. As a result we are forced for the most part to get along as best as we can with relatively coarse molar formulations derived from conditioned-reflex and other behavior experiments. From this point of view it appears that the processes of organic evolution have yielded two distinct but closely related means of effective behavioral adaptation. One of these is the laying down of unlearned receptor-effector connections ($_SU_R$) within the neural tissue which will directly mediate at least approximate behavioral adjustments to urgent situations which are of frequent occurrence but which require relatively simple responses. . . . The second means of effecting behavioral adjustment is probably evolution's most impressive achievement; this is the capacity of organisms themselves to acquire automatically adaptive receptor-effector connections. Such acquisition is *learning*.

LEARNING AND THE PROBLEM OF REINFORCEMENT

The substance of the elementary learning process as revealed by much experimentation seems to be this: A condition of need exists in a more or less complex setting of receptor discharges initiated by the action of environmental stimulus energies. This combination of circumstances activates numerous vaguely adaptive reaction potentials mediated by the unlearned receptor-effector organization ($_SU_R$) laid down by organic evolution. The relative strengths of these various reaction potentials are varied from instant to instant by the oscillation factor ($_SO_R$). The resulting spontaneous variability of the momentary unlearned reaction potential ($_SU_R$) produces the randomness and variability of the unlearned behavior evoked under given conditions. In case one of these random responses, or a sequence of them, results in the reduction of a need dominant at the time, there follows as an indirect effect what is known as reinforcement (G, of Figure (1)). This consists in (1) a strengthening of the particular receptor-effector connections which originally mediated the reaction and (2) a tendency for all receptor discharges (s) occurring at about the same time to acquire new connections with the effectors mediating the response in question. The first effect is known as primitive trial-and-error learning; the second is known as conditioned-reflex learning. In most adaptive situations both processes occur concurrently; indeed, *very likely they are at bottom the same process, differing only in the accidental circumstance that the first begins with an appreciable strength, whereas the second sets out from zero.* As a result, when the same need again arises in this or a similar situation, the stimuli will activate the same effectors more certainly, more promptly, and more vigorously than on the first occasion. Such action, while by no means adaptively infallible, in the long run will reduce the need more surely than would a chance sampling of the unlearned response tendencies ($_SU_R$) at the command of other need and stimulating situations, and more quickly and completely than did that particular need and stimulating situation on the first occasion. Thus the acquisition of such receptor-effector connections will, as a rule, make for survival; i.e., it will be adaptive.

Careful observation and experiment reveal, particularly with the higher organisms, large numbers of situations in which learning occurs with no associated primary need reduction. When these cases are carefully studied it is found that the reinforcing agent is a situation or event involving a stimulus aggregate or compound which has been closely and consistently associated with the need reduction. Such a situation is called a secondary reinforcing agent, and the strengthening of the receptor-effector connections which results from its action is known as secondary reinforcement. This principle is of immense importance in the behavior of the higher species.

The organization within the nervous system brought about by a particular reinforcement is known as a habit; since it is not directly observable, habit has the status of a symbolic construct. Strictly speaking, habit is a functional connection between *s* and *r;* it is accordingly represented by the symbol $_sH_r$. Owing, however, to the close functional relationship between *S* and *s* on the one hand, and between *r* and *R* on the other, the symbol $_SH_R$ will serve for most expository purposes; the latter symbol has the advantage that *S* and *R* both refer to conditions or events normally open to public observation. The position of $_SH_R$ in the chain of constructs of the present system is shown in Figure (1).

While it is difficult to determine the quantitative value of an unobservable, various indirect considerations combine to indicate as a first approximation that habit strength is a simple increasing growth function of the number of reinforcements. The unit chosen for the expression of habit strength is called the *hab,* a shortened form of the word "habit"; a hab is 1 per cent of the physiological limit of habit strength under completely optimal conditions.

CONDITIONS WHICH INFLUENCE THE MAGNITUDE OF HABIT INCREMENT PER REINFORCEMENT

A more careful scrutiny of the conditions of reinforcement reveals a number which are subject to variation, and experiments have shown that the magnitude of the habit increment (Δ_SH_R) per reinforcement is dependent in one way or another upon the quantitative variation of these conditions. One such factor concerns the primary reinforcing agent. It has been found that, quality remaining constant, the magnitude of the increment of habit strength per reinforcement is a negatively accelerated increasing function of the quantity of the reinforcing agent employed per reinforcement.

A second factor of considerable importance in determining the magnitude of Δ_SH_R is the degree of asynchronism between the onset of the stimulus and of the response to which it is being conditioned. This situation is complicated by whether or not the stimulus terminates its action on the receptor before the response occurs. In general the experimental evidence indicates that in case both the stimulus and the response are of very brief duration, the increment of habit strength per reinforcement is maximal when the reaction (and the reinforcement) occurs a short half second after the stimulus, and that it is a negatively accelerated decreasing function of the extent to which asynchronisms in either direction depart from this optimum. In case the reaction synchronizes with the continued action of the stimulus on the receptor, the increment of habit strength per reinforcement is a simple negative growth function of the length of time that the stimulus has acted on the receptor when the reaction occurs.

A third important factor in the reinforcing situation is the length of time elapsing between the occurrence of the reaction and of the reinforcing state of affairs (*G*, Figure (1)). Experiments indicate that this "gradient of reinforcement" is a negatively accelerated decreasing growth function of the length of time that reinforcement follows the reaction. The principle of secondary reinforcement, combined with that of the gradient of reinforcement, explains the extremely numerous cases of learning in which the primary reinforcement is indefinitely remote from the act reinforced. A considerable mass of experimental evidence indicates that a kind of blending of the action of these two principles generates a secondary phenomenon called the "goal gradient." Upon empirical investigation this turns out to be a decreasing exponential or negative growth function of the time (t) separating the reaction from the primary reinforcement for delays ranging from ten seconds to five or six minutes; delays greater than six minutes have not yet been sufficiently explored to make possible a quantitative statement concerning them.

There are doubtless other conditions which influence the magnitude of the increment of habit strength resulting from each reinforcement. Those listed above certainly are typical and probably comprise the more important of them. An adequate statement of the primary law or laws of learning would accordingly take the form of an equation in which $_SH_R$ would be expressed as a joint function not only of N but of the quantity and quality of the reinforcing agent, and of the temporal relationships of S to R and of R to G. A formula which purports to be a first approximation to such a general quantitative expression of the primary laws of learning is given as equations 16 and 17.*

A System of Behavior

B. F. Skinner

A DEFINITION OF BEHAVIOR

It is necessary to begin with a definition. Behavior is only part of the total activity of an organism, and some formal delimitation is called for. The field might be defined historically by appeal to an established interest. As distinct from the other activities of the organism, the phenomena of behavior are held together by a common conspicuousness. Behavior is what an organism is *doing*—or more accurately what it is observed by another organism to be doing. But to say that a given sample of activity falls within the field of behavior simply because it normally comes under observation would misrepresent the significance of this property. It is more to the point to say that behavior is that part of the functioning of an organism which is engaged in acting upon or having commerce with the outside world. The peculiar properties which make behavior a unitary and unique subject mat-

*Equations 16 and 17 are presented earlier in Hull's book but are not included in this excerpt. (Ed. note)

From Skinner, B. F. (1938). *The behavior of organisms*. New York: Appleton-Century-Crofts, pp. 6, 18–26.

ter follow from this definition. It is only because the receptors of other organisms are the most sensitive parts of the outside world that the appeal to an established interest in what an organism is doing is successful.

By behavior, then, I mean simply the movement of an organism or of its parts in a frame of reference provided by the organism itself or by various external objects or fields of force. It is convenient to speak of this as the action of the organism upon the outside world, and it is often desirable to deal with an effect rather than with the movement itself, as in the case of the production of sounds. . . .

TYPE S AND TYPE R CONDITIONING

In the course of this book I shall attempt to show that a large body of material not usually considered in this light may be expressed with dynamic laws which differ from the classical examples only in the nature of the operations. The most important instances are conditioning and extinction (with their subsidiary processes of discrimination), drive, and emotion, which I propose to formulate in terms of changes in reflex strength. One type of conditioning and its corresponding extinction may be described here.

The Law of Conditioning of Type S. The approximately simultaneous presentation of two stimuli, one of which (the 'reinforcing' stimulus) belongs to a reflex existing at the moment at some strength, may produce an increase in the strength of a third reflex composed of the response of the reinforcing reflex and the other stimulus.

The Law of Extinction of Type S. If the reflex strengthened through conditioning of Type S is elicited without presentation of the reinforcing stimulus, its strength decreases.

These laws refer to the Pavlovian type of conditioned reflex. . . . I wish to point out here simply that the observed data are merely changes in the strength of a reflex. As such they have no dimensions which distinguish them from changes in strength taking place during fatigue, facilitation, inhibition, or, as I shall show later, changes in drive, emotion, and so on. The process of conditioning is distinguished by what is done to the organism to induce the change; in other words, it is defined by the operation of the simultaneous presentation of the reinforcing stimulus and another stimulus. The type is called Type S to distinguish it from conditioning of Type R (see below) in which the reinforcing stimulus is contingent upon a response.

Before indicating how other divisions of the field of behavior may be formulated in terms of reflex strength, it will be necessary to consider another kind of behavior, which I have not yet mentioned. The remaining dynamic laws will then be taken up in connection with both kinds at once.

OPERANT BEHAVIOR

With the discovery of the stimulus and the collection of a large number of specific relationships of stimulus and response, it came to be assumed by many writers that all behavior would be accounted for in this way as soon as the appropriate stimuli could be identified. Many elaborate attempts have been made to establish the plausibility of this assumption, but they have not, I believe, proved convincing. There is a large body of behavior that does not seem to be *elicited,* in the sense in which a cinder in the eye elicits closure of the lid, although it may eventually stand in a different kind of relation to external stimuli. The original 'spontaneous' activity of the organism is chiefly of this sort, as is the greater part of the conditioned behavior of the adult organism, as I hope to show later. Merely to assert that there *must* be eliciting stimuli is an unsatisfactory appeal to ignorance. The brightest hope of establishing the generality of the eliciting stimulus was provided by Pavlov's demonstration that part of the behavior of the adult organism could be shown to be under the control of stimuli which had *acquired* their power to elicit. But a formulation of this process will show that in every case the response to the conditioned stimulus must first be elicited by an unconditioned stimulus. I do not believe that the 'stimulus' leading to the elaborate responses of singing a song or of painting a picture can be regarded as the mere substitute for a stimulus or a group of stimuli which originally elicited these responses or their component parts.

Most of the pressure behind the search of eliciting stimuli has been derived from a fear of 'spontaneity' and its implication of freedom. When spontaneity cannot be avoided, the attempt is made to define it in terms of unknown stimuli. Thus, Bethe says that the term 'has long been used to describe behavior for which the stimuli are not known and I see no reason why the word should be stricken from a scientific vocabulary.' But an event may occur without any observed antecedent event and still be dealt with adequately in a descriptive science. I do not mean that there are no originating forces in spontaneous behavior but simply that they are not located in the environment. We are not in a position to see them, and we have no need to. This kind of behavior might be said to be *emitted* by the organism, and there are appropriate techniques for dealing with it in that form. One important independent variable is time. In making use of it I am simply recognizing that the observed datum is the appearance of a given identifiable sample of behavior at some more or less orderly rate. The use of a rate is perhaps the outstanding characteristic of the general method to be outlined in the following pages, where we shall be concerned very largely with behavior of this sort.

The attempt to force behavior into the simple stimulus-response formula has delayed the adequate treatment of that large part of behavior which cannot be shown to be under the control of eliciting stimuli. It will be highly important to recognize the existence of this separate field in the present work. Differences between the two kinds of behavior will accumulate throughout the book, and I shall not argue the distinction here at any length. The kind of behavior that is correlated with specific eliciting stimuli may be called *respondent* behavior and a given correlation *a respondent*. The term is intended to carry the sense of a relation to a prior event. Such behavior as is not under this kind of control I shall call *operant* and any specific example *an operant*. The term refers to a posterior event, to be noted shortly. The term reflex will be used to include both respondent and operant even though in its original meaning it applied to respondents only. A single term for both is convenient because both are topographical units of behavior and because an operant may and usually does acquire a relation to prior stimulation. In general, the notion of a reflex is to be emptied of any connotation of the active 'push' of the stimulus. The terms refer here to correlated entities, and to nothing more. All implications of dynamism and all metaphorical and figurative definitions should be avoided as far as possible.

An operant is an identifiable part of behavior of which it may be said, not that no stimulus can be found that will elicit it (there may be a respondent the response of which has the same topography), but that no correlated stimulus can be detected upon occasions when it is observed to occur. It is studied as an event appearing spontaneously with a given frequency. It has no static laws comparable with those of a respondent since in the absence of a stimulus the concepts of threshold, latency, after-discharge, and the *R/S* ratio are meaningless. Instead, appeal must be made to frequency of occurrence in order to establish the notion of strength. The strength of an operant is proportional to its frequency of occurrence, and the dynamic laws describe the changes in the rate of occurrence that are brought about by various operations performed upon the organism.

OTHER DYNAMIC LAWS

Three of the operations already described in relation to respondent behavior involve the elicitation of the reflex and hence are inapplicable to operants. They are the refractory phase, fatigue, and conditioning of Type S. The refractory phase has a curious parallel in the rate itself, as I shall note later, and a phenomenon comparable with fatigue may also appear in an operant. The conditioning of an operant differs from that of a respondent by involving the correlation of a reinforcing stimulus with a *response*. For this reason the process may be referred to as of Type R. Its two laws are as follows.

The Law of Conditioning of Type R. If the occurrence of an operant is followed by presentation of a reinforcing stimulus, the strength is increased.

The Law of Extinction of Type R. If the occurrence of an operant already strengthened through conditioning is not followed by the reinforcing stimulus, the strength is decreased.

The conditioning is here again a matter of a change in strength. The strength cannot begin at zero since at least one unconditioned response must occur to permit establishment of the relation with a reinforcing stimulus. Unlike conditioning of Type S the process has the effect of determining the form of the response, which is provided for in advance by the conditions of the correlation with a reinforcing stimulus or by the way in which the response must operate upon the environment to produce a reinforcement. . . .

It is only rarely possible to define an operant topographically (so that successive instances may be counted) without the sharper delineation of properties that is given by the act of conditioning. This dependence upon the posterior reinforcing stimulus gives the term operant its significance. In a respondent the response is the result of something previously done to the organism. This is true even for conditioned respondents because the operation of the simultaneous presentation of two stimuli precedes, or at least is independent of, the occurrence of the response. The operant, on the other hand, becomes significant for behavior and takes on an identifiable form when it acts upon the environment in such a way that a reinforcing stimulus is produced. The operant-respondent distinction goes beyond that between Types S and R because it applies to unconditioned behavior as well; but where both apply, they coincide exactly. Conditioning of Type R is impossible in a respondent because the correlation of the reinforcing stimulus with a response implies a correlation with its eliciting stimulus. It has already been noted that conditioning of Type S is impossible in operant behavior because of the absence of an eliciting stimulus.

An operant may come to have a relation to a stimulus which seems to resemble the relation between the stimulus and response in a respondent. The case arises when prior stimulation is correlated with the reinforcement of the operant. The stimulus may be said to set the occasion upon which a response will be reinforced, and therefore (through establishment of a discrimination) upon which it will occur; but it does not elicit the response. The distinction will be emphasized later.

One kind of operation that affects the strength of reflexes (both operant and respondent) falls within the traditional field of drive or motivation. It would be pointless to review here the various ways in which the field has been formulated. In a description of behavior in terms of the present system the subject presents itself simply as a class of dynamic changes in strength. For example, suppose that we are observing an organism in the presence of a bit of food. A certain sequence of progressive, manipulative, and ingestive reflexes will be evoked. The early stages of this sequence are operants, the later stages are respondents. At any given time the strengths may be measured either by observing the rate of occurrence in the case of the former or by exploring the static properties in the case of the latter. The problem of drive arises because the values so obtained vary between wide extremes. At one time the chain may be repeatedly evoked at a high rate, while at another no response may be forthcoming during a considerable period of time. In the vernacular we should say that the organism eats only when it is hungry. What we observe is that the strengths of these reflexes vary, and we must set about finding the operations of which they are a function. This is not difficult. Most important of all are the operations of feeding and fasting. By allowing a hungry organism, such as a rat, to eat bits of food placed before it, it is possible to show an orderly decline in the strength of this group of reflexes. Eventually a very low strength is reached and eating ceases. By allowing a certain time to elapse before food is again available it may be shown that the strength has risen to a value at which responses will occur. The same may be said of the later members of the chain, the strengths of which (as respondents) must be measured in terms of the static properties. Thus, the amount of saliva secreted in response to a gustatory stimulus may be a similar function of feeding and fasting. A complete account of the strengths of this particular group of reflexes may be given in terms of this operation, other factors being held constant. There are other operations to be taken into account, however, which affect the same group, such as deprivation of water, illness, and so on.

In another important group of changes in reflex strength the chief operation with which the changes are correlated is the presentation of what may be called 'emotional' stimuli—stimuli which typically elicit changes of this sort. They may be either unconditioned (for example, an electric shock) or conditioned according to Type S where the reinforcing stimulus has been emotional (for example, a tone which has preceded a shock). Other operations which induce an emotional change in strength are the restraint of a response, the interruption of a chain of reflexes through the removal of a reinforcing stimulus (see later), the administration of certain drugs, and so on. The resulting change in behavior is again in the strength of reflexes. . . .

The operations characterizing drive and emotion differ from the others listed in that they effect concurrent changes in *groups* of reflexes. The operation of feeding, for example, brings about changes in all the operants that have been reinforced with food and in all the conditioned and unconditioned respondents concerned with ingestion. Moreover, a single operation is not unique in its effect. There is more than one way of changing the strength of the group of reflexes varying with ingestion or with an emotional stimulus. In addition to the formulation of the effect upon a single reflex, we must deal also with *the* drive or *the* emotion as the 'state' of a group of reflexes. This is done by introducing a hypothetical middle term between the operation and the resulting observed change. 'Hunger,' 'fear,' and so on, are terms of this sort. The operation of feeding is said to affect the hunger and the hunger in turn the strength of the reflex. The notion of an intermediate state is valuable when (a) more than one reflex is affected by the operation, and (b) when several operations have the same effect. Its utility may perhaps be made clear with the following schemes. When an operation is unique in its effect and applies to a single reflex, it may be represented as follows:

Operation I — ( ) — Strength of Reflex I,

where no middle term is needed. When there are several operations having the same effect and affecting several reflexes, the relation may be represented as follows:

Operation I ╲ ╱ Strength of Reflex I
Operation II — 'State' — Strength of Reflex II
Operation III ╱ ╲ Strength of Reflex III

In the present system hypothetical middle terms ('states') will be used in the cases of drive and emotion, but no other properties will be assigned to them. A dynamic law always refers to the change in strength of a single reflex as a function of a single operation, and the intermediate term is actually unnecessary in its expression.

An observation of the state of a reflex at any given time is limited to its strength. Since the data are changes in strength and therefore the same in all dynamic laws, the system emphasizes the great importance of defining and classifying operations. The mere strength of the reflex itself is an ambiguous fact. It is impossible to tell from a momentary observation of strength whether its value is due especially to an operation of drive, conditioning, or emotion. Suppose, for example, that we have been working with an operant that has been reinforced with food and that at a given time we observe that the organism does not respond (*i.e.*, that the strength is low). *From the state of the reflex itself,* it is impossible to distinguish between the following cases. (1) The organism is hungry and unafraid, but the response has been extinguished. (2) The response is conditioned and the organism is hungry but afraid. (3) The response is conditioned, and the organism is unafraid but not hungry. (4) The response is conditioned, but the organism is both not hungry and afraid. (5) The organism is hungry, but it is afraid, and the response has been extinguished. (6) The organism is not afraid, but it is not hungry and the response has been extinguished. (7) The response has been extinguished, and the organism is afraid but not hungry. We can decide among these possibilities by referring to other behavior. If we present the stimulus of an *unconditioned* reflex varying with hunger and fear (say, if we present food), the question of conditioning is eliminated. If the organism eats, the first case listed above is proved. If it does not eat, the possibilities are then as follows. (1) The organism is hungry but afraid. (2) It is unafraid but not hungry. (3) It is both not hungry and afraid. If we then test another reflex, the strength of which decreases in a state of fear but which does not vary with hunger, and find it strong, the organism is not afraid and must therefore not be hungry.

The strength of a reflex at any given time is a function of all the operations that affect it. The principal task of a science of behavior is to isolate their separate effects and to establish their functional relationships with the strength.

The development of dynamic laws enables us to consider behavior which does not invariably occur under a given set of circumstances as, nevertheless, reflex (*i.e.,* as lawful). The early classical examples of the reflex were those of which the lawfulness was obvious. It was obvious because the number of variables involved was limited. A flexion reflex could be described very early because it was controlled by a stimulus and was not to any considerable extent a function of the operations of drive, emotion, or conditioning, which cause the greatest variability in strength. The discovery of conditioning of Type S brought under the principle of the reflex a number of activities the lawfulness of which was not evident until the conditioning operation was controlled. Operants, as predictable entities, are naturally isolated last of all because they are not controlled through stimuli and are subject to many operations. They are not *obviously* lawful. But with a rigorous control of all relevant operations the kind of necessity that naturally characterizes simple reflexes is seen to apply to behavior generally. I offer the experimental material described later in this book in support of this statement.

Engineering Behavior: Project Pigeon, World War II, and the Conditioning of B. F. Skinner

James H. Capshew

During the Second World War the scientific outlook and professional goals of American psychologist B. F. Skinner underwent a remarkable metamorphosis. Wartime contingencies reshaped his research agenda and converted him to the cause of behavioral engineering. Before the war, Skinner was reluctant to venture very far outside the academic laboratory. He was a scientific purist who resisted extrapolating the results of his animal experimentation to the realm of human behavior. After the war, he attempted to make such connections boldly explicit, arguing that the scientific principles of behaviorism had widespread applicability to human affairs. By the 1950s Skinner had emerged as an advocate of the use of operant conditioning techniques for the control of individual and group behavior in a variety of settings and promoted applications ranging from teaching machines to the design of entire societies.

Skinner's transition from inventive scientist to social inventor can be traced to the circumstances of World War II, which provided him with opportunities to explore the technological ramifications of operant psychology. Years later he noted that three wartime projects had dramatically broadened his intellectual horizons by offering the first evidence that his system of behavioral science could engender a system of behavioral engineering.[1] The first was known as Project Pigeon—an attempt to construct a missile guidance system utilizing the conditioned pecking behavior of pigeons. Project Pigeon consumed much of Skinner's energy during the war, and, even though it was never brought to fruition, it played a pivotal role in reorienting his thinking toward the possibilities of behavioral engineering.[2] The second project was closer to home. Faced with the challenges of raising a second baby daughter, Skinner drew on his manual skills and invented the "baby-tender," a futuristic climate-controlled crib designed to promote the physical and psychological health of infants.[3] Featured in the *Ladies' Home Journal* shortly following the war, the device was later marketed commercially with little success as the "Aircrib."[4] Skinner's third novel project was precisely that—a novel. During the summer of 1945 he drafted the manuscript that would be published three years later as *Walden Two*.[5] The book was Skinner's attempt to conceive a utopian human society based on the principles of reinforcement that he had gleaned from his laboratory research on animal behavior.

Taken together, these efforts represent Skinner's initial forays into the realm of behavioral engineering, and they clearly demonstrate how the technocratic ideals embedded in his research practices found expression in the wartime context. Although Skinner's work was undeniably idiosyncratic, it reflected broader trends in American psychology that reached their fullest expression during the Second World War, with its overriding emphasis on military utility and the virtues of order, control, and effectiveness.[6]

Of the three projects, *Walden Two* became the most famous. It was the first step in Skinner's public transformation from experimental psychologist to social philosopher, and its description of an entire culture molded along behaviorist lines suggested the scope of Skinner's ambitions. As important as the novel was, it was only the most visible manifestation of a more fundamental change that had begun during Project Pigeon, when Skinner first confronted the

Capshew, J. H. (1993). Engineering behavior: Project Pigeon, World War II, and the conditioning of B. F. Skinner. *Technology and Culture, 34,* 835–857.

difficulties associated with conducting research outside the laboratory environment. The history of this unusual project is essential to understanding Skinner's profound intellectual shift from the development of a natural science of behavior in the laboratory toward its technological applications in a variety of real-life contexts. Project Pigeon encouraged Skinner to think about his research in new ways and reinforced his belief in the underlying orderliness of behavior. Skinner's behavioral engineering was characterized by the same kind of inventive activity he had engaged in as a professional psychologist, except that it took place beyond the confines of the laboratory.

From the start of his career, Skinner had been an inventor. His experimental work depended significantly on his ability to design, build, and repair laboratory apparatus. Devices such as the Skinner box were essential in providing the proper conditions for the manipulation of operant behavior; in fact, they can be regarded as machines for the production of behavior. When integrated with other elements of Skinner's research method, such as conditioning techniques, data recording, and interpretive schemes, such devices constituted part of a technological system for scientific research.[7] What was notable about Skinner's wartime projects was their common focus on controlling behavior in nonlaboratory settings. Because it was his first serious effort to construct a technological system to address a practical problem, Project Pigeon is worth examining in detail.

THE CONTROL OF BEHAVIOR

In 1938, a year before the war began in Europe, Skinner published his first book, *The Behavior of Organisms: An Experimental Analysis*.[8] The monograph synthesized nearly a decade of laboratory research on the conditioning of white rats and contained Skinner's program for establishing psychology as a natural science alongside biology, chemistry, and physics. The young psychologist was after nothing less than the foundations for a true science of behavior, one that treated behavior as a scientific datum in its own right. He was equally critical of both mentalistic theorizing and neurological reductionism. In his view, the goal of a naturalistic science of behavior was within reach, thanks largely to the legacy of Charles Darwin, Lloyd Morgan, and John B. Watson.

Skinner's scientific ambitions had been shaped by a long apprenticeship in the Laboratory of General Physiology at Harvard University. Arriving at the university as a graduate student in the mid-1920s, Skinner earned his Ph.D. in 1931. Although his degree was in psychology, he did the bulk of his work in physiology, where his primary mentor was W. J. Crozier, the architect of the Harvard laboratory's program. Under the influence of Crozier and other members of the laboratory, Skinner became an adherent of the engineering ideal in biology championed by Jacques Loeb and sought to extend similar principles and techniques to the control of behavior.[9] Following an intellectual agenda outlined in his doctoral dissertation, Skinner virtually lived in the laboratory for five years of postdoctoral research, first as a National Research Council fellow and then as a member of Harvard's Society of Fellows.

Skinner modeled his approach on Ernst Mach's philosophy of science, emphasizing the functional description of observed behavior and rejecting causal explanations as unnecessary. His laboratory practices followed the pattern laid down by Loeb and his disciples with their characteristic accent on the manipulation of biological organisms, and Skinner adopted "prediction" and "control" as his watchwords.

During this period Skinner gradually refined his concept of the operant. In simple terms, operant behavior was emitted by the organism spontaneously, rather than being elicited by particular stimuli as in the classical conditioning demonstrated by Ivan Pavlov. In classical conditioning, if a neutral stimulus (such as a bell) is paired with an unconditioned stimulus (such as food), eventually the unconditioned response (salivation) will occur upon presentation of the previously neutral stimulus. Although classical conditioning had yielded useful quantitative analyses of some kinds of behavior, it seemed to be limited to simpler, reflexive behavior. Skinner was interested in exploring the more complex kinds of behavior that were maintained through operant reinforcement.

Skinner developed relatively simple yet powerful experimental procedures for operant conditioning. The basic setup involved a single rat in a standard apparatus (what became known as the Skinner box), in which the animal would press a bar in order to receive reinforcing stimuli in the form of food or water. Measurements of the rat's bar-pressing behavior were recorded mainly in the form of graphs plotting the cumulative number of responses over a given period of time.

Skinner discovered many regularities in the response rates of his subjects under various stimulus protocols and reinforcement schedules. As an example of how an animal's behavior could be radically shaped by operant methods, he trained one rat, named Pliny the Elder, to perform a series of acrobatic tricks with a marble by reinforcing successive approximations of the desired responses. This provided a vivid demonstration of the power of operant conditioning to produce responses that were not in the original behavioral repertoire of the rat. Skinner was well aware that professional animal trainers relied on similar methods, which they had developed through trial and error rather than disciplined investigation. Skinner's work with Pliny came to the attention of the national media, and a story about it was published in *Life* magazine in 1937.[10]

By this time Skinner had left his monastic lab-centered existence at Harvard and was an assistant professor of psychology at the University of Minnesota. There he was exposed to the demands of teaching and to the array of scientific and professional concerns represented in a large midwestern psychology department. Although Minnesota was a noted center for applied psychology, Skinner hewed to his experimental program. In *The Behavior of Organisms,* he had studiously avoided commenting on the relevance of his work to human behavior until the last pages of the volume, where he admitted that "the importance of a science of behavior derives largely from the possibility of an eventual extension to human affairs. But it is a serious, though common, mistake to allow questions of ultimate application to influence the development of a systematic science at an early stage. I think it is true that the direction of the present inquiry has been determined solely by the exigencies of the system. . . . The book represents nothing more than an experimental analysis of a representative sample of behavior. Let him extrapolate who will."[11]

Not long afterward, the Second World War began, and Skinner himself was faced with the opportunity to extrapolate his system. Although a great number of other psychologists mobilized rapidly for the national emergency, nearly all, including those researchers in animal laboratories, addressed problems of human behavior. Skinner was unique, however, in that he found a way to continue working with animals in the unlikely field of guided missile technology.

THE GENESIS OF PROJECT PIGEON

Among the most disturbing aspects of the war in Europe was the emergence of aerial bombing as a terrible new weapon against which there was little reliable defense. Musing about the problem on a train bound for the Midwestern Psychological Association meeting in Chicago in 1940, Skinner was inspired with a solution: why not bomb the bombers with guided missiles dropped from planes flying at higher altitudes? The idea was hardly original—except for the guidance system, which would rely on the discriminative abilities of trained animals. As

Skinner described his first thoughts: "I saw a flock of birds lifting and wheeling in formation as they flew alongside the train. Suddenly I saw them as 'devices' with excellent vision and extraordinary maneuverability. Could they not guide a missile? Was the answer to the problem waiting for me in my own backyard?"[12]

Fifty years later Skinner's idea may appear outlandish since guided missile technology has become highly sophisticated, relying on the latest advances in electromechanics and electronics. At the time, however, the United States possessed virtually no expertise in guided missiles. The development of propulsion systems and warheads was confined to a few experimental projects in mechanical and electrical engineering laboratories, and guidance techniques based on servomechanisms were in the early stages of theoretical exploration. Work soon accelerated, however, when U.S. government authorities, realizing that the Nazis were well ahead in the area, started to mobilize American scientists and engineers.[13]

Skinner continued to ponder the idea, and by the spring of 1941 he was actively exploring its feasibility. Deciding that birds would be the most appropriate research subjects, he bought several pigeons and trained them to peck at a bull's-eye target. The birds were harnessed to a moveable hoist, and as they pecked their head movements operated electric motors that steered the hoist toward the target. Skinner demonstrated the experiment to John T. Tate, a well-known physicist and dean of the College of Science, Literature, and Art at Minnesota, who passed along the psychologist's "Description of a Plan for Directing a Bomb at a Target" to Richard C. Tolman, head of the physics department at the California Institute of Technology and vice chairman of the National Defense Research Committee (NDRC).[14]

Although Tolman called the plan "a new and unconventional approach to the problem," he rejected it, diplomatically claiming that the probable lack of interest by the armed services made it "hardly advisable" for the NDRC to develop it, even though the "suggestion may be perfectly feasible."[15] Skinner thanked Tolman for his interest and told him that he would continue to seek support for what was "admittedly a 'long shot.' "[16]

The entrance of the United States into the war after the attack on Pearl Harbor reactivated Skinner's interest, and on December 8, 1941, he began experiments on the guidance of offensive bombs directed toward stationary targets. With the help of a graduate student, Keller Breland, Skinner harnessed a pigeon in an apparatus that was guided by the bird's neck movements toward a target. After making a film demonstrating the device, he enlisted the aid of some of his colleagues in Washington and again approached the NDRC. Writing to Tolman once more, Skinner suggested that "if the United Nations could suddenly begin to sink ships with high altitude bombing, practically at the rate of one ship per bomb, the war would be won. And this is not a consequence to be sneezed at." He offered to send the demonstration film to the committee, joking that it would "at least . . . prove to be an entertaining 'short.' "[17] Tate also wrote to Tolman, avowing his "great confidence" in Skinner. In support of the unorthodox plan the physicist said, "If you have a steerable bomb, I feel fairly confident that a bird's vision and head movement constitute an instrument for guidance which is probably superior to anything which can be produced by the hand of man."[18]

In March 1942 Skinner traveled to New York to receive the prestigious Warren Medal of the Society of Experimental Psychologists. A chance encounter with a colleague led to a meeting between Skinner and the navy's chief of special devices in Washington. The official was supportive of Skinner's plan but was unable to provide financial backing.[19] Later the same month Tolman again rejected the proposal, in part because of the lack of suitable missiles. At that time only rudimentary research had been conducted on guided missile technology, and the

NDRC designated an entire division—Division 5—to foster its development.[20] Tolman encouraged Skinner to contact him if he performed more research and cautioned him against discussing the proposal in public.[21]

Skinner decided to continue on his own. Writing to Dean Tate about recent kamikaze attacks on Allied warships, he said it "looks as if the Japs were using men rather than birds. Perhaps we can get American morale that high, but if not, I can provide perfectly competent substitutes."[22] Through a fortuitous chain of circumstances, Skinner was able to obtain some research money from an unlikely source—the General Mills Company in Minneapolis. His work had come to the attention of the company's vice-president for research, Arthur D. Hyde, when it was mentioned by an inspired citizen in support of a scheme to use dogs to steer torpedoes by sound signals.[23] General Mills provided Skinner with a $5,000 grant to support his work during the summer of 1942.

General Mills also furnished the project with work space in an old flour mill, and another graduate student, Norman Guttman, volunteered to help. Skinner's group began working on an apparatus to translate a pigeon's pecking movements into a signal that could steer a gliding bomb. The pigeon's pecking behavior was shaped to the point where it would respond steadily and precisely to a sample visual target, which in this case was a particular street intersection in an aerial photograph of Stalingrad. At the same time Skinner worked with two more students, William K. Estes and Marian Breland, to carry out supplementary studies of possible environmental influences on the pigeon's behavior, including deprivation levels, reinforcement schedules, noise, and changes in temperature and pressure. The properly trained pigeon proved to be a stable performer under a wide range of conditions.[24]

Another demonstration film was sent to the NDRC, and the committee responded by dispatching an observer to Minnesota. Skinner was then invited to Washington to present his proposal in February 1943. The plan for what Skinner termed the "Bird's-Eye Bomb" was based on principles of operant conditioning, which could easily be applied to pigeons. The birds also made good subjects because of their excellent vision and their imperturbability in the face of acceleration and noise. The steering mechanism was straightforward and fairly simple. A plastic screen was placed behind a lens in the nose cone of the missile. As the bomb pointed downward toward the target, an image of the field was projected upward onto the screen. The bird, trained on a chosen target, would peck at the image on the screen, which was mounted on gimbal bearings. Electrical contacts were activated when the bird pecked at the off-center target image, which then generated signals to operate steering controls.[25]

This method simplified the stimulus-response situation. The target pattern appeared directly in front of the bird in such a way as to readily control the desired pecking response. Extraneous stimulation was minimized, and the pigeon's instinctive flight habits were bypassed by the use of a harness that restrained wing movements. Training the bird to peck at a target image, such as a boat or a landscape feature, was easily accomplished by using aerial photographs. (The project was provided with photos of the New Jersey coastline for training purposes.) By using variable-ratio conditioning schedules, Skinner was able to train birds to peck continuously for a period of several minutes, which would be necessary in the actual use of the missile. One bird, for example, made over 10,000 pecks in forty-five minutes without stopping. Factors that might disturb the birds were systematically studied. The pigeons could readily be adapted to loud noises, vibration, and acceleration. Temperature and pressure changes could easily be accommodated in the design of the device. Possible disturbing effects of variations in the target such as brightness and size, as well as of atmospheric interference such as clouds, could be avoided by means of appropriate training procedures.[26]

The proposal and demonstration film favorably impressed NDRC officials, and in March 1943 the chief technical officer of Division 5, electrical engineer Hugh S. Spencer, visited Minneapolis along with an assistant for a first-hand look at the project. They were pleased with what they saw, commenting that "aside from the pigeon racket, the organization seems exceptionally able, well staffed, and well equipped."[27] By April, Spencer informed the group that a contract was likely to be approved if quantitative data on the accuracy of the pigeon pecking could be provided. Skinner supplied the data in the form of plaster casts taken from modeling clay used to record the birds' pecking. The pigeons' marksmanship was excellent. Spencer also inquired about the available supply of birds. Skinner replied that practically all varieties of the species were usable and that pigeons could be obtained easily on the commercial market.[28]

An additional visit to the project laboratory by another NDRC staff member, physicist Alan C. Bemis, clinched the case for support. After spending a couple of hours with Skinner, Bemis reported, "As seems to be the case with most visitors, I went as a scoffer and came away somewhat converted."[29] Skinner discussed his need for assistance on the mechanical and electrical engineering aspects of the device. The only other visual guidance system under development by Division 5 was one that utilized television, and in consideration of the money spent on it Bemis commented, "Pigeons don't look too bad, but I still wouldn't know whether to vote yes or no on a contract."[30] His ambivalent endorsement epitomized the general attitude toward the project within the National Defense Research Committee. Even though the animal homing device had some promise, especially given the state of guidance-system technology, the NDRC officials clearly had trouble accommodating a psychological approach to an engineering problem.

By the end of May, Spencer wrote to Vannevar Bush, president of the Carnegie Institution and director of the Office of Scientific Research and Development (OSRD), the NDRC's parent body, to recommend support for the project, citing computations indicating that the system could guide a missile to within 20 feet of its target if the original azimuth error was less than 2,000 feet. Bush thanked Spencer for the project summary, stating, "I have the feeling that this whole subject is now for the first time on a basis of sound scientific examination from the angle of the physical as well as the organic elements."[31] On June 1, the NDRC awarded a $25,000 contract for an "organic homing device," to General Mills for the period from February 1 to December 31, 1943.[32]

REFINING THE DEVICE

Neither Skinner nor the NDRC engineers made much effort to enlist advice about the project from other psychologists. On a programmatic level, Skinner and his group received the endorsement of Princeton psychologist Charles W. Bray, soon to become head of the OSRD Applied Psychology Panel.[33] The panel, however, was oriented toward manpower and training problems and was preoccupied with the administration of its own contracts. Skinner had mentioned a number of psychologists as potential advisors, but the suggestion was never followed up.[34] Project Pigeon remained isolated both intellectually and institutionally from the tight-knit wartime psychology community.

At General Mills, the project was supervised by Arthur Hyde, vice-president and director of research. Hyde, who wanted to channel the company's broad program of engineering research on food-processing machinery into federal contract research, became an enthusiastic supporter of Skinner's group. Bemis, the NDRC official assigned to oversee the project, was located at Division 5's headquarters at the Massachusetts Institute of Technology (MIT). Deeply involved in overseeing a number of contracts for servomechanism research and development, he was not particularly interested in the Minnesota project, and its distant location reinforced his laissez-faire attitude. It was clear from the start that General Mills and Project Pigeon were on their own.

Problems soon arose as it became apparent that the main technical obstacles were mechanical rather than psychological. The birds' pecking provided an adequate signal for the servomechanism, but the development of mechanical linkages for translating the signal into steering movements proved difficult. Skinner was disappointed with the slow pace of the mechanical research saying, "I am not yet used to the low tempo of industry." Unfortunately, collaboration between the project's psychologists and engineers was hampered because the two groups were not under the same roof at General Mills, being housed in separate buildings nearly 4 miles apart. The NDRC's Spencer also expressed some reservations about the project's low-budget style, which he characterized privately as building on a "hay-wire-screen-door basis."[35]

Within a few months, however, the General Mills group constructed an improved signaling system that used pneumatic valves rather than electrical contacts. The target plate rested on four air valves at its edges. Depending on the location of the bird's pecking, the valves would allow air into the chamber and operate tambours that sent signals to the mechanism. As Skinner described it: "When the missile was on target, the pigeon pecked the center of the plate, all valves admitted equal amounts of air, and the tambours remained in neutral positions. But if the image moved as little as a quarter of an inch off-center, corresponding to a very small angular displacement of the target, more air was admitted by the valves on one side, and the resulting displacement of the tambours sent appropriate correcting orders directly to the servosystem."[36] By early September 1943 Project Pigeon had produced a workable model. At that time the project engineer at General Mills tried to get more information concerning the design and performance characteristics of the missile, which was under development at the MIT Servomechanisms Laboratory. The NDRC contract monitor was lackadaisical in responding to the queries, and, without proper specifications for their part of the servomechanism, Project Pigeon workers refined their system as best they could.[37]

The project was discussed at the next general meeting of NDRC Division 5. After hearing a report on its overall progress, the division chief could foresee eventual combat action, "not tomorrow, but in the not indefinite future."[38] This meeting was apparently the first time that many division officials had heard of the project, and Bemis told Hyde that there were favorable notices "in spite of the natural reaction which everyone has when learning about it for the first time to make light of it."[39]

By November contract funds were running out, and Skinner was anxious for NDRC officials to view his working model. In mid-December, shortly before the contract officially expired, Spencer and Bemis made another trip to Minnesota. They reviewed tracking data and observed the simulator—now with a three-bird control system to provide redundancy—following a target in the laboratory. Skinner later reported, "The only questions which arose were the inevitable consequence of our lack of information about the signal required to steer the [missile]."[40] The Minnesota group, without guidance from the NDRC or its vehicle contractors, had had to make arbitrary engineering decisions, such as compromising between smoothness and sensitivity in the vacuum-generated signal. Unfortunately, the chosen values had produced data that did not favorably impress the NDRC advisors. Bemis thought the birds' behavior looked erratic and was skeptical about the mechanics of the device. He favored extending the contract, "but," as he told Spencer, "let's can the thing in a hurry if they don't do a neat job on the oscillating target measurements."[41]

Project Pigeon came up for extended discussion at the next meeting of the NDRC, in January 1944. The MIT physicist Joseph C. Boyce, chief of the section, recommended the continuation of three projects, including the General Mills contract. The other two contracts—totaling $130,000—were quickly approved. Boyce began discussion of the third by saying, "I, having been previously skeptical, would now like to recommend an additional $25,000 for General Mills for the continuation of the studies on the organic homing project."[42] He noted that the latest version of the device used three pigeons rather than one for added efficiency and reliability. Boyce's positive opinion was undercut by Spencer, who told the group that he and Bemis were disappointed by their observations in Minnesota the month before. Concerned about the overextension of the project budget (it had run out of contract funds in November), Spencer had told Hyde then that the results were "not of sufficient promise to justify my asking him to go any farther or giving him any expectation of further support from NDRC."[43] Hyde had asked what kind of data the NDRC advisors would find conclusive; Spencer replied that they would like something quantitative that Albert C. Hall, a specialist at the Servomechanisms Lab, could analyze. General Mills complied, Spencer reported, but "unfortunately, the data shows just a little too much hope, so that you can't drop it out of hand. It is not quite good enough to be promising; it is not quite bad enough to throw away."[44]

An official from another section who had originally supported the contract changed his mind, saying that "if it doesn't look pretty good by this time I'm inclined to be a little cool."[45] Another committee member, aeronautical scientist Hugh Dryden, who was engaged in missile development, criticized the control mechanism as a "player piano movement type of thing" of the sort expected in a psychologist's laboratory.[46] J. C. Hunsaker, the National Advisory Committee for Aeronautics representative, maintained his original opposition. Although his vote did not count, Bemis, the project's technical monitor, voiced his opposition to extending the contract. In the face of dwindling support, Boyce was ready to withdraw his motion for $25,000, but the group went ahead and voted, rejecting the request for more funds for Project Pigeon.[47]

FIGHTING FOR CONTINUATION

Reacting to news of the termination, Skinner exploded with a long letter to Spencer: He began by saying that "the action of the Division regarding our project was very nearly a knockout blow" and that he found it "difficult to understand this decision." He went on to reiterate the rationale for the project and suggested that the device had not been "judged fully on its merits" because the division had not provided complete performance specifications. The signal system gave values within the verbal specifications supplied in November, but those had evidently changed. Skinner complained that "if more rigid specifications are now found to be necessary, we should at least have been given the chance to shoot for them." Responding to another question concerning the bird's accuracy at close range, Skinner told Spencer that the bird could be conditioned to focus on successively smaller details as the target approached. Furthermore, "the extraordinary possibilities of pattern selection could hardly have been correctly represented to the Division at the time action was taken, since we have not reported on them."[48] Skinner provided his own analysis of the decision:

> My guess is that certain technicalities have been invoked to support an underlying doubt concerning the reliability of the birds. I am quite sure that a non-organismic device which gave the same kind of signal with respect to any visual pattern

> would not be dropped at this stage. As a psychologist I can understand this (I have certainly seen enough of it during the past four years!), but I hate to accept it as the final word of men well acquainted with the history and methods of science. Any valid judgment of reliability must be made on the facts, not on random personal experiences. As you yourself must be able to testify, every competent person who has familiarized himself with our work has passed from a stage of amused skepticism to a serious belief that the scheme deserves to be tried. It is unfortunate that the final decision always seems to rest with men who have not had the benefit of close contact with the project.[49]

Skinner wanted to present his case directly to NDRC officials, hoping to persuade them to reopen the contract "up to the point of a field test." But he left the decision to Spencer, saying to him, "If you feel that such a step is hopeless, that the action would not be reconsidered, please say so frankly. In that case we shall immediately close up shop."[50] Under Hyde's signature additional supporting materials, including new data on the signal characteristics, were sent to Spencer from General Mills. In that report Hyde estimated that the device could be ready for a drop test in one month, at an estimated cost of $6,000. He repeated the group's plea that their work be more closely coordinated with the vehicle development team at MIT, complaining that "so far we have been working in the dark . . . with rather nebulous guesses and assumptions for guidance." In summary, he listed fourteen distinct advantages of the device, including its resistance to jamming, automatic close-up targeting, wide field of vision and small dead spot, easy construction, and short preparation time.[51]

Hyde also appealed to Spencer's superiors at the National Defense Research Committee. He arranged for the president of General Mills to contact Frank B. Jewett, an NDRC member and president of Bell Laboratories, and sent him a copy of the report. Ten days after the termination Jewett put Spencer "on the griddle" at a general NDRC meeting. Under pressure to justify the decision, Spencer requested more information from General Mills and asked Hall of the MIT Servomechanisms Lab to prepare a statement concerning the proper testing procedures for the device.[52]

The General Mills researchers responded with a three-part plan, covering drop tests, combat tests, and regular field use. The drop tests would use six pigeon units, costing $1,000 apiece, and could be ready to go in one week. For combat testing an estimated 200 units—employing 1,000 birds and fifty training devices—would be required, taking about three months of preparation time. Some forty unskilled workers would be needed to condition the pigeons under the supervision of five psychologists. Finally, plans for a regular field program projected sixteen units per day. For the necessary output of fifty birds per day, some 3,000 pigeons would participate in a general training program. Upon selection for a mission, they would be conditioned to the specific target. The basic conditioning work could be performed by the elderly or physically unfit, who could learn the procedures in a month or less. Compared to other military logistical operations, personnel requirements would be relatively modest, consisting of four experts, nine skilled group trainers (e.g., graduate students), 100 unskilled trainers, twenty caretakers, two repairmen, one pigeon specialist, one records clerk, one secretary, and a part-time installation crew. The report ended with a rhetorical flourish aimed at the NDRC engineers: "We again wish to emphasize our belief that the pigeon—an organism—is essentially an extremely reliable instrument, rugged in construction, simple and economical to obtain, and easily conditioned to be entirely predictable in behavior."[53]

Spencer received a five-page memorandum in early March from Hall regarding the device's technical feasibility. The servomechanism expert seemed impressed with its possibilities and stated that "at the present time I can see nothing which would lead me to believe that such a system should be inoperative."[54] On the basis of the new material Spencer pushed for reconsideration of the project. He wrote Hyde: "If the Division's action in terminating the project at its last meeting was premature, the fault was mine. I did not feel at that time assurance that the results obtainable by the system could be as substantially improved as your later work has shown possible."[55] Soon Spencer sent a memo to Division 5 members asking that the project be reconsidered. Citing the improved results reported by General Mills, Spencer apologized for "misleading" the group at the last meeting and admitted, "I am wholly candid in stating that the material furnished this office in these two reports is definitely more encouraging than anything that I expected to receive."[56] Skinner and his group were invited to present their case at the next meeting of Division 5, in March 1944.[57]

Spencer began the meeting's discussion by saying that he would have supported extension of the contract in January had the improved data been available then. Hall, harboring some doubts about the device, strongly recommended that thorough laboratory testing be completed before field testing. His mathematical calculations of the signal characteristics were inconsistent with the empirical data the project researchers had obtained. Various explanations of the inconsistency were offered, but, whatever reason for it, the signal seemed adequate for controlling the missile. Skinner thought the discrepancy had been satisfactorily resolved beforehand and was surprised when Hall told the group "that the signal we reported would cause the missile to 'hunt' wildly and lose the target."[58]

Skinner went on to enunciate the unique advantages of the organic device, pointing out the bird's ability to react to patterns rather than to the point sources or fields of force that radar and other systems relied on. Drawing on the language of engineering again, he said, "We have used pigeons, not because the pigeon is an intelligent bird, but because it is a practical one and can be made into a machine, from all practical points of view."[59]

Hoping that a live demonstration would dispel any doubts about the feasibility of the project, Skinner set up a simple simulation. A target was projected on a window in a small black box in which the pigeon was harnessed. A small tube would allow individual observation, but, since time was short, the top was taken off the box. As Skinner described the scene:

> The translucent screen was flooded with so much light that the target was barely visible, and the peering scientists offered conditions much more unfamiliar and threatening than those likely to be encountered in a missile. In spite of this the pigeon behaved perfectly, pecking steadily and energetically at the image of the target as it moved about on the plate. . . . It was a perfect performance, but it had just the wrong effect. One can talk about phase lag in pursuit behavior and discuss mathematical predictions of hunting without reflecting too closely upon what is inside the black box. But the spectacle of a living pigeon carrying out its assignment, no matter how beautifully, simply reminded the committee of how utterly fantastic our proposal was. I will not say that the meeting was marked by unrestrained merriment, for the merriment was restrained. But it was there, and it was obvious that our case was lost.[60]

Literally and figuratively unable to keep the lid on the black box, Skinner left the group to its deliberations.[61] Spencer suggested an additional $50,000 for the project, including $20,000 to cover the General Mills deficit as well as a budget for six additional months. Much discussion focused on the logistics of field deployment until it was pointed out that the army already used pigeons, as carriers for messages. Pigeons would also be simple to transport compared to other things already routinely moved, such as bombs or electronic equipment. But the officials seemed more interested in laying the matter to rest. It was clear that the project had not received good supervision or adequate technical support.

Boyce, the section chief, admitted, "I am perfectly free to confess that I have not supervised the thing in detail." Another official noted that project members were "working in ignorance of what is involved in a guided missile. We have been so long finding out."[62] These statements seemed designed more to assuage possible guilt feelings regarding the project's administration than to promote serious reconsideration. Continued support was voted down, four to two, on the basis of the perceived lack of armed forces interest and the problems of coordination with the missile development team at MIT.[63]

THE DEMISE OF PROJECT PIGEON

Project Pigeon was officially over. As Skinner wrote, "We had to show, for all our trouble, only a loftful [*sic*] of curiously useless equipment and a few dozen pigeons with a strange interest in a feature of the New Jersey coast."[64] In retrospect, it seems clear that the project failed, not for technical reasons, but because of fundamental differences in disciplinary outlook and research style between the Skinner team and the NDRC engineers. Coming from laboratory psychology, Skinner was at a disadvantage in trying to enter territory that was considered part of electrical and mechanical engineering. He lacked experience in dealing with extramural research funding agencies, even in his own field of psychology. Furthermore, he failed to mobilize the support of influential psychologists involved in government scientific circles. Instead, Project Pigeon members felt their way, eventually learning to articulate their work in engineering terms, as seen in the use of the metaphor of the bird as a machine. But that rhetorical ploy was tried only after NDRC officials had already begun to lose their initial enthusiasm for the novel guidance system. The contract administrators had tried to be open-minded about the project but proved unable to accommodate its unusual approach and eventually retreated behind traditional professional boundaries. In the official account of the project, NDRC staff members noted the prevailing mood: "Investigators in the physical sciences are inclined to discount unduly the findings of their colleagues in the field of psychological behavior. Such an attitude is far from scientific."[65]

The interests of the NDRC staff members were focused elsewhere on the development of more conventional hardware, and they devoted a minimum of supervision to Project Pigeon. Although the General Mills contract generated much discussion, it was a marginal item in the budget, receiving only $25,000 of the $13,000,000 spent by the division over the course of the war.[66] Other speculative projects, such as television-guided missiles, received major funding despite little demonstrable utility. None of the officials assigned to oversee the project spent much time doing so; more significant, none of them emerged as advocates for it, which was crucial to continued funding. Finally, logistical problems deepened the gulf between the two groups. The division was headquartered at MIT, a key center of wartime technological innovation, whereas Project Pigeon was isolated in a more limited research environment in the Midwest. The development of the missile vehicle went ahead at MIT without real consideration of the organic guiding mechanism. Communication between the groups was poor, and the lack of information clearly hampered the General Mills engineers.

The physical scientists and engineers of the National Defense Research Committee succeeded in closing the issue, and their postwar accounts became the official word on Project Pigeon. In *Guided Missiles and Techniques,* the Summary Technical Report of Division 5, less than four pages were devoted to "Organic Target Seeking." Asserting that "recognition by intelligence" was the simplest method of targeting, the report mentioned the effectiveness of Japanese kamikaze attacks as a prime example.[67] The main components of the pigeon device were described, and the summary concluded that the project "was given up because the mechanical engineering problem of developing an appropriate servo link seemed too difficult," especially in light of advances made with other missile systems.[68]

In the official public history of wartime guided missile research and development, NDRC section chief Joseph Boyce gave a brief but balanced review of Project Pigeon.[69] Another Division 5 member, physicist Louis N. Ridenour, satirized the project in the pages of the *Atlantic Monthly* in 1947 as one of "the more bizarre problems of wartime research." In a short piece entitled "Doves in the Detonator," he caricatured Skinner (under the pseudonym Ramsay) as an impractical dreamer and misrepresented several key aspects of the project. Among other inaccuracies, Ridenour claimed that homing pigeons were used and placed together in ten-bird units. In dismissing the work, he invoked the ultimate wartime fruit of physical science and engineering by concluding that perhaps "operational problems loomed so large that the Air Forces decided they'd rather wait for the atomic bomb, which you don't have to be very accurate with."[70]

BEYOND THE LABORATORY

With Project Pigeon over, Skinner returned to scholarly pursuits and took up a Guggenheim Fellowship to prepare a monograph dealing with verbal behavior. As he worked on the book during the 1944–45 academic year, Skinner explored other forms of behavioral technology. He built the baby-tender for his second daughter, and described it to the NDRC's Hugh Spencer as "a very different and more peaceful sort of behavioral engineering."[71] Extending his concerns to the rational management of society, Skinner drafted the manuscript for *Walden Two* during the summer of 1945, shortly before the end of the war. He later noted the connection between Project Pigeon and the book, saying, "that piece of science fiction was a declaration of confidence in a technology of behavior."[72]

The details of Project Pigeon remained classified for more than a decade following the war. Unable to comment directly on this research, Skinner continued to elaborate on the insights gained from his wartime experiences. In 1947, at a symposium on current trends in psychology, he punctuated his discussion of experimental psychology by stating, "It is not a matter of bringing the world into the laboratory, but of extending the practices of an experimental science to the world at large. We can do this as soon as we wish to do it."[73] Although Skinner resumed his research program in the experimental analysis of behavior, he devoted increasing amounts of time to applied projects, most notably teaching machines.[74] In *Science and Human Behavior,* published in 1953, he took a unified approach to behavioral science and engineering. Arguing that "the methods of science have been enormously successful wherever they have been tried," Skinner proposed to "apply them to human affairs" in the form of operant conditioning techniques.[75]

In 1958, after Project Pigeon was finally declassified, Skinner chose to discuss it in a highly visible forum when he accepted the Distinguished Scientific Contribution Award from the American Psychological Association. Instead of talking about his laboratory research, Skinner presented a history of Project Pigeon, characterizing it as "a crackpot idea, born on the wrong side of the tracks intellectually speaking, but eventually vindicated in a sort of middle class respectability."[76] He claimed that his efforts to develop a pigeon-guided missile generated techniques for shaping behavior that provided the foundation for a "technology of behavior."[77]

Over the course of two decades Skinner's perspective on the relation between his scientific research and its applications had changed considerably. In the 1930s he had drawn a sharp distinction between the pursuit of scientific discovery in the laboratory and any potential practical consequences. During World War II Skinner began to link his experimental research to various technical and social problems encountered in the wartime context. By the 1950s, he had integrated the scientific and technological elements in his system and used them to advance a behavioristic view of the world.

Skinner dramatized the consequences of his wartime research in his autobiography, published thirty-five years after the event: "Project Pigeon was discouraging. Our work with pigeons was beautifully reinforced, but all our efforts with the scientists came to nothing. . . . [However,] the research that I described in *The Behavior of Organisms* appeared in a new light. It was no longer merely an experimental analysis. It had given rise to a technology."[78] Project Pigeon became the opening wedge in what evolved into a campaign for behavioral engineering. The war provided Skinner with an opportunity to redefine the disparate problems associated with guiding a missile, raising a baby, and managing a society in terms of a common behavioral framework and to propose solutions based on techniques derived from the psychological laboratory. His wartime mechanical devices and literary constructions were designed with the same goals as his experimental apparatus: to control behavior predictably. Although Skinner's inventions received mixed reviews, he became convinced that behaviorism offered scientific methods equally applicable outside as well as inside the experimental work place. Faced with new contingencies, Skinner changed his behavior as a scientist during the war and began to discover how the laboratory could provide significant leverage in the wider realm of human affairs.[79]

NOTES

1. B. F. Skinner, "My Years at Indiana" (paper prepared March 31, 1988, for Indiana University Department of Psychology Centennial Celebration, Bloomington, April, 1988), p. 5; a copy is in the personal collection of the author.

2. B. F. Skinner, "Pigeons in a Pelican," *American Psychologist* 15 (1960): 28–37.

3. B. F. Skinner, *The Shaping of a Behaviorist* (New York, 1979), pp. 275 ff.

4. B. F. Skinner, "Baby in a Box," *Ladies' Home Journal* (October 1945), pp. 30–31, 135–36, 138.

5. B. F. Skinner, *Walden Two* (New York, 1948).

6. See James H. Capshew, "Psychology on the March: American Psychologists and World War II" (Ph.D. diss., University of Pennsylvania, 1986).

7. On the notion that technological systems include people and organizations as well as artifacts and processes, see Thomas P. Hughes, *American Genesis: A Century of Invention and Technological Enthusiasm, 1870–1970* (New York, 1989), pp. 184 ff.

8. B. F. Skinner, *The Behavior of Organisms: An Experimental Analysis* (New York, 1938).

9. Philip J. Pauly, *Controlling Life: Jacques Loeb and the Engineering Ideal in Biology* (New York, 1987), pp. 188–91. See also Laurence D. Smith, "On Prediction and Control: B. F. Skinner and the Technological Ideal of Science," *American Psychologist* 47 (1992): 216–23.

10. "Working Rat," *Life* (May 31, 1937), pp. 80–81.

11. Skinner, *Behavior of Organisms,* pp. 441–42.

12. Skinner, *Shaping of a Behaviorist* (n.3 above), p. 241. A similar account that is mistakenly dated 1939 is given in B. F. Skinner, "Autobiography," in *A History of Psychology in Autobiography,* ed. Edwin G. Boring and Gardner Lindzey (New York, 1967), 5:385–413, quote on 402.

13. Leaders of the wartime research and development establishment considered guided missile work a top priority, second only to the atomic bomb project. See Vannevar Bush and James B. Conant, "Foreward," in *Guided Missiles and Techniques,* Summary Technical Report, Office of Scientific Research and Development (OSRD), Division 5 (Washington, D.C., 1946), p. v.

14. Skinner, "Pigeons in a Pelican" (n. 2 above), pp. 28–29. Skinner recalled that psychological research using pigeons had hardly been attempted before and that he had bought the birds at a shop that sold them to Chinese restaurants (Skinner to J. H. Capshew, August 11, 1986; Skinner to Capshew, August 9, 1990; these letters are in the personal collection of the author). If Tolman was not particularly sympathetic toward psychology, he was certainly not ignorant of it since both his wife, Ruth S. Tolman, and his brother, Edward C. Tolman, were active professional psychologists in California.

15. Tolman to Skinner, June 9, 1941, Record Group 227, OSRD, National Defense Research Committee (NDRC), Records of Civilian Members, Tolman Files (hereafter cited as Tolman Files), Sk-Sm, National Archives, Washington, D.C.

16. Skinner to Tolman [June 1941], Tolman Files.

17. Skinner to Tolman, March 11, 1942, Tolman Files.

18. Tate to Tolman, March 19, 1942, Tolman Files.

19. Skinner, *Shaping of a Behaviorist* (n. 3 above), p. 257.

20. See *Guided Missiles and Techniques* (n. 13 above).

21. Tolman to Skinner, March 31, 1942, Tolman Files.

22. Quoted in Skinner, *Shaping of a Behaviorist,* pp. 256–57.

23. Skinner remembered only the man's first name—Victor. See Skinner, "Pigeons in a Pelican" (n. 2 above), p. 29.

24. For technical details, see Skinner "Pigeons in a Pelican," p. 30. Skinner noted that the technique of "shaping" behavior (i.e., reinforcing successive approximations of the desired response) had its origins in the flour mill during an attempt to teach a pigeon to bowl. See B. F. Skinner, "Reinforcement Today," *American Psychologist* 13 (1958): 94–99.

25. B. F. Skinner, K. B. Breland, and N. Guttman, "The Present Status of the 'Bird's-Eye Bomb,' " February 1, 1943, OSRD, NDRC Division 5, Spencer Files (hereafter cited as Spencer Files), 15, General Mills, Special Reports.

26. Ibid.

27. Spencer, "Visit," March 16, 1943, Spencer Files, 15, General Mills Correspondence.

28. Spencer to Hyde, April 10, 1943; Skinner to Spencer, April 12, 1943; Spencer to Skinner, April 30, 1943; Skinner to Spencer, May 6, 1943; all in Spencer Files.

29. Bemis characterized Skinner as "scientifically sound, able in his field though not of great caliber, and certainly a very pleasant individual personally." See Alan Bemis, "Diary," May 1, 1943, OSRD, NDRC Division 5, Bemis Files (hereafter cited as Bemis Files), 91, Diary 1943.

30. Ibid.

31. Spencer to Bush, May 27, 1943; Bush to Spencer, May 28, 1943; both in Spencer Files, 15, General Mills Correspondence.

32. Contract no. OEMsr-1068, Spencer Files, 15, General Mills Contracts and Vouchers.

33. Joseph Boyce, chief of Section 5.5, solicited Bray for some advice on the project, which they had previously discussed at the Cosmos Club in Washington. Bray was glad to oblige but apparently never did. See Boyce to Bray, July 13, 1943; Bray to Boyce, July 17, 1943; Boyce to Bray, July 21, 1943; all in Bemis Files, 96, General Mills Correspondence.

34. Spencer to Bemis, July 31, 1943, Bemis Files, 91, General Mills-Pigeons.

35. Ibid.

36. Skinner, "Pigeons in a Pelican" (no. 2 above), p. 31.

37. Bemis, perhaps feeling some guilt over his lack of help, was reassured by a visit from Charles Bray and Walter Hunter of the Applied Psychology Panel, who had a "positive opinion" of the project. See Bemis to Hyde, September 10, 1943, Bemis Files, 91, General Mills-Pigeons; and Bemis, "Diary," October 15, 1943, Bemis Files, 91, Diary 1943.

38. Meeting of Division 5, verbatim transcript, October 20, 1943, Richmond quoted on p. 46, OSRD, NDRC Division 5, Richmond Files (hereafter cited as Richmond Files), 62.

39. Bemis to Hyde, October 22, 1943, Spencer Files (n. 25 above), 15, General Mills Correspondence

40. Bemis to Hyde, November 20, 1943, Bemis Files (n. 29 above), 91, General Mills-Pigeons; Bemis to Spencer, December 3, 1943, Spencer Files, 15, General Mills Correspondence; Skinner, "Pigeons in a Pelican," p. 33.

41. Bemis to Spencer, December 13, 1943, Spencer Files, 15, General Mills Correspondence.

42. Meeting of Division 5, verbatim transcript, January 12, 1944, Boyce quoted on p. 130, Richmond Files, 62.

43. Ibid., p. 134.

44. Ibid.

45. Ibid., p. 135.

46. Ibid., p. 136.

47. Ibid., p. 140. After the vote, Spencer raised the nagging issue of reimbursing General Mills for its good faith in continuing to fund the project. He thought the NDRC's "no loss/no gain" principle regarding contractors implied some moral commitment to the company and pointed out that most contractors did not know how much they had spent until well past budget. Furthermore, the contract had come up for consideration without a thorough report from the contractor. Skinner and General Mills had complied with requests for data and results from their NDRC advisors, but no summary report had been requested. Apparently the Project Pigeon researchers had not been warned that their funding was in such jeopardy. After discussion, however, the reimbursement issue was dropped without a vote.

48. Skinner to Spencer, January 31, 1944, Spencer Files, 15, General Mills Correspondence.

49. Ibid.

50. Ibid.

51. Hyde to Spencer, January 31, 1944, OSRD, NDRC Division 5, Contractor's Reports (hereafter cited as Contractor's Reports), 648, General Mills Final Report, January 31, 1944.

52. Spencer to Boyce, "Memo," February 21, 1944, Bemis Files, 91, General Mills-Pigeons.

53. B. Skinner, E. Kuphal, G. Long, P. Christopherson, I. Boekelheide, "Cost of Homing Units, Personnel and Organization Required, Discussion and Analysis," February 21, 1944, Contractor's Reports, 648, General Mills Final Report, February 21, 1944. Kuphal to Spencer, February 25, 1944, Bemis Files, 91, General Mills-Pigeons.

54. Hall to Spencer, March 6, 1944, Spencer Files, (n. 25 above), 15, General Mills Correspondence. Spencer thanked Hall for his reports, commenting that he was sorry that a plan for using a mirror-centering system rather than the pneumatic signal was not picked up by the project. See Spencer to Hall, March 10, 1944, Bemis Files, 91, General Mills-Pigeons.

55. Spencer to Hyde, March 10, 1944, Spencer Files, 15, General Mills, Special Reports.

56. Spencer, "Memo to Division 5 Members," March 13, 1944, OSRD, NDRC Division 5, Dryden Files, 67, General Mills

57. "Minutes of Section 5.5 Meeting," March 21, 1944, Bemis Files (n. 29 above), 91, Minutes of Meetings.

58. Skinner, "Pigeons in a Pelican" (n. 2 above), p. 33. Meeting of NDRC Division 5, verbatim transcript, March 30, 1944, Richmond Files (n. 38 above), 62.

59. Meeting of NDRC Division 5, March 30, 1944, pp. 94–95, Richmond Files, 62.

60. Skinner, "Pigeons in a Pelican," p. 34. In an earlier summary of the project, Skinner noted only that "the questions which were put to us were random and for the most part trivial. It was clear to us that most of the men present had only the vaguest notion of the proposed system, and we left the meeting with the feeling that any decision, favorable or unfavorable, would have little to do with the facts of the case." See [B. F. Skinner], "History of the 'Project Pigeon' Contract with NDRC," HUG 60.20, Box 8, Folder 2, Project Pigeon, p. 5, Skinner Papers, Harvard University Archives, Harvard University, Cambridge, Mass.

61. On the notion of "black boxes" in the construction of knowledge claims, see Michel Callon and Bruno Latour, "Unscrewing the Big Leviathan: How Actors Macrostructure Reality and How Sociologists Help Them to Do So," in *Advances in Social Theory and Methodology: Toward an Integration of Micro- and Macro-Sociologies,* ed. Karin Knorr-Cetina and Aaron V. Cicourel (Boston, 1981), pp. 277–303.

62. Meeting of Division 5, March 30, 1944, pp. 151–53, Richmond Files, 62.

63. Ibid. pp. 154–55.

64. Skinner, "Pigeon in a Pelican" (n. 2 above), p. 34.

65. *Guided Missiles and Techniques* (n. 13 above), p. 201.

66. Irvin Stewart, *Organizing Scientific Research for War: The Administrative History of the Office of Scientific Research and Development* (Boston, 1948), pp. 86–87.

67. *Guided Missiles and Techniques,* p. 198.

68. Ibid., p. 201.

69. Joseph C. Boyce, ed., *New Weapons for Air Warfare: Fire-control Equipment, Proximity Fuzes, and Guided Missiles* (Boston, 1947), pp. 247–48.

70. Louis N. Ridenour, "Doves in the Detonator," *Atlantic Monthly* 179 (January 1947): 93–94.

71. Skinner to Spencer, August 23, 1945, Spencer Files (n. 25 above), 15, General Mills Correspondence. In an earlier letter Skinner had thanked Spencer for recommending James Burnham's recent book *The Managerial Revolution* (New York, 1941) and commented, "My faith in the success of a managerial society will not, however, reach a maximum until scientists become better managers." Skinner to Spencer, January 31, 1944, Spencer Files, 15, General Mills Correspondence.

72. Skinner, "Pigeons in a Pelican" (n. 2 above), p. 37.

73. B. F. Skinner, "Experimental Psychology," in *Current Trends in Psychology* (Pittsburgh, 1947), pp. 16–49, quote on p. 24.

74. B. F. Skinner, "The Science of Learning and the Art of Teaching," *Harvard Educational Review* 24 (1954): 86–97, and "Teaching Machines," *Science* 128 (1958): 969–77. Skinner noted a "direct genetic connection between teaching machines and Project Pigeon." See Skinner, "Pigeons in a Pelican," pp. 36–37.

75. B. F. Skinner, *Science and Human Behavior* (New York, 1953), p. 5.

76. Skinner, "Pigeons in a Pelican," p. 28.

77. Ibid., p. 37.

78. Skinner, *Shaping of a Behaviorist* (n. 3 above), p. 274. His students Marian Breland and Keller Breland also profited from their experience and in 1947 opened Animal Behavior Enterprises, a business based on the "mass production of conditioned operant behavior in animals" for circuses and other clients. See Keller Breland and Marian Breland, "A Field of Applied Animal Psychology," *American Psychologist* 6 (1951): 202–4, quote on 202. See also Keller Breland and Marian Breland, *Animal Behavior* (New York, 1966). For a brief account of postwar research on organic control at the Naval Research Laboratory, see U.S. Naval Research Laboratory, "Project ORCON: The Use of Pigeons to Guide Missiles," in *Report of NRL Progress, August 1959* (Washington, D.C.: U.S. Naval Research Laboratory, 1959); and Skinner, "Pigeons in a Pelican" (no. 2 above), pp. 34–36. For a review of the military uses of animals, see Robert E. Lubow, *The War Animals* (Garden City, N.Y., 1977).

79. See Bruno Latour, "Give Me a Laboratory and I Will Raise the World," in *Science Observed: Perspectives on the Social Study of Science,* ed. Karin Knorr-Cetina and Michael Mulkay (London, 1983), pp. 141–70. In the apt phrase of one historian, Skinner remained "above all a scientific preacher," preferring to proselytize from his university post rather than become a full-time behavioral engineer. See Pauly (n. 9 above), p. 196.

CHAPTER 13

PSYCHOANALYSIS

As Clark University in Worcester, Massachusetts, approached its twentieth anniversary, its president, G. Stanley Hall, was busy planning an academic gathering that is unique in the history of psychology (see Cromer and Anderson, 1970; Evans & Koelsch, 1985). Hall had wanted Wundt to visit the United States and give a special anniversary lecture, but Wundt declined, saying that he was committed to speaking at his own university in Leipzig, which would celebrate its five hundredth anniversary that same year. Even without Wundt, the 1909 gathering at Clark was an impressive one. William James was there, as was E. B. Titchener. Other dignitaries included William Stern, Franz Boas, Joseph Jastrow, James McKeen Cattell, Carl Seashore, and Carl Gustav Jung. The featured speaker at the conference was a 53-year-old physician from Vienna in his only visit to the United States—Sigmund Freud (1856–1939). Freud gave five pubic lectures at that conference. In those lectures he traced the intellectual history of his theory and method of psychoanalysis, giving initial credit to the work of another Viennese physician, Josef Breuer (1842–1925), whose most famous case Freud described to his American audience:

> Dr. Breuer's patient was a girl of twenty-one, of a high degree of intelligence. She had developed in the course of her two years' illness a series of physical and mental disturbances which well deserved to be taken seriously. She had a severe paralysis of both right extremities, with anesthesia, and at times the same affection of the members of the left side of the body, disturbance of eye-movements, and much impairment of vision; difficulty in maintaining the position of the head, an intense *Tussis nervosa,* nausea when she attempted to take nourishment, and at one time for several

> weeks a loss of the power to drink, in spite of tormenting thirst. Her power of speech diminished, and this progressed so far that she could neither speak nor understand her mother tongue; and finally, she was subject to states of "absence," of confusion, delirium, alteration of her whole personality. (Freud, 1910, p. 184)

This case history belongs to the most renowned patient in the history of psychoanalysis, a woman called "Anna O." Breuer had treated Anna during the period 1880–1882, at one time seeing her every day for a year. The hysterical symptoms described here were, according to Breuer, eliminated one by one until Anna was totally cured. This cure had been brought about by having Anna relive the experiences that had led to her symptoms, either by talking about them naturally or while in a hypnotic state. For example, she noted that her aversion to drinking water was similar to an aversion she had experienced as a child when she saw a dog drinking water from a glass. Once she had discussed this earlier incident with Breuer, the drinking aversion disappeared. Breuer referred to these cures as *cathartic*—the symptoms were reduced or eliminated through the release of the patient's pent-up anxiety.

Breuer had discussed this case with Freud, who viewed the cathartic method as an important tool in treating hysteria. Their friendship grew, and eventually they collaborated on a book published in 1895, entitled *Studies on Hysteria,* a book that some historians regard as the beginning of psychoanalysis (e.g., Kendler, 1987; Schultz & Schultz, 1996). The book contained five case studies, including that of Anna O. The importance of that case cannot be overstated; it was viewed as "the prototype of a cathartic cure and one of the basic occurrences that led Freud to the creation of psychoanalysis" (Ellenberger, 1972, p. 267).

Breuer was not the only important influence on Freud in the latter part of the nineteenth century; recall from Chapter 4 that Jean Martin Charcot exerted substantial influence in the four and one-half months that Freud studied with him in late 1885 and early 1886. Using nonhysterical patients, Charcot was able to demonstrate that under hypnosis, they could be made to exhibit the convincing physical symptoms of hysteria. That meant that conditions of the body could definitely be altered by conditions of the mind, an important realization for Freud's growing interest in psychiatry. Charcot's other principal influence on Freud was the result of a casual remark suggesting that sexual problems were the underlying cause of hysteria. Freud's emphasis on sex as a causative agent of paramount importance in neuroses led to the dissolution of his friendship with Breuer (Sulloway, 1979).

In developing his method of therapy, Freud eventually abandoned hypnosis, a technique that had figured prominently in the work of both Breuer and Charcot. He found that some subjects were very difficult to hypnotize and that, in fact, he was able to get valuable insights into a patient's behavior simply by having the patient talk spontaneously about anything that came to mind, a technique we know as *free association.* The free association of Freud's patients were often shocking to him, as they frequently described sexual seductions by their parents, usually the father, when they were very young. Freud decided that sexual abuse of children by their parents was much more common than anyone had imagined, and these patient revelations reinforced his belief in sex as a principal cause of neurosis. But then he had an insight that was to alter radically his interpretation of those events; the stories of sexual seduction revealed by his patients were, for the most part, just that—stories! They were fantasies of desired but not actual encounters (a fact disputed by at least one contemporary writer—see Masson, 1984).

Freud's emphasis on sex as an etiologic agent was not altered by this new interpretation. It made him even more aware of the powerful role of unconscious processes as determinants of behavior. He understood that for his patients, fantasy and reality were not easily distinguished. When reality was too difficult to face, the mind would create its own version of that reality, which Freud called *psychic reality*. The chief goal of psychoanalysis was to expose the psychic reality for the distortion that it was and to help the patient understand and accept the actual reality. These insights led to the development of Freud's view of personality, as well as to the refinement of his therapeutic technique of psychoanalysis, ideas that were defined more fully in what Freud and many historians regard as his most important book, *The Interpretation of Dreams* (1900).

The impetus for that book was Freud's own self-analysis, which he began in 1896. Realizing that he could not use the technique of free association for such an analysis, he began to make a record of his dreams to use in that task. A year earlier Freud began to argue for the significance of dreams as wish fulfillments. He regarded that insight as so important that he recorded the date of its occurrence: "In this House on July 24, 1895 the Secret of Dreams was revealed to Dr. Sigmund Freud" (E. Freud, 1960). He understood the value of dreams as the "royal road to the unconscious" and had used dream analysis with his patients.

The dream as told by the patient and Freud's recall of his own dreams were called the *manifest content* of the dream. But such content was the subject of dream recall in the waking state, when a person's defenses would be fully operative. The real meaning of the dream lay in what Freud called its *latent content*. It was there that the repressed wishes would be found. One of the repressed wishes first discussed in this famous book was the Oedipus complex, an idea that generated considerable controversy.

Freud's masterpiece on dreams was followed by the publication of *The Psychopathology of Everyday Life* (1901), a book that illustrated how slips of the tongue (*Freudian slips*), simple mistakes, and temporary losses of memory were actually revelations of unconscious conflicts. Thus, like the latent content of dreams, these everyday "errors" could give important insight into a person's personality. Four years later Freud published *Three Essays on the Theory of Sexuality* (1905), a book that further defined his ideas on psychoanalysis as a theory of personality, with particular emphasis on his growing realization of the nature of infantile sexuality.

In the brief introduction to this chapter it is simply not possible to cover much of the complexity and diversity of Freud's contributions in a life that spanned 83 years. No person since Darwin has so radically affected our intellectual world. Freud's ideas have found expression not only in psychology and psychiatry but also in art, literature, drama, education and the actions of everyday life. He was in his time, and continues to be, a figure of substantial controversy. Some of his ideas have been discarded in the light of contemporary psychological knowledge, but many contributions remain. Through his work he (1) focused awareness on unconscious processes in behavior, (2) defined a variety of defense mechanisms, such as repression, and showed how those are used as coping responses, (3) made the world cognizant of the importance of early experiences as determinants of later personality and adjustment, (4) helped to bring human sexuality out of its Victorian darkness, (5) shifted the emphasis from somatic to psychic causes of psychological disorders, and (6) generated great public interest in the questions of psychology, an interest that continues today.

THE READINGS

The initial selection in this chapter is Freud's opening lecture that he delivered at Clark University on September 7, 1909. The lecture focused on Josef Breuer's treatment of Anna O. and the insights that Freud gained from that case history that were important to the origins of psychoanalysis.

Freud delivered all five of his lectures in German, one each day. Back home in Vienna in October, 1909, Freud began to write out the lectures for publication. He sent the manuscripts to Hall in German, and they were then translated into English by an instructor at Clark University. The five lectures appeared together in the April 1910 issue of Hall's *American Journal of Psychology* (Freud, 1910). The version of the first lecture that appears in this chapter is a new translation by Saul Rosenzweig (1992), a psychologist whose book on Freud's American visit has added greatly to our understanding of the events surrounding that historic expedition and its significance for the growth of psychoanalysis in America.

The second selection, an example of historical detective work at its best, was written by historian of psychoanalysis H. F. Ellenberger, whose work on Charcot you read in Chapter 4. His historical search for the facts in this story even led him to enlist the services of the Montreal Police Department. In this article, Ellenberger dramatically revises the interpretation of the case of Anna O., relying heavily on a newly discovered document—a case report on Anna O. written by Breuer in 1882. That report and Breuer's later account in the book he coauthored with Freud give very different versions of the case. Ellenberger concludes that in the treatment of Anna O., both the catharsis and the cure are questionable.

The final selection is by Gail A. Hornstein, a psychologist at Mount Holyoke College. In this article, she traces the history of the relationship of psychology and psychoanalysis in America. She writes that when psychoanalysis arrived in the United States, "At first psychologists stood aside, astonished, as the analysts, bursting with self-importance and an almost frightening zealotry, pronounced themselves the real scientists of the mind. By the time the psychologists began to take this threat seriously, psychoanalysis had so captured the public imagination that even its pretensions could not be ignored" (Hornstein, 1992, p. 254). Hornstein's account illustrates how rapidly psychoanalytic ideas spread in America after Freud's visit to Clark University, and how American psychology was forced to change in reacting to this conceptual and epistemological threat from abroad. Today, the Division of Psychoanalysis is one of a number of special interest groups within the American Psychological Association.

REFERENCES

Breuer, J., & Freud, S. (1895). *Studien über Hysterie.* Vienna: Franz Deuticke.

Cromer, W., & Anderson, P. A. (1970). Freud's visit to America: Newspaper coverage. *Journal of the History of the Behavioral Sciences, 6,* 349–353.

Ellenberger, H. F. (1972). The story of "Anna O": A critical review with new data. *Journal of the History of the Behavioral Sciences, 8,* 267–279.

Evans, R. B., & Koelsch, W. (1985). Psychoanalysis arrives in America: The 1909 psychology conference at Clark University. *American Psychologist, 40,* 942–948.

Freud, E. (1960). *The letters of Sigmund Freud.* New York: Basic Books.

Freud, S. (1900). *The interpretation of dreams.* Available from Avon Books, New York, 1968.

Freud, S. (1901). *The psychopathology of everyday life.* Available from Avon Books, New York, 1965.

Freud, S. (1905). *Three essays on the theory of sexuality.* Available from Avon Books, New York, 1962.

Freud, S. (1910). The origin and development of psychoanalysis. *American Journal of Psychology, 21,* 181–218.

Hornstein, G. A. (1992). The return of the repressed: Psychology's problematic relations with psychoanalysis, 1909–1960. *American Psychologist, 47,* 254–263.

Kendler, H. H. (1987). *Historical foundations of modern psychology.* Chicago: Dorsey Press.

Masson, J. M. (1984). *The assault on truth: Freud's suppression of the seduction theory.* New York: Farrar Straus Giroux.

Rosenzweig, S. (1992). *Freud, Jung, and Hall the kingmaker: The historic expedition to America.* St. Louis: RANA House.

Schultz, D. P., & Schultz, S. E. (1996). *A history of modern psychology* (6th ed.). San Diego: Harcourt Brace.

Sulloway, F. J. (1979). *Freud: Biologist of the mind.* New York: Basic Books.

First Lecture on Psychoanalysis at Clark University: Breuer and the Treatment of Hysteria

Sigmund Freud

Ladies and Gentlemen: It is a novel and confusing experience for me to appear as lecturer before an eager audience in the New World. I assume that I owe this honor only to the connection of my name with the topic of psychoanalysis and, consequently, it is of psychoanalysis that I intend to speak. I shall attempt to give you in very brief compass a historical survey of the origin and further development of this new method of investigation and treatment.

If merit is due to the originator of psychoanalysis, the merit is not mine. I did not participate in its earliest beginnings. I was a student, occupied with the preparation for my final examinations, when another Viennese physician, Dr. Josef Breuer, applied this method for the first time in the case of a hysterical girl (1880–82). We shall start by examining the history of this case and its treatment. You can find it described in detail in *Studies on Hysteria* later published by Dr. Breuer and myself.

First, however, an incidental remark. I have discovered with satisfaction that the majority of my audience are not of the medical profession. Now have no concern that a medical education is necessary to follow my discourse. We shall at the outset accompany the physicians for a short time, but soon we shall separate from them and go with Dr. Breuer along a unique path.

Dr. Breuer's patient was a highly intelligent girl of 21. She had developed, in the course of her more than two years of illness, a series of physical and mental disturbances which well deserve to be taken seriously. She had a severe paralysis of both right extremities, with anaesthesia, and at times she had the same disturbance in the limbs of her left side; she had disordered eye-movements, and many visual restrictions; difficulty in keeping her head in an upright position, an intense *Tussis nervosa* (uncontrollable cough); nausea when attempting to take nourishment, and, at one time, during a period of several weeks, an inability to drink despite tormenting thirst. There was a reduction in her capacity for language which progressed to the point of her being unable either to speak or to understand her mother tongue; and, finally, she was subject to states of "absence," of confusion, delirium—alterations of her whole personality—which we shall later have to consider separately.

When one hears of such a syndrome one does not need to be a physician to incline to the opinion that one is here concerned with a serious illness, probably of the brain, for which there is little hope of recovery and which will probably lead to the early death of the patient. However, physicians inform us that in a certain type of case with such severe symptoms a different and quite favorable prognosis is justified. When such a syndrome appears in a young female whose vital internal organs (heart, kidneys) are shown by objective investigations to be normal but who has experienced intense *emotional* agitations, and if the individual symptoms are exceptional in certain of their minute characteristics, then physicians do not regard such a case too gravely. They maintain that an organic lesion of the brain is not present but, rather, an enigmatic condition, known since the time of Greek medicine as *hysteria,* which can simulate a large number of syndromes of serious illness. They then judge that the life of the patient is not threatened and that even a complete restoration

This lecture was published originally in the *American Journal of Psychology,* 1910, *21,* 181–218. This version is a new translation by Saul Rosenzweig, Copyright © 1992. Reprinted by permission from his book: *Freud, Jung, and Hall the Kingmaker: The Historic Expedition to America.* St. Louis: Rana House, 1992.

to health is probable. The differentiation of such a case of hysteria from one of severe organic illness is not always easy to make. But we do not need to know how a differential diagnosis of this kind is made; it is sufficient for us to be assured that Breuer's patient was just such a case in which no competent physician would fail to make a diagnosis of hysteria. We can also at this point add from the case report that her illness arose while she was nursing her dearly loved father, during his serious and fatal illness, and that she had to withdraw from this duty as a consequence of falling ill herself.

Thus far it has been an advantage to go along with the doctors, but we shall soon take leave of them. You should not, indeed, expect that the prospects of a patient to receive medical aid are, in fact, increased by a diagnosis of hysteria instead of serious brain disease. Medical skill is powerless in most cases involving serious brain disease, but the physician is likewise helpless in combating hysterical illness. He is obliged to rely upon benign Nature as to when and how the hopeful prognosis is to be realized.

Hence, with the diagnosis of hysteria little is changed for the patient, though for the physician a great deal is thereby altered. We can observe that he orients himself quite differently toward a hysterical patient as compared to one with an organic illness. He will not take the same interest in the former as in the latter because, though his suffering is much less intense, the patient yet seems to demand that he be taken just as seriously. But there is still another element involved here. The physician who, through his studies, has learned so many things that are hidden from the layman, is able to visualize the causes of disease and the changes brought about by it (e.g., in the brain of a patient suffering from apoplexy or neoplasm). This must, up to a certain point, meet the situation since it suffices to give him an understanding of the disease picture. However, in the presence of the particulars of hysteria, all his knowledge, all his anatomic-physiological and pathological conceptualizations leave him in the lurch. He cannot comprehend hysteria; in its presence he is himself like a layman. And this situation is, of course, not agreeable for anyone who usually sets such great store by his knowledge. Hysterical patients are, accordingly, deprived of his sympathy. He regards them as persons who overstep the laws of his science—just as the orthodox believer regards the heretic. He attributes all possible evil to them, blames them for exaggeration and intentional deception, for malingering; and he punishes them by withholding his interest.

But Dr. Breuer in his relation to his patient does not merit this reproach. He offered her sympathy and interest although he did not at first understand how to help her. She apparently lightened his task through the distinguished characteristics of mind and character to which he bears witness in his graphic case history. His solicitous mode of observation also soon found the method by which the first effective relief became possible.

It had been noticed that the patient in her states of absence—alterations of consciousness with confusion—used to mutter a few words to herself which appeared to derive from some connection with the thoughts preoccupying her. The doctor, after recovering these words, put her into a kind of hypnosis and reiterated these words in order to encourage her associations to them. The patient complied and reproduced for the physician the mental images which controlled her mind during her states of absence and had betrayed themselves in the mentioned fragmentary utterances. These were deeply tragic, often poetically beautiful fantasies—we might call them daydreams—which usually took as their starting point the situation of a girl at the sickbed of her father. Once she has narrated a number of such fantasies, she seemed to be set free and restored to her normal mental condition. The state of ensuing wellbeing, which continued for several hours, yielded on the next day to a new state of absence which would be removed in the same manner through the narration of other fantasies. One could not escape the impression that the mental alterations which expressed themselves in the states of absence were a consequence of stimuli derived from these highly emotional fantasy formations. The patient herself, who at this stage of her illness, rather remarkably spoke and understood only English, named this novel method of treatment "talking cure" or, as a joke, designated is as "chimney sweeping."

It was soon realized that by such purging of the mind more could be accomplished than a temporary removal of the constantly recurring mental turbulence. Symptoms of the illness could be brought to disappear when during the hypnosis the patient recalled on what occasion and in which connections the symptoms had first appeared if at the same time she gave vent to her feelings. "During the summer there had been a time of intense heat and the patient was suffering very severely from thirst; for, without being able to assign any reason, it had suddenly become impossible for her to drink. She reached for a desired glass of water but as soon as it touched her lips she pushed it away from her like a hydrophobiac. As she did so, she was for a few seconds clearly in a state of absence. She took only fruit, melons and the like, in order to assuage her tormenting thirst. After this condition had lasted for about six weeks, she was once ruminating, under hypnosis, about her English lady companion, whom she did not like. She related with every sign of disgust how she had come into that lady's room and had seen her little dog, a nauseating creature, drinking out of a glass. She had said nothing for she wanted to be polite. After she had given energetic expression to her stifled anger, she asked for water, drank a large quantity of it uninhibitedly, and woke from hypnosis with the glass at her lips. Thereupon the disturbance disappeared forever."

Permit me to dwell on this experience for a moment. No one had ever previously cured a hysterical symptom by such means or had, by doing so, entered so deeply into the understanding of its causation. It would have to be a discovery of great consequence if one were able to confirm the expectation that still other symptoms, perhaps the majority of them, arose in the patient in such a manner and could be removed in this way. Breuer spared no pains to convince himself of this assertion and he methodically investigated the pathogenesis of the other and more serious symptoms. Such was actually the case; almost all the symptoms had arisen in this way, as residues, as precipitates—if you will—of affect-laden events which we later labeled "psychic traumas," the peculiarity of which was explained through their relationship to the causative injurious situations. They were, to use the technical term, *determined* by the scenes, the memory traces of which they embodied, and need not any longer be described as capricious or enigmatic aspects of neurosis. Only one qualification must be noted: it was not always a single event which left the symptom behind. Most symptoms, instead, arose through the effective convergence of numerous, often very many similar, repeated traumas. This entire chain of pathogenic memories would then have to be reproduced in chronological order, but, in fact, reversed, the last ones first, and the first ones last. It was quite impossible to push through to the earliest, and often most cogent trauma, by skipping those which came later.

You will certainly now want to hear about other examples of the origin of her hysterical symptoms in addition to the one concerning the drinking inhibition which resulted from her disgust at seeing the dog drink from a glass. However, if I am to adhere to my program, I must limit myself to very few instances. Breuer relates that her visual disturbances could be traced to occasions "such as when the patient, sitting at her father's sickbed with tears in her eyes, was suddenly asked by him what the time was, whereupon trying to look but seeing only indistinctly, she brought the watch up so close to her face that the dial appeared much enlarged (compare the later macropsia and convergent squint). Again, she exerted herself to suppress her tears so that the sick man would not see them." In like manner, all the pathogenic impressions stemmed from the period when she shared in the care of her sick father. "Once, at night, she was very anxiously attending the sick man, who had a high fever, and she was in suspense because a surgeon was expected from Vienna to perform an operation. Her mother had gone out for a while and Anna was sitting by the sickbed with her right arm over the back of the chair. She fell into a state of daydreaming in which she saw a black snake approaching the sick man as if to bite him. (It is very probable that in the meadow behind the house there actually were some snakes which had previously frightened the girl and thus furnished the material for the hallucination.) She wanted to drive away the animal but seemed paralyzed. Her right arm, hanging over the back of the chair had 'fallen asleep.' It had become anaesthetic and paretic, and when she looked at it, the fingers were transformed into little snakes with death-heads (fingernails). She probably made an attempt to drive off the snake with her paralyzed right hand and in this way the anaesthesia and the paralysis became associated with the snake hallucination. When this image vanished, she tried in her anxiety to pray, but all speech failed her. She could not talk in any language until at last an *English* children's verse occurred to her and thereafter she continued to think and to pray in that language." With the recall of this scene under hypnosis, the paralysis of the right arm which had existed since the start of the illness, was eliminated, and the treatment came to an end.

When, a number of years later, I began to employ Breuer's method of investigation and treatment with my own patients. I discovered that my experience agreed completely with his. A woman about 40 years of age had a tic, a peculiar smacking sound which she uttered without appropriate cause whenever she became excited. It had its origin in two events during both of which she had determined to make no sound and both times, by a kind of counter-will, this sound came from her mouth to break the stillness. The first time she had, after much effort, finally managed to get her child, who was ill, to fall asleep, and she told herself that she must now remain absolutely quiet in order not to awaken it. On the second occasion, during a carriage ride with her two children, a thunderstorm arose, the horses bolted, and she carefully avoided making any sound in order not to frighten the animals still more. I give you these examples from among many others which are cited in the *Studies on Hysteria*.

Ladies and Gentlemen, if you will permit me a generalization, which is inescapable in so abbreviated a presentation, we can summarize our findings up to this point in the formula: *Our hysterical patients suffer from reminiscences*. Their symptoms are residues and memory symbols for certain (traumatic) events. A comparison with other memory symbols in other areas will perhaps lead us to a deeper understanding of this symbolism. The memorials and monuments with which we decorate our large cities are just such symbols. If you take a walk through London, you find in front of one of the largest railway stations of the city an elaborately decorated gothic pillar—*Charing Cross*. One of the old Plantagenet kings in the XIIIth century, who had the body of his beloved Queen Eleanor carried to Westminster, erected gothic crosses at each of the stations where the coffin was set down, and *Charing Cross* is the last of the monuments preserving the memory of the sad procession. At another place in the city, not far from London Bridge, one sees a more modern, lofty pillar which is merely called "The Monument." It commemorates the great fire which broke out in that neighborhood in the year 1666 and destroyed a great part of the city. These monuments are therefore memory symbols similar to the symptoms of hysteria, and up to this point the comparison seems justified. But what would you say to a Londoner who today stood in sorrow before the monument to the funeral of Queen Eleanor instead of going about his business, with the haste demanded by modern industrial conditions while rejoicing in the youthful queen of his own heart? Or to another who, standing before the "Monument," bemoaned the burning down of his beloved native city which has long since been restored in more splendor than before? Hysterical patients, indeed all neurotics, behave like these two impractical Londoners, not only in that they remember the painful experiences of the distant past but because they are still strongly affected by them. They cannot free themselves from the past; by dwelling on it they neglect the reality of the present. This fixation of the mental life on pathogenic traumas is one of the most important and practically significant characteristics of neurosis.

I am willing to yield to an objection which you are probably framing as you think over the case history of Breuer's patient. All traumas stemmed from the time when she was nursing her sick father, and her symptoms can be regarded as memory traces of his illness and death. They therefore express a state of mourning, and fixation on memories of the dead person such a short time after his decease signify nothing pathological. Instead, such conduct is a normal expression of feeling. I concede this point; the fixation on such traumas in the case of Breuer's patient is not all surprising. But in other cases, as in the one treated for tic, the precipitations of which were distant by ten or fifteen years, the mark of an abnormal adherence to the past is very clear, and Breuer's patient would probably also have developed it had she not benefited from the *cathartic* treatment so soon after experiencing the traumas and developing the symptoms.

We have thus far discussed only the relationship of the hysterical symptoms to the life history of the patient. By considering two further aspects which Breuer observed, we can gain a clue as to how to conceptualize the process of falling ill and of recovering. With regard to the first, it is especially to be noted that in almost all pathogenic situations Breuer's patient had suppressed any strong excitement instead of permitting its discharge by appropriate emotion, by word and deed. In the minor episode of the lady companion's dog, the patient suppressed, out of deference, every manifestation of her very intense disgust. While she was sitting by the bed of her father she was continually careful not to let the sick man observe any sign of her anxiety or of her sorrowful mood. When she later reproduced the same scene for the physician, the emotion which she had previously inhibited burst forth with special intensity as though it had been long pent up. In fact, the symptom which had been left over from that scene achieved its highest intensity when the doctor got close to the cause of it, and it vanished after the cause had been fully aired. On the other hand, experience shows that the recollection of a scene in the presence of the physician remained without effect if, for any reason whatever, it occurred without emotional expression. The fate of these affects, which can hence be conceived as displaceable quantities, were thus the decisive basis for the development of the illness as well as for the recovery. One is impelled to the assumption that the illness came into existence because the emotions developed in the pathological situations were denied a normal outlet; the essence of the illness consisted in an abnormal use of this underlying "strangulated" affect. In part they remained as a persisting burden on the psychic life and constituted a source of constant excitement for it; in part they underwent a transformation into unusual physical *innovations* and *inhibitions* which manifested themselves as the somatic symptoms of the case. We have coined the term "hysterical conversion" for this latter process. A certain portion of our own psychical excitement is, apart from this special process, led into the path of somatic innovation and yields what we know as "the expression of emotions." Now, hysterical conversion exaggerates that portion of the discharge of an affectively cathected mental process; it bespeaks a much more intensive expression of the emotions directed into new paths. If the bed of a stream flows in two channels, there will be an overflow of one of them as soon as the stream meets with an obstruction of the other.

You will note that we have arrived in our thinking at a purely psychological theory of hysteria in which we assign the affective processes the chief place. But now a second observation of Breuer obliges us to assign a role of great significance to the condition of consciousness in characterizing the pathological proceedings. Breuer's patient displayed numerous peculiar mental states—conditions of absence, confusion, and character alterations along with her normal condition. In the normal state she knew nothing of the pathogenic scenes and of their relation to her symptoms; she had forgotten these events or, at any rate, had split away the pathogenic connection. When she was hypnotized, it became possible, but only after considerable exertion, to recall these scenes to her memory, and by this process of recall the symptoms were removed. One would have encountered great difficulty in finding a way to interpret this situation had not previous experiences and experiments in hypnotism pointed the way. Through the investigation of hypnotic phenomena the conception had become familiar, though it seemed at first preposterous, that in one and the same individual mind several mental groupings are possible and that these can remain quite independent of one another, "know nothing" of one another, and can, by splitting, alternate in consciousness. Cases of this kind, known as "double conscience" [French for dual personality], occasionally come under observation as spontaneous occurrences. When in such splitting of the personality consciousness remains persistently attached to one of these two states, it is called the *conscious* mental condition, and the split-off portion is termed *unconscious*. In the well-known phenomenon of posthypnotic suggestion, in which a command given in hypnosis is involuntarily carried out in the later normal state, one has an excellent prototype of the influence which can be exerted upon consciousness by what is unconscious. Moreover, on this model one can interpret the phenomena of hysteria. Breuer arrived at the postulate that hysterical symptoms originate in such special mental states, which he called *hypnoidal*. Affective stimulation which occurs in such hypnoidal states readily becomes pathogenic because such states do not provide the conditions for a normal discharge of aroused emotion. There ensues, after the emotional arousal, an unusual product, namely, the symptom, which intrudes itself like a foreign body into the normal state of consciousness and the latter lacks any knowledge of the hypnoidal, pathogenic situation. When a symptom arises one thus finds an amnesia, a memory gap, and the closing of the gap is accomplished by the removal of the originating conditions of the symptom.

I am afraid that this part of my exposition may not have seemed very clear. However, you must bear in mind that we are dealing here with new and difficult views which can perhaps not be made much clearer. This circumstance proves that we have not yet advanced very far in our knowledge. Breuer's concept of the *hypnoidal* states has, moreover, proved to be a handicap, and to be superfluous, and it has been dropped from contemporary psychoanalysis. Presently you will learn at least something of the influences and processes discovered behind the dubious construct of hypnoidal states advanced by Breuer. You may also quite rightly have received the impression that Breuer's formulation was able to give only a very incomplete and unsatisfying explanation of the observed phenomena. But complete theories do not fall from heaven, and you would be even more justified to be skeptical if anyone at the beginning of his observations offered you a well-rounded theory without any gaps. Such a theory could certainly be only a child of speculation, not the product of an unprejudiced and objective investigation.

The Story of "Anna O": A Critical Review with New Data

H. F. Ellenberger

To this day, the most elementary account of psychoanalysis begins with the story of a mysterious young woman, "Anna O", whose numerous hysterical symptoms disappeared one by one as Josef Breuer was able to make her evoke the specific circumstances that had led to their appearance. The patient herself called this procedure "talking-cure" or "chimney sweeping," but Breuer termed it "catharsis." Anna O's cure took place in 1880–1882, but the case history was published thirteen years later, that is, in 1895 in Breuer and Freud's *Studies in Hysteria.* From that time on, Anna O's story was given as the prototype of a cathartic cure and one of the basic occurrences that led Freud to the creation of psychoanalysis.

Today, the veil of legend surrounding the foundation of psychoanalysis has been only partly lifted up by objective research. In the following we will examine Anna O's story in the light of the historical-critical method in order to ascertain what can be considered historically certain, possible but doubtful, definitely legendary. After a brief summary of Breuer's original report of 1895, we will make a survey of all subsequent researches about Anna O, following the chronological sequence of the investigations. We will bring two newly discovered documents, one being a hitherto unknown case history of the patient, written by Breuer himself in 1882, and the second one a follow-up written in the Sanatorium Bellevue, Kreuzlingen, where Anna O was transferred in July 1882. We will try to see what new light these documents throw upon Anna O's story.

Ellenberger, H. F. (1972). The story of "Anna O": A critical review with new data. *Journal of the History of Behavioral Sciences, 8,* 267–279.

BREUER'S ORIGINAL REPORT OF 1895

According to Breuer, Anna O was 21 years old at the time when she fell ill, that is, in 1880. She belonged to a well-to-do family. She was very intelligent, attractive, kind, charitable, but moody and stubborn. The family was extremely puritanical and, Breuer says, "the sexual element was surprisingly undeveloped" in Anna. There was, he added, a marked contrast between the refined education she had received and the monotonous home life she led. This brought her to escape into long daydreams that she called her "private theater." However these daydreams did not interfere with her daily activities and her family were not aware of them.

Her illness, as described by Breuer in 1895,[1] went through four chronologically sharply delimited periods.

1) The *period of latent incubation,* from July 1880 to December 10, 1880. The starting-point was a severe physical illness of her beloved father. She gave him intensive care, staying up during the night and resting in the afternoon. But she became exhausted and had to be kept away from the sick father. Thereupon she began to suffer from an intensive coughing and she had long episodes of sleepiness and agitation in the afternoon. According to Breuer, Anna O had at that time all kinds of hidden symptoms that neither her family nor she herself suspected. But Breuer did not see her during that period; his description of her symptoms—overt or hidden—was a later reconstruction.

2) The *period of manifest psychosis,* went from December 1880 to April 1881. During the period Anna O was under Breuer's care and she remained in bed from December 11, 1880 to April 1, 1881. A great variety of symptoms appeared within a short time, beginning with ocular disturbances, followed with paralyses, con-

tractions, zones of tactile anesthesia, and linguistic disorganization. She spoke an agrammatical jargon composed of a mixture of four or five languages. Her personality, now, was split into one "normal," conscious, sad person, and one morbid, uncouth, agitated person who had hallucinations of black snakes. It happened that for two weeks she remained completely mute, but Breuer knew that this had followed a certain painful incident; and after he could bring her to talk about this incident, the patient started to speak again. Now, however, she talked only in English, though still understanding what people told her in German. On late afternoons she had what she called (in English) her "clouds," that is a kind of drowsiness; then she could be easily hypnotized. Breuer usually visited her in these moments; she told him her daydreams; they were mostly stories of an anxious girl around sick persons. During the month of March there came a gradual improvement and she left her bed for the first time on April 1, 1881.

3) The *period of "continuous somnambulism alternating with more normal conditions"* went from April 5 to December 1881. The death of her father, on April 5, 1881, was severe shock. After two days of deep stupor, a new set of severe symptoms appeared. She manifested a "negative instinct" against her close relatives and recognized no one, except Breuer; he had to feed her for some time. She spoke nothing but English, and now, apparently she was unable to understand what was told or written in German.

About ten days after her father's death, a consultant was called. She manifested "negative hallucinations" toward him; in other words she behaved as if she did not perceive his presence. The consultant tried to force her attention by blowing some smoke toward her face. This attempt was followed by a terrific attack of anger and anxiety. On the same evening, Breuer had to leave for a journey. When he came back he found that Anna O's condition was much worse. During his absence she had refused to eat, she had fits of intense anxiety and ghastly hallucinations. Breuer began to hypnotize her again on the evening; she told him about her recent hallucinations, whereupon she was relieved. The personality contrast was now between the disturbed mind of the daytime and the clear mind of the night.

Because Anna O had manifested suicidal impulses, it was felt that she could no longer be kept at home, and—much against her will—she was transferred into a country-house near Vienna, on June 7, 1881. After three days of great agitation, she quieted down. Breuer visited her every three or four days. Her symptoms now appeared in a regular cycle and were relieved by Breuer's hypnotic sessions. She remained quiet after Breuer's visits; but during the intervals had to be given fairly high amounts of chloral.

It was found that no one but Breuer could practice what she now called her "talking cure" or "chimney sweeping." While Breuer was on a vacation trip, one of his colleagues attempted to give her the same treatment but failed. Nevertheless her condition gradually improved. She played with a Newfoundland dog and visited a few poor people in the neighborhood. In the fall, she went back to Vienna, where her mother had moved to another house. However her condition became worse in December 1881, so that she had to be taken back to the country-house.

4) The *fourth period,* extended from December 1881 to June 1882. A very remarkable, twofold change occurred in the illness. First, a difference in regard to the multiple personality. There still were the "normal" and "sick" personalities, but the main feature was that the sick personality lived 365 days earlier than the healthy one. Thanks to the diary her mother had kept about her illness, Breuer was able to check that the events she hallucinated had occurred, day by day, exactly one year earlier. She sometimes shifted spontaneously and rather abruptly from one personality to the other; Breuer could provoke the shifting by showing her an orange. The second modification concerned the nature and content of the talking-cure. Once, under

hypnosis, she told Breuer how her difficulties in swallowing water had started after she had seen a dog drinking from a glass. Having told Breuer this, the symptom disappeared. This initiated a new kind of treatment. She told Breuer, in reverse chronological order, each appearance of a given symptom with exact dates, until she reached the original manifestation and initial event, and then the symptom disappeared. Obviously, this was an extremely time-consuming procedure. Breuer gives as an example one of the symptoms, the patient's transient states of deafness; he found seven subforms of this symptom and each one of them constituted one of the "series" that Breuer had to treat separately. The first subform, "not hearing when someone came in" had occurred 108 times, and the patient had to tell the detail of each one of these 108 occurrences in reverse chronological order, until Breuer reached the first manifestation: she once had not heard her father coming in. But the six other subforms of the "not hearing" symptom as well as each other symptom had to be treated for itself with a similar procedure. Breuer eradicated each symptom in that tedious way. Finally, the last symptom was traced back to a specific incident: while nursing her sick father she had had a hallucination of a black snake, had been upset, had muttered a prayer in English, the only one that came to her mind. As soon as Anna had recovered that memory, the paralysis left her arm and she was able to speak German. The patient had decided and announced in advance that she would be cured in June 1882, on the anniversary of her transfer to the country-house, and in time for her summer vacation. Then, Breuer says, "she left Vienna for a trip, but needed much more time until she recovered her psychic equilibrium. Since then she enjoys a fully good health."

The current accounts of Anna O's illness do not emphasize the unusual features of that story, such as the peculiar form of multiple personality during the fourth period (one person living in the present and the other 365 days earlier). Above all, it is absolutely not so that "it sufficed to recall the circumstances under which the symptom had appeared" (this point is explicitly stated by Breuer): Anna had to recall each instance when the symptom had occurred, whatever the number, in the exact reverse chronological order. Anna O's illness was not a "classical case of hysteria" but a unique case of which, to the author's knowledge, no other instance is known, either before or after her.

FROM BREUER TO JONES

Anna O's story remained for a long time an anonymous case history which psychoanalysts and non-psychoanalysts faithfully copied from book to book, with a certain tendency to oversimplification. It was proclaimed as being the prototype of a cathartic cure. Janet's claims to priority, based on his cases of Lucie (1886), Marie (1889) and a few other ones after 1890 were rejected on the ground that he had been anticipated by Breuer. At times, a few doubts were expressed about the diagnostic. Goshen,[2] in 1952, contended that Anna, as well as the other patients described in the *Studies in Hysteria* had been schizophrenics.

For many years, very few new details emerged about Anna O's case. In 1924 Freud[3] suggested that Breuer had been the unaware victim of "transference love." In a seminar given in Zurich in 1925, Jung[4] revealed that Freud had told him that the patient had actually not been cured. Jung stated that this famous first case "so much spoken about as an example of brilliant therapeutic success, was in reality nothing of the kind. . . . There was no cure at all in the sense of which it was originally presented." And yet, Jung added, "the case was so interesting that there was no need to claim for it something that did not happen."

In 1953, Ernest Jones revealed—much to the family's displeasure—the true name of the patient: Bertha Pappenheim. In his biography of Freud, Jones[5] published a new version of the story. Unfortunately it is not clear to what extent Jones documented himself in Freud's unpublished correspondence, or simply reported from memory details which he had heard many years earlier. According to Jones's version, Freud had told him that Breuer had developed a strong "counter-transference" toward his patient so that Mrs. Breuer became jealous and Breuer decided to bring the treatment to its end. But on that same evening he was called to the patient to find her in the throes of an hysterical childbirth, the logical termination of phantom pregnancy that had slowly developed without Breuer's awareness; Breuer hypnotized her and then "fled the house in a cold sweat." On the next day he left with his wife for Venice to spend a second honeymoon which resulted in the conception of a daughter, Dora. The patient was removed to an institution in Gross Enzersdorf and remained very sick for several years. In the sanitarium she inflamed the heart of the psychiatrist in charge, so that her mother came from Frankfurt and took her back there. Later she recovered, developed a remarkable social activity, and devoted her life to the cause of the emancipation of women and the care of orphan children.

Jones's version is in many points incompatible with that of Breuer, but owing to the revelation of the patient's true identity it could be expected that new tracks were open toward objective biographical research.

WHO WAS BERTHA PAPPENHEIM?

Bertha Pappenheim was not an unknown figure among Jewish circles. A short biographical note on her was already to be found in the *Grosse Jüdische National Biographie,* edited by S. Winiger. Her death in 1936 was commemorated with a 40-page special issue of a journal she had founded, the *Blätter des Jüdischen Frauen bundes,*[6] with introductory notes from Martin Buber and Max Warbi and substantial accounts of her life, writings, and social activities. Material toward her biography had been gathered but was destroyed during World War II. A number of biographic details were collected by Mrs. Ellen Jensen[7] in Denmark, and a little monograph was published by Mrs. Dora Edinger in 1963.[8]

Bertha Pappenheim belonged to a distinguished old Jewish family. Her grandfather, Wolf Pappenheim, a prominent personality of the Pressburg ghetto, had inherited a great fortune. Her father, Siegmund Pappenheim, was a well-to-do merchant in Vienna. The family belonged to the strictly orthodox Jewish community. Little is known of her childhood and youth. She spoke English perfectly, read French and Italian. According to her own account, she led the usual life of a young lady of high Viennese society, with outdoor activities including horseback riding, and doing a great deal of needlework. It was reported that after her father's death in 1881 she and her mother left Vienna and settled in Frankfurt on the Main. In the later 1880's Bertha devoted herself fully to philanthropic activities. For about twelve years she was the director of an orphanage in Frankfurt. She traveled in the Balkan countries, the Near East, and Russia, to inquire into prostitution and white slavery. In 1904 she founded the *Jüdischer Frauenbund* (League of Jewish Women), and in 1907 she founded a teaching institution affiliated with that organization. Among her writings are travel reports, studies on the condition of Jewish women and on the criminality among Jews, and a number of short stories and theatricals (which reveal more concern with social problems than true literary talent). In her late years she re-edited ancient Jewish works into modernized form, including a history of a prominent ancestor. Toward the end of her life she was depicted as a deeply religious, strict and authoritarian person, utterly selfless and devoted to her work, who had retained from her Viennese education a lively sense of humor, a taste for good food, and the love of beauty, and who possessed an impressive collection of embroideries, china and glassware. When Hitler seized power and began to persecute the Jews she discouraged their emigration to Palestine or other countries. She died in March 1936, perhaps too early to realize that she had been mistaken in that regard. After World War II she was remembered as an almost legendary figure in the field of social work, to the extent that the government of Western Germany honored her memory by issuing a postage stamp with her picture.

In the biographic notices of 1936 there was no mention of a nervous illness in Bertha's youth. Bertha was said to have left Vienna for Frankfurt with her mother after the father's death in 1881. There is a wide gap indeed between the descriptions of the philanthropist and pioneer social worker, Bertha Pappenheim, and of Breuer's hysterical patient, Anna O.

One means for filling this gap could have been to replace the person into the context of Viennese life of the early 1880's. Obviously Bertha Pappenheim had nothing in common with the "sweet girl" (*das süsse Mädel*) of Schnitzler's theaticals and novels. Many Jews of the higher social strata kept the strict puritanical mores that had been those of their parents or grandparents in the ghetto. However they had access to the privilege and pleasures of the Austrian wealthy bourgeoisie. Bertha had received a fine education, she enjoyed outdoor activities and theater, but all this could not lead her to an independent or professional life; universities were still closed to women. We thus find in her situation a contrast between the ambitions and the obstacles set to ambitions; the same contrast is found in the story of several prominent hysterical women of that time.[9]

It is Juan Dalma[10] who showed the connection between Anna O's cure and the widespread interest in catharsis that followed the publication in 1880 of a book on the Aristotelian concept of catharsis by Jacob Bernays[11] (the uncle of Freud's future wife). For a time catharsis was one of the most discussed subjects among scholars and one of the topics of conversation in sophisticated Viennese salons. A historian of literature complained that, following the treatise by Bernays, there had been such a craze for the topic of catharsis that few people remained interested in the history of drama.[12] The time was ripe for catharsis to become a psychotherapeutic procedure.

THE AUTHOR'S OWN RESEARCH

During the preparation of my book, *The Discovery of the Unconscious,* I conducted in Vienna an inquiry about Bertha Pappenheim. The first task was to exactly identify the characters of the story. In the *Heimat-Rolle* (in the Community Archives) I found the following indications. Bertha's father, Siegmund Pappenheim, merchant, was born in Pressburg on June 10, 1824; he died in Vienna on April 5, 1881 (this is exactly the date given by Breuer as that of the death of Anna O's father, thus a confirmation of the identity between Anna O and Bertha Pappenheim). Her mother, Recha Goldschmidt, was born in Frankfurt on the Main on June 13, 1830. They had three children, all of them born in Vienna: Henriette, born on September 2, 1849, Bertha, born on February 27, 1859, Wilhelm, born on August 15, 1860. Henriette, who was ten years older than Bertha, died in early youth. The family lived for many years in the Jewish quarter of Leopoldstadt, but moved to Liechtensteinerstrasse in 1880 (incidently this street was near to the Berggasse where Freud was to live from 1891 to 1938).

A few details about Pappenheim can be found in the *Memoirs* of Sigmund Mayer.[13] He had been acquainted in the ghetto with old Wolf Pappenheim, a man of a rather humble condition who, following an unexpected inheritance had been metamorphosed into a wealthy patrician. All the Pappenheims were distinguished people, Mayer says. Mayer was well acquainted with Wilhelm (Bertha's brother), whom he depicts as an accomplished gentleman, strongly identified with the Jewish tradition but open to all modern ideas, who owned perhaps the most complete library on socialism to be found in Europe.

Bertha Pappenheim was related to prominent Jewish families from her mother's side too. This is shown in an extremely rare book that she and her brother Wilhelm published in private print in 1900. It is a German translation of the memoirs of an illustrious ancestor, Glückel von Hameln (1645–1724).[14] The translation is supplemented with a series of genealogical tables. One sees the connections of the Goldschmidts with numerous well-known Jewish names (such as the families Gomperz, von Portheim, Homburger, Friedländer, Oppenheim, etc.).

Coming now to Jones's version of Bertha's illness, we find difficulty reconciling it with the facts. First, Breuer's last child, Dora, was born on March 11, 1882 (as evidenced by the *Heimat-Rolle* in Vienna). Thus she could not possibly have been conceived after the supposed terminal incident of June 1882. The approximate time of Dora's conception (June 1881) would rather coincide with the date of Bertha's transfer to the country-house, but there is no evidence that Breuer interrupted the treatment at this time. (It was the beginning of the period when he went to visit her every few days, when her symptoms developed in the form of a regular cycle.) Second, there was never a sanitarium in Gross-Enzersdorf. Mr. Schramm, who wrote a history of the locality, told the author that it must have been confused with Inzersdorf, where there was a fashionable sanitarium. Upon inquiry, the author learned that it had been closed, and its medical archives transferred to the Viennese Psychiatric Hospital. No case history of Bertha Pappenheim could be found there.[15]

In Dora Edinger's biography of Bertha Pappenheim there was a photograph of Bertha with the date 1882, showing a healthy-looking, sporting woman in riding habit, in sharp contrast to Breuer's portrait of a home-bound young lady who had no outlets for her physical and mental energies. Thanks to the help of Mrs. Dora Edinger, I received the authorization to examine the original of that picture. As was usual in that time, the picture was stuck on a piece of cardboard. The date 1882 had been embossed by the photographer. The name and address of the photographer could no longer be deciphered. However, when the picture was examined under special light in the laboratory of the Montreal City Police, the name of the town, *Constanz,* appeared, with a part of the address.[16] This discovery led to the question: What was Bertha doing in riding habit in Konstanz, Germany, at the time when she was supposed to be severely sick in a sanitarium near Vienna? Mrs. Edinger suggested that she could have been treated in one of the sanitariums which existed in that part of Europe. Actually, there was one famous sanitarium, in the little Swiss town of Kreuzlingen, quite close to Konstanz: the Sanitorium Bellevue. I asked the present director, Dr. Wolfgang Binswanger, if the medical archives contained a case history of Bertha Pappenheim. I learned from him that Bertha Pappenheim had actually sojourned there as a patient from July 12 to October 29, 1882. The patient's file contained two documents: a copy of a case history written by Breuer himself in 1882, and a follow-up written by one of the doctors of the Sanitorium Bellevue.

BREUER'S UNKNOWN REPORT OF 1882

The name of Breuer does not appear in the document, but it quite obviously originates from him: it is the story of the same patient told by the same physician; whole sentences are almost identical with those of the *Studies in Hysteria.* It is a manuscript of $21^1/_2$ pages of large size, manifestly a copy written by a lay person; a number of difficult words were misunderstood, left blank, or corrected by another hand.

The report of 1882 contains numerous details which were left out in the later version, but it ends rather abruptly at the end of the "third period" of Bertha's illness. The time has not yet come for a publication of the complete document, but we will give a cursory view of the early case history, stressing the points where it gives new information or differs from the 1895 report.

The 1882 report provides a more complete picture of the family constellation. Bertha had difficulties with her "very serious" mother. Her brother (never mentioned in the *Studies in Hysteria*) plays a certain role; she sometimes had quarrels with him. There are several mentions of her "passionate love for her father who pampered her."[17] Breuer confirms that the sexual element was "astonishingly undeveloped" in Bertha and says that he had never found it represented in the immense amount of her hallucinations. She had never been in love, "insofar her relationship to her father did not replace it, or rather was replaced by it."[18] Two other features in Bertha's character are stressed: her stubborn, childish opposition against medical prescriptions; and her opposition against religion: "She is thoroughly unreligious. . . . Religion played a role in her life only as an object of silent struggles and silent opposition,"[19] although, for her father's sake, she outwardly followed all the religious rites of her strictly orthodox Jewish family.

As early as in the spring of 1880, we learn, Bertha began to suffer from facial neuralgia and muscular jerks. What Breuer called the "first period of the illness" went from July 17 to December 10, 1880. Breuer states that he did not see her during that time. All of what he related about her symptoms during that period, he learned later from the hypnotized patient, and the patient herself, in her conscious state, knew only what Breuer told her about it. To these hypnotic revelations belong to the story of the initial symptom. During the night of July 17 to 18, while the father was sick and the family waited for the arrival of a surgeon from Vienna, it happened that Bertha had a hallucination of a black snake crawling out of the wall to kill her father. She wanted to drive it away, but could not move her right arm; she saw her fingers as transformed into as many little snakes with tiny skulls, instead of the nails. She was filled with anguish, tried to pray, but could not speak until she found an English sentence. At this point the spell was interrupted by the whistling of an engine: it was the train that brought the surgeon from Vienna. A great number of other symptoms are described; many of them occurred during a peculiar state of absent-mindedness which she termed (in English) "time-missing." Her visual perceptions were strangely distorted. Looking upon her father, she saw him as a skeleton and his head as a skull. After having once been shaken by her brother she became momentarily deaf but from that time on a transient deafness always appeared whenever she was shaken. A great number of other symptoms appeared, but, Breuer says, no one around her ever noticed anything of them.

At the beginning of September 1880, the family went back to Vienna (it is not stated where they were before). Bertha devoted herself to nursing her sick father. Her symptoms were aggravated, a "nervous cough" appeared. Breuer saw her for the first time at the end of November on account of an "hysterical cough"; he recognized at once that she was mentally sick—something that had escaped her family's notice.

The second period (the "manifest illness" of Breuer's report of 1895), thus began shortly after Breuer's first visit. Bertha remained in bed from December 11, 1880, to April 1, 1881. Breuer gives a lengthy description of that period of the disease, which does not add very much to what he reported in 1895. In 1882, however, he laid more emphasis upon Bertha's "truly passionate love for her father."[20] The period when she remained mute for two weeks (in 1882 Breuer called it an "aphasia") occurred, Breuer says, after she had once been hurt (*gekränkt*) by her father. After being excluded from seeing her father, she felt a longing (*Sehnsucht*) for him. During that period of the illness Breuer was concerned with an anatomical diagnosis; he considered the possibility of a tubercle in the left *fossa Sylvii* with a slowly expanding chronic meningitis. However, the "nervous" character of her cough, and the tranquillising effect of Breuer's listening to the stories she told him evenings led him to think of a "purely functional ailment."[21]

Breuer's report of 1882 gives a great number of hitherto unknown data about the third period of Bertha's illness. First, we learn why her father's death was such a shock to her. During the previous two months she had not been allowed to see him and had continuously been told lies about his condition. In spite of her lasting anxiety, there had been some improvement in Bertha's illness and she had got up for the first time on April 1. On April 5, at the moment when her father was dying, she called her mother and asked for the truth, but was appeased and the lie went on for some time. When Bertha learned that her father had died, she was indignant: she had been "robbed" of his last look and last word. From that time on, a marked transformation appeared in her condition: anxiety replaced by a kind of dull insensitivity with distortions in her visual perceptions. Human beings appeared to her as wax figures. In order to recognize someone she had to perform what she called (in English) a "recognizing work." The only person she immediately recognized was Breuer. She manifested an extremely negative attitude toward her mother and to a lesser degree, toward her brother.

We learn that the consulting psychiatrist who came about ten days after the father's death was none other than Krafft-Ebing. The story of his intervention is related with the same details (save that we learn the fact that the smoke he blew into her face was from a burning piece of paper!). Unfortunately nothing is said of Krafft-Ebing's diagnosis and recommendations.

In view of the difficulty of keeping Bertha at home and because of several suicidal attempts, it was decided to transfer her to Inzersdorf. However it was not in the fashionable sanitarium of the Drs. Fries and Breslauer,[22] but in a kind of cottage close to the sanitarium (Breuer called it in 1882 a *Villa,* in 1895 a *Landhaus*), so that she could be kept under the daily care of the psychiatrists of that institution, while still visited by Breuer every few days. The transfer was performed "without deceit, but by force" on June 7, 1881.

Bertha's illness had reached its acme in that month of June, and from that time on there were periods of slow improvement and relapses. Breuer, as we know, came frequently; he was able to soothe her by listening to her stories. But his task was not always easy; he had to use much persuasion and to introduce the story with the sentence (in English): "And there was a boy . . ." and she had to feel his hands to make sure of his identity. Dr. Breslauer did not enjoy the same success and had to give her chloral.

Breuer tells of a five-week vacation from whence he came back in the middle of August (whether he went to Venice is not mentioned in the report). On his return, he found Bertha in a pitiful condition: "emotionally very bad, disobedient, moody, nasty, lazy."[23] It also looked as if her fantasy was exhausted. She gave distorted accounts of what had irritated her during the last days. There was an unexpected development at this point. Breuer's report of 1882 brings a new, more complete version of the discovery of the "talking-cure." He found that certain of the patient's whims or fancies (he called them by the French word *caprices*) could disappear when traced back to the "psychic incitements" (*psychische Reize*) which had been at their origin. (Let us recall that even earlier Bertha's "aphasia" had disappeared when Breuer could get the patient to tell that it started after having been offended by her father.) But the patient had taken to quite a few other "fancies." Thus, she went to bed with her stockings on; sometimes she woke up at 2 or 3 in the morning and complained that she had been left to go to bed in her stockings. One evening she told Breuer that while her father was sick and she had been forbidden to see him, she used to get up in the night, put her stockings on and go to listen at his door, until one night she was caught by her brother. After she told Breuer of this incident, the stockings "fancy" disappeared. The following occurrence (described as being the first one in the *Studies in Hysteria*) was the story of the little dog: for six weeks Bertha refused to drink water and quenched her thirst with fruits and melons; she told Breuer that it had started after seeing her lady companion's dog drinking water from a glass; she had been disgusted but had said nothing. Five minutes after telling Breuer the story she was able to drink water and the "drinking inhibition" (*Trink hemmung*) disappeared forever. Breuer found that certain "caprices" could be traced back, simply to some "fantastic thought" which the patient had imagined; such was her refusal to eat bread. The next step in the progress of the treatment was Breuer's discovery that not only "caprices," but also seemingly neurological symptoms could be made to disappear in the same way.

The end of the case history is disappointing. Breuer tells in a few lines that Bertha came back to her mother in Vienna at the beginning of November 1881, so that he was able to give her her talking-cure every evening. However, "for unaccountable reasons" her condition became worse in December. At the end of December, during the period of the Jewish Holidays, she was agitated; during that whole week she told Breuer every evening the fantastic stories that she had imagined at the same period of the preceding year; they were, day by day, the same stories.

The report contains nothing about the "fourth period" of the illness, although it is stated at the beginning of the report that it extended from December 1881 to the middle of June 1882. It ends with that enigmatic sentence: "After termination of the series great alleviation."[24] It should also be noted that there is nowhere any mention of a hysterical pregnancy and that the word catharsis appears nowhere in the 1882 report.

THE FOLLOW-UP OF THE SANITORIUM BELLEVUE

The copy of Breuer's long report is immediately followed on its last page by the beginning of a 2½ page follow-up, obviously written at the end of Bertha's sojourn by one of the doctors of the Sanitorium Bellevue. It bears the title: "Evolution of the illness during the sojourn in Bellevue from July 12, 1882 to October 29, 1882."

This follow-up is in many regards very instructive, in other regards disappointing. Someone who would know of Anna O only what Breuer related in the *Studies in Hysteria* would hardly guess that it is a follow-up of the same patient just after she had undergone Breuer's "cathartic cure." The follow-up consists of a long enumeration of medications given to the patient on account of severe facial neuralgia. We learn that the facial neuralgia had been exacerbated during the past six months (that is, the "fourth period" of her illness) and that during that period high amounts of chloral and of morphine had been prescribed. On her admission the amount of morphine was reduced to 7 to 8 centigrams of morphine in two daily injections. But the pains were at times so intolerable that one had to give her 10 centigrams. When she left the sanitarium she still received injections amounting to a total of 7 to 10 centigrams *pro die*. The follow-up, however, contains mention of "hysterical features" (*hysterische Merkmale*) in the patient, of her "unpleasant irritation against her family,[25] of her "disparaging judgments against the ineffectiveness of science in regard to her sufferings,"[26] of her "lack of insight into the severity of her nervous condition."[27] She often remained for hours under the picture of her father and told of visiting his tomb in Pressburg. In the evening, she regularly lost the use of the German language as soon as she had put her head on the pillow; she would even terminate in English a sentence that she had begun in German. The follow-up ends with this sentence: "Here, she did understand and speak French, though it was difficult to her on certain evenings." There is no mention of where the patient went after leaving Bellevue.

COMMENTARY

The time has not yet come for a complete and truly objective appraisal of Anna O's story. The two newly discovered documents may however shed some light upon a few points.

We know, now, that when Breuer published Anna O's story in 1895 he had under his eyes a previous report he had written in 1882 (whole lines are sometimes almost identical). This report, however, relates the story of the patient up to December 1881 and leaves out the "fourth period" of her illness. On the other hand, it seems that during the period when Breuer treated his patient he did not write daily notes about her. There are good reasons to think that the 1882 report was written from memory: there are no precise dates, aside from those of the father's death and of Bertha's transfer to the country-house. (Breuer does not even mention the date of his first visit to Bertha, nor that of the consultation with Krafft-Ebing). This might also be the reason why Breuer tells in 1895 of his "incomplete notes," when referring to the "fourth period" of the illness.

Breuer's report of 1882 brings a more complete picture of the patient's family and environment. Breuer draws a connection between the fact that Bertha had never been in love and her "truly passionate love to her father." We learn of her difficulties with her "very serious mother" and her quarrels with her brother. There is also a passing mention of an aunt.

Bertha's stubborn character is emphasized in the 1882 report, with her "childish opposition" to the doctors. Unexpected is the fact that Bertha was "thoroughly unreligious" in the midst of her strictly orthodox Jewish family. One would wish to know how and when she returned to the faith of her ancestors and became the ardent religious personality of the later years. We also learn of Bertha's visits to the theater and her interest in Shakespeare's plays.

The problematic features of the "first period" of Bertha's illness appear more clearly in the 1882 report than in the 1895 case history. Breuer did not see Anna during that first period and he emphasizes that her illness was completely unnoticed by her family. She did not remember her symptoms of that period and knew about them only what Breuer had learned from her under hypnosis and told her afterwards. One may wonder how Breuer could take at face value all the revelations of the hypnotized patient, whereas he expressly notes that—on the conscious level—she "gave distorted accounts of what had irritated her during the last days."

In the 1882 report the course of Bertha's illness appears as having been somewhat more stormy than in the narrative of 1895. We learn why the father's death was such a severe psychic trauma for the patient. We see more clearly that there was a succession of ups and downs, with at least four periods of worsening: (1) after the father's death; (2) after the transfer to the country-house; (3) during Breuer's vacation of July–August 1881; (4) and "for unaccountable reasons" in November 1881. We see more clearly the origin and development of what was called later "cathartic" treatment: at first and for a long time the "chimney-sweeping" merely meant that Bertha unburdened her mind from the stories she had imagined during the past days. But there came a time (in August 1881) when her fantasy was exhausted, and then she started to tell about the events that had been the starting-point of her (quite conscious and voluntary) "caprices." Later, she extended this procedure to the more serious, seemingly neurological symptoms. It is also noteworthy that the neurological symptoms, particularly the facial neuralgia, stand out more clearly in the 1882 report than in the 1895 case history. Breuer's concern with the brain-anatomical seat of the illness is noted in two places in the 1882 report.

Unfortunately the "fourth period" of Bertha's illness keeps its mystery entirely. The case history of 1895 tells of a strange, indeed unique, condition, and of two personalities, one living exactly 365 days before the other, and of the extraordinary therapeutic method of curing the illness by having the patient tell in reverse chronological order all occurrences of a given symptom, whatever the number, until one came to the first manifestation with the circumstances of its appearance. But Breuer's report of 1882 is almost completely silent about these strange facts. The Kreuzlingen follow-up does not mention anything of all this and merely refers to the fact that the patient had gotten used to taking high doses of chloral and morphine. In this follow-up the patient is depicted as a neurological case of a rather unpleasant person showing some hysterical features.

Thus, the newly discovered documents confirm what Freud, according to Jung, had told him: the patient had not been cured. Indeed, the famed "prototype of a cathartic cure" was neither a cure nor a catharsis. Anna O had become a severe morphinist and had kept a part of her most conspicuous symptoms (in Bellevue she could no longer speak German as soon as she had put her head on the pillow). Jones's version of the false pregnancy and hysterical birth throes cannot be confirmed and does not fit into the chronology of the case.

In *The Discovery of the Unconscious* I proposed the hypothesis that Anna O's illness was similar to one of those great "magnetic diseases" of the early 19th century such as that of the "Seeress of Prevorst." This would mean that the illness was a creation of the mythopoetic unconscious of the patient with the unaware encouragement and collaboration of the therapist. However, there must have been in Bertha's case more than just a "romance of the subliminal self" (to use Frederick Myers' terminology). Anna O's illness was the desperate struggle of an unsatisfied young woman who found no outlets for her physical and mental energies, nor for her idealistic strivings. It needed much time and effort before she succeeded in sublimating her personality into the respectable figure of a pioneer of social work, fighter for the rights of women and the welfare of her people—Bertha Pappenheim.

NOTES

1 Joseph Breuer und Sigmund Freud: *Studien über Hysterie,* Leipzig und Vienna, Deuticke, 1895, pp. 15–37.

2 Charles E. Goshen: The Original Case Material of Psychoanalysis. *American Journal of Psychiatry,* vol. 108, 1951–1952, pp. 830–834.

3 Sigmund Freud: *Medizin in Selbstdarstellung,* IV, 1924, p. 15.

4 *Notes on the Seminar in Analytical Psychology Conducted by C. G. Jung,* Zurich, March 23–July 6, 1925. Arranged by Members of the Class, Zurich, 1926 (unpublished typescript).

5 Ernest Jones: *The Life and Work of Sigmund Freud,* vol. I. New York, Basic Books, 1953, pp. 223–226.

6 *Blätter des Jüdischen Frauenbundes für Fraue-nar beit und Frauenbewegung,* vol. XII, no. 7/8, July–August, 1936.

7 Ellen Jensen: Anna O. Ihr späteres Schicksal. *Acta psychiatrica et neurologica scandinavica,* vol. 36, no. 1, 1961, pp. 119–131. See also: Allen M. Jensen: Anna O.—A Study of Her Later Life. *Psychoanalytic Quarterly,* vol. 39, no. 2, 1970, pp. 269–293.

8 Dora Edinger (Ed.): *Bertha Pappenheim: Leben und Schriften.* Frankfurt-am-Main, Ner-Tamid-Verlag, 1963.

9 See the stories of Catherine Muller and of Helene Preiswerk in the author's book, *The Discovery of the Unconscious,* New York, Basic Books, 1970, pp. 315–317, 689–691.

10 Juan Dalma: La catarsis en Aristoteles, Bernays y Freud. *Revista de Psiquiatría y Psicología Medical,* vol. 6, 1963, pp. 253–269. Reminiscencias Culturales Clásicas en Algunas Corrientes de Psicologia Moderna, *Revista de la Facultad de Medicina de Tucuman,* vol. 5, 1964, pp. 301–332.

11 Jacob Bernays: *Zwei Abhandlungen über die Aris totelische Theorie des Drama.* Berlin, Wilhem Hertz, 1880.

12 Wilhelm Wetz: *Shakespeare vom Standpunkt der vergleichenden Literaturgeschichte.* Hamburg, Haendeke, Lehmkübe, 1897, vol. 1, p. 30.

13 Sigmund Mayer: *Ein jüdischer Kaufmann, 1831 bis 1911. Lebenserinnerungen.* Leipzig, Duncker und Humblot, 1911, pp. 49–50.

14 *Die Memoiren des Glückel von Hameln . . . Autorisierte Uebertragung nach der Ausgabe des Prof. Dr. David Kaufman von Bertha Pappenheim.* Wien, 1910. Verlag von Dr. Stefan Meyer und Dr. Wilhelm Pappenheim.

15 For assistance in the author's inquiries he is indebted to Mr. Schramm, of Gross Enzersdorf, Mr. Karl Neumayer, Mayor of Inzersdorf, and Dr. W. Podhajsky, Director of the Viennese Psychiatric Hospital.

16 Thanks are due to Dr. Jörg Schuh-Kuhlmann who performed that investigation and to the Montreal City Police Laboratory for this valuable contribution to a point of psychiatric history.

17 "*. . . in leidenschaftlicher Liebe zu dem sie verhät schelnden Vater.*"

18 "*. . . soweit nicht ihr Verhältnis zum Vater dieses ersetzt hat oder vielmehr damit ersetzt war.*"

19 "*Sie ist durchaus nicht religiös. . . . Eine Rolle in ihrem Leben spielte Religion nur als Gegenstand stiller Kämpfe und stiller Opposition.*"

20 "*. . . ihre wahre leidenschaftliche Liebe.*"

21 "*. . . dass es sich doch um rein funktionnelles Lei den handle.*"

22 Details about the Inzersdorf sanitarium may be found in Heinrich Schlöss (Ed.): *Die Irrenpflege in Oesterreich in Wort und Bild.* Halle, Carl Marhold, 1912, pp. 241–253. The institution had been founded in 1872 by Hermann Breslauer (a former assistant of Prof. Leidensdorf) and Dr. Fries. The main building was the former castle of a noble family; there was a large English park. All kinds of psychotic and neurotic patients were treated.

23 "*. . . moralisch recht schlecht, unfügsam, launisch, boshaft, träge.*"

24 "*Nach Beendigung der Serie grosse Erleichte rung.*"

25 "*. . . geradezu unliebenswürdigen Gereiztheit gegen Angehörige.*"

26 "*So beurtheilte sie in abfälliger Weise die Unzuläng lichkeit der Wissenschaft gegenüber ihren Leiden.*"

27 "*Die fehlende Einsicht in die Schwere ihres Stat. nervosus.*"

The Return of the Repressed: Psychology's Problematic Relations with Psychoanalysis, 1909–1960.

Gail A. Hornstein

Freud and Jung were having dinner in Bremen. It was the evening before they set sail for the Clark conference, the occasion of Freud's only visit to America. Jung started talking about certain mummies in the lead cellars of the city. Freud became visibly disturbed. "Why are you so concerned with these corpses?" he asked several times. Jung went on talking. Suddenly, without warning, Freud fell to the floor in a faint. When he recovered, he accused Jung of harboring death wishes against him. But it was not Jung who wanted Freud dead. Had Freud only known what American psychologists were about to do to psychoanalysis, he might never have gotten up off the floor.

There is no easy way to talk about psychology's relations with psychoanalysis.[1] It is a story dense with disillusionment and the shapeless anger of rejection. Each side behaved badly, and then compounded its insensitivity with disdain. Their fates bound together like Romulus and Remus, psychology and psychoanalysis struggled to find their separate spheres, only to end up pitted against one another at every turn. Too much was at stake—property lines, areas of influence, and a deeper question: Which field

Hornstein, G. A. (1992). The return of the repressed: Psychology's problematic relations with psychoanalysis, 1909–1960. *American Psychologist, 47,* 254–263.

would ultimately dictate the ground rules for a science of the mind?

In the 1890s, when this struggle began, there was little sign that it would become another Hundred Years' War. Psychologists had just begun to apply experimental methods to some of the classic problems of metaphysics, with the hope of answering questions that had bedeviled philosophers for centuries. By systematically organizing the psychological world into a set of discrete variables, these methods brought the unruly phenomena of mind within the purview of science. It was a heady time, a time of possibility and change and the reckless felicity of the new. American psychologists raced around founding laboratories at every college that would let them, in closets, basements or wherever they could snatch a little space, setting up apparatus in their own homes if necessary. They invented new forms of measurement, odd devices, tests of all sorts. Reports of their findings poured into the journals that sprang up suddenly to fill the need. The *new psychology,* as they liked to call it, seemed destined even in its infancy to do what had been declared since Kant to be impossible—to create a truly scientific approach to mind.

Psychoanalysts thrust themselves directly into the middle of this scene, brazenly trying to supplant the new psychology at the moment of its greatest promise. At first psychologists stood aside, astonished, as the analysts, bursting with self-importance and an almost frightening zealotry, pronounced themselves the real scientists of the mind. By the time psychologists began to take this threat seriously, psychoanalysis had so captured the public imagination that even its pretensions could not be ignored.[2]

The question was how to define science. To the analysts, science had nothing to do with method, with controlling variables or counting things. What made something scientific was that it was true. Constructing a science of the mind could mean one thing—finding some way to peer through the watery murk of consciousness to the subaquean reality that lay beyond. The efforts of psychologists, with their bulky equipment and piles of charts and graphs, seemed superficial and largely irrelevant to this goal.[3]

For their part, psychologists initially saw psychoanalysis as just another of the "mind cures" that flashed across the American landscape in the 1890s—like Christian Science or the Emmanuel movement—a popular craze that had nothing to do with the scientific study of mind. Most psychologists who attended Freud's Clark lectures in 1909 saw his speculations about dreams and sex as a pleasant diversion, about as relevant to their work as Mrs. Eddy's epistles. The occasional articles about psychoanalysis that appeared in psychology journals before 1910 (e.g. Putnam, 1906; Scott, 1908) made it seem mildly interesting, but not essentially different from related methods like suggestion.

By 1915, readers of a publication like *The Journal of Abnormal Psychology* had an opportunity for more varied exposure to psychoanalytic ideas.[4] Books by Freud, Jung, and A. A. Brill were regularly reviewed. Articles demonstrating the therapeutic effectiveness of psychoanalytic techniques began to appear, along with some discussion of the theory itself (see, e.g., Coriat, 1910; Emerson, 1912–1913; Gordon, 1917; MacCurdy, 1913; Maeder, 1910; Putnam, 1909–1910). Criticisms, when made, were fair-minded and well within the spirit of scientific repartee. Donley (1911), for example, suggested that anxiety neurosis might have other causes beyond those considered by Freud. Bellamy (1915a) argued that dreams fulfill fears or states of anger just as often as they represent wishes. Taylor (1911) noted that there were cases of neurosis in which patients recovered without having had their childhood or sexual life dissected. Even critics with a broader focus expressed little ire. Wells (1913) was concerned about "looseness in the formulation of psychoanalytic theories" (p. 227). Solomon (1916) argued that the term *sexual* was used inconsistently by analytic writers. The psychiatrist Morton Prince (1910) expressed the common view that psychoanalysts "fit the facts to the universal concepts which dominate the school" (p. 349).

There were occasional writers who became exasperated and called psychoanalysis "weird" (Donley, 1911), "esoteric" (Carrington, 1914), or "grotesque" (Bellamy, 1915a), its assumptions "fantastic" or "sheer nonsense" (Humphrey, 1920b), but these imprecations were unusual in the early years. The sexual nature of psychoanalytic interpretation was a problem for some; Bellamy (1915b), for example, in reviewing a book by Coriat, made plain his relief that "there is not a word or sentence in this book that a precise maiden lady need hesitate to read to her Sunday school class or at a pink tea" (p. 434). On the whole, however, psychologists were initially so supportive of psychoanalysis that when Roback reviewed Dunlap's (1920) *Mysticism, Freudianism and Scientific Psychology,* he felt he had to defend its critical tone on grounds of balance: "Freud has had so many warm advocates of his views in this country and so few systematic critics among the psychologists that Dunlap's discussion is both timely and important" (Roback, 1921, p. 406).

These positive attitudes might well have resulted from more than psychologists' open-mindedness. Analysts, ever worried about their public image, left little to chance. Soon after the Clark conference they embarked on a systematic campaign to win Americans to their cause. A. A. Brill, the founder of the New York Psychoanalytic Society, was charged with disseminating information about psychoanalysis in that city; Ernest Jones, Freud's scrappy lieutenant, took the rest of the country for himself (Burnham, 1967, pp. 134–137). Psychologists were among the major recipients of Jones's educational largess; by 1916, they had been treated to 20 of his articles, abstracts, reviews, and comments in the *Journal of Abnormal Psychology* alone. Most of these pieces were patient expositions of psychoanalytic concepts, designed to lead the uninitiated to a correct understanding of the theory. But Jones also maintained a vigilant watch over what psychologists were writing about psychoanalysis, and shot back a tart riposte whenever he encountered an "erroneous" statement (see also Tannenbaum, 1916, 1917).

Neither Jones nor his colleagues gave serious attention to the careful criticisms that psychologists leveled against psychoanalysis in the early years. Acutely aware of the tenuous status of their own new field, psychologists found this highly disconcerting. After all, they were constantly obliged to defend their science against attacks from philosophy and biology; what gave analysts the right not only to ignore legitimate criticism but to patronize their opponents? Who knows what might have happened had analysts been more responsive; what did happen was that psychologists sharpened their pencils and began to fight.

The first skirmish actually occurred as early as 1916, when the Princeton philosopher Warner Fite reviewed Jung's *Psychology of the Unconscious* for *The Nation* (Fite, 1916). His surprisingly nasty tone incited a riot of response from psychologists. In her letter to the editor, Christine Ladd-Franklin, the eminent experimentalist, characterized psychoanalysis as a product of the "undeveloped . . . German mind" (hardly a compliment in 1916), and concluded ominously that "unless means can speedily be found to prevent its spread . . . the prognosis for civilization is unfavorable" (Ladd-Franklin, 1916, p. 374). R. S. Woodworth of Columbia (1916), a bit more circumspect, called psychoanalysis an "uncanny religion" (probably not the psychologist's highest accolade) that led "even apparently sane individuals" to absurd associations and nonsensical conclusions. In a telling illustration, he showed how the words *Freudian principles* led to a train of thought that revealed his own "deep-seated wish . . . for a career of unbridled lust" (p. 396).

Woodworth went on to publish an extensive critique of "Freudism" in the 1917 volume of the *Journal of Abnormal Psychology.* Adopting the peevish tone that soon became commonplace in these sorts of articles, he complained that analysts disregarded psychological research, contemptuously dismissed it as superficial, and treated psychologists "shabbily" (Woodworth, 1917, p. 175). What most annoyed Woodworth was the analysts' slippery dodge, their way of attributing any criticism of psychoanalysis to unconscious resistance on the part of the critic.

Other writers echoed these complaints, often with less poignancy and considerably more pique than Woodworth. But what soon emerged as the real irritant for psychologists was the analysts' insistence, at times moralistic, at times snide, that only those who had themselves undergone a personal psychoanalysis were qualified to evaluate the theory. To an experimental psychology whose raison d'etre was to differentiate itself from religion, this talk of initiation rites and secret knowledge was anathema. Such a rule also conveniently disenfranchised just about every psychologist from serving as a potential critic; even those Americans who sought analysis had a hard time finding it in this country before 1920. Of course the real issue here was not who had been analyzed and who had not (a good thing, since Freud and his closest colleagues would have had to disqualify themselves); what was at stake was the fundamental question of subjectivity in science.

For experimental psychologists, being scientific meant creating distance. It meant opening up a space, a "no man's land," between themselves and the things they studied, a place whose boundary could be patrolled so that needs or desires or feelings could never infiltrate the work itself. Every aspect of the experimental situation was bent toward this goal—the "blind subjects," the mechanized recording devices, the quantified measures, and statistically represented results (Danziger, 1990; Hornstein, 1988; Morawski, 1988). What united experimental psychologists more than anything else was a distrust of personal experience, a sense that feelings in particular were dangerous and had to be held carefully in check lest they flood in and destroy the very foundations of the work. They were willing to make a number of sacrifices to protect psychology from this threat, including a radical narrowing of the field to include only phenomena that could be studied "objectively."

Having gone to these lengths, psychologists found it profoundly disquieting to have analysts claim that being psychoanalyzed was what made someone a credible scientist. This implied that science was subjective, that is was ultimately about personal experience rather than rigorous method. Even worse, it suggested that the unconscious was so powerful a part of mind that its force had to be experienced directly, in one's own life, in order to understand the psychology of others.

Such a view could not go unchallenged. "Voodooism," Watson (1927, p. 502) called it. "A delusion," echoed Jastrow (1932, p. 285). The very idea of an unconscious conjured up the chaos and irrationality that psychologists had banded together to escape. If analysts wanted to plunge into that nightmare world and call it science, so be it, but they could not be allowed to drag everyone else down with them.

The technique of free association came in for particular scorn (Heidbreder, 1933). It struck psychologists as an elaborate subterfuge, a way for analysts to appear not to influence patients when of course they did. Interpretation, they argued, was nothing but a new name for suggestion; that patients were gullible enough to mistake it for truth was hardly proof of its scientific status. Analysts were "free," all right—free to define as evidence whatever would meet their needs, free to label any challenge "resistance," free to pretend that they were doing nothing of the sort.

Heidbreder (1933), in her typically fair-minded way, struggled to make these practices sound reasonable. But even she could muster only this faint defense: Just because "psychoanalysts offer a different kind of evidence from that accepted by science . . . does not mean that they offer *no* evidence" (p. 402). To most psychologists, calling an analyst's retrospective musings about events that occurred in the secrecy of the consulting room evidence was an insult to science. Even first-year students knew that the cardinal rule of scientific proof was publicly verifiable data. Knight Dunlap (1920, p. 8) put it bluntly: "psychoanalysis attempts to creep in wearing the uniform of science, and to strangle it from the inside."[5]

By the mid-1920s, psychologists seem to have decided that the best way to defend science was simply to do it. Critiques of psychoanalysis began to be displaced in the literature by enthusiastic works like *Great Experiments in Psychology* (Garrett, 1930). Any remaining aggressive tendencies were easily absorbed by the interminable debates over behaviorism and Gestalt psychology.[6] Psychologists did not need psychoanalysis, and it surely did not need them.

Or so it seemed, until one day in the fall of 1934 when the rumor got out that Edwin Garrigues Boring, the self-acknowledged dean of experimental psychology, had entered analytic treatment. To preserve his reputation, he told colleagues that he was studying the relation between the two fields; actually, he was depressed, frightened, and unable to work. The strange saga of Boring's analysis gives a glimpse into psychologists' continuing ambivalence about psychoanalysis.

Boring chose as his analyst the emigré Berliner, Hanns Sachs, who had been a member of Freud's inner circle and was therefore above reproach. Despite his depression, Boring embarked on the analysis with customary gusto, quickly absorbing the daily analytic sessions into the swirl of his 80-hour work week.

Boring struggled to make the analysis a success. He missed no sessions. He wept. He threw things. He made enough of a financial sacrifice to demonstrate the seriousness of his commitment. He discussed his childhood, explored his dreams, and scrutinized the motivations for his actions. Then, at the end of 10 months, he ran out of money, time, and desire. He had completed 168 sessions, for which he had paid $1,680, more than a fifth of his yearly salary. But his efforts brought little relief:

> [A]ll that happened was that the analysis petered out in an uneventful session on June 21st and my analyst went abroad! . . . I was distraught. I had tried a last resource, and it had failed. Yet, unwilling to accept so bitter a conclusion, I found myself seizing on the analyst's casual statement that I ought to wait a month. I waited anxiously, hoping for a new personality by July 21st. None came. Finally I sought out my psychologist-friends who believe in psychoanalysis, and we sat in conference discussing this sad immutability of my personality—on August 21st, as I suddenly realized. Their advice was patience, the less haste the more speed; wait at least until December 21st, they urged. So I waited. . . . And finally I ceased to expect a miracle. (Boring, 1940, pp. 9–10)[7]

How could a man like Boring, whose name was practically synonymous with hard-nosed experimentation, have such childlike faith in psychoanalysis? He actually seemed to expect that he would wake up a new man, that "a light from heaven" would change him "from Saul to Paul" (p. 9). There are certainly no hints of these hopes in his published writings. In the first edition of his classic *History of Experimental Psychology* (Boring, 1929), published just five years before the analysis, there were only four brief mentions of Freud in almost 700 pages. Psychoanalysis did not even appear in the index of *Psychology: A Factual Textbook,* the text Boring published with Langfeld and Weld in 1935, the same year he saw Sachs.

Yet in his own life, Boring kept searching for some sign that the analysis might have worked. Five years passed. Still no light. In 1940, he tried a new strategy. He proposed to the *Journal of Abnormal and Social Psychology* that it locate other well-known psychologists who had been analyzed, solicit reports of their experiences, and publish them in a special issue. Perhaps they would reveal something that he had missed. Leaving nothing to chance, Boring even persuaded Sachs to write a companion piece to his own account, evaluating the analysis from the analyst's perspective.

Psychologists turned out to be surprisingly excited by the prospect of reading about their colleagues' adventures on the couch. The American Psychological Association even reprinted the articles and sold them as a set, exhausting the entire edition within a few months. Boring, ever hopeful, titled his piece "Was This Analysis a Success?" Sachs (1940) replied with a tactful "no." Wistful and perplexed by the whole experience, Boring struggled to come to terms with his sense of loss: "There is so much about this personality of mine that would be better if different, so much that analysis might have done and did not!" (Boring, 1940, p. 10). Yet he refrained from attacking psychoanalysis directly. His colleagues, however, knew where to lay the blame for their own failed attempts. Carney Landis of Columbia parodied his experience with a statistical analysis of how much time he had allocated to each of eight topics during free association. To Landis, analysts were scientific illiterates who did little but mouth received dogma in order to make themselves rich. Hinting that his "neurosis" was created by the analysis itself, Landis (1940) concluded his tirade by warning that psychoanalysis was safe only when used by experimental psychologists to produce psychopathic phenomena in the laboratory.

The editor of the *Journal of Abnormal and Social Psychology,* apparently concerned about the lack of balance in these articles, invited the eminent analyst Franz Alexander to contribute a rejoinder. Instead of critiquing the other papers, Alexander (1940) made a parable of his own life. Like his readers, he had spent his youth as a devotee of laboratory science. When he first tried to read Freud's work, he found its "vague and ambiguous mental excursions . . . equal almost to physical pain" (p. 312). He turned to psychoanalysis only when the evidence in support of it became undeniable. This meant sacrificing his promising academic career, enduring the opprobrium of his colleagues, and being forced from home by his irate philosopher father, who considered psychoanalysis a "spiritual gutter." But for Alexander, there was no choice—having committed himself to empiricism, he had to adopt whatever view had the most evidence, regardless of how distasteful it might be on other grounds. Of course, in the end, his quest for truth was vindicated when his father, near death, gave up his own lifelong belief in the superiority of natural science to express the fervent wish that "psychoanalysis will enthrone again real understanding in place of fumbling—the rule of thought in place of that of the gadget" (p. 314).

Alexander's inspiring tale fell on closed ears. Distrusting subjectivity in all its forms, psychologists put little stock in personal testimony, even that of fellow scientists. This series of articles clearly had less to do with evaluating psychoanalysis than it did with assuaging the anxiety of its contributors, many of whom were worried, like Boring, that their analyses had failed. What they needed was reassurance. But the tangible benefits of this kind of therapy are always elusive. Recall Janet Malcolm's (1984) sardonic comment: "The crowning paradox of psychoanalysis is the near-uselessness of its insights. To 'make the unconscious conscious' . . . is to pour water into a sieve. The moisture that remains on the surface of the mesh is the benefit of analysis" (p. 25). Ultimately, these articles were exercises in self-persuasion, attempts by the contributors to convince themselves that psychoanalysis was too ridiculous or too ineffectual to be taken seriously. If they managed in the process to warn off colleagues who might have been tempted to try the thing themselves, so much the better.

By the early 1940s, the situation had reached a critical stage. Psychoanalysis was becoming so popular that it threatened to eclipse psychology entirely. Journalists seemed oblivious to the differences between the two fields, and exasperated psychologists often found their discipline being portrayed as if it were nothing but a branch of psychoanalytic inquiry. This was especially galling because most psychologists assumed that psychoanalytic claims were not even true. But how could they prove this? The critiques of the early years had not worked. Attacking psychoanalysis from the couch had simply allowed Alexander to make psychologists look foolish. There had to be a better way.

The solution turned out to be so obvious that it is hard to believe it took until the mid-1940s to appear. Psychologists would set themselves the job of determining through carefully controlled experiments which, if any, psychoanalytic concepts were valid. This reinstated psychologists as arbiters of the mental world, able to make the final judgment about what would and would not count as psychological knowledge. It allowed them to evaluate psychoanalysis, rather than be overshadowed or absorbed by it. Most important, it restored the objective criterion of the experiment as the basis for making claims and settling disputes, undermining the analysts' attempts to substitute a new, subjective standard for psychological truth.

Psychologists took to their new role with a vengeance. Every conceivable psychoanalytic concept was put to the test, in hundreds of studies whose creativity was matched only by the uselessness of their findings. Mowrer (1940) demonstrated that regression and reaction formation could be produced in rats. Blum and Miller (1952) found that children who were categorized as having an "oral character" ate significantly more ice cream than did other children. Scodel (1957) showed that "high-dependency" men did not manifest the predicted preference of women with large breasts. Schwartz (1956) found more castration anxiety among men than women, with homosexual men scoring the highest of all. Sarnoff and Corwin (1959) reported that "high castration anxious" men showed a greater increase in fear of death than did "low anxious" men after being exposed to photographs of nude women. And Friedman (1952) found that when children were shown a picture of a father and a child near some stairs, more girls than boys fantasized that the father would mount the stairs and enter the room.

Topics like oedipal relations and anal personality had their aficionados, but it was *perceptual defense* that really captured the imagination of psychological researchers. Their hypothesis was a simple one: If the mind did defend against forbidden material, then words with disturbing or salacious associations should be recalled less easily than more neutral stimuli. Fresh-faced graduate students spent hours making certain that items like *whore* and *bugger* were matched in length and salience with their sexless counterparts. Controversies erupted left and right: Were taboo words difficult to recognize just because they were not used very frequently? Weiner's (1955) famous "pussy–balls" study dispatched that idea by demonstrating that the context, not the words themselves, made certain stimuli threatening. But was exposure to a list of scatological words really analogous to the sort of trauma that necessitated repression? Blum (1954) addressed that problem with a new methodology based on the Blacky Pictures, a set of cartoon images of a dog depicted in various psychoanalytically relevant poses (licking his genitals, observing his parents having sex, defecating outside their kennel). When studies with Blacky were found to support the earlier word-item findings, repression gained the sort of empirical reality that only psychologists could give it.

By the 1950s, research on psychoanalysis had become so popular that psychologists were drowning in it. No one could possibly read all the studies that were being published, much less keep track of their results.[8] A new cottage industry was born of this need, with workers who did nothing but summarize and evaluate these studies. Robert Sears had been the first such laborer, commissioned in 1943 by the Social Science Research Council to write an objective review of the scientific literature on psychoanalytic theory. Sear's approach, used by all subsequent evaluators, was straightforward: Having first divided the literature into topic categories (fixation, sexuality, object choice), he then counted how many studies in each area supported Freud's claims. The larger the number, the more scientific the claim. Taken together, these individual scores were supposed to provide an answer to the overall question of whether psychoanalytic theory was valid.

Sears (1943) hedged, saying that some of it was, and some of it was not. Such caution soon vanished. The self-appointed judges whose reports appeared up through the early 1970s placed themselves squarely on one side of the debate or the other. Evaluation studies quickly became as difficult to sort out as research on psychoanalysis itself, and much less fun to read (see, for example, Fisher & Greenberg, 1977; Kline, 1972). Each report took a tone yet more strident than the last, and the original goal of providing an objective review was lost entirely. This was nowhere more evident than in Eysenck and Wilson's (1973) polemic. Every shred of evidence seeming to support psychoanalysis was scrutinized for methodological flaws, whereas studies opposing the theory were flaunted as examples of good science.

No one especially cared that the evaluation literature was becoming debased. It made little difference what the findings were; as long as psychoanalytic phenomena were made subservient to empirical test, empiricism was vindicated.[9] That much of this research supported Freud's theory was an irony appreciated by few. It was the act of doing these studies, of piling them up and sorting them out and arguing about them that was important, not what they revealed about psychoanalysis. Some psychologists found these activities so salubrious that they recommended them even to analysts. As Albert Ellis (1950) cheerfully noted, "sociologists, who but a decade or two ago were mostly concerned with pure theory, now frequently design and execute crucial experiments which enable them to support or discredit hypotheses. There is no basic reason why psychoanalysts cannot do likewise" (p. 190).

Analysts were in no position to point out that the content of these psychological studies had only the dimmest relation to Freud's theory. "Every country creates the psychoanalysis it [unconsciously] needs," said Kurzweil (1989, p. 1), and disciplines surely do the same. Research on psychoanalysis was invigorating because it gave psychologists a sense of mastery: They had ventured onto the battlefield of the unconscious and returned, triumphant, with a set of dependent variables. Some psychologists even managed to convince themselves that the danger had been exaggerated all along, that they had really been in control. They scoffed that psychoanalysis had never been much more than an inflated way of talking about conditioning, one of psychology's oldest topics. By the time Dollard and Miller (1950) actually began translating every psychoanalytic concept into its learning theory equivalent, their efforts were almost redundant.

These behaviorist reworkings of Freud, although often clumsy, did signal a new strategy in dealing with psychoanalysis—co-optation. More satisfying than silence, with none of the pitfalls of criticism, the appropriation of psychoanalytic concepts into mainstream psychology seemed an ideal compromise. Like the Christianizing of paganism, the dangerous parts were still there somewhere, but in such diluted form as to pose no real threat.[10]

Watson had tried to move in this direction as early as the 1920s. By relabeling the *unconscious* as the *unverbalized,* he could sweep most psychoanalytic phenomena into the neat piles of behaviorist theory. Emotions became sets of habits; neurosis was conditioning; therapy, unconditioning. Watson never denied the reality of Freud's findings; he simply cast them in his own terms (e.g., when he warned [1928, p. 80] that sexual frustration made mothers want to kiss rather than shake hands with their children). At times, Watson even took to calling himself an analyst, as if, like some ancient warrior, he could magically disarm his enemy by assuming his name.[11]

Other behaviorists continued where Watson left off. Humphrey (1920a), following Holt's (1915) earlier lead, dissolved wishes into conditioned reflexes. Keller and Schoenfeld (1950) laid claim to such psychoanalytic staples as the slip of the tongue (yet another reflex) and the oedipal complex (a consequence of early conditioning). But it was Skinner who took the task of appropriating Freud most seriously. In *Science and Human Behavior* (1953), he systematically redefined each of the defense mechanisms in operant terms (*repression:* a "response which is successful in avoiding the conditioned aversive stimulation generated by punishment," p. 292; *reaction formation:* "an extension of a technique of self-control in which the environment is altered so that it becomes less likely to generate punished behavior," p. 365). By the end of the book, even symbols and dreams had taken on the veneer of conditioned responses. Artful as these efforts were, they did not really solve the problem. Freud was still there. His new operant outfit gave him a natty American look, but there was no mistaking that sardonic smile. As long as psychoanalytic concepts remained identifiable as such, they were potential rivals to psychology's own constructs.

Help with this problem came from an unlikely source—introductory textbook writers. Typically dismissed as nothing but purveyors of pabulum for college students, these authors, many of them prominent psychologists, played a major role in advancing the co-optation of psychoanalytic theory. This is not so surprising. As Morawski (1992) shows, introductory texts exist in a liminal space, neither popular nor professional, yet somehow both. They function simultaneously as translators of standard doctrine and contributors to it. Because new texts constantly supplant older ones, they become disciplinary artifacts, frozen moments of taken-for-granted knowledge, X rays of the uncontroversial.

Textbook writers took advantage of their role by assimilating psychoanalytic concepts into mainstream psychology without mentioning their origins. An early example was Walter Hunter's 1923 text, *General Psychology,* in which the various defense mechanisms were stripped of any connection to the unconscious, much the way bagels now appear in the frozen-food sections of Peoria supermarkets. Other writers soon adopted this practice, sometimes using the term *adjustment mechanisms* to expunge any remaining whiff of psychodynamics (Guthrie & Edwards, 1949; Kimble, 1956).

These appropriations took place amidst a general silence in these texts about psychoanalytic theory itself. Many writers ignored the topic entirely: Robinson and Robinson's 665-page *Readings in General Psychology* (1923) included the contributions of every conceivable psychologist, even Helen Keller and the Lord Archbishop of York, but had nothing by Freud or any other psychoanalyst (the section titled "Dreams as a Vehicle of Wish Fulfillment" was written by Watson). Readers of well-known texts like Seashore's (1923) *Introduction to Psychology* or Warren and Carmichael's (1930) *Elements of Human Psychology* would never have known that psychoanalysis existed. Even as late as 1958, a classic like Hebb's *Textbook of Psychology* barely mentioned the topic. When Freud did make an appearance, it was more likely to be in the section on punishment or motivation—topics dear to the heart of experimentalists—than in expected places like the chapter on abnormality.

Of course some textbook writers did discuss psychoanalysis in more depth, but few besides Hilgard (1953) did so sympathetically.[12] Kimble (1956) went to the trouble of including a special section in his introduction warning readers not to make the common error of confusing psychology with psychoanalysis. It was not that

Freud had no value: Kimble called his work "one of the great milestones in the history of human thought" with "insights [that] have never been equaled" (pp. 369–370). Psychoanalysis just happened to be "entirely literary and not worth discussion" in a scientific text (p. 370).

In 1956, Gardner Murphy was asked to determine the extent of Freud's impact on the various subfields of psychology. He likened the overall effect to the erosion of the rocky coastline in Maine, but admitted that some areas had remained untouched by the psychoanalytic current. His results, on a numerical scale, of course, constitute what one might call an *index of intro-gression,* ranging from 0, Freud never had a chance, to 6, he made it all the way in. Here are Murphy's ratings: intelligence and physiological = 0; comparative, learning, thinking, perception, and vocational = 1; memory, drive and emotion, child and adolescent = 2; social and industrial = 3; imagination = 4; abnormal = 5; personality and clinical = 6.

What is surprising about these results is that there are any high scores at all. How could a discipline that had spent 50 years protecting its chastity end up seduced by a ladykiller like Freud? Of course the problem was really only with the clinicians, but there were thousands of them, and more every year (Gilgen, 1982; Kelly, 1947). When the American Psychological Association surveyed a sample of its members in 1954, asking who had influenced them to enter the field, Freud, of all people, got the greatest number of mentions (Clark, 1957, pp. 17–18). True, by that time, 37% of APA members were clinicians (p. 116), but how had that happened? Why were so many psychologists fleeing the laboratory?

Perhaps it was just the money. Or the effects of the war. But what if this exodus had a more ominous meaning?

Repression is a perverse process. It appears to efface the offending material, but this is an illusion—the contents of the unconscious are indestructible. Repressed material, like radioactive waste, lies there in leaky canisters, never losing potency, eternally dangerous. What is worse, it actively presses for expression, constantly threatening to erupt into consciousness. No one can control these forces; the best we can do is try to deflect them. It is a sign of health if we can accomplish this with a few judiciously used defenses. We know we're in trouble when we have to resort to the rigidity of symptoms.

Experimentalists took a calculated risk in trying to create a psychology in which subjective phenomena were banned from study. They knew that this would be difficult, that it would require erecting a set of defenses (the experimental method and all its appurtenances) and being vigilant about their use. But subjectivity creeps through every crevice and finds its way around even the strongest barricade. In the early years, this threat was manageable and psychology was wiling to tolerate some narrowing of its operations in exchange for the reduction of anxiety its defenses allowed. Psychoanalysis tore this fragile equilibrium to pieces. By embracing subjectivity—sometimes even reveling in it—while still proclaiming itself a science, psychoanalysis forced psychology to define itself in ever more positivist terms. This was no ordinary battle over intellectual turf. It was more like a nightmare, in which psychologists watched, horrified, as the very phenomena they had sought to banish now returned to haunt them. They did what they could to contain the threat, but each new tactic only made things worse. Co-opting analytic concepts proved to be especially disastrous because it let the banned phenomena inside psychology itself. Even in scientific disguise, they were still dangerous, like a well-dressed hitchhiker who pulls a knife after getting into the car. With the threat now internal as well as external, experimental psychology was forced to harden itself still further. What had once been science became scientism, the neurotic symptom of a frightened discipline.

In retrospect, we might say that this was all to the good. The psychology that emerged from these wrenching experiences was stronger and more resilient, able to tolerate a degree of diversity among its members that would once have been unthinkable. The past 30 years have been a time of exponential growth, as older areas like learning have reorganized and newer ones like clinical have matured. The "cognitive revolution" that brought the mind back to psychology transformed even the most hard-core behaviorist, and terms like *self-perception* are now bandied about the laboratory as if they had been there all along. The rigid experimentalism of the 1940s now seems vaguely embarrassing, one of those righteous crusades of adolescence that pales before the complex realities of middle age.

There were many reasons for these changes, and certainly the threat from psychoanalysis was only one of a host of factors pushing psychology toward greater flexibility. But, as Burnham (1978) has argued, psychoanalysis did represent an extreme position against which more conservative disciplines like psychology and psychiatry had to define themselves. The willingness of analysts to occupy the radical frontiers of subjectivity gave psychologists room to maneuver, to create a middle ground in which previously excluded phenomena could enter without threatening the scientific standards psychologists had fought so hard to establish.

Equally important were the changes in psychoanalysis itself. During the period from 1940 to 1960, internecine warfare reached new heights among American analysts. The purges in the New York Psychoanalytic Institute were only the most visible sign that the field had become increasingly intolerant of dissent, and the huge influx of candidates after the war accelerated this slide toward conformity and conservatism (Hale, 1978; Jacoby, 1983). Psychoanalysis in 1950 was fundamentally different from what it had been in 1920, and its new mainstream mentality made it far easier for psychologists to accept.

The Second World War also played a significant role in these dynamics. Psychologists made substantive contributions to the diagnosis and treatment of war-related disturbances, as well as to myriad other problems from personnel selection to instrument design. These efforts enhanced the reputation of professional psychology and stimulated a massive increase in funding for psychological research. The war also brought to America European refugee psychologists, many of whom saw psychoanalytic ideas as part of the psychological canon. Psychologists began to spend less time worrying about whether analysts were eroding the fragile boundary between legitimate and popular psychology (Morawski & Hornstein, 1991) and took advantage of opportunities to get some favorable press of their own.[13]

American psychology has always been distinguished by an uncanny ability to adapt itself to cultural trends as quickly as they emerge. Once it became clear that the public found psychoanalysis irresistible, psychologists found ways of accommodating to it. Instead of concentrating all their efforts on criticism, they identified those parts of the theory that were potentially useful to their own ends and incorporated them. As psychoanalysis became less threatening, psychologists were able to notice that the two fields actually shared many of the same basic assumptions: a commitment to psychic determinism, a belief in the cardinal importance of childhood experience, and an optimistic outlook about the possibility of change.

It has been only 70 years since James McKeen Cattell rose from his seat at the annual meeting of the American Psychological Association to castigate a colleague for having mentioned Freud's name at a gathering of scientists (Dallenbach, 1955, p. 523). Today that same APA celebrates the success of its lawsuit against the psychoanalytic establishment, a suit which gave psychologists the right to become bona fide candidates at the analytic institute of their choice (Buie, 1988). As the moribund institutes prepare to be enlivened by a rush of eager psychologists, perhaps it is not too much to suggest that psychology itself has benefited from having had the psychoanalytic wolf at its door.

NOTES

1 The standard reference on this whole topic is Shakow and Rapaport (1964). Their study remains invaluable as a thoughtful, systematic review of much of what psychologists have had to say about psychoanalysis. However, because their goal was to document Freud's influence on American psychology, they focused more on positive effects than on negative ones. My goal is to characterize psychologists' attitudes toward psychoanalysis. Many psychologists saw psychoanalysis as a threat and not as a positive influence, and thus my version of the story is inevitably more conflicted than Shakow and Rapaport's.

2 A discussion of the popular reception of psychoanalysis in America is beyond the scope of this article. See Hale (1971, 1978) and Burnham (1968, 1978, 1979, 1987) for detailed treatments of this issue.

3 Psychologists were not alone in having to struggle with competing definitions of science. Kuklick's (1980) analysis of boundary maintenance in sociology offers a general model for understanding how each of the social sciences resolved this dilemma.

4 Of all major psychology journals of the period, the *Journal of Abnormal Psychology* was the one with the greatest number of articles relevant to psychoanalysis (both pro and con). Not all were written by psychologists, but they were clearly intended for this audience. G. Stanley Hall published the text of Freud's, Jung's, and Ferenczi's Clark lectures in his *American Journal of Psychology* in 1910, but from then on that journal concentrated primarily on reviews of the psychoanalytic literature (both German and English) and carried very few original articles by psychologists.

5 With characteristic irony, Dunlap (1920) concluded that psychoanalysis might ultimately prove beneficial to psychology: "Just as Christian Science has tremendously accelerated the progress of Scientific Medicine, so Psychoanalysis, by compelling psychology to put its house in order, will eventually help in the development of the Scientific Psychology it aims to thrust aside" (p. 9).

6 See, for example, a classic work like *Psychologies of 1925* (Murchison, 1926), which allots four chapters to behaviorism, three to Gestalt, and even three to the dying gasps of structuralism, but none to psychoanalysis.

7 Among those Boring consulted was his colleague Henry Murray, who advised him to let Sachs have it "right between his eyes. . . . give him the works—don't omit a single grievance, not one." (H. Murray to E. G. Boring [n.d., August 1935?], Box 43, Folder 919, E. G. Boring Papers, Harvard University Archives quoted by permission). There is no evidence that Boring took this advice: He and Sachs maintained a cordial relationship for some time thereafter, dining together at the Harvard Club and exchanging papers and letters on professional topics.

8 Fisher and Greenberg's (1977) review includes more than 400 studies from the 1940s and 1950s alone. By the mid-1970s, there were at least 1,000 more.

9 Hilgard (1952) was the only evaluator who seemed willing to grant this point. He chastised psychologists for doing experiments that "give merely trivial illustrations of what psychoanalysts have demonstrated . . . in clinical work," and argued that although "such illustrations may be useful as propaganda," they "do not really do much for science." In his view, psychoanalytic research "ought to *advance* our understanding, not merely *confirm* or *deny* the theories that someone [else] has stated" (p.43).

10 Precisely the same thing was done with Gestalt psychology. At first, the philosophic assumptions of the theory were seen as a challenge to American (behaviorist) psychology, and Gestalt was explicitly opposed. Then the dangerous aspects were simply stripped away, making it appear as if the principles of organization were empirical observations that had arisen out of nowhere. A contemporary student of perceptual psychology would have no idea that these principles were originally formulated in opposition to behaviorist thought.

11 "I venture to predict that 20 years from now an

analyst using Freudian concepts and Freudian terminology will be placed upon the same plane as a phrenologist. *And yet analysis based upon behavioristic principles is here to stay and is a necessary profession in society—to be placed upon a par with internal medicine and surgery*" (Watson, 1925, p. 243). The comparison of psychoanalysis to phrenology was a favorite among psychologists; Dallenbach (1955) later wrote an entire article on this theme.

12 Buys (1976) has argued that it was only in the 1970s that positive portrayals of psychoanalysis became common in introductory texts. See also Herma, Kris, & Shor (1943), whose study focused on how Freud's theory of dreams was presented in such texts. They found such a high degree of criticism that they were forced to make separate tallies for *ridicule, rejection on moral grounds,* and *sheer denial.*

13 See, for example, Gengerelli's (1957) rhetorical romp in the *Saturday Review,* which painted psychologists as tireless laborers in the "scientific vineyard" and analysts as "muddle-headed, sob-sisters" (p. 11) who are the cause of every social ill from delinquency to early marriage.

REFERENCES

Alexander, F. (1940). A jury trial of psychoanalysis. *Journal of Abnormal and Social Psychology, 35,* 305–323.

Bellamy, R. (1915a). An act of everyday life treated as a pretended dream and reinterpreted by psychoanalysis. *Journal of Abnormal Psychology, 10,* 32–45.

Bellamy, R. (1915b). Review of Coriat's *The meaning of dreams. Journal of Abnormal Psychology, 10,* 433–434.

Blum, G. S. (1954). An experimental reunion of psychoanalytic theory with perceptual vigilance and defense. *Journal of Abnormal and Social Psychology, 49,* 94–98.

Blum, G. S., & Miller, D. R. (1952). Exploring the psychoanalytic theory of the "oral character." *Journal of Personality, 20,* 287–304.

Boring, E. G. (1929). *A history of experimental psychology.* New York: Century.

Boring, E. G. (1940). Was this analysis a success? *Journal of Abnormal and Social Psychology, 35,* 4–10.

Boring, E. G., Langfeld, H. S., & Weld, H. P. (1935). *Psychology: A factual textbook.* New York: Wiley.

Buie, J. (1988). Psychoanalytic group bolstered by legal win. *APA Monitor, 19,* 21.

Burnham, J. C. (1967). *Psychoanalysis and American medicine, 1894–1918.* New York: International Universities Press.

Burnham, J. C. (1968). The new psychology: From narcissism to social control. In J. Braeman, R. H. Bremmer, & D. Brody (Eds.), *Change and continuity in twentieth-century America: The 1920s* (pp. 351–398). Columbus: Ohio State University Press.

Burnham, J. C. (1978). The influence of psychoanalysis upon American culture. In J. M. Quen & E. T. Carlson (Eds.), *American psychoanalysis; Origins and development* (pp. 52–72). New York: Brunner/Mazel.

Burnham, J. C. (1979). From avant-garde to specialism: Psychoanalysis in America. *Journal of the History of the Behavioral Sciences, 15,* 128–134.

Burnham, J. C. (1987). *How superstition won and science lost: Popularizing science and health in the United States.* New Brunswick, NJ: Rutgers University Press.

Buys, C. J. (1976). Freud in introductory psychology texts. *Teaching of Psychology, 3,* 160–167.

Carrington, H. (1914). Freudian psychology and psychical research. *Journal of Abnormal Psychology, 9,* 411–416.

Clark, K. E. (1957). *America's psychologists: A survey of a growing profession.* Washington, DC: American Psychological Association.

Coriat, I. H. (1910). The psycho-analysis of a case of sensory automatism. *Journal of Abnormal Psychology, 5,* 93–99.

Dallenbach, K. M. (1955). Phrenology versus psychoanalysis. *American Journal of Psychology, 68,* 511–525.

Danziger, K. (1990). *Constructing the subject: Historical origins of psychological research.* New York: Cambridge University Press.

Dollard, J., & Miller, N. E. (1950). *Personality and psychotherapy.* New York: McGraw-Hill.

Donley, J. E. (1911). Freud's anxiety neurosis. *Journal of Abnormal Psychology, 6,* 126–134.

Dunlap, K. (1920). *Mysticism, Freudianism and scientific psychology.* St. Louis, MO: Mosby.

Ellis, A. (1950). An introduction to the principles of scientific psychoanalysis. *Genetic Psychology Monographs, 41,* 147–212.

Emerson, L. E. (1912–1913). A psychoanalytic study of a severe case of hysteria. *Journal of Abnormal Psychology, 7,* 385–406; *8,* 44–56, 180–207.

Eysenck, H. J., & Wilson, G. D. (1973). *The experimental study of Freudian theories.* London: Methuen.

Fisher, S., & Greenberg, R. P. (1977). *The scientific credibility of Freud's theories and therapy.* New York: Basic Books.

Fite, W. (1916). Psycho-analysis and sex-psychology. *The Nation, 103,* 127–129.

Friedman, S. M. (1952). An empirical study of the castration and Oedipus complexes. *Genetic Psychology Monographs, 46,* 61–130.

Garrett, H. E. (1930). *Great experiments in psychology.* New York: Century.

Gengerelli, J. A. (1957, March 23). The limitations of psychoanalysis: Dogma or discipline? *The Saturday Review,* pp. 9–11, 40.

Gilgen, A. R. (1982). *American psychology since World War II: A profile of the discipline.* Westport, CT: Greenwood Press.

Gordon, A. (1917). Obsessive hallucinations and psychoanalysis. *Journal of Abnormal Psychology, 12,* 423–430.

Guthrie, E. R., & Edwards, A. L. (1949). *Psychology: A first course in human behavior.* New York: Harper.

Hale, N. G. (1971). *Freud and the Americans: The beginnings of psychoanalysis in the United States, 1876–1917.* New York: Oxford University Press.

Hale, N. G. (1978). From Berggasse XIX to Central Park West: The Americanization of psychoanalysis, 1919–1940. *Journal of the History of the Behavioral Sciences, 14,* 299–315.

Heidbreder, E. (1933). *Seven psychologies.* Englewood Cliffs, NJ: Prentice-Hall.

Hebb, D. O. (1958). *A textbook of psychology.* Philadelphia: W. B. Saunders.

Herma, H., Kris, E., & Shor, J. (1943). Freud's theory of the dream in American textbooks. *Journal of Abnormal and Social Psychology, 38,* 319–334.

Hilgard, E. R. (1952). Experimental approaches to psychoanalysis. In E. Pumpian-Mindlin (Ed.), *Psychoanalysis as science* (pp. 3–45). New York: Basic Books

Hilgard, E. R. (1953). *Introduction to psychology.* New York: Harcourt, Brace.

Holt, E. B. (1915). *The Freudian wish and its place in ethics.* New York: Holt.

Hornstein, G. A. (1988). Quantifying psychological phenomena: Debates, dilemmas, and implications. In J. G. Morawski (Ed.), *The rise of experimental psychology* (pp. 1–34). New Haven, CT: Yale University Press.

Humphrey, G. (1920a). The conditioned reflex and the Freudian wish. *Journal of Abnormal Psychology, 14,* 388–392.

Humphrey, G. (1920b). Education and Freudianism. *Journal of Abnormal Psychology, 15,* 350–386.

Hunter, W. (1923). *General psychology.* (Rev. ed.). Chicago: University of Chicago Press.

Jacoby, R. (1983). *The repression of psychoanalysis: Otto Fenichel and the political Freudians.* New York: Basic Books.

Jastrow, J. (1932). *The house that Freud built.* New York: Chilton.

Keller, F., & Schoenfeld, W. (1950). *Principles of psychology: A systematic text in the science of behavior.* New York: Appleton-Century-Crofts.

Kelly, E. L. (1947). Clinical psychology. In W. Dennis et. al. (Eds.), *Current trends in psychology.* (pp. 75–108). Pittsburgh, PA: University of Pittsburgh Press.

Kimble, G. A. (1956). *Principles of general psychology.* New York: Ronald Press.

Kline, P. (1972). *Fact and fantasy in Freudian theory.* London: Methuen.

Kuklick, H. (1980). Boundary maintenance in American sociology: Limitations to academic "professionalization." *Journal of the History of the Behavioral Sciences, 16,* 201–219.

Kurzweil, E. (1989). *The Freudians: A comparative perspective.* New Haven, CT: Yale University Press.

Ladd-Franklin, C. (1916). Letter to the editor. *The Nation, 103,* 373–374.

Landis, C. (1940). Psychoanalytic phenomena. *Journal of Abnormal and Social Psychology, 35,* 17–28.

MacCurdy, J. T. (1913). The productions in a manic-like state illustrating Freudian mechanisms. *Journal of Abnormal Psychology, 8,* 361–375.

Maeder, A. (1910). Psycho-analysis in a case of melancholic depression. *Journal of Abnormal Psychology, 5,* 130–131.

Malcolm, J. (1984). *In the Freud archives.* New York: Knopf.

Morawski, J. G. (1988). Introduction. In J. G. Morawski (Ed.), *The rise of experimentation in American psychology* (pp. vii–xvii). New Haven, CT: Yale University Press.

Morawski, J. G. (1992). There is more to our history of giving: The place of introductory textbooks in American psychology. *American Psychologist, 47,* 161–169.

Morawski, J. G., & Hornstein, G. A. (1991). Quandary of the quacks: The struggle for expert knowledge in American psychology, 1890–1940. In D. van Keuren & J. Brown (Eds.), *The estate of social knowledge* (pp. 106–133). Baltimore: Johns Hopkins University Press.

Mowrer, O. H. (1940). An experimental analogue of "regression" with incidental observations on "reaction-formation." *Journal of Abnormal and Social Psychology, 35,* 56–87.

Murchison, C. (1926). *Psychologies of 1925.* Worcester, MA: Clark University Press.

Murphy, G. (1956). The current impact of Freud upon psychology. *American Psychologist, 11,* 663–672.

Prince, M. (1910). The mechanism and interpretation of dreams—A reply to Dr. Jones. *Journal of Abnormal Psychology, 5,* 337–353.

Putnam, J. J. (1906). Recent experiences in the study and treatment of hysteria at the Massachusetts General Hospital with remarks on Freud's method of treatment by "psycho-analysis." *Journal of Abnormal Psychology, 1,* 26–41.

Putnam, J. J. (1909–1910). Personal impressions of Sigmund Freud and his work, with special reference to his recent lectures at Clark University. *Journal of Abnormal Psychology, 4,* 293–310, 372–379.

Roback, A. A. (1921). Review of Dunlap's *Mysticism, Freudianism and scientific psychology. Journal of Abnormal and Social Psychology, 16,* 406–408.

Robinson, E. S., & Robinson, F. R. (1923). *Readings in general psychology.* Chicago: University of Chicago Press.

Sachs, H. (1940). Was this analysis a success?: Comment. *Journal of Abnormal and Social Psychology, 35,* 11–16.

Sarnoff, I., & Corwin, S. M. (1959). Castration anxiety and the fear of death. *Journal of Personality, 27,* 374–385.

Schwartz, B. J. (1956). An empirical test of two Freudian hypotheses concerning castration anxiety. *Journal of Personality, 24,* 318–327.

Scodel, A. (1957) Heterosexual somatic preference and fantasy dependency. *Journal of Consulting Psychology, 21,* 371–374.

Scott, W. D. (1908). An interpretation of the psychoanalytic method in psychotherapy with a report of a case so treated. *Journal of Abnormal Psychology, 3,* 371–379.

Sears, R. R. (1943). *Survey of objective studies of psychoanalytic concepts.* New York: Social Science Research Council.

Seashore, C. E. (1923). *Introduction to psychology.* New York: Macmillan.

Shakow, D., & Rapaport, D. (1964). *The influence of Freud on American psychology.* New York: International Universities Press.

Skinner, B. F. (1953). *Science and human behavior.* New York: Macmillan.

Solomon, M. (1916). Critical review of the conception of sexuality assumed by the Freudian school. *Journal of Abnormal Psychology, 11,* 59–60.

Tannenbaum, S. A. (1916). Letter to the editor. *The Nation, 103,* 218–219.

Tannenbaum, S. A. (1917). Some current misconceptions of psychoanalysis. *Journal of Abnormal Psychology, 12,* 390–422.

Taylor, E. W. (1911). Possibilities of a modified psychoanalysis. *Journal of Abnormal Psychology, 6,* 449–455.

Warren, H. C., & Carmichael, L. (1930). *Elements of human psychology* (Rev. ed.), Boston: Houghton Mifflin.

Watson, J. B. (1925). *Behaviorism.* New York: Norton.

Watson, J. B. (1927). The myth of the unconscious. *Harpers, 155,* 502–508.

Watson, J. B. (1928). *Psychological care of the infant and child.* New York: Norton.

Wells, F. L. (1913). On formulation in psychoanalysis. *Journal of Abnormal Psychology, 8,* 217–227.

Wiener, M. (1955). Word frequency or motivation in perceptual defense. *Journal of Abnormal and Social Psychology, 51,* 214–218.

Woodworth, R. S. (1916). Letter to the editor. *The Nation, 103,* 396.

Woodworth, R. S. (1917). Some criticisms of the Freudian psychology. *Journal of Abnormal Psychology, 12,* 174–194.

CHAPTER **14**

GESTALT PSYCHOLOGY

In 1912, Edward L.Thorndike was delivering his presidential address in Cleveland, Ohio, before the twenty-first annual meeting of the American Psychological Association; G. Stanley Hall's student, Henry Herbert Goddard, was publishing his famous book on the Kallikak family showing the relationship between heredity and feeblemindedness; William Stern was introducing the concept of the intelligence quotient (IQ) to mental testing; and John B. Watson was writing his Behaviorist Manifesto. In that same year, a German journal of psychology published an article entitled "Experimentelle Studien über das Sehen von Bewegung" (experimental studies on the perception of movement). That article was to signal the beginning of a new school of thought in psychology, a system known as *Gestalt psychology*.

The author of that 1912 paper was Max Wertheimer (1880–1943), a German psychologist who is viewed as the founder of Gestalt psychology. The source of those studies on the perception of movement is the subject of one of the most famous anecdotes in the history of modern psychology. The idea came to Wertheimer when he was traveling on a train in 1910 during his vacation. He got off the train in Frankfurt, purchased a toy stroboscope (a device that presents a series of successive pictures producing apparent motion), and tested his ideas in his hotel room. He continued his research at the Frankfurt Psychological Institute, where he was joined in his efforts by two recent doctoral graduates from the University of Berlin: Kurt Koffka (1886–1941) and Wolfgang Köhler (1887–1967). These three would become the triumvirate of Gestalt psychology, launching their fight against a German psychology whose atomistic approach was antithetical to their views of consciousness.

Wertheimer's initial experiments in Frankfurt involved a type of apparent movement he labeled the *phi phenomenon.* Two black lines were stroboscopically presented against a white background. The first line was vertical, the second horizontal, and the two were positioned so that if they were seen simultaneously they would form a right angle. The first line would appear briefly and then disappear, followed by the appearance of the second line. The position of the lines was held constant, as was their time of exposure. Only the temporal interval between the offset of the first line and the onset of the second line was varied. When the interval was approximately 30 milliseconds, the observer reported that the lines appeared and disappeared simultaneously. If the interval was increased to 60 milliseconds, the observer reported seeing movement; that is, the observer saw a single line moving from the vertical position to the horizontal position, rather than two separate lines appearing in succession (Max Wertheimer, 1912).

This form of apparent movement was not new to the scientific world. What was new was Wertheimer's interpretation of the movement; he viewed it as an experience that was not reducible to its component elements. Not only was it impossible to make such a reduction by even the most deliberate of introspections, but the seen movement could not be readily explained by describing the appearance and disappearance of the two static lines. There was something *more* to the experience than was evident in those line stimuli (see O'Neil & Landauer, 1966). This awareness is indicated in the Gestalt maxim that "the whole is different from the sum of its parts"; that is, there is a quality of experience that is often independent of the collection of stimulus elements that make up that experience—an idea anticipated by Christian von Ehrenfels (1859–1932), with whom Wertheimer had studied.

Ehrenfels was at Graz University in Austria in 1890 when he published his criticism of the incompleteness of Wundt's atomistic psychology. His objection was not to the study of elements; rather it was that Wundt's analysis was ignoring important elements—that were beyond the mere sensory elements. He called these elements form qualities (*Gestaltqualitäten*) and described their existence with the example of a musical melody. A melody, he argued, is more than just the collection of individual notes; it is also the patterning or configuration of those notes. Thus a melody played at either end of a piano keyboard would be recognizable as the same melody even though each version would consist of entirely different sound frequencies. For Ehrenfels, the configuration of the notes (the form quality of the melody) was one more element to be added to the individual elements (notes) in the conscious experience of a melody.

Wertheimer built on Ehrenfels's work, but with an interesting and insightful twist:

> The whole quality is not just one more added element. The qualities of the whole determine the characteristics of the parts. . . . the nature of the parts is determined by the whole rather than vice versa; therefore analysis should go "from above down" rather than "from below up." One should not begin with elements and try to synthe-

> size the whole from them, but study the whole to see what its natural parts are. (Michael Wertheimer, 1987, p. 136)

Thus, for Wertheimer, Wundt's approach was not just incomplete, it was wrong. Its reductionism produced a view of consciousness that was distorted, artificial. The Gestalt psychologists argued for the study of immediate experience, which they defined very differently from Wundt. Immediate experience consists of wholes, usually segregated wholes seen against a background, not the batches of sensations they saw as artificially created by the methods of the Wundtians: "analysis destroys the very reality it seeks to explain; . . . to reduce a thing to its elements and study it piecemeal is to lose sight of the thing itself" (Heidbreder, 1933, p. 373).

The holistic approach of the Gestalt psychologists was in direct opposition to the prevailing view of German psychology at the beginning of the twentieth century. They struggled to gain their place, and what began as a foothold eventually supplanted Wundtian psychology, as perhaps best indicated by the ascendancy of Wolfgang Köhler to German psychology's premier position as head of the Psychological Institute at Berlin University in 1921.

For most American psychologists initial exposure to Gestalt psychology came from an article published by Kurt Koffka in a 1922 issue of the *Psychological Bulletin*. The article, entitled "Perception: An Introduction to Gestalt-Theorie," led many American psychologists to see Gestalt psychology as a perceptual theory. But Gestalt theory was in fact much broader, emphasizing particularly the areas of thinking and learning. The reason for much of the early work on perception was that Wundt and his followers had focused on perception. Thus the Gestalt psychologists attacked the older theory in its stronghold (Michael Wertheimer, 1987).

In the 1920s and early 1930s, Gestalt psychology enjoyed considerable success in Germany (see Ash, 1995). But all that would come to a sudden, and sometimes tragic, end when the Nazis came to power in 1933. Koffka had already left Germany, taking a position at Smith College in Northampton, Massachusetts, in 1927. Wertheimer, who was Jewish, fled Germany in 1933, taking a university position at the New School for Social Research in New York City. Two years later, after tense confrontations with the Nazis, Köhler followed him to the United States, accepting a position at Swarthmore College in the Philadelphia area.

Wertheimer and Köhler were two of many German and Austrian émigré-psychologists who came to the United States to escape the Nazis. They left prestigious professorships in the best German universities to take lesser positions in the United States. The 1930s were hard times in the United States, the era of the Great Depression; jobs were scarce for American doctorates, much less for the wave of European immigrants. For these newly arrived psychologists, the culture was unfamiliar, the language was a problem, and the dominant psychology of behaviorism was as objectionable as that of the Wundtians.

In behaviorism, the Gestalt psychologists found another atomistic approach to psychology—complex behaviors were the result of combinations of simple reactions. Behaviorism was just one more molecular approach, filled with the artificiality inherent in such approaches. Its artificiality was clearly indicated by its denial of consciousness as a valid topic for scientific study. On the other side, the Americans, too, were dismayed by this foreign psychology that espoused the study of consciousness using introspective methods. It sounded too much like the mentalism they had so recently discarded.

Although Gestalt psychology did not displace behaviorism, tenets of Gestalt theory found their way into the psychology of perception and learning (recall the comments on Edward C. Tolman in Chapter 12). Its greatest influence, however, was evident in the emergence of the cognitive revolution in American psychology beginning in the 1950s. Much of the contemporary work on thinking, problem solving, language, and information processing has antecedents in Gestalt psychology.

THE READINGS

The philosophy and history of Gestalt psychology are surveyed in the three articles in this chapter. The first selection, by Wolfgang Köhler, was written shortly before his death—his last scientific paper. It represents an intellectual history of the Gestalt movement and a defense against its German and American critics. In it, Köhler describes the early work in Germany as well as the continuation of the research in the United States. The reader should be aware that this article benefits from the first-hand experiences of Köhler as part of Gestalt psychology's origin, but it also represents recollections of events that sometimes happened more than 50 years earlier than its writing. Although some historians would question its accuracy on grounds of personal bias and possible memory distortions, this history according to Köhler is a lucid and interesting account.

The second selection is by Mary Henle. In this article, she tells the fascinating story of the final days of the Psychological Institute at Berlin University and how Köhler fought to keep it going in the face of growing Nazi pressures. It is a tale of great human courage and an example of archival research and storytelling at their best.

The final selection is by Michael M. Sokal, whose work on James McKeen Cattell appears in Chapter 8. In this selection, Sokal describes the treatment of Gestalt psychology in the behaviorist America, arguing that understanding the outcome of the intellectual migration requires a differentiation of reactions to Gestalt psychology, the Gestalt movement, and the Gestalt psychologists themselves. He concludes that American psychology was more open to Gestalt ideas and the Gestalt psychologists than many previous histories have implied. That view is not without its opponents (see Henle, 1977).

Personalities often play an important role in shaping any discipline, including the science of psychology. This chapter probably illustrates that more clearly than any other chapter in this book. All three selections demonstrate how personalities have affected the history of Gestalt psychology on both sides of the Atlantic Ocean.

REFERENCES

Ash, M. G. (1995). *Gestalt psychology in German Culture, 1890–1967: Holism and the quest for objectivity*. New York: Cambridge University Press.

Heidbreder, E. (1933). *Seven psychologies*. New York: Appleton-Century-Crofts.

Henle, M. (1977). The influence of Gestalt psychology in America. *Annals of the New York Academy of Sciences, 291,* 3–12.

Koffka, K. (1922). Perception: An introduction to Gestalt-theorie. *Psychological Bulletin, 19,* 531–585.

O'Neil, W. M., & Landauer, A. A. (1966). The phi-phenomenon: Turning point or rallying point. *Journal of the History of the Behavioral Sciences, 2,* 335–340.

Wertheimer, Max (1912). Experimentelle studien über das Sehen von Bewegung. *Zeitschrift fur Psychologie, 61,* 161–265. English translation appears in T. Shipley (Ed.), *Classics in psychology*. New York: Philosophical Library, 1961.

Wertheimer, Michael (1987). *A brief history of psychology* (3d ed.). New York: Holt, Rinehart and Winston.

Gestalt Psychology

Wolfgang Köhler

What we now call Gestalt psychology began to develop in 1910. At the time, there was not much psychology anywhere in Germany. People were doing experiments on memory, with the technique introduced by Ebbinghaus, and on the problems of psychophysics. Fechner, a physicist-philosopher, somewhat optimistically regarded difference limens, as investigated by Weber, and the quantitative relation between stimulus and sensation from his own studies, as the beginning of a real science of the mind. Max Wertheimer, in 1910, was disturbed by the narrowness of such enterprises. He tried to study more interesting psychological facts and, as a first example, he chose apparent movement, the movement seen when two objects appear in fairly rapid succession, one in one place and another in a different location.

Apparent movement as such was known; but many psychologists regarded it as a mere cognitive illusion. Since no real objective movement occurs under these conditions, it was believed that apparent movement could not be a real perceptual fact. Rather, it was felt, it must be a product of erroneous judging. The explanation went like this. First, I see one object; immediately afterwards I see an object of the same kind in a somewhat different place. Naturally, I regard this second object as identical with the first, and conclude that the first has simply moved from the one place to the other.

This is a tranquilizing explanation. No longer need we worry about apparent movement. But this is also what we would now call a case of "explaining away." A striking perceptual fact is observed which we cannot immediately explain. Then we invent an explanation for which there is no factual evidence, an explanation according to which there simply is no perceptual fact that has to be explained, but only a curious cognitive blunder.

"Explaining away" has not entirely disappeared from psychology even now, although such extraordinary constructions as the one just mentioned are no longer used for the purpose. The procedure may kill important problems. When tempted to do this kind of thing, we therefore ought immediately to test our proposed explanation in experiments.

This is what Wertheimer did. He studied the conditions under which apparent movement is seen. He varied the spatial locations of the objects involved, and the rate at which they followed each other; he observed the variations of the movement itself which occurred under such conditions, and so on. He also showed his subjects optimal apparent movement and similar movement of a real object, side by side and simultaneously. He found that the two could not be distinguished by the observer. Eventually he added a most important test which, it was afterwards discovered, had once before been done by a physiologist. First, a great many repetitions of apparent movement are shown in a given place. Later, when a stationary pattern is shown in the same place, subjects clearly see a negative afterimage of the apparent movement, just as negative afterimages are seen after repeated presentations of a physically real movement.

Wertheimer's was a masterpiece of experimental investigation in the field of perception. It was also the beginning of extremely fruitful studies in general Gestalt psychology. Much thinking and many discussions followed. The number of basic questions which Wertheimer now began to consider increased rapidly. At the time, he did not publish what he found; rather, he told Koffka about his questions and his tentative answers, and Koffka in turn began to tell his students what he had learned from Wertheimer and about further ideas that he himself had developed in the same productive spirit.

Köhler, W. (1967). Gestalt psychology. *Psychologische Forschung, 31.* xviii–xxx.

These students investigated one interesting possibility after another in the new field. For a brief time I was able to take part in this development. It was Koffka, who, realizing that Wertheimer hesitated to write down what he was thinking, formulated first principles of Gestalt psychology in an excellent article which was published in 1915.

Similar questions had begun to be discussed in Austria. Years before Wertheimer began his work, von Ehrenfels had called attention to a serious omission in the customary treatment of perceptual facts. We are accustomed, he said, to regard perceptual fields as collections of local sensations whose qualities and intensities are determined by corresponding local physical stimuli. This simple assumption, he added, cannot explain a large number of particularly interesting perceptual phenomena. For, quite apart from such local sensations, we often find in perceptual fields phenomena of an entirely different class—Gestalt qualities such as the specific shapes of objects, the melodic properties of this or that sequence of tones, and so forth. These Gestalt qualities remain practically unaltered when the stimuli in question are transposed. They seem to depend upon relations among the stimuli rather than upon the individual stimuli as such.

From these, and other obvious perceptual facts, the Austrian psychologists developed an interpretation of perception which differed radically from the views developed by Wertheimer. Since the Gestalt qualities could not be derived from the properties of individual sensations, the psychologists in Austria felt that they must be products of higher mental operations which the mind constantly imposes on mere sense data. This theoretical approach, the so-called production theory, did not seem particularly inviting to Wertheimer and Koffka. Nevertheless one has to admit that at least one member of the Austrian School, Benussi, sometimes seemed to forget the curious production theory, and then invented most original experiments.

At this point, I have to say a few words about my own experiences during this period. I was aware of what Wertheimer was trying to do and found it not only objectively interesting but also most refreshing as a human endeavor. He observed important phenomena regardless of the fashions of the day and tried to discover what they meant. I had a feeling that his work might transform psychology, which was hardly a fascinating affair at the time, into a most lively study of basic human issues. My own work, however, was not yet related to Wertheimer's investigations, although I did write a fairly energetic paper against the tendency of others to invent explanations which served to get rid of many most interesting facts. Just when Wertheimer's work came near its most decisive stage, I became separated from my friends in Germany when I was sent to Spanish Africa by the Prussian Academy of Science. They wanted me to study a group of chimpanzees, just captured for the purpose in western parts of the African continent.

The chimpanzees proved to be extremely interesting creatures. I studied their sometimes strangely intelligent behavior and also the curious restrictions to which such achievements were often subject. Somewhat later, I occasionally interrupted these studies and investigated the perception of chimpanzees and, for the sake of comparison, that of chickens. It soon became clear that in the visual field of both species constancies of size and of brightness are almost as obvious as they are in humans. In further experiments these animals, particularly the chimpanzees, learned to choose between two objects of different size or brightness. I was able to show in tests of transposition that what they had learned was relationally determined. (I later discovered that experiments of the same kind had been done, a short time before, by American psychologists.)

I was kept in Africa for more than six years by the First World War. During that long period I did not always feel inclined to continue my work in animal psychology. Ideas with which I had become acquainted in Europe would come back to me, most often the changes in psychological thinking which Wertheimer had just introduced. But I was also very much aware of what I had learned as a student of Max Planck, the great physicist. He had just discovered the quantum of electromagnetic radiation, but at the time taught us mainly what physicists called field physics. Under Planck's influence I had dimly felt that between Wertheimer's new thinking in psychology and the physicist's thinking in field physics there was some hidden connection. What was it? I now began to study the important works on field physics. The first discovery I made was that, fifty years before Wertheimer, some of his basic questions had already been asked not by psychologists but by physicists, first of all by Clerk Maxwell, the greatest physicist of that period. The Gestalt psychologists, we remember, were always disturbed by a thesis which was widely accepted by others. One psychologist, strongly influenced by traditional convictions, had formulated it in the following words: "I do not know whether perceptual fields actually consist of independent local elements, the so-called sensations. But, as scientists, we have to proceed as though this were true." An extraordinary statement—an a priori general conviction about the right procedure in science is assumed to be more important than the nature of the facts which we are investigating.

From its very beginning, Gestalt psychology ignored this thesis and began its work with simple and unbiased observations of facts. Independent local sensations? Consider again what happens in apparent movement. After a first visual object has appeared in one place, a second visual object does not appear in its normal location but nearer the place where the first has just disappeared, and only then moves towards what I just called its normal location. Clearly, therefore, the process corresponding to the second object has been deflected, has been attracted by a remnant of what has just happened in another place, the place of the first object, and has only then approached its "normal" location. Consequently, under the conditions of such experiments, the second object does not behave as though it were an independent local fact at all. The statement, quoted earlier, that perceptual fields must be assumed to consist of independent local sensations, is therefore at odds with the behavior of percepts even under such fairly simple conditions. Or take any of the well-known perceptual illusions, say the Müller-Lyer illusion. Can there be any doubt that in this case two lines of objectively equal length become lines of different length under the influence of the angles added at the ends of the distances to be compared? And so on, in a long list of examples, all of them incompatible with the statement about the nature of perceptual fields.

Ours was an uphill fight. I felt greatly relieved, as mentioned above, to find so fundamentally similar an approach from the side of physics. In his great treatise, *Electricity and Magnetism,* Clerk Maxwell had remarked that we are often told that in science we must, first of all, investigate the properties of very small local places one after another, and only when this has been done can we permit ourselves to consider how more complicated situations result from what we have found in those elements. This procedure, he added, ignores the fact that many phenomena in nature can only be understood when we inspect not so-called elements but fairly large regions. Similarly, in 1910, Max Planck published lectures which he had just delivered in New York. In one of these, when discussing the second principle of thermodynamics, the entropy principle, the author states emphatically that those who try to build up physics on the assumption that a study of local elements has to precede any attempt to explain the behavior of larger systems will never understand the entropy principle, the principle which deals with the direction of physical processes. Or take Eddington, the astronomer, who once wrote the following sentences: "In physics we are often invited to inspect all tiny elements of space in succession in order to gain a complete inventory of the world." But, the author objects, if we were to do this, "all properties of the physical world would be overlooked which cannot be found or understood as matters of tiny elements in space."

I was greatly surprised by these statements of eminent scientists which so obviously agreed with statements made by Gestalt psychologists. Did these great physicists merely add further mysteries to the mysteries in which, according to many critics, the Gestalt psychologists were mainly interested? Actually, these physicists did not refer to mysteries at all. Rather, they studied a great many specific physical situations and did so in an extraordinarily clear fashion. They handled these situations as wholes rather than as collections of small, local, independent facts; they had to because of the nature of such situations, the parts of which are all functionally related (or interdependent) so that what happens at a given moment at a place happens only so long as conditions and events everywhere else in the system are not altered, so long, that is, as all interactions within the whole system remain the same.

Most of us are probably familiar with Kirchhoff's laws which describe the distribution of a steady electric flow in a network of wires. When looking at the fairly simple expression which indicates what occurs within a particular local branch of the network, we see at once that this expression refers to the conditions of conduction not only in this particular local branch but also to conditions in all other branches. This is, of course, necessary because, in the steady state, the local currents throughout the network must balance one another—which means that, while a current develops in the local branch, its flow is influenced by the flow in all other branches as much as by the condition in the interior of its branch. What could be more natural when function is balanced everywhere within the system as a whole? Obviously, there is no mystery in this behavior of physical systems. And there would be no mystery either if the same kind of thing happened in a brain rather than in a network of wires. To be sure, networks of wires are exceptionally simple examples; other systems in which functional interrelations determine local facts in a far more radical fashion are not so easy to handle.

I was much impressed by such facts in physics. They offered a striking lesson to psychology in general and seemed to give Gestalt psychology a most welcome justification. I wrote, in Africa, a book about this part of exact physics and its possible application to psychology and to the understanding of brain function. The book has remained practically unknown in this country, partly, I think, because it uses the language and the logic of field physics, a part of physics with which not all of us are familiar.

When the book was published in 1920, both Wertheimer and Koffka greatly enjoyed its content. It showed that the alleged mysteries of Gestalt psychology agreed with perfectly clear procedures and facts in natural science. In a sense, Gestalt psychology has since become a kind of application of field physics to essential parts of psychology and of brain physiology.

When I was able to return to Germany, I found a most lively group of students just appearing at the Psychological Institute of the University of Berlin. They were attracted by Wertheimer, by Kurt Lewin, and to a degree, by what I had discovered when experimenting with chimpanzees and reading physics in Africa. Not all our work referred to Gestalt psychology. For instance, we managed to prove that the famous moon illusion is by no means restricted to situations in which the sky and the moon play the decisive role. But Gestalt psychology remained the central issue. A few simple examples. One student, Scholz, examined the distance between two successively shown parallel lines when the rate of their succession was varied. He found that the second line appeared clearly too near the first line long before the rate of the succession approached that was needed for apparent movement. Hence, the second line was attracted by some remnant of the first, just as Wertheimer had said. Or again: in an attempt to investigate time errors in the comparison of shapes, and the connection of such errors with the fate of young memory traces, Lauenstein did some beautiful experiments. Also, just about the same time, von Restorff and I applied Gestalt principles of perception to problems of memory, and in doing so discovered the so-called isolation effect. Kurt Lewin, too, did experiments in memory. But his main achievements were experiments in which he boldly transferred psychological situations from ordinary life to the laboratory and thus enlarged the range of psychological investigations in a highly productive fashion.

The most important person of our group, however, remained Wertheimer, who at the time was completing his most significant study in perception, his investigation of the way in which objects, figures, and patches are segregated from their environment as circumscribed entities. Perhaps it was not emphasized at the time, but for most of us it became the main result of his observations that, in this fashion, he gave a perfectly clear meaning to the term "perceived wholes" which, before, had sounded so mysterious to many colleagues. Obviously, the appearance of wholes of this kind is just as much a matter of division or separation within the visual field as it is of their coherence, their unitary character.

So long as Wertheimer's observations referred only to well-known unitary things, many authors were inclined to believe that it was merely learning ("previous experience") which makes them appear as firm units detached from their environment. But Wertheimer continued his investigation of perceptual wholes when the units in question were unitary groups of individual objects rather than simple things. In such situations one can often demonstrate that the formation of specific group units is not a matter of prior learning. Wertheimer did not deny that sometimes past experience does influence perceptual grouping. But, on the other hand, one should not forget what Gottschaldt once demonstrated: that, in many cases, purely perceptual organization is too strong to be affected by past experience, even when this past experience is, as such, most powerful.

In the meantime, several European and American psychologists who were not members of the Gestalt group became intensely interested in its work. They had begun independently to work on similar problems. One such person was Edgar Rubin who concentrated on what he called the relation of "figure" and "ground" in perception. For instance, even when an object is part of a large frontal-parallel plane, this object appears slightly separated from the ground and stands out in the third dimension. We now know that this separation is not only a qualitative curiosity but a real perceptual depth effect which can easily be varied in a quantitative fashion, and may then establish quite specific shapes in three dimensional space.

Other psychologists who turned in the same direction were David Katz and Albert Michotte in Europe, Lashley, Klüver and, to a degree, Gibson in America. I wish more people would study Michotte's marvelous publications, and also a lecture which Lashley delivered in 1929, when he was president of the American Psychological Association. The spirit of this lecture was throughout that of Gestalt psychology; later, it is true, Lashley became a bit more skeptical. Once, when we discussed the main tenets of Gestalt psychology, he suddenly smiled and said, "Excellent work—but don't you have religion up your sleeve?"

Time is too short for a discussion of the great achievements of Wertheimer and Duncker in the psychology of thinking. Their work in this field may be regarded as the last great development in Gestalt psychology that occurred in those years. Since then almost all members of the old school have died, and only a few younger psychologists are left whose investigations are clearly related to those of the earlier period: Asch, Arnheim, Wallach, Henle, Heider—all of whose work is well known to us.

When the Nazi regime became intolerable, I emigrated to the United States which I knew well from earlier visits. In America, I tried to continue the investigations which had been started in Berlin. For instance, when actual perceptions have disappeared, traces of them must be left in the nervous system. They are supposed to be the factual condition which makes recall of those perceptions possible. My first question was: traces of what in perception? Perceptual fields contain not only individual objects but also other products of organization such as segregated groups, sometimes groups which contain only two members. Grouping of this kind may be just as obvious in perception as are the individual members of the groups. Now, this means a perceptual unification or connection within the group, and there is no reason why, in the realm of memory traces, this connection or unification should not be just as clearly represented as are the members of the group. Consequently, when the group has only two members, we must expect these members to be connected not only in perception but also as traces. How would this fact manifest itself in memory?

Among the concepts used in the psychology of memory, the concept "association" may mean, for instance, that two items in a perceptual field are functionally so well connected that, when one of them is reactivated, the same happens also to the other item. This is precisely what one has to expect if, in perception, the two items form a pair-group, and if the unitary character of the perceived pair is represented as a correspondingly unitary entity in the realm of traces. If this were true, the concept of association would be directly related to the concept of organization as applied to pairs in perception.

This assumption can be tested in simple experiments in the following manner. The formation of pairs in perception depends upon the characteristics of the objects involved; it is, for instance, most likely to occur when these objects resemble each other—or when both belong to the same class of objects. Consequently, if association is an aftereffect of pair formation in perception, association must be most effective precisely when the objects are similar or at least obviously members of the same general class. Tests of this conclusion could be quite easily arranged and showed, for instance, that association of members of a given class is far more effective than association of objects dissimilar in this sense. I fully realize—and some, Postman in particular, have emphasized—that this result may still be explained in another fashion; therefore, I have just begun to do further experiments which ought to tell us whether or not the organizational interpretation of our results is correct. Work in a young science is an exciting affair. It becomes particularly exciting when new functional possibilities have just been introduced. I am grateful to those who make the present issue even more exciting by their objections. They force me to do further experiments which will decide whether the concept of organization is applicable to basic facts in memory.

Objections have also been raised against the Gestalt psychologist's organizational explanation of the isolation effect, or the Restorff effect. Here again, some investigators, including Postman, believe that the intrusion of dangerous concepts developed in the study of perception may be avoided and replaced by older, well-known, and therefore (according to them) healthier ideas. I recently constructed sets of experiments which had to have one result if the Restorff effect can be understood in the conservative way, but just the opposite result if this effect must be interpreted as a consequence of organization in perception and in memory. The results prove that, in this case, the unhealthy organizational explanation is undoubtedly correct.

Another more recent investigation referred to a problem in perception. Wallach and I tried to discover whether, after prolonged presentation of visual objects in a given location, these objects (or others) show any aftereffects such as changes of size or of shape. When numerous objects and combinations of objects had been used for the purpose, it became perfectly clear that prolonged presence of a visual object in a given place causes not only distortion of this object but also displacements of other test objects, displacements away from the previously seen inspection objects. Practically any visual objects may serve as inspection objects in such experiments. Eventually it became obvious that the well-known distortions observed by Gibson in the case of some particular figures such as curves and angles were special examples of a veritable flood of what we now call figural aftereffects.

When we had studied the figural aftereffects which occur in a frontal-parallel plane before the observer, Wallach and I asked ourselves whether there are not similar distortions and displacements in the third dimension of visual space. These experiments clearly showed that there are displacements of test objects in the third dimension, and that these are often even more conspicuous than the displacements which occur in the first two dimensions. Next, I tried another perceptual modality, namely kinesthesis, where Gibson had already observed a figural aftereffect. We could not only corroborate Gibson's findings, but could also observe such effects in further kinesthetic situations. Again, not only in the kinesthetic modality, but also in simple touch were examples of figural aftereffects immediately observable. Once, when I tried auditory localization, displacements of the same kind seemed to occur. Obviously, then, figural aftereffects can be demonstrated in most parts of the perceptual world. This made us look with some suspicion at facts in perception which had generally been regarded as facts of learning. The Müller-Lyer illusion, for instance, can be abolished or greatly reduced when the pattern is shown repeatedly. This fact had previously always been regarded as a matter of learning how to observe the pattern better and better. But one look at this pattern suggests that it is most likely to develop considerable aftereffects, effects which would surely reduce the size of the illusion under conditions of continued or often repeated observation. Fishback and I found that such aftereffects, not learning in the usual sense, were probably the right explanation of the reduction of the illusion so often found by other psychologists.

Now, what kind of change in the nervous system is responsible for all these aftereffects? Or, what kind of process occurs in so many parts of the nervous system and always has about the same result? This question I regarded as particularly important because it seemed probable that the very process which is responsible for normally organized perception also causes the figural aftereffects when perception continues to occur in a given place for some time.

The nature of figural aftereffects in the visual field made it fairly easy to discover a good candidate for this fundamental role. The candidate must be able to explain the following facts:

1 The figural aftereffects are the result of an obstruction in the nervous system. Why else should test objects recede from the places where inspection objects have been seen for some time?

2 The process in question and the obstruction which it causes cannot be restricted to the circumscribed area in which the inspection object is seen. Otherwise, why does even a fairly remote test object recede from that area?

3 The intensity of the process which causes the obstruction has to be particularly great near the boundary between the inspection object and its background. For simple observations show that the displacements of test objects are particularly conspicuous just inside and outside this contour, in both cases, of course, away from the contour.

These simple statements almost tell the physiologist what kind of process occurs in the brain when we see visual objects, and which then produces the figural aftereffects. Among the processes possible in the brain, only steady electrical currents spreading in the tissue as a volume conductor have the functional characteristics just mentioned. Such currents would originate when a circumscribed area with certain characteristics is surrounded by a larger area with different properties. The current would pass through the circumscribed area in one direction, and would then turn and pass through its environment in the opposite direction, so that a closed circuit and current result. Consequently all together just as much current would pass through the environment as flows through this circumscribed area, a behavior which fits our condition 2. The current would be most intense near the boundary of the two regions, because here the lines of flow will be shortest and thus the resistance lowest—a behavior which fits our condition 3. Condition 1, the fact that the processes in question must cause an obstruction in the tissue, is satisfied by any currents which pass through layers of cells. In fact, the flow has several kinds of effects on the tissue, all of them well known to the electro-physiologists. When the flow continues for some time, these effects are obstructions. Physiologists in Europe call these obstructions electro-tonus, a name which (for unknown reasons) has not become popular in the United States. The term means that where currents enter cells, a kind of resistance or, better, obstruction develops in the surface layers of the cells, and this reduces the local flow—whereupon the current is forced to change its own direction and distribution. Thus the current has precisely the effects which appear in perception as distortions and displacements, in other words, as figural aftereffects.

We have now returned to field physics, but field physics applied to the neural medium. I need not repeat what I explained in the beginning of my report. What happens locally to a current that flows in a volume conductor is not an independent local event. What happens locally is determined and maintained within the total distribution of the flow.

Although this explanation seemed plausible enough, could we be sure that the brain is really pervaded by quasi-steady currents when we perceive? We could not, and therefore I tried to record such brain currents when visual objects appeared before human subjects or animals. This was not an easy task. To be sure, several physiologists (in England) had recorded steady currents from other active parts of the nervous system, but not from the striate area, the visual center of the brain. After initial attempts made in order to discover optimal conditions for what we planned to do, we did succeed, and could record many such currents not only from the visual, but also from the auditory cortex. I am surprised to see that, so far, no physiologists have repeated or continued our work. Too bad: the microelectrode inserted in an individual cell seems to have abolished all interest in more molar functions of the nervous system.

Our observations lead to one question after another. For instance, how do currents of the visual cortex behave when the third dimension of visual space is conspicuously represented in what we see? Or also, are currents of the brain capable of establishing memory traces in the brain? And so forth. The situation is exciting. What we now need more than anything else are people who get excited. Sooner or later there will be some people who enjoy the atmosphere of adventure in science, the atmosphere in which we lived when Gestalt psychology just began its work. If that could develop in Germany, why should it not also happen in America, the country which once produced so many pioneers?

One Man Against the Nazis—Wolfgang Köhler

Mary Henle

In the 1920s and early 1930s, psychology was flourishing at the Psychological Institute of Berlin University under the direction of Wolfgang Köhler. There was truly an all-star cast of characters. In addition to the director, Max Wertheimer had been there from about 1916 until 1929, when he left to accept the chair at Frankfurt. Kurt Lewin, too, came to Berlin after World War I and remained until his resignation in 1933. Köhler's last assistants in Berlin are still known, although all of them died young: Karl Duncker, whose studies of problem solving and of induced movement remain classics; von Lauenstein, who is known mainly for his theory and investigation of time errors—an important problem, since time errors offer a good opportunity to study the behavior of young memory traces; von Restorff, whom we know for her work with Köhler on the isolation effect (sometimes called the Restorff effect) and on theory of recall. The Chief *Assistent* at the institute, Hans Rupp, chief by virtue of seniority, will hardly figure in our story.*

Berlin, with Köhler and Wertheimer, was the seat of Gestalt psychology in those days, along with another highly productive seat at Giessen under Koffka until 1924, when Koffka came to America. Berlin had seen the publication of major theoretical and experimental contributions to Gestalt psychology. Wertheimer published, among others, major papers on Gestalt theory, including the paper on perceptual grouping. Köhler's *Die physischen Gestalten in Ruhe und im stationären Zustand* appeared in 1920. His work on chimpanzees was still appearing, and there were numerous papers, both theoretical and experimental, many of them in perception but also in other fields. His translation of his book, *Gestalt Psychology,* into German was published in 1933. Lewin's early papers on perception and on association appeared, and then the long and influential series, published with his students, on *Handlungs- und Affektpsychologie*.

Among the students at the institute, I will mention only a few, mainly names we know today. Rudolf Arnheim and later Werner Wolff worked in the field of expression; Metzger's work on visual perception was under way, including the work on the *Ganzfeld*. Gottschaldt's studies on the influence of past experience on visual form perception came out of the institute; his figures are still in use in the Embedded Figures Test. Hans Wallach did his first work there. Kopfermann's beautiful experiments on depth perception, Ternus's on phenomenal identity, von Schiller's on stroboscopic movement, and much, much more excellent work were all products of the Psychological Institute. A number of young American PhDs came to study and work at the institute, for example, Robert B. MacLeod, Donald K. Adams, Karl Zener, Carroll Pratt, Leonard Carmichael, and others.

On January 30, 1933, the Nazis came to power. The first effects on German universities were dismissals of Jewish professors and others considered to be hostile to the new regime. This story is well known. The dismissals ranged from Nobel laureates (including Einstein, Haber, Franck, Hertz) to *Assistenten*. Hartshorne relates an anecdote which he says was widely believed—that Max Planck, the great physicist, petitioned Hitler to stop the dismissal of scientists for political reasons; he stressed the importance of science for the country. Hitler is said to have replied, "Our national policies will not be

Henle, M. (1978). One man against the Nazis: Wolfgang Köhler. *American Psychologist, 33,* 939–944.

*It should be mentioned that at that time an *Assistent* in a German university already had the PhD but was not yet *habilitiert,* that is, had not yet the so-called right to teach, which was conferred after a second dissertation.

revoked or modified, even for scientists. If the dismissal of Jewish scientists means the annihilation of contemporary German science, then we shall do without science for a few years!" (Hartshorne, 1937, pp. 111–112).

About the dismissed scholars, their university colleagues kept silent. As Köhler remarked years later, "Nothing astonished the Nazis so much as the cowardice of whole university faculties, which did not consist of Nazis. Naturally this corroborated the Nazis' contempt for the intellectual life" (Köhler, Note 1).

The future of an independent professor was, of course, uncertain. As early as April 1, 1933, Köhler, briefly outside of Germany, wrote to Ralph Barton Perry:

> Nobody in Germany with any decency in his bones . . . knows very much about his near future. If nothing happens, I shall be in Chicago for the meeting of the American Association. . . .
>
> As to myself, my patriotism expects the Germans to behave better than any other people. This seems to me a sound form of patriotism. Unfortunately it is very different from current nationalism which presupposes that the own people are right and do right whatever they are and do. However, there will still be some fight during the next weeks. Don't judge the Germans before it is over.

With the dismissal of James Franck, the great experimental physicist, Köhler made public his stand. The fight had begun. On April 28, 1933, he wrote, for the *Deutsche Allgemeine Zeitung,* the last anti-Nazi article to be published openly in Germany under the Nazi regime, "Gespräche in Deutschland" (Conversations in Germany). The courage of such an act may be indicated by the fact that everybody expected Köhler to be arrested for it.

Why, ask the powerful men who rule Germany, have many valuable people not joined the Nazi party? Of them Köhler comments, "Never have I seen finer patriotism than theirs." Regarding the wholesale dismissal of Jews from universities and other positions, he continues,

> During our conversation, one of my friends reached for the Psalms and read: "The Lord is my shepherd, I shall not want. . . ." He read the 90th Psalm and said, "It is hard to think of a German who has been able to move human hearts more deeply and so to console those who suffer. And these words we have received from the Jews."
>
> Another reminded me that never had a man struggled more nobly for a clarification of his vision of the world than the Jew Spinoza, whose wisdom Goethe admired. My friend did not hesitate to show respect, as Goethe did. Lessing, too, would not have written his *Nathan the Wise* unless human nobility existed among the Jews? . . . It seems that nobody can think of the great work of Heinrich Hertz without an almost affectionate admiration for him. And Hertz had Jewish blood.
>
> One of my friends told me: "The greatest German experimental physicist of the present time is Franck; many believe that he is the greatest experimental physicist of our age. Franck is a Jew, an unusually kind human being. Until a few days ago, he was professor at Göttingen, an honor to Germany and the envy of the international scientific community."

Perhaps the episode of Franck's dismissal

> shows the deepest reason why all these people are not joining [the Party]: they feel a moral imposition. They believe that only the quality of a human being should determine his worth, that intellectual achievement, character, and obvious contributions to German culture retain their significance whether a person is Jewish or not.

Expecting arrest, the Köhlers and members of the institute spent the night of April 28 playing chamber music. But the Nazis did not come.

Four months later, reprints of this article were still being circulated. Letters poured in, for the most part from strangers, occasionally critical, but the overwhelming majority was full of admiration for Köhler's courageous stand. Warm thanks were expressed by Jew and non-Jew alike. The following letter, as a single example, was signed only "A German Jew":

> Today I read your article, "Conversations in Germany." I am not ashamed to admit that, despite my 65 years, I was deeply moved by it and tears came to my eyes. I asked myself: Are there really Germans in Germany who can still muster such courage?
>
> I am a Jew, born in Germany as were my father and grandfather. I am a simple merchant, not a politician, who formerly for many years employed hundreds of Christian workers of all parties and religions and who enjoyed the greatest respect and recognition from them.
>
> These lines are simply intended to express to you my respect for your straightforward, fearless way of thinking.
>
> I omit my name since it is not relevant. I feel that in spirit I want to shake your hand, since I have children who now may no longer look upon Germany as their homeland.

On November 3, 1933, the government decreed that professors must open their lectures with the Nazi salute. Köhler flipped his hand in a caricature of the salute and said:

> Ladies and gentlemen, I have just saluted you in a manner that the government has decreed. I could not see how to avoid it.
>
> Still, I must say something about it. I am professor of philosophy in this university, and this circumstance obligates me to be candid with you, my students. A professor who wished to disguise his views by word or by action would have no place here. You could no longer respect him; he could no longer have anything to say to you about philosophy or important human affairs.
>
> Therefore I say: the form of my salute was until recently the sign of very particular ideas in politics and elsewhere. If I want to be honest, and if I am to be respected by you, I must explain that, although I am prepared to give that salute, I do not share the ideology which it usually signifies or used to signify.
>
> The National Socialists among you will particularly welcome this explanation. Nobility and purity of purpose among the Germans are goals for which the National Socialists are working hard. I am no National Socialist. But out of the same need to act nobly and purely, I have told you what the German salute means in my case and what it does not mean. I know you will respect my motives.

A witness reports that the audience of 200 greeted these remarks with thunderous applause, despite the presence of numerous brownshirts and many Nazi sympathizers (Crannell, 1970).

There was no real interference with the work of the institute until one evening in the beginning of December 1933, when Köhler gave the psychological colloquium. The doors to the colloquium room were guarded by troops, some in uniform, others in civilian clothes. When the students and assistants wanted to leave after the colloquium, they were stopped and their student cards examined.

Köhler did not then interfere with the inspection. When it was over, he telephoned the rector of the university, Eugen Fischer, protesting the unannounced raid. A discussion was arranged: The rector, who admitted that the procedure had been incorrect, agreed to exempt the Psychological Institute from further inspections of this kind. He had no objection to Köhler's informing the psychological colloquium of this agreement, and Köhler did so.

In the rector's absence, on February 26, 1934, Deputy Rector Bieberbach ordered another inspection of the institute. In accordance with his agreement with the rector, Köhler refused permission, and the inspection was not carried out. The rector was informed and offered no objection.

But trouble was ahead. A trip to Norway the next month gave Köhler another opportunity to write freely to Perry:

> I am trying to build up a special position for myself in which I might stay with honour. As yet it seems to work, but the end may come [any] day. Quite exciting sometimes, not a life of leisure, occasionally great fun. The art is not to act in passion, but to make at once use of any occasion when the others make a mistake; then it is time to push a foot forward or to hit without serious danger for oneself. You will say that such is the

> method of cowards. But think of the difference in strength!. . .
>
> Good work is being done in Berlin, as though we had to do what the emigrants are no longer able to do in Germany. Unfortunately my assistants have been in serious danger several times because of political denunciations—a denunciation a month is more or less our current rate; as yet, however, it has always been possible to save them.

Again the rector left town, and on April 12, 1934, Bieberbach ordered a new inspection "despite the agreement between Rector Fischer and Professor Köhler." The search of the institute was carried out under the leadership of a law student named Hennig, who submitted a report full of suspicions, innuendoes, and accusations but no more hard evidence than the discovery of a couple of foreign newspapers in an office (newspapers not banned by the regime) and the smell of cigarette smoke in an unoccupied room. His impertinent report insulted Professor Köhler and ended with the recommendation that two assistants, Drs. Duncker and von Lauenstein, as well as three employees, be dismissed. He recommended that the institute be moved to new quarters which would be easier to supervise and even suggested the need for another structure of the institute "which corresponds better to our time and spirit."

Köhler angrily informed the rector on April 13 that he was, for the time being, unable to continue to direct the institute and that he had therefore transferred the directorship to his chief assistant, Professor Rupp. He reminded Rector Fischer that the agreement between them had been violated and that his authority as director had been seriously undermined; only when the situation was rectified would he resume his duties as director.

Bieberbach, the deputy rector, replied (April 14), reaffirming his "self-evident right" to inspect every part of the university. Köhler telephoned the Minister of Science, Art, and Education, Dr. Achelis, and on April 18 sent him a copy of the whole correspondence, including Hennig's report along with his own detailed reply. He requested an immediate end to a situation which he could not regard "as compatible with the dignity of the University of Berlin."

On the same date, Rector Fischer replied to Köhler's letter of April 13, denying that there had ever been any agreement that the Psychological Institute be exempted from inspections. He expressed the desire to settle the disagreement without the intervention of the Ministry and requested an oral reply from Köhler.

Köhler's reply was *written* (April 20, 1934). In his letter he assures the rector that he welcomes an oral discussion when clarification has been achieved on the earlier one in which the agreement had been made, but he makes it altogether clear that the rector's account does not correspond with the facts:

> With the greatest astonishment I read in your letter the sentence: "Of an agreement between us that there would be no inspection of students in your Institute there was obviously never any question," as well as the further one: "I have only said to you that the inspecting student had to announce himself to the Director of the Institute on his appearance" . . . Something of value is to be expected from an oral discussion with you only when you recall how we came to this agreement and how, until a short time ago, it was taken for granted by both of us.

Köhler concludes that as soon as the rector and he agree again about that earlier agreement, he will welcome an oral discussion.

Two weeks later, May 3, Fischer expresses his disagreeable surprise that Köhler attaches a condition to an oral discussion to try to settle the issues between them. He asserts that it is "a matter of one opinion against another."

Köhler's reply on May 8, even less than the others in this series, hardly corresponds to the kind of communication normally expected from a professor to the rector of his university.

> I can give the following explanation: If another person, in a discussion with me, makes a detailed

and completely unmistakable agreement with me, if for months afterwards this agreement is carried out on both sides, but one day the other declares that the agreement was never made, then prudence forbids me to have another discussion with this person before he has corrected his mistake in a manner that produces confidence again. For who would protect me from a mistake of the same kind which could result from a further discussion? This holds for discussions with the Rector Magnificus exactly as for anyone else.

He points out that the rector has simply continued to renounce his agreement without giving any thought to the actual facts of the case.

> This cannot continue. . . . It is . . . extremely important, even if it has until now been taken for granted, that the administration make no error in memory which concerns matters of morals. I therefore ask you to communicate with me in writing by May 19 whether you have, in the meantime, recalled our agreement. I assume that in the meantime you will also find words of reproach and regret about the behavior of Hennig as authorized by the Rectorate and about his incredible report.

Thus Köhler is again in effect calling the Rector Magnificus of his university a liar, he makes clear that a matter of morals is involved, and he delivers what can only be called an ultimatum.* A copy of this letter and of Fischer's letter of May 3 was sent to the minister with the following remark:

> It is unusual for a professor to behave in this way toward the Rector. But the behavior of the Rector which leads me to do so is much more unusual. The dilatory handling of the matter I can no longer permit, and I must therefore insist that an untenable situation come to an end in a reasonable time.

Apparently no reply was received, either from the rector or from Dr. Achelis. On May 21, after the expiration of the ultimatum, Köhler (now in Scotland on a brief lecturing tour) sent to the Ministry and to the Dean of the Philosophical Faculty a request for retirement.

On the same day he wrote to Perry:

> My resignation is most likely to be final. Since most of the serious workers in psychology had to leave before, and since my excellent assistants would not stay without me, this means the abolition of German psychology for many years. I do not regard myself as responsible. If only 20 professors had fought the same battle, it would never have come so far with regard to German universities.

The reply to Köhler's request for retirement was a letter from an official of the Ministry to the effect that the transfer of civil service personnel to retirement status cannot simply be done upon request. Köhler is asked to discuss the matter with Dr. Achelis.

Meanwhile, the situation was deteriorating at the institute. A handyman, one Herr Schmidt, whose denunciation was apparently responsible for the dismissal of von Lauenstein, refused to carry out instructions, claiming the protection of the rector. Representatives of the German Student Organization (Nazis, of course) interfered in the administration of the institute, and the rector did nothing about it. In June 1934 a torchlight procession planned by students at the institute to honor Professor Köhler was forbidden. Students were called to the Department for Political Education and threatened when they tried to defend the institute. Two students, in an interview with the leader of the German Student Organization, heard Köhler attacked as a man who does not "stand on the ground of National Socialism" and who "identifies with the Jew Wertheimer." They learned that Duncker's habilitation would be prevented and that the attack on Köhler and his assistants was just the beginning.

In July 1934, matters had temporarily improved: The Ministry had intervened. On July 21, after a morning meeting, Köhler wrote to thank the *Ministerialdirektor* for his "interven-

*The letters lose something in translation. For example, the form of address to the rector was not simply "you," but, "your Magnificence."

tion and benevolent justice." He assured him that he would withdraw his resignation as soon as the following conditions were met: the reinstatement of von Lauenstein, the granting of leave and subsequent transfer of the handyman Schmidt, the dismissal of the leader of psychology students of the German Student Organization, and a public statement from the Ministry.

It was not until September 24, 1934, that the Ministry, represented by Vahlen, wrote to the rector of the University of Berlin the conclusions of his investigation of the Psychological Institute. Vahlen expresses his conviction that the personal attacks on Professor Köhler were unjustified, nor can he approve of the measures taken, with the Rector's permission, by the student organization. No action was taken against Hennig, the student leader of the raid on the institute, only because he had been removed from his position for other reasons. The Ministry considered justified Köhler's objections to the methods used by the leader of the student group.

On the other hand, Vahlen finds reason to criticize Köhler's refusal to discuss matters with the rector as well as the tone of his letters. He disapproves in particular of Köhler's interruption of his duties as director of the institute and of his activities there. He assures the rector that Professor Köhler has his confidence, and he expects all measures aimed at discrediting the institute to stop immediately.

The public statement made by the Ministry is the following:

> Accusations which have been raised against the Psychological Institute force me to point out that Professor Köhler has the confidence of the Minister. I expect from the Student Organization that no more cases of hostile behavior take place against Professor Köhler, his Institute, and his students.

A copy of this letter was sent to Köhler, along with a repetition of criticisms of Köhler's behavior toward the rector, with whom Vahlen asks him to cooperate in the future.

A month later Köhler was in the United States, delivering the William James Lectures at Harvard. Here he received a letter from Bieberbach, the deputy rector, asking him to sign an oath of loyalty to Adolf Hitler. The letter went unanswered until February. In the meantime, on January 7, 1935, Vahlen wrote to Köhler that the vacancy created by the departure of Professor Kurt Lewin had been filled. Dr. Keller of Rostock had been appointed in December, although Köhler had not been consulted. Vahlen assumes that Köhler will give his consent retroactively, and he is reassured by the opinion of the acting director, Rupp, that Köhler would have no objection. The minister asks for Köhler's opinion and wants to know whether, under these circumstances, Köhler's request to resign still holds.

On February 2, Köhler wrote that the law requiring a loyalty oath does not apply to him, since he has submitted his resignation to the Ministry. On the next day he replied to Vahlen's communication of January 7. He refers to the minister's earlier criticisms of the intrusions into the administration of the institute, for which he is grateful. But that same letter had contained reference to the "peculiar composition" of the circle close to Professor Köhler and had criticized the manner in which he had defended himself against the rector. He takes exception to both points, and on the basis of them had been considering for some time whether to renew his request to resign. Then he received the news of Dr. Keller's appointment. He can only see this as a continuation of the measures that first led him to request retirement: It is totally impossible for him to direct the institute when, time after time, important decisions are made without even consulting him. He can therefore not withdraw his request for resignation. For this, as he writes to the minister, he would need a most dramatic and binding assurance that he could be Director of the Psychological Institute of the University of Berlin "without repeatedly being subjected to the kind of treatment that only a weakling with no sense of honor could tolerate."

Apparently Köhler again requested reinstatement of his assistants, and this request was denied. Accordingly, a new request to resign was addressed to the minister on August 22, 1935, when Köhler was again in Germany. In it he points out that it is impossible for him to continue his work without these assistants, who represent new points of view now beginning to spread to all countries.

And so ended the great days of the Psychological Institute of the University of Berlin. Even before his final resignation, Köhler wrote an obituary notice to an American friend, Donald K. Adams:

> I feel obliged to announce to all those who have taken a friendly interest in the Psychological Institute at Berlin that this institute does not exist any more—though the rooms and the apparatus and Mr. Rupp are still there. The government has decided in May to dismiss all the assistants who were trained by me and in June, during the term, they were suddenly forbidden to continue their work and their teaching: Duncker, von Lauenstein and von Restorff. Since, at my last visit in Berlin, I had expressly stated orally and in official documents that I could not possibly remain as director without the help of my young friends and since this is a clear case of their modern brutality (another man uses this method in order to push *me* out), the measure is morally equivalent to my own dismissal too. I shall have a last interview with the Nazi authorities in August. But there is not one chance in a hundred for my staying on in Germany. . . . We were depressed for some days but have come back to the fighting spirit once more. Personally, I shall be glad when I have no contact with the official Germany of today, and I have so many good friends in this country, more indeed than over there. My deepest anxiety refers to the assistants. I am not yet sure whether I shall be able to place them somewhere.

The new Nazi director of the institute would not allow Köhler's students to remain (Wallach, Note 2); and of course his assistants were gone. A few went to other universities, some emigrated, some died. The young generation of Gestalt psychologists was effectively wiped out.

It is difficult to guess what would have been the effect on psychology in Germany, and indeed in the world, if the Psychological Institute had been allowed a few more productive years. It was perhaps the outstanding psychological institute of its time. Max Planck, in a letter to Köhler in the midst of the struggle, speaks of the importance of its preservation "in its unique significance for science and for our university." The institute attracted students from many countries; and the ideas of Gestalt psychology were respected and were spreading in Germany and in other countries. It is possible that our science would be different today if that institute had been able to continue its work.

The courageous struggle of Wolfgang Köhler against the Nazis could not save the Psychological Institute. Was that struggle in vain? I think not. For as we look back on it, it shows us once more what a human being can be.

REFERENCE NOTES

1 Köhler, W. *Peace and education.* Unpublished lecture given during World War II. In the Library of the American Philosophical Society, Philadelphia, Pennsylvania.

2 Wallach, H. Personal communication, September 10, 1973.

REFERENCES

Crannell, C. W. Wolfgang Köhler, *Journal of the History of the Behavioral Sciences,* 1970, 6, 267–268.

Hartshorne, E. Y. *The German universities and National Socialism.* Cambridge, Mass.: Harvard University Press, 1937.

Mandler, J. M., & Mandler, G. The diaspora of experimental psychology: The Gestaltists and others. *Perspectives in American History,* 1968, *2,* 371–419.

The Gestalt Psychologists in Behaviorist America

Michael M. Sokal

To many people in the United States, . . . Gestalt psychology in the 1920s and early 1930s meant primarily the work of Wolfgang Köhler, and the history of his interaction with American psychologists through the mid-1930s reveals much about the way in which Gestalt ideas and the Gestalt psychologists were received. . . . This fact, as well as the many rumors that still circulate concerning Köhler's relations with several American psychologists, especially those at Harvard, justifies an extensive treatment of his role. It is not generally known that Köhler had contacts with American psychology as early as 1914, when he was working with chimpanzees at Tenerife. Early that year, Robert M. Yerkes, then a young assistant professor at Harvard, wrote to Köhler, expressing interest in his work, asking for further information about it, and hoping to be able to join the German professor off the coast of Africa. The outbreak of the European war and Köhler's internment on Tenerife ended Yerkes's travel plans. But the two psychologists soon began to exchange offprints, and the American even asked John B. Watson to send Köhler a set of his articles. Yerkes also had Köhler's motion picture films of his chimpanzee experiments processed in the United States when this became impossible on the islands. But this friendly and mutually profitable exchange was marred in 1916, when Yerkes published *The Mental Life of Monkeys and Apes* and did not cite Köhler's work. And with American entry into the war in 1917, the relationship came to a temporary close.(1)

Shortly after the war, Yerkes used his temporary position with the National Research Council to try to re-establish contact with Köhler. He accomplished this by 1921, and soon the two psychologists exchanged books, offprints, and congratulations on each other's appointments: Köhler's at Berlin and Yerkes's at Yale. Yerkes even offered to send money to Köhler to cover the cost of the books and offprints, in view of the deterioration of the economic situation in Germany and the "unfairness of the exchange situation," but Köhler would not accept. By 1923, the two men were again learning much from a correspondence they both apparently enjoyed. And in 1924, Yerkes reviewed Köhler's *Mentality of Apes* most positively, writing that both its "observations and conclusions . . . are important" and hoping "that it may also achieve wide influence."(2)

Later in 1924 Carl Murchison at Clark University arranged for Köhler to serve as visiting professor at the Worcester institution during 1925, and the reaction of many American psychologists was enthusiastic. Terman, a Clark alumnus who had been bemoaning the condition of psychology at his alma mater, was especially pleased. As he wrote to a Clark official, "It was a splendid stroke to get Dr. Köhler to come over." Boring and Yerkes congratulated Köhler on his appointment and were among the first to welcome him to America. Boring, of course, had been studying Gestalt psychology at the time, and his welcome was particularly enthusiastic. "The psychological stock of America took a jump upward as soon as I heard you were safely on shore."(3) Once Köhler was at Worcester, Boring and Yerkes saw him regularly, and the visitor spoke at least once at both Harvard and Yale. Boring even attended weekly seminars led by Köhler at Clark, which he described as "great fun," at least in part because the meetings included extensive discussions of Köhler's experimental work. These seminars in turn led

Adapted from Sokal, M. M. (1984). The Gestalt psychologists in behaviorist America. *American Historical Review, 89,* 1240–1263.

to Köhler's influential chapters in *Psychologies of 1925*, published by Clark University Press.[4] Meanwhile, Köhler met with other members of the American psychological community and impressed most of them. He and Koffka attended a meeting of the Society of Experimental Psychologists as guests, two of the few ever so honored. . . . During a later visit to Stanford, Köhler impressed Terman as "an intellectually active man" with "youth and vigor." Yerkes also recommended Köhler and Koffka to the home secretary of the National Academy of Sciences as "two of the foremost German psychologists" in an effort to get for them a place on the academy's programs. In 1926 Ogden sought the translation and publication in English of other books by Köhler. Although unsuccessful, the attempt shows how important to American psychology Köhler's ideas had become.[5]

Soon after Köhler started lecturing at Clark in January 1925, Boring and James H. Woods, chairman of the joint Department of Philosophy and Psychology at Harvard, proposed to invite Köhler to Cambridge the following fall as visiting professor. The idea had the support of Harvard philosophers—Ralph Barton Perry was then reviewing favorably *Mentality of Apes*, and Woods even told the Harvard administration that he himself would raise the funds to pay for Köhler's salary. As director of the Harvard Psychological Laboratory, Boring exchanged letters with Köhler about the position. Köhler was interested, for he wanted to work with Harvard graduate students.[6]

But in late April 1925 Köhler spoke at Cambridge under the auspices of the Harvard Philosophical Club, and his talk disappointed Boring greatly. He later described it as being full of "general theoretical analogies [and] unformulated psychological events [with] not [one] bit of experimentation." In another letter, he expressed dissatisfaction with the "vagueness of [Köhler's] speculation." He had hoped to find in Köhler the experimentalist that he strongly believed the Harvard department needed, only to discover that the Gestaltist was moving away from the laboratory.[7]

Personal concerns may also have figured in Boring's reversal. He was a moody and oversensitive man, highly conscious of his status as Harvard's leading psychologist, which would have been threatened by Köhler's appointment. But at the same time he was jealous of Harvard's position in the American psychological community and knew that it would be generally enhanced if Köhler lectured at the university.[8] His continuing correspondence with Köhler mirrors Boring's ambivalence. In June he listed in detail the facilities available at Harvard, and added, "I am very anxious for you to come." And yet he stressed the space and financial limitations at Harvard and feared Köhler might "be disappointed" at not having "what you could have had at Berlin." In response Köhler began to express doubts about the visiting appointment and finally begged off in the summer of 1925, citing his responsibilities to his colleagues in Berlin that prevented an extension of his leave. "Just about the time that Köhler got an inkling that Harvard might do something to get him here," Boring wrote several years later, "he stiffened up towards me."[9]

Köhler's relations with Boring were undoubtedly "stiff." Boring's ambivalence probably set him on edge, but more than Boring's attitude was involved. Köhler was a difficult man to get to know, and he, too, enjoyed status as a professor at Germany's leading university. He believed his psychology vastly superior to any yet developed and urged its merits on Americans with a confidence that some saw as arrogance. He had high standards of propriety and was easily put off by anything he considered improper. According to an American student in Berlin, even his German friends thought him "a little too temperamental" and inclined to be rigidly formal on even informal occasions. Before transcending the formal "Sie" to the intimate "Du," Köhler had to know somebody socially for ten years or more. American friends attributed Köhler's constraint to discomfort in speaking English, his unbending need to do the proper thing socially, and his basic shyness. Whatever its cause, it did "put off" many Americans and complicated his relations with many people in this country, especially Boring, whose own personality did not ease the situation. The two men apparently never understood one another and found the negotiations difficult. Both tried to be cordial and conciliatory throughout their correspondence, and their letters to each other were always polite. But Boring, at least, disliked Köhler and felt disliked in turn. The depth of his feelings bothered him, however, and Boring once even wrote of them to his colleague, Perry, describing his letter as "the confession of a divided neurotic soul."[10] But neurotic or not, the relationship between the two men affected the history of American psychology.

Despite the personal feelings involved, Köhler did not close the door in the summer of 1925 to a visiting position at Harvard and hinted that he would welcome an invitation to Cambridge in the future. Boring and Woods apparently discussed this possibility with Abbot Lawrence Lowell, Harvard's president. Köhler's fame in America in the mid-1920s was such that he had already been recommended strongly to Lowell by a member of the university's Board of Overseers. Henry Osborn Taylor, the New York philosopher and historian, had described Köhler in a letter to Lowell as "a light in a dark night." Lowell, intrigued by these recommendations, made inquiries of his own, writing to Edward Bradford Titchener, the leading structuralist. Titchener responded that he had been impressed by Köhler's experimental work in Germany before World War I but found his later theoretical work so disappointing that he feared "Köhler's health may have been seriously impaired by his four years' residence on Tenerife." Furthermore, Köhler in person impressed Titchener even less favorably, appearing "apathetic and uninspiring," a reaction shared, he said, by other Americans. The Cornell psychologist warned Lowell against offering Köhler a permanent chair but thought that a one-year visiting professorship would be a good test of the Gestaltist's health and ability.[11] Boring was not the only psychologist of the mid-1920s who believed that Köhler's major scientific achievements lay behind him.

Lowell apparently did not tell Boring and Woods of Titchener's opinion, and in January 1926 the two men again made plans to approach Köhler about a visiting professorship. Although these plans fell through,[12] a possibility appeared in December for a permanent appointment. In that month William McDougall, the English psychologist who had been teaching at Harvard since 1920, resigned his position and left Cambridge for Duke University. Woods immediately thought of Köhler as McDougall's successor and was supported by Perry and other Harvard philosophers. Boring, however, told his colleagues that what Harvard psychology required was a leading experimentalist and that Köhler, having left the laboratory for theoretical exploration, did not fill this need. He strongly favored the appointment of an American, such as Lashley or Tolman. He also told Perry, and perhaps others, of his personal feelings about Köhler. But he still believed that the Gestaltist's appointment at Harvard would do much for the university's standing in psychology, and, as he phrased it, he did not "think that [Köhler's] dislike of me . . . [was] a reason for not calling him, but [was] rather sorry to have this personal reaction to render me unsure of my other professional judgment." He therefore went along with Woods and Perry and agreed to ask Köhler to join the Harvard faculty, at least on a temporary basis.[13]

Köhler, however, did not respond to two of Boring's letters on the subject. A third letter from Boring, and one from Woods, did bring a reply, but it did not clarify the situation. To be sure, some of the correspondence between these three men has apparently been lost or destroyed, so the details of the episode are unclear. Those letters that survive are polite and even friendly, and yet those who saw all the correspondence were not sure of what Köhler, who hated financial negotiations connected with jobs, intended. Boring wrote to Terman, "My own interpretation of the correspondence is that he will not accept . . . [but] some at Harvard interpret the same letters as meaning that he is coming." The one letter from Köhler to Boring that survives illustrates the problem of determining the former's intentions. "When I think of you and my other friends at Harvard the choice looks simple. But when I look at the economic situation and the number of lectures to which an American Professor tends to be obligated, then my face drops."(14) Not until the fall of 1927 did Köhler definitely notify Harvard that he would stay in Berlin. Apparently he apologized to Boring for the long suspense. In reply Boring tried to be conciliatory, but his annoyance is evident. "After all what is Harvard against Berlin? . . . That you have left us in the lurch and we are still limping along is certainly not your fault, but is entirely our responsibility." It is no wonder then that he later described this period as "the summer that Köhler blew up on us."(15)

Harvard still had to appoint a successor to McDougall, and the philosophers continued to urge that a European be chosen for the position. They kept hoping that Köhler might be persuaded to come to Cambridge. But Boring still argued for an American and an experimentalist, and he found that other American psychologists shared his, and Titchener's, low opinion of Köhler's post-1920 work, which was too grandly speculative for their tastes. Terman noted, "I doubt . . . he will ever do much more experimenting." Boring complained to his philosophical colleagues about their preference for European psychologists, who performed "the scissors and cardboard kind of experiments that do not reflect favorably upon Harvard's psychology in America." His concern for Harvard's reputation meshed with his antipathy toward Köhler's work. He cited the "criticism from the men whose opinion I respect and in whose judgment I concur." In the spring of 1928 Köhler's name was again mentioned for the position at Harvard, and Boring blew up. "American psychologists who felt that Harvard had made a mistake with both [Hugo] Münsterberg and McDougall would feel that it again erred."(16) But Boring's outburst got him nowhere, since many Harvard philosophers wanted Köhler. In the fall of 1928 he analyzed the situation:

> The issue is out in the open. It is between A and B.
> A. Breadth of interest, vision and imagination.
> B. Technical skill and knowledge within a given field.
> We want both. We can not have them. Actually they are negatively correlated. . . .
> Hocking, Perry and Woods are for A and thus for a renewal of the offer to Köhler.
> I am for the B and thus can not conscientiously agree to Köhler.(17)

Boring was also annoyed that philosophers were trying to tell psychologists how to manage their own affairs. His protests over the way in which the entire situation had been handled were later a major reason why philosophy and psychology at Harvard were reorganized in the mid-1930s as separate departments within a joint division.(18)

Meanwhile, Boring had been devoting all of the time that he could spare from Harvard matters to the study of the history of psychology, in preparation for the writing of his well-known book, *History of Experimental Psychology,* published in 1929. This research, his quarrels with his Harvard colleagues, and his feelings about Köhler's experimental work, all led him to reconsider his early enthusiasm for Gestalt psychology, which he had never expressed in print. Several of his friends—for example, Margaret Floy Washburn—had always been critical of the school, and Boring had always been sensitive to the opinions of other psychologists. Some thought highly of the work of individual Gestaltists but criticized that of others. Terman, for example, found Lewin's work exciting but had qualms about Koffka's and Köhler's. He described a talk by Koffka at Stanford as "piffle" and, though somewhat impressed by Köhler's early writings, thought little of Köhler's future as an experimental psychologist. Terman felt that propagandizing by Gestalt psychologists detracted from the merit of their ideas, and Boring began to be concerned about this aspect of his relationships with Koffka and Köhler.(19)

Gestaltists were not the only psychologists of the 1920s to argue that the school to which they belonged possessed the only valid approach to psychology. And yet American psychologists were especially bothered by the attitude of the Gestaltists. As shown earlier, some felt that the Gestaltists had come to the United States almost as intellectual missionaries, spreading a new gospel. And Köhler's stiffness did nothing to ease the situation. Recently the term "Mandarin" has been used to characterize the attitudes and behavior of many of the German university professors of the period. In some ways the entire Gestalt movement represented a revolt against traditional German university culture, but in other, deeper ways the Gestaltists shared many traits typical of the faculties of German universities.(20) Although they never heard the term "Mandarin" applied to the Gestaltists, many American psychologists would have easily recognized the characterization.

When Boring's *History of Experimental Psychology* appeared, his ten-page discussion of Gestalt psychology was negative in tone. Apparently he felt that he had tried to be fair. "It is a question as to whether I have been favorable or unfavorable." But friends of Gestalt psychology like Ogden had little doubt about Boring's actual opinion. His analysis of the school continually stressed its origins as a "psychology of protest" against the older, atomistic theories of psychology. Although he admitted that, "if this negative element were all that there is to *Gestalt* psychology, it would never have become an important movement," most of his discussion revolved around its criticisms of older ideas. Furthermore, he emphasized the continuity of Gestalt ideas with older theories and criticized the Gestaltists because they "made little effort to show the antiquity of the[ir] objection."(21) One can readily see why Ogden felt attacked.

The year 1929 also saw the publication of Köhler's *Gestalt Psychology,* which he wrote in English and intended as a general introduction to his science for American psychologists. To show his readers what Gestalt psychology was not, he opened his presentation with a long critique of behaviorism. But the psychology that these chapters attacked was almost a caricature of the American science, since they neither mentioned (with one exception in a single sentence) any behaviorist nor included a detailed discussion of any behaviorist study, even by way of example. (A bibliography did list three works by behaviorists, but only one by Watson, and that a short article.) The book also included chapters on sensory organization, association, recall, and insight, which explained quite clearly the Gestalt perspective on these topics.(22) The volume was at least partially successful, but it did not win many friends for the Gestalt school.

Although not a behaviorist, Boring believed that he had to respond to the book, and he criticized Köhler's vague and slanted account of the American school. But he made sure to comment favorably on the most substantive chapters. Boring's review was entitled "The *Gestalt* Psychology and the *Gestalt* Movement," and it praised the former, while criticizing the latter. But despite his belief that Köhler's book required his response, he felt uneasy about it and attempted, before it was published, to soften its impact. He asked a friend to read a draft to make sure it was not too "violent." He sent galley proofs of the note to Köhler in Berlin and tried in a cover letter to explain his ambivalence. "Sometimes I seem to be so enthusiastic about it and sometimes so negative." He wrote of his "enthusiasm for the research that has come out under this label" but admitted, "I get very angry about the label of *Gestalt* psychology and its solidarity as a new movement."(23)

If Köhler responded to Boring's letter or to the review, his answer has been lost, but Koffka's reaction was calm, reasoned, and cordial. He argued "that the Gestalt *movement* has been created not by the Gestalt psychologists but by their opponents" and claimed that "many misunderstandings may have been caused by the fact that Köhler and I were invited to give so many public lectures," from which "concrete details" had to be omitted. There was some validity to Koffka's points, especially in view of the long list of papers criticizing Gestalt psychology that Boring presented in his history, and Koffka's attitude toward his public lectures might certainly explain why Terman thought the one he heard was "piffle." Boring found at least some truth in Koffka's rebuttal. But at the same time he harked back to the talk that Köhler had given in 1925 at the Harvard Philosophical Club, which had impressed him so unfavorably. Boring made sure to stress that these specific criticisms did not apply to Koffka, but, though cordial, Boring clearly was unhappy with Gestalt psychology, or at least with the Gestalt school.(24)

Boring's note was not the only response to Köhler's book critical of the Gestalt movement. The *New Republic,* for example, published an article by Edward S. Robinson, a Yale psychologist, on "A Little German Band," which was subtitled "The Solemnities of Gestalt Psychology." The essay was important in that it apparently marked the first time that Köhler and Koffka were referred to in print as Gestaltists. Previously Americans called them Gestalt psychologists or Gestalt theorists, but after its appearance in this article "Gestaltist" passed into general usage, analogous to behaviorist or structuralist and usually, despite Robinson's intent, without disparaging implications. But Köhler and other Gestalt psychologists always saw the term as an insult to them and their work and decried its use. Boring avoided it, at least partly in deference to their feelings. But even today, when many psychologists speak fondly of their teachers as Gestaltists, those still annoyed by the term blame its coinage on Boring.(25)

By clarifying Gestalt psychology and its concepts for an American audience, Köhler's *Gestalt Psychology* made it easier for behaviorists and other non-Gestalt psychologists to attack his point of view. And in the following years, such attacks multiplied. For example, an article on "The Phantom of the Gestalt" concluded that "the Gestalt . . . has no assignable value in psychological description nor any real existence within the experimental sequence." Similarly, in "Materializing the Ghost of Köhler's Gestalt Psychology," an American psychologist argued that Gestalt concepts, if reinterpreted within the framework of Washburn's motor theory of consciousness, would be immediately subsumed within the mainstream of American psychology. These critiques and others like them are difficult to interpret, but all indicate a growing familiarity with, if not a deep understanding of, Gestalt ideas among American psychologists. By 1933, when it was included as one of the *Seven Psychologies* in Edna Heidbreder's classic survey of American schools of psychology, Gestalt psychology was clearly a part of the American psychological scene. (26)

Meanwhile, Koffka remained at Smith, Boring at Harvard, and Köhler at Berlin. These three men continued to correspond regularly with each other, and all went on with their scientific work. Boring drifted toward behaviorism and published *The Physical Dimensions of Consciousness,* an attack on dualism that he later admitted was "immature" and a friendly colleague called a "silly little thing." Koffka began work on his very influential book, *Principles of Gestalt Psychology,* which went far beyond Köhler's introduction. In Germany, the rise of Hitler did not immediately affect Köhler, as he was an "Aryan," but he greatly disliked the Nazis and what they stood for and was one of the few non-Jewish scientists in Germany to oppose the regime actively.[(27)] In the mid-1930s developments at Harvard led to another invitation to Köhler. The Division of Philosophy and Psychology sponsored the William James lectures and decided—after hearing two distinguished American philosophers, John Dewey and Arthur O. Lovejoy—to invite a foreign, or at least foreign-born, psychologist as the next lecturer. After considering Carl Gustav Jung, the faculty soon focused on Koffka and Köhler. In comparing the two, the Harvard psychologists found that each had different strengths; they had to determine just what they wanted. As Boring summarized their deliberations, the Harvard professors decided "that the most distinguished and appropriate appointment that could be made at the present time would be Köhler and that the most useful appointment in the effect it would have upon the atmosphere of the laboratory would be Koffka. I have lent my support to the view that we must in such an appointment weight distinction very heavily, and that we ought therefore to ask Köhler."[(28)]

In December 1933, Harvard invited Köhler to be the third William James lecturer, to deliver a course of ten or twelve public lectures, and to conduct a seminar for graduate students. Boring wrote to Köhler that *both* the philosophers and the psychologists in the division wanted the Gestaltist to accept the appointment and that he was especially hopeful of hearing Köhler again. Köhler responded as he had to so many previous invitations from Harvard, writing that he would love to accept "this invitation, which I regard as an unusual honour," and stressing that "it should have been impossible for me to accept without knowing about your point of view." He did not agree to the proposal immediately, citing the difficult problems he faced at the University of Berlin with regard to the Nazi-controlled administration.[(29)]

But Köhler soon afterwards accepted and arrived at Cambridge in September 1934. Boring attended the lecture series and, burying his misgivings, apparently hoped to see a good deal of Köhler, arranging at least one social event for the visitor and his wife. But on the whole he was greatly disappointed; Köhler spent most of his time with Harvard's distinguished philosophers, especially Perry. In planning for Köhler's visit, Boring assumed that the Gestaltist would not need an office near the psychology laboratory, but his colleagues in philosophy convinced him otherwise. Once in Cambridge, Köhler hardly used the office, and the two psychologists rarely met. By November, the situation became so bad that Boring felt he had to write to Köhler, if he was to have an opportunity to discuss some points raised in the lectures. "Things are so disposed that we are not thrown together for conversation."[(30)] In all, Boring seems to have come across as a pushy American, and Köhler seems to have retreated into his personal shell. Both psychologists acted with the best intentions, but neither knew how to improve the relationship.

Boring had other reasons to be annoyed. The lectures that Köhler gave—published four years later as *The Place of Value in a World of Fact*—extended various philosophical implications of Gestalt theory into the realm of ethics and aesthetics and focused much attention on epistemological and metaphysical problems. Köhler's English was good, but the lectures were not as easily followed as were the substantive chapters of *Gestalt Psychology,* which perhaps merely reflected the complexity of the topics on which he spoke. Later reviews in philosophy journals and the popular press praised the book as, for example, "keen, wide-ranging, and original." But most reviews of it by psychologists—especially those taking some sort of behaviorist perspective—were extremely negative.[(31)] And Boring was one who decried what Köhler had done. He knew that the lectures would not focus on experimental studies and their implications, but apparently he had expected Köhler to talk about psychology, even if from a theoretical perspective. Instead, Köhler spoke on epistemology and metaphysics, and Boring was angry. At issue, too, was more than a simple tension between philosophy and psychology. In 1934, at least one psychologist wrote to Boring that the single lecture by Köhler that he had heard did not impress him, and Boring's reply reveals much. "You commented on being disappointed in a lecture which you heard recently. I can say only that I heard the whole series and am terribly disappointed, and a little humiliated at the knowledge that I took the time to go to them. The content was not well informed nor related to current knowledge. The ideas were not important or clear. Most of the argument was childishly elementary, although I caught suggestions of something sinister behind the scenes once in a while—but I was never sure. The vocal presentation was dull and tiresome, although the literary was, if you could grasp it, exceptionally able. This then is what we applaud so heartily!"(32)

To be sure, Boring was at a critical point in his life and about to undergo psychoanalysis in an attempt to free himself from the despondency that plagued him throughout the mid-1930s.(33) But his criticisms of Köhler were as much intellectual as personal. Apparently, soon after Köhler completed his William James lectures, the philosophers at Harvard urged that he be appointed professor at the university, and, with the situation in Germany worsening, Köhler was more open to such an appointment than ever before. But Boring, as director of the psychological laboratory and head of the Department of Psychology within the Division of Philosophy and Psychology, adamantly opposed the appointment. This position also gave Boring easier access to James B. Conant, a chemist who was Harvard's new president, and he was, at last, able to convince the Harvard administration to close the door permanently to Köhler. In all, Boring's opposition was final, and in 1935 he was able to appoint Lashley to a Harvard professorship, thus bringing to Cambridge the type of experimentalist he always wanted. (An earlier offer to Tolman fell through, in part because the Californian "loved[d] Berkeley and dislike[d] Cambridge.")(34) Despite this success, Boring's despondency grew, as his role in this incident apparently cost him several friends at Harvard. Even in the 1980s rumors still circulate about the feud between Boring and Köhler, and how it cost Köhler a Harvard professorship.(35) In any event, by the end of 1935 Köhler had settled at Swarthmore College, where he established an institutional base for his work comparable to Koffka's at Smith. There he was a major influence on the development of such distinguished psychologists as Mary Henle, Solomon Asch, and Robert B. MacLeod. Within a year or two Boring and Köhler were again corresponding cordially, and after World War II Boring readily admitted Köhler's great influence on American psychology. In the 1950s Köhler was honored by election to the National Academy of Sciences—in fact, he was elected as soon as he became eligible through naturalization(36)—and to the presidency of the American Psychological Association.

The transmission of Gestalt psychology was a complicated affair, but several points are especially striking. One major conclusion is that, like the transit of the new physics to America,(37) the diffusion of Gestalt psychology from Germany to the United States began long before Hitler came to power. Americans were too interested in German ideas and Germans too interested in American opportunities to wait until political events forced them into contact. By 1930 Gestalt psychology was firmly established in the United States as a psychological school, and graduate students interested in a Gestalt-focused education in psychology knew where to study. The rise of the Nazis certainly contributed to the completion of the migration, but it did not determine the direction in which American psychology developed. Another point worth noting is that Americans found that they had to react to at least three different factors—Gestalt psychology, the Gestalt movement, and the Gestalt psychologists themselves. They responded differently to each. Some, like Boring, were attracted by Gestalt experimental work but reacted negatively to Gestalt theory. And clearly, despite Koffka's disclaimer, the protagonists of Gestalt theory constituted a movement that tried to convert Americans to their view of the world. Americans quite naturally resented their missionary efforts.

The personalities of the psychologists involved—both German and American—also helped shape the course of the migration. Certainly Köhler's formality, Boring's oversensitivity, and the concern for status that both men shared affected their interactions. And yet, despite the dominance of behaviorism, American psychology was open to Gestalt ideas, and today many Gestalt interpretations of psychological phenomena have joined the mainstream of modern American psychology. Certainly perception is an area of research molded by Gestalt ideas. Even in the 1920s and 1930s, the experimental work of leading American psychologists strongly exhibited the influence of the Gestalt approach to their science. Lashley's stress on basic neural mechanisms and, especially, Tolman's "Purposive Behaviorism"—one of the most influential approaches to psychology in the 1930s—clearly owed much to Gestalt theory. That both were offered positions at Harvard at a time when Köhler's suitability for such a position was being debated further illustrates how Americans differentiated between the psychologists and the ideas. In other areas of psychology, too, Gestalt concepts have been influential. Lewin's work, for example, with its stress on an individual's interaction with his or her "life space" or social field, has done much to shape modern social psychology.

Finally, and perhaps most controversially, I think we can conclude that the Gestalt psychologists themselves were well received in the United States. To be sure, the few who still define themselves as Gestalt psychologists argue that America did not give their teachers what it should have. But in many ways, this attitude is reminiscent of the situation of the 1920s and early 1930s when Koffka and Köhler allowed their movement to get the better of their ideas and preached to the Americans, trying to convert the heathen to the true gospel. In any event, all major Gestalt psychologists found positions in America in the middle of the depression and were able to carry on with the work they had started in Germany. This work enriched American psychology greatly and did much to counter the attractions of extreme behaviorism. If Gestalt psychology has today lost its identity as a school of thought—and very few of Koffka's, Köhler's, Wertheimer's, or Lewin's students call themselves Gestalt psychologists—it is not because the mainstream of American psychology has swamped their ideas. Rather, their work has done much to redirect this mainstream, which adopted many of their points of view. Few other migrating scientific schools have been as successful.[38]

NOTES

(1) Yerkes to Köhler, March 27, May 20, 1914, July 17, October 10, December 21, 1916, January 10, 1917; Köhler to Yerkes, April 17, 1914, February 15, May 19, 1916, September 10, 1917, December 13, 1916, March 2, 1917, Yale University Archives, New Haven, Robert M. Yerkes Papers [hereafter, Yerkes Papers].

(2) Yerkes to U.S. Department of State, February 14, 1921; Yerkes to Köhler, April 13, October 8, 1921, March 6, 1922, November 6, 1923; Köhler to Yerkes, May 19, October 23, 1921, January 29, 1922, Yerkes Papers; and Yerkes, review of Köhler's *Mentality of Apes,* in *International Book Review,* June 1925, p. 461.

(3) Terman to C. H. Thurber, May 26, 1924, Stanford University Archives, Stanford, CA, Lewis Terman Papers [hereafter Terman Papers]; Boring to Köhler, June 9, 1924, February 6, 1925, Harvard University Archives, Cambridge, MA, Edwin G. Boring Papers [hereafter Boring Papers]; and Yerkes to Köhler, October 22, 1924, January 26, 1925, May 7, 1924; Köhler to Yerkes, February 8, 1924, February 15, 1925, Yerkes Papers.

(4) Boring to Yerkes, October 28, 1925; Yerkes to Köhler, May 7, 1925, Yerkes Papers; Boring to Köhler, March 31, 1925, Köhler to Boring, April 2, April 20, 1925, Boring Papers; and Köhler, "An Aspect of Gestalt Psychology," and "Intelligence in Apes," in Carl Murchison, ed., *Psychologies of 1925* (Worcester, Mass., 1926), 129–43, 145–61.

(5) Terman to Boring, January 26, 1927, Terman Papers; Yerkes to David White, March 5, 1925, Yerkes Papers; Kegan Paul Trench Trubner and Company to Köhler, November 16, 1926, January 19, February 15, June 14, July 22, October 11, 1927, American Philosophical Society Library, Philadelphia, Wolfgang Köhler Papers [hereafter, Köhler Papers]; and Boring, "The Society of Experimental Psychologists, 1904-1938," *American Journal of Psychology,* 51 (1938): 410–21. . . . The Society of Experimental Psychologists, [an] exclusive group, first brought together in 1904 by Edward B. Titchener of Cornell and not formally organized until after his death in 1927, limited attendance at its meetings to the directors of American university psychological laboratories and their entourages of junior colleagues and graduate students. Attendance in 1925 was higher than at any previous meeting; American psychologists came both to celebrate the dedication of Eno Hall, the new psychological laboratory at Princeton, and to meet with and hear Köhler and Koffka, the honored guests.

(6) Woods to Abbot Lawrence Lowell, March 17, 1925, Harvard University Archives, Cambridge, Mass., Abbot Lawrence Lowell Papers [hereafter, Lowell Papers]; and Boring to Woods, April 15, April 16, 1925; Boring to Köhler, March 25, March 31, 1925; Köhler to Boring, April 2, 1925, Boring Papers.

(7) Boring to Koffka, April 23, 1930; Boring to Raymond H. Wheeler, March 3, 1927, Boring Papers.

(8) Boring, *Psychologist at Large: An Autobiography and Selected Essays* (New York, 1961); and Julian Jaynes, "Edwin Garrigues Boring, 1886–1968," *Journal of the History of the Behavioral Sciences,* 5 (1969): 99–112.

(9) Boring to Köhler, June 4, 1925; Köhler to Boring, July 12, 1925, Boring Papers; Boring to Yerkes, October 28, 1925, Yerkes Papers; Boring to Wheeler, March 3, 1927, Boring Papers; and Köhler to Woods, [July 10, 1925], Köhler Papers.

(10) Jean M. Mandler and George Mandler, "The diaspora of experimental psychology: The Gestaltists and others." In D. Fleming & B. Bailyn (Eds.), *The Intellectual Migration: Europe and America, 1930–1960,* Cambridge, MA, 1969, pp. 371–419; interview with Edwin B. Newman, October 3, 1979; and Carroll C. Pratt to Boring, April 19, 1931, as quoted in Boring to Terman, July 31, 1931; Boring to Perry, [1928], Boring Papers.

(11) Taylor to Lowell, February 28, 1926; Lowell to Taylor, March 2, 1926; Lowell to Titchener, April 17, 1926, Lowell Papers; and Titchener to Lowell, April 19, 1926, Cornell University Archives, Ithaca, N.Y., Edward Bradford Titchener Papers [hereafter, Titchener Papers].

(12) Boring to Woods, January 6, January 21, March 18, 1926, Boring Papers; and Köhler to Woods, March 15, 1926, [April 1926], Köhler Papers.

(13) Boring to Perry, [1928], Boring Papers; Woods to Boring, December 17, 1926; Boring to Woods, December 27, 1926, Boring Papers; Boring to Terman, January 17, 1927, Terman Papers; and Boring to Clarence I. Lewis, August 14, 1927, December 4, April 4, 1928, Harvard University Archives, Cambridge, Mass., Department of Philosophy Papers [hereafter, Department of Philosophy Papers].

(14) Boring to Terman, July 11, 1927, Terman Papers; and Boring to Woods, January 13, 1927; Köhler to Boring, May 13, 1927 (my translation from the German), Boring Papers.

(15) Boring to Köhler, January 6, 1928, Boring Papers; and Boring to Terman, August 9, December 14, 1927, Terman Papers. Also see Boring to Lewis, August 2, August 14, 1927, Department of Philosophy Papers.

(16) Terman to Boring, January 26, 1927, Terman Papers; and Boring to Lewis, December 4, December 7, 1927, April 4, October 30, 1928, Department of Philosophy Papers.

(17) Boring to Lewis, October 30, 1928, Department of Philosophy Papers.

(18) Boring to Perry, November 15, 1928, Department of Philosophy Papers.

(19) Terman to Boring, August 3, January 26, 1927, Terman Papers; Washburn, "Gestalt Psychology and Motor Psychology," *American Journal of Psychology,* 37 (1926): 516–20; and Washburn to Boring, September 16, 1925; Boring to Carl E. Seashore, June 25, August 21, 1928, Boring Papers.

(20) Fritz K. Ringer, *The Decline of the German Mandarins: The German Academic Community, 1890–1933* (Cambridge, Mass., 1969); and Mitchell G. Ash, "The Emergence of Gestalt Theory: Experimental Psychology in Germany, 1890–1920 (Ph.D. dissertation, Harvard University, 1982).

(21) Boring to Köhler, February 27, 1930, Boring Papers, and *A History of Experimental Psychology* (New York, 1929), 570–80, 591–93.

(22) Köhler, *Gestalt Psychology* (New York, 1929).

(23) Boring to Joseph Peterson, January 13, 1930; Boring to Köhler, February 27, 1930, Boring Papers; and E. G. Boring, "The *Gestalt* Psychology and the *Gestalt* Movement," *American Journal of Psychology, 42* (1930): 308–15.

(24) Koffka to Boring, April 22, 1930; Boring to Koffka, April 23, 1930, Boring Papers; and Boring, *History of Experimental Psychology,* 593.

(25) Robinson, "A Little German Band," *New Republic,* November 27, 1929, pp. 10–14. James R. Angell, president of Yale and a psychologist, apparently criticized Robinson sharply for the tone of his review; see Robinson to Angell, December 10, 1929, Yale University Archives, New Haven, Conn., James R. Angell Presidential Papers. Also see Grace Heider to Jean and George Mandler, December 21, 1927, Archives of the History of American Psychology, Akron, Ohio, Jean Mater Mandler and George Mandler Papers [hereafter Mandler Papers].

(26) Frederick H. Lund, "The Phantom of the Gestalt," *Journal of General Psychology,* 2 (1929): 307–23; F. M. Gregg, "Materializing the Ghost of Köhler's Gestalt Psychology," *Psychological Review,* 39 (1932): 257–70; and Edna Heidbreder, *Seven Psychologies* (New York: Appleton-Century-Crofts, 1933). Also see William McDougall, "Dynamics of Gestalt Psychology," *Character and Personality,* 4 (1930): 232–44, 319–34; and S.C. Fisher, "A Critique of Insight in Köhler's Gestalt Psychology, 43 (1931): 131–35.

(27) Boring, *The Physical Dimensions of Consciousness* (New York, 1933); Jaynes, "Edwin Garrigues Boring"; Mary Henle, "One Man against the Nazis—Wolfgang Köhler," *American Psychologist,* 33 (1978): 939–44; and Ash, "The Struggle against the Nazis," *ibid.,* 34 (1979): 363–64.

(28) Boring to Perry, March 22, October 14, 1933, Boring Papers.

(29) Köhler to Boring, January 22, 1934; Boring to Köhler, December 7, 1933; Boring to Koffka, December 13, 1933, Boring Papers.

(30) Boring to Köhler, March 19, October 2, November 7, 1934; Boring to Perry, April 13, 1934, Boring Papers; and Boring to Jean and George Mandler, February 14, 1968, Mandler Papers.

(31) See *Journal of Philosophy,* 36 (1939) 107–08; *New York Times,* February 5, 1939, p. 6; Harry L. Hollingworth, review of Köhler's *Place of Value in a World of Facts,* in *American Journal of Psychology,* 53 (1940): 146–52; and J. R. Kantor, review of Köhler's *Place of Value in a World of Facts,* in *Psychological Bulletin,* 36 (1939): 292–96; and Köhler, *The Place of Value in a World of Facts* (New York, 1938).

(32) Boring to Leonard Carmichael, [December 20, 1934]; Carmichael to Boring, December 15, December 22, 1934, American Philosophical Society Library, Philadelphia, Leonard Carmichael Papers.

(33) Boring, *Psychologist at Large,* 53–54; and Jaynes, "Edwin Garrigues Boring," 107. Also see Boring and Hanns Sachs, "Was This Analysis a Success?" *Journal of Abnormal and Social Psychology,* 35 (1940): 4–16.

(34) Boring to Terman, March 27, 1928, Terman Papers; and Frank A. Beach, "Karl Spencer Lashley," in National Academy of Sciences *Biographical Memoirs, 35* (1961): 163–204.

(35) Harry Helson to Jean and George Mandler, February 27, 1968, Mandler Papers; Boring to Perry, November 28, 1933; Perry to Boring, October 28, December 1, 1933, Boring Papers; and Jaynes, "Edwin Garrigues Boring," 107.

(36) Boring to Terman, March 7, 1947, Terman Papers; and Boring to Jean and George Mandler, February 14, 1968, Mandler Papers.

(37) Stanley Coben, "The Scientific Establishment and the Transmission of Quantum Mechanics to the United States, 1919–32," *AHR,* 76 (1971): 442–66.

(38) Several distinguished scholars will disagree with most of these conclusions and have, in fact, drawn others directly opposed to them. For example, see Mary Henle, "The Influence of Gestalt Psychology in America," in R. W. Reiber and Kurt Salzinger, eds., *The Roots of American Psychology: Historical Influences and Implications for the Future* (New York, 1977), 3–12.

CHAPTER **15**

THE BEGINNINGS OF AMERICAN APPLIED PSYCHOLOGY

In the United States today, most psychologists work as applied psychologists in schools, hospitals, businesses, government agencies, and in private practice. Yet, it is clear from the previous chapters that psychology did not start out that way. This chapter tells the story of how American psychology moved from doing experiments in the university laboratory to solving the problems of everyday life.

Psychology, including applied psychology, benefited enormously by the changing American social fabric at the turn of the century. Historian Frederick Jackson Turner (1893) wrote that the end of the first period of American history was marked in 1890 by the disappearance of an American frontier. What followed in the next three decades was unprecedented in terms of social upheaval: the growth of industrialization, vast new waves of immigration, growth of the cities, and accelerated demands on public education, including laws of compulsory education. It is easy to imagine the psychological consequences of such rapid social change.

The end of the frontier meant an end to an important American concept, that of "pioneer individualism." Government recognized the conflicts between the practice of individual liberties and the cooperative demands of society. And laws were passed to limit individual and corporate freedoms. This social metamorphosis demanded an understanding of the nature of mind, particularly of individual differences, and an applied science capable of solving the problems inherent in such social upheaval. Psychology's time had come, and there were those ready to pursue the promise of their new science. Regarding this transformation, historian Donald Napoli (1981) wrote that:

> Applied psychology was primarily an urban phenomenon. Most of the practitioners lived in the cities, and the problems they addressed—delinquency, unassimilated immigrants, nonconforming school children—were largely urban problems. . . . [With] the formation of large industrial empires . . . came new management problems and a growing preoccupation with efficiency. Applied psychologists, with their widening variety of psychological tests, provided a timely management tool that attracted attention among the leaders of some of America's largest corporations. . . . [And the growth of power in the federal government, allowing the military] to measure the psyches of its recruits, gave applied psychology a potent impetus that it could have received no other way. (p. 28)

American psychology, imported largely from Germany and Britain in the late 1800s, became preeminent in the world by the 1920s. Arguably, that preeminence was deserved. Although deficient in theoretical accomplishments, American psychology enjoyed huge successes in methodological achievements and particularly in the realm of applied science. One of the principal myths about the history of American psychology is that applied psychology began following the First World War. But nothing could be farther from the truth. In its worst form, this mythical tale alleges that American psychologists remained true to the laboratory, but when they were called to military duty during World War I, they were required to apply their psychology to the solution of military problems, realized that they enjoyed the applied work, and then founded an applied psychology that made them happy ever after. In fact, American psychology is, and always has been, characterized by application, and not by just applied research, but by application in terms of consultation and practice.

The need for psychological services is much older than the new scientific psychology. Fifty years earlier, in the mid-nineteenth century, American phrenologists had been much in demand as mental testers, evaluating cranial shapes to advise companies on hiring and promoting, to advise individuals on the selecting of mates for marriage, and to identify individuals suited for the teaching profession. In 1890, James McKeen Cattell coined the term *mental test* and began the development of a series of such tests, many of which would be used in applied work. Thus mental testing tools of the beginning twentieth-century psychologists were new, but the objectives were much the same as they had been for the American phrenologists.

While the paint on the laboratory walls was still drying, American psychologists were applying their new science to the problems of their world. You may recall from Chapter 8 that G. Stanley Hall sought to use psychology to improve education. He wrote, in 1894 that "The one chief and immediate field of application for all this work [psychology] is its application to education" (Hall, p. 718). And it was through the child study movement that Hall pursued his agenda in educational psychology, attempting to learn all there was to know about children in order to improve the training of teachers and the pedagogical strategies used in the classroom.

At the same time that Hall was promoting the study of children, Lightner Witmer (1867–1956) was also showing interest in the educational problems of children. Witmer (who was mentioned briefly in Chapter 5) had studied with Cattell and then had gone to Leipzig where he received his doctorate from Wundt in 1892. After graduation, Witmer returned to his native city of Philadelphia to head the psychology program at the University of Pennsylvania, which Cattell had abandoned a year earlier to take charge of the department at Columbia University (McReynolds, 1987).

Witmer had shown an interest in problems associated with learning as early as 1889 when he studied with Cattell, and he continued that interest on his return to Pennsylvania. Then in March, 1896, an event took place that changed Witmer's career and the nature of applied psychology. A local school teacher brought a 14-year-old boy to see Witmer. The boy was described as a bad speller, and the teacher reasoned that if psychology was truly the science of the mind, then it ought to be able to deal with a problem of that sort. Witmer did deal with it successfully, and that case led to his founding the first psychological clinic in America, indeed, perhaps the first psychological clinic anywhere in the world. Later that year, Witmer addressed the American Psychological Association about the possibilities of using psychology to solve learning difficulties in school children.

The clinic grew, slowly at first, and Witmer handled much of the caseload himself. After a decade of this work, he felt the need for a journal to publish reports on the kinds of cases he was seeing in the clinic. Thus *The Psychological Clinic* was founded in 1907, with Witmer as editor (more about this later). The initial article in that journal was entitled "Clinical Psychology," and in it, Witmer named a new field of applied psychology that he called by the same name. As the clinic continued its growth, specialty clinics were added, first on speech defects in 1914, and then on vocational and industrial guidance in 1920. The idea of psychology clinics caught on elsewhere, and by 1914, there were nineteen university-based clinics in the United States, all involving psychologists.

Today, Witmer's pioneering achievement has earned him recognition as the founder of clinical psychology. (See the March, 1996, issue of the *American Psychologist* for a special section of articles honoring the centennial of Witmer's psychological clinic.) In fact, Witmer's early work is quite similar to the kinds of problems dealt with by school psychologists today, and for that reason, he is also usually labeled the founder of school psychology (see Baker, 1988; Fagan, 1992). Clearly, his work anticipated two of the largest applied specialties in contemporary psychology.

Shortly after Hall and others began to apply psychology to education, and Witmer and others began to apply psychology to the amelioration of learning and behavioral problems, still other psychologists decided that psychology was relevant to the business community. From this effort evolved a field initially called business psychology and later named industrial psychology. One of the first psychologists to apply psychology to the problems of business was Walter Dill Scott (1869–1955), who, like Witmer, had earned his doctorate with Wundt in 1900.

Scott, who was on the faculty of Northwestern University, began his career in applied psychology with a lecture he gave at a meeting of advertising executives in Chicago in late 1901. One of those in attendance was John L. Mahin, head of a major Chicago advertising agency. He was intrigued by Scott's remarks and met with him later to discuss the potential contribution of psychology to advertising. Mahin offered to start publication of a magazine on advertising if Scott would write a series of twelve articles on psychology for that publication. Scott agreed, and the magazine, *Mahin's Magazine,* began monthly publication in 1902, with Mahin's promise to his readers to work toward developing advertising as an exact science. Scott's initial contribution was a brief discussion of the laws of association of ideas: habit, recency, vividness (Scott, 1902).

The article on association was followed by others on suggestion, on the direct command as a form of argumentation, on the psychological value of the return coupon, on perception and apperception, on illusions, and on individual differences in mental imagery (Ferguson, 1962). Only one of those contributions—a study on the legibility of typefaces of timetables for the Burlington Railroad—was based on any research by Scott. The majority were grounded in his own armchair theorizing, which seemed to appeal to Mahin and his readers. Those dozen articles from *Mahin's Magazine* were republished as Scott's first book, *The Theory of Advertising* (1903). Scott's contributions were quite popular, and Mahin convinced him to continue his articles. Scott wrote another twenty-one articles through the end of 1904, and these were collected in a second book, *The Psychology of Advertising* (1908).

By 1905, Scott was engaged in some applied research, mostly investigating practical problems supplied to him by businesses that were willing to pay for the research to be done. Yet most of the articles he was writing were not based on any of his research. The content represented quite accurately the current knowledge base in psychology, but the applications to advertising were largely speculative. In engaging in such speculation, Scott was not alone among his psychologist colleagues. He stayed active in business psychology, publishing two more books in 1911: *Increasing Human Efficiency in Business* and *Influencing Men in Business.*

Scott was not the only psychologist lured into the business world. Another Wundt doctorate, Hugo Münsterberg (1863–1916), was brought by William James from Germany to Harvard University to head Harvard's psychology laboratory. Münsterberg was a psychologist with wide-ranging interests who wrote on a number of applied topics, including the psychology of motion pictures, psychotherapy, the psychology of teaching, and the psychology of the courtroom. He published on business psychology as early as 1909 with an article on psychology in the marketplace, but his most important work would appear four years later, a book entitled *Psychology and Industrial Efficiency* (1913). You may recall from the quotation from Donald Napoli earlier in this chapter that early twentieth-century America was preoccupied with efficiency. Thus it is no accident that it was the subject of books by both Scott and Münsterberg. Efficiency meant more effective advertising, better training of workers, more scientific management, improved employee selection procedures, better accounting methods, and better ways to control the performance of workers and the quality of their output. One of Münsterberg's chief interests was in matching worker abilities to the requirements of the job. He argued that when job and worker were matched, an employer got a very satisfied employee and a good work output. And psychology, he believed, had the tools (for example, mental tests) to help create that perfect match by determining the mental traits required for any job.

Münsterberg's 1913 book was exceptionally popular, even appearing, for a short time, on the best-seller list for nonfiction (Hale, 1980). His focus on hiring and training the best worker, to do the best work, with the best possible outcome (the three principal subheads in his book) established Münsterberg as the leading authority on the psychology of efficiency in the workplace. The book is of such historical significance that several historians have named Münsterberg the founder of industrial psychology even though others were working in the field before he arrived.

Another of the important pioneers in applied psychology is Harry Hollingworth (1880–1956). Hollingworth completed his doctorate with Cattell at Columbia University in 1909 and spent his career as a professor at Columbia's Barnard College. His career in applied work began with a night class he taught in Columbia's Extension Division. The course was attended mostly by businesspeople, and so Hollingworth lectured about the relevance of psychological science to business, especially advertising. The contacts he made through the class resulted in his giving a series of lectures in 1910 to the Advertising Men's League of New York City, which led to his 1913 book entitled *Advertising and Selling*. Like Münsterberg, Hollingworth's applied interests were wide ranging, and in his career as an applied psychologist, he published books on educational psychology, clinical psychology, vocational psychology, and the psychology of public speaking. Yet the work that seemed to set him on his course as an applied psychologist was a study that he undertook for the Coca-Cola Company in 1911 to determine the effects of caffeine on human behavior and cognitive processes. At the time of the research, Coca-Cola was being sued by the federal government for marketing an adulterated beverage with a deleterious ingredient, namely caffeine. Coca-Cola hoped that Hollingworth's research could be used in the trial to show that caffeine was harmless. The outcome of that trial is discussed in one of the readings in this chapter.

This brief introduction has presented some of the principal figures in the history of applied psychology. They are not the whole story, but through their work, you should get a good picture of how psychology moved from the laboratory to the real world in the early part of the twentieth century. These individuals founded a profession of psychology that ultimately enjoyed successes that likely far exceeded even the greatest expectations of these pioneers.

THE READINGS

The first selection is by Lightner Witmer and is the inaugural article in his journal on clinical psychology. It is in this article that he names the field of clinical psychology, discusses some of the cases in his own clinic, and provides a description of how psychologists could be trained to function in clinical work.

The second selection, by historian John M. O'Donnell, is an analysis of Witmer's clinical work in the context of turn-of-the-century American culture and the psychology of that time. It is an example of excellent external history. O'Donnell is critical of contemporary psychologists who have argued for a minimal role for Witmer, claiming that Witmer failed to anticipate the current nature of clinical psychology. O'Donnell shows why these critics have misunderstood the critical role that Witmer played in the development of applied psychology.

The third selection is by Hugo Münsterberg and is from his 1913 book *Psychology and Industrial Efficiency*. The excerpt begins with a section from the book's introduction in which he talks about the importance of applied psychology. It is followed by a later section in the book that deals with Münsterberg's study of trolley operators (motormen) for the Boston Elevated Railway Company. The company was in trouble because the trolley drivers had been in a number of fatal accidents involving pedestrians. Münsterberg was hired in the spring of 1912 to develop a test that would allow the company to weed out those drivers who were accident-prone. His account of this research project is an excellent example of the early studies of business psychology.

The final selection, by Ludy T. Benjamin, Jr., Anne M. Rogers, and Angela Rosenbaum, is a historical treatment of Harry Hollingworth's caffeine studies and the Coca-Cola trials. The story is an inherently interesting one, as many trials are. But the subject of the story is also important in raising several issues that psychologists faced in doing applied work, such as the stigma of applied work, the use of research results in advertising, and the pressure to produce results that would be in line with the needs of the corporate sponsor of the research. Hollingworth's caffeine studies were a model of good applied research, and the quality of those studies continues to be recognized today.

REFERENCES

Baker, D. B. (1988). The psychology of Lightner Witmer. *Professional School Psychology, 3,* 109–121.

Fagan, T. K. (1992). Compulsory schooling, child study, clinical psychology, and special education: Origins of school psychology. *American Psychologist, 47,* 236–243.

Ferguson, L. (1962). *The heritage of industrial psychology: Walter Dill Scott, first industrial psychologist.* Privately printed.

Hale, Jr., M. (1980). *Human science and social order: Hugo Münsterberg and the origins of applied psychology.* Philadelphia: Temple University Press.

Hall, G. S. (1894, August). The new psychology as a basis of education. *Forum,* pp. 710–720.

Hollingworth, H. L. (1913). *Advertising and selling: Principles of appeal and response.* New York: D. Appleton and Co.

McReynolds, P. (1987). Lightner Witmer: Little-known founder of clinical psychology. *American Psychologist, 42,* 849–858.

Münsterberg, H. (1913). *Psychology and industrial efficiency*. Boston: Houghton Mifflin.
Napoli, D. S. (1981). *Architects of adjustment: The history of the psychological profession in the United States*. Port Washington, NY: Kennikat Press.
Scott, W. D. (1902). Association of ideas. *Mahin's Magazine, 1,* 10–13.
Scott, W. D. (1903). *The theory of advertising*. Boston: Small, Maynard & Co.
Scott, W. D. (1908). *The psychology of advertising*. Boston: Small, Maynard & Co.
Scott, W. D. (1911). *Increasing human efficiency in business*. New York: Macmillan.
Scott, W. D. (1911). *Influencing men in business*. New York: Ronald Press.
Turner, F. J. (1893). The significance of the frontier in American history. *Report of the American Historical Association,* pp. 199–227.
Witmer, L. (1907). Clinical psychology. *The Psychological Clinic, 1,* 1–9.

Clinical Psychology

Lightner Witmer

During the last ten years the laboratory of psychology at the University of Pennsylvania has conducted, under my direction, what I have called "a psychological clinic." Children from the public schools of Philadelphia and adjacent cities have been brought to the laboratory by parents or teachers; these children had made themselves conspicuous because of an inability to progress in school work as rapidly as other children, or because of moral defects which rendered them difficult to manage under ordinary discipline.

When brought to the psychological clinic, such children are given a physical and mental examination; if the result of this examination shows it to be desirable, they are then sent to specialists for the eye or ear, for the nose and throat, and for nervous diseases, one or all, as each case may require. The result of this conjoint medical and psychological examination is a diagnosis of the child's mental and physical condition and the recommendation of appropriate medical and pedagogical treatment. The progress of some of these children has been followed for a term of years.

To illustrate the operation of the psychological clinic, take a recent case sent to the laboratory from a city of Pennsylvania, not far from Philadelphia. The child was brought by his parents, on the recommendation of the Superintendent of Schools. Examination revealed a boy ten years of age, without apparent physical defect, who had spent four years at school, but had made so little progress that his ignorance of the printed symbols of the alphabet made it necessary to use the illiterate card to test his vision. Nothing in the child's heredity or early history revealed any ground for the suspicion of degeneracy, nor did the child's physical appearance warrant this diagnosis. The boy appeared to be of normal intelligence, except for the retardation in school work. The examination of the neurologist to whom he was sent, Dr. William G. Spiller, confirmed the absence of conspicuous mental degeneracy and of physical defect. The oculist, Dr. William C. Posey, found nothing more serious than a slight far-sighted astigmatism, and the examination of Dr. George C. Stout for adenoids, gave the child a clean bill of health, so far as the nose and pharynx were concerned. On the conclusion of this examination he was, necessarily, returned to the school from which he came, with the recommendation to the teacher of a course of treatment to develop the child's intelligence. It will require at least three months' observation to determine whether his present pedagogical retardation is based upon a arrest of cerebral development or is merely the result of inadequate methods of education. This case is unequivocally one for the psychologist.

My attention was first drawn to the phenomena of retardation in the year 1889. At that time, while a student of psychology at the University of Pennsylvania, I had charge of the English branches in a college preparatory school of Philadelphia. In my classes at this academy I was called upon to give instruction in English to a boy preparing for entrance to college, who showed a remarkable deficiency in the English language. His compositions seldom contained a single sentence that had been correctly formed. For example, there was little or no distinction between the present and the past tenses of verbs; the endings of many words were clipped off, and this was especially noticeable in those words in which a final ending distinguished the plural from the singular, or an adverb from an adjective. As it seemed doubtful whether he would ever be able to enter college without special instruction in English, I was engaged to tutor him in the English branches.

Witmer, L. (1907). Clinical psychology. *The Psychological Clinic, 1,* 1–9.

I had no sooner undertaken this work than I saw the necessity of beginning with the elements of language and teaching him as one would teach a boy, say, in the third grade. Before long I discovered that I must start still further back. I had found it impossible, through oral and written exercises, to fix in his mind the elementary forms of words as parts of speech in a sentence. This seemed to be owing to the fact that he had verbal deafness. He was quite able to hear even a faint sound, like the ticking of a watch, but he could not hear the difference in the sound of such words as *grasp* and *grasped*. This verbal deafness was associated with, and I now believe was probably caused by, a defect of articulation. Thus the boy's written language was a fairly exact replica of his spoken language; and he probably heard the words that others spoke as he himself spoke them. I therefore undertook to give him an elementary training in articulation to remedy the defects which are ordinarily corrected, through imitation, by the time a child is three or four years old. I gave practically no attention to the subjects required in English for college entrance, spending all my time on the drill in articulation and in perfecting his verbal audition and teaching him the simplest elements of written language. The result was a great improvement in all his written work, and he succeeded in entering the college department of the University of Pennsylvania in the following year.

In 1894–1895, I found him as a college student in my classes at the University of Pennsylvania. His articulation, his written discourse and his verbal audition were very deficient for a boy of his years. In consequence he was unable to acquire the technical terminology of my branch, and I have no doubt that he passed very few examinations excepting through the sympathy of his instructors who overlooked the serious imperfections of his written work, owing to the fact that he was in other respects a fair student. When it came to the final examinations for the bachelor's degree, however, he failed and was compelled to repeat much of the work of his senior year. He subsequently entered and graduated from one of the professional departments of the University. His deficiencies in language I believe, have never been entirely overcome.

I felt very keenly how much this boy was losing through his speech defect. His school work, his college course, and doubtless his professional career were all seriously hampered. I was confident at the time, and this confidence has been justified by subsequent experience with similar cases, that if he had been given adequate instruction in articulation in the early years of childhood, he could have overcome his defect. With the improvement in articulation there would have come an improved power of apprehending spoken and written language. That nothing was done for him in the early years, nor indeed at any time, excepting for the brief period of private instruction in English and some lessons in elocution, is remarkable, for the speech defect was primarily owing to an injury to the head in the second year of life, and his father was a physician who might have been expected to appreciate the necessity of special training in a case of retardation caused by a brain injury.

The second case to attract my interest was a boy fourteen years of age, who was brought to the laboratory of psychology by his grade teacher. He was one of those children of great interest to the teacher, known to the profession as a chronic bad speller. His teacher, Miss Margaret T. Maguire, now the supervising principal of a grammar school of Philadelphia, was at the time a student of psychology at the University of Pennsylvania; she was imbued with the idea that a psychologist should be able, through examination, to ascertain the causes of a deficiency in spelling and to recommend the appropriate pedagogical treatment for its amelioration or cure.

With this case, in March, 1896, the work of the psychological clinic was begun. At that time I could not find that the science of psychology had ever addressed itself to the ascertainment of the causes and treatment of a deficiency in spelling. Yet here was a simple developmental defect of memory; and memory is a mental process of which the science of psychology is supposed to furnish the only authoritative knowledge. It appeared to me that if psychology was worth anything to me or to others it should be able to assist the efforts of a teacher in a retarded case of this kind.

"The final test of the value of what is called science is its applicability" are words quoted from the recent address of the President of the American Association for the Advancement of Science. With Huxley and President Woodward, I believe that there is no valid distinction between a pure science and an applied science. The practical needs of the astronomer to eliminate the personal equation from his observations led to the invention of the chronograph and the chronoscope. Without these two instruments, modern psychology and physiology could not possibly have achieved the results of the last fifty years. If Helmholtz had not made the chronograph an instrument of precision in physiology and psychology; if Fechner had not lifted a weight to determine the threshold of sensory discrimination, the field of scientific work represented to-day by clinical psychology could never have been developed. The pure and the applied sciences advance in a single front. What retards the progress of one, retards the progress of the other; what fosters one, fosters the other. But in the final analysis the progress of psychology, as of every other science, will be determined by the value and amount of its contributions to the advancement of the human race.

The absence of any principles to guide me made it necessary to apply myself directly to the study of these children, working out my methods as I went along. In the spring of 1896 I saw several other cases of children suffering from the retardation of some special function, like that of spelling, or from general retardation, and I undertook the training of these children for a certain number of hours each week. Since that time the psychological clinic has been regularly conducted in connection with the laboratory of psychology at the University of Pennsylvania. The study of these cases has also formed a regular part of the instruction offered to students in child psychology.

In December, 1896, I outlined in an address delivered before the American Psychological Association a scheme of practical work in psychology. The proposed plan of organization comprised:

1. The investigation of the phenomena of mental development in school children, as manifested more particularly in mental and moral retardation, by means of the statistical and clinical methods.

2. A psychological clinic, supplemented by a training school in the nature of a hospital school, for the treatment of all classes of children suffering from retardation or physical defects interfering with school progress.

3. The offering of practical work to those engaged in the professions of teaching and medicine, and to those interested in social work, in the observation and training of normal and retarded children.

4. The training of students for a new profession—that of the psychological expert, who should find his career in connection with the school system, through the examination and treatment of mentally and morally retarded children, or in connection with the practice of medicine.

In the summer of 1897 the department of psychology in the University of Pennsylvania was able to put the larger part of this plan into operation. A four weeks' course was given under the auspices of the American Society for the Extension of University Teaching. In addition to lecture and laboratory courses in experimental and physiological psychology, a course in child psychology was given to demonstrate the various methods of child psychology, but especially the clinical method. The psychological clinic was conducted daily, and a training school was in operation in which a number of children were under the daily instruction of Miss Mary E. Marvin. At the clinic, cases were presented of children suffering from defects of the eye, the ear, deficiency in motor ability, or in memory and attention; and in the training school, children were taught throughout the session of the Summer School, receiving pedagogical treatment for the cure of stammering and other speech defects, for defects of written language (such as bad spelling), and for motor defects.

From that time until the present I have continued the examination and treatment of children in the psychological clinic. The number of cases seen each week has been limited, because the means were not at hand for satisfactorily treating a large number of cases. I felt, also, that before offering to treat these children on a large scale I needed some years of experience and extensive study, which could only be obtained through the prolonged observation of a few cases. Above all, I appreciated the great necessity of training a group of students upon whose assistance I could rely. The time has now come for a wider development of this work. To further this object and to provide for the adequate publication of the results that are being obtained in this new field of psychological investigation, it was determined to found this journal, *The Psychological Clinic*.

My own preparation for the work has been facilitated through my connection as consulting psychologist with the Pennsylvania Training School for Feeble-Minded Children at Elwyn, and a similar connection with the Haddonfield Training School and Miss Marvin's Home School in West Philadelphia.

Clinical psychology is naturally very closely related to medicine. At the very beginning of my work I was much encouraged by the appreciation of the late Provost of the University of Pennsylvania, Dr. William Pepper, who at one time proposed to establish a psychological laboratory in connection with the William Pepper Clinical Laboratory of Medicine. At his suggestion, psychology was made an elective branch in what was then the newly organized fourth year of the course in medicine. At a subsequent reorganization of the medical course, however, it was found necessary to drop the subject from the curriculum.

I also desire to acknowledge my obligation to Dr. S. Weir Mitchell for co-operation in the examination of a number of cases and for his constant interest in this line of investigation. I have also enjoyed the similar co-operation of Dr. Charles K. Mills, Dr. William G. Spiller, the late Dr. Harrison Allen, Dr. Alfred Stengel, Dr. William Campbell Posey, Dr. George C. Stout, and Dr. Joseph Collins, of New York. Dr. Collins will continue this co-operation as an associate editor of *The Psychological Clinic*.

The appreciation of the relation of psychology to the practice of medicine in general, and to psychiatry in particular, has been of slow growth. The first intelligent treatment of the insane was accorded by Pinel in the latter part of the eighteenth century, a century that was marked by the rapid development of the science of psychology, and which brought forth the work of Pereire in teaching oral speech to the deaf, and the "Emile" of Rousseau. A few medical men have had a natural aptitude for psychological analysis. From them has come the chief development of the medical aspects of psychology,—from Seguin and Charcot in France, Carpenter and Mandsley in England, and Weir Mitchell in this country. Psychological insight will carry the physician or teacher far on the road to professional achievement, but at the present day the necessity for a more definite acquaintance with psychological method and facts is strongly felt. It is noteworthy that perhaps the most prominent name connected with psychiatry to-day is that of Kraepelin, who was among the first to seek the training in experimental psychology afforded by the newly established laboratory at Leipzig.

Although clinical psychology is closely related to medicine, it is quite as closely related to sociology and to pedagogy. The school room, the juvenile court, and the streets are a larger laboratory of psychology. An abundance of material for scientific study fails to be utilized, because the interest of psychologists is elsewhere engaged, and those in constant touch with the actual phenomena do not possess the training necessary to make their experience and observation of scientific value.

While the field of clinical psychology is to some extent occupied by the physician, especially by the psychiatrist, and while I expect to rely in a great measure upon the educator and social worker for the more important contributions to this branch of psychology, it is nevertheless true that none of these has quite the training necessary for this kind of work. For that matter, neither has the psychologist, unless he has acquired this training from other sources than the usual course of instruction in psychology. In fact, we must look forward to the training of men to a new profession which will be exercised more particularly in connection with educational problems, but for which the training of the psychologist will be prerequisite.

For this reason not a small part of the work of the laboratory of psychology in the University of Pennsylvania for the past ten years has been devoted to the training of students in child psychology, and especially in the clinical method. The greater number of these students have been actively engaged in the profession of teaching. Important contributions to psychology and pedagogy, the publication of which in the form of monographs has already been begun, will serve to demonstrate that original research of value can be carried on by those who are actively engaged in educational or other professional work. There have been associated in this work of the laboratory of psychology, Superintendent Twitmyer, of Wilmington; Superintendent Bryan, of Camden; District Superintendent Cornman, of Philadelphia; Mr. J. M. McCallie, Supervising Principal of the Trenton Schools; Mr. Edward A. Huntington, Principal of a Special School in Philadelphia; Miss Clara H. Town, Resident Psychologist at the Friends' Asylum for the Insane, and a number of special teachers for the blind, the deaf, and mentally deficient children. I did not venture to begin the publication of this journal until I felt assured of the assistance of a number of fellow-workers in clinical psychology as contributors to the journal. As this work has grown up in the neighborhood of Philadelphia, it is probable that a greater number of students, equipped to carry on the work of clinical psychology, may be found in this neighborhood than elsewhere, but it is hoped that this journal will have a wider influence, and that the co-operation of those who are developing clinical psychology throughout the country will be extended the journal.

The phraseology of "clinical psychology" and "psychological clinic" will doubtless strike many as an odd juxtaposition of terms relating to quite disparate subjects. While the term "clinical" has been borrowed from medicine, clinical psychology is not a medical psychology. I have borrowed the word "clinical" from medicine, because it is the best term I can find to indicate the character of the method which I deem necessary for this work. Words seldom retain their original significance, and clinical medicine, is not what the word implies,—the work of a practicing physician at the bedside of a patient. The term "clinical" implies a method, and not a locality. When the clinical method in medicine was established on a scientific basis, mainly through the efforts of Boerhaave at the University of Leiden, its development came in response to a revolt against the philosophical and didactic methods that more or less dominated medicine up to that time. Clinical psychology likewise is a protestant against a psychology that derives psychological and pedagogical principles from philosophical speculations and against a psychology that applies the results of laboratory experimentation directly to children in the school room.

The teacher's interest is and should be directed to the subjects which comprise the curriculum, and which he wishes to impress upon the minds of the children assigned to his care. It is not what *the child is,* but *what he should be taught,* that occupies the center of his attention. Pedagogy is primarily devoted to mass instruction, that is, teaching the subjects of the curriculum to classes of children without reference to the individual differences presented by the members of a class. The clinical psychologist is interested primarily in the individual child. As the physician examines his patient and proposes treatment with a definite purpose in view, namely the patient's cure, so the clinical psychologist examines a child with a single definite object in view,—the next step in the child's mental and physical development. It is here that the relation between science and practice becomes worthy of discrimination. The physician *may* have solely in mind the cure of his patient, but if he is to be more than a mere practitioner and to contribute to the advance of medicine, he will look upon his efforts as an experiment, every feature of which must indeed have a definite purpose—the cure of the patient—but he will study every favorable or unfavorable reaction of the patient with reference to the patient's previous condition and the remedial agents he has employed. In the same way the purpose of the clinical psychologist, as a contributor to science, is to discover the relation between cause and effect in applying the various pedagogical remedies to a child who is suffering from general or special retardation.

I would not have it thought that the method of clinical psychology is limited necessarily to mentally and morally retarded children. These children are not, properly speaking, abnormal, nor is the condition of many of them to be designated as in any way pathological. They deviate from the average of children only in being at a lower stage of individual development. Clinical psychology, therefore, does not exclude from consideration other types of children that deviate from the average—for example, the precocious child and the genius. Indeed, the clinical method is applicable even to the so-called normal child. For the methods of clinical psychology are necessarily invoked wherever the status of an individual mind is determined by observation and experiment, and pedagogical treatment applied to effect a change, *i.e.,* the development of such individual mind. Whether the subject be a child or an adult, the examination and treatment may be conducted and their results expressed in the terms of the clinical method.

The Clinical Psychology of Lightner Witmer: A Case Study of Institutional Innovation and Intellectual Change

John M. O'Donnell

In his 1895 presidential address to the American Psychological Association, James McKeen Cattell announced, "In the struggle for existence that obtains among the sciences psychology is continually gaining ground." The purpose of this nascent organization inhered in what Cattell perceived to be its precocious achievement: "This Association demonstrates the organic unity of psychology, while the wide range of our individual interests proves our adjustment to a complex environment."[1] Seated in the Philadelphia audience was one of Cattell's former students, Lightner Witmer. "One of the all-but-forgotten names in American psychology,"[2]

O'Donnell, J. M. (1979). The clinical psychology of Lightner Witmer: A case study of institutional innovation and intellectual change. *Journal of the History of the Behavioral Sciences, 15,* 3–17.

Witmer was shortly to exhibit one aspect of its wide-ranging interests by founding the world's first psychological clinic. His anonymity reinforces the appropriateness of Cattell's Darwinian rhetoric, and the extinction of Witmer's clinical species provokes inquiry into the complexity of American psychology's intellectual, social, and professional environment.

Unfortunately, such complexity is often oversimplified by evolutionary assumptions implicit in disciplinary history.[3] In historiography as in nature, the fittest seem tautologically to survive and, therefore, to merit recognition. Consequently, Witmer, one of the earliest proponents of utilitarian psychology, has attracted little historical attention because institutionally his efforts were ultimately unsuccessful. His career seems negligible because he remained outside his disciplinary elite, failed to create a role that perpetuated itself, and created no coherent intellectual system.[4]

History usually attends the victor. Hence, psychologist-historians who have attempted to elucidate their field's scientific and theoretical consistency have relegated Witmer to the periphery of psychology's development. And from their perspective rightly so. Opposed to what he considered the sterility of "brass instrument psychology," Witmer emerges in the words of a recent intellectual historian as "a voice crying in the wilderness."[5] Similarly, modern-day clinicians, seeking historical validation for their contemporary scientific procedures and professional styles, have treated Witmer in more breadth but with more disparagement, for the intellectual tributaries that formed clinical psychology in fact did not flow through his terrain.[6] These disciplinary chroniclers have deprecated Witmer for his failure to achieve for psychology professional hegemony over the "problem child." The fact that the original applications of experimental and scientific psychology to the mental and behavioral problems of individuals were eventually subsumed under a more general medical and psychiatric point of view has led to a repudiation of clinical psychology's progenitor. Thus, David Shakow concludes that "Witmer failed to make the contributions which he was in such a strategic position to make, with the result that clinical psychology passed him by."[7]

In fact, Witmer was in no such strategic position and must therefore be excused for not charting the ideal course so apparent to those blessed with 20-20 hindsight. Yet the chief concern of this article is not to restore Witmer to the position of initiator of all that followed. Nor is it my intention to exonerate him of deficiencies of intellectual and professional imagination. What I wish to suggest is that ventures which in Joseph Ben David's phrase fail to "take off" constitute extremely illuminating historical indicators of a discipline's shifting ideas, styles, and roles. Witmer's importance is not diminished by his inability to invest present-day psychology with adducible precedent. Failure to sire a fertile lineage, in other words, does not imply lack of contemporary relevance. To the contrary, precocious subgroups of larger disciplines—social manifestations of what Cattell called "our individual interests"—should become loci of investigation for historians seeking to uncover the process of intellectual change. Efforts to explain the decline of evolutionary naturalism or the demise of recapitulation theory within psychology through the explication of textbooks and theoretical tracts describe change rather than explain it.[8] Cross-disciplinary efforts to account for oscillating psychologistic tendencies toward hereditary and environment by invoking innovations in biological theory often overlook the fact that psychologists usually enlisted biology to validate a point of view rather than to inform it. Furthermore, such historical procedure merely shifts the ultimate burden of explanation to a neighboring discipline.

By examining in more detail subgroups of larger disciplines, one often finds that new trends are not created by new ideas but rather by a growing conviction that old ideas can be put to new uses. This depends not so much upon the implementation of new thought as upon the creation of innovative roles—products of social demands, professional opportunities, and economic exigencies.[9] Precisely at this point intellectual history becomes social history. In the case of clinical psychology, the conscription of extant scientific ideas and procedures in behalf of diagnosing and treating children with what we would nowadays label learning disabilities led to the formulation of novel problems, the solutions of which required the development of new viewpoints and the discarding of old theories. This process does not imply that older theories were necessarily disproved; rather they simply became irrelevant to tasks at hand. Paradigms need not be destroyed in order to become defunct.

One final disavowal. This article makes no attempt to deal with the fascinating social aspects of what may be called the "mainstream" of clinical psychology's professional development. Simultaneously with Witmer's creation there arose a tradition in clinical treatment centered around concepts of mental illness, sponsored by individuals often possessing both medical and psychological training, and located within hospitals, medical schools, and state asylums.[10] Modern clinical and consulting psychology emerged from this latter tradition, whereas Witmer's interests evolved into the comparatively low-status school psychology and remedial education. Much of the historical polemic that surveys the growth of clinical psychology involves criticisms of Witmer for his excessive reliance on psychometrics, his unreceptivity toward dynamic trends in psychiatry, and his consequent failure to treat the conative and affective aspects of the child's personality and behavior.[11] On the positive side, however, Witmer's establishment of a novel social function—the "restoration" of the "retarded" school child—discloses to the historian early tendencies within academic psychology which subsequently informed other areas of pure and applied endeavor: a growing environmentalism, a quest to make psychology serviceable, an increasing skepticism of the value of intelligence tests, the growing disenchantment with genetic psychology, and an emphasis on psychology as the study of behavior.[12] These tendencies became important trends, and Witmer's articulation of them came not so much from theoretical investigations as from two decades of clinical experience.

While a graduate student at the University of Pennsylvania, Lightner Witmer became the assistant of psychologist Cattell, who in Germany in 1883 had himself become Wilhelm Wundt's first assistant.[13] At Leipzig, Cattell applied reaction time experiments to the problem of "mental measurement." Whereas scientific psychology at the time was primarily interested in such experiments in order to provide generalizations about the normal mind, Cattell was interested in them from the point of view of individual differences. In 1888 he lectured at Cambridge, where he came in close contact with Francis Galton and the Gaussian normal distribution curve. A familiar verbalism among psychologist-historians relates Galton's interest to "the central values of this curve" while applauding Cattell's attention to the "tails."[14] In 1890 Cattell coined the term "mental test" in an article dealing with the results of his experiments upon students at Pennsylvania.[15] The following year he left Pennsylvania for Columbia and historians of psychology have, in a sense, followed him there, leaving behind the laboratory which he developed and its new director, Lightner Witmer, recently returned from Leipzig (1892) with a doctorate in psychology and an interest in individual differences. Four years later Witmer founded the first psychological clinic.

The catalytic event which prompted the birth of the Psychological Clinic came in the form of a challenge. In March 1896, a teacher in the Philadelphia public school system, Margaret Maguire, brought to Witmer's laboratory a fourteen-year-old boy described as a "chronic bad speller." The implication of Miss Maguire's challenge involved the practical assumption that if psychology were worth anything it should be able to diagnose the boy's problems. Happily, the "mental deficiency" retarding the pupil's academic progress was remediated through optometrical prescription.[16] In short, eyeglasses seemed to improve intellect. The ramifications of what might otherwise be recalled as a cute pedagogical success story were not lost upon Witmer. Within months he published an article proposing the establishment both of a practical laboratory capable of examining the physical and mental conditions of school children and also a training school for the remedial treatment of those psychologically or physiologically diagnosed as deviates or defectives.[17] In December 1896, Witmer proposed before the annual meeting of the American Psychological Association (APA) a more detailed program for "The Organization of Practical Work in Psychology."[18] Repeating the call for diagnostic laboratories and training schools, he urged, "the direct application . . . of psychological principles to therapeutics and to education." This plan involved extending instruction in psychology to doctors and teachers and demanded a closer relationship between departments of psychology and public schools, medical schools, and departments of education. The statement of one of Witmer's admirers to the effect that the professional response to his suggestion that the pure science of psychology should engage in utilitarian pursuits was a polite round of apathy underestimates the vitality of certain applied trends in psychology and the strength of various professional pressures and aspirations.[19] Had these tendencies not been present in 1896 it is doubtful that Maguire would have approached an academic psychologist with her pupil's problem.

The reasons for a growing tendency on the part of many psychologists to define for themselves utilitarian roles can only be hinted at here.[20] Backed by the reform presidents of many of the major universities,[21] reinforced by a growing professional awareness of a crisis in public education and by educator's wishes to enhance their professional status by scientizing their pursuits,[22] and recognizing the growing need to justify their own scientific endeavor in order to secure institutional and financial supports,[23] many psychologists began to see themselves as reformers and looked to the field of education as a legitimating arena and occupational haven for their expertise.[24] Inaugurated by G. Stanley Hall, the child study movement represented an early association of educators and psychologists.[25] One of Hall's foremost students, William Lowe Bryan, warned of the professional dangers of pursuing pure science unresponsive to utilitarian demand when he declared before the National Education Association in 1893, "We promise a science of conscious life. . . . But we shall be false to all our promise, and we shall turn the confidence and sympathy which has endowed chairs and built laboratories, into derision and rejection if we confine our science to a little round of testing in the laboratory."[26] Witmer shared Bryan's sensibilities but not his program. The child study movement was a relatively conservative scientific venture involving a massive empirical compilation of the results of mental tests, questionnaires, and reports from teachers and parents aimed at producing a statistical composite of the cognitive and emotional development of the normal child.[27] Upon this basis pedagogy would be reformed to coincide with the developmental sequence of the child's mental growth. Witmer, however, was concerned with children's minds, not the Mind of the Child. His more radical plan met with resistance within the APA because it prescribed to psychologists a therapeutic function which most thought premature and a role not yet legitimated for the academic scientist.[28]

Undeterred, Witmer returned to Philadelphia and established his plan of operation, conducting a summer school for the treatment of "backward children."[29] The success of this program prompted University officials in 1907, during what has been described as an "era of expansion,"[30] to enlarge the clinic. Monies were procured to inaugurate publication of a specialized journal, *The Psychological Clinic,* partially patterned after Hall's important *Pedagogical Seminary*. In 1909 the University allocated to the clinic an enlarged budget and increased physical plant, and designated it a distinct administrative unit directly responsible to the Trustees.[31]

Though the organization of the clinic expanded with increased funding, the operational format remained basically unchanged throughout its history. Children would be referred to the clinic through the school system. Following medical diagnosis, subjects would undergo anthropometric, optometric, and psychometric examination. The latter testing is particularly interesting because it illustrates ways in which old technology was adapted to new uses. Witmer converted such experimental apparatus as the chronoscope, kymograph, ergograph, and plethysmograph into diagnostic devices merely by substituting the child for the trained introspectionist. Similarly, the Seguin form board—formerly used as a pedagogical tool—was transformed into an instrument for testing a child's powers of memory, visual discrimination, and muscular coordination. Complementing psychologist and physician, the social worker would prepare a case study of the child's background. Clinical records were compiled with the threefold purpose of correlating case histories in order to produce generalizations, of standardizing tests, and of establishing new diagnostic techniques.[32] Testing completed, a final diagnosis would be made, followed by attempts at remedial treatment.

Contrary to the frequently raised charge that the founder of clinical psychology was inordinately preoccupied with narrow concerns narrowly conceived,[33] the hallmark of Witmer's approach was his catholicity. At a time when nascent social sciences and services were busy erecting boundaries about their peculiar specialties, Witmer's liberal eclecticism exhibited in his attitude toward training, organization, research, diagnosis, and remediation enabled him to interact with medical practitioners, educators, school administrators, sociologists, and social workers, and even to advocate a close connection between clinical psychology and psychiatry, psychoanalysis and anthropology.[34] Witmer's new role can be pronounced narrow only in one sense: he focused unremittingly upon the individual child and upon the possibility of his or her educational rehabilitation.[35] From such constriction of focus came breadth of approach, for an ethical element implicit in the clinical goal of effecting a cure involved a pragmatic attitude toward diagnosis and an openness to nonpsychological sources of assistance. Such openness was undoubtably facilitated by the fact that "special" teachers often possessed greater expertise in remedial matters than did the psychologist himself. Eclectic rather than experimental attitudes were required. The clinician confronted children in pedagogical disarray, not chickens in puzzle-boxes. He had neither the time nor the right to relegate some subjects to control groups for purposes of comparative analysis. Witmer's diagnostic data included, as I have mentioned, medical examinations and social case studies as well as mental tests. Often following the surgical removal of sources of physical discomfort such as impacted teeth or adenoids, the restoration of defective vision, or the improvement of the subject's environment by means of proper hygienic and dietary care, the subject would be retested in the various psychological examinations and would show marked improvement. Hence, the eclecticism implicit in Witmer's new role added a new dimension—though not yet a conclusively environmental one—to the diagnosis of the so-called feebleminded.

The implications of that new dimension for a changing psychological theory become more apparent when Witmer's approach is compared with that of his eugenically minded colleague in neighboring Vineland, H. H. Goddard. For Witmer the battery of mental examinations which he employed were, in a way "before-and-after" tests of the child's performance. For the Vineland psychologist, on the other hand, his revisions of the Binet test were strictly post hoc results. His tests were administered to groups of delinquents who, in Witmer's phrase, were already "socially diagnosed."[36] Goddard's task was merely to account for this moral delinquency by correlating criminality with low intelligence; a secondary and practical aspect of this endeavor involved the placement of delinquent individuals within institutions according to their trainability.[37] Goddard's conviction that intelligence was an hereditary unit-character explicable in terms of Mendelian genetics would appear to be substantiated as long as his testing took place—as one of Witmer's students perceptively pointed out[38]—in the relatively unchanging, regimented environment of the detention home. The antipodal social locations and antithetical social functions of their respective clinics continually reinforced Goddard's and Witmer's diametrically opposed intellectual assumptions and social perceptions.

Goddard, the Philadelphia clinician argued, dismissed the influence of environment without examining it. But despite assertions of social and intellectual historians that between 1910 and 1920 hereditarians prevailed,[39] it must be emphasized that they did so over determined opposition. In 1911, shortly before Goddard released the final results of his first testing of delinquents, Witmer, in an article pointedly entitled "Criminals in the Making," unleashed a scathing attack on the dismal implications of Goddard's approach.[40] Confronted with a case of juvenile delinquency, Witmer brought extensive medical, genealogical, and sociological evidence to bear upon and to reinforce his conclusion that his subject, the pseudononymous Harry, was "the product of his environment." Witmer's argument is of special interest since it marks his apparent acceptance of the Weismannian dualism and the consequent repudiation of Neo-Lamarckianism which, as will be later shown, was so much a part of the genetic psychology that formed the basis of his early educational theory. "Feeblemindedness, insanity, moral degeneracy," claimed Witmer,

> . . . these are doubtless in a certain proportion of cases the direct result of an inherited factor. Nevertheless, mental and moral degeneracy are just as frequently the result of the environment. In the absence of the most painstaking investigation, accompanied by a determined effort at remedial treatment, it is usually impossible to decide, when confronted by an individual case, whether heredity or environment has played the chief role. Who can improve a man's inheritance? And what man's environment can not be bettered? In the place of the hopeless fatalism of those who constantly emphasize our impotence in the presence of the hereditary factor, we prefer a hopeful optimism of those who point out the destructive activity of the environment. To ascribe a condition to the environment, is a challenge to do something for its amelioration; to ascribe it to hereditary too often means that we fold our hands and do nothing.
>
> Take for instance the belief in human depravity and criminal instincts. Public opinion, even scientific opinion, is clearly fatalistic. In this country the treatment of the criminal is still conducted with a view only to punish and segregate, scarcely ever to educate or cure.[41]

This passage has been quoted at length to illustrate the ideological flavor of Witmer's vision with its typically progressive faith in the efficacy of the environment and in the plasticity of the human being. Regardless of the *ultimate* source of this faith, it was undoubtably invigorated by fifteen years of successful remediation of children who elsewhere and on different scales of intelligence might have been diagnosed as permanently feebleminded. Likewise, it was reinforced by the vast numbers of case studies surrounding Witmer's articles in his journal, *The Psychological Clinic*.[42] Written by psychological examiners and social workers at the exact time when the genre of muckraking journalism was filling the more popular magazine, many of these short pieces were rhetorically identical (if less polished stylistically) with the offerings appearing in *McClure's Magazine,* which began its sensationalist version of literary progressivism the year before Witmer's journal began its scientific one. It is appropriate that Witmer referred to the "destructive activity of the environment" as opposed to its more salutary aspects. Social perception has a way of adjusting scientific focus.

Programmatically, Witmer's focus was still upon the individual as the proper object of psychological study and upon insistence that environmental influences must be observed before they are counted or discounted. More important, the above passage enunciates a second major purpose of clinical practice. It is to fulfill not only a remedial but a research function and so reorient public and scientific opinion away from fatalism. Witmer sought to correct both children's performance and psychological assumptions by bridging the gap between research and clinical activity. A "determined effort at remedial treatment" becomes a way of assessing the relative importance of nature and nurture identified as they seemed to be with organic and nonorganic etiologies of abnormal behavior. Throughout the decade that ostensibly belonged to the Neo-Darwinian determinists in psychology, Witmer would elaborate his empirical results into a theoretical formulation involving modification of current theories of genetic and educational psychology. So long as animals and introspectionists remained the subjects of experimentation such reformulations would not emerge.

In the 1890s psychologists increasingly looked to evolutionary explanations of mental processes. The older physiological psychology of the structuralists, essentially descriptive, could not answer questions of causation and, hence, could never provide the dynamic explanation of behavior which psychologists needed in order to distinguish their experimental programs from those of physiologists. G. Stanley Hall saw in the extension of biological explanations of the evolution of the race to an understanding of the evolution of mental life of the individual the hope for a theoretical reconstruction of the science of mind. The recapitulation theory, explicit in the works of Herbert Spencer and E. H. Haeckel, was given added impetus by the comparative psychology of George John Romanes in England and the philosophical psychology of James Mark Baldwin in America.[43] The study of a child's mental development, thought Hall, would become the basis for a synthetic evolutionary psychology. A comparison of the mental growth of the child with the instinctive development of animals would then provide answers to the central problem of educational psychology; namely, what traits are innate and what characteristics are acquired.

Involving the idea that habits might become organized as instincts, Hall's genetic psychology was distinctly Lamarckian.[44] Hall was au courant with the biological thought of the day and, as George Stocking, Jr., has pointed out, he was gradually forced without ever fully discarding his Lamarckianism toward an accommodation with August Weismann's position.[45] In addition to biological objections to Hall's theories, psychologists enamored with the vogue of experimentalism were increasingly anxious to discredit Hall's unscientific procedures of using analogous records of parallel development to account for mental growth in humans.[46] Such assaults manifestly constituted the preconditions for repudiating the last great systematic articulation of naturalistic psychology. Understandably, such assaults form the investigative locus for historians attempting to explain intellectual change. The fascinating aspect of early twentieth-century psychology, however, is that naturalistic theories were not so much overwhelmed as they were overlooked. Overlooked because a new generation of psychologists was no longer seeking solutions to the problems that had motivated its mentors. The historian who would account for the demise of naturalistic psychology need not look for smoldering ruins but for evidences of new and ongoing construction in areas once considered the outer provinces of psychology. The new psychological clinic was one such structure.

Often the new would resemble the old architecturally. In 1907, for example, Witmer announced a course offering by Herbert Strotesbury of Temple College in genetic psychology. Strotesbury would discuss the inheritance of acquired characteristics.[47] Four years later Witmer offered a summer course in developmental psychology which would attend to "the problem of heredity by tracing the individual growth from the remotest period of its genesis in the germ-cell—the physical basis of heredity, in which are focused all the influences, actual and potential, of remote and immediate ancestry, and from which emerges the future human being."[48] By 1914 he was still insisting that the "whole problem of the mental development of the individual personality belongs to genetic psychology. . . ."[49] This, however, was genetic psychology with a difference. The developmental model to which Witmer adhered was strictly ontogenic. Recapitulation and evolution had dropped out of the picture. And why should they not? The scales with which Witmer was concerned were not phylogenic but pedagogical. Recapitulation, as Dorothy Ross has pointed out, "seemed most plausible for those aspects of child behavior most removed from the central learning experiences of children."[50] Concentrating on these more germane and manifest experiences, Witmer seems also to have obviated Lamarckianism. Strotesbury, for example, was scheduled to discuss inheritance of acquired characteristics through "congenital factors (nonhereditary)."[51] This appears at first to be self-contradictory, but it is safe to conclude that Witmer was here making a distinction between those acquirements of an individual organism in the course of uterine development subsequent to genetic action but prior to delivery (congenital) and genetic endowment (hereditary). In this view, not uncommon among contemporary biologists, the word inheritance assumes the pejorative meaning of the combined endowment of congenital and hereditary factors with which the organism is presented at birth.[52]

"Whether the existence of a congenital ability can be explained as the effect of causes acting through heredity or derived from the environment," quips the pragmatic Witmer, "I leave to philosophers and biologists. The starting point in psychology is the assumption of a number of congenital abilities. . . ."[53] The disclaimer is, of course, rhetorical. By moving the psychologist's frame of reference from the genetic to the congenital in this era of hereditary determinism, Witmer was able to leave open the possibility of environmental influences without having to plead guilty to Lamarckianism. Indeed, it had been his experience that medical examinations and clinical biographies of retarded children often uncovered evidence of intrauterine accidents, maternal disease during pregnancy, attempted abortions, miscarriages, and so forth.[54] Moreover, therapy often succeeded in overcoming these handicaps which affected the child's ability to learn. A pregnant mother's inclination toward alcoholic beverages can surely have an adverse effect upon the fetus. Witmer did not believe, however, that this habit would result in degenerate grandchildren. More to the point, the problem was irrelevant to clinical aims.

Having discarded the evolutionary brand of genetic psychology, Witmer found it easier to downplay the significance of instincts. In his course in developmental psychology he stated that individual inheritance, "as typified in the instincts, will receive the large attention they demand as congenital sources of habits and as primary springs of conduct during much of the child's life."[55] He continued: "Their origin, nature, variableness and transitoriness . . . will be treated in their psychological aspect as impulses to conduct."[56] Transitoriness is the key word.

Nowhere does Witmer suggest that instincts are modified; on the contrary, like old psychological theories, they seem to fade away as the environment assumes command. "By the age of six," concluded Witmer, "the child is more or less affected by his environment. . . . Upon inherited tendencies, habits have been grafted."[57] In a sense the child is continually trading instinct psychology for associationism, and the answer to the question of whether instinct or habit is more influential depends upon either the age of the subject or the tense of the application.

Witmer's genetic psychology embodied an uncomplex version of the familiar and bothersome idea of psychophysical parallelism. The organism is presented at birth with a set of congenital mental givens which develop—that is, become modified and "complexified"—at first through "the genetic process alone," or, in other words, by responding to internal physiological changes in organic structure, size, and function. Later, as we have seen, the mind is sufficiently developed to let the environment take over. As the body grows, so grows the mind. Any obstacle to physiological growth will probably frustrate mental development by depriving mind of the genetic stimulation which normal physical growth supplies.[58] The practical psychology enlisted to remove these obstacles or to reinvigorate retarded mental functions Witmer labelled "orthogenics," "the science of normal development [which] comprehends within its scope all the conditions which facilitate, conserve, or obstruct the normal development of mind and body."[59] Witmer was enough of an hereditarian to realize that people vary in their provisions of innate mental capacities and enough of an egalitarian to insist that everyone had the right to achieve his or her level of normal development. But what constituted a retardate's normal development—the essential question for the clinician—would depend upon a determination of the *extent* of hereditary endowment. Such a determination, however, would have to be based on statistical probability and Witmer had always divided applied psychology into two exclusive approaches according to method: the statistical and the clinical.[60] His attempt to resolve this dilemma by formulating a definition of normality from within the clinical tradition would lead him to downplay the concept of intelligence altogether and to emphasize a behavioral interpretation of test results.

Binet testers in the Goddard mold administered tests to *groups* of children in an attempt to correlate statistically mental with behavioral abnormalities. What Goddard considered the benefits of such compilation Witmer considered its drawbacks. Both found interpretations and methods of administration which coincided with their respective roles. Even the colleague of Witmer most sympathetic to Goddard's work realized that:

> while it may be possible to tabulate statistics of the percentage of moral degenerates that will spring from morally degenerate or imbecile stock, it by no means follows that any particular individual can be pronounced a moral imbecile from heredity alone, nor can it be predicted with any certainty that particular parents like A and B will have particular children like a and b who may be morally deficient.[61]

Unlike Goddard, Witmerians used so-called intelligence tests as structured opportunities to observe the subject perform certain mental tasks. The clinician observed performance and, in the process, those things which inhibited performance. For example, attention was considered a mental ability readily improvable with practice. All things being equal, an inattentive child would not achieve the same results in a testing situation as an attentive child. Raw scores from group tests can not only be deceiving but also damaging to accurate prognosis. Witmer claimed that his "very early experience . . . revealed the necessity for keeping the examination in a fluid state. I acquired a fear of the formalism of the blank . . . ."[62]

Tests were, therefore, clinically useful but

statistically dangerous and throughout the period in which clinical psychologists were increasingly coming to be identified with mental tests, Witmer repeatedly sounded the call for skepticism and caution.[63] Once again, it was a caution based upon experience. For example, Witmer had examined a delinquent boy whose father had a record of alcoholism. There was a place on clinical examination forms for such information, but such information, claimed Witmer, would be misleading. In this particular case, five of the boy's brothers and sisters born after his father's drinking became excessive were quite normal. Such findings were the result of individual examinations and they led Witmer to "look with skepticism on family and social statistics reported by physicians or gathered by eugenicists."[64] The clinician's melioristic orientation precluded facile correlations between statistical probability and clinical prognosis. Witmer was preoccupied with assessing the relative importance of nature and nurture. For the clinician, however, the issue was more of practical than theoretical significance. The clinic was a social and educational service and in the interests of efficiency and alumni funds it should not spend time attempting to retrieve the irretrievable or to reform the incorrigible.[65] Witmer's procedure was therefore to work backwards from the most probable proximate cause of defect until remediation produce an improvement. At that point the etiological significance of the ailment might possibly make itself known. Lengthy Galtonian genealogical recording would simply constitute "wasting paper, ink, and my assistant's time," complained Witmer, "besides producing statistics which may be misused, as so many statistics of heredity are misused today, to uphold unsound contentions and to urge legislation of doubtful social value."[66]

Eschewing eugenicist data and turning, therefore, to E. L. Thorndike's educational psychology for an estimation of the role of heredity in mental development, Witmer subscribed to the idea of innate intelligence. The discovery, however, of wide-ranging test scores administered to an individual before and after medical, hygienic, or pedagogical treatment convinced him that intelligence tests do not, in fact, measure intelligence. This conclusion had been reached by a number of clinical investigations between 1912 and 1920 and Witmer was quick to draw upon the results.[67] Herein rests the strongest argument for historical focus upon institutions as catalysts for intellectual change: *the clinic provided an arena in which generalizations were made visible and theory tangible.* As such it quickened the pace of psychology's development in a way that nonapplied branches could never duplicate. When, for example, the eugenicist Lewis Terman retested a group of geniuses in 1927–1928, he discovered a striking downward deviation in the group's I.Q. that led him to conclude that factors of environment, personality, and health played a role in the measurement of intelligence. What is remarkable about this revision is that the original testing of the group occurred in 1921. The earlier conclusions of his *Genetic Studies in Genius* were allowed to stand authoritatively for over six years.[68] Within the clinic, however, where timely retesting was required, results were allowed to stand for only a number of weeks. To be sure, it would take years to produce a significant statistical deviation within a large group; but this justification can also be taken to indicate the remedial drawbacks rather than the benefits of statistical compilations.[69]

It is no coincidence that prior to World War One the two chief attacks upon the hereditarian implications of psychological testing came from William Healy and J. E. Wallace Wallin.[70] In 1906 Wallin visited Witmer's clinic and carried away with him the approach which was to emerge in his own clinic a few years later.[71] Healy likewise explored Witmer's organization and later commented that the creation of his psychiatric clinic in Chicago—which constituted the institutional beginnings of the child guidance movement in the United States—was partially modeled after Witmer's establishment.[72] Thus, it was from the psychological clinics, those supposed centers for eugenicist propaganda, that the earliest complaints about eugenics appeared.[73]

By 1920 the institutional vulnerabilities of Witmer's brand of clinical psychology were becoming apparent. Alliances with medical departments broke down as psychiatry came into closer contact with the universities.[74] Psychiatric clinics were steadily growing and psychiatrists, in a better position to assert their therapeutic claims, began to complain the psychologists were encroaching upon their legitimate territory while ironically adapting the program of clinical psychology to their own operational procedures. Aware of their comparative institutional weaknesses and lacking sufficient support from the American Psychological Association, clinical psychologists tenaciously held onto the one aspect of clinical practice over which they could reasonably claim authority. They insisted that psychiatrists were unqualified to administer psychological tests. Implemented at the highest levels of their respective professional organizations, the resultant compromise was decidedly adverse to clinical psychology's status. Psychologists gained hegemony over testing but little else. Diagnosis is not as prestigious a function as cure and clinical psychologists after 1920, as psychometricians, became subordinate components within psychiatric clinics. By 1935 only seven of the original psychological clinics cited by Wallin in 1911 were still in existence.[75] In that year there were 87 child clinics directed by psychologists in comparison to 755 psychiatric clinics.[77]

In professional terms, however, psychologists did not suffer. Though they lacked the legitimacy of the therapeutic role neither were their activities circumscribed by that exclusive function. Their clinical training served them well in other areas of applied endeavor. The success of the testers during the war broadened their occupational horizons after the Armistice. In the twenties the business of psychology, like that of the country, was business. Led by Morris Viteles, many of Witmer's students, admirably prepared, went into personnel work or into industrial psychology.[77] Others converted their associations with educators into positions as school administrators. Their individual careers were not unlike those of the Peace Corps volunteers of the sixties—those corporation men of the seventies. Clinical psychology of the educational variety went the way of the Progressive Movement. Its larger concerns were assimilated into increasingly viable departments of education, whose prestige in the first decade of the century psychology had helped enhance.

In many respects, the psychologist-historian Robert I. Watson is correct to have dismissed Witmer as a man "of historical significance only."[78] Yet those of us from whom that verdict holds significance enough should be suspicious of his assertion that Witmer's articles—from which much of the above analysis is drawn—"are chiefly of antiquarian interest today."[79] The nature of Witmer's work and the requirements of his role prompted him to discard the genetic model of recapitulation, to regard intelligence tests as indicators of performance, to adopt environmental explanations of human behavior, and to call for a psychology that takes into account nature and culture as mutually exclusive categories.[80] To assume that Witmer transformed American psychology is to go to the opposite extreme, for in crucial ways his pursuits were parochial. But to assert that his activities were irrelevant to essential changes within American psychology because "his influence did not spread beyond Philadelphia to any considerable degree"[81] likewise misses the point. Such a conception of intellectual change as rooted in patterns of linear influences serves to keep disciplinary history at an essentially descriptive level of analysis. If Witmer's institutional situation, social location, role identification, and social function caused him to alter his intellectual suppositions and if the locations, roles, and functions of clinical (or, for that matter, of any applied) psychologists elsewhere were analogous,[82] then new ideas need not the postal service and the annual meeting to obtain salvation. Similar undertakings will tend to produce similar responses. The cumulative effect upon theory of changing ideas emerging simultaneously in disparate geographical and institutional locations and connected by a novel similarity of roles will go a long way toward explaining a discipline's general susceptibility to new paradigms.

Regardless of the institutional fate of that variety of clinical psychology which Witmer initiated, the intellectual viewpoints of those who participated in that and similar disciplinary episodes remained intact to inform associated endeavors. That Lightner Witmer failed to perpetuate his particular role does not diminish his relevance, for while others called for an applied psychology, Witmer enacted one. His theoretical formulations may have been incomplete and, in retrospect, roughhewn and hidebound, but they were never irrelevant. Although his intellectual contributions may seem imperceptible to us today, we must not forget that he prescribed and performed a social function which remains his legacy.

NOTES

1. *Psychological Review 3* (1896): 134.

2. A. A. Roback, *A History of American Psychology,* rev. ed. (New York: Collier, 1964), p. 230.

3. Henrika Kuklick, "The Organization of Social Science in the United States," *American Quarterly* 28 (1976): 129.

4. Employing the sociological surrogate of evolutionary theory, the professionalization model, historians often adduce the creation of viable social roles as proof of a discipline's intellectual legitimacy. If a movement fails to perpetuate itself, we are thereby absolved of the obligation to look at its ideas. I call this assumption "intellectual Darwinism" and attempt in this article to develop an argument for circumventing it.

5. Hamilton Cravens, "American Scientists and the Hereditary-Environment Controversy, 1883–1940" (Ph.D. dissertation, University of Iowa, 1969), p. 266. At the risk of formulating a frontier thesis of disciplinary history, I am suggesting that crucial developments within American psychology have occurred exactly in such "wilderness" areas.

6. C. M. Louttit, "The Nature of Clinical Psychology," *Psychological Bulletin* 36 (1939): 366; Robert I. Watson, "A Brief History of Clinical Psychology," ibid. 50 (1953): 327–328; David Shakow, "Clinical Psychology: An Evaluation," in *Orthopsychiatry, 1923–1948: Retrospect and Prospect,* ed. L. G. Lowrey and Victoria Sloane (New York: American Orthopsychiatric Association, 1948), p. 234; Shakow, "Clinical Psychology," in *International Encyclopedia of the Social Sciences,* ed. David L. Sills, vol. 2 (New York: Macmillan and Free Press, 1968), p. 514.

7. Shakow and David Rapaport, *The Influence of Freud on American Psychology (Psychological Issues,* Monograph 13, Vol. 4, No. 1), p. 85, n. 37.

8. See, for example, Charles Everett Strikland, "The Child and the Race: The Doctrines of Recapitulation and Culture Epochs in the Rise of the Child-Centered Ideal in American Educational Thought, 1875–1900" (Ph.D. dissertation, University of Wisconsin, 1963). An excellent study which partially attends to the relationship of psychological thought to psychological practice is John C. Burnham and Hamilton Cravens, "Psychology and Evolutionary Naturalism in American Thought, 1890–1940," *American Quarterly* 23 (1971): 635–657.

9. For a systematic approach to the impact of institutional change upon intellectual innovation, see Thomas C. Cochran, *Social Change in America: The Twentieth Century* (New York: Harper Torchbooks, 1972), pp. 11–29.

10. The instable mixture of psychiatry and psychology which was distilled in such institutional settings required the establishment of novel interprofessional arrangements and the elaboration of consensualized theory. Though the history of this relationship has not yet been written, cursory investigations can be found in Thomas Verner Moore, "A Century of Psychology in its Relationship to American Psychiatry," in *One Hundred Years of American Psychiatry,* ed. J. K. Hall et at. (New York: Columbia University Press, 1944), pp. 443–477. For a general account, see John M. Reisman, *The Development of Clinical Psychology* (New York: Appleton-Century-Crofts, 1966).

11. Shakow, "Clinical Psychology," p. 514 summarizes this critique. Witmer's actual awareness of these trends reinforces this retrospective verdict.

12. John C. Burnham, "On the Origins of Behaviorism," *Journal of The History of the Behavioral Sciences* 4 (1968): 151, reminds us that "the evolution of Watson's thinking, on the one hand, is not necessarily relevant to the origins of behaviorism, on the other hand." As a complementary thesis, I am suggesting that behaviorism, broadly construed, represented the theoretical rationalization of trends within American psychology toward application, service, and social control. Watson seemed to provide intellectual legitimacy for psychologists whose social roles involved them in practical problems of human behavior. Much of his support came from these academically marginal areas. This essay constitutes a case study of one such outpost. The cumulative impact upon psychological thought of "practising" psychologist' engagements with actual social and behavioral problems partially accounts for the widespread acceptance of behaviorism after World War One.

13. Although is usually assumed that Witmer was a student in philosophy, he had actually changed his major from political science under Edmund James to experimental psychology in exchange for an assistantship offered by the philosopher George Fullerton, one of James's academic rivals. Witmer states that later his salary was significantly increased "on condition that I would go to Leipzig and remain there eighteen months." Witmer to Edwin G. Boring, 18 March 1948, Boring Correspondence, Harvard University Archives, Cambridge, Massachusetts. Both incidents are herein related as antidotes (though not, of course, contradictions) to the heroic historiographic portrayals of vocational motivation as a product of altruistic inspiration. See, for example, Edna Heidbreder, *Seven Psychologies* (New York: Appleton-Century-Crofts, 1933), pp. 94–95.

14. Edwin G. Boring, *A History of Experimental Psychology,* 2d ed. (New York: Appleton-Century-Crofts, 1950), pp. 533–534; Samuel W. Fernberger, "The Training of Mental Hygienists," *Psychological Clinic* 19 (1930): 139.

15. James McKeen Cattell, "Mental Tests and Their Measurements," *Mind* 15 (1890): 373–380.

16. Witmer, "The Psychological Clinic," *Old Penn* 8 (1909): 100; Arthur Holmes, *The Conservation of the Child: A Manual of Clinical Psychology Presenting the Examination and Treatment of Backward Children* (Philadelphia: Lippincott, 1912), pp. 28–29. The title of Holmes's volume is indicative of the progressive rhetoric that informed and inspired turn-of-the-century clinical practice.

17. Witmer, "Practical Work in Psychology," *Pediatrics* 2 (1896): 462–471.

18. *Psychological Review* 4 (1897): 116–117.

19. Joseph Collins, "Lightner Witmer: A Biographical Sketch," in *Clinical Psychology: Studies in Honor of Lightner Witmer,* ed. Robert A. Brotemarkle (Philadelphia: University of Pennsylvania Press, 1931), p. 5; Reisman, *Clinical Psychology,* p. 46.

20. See John M. O'Donnell, "The Transformation of American Psychology, 1890–1920" (M.A. thesis, University of Delaware, 1974), esp. chap. 4; John C. Burnham, "Psychiatry, Psychology and the Progressive Movement," *American Quarterly* 12 (1960): 457–465; David Bakan, "Behaviorism and American Urbanization," *Journal of the History of the Behavioral Sciences* 2 (1966): 5–28.

21. Laurence R. Veysey, *The Emergence of the American University* (Chicago: University of Chicago Press, 1965), pp. 57–120, 159, 177.

22. Lawrence A. Cremin, *The Transformation of the School: Progressivism in American Education, 1876–1957* (New York: Knopf, 1961), pp. 168–176; Arthur G. Powell, "Speculations on the Early Impact of Schools of Education on Educational Psychology," *History of Education Quarterly 11* (1971): 406–412.

23. George H. Daniels, "The Process of Professionalization in American Science: The Emergent Period, 1820–1860," *Isis* 58 (1967): 151–166.

Daniels regards such justification (legitimation) as an essential step in the institutional growth of new sciences. The dramatic increase in public financial support of education in the United States between 1880 and 1900 surely helped psychologists focus their professional and intellectual attentions; Albert Fishlow, "Levels of Nineteenth-Century American Investment in Education," *Journal of Economic History* 26 (1966): 418–436.

24. Of the 160 individuals who listed psychology as their primary or exclusive field in the second edition of Cattell's *American Men of Science,* 67 or nearly 42% indicated educational concerns and interests. The 1910 edition was selected for its temporal proximity to Watson's 1913 behaviorist manifesto and because it encompasses the period of the Psychological Clinic's most rapid institutional growth.

25. James Dale Hendricks, "The Child-Study Movement in American Education, 1880–1910: A Quest For Educational Reform Through A Scientific Study of the Child" (Ph.D. dissertation, Indiana University, 1968): Dorothy Ross, *G. Stanley Hall: The Psychologist as Prophet* (Chicago: University of Chicago Press, 1972), pp. 279–308, 350–367.

26. "A Plea For Special Child Study," *Proceedings of the International Congress of Education, 1883* (New York: Little, 1884), p. 778.

27. Hendricks, "Child-Study Movement," pp. 138–140, 186–198; Jason R. Robarts, "The Quest for a Science of Education in the Nineteenth Century," *History of Education Quarterly* 8 (1968): 431–446.

28. Robert L. Church, "Educational Psychology and Social Reform in the Progressive Era," *History of Education Quarterly* 11 (1971): 390–405, attempts to explain why educational psychologists did not share the reform concerns of educators. Implicitly, Church (esp. pp. 396–397) argues for psychologists' need to create a new role, a role which I maintain was defined by Witmer as the clinical psychologist.

29. Witmer, et al., *The Special Class for Backward Children* (Philadelphia: The Psychological Clinic Press, 1911); Holmes, *Manual,* p. 30.

30. Edward Potts Cheyney, *History of the University of Pennsylvania* (Philadelphia: University of Pennsylvania Press, 1940), pp. 353–355, 401.

31. Fernberger, "History of the Psychological Clinic," in Brotemarkle, *Clinical Psychology,* pp. 14, 15.

32. These records have recently been microfilmed and surveyed. See Murray Levine and Julius Wishner, "The Case Records of the Psychological Clinic at the University of Pennsylvania (1896–1961)," *Journal of The History of the Behavioral Sciences* 13 (1977): 59–66.

33. This criticism has been invoked not only retrospectively but contemporaneously as well; R. H. Sylvester, "Clinical Psychology Adversely Criticized," *Psychological Clinic* 7 (1913): 182.

34. Witmer, "Clinical Psychology," *Psychological Clinic* 1 (1907): 6–7; "Courses at the Summer School of the University of Pennsylvania," ibid. 4 (1911): 246; "The Scope of Education as a University Department," ibid. 7 (1914): 245, 246; Sylvester, "Clinical Psychology," pp. 182, 186; Holmes, *Manual,* pp. 40–41, 91, 299.

35. Witmer, "Clinical Records," *Psychological Clinic* 9 (1915): 3, "The Exceptional Child at Home and at School," *University Lectures Delivered by Members of the Faculty in the Free Public Lecture Course, 1913–1914* (Philadelphia: University of Pennsylvania Press, 1915), p. 538; "Psychonomic Personeering," *Psychological Clinic* 19 (1930): 73.

36. Quoted in Francis M. Maxfield, "Mental Deficiency," in Brotemarkle, *Clinical Psychology,* p. 44.

37. Mark H. Haller, *Eugenics: Hereditarian Attitudes in American Thought* (New Brunswick: Rutgers University Press, 1963), pp. 95–96.

38. M. S. Viteles, "The Children of a Jewish Orphanage," *Psychological Clinic* 12 (1918): 254.

39. Haller, *Eugenics,* p. 112; Cravens, "American Scientists," p. 265. Witmer's interpretation of Goddard sounds unduly harsh to historians of mental retardation. Such hyperbole, however, constitutes early evidence of polarization of debate between hereditarians and environmentalists.

40. *Psychological Clinic* 4 (1911): 221–238.

41. Ibid., pp. 231–232.

42. While Witmer's articles represented the clinic's viewpoint, his writings largely constituted theoretical generalizations based upon the findings of social workers, educators, and graduate students whose writings formed a large portion of the journal's commentary.

43. Ross, *G. Stanley Hall,* p. 261. My debt to Ross in this passage will be obvious to those familiar with her excellent biography. See also Robert E. Grinder, *A History of Genetic Psychology: The First Science of Human Development* (New York: John Wiley, 1967).

44. Ross, *G. Stanley Hall,* p. 371.

45. George W. Stocking, Jr., *Race, Culture, and Evolution: Essays in the History of Anthropology* (New York: Free Press, 1968), pp. 254–255.

46. Ross, *G. Stanley Hall,* p. 371.

47. Witmer, "University Courses in Psychology," *Psychological Clinic* 1 (1907): 32.

48. Witmer, "Courses in Psychology at the Summer School," pp. 259–260.

49. Witmer, "The Scope of Education," p. 239.

50. Ross, *G. Stanley Hall,* p. 350.

51. Witmer, "University Courses in Psychology," p. 32.

52. Charles E. Rosenberg has stated that after 1900 "the reformist in temperament tended, as their emotional position dictated, to disassociate behavioral characteristics entirely from a possible genetic basis." Rosenberg, *No Other Gods: On Science and American Social Thought* (Baltimore: Johns Hopkins University Press, 1976), p. 10. The clinics social function likewise required such a dissociation in an era of hereditary determinism.

53. Witmer, "Performance and Success: An Outline of Psychology for Diagnostic Testing and Teaching," *Psychological Clinic* 12 (1919): 150.

54. See, for example, Witmer, "Clinical Records," pp. 5–6.

55. Witmer, "Courses in Psychology at the Summer School," p. 260.

56. Ibid.

57. Ibid.

58. Witmer, "Retardation Through Neglect in Children of the Rich," *Psychological Clinic* 1 (1907): 157.

59. Frontispiece, *Psychological Clinic;* Witmer, "Diagnostic Education—An Education For the Fortunate Few," ibid. 11 (1917): 70.

60. Witmer, "Courses in Psychology at the Summer School," p. 271.

61. Holmes, *Manual,* pp. 273–274.

62. Witmer, "Clinical Records," p. 2.

63. Ibid., p. 5; Witmer, "Performance and Success," p. 155.

64. Witmer, "Clinical Records," p. 6.

65. Witmer, "The Scope of Education," p. 246.

66. Witmer, "Clinical Records," p. 5.

67. Sylvester, "Clinical Psychology," p. 182; Witmer, "Performance and Success"; "On the Relation of Intelligence to Efficiency," *Psychological Clinic* 9 (1915): 61–86; Fernberger, "Statistical and Non-Statistical Interpretations of Test Results," ibid. 14 (1922): 68–72; William Filler Lutz, "The Relation of Mental to Physical Growth," ibid. 15 (1924): 125–129; Witmer, "What is Intelligence and Who Has It?" *Scientific Monthly* 15 (1922): 57–67.

68. Alice M. Jones (Rockwell), "The Superior Child," in Brotemarkle, *Clinical Psychology,* pp. 46–55.

69. I am not, of course, arguing that individualized clinical conclusions are necessarily more scientific or more accurate than longitudinal statistical ones. Nevertheless, for an amusing experimental account of how applied psychologists jump to conclusions often fortuitously correct, see H. J. Eysenck, *Uses and Abuses of Psychology* (Baltimore: Penguin Books, 1953), p. 11.

70. Haller, *Eugenics,* pp. 112–113.

71. J. E. W. Wallin, *The Odyssey of a Psychologist* (Wilmington, Delaware: by the author, 1955), p. 32.

72. William Healy, *Twenty-Five Years of Child Guidance Studies From the Institute For Juvenile Research* (Chicago: Illinois Dept. of Public Welfare, 1934), p. 46.

73. Haller, *Eugenics,* pp. 92, 101. Haller's depiction of psychological clinics as centers of eugenicist preachings is somewhat misleading in that he tends to equate clinical psychology at large with clinical psychology at Vineland. Witmer's clinic was prototypical of developments in the United States. It is hardly surprising that in a period of increasing hereditary determinism those institutions attempting remediation would tend to criticize the pessimistic implications of eugenicist thought. For synopses of the growth (and, more important, of the typology) of psychological clinics, see Theodate L. Smith, "The Development of

Psychological Clinics in the United States," *Pedagogical Seminary* 21 (1914): 143–153; Wallin; "The New Clinical Psychology and the Psycho-Clinicist," *Journal of Educational Psychology* 2 (1911): 121–132, 191–210; and the American Psychological Association's Clinical Section's "Guide to the Psychological Clinics in the United States," reprinted in *Psychological Clinic* 23 (1935): 9–140.

74. The literature encompassing the furious debate between psychologists and psychiatrists in the second decade of this century is too vast to be cited here. The nature of the controversy can be apprehended from the psychologists' side in Carl E. Seashore, *Pioneering in Psychology* (Iowa City: University of Iowa Press, 1942), pp. 128–134 and from the psychiatrists' viewpoint in Moore, "A Century of Psychology in its Relationship to American Psychiatry," pp. 468–477. See also William J. Goode, "Encroachment, Charlatanism, and the Emerging Profession: Psychology, Sociology, and Medicine," *American Sociological Review* 25 (1960): 907–913; John C. Burnham, "The Struggle between Physicians and Paramedical Personnel in American Psychiatry, 1917–1941," *Journal of the History of Medical and Allied Sciences 29* (1974): 93–106.

75. Louttit, "The Nature of Clinical Psychology," p. 372.

76. M. A. Clark, "Directory of Psychiatric Clinics in the United States," *Mental Hygiene* 20 (1936): 66–129.

77. Viteles himself discusses the linkage between clinical and industrial psychology in *Industrial Psychology* (New York: Norton, 1932), pp. 34–36. Industrial psychology has other roots; see Leonard W. Ferguson, *The Heritage of Industrial Psychology* (n. p., 1963–1965) and Loren Baritz, *Servants of Power: A History of the Use of Social Sciences in American Industry* (Middletown, Conn.: Wesleyan University Press, 1960).

78. Watson, "A Brief History of Clinical Psychology," p. 329.

79. Ibid., p. 328.

80. Witmer, "Performance and Success," p. 148.

81. Watson, "A Brief History," p. 328.

82. I have chosen to concentrate in depth on one case study. Nevertheless, even a casual reading of Wallin's descriptions of clinics elsewhere, which he gathered together in *The Mental Health of the School Child* (New Haven: Yale University Press, 1914), reinforces the conviction that many psychologists' experiences were not only analogous but very nearly identical.

Psychology and Industrial Efficiency

Hugo Münsterberg

APPLIED PSYCHOLOGY

Our aim is to sketch the outlines of a new science which is to intermediate between the modern laboratory psychology and the problems of economics: the psychological experiment is systematically to be placed at the service of commerce and industry. So far we have only scattered beginnings of the new doctrine, only tentative efforts and disconnected attempts which have started, sometimes in economic, and sometimes in psychological, quarters. The time when an exact psychology of business life will be presented as a closed and perfected system lies very far distant. But the earlier the attention of wider circles is directed to its beginnings and to the importance and bearings of its tasks, the quicker and the more sound will be the development of this young science. What is most needed to-day at the beginning of the new movement are clear, concrete illustrations which demon-

Excerpted from Münsterberg, H. (1913). *Psychology and Industrial Efficiency*. Boston: Hougton Mifflin, pp. 3–10, 63–82.

strate the possibilities of the new method. In the following pages, accordingly, it will be my aim to analyze the results of experiments which have actually been carried out, experiments belonging to many different spheres of economic life. But these detached experiments ought always at least to point to a connected whole; the single experiments will, therefore, always need a general discussion of the principles as a background. In the interest of such a wider perspective we may at first enter into some preparatory questions of theory. They may serve as an introduction which is to lead us to the actual economic life and the present achievements of experimental psychology.

It is well known that the modern psychologists only slowly and very reluctantly approached the apparently natural task of rendering useful service to practical life. As long as the study of the mind was entirely dependent upon philosophical or theological speculation, no help could be expected from such endeavors to assist in the daily walks of life. But half a century has passed since the study of consciousness was switched into the tracks of exact scientific investigation. Five decades ago the psychologists began to devote themselves to the most minute description of the mental experiences and to explain the mental life in a way which was modeled after the pattern of exact natural sciences. Their aim was no longer to speculate about the soul, but to find the psychical elements and the constant laws which control their connections. Psychology became experimental and physiological. For more than thirty years the psychologists have also had their workshops. Laboratories for experimental psychology have grown up in all civilized countries, and the new method has been applied to one group of mental traits after another. And yet we stand before the surprising fact that all the manifold results of the new science have remained book knowledge, detached from any practical interests. Only in the last ten years do we find systematic efforts to apply the experimental results of psychology to the needs of society.

It is clear that the reason for this late beginning is not an unwillingness of the last century to make theoretical knowledge serviceable to the demands of life. Every one knows, on the contrary, that the glorious advance of the natural sciences became at the same time a triumphal march of technique. Whatever was brought to light in the laboratories of the physicists and chemists, of the physiologists and pathologists, was quickly transformed into achievements of physical and chemical industry, of medicine and hygiene, of agriculture and mining and transportation. No realm of the external social life remained untouched. The scientists, on the other hand, felt that the far-reaching practical effect which came from their discoveries exerted a stimulating influence on the theoretical researches themselves. The pure search for truth and knowledge was not lowered when the electrical waves were harnessed for wireless telegraphy, or the Roentgen rays were forced into the service of surgery. The knowledge of nature and the mastery of nature have always belonged together.

The persistent hesitation of the psychologists to make similar practical use of their experimental results has therefore come from different causes. The students of mental life evidently had the feeling that quiet, undisturbed research was needed for the new science of psychology in order that a certain maturity might be reached before a contact with the turmoil of practical life would be advisable. The sciences themselves cannot escape injury if their results are forced into the rush of the day before the fundamental ideas have been cleared up, the methods of investigation really tried, and an ample supply of facts collected. But this very justified reluctance becomes a real danger if it grows into an instinctive fear of coming into contact at all with practical life. To be sure, in any single case there may be a difference of opinion as to when the right time has come and when the inner consolidation of a new science is sufficiently advanced for the technical service, but it ought to be clear that it is not wise to wait until the scientists have settled all the theoretical problems involved. True progress in every scientific field means that the problems become multiplied and that ever new questions keep coming to the surface. If the psychologists were to refrain from practical application until the theoretical results of their laboratories need no supplement, the time for applied psychology would never come. Whoever looks without prejudice on the development of modern psychology ought to acknowledge that the hesitancy which was justified in the beginning would to-day be inexcusable lack of initiative. For the sciences of the mind, too, the time has come when theory and practice must support each other. An exceedingly large mass of facts has been gathered, the methods have become refined and differentiated, and however much may still be under discussion, the ground common to all is ample enough to build upon.

Another important reason for the slowness of practical progress was probably this. When the psychologists began to work with the new experimental methods, their most immediate concern was to get rid of mere speculation and to take hold of actual facts. Hence they regarded the natural sciences as their model, and, together with the experimental method which distinguishes scientific work, the characteristic goal of the sciences was accepted too. This scientific goal is always the attainment of general laws; and so it happened that in the first decades after the foundation of psychological laboratories the general laws of the mind absorbed the entire attention and interest of the investigators. The result of such an attitude was, that we learned to understand the working of the typical mind, but that all the individual variations were almost neglected. When the various individuals differed in their mental behavior, these differences appeared almost as disturbances which the psychologists had to eliminate in order to find the general laws which hold for every mind. The studies were accordingly confined to the general averages of mental experience, while the variations from such averages were hardly included in the scientific account. In earlier centuries, to be sure, the interest of the psychological observers had been given almost entirely to the rich manifoldness of human characters and intelligences and talents. In the new period of experimental work, this interest was taken as an indication of the unscientific fancies of the earlier age, in which the curious and the anecdotal attracted the view. The new science which was to seek the laws was to overcome such popular curiosity. In this sign experimental psychology has conquered. The fundamental laws of the ideas and of the attention, of the memory and of the will, of the feeling and of the emotions, have been elaborated. Yet it slowly became evident that such one-sidedness, however necessary it may have been at the beginning, would make any practical application impossible. In practical life we never have to do with what is common to all human beings, even when we are to influence large masses; we have to deal with personalities whose mental life is characterized by particular traits of nationality, or race, or vocation, or sex, or age, or special interests, or other features by which they differ from the average mind which the theoretical psychologist may construct as a type. Still more frequently we have to act with reference to smaller groups or to single individuals whose mental physiognomy demands careful consideration. As long as experimental psychology remained essentially a science of the mental laws, common to all human beings, an adjustment to the practical demands of daily life could hardly come in question. With such general laws we could never have mastered the concrete situations of society, because we should have had to leave out of view the fact that there are gifted and ungifted, intelligent and stupid, sensitive and obtuse, quick and slow, energetic and weak individuals.

But in recent years a complete change can be traced in our science. Experiments which refer to these individual differences themselves have been carried on by means of the psychological laboratory, at first reluctantly and in tentative forms, but within the last ten years the movement has made rapid progress. To-day we have a psychology of individual variations from the point of view of the psychological laboratory. This development of schemes to compare the differences between the individuals by the methods of experimental science was after all the most important advance toward the practical application of psychology. The study of the individual differences itself is not applied psychology, but it is the presupposition without which applied psychology would have remained a phantom.

EXPERIMENTS IN THE INTEREST OF ELECTRIC RAILWAY SERVICE

The problem of securing fit motormen for the electric railways was brought to my attention from without. The accidents which occurred through the fault, or at least not without the fault, of the motormen in street railway transportation have always aroused disquietude and even indignation in the public, and the street railway companies suffered much from the many payments of indemnity imposed by the court as they amounted to thirteen per cent of the gross earnings of some companies. Last winter the American Association for Labor Legislation called a meeting of vocational specialists to discuss the problem of these accidents under various aspects. The street railways of various cities were represented, and economic, physiological, and psychological specialists took part in the general discussion. Much attention was given, of course, to the questions of fatigue and to the statistical results as to the number of accidents and their relation to the various hours of the day and to the time of labor. But there was a strong tendency to recognize, as still more important than the mere fatigue, the whole mental constitution of the motormen. The ability to keep attention constant, to resist distraction by chance happenings on the street, and especially the always needed ability to foresee the possible movements of the pedestrians and vehicles were acknowledged as extremely different from man to man. The companies claimed that there are motormen who practically never have an accident, because they feel beforehand even what the confused pedestrian and the unskilled chauffeur will do, while others relatively often experience accidents of all kinds because they do not foresee how matters will develop. They can hardly be blamed, as they were not careless, and yet the accidents did result from their personal qualities; they simply lacked the gift of instinctive foresight. All this turned the attention more and more to the possibilities of psychological analysis, and the Association suggested that I undertake an inquiry into this interesting problem with the means of the psychological laboratory. I felt the practical importance of the problem, considering that there are electric railway companies in this country which have up to fifty thousand accident indemnity cases a year. It therefore seemed to me decidedly worth while to undertake a laboratory investigation.

It would have been quite possible to treat the functions of the motormen according to the method which resolves the complex achievement into its various elements and tests every function independently. For instance, the stopping of the car as soon as the danger of an accident threatens is evidently effective only if the movement controlling the lever is carried out with sufficient rapidity. We should accordingly be justified in examining the quickness with which the individual reacts on optical stimuli. If a playing child suddenly runs across the track of the electric railway, a difference of a tenth of a second in the reaction-time may decide his fate. But I may say at once that I did not find characteristic differences in the rapidity of reaction of those motormen whom the company had found reliable and those who have frequent accidents. It seems that the slow individuals do not remain in the service at all. As a matter of course certain other indispensable single functions, like sharpness of vision, are examined before the entrance into the service and so they cannot stand as characteristic conditions of good or bad service among the actual employees.

For this reason, in the case of the motormen I abstracted from the study of single elementary functions and turned my attention to that mental process which after some careful observations seemed to me the really central one for the problem of accidents. I found this to be a particular complicated act of attention by which the manifoldness of objects, the pedestrians, the carriages, and the automobiles, are continuously observed with reference to their rapidity and direction in the quickly changing panorama of the street. Moving figures come from the right and from the left toward and across the track, and are embedded in a stream of men and vehicles which moves parallel to the track. In the face of such manifoldness there are men whose impulses are almost inhibited and who instinctively desire to wait for the movement of the nearest objects; they would evidently be unfit for the service, as they would drive the electric car far too slowly. There are others who, even with the car at high speed, can adjust themselves for a time to the complex moving situation, but whose attention soon lapses, and while they are fixating a rather distant carriage, may overlook a pedestrian who carelessly crosses the track immediately in front of their car. In short, we have a great variety of mental types of this characteristic unified activity, which may be understood as a particular combination of attention and imagination.

My effort was to transplant this activity of the motormen into laboratory processes. And here I may include a remark on the methodology of psychological industrial experiments. One might naturally think that the experience of a special industrial undertaking would be best reproduced for the experiment by repeating the external conditions in a kind of miniature form. That would mean that we ought to test the motormen of the electric railway by experiments with small toy models of electric cars placed on the laboratory table. But this would be decidedly inappropriate. A reduced copy of an external apparatus may arouse ideas, feelings, and volitions which have little in common with the process of actual life. The presupposition would be that the man to be tested for any industrial achievement would have to think himself into the miniature situation, and especially uneducated persons are often very unsuccessful in such efforts. This can be clearly seen from the experiences before naval courts, where it is usual to demonstrate collisions of ships by small ship models on the table in the courtroom. Experience has frequently show that helmsmen, who have found their course a life long among real vessels in the harbor and on the sea, become entirely confused when they are to demonstrate by the models the relative positions of the ships. Even in the naval war schools where the officers play at war with small model ships, a certain inner readjustment is always necessary for them to bring the miniature ships on the large table into the tactical game. On the water, for instance, the naval officer sees the far-distant ships very much smaller than those near by, while on the naval game table all the ships look equally large. On the whole, I feel inclined to say from my experience so far that experiments with small models of the actual industrial mechanism are hardly appropriate for investigations in the field of economic psychology. The essential point for the psychological experiment is not the external similarity of the apparatus, but exclusively the inner similarity of the mental attitude. The more the external mechanism with which or on which the action is carried out becomes schematized, the more the action itself will appear in its true character.

In the method of my experiments with the motormen, accordingly, I had to satisfy only two demands. The method of examination promised to be valuable if, first, it showed good results with reliable motormen and bad results with unreliable ones; and, secondly, if it vividly aroused in all the motormen the feeling that the mental function which they were going through during the experiment had the greatest possible similarity with their experience on the front platform of the electric car. These are the true tests of a desirable experimental method, while it is not necessary that the apparatus be similar to the electric car or that the external activities in the experiment be identical with their performance in the service. After several unsatisfactory efforts, in which I worked with too complicated instruments, I finally settled on the following arrangement of the experiment which seems to me to satisfy those two demands.

The street is represented by a card 9 half-inches broad and 26 half-inches long. Two heavy lines half an inch apart go lengthwise through the centre of the card, and accordingly a space of 4 half-inches remains on either side. The whole card is divided into small half-inch squares which we consider as the unit. Thus there is in any cross-section 1 unit between the two central lines and 4 units on either side. Lengthwise there are 26 units. The 26 squares which lie between the two heavy central lines are marked with the printed letters of the alphabet from A to Z. These two heavy central lines are to represent an electric railway track on a street. On either side the 4 rows of squares are filled in an irregular way with black and red figures of the three first digits. The digit 1 always represents a pedestrian who moves just one step, and that means from one unit into the next; the digit 2 a horse, which moves twice as fast, that is, which moves 2 units; and the digit 3 an automobile which moves three times as fast, that is, 3 units. Moreover, the black digits stand for men, horses and automobiles which move parallel to the track and cannot cross the track, and are therefore to be disregarded in looking out for dangers. The red digits, on the other hand, are the dangerous ones. They move from either side toward the track. The idea is that the man to be experimented on is to find as quickly as possible those points on the track which are threatened by the red figures, that is, those letters in the 26 track units at which the red figures would land, if they make the steps which their number indicates. A red digit 3 which is 4 steps from the track is to be disregarded, because it would not reach the track. A red digit 3 which is only 1 or 2 steps from the track is also to be disregarded, because it would cross beyond the track, if it took 3 steps. But a red 3 which is 3 units from the track, a red 2 which is 2 units from the track, and a red 1 which is 1 unit from the track would land on the track itself; and the aim is quickly to find these points. The task is difficult, as the many black figures divert the attention, and as the red figures too near or too far are easily confused with those which are just at the dangerous distance.

As soon as this principle for the experiment was recognized as satisfactory, it was necessary to find a technical device by which a movement over this artificial track could be produced in such a way that the rapidity could be controlled by the subject of the experiment and at the same time measured. Again we had to try various forms of apparatus. Finally we found the following form most satisfactory. Twelve such cards, each provided with a handle, lie one above another under a glass plate through which the upper card can be seen. If this highest card is withdrawn, the second is exposed, and from below springs press the remaining card against the glass plate. The glass plate with the 12 cards below lies in a black wooden box and is completely covered by a belt 8 inches broad made of heavy black velvet. This velvet belt moves over two cylinders at the front and the rear ends of the apparatus. In the centre of the belt is a window 4 1/2 inches wide and 2 1/2 inches high. If the front cylinder is turned by a metal crank, the velvet belt passes over the glass plate and the little window opening moves over the card with its track and figures. The whole breadth of the card, with its central track and its 4 units on either side, is visible through it over an area of 5 units in the length direction. If the man to be experimented on turns the crank with his right hand, the window slips over the whole length of the card, one part of the card after another becomes visible, and then he simply has to call the letters of those units in the track at which the red figures on either side would land, if they took the number of steps indicated by the digit. At the moment the window has reached Z on the card, the experimenter withdraws that card and the next becomes visible, as a second window in the belt appears at the lower end when the first disappears at the upper end. In this way the subject can turn his crank uninterruptedly until he has gone through the 12 cards. The experimenter notes down the numbers of the cards and the letters which the subject calls. Besides this, the number of seconds required for the whole experiment, from the beginning of the first card to the end of the twelfth, is measured with a stopwatch. This time is, of course, dependent upon the rapidity with which the crank is turned. The result of the experiment is accordingly expressed by three figures, the number of seconds, the number of omissions, that is, of places at which red figures would land on the track which were not noticed by the subject; and thirdly, the number of incorrect places where letters were called in spite of the fact that no danger existed. In using the results, we may disregard this third figure and give our attention to the speed and the number of omissions.

The necessary condition for carrying out the experiments with this apparatus is a careful, quiet, practical explanation of the device. The experiment must not under any circumstances be started until the subject completely understands what he has to do and for what he has to look out. For this purpose I at first always show the man one card outside of the apparatus and explain to him the differences between the black and the red figures, and the counting of the steps, and show to him in a number of cases how some red figures do not reach the track, how others go beyond the track, and how some just land in danger on the track. As soon as he has completely understood the principle, we turn to the apparatus and he moves the window slowly over a test card and tries to find the dangerous spots, and I turn his attention to every case in which he has omitted one or has given an incorrect letter. We repeat this slowly until he completely masters the rules of the game. Only then is he allowed to start the experiment. I have never found a man with whom this preparation takes more than a few minutes.

After developing this method in the psychological laboratory, I turned to the study of the men actually in the service of a great electric railway company which supported my endeavors in the most cordial spirit. In accordance with my request, the company furnished me with a number of the best motormen in its service, men who for twenty years and more had performed their duties practically without accidents, and, on the other hand, with a large number of motormen who had only just escaped dismissal and whose record was characterized by many more or less important collisions or other accidents. Finally, we had men whose activity as motormen was neither especially good nor especially bad.

The test of the method lies first in the fact that the tried motormen agreed that they really pass through the experiment with the feeling which they have on their car. The necessity of looking out in both directions, right and left, for possible obstacles, of distinguishing those which move toward the track from the many which move along the track, the quick discrimination among the various rates of rapidity, the steady forward movement of the observation point, the constant temptation to give attention to those which are still too far away or to those which are so near that they will cross the track before the approach of the car, in short, the whole complex situation with its demands on attention, imagination, and quick adjustment, soon brings them into an attitude which they themselves feel as identical with that in practical life. On the other hand, the results show a far-reaching correspondence between efficiency in the experiment and efficiency in the actual service. With a relatively small number of experiments this correspondence cannot be expected to be complete, the more as a large number of secondary features must enter which interfere with an exact correlation between experiment and standing in the railway company. We must consider, for instance, that those men whom the company naturally selects as models are men who have had twenty to thirty years of service without accidents, but consequently they are rather old men, who no longer have the elasticity of youth and are naturally less able to think themselves into an artificial situation like that of such an experiment, and who have been for a long time removed from contact with book work. It is therefore not surprising, but only to be expected, that such older, model men, while doing fair work in the test, are yet not seldom far surpassed by bright, quick, young motormen who are twenty years younger, even though they are not yet ideal motormen. Moreover, the standing in the company often depends upon features which have nothing to do with the mental make-up of the man, while the experiment has to be confined to those mental conditions which favor accidents. It is quite possible that a man may happen to experience a slight collision, even though no conditions for the accident were lying in his mental make-up. But we may go still further. The experiment refers to those sides of his mind which make him able to foresee the danger points, and that is decidedly the most essential factor and the one from which most can be hoped for the safety of the public. But this does not exclude the possibility that some other mental traits may become causes of accidents. The man may be too daring and may like to run risks, or he may still need discipline, or he may not be sufficiently acquainted with the local conditions. Any such secondary factors may cause some slight accidents with the man who shows rather fair results in the experimental test of his foresight. Finally, we must not forget that some men enter into such tests under a certain nervous tension and therefore may not show so well at the very first test as their mental equipment should allow. Hence it is decidedly desirable not to rely on the first test, but to repeat it. If those various interferences are taken into account, the correspondence between efficiency and the results of the tests is fairly satisfactory. It justified me in proposing that the experiments be continued and in regarding it as quite possible that later tests on the basis of this principle may be introduced at the employment of motormen.

A difficulty is presented by the valuation of the numerical results. The mere number of omissions alone cannot be decisive, as it is clear that no intelligent man would make any omission if he should give an unlimited amount of time to it; for instance, if he were to spend fifteen minutes on those 12 cards. But this is the same thing as to say that a motorman would not run over any one if he were to drive his car one mile in an hour. The practical problem is to combine the greatest possible speed with the smallest number of oversights, and both factors must therefore be considered. The subject who makes relatively many mistakes but uses a very short time must be acknowledged to be as good as the man who makes fewer mistakes but takes a longer time. In the results which I have gathered in experiments with motormen, no one has gone through those 12 cards in a shorter time than 140 seconds, while the longest time was 427 seconds. On the other hand, no one of the motormen made less than 4 omissions, while the worst ones made 28 omissions. I abstract from one extreme case with 36 omissions. On the whole, we may say that the time fluctuates between 180 and 420, the mistakes between 4 and 28. The aim is to find a formula which gives a full value to both factors and makes the material directly comparable in the form of one numerical value instead of two. If we were simply to add the number of seconds and the number of omissions, the omissions would count far too little, inasmuch as 10 additional omissions would then mean no more than 10 additional seconds. On the other hand, if we were to multiply the two figures the omissions would mean by far too much, as the transition from 4 mistakes to 8 mistakes would then be as great a change as the transition from 200 to 400 seconds, that is, from the one extreme of time to the other. Evidently we balance both factors if we multiply the number of omissions by 10 and add them to the number of seconds. The variations between 4 and 28 omissions are 24 steps, which multiplied by 10 correspond to the 240 steps which lie between 180 and 420 seconds. On that basis any additional 50 seconds would be equal to 5 additional omissions. If of two men one takes 100 seconds less than his neighbor, he is equal to him in his ability to satisfy the demands of the service, if he makes 10 mistakes more.

On the basis of this calculation I find that the old, well-trained motormen come to a result of about 450, and I should consider that an average standard. This would mean that a man who uses 400 seconds would not be allowed to make more than 5 omissions, in 350 seconds not more than 10, in 300 not more than 15, in 250 not more than 20, under the condition that these are the results of the first set of experiments. Where there are more than 20 omissions made, mere quickness ought not to be allowed as a substitute. The man who takes 150 seconds and makes 30 mistakes would come up to the same standard level of 450. Yet his characteristics would probably not serve the interests of the service. He would speed up his car, and would make better time than any one else, but would be liable to accidents. I should consider 20 mistakes with a time not longer than 250 as the permissible maximum. Among the younger motormen whom I examined, the best result was 290, in which 270 seconds were used and only 2 omissions made. Results below 350 may be considered as very good. One man, for instance, carried out the experiment in 237 seconds with 11 mistakes, which gives the result 347. From 350 to 450 may be counted as fair, 450 to 550 as mediocre, and over 550 as very poor. In the case of old men, who may be expected to adjust themselves less easily to artificial experiments, the limits may be shifted. If the experiments are made repeatedly, the valuation of the results must be changed accordingly. The training of the men in literary and mathematical work or in experimentation may be considered, as our experiments have shown that highly educated young people with long training in experimental observations can pass through the test much more quickly than any one of the motormen could. Among the most advanced graduate students who do research work in my Harvard laboratory there was no one whose result was more than 275, while, as I said, among all the motormen there was no one whose result was less than 290. The best result reached was by a student who passed through the test in 223 seconds with only 1 mistake, the total therefore being 233. Next came a student who did it in 215 seconds with 3 mistakes, total, 245; then in 228 seconds with 2 omissions, total 248, and so on.

I recapitulate: With men on the educational level and at the age that comes in question for their first appointment in the service of an electric railway company, the test proposed ought to be applied according to this scheme. If they make more than 20 mistakes, they ought to be excluded; if they make less than 20 mistakes, the number of omissions is to be multiplied by 10 and added to the number of seconds. If the sum is less than 350, their mental fitness for the avoidance of accidents is very high, between 350 and 450 fair, and more than 550 not acceptable under any conditions. I submit this, however, with the emphasis on my previous statement that the investigation is still in its first stage, and that it will need a long coöperation between science and industry in order to determine the desirable modifications and special conditions which may become necessary in making the employment of men partly dependent upon such psychological tests. There can be no doubt that the experiments could be improved in many directions. But even in this first, not adequately tested, form, an experimental investigation of this kind which demands from each individual hardly 10 minutes would be sufficient to exclude perhaps one fourth of those who are nowadays accepted into the service as motormen. This 25 per cent of the applicants do not deserve any blame. In many other occupations they might render excellent service; they are neither careless nor reckless, and they do not act against instructions, but their psychical mechanism makes them unfit for that particular combination of attention and imagination which ought to be demanded for the special task of the motorman. If the many thousands of injury and the many hundreds of death cases could be reduced by such a test at least to a half, then the conditions of transportation would have been improved more than by any alterations in the technical apparatus, which usually are the only objects of interest in the discussion of specialists. The whole world of industry will have to learn the great lesson, that of the three great factors, material, machine, and man, the man is not the least, but the most important.

Coca-Cola, Caffeine, and Mental Deficiency: Harry Hollingworth and the Chattanooga Trial of 1911

Ludy T. Benjamin, Jr., Anne M. Rogers, and Angela Rosenbaum

On 20 October 1909, agents of the United States Government stopped a truck outside of Chattanooga, Tennessee, and under federal authority over interstate commerce, seized its freight. The contraband consisted of forty barrels and twenty kegs of Coca-Cola syrup on its was from the headquarters plant in Atlanta, Georgia, to the principal bottling plant in Chattanooga. The seizure was directed from Washington, D.C., under the recently passed Federal Food and Drug Act (1906), commonly known as the Pure Food and Drug Act. In the lawsuit that was to follow, the Coca-Cola Company would be charged with marketing and selling an adulterated beverage that was injurious to health because it contained a deleterious ingredient, namely, caffeine.

In early 1911 the Coca-Cola Company was preparing its defense for the upcoming trial in Chattanooga, only several months away, when Hobart Amory Hare, a noted physician, toxicologist, medical textbook author on the faculty of Jefferson Medical College in Philadelphia, and head of Coca-Cola's team of scientific experts, realized that they had almost no evidence on the behavioral effects of caffeine on human beings. He proposed that a psychologist be hired to conduct the needed research and asked a friend, Dickinson Miller, who taught philosophy and psychology at Columbia University, for a recommendation. Miller suggested Columbia's eminent psychologist, James McKeen Cattell, who declined. Others may have been approached subsequent to Cattell, but eventually the offer fell to Harry Levi Hollingworth (1880–1956), a young instructor at Barnard College who had completed his doctorate in psychology with Cattell two years earlier. Hollingworth accepted this questionable assignment because, as he described it, he "had as yet no sanctity to preserve."[1] Writing in 1940 in an unpublished autobiography he recalled this decision:

> Here was a clear case where results of scientific importance might accrue to an investigation that would have to be financed by private interests. No experiments on such a scale as seemed necessary for conclusive results had ever been

Benjamin, Jr., L. T., Rogers, A. M., & Rosenbaum, A. (1991). Coca-Cola, caffeine, and mental deficiency: Harry Hollingworth and the Chattanooga trial of 1911. *Journal of the History of the Behavioral Sciences, 27,* 42–55.

> staged in the history of experimental psychology. . . .
>
> With me there was a double motive at work. I needed money, and here was a chance to accept employment at work for which I had been trained, with not only the cost of the investigation met but with a very satisfactory retaining fee and stipend for my own time and services. I believed I could conscientiously conduct such an investigation, without prejudice to the results, and secure information of a valuable scientific character as well as answer the practical questions raised by the sponsor of the study.[2]

As 1911 began, Harry Hollingworth certainly needed money. He was in his second year of teaching at Barnard earning an annual salary of $1,000, the same salary he had received the previous year.[3] Like many new faculty, especially those living in Manhattan, his standard of living was meager and he looked for ways to ameliorate that situation. He had married his college classmate from Nebraska, Leta Stetter, in 1908. She had hoped to teach as she had done for the past two years in Nebraska, and thus provide a much-needed second income. However, New York City barred married women from teaching.

Leta Hollingworth, who had graduated first in her class at the University of Nebraska, hoped to pursue graduate work but they lacked the money to do so.[4] Borrowing from their families was an impossibility because both families had less than modest incomes. So Leta kept house, shopped, cooked, sewed her own clothes and some of her husband's, and wrote short stories that she was unsuccessful in selling to magazines. Harry worked extra jobs, such as proctoring exams for fifty cents an hour, and for a while, he taught in the night school of Columbia University until the administration discovered that he was on the payroll twice and made him resign his evening faculty job. He also had begun to give workshops on the psychology of advertising to members of the Men's Advertising League of New York City.[5] Thus extra funds accumulated. Yet just when there seemed enough for Leta Hollingworth to begin graduate study, a family need in Nebraska would arise that would exhaust all of their savings. Referring to their desire for Leta to pursue her own intellectual pursuits, Harry wrote, ". . . it did not yet appear how soon, if ever, it was going to be her turn to get her feet on the glory road."[6]

The offer from Coca-Cola proved to a windfall for the Hollingworths. The exact sum of the contract is not known although it must have been a substantial amount. It funded Harry as director of the studies and Leta as assistant director, and according to Harry, assured all of Leta's graduate school expenses.[7]

Despite his desperate need of money in 1911, Harry Hollingworth was nevertheless cautious about undertaking this research for Coca-Cola. He was clearly aware of the stigma attached to applied work, and the "unclean" nature of those efforts had been made apparent in reactions from colleagues to his earlier work on the psychology of advertising with the New York City business community.[8] However, the hesitancy in the case of this research was more than just its applied nature; there was concern about scientific integrity raised by a large company spending a lot of money for research it hoped would be favorable to its legal and commercial needs.

According to Hollingworth, he sought to minimize that concern in his contractual arrangement with the Coca-Cola Company. The contract specified that Hollingworth would be allowed to publish the results of his studies regardless of their outcome. Further, Coca-Cola was not to use the results of the research in its advertising, nor was there to be any mention of Hollingworth's name or that of Columbia University in any promotion of Coca-Cola.[9] Still, he was aware that the questions surrounding integrity would not go away. In the preface to his published report of the research he wrote:

> The writer is well aware of a popular tendency to discredit the results of investigations financed

> by commercial firms, especially if such concerns are likely to be either directly or indirectly interested in the outcome of the experiments. He is also aware of a similar human impulse at once to attribute interpretive bias to the investigator whose labors are supported and made possible by the financial aid of a business corporation, and hence do not represent a vicarious sacrifice of time and effort on his own part.[10]

He hoped to reduce the potential for claims of bias in the research by instituting a series of experimental controls, including blind and double-blind conditions.

HARVEY WILEY AND THE FIGHT FOR PURE FOOD

The urgent necessity of Hollingworth's research and the Coca-Cola trial had come about largely because of the efforts of one man, a sixty-five-year-old chemist and long-time federal government bureaucrat—Harvey Washington Wiley (1884–1930).[11] In 1911 he was serving as Chief of the Bureau of Chemistry for the U.S. Department of Agriculture. He had gone to Washington in 1883 to join the bureau as a chemist, leaving a joint position as professor at Purdue University and chief chemist for the state of Indiana.

A trip to Germany in 1878 interested Wiley in the chemistry of food, specifically the adulteration of food. His first published report in that field, in 1881, concerned the adulteration of syrups with glucose.[12] From his post in Washington, Wiley assumed the leadership of a national effort to establish a federal law that would protect consumers from foods that were mislabeled, falsely advertised, and most important, adulterated with substances that were injurious to health. With the fervor and zeal of his strict religious upbringing, he stumped the country for the needed legislation—"every rostrum [became] a pulpit for the gospel of pure food."[13]

Wiley became a powerful figure in the federal government gathering much support from an admiring public who viewed him as their protector in Washington. He also enjoyed strong support from sections of agriculture and the food industry. However, he also had opponents, some of whom opposed him on business grounds and others who felt he had ceased being a scientist in his passion for pure foods.[14] Nevertheless, his efforts were finally rewarded on 30 June 1906 when Theodore Roosevelt signed the Pure Food and Drug Act. The bill was the result of more than twenty years of campaigning by Wiley and others, and it passed, not surprisingly, with considerable opposition. Its detractors often referred to the new law as "pure foolishness."[15]

Some of Wiley's opponents believed that his pursuit of the Coca-Cola Company was revenge against the South from whence had come the largest Congressional opposition to the passage of the pure food act. By 1910, Coca-Cola was sold in every state and territory and was, arguably, the most successful industry in the post-Reconstruction South. Thus it was a very visible target.[16] However, there seems little evidence to support a motive of vengeance. Instead, Wiley's actions can be more plausibly traced to a long-standing distaste for caffeine and his belief that it poisoned the body. As a twenty-year-old member of the Indiana Volunteers, his Civil War diary contains the following passage: "Passed outside the lines today and exchanged coffee for milk. [I am] in much better condition since I quit drinking coffee. . . ."[17]

As early as 1902, Wiley had testified before Congress that caffeine was a poison and a habit-forming drug.[18] Although he was not a proponent of coffee or tea, he was willing to tolerate public consumption of those beverages because the caffeine was a natural part of those drinks. However, caffeine was an additive in Coca-Cola which made it a beverage adulterated with a harmful ingredient. Moreover, he objected to Coca-Cola because, unlike coffee or tea, it was marketed and sold to children. He conducted investigations of Coca-Cola consumption that convinced him that there were Coca-Cola addicts. For Wiley, Coca-Cola was a serious health threat to the American public and the new law made it possible, he thought, to eradicate such products.

Wiley wanted to bring the Coca-Cola Company to court in early 1907, shortly after the Pure Food and Drug Act became law. However, he was blocked by Secretary of Agriculture James Wilson who ordered him to cease his investigations of Coca-Cola. When, in 1909, an Atlanta newspaper editor threatened to publish a story that Wilson was protecting Coca-Cola, Wilson withdrew his order. Wiley began working with the Justice Department to plan the seizure and subsequent case.[19]

The two principal charges in the suit against Coca-Cola were that it was mislabeled because it contained negligible or nonexistent quantities of either coca or cola and, of greatest significance, that it contained an *added* ingredient, caffeine, that was injurious to health. Wiley's principal objection to caffeine was its function as a stimulant. He wrote:

> . . . stimulation means increased exertion. . . . All increased energy implies increased consumption of tissue and fuel. Fatigue is nature's danger signal, to show that muscles, brain, nerves, et cetera, need rest and recreation. Any drug that strikes down the danger signal without removing the danger must of necessity be a threat. The thing to do when one is tired is to rest, to sleep, and to take real food. The thing not to do is to take a drug that makes one forget he is tired.[20]

Wiley was particularly incensed by Coca-Cola's advertisements touting the stimulant properties of the beverage. One claimed that the drink could be used to "invigorate the fatigued body and quicken the tired brain." Another said it "relieves mental and physical exhaustion." Although marketed largely as a beverage, and not a drug, advertising often conveyed the latter in proclaiming Coca-Cola as "the ideal brain tonic."[21]

HARRY HOLLINGWORTH'S CAFFEINE STUDIES

Hollingworth was not the first psychologist to investigate the behavioral effects of caffeine; however, the earlier research was inadequate on one or two grounds: (a) the studies concentrated largely on motor responses with little or no attention to cognitive processes, and (b) the studies did not use appropriate experimental controls.[22] The Coca-Cola Company believed it had adequate data about the effects of caffeine on human physiology; instead, it was looking for evidence of caffeine's effects on mental functioning. Specifically, was there any mental deficiency associated with its use, at least in terms of the quantities of caffeine that might be consumed by a drinker of Coca-Cola?

When Hollingworth was contacted to conduct the research, the trial date in Chattanooga was a little more than two months away. Thus the time pressures were considerable. Yet Hollingworth planned an extensive series of studies to run for approximately forty days, employing a scope of testing and a sophistication of methodology that had not been seen before in applied psychology. It is not surprising that Hollingworth was an excellent student of experimental method given that his graduate school mentors were Cattell, Edward L. Thorndike, and Robert S. Woodworth.

Clearly Cattell had some influence on the Hollingworth research, either directly or indirectly. The research design called for ten different major tests and a score of minor ones. Many of these were tests that had been recommended by Cattell for mental measurement.[23] Some were motor tests that measured speed, steadiness, and coordination. But most of the tests involved mental measurements in tasks of perception, association, attention, judgment, and discrimination, for example, color naming, identifying word opposites, mental calculations, and discrimination reaction times. These tests were selected to measure mental processes alone and in combination with other mental and motor processes.

Some tests combined several cognitive processes at once, for example, the cancellation test that combined attention and discrimination. In this test, subjects were given a sheet of paper with twenty rows of numbers, fifty numbers in each row. All digits from 0 to 9 were represented an equal number of times in a random order. The subjects were instructed to cross out all 7s on the page, beginning the task in the upper left hand corner of the page and proceeding systematically down the columns from that point. Thus it was possible to measure the accuracy of performance over time as well as the speed of the task. This test was selected largely because of its use as a measure of mental fatigue, and Hollingworth used it at varying intervals following caffeine administration to determine the period of effectiveness of the drug.[24]

The laboratory for this study was a six-room Manhattan apartment, rented specifically for this research. The kitchen was used to prepare the dosages, and several rooms were equipped with some of the specialized apparatus used in the testing. Sixteen subjects were selected, ten men and six women, ranging in age from nineteen to thirty-nine. They were selected to be a cross-section of the age group that made up most of Coca-Cola's consumers. Further, they were selected because of their normal caffeine consumption habits, and were classified as abstainers, occasional users, moderate users, and regular users.

Subjects were paid for their participation in the research and had to sign an agreement listing nine conditions to which they would adhere throughout the course of the study. These included prohibitions against any caffeine or alcohol usage during the study, except that administered as part of the research. A physician was hired to take periodic measurements on the subjects during the course of the study. All subjects kept daily records on their level of alertness, other measures of general health, and on the amount and placement of their sleep.

The research actually involved three separate studies. The first, and longest, began on 3 February 1911 and lasted four weeks. Subjects went through all the principal tests five times per day. The first testing began at 7:45 each morning and the last began at 5:30 in the afternoon. With Harry at his daily routine at Barnard, Leta Hollingworth was in charge of the research. Five different experimental stations existed in the apartment, each staffed by a different experimenter. Subject groups rotated among the experimental stations in a testing period until all five had been completed. Each testing station required about an hour to complete and all testing orders were counterbalanced over the course of the studies. Between testing periods, subject relaxed, read, sewed, or worked in a room in the apartment reserved for those purposes.

For the first week no subjects were given caffeine. Instead, they received daily capsules of milk-sugar solution as a placebo. This period allowed for adaptation to the testing routine and collection of baseline data on the various tests. For most subjects, caffeine doses began in the second week. At that time, subjects were divided into four groups, one of which was a milk-sugar placebo group. The three experimental groups all received caffeine of differing dosages, at different times of the day, and sometimes caffeine days were alternated with placebo days.

The study was a classic double-blind experiment. Experimenters working with the subjects did not know whether the subject had been given caffeine or the placebo. And because the substances were swallowed in capsule form, thus preventing taste, subjects were also unaware of what they were receiving. Dosage rates extended over a reasonable range on either side of the amount of caffeine a moderate drinker of Coca-Cola might consume in a day.

The second study was an intensive experiment of three days duration. This study sought specifically to determine the time course of the drug's action. All subjects were fed lunch and supper in the laboratory-apartment to control the diet. Dosage rates differed and placebos were used again. Each of the principal tests was run fifteen times on each subject, across a range of post-drug intervals. Four groups were used again, one of which took its caffeine in a mixture of soda fountain syrup and carbonated water.

The third study lasted seven days and administered differing caffeine dosages in specially prepared Coca-Cola syrup that was decaffeinated. Again, subjects and experimenters were blind as to whether the drinks did or did not contain caffeine. This study was designed to test the effects of caffeine when taken with food, namely, the sugar content of Coca-Cola and to compare the effects of the carbonated beverage with and without caffeine.

The subjects were usually gone by 6:30 each evening, yet the work for the experimenters continued. The studies were generating an enormous amount of data and Hollingworth understood that to have any results ready for the trial, it would be necessary to spend evenings analyzing the data. For that task he drew on the help of several graduate students—John Dashiell, Albert T. Poffenberger, and Edward K. Strong, Jr.—who spent their evenings together in the laboratory-apartment, generating curves, graphs, and tables. By the conclusion of the studies, more than 64,000 separate measurements had been recorded. Because of Hollingworth's "catastrophobia," each night he and a colleague made a duplicate set of the day's data which would then be housed in a separate location.

THE TRIAL IN CHATTANOOGA

The trial, which began on 16 March 1911 was already underway when Hollingworth completed the analyses of his studies. It was a major media event in Chattanooga, not only because of a company so visible as Coca-Cola being the defendant in the suit, but also because of the presence of Harvey Wiley. Wiley, age sixty-five and a life-long bachelor, was married only a few days prior to the start of the trial. His wife accompanied him to Chattanooga for their honeymoon and according to Wiley, "attended all the sessions of the court and also took great interest in the proceedings."[25] (One wonders if she had any other choice.)

Wiley had wanted to have the trial in Washington, D.C., instead of Chattanooga where the sentiment would be favorable to Coca-Cola, but he was overruled by officials in the Department of Agriculture. Upon his arrival in Chattanooga he learned, to his dismay, that the Hotel Patten, where he and his wife were staying, was owned by the Coca-Cola Company.

An impressive force had been assembled to try the government's case. There were three attorneys and a host of expert witnesses from science and medicine. Of course the Coca-Cola Company had the financial resources to respond in kind. Wiley would later complain that Coca-Cola had outbid the government for the services of some of its expert witnesses. Attorneys for both sides sat on opposite sides of the courtroom with their scientific and medical experts behind them. Occasionally one of the experts would suggest a question to be asked of one of the witnesses. The trial began with the government presenting its case. Its witnesses:

> . . . swore to the dangers of caffeine, saying it disguised fatigue and led to exhaustion, overstimulated the heart, overworked the kidneys, brought addiction, nervous debility, sometimes—though rarely—death. . . . Animal experiments with rabbits, mice, frogs, guinea pigs, and dogs, pharmacologists testified, demonstrated the debilitating, even the lethal, potential of caffeine.[26]

The proceedings were not without moments of humor. One physician, testifying for the government, described how caffeine had produced congestion in the cerebral arteries of his rabbits. When asked, in cross examination, how he had killed his animals, he admitted that he had hit them on the head with a stick.[27]

Not surprisingly, Coca-Cola's witnesses presented a very different picture of caffeine in their testimony. They acknowledged that caffeine could be harmful if consumed in large doses; however, they argued that even a frequent drinker of Coca-Cola could not consume anywhere near the quantity of caffeine that could be considered harmful. Testimony focused on the benefits of caffeine as a mild stimulant that allowed individuals to avoid muscular or mental fatigue. Coca-Cola's experts could find no evidence of depression, either muscular or mental, once the effects of the caffeine wore off. Nor was there any evidence that caffeine was habit forming.

Based on the transcript of the trial, most of the research presented on both sides appears to be poor science.[28] That was particularly true of the medical research which tended to be anecdotal—physicians reporting on observations of their patients or on their own experiences with coffee or Coca-Cola. Even among the scientists in physiology, chemistry, and pharmacology the research was frequently flawed in design or interpretation or both, for example, few subjects, inadequate controls, qualitative measurements where quantification was possible, interpreting significant differences where none likely existed, excessive caffeine doses, and confounding of caffeine with other drugs. That Hollingworth's research was an exception is evident in the trial transcript, and it was evident to the reporters who were in court each day.[29]

Hollingworth testified on 27 March 1911 as the trial began its third week. He was the ninth scientific witness called by Coca-Cola's attorneys. Armed with pieces of scientific apparatus he had brought with him from New York and numerous charts, his testimony occupied most of the morning. It was noticeably more quantitative than the testimony of earlier witnesses, a fact cited in most newspaper accounts of the trial. The Chattanooga *Daily Times* which had covered each day of the trial with a front-page story, paid high tribute to Hollingworth (even if they did misspell his name): "His testimony was by far the most interesting and technical of any yet introduced. Cross-examination failed to shake any of his deductions."[30]

Hollingworth's testimony described caffeine as a mild stimulant whose effect on motor performance was rapid and transient, whereas the effect on cognitive performance appeared more slowly but was more persistent. Of particular importance, given the fatigue arguments of Wiley, was that Hollingworth found no evidence of secondary fatigue or depression as a result of the caffeine at any dosage in his studies. He argued that the enhanced performance produced by the caffeine was a genuine drug effect and not due to some other cause such as arousal, expectation, interest, suggestion, or sensory stimulation. He noted that his studies did not address the physiological mechanisms underlying this effect.

> But whether this increased capacity comes from a new supply of energy introduced or rendered available by the drug action, or whether energy already available comes to be employed more effectively, or whether the inhibition of secondary afferent impulses is eliminated, or whether fatigue sensations are weakened and the individual's standard of performance thereby raised, no one seems to know.[31]

In his testimony, Hollingworth concluded that there was no evidence in his studies that caffeine produced any deleterious effects in mental or motor performance. He believed that if caffeine was harmful, surely that would have been demonstrated given the wide array of tests, dosages, subjects, and times and conditions of drug administration used in his studies. The only negative results he reported had to do with some subjects' ratings of poorer sleep quality following days when they had received the larger caffeine dosages.[32] No doubt the Coca-Cola Company must have been pleased with those conclusions.

The trial lasted another week beyond Hollingworth's testimony but it never reached the jury decision stage.[33] Once all of the testimony had been presented, Coca-Cola's attorneys introduced a motion to dismiss the case, arguing that the case was based on caffeine being an added ingredient, but the Coca-Cola Company contended that caffeine was one of several ingredients *inherent* in Coca-Cola. Why that motion was not made earlier in the trial is a mystery, because it was a claim that Coca-Cola made from the beginning in challenging the government's case. Judge Edward T. Sanford's ruling on the motion came as a shock to the government attorneys and Wiley, and likely to Coca-Cola's attorneys as well. In his twenty-five-page opinion on the meaning of the word "added" in the Pure Food Act, Judge Sanford stated:

> The conclusion is to my mind unavoidable that by the use of this language Congress intended to provide that a compound article of food thus known, labeled, and sold under its own distinctive name, should be assimilated to a natural product and not be deemed to be adulterated whatever the character of its ingredients . . . the caffeine contained in the article Coca-Cola is one of its regular, habitual, and essential constituents, and that without its presence, that is, if it were de-caffeinized, so to speak, the product would lack one of its essential elements and fail to produce upon the consumer a characteristic if not the most characteristic effect which is obtained from its use. In short Coca-Cola without caffeine would not be "Coca-Cola" as it is known to the public.[34]

In concluding his statement, Sanford declared the government's case invalid and directed the jury to return a verdict in favor of the claimant, the Coca-Cola Company. Thus the key question, whether or not caffeine was a substance injurious to health, was never decided by the jury.

THE BATTLE CONTINUES

The Coca-Cola Company, having endured the adverse publicity of the past years, began an advertising and consumer relations blitz touting the "vindication" of their product. Coca-Cola's president, Asa Griggs Candler, was the architect of this campaign. Candler, a long-time enemy of Wiley, must have relished the opportunity to strike back with the law on his side. Coca-Cola published several pamphlets to distribute their message to consumers and retailers. These bore such titles as "The Truth about Coca-Cola" and "The Truth, the Whole Truth, and Nothing but the Truth about Coca-Cola."[35] These pamphlets cited the research of the authorities that testified on behalf of Coca-Cola at the trial. But Hollingworth's research was rarely mentioned, perhaps due to his agreement with the company about use of his research in advertising. When his research did appear, it was a reprinted excerpt of the newspaper coverage of the trial.[36]

While this advertising campaign was ongoing, the government attorneys were preparing for an appeal filed before the United States Circuit Court of Appeals in Cincinnati. Wiley was involved in the initiation of the appeal, but resigned from the bureau in early 1912 because of political issues he was unable to resolve to his satisfaction.[37] However, he continued his fight for pure food, including his crusade to eliminate caffeine in Coca-Cola. Prior to his resignation he had arranged to assume a position with *Good Housekeeping* magazine, which he did immediately. As director of the Good Housekeeping Bureau of Food, Sanitation, and Health, his duties chiefly entailed writing a monthly column. In these he warned about the dangers of bleached flour, white rice, and alum in baking powder. Among his strongest attacks were those directed at Coca-Cola, for example, one that objected vociferously to Coca-Cola's use of the label "soft drink." He argued that "no beverage which has added to it any stimulating or stupefying drug is properly classed under the term 'soft drinks'."[38] Thus he continued his pubic claim of the noxious nature of caffeine.

Three years passed before the Appeals Court in Cincinnati reached a decision. And when they did, they upheld the lower court decision. The Coca-Cola Company, elated once more, produced a new pamphlet entitled, "Truth, Justice, and Coca-Cola," whose cover pictured the scales of justice over the trademark for the company. Its opening page read:

> On Saturday, June 13, 1914, the Court of Appeals rendered its verdict in favor of Coca-Cola settling the case forever and completely vindicating Coca-Cola. This means that Coca-Cola emerges with a clean bill of health—in effect the highest and final court decides that Coca-Cola is just exactly what we have always claimed—a wholesome, harmless, and non-habit forming beverage. And note this—this case was not decided on eloquence of counsel, or on petty technicalities. No arguments were made before jury, no play to sympathies or emotions was made, because it was the judges themselves who settled the case by a cold, critical review of the Chattanooga trial . . . The victory is absolutely one of cold justice—law and the right.[39]

The pamphlet also listed the witnesses to testify for both sides in the Chattanooga trial. Wiley is listed for the government and after his name it says in italics "who, however, failed to testify." Hollingworth is the *only* one of the Coca-Cola witnesses not listed, again, presumably because of his prior agreement with the company.

The pamphlet is clearly not very truthful. The Appeals Court did not rule on the safety of Coca-Cola as a beverage, rather it supported Judge Sanford's decision that the federal suit alleged something that was not true, that is, it upheld the opinion that caffeine was not an added ingredient. The author of the pamphlet should have known better than to say that anything is settled forever, and should have been better educated about the upper level of the judicial system of the United States. Because the U.S. Department of Justice immediately appealed the case to the Supreme Court.

Wiley, from his post at *Good Housekeeping,* was not about to let this new pamphlet of "truth" pass without comment. In a 1914 column in the magazine, he argued correctly about the meaning of the two court rulings and warned again about the dangers of Coca-Cola. The following passage is indicative of his crusading appeal:

> A bright-eyed small boy of ten was turned over to me by his mother, the other day, for a few plain words as to why he had better drink lemonade and grape juice instead of Coca-Cola. I told him the story, without exaggeration; just what was in it, and why caffeine in either coffee or Coca-Cola, was not good for a growing boy. His eyes grew steadily larger, and at the end he said with great earnestness: "But why do they let them make it? The signs all say 'Delicious, Refreshing'." Why indeed?[40]

The issue that had been "settled forever" was unsettled in 1916 in a Supreme Court decision written by Justice Charles E. Hughes that stated caffeine *was* an added ingredient within the meaning of the Pure Food and Drugs Act. The case was remanded to the district court in Chattanooga to be retried on the question of whether or not the beverage contained a substance that was injurious to health. However, before the case could come to trial again, Coca-Cola changed its formula, reducing the caffeine content by half.[41] Thus at the trial, the Coca-Cola Company entered a plea of *nolo contendere,* arguing that a trial based on the seized syrup—the famous forty barrels and twenty kegs—would not be appropriate because the decision would be based on a formula that was no longer used. The judge agreed and dismissed the charges, although Coca-Cola was required to pay all court costs, which it did.[42]

THE LEGACY OF THE CAFFEINE STUDIES FOR HOLLINGWORTH

Harry Hollingworth published the caffeine research funded by the Coca-Cola Company in April 1912 as a 166-page monograph in Robert Woodworth's series, *Archives of Psychology.*[43] It was the first of twenty-five books that he would write in his career, most of them in the field of applied psychology. Given the controversy over caffeine, whose flames Wiley continued to fan, it is not surprising that the book got a lot of attention, particularly in the medical and pharmacological communities. No behavioral studies of such comprehensiveness, in terms of independent and dependent variables, had ever been conducted.

Reviews of the book appeared in many of the medical, pharmacological, and psychological journals which offered high praise not only for the valuable findings but also for the sophistication of the experimental design. The caffeine research on human beings, prior to Hollingworth's work, consisted largely of demonstrations of its effectiveness as a stimulant in ergographic studies or studies of reaction time. Thus the wealth of cognitive tests in Hollingsworth's research added substantially to the knowledge of caffeine effects.[44] One medical journal reviewing the caffeine monograph commented:

> The careful description of methods, the presentation of a mass of entirely new data, and the obviously frank, if not actually objective, discussion of the data make this paper a very important contribution to the pharmacology of caffeine.[45]

An editorial in the *Journal of the American Medical Association* praised the studies for their rigor and argued that such thoroughness was the only way to provide "an adequate basis for correct conclusions as to the possible dangers of the use of caffeine-containing beverages."[46] One arrogant review in the *New York Medical Journal* lauded the accomplishments and conclusions of the research but cautioned ". . . it must be remembered that the author is a psychologist and that his experiments should be taken only from the psychological point of view."[47]

In the years that followed, Hollingworth's caffeine monograph was cited frequently in the pharmacological literature. As interest in psychopharmacology grew, it was cited in the newer literature on caffeine, and in other articles it was portrayed as a model of good research. It is still cited in current literature, mostly in pharmacological journals.[48]

The research seems to have had little impact on psychology during its time, largely because of psychology's disinterest in drug effects. The psychology textbooks of the 1910s and 1920s rarely cited Hollingworth's monograph. When it did appear, it was either in a discussion of experimental issues (mostly control) in which it was included as an example of rigorous research, or it was part of a discussion of drug effects on behavior. Nearly thirty years after conducting the studies, Hollingworth wrote:

> I have always been glad that we took on this project, which in the beginning appeared to all concerned to be a somewhat dubious undertaking. It did yield results of scientific value and they have stood the test of time and of such repetition as has been accorded them. . . . The investigation, and its report, did I believe its bit to break down some of the taboos then prevalent and to encourage cooperative investigation in which science provides the insight and technique and industry offers the problems and the means.[49]

Hollingworth's assertion that the caffeine studies helped to build the bridge between academic psychology and industry is difficult to document. Clearly such cooperative ventures in psychology increased in frequency, and the stigma associated with industry-sponsored research diminished over time. The quality of the caffeine research was generally acknowledged in the scientific community of psychology, and certainly Hollingworth's reputation as a scientist grew, earning him the presidency of the American Psychological Association in 1927 and membership in the Society of Experimental Psychologists. And maybe it increased the acceptability of such applied research.

The greatest impact of the caffeine research was on Harry Hollingworth himself. It erased the deficit line that had become an annual fixture in the Hollingworth family budget. And it showed him how he could supplement his modest faculty salary. In his autobiography he says there were two dominating "goads" in his life: one was intellectual hunger and the other was poverty. In the beginning the Hollingworths struggled to be able to afford food and decent clothing. But as those needs were met, Harry longed for the ability to "participate in life": traveling throughout the world and enjoying the many cultural opportunities in New York City.[50] The funds from the caffeine investigation, which permitted him and his wife to spend much of their summer of 1911 in Europe, provided a taste of life that drew him into a profitable career as an applied psychologist.[51]

In assessing Hollingworth's life, the caffeine research is arguably the most significant event in his career. As an immediate outcome, it provided the financial means for Leta Hollingworth's graduate education. For Harry it was a vision of his future in psychology and a means to a comfortable life. It marked an auspicious beginning to a career of substantial achievement. Thus it is a significant chapter in his life, if not, in fact, in the history of industrial psychology.

NOTES

1. Harry L. Hollingworth, "Memories of the Early Development of the Psychology of Advertising," *Psychological Bulletin* 35 (1938): 308.
2. H. L. Hollingworth, "Years at Columbia," unpublished autobiography written in 1940. Collection of the Nebraska State Historical Society, Lincoln, Nebraska, p. 65.
3. Salary page showing Hollingworth's Barnard salaries from 1909–1946. In Hollingworth Papers, Archives of the History of American Psychology, University of Akron, Akron, Ohio.
4. For biographical material on Leta S. Hollingworth (1886–1939) see H. L. Hollingworth, *Leta Stetter Hollingworth: A Biography* (Lincoln: University of Nebraska Press, 1943). Reissued by Anker Publishing Company, Bolton, Mass., 1990. See also the special issue of *Roeper Review* (1990, vol. 12) that contains twenty-one articles on the life and work of Leta Hollingworth.
5. H. L. Hollingworth, "Years at Columbia," pp. 56–58.
6. Ibid., p. 53
7. Ibid., p. 96. A letter from Leta Hollingworth to Anna Stetter Fischer (Leta's cousin) dated 28 April 1911 states "We did a big experiment for the Coca-Cola Company and made quite a neat little 'wad' of money." Copy in possession of Ludy T. Benjamin, Jr.; original in family papers in Garland, Nebraska.
8. See H. L. Hollingworth, "Memories of the Early Development of the Psychology of Advertising."
9. H. L. Hollingworth, "Years at Columbia," p. 66. No copy of the contract has been located, either in the Hollingworth Papers at the Archives of the History of American Psychology or in the Coca-Cola Archives in Atlanta.
10. H. L. Hollingworth, "The Influence of Caffein on Mental and Motor Efficiency," *Archives of Psychology* 22 (April 1912): iii.
11. For biographical information on Wiley see Oscar E. Anderson, Jr., *The Health of a Nation: A Biography of Harvey Wiley,* (Chicago: University of Chicago Press, 1958); Harvey W. Wiley, *An Autobiography* (Indianapolis: Bobbs-Merrill, 1930); and Maurice Natenberg, *The Legacy of Doctor Wiley* (Chicago: Regent House, 1957).
12. Harvey W. Wiley, "The Adulteration of Syrups in Indiana," report to the Indiana Department of Agriculture, 1881. See Chapter 2 of Anderson, *The Health of a Nation.* Wiley achieved his federal government post, in part, because of his expertise in sugar at a time when the government was seeking to improve sugar production, thus reducing reliance on foreign imports. See William L. Fox, "Harvey W. Wiley's Search for American Sugar Self-sufficiency," *Agricultural History* 54 (1980): 516–526.
13. James Harvey Young, "Three Southern Food and Drug Cases," *The Journal of Southern History* 49 (1983): 4.
14. See "Review of the Wiley Investigation," *The American Food Journal* (15 November 1911): 1–4; "Dr. Wiley's Resignation," *Scientific American* (30 March 1912): 36; "Dr. Wiley, A Zealot," *The Medical Herald* 31 (1912): 187–188.
15. For an excellent history of the law see James H.

Young, *Pure Food: Securing the Federal Food and Drugs Act of 1906* (Princeton, N.J.: Princeton University Press, 1989). Wiley's version of the law's history and its aftermath is presented in his book, *The History of a Crime Against the Food Law* (privately printed in 1929 and reprinted in 1976 by Arno Press, New York). The lengthy subtitle of the book is descriptive of Wiley's dissatisfaction with the subsequent enforcement and interpretation of the law—"The Amazing Story of the National Food and Drugs Law Intended to Protect the Health of the People, Perverted to Protect Adulteration of Food and Drugs." In 1956, on the fiftieth anniversary of the Pure Food and Drugs Act, the United States Postal Service issued a three-cent commemorative postage stamp featuring Wiley's picture.

16. Young, "Three Southern Food and Drug Cases," pp. 8–9. The success of soft drinks in America at the time of the seizure is indicated by the existence of 4,916 bottling plants and annual sales of $43 million in 1910. See John J. Riley, *A History of the American Soft Drink Industry: 1807–1957* (New York: Arno Press, 1972; originally published by the American Bottlers of Carbonated Beverages in 1958).

17. 27 June 1864 entry in Wiley's Civil War diary. Wiley Papers, Box 213, Manuscript Division, Library of Congress, Washington, D.C., (hereafter "Wiley Papers").

18. In speeches, Wiley regularly linked caffeine with other habit-forming drugs such as opium and cocaine, and he often indicated that he viewed caffeine as the most serious public health hazard. In a 1909 lecture he stated, "It seems to me that the traffic in cocaine and opium and their products may be easily controlled because they are not produced in any quantity in the United States, nor are they generally purchased by the people. On the other hand, the beverages containing caffeine are universally employed, almost in every family. . . ." From "Abstract of Remarks Given before the Temperance Conference of the International Reform Bureau," Washington, D.C., 16 and 17 December 1909. Wiley Papers.

19. H. W. Wiley, *Autobiography,* pp. 261–262. This incident marked Coca-Cola's third clash with the federal government since the company was founded in 1886. The first trouble resulted from the small amount of cocaine in the beverage, and that was eliminated by changing the manufacturing process in 1898. The second difficulty stemmed from exaggerated reports of its alcoholic content in 1907, a time of campaigns to establish prohibition. The U.S. Army was concerned enough to ban Coca-Cola sales on all of its bases. But the alcohol content proved to be a negligible trace. The Army ban was lifted after a few months, and the alcohol furor largely disappeared. See Young, "Three Southern Food and Drug Cases," pp. 5–8.

20. H. W. Wiley, "The Coca-Cola Controversy," *Good Housekeeping* 55 (1912): 392.

21. These slogans were used in advertisements from 1898 to 1911. From the Archives of the Coca-Cola Company, Atlanta, Georgia (Hereafter, "Coca-Cola Archives"). For a collection of older Coca-Cola advertisements, see Pat Watters, *Coca-Cola: An Illustrated History* (Garden City, N.Y.: Doubleday, 1978). Psychologist John B. Watson may have believed Coca-Cola's claim as "the ideal brain tonic." Recalling his senior year at Furman University in 1898, Watson wrote, "I was the only man who passed the final Greek exam. I did it only because I went to my room at two o'clock the afternoon before the exam, took with me one quart of Coca-Cola syrup, and sat in my chair and crammed until time for the exam next day." From John B. Watson, "Autobiography," in *A History of Psychology in Autobiography,* ed. Carl Murchison (Worcester, Mass.: Clark University Press, 1936), vol. 3, pp. 271–272.

22. The notable exception was a study on the effects of caffeine on muscular and mental fatigue performed by British psychologist W. H. R. Rivers. Although the study employed good controls, it suffered in terms of generalizability using only two subjects, three dependent variables, and a short time course. W. H. R. Rivers, *The Influence of Alcohol and Other Drugs on Fatigue* (London: Edward Arnold, 1908), pp. 22–49.

23. See Michael M. Sokal, ed., *Psychological Testing and American Society, 1890–1930* (New Brunswick, N.J.: Rutgers University Press, 1987).

24. H. L. Hollingworth, "The Influence of Caffein," pp. 121–131.

25. Wiley, *Autobiography,* p. 282. Anna Kelton Wiley kept a diary during the course of the trial. In it she gives an account of the people she and her husband met on the train to Chattanooga. They included Judge Edward T. Sanford, who would preside in the trial, and John W. Mallett, a professor emeritus of chemistry from the University of Virginia and Confederate Army veteran who was one of Coca-Cola's star witnesses. The other diary entries on the trial consist of daily newspaper clippings. See "Account of the Coca-Cola Trial," Wiley Papers.

26. Young, "Three Southern Food and Drug Cases," p. 13.

27. Hollingworth, "Years at Columbia," p. 70.

28. Transcript for "The United States vs. Forty Barrels and Twenty Kegs Coca-Cola," in the National Archives, Atlanta Regional Archives Branch, Atlanta, Georgia, Record Group No. 21, Box 121.

29. The quality of his research was recognized by Hollingworth who wrote, somewhat immodestly, in his autobiography, "And how different were our carefully controlled experimental findings from much of the anecdotal and misguided testimony that appeared on both sides," "Years at Columbia," p. 70.

30. "Coca-Cola Compared to Other Drinks," *The Daily Times* (Chattanooga) (28 March 1911), p. 1. Wiley may not have been as impressed with Hollingworth's research or perhaps he did not like the conclusions drawn from the studies. Whatever the reason, Wiley did not include Hollingworth's research in a summary he wrote of the evidence for and against caffeine. See "The Effects of Caffein Upon the Human Organism," June 1915, Wiley Papers.

31. H. L. Hollingworth, "The Influence of Caffein," p. 165.

32. See Hollingworth's testimony in the trial transcript, National Archives, Atlanta Regional Archives Branch, pp. 1097–1119. See also H. L. Hollingworth, "The Influence of Caffein."

33. Harvey Wiley did not testify in the trial and he was soundly criticized in the press for failing to do so. Wiley said he decided not to testify because he would have been disqualified as an expert witness because he had no actual experience in caffeine research. See Anderson, *The Health of a Nation,* p. 237. The critics were especially upset that government funds had been used to send Wiley to Chattanooga explicitly as an expert witness. See letter from H. L. Harris to G. C. Morehead, 18 October 1911, Wiley Papers.

34. Chattanooga trial transcript, National Archives, Atlanta Regional Branch, pp. 3180 and 3185.

35. Copies of the pamphlets are in the Coca-Cola Archives.

36. In published accounts of the trial, Hollingworth's research was often prominently featured. See, for example, "Coca-Cola Litigation Ends with Defeat for the Government," *The American Food Journal* (15 April 1911): 1–8. The Coca-Cola Company cited Hollingworth's research in four places in a thirty-two page document it prepared in 1912 for the Committee of the House of Representatives on Interstate and Foreign Commerce. That document was written in response to two House bills that would amend the Pure Food Act by adding caffeine to the list of substances deemed "habit forming" and "deleterious." Hollingworth's research was cited as "proving" that caffeine was neither. See "Statement on Behalf of the Coca-Cola Company in Regard the Caffeine Contents of Coca-Cola." Coca-Cola Archives.

37. See Anderson, *The Health of a Nation,* pp. 248–253. Editorial responses to Wiley's resignation were mixed, but most journals and magazines felt that the American public had lost an important ally and protector. See *The Literary Digest* (23 March 1912): 578; *Journal of the American Medical Association* (23 March 1912): 129; *The Pacific Pharmacist* (April 1912): 327–329.

38. H. W. Wiley, "Soft Drinks and Dope," *Good Housekeeping* 55 (1912): 244. See also H. W. Wiley, "The Coca-Cola Controversy," *Good Housekeeping* 55 (April 1912): 386–394.

39. "Truth, Justice, and Coca-Cola," published by the Coca-Cola Company in 1914. Coca-Cola Archives.

40. H. W. Wiley, "Coca-Cola and the Circuit Court of Appeals," *Good Housekeeping* 59 (1914): 495–497.

41. Although the Coca-Cola attorneys testified to the reduction in caffeine in the manufacture of Coca-Cola, Wiley doubted the truth of the company's claim. He wrote to the U.S.D.A. Bureau of

Chemistry asking for its data on the caffeine content of Coca-Cola taken over a ten-year span of assessing the beverage. But the bureau would not release the information to Wiley, prompting a lengthy letter of complaint to President Calvin Coolidge on 3 June 1925. Wiley Papers.

42. Coca-Cola's expenses for the three trials totaled more than $85,000. See Charles H. Candler, *Asa Griggs Candler* (Atlanta: Emory University Press, 1950), pp. 147–152.

43. See H. L. Hollingworth, "The Influence of Caffein." Hollingworth's initial presentation of the data (other than the court testimony) was at a meeting of the College of Physicians of Philadelphia on 23 October 1911. That address, which bore the same title as the 1912 monograph, was published in *The Therapeutic Gazette* (15 January 1912): 1–16. Subsequently he used additional analyses of the caffeine data to publish three other articles: on quality and amount of sleep, *American Journal of Psychology* 23 (1912): 89–100; on typewriting performance, *Psychological Review* 19 (1912): 66–73; and on a comparison with alcohol, *The Therapeutic Gazette* (15 February 1921): 1–10.

44. See Vivian A. C. Henmon's review of the monograph in *Journal of Philosophy, Psychology, and Scientific Methods* 10 (1913): 681–682.

45. *The Post Graduate: A Monthly Journal of Medicine, Surgery, and Medical Education* (July 1912): 155.

46. "The Influence of Caffeine on Mental and Motor Efficiency and on the Circulation," *Journal of the American Medical Association* 58 (1912): 784–785.

47. "The Toxicity of Caffeine," *New York Medical Journal* (May 1912): 1052.

48. A search of the 1983–1988 annuals of the *Science Citation Index and Social Science Citation Index* yielded twenty-two citations of Hollingworth's 1912 monograph.

49. H. L. Hollingworth, "Years at Columbia," p. 72.

50. Ibid., p. 48.

51. In his career, Hollingworth accepted many consulting jobs from a wide variety of companies. Income from this work and his book royalties made him moderately wealthy. Evidence of that is the scholarship he established at Columbia University in memory of his wife with a cash gift of $51,000 in 1944. Hollingworth Papers.

CHAPTER **16**

AMERICAN PSYCHOLOGY'S SOCIAL AGENDA: THE ISSUE OF RACE

When the American Psychological Association (APA) was founded in 1892, its sole objective, according to its bylaws was to advance psychology as a science. That statement of objectives has been changed only once in the more than 100-year existence of the Association. When the APA was reorganized in 1945 and established its newly created Central Office in Washington, D.C., its new bylaws contained an expanded objectives statement: "The object of the American Psychological Association shall be to advance psychology as a science, as a profession, and as a means of promoting human welfare" (Wolfle, 1946, p. 3). Those two additions recognized significant roles for psychologists in the application of psychological science.

To *advance psychology as a profession* acknowledged the growing importance of applied psychology, far beyond the beginnings discussed in the previous chapter. For years, many psychologists had been working outside the traditional university setting. The APA had been reluctant to recognize that side of psychology and had prevented applied psychologists, often called consulting psychologists, from using the APA to further their interests. But by the end of World War II, the number of applied psychologists had reached a critical mass, and their number promised to get significantly larger with the need for psychological services for hundreds of thousands of veterans returning from the war. This end-of-war demand led to the founding of the modern profession of clinical psychology, initially through the cooperation of the APA and the Veterans Administration (VA), in establishing clinical psychology training programs in universities and internship training sites in the VA hospitals. Significant developments included the establishment by APA, in 1946, of procedures to accredit clinical psychology programs in university psychology departments and, in 1952, similar procedures for counseling psychology programs. Also of great significance was a conference sponsored by the APA in Boulder, Colorado, in the summer of 1949 that created a new training model for clinical psychologists that required them to be knowledgeable about scientific research in psychology as well as clinical practice (see Raimy, 1950). This training model, often referred to as the scientist–practitioner model or the Boulder model, is still the principal training model used today in doctoral programs of clinical, counseling, and school psychology.

To *advance psychology as a means of promoting human welfare* described a third role for psychologists, one that included psychologists in research as well as those in practice. Early in the twentieth century, American psychologists had seen their research and theories used in the debates over social issues such as child labor, co-education, immigration, and prohibition. Some of these early psychologists actually initiated research programs specifically aimed at social issues; recall (from Chapter 9) the work of Leta Hollingworth (1886–1939), who investigated the assertions of the biological inferiority of women. Her work occurred at a time in American history when women were struggling to gain the right to vote, a right eventually achieved in 1920 by the Nineteenth Amendment to the U.S. Constitution.

Psychological research on social issues was not widespread before the 1930s, nor was it popular in the community of academic psychologists. Applying psychology to social problems was stigmatized, in the same way that all applied psychology was viewed, as less important than the "pure" research of the laboratory. Many in psychology felt that application was not the role of the psychologist, that psychologists ought to remain true to research, allowing the application to be done by lawyers, educators, politicians, physicians, and so forth. To be a scientist meant a life engaged in the pursuit of truth, a kind of holy crusade. This attitude was expressed quite well by sociologist Albion Small who wrote that "The prime duty of everyone connected with our graduate schools is daily to renew the vow of allegiance to research ideals. . . . The first commandment with promise for graduate schools is: Remember the research ideal, to keep it holy!" (Storr, 1973, pp. 48–49). For those who agreed with Small, applied psychology was bad enough; applied psychology aimed at social issues was even worse. And yet there was a growing awareness among American psychologists that the science of psychology was important for improving human welfare, and they were interested in engaging in that kind of work. A twist of fate in American history was soon to give them their chance.

The good times of the 1920s in America came to an end at the close of that decade with the crash of the stock market, signaling the beginning of the Great Depression. In contrast to the public euphoria of the 1920s, the 1930s brought social problems to the awareness of many: unemployment, hunger, racism, labor–management disputes, poverty, and impending war.

Amid the Great Depression, a new psychological organization was formed.

An extremely controversial organization, its founding represented an act of courage because many psychologists saw the society as a communist or socialist organization; indeed, the FBI established a file on the organization in the 1930s (see Harris, 1980). The organization was named the Society for the Psychological Study of Social Issues (SPSSI), and it continues today as one of the more than fifty divisions of the APA.

The beginnings of SPSSI can be traced to 1935, when psychologists Ross Stagner and Isadore Krechevsky (later David Krech) talked about common frustrations such as the avoidance of political questions by psychologists and the lack of opportunity for psychology to contribute solutions to the social ills of the day (Stagner, 1986). They also were frustrated by the problems of unemployment faced by new psychologists, a problem exacerbated by the influx of European psychologists fleeing the Nazi regime. It has been suggested that some of the SPSSI organizers hoped to manufacture jobs for psychologists by creating a social agenda for behavioral research (see Finison, 1976, 1979).

The discussions between Stagner and Krechevsky led to a plan of action to organize psychologists with similar interests. In February of 1936, Krechevsky wrote to a small number of psychologists he felt might be kindred spirits. Sixteen in addition to Stagner and Krechevsky agreed to be part of an organizing committee, including social psychologist Gordon Allport (who would, in 1954, publish an important book on the psychology of prejudice) and learning theorist Edward C. Tolman (whose work was discussed in Chapter 12). Acting as secretary, Krechevsky mailed a letter to several hundred members of APA, describing the plans for the new organization and asking for indications of interest. He wrote: "In general, we wish to establish an organization of accredited psychologists to promote specific research projects on *contemporary* psychological problems; to collect, analyze, and disseminate data on the psychological consequences of our present economic, political and cultural crisis; to encourage the participation of psychologists *as psychologists* in the activities of the day" (Benjamin, 1993, p. 170). Most replies supported the goals of the new society, but several were quite critical, such as the one from Colgate University's G. H. Estabrooks: "With reference to your mimeographed sheets concerning participation of psychologists in the contemporary political world, allow me to register my hearty dissent with approximately everything contained therein" (Benjamin, 1993, p. 174).

The initial organizing meeting of SPSSI was held in September, 1936, in conjunction with the annual meeting of the APA, and more than 100 people attended. Following this meeting, another letter was sent to the nearly 2,000 members of the APA, explaining the two goals of the new society as follows:

> One is to encourage research upon those psychological problems most vitally related to modern social, economic and political policies. The second is to help the public and its representatives to understand and to use in the formation of social policies, contributions from the scientific investigation of human behavior. (Krech & Cartwright, 1956, p. 471)

More than 330 psychologists accepted the invitation to join SPSSI as charter members, including Kurt Lewin (1890–1947), whose program of "action research" on social issues, so clearly consistent with SPSSI's goals, would define the field of social psychology for more than three decades. In the years that followed, SPSSI encouraged research on social issues and even founded its own journal, *The Journal of Social Issues,* to publish such research. It supported the application of psychological knowledge to a multitude of social problems such as divorce, war, pornography, drug addiction, violence, and racial prejudice. The last of these subjects is the focus of this chapter. Further, that focus is mostly about racial comparisons of blacks and whites because most of the psychological and popular literature dealt with that racial comparison.

When the science of psychology emerged in the late nineteenth century, the Western world already was clear on the question of the comparative worth of the races. In his classic book, *Hereditary Genius* (see the excerpt in Chapter 7), Galton (1869) had, via his own observations during a trip to Africa, determined that the black race was substantially inferior to the white race on a number of intellectual and behavioral dimensions. Those comments merely confirmed what almost all of white Europe already believed to be the truth. By the time that psychology laboratories were being founded in America, the "race question" had already been answered there as well—blacks, Hispanics, and Native Americans were believed to be inferior to whites. This conclusion was not based on any research. In fact, the idea of doing research to discover if there were differences among the races would have been considered incredibly absurd. Most whites believed that the differences among races were so patently obvious that to have subjected people to scientific investigation would clearly have been a waste of time (see Duckitt, 1992). So for whites, the race question had already been answered. What remained was how to deal with what was viewed as the inferior races, the so-called "race problem."

The race question, though answered, would not stay answered. There were dissenters, growing in number in the twentieth century, who questioned the agreed-upon conclusion. Among them were William James, who spoke and wrote about racial injustice in America (Plous, 1994), and E. B. Titchener (Beardsley, 1973). Clearly, some scientific data were needed to show these nonbelievers the nature of their folly. Perhaps the first research to be conducted in race psychology was an 1895 study of reaction time published in the *Psychological Review* by R. M. Bache. The data were actually collected, at Bache's suggestion, by Lightner Witmer in his psychology laboratory at the University of Pennsylvania. Witmer tested the reaction times of twelve whites, eleven blacks, and eleven Native Americans to auditory, visual, and tactile stimuli, and found that Native Americans had the fastest reaction times in all three conditions, followed by blacks, and then by the whites. Thus whites had the *slowest* reaction times; clearly, these data did not fit with a notion of white superiority. However, for Bache they did. He reasoned that the faster reaction time for Native Americans and blacks indicated that their minds operated automatically and reflexively as opposed to the contemplative nature of white minds. Thus the slower reaction times did, after all, indicate the mental superiority of whites.

In the first couple of decades of the twentieth century, a number of prominent American psychologists offered their views on the nature of African Americans. G. Stanley Hall referred to black Americans as primitive people whose mental development approximated that of a white adolescent, and for Native Americans, that of a child (Hall, 1905; Muschinske, 1977). Columbia University's Robert S. Woodworth (1916) and Stanford University's Lewis Terman (1916), the creator of the Stanford-Binet intelligence test, also wrote about the mental inferiority of black Americans.

Had you been reading the American psychology journals at this time, you would have encountered a number of articles that testified to the inferiority of blacks. This excerpt from the *Psychological Bulletin* in 1912 is from a review of the psychology of racial differences and is typical of the dominant beliefs of that time:

> . . . the mental qualities of the Negro [may be summarized] as: lacking in filial affection; strong migratory instincts and tendencies; little sense of veneration, integrity, or honor; shiftless, indolent, untidy, improvident, extravagant, lazy, untruthful, lacking in persistence and initiative, and unwilling to work continuously at details. Indeed, experience with the Negro in class rooms indicates that it is impossible to get the child to do anything with continued accuracy, and similarly in industrial pursuits, the Negro shows a woeful lack of power of sustained activity and constructive conduct . . (Bruner, 1912, pp. 387–388).

With the emphasis on mental tests, and particularly intelligence tests in the 1910s and 1920s, a number of studies reported race differences that supported beliefs in white superiority. But in the 1930s, those views began to be altered dramatically, partly because many Americans looked at racial issues in the new light cast by Adolph Hitler's notion of racial superiority. By the 1940s, many American psychologists had abandoned their belief in inherent racial differences and were arguing instead that the differences were the result of prejudice and bias in American society or within the psychological studies themselves. What brought about such a dramatic and rapid change in psychological thought is the subject of one of the readings in this chapter.

It should not be surprising that attitudes purporting the intellectual inferiority of blacks would prevent them from access to higher education. Between 1876 and 1920, it is estimated that 10,000 Ph.D. degrees had been awarded in America. Yet only eleven of those had gone to blacks (Guthrie, 1976). One of those eleven was Francis Cecil Sumner (1895–1954), who earned his doctorate at Clark University, where G. Stanley Hall chaired his thesis committee. Sumner is considered the father of black American psychologists, not just because he was the first black psychologist but also because, as head of the Psychology Department at Howard University in Washington, D.C. from 1928 to 1954, he was responsible for encouraging a number of black Americans to pursue advanced study in psychology. One of those students was Kenneth B. Clark

(1914–) who completed his baccalaureate and master's degrees with Sumner at Howard before going to Columbia University for his doctorate, which he received in 1940. At Columbia, Clark was most influenced by social psychologist Otto Klineberg (1899–1992), whose 1935 book, *Race Differences,* concluded that "there is no adequate proof of fundamental race differences in mentality, and that those differences which are found are in all probability due to culture and the social environment . . ." (p. vii).

While a graduate student at Columbia, Clark collaborated on a series of studies initiated by Mamie Phipps (1917–1983; then a graduate student at Howard University, and who would later marry Kenneth Clark) on racial identification in black preschool children. These studies investigated self-awareness and self-esteem in black children and were published jointly by the Clarks in the 1930s and 1940s. When they completed these studies, the Clarks could never have imagined how important they would be. Approximately fifteen years later, their research would play a part in what is arguably the most important Supreme Court decision of the twentieth century. The case was *Brown v. Board of Education, Topeka, Kansas* (1954), and the unanimous decision from the justices declared school segregation illegal. The head attorney for Brown, the plaintiff in the case, was Thurgood Marshall (later a distinguished Supreme Court Justice), who was employed by the Legal Defense Fund of the National Association for the Advancement of Colored People (NAACP). SPSSI was active in helping Marshall with the testimony, and Kenneth Clark and several other prominent SPSSI members testified before the Court for the plaintiff. In the Court's written decision, the research of the Clarks was cited as influential in demonstrating scientifically the harmful effects of segregation. It was not only a great victory for all Americans who opposed school segregation, but it was an important accomplishment for the science of psychology as well because it marked the first time that psychological research had ever been cited in a Supreme Court decision. And it was a dream come true for the members of SPSSI to see one of their goals realized—to have psychological research affect national social policy.

One of the Clark and Clark studies presented to the Court appears as a selection in this chapter. In 1960, Kenneth Clark was elected president of SPSSI, and in 1970, he became the first black American to be elected president of the American Psychological Association. Mamie Phipps Clark, whose master's thesis work at Howard University had begun the studies that the Supreme Court found so compelling, suffered the double discrimination of being both female and black. She was never able to secure an academic position, and instead, worked in various government and private agency positions. In 1946, she and her husband started the Northside Center for Child Development in Harlem, which assisted children with all kinds of educational and psychological needs. From 1946 until 1979, she served as executive director of that center. She died in 1983 (see Guthrie, 1990, for a biographical sketch of her life and work).

This brief account of psychology's social agenda has focused on only one social issue, that of race, and mostly on only one race. Even with such a focus, this introduction cannot do justice to such a complex topic. It is hoped that, combined with the readings, this introduction will give the reader a sense of the evolution of American psychology's treatment of race. For those seriously interested in this topic, the reference section for this introduction contains a number of important readings. Particularly recommended for a broad overview of racial issues and African Americans in psychology is the book by Robert Guthrie, *Even the Rat was White: A Historical View of Psychology* (1976).

THE READINGS

The first selection is by Otto Klineberg, who was elected president of SPSSI in 1943. It is the final chapter of his classic book on racial differences, which offers his conclusions after reviewing all the extant data and theory on racial differences and finally, the practical implications for the conclusions reached in his book. This book would shape the course of psychological thought on race for the next thirty years.

The second selection is by Kenneth B. Clark and Mamie P. Clark, a study conducted in 1940–1941 using black children from segregated schools in Arkansas and black children from integrated schools in Massachusetts. The results are disturbing in what they reveal about the impact of segregation on children's self-awareness and self-esteem. These data helped convince the Supreme Court justices that "separate but equal" schools were, in reality, not equal.

The third selection is also by Klineberg. It was written in 1986, a little more that fifty years after the publication of his book on race relations. In this article, Klineberg provides a personal account of SPSSI's involvement in the *Brown v. Board of Education* case and the course of race relations in the years that followed. It is interesting to read that, after fifty years of activism, Klineberg continued to be optimistic about the improvement of race relations and the role that psychology can play in accomplishing that.

The final selection is by historian of psychology Franz Samelson, whose work you encountered in Chapter 11 describing the slow spread of Watsonian behaviorism. In this article, Samelson describes the rather abrupt shift in psychological thinking about race that occurred in the first half of the twentieth century. The article also addresses the evolution of the field of social psychology during this time.

REFERENCES

Allport, G. W. (1954). *The nature of prejudice*. Reading, MA: Addison-Wesley.

Bache, R. M. (1895). Reaction time with reference to race. *Psychological Review, 2,* 475–486.

Beardsley, E. H. (1973). The American scientist as social activist: Franz Boas, Burt G. Wilder, and the cause of racial justice, 1900–1915. *ISIS, 64,* 50–66.

Benjamin, L. T., Jr. (1993). *A history of psychology in letters*. Dubuque, IA: Brown & Benchmark.

Bruner, F. G. (1912). The primitive races in America. *Psychological Bulletin, 9,* 380–390.

Duckitt, J. (1992). Psychology and prejudice: A historical analysis and integrative framework. *American Psychologist, 47,* 1182–1193.

Finison, L. J. (1976). Unemployment, politics, and the history of organized psychology. *American Psychologist, 31,* 747–755.

Finison, L. J. (1979). An aspect of the early history of the Society for the Psychological Study of Social Issues: Psychologists and labor. *Journal of the History of the Behavioral Sciences, 15,* 29–37.

Galton, F. (1869). *Hereditary genius.* London: Macmillan.

Guthrie, R. V. (1976). *Even the rat was white: A historical view of psychology.* New York: Harper & Row.

Guthrie, R. V. (1990). Mamie Phipps Clark (1917–1983). In A. N. O'Connell & N. F. Russo (Eds.), *Women in psychology: A bio-bibliographic sourcebook* (pp. 66–74). New York: Greenwood Press.

Hall, G. S. (1905). The Negro in Africa and America. *Pedagogical Seminary, 12,* 350–368.

Harris, B. (1980). The FBI's files on APA and SPSSI: Description and implications. *American Psychologist, 35,* 1141–1144.

Klineberg, O. (1935). *Race differences.* New York: Harper & Brothers.

Krech, D., & Cartwright, D. (1956). On SPSSI's first twenty years. *American Psychologist, 11,* 470–473.

Muschinske, D. (1977). The nonwhite as a child: G. Stanley Hall on the education of nonwhite peoples. *Journal of the History of the Behavioral Sciences, 13,* 328–336.

Plous, S. (1994). William James' other concern: Racial injustice in America. *The General Psychologist, 30,* 80–88.

Raimy, V. C. (Ed.) (1950). *Training in clinical psychology.* New York: Prentice Hall.

Stagner, R. (1986). Reminiscences about the founding of SPSSI. *Journal of Social Issues, 42 (1),* 35–42.

Storr, R. J. (1973). *The beginning of the future: A historical approach to graduate education in the arts and sciences.* New York: McGraw-Hill.

Terman, L. M. (1916). *The measurement of intelligence.* Boston: Hougton Mifflin.

Wolfle, D. (1946). The reorganized American Psychological Association. *American Psychologist, 1,* 3–8.

Woodworth, R. S. (1916). Comparative psychology of races. *Psychological Bulletin, 13,* 388–397.

Race Differences

Otto Klineberg

The preceding discussion has shown that race cannot be regarded as the cause of a particular culture, or as the cause of culture in general. Ignoring the question of cultural values for the time being, we have seen that folkways may differ fundamentally in the case of peoples who are racially identical. Among the American Indians, for example, we find many extremes of behavior; the Plains Indians have been described as introvert, and the Eskimo as extrovert; the Pueblos are peaceful and the Apache very warlike; the Sioux are stoical and reserved, the Huichol lively and emotional. These are only a few of the cases that might be cited. The group differences are very important, but they seem to have no relation to race.

If in spite of this the attempt is made to evaluate the cultural contributions of the various races, there arises the apparently insoluble problem of finding an adequate criterion. Value-judgments are necessarily subjective, and there appears to be no way of making them scientifically acceptable. The Chinese invented gunpowder, but instead of using it as a weapon of war they amused themselves by making fireworks. The Westerners adopted it to make themselves masters of a large part of the world. If we use power as a criterion we shall regard the Westerners as superior; if our values are aesthetic rather than political, at least as good a case can be made for the Chinese.

There are simple people who have moral standards which must be considered superior even by our own criteria; as we have seen, the Yakuts of Siberia could not understand how it is possible in our cities for some to be starving while others have more than enough to eat. The Yakuts have the custom of sharing their food with the hungry, and a Yakut moralist might make a good case for the inferiority of our civilization. The same may be said also of the Eskimo who offered to teach the White men how to live at peace with one another. We have the right to speak of our civilization as more complex, but we have no evidence of its general superiority.

Even on the basis of our own standards it is difficult to make a clear case for the superiority of any race over another. We happen now to be in a period of history in which a great deal of political power is in the hands of northwest Europeans. If we take a longer historical view, however, their superiority even in that respect may certainly be questioned. We have seen how Aristotle doubted the abilities of the northern barbarians; Julius Caesar spoke of them just as contemptuously. The Chinese had a rich culture, with a highly developed art and philosophy, at a time when most White peoples had not made any of the contributions which are now regarded as proving their superiority. One of the earliest and most important of all civilizations, the Egyptian, from which the western world borrowed so profusely, was the creation of Mediterraneans with a strong Negroid intermixture. The Renaissance, in spite of Woltmann and Chamberlain, was certainly much more a Mediterranean than a Nordic product. We cannot judge the superiority of a race by its supremacy at any given moment, and we can say nothing about the hierarchy of races in the future.

It becomes especially difficult to assume an intimate relation between race and cultural contributions when we note the tremendous difference in level of complexity of groups belonging to the same race. The highly developed Chinese and the simple North Siberian are both Mongoloid; the Mayas and the Incas of Central and South America were of the same race as the simplest tribes of California. Race, therefore, cannot be responsible. It is not easy to say why these differences developed. The answer may be found in a host of contributing factors—the physical environment, the history, the economic life, contact with other peoples, the presence of outstanding individuals, the fortunes of war, etc. An analysis of these is outside the scope of the present volume.

In one sense, the end of this investigation finds us not much farther advanced than its beginning. The subjective judgments of race differences, reviewed in the introductory chapter, were dismissed as having little significance for a scientific, impartial study. The search for something more objective led through a considerable quantity of material, collected by all the methods at the disposal of both the natural and the social scientist, and presumably not too directly influenced by the personal whims and prejudices of the investigators. The findings, however, though rich and varied, are either inconsistent or inconclusive, and the general conclusion can be only that the case for psychological race differences has never been proved. This is perhaps a negative result, but it has certain very definite and positive implications.

RATIONALIZATIONS

When the Spanish writers justified the exploitation of the American Indians on the grounds that they were racially distinct from and inferior to the Whites, they set a fashion which was widely followed. In the history of the treatment of the American Negro, for example, the notion of a racial inferiority played an important part, though it is not difficult to see in it the consequence of an economic system based upon slavery, rather than an honest attempt to evaluate the abilities of a people. The arguments in common use were often based on concepts which are now outworn, like that which saw in the inferiority of the Negroes a punishment for the sin their ancestor Ham had committed against his father Noah. (Priest, 3.) With a change in habits, the Bible was no longer considered adequate evidence; but the shift to the language of a more modern scientific era added very little soundness or objectivity. (Johnson, 2.) The conclusion came first, and the "facts" were found to justify it.

The wholly artificial character of the argument is clearly illustrated in the attitude toward Negro skilled labor after Emancipation. During slavery, a large part of the skilled mechanical work in the South was in the hands of Negro slaves. There are accounts of bitter protests made by White artisans against the practice of turning over the bulk of this skilled work to Negroes. After Emancipation, however, the theory was advanced and accepted that Negroes were constitutionally incapable of filling the very positions they had held during slavery! (Weatherford and Johnson, 5.) It would be difficult to find a clearer case of belief motivated by self-interest. In this instance there are historical facts which show the belief to be false, but these are conveniently ignored or forgotten.

There are many other examples of this type of rationalization. Professor Strong (4) has shown how, in the case of the Japanese on the Pacific Coast, every significant fact about them was seized upon and twisted about until it made a suitable weapon for causing them injury. "Hence, if they asked less than the going wage, they were threatening the American standard of living; if they demanded better wages, they were avaricious; if they were successful in farming and saved enough to buy their own ranch, they were driving the whites out; if they were unsuccessful, they were 'wearing out the land' " (p. 125). This is the stuff out of which racial theories are made. Man is a rationalizing, not a rational, animal.

That being the case, there may not seem to be much hope of affecting behavior by an appeal to science and objectivity. The materials presented in this volume and the conclusions to which they lead have certain implications for the practical problems of human relations, but making these implications felt is quite a different matter. It may still be of interest, however, to analyze them a little further.

SOME PRACTICAL IMPLICATIONS

The general conclusion of this book is that there is no scientific proof of racial differences in mentality. This does not necessarily mean that there are no such differences. It may be that at some future time, and with the aid of techniques as yet undiscovered, differences may be demonstrated. In the present stage of our knowledge, however, we have no right to assume that they exist.

There is no reason, therefore, to treat two people differently because they differ in their physical type. There is no justification for denying a Negro a job or an education because he is a Negro. No one has been able to demonstrate that ability is correlated with skin color or head shape or any of the anatomical characteristics used to classify races. A man must be judged as an individual, not as a member of a group whose limits are arbitrary and artificial. Our racial and national stereotypes—the "pictures in our minds" of the Oriental, the Italian, the Jew, the Mexican—will be wrong much more often than right; they are based on current opinions which have never been verified, and they cannot be trusted in the treatment of human beings.

There is no reason to make immigration laws stricter for one people than for another. It has never been demonstrated that groups differ fundamentally in their ability to adapt themselves to a new culture, or to make a contribution to their new country. If their culture resembles ours more closely, the process of adaptation may not take quite so long, but the whole history of the United States has shown that these differences are negligible. There is nothing more illuminating in this connection than the report of a congressional committee in 1838, which charged that "the country is being flooded with the outcasts of the jails, alms-houses, and slums of pauper-ridden Europe," that the newcomers were "the most idle and vicious classes, in personal appearance most offensive and loathsome," and that the prisons were filled with them. There were, however, the ancestors of the Irish and German and British Americans who are now (or were until recently) most concerned about the character of the new immigrants. (See Feldman, 1, pp. 134–136). There is something to be said for the careful examination of each individual immigrant, but no valid reason for accepting or rejecting an applicant because of his national origin.

There is no reason to pass laws against miscegenation. The human race is one, biologically speaking. There are no subvarieties whose genes are mutually incompatible, or whose crossing will necessarily lead to degeneration. Race mixture is not in itself harmful if the parent stocks are healthy, and if the hybrids suffer no special social disabilities. Certain groups may prefer, for reasons of cultural or religious loyalty, not to intermarry with others, but that is a matter of sentiment and not of biology. If two individuals of different stock wish to marry, any objection by the state is an unwarranted interference in a matter which concerns them alone, and which in any case has not been shown to have any harmful consequences. Laws directed against mixture in order to maintain race purity have no meaning, since every large population in the world already contains within it a varied assortment of physical types.

There is no innate aversion of races to one another. The very fact that race mixture has taken place everywhere and at all times is the best possible indication that this is so. Racial antagonisms must be understood in their historical and social setting; they have no basis in biology. The assumption that they are the inevitable result of group differences merely serves to hide their true causes.

THE RACE PROBLEM

What these causes are is by no means easy to determine, and it would be presumptuous on the part of the writer to attempt to analyze them in a few closing sentences. There is an increasing tendency to see in the race problem merely one aspect of the class war, in which those who are in a position of privilege make of unimportant differences in skin color or religion or language a convenient excuse for their own continued domination. Those who look upon race relations from this point of view see little hope of any real improvement until the present competitive system has been replaced by a new social order. They point with conviction to Russia, where the economic change has been accompanied by a more sympathetic treatment of minorities, and where the class struggle and the race problem seem to have disappeared together.

On this point the writer must reserve judgment. It may be that the analysis in terms of economics is an oversimplification, and that racial antipathies have a life and momentum which are to some degree independent of the economic structure. It may be, on the other hand, that these antipathies are entirely secondary, and that if nothing more were to be gained by them, they would disappear of themselves.

In any case, that is not really our problem. Most of us live in a competitive society. We have no means of knowing whether in the near or distant future this competition will be replaced by something radically different. We are dealing with race conflict under conditions of competition, and we cannot wait for this conflict to be removed by an upheaval in our whole social structure. Even under conditions of competition there is something that can be done. It is quite possible, for example, to concede the irrelevance of cephalic index and pigmentation and nasal width, while maintaining a firm faith in "rugged individualism."

If the material collected in this volume were accepted as demonstrating the absence of any valid proof of racial differences in intelligence or character, it might conceivably lead to a more favorable attitude toward groups usually regarded as inferior. In time there might even be a change in race relations. This seems to assume that people do reason, although a little earlier it was suggested that they usually rationalize. There is hope, however, even in rationalization. The very search for reasons, even if that search is secondary, makes it possible for opinions to change, if one by one the foundations on which they rest are shown to be illusory.

Once science has demonstrated that there is nothing in the brain or blood of other races which justifies our ill-treatment of them, it becomes important to see that this knowledge is disseminated. In this respect, the schools have a particularly important function to perform. If attitudes are to be changed in the face of the forces tending to perpetuate them, the only hope is to reach them early, and to give to children habits of favorable reactions to other races which will stay with them through life. These habits may possibly result, in part at least, from the knowledge that every single one of the arguments used in order to prove the inferiority of other races has amounted to nothing. In any case, the educational experiment seems to the writer to be worth trying.

BIBLIOGRAPHY

1. Feldman, H. *Racial Factors in American Industry.* New York, 1931.
2. Johnson, C. S., and Bond, H. M. "The Investigation of Racial Differences Prior to 1910." *J. of Negro Education,* Yearbook III, July, 1934.
3. Priest, Josiah. *Bible Defense of Slavery.* Glasgow, Ky., 1852.
4. Strong, E. K., Jr. *The Second-Generation Japanese Problem.* Stanford University, 1933.
5. Weatherford, W. D., and Johnson, C. S. *Race Relations: Adjustment of Whites and Negroes in the United States.* New York, 1934.

Racial Identification and Preference in Negro Children

Kenneth B. Clark and Mamie P. Clark

PROBLEM

The specific problem of this study is an analysis of the genesis and development of racial identification as a function of ego development and self-awareness in Negro children.

Race awareness, in a primary sense, is defined as a consciousness of the self as belonging to a specific group which is differentiated from other observable groups by obvious physical characteristics which are generally accepted as being racial characteristics.

Because the problem of racial identification is so definitely related to the problem of the genesis of racial attitudes in children, it was thought practicable to attempt to determine the racial attitudes or preferences of these Negro children—and to define more precisely, as far as possible, the developmental pattern of this relationship.

PROCEDURE

This paper presents results from only one of several techniques devised and used by the authors to investigate the development of racial identification and preferences in Negro children.[1] Results presented here are from the Dolls Test.

Dolls Test

The subjects were presented with four dolls, identical in every respect save skin color. Two of these dolls were brown with black hair and two were white with yellow hair. In the experimental situation these dolls were unclothed except for white diapers. The position of the head, hands, and legs on all the dolls was the same. For half of the subjects the dolls were presented in the order: white, colored, white, colored. For the other half the order of presentation was reversed. In the experimental situation the subjects were asked to respond to the following requests by choosing *one* of the dolls and giving it to the experimenter:

1. Give me the doll that you like to play with—(*a*) like best.
2. Give me the doll that is a nice doll.
3. Give me the doll that looks bad.
4. Give me the doll that is a nice color.
5. Give me the doll that looks like a white child.
6. Give me the doll that looks like a colored child.
7. Give me the doll that looks like a Negro child.
8. Give me the doll that looks like you.

Requests 1 through 4 were designed to reveal preferences; requests 5 through 7 to indicate a knowledge of "racial differences"; and request 8 to show self-identification.

It was found necessary to present the preference requests first in the experimental situation because in a preliminary investigation it was clear that the children who had already identified themselves with the colored doll had a marked tendency to indicate a preference for this doll and this was not necessarily a genuine expression of actual preference, but a reflection of ego involvement. This potential distortion of the data was controlled by merely asking the children to indicate their preference first and then to make identifications with one of the dolls.

Clark, K. B., & Clark, M. P. (1947). Racial identification and preference in Negro children. In T. N. Newcomb & E. L. Hartley (Eds.), *Readings in Social Psychology*, pp. 169–178. New York: Henry Holt. Reprinted by permission of the author.

SUBJECTS

Two hundred fifty-three Negro children formed the subjects of this experiment. One hundred thirty-four of these subjects (southern group) were tested in segregated nursery schools and public schools in Hot Springs, Pine Bluff, and Little Rock, Arkansas. These children had had no experience in racially mixed school situations. One hundred nineteen subjects (northern group) were tested in the racially mixed nursery and public schools of Springfield, Massachusetts.

Age distribution of subjects:

Age, years	North	South	Total
3	13	18	31
4	10	19	29
5	34	12	46
6	33	39	72
7	29	46	75
Total	119	134	253

Sex distribution of subjects:

Sex	North	South	Total
Male	53	63	116
Female	66	71	137

Skin color of subjects:

Skin color	North	South	Total
Light[a]	33	13	46
Medium[b]	58	70	128
Dark[c]	28	51	79

[a]light (practically white)
[b]medium (light brown to dark brown)
[c]dark (dark brown to black)

All subjects were tested individually in a schoolroom or office especially provided for this purpose. Except for a few children who showed generalized negativism from the beginning of the experiment (results for these children are not included here), there was adequate rapport between the experimenter and all subjects tested. In general, the children showed high interest in and enthusiasm for the test materials and testing situation. The children, for the most part, considered the experiment somewhat of a game.

RESULTS

Racial Identification

Although the questions on knowledge of "racial differences" and self-identification followed those designed to determine racial preference in the actual experimental situation, it appears more meaningful to discuss the results in the following order: knowledge of "racial differences," racial self-identification, and finally racial preferences.

The results of the responses to requests 5, 6, and 7, which were asked to determine the subjects' knowledge of racial differences, may be seen in Table 1. Ninety-four percent of these children chose the white doll when asked to give the experimenter the white doll; 93 percent of them chose the brown doll when asked to give the colored doll; and, 72 percent chose the brown doll when asked to give the Negro doll. These results indicate a clearly established knowledge of a "racial difference" in these subjects—and some awareness of the relation between the physical characteristic of skin color and the racial concepts of "white" and "colored." Knowledge of the concept of "Negro" is not so well developed as the more concrete verbal concepts of "white" and "colored" as applied to racial differences.

The question arises as to whether choice of the brown doll or of the white doll, particularly in response to questions 5 and 6, really reveals a

TABLE 1
CHOICES OF ALL SUBJECTS

	Request 5 (for white)		Request 6 (for colored)		Request 7 (for Negro)		Request 8 (for you)	
Choice	**No.**	**Percent**	**No.**	**Percent**	**No.**	**Percent**	**No.**	**Percent**
Colored doll	13	5	235	93	182	72	166	66
White doll	237	94	15	6	50	20	85	33
Don't know or no response	3	1	3	1	21	8	2	1

knowledge of "racial differences" or simply indicates a learned perceptual reaction to the concepts of "colored" and "white." Our evidence that the responses of these children *do* indicate a knowledge of "racial difference" comes from several sources: the results from other techniques used (i.e., a coloring test and a questionnaire) and from the qualitative data obtained (children's spontaneous remarks) strongly support a knowledge of "racial differences." Moreover, the consistency of results for requests 5 through 8 also tends to support the fact that these children are actually making identifications in a "racial" sense.

The responses to request 8, designed to determine racial self-identification follow the following pattern: 66 percent of the total group of children identified themselves with the colored doll, while 33 percent identified themselves with the white doll. The critical ratio of this difference is 7.6.[2]

Comparing the results of request 8 (racial self-identification) with those of requests 5, 6, and 7 (knowledge of racial difference) it is seen that the awareness of racial differences does not necessarily determine a socially accurate racial self-identification—since approximately nine out of ten of these children are aware of racial differences as indicated by their correct choice of a "white" and "colored" doll on request, and only a little more than six out of ten make socially correct identifications with the colored doll.

Age Differences

Table 2 shows that, when the responses to request 5 and 6 are observed together, these subjects at each age level have a well-developed knowledge of the concept of racial difference between "white" and "colored" as this is indicated by the characteristic of skin color. These data definitely indicate that a basic knowledge of "racial differences" exists as a part of the pattern of ideas of Negro children from the age of three through seven years in the northern and southern communities tested in this study—and that this knowledge develops more definitely from year to year to the point of absolute stability at the age of seven.

A comparison of the results of requests 5 and 6 with those of request 7, which required the child to indicate the doll which looks like a "Negro" child, shows that knowledge of a racial difference in terms of the word "Negro" does not exist with the same degree of definiteness as it does in terms of the more basic designations of "white" and "colored." It is significant, however, that knowledge of a difference in terms of the word "Negro" makes a sharp increase from the five- to six-year level and a less accelerated one between the six- and seven-year levels. The fact that all of the six-year-olds used in this investigation were enrolled in the public schools seems to be related to this spurt. Since it seems clear that the term "Negro" is a more verbalized designation of "racial differences," it is reason-

TABLE 2
CHOICES OF SUBJECTS AT EACH AGE LEVEL*

Choice	3 yr.		4 yr.		5 yr.		6 yr.		7 yr.	
	No.	Percent	No.	Percent	No.	Percent	No.	Percent	No.	Percent
Request 5 (for white)										
colored doll	4	13	4	14	3	7	2	3	0	
white doll	24	77	25	86	43	94	70	97	75	100
Request 6 (for colored)										
colored doll	24	77	24	83	43	94	69	96	75	100
white doll	4	13	5	17	3	7	3	4	0	
Request 7 (for Negro)										
colored doll	17	55	17	59	28	61	56	78	64	85
white doll	9	29	10	35	14	30	12	17	5	7
Request 8 (for you)										
colored doll	11	36	19	66	22	48	49	68	65	87
white doll	19	61	9	31	24	52	23	32	10	13

*Individuals failing to make either choice not included, hence some percentages add to less than 100.

able to assume that attendance at pubic schools facilitates the development of this verbalization of the race concept held by these children.

In response to request 8 there is a general and marked increase in the percent of subjects who identify with the colored doll with an increase in age—with the exception of the four- to five-year groups.[3] This deviation of the five-year-olds from the general trend is considered in detail in the larger, yet unpublished study.

Identification by Skin Color

Table 3 shows slight and statistically insignificant differences among the three skin-color groups in their responses which indicate a knowledge of the "racial difference" between the white and colored doll (requests 5 through 7).

It should be noted, however, that the dark group is consistently more accurate in its choice of the appropriate doll than either the light or the medium group on requests 5 through 7. This would seem to indicate that the dark group is slightly more definite in its knowledge of racial differences and that this definiteness extends even to the higher level of verbalization inherent in the use of the term "Negro" as a racial designation. In this regard it is seen that 75 percent of the dark children chose the colored doll when asked for the doll which "looks like a Negro child" while only 70 percent of the light children and 71 percent of the medium children made this response. The trend of results for requests 5 and 6 remains substantially the same.

These results suggest further that correct racial identification of these Negro children at these ages is to a large extent determined by the concrete fact of their own skin color, and further that this racial identification is not necessarily dependent upon the expressed knowledge of a racial difference as indicated by the correct use of the words "white," "colored," or "Negro" when responding to white and colored dolls. This conclusion seems warranted in the light of the fact that those children who differed in skin color from light through medium to dark were practically similar in the pattern of their re-

TABLE 3
CHOICES OF SUBJECTS IN LIGHT, MEDIUM, AND DARK GROUPS*

	Light		Medium		Dark	
Choice	No.	Percent	No.	Percent	No.	Percent
Request 5 (for white)						
colored doll	2	5	8	6	3	4
white doll	43	94	118	92	76	96
Request 6 (for colored)						
colored doll	41	89	118	92	76	96
white doll	4	9	8	6	3	4
Request 7 (for Negro)						
colored doll	32	70	91	71	59	75
white doll	9	20	27	21	14	18
Request 8 (for you)						
colored doll	9	20	93	73	64	81
white doll	37	80	33	26	15	19

*Individuals failing to make either choice not included, hence some percentages add to less than 100.

sponses which indicated awareness of racial differences but differed markedly in their racial identification (responses to request 8 for the doll "that looks like you") only 20 percent of the light children, while 73 percent of the medium children, and 81 percent of the dark children identified themselves with the colored doll.

It is seen that there is a consistent increase in choice of the colored doll from the light to the medium group; an increase from the medium group to the dark group; and, a striking increase in the choices of the colored doll by the dark group as compared to the light group.[4] All differences, except between the medium and dark groups, are statistically significant.

Again, as in previous work,[5] it is shown that the percentage of the medium groups' identifications with the white or the colored representation resembles more that of the dark group and differs from the light group. Upon the basis of these results, therefore, one may assume that some of the factors and dynamics involved in racial identification are substantially the same for the dark and medium children, in contrast to dynamics for the light children.

North-South Differences

The results presented in Table 4 indicate that there are no significant quantitative differences between the northern and southern Negro children tested (children in mixed schools and children in segregated schools) in their knowledge of racial differences.

While none of these differences is statistically reliable, it is significant that northern children know as well as southern children which doll is supposed to represent a white child and which doll is supposed to represent a colored child. However, the northern children make fewer identifications with the colored doll and more identifications with the white doll than do the southern children. One factor accounting for this difference may be the fact that in this sample there are many more light colored children in the North (33) than there are in the South (13). Since this difference in self-identification is not

TABLE 4
CHOICES OF SUBJECTS IN NORTHERN (MIXED SCHOOLS) AND SOUTHERN (SEGREGATED SCHOOLS) GROUPS*

Choice	North percent	South percent
Request 5 (for white)		
colored doll	4	6
white doll	94	93
Request 6 (for colored)		
colored doll	92	94
white doll	7	5
Request 7 (for Negro)		
colored doll	74	70
white doll	20	19
Request 8 (for you)		
colored doll	61	69
white doll	39	29

*Individuals failing to make either choice not included, hence some percentages add to less than 100.

statistically significant, it may be stated that the children in the northern-mixed-school situation do not differ from children in the southern segregated schools in either their knowledge of racial differences or their racial identification. A more qualitative analysis will be presented elsewhere.

Racial Preferences

It is clear from Table 5 that the majority of these Negro children prefer the *white* doll and reject the colored doll.

Approximately two thirds of the subjects indicated by their responses to request 1 and 2 that they like the white doll "best," or that they would like to play with the white doll in preference to the colored doll, and that the white doll is a "nice doll."

Their responses to request 3 show that this preference for the white doll implies a concomitant negative attitude toward the brown doll. Fifty-nine percent of these children indicated that the colored doll "looks bad," while only 17 percent stated that the white doll "looks bad" (critical ratio 10.9). That this preference and negation in some way involve skin color is indicated by the results for request 4. Only 38 percent of the children thought that the brown doll was a "nice color," while 60 percent of them thought that the white doll was a "nice color" (critical ration 5.0).

The importance of these results for an understanding of the origin and development of racial concepts and attitudes in Negro children cannot be minimized. Of equal significance are their implications, in the light of the results of racial identification already presented, for racial mental hygiene.

Age Differences

Table 6 shows that at each age from three through seven years the majority of these children prefer the white doll and reject the brown doll. This tendency to prefer the white doll is not as stable (not statistically reliable) in the three-year-olds as it is in the four- and five-year-olds. On the other hand, however, the tendency of the

TABLE 5
CHOICES OF ALL SUBJECTS

	Request 1 (play with)		Request 2 (nice doll)		Request 3 (looks bad)		Request 4 (nice color)	
Choice	No.	Percent	No.	Percent	No.	Percent	No.	Percent
Colored doll	83	32	97	38	149	59	96	38
White doll	169	67	150	59	42	17	151	60
Don't know or no response	1	1	6	3	62	24	6	2

TABLE 6
CHOICES OF SUBJECTS AT EACH AGE LEVEL*

Choice	3 yr.		4 yr.		5 yr.		6 yr.		7 yr.	
	No.	Percent	No.	Percent	No.	Percent	No.	Percent	No.	Percent
Request 1 (play with)										
colored doll	13	42	7	24	12	26	21	29	30	40
white doll	17	55	22	76	34	74	51	71	45	60
Request 2 (nice doll)										
colored doll	11	36	7	24	13	28	33	46	33	44
white doll	18	58	22	76	33	72	38	53	39	52
Request 3 (looks bad)										
colored doll	21	68	15	52	36	78	45	63	32	43
white doll	6	19	7	24	5	11	11	15	13	17
Request 4 (nice color)										
colored doll	12	39	8	28	9	20	31	43	36	48
white doll	18	58	21	72	36	78	40	56	36	48

*Individuals failing to make either choice not included, hence some percentages add to less than 100.

three-year-olds to negate the brown doll ("looks bad") is established as a statistically significant fact (critical ratio 4.5.).

Analyzing the results of requests 1 and 2 together, it is seen that there is a marked *increase* in preference for the white doll from the three- to four-year level; a more gradual *decrease* in this preference from the four- to the five-year level; a further decrease from the five- to the six-year level; and a continued decrease from the six- to the seven-year level. These results suggest that although the majority of Negro children at each age prefer the white doll to the brown doll, this preference decreases gradually from four through seven years.

Skin color preference of these children follow a somewhat different pattern of development. The results of request 4 show that while the majority of children at each age below 7 years prefer the skin color of the white doll, this preference increases from three through five years and decreases from five through seven years. It is of interest to point out that only at the seven-year level do the same number of children indicate a preference for the skin color of the colored doll as for that of the white doll.

The majority of these children at each age level indicate that the brown doll, rather than the white doll, "looks bad." This result shows positively the negation of the colored doll which was implicit in the expressed preference for the white doll discussed above.

The evaluative rejection of the brown doll is statistically significant, even at the three-year level, and is pronounced at the five-year level. This indicated preference for the white doll is statistically significant from the four-year level up to the seven-year level.

It seems justifiable to assume from these results that the crucial period in the formation and patterning of racial attitudes begins at around four and five years. At these ages these subjects appear to be reacting more uncritically in a definite structuring of attitudes which conforms

TABLE 7
CHOICES OF SUBJECTS IN LIGHT, MEDIUM, AND DARK GROUPS*

Choice	Light		Medium		Dark	
	No.	Percent	No.	Percent	No.	Percent
Request 1 (play with)						
colored doll	11	24	41	32	31	39
white doll	35	76	86	67	48	61
Request 2 (nice doll)						
colored doll	15	33	50	39	32	40
white doll	31	67	72	56	47	60
Request 3 (looks bad)						
colored doll	31	67	73	57	45	57
white doll	6	13	22	17	14	18
Request 4 (nice color)						
colored doll	13	28	56	44	27	34
white doll	32	70	68	53	51	65

*Individuals failing to make either choice not included, hence some percentages add to less than 100.

with the accepted racial values and mores of the larger environment.

Preferences and Skin Color

Results presented in Table 7 reveal that there is a tendency for the majority of these children, in spite of their own skin color, to prefer the white doll and to negate the brown doll. This tendency is most pronounced in the children of light skin color and least so in the dark children. A more intensive analysis of these results appears in a larger, yet unpublished study.

North-South Differences

From Table 8 it is clear that the southern children in segregated schools are less pronounced in their preference for the white doll, compared to the northern children's definite preference for this doll. Although still in a minority, a higher percentage of southern children, compared to northern, prefer to play with the colored doll or think that it is a "nice" doll. The critical ratio of this difference is not significant for request 1 but approaches significance for request 2 (2.75).

A significantly higher percentage (71) of the northern children, compared to southern children (49) think that the brown doll looks bad (critical ratio 3.68). Also a slightly higher percent of the southern children think that the brown doll has a "nice color," while more northern children think that the white doll has a "nice color."

In general, it may be stated that northern and southern children in these age groups tend to be similar in the degree of their preference for the white doll—with the northern children tending to be somewhat more favorable to the white doll than are the southern children. The southern children, however, in spite of their equal favorableness toward the white doll, are significantly less likely to reject the brown doll (evaluate it negatively), as compared to the strong tendency for the majority of the northern children to do so. That this difference is not primarily due to the larger number of light children found in the northern sample is indicated by more intensive analysis presented in the complete report.

Some Qualitative Data

Many of the children entered into the experimental situation with a freedom similar to that of play. They tended to verbalize freely and

TABLE 8
CHOICES OF SUBJECTS IN NORTHERN (MIXED SCHOOLS) AND SOUTHERN (SEGREGATED SCHOOLS) GROUPS (REQUESTS 1 THROUGH 4)*

Choice	North percent	South percent
Request 1 (play with)		
colored doll	28	37
white doll	72	62
Request 2 (nice doll)		
colored doll	30	46
white doll	68	52
Request 3 (looks bad)		
colored doll	71	49
white doll	17	16
Request 4 (nice color)		
colored doll	37	40
white doll	63	57

*Individuals failing to make either choice not included, hence some percentages add to less than 100.

much of this unsolicited verbalization was relevant to the basic problems of this study.

On the whole, the rejection of the brown doll and the preference for the white doll, when explained at all, were explained in rather simple, concrete terms: for white doll preference—"'cause he's pretty" or "'cause he's white"; for rejection of the brown doll—"'cause he's ugly" or "'cause it don't look pretty" or "'cause him black" or "got black on him."

On the other hand, some of the children who were free and relaxed in the beginning of the experiment broke down and cried or became somewhat negativistic during the latter part when they were required to make self-identifications. Indeed, two children ran out of the testing room, unconsolable, convulsed in tears. This type of behavior, although not so extreme, was more prevalent in the North than in the South. The southern children who were disturbed by this aspect of the experiment generally indicated their disturbance by smiling or matter of factly attempting to escape their dilemma either by attempted humor or rationalization.

Rationalization of the rejection of the brown doll was found among both northern and southern children, however. A northern medium six-year-old justified his rejection of the brown doll by stating that "he looks bad 'cause he hasn't got a eyelash." A seven-year-old medium northern child justified his choice of the white doll as the doll with a "nice color" because "his feet, hands, ears, elbows, knees, and hair are clean."

A northern five-year-old dark child felt compelled to explain his identification with the brown doll by making the following unsolicited statement: "I burned my face and made it spoil." A seven-year-old northern light child went to great pains to explain that he is actually white but: "I look brown because I got a suntan in the summer."

NOTES

1. Condensed by the authors from an unpublished study made possible by a fellowship grant from the Julius Rosenwald Fund, 1940–1941.
2. These results are supported by those from the use of the Horowitz line drawing technique.
3. These results are supported by those from the use of the Horowitz line drawing technique.
4. These results substantiate and clearly focus the trend observed through the use of the Horowitz line drawing technique.
5. K. B. and M. P. Clark, "Skin Color as a Factor in Racial Identification of Negro Preschool Children," *J. Soc. Psychol.*, 1940, XI, 159–169; "Segregation as a Factor in the Racial Identification of Negro Preschool Children: a preliminary report," *J. Exper. Educ.*, 1939, IX, 161–163; "The Development of Consciousness of Self and the Emergence of Racial Identification in Negro Preschool Children," *J. Soc. Psychol.*, 1939, X, 591–599.

SPSSI and Race Relations, in the 1950s and After

Otto Klineberg

If there is any social issue on which psychologists can claim to have made a contribution, it is in the field of intergroup relations and race. Many of us were involved in the activities that led up to the unanimous 1954 decision of the U.S. Supreme Court that the segregation imposed on black children in U.S. schools was in conflict with the principles of the U.S. Constitution. We were all proud that psychological research findings were included in the social science statement that accompanied the legal brief and to which Chief Justice Earl Warren made approving reference. This pride increased when Warren justified the decision in *Brown v. The Board of Education,* in part, by developments in the field of psychology. Referring to the Supreme Court's finding in the 1896 case of *Plessis v. Ferguson,* that "enforced separation of the races was not necessarily a badge of inferiority," Warren added that "whatever may have been the extent of psychological knowledge [at the time, the reverse position] is amply supported by modern authority" (Kluger, 1975, p. 782). This has justifiably been regarded as the greatest compliment ever paid to psychology by the powers-that-be in our own or any other country.

This aspect of the Supreme Court's decision which has pleased us so much has, however, been criticized for its introduction of nonlegal considerations into a situation clearly legal in character. I had the good fortune to meet Chief Justice Warren a few years later in San Francisco, where I had a chance to talk with him about this aspect of the 1954 decision. He told me that the members of the Court would probably have come to the same conclusion in any case, but they (and he in particular) felt their position was strengthened by the clear support of the present generation of psychologists.

I would like to raise a difficult question. Was this a contribution by SPSSI or by social psychologists, or more broadly by social scientists in general? At the time of the decision I was a member of the secretariat of UNESCO (the United Nations Educational, Scientific, and Cultural Organization) in Paris. On May 18, the day after the Court's decision had been reported, I received a telegram from Robert Carter of the Legal Defense Fund, informing me of what had happened. During the whole day following, my telephone was busy with calls of congratulations from UNESCO colleagues, not to me personally, but to me as the local representative of the social sciences. What role did SPSSI play?

Some of the contributions by social psychologists might have been made in any case but, in my judgment, the role of SPSSI was unmistakable. SPSSI helped create an environment in which it was easier to act because of the support of this large body of social scientists. It helped provide an atmosphere of acceptance by our colleagues. In a recent address on social sciences and desegregation, Kenneth Clark (1986) mentioned the names of those psychologists who testified at the trials that preceded the epochmaking finding of 1954. They include at least six former SPSSI presidents as well as other SPSSI members.

A quantitative analysis of the roles played by former SPSSI presidents is reported by James Capshew (1986). His collective biography, or "prosopography," reveals not only "a substantial overlap between the presidency of SPSSI and the APA" (p. 85), but also that SPSSI presidents have been well represented among recipients of awards from the APA and the American Psychological Foundation (APF). This may help us

Klineberg, O. (1986). SPSSI and race relations, in the 1950s and after. *Journal of Social Issues, 42(4),* 53–59.

understand the striking convergence in policy between SPSSI and APA as a whole in connection with many social issues, including the issues of race relations and international policy.

In regard to race relations, the most direct and effective contribution by SPSSI is represented by its collective role in the 1954 decision. After the preliminary court cases in South Carolina, Kansas, Delaware, and Virginia, at which psychologists and other social scientists had testified, the NAACP (National Association for the Advancement of Colored People) lawyers asked the psychologists to prepare a summary of the testimony previously presented, as well as other pertinent material to be submitted to the U.S. Supreme Court. At this point SPSSI became directly involved. It appointed a committee chaired by Gerhart Saenger—then a professor at New York University and later author of *The Social Psychology of Prejudice* (1963)—with Kenneth Clark and Isidor Chein as members, joined by Stuart Cook in the preparation of the final version of the statement. The statement was signed and endorsed by 32 social scientists and submitted as an appendix to the legal brief.

I here take the liberty of mentioning my own contribution to these developments. I had been consulted at an early stage by R. L. Carter of the Legal Defense Fund about the possibility of making use of social science material, and I informed him about the research data collected and analyzed by Kenneth Clark, presented at the White House Conference on Children in 1950 that I had attended. Carter and Thurgood Marshall then made contact with Clark, which changed the whole course of developments in this area. It also changed the course of Clark's life and prepared the way for the debt of gratitude owed to him by all of us concerned with racial prejudice and discrimination. As I have said on other occasions, my own contribution to the case was the suggestion to ask Clark to work with the lawyers. The rest is history.

SPSSI's role in all this was crucial and prepared the way for what many of us at that time regarded as a great victory. Our general reaction was one of optimism; we thought if the barriers to equal education were removed, all the other barriers to full equality would also disappear. The sequel was on the whole somewhat disappointing. The various investigations of the consequences of desegregation, some of which have been presented in the *Journal of Social Issues,* are not sufficiently clear in their findings or implications to warrant complete confidence in the prediction of the changes that had seemed ensured by the Supreme Court decision. There were debates and discussions, which continue to this day, sometimes very acrimonious, regarding such issues as affirmative action, quotas, further desegregation in the schools by busing and related techniques, and the values and limitations of compensatory education. There were also a number of critical reactions to the content and role of the social science statement, notably and most recently by Gerard (1983) in the *American Psychologist.* This was answered by Stuart Cook's (1984) excellent article, which I feel effectively defended the content of the original statement.

Although nothing in the following decades was quite so spectacular as what happened in 1954, I want to make a brief additional comment regarding compensatory education. This, of course, was the issue that formed the cornerstone of the first of the series of Arthur Jensen's publications, which was entitled "How Much Can We Boost the I.Q. and Scholastic Achievement?" (1969); Jensen's answer, of course, was "very little." In that same year I participated in a Nobel symposium in Stockholm, at which another participant was Gunnar Myrdal. The subject of Myrdal's address was biases in social research (1970). Referring to a former bias that he thought no longer existed, Myrdal stated that "the racial inferiority doctrine has disappeared" (p. 158). Ironically, Myrdal's "former bias" remark was made just at the time that Jensen's 1969 monograph appeared, proving Myrdal wrong. The monograph was soon followed by further Jensen publications, as well as by support from Eysenck in the United Kingdom.

SPSSI did not remain quiescent on this issue. In 1968–1969 Martin Deutsch was SPSSI president; on the basis of his extensive research on compensatory education, he played an important role in the preparation of a statement issued by SPSSI on this topic. In 1971, I myself wrote an updated chapter on race and psychology, which was first published in the UNESCO *Courier* and later as part of a 1975 book entitled *Race, Science, and Society*. Since the *Courier* was published in 15 languages, and the book in English and French, SPSSI received international publicity, because the following part of its statement appeared in both publications:

> One of our most serious objections to Jensen's article is to his vigorous assertion that compensatory education has apparently failed. The major failure in so-called compensatory education has been in the planning, size, and scope of the program. We maintain that a variety of programs planned to teach specific skills have been effective and that a few well-designed programs which teach problem-solving and thinking have also been successful. The results from these programs strongly suggest that continuous and carefully planned intervention procedures can have a substantially positive influence in the performance of disadvantaged children. (Klineberg, 1971, 1975)

Some years later there appeared the SPSSI-sponsored volume *Genetic Destiny: Scientific Controversy and Social Conflict* (1976), edited by Ethel Tobach and Harold M. Proshansky, which may be regarded as another answer to Jensen's position. I shall not repeat here the arguments presented in this publication, or in my own use of it. I only add that it seems that no striking practical consequences have followed from Jensen's publications; for example, his argument in favor of separate and different education for black and white children has found little direct public echo in the educational world. It is, of course, difficult to assess that recommendation's use at the private level to justify discrimination against minority groups.

There can be no doubt that educated, middle-class blacks have made enormous progress economically and politically, but conditions in black ghettos remain deplorable. On the positive side, there is now little public appeal to fundamental racial differences as a justification for discrimination. With this stumbling block removed, there are no limits to what can be accomplished.

In conjunction with the subject of race relations is the relation between psychology and international affairs, an issue that occupied the attention of SPSSI in the 1950s and at other periods. SPSSI issued its first major publication in the field of international relations with a 1945 yearbook entitled *Human Nature and Enduring Peace,* under the editorship of Gardner Murphy. This was followed by a number of public statements as well as a series of volumes by individual SPSSI members. There was another yearbook in 1965, edited by Herbert Kelman, *International Behavior: A Social-Psychological Analysis*.

There is considerable overlap between the two issues of international relations and racism. Both use the dehumanization of the "enemy" to justify their actions. The most extreme such example is the present tragedy in South Africa, with its threat of global involvement and its foundation in racist attitudes symbolized by the phenomenon of apartheid.

Even though psychological findings have not yet had an appreciable impact on international affairs, there have been numerous applications of psychological research and principles by scholars not directly identified with psychology; this gives us the right to a modest optimism regarding the role of psychology in this area. That nonpsychologists are now using psychological materials in writing about race *and* international relations is significant. It is not entirely true that what we write and what SPSSI stands for are known only to our colleagues and our students. There has clearly been a wider degree of diffusion, of which I would like to cite a few examples.

The notion of dehumanization of the enemy, mentioned earlier, was developed by psychiatrists and psychologists and is used by George Kennan, historian and diplomat, in his 1982 book *The Nuclear Delusion.* He also mentions the importance of perception and misperception in international relations with reference to the self-fulfilling prophecy. M. D. Shulman (1984), political scientist and Soviet specialist Columbia University, has also applied to Soviet–American relations some of the insights arising from psychological research on perception, such as the mirror image, the Rorschach test, and national stereotypes, although in this last respect his source is Walter Lippmann rather than more recent specialists. In addition, Robert Jervis, a political scientist now at Columbia, has written an influential volume, *Perception and Misperception in International Politics* (1976), described recently by Ralph White (1984) as a "classic."

A somewhat similar development has occurred in the area of race, in which psychological research has been used by nonpsychologists in a number of important publications. I would like to mention three such works.

The first is the book *Simple Justice: The History of Brown v. the Board of Education and Black America's Struggle for Equality* (1975) by Richard Kluger, a former journalist and editor. In my opinion, this is the most complete account of the background of the litigation undertaken by the lawyers of the NAACP, with full details of the testimony presented by psychologists and other social scientists in the preliminary trials that prepared the way for the Supreme Court hearings. Kluger also discusses how the psychological material was used and the general atmosphere that prevailed in the courts in connection with the psychological material presented. No direct mention is made of SPSSI but there is a general discussion of the social science statement.

The second book is by Allan Chase, an independent scholar; it is entitled *The Legacy of Malthus: The Social Costs of the New Scientific Racism* (1979). This book gives a detailed account of attempts to analyze racial discrimination scientifically, and the uses and abuses to which such analyses have been subjected. There is also a treatment of recent positive reactions in psychological and biological research with emphasis on the developments that have helped create a more scientifically acceptable attitude toward the poor, the deprived, and toward racial minorities.

Most recent is the important book by Daniel J. Kevles, *In the Name of Eugenics: Genetics and the Uses of Human Hereditary* (1985). Kevles is a professor of the history of science at the California Institute of Technology.

None of these three books makes any mention of SPSSI, but there is in them a general substantial agreement between the position of SPSSI and the three authors, and there are a number of references to the work of psychologists who have been active in SPSSI affairs through the years. I regard this as a positive development, and I hope it may lead to further cooperation with representatives of other disciplines in the future.

About 30 years ago I had the honor of addressing SPSSI on the role of the psychologist in international affairs. I concluded with the following words: "As I read over what I have written, I am struck by the large number of international activities in which SPSSI members have played a significant part." Today I can say the same with regard to race relations, and I can only hope this survey gives you, as it does me, grounds for satisfaction. Our society has been fortunate in its leadership and its membership.

I should like to conclude by briefly acknowledging some of those who are no longer with us; all of them contributed to SPSSI's work on race or international affairs or both. I start with the name of Gardner Murphy, my very dear friend and teacher, and my Rock of Gibraltar when we were both at Columbia; Gordon Allport, who with Gardner was one of the true builders of social psychology; Goodwin Watson, my close colleague in the attempt to build up social psychology at Columbia in the 1950s; Ted Newcomb, my partner in so many undertakings; David Krech, who first had the idea of creating SPSSI; Isidor Chein, whose role has already been mentioned; and Mamie Clark, whose early research played an important part in the psychological testimony on the effects of segregation and discrimination. It has been a privilege to work with them and others still with us, under the auspices of SPSSI and the APA.

This moment in American history reminds us that progress is often accompanied by setbacks. We are experiencing a diminution of concern for human rights in our society that may even reach the Supreme Court. We must continue to work, together with like-minded colleagues in other disciplines, toward a solution of the social problems that still exist.

REFERENCES

Capshew, J. H. (1986). Research on leadership: A quantitative study of SPSSI presidents, 1936–1986. *Journal of Social Issues, 42(1),* 75–106.

Chase, A. (1979). *The legacy of Malthus: The social costs of the new scientific racism.* New York: Alfred A. Knopf.

Clark, K. B. (1986). An analysis of the social sciences and *Brown v. Board of Education.* Unpublished paper presented at 25th anniversary of the Graduate Center-City University of New York.

Cook, S. W. (1984). The 1954 social science statement and school desegregation: A reply to Gerard. *American Psychologist, 39,* 819–832.

Gerard, H. B. (1983). School desegregation: The social science role. *American Psychologist, 38,* 869–877.

Jensen, A. R. (1969). How much can we boost I.Q. and scholastic achievement? *Harvard Educational Review, 39,* 1–123.

Jervis, R. (1976). *Perception and misperception in international politics.* Princeton: NJ: Princeton University Press.

Kelman, H. C. (Ed.) (1965). *International behavior: A social-psychological analysis.* New York: Holt, Rinehart & Winston.

Kennan, G. (1982). *The nuclear delusion.* New York: Pantheon.

Kevles, D. J. (1985). *In the name of eugenics: Genetics and the uses of human hereditary.* New York: Alfred A. Knopf.

Klineberg, O. (1971, November). Race and I.Q. *UNESCO Courier, 26,* pp. 5–13.

Klineberg, O. (1975). Race and psychology. In L. Kuper (Ed.), *Race, science and society.* Paris: UNESCO Press; London: Allen & Unwin. (Reprint of "Race and I.Q.")

Kluger, R. (1975). *Simple justice: The history of Brown v. Board of Education and black America's struggle for equality.* New York: Alfred H. Knopf.

Murphy, G. (Ed.) (1945). *Human nature and enduring peace.* Boston: Houghton mifflin.

Myrdal, G. (1970). Biases in social research. In A. Tiselius & S. Nilsson (Eds.), *The place of values in a world of facts: Nobel symposium 14.* (pp. 155–164). Stockholm: Almquist & Wiksell.

Saenger, G. (1963). *The social psychology of prejudice.* New York: Harper & Row.

Shulman, M. D. (1984, April). A rational response to the Soviet challenge. *Harper's Magazine,* pp. 63–71.

Tobach, E., & Proshansky, H. M. (Eds.) (1976). *Genetic destiny: Race as a scientific and social controversy.* New York: AMS Press.

White, R. K. (1984). *Fearful warriors: A psychological profile of the U.S.—Soviet relations.* New York: Free Press

From "Race Psychology" to "Studies in Prejudice": Some Observations on the Thematic Reversal in Social Psychology

Franz Samelson

The aim of this article is threefold: to describe briefly the fairly abrupt reversal in the definition of the "race problem" by psychologists; to suggest some of the factors involved in this change; and thereby to contribute to a wider perspective for understanding the achievements and failures of our discipline.

RACE PSYCHOLOGY

In 1912, the *Psychological Index* (the forerunner of the *Psychological Abstracts*) revised its classification system, in the process giving greater emphasis to the concept of race. The earlier volumes had carried only one subsection—the very last one—entitled "Race Pathology" (divided in "a. Criminology, b. Degeneration and Sex Pathology"). The new system changed a major heading from "Genetic, Individual, and Social Psychology" to "Individual, Racial, and Social Phenomena," and introduced the subsection, "Race Psychology and Anthropology." The reason for this change is not obvious.[1] It was certainly not a wave of empirical studies in race psychology; in the first two years, the entries in this new category were mostly European (largely German) and consisted of anthropological material. In any case, the new headings seem to reflect a shift in emphasis, from the unity of the human race to the uniqueness of different races.

Two years earlier, in a marvelously cautious and evenhanded discussion, "Racial Differences in Mental Traits," Robert Woodworth made reference to only two sets of empirical data: those from the Torres Straits expedition, and the data he had collected at the 1904 St. Louis Fair. Emphasizing the dangers of "typing" groups of men, the greater importance of the *range* than of the average in group measurements, and the difficulty of making fair comparisons between "primitives" and whites, he concluded that so far most of the data showed no important differences. The testing psychologists had as yet only a "crumb" to offer on the question of racial differences in intelligence.[2] Similar views were expressed by others. The First Universal Races Congress, held in London in 1911, heard many speakers denounce the notions of innate race superiority and inferiority and warn about the dangerous consequences of race antipathies.[3]

But majority opinion in the Western world was different. In a chapter entitled "The Comparative Worth of Different Races," Francis Galton had argued, forty years earlier, for the existence of innate intelligence differences between races, and had estimated that "the negro race is some two grades [in modern terms, roughly one standard deviation] below our own"—an estimate not based on experimental data but on his study of eminent men and on the observations of Negroes on a trip to Southwest Africa.[4] (Seventy-five years of empirical research do not seem to have improved this crude guess; was it perhaps a self-fulfilling prophecy?) By 1895, the *Psychological Review* had reported empirical evidence for the superiority of the white over the Negro race: whites (a total of twelve subjects) had *slower* reaction times than (eleven) "Africans"; and quickness of automatic, reflexive action was obviously a mark of primitiveness and inferiority, inversely related to intelligence.[5]

Still, in the main the nineteenth century had looked to physical anthropology to demonstrate

Samelson, F. (1978). From "race psychology" to "studies in prejudice": Some observations of the thematic reversal in social psychology. *Journal of the History of the Behavioral Sciences, 14,* 265–278.

scientifically the inferiority of the Negro race. The failure to produce reliable and convincing evidence to this effect through anthropometric measurements, together with the introduction of a new psychological tool, the intelligence test, had changed the situation by 1910. The original purpose of testing had been the study of *individual* differences. Soon, however, some testers began collecting data on *race* and found differences—or, if they did not, insisted that further research would.[6] The initial focus of such studies was on black-white comparisons; a number of authors published empirical demonstrations of white superiority, the inferiority of blacks (and Indians), and the increase in native intelligence with increasing admixture of white blood.[7] But the development of race theorizing, from Anglo-Saxonism to Teutonism to Nordicism—at least in part stimulated by the changing composition of immigrants to this country and the resulting efforts to restrict the influx of southeastern Europeans—produced additional interest in differences among European races.[8] By the early twenties, several testing studies had obtained evidence that, beyond the "obvious" inferiority of the Negro, a number of European nationalities were inferior to the northern Europeans; at least some of them interpreted these differences as showing the superiority of the Nordic race[9] or the need for selective immigration restriction.[10]

In 1923, E. G. Boring summarized the status of the nature-nurture debate by saying that "in general, psychologists believe in inheritance [of intelligence] though the belief is perhaps a little weaker than it was a few years ago." In a "Review of Racial Psychology" for the *Psychological Bulletin* in 1925, Thomas Garth surveyed seventy-three studies and, besides citing the findings of Nordic superiority and the inferior scores of the Latins/Mediterraneans, concluded that the "studies taken all together seem to indicate the mental superiority of the white race."[11]

It is not quite clear how the relation between "race psychology" and the ill-defined but growing field of social psychology was perceived by contemporaries. Although the labels seem to have been almost synonymous in the eyes of some psychologists (for example, Lewis Terman), the topics of intelligence, race, and testing did not receive much emphasis in the early textbooks of social psychology. Yet in other writings, some prominent "fathers" of social psychology, beginning with Gustave LeBon, had given a good deal of support to racist notions even if occasionally deploring crude race prejudice. E. A. Ross, author of the first American text on social psychology, produced a series of articles about immigrants in 1912 (collected in *The Old World in the New*), which supported notions of stock, blood, and race differences and gave some vivid illustrations of the undesirable characteristics of immigrants from southeastern Europe: "These oxlike men[,] descendants of those *who always stayed behind.*"[12] Presumably, Ross's articles produced popular support for the first immigration restriction effort, the Literacy Test Law, passed in 1917.[13] William McDougall, another classic author on social psychology, published a similar book in 1921; entitled *Is America Safe for Democracy?,* it argued for inherited intelligence differences in social class and race and supported eugenics as well as differential immigration restriction.[14] Finally, Floyd Allport's seminal book, *Social Psychology,* although devoting little space to the issue, found it "fairly well established . . . that the intelligence of the white race is of a more versatile and a complex order than that of the black race."[15] His only comment on the immigration issue was restricted to a complaint about the narrowness and provincialism of the "Americanizers."[16] But a few months later, he expressed his opinions a bit more fully in a review of Carl Brigham's book on immigrant races and the superior intelligence of the Nordics. While pointing out some of the methodological weaknesses of the study and warning against overgeneralization, he wondered about the reasons for the strong resistance to Brigham's "suggestive" though not "authoritative" conclusions. A final comment summed up his position: "Though we may still raise our eyebrows when someone dogmatically states his convictions upon racial differences, we can no longer close our eyes to the fact that very significant differences have already been found, and that further differences may merely be waiting for the perfecting of technique and the patience necessary for their discovery."[17]

The notion of Nordic superiority, rather widespread in the United States in the early twenties—the time Hitler was developing his own version of it—seems to have lost popularity fairly quickly in the country at large and among psychologists. The attempts to test for intelligence differences between European races were disappearing by 1930, even though as late as 1937 Gardner Murphy, Lois Murphy, and Theodore Newcomb in their new *Experimental Social Psychology* handbook, did not "regard as closed the question" of innate differences between Nordic, Alpine, and Mediterranean races. This was probably more an attempt to display their scientific openmindedness than an expression of their personal convictions.[18] The belief in black inferiority showed considerably more resilience.

Explicit attacks on the psychologists' race data began in 1921, at first coming not from within the profession but from critics without, and directed against the most prominent set of relevant data, the results of the testing of United States Army recruits in World War One. Soon, psychologists joined in the criticism. By 1928, C. C. Brigham—who had published the most explicitly racist interpretation of the army data in 1923—had changed his mind; in 1930, he publicly retracted his earlier conclusions as having been "without foundation." In the same year, a follow-up review of "Race Psychology" by Garth in the *Psychological Bulletin* concluded that the race difference hypothesis was "no nearer [to] being established than it [had been] five years ago. In fact many psychologists seem practically ready for another, the hypothesis of racial equality."[19] A survey carried out at this time showed Garth's judgment a bit optimistic, but not wrong. Of one hundred psychologists, selected for their contact with the problem area, only twenty-five percent still indicated a belief that the Negro was inferior in intelligence (with some qualifications of this statement in their written comments), eleven percent believed in the equality of the Negro, and sixty-four percent thought the data to bc inconclusive.[20]

STUDIES IN PREJUDICE

Meanwhile, a different but clearly related issue was beginning to come into focus. Instead of trying to determine the *objective* mental differences between nonwhite and white, as well as among the white races, psychologists became interested in the subjective side, the *attitudes* of the "racial" groups toward each other. In 1927, L. L. Thurstone (an engineer-turned-psychologist concerned with making psychology into a quantitative rational science) decided that instead of asking his subjects about dull psychophysical problems such as differences between weights, it would be more interesting to ask which nationalities they preferred to associate with.[21] Such judgments, "saturated with prejudice and bias," would present a severe test of his new method of paired comparisons. Not long afterward, the new *Journal of Social Psychology* (subtitled *Political, Racial, and Differential Psychology*) published J. P. Guilford's study, "Racial Preferences of a Thousand American University Students." The main purpose of Guilford's experiment was, like Thurstone's, the testing of new psychometric scaling methods. However, he saw a secondary purpose. Trying to stem the tide of immigration, the country had been wrestling with the problem of preferential treatment for members of certain races. In a representative democracy, it was reasonable that the "preferences of the people themselves should have something to say in determining the source of their newest adopted countrymen."[22] Instead of tests of innate intelligence, which had become problematic, psychologists were now offering "scientifically scaled" popular biases for the selection of immigrants. The change in methods did not make much difference, however, because the new ranking was almost the same as the old one, except perhaps in regard to the Jews.

This peripheral involvement of the psychometricians, ready to turn their instruments on targets of opportunity, was soon superceded by substantive concern with the problem of race or ethnic relations. Although devising new measuring methods remained an important aspect of the work, psychologists became concerned with the description and explanation of the social problem of prejudice in an attempt to contribute to its solution. The 1931 compendium of *Experimental Social Psychology* clearly shows this development. The longest section in its chapter on attitudes, and the first content-oriented one, was entitled "Interracial Attitudes"; other parts, on measuring and changing attitudes, etc., contained additional studies on this topic.[23] Race prejudice was on its way to becoming an important problem of the developing empirical social psychology.

Of course, just as the notion of *real* race superiority had not originated with the psychologists, the issue of race *prejudice* had been raised long before the psychologists became involved in it. Apart from the aforementioned Universal Race Congress, a black social scientist, W. E. B. DuBois, and a white sociologist, W. I. Thomas, the latter in a paper entitled "The Psychology of Race-Prejudice," had called attention to the problem in its practical and theoretical aspects shortly after the turn of the century.[24] In 1915, another black, George W. Ellis, presented a critical and hard-hitting description of the psychology of American race prejudice in G. S. Hall's new *Journal of Race Development*.[25] In the early twenties, stimulated by Robert Park's discussion of "spontaneous" if not "instinctive" race prejudice, another sociologist, Emory Bogardus—who had been involved in Americanization work during the war—developed an empirical tool, the "social distance scale"; applying this instrument, he explored the distribution and origins of prejudice in a number of studies, largely in the context of Caucasian-Oriental relations on the Pacific coast. Some social-problems-oriented religious organizations also became concerned with practical race relations after the war; one of them, The Inquiry, began a research project which produced the first large-scale treatment of the ontogentic development of prejudice, in Bruno Lasker's book *Race Attitudes in Children*.[26]

Even Goodwin Watson, apparently the first *psychologist* attempting to measure race prejudice, seems to have been stimulated by his involvement in religious education. At the time Watson was moving from Union Theological Seminary to the psychologists at Teachers College. In his dissertation, *Measurement of Fairmindedness,* which included opinions about racial groups, he combined his social-religious concerns with the psychologists' interest in the methodological problems of attitude measurement.[27] Another early psychological study, Daniel Katz's investigation of student attitudes at Syracuse University, carried out in 1926, seems to have included the topic of race prejudice almost by accident,[28] in an attempt to measure what the book called "snobbishness," the exclusionary attitude of students, especially fraternity men, toward outgroups.[29]

The beginning of the next decade saw Katz and Kenneth Braly produce their classic study of racial stereotypes of Princeton students. Although the category of "Race Psychology" in the index of the *Psychological Abstracts* shows only few, by and large German, entries in the thirties, and although surprisingly few entries are found under the label "Prejudice" (even the second Katz and Braly paper appeared, for unfathomable reasons, under the heading "Race

Attitudes"), the social psychology of race prejudice was growing.[30] It became one of the cornerstones of the developing discipline of empirical social psychology, giving some theoretical focus to attitude research, providing perhaps the close link between the academic enterprise and the "real world," and often serving as its moral legitimation. The sections on applied social psychology in the major works of the field began with chapters on prejudice.[31]

The Katz and Braly study had implicitly defined prejudice as irrational: because the possession of any *real* trait would vary among members of *any* group, the attribution of a trait to *all* members of a race or nationality—a result at least in part imposed by the data collection method—could not be based on actual experience and was nonveridical. With the absorption of more psychoanalytic thinking, through John Dollard, the frustration-aggression theory, and finally the Berkeley study of the Authoritarian Personality, into social psychological theorizing,[32] prejudice became more explicitly defined as rooted in personality dynamics and irrationality; the extreme position was represented in the argument that "anti-Semitism has nothing to do with the Jews." Researchers in a score of studies on prejudice sought the intrapsychic roots of bigotry and intolerance, forgetting that not long ago psychological science had certified the inferiority of the rejected groups. The last step was taken; the issue had moved from one pole to the other, from the real race superiority of the Anglo race (and the Anglo psychologists) to the irrational prejudices of the psychologists' new subjects. The superior rationality of the professional researchers had been maintained.

WHY THE CHANGE?

In a traditional view as expounded in our textbooks, this outline history (which is not intended to be complete) looks like a beautiful example of the progress of empirical science: objective data triumph over prejudices and speculation and overcome, in self-corrective fashion, even the misconceptions and biases of the first generation of researchers. Francis Bacon could not be more pleased with this emergence of truth out of error. Unfortunately, however, it may be a myth. Empirical data certainly did not settle the issue, one way or the other, as the current controversy about the heritability of intelligence between respected psychologists at Harvard, Berkeley, and Princeton shows;[33] the vast majority of psychologists have never taken a close look at all the data, but accepted, by and large, received opinion supported by appropriate pieces of the evidence, then and now. (It is tempting to extend the argument to claim that *no* important psychological issue has been settled by empirical data.)

Another view would see these historical developments, in the currently popular terms of Thomas Kuhn,[34] as a shift in the dominant paradigm for the social psychological study of groups and group relations. Just as empirical data were not irrelevant to the issue, the notion of a paradigm shift from evolutionary genetics to the culture concept, from Darwin to Boas (and in psychology from instincts to learning),[35] is not without its attractions. Unfortunately, even before Kuhn psychologists were well aware of historical shifts in their theoretical and methodological orientations toward their subject matter, from introspection to functionalism, to behaviorism, and so on. Although, superimposing Kuhn's labels on such changes may seem to legitimize them (after all, it happened even in physics), it avoids the difficulties of dealing with the more original parts of Kuhn's argument; for instance, what precisely was the old and the new paradigm-exemplar: Mendel's peas versus Boas's cranial measurements of immigrant children? the Stanford-Binet versus the social distance scale? mental tests versus attitude measures? Furthermore, such labeling only appears to give an explanation and adds little to our understanding of the actual historical process and its implications.

What is clear, however, is that we may have to break out of a purely internalist treatment of our history, dealing only with scientific data, the abstract theoretical concepts, and their interplay. From the very beginning, the problem was not just one of pure or idle scientific curiosity and the search for abstract truth; it was enmeshed in the real world from the start, in ways which are more obvious if perhaps not more important than is true of other, seemingly more esoteric problems of psychology.

It seems unnecessary to document the relation between the question of black inferiority and political issues of slavery, colonialism, and emancipation. The interest in the "comparative worth" of the different white races, as well as of the Orientals, also was clearly related to political issues, especially the immigration question in the United States, exacerbated by the problem of divided loyalties in World War One. Details of the involvement of psychologists in the immigration issue have been presented elsewhere.[36] Here I will focus on some of the factors contributing to the historical sea change from Race Psychology to Studies in Prejudice.

The first external factor was the passage of the permanent Immigration Restriction Law of 1924, which dramatically reduced, through the use of the 1890 census as quota base, the inflow of southeastern Europeans both in absolute and relative numbers. It was no longer necessary to justify scientifically the exclusion of these undesirable and inferior aliens. Although the study of Negro intelligence remained at a steady rate for the decade from 1919 to 1929—according to Garth's tabulations in 1925 and 1930—studies of differences between European nationalities and "races" increased during the debate about immigration restriction (1920–1924) and fell off sharply soon after its passage. At least two of the larger studies published afterward involved work begun or data collected before the enactment of the law.[37]

This was hardly a coincidence. In an analysis of fifteen popular magazines, Thomas Woofter found a similar drop, from 1925 on, in the volume of discussion of immigration, reflecting "a rapidly decreasing interest in immigration."[38] And in a conference of the National Research Council's Committee for the Scientific Study of Human Migration (itself originating in the eugenicists's concern over immigration problems), sociologist H. P. Fairchild—a staunch supporter of immigration restriction and president of the Eugenics Society—remarked, "We as American citizens may have been influenced by our permanent restriction law to feel that the problem is not so acute—not so menacing as it has been in the last few years. We find our minds somewhat satisfied with regard to the situation in our country." The "scientific" question was by no means settled, but the practical one was. The NRC Committee itself was fading away into inactivity. As F. H. Hankins in the new journal *Industrial Psychology* (by then denouncing the "Nordic Myth" which had served its purpose) was arguing in 1926, the remaining problems were (1) a higher standard of admission for *individual* immigrants within national quotas, preferably based on mental tests, and (2) "a wider spirit of racial toleration between native and foreign elements now in the country, particularly a greater appreciation on the part of the native stock of the cultural contributions of their foreign-born neighbors."[39]

The first item remained a recommendation of the Immigration Committee of the Eugenics Society for a long time and sporadically attracted the attention of psychologists, but failed to gain much public support.[40] The second one, how to maintain peace and tranquility among the peoples already here, has occupied an important place on the agenda of the nation ever since, even if waxing and waning in its visibility, and has absorbed a good deal of the energy and moral fervor of the social sciences. While earlier the deterioration of American intelligence and genetic potential had been called the problem of overriding importance, by 1928 Bogardus's book opened with the claim that the greatest single issue confronting America was that of race relations. Bogardus provided the early link between the failed Americanization movement of the war years and the study of prejudice, which became the major contribution of social psychologists.

But apart from the shift in public interest from racial homogeneity to interracial harmony, another factor becomes relevant when we ask *how* the shift took place in psychology: Did individuals change their stand on the issue or did new professionals enter the arena with a different perspective? It appears that some individuals changed their minds (for example, Brigham, Garth, Kimball Young); others weakened their stand slowly and gradually (Terman, Robert Yerkes); some remained adamant (Henry E. Garrett). It is not easy to obtain the raw data or to demonstrate clearly their relevance, yet it seems arguable that a change in the pattern of ethnic backgrounds among psychologists contributed significantly to the shift. Looking at any list of prominent early psychologists, one is struck by the character of their names. American psychology up to 1920 was lily-white, consisting essentially of native or imported Anglo-Saxons (if we do not take the definition of this term too literally), with an occasional Jew or half-Jew thrown in who, like Hugo Muensterberg, was more German than Jew. There is nothing peculiar about psychology in this; as James McKeen Cattell and others have shown in their analysis of American scientists, early American science was predominantly "Puritan" or at least Anglo-Saxon.[41] From the twenties on, however, ethnics began to move into the profession in ever-increasing numbers, at first primarily with recruits from Jewish backgrounds. It was not until the sixties that Italian, Greek, and all the other "ethnic" names showed up in large numbers among our journal authors. Blacks were, of course, even further behind. The first black Ph.D. in psychology was apparently awarded in 1920. By 1940, the number of black Ph.D.'s had increased to nine, according to Robert Guthrie. Although between 1920 and 1966 the ten leading departments produced over 3700 Ph.D.s in psychology, a survey found only eight of them to have been blacks.[42]

If this estimate of the ethnic origins of American psychologists is indeed accurate, what is its significance for an empirical science carried on by professionals trained to be objective? Apart from the fact that such a question is in bad taste—if not worse—it is not easy to document that such differences in background affected the sensitivities and insensitivities of scientists to the issues. E. A. Ross's autobiography, with its frank admission of early Anglo-Saxon bias and distaste for immigrants, as well as the subsequent regret over his chauvinism and lack of empathy, provides the best example, though even he distorted retrospectively the recency of his nativist utterances.[43] Other (auto)biographies—Terman, Yerkes, Walter D. Scott—are less frank or at least less illuminating on this point, and also marked by significant omissions (for instance, membership in eugenics organizations).[44] They *do* contain an emphasis similar to Ross's on family origin and pedigree (Anglo), childhood on the farm, and their successful movement up the social structure apparently based on native endowment and individual effort.[45]

Other clues are sparse and consist mainly of expressions about Jews. (Both Ross's and McDougall's books had been attacked as anti-Semitic in their description of the Jewish race; both had protested against such accusations and deplored "crude race prejudice.") Jewish students were receiving doctorates in psychology in the twenties, a few even earlier; but they did not seem to fare too well in terms of jobs. The correspondence of Terman, Yerkes, and Boring indicates an awareness of the "Jewish problem," in references to students' origins and to the fact that a particular person did not, or on occasion did, posses the undesirable traits of the Jewish race. Several decades later, A. A. Roback chided Terman for having accepted, in the Stanford-

Binet vocabulary items, the answer "Jewish" as a correct definition of the word "shrewd." Although Terman replied with a clarification, he also admitted that he was "sorry now that we included this as a plus response."[46] Probably, a Jewish test constructor would not have been insensitive to this usage.

In fairness, it should be stated clearly that, whatever such expressions indicate, they were far different in tone from the more virulent anti-Semitism in Madison Grant's "Nordic" camp.[47] Terman, for example, brought Kurt Lewin to Stanford in 1931 (and later tried hard to help him with his emigration from Germany in 1933) even though he had learned in a rather comic exchange of letters with Boring that Lewin was Jewish.[48]

Such evidence is rather incomplete at this point and far from satisfactory, yet it seems at least plausible that ethnic-cultural backgrounds and their ramifications were not entirely unrelated to professional activities. In any case, it appears that the first psychologist who tested "white and negro" children and did not simply conclude that blacks were intellectually inferior, was an immigrant and a female.[49] Instead, she found her black children superior in a number of abilities, saw no definite race differences in tests of reasoning, and concluded that individual capacity was at least as important as race and sex. The first questioning, in professional journals, of the army tests on blacks came from Howard University.[50] Another—Jewish—immigrant had criticized the racial interpretation of the army tests in the *Yale Review* a year earlier.[51]

In the subsequent shift from race psychology to concern with prejudice, one finds names like Klineberg, Herskovits, Feingold, Hirsch, Viteles, Lasker, Katz, Lehman, Horowitz, Fukuda, and Yeung. They were not the only ones taking up the culture argument; certainly, no claim is made that researchers split cleanly along racial or ethnic lines on the issues.[52] It seem likely, however, that personal experience sensitized individuals to different aspects of the problem, and led some to question the assumptions taken as self-evident by others lacking such experience.[53] One of the earliest empirical studies of race differences (by M. J. Mayo) found the school performance of New York blacks inferior to that of whites. This difference could be a matter of opportunity or of hereditary, the author conceded. But "it is hard to escape the conclusion that [it was] mainly . . . the factor of race heredity . . . in as much as everything in the power of the educator, philanthropist, and law giver has been done for the equalization of opportunity. . . ." Most black researchers would have known better. In fact, the first volume of the Urban League's journal *Opportunity* carried an article attacking Mayo's study and its insensitivity to the disadvantaged position of Negroes.[54]

As Horace Mann Bond wrote in the NAACP journal, *The Crisis,* in reply to the same type of argument as Mayo's but based on the army data, "The time has passed for opposing these false ideas with silence; . . . There is no longer any justification for the silence of the educated Negro, when confronted with these assertions; and only through his activity and investigation will the truth be disclosed and the ghosts of racial inferiority, mental or physical, set at rest forever." But there were almost no black psychologists; Bond's and other black voices were not heard by many. (One of the first black psychologists with a doctor's degree, Howard H. Long, was among the earliest critics of the army tests; but his articles appeared in *Opportunity* and the *Howard Review*—journals not searched for the *Psychological Index.*)[55] The battle in academics was fought by nonblacks, with some consequences for the definition of the issue at stake.

The questioning of theories of innate race differences and the interest in race prejudice did not originate exclusively with members of ethnic minorities. Yet the shift of the *majority* opinion in the profession was probably supported by a third factor, the political developments of the thirties and forties. The Depression seems to have given many psychologists a powerful push toward the left.[56] By 1939, a survey of psychologists attending the APA convention found "a plurality or majority of psychologists select[ing] the answers that are liberal, progressive, democratic."[57]

Soon World War Two was to impose the need to unite the country in the fight against a powerful enemy who proclaimed racial superiority as one of the main sources of his strength. By the time the war was over, there existed hundreds of organizations dedicated to the promotion of racial tolerance and intergroup harmony—as reported in the *Annals of the Academy of Political and Social Science,* which devoted the whole issue of March 1946 to the topic "Controlling Group Prejudice." Harvard psychologist Gordon Allport, in his introduction to this issue, declared that many of the problems of the world were largely caused by a "primary weakness in human nature . . . . *group prejudice.*"[58] In twenty-five years, the psychologists' diagnosis of the ills of mankind had changed dramatically in its manifest content.

FROM AMOS 'N ANDY TO ARCHIE BUNKER

More than two decades later, the chapter entitled "Prejudice and Ethnic Relations" in the new *Handbook of Social Psychology* stated that it would focus on the topic of attitudes, and furthermore, on attitudes of the so-called majority group toward ethnic minorities. "These emphases do not represent an arbitrary selection of topics on our part; they reflect rather the major preoccupations of social-psychological research in this area. . . ."[59] The reasons for this focus seem obvious. But are they perhaps problematic in their obviousness? And what were the consequences? Only a brief indication of the answers to such questions is possible here.

The selection of the crudely prejudiced white, and the psychological bases for his prejudice, as the (easy?) target left other issues largely untouched. In a society where, despite protestations, inequality and discrimination were part of the fabric of daily life, where in many studies the majority had expressed some negative reactions to blacks,[60] might not the problem be one of understanding how some individuals developed (or became) free of race prejudice—rather than trying to find complex psychological reasons why the majority did not? Yet this problem was rarely raised.

The attitudes of blacks toward the race problem and integration were usually taken for granted. The classic studies of integration in the army and in housing either did not even ask the black participants about their feelings[61] or, having undersampled the black housewives to begin with (at a one to four ratio), concentrated on the reactions of the white subjects.[62] The implicit liberal assumption was that the right and natural end state would be reached when all ethnics had been assimilated into a universalistic culture (coinciding with middle-class standards), and everybody would politely overlook the existence of darker skin colors. It received a rude shock with the emergence of black nationalism into white awareness in the sixties. We have not yet found a realistic solution to this dilemma.

The old question, whether race discrimination was a phenomenon sui generis or only a correlate of a society divided by social classes, was hardly raised and never pursued systematically, perhaps because it was tainted by its Marxist origins. And finally, the professional self-limitation to "psychological" issues typically led the social psychologists to ignore, after cursory acknowledgment of the relevance of social conditions, the possibility that societal forces might keep the Archie Bunkers locked into their discriminatory behaviors in order to defend what little they had.

Certainly, social psychologists have made valuable contributions to our understanding of "race relations." But could even greater contributions have been vitiated by an unreflected attitude toward their own role? Based on the personal experience of inequities in the social system, outsiders had raised some important questions about it and the attendant orthodoxies. But having become insiders, had they limited their questioning to the more superficial and comfortable issues which would not threaten their newly achieved professional status? What happened to social psychology in the forties and fifties, perhaps epitomized by the changing conceptions and contexts of what became known as the *Authoritarian Personality,* as well as the professional reaction to it, seems crucial to an understanding of these developments.[63] But this story remains to be worked out.

NOTES

1. In general, the changes made in this year were the result of coordinating the classification system of the *Index* with the *Bibliographie* of the *Zeitschrift fuer Psychologie und Physiologie der Sinnesorgane,* ee *Psychological Index,* No. 18, Index for the Year 1911 (1912): III. However, the *Bibliographie* did not have any classification containing the word "Rasse" before this date.

2. Robert S. Woodworth, "Racial Differences in Mental Traits," *Science* 31 (1910): 171–186.

3. Gustav Spiller, ed., *Papers on Inter-Racial Problems Communicated to the First Universal Races Congress* (London: King and Son, 1911).

4. Francis Galton, *Hereditary Genius,* rev. ed. (New York: Appleton, 1884; originally published 1869), p. 338.

5. R. Meade Bache, "Reaction Time with Reference to Race," *Psychological Review* 2 (1895): 475–486.

6. See Robert M. Yerkes, James W. Bridges, and Rose S. Hardwick, *A Point Scale for Measuring Mental Ability* (Baltimore: Warwick and York, 1915), p. 86.

7. For instance, George O. Ferguson, "The Psychology of the Negro," *Archives of Psychology,* No. 36 (1916).

8. See John Higham, *Strangers in the Land* (New Brunswick: Rutgers University Press, 1955); Barbara M. Solomon, *Ancestors and Immigrants* (Cambridge: Harvard University Press, 1956); and a number of other authors.

9. Carl C. Brigham, *A Study of American Intelligence* (Princeton: Princeton University Press, 1923); Kimball Young, "Intelligence Tests of Certain Immigrant Groups," *Scientific Monthly* 15 (1922): 417–434.

10. Clifford Kirkpatrick, *Intelligence and Immigration* (Baltimore: Williams and Wilkins, 1926).

11. Edwin G. Boring, "Intelligence as the Tests Test It," unpublished manuscript (1923), p. 14, Edwin G. Boring Papers, Harvard University Archives; Thomas R. Garth, "A Review of Racial Psychology," *Psychological Bulletin 22* (1925): 359.

12. Lewis M. Terman, "Mentality Tests: A Symposium," *Journal of Educational Psychology* 7 (1916): 348–360; Gustave LeBon, *The Psychology of Peoples* (London: Fischer Urwin, 1899); Edward A. Ross, *The Old World in the New* (New York: Century, 1914), p. 286, emphasis in the original.

13. See Edward A. Ross, *Seventy Years of It* (New York: Appleton-Century, 1936), p. 223; see also Julius Weinberg, *Edward Alsworth Ross and the Sociology of Progressivism* (Madison: State Historical Society of Wisconsin, 1972), especially chapter 7 on Ross's nativism.

14. William McDougall, *Is America Safe for Democracy?* (New York: Scribner, 1921).

15. Floyd H. Allport, *Social Psychology* (Boston: Houghton Mifflin, 1924), pp. 386–387. Yet he went on to say that the difference in mental ability was not enough to account for the Negro problem; rather, it was caused by the Negro's insufficient socialization—perhaps an early version of the "blaming the victim" strategy in social science.

16. Ibid., pp. 387–388.

17. Floyd H. Allport, "Social Aspects of the Measurement of Intelligence," *Journal of Abnormal and Social Psychology* 19 (1924–1925): 313.

18. Gardner Murphy, Lois B. Murphy, and Theodore M. Newcomb, *Experimental Social Psychology,* rev. ed. (New York: Harper, 1937), p. 68.

19. Carl C. Brigham, "Intelligence Tests of Immigrant Groups," *Psychological Review* 37 (1930): 158–165; Thomas R. Garth, "A Review of Race Psychology," *Psychological Bulletin* 27 (1930): 348.

20. Of the anthropologists and sociologists asked, only five percent still believed in the inferiority, and thirty-eight percent in the equality of Negroes. Charles H. Thompson, "The Conclusions of Scientists Relative to Racial Differences," *Journal of Negro Education* 3 (1934): 499. Of course, by now there is an extensive secondary literature on this first period of scientists' involvement with race, immigration, and IQ differences, beginning with Higham, *Strangers in the Land* and Solomon, *Ancestors and Immigrants.* See also Franz Samelson, "World War I Intelligence Testing and the Development of Psychology," *Journal of the History of the Behavioral Sciences* 13 (1977): 274–282.

21. Louis L. Thurstone, "An Experimental Study of Nationality Preferences," *Journal of General Psychology* 1 (1928): 405–423. Thurstone was the son of Swedish immigrants and himself a quasi-immigrant, having spent part of his childhood in Sweden.

22. J. Paul Guilford, "Racial Preferences of a Thousand American University Students," *Journal of Social Psychology* 2 (1931): 199.

23. Gardner Murphy and Lois Barclay Murphy, *Experimental Social Psychology* (New York: Harper, 1931), chap. 11.

24. W. E. Burkhardt DuBois, "The Relation of the Negroes to the Whites in the South," *Annals of the American Academy of Political and Social Science 18* (1901): 121–140; William I. Thomas, "The Psychology of Race-Prejudice," *American Journal of Sociology* 9 (1904): 593–611. There were others, too, such as Jean Finot, *Race Prejudice,* trans. Florence Wade-Evans (New York: Dutton, 1907): and Josiah Royce's essay on race prejudices in his *Race Questions, Provincialism, and Other American Problems* (New York: Macmillan, 1908), pp. 1–53.

25. George W. Ellis, "The Psychology of American Race Prejudice," *Journal of Race Development* 5 (1914–1915): 297–315. The major concern of this journal had been, from the beginning, the affairs of the colonial countries in Asia and Africa. Its ambiguous title was changed, in 1919, to *Journal of International Affairs.*

26. Emory S. Bogardus, "Social Distance and its Origins," *Journal of Applied Sociology* 9 (1925): 216–226; Bogardus, *Immigration and Race Attitudes* (Boston: Heath, 1928); Bruno Lasker, *Race Attitudes in Children* (New York: Holt, 1929). For the beginnings of this effort, see The Inquiry, *And Who is My Neighbor? An Outline for the Study of Race Relations in America* (New York: Association Press, 1924).

27. Goodwin B. Watson, Oral History (1963, pp. 35–40). Oral History Collection, Columbia University; Watson, *The Measurement of Fairmindedness* (New York: Columbia Teachers College, 1925).

28. Though a year earlier he had collected data on the exclusion of Negroes and immigrants from trade unions, in the context of a study of the effects of race and nationality on industrial relations in Buffalo. The study had been suggested by The Inquiry. See Niles Carpenter, *Nationality, Color, and Economic Opportunity in the City of Buffalo* (Buffalo: University of Buffalo, 1927).

29. Daniel Katz and Floyd H. Allport, *Students' Attitudes* (Syracuse: Craftsman Press, 1931).

30. Daniel Katz and Kenneth Braly, "Racial Stereotypes of One Hundred College Students," *Journal of Abnormal and Social Psychology* 28 (1933): 280–290; Katz and Braly, "Racial Prejudice and Racial Stereotypes," *Journal of Abnormal and Social Psychology* 30 (1935): 175–193.

31. David Krech and Richard S. Crutchfield, *Theory and Problems of Social Psychology* (New York: McGraw-Hill, 1948); Gardner Lindzey, ed., *Handbook of Social Psychology* (Cambridge, Mass.: Addison-Wesley, 1954), vol. 2; 2nd ed., Gardner Lindzey and Elliot Aronson, eds., *Handbook* (Reading, Mass.: Addison-Wesley, 1969), vol. 5.

32. John Dollard, *Caste and Class in a Southern Town* (New Haven: Yale University Press, 1937); John Dollard, Leonard W. Doob, Neal E. Miller, O. Hobart Mowrer, and Robert R. Sears, *Frustration and Aggression* (New Haven: Yale University Press, 1939); Theodore W. Adorno, Else Frenkel-Brunswik, Daniel J. Levinson, and R. Nevitt Sanford, *The Authoritarian Personality* (New York: Harper, 1950).

33. Richard J. Herrnstein, *I.Q. in the Meritocracy* (Boston: Little, Brown, 1973); Arthur R. Jensen, *Genetics and Education* (New York: Harper and Row, 1972); Leon J. Kamin, *The Science and Politics of I.Q.* (Potomac, Md.: Erlbaum, 1974).

34. Thomas S. Kuhn, *The Structure of Scientific Revolutions* (Chicago: University of Chicago Press, 1962).

35. For a rather comprehensive overview and interesting discussion of this shift in genetics and the social sciences, presented from a more internalist point of view, see Hamilton Cravens's Ph.D. dissertation. *American Scientists and the Heredity-Environment Controversy. 1883–1940* (University of Iowa, 1969. University Microfilm, order no. 69-21678). Cravens is certainly correct in pointing out the problems created for a simplistic hereditarian view by the experimental and theoretical advances in genetics and by new empirical and methodological results in mental testing. However, he seems to overestimate the quality of the new psychological data in support of environmentalism, which were not all that superior to the older data; the new evidence was convincing only if one had already accepted the new paradigm.

36. Franz Samelson, "On the Science and Politics of the I.Q.," *Social Research* 42 (1975): 467–488; Samelson, "Putting Psychology on the Map," in *The Social Context of Psychology,* ed. Allen R. Buss (New York: Irvington, in press).

37. Garth, "Race Psychology"; Nathaniel D. M. Hirsch, "A Study of Natio-Racial Mental Differences," *Genetic Psychology Monographs* 1 (1926): 239–406; Kirkpatrick, *Intelligence and Immigration.*

38. Thomas J. Woofter, Jr., "The Status of Racial and Ethnic Groups," in *Recent Social Trends,* Report of the President's Research Committee on Social Trends (New York: McGraw-Hill, 1933), chap. 11: 557.

39. Henry P. Fairchild, in minutes of conference, 1 and 2 January 1925, p. 8. Conferences, Committee on Scientific Problems of Human Migration, Anthropology and Psychology, Archives of the National Research Council, Washington, D.C.: Frank H. Hankins, "Racial Differences and Industrial Welfare," *Industrial Psychology* 1 (1926): 98.

40. See *Organized Eugenics* (New Haven: American Eugenics Society, Inc., January 1931), p. 20.

41. J. McKeen Cattell, as cited in Stephen S. Visher, *Scientists Starred 1903–1943 in "American Men of Science"* (Baltimore: Johns Hopkins Press, 1947), p. 540.

42. Robert V. Guthrie, *Even the Rat was White* (New York: Harper and Row, 1976); Lauren G. Wispé, Philip Ash, Joseph Awkward, Leslie H. Hicks, Marvin Hoffman, and Janice Porter, "The Negro Psychologist in America," *American Psychologist 24* (1969): 142–150.

43. Ross, *Seventy Years,* pp. 93, 276–278.

44. Cf. Edwin G. Boring, *A History of Experimental Psychology* (New York: Century, 1929), p. 558, and the second edition (New York: Appleton-Century-Crofts, 1950), p. 628. In the first edition, Boring mentioned Yerkes's leadership in the army intelligence testing. "Afterward he supported various projects that had to do with racial psychology." By 1950 the same paragraph, rewritten, described Yerkes as "chief of the psychological services [in the war], and not long after he got his ape studies under way . . . ." The reference to the projects in racial psychology had dropped out of the paragraph, and out of the history of psychology. (For some details of Yerkes's involvement in race and immigration, see Samelson, "Putting Psychology on the Map.").

45. Lewis M. Terman, "Trails to Psychology," in *A History of Psychology in Autobiography,* vol. 2, ed. Carl Murchison (Worcester, Mass.: Clark University Press, 1932), pp. 297–331; Robert M. Yerkes, "Psychobiologist," ibid., pp. 381–407; Yerkes, *Testament,* unpublished manuscript (c. 1949), Robert M. Yerkes Papers, Historical Library, Yale Medical Library, New Haven, Conn.; Jacob Z. Jacobson, *Scott of Northwestern* (Chicago: L. Mariano, 1951). See also Edwin G. Boring, *Psychologist at Large* (New York: Basic Books, 1961); Matthew T. Downey, *Carl Campbell Brigham, Scientist and Educator* (Princeton: Educational Testing Service, 1961)—although their background was not rural.

46. For instance, Boring to Terman, 1 February 1923 and 25 February 1932, Correspondence Files, Boring Papers; Herbert S. Langfeld to Yerkes, 17 June 1915; Yerkes to secretary, Board of National Research Fellowship in Biology, 29 May 1923, Correspondence Files, Yerkes Papers; Yerkes to Terman, 21 July 1921, p. 3, Box 17; Abraham A. Roback to Terman, 12 November 1950, and Terman to Roback, 27 November 1950, Box 15, Lewis M. Terman Papers, Stanford University Archives, Stanford, Calif.

47. See Samelson, "Science and Politics," p. 467,

and other material in the Files of the Immigration Restriction League, Houghton Library, Harvard University. On Madison Grant, see Charles C. Alexander, "Prophet of American Racism: Madison Grant and the Nordic Myth," *Phylon* 23 (1962): 73–90.

48. Exchange of letters between Boring and Terman, July to October 1931, Correspondence Files, Boring Papers, Box 13, Terman Papers.

49. Dagny Sunne, "A Comparative Study of White and Negro Children," *Journal of Applied Psychology* 1 (1917): 71–83.

50. Martha McLear, "Sectional Differences as Shown by Academic Ratings and Army Tests," *School and Society* 15 (1922): 676–678. McLear was neither black nor an immigrant, but a Quaker who had taught at Howard University for a decade or more—and also a feminist, to judge from her Ph.D. dissertation. McLear, *The History of the Education of Girls in New York and New England. 1800–1870* (Washington, D.C.: Howard University Press, 1926).

51. Franz Boas, "The Problem of the American Negro," *Yale Review* 20 (1921): 384–395.

52. Cf. David Hollinger's recent argument that the American liberal intelligentsia emerging in the thirties was composed of an alliance between disaffected Anglo-Saxons and Jewish intellectuals. See David A. Hollinger, "Ethnic Diversity, Cosmopolitanism, and the Emergence of the American Liberal Intelligentsia," *American Quarterly* 27 (1975): 133–151. I am indebted to John Burnham for the reference to this article; while the individuals and the specific context are different, the general issue is clearly related.

53. For a more recent description of such sensitivities, see Seymour B. Sarason, "Jewishness, Blackishness, and the Nature-Nurture Controversy," *American Psychologist* 28 (1973): 962–971.

54. Marion J. Mayo, "The Mental Capacity of the American Negro," *Archives of Psychology* No. 28 (1913): 67; Charles S. Johnson, "Mental Measurement of Negro Groups," *Opportunity* 1 No. 2 (1923): 21–25.

55. Horace M. Bond, "Intelligence Tests and Propaganda," *The Crisis* 28 (1924): 64; for example, Howard H. Long, "Race and Mental Tests," *Opportunity* 1, No. 3 (1923): 22–28. Beginning with vol. 3 (1929), the *Psychological Abstracts* listed both *Opportunity* and *Crisis* among the journals abstracted.

56. See Lorenz J. Finison, "Unemployment, Politics, and the History of Organized Psychology," *American Psychologist* 31 (1976): 747–755; David Krech, (Autobiography), in *A History of Psychology in Autobiography,* vol. 6, ed. Gardner Lindzey (Englewood Cliffs, N.J.: Prentice-Hall, 1974), pp. 221–250; Goodwin B. Watson, Oral History.

57. Ralph H. Gundlach, "The Psychologists' Understanding of Social Issues," *Psychological Bulletin* 37 (1940): 620.

58. Gordon W. Allport, ed., "Controlling Group Prejudice," *Annals of the American Academy of Political and Social Science* 244 (1946): VII, emphasis in the original.

59. John Harding, Harold Proshansky, Bernard Kutner, and Isidor Chein, "Prejudice and Ethnic Relations," vol. 5, p. 2.

60. Cf. Frank R. Westie, "The American Dilemma: An Empirical Test," *American Sociological Review* 30 (1965): 537–538.

61. Samuel Stouffer, Edward A. Suchman, Leland C. DeVinney, Shirley A. Star, and Robin M. Williams, *The American Soldier: Adjustment during Army Life,* vol. 1 (Princeton: Princeton University Press, 1949), p. 588; see also p. 488.

62. All twenty-six tables presented only data for whites; in the text, an occasional paragraph referred to the Negro women or children, usually describing their responses as similar. Morton Deutsch and Mary E. Collins, *Interracial Housing* (Minneapolis: University of Minnesota Press, 1951).

63. Adorno et al., *Authoritarian Personality*; for some earlier, and inadequate, comments on this problem, see Franz Samelson and Jacques F. Yates, "Acquiescence and the F Scale: Old Assumptions and New Data," *Psychological Bulletin* 68 (1967): 91–103.

NAME INDEX

Achilles, P. S., 427
Acord, J., 123
Adams, D. K., 538, 544
Adams, F., 453
Adams, H., 253
Adler, H. E., 121, 124
Agger, E. E., 373
Agger, L. D., see Kellogg, L. A.
Albert B. ("Little Albert"), 393, 411
Alexander, F., 89, 515–516
Allen, C. N., 320, 331
Allen, G. W., 253
Allport, F. H., 409, 414, 634
Allport, G. W., 194, 409, 609, 632, 641
Amsel, A., 437
Anderson, P. A., 488
Andral, G., 77, 78
Angell, F., 168, 189
Angell, G. T., 354, 360
Angell, J. R., 196, 269, 297–309, 313, 314, 359, 362–364, 390, 391, 402–404, 406
Angier, R. P., 406
Anna O, 489, 491, 493–510
Aristotle, 23, 300, 615
Arnheim, R., 535, 538
Aronson, L., 366
Artz, T., 56
Asch, S., 535, 552
Ash, M. G., 527
Aubertin, S. A. E., 78

Babcock, M. E., 320
Babinski, J., 111, 112
Babkin, B. P., 364
Bache, R. M., 610
Bacon, F., 26, 34, 37, 38, 637
Bailey, D. E., 460
Baillarger, J. G. F., 80
Bain, A., 318, 330
Bakan, D., 64
Baker, D. B., 123, 559
Balance, W., 158
Baldwin, J. M., 180, 290, 362–363, 391, 575
Barger, A. C., 354
Barnes, E., 272
Barzun, J., 249
Bascom, J., 359–360
Basset, G. C., 451
Bateson, W., 450
Baudouin, A., 111
Baum, W. K., 15

Beach, F. A., 385
Beard, G. M., 109
Beardsley, E. H., 610
Belais, D., 362
Belenky, M. F., 199
Bell, A. G., 243
Bell, C., 62, 366
Bellamy, R., 511, 512
Bemis, A. C., 477–479
Ben-David, J., 314
Benedek, T., 331
Benedikt, Meynert, 108
Benedikt, Moritz, 108
Benison, S., 354, 357, 358, 364
Benjamin, L. T., Jr., 2, 10, 13, 88, 123, 241, 242, 338, 372–389, 562, 593–606, 609
Bensley, R. R., 364
Bentley, M., 235, 366, 367
Benussi, V., 531
Bergh, H., 354
Berkeley, G., 24, 305
Berker, A. H., 79
Berker, E. A., 79
Bernard, C., 353, 354
Bernays, J., 503
Bernays, M., see Freud, M. B.
Bethe, H., 468
Binet, A., 290–291, 293, 409
Bingham, H. C., 409
Bingham, W. V. D., 405, 414, 424
Binswanger, W., 504
Bjork, D., 249, 252, 253
Blanchard, P., 275–278
Blum, G. S., 516
Blumenthal, A. L., 123–125, 158–167, 169, 179, 184
Boas, F., 288, 291–292, 488, 637
Bogardus, E. S., 636, 638–639
Boggs, L. P., 276, 277, 279
Bois, J., 112
Bolton, T. L., 264
Bond, H. M., 640
Boring, E. G., 121, 153, 160, 161, 170, 184, 190, 191, 194, 195, 198, 235–237, 266, 270, 402, 420, 514–515, 545–553, 634, 639, 640
Bouillaud, J.-B., 77–79
Bourdieu, P., 415
Bowers, F., 357
Boyce, J. C., 479, 482, 483
Boyle, R., 39
Braly, K., 636–637
Bray, C. W., 477
Bregman, E. O., 411
Breland, K., 475
Breland, M., 476
Brentano, F., 338
Brett, G. W., 312
Breuer, J., 488, 489, 491, 493–510
Brewer, M., 366
Bridgman, P., 436
Brie, S., 155–156
Brigham, C. C., 634–635, 639
Brill, A. A., 511, 512
Bringmann, N. J., 125, 151–157
Bringmann, W. G., 125, 151–158, 165
Britt, S. H., 381, 382
Broadbent, D., 163
Broca, P., 63, 64, 73–81, 319
Brodie, B. C., 105
Brown, A., 276
Brown, W., 452, 453
Broyles, J. W., 123
Brozek, J., 12, 18
Bruce, D., 338, 372–389
Brücke, E., 114
Brueghel, P., 9
Bruner, F. G., 611
Brunswik, E., 459
Brunton, L., 355
Bryan, A. I., 270
Bryan, W. L., 572
Buber, M., 502
Buckley, K. W., 394, 420–434
Buie, J., 520
Bullock, G., 275
Burghardt, G. M., 386
Burkhardt, F. H., 357
Burks, B. S., 453
Burnham, J. C., 336, 392, 512, 520
Burrow, J. W., 220
Burt, C., 163
Burtt, E. A., 185
Butterfield, H., 5, 7

Cadwallader, T. C., 12
Calkins, M. W., 14, 264, 270, 275, 288, 304, 326, 403, 408
Candolle, de, A., 85

Cannon, W. B., 354, 357, 358, 360, 364–366
Capshew, J. H., 440, 472–487, 628
Cardno, J. A., 17
Carlson, A. J., 366
Carmichael, L., 518, 538
Carr, E. H., 2, 5, 6, 8
Carr, H. A., 298, 407, 409, 414
Carrington, H., 512
Carter, R. L., 628, 629
Cartwright, D., 609
Cason, H., 387, 411
Casson, H. N., 365
Castle, C. A., 325
Castle, I., see McLaughlin, I. C.
Castro, M., 196
Cattell, J. M., 11, 14, 123, 232–237, 240–244, 282–295, 311, 325, 391, 406, 407, 413, 422, 488, 520, 558, 559, 569, 571, 593, 596, 639
Chambers, R., 219–221
Chappell, M. N., 381
Charcot, J. B., 106, 112
Charcot, J. M., 89, 91, 97–119, 489
Chase, A., 631
Chase, S., 430
Chein, I., 629, 632
Chomsky, N., 162, 179
Claretie, J., 108
Clark, J. G., 274, 360
Clark, K. B., 14, 611–613, 619–629
Clark, K. E., 519
Clark, M. P., 612, 613, 619–627, 632
Clark, R. W., 355
Clarke, E., 271, 323
Clerk Maxwell, J., 532
Clinchy, B. M., 199
Coan, T. M., 357
Cobbe, F. P., 354–357
Cohen, D., 360–361
Collingwood, R. G., 2, 3
Collins, R., 314
Commager, H. S., 4, 5, 7–9
Comte, A., 6, 24–25, 164, 170, 435
Conant, J. B., 552
Cook, S. W., 629
Coriat, I. H., 511, 512
Corwin, S. M., 516
Crannell, C. W., 540
Cristy, A. P., 360
Cromer, W., 488
Cronan-Hillix, W. A., 123, 438
Crozier, W. J., 473
Cruveilhier, J., 78
Culler, E., 382
Cuny, H., 364
Cuvier, G., 85

Dallenbach, K. M., 520
Dalma, J., 503
Daniel, R. S., 376
Daniels, R. V., 7
Danziger, K., 123, 513
Darwin, C., 82, 170, 203–226, 242, 244, 254, 299, 300, 320, 321, 335, 354–356, 450, 473, 637
Darwin, E., 204
Darwin, F., 219, 355, 356
Darwin, W., 355
Dashiell, J. F., 409, 598
Daudet, A., 106
Daudet, L., 106, 112
Davidson, E. S., 242
Davis, F. C., 455
Dax, G., 79
Dax, M., 79
Deese, J., 373, 382
Delboeuf, J., 109, 155
Descartes, R., 23–48, 57, 85
Deutsch, M., 630
Dewey, J., 170, 232, 249, 269, 276, 297–299, 309, 311–314, 331, 359, 390, 404, 407, 414, 551
Dewsbury, D. A., 338, 353–372, 387, 391
Diamond, S., 205, 206, 231–239, 241
Diehl, L. A., 243–244, 266–282, 299
Dixon, E., 275
Dodge, R., 194, 405
Dollard, J., 517, 637
Donaldson, H. H., 311, 362, 390
Donders, F. C., 18, 164
Donley, J. E., 511, 512
Downey, J. E., 198, 331
Drucker, R., 156
Dryden, H., 479
DuBois, W. E. B., 636
Duckitt, J., 610
Duncker, K., 534, 538, 541, 542, 544
Dunlap, J., 330
Dunlap, K., 14, 366, 392, 404, 408, 452, 512, 514
Durkin, M., 123

Duval, A., 79
Dykman, R. A., 382

Eagleson, B. M., 374
Ebbinghaus, H., 121, 181, 190, 314, 392, 530
Eddington, A. S., 532
Eddy, M. B., 511
Edinger, D., 502, 504
Edwards, A. L., 518
Ehrenfels, von, C., 526, 531
Einstein, A., 538
Eliot, C., 236
Ellenberger, H. F., 91, 104–114, 116, 489, 491, 499–510
Elliott, H. C., 318
Elliott, R. M., 409
Ellis, A., 517
Ellis, G. W., 636
Ellis, H., 267, 272, 319, 321, 322, 325, 331
Ellison, L., 275
Emerson, L. E., 511
Emerson, R. W., 251, 252, 254
Estabrooks, G. H., 609
Estes, W. K., 476
Evans, R. B., 158, 170, 488
Exner, S., 233
Eysenck, H. J., 517, 630

Faderman, L., 272
Fagan, T. K., 559
Fairchild, H. P., 638
Fancher, R. E., 64, 81–87, 205
Farrand, L., 288
Fechner, G. T., 120–124, 127–144, 165, 240
Feinberg, M., 382
Feinstein, H., 249, 252, 253
Feldman, H., 617
Fensch, D., 156
Ferguson, L., 123, 560
Fielde, A. M., 365
Filene, P. G., 272
Finger, S., 64, 77–81
Finison, L. J., 609
Fischel, W., 163
Fischer, E., 540, 541
Fisher, S., 517
Fiske, J., 236
Fite, W., 512
Flourens, P., 63, 64, 78, 81, 85–87
Franck, J., 538, 539
Franklin, F., 197
Franz, S. I., 80
French, R. D., 353
Freud, M. B., 116
Freud, S., 88, 91, 109, 114–119, 180, 242, 488–524
Friedman, S. M., 516
Friedrich, M., 152–154
Fulcher, R., 88
Fuller, J. L., 451
Fuller, P. R., 375
Furumoto, L., 18, 171, 188–202

Galileo, 22, 26, 38, 39, 223
Gall, F. J., 64, 77, 78, 81–87, 317, 318
Gallinger, J., 354, 359
Gallistel, C. R., 366
Galton, F., 204–206, 226–239, 241–244, 267, 284, 287, 288, 320, 571, 610, 633
Gamble, E. A. M., 195
Gantt, W. H., 364
Gardner, R. W., 162
Gardner, S., 270, 273, 274
Garfield, E., 17
Garrett, H. E., 514, 639
Garth, T. R., 634, 635, 638, 639
Geddes, P., 267, 321, 324
Gerard, H. B., 629
Gibson, E. J., 198
Gibson, J. J., 534, 536
Gifford, R., 362
Gilbreth, F. B., 414
Gilbreth, L. M., 414
Gilderhus, M. T., 4, 7, 9
Gilgen, A. R., 519
Gillispie, C. C., 219, 222, 223
Gilman, C., 153
Ginsburg, B., 366
Goddard, H. H., 14, 293, 525, 573–574, 577
Godwin, M. W., see Wollstonecraft, M.
Goldberger, N., 199
Goncourt, de, E., 106, 109
Goncourt, de, J., 106, 107
Good, R., 220, 222
Goodnow, F. J., 423

Goodwin, C. J., 192–193
Gordon, A., 511
Goshen, C. E., 501
Gossel, P. P., 354
Gottlieb, G., 337, 385
Gottschaldt, K., 534, 538
Gould, S. J., 206, 220, 267
Gowers, W. R., 80
Grant, M., 640
Gratiolet, P., 78, 80
Graves, R., 332
Greenberg, R. P., 517
Grob, G. N., 91
Gruber, H., 204, 220
Guilford, J. P., 635
Guillain, G., 108, 110, 112
Guthrie, E. R., 409, 518
Guthrie, R. V., 611–613, 639
Guttman, N., 476

Haeckel, E. H., 575
Haggerty, M. E., 405, 407, 409
Hahn, E., 378
Hale, M., Jr., 561
Hale, N. G., 520
Hall, A. C., 479–481
Hall, C. S., 451, 456, 459
Hall, G. S., 19, 123, 141, 142, 151–153, 192, 232–234, 240–244, 249, 263–282, 287, 293, 297, 299, 310, 311, 313, 314, 323, 360, 390, 404, 408, 488, 558, 559, 572, 575, 611, 636
Halleck, R. P., 328
Hamilton, G. V., 406
Hankins, F. H., 638
Hannush, M. M., 364
Hanson, N. R., 185
Hardy, K. A., 17
Hare, H. A., 593
Harper, R. S., 240
Harper, W. R., 278, 359, 390
Harris, B., 393, 609
Harris, G. W., 331
Harris, M., 54, 60
Hartley, D., 24
Hartshorne, E. Y., 539
Hartwell, E. M., 232
Harvey, W., 26, 38
Hayes, C., 379
Hayford, J. F., 362
Head, H., 77, 78
Healy, W., 578
Hebb, D. O., 518
Hegel, G. W. F., 310, 313, 317
Heidbreder, E., 121, 296, 513, 527, 550
Heider, F., 535
Helmholtz, von, H., 63, 155, 197, 240, 246, 314
Henle, M., 528, 535, 538–544, 552
Henri, V., 291
Herbart, J. F., 160–162, 165
Hering, E., 311
Hermann, I., 138–141
Heron, W. T., 367, 459
Herrick, C. J., 407
Hertz, H., 538, 539
Hilgard, E. R., 19, 296, 411, 518
Hill, M. R., 12, 14
Hillix, W. A., see Cronan-Hillix, W. A.
Himmelfarb, G., 219
Hirsch, J., 450, 451, 460
Hitler, A., 502, 538, 543, 550, 611, 635
Hobbes, T., 26, 34, 43
Hobhouse, L. T., 328
Hodge, C. F., 360
Hollingworth, H. L., 10–11, 14, 560, 562, 593–606
Hollingworth, L. S., 14, 269, 279, 326–327, 594, 597, 603, 608
Holmes, S. J., 359
Holmgren, F., 356
Holsti, O. R., 17
Holt, E. B., 405, 407–409, 518
Holzman, P. S., 162
Hooker, J. D., 207, 219, 356
Hoopes, J., 15
Hornstein, G. A., 491–492, 510–524
Hothersall, D., 90
Huarte, J., 320
Hughes, H. S., 165
Hughes, R., 368
Hull, C. L., 386, 409, 437–439, 462–466
Humboldt, von, W., 162
Hume, D., 24, 55, 305
Humphrey, G., 512, 518
Hunsaker, J. C., 479
Hunt, W. M., 249, 252, 253
Hunter, W. S., 298, 407, 409, 518

Hurvich, D. J., 198
Husserl, E., 47
Huxley, L., 356, 357
Huxley, T. H., 219, 220, 356
Hyde, A. D., 476–481

Innis, N. K., 439, 450–461
Itard, J. M. G., 376
Ivy, A. C., 366

Jackson, H., 318
Jackson, S. W., 89
Jacobsen, C. F., 379
Jacobsen, M. M., 379
Jacoby, R., 520
James, H., 241, 252, 253, 258
James, W., 14, 123, 142, 155, 160, 240–243, 245–262, 284, 298, 310, 312, 313, 328, 357–358, 413, 488, 560, 610
Janet, J., 111
Janet, P., 105, 110–111, 501
Jarausch, K. H., 17
Jastrow, J., 206, 232, 234, 238, 284, 287–293, 311, 325–326, 328, 407, 488, 513
Jefferson, T., 233, 366
Jeffress, L., 456, 457
Jenkins, H. M., 436
Jennings, H. S., 366, 392
Jensen, A. R., 629–630
Jensen, E., 502
Jervis, R., 631
Jewett, F. B., 480
Johnson, C. S., 616
Johnson, E., 141
Jones, E., 115, 116, 118, 501–502, 504, 509, 512
Jones, M., 88
Jones, Mary Cover, 393
Jordan, D. S., 323–324
Judd, C. H., 123
Judson, H. P., 363, 364
Jung, C. G., 488, 509, 510, 512, 551

Kahneman, D., 163
Kalish, D., 448
Kant, I., 310, 317, 511
Katz, Daniel, 636–637
Katz, David, 194, 534
Keen, W. W., 358
Keller, F. S., 184, 518
Kellogg, D., 376, 378–380, 387
Kellogg, L. A., 338, 372–389
Kellogg, W., 338, 372–389
Kelly, E. L., 519
Kelman, H. C., 630
Kendler, H. H., 205, 336, 489
Kennan, G., 631
Kevles, D. J., 631
Kidd, B. E., 368
Kimble, G. A., 382, 518–519
Kingsland, S., 366
Kirchhoff, G. R., 533
Kirschmann, A., 196
Klein, G. S., 162
Kline, P., 517
Klineberg, O., 612, 613, 615–618, 628–632
Kluger, R., 628, 631
Klüver, H., 534
Koch, S., 185
Koelsch, W. A., 360, 488
Koffka, K., 14, 525, 527, 530–531, 533, 538, 545–546
Köhler, W., 379, 525, 527, 528, 530–556
Konig, A., 197
Kornfeld, A. D., 392, 393
Kraepelin, E., 89, 153, 154, 163
Krafft-Ebing, von, R., 506, 508
Krantz, D. L., 296
Krech, D., 459, 609, 632
Krechevsky, I., see Krech, D.
Kuhn, T. S., 185, 223, 409–410, 412, 415, 637
Kuker-Reines, B., 365
Külpe, O., 170, 179–181, 183, 190
Kuntze, J. E., 138–142
Kuo, Z. Y., 452, 453
Kurzweil, E., 517
Kussmaul, A., 77

Ladd, G. T., 121, 284, 343
Ladd-Franklin, C., 14, 196–198, 512
La Farge, J., 249, 252, 253
Lallemand, C.-F., 77
Lamarck, J. B., 204
Landauer, A. A., 526
Landis, C., 515
Langfeld, H. S., 194, 402, 407, 514

Larsen, J. C., 12
Larson, C. A., 406
Lashley, K. S., 409, 411, 447, 534, 552, 553
Lasker, B., 636
Lasswitz, K., 141, 142
Lavater, J. K., 82
Leahey, T. H., 23, 122, 123, 125, 171, 178–188, 297, 436
Leary, D. E., 19, 243, 249–262
LeBon, G., 634
Leborgne ("Tan"), 64, 73–76, 78
Leffingwell, A., 357, 365
Leibniz, G. W., 129
Leuba, J., 196
Leuret, F., 80
Levine, S., 331
Lewin, K., 533, 534, 538, 543, 549, 553, 610, 640
Liebig, J., 236, 289
Lind-af-Hageby, E. A. L., 364, 365
Link, H. C., 414, 426–427
Link, M., 123
Linnaeus, 211
Linton, H., 162
Lippitt, R., 445
Lippmann, W., 631
Lloyd Morgan, C., 335, 336, 473
Lockard, R. B., 385
Locke, J., 23–26, 35, 39, 48–61, 120
Loeb, J., 336, 337, 365, 390, 413, 473
Lombroso, C., 82
Long, H. H., 640
Lotze, R. H., 232, 248
Lovejoy, A. O., 551
Lowell, A. L., 547
Luckhardt, A. B., 366
Ludwig, C., 153
Ludwig, K., 240
Lummis, T., 15, 16
Lyell, C., 204, 207, 210, 219
Lyubimov, A., 104, 106, 108, 109, 112

MacCurdy, J. T., 511
Mach, E., 155, 182, 185, 435, 473
Mackenzie, B., 182
MacLeod, R. B., 47, 538, 552
MacMechan, A., 270
Maeder, A., 511
Magendie, F., 62, 77, 353–354, 356, 366
Magruder, E., 422–423
Maguire, M. T., 565, 571–572
Maher, B. A., 89
Maher, W. B., 89
Mahin, J. L., 560
Malcolm, J., 515
Malebranche, de, N., 318
Mall, F. P., 319
Malthus, T., 203, 208, 211, 218
Manchester, W., 366
Marquis, D. G., 411
Marshall, H. R., 404
Marshall, M. E., 124, 137–144
Marshall, T., 612, 629
Martin, R., 353
Marx, M., 438
Maslow, A. H., 14
Masserman, J., 366
Masson, J. M., 490
Maxwell, J. C., 532
Mayer, S., 503
Mayo, M. J., 640
McClearn, G. E., 451, 456, 459
McDougall, W., 328, 329, 392, 403, 408, 413, 547, 634, 639
McGuire, G. R., 19
McGuire, T., 450
McLaughlin, I. C., 366
McLellan, J. A., 312
McMillan, J., 354
McPherson, M. W., 2
McReynolds, P., 559
Mead, G. H., 309, 313–314, 362
Mendel, G. J., 450, 637
Metzger, W., 538
Meyer, A., 181, 182, 392, 423, 424
Meyer, M. F., 319, 392, 403, 405
Meynert, T., 109, 319
Michotte, A., 534
Miles, C. C., 331
Miles, W., 14
Mill, James, 24
Mill, John Stuart, 24–25, 161, 184, 322, 323
Miller, D., 516, 593
Miller, J. C., 366
Miller, N. E., 517
Mills, T. W., 358–359
Mischel, T., 158, 160
Mitchell, J. A., 354

Mitchell, P. C., 236
Mobius, P. J., 319, 320
Money, J., 331
Monzie, de, A., 111
Morawski, J. G., 513, 518, 520
Moray, N., 163
More, H., 323
Morgan, C. L., 335, 336, 473
Morgan, J. J. B., 393
Morgulis, S., 338, 345–353
Morris, G. S., 299, 310–312
Mott, F. L., 354
Mowrer, O. H., 516
Müller, G. E., 197
Müller, J., 63, 64, 66–73, 122
Münsterberg, H., 14, 193, 290, 313, 404, 407, 451, 548, 560–562, 584–593, 639
Munthe, A., 112
Murchison, C., 545
Murphy, G., 519, 630–632, 635
Murphy, L., 635
Muschinske, D., 611
Myers, F., 111, 509
Myers, G. E., 250
Myrdal, G., 629

Napoli, D. S., 557, 560
Neisser, U., 163, 183, 184
Newcomb, T., 632, 635
Newton, I., 23
Nicholson, E. B., 368
Niven, C. D., 353, 364
Novick, P., 6
Nyswander, D. B., 455–457

O'Donnell, J. M., 64, 89, 122, 123, 296, 337, 392, 562, 569–584
Obersteiner, H., 233
Ogden, R. M., 546, 549
Ombredane, A., 77
O'Neil, W. M., 526
Osborne, C., 275
Osgood, C. E., 163, 382

Palmer, G. H., 313
Pappenheim, B., 501–510; see also Anna O.
Park, R., 636
Parmelee, M., 392, 402, 403, 405
Parrott, J., 79
Parsons, F., 293
Pasteur, L., 356, 359
Patrick, G. T. W., 319
Pavlov, I. P., 337, 338, 345–353, 364–365, 404, 411, 473
Pawlow, J. P., see Pavlov, I. P.
Payne, B., 374
Pearson, K., 231, 237, 321, 322
Peirce, C. S., 121, 170, 299, 310, 311, 314
Perry, R. B., 240, 249, 252–254, 409, 539, 540, 542, 546, 547, 551
Petryszak, N. G., 26, 53–61
Pillsbury, W. B., 169, 190, 191, 330, 400, 407
Pinel, P., 89–91, 93–97, 107, 117
Planck, M., 532, 538, 544
Plato, 250, 265
Playfair, L., 354, 355
Plous, S., 610
Poffenberger, A. T., 598
Pomeroy, W. B., 374
Popplestone, J. A., 2
Porteus, S., 320
Pratt, C., 538
Priest, J., 616
Prince, M., 407, 511–512
Pronko, N. H., 382
Proshansky, H. M., 630
Putnam, F. W., 288
Putnam, J. J., 249, 511

Rafail, P. A., 12
Raimy, V. C., 608
Rambo, L. R., 357
Randall, J. H., Jr., 47
Raphelson, A. C., 299, 309–315
Rashotte, M. E., 437
Rausch, F. A., 327
Rayner, R., 393
Reed, C. I., 366
Reisman, J. M., 89
Resor, S., 428
Reynolds, R., 105
Rheingold, J., 330
Rice, C. E., 375, 384
Richards, R. J., 206, 218–226

Richer, P., 104, 115
Richet, C., 104
Ridenour, L. N., 483
Riese, W., 78
Ringer, F., 181, 182
Riopelle, A., 378
Ritchie, B. F., 447–448
Roback, A. A., 309, 512, 639
Robinson, D., 184
Robinson, E. S., 518, 550
Robinson, F. R., 518
Rogers, A. M., 10, 562, 593–606
Romanes, E., 356
Romanes, G. J., 233, 318, 335–337, 356, 575
Rosenbaum, A., 10, 562, 593–606
Rosenberg, C., 266
Rosenberg, R., 266, 269, 270, 274, 278, 279
Rosenzweig, S., 491
Ross, D., 266, 274, 278, 360, 576
Ross, E. A., 634, 639
Rostan, L. L., 77
Rowley, F. H., 357
Royce, J., 313
Rubenstein, B. B., 331
Rubin, E., 534
Rupp, H., 538, 541, 543, 544
Ruse, M., 220–221
Russell, B., 423, 424
Ryan, M. P., 272
Ryan, W. C., 276, 278

Sachs, H., 514–515
Saenger, G., 629
Sahakian, W., 184
Salt, H. S., 368
Samelson, F., 18, 391, 394, 402–419, 613, 633–645
Sanderson, J. S. B., 189, 354, 356
Sanford, E. C., 196, 234, 277, 287, 290, 311
Santayana, G., 249
Sarnoff, I., 516
Scarborough, E., 18
Schaub, E., 164
Schiller, von, J. C. F., 538
Schlesinger, A., Jr., 9
Schlosberg, H., 163
Schoenfeld, W., 518
Schopenhauer, A., 248, 317
Schultz, D. P., 184, 296, 489
Schultz, S. E., 296, 489
Schulze, M., 140
Schusterman, R., 375
Schwartz, B. J., 516
Schwendinger, H., 266
Schwendinger, J., 266
Scodel, A., 516
Scott, W. D., 123, 422, 425–426, 511, 559–560, 639
Scripture, E. W., 123, 287, 290–293
Sears, R. R., 516–517
Seashore, C. E., 293, 488, 518
Sechzer, J. A., 353, 366
Selesnick, S. T., 89
Selye, H., 366
Shakow, D., 570
Shand, A. F., 328, 329
Sharp, S. E., 291
Shaw, G. B., 365
Shields, S. A., 266, 267, 299, 316–334
Shortall, J., 357, 361, 363
Shulman, M. D., 631
Shurrager, P. S., 382
Siegel, A. W., 268
Silverman, J., 163
Simon, B., 89
Simonton, D. K., 18
Sinclair, A., 323
Singer, P., 366
Skinner, B. F., 14, 185, 186, 437–440, 466–487, 518
Skrupskelis, I. K., 357
Slade, H., 142–143
Small, A., 608
Smith, A., 79
Smith, L. D., 435
Smith, P., 323
Smith-Rosenberg, C., 266
Sohen, J., 273
Sokal, M. M., 12, 19, 122, 123, 240, 243, 244, 287–295, 528, 545–556
Solomon, M., 511
Sondhaus, E., 78
Souques, A., 104
Spence, D. P., 162
Spence, K. W., 445
Spencer, Herbert, 236, 300, 327, 328, 357, 575
Spencer, Hugh, 477–481, 483
Sperling, G., 163
Sperling, S., 353, 368

Spurzheim, J., 317–318
Squires, P. C., 376
Stagner, R., 609
Stannard, U., 332
Stapp, J., 88
Stern, W., 488, 525
Sternberg, S., 164
Stetter, L., see Hollingworth, L. S.
Stevens, G., 270, 273, 274
Stevens, S. S., 382, 436
Stieda, W., 153
Stocking, G. W., Jr., 7, 575
Stone, C. P., 366
Stookey, B., 77
Storm, M., 366
Storr, R. J., 608
Strong, E. K., Jr., 598, 616
Strotesbury, H., 576
Stumpf, C., 155
Suci, G., 163
Sullivan, J. J., 406
Sulloway, F. J., 91, 114–119, 489
Sumner, F. C., 611, 612
Sutherland, A., 328

Taber, S., 357
Tannenbaum, P., 163
Tannenbaum, S. A., 512
Tanner, A., 276–277
Tarule, J. M., 199
Tate, J. T., 475, 476
Taylor, E. W., 511
Taylor, F. M., 311
Taylor, F. W., 429
Taylor, H. O., 547
Terman, L. C., 235, 331, 545, 546, 549, 578, 611, 634, 639, 640
Thomas, M. C., 268, 270
Thomas, R. F., 364
Thomas, W. I., 424, 636
Thompson, H. B., see Woolley, H. B. T.
Thompson, T., 439
Thompson, W. R., 451
Thomson, J. A., 267, 321, 324
Thorndike, E. L., 235, 241, 243, 268, 269, 276, 325, 328–329, 336, 337, 340–345, 365, 404–407, 412–414, 436–438, 525, 578, 596
Thurstone, L. L., 635
Titchener, E. B., 26, 123, 125, 160, 168–202, 233, 234, 241, 289, 291, 296–298, 304, 390, 406, 409, 410, 413, 414, 488, 547, 610
Tobach, E., 630
Tolman, E. C., 367, 409, 437–461, 552, 553, 609
Tolman, R. C., 440, 475
Trecker, J. L., 266, 278
Trousseau, A., 79–80
Tryon, R. C., 439, 450, 451, 455–461
Tufts, J. H., 309, 312–314
Turner, F. J., 557
Turner, J., 353

Ungerer, G. A., 125, 151–157
Urch, G., 13

Veatch, H. B., 183
Vestal, M., 123
Virchow, R., 356
Viteles, M., 579
Volkmann, A. W., 311

Wade, N., 366
Waite, M. A., 276
Walker, A., 317, 318
Walker, H. M., 233
Wallace, A. R., 207, 218
Wallach, H., 535, 536, 538, 544
Wallin, J. E. W., 578–579
Walsh, A. A., 64
Warbi, M., 502
Warden, C. J., 338, 367
Warren, A., 143
Warren, H. C., 190, 402, 404–407, 518
Washburn, M. F., 169, 195, 196, 198, 406, 407, 409, 548, 550
Watson, G., 632, 636
Watson, James B., 221, 364
Watson, John B., 182, 198, 298, 330, 338, 360–364, 390–394, 396–438, 451, 453, 473, 513, 517–518, 525, 545, 549
Watson, R. I., 25–26, 34–48, 184, 266, 579
Watson, R. R., 393
Weatherford, W. D., 616
Weber, E. H., 120–121, 134–135, 530
Weber, W., 143

Weidensall, J., 403
Weiner, H., 89
Weiner, M., 516
Weininger, O., 320
Weismann, A., 575
Weiss, A. P., 408
Weisse, C., 140
Welch, W. H., 354
Weld, H. P., 514
Wellek, R., 143
Wells, F. L., 403, 405, 409, 511
Wells, H. G., 365
Wells, L., 233
Wendt, R. A., 143
Werner, H., 162, 164
Wertheimer, Max, 525–527, 530–534, 538, 542, 553
Wertheimer, Michael, 527
Wever, E. G., 367
Whipple, G. H., 366
White, C. E., 354
White, R. K., 631
White, S. H., 268
Whitman, C. O., 359
Wicherski, M., 88
Wiley, H. W., 10–11, 595–596, 598–602
Willis, T., 81
Wilson, G. D., 517
Windholz, G., 337
Wishard, G. W., 362
Wissler, C., 291–293, 325
Witmer, L., 89, 123, 192, 196, 290–293, 377, 558–559, 561–562, 564–584, 610
Wittmann, B., 111, 112
Wolf, C., 79
Wolfe, E. L., 354
Wolfe, H. K., 123, 263, 287
Wolff, W., 538
Wolfle, D., 607
Wollstonecraft, M., 322
Wood, I., 276
Wood, W., 88
Woods, J. H., 546, 547
Woodworth, R. S., 194, 197, 235, 338, 343, 373, 410, 452, 453, 512–513, 596, 601, 611, 633
Woody, T. A., 270, 273, 279
Woofter, T. J., Jr., 638
Woolley, H. B. T., 269, 279, 316, 319, 324–326
Wordsworth, W., 251, 252, 254
Wundt, M., 151, 161
Wundt, W., 25, 89, 121–125, 141–143, 145–171, 178–190, 232–234, 236, 240, 242, 243, 284, 287, 290, 310, 314, 316, 488, 526–527, 559, 560
Wyckoff, A. E., 264
Wyzewa, de, T., 111

Yerkes, A. W., 379, 451, 452
Yerkes, R. M., 338, 341, 345–354, 359, 360, 366, 367, 378, 379, 402–413, 422, 451, 545, 639
Yoshioka, J. G., 379
Young, K., 639
Young, P. T., 367

Zenderland, L., 366
Zener, K., 538
Zilboorg, G. A., 89, 90
Zollner, J. F. C., 142, 143

SUBJECT INDEX

Ablation technique, 85–86
Abnormal psychology, 163,
Accident proneness, 562, 587
Adaptation, biological, see Evolutionary theory
Adolescent development, 267–273
Advertising, psychology of, 420–434, 560, 561
Affective processes, 42, 145–150, 163, 204, 393, 398, 411
African Americans, 610–645
Albert study of conditioned fear, 393, 411
American Historical Review, 1
American Journal of Psychology, 242
American Psychological Association, 170, 192–193, 242
  and animal experimentation, 338, 353–372
  archives, 2, 16
  Division 26, 1
  goals, 607–608
  and mental testing, 290
  and terminology, 408
Animal learning, 335–389, 391, 436, 531
Animal rights movement, 367–368
Anna O case, 489, 491, 493–510
Anthropometric testing, 205, 232–236, 243, 244, 282–295
Antivivisection movement, 338, 353–372
Aphemia, 73–76
Apparent movement (phi) phenonenon, 526, 530
Apperception, 160, 162, 163, 165, 169
Applied psychology, 89, 242, 274, 557–562
Archival research, 2, 10–15, 125, 151–157
Archives of the History of American Psychology, 2, 11, 14, 16
Army Alpha and Beta tests, 422
Associationism, 24–26, 160–162, 169
  See also Learning
Atomism, 124, 160–162
Attention, 163–164, 243, 245–248
Authoritarian personality, 642

Behavior genetics, 439, 450
Behavior modification, 437
Behaviorism, 182, 185, 329–330, 390–394, 396–419, 435–440, 527–528
Bell-Magendie law, 62
Bicêtre asylum, 90
Bias issue, 5–8, 19
Biographical research, 124, 137–144
Biological adaptation, see Evolutionary theory
Black Americans, 610–645
Blacky Pictures, 516

Boulder training model, 608
Brain functioning, 44, 62–64, 66–87
sex differences in, 317–320
British empiricism, 23–25, 63
Broca's area, 63, 73–81
Brown v. Board of Education case, 612, 613, 628–632
Bulletin of the History of Medicine, 1
Business psychology, 559–562, 584–593

Caffeine, effects on behavior, 561, 562, 593–606
Cartesian dualism, 23, 27–38
Catharsis, 489, 495, 497, 499
Cheiron (International Society for the History of the Behavioral and Social Sciences), 1
Chicago functionalist school, 269, 296–299, 309–315, 390
Child abuse, 489–490
Child study movement, 242, 243, 263–265, 267, 558
Childrearing techniques, 427
Children, race awareness in, 619–627
Chimpanzee-child study, 376–381
Christian doctrine, influence of, 27–34, 51, 53–61
Citation analysis, 17–18
Clark University, 242, 488
education for women, 273–280
Classical conditioning, 337, 345–353, 411, 440, 466–471
Clinical autopsy method, 63, 64
Clinical psychology, 88–91, 291, 558–562, 564–584, 608
Coca-Cola trial, 561, 562, 593–606
Coeducation, 244, 266–281, 323–324
Cognitive control, 162
Cognitive maps, 437, 441–450
Cognitive psychology, 162–166, 437, 439
Comparative psychology, 335–338
Complex ideas, 24, 26, 48–53
Conditioned fear, 393, 411
Conditioned reflexes, 337, 345–353, 393, 411
Consciousness, 29–30, 44, 300–309, 391–392, 396–402
elements of, 123–124, 145–150, 169–170, 172–178, 301
stream of, 245–248, 254–258
Consumer behavior, 420–434
Content analysis, 17
Correlational method, 232, 236
Cortical localization, 62–64, 66–87
Craniometry, 82
Creative synthesis, 161, 169
Critical history, 18–19
Cultural psychology, 164

Darwinian theory, 203–226, 241–242, 266–269, 299, 316–334, 450
Deductive rationalism, 35–38
Defense mechanisms, 491, 518
Derived ideas, 23, 48–53
Difference threshold, 121
Dolls Test, 619
Dreams, 34, 490
Dynamic psychiatry, 88–91, 110–111

Echolocation, 382–385
Electrical stimulation, 63, 68
Elements of consciousness, 123–124, 145–150, 169–170, 172–178, 301
Elements of Psychophysics (Fechner), 121, 124
Eminence, 205, 321, 325, 610
Emotions, 42, 145–150, 163, 204, 393, 398, 411
Empiricism, 23–25, 35, 63
Empty-organism psychology, 438
Enlightenment period (17th-18th centuries), 26, 53–61
Environmentalism, 393, 452
See also Nature-nurture issue
Eugenics, 204–205, 237, 573–574
Evolutionary theory, 203–226, 241–242, 266–269, 299, 316–334, 450
Experimental Psychology (Titchener), 170, 191
Externalism issue, 19
Extinction, 337, 467, 469

Factor-analytic method, 162
Fear, conditioned, 393, 411
Feelings, see Emotions
Feral children, 376–377
Figural aftereffects, 536–537
Figure-ground perception, 534
Folk psychology, 164
Form qualities, 526, 531
Free-association technique, 489, 490, 513
Freudian slips, 490
Functionalism, 170, 205, 240–244, 296–309, 390–391

Genius, 578
  See also Eminence
Genetic counseling, 237
Geriatrics, 110
Gestalt psychology, 161, 169, 181, 525–537, 545–556
Gestalt qualities, 526, 531
Goal gradient hypothesis, 466

Habits, 400–401, 465–466
Hereditary factors, 205, 226–231, 564–584
Historical models, 218–226
Historiography, 3–20
Historiometry, 18
History, definition, 2–5
History of Human Sciences, 1
History of Psychiatry, 1
History of psychology courses, 1–2
History of science, 10, 221–224
Holistic approach, 161, 169
Hypnosis, 104, 109–111, 115–118, 489
Hypothetico-deductive method, 34–38
Hysteria, 91, 104–105, 110–112, 115–118, 489, 493–498
  in males, 97–103

Ideas, 23–24, 36, 44, 48–53, 55, 58
Imageless-thought controversy, 409–410
Imagination, 27, 41
Immediate experience, 123, 158
Immigration issue, 634–638
Individual differences, 203–206, 226–235, 243, 291–293
Industrial psychology, 559–562, 584–593
Infantile sexuality, 489–490
Innate ideas, 23, 36, 55, 58
Instinct theory, 453–454
Intelligence, 436
  race differences, 611, 633
  sex differences, 317–327
Intelligence testing, 243, 244, 422, 577–578
  See also Mental testing
Internalism issue, 19
International Congress of Psychology, 194
Interpretation of Dreams (Freud), 490
Intervening variables, 437
Introspection methods, 123, 159, 169, 174–176, 183–184, 233, 298, 391, 392, 398, 410
Introspection-by-analogy, 335–336

Isis, 1
Isolation (Restorff) effect, 534, 544

Journal of Applied Psychology, 242
Journal of Genetic Psychology, 242
Journal of the History of the Behavioral Sciences, 1
Journal of the History of Ideas, 1
Journal of Religious Psychology, 242
Journal of Social Issues, 610
Just noticeable difference (jnd), 121

Kuhnian paradigms, 223, 409–412, 415, 637

Laryngeal movements, 412
Latent learning, 445–447
Law of effect, 336, 340–345
Law of exercise, 340–345
Law of readiness, 340–345
Law of reinforcement, 336
Learning, 24, 298, 335–338, 436–439, 441–466
Learning disabilities, 564–584
Lefthandedness, 80
Leipzig laboratory, 122, 151–157
Library of Congress, 2, 11, 14, 16
Logical positivism, 435–436

Magnetism, 105
Manuals (Titchener), 170, 191
Manuscript collections, 2, 10–15
Marketing, psychology of, 420–434
Masculinity, 272–273, 316–322, 331
Maternal instinct, 323, 327–330
Mathematico-deductive theory, 438
Maze learning, 336, 340–345, 439, 441–461
Mechanism, 22–25, 32, 47, 164
Mediate experience, 123
Meditative method, 25, 43
Mental chemistry, 161, 169
Mental disorders, 88–91, 177–178
  early treatment, 93–97
Mental elements, 123–124, 145–150, 169–170, 172–178, 301
Mental hospitals, 90, 93–97
Mental testing, 243, 244, 282–295, 558, 587
  sex differences, 324–327

Mind-body interaction, 23, 25, 27–48, 120, 127–137, 159, 304–305
Morgan's Canon, 335
Müller-Lyer illusion, 162, 532, 536

National Archives, 11
National Library of Medicine, 16
National Union Catalog of Manuscript Collections, 11–12
Native Americans, 610, 615–618
Natural selection, see Evolutionary theory
Nature-nurture issue, 237, 325, 338, 453, 634
Neobehaviorism, 435–440
Neorealism, 437
Nerve energies doctrine, 63, 64, 66–73
Neurological functioning, 62–64, 66–87
Neuroses, 488–492
Normal distribution, 232

Objectivity issue, 5–8, 39, 47
Oedipus complex, 490
On the Origin of Species (Darwin), 203–206, 218–226, 300
Operant conditioning, 440, 466–471
Operationism, 436
Oral history, 15–17

Paradigms, 409–412, 637
Paralysis, hysterical, 104–114
Parental instinct, 328–330
Passions, see Emotions
Pavlovian conditioning, 337, 345–353, 411, 440, 466–471
Pedagogical techniques, 242, 243, 263–265
Perception, 27–34, 41
  Gestalt approach, 527, 530–537
Perceptual defense, 516
Perceptual illusions, 532
Phi phenomenon, 526, 530
Philosophy, 120, 160
Phrenology, 64, 77, 78, 81–87
Physics, 120, 160, 532–533
Physiology, 62–65
Pigeon project (Skinner), 440, 472–487
Positive reinforcement, 336–337, 437–439, 462–466
Positivism, 169, 182, 185–186
Prejudice, 635–641
Prescriptive analysis, 25–26
Presentism issue, 19
Primary qualities, 24, 120
Principles of Physiological Psychology (Wundt), 122
Principles of Psychology (James), 241, 245–258, 312, 313, 390
Project Pigeon, 440, 472–487
Psychiatry, 88–91
Psychic reality, 490
Psychic reflexes, 337
Psychic theory of mental illness, 88, 90
Psychical compounds, 149–150
Psychical elements, see Mental elements
Psychoanalysis, 204, 329–332, 488–492, 510–524
Psychogenetics, 451
Psycholinguistics, 162–163
Psychological clinics, 89, 291, 293, 558–559, 561–562, 564–584
Psychological Corporation, 243, 291–292, 422, 426
Psychology of women, 299, 316–334, 608
Psychonomic Society, 2
Psychopathology, 88–92, 488–492
Psychophysics, 120–121, 123, 124, 127–137, 303
Punishment, 336
Purposive behaviorism, 437, 453
Puzzle-box experiments, 336–337, 340–345

Quantitative methods, 17–18, 231–239
Questionnaires, 232, 242, 267, 276

Racial identification research, 619–627
Racial issues, 228–231, 237, 610–645
Radical behaviorism, see Skinnerian behaviorism
Rationalism, 22–23, 25, 34–38, 57
Reaction time, 164, 242, 392
  race differences, 610, 633
Recapitulation theory, 242, 244, 266–281
Reflex arc, 297–298, 312, 314
Reflexive behavior, 23, 469–471
Regression analysis, 232, 236
Reinforcement, 336–337, 437–439, 462–466
Renaissance period (14th-17th centuries), 22
Repressed memories, 496
Restorff effect, 534, 544

Salivary reflex, 337, 345–353, 411
Salpêtrière asylum, 90, 91, 104–118
Schizophrenia, 163
School psychology, 559
School segregation, 612, 619–632
Scientific management, 429–430, 560
Scientific method, 22
Scott Company, 422
Secondary qualities, 24, 120
Selective attention, 163–164, 243, 245–248
Selective breeding (rats), 452, 456
Self-consciousness, 43–45
Sensations, 27–34, 41, 48–49, 66–73, 127–137
Sensory capacities, see Mental testing
Set (attitude), 343
Sex differences, 244, 266–281, 299, 316–334
Sexual factors in neurosis, 489–491
Sign-gestalts, 437
Simple ideas, 24, 26, 48–53
Skinnerian behaviorism, 185, 437–439, 466–471, 472–487
Social history, 9–10, 19
Social issues research, 608–613, 628–632
Social philosophy, 53–61
Society of Experimental Psychologists, 170, 171, 188–202, 405
Society for the Psychological Study of Social Issues (SPSSI), 608–613, 628–632
Somatic theory of mental illness, 88, 90
Soul, 44, 50–51
Spatial orientation research, 447–449
Specific nerve energies doctrine, 63, 64, 66–73
Speech, 73–76
Spinal cord, 62–63
Stimulus-response (S-R) psychology, 297, 336, 391, 438, 441–442
Stream of consciousness, 245–248, 254–258
Structuralism, 160, 168–178, 296–297, 390–391
  and Wundtian psychology, 178–188
Subjectivity issue, 5–8, 39, 47
Symbolic constructs, 462

Tabula rasa, 23, 26, 53–61
Threshold measurement, 121
Titchener's Experimentalists, 170, 171, 188–202, 405
Trial-and-error learning, 336, 437
Tropism, 336–337
Twin-comparison method, 232
Two-point threshold, 121

Unconscious processes, 491, 498

Variability hypothesis, 320–327
Verbal report method, 123, 392
  See also Introspection methods
Veterans Administration (VA) hospitals, 607
Vivisection, 338, 353–372
Vocational guidance and testing, 293, 559
Volition, 160, 162, 303–305
Voluntarism, 160

Weber's law, 121
Wish fulfillment, 490
Women, education, 244, 266–281, 322–327
  hysteria in, 104–105, 110–112, 115–118
  intelligence, 317–320
  in psychology, 89, 171, 188–202, 273–280
Women's colleges, 273–274
Word association, 231
Wundtian psychology, 122–125, 145–167, 178–188, 526–527

Young-Helmholtz theory, 118

Zeitgeist, 165